Shooter's Bible
No. 94 2003 Edition

Stoeger Publishing Company, Accokeek, Maryland

STOEGER PUBLISHING

NEW FOR 2002

25th Edition
For almost half a century, millions of gun buffs have chosen "Gun Trader's Guide" as their primary reference tool for firearms identification and pricing. A comprehensive guide, "Gun Trader's Guide" gives comparisons for sporting, military and law enforcement models, including rare and unusual collectibles and commemoratives.

This upcoming edition will feature more listings than ever before, with completely updated specifications, dates of manufacture, and current market average values for over 6,000 handguns, rifles, and shotguns, both domestic and foreign.

World-Class Recipes for the Game Connoisseur
Venison is the most widely-sought game meat throughout the world and has been since the dawn of time. Venison, low in fat and cholesterol, is lauded as a wise, health-conscious choice to create a wide variety of tasty dishes.

"Wild About Venison" features 70 exquisite recipes from some of the top chefs in the culinary arts. Distinctively different in flavor, recipes for white-tailed deer, mule deer, elk, moose, caribou and antelope are sure to please the most discriminating tastes. More than 100 color photos showcase fabulous gourmet presentations and offer helpful serving hints.

by David Alderton
"Hounds of the World" concentrates solely on this popular group of breeds, many of which are now widely kept as companion dogs because of their friendly and intelligent natures. It features superb photographs of hounds outdoors in their natural environments, as well as close-up portrayals of individual dogs. All photographs have been taken especially for this book. The text adopts a chronological approach to its subject, explaining the development of the hound lineage and the different types of hounds that have been bred down the centuries.

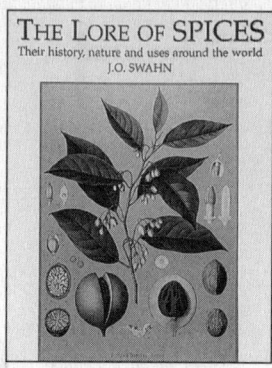

Their History, Nature and Uses Around the World

by J.O.Swahn
"The Lore of Spices" explores the cultural history of man's use of spices, in addition to describing the plants and their origins. From anise, coriander and ginger to laurel, rosemary, wormwood and vanilla, the informative text describes forty main spices and includes anecdotes and recipes. Complemented with finely reproduced botanical art, "The Lore of Spices" is a feast for the senses.

by Jay Langston
"Turkey Hunter's Tool Kit: Shooting Savvy" shares Jay Langston's tips for picking the best gun and load, and, some sage advice on the right moves when a gobbler steps in range. In-depth, hands-on experience with a wide variety of popular action types make this book a must read for the rookie and veteran alike in pursuit of a new turkey gun. The latest developments in ammunition and accessories round out the vital information shared in this book.

Revised Edition

by John J. Donnelly
All the physical data, how-to details, drawings, and tools needed to convert over 900 obsolete cartridge cases into shootable centerfire ammunition.

by Monte Burch
Today, more than 10 million anglers pursue these finny fighters throughout North America. A common thread among bass anglers is the use of watercraft to hunt for the perfect spot to cast a lure to a waiting fish. Author Monte Burch is one of the industry's leading authorities on fishing boats and their use. "Ultimate Bass Boats" is a collection of Burch's practical experience in a "how-to" format so fishermen - from rookie to aspiring pro - can rig their boats for maximum fishing performance.

A large section will be devoted to a visual tour of several pro anglers' boats. See how they rig their boats for maximum fishing performance.

MORE BOOKS FROM STOEGER PUBLISHING

COWBOY ACTION SHOOTING

SPORTING COLLECTIBLES

FN BROWNING ARMORER TO THE WORLD

HECKLER & KOCH:

LEGENDARY SPORTING RIFLES

MODERN BERETTA FIREARMS

P-38 AUTOMATIC PISTOL

RIFLE GUIDE

THE BOOK OF THE TWENTY-TWO

THE ULTIMATE IN RIFLE ACCURACY

THE WALTHER HANDGUN STORY

ANTIQUE GUNS

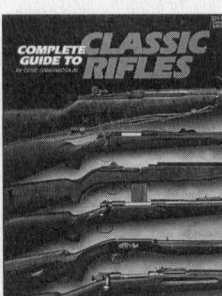
COMPLETE GUIDE TO CLASSIC RIFLES

COMPLETE GUIDE TO COMPACT HANDGUNS

FIREARMS DISASSEMBLY WITH EXPLODED VIEWS

GUNSMITHING AT HOME

HOW TO BUY & SELL USED GUNS

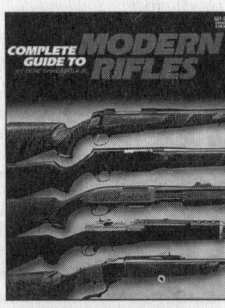
COMPLETE GUIDE TO MODERN RIFLES

COMPLETE GUIDE TO SERVICE HANDGUNS

SPANISH HANDGUNS

Great Outdoor Books Since 1925

STOEGER PUBLISHING COMPANY
is a division of Benelli U.S.A.

Benelli U.S.A.
Vice President and General Manager: Stephen Otway
Director of Brand Marketing and Communications:
   Stephen McKelvain
Vice President of Sales/Strategic Marketing: Jack Muety

Stoeger Publishing Company
President: Jeffrey K. Reh
Publisher: Jay Langston
Art Director: Cynthia T. Richardson
Copy Editor: Kate Baird

Cover Photography: Ray and Matt Wells

© 2002 by Stoeger Publishing Company. All rights reserved.

No part of this book may be reproduced or transmitted in any form or by any means, electronic or mechanical, including photocopying, recording, or by any information storage and retrieval system, without permission in writing from the Publisher.

Published by:
Stoeger Publishing Company
17603 Indian Head HIghway, Suite 200
Accokeek, Maryland 20607-2501

ISBN:0-88317-243-7   BK6473
Library of Congress Control Number: 2002105785

Manufactured in the United States of America

Distributed to the book trade and the sporting goods trade by:
Stoeger Industries, Stoeger Publishing Company
17603 Indian Head HIghway, Suite 200
Accokeek, Maryland 20607-2501
301 283-6300   Fax: 301 283-6986

Note: Every effort has been made to record specifications and descriptions of guns, ammunition and accessories accurately, but the Publisher can take no responsibility for errors or omissions. The prices shown for guns, ammunition and accessories are manufacturers' suggested retail prices (unless otherwise noted) and are furnished for information only. These were in effect at press time and are subject to change without notice. Purchasers of the book have complete freedom of choice in pricing for resale.

Front Cover: This year's front cover features three high-quality guns: the Benelli Super Black Eagle 12 gauge 3 1/2-inch magnum dressed in Advantage High Definition camouflage; a Para-Ordnance .45 Auto single-stack Light Double Action (LDA); and a Sako Safari 80th Anniversary Model 75 chambered in .375 H&H. This limited-edition rifle includes a Swarovski PV-1 1.25-4 x 24 scope and retails for $15,960.

OTHER PUBLICATIONS:

Gun Trader's Guide – 25th Edition
"Complete Fully Illustrated Guide to Modern Firearms with Current Market Values"

Hunting & Shooting
Hounds of the World
The Turkey Hunter's Tool Kit: Shooting Savvy
Complete Book of Whitetail Hunting
Hunting and Shooting with the Modern Bow
The Ultimate in Rifle Accuracy
Advanced Black Powder Hunting
Labrador Retrievers
Hunting America's Wild Turkey
Taxidermy Guide
Cowboy Action Shooting
Great Shooters of the World

Collecting Books
Sporting Collectibles
The Working Folding Knife
The Lore of Spices

Firearms
Antique Guns
P-38 Automatic Pistol
The Walther Handgun Story
Complete Guide to Compact Handguns
Complete Guide to Service Handguns
America's Great Gunmakers
Firearms Disassembly with Exploded Views
Rifle Guide
Gunsmithing at Home
The Book of the Twenty-Two
Complete Guide to Modern Rifles
Complete Guide to Classic Rifles
Legendary Sporting Rifles
FN Browning Armorer to the World
Modern Beretta Firearms
How to Buy & Sell Used Guns
Heckler & Koch: Armorers of the Free World
Spanish Handguns

Reloading
The Handloader's Manual of Cartridge
   Conversions
Modern Sporting Rifles Cartridges
Complete Reloading Guide

Fishing
Ultimate Bass Boats
The Flytier's Companion
Deceiving Trout
The Complete Book of Trout Fishing
The Complete Book of Flyfishing
Peter Dean's Guide to Fly-Tying
The Flytier's Manual
Flytier's Master Class
Handbook of Fly Tying
The Fly Fisherman's Entomological Pattern Book
Fiberglass Rod Making
To Rise a Trout

Motorcycles & Trucks
The Legend of Harley-Davidson
The Legend of Indian
Best of Harley-Davidson
Classic Bikes
Great Trucks
4X4 Vehicles

Cooking Game
Fish & Shellfish Care & Cookery
Game Cookbook
Dress 'Em Out
Wild About Venison

CONTENTS

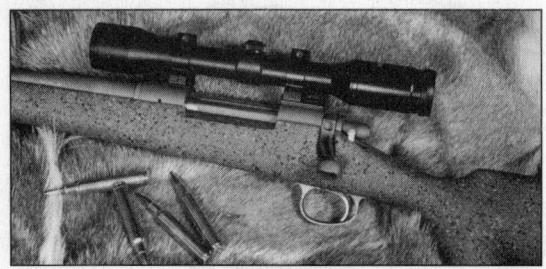

FOREWORD	**6**
FEATURE ARTICLES	**7**
WHAT WOULD JACK THINK?	8
THE NORMA STORY	18
ACCESS THROUGH TECHNOLOGY—MODERN TOOLS	24
MAUSER'S REMARKABLE "BROOMHANDLE" PISTOL	30
HEARING LOSS	36
NO SWAN SONG FOR THE 16	42
SHOPPING FOR A STACKBARREL	48
HUNTING WITH REMINGTON'S NEW SHORT ACTION ULTRA MAG	54
THE SABOTED MUZZLE-LOADED HUNTING PROJECTILE	60
ONE CARTRIDGE, MANY BULLETS	68
MANUFACTURER'S SHOWCASE	**42**
FIREARMS SPECIFICATIONS	**48**
CUSTOM GUNMAKERS	80
RIFLES	111
SHOTGUNS	221
HANDGUNS	278
BLACK POWDER	351
SIGHTS & SCOPES	391
AMMUNITION	449
BALLISTICS	467
RELOADING	505
REFERENCE	**560**
DIRECTORY OF MANUFACTURERS & SUPPLIERS	561
GUNFINDER INDEX	572

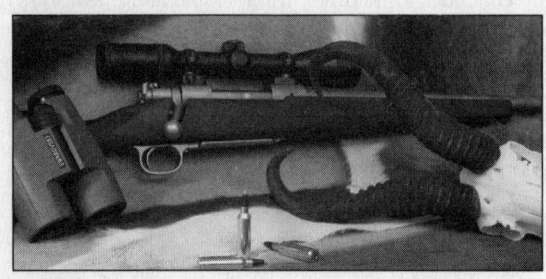

FOREWORD

Feature Articles Editor

A good old-fashioned American tradition continues with the 94th Edition of the Shooter's Bible. I find it interesting to see how some things come full circle.

I didn't have a clue at the time, but thinking back, I can remember the day Jerry Wood's father came home with a copy of the "Shooter's Bible." My best friend and I became unlettered gun scribes, spending hours memorizing the text and photos while sitting at Mrs. Wood's kitchen table. The day I hocked a mint condition Bobby Bonds rookie card so Jerry would lend me his "Shooter's Bible," I felt like I got the better end of the deal. Picture, if you will, an 11-year-old with one of Mrs. Wood's liberated pillowcases tied to the handlebars of his bike, peddling toward home with that near-sacred cargo of the 1973 edition of the "Shooter's Bible."

My passion for guns, shooting and hunting burns just as brightly today as it did for that pre-adolescent boy. As the new publisher for Stoeger Publishing, and Editor of "Shooter's Bible," I am proud to present this latest edition of the shooter's most popular gun book.

A milestone has been eclipsed with the printing of this edition of "Shooter's Bible." Today, more than 4 million copies have been printed in its 78-year history.

In this Edition

In addition to the ever-popular technical section compiled and edited by famous gun writer Wayne van Zwoll, a wide range of topics are covered in the feature section.

Noted writer Bryce Towsley leads off with the question, "What Would Jack Think?" This feature explores what legendary gun scribe Jack O'Connor would have thought about the new .270 Winchester Short Magnum.

Technical Editor Wayne van Zwoll has two features in this edition. "The Norma Story" takes an in-depth look at the people behind the success of Norma Ammunition. His other article is a buyer's guided to purchasing an over-and-under shotgun. Take a look at "Shopping for a Stack Barrel" to help decide which model fits your needs.

Outdoor Life Magazine Hunting Editor Jim Zumbo shares his experience with the latest from Remington, the Short Action Ultra Mags.

Author of several Stoeger books, Gene Gangarosa, takes a step back in history with his feature on Broomhandle Mausers.

Muzzleloading expert Toby Bridges shares his vast knowledge of cutting edge technology for front-stuffers. His latest findings will help you decide which projectile will fit your black powder hunting needs.

Check out these features and more to get an insider's look at the gun industry today.

Shoot straight,

Jay Langston, Publisher
Stoeger Publishing Company

Specifications Editor

Stoeger Publishing has a new owner, but we who catalog shooting gear for Shooter's Bible are still aboard, committed to making each book the best yet! Improvements include ballistics tables for handguns with the readable format introduced in our rifle section last year. There's up-to-date information here on rifles chambered for the short magnum cartridges from Winchester and Remington: two .300s, a .270 and a 7mm. Modern bolt rifles share century-old technology with the Mauser 98, but new chamberings listed here make them more effective. Savage now chambers Lazzeroni short magnums in its affordable 110.

In Shooter's Bible 2003 you'll see the two trends in rifles. One, defined by slim lines and lighter weight, is popular where hiking gets more attention than shooting. The other drift is to heavy rifles for hitting at long range. Then there's the Cowboy Action game, requiring rifles (and handguns and shotguns) of 19th-century design. Marlin dominates in this arena – and this year has dropped the porting on its popular Guide and Outfitter carbines. Ye whose ears still ring, rejoice! Pistol shooters will find new guns and loads here for the potent .480 Ruger and .454 Casull. Autoloaders on the timeless M1911 Colt frame continue to sell. Ace pistolsmiths like Jim Clark Jr. make them shoot better (find him in our expanded custom section).

With a boldness bred of experience, Weatherby has announced affordable side-by-side shotguns, and Ruger an American-built Gold Label double. Not that over/unders are dead. Browning's Lightning Feather (alloy receiver with steel hinge) delivers strength in a cat-quick package. Remington has improved the 300 Ideal, recontouring the stock to mimic the company's famous Model 32. The 332 looks and feels like the over/under you've always wanted. Remington has also re-introduced the 16-bore 870 – my first shotgun when Shooter's Bible listed the price at under $100.

Hornady continues to innovate in the ammunition field, now with loads for the .405 Winchester and .458 Lott. The .444 Marlin gets more muscle. Then there's the .17 HMR, probably the biggest news in ammodom for 2003. Its tiny 17-grain bullet at 2550 fps has delivered half-minute accuracy from test rifles. Muzzleloaders are now weatherproof rifles, with 200-yard reach and super-charged ignition. To help you see better what you're shooting, Leupold has introduced two lines of scopes to straddle its defunct Vari-X II. The VX-1 is essentially the Vari-X II – in 2-7x, 3-9x or 4-12x only. Many more models of VX-2 are cataloged, each with Multi-Coat 4 lens coatings and click adjustments. Burris and Nikon have new 6x scopes, Sightron a 12x, Bushnell a 10x. Zeiss and Kahles offer new variable scopes for 2003.

As usual, you'll find the latest in loading equipment in these pages, from Redding, RCBS, Lyman and other prestigious names. Components are here too: hunting bullets from Barnes, Hornady, Nosler, Speer and Sierra, Berger, Swift and Woodleigh - with powders from Accurate, Alliant, Hodgdon, IMR and Ramshot. So if you want to know more about shooting equipment, you've come to the right place. We hope you enjoy reading Shooter's Bible 2003 as much as we've enjoyed putting it together.

Wayne Van Zwoll,
Specifications Editor

FEATURE ARTICLES

WHAT WOULD JACK THINK? BY BRYCE M. TOWSLEY	8
THE NORMA STORY BY WAYNE VAN ZWOLL	18
ACCESS THROUGH TECHNOLOGY— MODERN TOOLS BY JAMES POWELL, NWTF	24

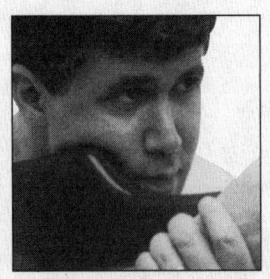

MAUSER'S REMARKABLE "BROOMHANDLE" PISTOL BY GENE GANGAROSA, JR.	30
HEARING LOSS BY PHIL W. JOHNSON	36
NO SWAN SONG FOR THE 16 BY STAN WARREN	42

SHOPPING FOR A STACKBARREL BY WAYNE VAN ZWOLL	48
HUNTING WITH REMINGTON'S NEW SHORT ACTION ULTRA MAG BY JIM ZUMBO	54

THE SABOTED MUZZLE-LOADED HUNTING PROJECTILE BY TOBY BRIDGES	60
ONE CARTRIDGE, MANY BULLETS BY SAM FADALA	68

What Would Jack Think?
by Bryce M. Towsley

Jack O'Connor, the former Shooting Editor of *Outdoor Life Magazine*, in his later years.

In 1925, Winchester introduced a new bolt-action rifle called the Model 54. At the same time, they also introduced a new cartridge, the .270 Winchester. The first generation of hunters conditioned to small-bore, high-velocity cartridges was just coming of age and the timing couldn't have been better. While their fathers and grandfathers had used big-bore, black powder guns, these Young Turks used smokeless powder and small bullets that hid the secret of their power deep in the magic of high velocity. These new-fangled cartridges had changed the world of hunting. Now Winchester smashed yet another barrier with their new cartridge. With a 130-grain bullet exiting the muzzle at an unheard of 3,100 ft/s, the .270 Winchester was a wonder to behold.

A few years later, a youthful Irishman from Arizona graduated from college and was soon making his name as a writer. Jack O'Connor was a hunter before he was a writer, so he wrote about hunting. He also took a shine to the .270 Winchester. In 1939 O'Connor started his long association with Outdoor Life Magazine, where he soon rose to national prominence. There were very few outdoor or gun writers back then, and only a small handful of magazines to publish their work. Outdoor Life was a giant and the influence that O'Connor would wield as their shooting editor was immense. If he liked the .270 Winchester, then by God, America would damn well like the .270 Winchester too. And they did.

Why Winchester chose the .270 bullet diameter is a bit of a mystery. No other cartridge had been introduced in that size, and in the years since, only the .270

A collection of O'Connor books and other publications.

Weatherby has joined the Winchester with any sort of commercial success. Weatherby's first cartridge is a good one, but it has always been outshone by its younger sibling, the .300 Weatherby Magnum. In terms of mainstream popularity, the .270 Winchester has stood alone. Conventional thinking says that without Jack O'Connor to sing its praises, the .270 Winchester would probably have been relegated to the junk heap of obsolescence along with so many other great rifle cartridges.

But, as any shooter knows, the .270 Winchester never looked back and is currently one of the most popular rifle cartridges on the market, a position it's held for a very long time. In a survey a few years ago of ammo and reloading die sales for rifle cartridges, the .270 Winchester came in third. Only the .30-06 Springfield and the .223 Remington sold more. Unquestionably, it owes much of that popularity to Mr. O'Connor.

Now, 77 years later, Winchester is introducing its second .270 rifle cartridge, the .270 Winchester Short Magnum. The obvious question begging to be asked about this .270 for the new millennium is, "What would Jack think?"

Truth is, I don't really know. At least not for sure. I never met the man and I can tell you from long experience that people who think they know a writer from reading his work are actually clueless. Most of the gun writers I know in "real life" are not much like the personalities they project in their words. Writing is a very personal thing if it's to be done well. And while it might reflect the core of a man, the shields he builds to protect himself almost always mask something of his true personality. From all the stories I have heard from men who knew him well, this was the case with O'Connor. However, he was a very experienced worldwide hunter and a knowledgeable gun guy. He had a talent for expressing himself and strong opinions about what to say. I have read a lot of his work and I think I can make an educated guess.

A clue might be found in writer Jim Casada's answer when I put the question to him. Jim is an historian with a passion for sporting writers. He has studied O'Connor and the first thing he said to me was, "He would have hated it!"

"Why," I asked.

"Because he was too much of a traditionalist."

"Yes," I argued, "But he was also a man who recognized quality and performance. When he first used the .270 Winchester it too was a radical new cartridge, a departure from the tradition. But, he recognized how good it really was and went on to become its biggest cheerleader."

Jim and I then talked about the new .270 WSM, and I told him how I thought it was a modern day version of the old .270 and how the performance in the perspective of today mirrored that of the .270 Winchester in O'Connor's time.

"Well then by golly, when we look at it that way, I think he would have liked it," Jim chuckled. "One thing about O'Connor and the .270 Winchester is that he shot the fool out of it and decided it worked.

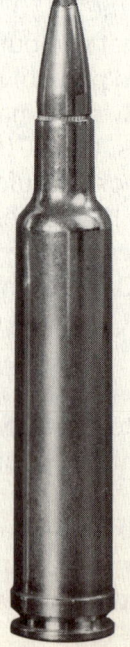

Left to Right:
.270 Winchester, .270 Winchester Short Magnum & .270 Weatherby Magnum.

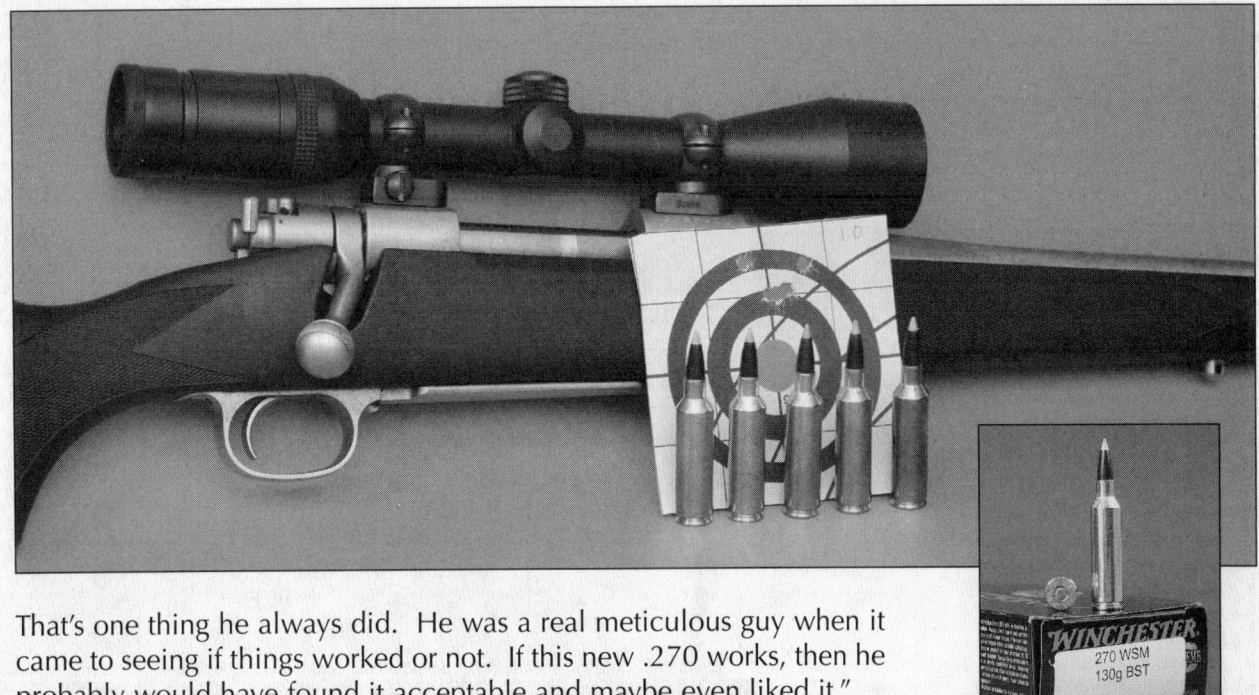

That's one thing he always did. He was a real meticulous guy when it came to seeing if things worked or not. If this new .270 works, then he probably would have found it acceptable and maybe even liked it."

I have to agree. I think O'Connor would have tried this cartridge and deemed it "a keeper."

In many ways the .270 Winchester was the "super magnum" of its day. It was a fire breathing, screaming-fast, trendsetter in 1925. It was accurate with good bullets, it shot extremely flat and it killed game like lightning reached out from the sky to smite them down. But, today's new cartridges have passed it by ballistically. While I don't think O'Connor would have liked some of the cavernous "super magnums" with the case capacity of a town water tower, I believe he would have

Winchester Model 70 S/S in .270 WSM. Kahles scope blue. Five cartridges and 100-yard target showing 1-inch five shot group.

Inset:
.270 WSM Winchester Short Magnum

Center is Nathan Towsley (age 12) with a 14-1/2 inch antelope taken in S-E Montana October 7, 2001. On left is Pat West, his guide, and on right is Nathan's sister, Erin (age 15). This is the first antelope ever taken with the .270 Winchester Short Magnum cartridge.

Winchester's Supercharged 270 WSM

Winchester Ammunition Public Relations man Kevin Howard scored on this whitetail on a South Texas hunt with one of the new Winchester Short Magnum cartridges.

On the heels of one of the most successful new rifle cartridge introductions in recent years, the 300 Winchester Short Magnum, Winchester Ammunition, in cooperation with Browning, and U.S. Repeating Arms Company, is adding the .270 caliber to the WSM line. The new 270 Winchester Short Magnum, or .270 WSM, takes this popular caliber to new heights.

The .270 WSM is based on the original 300 WSM case. This case was developed by Winchester and Browning. The short, fat, beltless case has already become a hit with shooters and reloaders looking for ultimate accuracy and superior velocities, all with lower felt recoil. Like the 300 WSM, the 270 WSM provides precise head spacing on the shoulder and reliable feeding in the short action rifles for which it was designed.

Initial offerings from Winchester include a 130 grain Ballistic Silvertip bullet and a 140 grain Fail Safe bullet, both in the Supreme line of rifle cartridges. A 150 grain Power-Point bullet is offered in the Super-X line.

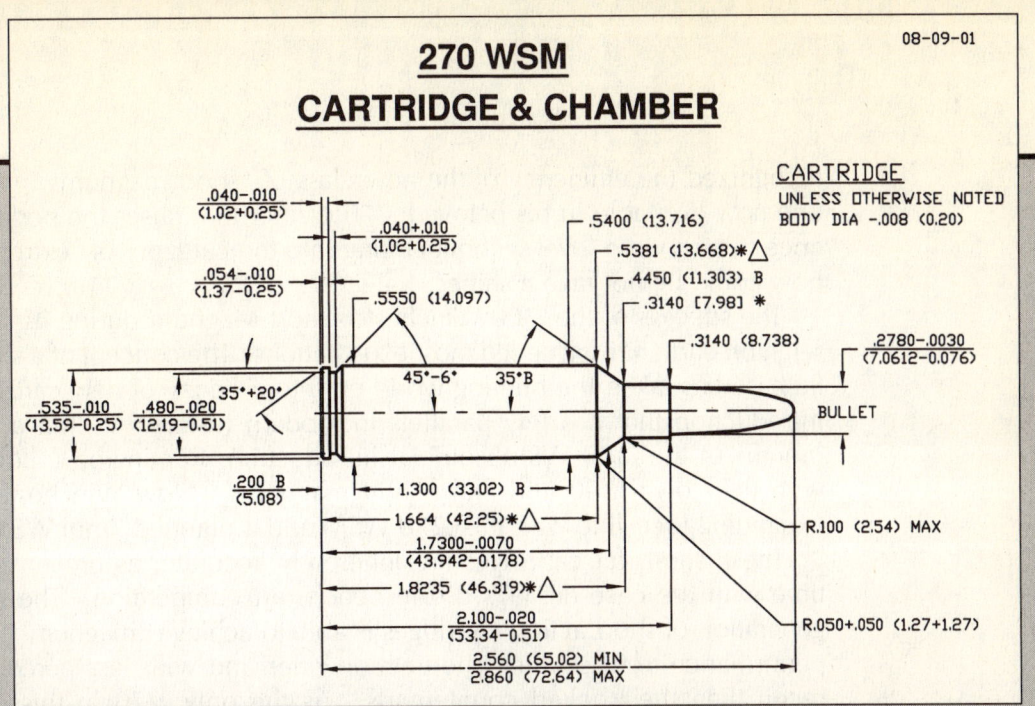

.270 WSM LOAD	VELOCITY IN FEET PER SECOND (FPS)					
	MUZZLE	100	200	300	400	500
SUPREME 130-GRAIN BALLISTIC SILVERTIP	3275	3041	2820	2609	2408	2215
SUPREME 140-GRAIN FAIL SAFE	3125	2865	2619	2386	2165	1956
SUPER-X 150-GRAIN POWER-POINT	3150	2867	2601	2350	2113	1890
.270 WSM LOAD	ENERGY IN FOOT POUNDS (FT-LBS)					
	MUZZLE	100	200	300	400	500
SUPREME 130-GRAIN BALLISTIC SILVERTIP	3096	2669	2295	1964	1673	1416
SUPREME 140-GRAIN FAIL SAFE	3035	2550	2132	1769	1457	1189
SUPER-X 150-GRAIN POWER-POINT	3304	2737	2252	1839	1487	1190
.270 WSM LOAD	TRAJECTORY, LONG RANGE YARDS					
	100	150	200	300	400	500
SUPREME 130-GRAIN BALLISTIC SILVERTIP	1.1	1.1	0	-5.5	-16.1	-32.8
SUPREME 140-GRAIN FAIL SAFE	1.4	1.3	0	-6.5	-19.0	-39.1
SUPER-X 150-GRAIN POWER-POINT	1.4	1.3	0	-6.5	-19.4	-40.1

recognized the efficiency of the new class of "short magnums." With one now available in his beloved .270 caliber that raises the performance to a modern level without edging into the category of "extreme," how could he not take a shine?

The success of the .300 Winchester Short Magnum during its short reign on earth has exceeded most expectations. The concept of a short-fat case has taken the hunting world up into a frenzy of new cartridge introduction that has few parallels in modern history. Within a few months of the .300 WSM's official introduction, Remington followed with their own .300 and 7mm short magnums. Now Winchester is expanding their line with this .270 WSM and a planned 7mm WSM.

These short, fat cartridges are inherently accurate, as proven over time with the case design's use in bench rest competition. The new generation of short action cartridges is able to achieve "magnum" type performance from smaller, short-action rifles and with less perceived recoil then their belted counterparts. As the only .270 in this new "class," the .270 WSM sets a new standard for performance.

The .270 Winchester Short Magnum doesn't stray far from its parent case. The case is 2.100-inches long and has an overall cartridge length of 2.860-inches. The case body at the head is .555-inch diameter and

Bryce M. Towsley shooting Winchester Model 70 S/S in .270 WSM. Kahles scope.

tapers to .540-inch behind the shoulder, so its body is very straight. The case has a rebated .535-inch rim diameter that fits a standard magnum size bolt face and a shoulder angle of 35 degrees. Of course, there is no belt, so the case headspaces off the shoulder. Like almost all of the new magnum cartridges, the .270 WSM is loaded to 65,000 psi Maximum Average Pressure (MAP), the limit currently allowed by SAAMI standards.

The Winchester short magnum line up. Left to right: .270 WSM, 7mm WSM & .300 WSM.

The .270 Winchester Short Magnum (WSM) will be initially offered in three different factory loads. A 130-grain Ballistic Silvertip Supreme with a muzzle velocity (MV) of 3,275 ft/s. A 140-grain Fail Safe Supreme with a MV of 3,125 ft/s and a Super-X 150-grain Power Point at 3,150 ft/s. Browning and Winchester (USRAC) will offer the cartridge in a wide selection of short action rifles.

While the .270 Winchester factory load has a 130-grain bullet with a muzzle velocity of 3,050 ft/s, the new .270 WSM launches the same bullet 225 ft/s faster. That's a 14% increase in energy and a 15% decrease in bullet drop. While the .270 Winchester has 2,686 ft-lbs of

Winchester Model 70 S/S in .270 WSM with Kahles scope.

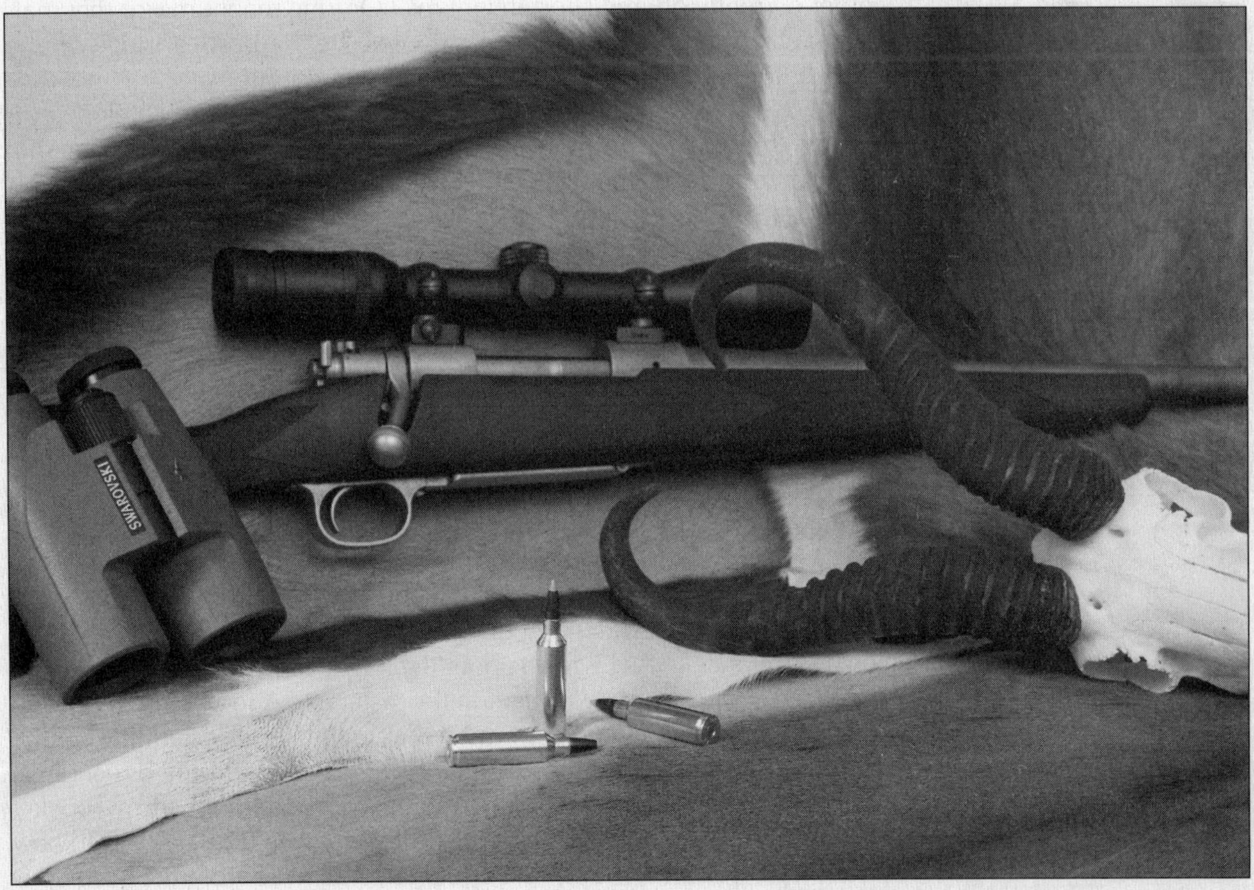

Features Articles • 15

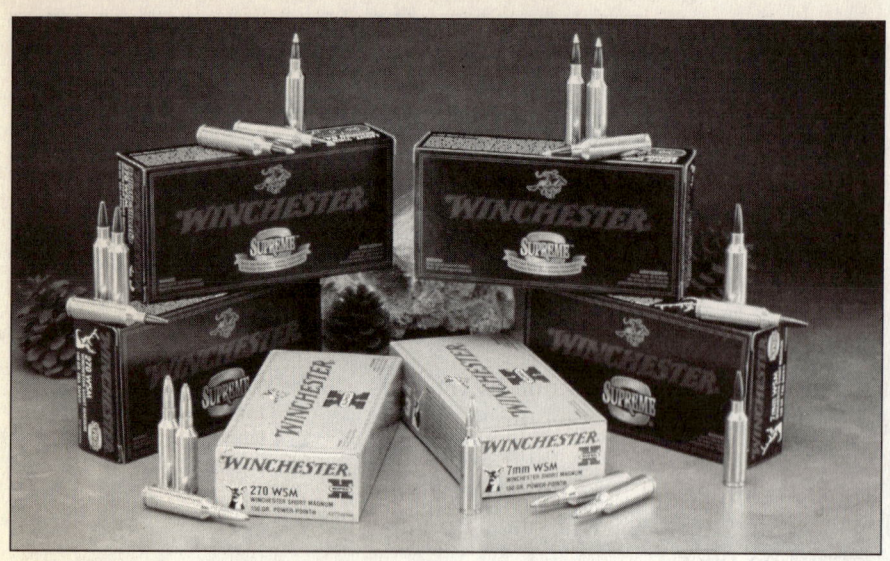

.270 WSM & 7mm Winchester Short Magnums.

energy at the muzzle, the .270 WSM has 3,097 ft-lbs, a jump of 23% in bullet energy.

With a 200 yard zero, the .270 Winchester is 6.51 inches low at 300 yards. With the same zero and bullet, the .270 WSM is 5.51 inches low at 300 yards. With a six-inch target zone the maximum point blank range, that is, the distance where the bullet will not go above or below the line of sight by more than three inches, is 298 yards for the .270 Winchester and 319 yards for the .270 WSM.

What it all means is that the .270 WSM is one of the flattest shooting big game cartridges around. It is certainly the flattest shooting of the new short magnums. It also produces less recoil than any of the other currently offered short magnums. Or long magnums for that matter. In that light, the .270 WSM may well be the best cartridge on the market for hunting deer or antelope in open country.

My twelve-year-old son Nathan took the first pronghorn antelope ever shot with the .270 WSM in early October, 2001. It was a longer shot through more Montana wind than I would have liked, but that's what this cartridge was born to do. The stalk was hours old already and we could get no closer, so I gave the green light to shoot. Nathan tickled the Model 70's trigger and created his own small piece of hunting history.

A couple of months later, I was able to use the .270 WSM on the famed King Ranch in south Texas. A couple of deer, some coyotes and a javelina later I put it back in its case knowing I had witnessed the birth of a great hunting cartridge. On that trip the .270 WSM accounted for around twenty big game animals for our group, including some big and tough feral hogs. At the end it had gained the universal approval from that gathering of experienced big game hunters.

On the last morning of our trip, I found myself with all my big game tags filled. So, an hour into daylight I was sitting in the coastal grasslands wedged underneath a tipped over oak tree and singing the blues on a varmint call. As I wailed about the tragedy of a rabbit dying young, I noticed a pair of pointy ears off in the distance. A look through the ten power Kahles binoculars confirmed that a coyote was standing on the far edge of a large opening and staring suspiciously in my direction. I should have checked the distance with the rangefinder in my pocket before starting to call, but I didn't and then it was too late. All I knew was that it was a very long shot and a coyote's head from the nose up is

Veteran gun scribe John Wooters put the .270 Winchester Short Magnum through its paces on a South Texas hunt last fall.

a very small target. When the .270 WSM made its music, the 140-grain Fail Safe bullet struck exactly between his eyes. I suppose a lot of cartridges could have done as well, but none could have done it better.

The concept of a high performance, flat shooting, big game cartridge in a compact and accurate short action rifle is, of course, well suited for almost any of today's big game hunting from elk to black bears. But this cartridge might well appear to be the perfect design for hunting the thin-air mountains that are home to wild sheep. If Jack O'Connor is remembered best for his love affair with the .270 Winchester, a close second was his love for sheep hunting. Time will of course prove the truth, but this new Winchester .270 may well also be the best sheep-hunting cartridge ever put in a rifle. To think that would have been lost on a man like Jack O'Connor is a foolish thought.

The Norma Story
by Wayne Van Zwoll

Norma was founded in 1895; the current factory in Amotfors, Sweden dates to 1967.

Norma's corporate offices are unpretentious. Efficiency matters almost as much as product excellence. Note the American flag. About a quarter of Norma's production is exported to the U.S.

You'd think that a firm founded in 1895 would have long since become uninteresting. Norma, a centenarian ammunition firm, remains enigmatic. Not many shooters, for example, know that the name derives from an opera by Bellini.

"We work hard to stay ahead of predictions," chuckles Torbjorn Lindskog, the firm's CEO. He likes to quote famous military leaders – and follow their example. "You can't adopt circumstance to plan, but you can adopt plan to circumstance. That's from George Patton. We've tried to keep Norma nimble, to succeed in changing markets."

Change has marked both the industry and the company. Norma started making ammo shortly after the debut of smokeless powder. In 1902 the firm had one employee tending two machines in a small shop in Amotfors, a tranquil community surrounded by forests and lakes. Sweden's Varmland region has since blossomed, but it retains a bucolic innocence. Norma is still in Amotfors.

By 1906, the union binding Norway and Sweden had collapsed. Norway's bonanza in offshore oil was still decades from discovery; the country had little wealth. Sweden, on the other hand, became a center of industry. In 1911 Norma built a new ammunition factory. Over the next decades the firm prospered, its fortunes enhanced by World War II. In 1940 the company added 10 buildings, and by 1942 its workforce had grown to 800. "Nils Kavle, a retired military man from Norway, was marketing director then," recalls Torb. "He took full advantage of the temporary demand for munitions; but it wasn't until 1950 that Norma started exporting hunting ammo."

Expansion continued thereafter, and by 1965, Norma had 420 employees on the payroll. Annual production exceeded 40 million cartridges. Two years later 530 people were at work, rolling out 64 million rounds. In 1975 Hasselfors Burks AB bought Norma. Within four years the company changed hands again to become a subsidiary of FFV. In 1990 Dynamit Nobel AG bought the firm. Production scaled back. By the mid 1990s, Norma was down to 175 employees. But automation yielded more product per worker. The company grew leaner still. By the year 2000, 135 Norma workers were cranking out 25

The Making of Norma Ammunition

million cartridges, plus the same numbers of bullets and cases. Gross revenue totaled 134 million Swedish Crowns.

Now Norma controls 70 percent of the ammunition market in Scandinavia, excluding Finland. It also owns 30 percent of the European market, mainly Germany, France and Spain. About 25 percent of the annual production stays in Sweden; another 25 percent goes to the U.S. Just over half is hunting ammo; 17 percent goes to target shooters. The company offers 70 centerfire cartridges (and 275 loads), from .223 to .470 Nitro Express. "Two percent of Norma production is rimfire," says Torb. "The remainder of civilian munitions is OEM." The acronym? Original Equipment Manufacturer, according to Paul Coil, Nosler's liason with Norma. Paul accompanied me to the Norma plant last year.

We met some of Norma's staff in the Norwegian highlands, where they'd come to hunt reindeer. These animals are more like Barren Ground caribou than the harnessed reindeer we envision. They're as big as caribou in body and antler and seemed to me more wary. One look at a hunter – no matter how far away – and they run off!

Paul and I, and Alan Corzine, formerly a ballistician with Winchester, had the privilege of hunting with Torb and two other Norma people: Karl-Erik Backman, in charge of quality assurance, and Kenneth Skoglund, area sales manager. Both had worked a long time at Norma (Karl-Erik 25 years, Kenneth 29). "My job is to make sure Norma ammunition is uniformly perfect," said Karl-Erik. "I also work with CIP, the equivalent of SAAMI in the U.S." Founded in 1916 in Belgium to regulate rifle manufacture, it's the organization that sets pressure levels for ammo produced in member countries. "Sweden is not a member," Karl-Erik explained. "But we must have CIP approval to export to member countries." He said that Weatherby specifies its own pressure ceilings. As most shooters know, Norma has loaded Weatherby ammunition for decades. The hotrod performance of those cartridges is due partly to their design, but also to the high pressure ceilings made possible by the Mark V Weatherby action. "Of course, cartridges that might be used in old military rifles can't be loaded so ambitiously." Karl-Erik noted that case life figures into established pressure limits. "We think a case should last 10 reloadings."

1. A roll of brass awaits the punch press at the Norma factory, Amotfors, Sweden.
2. Norma buys some if its brass in disc form. Three draws later, the discs become belted magnum cases.
3. Following two preliminary draws, the cups are annealed before a third. Despite tight quality control, rejection rate hovers at a low 3 percent.
4. Polished cases tumble into a bin prior to boxing. Norma ships 39 million cases a year.

The loading room features a variety of sophisticated and dated (but still useful!) machines. Powder is stored above, for safety.

Below: Primers come from a number of sources, including Federal. Weatherby ammo features Hirtenbergers.

Below Right: No pulling targets here! The group appears on-screen instantly at Norma's test range.

Rifles can influence pressures. "In the mid 1990s, some 7mm Remington Magnum rifles with 3-degree throats showed signs of excess pressure, so we had to ease back on the loads," Karl-Eric recalled. He keeps tabs on how customers perceive Norma products, with cards that fill a huge file. "We have to be efficient," he pointed out. "My goals are 3 percent scrap for cases and bullets, 1 percent for cartridges." Norma uses Bofors powders, under the Norma labels of 200, 201, 203B, 204, MRP and MRP2. About 80 percent of primers used are RWS, with some Hirtenberger, some Federal. "The Federal 215 is especially good in big cases with slow powders," Karl-Eric noted. "Weatherby specifies the Hirtenberger 1204."

Like many Norma people, Kenneth is a keen shooter. Norwegian-born and still living in Norway a short drive from Amotfors, Kenneth was 15 years on his country's Olympic team in running boar events. He now competes with fellow Scandinavians in local "running moose" matches and was among the first shooters to try two post reticles to build in lead with standard-velocity rounds, rather than employ a single reticle with high-speed cartridges. He uses a Mauser M59 in 6.5x55 – the original smokeless round for the Swedish military. "For 300-meter shooting, I like a 130-grain VLD load at 800 meters per second (about 2600 fps). It bucks the wind better than most 7.62 (.308) bullets. For unknown distances from 150 to 600 meters, I prefer a 130-grain bullet at 900 m/sec." In that event, each of 20 shooters on the team fire six shots from five stations. "Some targets are shot prone, some kneeling," Kenneth explained. "You get 35 seconds for prone strings, 50 seconds for kneeling." Running moose matches are popular partly because they satisfy government requirements for practice. "To get a hunting license in Norway, you must fire at least 15 shots in training each year, then qualify with a five-shot group in a 25-centimeter circle (about 10 inches). Any position."

A Norma machinist before taking on his sales job, Kenneth grew up on a small farm, helping his father log with horses. He now owns 200 acres of forest, part of a 1250-acre hunting preserve managed for moose. Though he still favors the 6.5x55 for competition, and has good things to say about the .30-06, he has turned to the .338 Winchester Magnum for most of his big game hunting.

"The 6.5x55 remains our biggest

seller," he said. "It's a required round for rifle competition in Scandinavia, and the most popular hunting cartridge. But demand for it is waning. In 1975 we produced 11 million 6.5x55s for target shooting alone. Though we can make 75,000 cases per shift, our output now totals less than 4 million." As in the U.S., the shooting public is aging. "Our average customer is 58 years old."

Norma still produces 25 million rounds of target ammunition each year, twice as much as RWS or the Finnish company Lapua. Winchester, Remington and Federal each sell between 120 and 160 million rounds of target ammo.

"We like to think our competition cartridges are the best you can get," said Kenneth. "It's not that we have the most modern machines. In fact, much of our 6.5x55 match ammo comes off a 1928 machine that loads 210 rounds a minute. A lot of our hardware dates from between the world wars. It still produces top-notch ammo. Quality control is the key. We hew to close tolerances."

Quality translates to success on the range. At the CISM World Championships in Ankara, Turkey two years ago, Norma 6mm BR ammunition took 11 of the 12 top medals. Torb Lindskog would quote MacArthur: "There's no substitute for victory."

The care lavished on target ammo is not lost on hunting cartridges. Norma buys its raw material from the best sources – Diehl for brass and copper, Sala Bly and SM for lead – and its components from respected houses like RWS and Bofors, to assemble ammunition that's world-renowned for its uniformity. Norma has OEM contracts with 14 companies, including Dakota, Federal, Winchester, Weatherby, RWS, Blaser, Sako and Hirtenberger. Cor-bon too. At this writing, Remington and Lapua are expected to join the list. Even the Dutch Army buys its .338 Lapua sniper cartridges from Norma. Tactical .308 and .300 Winchester rounds also go abroad. In the research and development department, Christer Larsson is at work on new loads to serve both hunters and soldiers.

Norma limits its focus to rifle ammunition. "We still make 9mm and .32 pistol ammo for military contracts," says Torb. "But the

Top Left: **Weatherby's magnums owe much of their high-octane performance to Norma's loadings.**

Top Right: **The 6.5x55 is still Norma's biggest seller, but hunters, target shooters and tactical units also buy .308s in quantity. These are loaded with Nosler bullets.**

Above: **The .308 and .358 Norma Magnums appeared around 1960 but failed to win over American shooters soon to be blessed with the 7mm Remington and .300 Winchester Magnums.**

Remington's 6mm BR is almost identical to the Norma version, a stellar performer in European rifle competition. The Finnish company Lapua is one of Norma's chief competitors.

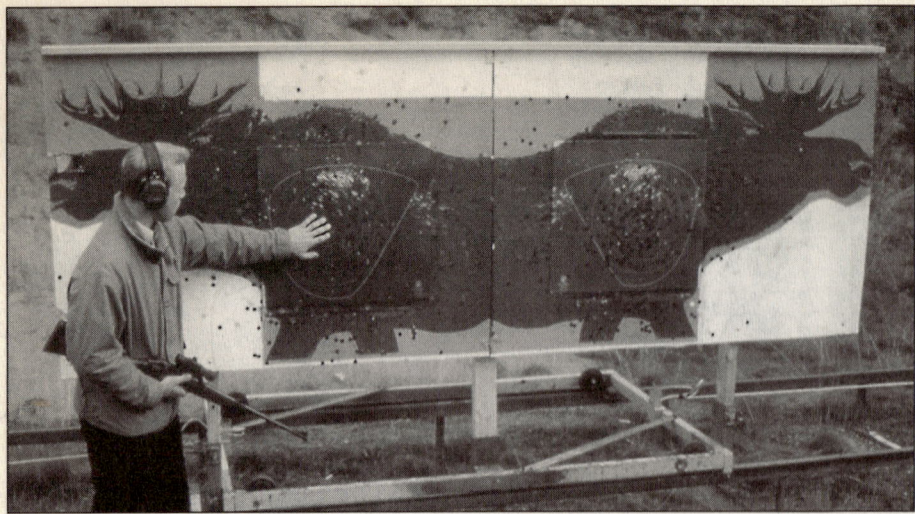

Running moose matches are popular in Scandinavia, where hunters qualify on targets like this.

Danes haul a moose from a Swedish forest. Moose hunting is very popular among Norma employees.

rest of our pistol line has been dropped." He tells me that some rifle rounds are quite difficult to manufacture: "The 7x57R, for example. But it sells well. A lot of Swedish hunters use it in drillings. Another rimmed case, the .303 British, is likewise costly to make, and its market isn't so big. But there are still many SMLE rifles floating around in countries that buy from us."

We visited the factory floors, spotless under a curious mix of wartime presses chugging smoothly in the shadow of boxy CNC machines. Norma buys cups from which to make most of its cartridges, but it imports discs for the magnums. "There are two draws after the initial cup," shouts Torb over the hum and clang of the machines. "Then we anneal the brass, draw it a third time, trim, pre-punch the primer pocket to ensure the strength of the head and send it to the header, which cuts an extractor groove. Necking comes next, then the flash-hole finishing." Some holes at Norma are punched, some drilled.

The factory was built in 1967 and includes a loading room with eight commercial machines, some of which have been in service since 1928. Together, the machines hold no more than 20 kg of powder – 44 pounds. Propellant storage is in the ceiling, with drop tubes running to the machines. "Lapua had a serious fire in 1977," explains my host. "We wanted to isolate the powder magazine from the workers. A fire here would be survivable."

Torb, a positive thinker and obviously delighted to be at the Norma helm, is optimistic about the business. "Retailers need ammunition more than they do rifles now," he says. "We're committed to long-term growth. Of course," – here he pauses to choose his words carefully – "what we do depends in large part on who owns Norma. Our most ambitious and profitable strategies can be scuttled by a parent firm on another mission." As for his goals, Torb wants to expand the OEM business, outsource the manufacture of pistol ammo to Finland (Lapua) or Germany (RWS), boost selection and sales of high-performance rounds, cement more cooperative agreements with U.S. bullet makers and embark on joint distribution ventures with industry giants. "I attack; I don't want to defend," he finishes, quoting Erwin Rommel. His target: $150 million in sales by 2003, and $25 in profits.

"Our fortunes depend on the world's economic climate," Torb concedes. "We're in the dream business. People want what we make, but very few customers need it. Our job is to keep the dream alive and keep Norma's name up front."

My last stop in Norma's plant: the gun vault, a huge underground room near the shooting tunnels, which boast the latest electronic ballistic equipment. Twenty firing points span 30-, 50- and two 100-yard ranges. Pelleted rubber aprons allow for bullet recovery. To measure penetration, Norma uses gelatin.

The gun vault is impressive. Not many munitions companies have a collection like this one! "We need at least one rifle for each chambering, of course," says Christer Larsson. But the wall racks hold more than 200 rifles, some of them in such condition as to make a collector salivate. Early Sakos, including the lever-action Finnwolf, stand beside Schultz and Larsens, Weatherbys, Brownings, Remingtons, Mausers, Winchesters and Savages – many of pre-1960 vintage. There are pumps and autoloaders and lever rifles as well as the bolt guns you expect in a test battery. Spotless Husqvarnas and Mannlicher-Schoenauers make me wish I'd allocated more time for this visit. Military weapons include broomhandle Mauser pistols and Thompson submachine guns, plus modern models in truly short supply these days, like a Navy M-16.

Norma remains an unusual company, a major munitions firm nestled in the forest and staffed by people of rural heritage. It draws its own brass but loads American rounds with American bullets for sale in America and gets a 20 percent subsidy from the Swedish government for capital investment. Norma's name is known to every shooting enthusiast Stateside, but few can tell you where to buy Norma products.

"That's a situation we hope to correct," says Marketing Director Lennart Falk, who has graciously driven us to and from our hotel. "The owners determine our distribution network and limit our outlets and the names under which we can put our brand. American shooters haven't been well served. Our products are the best you can buy – if you can find them. They're not as readily available as we'd like them to be."

Torb Skoglund adds, as I finish my interviews, that clearing the path of marketing roadblocks is a top priority. "We're committed to improving the flow of Norma products to the U.S. We can deliver." He sighs, thinking of things he won't tell me. "Chesty Puller once said that paperwork will ruin an army. He was right."

If Torb and his crew have their way, shipments of Norma ammunition and components will grow, giving American hunters and target shooters an expanding line of some of the world's best ammunition.

The author killed this fine reindeer at 80 yards with Norma's Oryx bullet from a Sako rifle in .30-06.

Suppliers for Norma products:

Black Hills Shooters Supply,
2875 South Creek Dr.,
Rapid City, SD 57703,
605-348-4477.

Graf & Sons, Inc., 2050
South Clark St.,
Mexico, MO 65265,
573-581-2266.

Huntington Dies Specialties,
601 Oro Dam Blvd.,
POB 991,
Oroville, CA 95965,
530-534-1212.

MidwayUSA,
5875 W. Van Horn Tavern Rd.,
Columbia, MO 65203,
573-445-6363.

NECO,
536-C Stone Rd.,
Benicia, CA 94510,
707-747-0897.

Sinclair International,
2330 Wayne Haven St.,
Ft. Wayne, IN 46803,
219-493-1858.

Widener's Reloading & Shooting Supply,
POB 3009 CRS,
Johnson City, TN 37602,
423-282-6786.

Access Through Technology—Modern Tools
by James Powell, NWTF

Disabled hunter Micheal Glaser with guide and deer during 2001 Wheelin' Sportsmen Ultimate Team Up.

Walking through the woods on the way to a hunting blind or food plot is something most hunters take for granted. In fact, for many hunters, getting there is half the fun. Hopping logs, crossing creeks and climbing hills are all obstacles a hunter typically encounters. Now imagine not being able to walk through the woods. Each obstacle that you previously overcame with relative ease now becomes a difficult, even overwhelming barrier to your hunt.

For a surprising number of hunters, especially disabled hunters that can't walk or otherwise get around on their own, that's exactly what they face each time they head afield on a hunting trip. The National Rehabilitation Association, the organization that tracks and compiles statistics on the disabled, estimates that there are over 50 million disabled people in the United States—thousands of which are or were hunters before becoming disabled—and their major obstacle to enjoying hunting and other forms of outdoor recreation is access.

Sound like a bleak outlook? It used to be. But today's disabled hunters now have an arsenal of equipment and technology at their disposal that allows them to get out and hunt, oftentimes right alongside able-bodied hunters. In fact, the number of disabled hunters heading to the woods each fall is increasing, thanks to modern technology and new opportunities provided by state and federal wildlife management agencies and hunter's organizations across the country.

Virtually every state in the country now offers special licenses and regulations to make hunting easier for disabled sportsmen. Mike Willis, Communications Director for the South Carolina Department of Natural Resources, says his state, like many others, works hard to provide hunting opportunities. "Currently, we have 26,387 disabled license holders in South Carolina, and I can only see that number increasing in the future. We're doing all we can to get the disabled involved in hunting and outdoor recreation. Providing opportunities and access is the best way to get disabled hunters involved."

Getting There

As the saying goes, "getting there is half the battle." That's where technology comes into play. Disabled hunters use the same rifles, shotguns, bows and even crossbows that able-bodied hunters use. What has changed is that disabled hunters now have unprecedented access to high-quality, specialized equipment to transport themselves, and their gear, to the hunt. A quick search of the Internet will bombard a disabled hunter with dozens, if not hundreds, of products ranging from hand-operated or motor-driven wheelchairs to full-blown ATVs and beyond.

Wheelin' Spotrsmen NWTF National Cordinator Kirk Thomas getting on Bombardier ATV from wheelchair.

Below: Kirk Thomas in wheelchair before camo cover and after with camo skirt covering wheelchair.

Many disabled sportsmen, like their able-bodied friends, have discovered the convenience and utility of ATVs. Kirk Thomas, National Coordinator for Wheelin' Sportsmen NWTF, the National Wild Turkey Federation's outreach program for disabled hunters—and would-be hunters—has become an expert on the subject through years of personal experience. "As a disabled hunter, I know how difficult moving around during a hunt can be. I've found that using an ATV is often the best way for me to hunt because I can travel and hunt out of the same vehicle. I have an ATV rigged up both as a transport and as a portable blind,

Disabled youth sighting in rifle.

and it allows me to hunt just as effectively as the next guy."

Other disabled hunters, like Thomas, are catching on to the practical uses of ATVs for hunting, fishing or doing chores around the house or deer lease. Many manufacturers, like Bombardier, maker of the Quest 500 4x4 and other models, have pushed the envelope of cutting edge technology in the industry, allowing almost any hunter access to places previously out of reach. Another Bombardier model, the Traxter XL, features a high-impact polyethylene rear box bed to store hunting gear, and a unique "step through" seat design that is especially helpful for disabled riders who can't step over a typical ATV's saddle-style seat. Models from other manufacturers such as Kawasaki, EZ-GO and John Deere also feature disabled-friendly seating and plenty of storage for guns, blinds, wheelchairs and other gear.

Another segment of the transport industry is specializing in taking wheelchair and power scooter technology to the next level. Already proven performers on city streets, wheelchairs and power scooters have been modified and adapted to life on the wild side. Wheelchairs with ultralight, ultratough frames and all-terrain balloon tires are now available. Models such as Colours 'N Motion's Tremor All-Terrain wheelchair or Natural Access's Landeez All-Terrain Beach Wheelchair can be used on challenging surfaces such as sand, gravel and snow, and can be easily outfitted and camouflaged for hunting or fishing.

Power scooters are another option for those who want a motorized vehicle in the woods, but can't or don't want to move up to a full-blown ATV. Magic Mobility offers the EXTREME 4x4, a four-wheel drive power wheelchair designed to tackle tough off-road conditions. With four motors, large all-terrain wheels and steering control and seating options to suit a variety of users and their special needs, the EXTREME 4x4 is a wheelchair in name only.

How does someone choose from so many styles and options? It depends on the hunter's disability, their personality and the type of hunting they'll be doing. On relatively level and firm terrain, where most travel will be on packed trails or dirt roads, many of the wheelchair models will suffice. But if an outing will include rough terrain, traveling long distances, hauling heavy gear or dealing with steep climbs or fallen rocks and logs, consider a motorized scooter or ATV. Remember, the idea is to enjoy the hunt.

Hide and Seek

Hunting is more than just getting to your favorite spot. Fortunately, disabled hunters have even more tools available once they arrive at their hunting destination. To be successful, a disabled hunter, like any other hunter, needs to stay hidden, quiet, comfortable and ready. Today's modern hunting gear, made with high-tech materials and innovative designs, evens the odds for disabled hunters.

Pop up blinds, like Ameristep's Outhouse are a good start and a snap to set up. With one hand, a hunter can throw it in the air where it pops open and takes shape in less than five seconds. The blind weighs only 8 pounds and is constructed of spring-steel and weather-resistant nylon, breaks down in about 10 seconds and has enough room inside for a wheelchair hunter and a partner. It's available in Ameristep Tangle or Mossy Oak Breakup camouflage patterns.

Wheelin' Sportsmen NWTF: Getting Involved

For great hunting tips and information for disabled hunters try the National Wild Turkey Federation's website (www.nwtf.net) where you'll find Wheelin' Sportsmen NWTF, an outreach program of the National Wild Turkey Federation dedicated to helping disabled people enjoy outdoor recreational opportunities. "To me, this is the greatest thing in the world," Bauer said. "There are two things I know in this world: hunting and being disabled. Wheelin' Sportsmen has been very rewarding to me. Getting people out in the woods hunting and fishing is where the magic of this program lies."

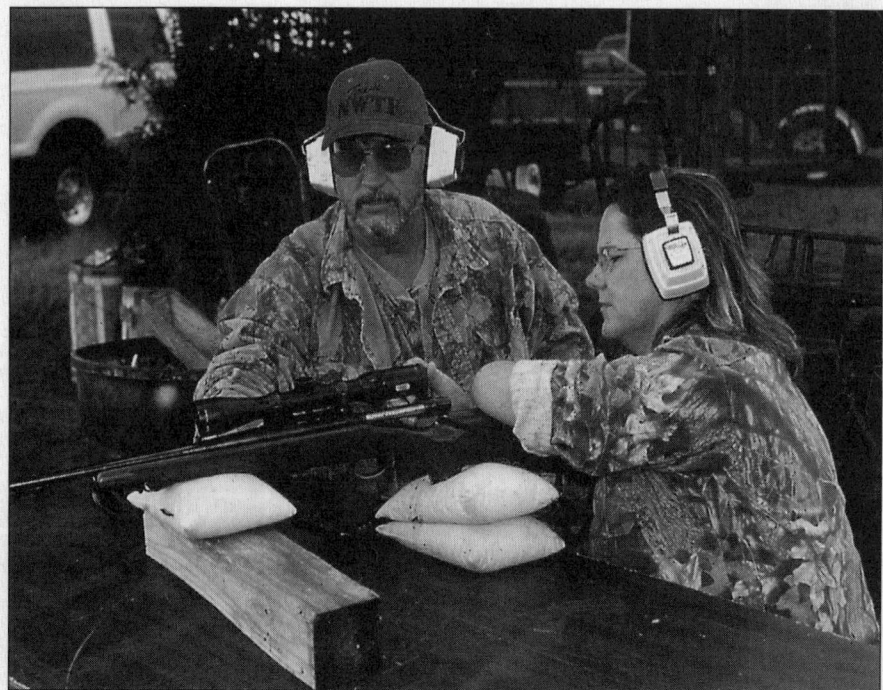

Young woman sighting in rifle at Wheelin' Sportsmen NWTF event.

Internet Resources for Disabled Hunters

There are some great resources for the disabled hunters looking to buy new equipment or share tips and information with others. For specialty equipment, try these websites:

- Access To Recreation www.accesstr.com – (product retailer website with some hard to find, useful products)
- Allegromedical.com www.allegromedical.com – (retailer specializing in wheelchairs, scooters, and other products for the disabled)
- Bombardier (www.bombardier-atv.com) – (ATV manufacturer that offers a wide range of models and features)
- Vestil Manufacturing (www.vestil.com) – (retail website for Vestil's Innovation in Motion products, including a link to their EXTREME 4x4.
- Ameristep, Inc. (www.ameristep.com) – (hunting products manufacturer offering a huge selection of hunting blinds and hunting accessories)
- Bass Pro Shops (www.basspro.com) – (Well-known hunting, fishing and outdoor recreation retailer offering a huge variety of products, and services, for hunters)
- Cabela's (www.cabelas.com) – (Another well-known hunting, fishing and outdoor recreation retailer with a complete line of products and services)

John Bauer, a dedicated turkey hunter who was left paralyzed from the waist down after a fall from a tree in 1981, hunts from a four-wheeler he camouflaged himself. "Every bird I've taken has been from a four wheeler," Bauer said. "You want it to look like a rolling brush pile—you do everything in your power to accomplish this. And when you ride to the store to get a soda in your ATV bush, people really give you some strange looks."

Modern technology is also helpful when it comes to hunting clothes. High-performance materials like polypropylene and Gore-Tex have made it easier, and safer, for disabled hunters to be out during bad weather. Many disabled hunters prefer synthetic materials because they wick moisture away from the skin and provide warmth without bulk. And innovations in camouflage clothing have made it easier for disabled hunters and their equipment to blend into the woods.

"I like to hunt in a blind or from my ATV, which I have camouflaged," said Thomas. "But there are times when I want to sneak into position with my wheelchair. I use a camouflage net suit I helped design that covers both me and my wheelchair."

Similar suits, which have real-looking cut leaf shapes and are sometimes called "Ghillie Suits" are available through companies like Bass Pro Shops and Cabela's. Make sure to order the biggest size available for the best coverage.

One of the biggest stumbling blocks for disabled hunters is finding specialized hunting and fishing equipment that actually works and will stand up to the abuse of the outdoors. In recent years, that alone was enough to keep disabled sportsmen out of the game. Not anymore. There are several companies out there that make or sell specialized products for disabled sportsmen and women.

The Internet is a great place to start. Many sites, including Access To Recreation (accesstr.com), feature special sections on fishing and hunting products for the disabled. Offerings include everything from specialized exercise equipment for pre-season workouts to trigger activators for firearms and all terrain wheelchairs.

"Our hunting and fishing products are some of our most popular items," said Don Krebs, a C-6 quadriplegic and president of Access to Recreation, Inc. "I can really tell by our sales when the fishing and hunting seasons rolls around."

One really useful item for hunters who use wheelchairs is Blackberry's Uni-Mount System, a mechanical arm that mounts to a wheelchair, tree stand, vehicle or almost anything else and holds a rifle or shotgun firmly in place for shooting or hunting.

Keeping in Touch

Some of the biggest technological innovations in recent history have come in the communications industry. As today's disabled hunters go deeper and deeper into the woods in pursuit of game, communicating with a partner or the outside world becomes more important. Handheld radios and cell phones make it easier to reach help if there's an emergency, and they can be great hunting tools when used with a partner. Affordable handheld units by Cobra, Motorola and others allow disabled hunters to stay in contact with an able-bodied partner hunting nearby.

Even able-bodied hunters have taken advantage of the ability to keep in touch with a partner in the woods. Karen Roop, editor of Wheelin' Sportsmen magazine, finds them handy in the woods. "I'm fairly new to bow hunting for deer, so having the ability to call a more experienced hunting partner on a handheld radio while I'm in the woods is really helpful."

A Low-Tech Tool

Even with all the modern advancements in equipment that a disabled hunter can take advantage of, having a good, old-fashioned hunting partner may be the best tool. John Bauer's hunting buddies were responsible for getting him back in the woods after his accident in 1981. "After the accident, I secluded myself from people, from hunting, from everything," said Bauer. Concerned for his well-being, Bauer's buddies were determined to get him back into the wild. "None of us knew what we were doing; we probably had no business being out there in the first place. But they came and took me hunting. I don't think I would have made it without them. Looking back, I can see how vital it was."

The Internet is one of the best ways to find a good hunting partner. It's opened up a whole new world to disabled hunters where they can exchange hunting tips and experiences on message boards, and can download the latest articles and information from websites like the NWTF's Wheelin' Sportsmen site (www.nwtf.org).

Today's disabled hunter has come a long way thanks to modern technology and equipment. Access is where it's at for disabled hunters, and modern transportation, communications and concealment technology—combined with a good, old fashioned hunting partner—has proven the right combination to put disabled hunters back in the woods.

Disabled hunter looks on as hunting partner sets up a pop-up blind.

Below: Disabled hunter and hunting partner/guide using pop-up blind to conceal themselves, wheelchair and other gear.

Features Articles • 29

Mauser's Remarkable "Broomhandle" Pistol
by Gene Gangarosa, Jr.

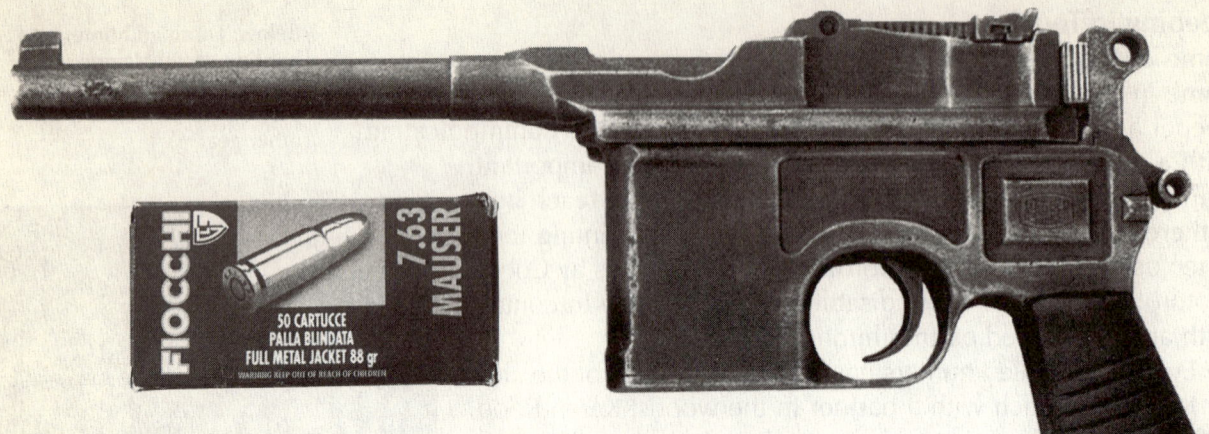

The Mauser Model 1896's left-side view shows its oddly-shaped grip which gives rise to the nickname "Broomhandle Mauser." This is the Model 1930, the latest fixed-magazine variant to remain in production. Fiocchi is the only major manufacturer currently producing ammunition for this pistol.

The Broomhandle Mauser, right side view, shows the rear-sight adjustment cursor and the bolt retainer just underneath it. Notice the receiver's distinctive recessed sides, a cosmetic touch included on all but a very few early pistols.

The Mauser Model 1896, nicknamed the "Broomhandle" because of its distinctively-shaped grip, was one of the most important early automatic pistols. The Feederle brothers, employees of Germany's famous Mauser factory, developed the prototype on their own time until Paul Mauser became aware of it and asked the Feederles to finish its development for the company. The prototype was first fired on March 15, 1895, series production beginning the next year. In a forty-year production run, Mauser built about a million Model 1896 pistols. Moreover, the 7.63mm Mauser cartridge (also known as the 7.62x25mm or .30 Mauser) Mauser developed for the Model 1896 became even more popular than the pistol. When the Soviet Union adopted it for its Tokarev pistol in 1930 and for its World War Two submachine guns, the .30 Mauser cartridge joined the ranks of top military cartridges.

Mauser created many variants of its Model 1896 pistol. The first prototype used a spur hammer, but early production models used the famous rounded "conehead hammer." In later production a ring hammer became standard. Before 1903 this hammer was large enough to obscure the rear sight when uncocked; afterwards a smaller hammer came into use. While some early Model 1896 pistols used a fixed rear sight, a rear sight adjustable to 1000 meters is most common. Early on Mauser experimented with a six-round magazine but settled on a 10-shot integral (non-detachable) magazine reloaded through the top of the action by a stripper clip. For Model 1896 variants made after 1931 a detachable magazine came on line. A 5.5-inch (140mm) barrel length became standard early on.

Most Model 1896s were not just pistols, but rather convertible pistol-carbines. A slot in the back of the grip accepted a hollow detachable shoulder stock for improved stability and accuracy, particularly at extended ranges. When removed from the pistol this stock doubled as a holster.

The first big military order for Model 1896s came in 1899, when the Italian navy bought 5000. Another big order came from Turkey. Dozens of military forces, including the British, Russia, Switzerland and the United States, bought small quantities for testing and evaluation. While these buys rarely led to large orders, Model 1896 sales were strong nevertheless, the pistol selling well among private citizens and with military officers permitted to use privately-owned handguns, such as was the case in the British armed forces. Winston Churchill carried a Model 1896 at the Battle of Omdurman in 1898 and in the Boer War shortly after.

Mauser built about 100,000 true Model 1896s before switching to the Model 1912 variation. This used 6-groove instead of 4-groove rifling, and adopted the Neues Sicherung (New Safety) manual safety which could be moved back to its safe position only with the hammer cocked. All Broomhandle Mauser pistols made from 1912 to 1930 used the New Safety, marked with an intertwined NS logo on the hammer.

During World War One Mauser scored a major commercial coup when the German armed forces, which had

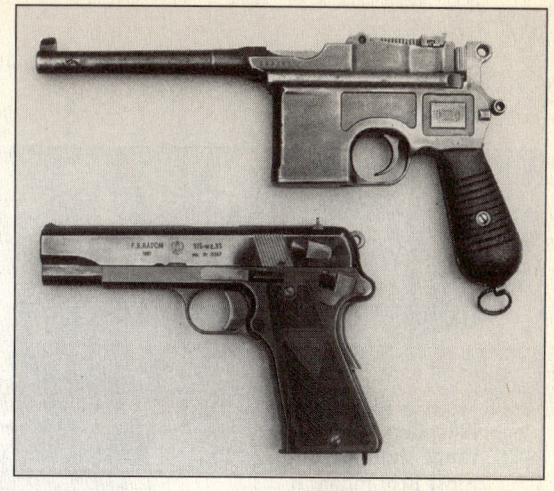

The Broomhandle Mauser's unusual shape, which places the magazine ahead of the grip instead of within it, makes for an unusually long pistol. With a 5 1/2-inch barrel the Mauser Model 1896 pistol (top) goes 12 1/4 inches overall, while the VIS 35 Radom with a 4.8-inch barrel (bottom) is just over 8 inches long.

The early Broomhandle Mausers all reloaded via stripper clips inserted through the top of the open action, while the later Model 711 and 712 variants could either reload this way or by swapping their detachable magazines.

Features Articles • 31

Mauser's Holstered Pistol Stock

A further aid to long-range shooting in most Broomhandle Mausers was a slot in the frame which allowed the shooter to attach a shoulder stock to steady the pistol, converting it into a small carbine.

The Broomhandle Mauser usually came with a hollow combination shoulder stock/holster which securely held the pistol and associated tools on a belt. Today original shoulder stock/holsters are quite uncommon.

The fieldstripped Broomhandle Mauser consists of (top to bottom) barrel extension, bolt, locking block, bolt retainer, recoil spring, firing pin, subframe, magazine assembly and frame.

The pistol fits into the hollow shoulder stock/holster as shown. Note the slot at the rear of the pistol's frame to attach the stock, and the lanyard loop at the bottom of the Broomhandle Mauser's odd grip, which allows the shooter to keep up with the pistol more easily.

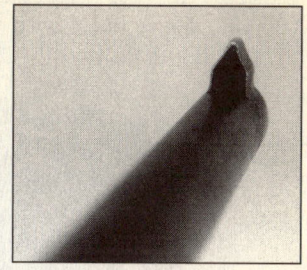

remained aloof from the Broomhandle pistol, found themselves short of weapons and ordered 150,000 Model 1912s rechambered for the 9mm Parabellum cartridge in 1915. Mauser-Werke made an estimated 138,000 of these by 1918. The 9mm Model 1912 pistol features a number 9 carved into the grip pieces and painted red, giving the pistol its nickname of "Red Nine." In addition to the 9mm pistols, Mauser made an equal number of standard 7.63mm Model 1912s for issue to the wartime German armed forces.

After World War One the victorious Allies forbade German manufacture of pistols firing the 9mm Parabellum cartridge or pistols having barrels over 4 inches long. Therefore, in 1922 Mauser-Werke introduced its so-called Bolo model. Chambering the 7.63mm Mauser round in a 3.9-inch (99mm) barrel, this proved popular in Russia, where a civil war raged between the communist Bolsheviks ("Reds") and various opposing "White" factions. "Bolo," slang for Bolshevik, became the nickname by which this variant, and by extension any short-barreled Mauser Model 1896-type pistol, has become known. Despite its short barrel, the Bolo Mauser retained the shoulder stock attachment slot and adjustable rear sight. Mauser-Werke made about 500,000 Bolo Models. In addition to Russia, many went to war-torn China, a lucrative market with its huge population and insatiable demand for weapons. Production stopped in 1930 in favor of the Model 1930. This, the last semiautomatic Broomhandle variation to include an integral magazine, featured a longer 5.7-inch barrel. Abandoning the New Safety, Mauser introduced the Universal Safety with the Model 1930. This offered three positions. Pulled down alongside the cocked hammer, was the manual safety's fire position. Pushed halfway up, the manual safety locked the hammer, trigger and bolt, while pushed fully up against the frame the manual safety blocked the hammer.

Mauser made about 160,000 Model 1930s. Most were sold in China, while many were sold to private citizens. The Norwegian armed forces also bought Model 1930s. The German armed forces used sev-

Far Left: Most Broomhandle Mauser pistols employed a long-range adjustable rear sight, generally adjustable to settings of up to 500 yards or even 1000 yards as shown.

Left: Mauser created the Broomhandle Mauser's v-notch rear sight for long-range accuracy, but a wider square notch would have been more useful.

Right: The Broomhandle Mauser's oddly-shaped front sight allows rapid sight acquisition, a particularly valued feature in a combat shooting situation.

Below Left: The Mauser Model 1930 introduced the Universal Safety, which pushed forward as shown, exposing a letter "S," to its safe setting.

Below: The Universal Safety as introduced on the Model 1930 variant went into its fire setting by being pulled back alongside the cocked hammer as shown.

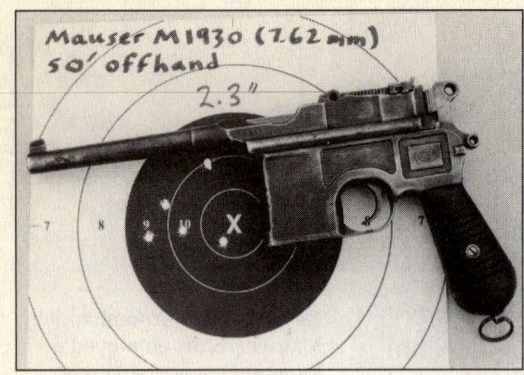

This Broomhandle Mauser (Model 1930) tested by the author proved quite accurate, putting a 5-shot offhand group into just 2.3 inches from a distance of 50 feet.

This Model 1930 test pistol delivered a 5.6-inch group from a 50-yard benchrested position, a solid performance for a handgun.

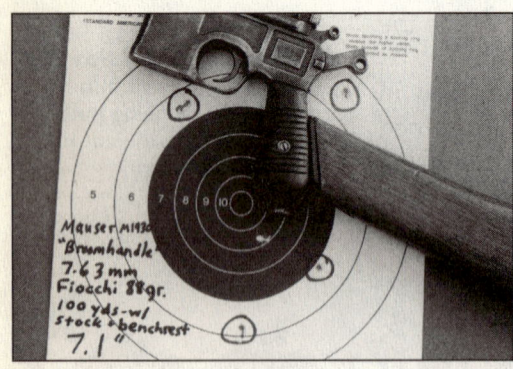

The attached shoulder stock enabled the author to fire a 7.1-inch group from 100 yards using this Model 1930 test pistol.

eral thousand in World War Two, along with older Broomhandle types. Model 1930 production continued until 1939.

Meanwhile two Spanish manufacturers copied the Broomhandle Mauser to horn in on the lucrative trade in these weapons, particularly in China and in Latin America. Bestegui Hermanos' Mauser copy, the "Royal," entered production in 1926 and enjoyed immediate success. Bestegui then made a selective-fire variant which fired at a cyclic rate of 850 rounds per minute. Some variants used integral 10-shot or 20-shot magazines, while others fired from detachable magazines holding 10, 20 or 30 rounds. Astra-Unceta y Cia's first Broomhandle Mauser copy, the Astra Model 900, fired semi-automatically only. It appeared in 1927. Unceta then introduced the selective-fire Model 901 in 1928 with 10-shot integral magazine, dropped in favor of the Model 902 which used a 20-round integral magazine. The Model 903, introduced in 1932, introduced a detachable magazine of 10- or 20-round capability. Unceta's Model 904, introduced in 1934, incorporated a clever flywheel device to reduce the rate of fire from 900 rounds per minute to a more manageable 350 rpm. In all, Astra-Unceta y Cia produced almost 35,000 Broomhandle copies before production stopped in 1960, while Bestegui's production numbered about 30,000.

The growing popularity of Spanish copies forced Mauser-Werke to respond in 1930 with the Model 711. This was basically a Model 1930 with a detachable 10-, 20- or 40-round box magazine and was limited to semiautomatic fire. Mauser followed this up with the selective-fire Model 712 Schnellfeuerpistole (Rapid-Fire Pistol) in 1932. This proved a great success. Mauser-Werke manufactured about 95,000 Schnellfeuerpistolen before stopping production in 1938. Tens of thousands went to the Chinese, several hundred to the Yugoslav armed forces in 1933 and the entire remaining stock to the German army and Waffen-SS in 1939.

The A.F. Stoeger Company, forerunner of today's Stoeger Industries, handled the Mauser line including the Models 711 and 712. A 1932 Stoeger ad, reproduced in this article, gave a glowing testimonial to the Mauser pistol series and warned the buyer to "avoid spurious imitations."

The Chinese Shensi and Shantung arsenals made thousands of Mauser pistol copies in the late 1920s, some chambered for .45 ACP. In 1980 the Chinese revived the Mauser 712 design as their Type 80 Submachine Gun. Internally the 7.63mm/.30 Mauser caliber Type 80 faithfully follows the Mauser design, though its external appearance is modified somewhat by an enlarged pistol grip, a forward-angled magazine housing, and a bayonet.

The Broomhandle Mauser showed the world that an automatic pistol could be a viable service weapon. Despite its odd appearance it balances and shoots well. A specimen in good shape remains a viable combat handgun. Meanwhile, the effectiveness of Broomhandle-type machine pistols in fully-automatic fire has been intensely debated since they first appeared. In 1967 personnel at the U.S. Army's Center for Special Warfare at Fort Bragg, North Carolina, thoroughly tested the concept. Using Model 712s with the shoulder stock attached, a team of testers attained accurate fire on man-sized targets at ranges as great as 100 meters (109 yards) in fully-automatic fire. They discovered that the trick to mastering this weapon in fully-automatic fire involves using the support hand to hold the wrist of the shooting hand firmly against the wooden stock. Then press and immediately release the trigger, thereby shooting a quick burst of perhaps three or four shots instead of emptying the entire magazine. In semi-automatic fire, the Army testers demonstrated the gun's ability to engage man-sized targets as far away as 200 meters effectively. Thus the adjustable rear sight and shoulder stock/holster that seem foolish affectations actually are not.

The Broomhandle Mauser's clever design, outstanding workmanship and efficient features helped give it a worldwide distribution. One of the most popular collectible firearms, the exotic "Broomhandle" qualifies as a true classic of firearms history.

Fully-automatic firing technique as developed by the U.S. Army's Center for Special Warfare at Fort Bragg, North Carolina, involves using the support hand to hold the wrist of the shooting hand firmly against the wooden stock. The shooter presses the trigger and immediately releases it, thereby shooting a quick burst of perhaps three or four shots instead of emptying the entire magazine. Note the shooter's forward-leaning stance, a great aid to controlling recoil in a lightweight automatic weapon.

A left-side view of the Center for Special Warfare's fully-automatic firing technique shows the shooter using his support hand to hold the wrist of his shooting hand firmly against the wooden stock. This technique makes the weapon more controllable.

Features Articles

Hearing Loss
by Phil W. Johnston

Going...Going...Gone! Once your hearing is lost, prevention is too late. Learn more about how to safeguard your hearing.

Suddenly the buck appeared in my peripheral vision, immediately below me and it was too late to draw the bow. Silently, or seemingly so, he moved out of the shooting lane I'd cleared quickly and the opportunity for a shot was gone. How had he gotten so close without being heard? Oh, I knew only too well. Over the years I've turned myself into a handicapped hunter.

While I work out three to 4 times a week and pride myself in being able to "walk the younger guys into the ground" at the age of 54, I've handicapped myself in another way. Tragically there's nothing I can do to regain my ability to hear game in the field, or understand my daughter on an un-amplified phone. All because as a young man I didn't value my hearing as much as I should have.

Although we don't wish to turn this into a science or health class, if we're to understand hearing and sound, it's imperative that we take a look first at what sound is and then look at the way our hearing interprets sound.

Webster's New World Dictionary, Third College Edition defines sound thusly: "1 a) vibrations in air, water, etc. that stimulate the auditory nerves and produce the sensation of hearing…" Thus, as most of us learned in grade school, by definition, unless someone is in the woods to hear the tree fall, there is no sound. At any rate a sound is generated by a disturbance of the medium that surrounds the sound source. As a submarine sonarman during the late 1960s I routinely got the chance to listen to sound sources that ranged from whales and shrimp (biologics) to distant surface and underwater craft at distances that varied from far too

Sound Waves are Measured in Two Ways:

- We measure the frequency of sound in Hertz (or cycles per second if you're from the "old school") and amplitude (strength).
- We measure the amplitude of a sound source in Decibels or dB.

close to hundreds of miles away. Sound travels far more efficiently through water than it does through the air. If ever you put your ear to the railroad tracks to listen for an approaching train you know that it also travels very well through metal. It was easy to hear a train in this manner long before it appeared, although the practice isn't to be encouraged, either.

A sound source disturbs the surrounding medium and for our purposes we'll deal with sound sources disturbing the surrounding air. Sound waves are measured in two ways: we measure the frequency of sound in Hertz (or cycles per second if you're from the "old school") and amplitude (strength). We measure the amplitude of a sound source in Decibels or dB. Decibels express the amplitude of a sound in a logarithmic scale and it's important to remember that for each increase of 3 dB the amplitude or strength of a sound has doubled while a similar decrease of 3 dB represents a signal half as loud. In our opinion, this logarithmic scale tends to downplay the level of sound that we measure. For instance, if we were faced with a price increase that went from $100.00 to $103.00 we might not be alarmed while a sound that went from 100 dB to 103dB increased two-fold in amplitude! Bear this in mind when we get down the road a bit. A sound that increased by 10 dB increased by 10 times!

If we could see sound, it would look much like the waves that appear in a puddle when you drop a stone in the middle. It radiates outward in a 360∞ direction and decreases in amplitude as it moves away from the source of the disturbance, although the frequency stays the same.

Since a sound has to be heard by definition, our ears make up the second portion of the equation. While many of us tend to think of the protuberances on the sides of our head as a place to hang things, they are part of a complex system that makes up our sense of hearing. The sometimes less than attractive attachments to our head serve only to collect and direct sound energy first to the auditory canal and ultimately to the eardrum, in the middle ear where the magic begins to take place. Before we leave the outer ear, one last note is worth mentioning. Because our hearing capacity tends to diminish with age our body tries to compensate by enlarging the outer ear. If you've got big ears now, nah, better not go there.

Our eardrum is the doorway to

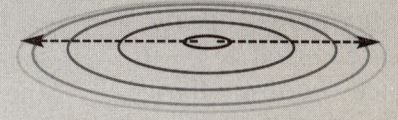

If We Could See Sound

It would look much like the waves that appear in a puddle when you drop a stone in the middle. It radiates outward in a 360 degrees direction and decreases in amplitude as it moves away from the source of the disturbance, although the frequency stays the same.

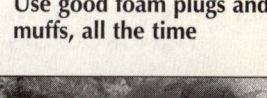

Use good foam plugs and muffs, all the time

Because gunfire generates "white" noise that covers the entire spectrum, and our high frequency hearing is so sensitive, our high-end hearing is the first to go if we shoot anything without protecting our hearing.

the middle ear, if you will, and it deflects when sound energy strikes this fragile membrane. The middle ear contains three small bones that amplify sound energy and transfer the energy to the inner ear. The hammer is attached directly to the eardrum, while the anvil transfers amplified energy to the stirrup. The hammer, anvil and stirrup tend to amplify sound energy by 20 times or so. The stirrup bears directly on the oval window, a membrane over the inner ear.

The portion of the inner ear that refers to hearing is the cochlea, a spiral shaped, fluid-filled chamber imbedded in bone behind the ear. The cochlea is divided into two parts-an upper and lower chamber separated by the basilar membrane. The fluid in the inner ear transfers energy to the organ of Corti where hair-like cells or nerve endings transform physical movement into electrical energy that moves through the auditory nerve to the brain.

Permanent, shooting related hearing damage occurs within the organ of Corti. Here, when noise forces are sufficient to deflect these nerves to an abnormal degree, the nerves can be permanently damaged. The nerve cells that respond to high frequencies are the most delicate by design because they have to vibrate the fastest when responding to a high frequency. Because gunfire generates "white" noise that covers the entire spectrum, and our high frequency hearing is so sensitive, our high-end hearing is the first to go if we shoot anything without protecting our hearing. This explains why our senior shooters might have a difficult time hearing the phone ring or the birds sing. Read on.

Frequencies The Human Ear Hears

AT BIRTH	= 16 Hertz to 20,000
HEALTHY EARS	= 1 dB
LEAF RUSTLING	= 10 dB of sound
WHISPER	= 30 dB
NORMAL VOICE CONVERSATION	= 60 dB or so
DISCOMFORT	= 120 dB or so
PERMANENT HEARING DAMAGE OCCURS	= 140 dB

Remember, that an increase of 3 dB is a doubling of sound intensity. An increase of 10 dB represents a tenfold increase in sound pressure!

What firearm can you shoot without hearing protection? In a nutshell, nothing but an air gun or BB gun may safely be fired without hearing protection, anytime, anyplace. According to information adapted from NOISE OF POLICE FIREARMS, by P.G. Weissler, every firearm measured thus far exceeds safe levels for the human ear.

Although it might be far too little, too late, you won't catch me taking a shot with anything, anytime without hearing protection. This isn't to say that you'll see me with shooting muffs on all the time, but you will find me wearing some type of hearing protection, even when working my chocolate Labrador on pheasant this fall. It's too bad I didn't do this years ago. Unfortunately, I'm not alone.

Garry G. Gordon, MS, Audiologist with E.A.R., Inc., Box 2146, Boulder, Colorado, 80306 has been a long-time friend and he must be regarded as one of the shooter's best friends. In his work with E.A.R. he's traveled throughout the world attending sports shows, major competi-

In a nutshell, nothing but an air gun or BB gun may safely be fired without hearing protection, anytime, anyplace.

tions, and generally being available whenever a large number of shooters get together. Over the years he's managed to compile a large amount of information that points out just how extensive this problem is. Gordon's research points out that when 852 people were asked about their hearing (or lack thereof), 47% reported that that they were aware of a hearing loss. 36% reported that they hear better out of one ear than the other and 34% reported that they had a ringing or buzzing in their ears (we'll talk more about this later). If you're still not alarmed about the problem, 32% of those questioned by Gordon reported that they have problems understanding speech and were experiencing a reduction in the ability to communicate! In my case, several family members as well as close friends now rely on e-mail to communicate with me because I tend to answer unasked questions on the phone or otherwise fail to communicate.

As we said earlier, because our high-end hearing is the most fragile, it tends to be the first that goes when we expose our hearing to loud noise. As the nerve cells in the inner ear get damaged, in many cases they begin emitting false electrical signals. These false noise signals often take the form of a buzzing or ringing that never ceases. Called tinnitus, one of the best definitions comes from Dr. Timothy C. Hain, MD, of the Northwestern University Medical School in Chicago, IL. "Tinnitus (Tin-it-tus) is an abnormal noise in the ear". He reports that nearly 36,000,000 humans have tinnitus and in 20% of these cases, "…the individuals are so impacted by the disease that they cannot lead normal lives." In many cases this definition is understated to say the least.

Shooting related hearing loss or tinnitus does indeed impact one's lifestyle. A few years back we heard about a 16-year old trapshooting champion who had to leave a vacuum cleaner running by his bed to drown out his tinnitus and allow sleep to come! In other cases, permanent shooting related hearing damage has been the basis for law suits being leveled at individuals as well as companies. In many cases they're based on exposure to firearms equipped with muzzle brakes. We don't have access to noise measurements that contrast a standard barreled arm against an identical one sporting a brake but Dr. Bill Krammer, Ph.D., Ball State University, Muncie, Indiana has looked at a .375 H&H that sported an 18" barrel and a muzzle brake and found that it generated an average level of 170 dB. An 18" .30-06 without a brake manages a paltry 163.2 dB. Although neither level is "safe", anyone who needs a brake to reduce felt recoil would be well advised to choose instead a cartridge/firearm combination that generates less recoil in the first place, rather than trying to tame a hard kicker with a muzzle brake. Brakes have no place on sporting firearms. Period. Although you might dispute these words, be advised that hunters have

Every Firearm Exceeds Safe Levels

.22 rimfire rifle = 134-144 dB

.22 rimfire pistol = 150-152 dB.

12-gauge shotgun = 154-156 dB

Information adapted from *NOISE OF POLICE FIREARMS*, by P.G. Weissler

Because our hearing capacity tends to diminish with age our body tries to compensate by enlarging the outer ear.

This is a culprit, any way you cut it in the author's opinion. Using a brake van be tough on the shooter to be sure but it is even tougher on bystanders or shooters on the same firing line. Don't use one and if you have a rifle or handgun equipped with one, remove it.

Percentage of Hearing Loss

852 people surveyed

47% aware of hearing loss
36% better out of one ear
34% ringing or buzzing
32% problems understanding speech

Research compiled by Gary G. Gordon, MS, Audiologist with E.A.R., Inc.

---

been successfully sued by guides/outfitters that were exposed to shots in the field from rifles equipped with muzzle brakes.

Preventing permanent hearing damage requires that we pay constant attention to our surroundings and if there's a ghost of a chance that we'll be exposed to a loud noise, hearing protection must be in place before it occurs. While hearing protection must be effective in reducing the levels of sound that reach our ears, it must be worn for every shot and thus must be practical and comfortable. In this light, the most difficult situation occurs with the hunter because he or she needs every speck of hearing that is possible before the shot as well as after the shot, while requiring great protection during the shot. Today there are several electronic hearing protection systems on the market that amplify sounds below a certain level and cut off any noise level over a certain level, making it entirely possible for the hunter to have his or her cake and eat it too, as the old saying goes. I've used models from several manufacturers and caution readers that one often gets exactly what one pays for. In other words, make sure that the system you choose has the ability to attenuate or cut the sound level that reaches your ear to an acceptable level and that it seals either inside your auditory canal or on the outside of your head, completely. Leakage of any kind defeats the protection device in an instant. This is a good place to point out that when hearing protection consists of the hard muffs worn over the ears, glasses, heavy hair, or a cap could indeed mess up the seal between the device and the ear.

Typically we'll see hearing protection that is assigned a noise reduction number (NRR) of 25 to 30 dB or slightly more. The NRR of a system may be deducted from the expected noise exposure level to determine the level of protection that is necessary. In the case of the .30-06 that generates 163.2 dB, a protection system that provides a NRR of 30 or so takes the level just below the level of potential damage. As we pointed out earlier, no level of protection below 40 will protect against the noise generated by a muzzle brake.

When we were actively involved in NRA Bullseye competition, we used two different types of hearing protection. We started by inserting a custom molded earplug into each ear and finished the package off with a set of shiny, hard muffs over the ears on the outside. Using two different types of hearing protection at the same time does afford increased protection but the two NRRs can't be added together to arrive at the level of total protection. In other words, using ear plugs rated at a NRR of 29 being used in concert with muffs rated at 30 doesn't add up to a combined NRR of 59. The protection will be somewhere between 30 and

The Danger of Handguns

Handgun puts the muzzle blast just that much closer to the shooter's ears, they are notorious for producing huge hearing losses.

.38 SPECIAL REVOLVER	57-158 dB
.357 MAGNUM cartridge in the chamber	164-166 dB
.44 MAGNUM	164-170 dB
.41 MAGNUM	163-167 dB
.454 CASULI	170 & 173 dB

The big half-inch handguns sound even louder

VARIOUS RIFLES	160-172.5 dB
A JET PLANE	160 dB

59. We strongly urge anyone shooting under range conditions to use two forms of hearing protection, all the time.

While it's easy, practical and wise to use several forms of hearing protection on the range, practical protection in the field demands the use of the electronic devices that amplify low noise levels and cut off the high levels. These devices should be worn at all times and become second nature.

What can you do if you learned of this danger too late, as I did? Sadly, there is no outright cure for tinnitus, yet, although work continues in that direction. There is equipment that works to mask the constant ringing but as far as we know it is designed not to eliminate tinnitus, rather covering it with some other type of noise. That's not a fix in our mind. We strongly suggest that anyone so afflicted contact the American Tinnitus Association at www.ata.org and request membership material that includes a periodical publication that could help. Also don't be afraid to consult with your local audiologist to seek help. If hearing aids are suggested, remember that again one tends to get what one pays for and let the buyer beware. We also strongly urge shooters to hit two informative pages on the Internet, as well. Check out www.freehearingtest.com and www.earinc.com to keep abreast of news that is vital to our sport as well as our life.

It's completely possible to enjoy a lifetime of shooting and hunting and hang on to one of the greatest gifts of life-our hearing. It takes but seconds to don several hearing protection systems before the first shot and remove them after the last shot of the day that there's no excuse for not doing so. By the same token, taking but one shot without hearing protection in place can permanently damage your hearing. Protect yourself and protect those around you.

The alternative just could be the vacuum cleaner by the bed-or worse-having to learn sign language. It's your call.

Taking but one shot without hearing protection in place can permanently damage your hearing. Protect yourself and protect those around you.

Jason Gelling, the author's son-in-law, getting ready to tackle a distant praire dog. Note the use of hearing protection which includes plugs as well.

No Swan Song for The 16
by Stan Warren

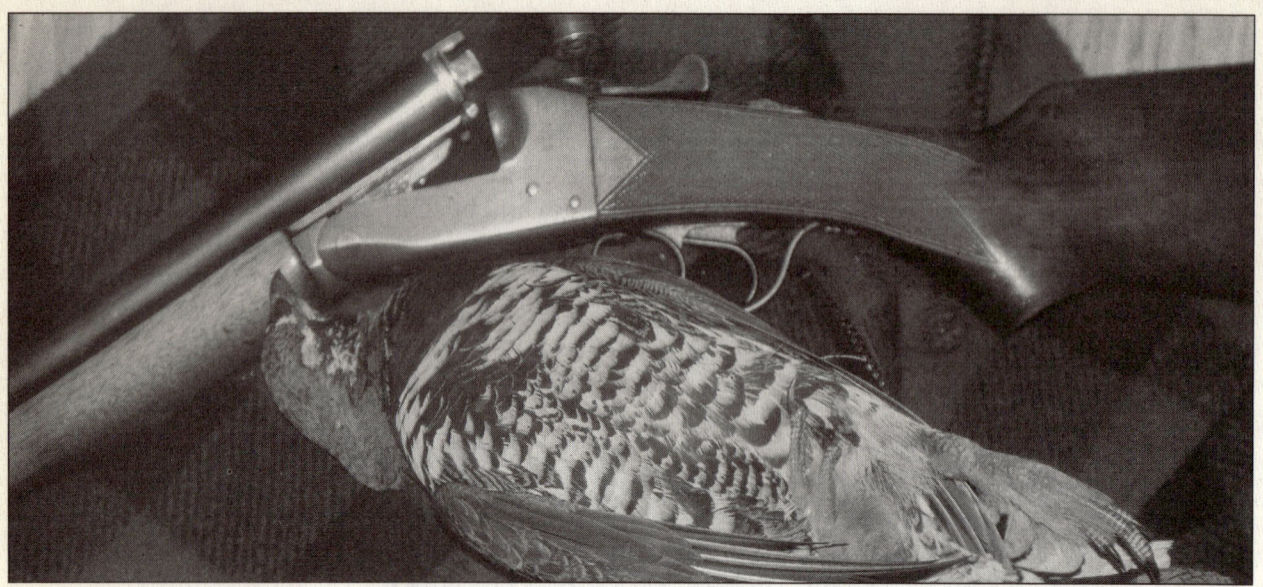

The author's Stevens Model 311A 16-bore double dates back to 1963 and has been completely rebuilt internally due to extensive use. Its improved cylinder/modified barrels still make it suitable for various applications such as taking birds like this spruce grouse.

Ruffed grouse tend to leave without preamble and this Alberta specimen was no different than his brethren to the south. He burst toward the thickest part of the surrounding poplars. I shouted, There he goes, to my gunning companion, then let the side-by-side do the magical thing that it has done for more years than I care to remember. The ruffie tumbled to earth trailing a mini-cloud of feathers in his wake.

Mike Jordan, the ammunition guru from Winchester claimed that he had been fouled. It seems that he had just about pushed the safety off on his new autoloader when the bird bumped into an ounce of #8 shot. Maybe using a gun for almost four decades does give one a slight advantage, I decided. An hour later the same smoothbore, different loading, dumped a couple of sharptails, one around the 40-yard mark and moving out.

Back at the truck Mike asked to examine the well-worn Stevens double. Never fancy, it has been polished, carried and shot so much that the firing pins and springs have been replaced and it is on its third stock refinishing. He swung on an imaginary target and a smile reached all the way to his eyes.

The first shotgun that I ever bought was just like this one, he said. Same gun, same barrel length and chokes, everything. I figured then that it was just about perfect for most any kind of wingshooting. Come to think about it, maybe I wasn t so very far from correct.

As the guest of an Alberta lodge catering to waterfowl and grouse hunters, Mike had brought along his company s latest shotgun loadings. Geese were number one on the list because some new big boomers were being introduced. During the planning stages I had mentioned that he should bring along a skeet oong came the 3-inch magnum 20 gauge and shooting pundits declared that, except for the 12- and 20-gauges for hunting and the 28- and .410 for non-serious duty, everything else was dead. Dead? The 16 was never even sick.

Let me quickly insert that I am not advocating a boycott of the other shotshell diameters or loadings. I absolutely love a lightweight twenty or even a twenty-eight when trekking some particularly nasty grouse country, and when big-water waterfowling or pass shooting is the order of the day give me a twelve or even a ten with all possible horsepower. This does not mean, however, that either is truly a better all-around choice than the sixteen. Now before the uprising starts and the lynch mob forms, let s take an open and impartial look at a few things.

One argument states that the twenty is a better upland choice because it can be made lighter and more portable. That does not really hold up when you consider that the famous Model 12 used the same frame for both bores and many other makers did likewise. You can right now wrap your hands around a quick and graceful Arrietta double gun of my acquaintance, even shoot it, and never know that it is a member of the dying gauge community. Using one-ounce loads of #8 shot it prompted a friend to liken it to a magic wand for woodland quail and woodcock. On the outside its dimensions vary minutely if at all from the maker s 20-bore and I believe that the receivers are identical. I once owned a Winchester Model 24 with two sets of barrels, one set in 16 gauge and the other in 20 gauge. You can quickly guess how small the weight difference was.

Bill Teasdale, the gun-wise smoothbore specialist at Wingshooting Adventures which specializes in both high-dollar shotguns and appropriate hunts explained the weight difference from a practical level. He said, Since all of our better guns are made to order (Arrietta), we control most factors. The one that we can t control is the weight factor in the sense that everything comes down to balance. Our upland models vary less than

To prove the effectiveness of a full-choke 16 gauge shotgun with today's heavier loadings the author took a Merkel double on a Texas turkey hunt. In three days he bagged two dandy Rio Grande gobblers in as many shots, knocking that as flat as any magnum 12-gauge round could have done.

With his Arrietta double, a sweetheart weighing right at six and one-half pounds, the author collected these woodland bobwhites. Fast handling and excellent pattern qualities make his gun a grand choice when a quick shot is needed.

Features Articles • 43

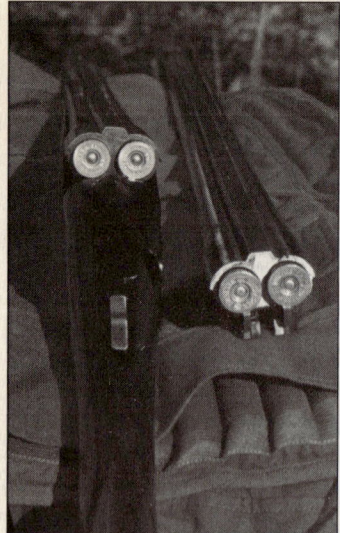

The author found this Winchester Model 24 two-barrel set in the Cabela's Gun Library. The 20-gauge tubes were choked full and modified while the 16-gauge versions were more open, but both pairs fit the same receiver perfectly.

The author's daughter frequently confiscates his Stevens double for use on upland birds such as quail and woodcock. Both members of the family like the sling that has been installed for European-style practicality.

you might think between the 20- and 16 gauge. The former weighs in at around six and one-quarter pounds while the latter tips the scale at six and one-half on average. Variations will be less than an ounce either way regardless of the density of the wood, a deciding factor. In all honesty, I don t believe anyone but the most discriminating or persnickety person could tell the difference even after a long day chasing grouse and woodcock.

The twenty has less recoil and is therefore better for lightly-built or young shooters, or just when you plan on burning a bunch of ammo in a short period of time. To that I can only say carry two similar guns, one in each bore diameter, to a good dove field. Using factory ammunition with 2-1/2 dram equivalent powder charges, try to tell the difference between and ounce of shot and seven-eights of an ounce. Most mortals simply cannot. My daughter began carrying my old Stevens Model 311 when barely into her teens, preferring it to a 20-gauge autoloader available to her at the time. She would certainly have opted for less kick (and there must have been some difference) had it been substantial enough to make a difference. The fact that she liked the handling qualities of the side-by-side was probably a factor as well, but in any event she never seemed to feel that the gun punished her even in a dove field where the shooting was of the rapid sort.

The twelve gauge is more versatile than any other bore. No argument there; some models will carry anything from an ounce to two ounces of shot effectively. It is worthwhile to note that smoothbores that thrive on the heavy stuff are not quite as portable as an upland gunner might like, and something that carries well on a long afternoon will probably not be very pleasant when you try a high overhead shot with a magnum goose load. Every choice in the do-it-all shotgun category has strengths and weaknesses. Certainly Mike Jordan s magnum autoloader gave him an edge on distant geese even though it could not compete in terms of handling speed with the shorter, lighter and more compact double when chasing grouse in thick cover.

Since the twenty in its 3-inch form is what set the other into its downhill skid, a closer look at how they compare is in order. First a general look at lead shot loadings shows that both are practically the same on the light end but on the upper side of things, the sixteen has an edge in the 2-3/4 inch loadings. In the 3-inch, the twenty takes over: right? Sorry, even in its longer version it still has less bird-dropping potential than the other's heavy field combination. If you doubt it, check the ammunition makers catalogs yourself. Then shoot a few of the heavier rounds as I did over my Pro Chrono and you will find that the sixteen in the high-brass department commonly has more speed than the 3-inch twenty gauge. This is fact, not fiction.

Most of today's 16-gauge factory loads carry from an ounce to one and one-eighth ounces of shot. Specialty loads both heavier and lighter are encountered, but do not expect to find them at just any gun shop.

The only place that I can find where the smaller bore carries more shot is in steel shot loadings (which are precious few if you shoot a sixteen) where the magnum twenty supposedly handles a full one-sixteenth ounce more pellets. This is a bit of a puzzle since the internal capacity of the shot area is pretty much the same on both. Something to do with shot cup thickness and wad column length, possibly. The few that I cut open and checked were so close together that I doubt any bird addressed with either would have known the difference.

Handloaders can bring the smaller bore up to the same powder equivalent and shot levels with non-steel pellets when using a few hulls, notably Winchester's AA-type. For reasons unknown to me, the velocity here in magnum land never quite catches up with the sixteen-gauge heavy field loads. The longer case is occasionally more aggravating to load, by the way.

During the actual testing of different load combinations I turned to Winchester's Mike Jordan once again since he has access to equipment that is somewhat more sophisticated than my chronograph and patterning boards. His first sentence confirmed what I had long suspected.

One overlooked detail when making comparisons of the two shotshells is the length of the shot column involved. A 16-gauge loading in any charge weight has a shorter shot column than the 20. This simply means that there is less of a time lag between when the first pellets hit the target and the last ones, so a short column is more efficient. It may not seem to make much difference and doesn't show up on a stationary pattern board, but if you have to take a crack at a fast-moving target coming straight across at an appreciable distance, say over 30 yards, the difference can be important.

Just for the fun of it, I measured the internal length of two plastic shot cups. The first was from a Federal 3-inch 20-gauge for use with 1-1/4-ounce loads of lead shot. It measured about 38 millimeters. A 16-gauge shot cup for the same payload measured just 24 millimeters. Since all shot charges string upon firing it would appear that the 16 starts out with a fair advantage that physics dictates will become more pronounced as distance increases. A 3-inch 20-gauge

The Fox Model B shown here is heavier thatn a 16-bore double needs to be but the guns were quite popular for a time. This 25-year old version is still capable of dropping fast-moving targets like these woodcock

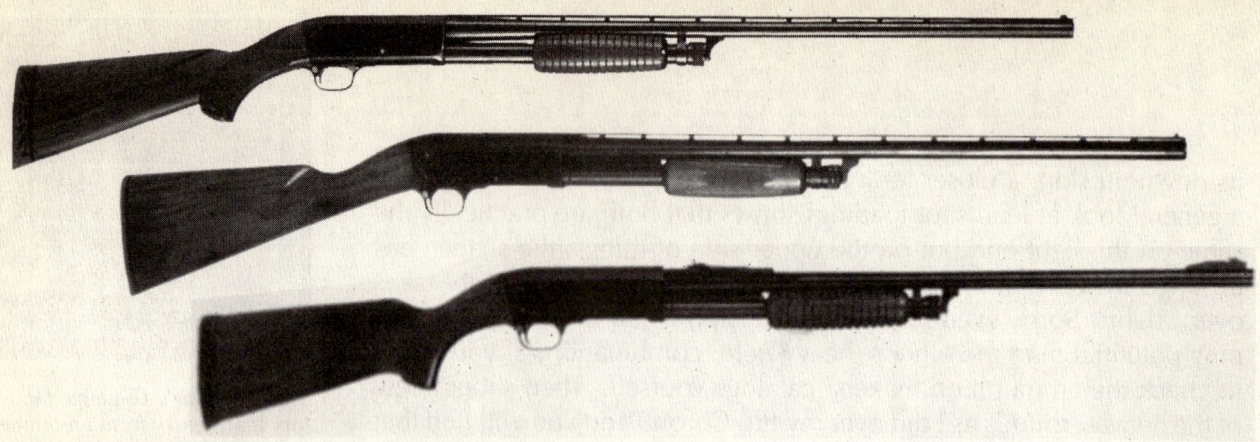

For a 16-gauge repeater of modern design there is the Ithaca Model 37. This time-proven design is available in Classic, English and Deerslayer configurations.

Comparisons between the 16 and 20 gauges are generally matters of opinion, especially in upland applications. However, hard data still shows that the 16 can do things that the smaller guage cannot.

shot cup for use with steel makes the stack even taller and, according to logic, would mean a still longer string.

Jordan also added, The 16 gauge has always enjoyed wonderfully balanced loadings. In the 2-1/2 dram, 1-ounce configuration it s a low-recoil delight for upland use. Put in a 3-1/4, 1-1/8 combination and you have an effective choice for general gunning on pheasant, big rabbits and such, even waterfowl in the days of lead shot, or now with Bismuth or other non-toxic shot. For this reason you will still see a lot more of these guns used in Europe than in the United States. Maybe the gunners there are more impressed by performance than the hype that is part of our shooting press.

Following up on his comment concerning European gunning I contacted the redoubtable Jack Jansma, head of Wingshooting Adventures. He is also a marvelous shotgun man and a fan as well as importer of the elegant Arrietta double guns made in Spain. I had been fortunate to hunt that country with him for driven partridge, plus a couple of times for driven pheasant in Hungary. On all three trips, some members of our parties had been shooting 16-bore guns alongside the more common 12-gauge smoothbores.

One old phrase that runs through my head states that pattern fails before penetration , and anyone who shoots should be able to feel confident with that idea, he stated. If you will remember back to the second Hungarian shoot we had three sixteens out of eight guns on the line and any difference in their success figures came from the shooter s ability rather than the hardware. The reason is simple: both loadings were similar, in fact identical in terms of shot charge weight. With the same choke combinations one bore size was just as effective as the other under those conditions. Since the targets were fully-flighted, mature pheasants at various ranges out to as far as 50 yards, maybe a little over sometimes, the idea that one is innately superior to the other just doesn t make sense.

While we were on the topic of bores and chokes, Jack dredged up another historical detail from his store of knowledge. While it had more to do with the latter than the former, it was a 16-gauge gun that got the credit. It seems that back in the days of community turkey or ham shoots, one of the common games was shooting the card in which playing cards were placed on stakes at a particular distance and each contestant took a crack at one. The shooter putting the most pellets in the pasteboard won. Anytime that a shooter was toting a 16-bore Browning Auto-5, no less than the famous Sweet Sixteen as a rule, with a full choke barrel, he usually took home the meat. It seems that Browning s Belgian-produced full was a bit tighter than the various designs made in America. It proves nothing in the which-gauge-is-best affair although it does make an interesting footnote.

The most popular pump shotgun of all time has returned in 16 gauge: Remington's Model 870. What began as a custom and semi-custom trend has spread across the shotgun spectrum in the last few years.

How bad is the 16-bore actually faring? While things may look grim in terms of standard production offerings from the Big Name American makers, things are different elsewhere in the industry. Perazzi made a run of elegant over-and-under guns which is doing well with the United States gunning public. Obviously these are not competition smoothbores, either. Another Italian gunmaker, I. Rizzini offers a snazzy stack-barreled version and others in the semi-custom and custom business are following suit.

Even the resurrected Ithaca in its Ithaca Classic Double persona is out in a 16-gauge model and there are others. Remember the graceful Ithaca Model 37 pump? It s back in 16-gauge form, too. Following what seems to be a rather definite trend, Remington announced the return of the 870 series in 16 gauge in time for the 2002 hunting season. Choose from the elegant to the workmanlike.

One of the most telling comments came from Bill Teasdale, a man who writes a lot of orders for elegant, custom and semi-custom guns.

Over the past three years or so the demand for these shotguns has shown a real upward trend. Somewhere between 35% and 40% of the confirmed orders that I get now are for 16-gauge double guns. Because we book a number of driven-bird shoots to various locations it would be easy to assume that the European influence has something to do with it, but I don t think so. Many of the buyers have never been on a driven shoot, never been to Europe, and have no intention of doing either, realistically. I think it is just that shooters today are better educated than ever and a lot of them simply want a gun that is best suited for their type of hunting. Some folks are rediscovering what a few of us have known all along. If you think that the 16-gauge is fading, just take its pulse. There s a lot of life left.

Bill, my friend, I could not have said it better. The 16 may not be the perfect gun for all purposes, but it sure does a lot of things well.

What's Available in the Ammunition Line:

- Remington - 1-ounce load at 1,200 fps, an express 1-1/8-ounce load at 1,295 and a 15/16-ounce steel load at 1,300 fps.
- Winchester - 1-ounce load at 1,165 fps, 1-1/8 ounce load at 1,295 fps.
- Federal - 1-1/8-ounce load at 1,185 fps a 1-1/8-ounce magnum load at 1,295, and a 15/16-ounce steel load at 1,300 fps.
- Polywad - These are two-and-a-half inch shells carrying a payload of 7/8-ounce with either a spreader or conventional wad. Both run about 1,200 fps.
- Baschieri & Pellagri - 67mm (okay in either 2/34 or 2-1/2 inch chambers) with 1-1/32 ounce shot charges at 1,320 fps and a one-ounce load at 1,230 fps.
- Bismuth - 1-1/8 ounce load at 1,200 and a new one-ounce load should be here by `the time that you read this.
- Kent - 1-1/16 ounces of nontoxic tungsten/matrix at 1,315 and a one-ounce load at 1,250. They also have a lead shot charge of one ounce at 1,250.

Shopping for a Stackbarrel
by Wayne Van Zwoll

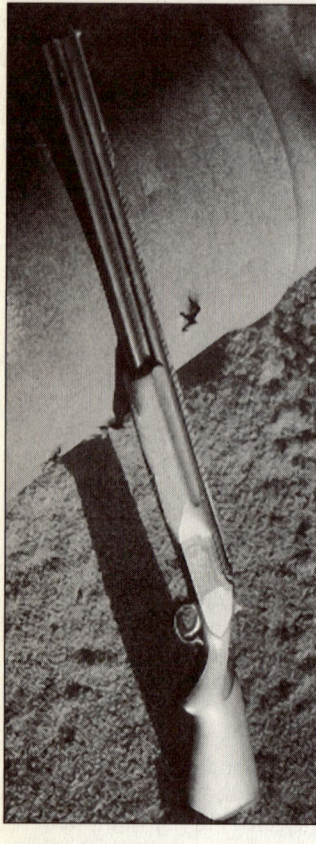

Right: Wayne shot these South Dakota pheasants with a Remington 300 Ideal, a followup to the Model 3200. It proved easy to load with gloved hands.

The over-under lacks the slim profile of a side-by-side but is a functional equal. Many shooters prefer the single sighting plane.

An over/under shotgun may be the ticket to better field shooting.

The smallbore gun whisked itself to my shoulder. Its bead appeared instantly where I looked, the delicate rip as straight and obedient as a flashlight beam. No matter where I swung my arms, the shotgun seemed to get there first. It never lagged or overshot my vision. It felt neither heavy nor light, just eager. "How much?" I asked. The engraving was very good, but I hoped the fellow wouldn't price it to the engraving. Or the marble cake French walnut.

He shrugged. Then he pointed to the silver oval in the stock. I'd paid no attention to it. "JOC," he said. "Not many shotguns around that were owned by Jack O'Connor."

The shotgun went to another home, where pockets were deeper. Perhaps I should have sold a few rifles and bought it. That over/under was surely not the first lovely smoothbore to slip through my fingers – though it remains the only O'Connor gun I've been offered.

While Jack wrote quite a bit about Winchester's 21, I like to think he quietly admired stackbarrel shotguns. Finely made and strong, the 21 is a heavy gun, and like all side-by-sides puts too much steel in front of my eye. Those tubes look as wide as a parking lot. Having learned to shoot with rifles, I'm much too deliberate for any double-barrel. Accomplished shotgunners don't let their eye dwell on all that acreage below the bead. Or fret because their left hand swallows the tubes and obscures the target. They just shoot. I'm still minding things that shouldn't get my attention at all, which is probably why I miss so often.

It's also why I prefer over/under shotguns. That single sighting plane is delightfully precise and unequivocal, more so when the bore is small and the rib narrow. It leads my eye quickly to the target. No guesswork. I shoot faster as a result.

Over/under shotguns have been around for a long time, though most old black-powder doubles you find will be side-by-sides. The British have worked very hard over many generations perfecting the side-by-side and seem content to continue. Some fine over/unders have come from London shops, but the stackbarrel is more common on the Continent, where drillings (three-barrel combination guns) and Cape guns (two-barrel combination guns) evolved. In the U.S., the over/under has gathered a bigger following than the side-by-side, despite the latter's long use by nineteenth-century market hunters. Both still have a couple of advantages over repeaters: shorter overall length (because there's no bolt to move back and forth) and instant choice of two loads and/or chokes.

Advocates of side-by-side guns point out that these doubles are slimmer in profile and, given the same barrel weights and buttstocks, lighter than over/unders. A sliver forend looks fine on a side-by-side but is hardly practical with the barrels stacked. The deep receiver of an over/under adds weight and bulk absent on the trimmest side-by-sides (though weight differences between types can be small indeed). A legitimate complaint about over/unders is the sharp opening angle necessary for bottom-barrel ejection and loading. So loading is slower. It can be slower still if the barrels "rebound" slightly after they reach the limit of the hinge. Such rebounding is less apparent in the showroom than when you're trying to stuff a pair of heavy 4s down the tubes to catch a late-flaring squadron of mallards, or reloading to tag a laggard chukar.

A budding Sporting Clays shooter gets some coaching. Many over/unders are available in special configurations for Sporting Clays competition.

Pattern both barrels of your over/under to check load performance and the placement of pattern centers. The gun must shoot where you look!

The criticism that over/unders catch wind has less merit. Sure, there's more steel to catch breeze. But even with solid side rails, you'll probably have no trouble swinging into the wind or maintaining a lead in gusty conditions. Only when the wind is very strong do I notice a tug on the tubes. And then a light side-by-side is apt to bounce around a little too. To my mind, an over/under should have no side rails, even ventilated slats. Rather, the barrels should be free of each other from the monobloc to the forward barrel attachment. Remington's old Model 32 was designed this way, giving the wind much less surface to push, and

Features Articles • 49

This Sig Apollo has the slim profile and long, open grip Wayne prefers.

Ted Hatfield found the Winchester Supreme a good choice for Alaska's ptarmigan.

enabling the barrels to cool faster. The 32, incidentally, was a livelier gun than the subsequent 3200 and the later Model 300 Ideal. After polling knowledgeable shotgunners, Remington decided in 2002 to reintroduce the 32, slightly modified, as the 332.

Over/under fans are quick to champion the single sighting plane, and to point out that recoil from both barrels is directly in line with the grip's lateral axis. Like wind-sensitivity of stackbarrel guns, the tendency of side-by-sides to "whip" to the side on recoil is hard to document. You'll probably not notice it on most high-quality doubles. I've never found it an impediment to quick second shots. Given equal gun weights, shot charges and stock dimensions, you'd be hard pressed to confirm any difference in the nature or severity of recoil between the two designs. On the other hand, the low, on-axis punch from the o/u's bottom barrel brings the gun straight back. Because there's little muzzle jump, you're on target quicker with the top barrel. That's one reason competitive clay bird shooters overwhelmingly favor the over/under.

Strength? That depends on the breech design, materials and fitting tolerances. A well-built side-by-side will last for decades of field shooting. Ditto an over/under. Either can eventually be worn down on the trap, skeet or Sporting Clays circuit; but it will take more shooting than most of us have time for. Even super-lightweight guns can be as tough as a whaler's oar. The Browning Citori Feather guns feature alloy breeches. A steel insert, dovetailed into the breech face, reinforces the area that establishes headspace, gets the brunt of the recoil energy and houses the firing pins. A steel hinge-pin ensures durability at that critical wearpoint. The alloy shaves about half a pound off the shotgun's weight. The Citori Superlight Feather, in 20 gauge with 26-inch barrels, scales only 5 pounds 11 ounces!

Like repeaters, over/unders are now available with screw-in chokes. The advantage is bigger for fixed-breed shotguns, because additional barrel sets are many times more expensive than spare barrels for pumps and autoloaders. The evolution of strong but thin-walled tubes has enabled manufacturers to keep barrels as slim as on traditional integral-choke guns.

There's no guarantee that an over/under will throw patterns where you're looking, or that the shot from any given load will distribute itself the way you want it to. The only way to check is by firing at a big sheet of white paper 40 yards away, aiming at a mark in its center. Circle with a felt pen every pellet hole. Calculate pattern percentage by drawing a 30-inch circle around the pattern's center and divide the number of hits inside the circle by the number of pellets in the shell. Five trials per load provide a useful average. Measure also the distance between pattern center and the aiming point. If it's more than 3 inches or so, I get uncomfortable. Maybe another load will do better. Maybe some stock work is necessary, to put your eye (essentially the rear sight on a shotgun) at a different place. Before altering any stock, you're wise to consult with veteran shooters, who might point out flaws in your form as causing pattern displacement.

Both barrels should shoot to the same place. If they don't, you're handicapping yourself. It's odd that few bird hunters check their double guns for this consistency – though hunters using double rifles for dangerous game insist on precise "regulation" of the barrels. If you want to learn to shoot better, every shot must be predictable. If you make a mistake, you should miss the target. If you shoot perfectly, you should hit. Barrels not shooting to the same place will give you erratic results.

Ralph Walker of Selma, Alabama, pioneered after-market lengthening of forcing cones to boost pattern uniformity. Now it's a common operation. Long forcing cones ease the passage of shot into the bore. Manufacturers are also building longer forcing cones into their guns. Back-boring is another way to reduce pellet deformation and improve patterns. It's an old process, dating to the 1920s and then called overboring. The Ansley H. Fox Gun Company of Philadelphia built what was called the Super Fox for the first 3-inch 12-gauge shells. It had bores larger than the standard .730 diameter. Remington backbored the barrels for its Model 11 autoloader and Model 31 pump guns during the 1930s. The over/under followed as this trend gained steam. Stan Baker, of Seattle, Washington, became known for backboring trap guns for less recoil. Backboring was made practical by the development of polymer wads whose skirts expanded to seal gas behind the shot charge. The card and fiber wads of decades past would disappoint in backbored barrels with long forcing cones.

In my youth, the over/under of every boy's dream was the Browning Superposed, mainly because there were few other choices but also because Browning published a color catalog with cheesecake images of the lovely guns. Enlarged insets detailed the fine engraving on Pigeon, Pointer, Diana and Midas grades. They've been replaced by a bevy of Citori over/unders, the Japanese-built replacement for the Superposed. These days, shotgunners have many more over/unders to choose from than they had in the 1960s. In fact, there are enough to be confusing. So not long ago I telephoned a fellow whose enduring passion for stackbarrels has filled several racks in his gun room. "Which is the best?" I asked. "Ruling out a built-to-order Perazzi or a London equivalent, where can a shooter get top value and durability in

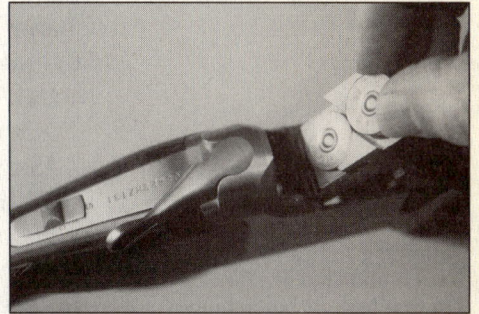

Weatherby's Orion SSC shows the steep grip and substantial buttstock common on Sporting Clays shotguns.

Most high-quality over/unders give you automatic ejectors, meaning that fired shells are kicked out, while unfired shells are elevated for easy unloading.

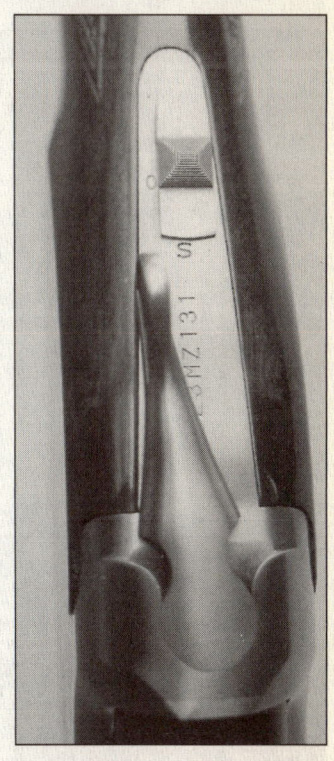

Over/under barrel selectors are commonly incorporated in the safety, as on this Browning Citori.

Smallbore over/unders like this Sig Apollo 28-bore are particularly fetching. A shallow breech is a requisite if that straight grip is to look proper.

Patterning tests a shotgun's barrels and chokes. Bird hunting tests its pointability.

a stackbarrel?" My friend hesitated only a second. "You can hardly go wrong," he said. "Stay away from cheap guns made in Brazil and Russia. They're functional and probably fine for beginning shooters. But they don't have the feel, fit or looks of a Ruger Red Label or a Browning Citori."

"How about the Winchester Supreme? The Remington Ideal and 332?"

"Fine guns."

"The Beretta 686 and 687? The Marocchi Conquista?"

He nodded. "And don't forget the Weatherbys. They and SKB 505s give you first-rate handling and workmanship. They're made in Japan. The Citori too." He reminded me that in the 1960s Japanese-built Charles Dalys imported by Sloans helped re-establish the over/under Stateside, after the Savage 430 disappeared in the 1940s, the Marlin Model 90 in 1958.

"Other good buys?"

"Sig's Apollo. The Merkel 2000. The old Winchester 101."

"What should a shooter look for in an over/under?"

He ticked off personal preferences that pretty much matched mine: Trim stock lines – particularly a long, slim grip; neat, clean checkering and tight wood-to-metal fit; mechanically-activated single trigger (one that fires the second barrel with the second tug of your finger, whether the first barrel has fired or not, as opposed to a recoil-activated trigger); trigger selector on the tang; vault-snug lock-up with a hinge that lets the barrels fall open smoothly but not loosely, and with no rebound; snappy automatic ejectors (fired shells are ejected, unfired rounds raised by the extractor); good "pointability" – that feeling you get when the gun leaps to your shoulder and tracks the target without your conscious help, a fit that makes pointing the shotgun off-target harder than pointing it at the target.

Some of these features – a mechanical trigger, for instance – are negotiable. But not pointability. It depends a great deal on stock fit and the gun's balance. To check stock fit, shoulder the shotgun several times with your eyes closed, opening them when your cheek settles on the comb. You should be looking straight down the rib, with just enough rib showing to center the pattern where the bead appears. Of you have to move

Necessary hardware is hidden in the forend of any over/under, making slim forward profiles hard to engineer.

your head to get the right picture, the stock does not fit you.

Balance is harder to measure. There's no saying where the balance point should be. Besides, the distribution of weight either side of the balance point also affects the way a shotgun points. Good balance is one of those things you'll recognize but have a hard time describing.

Shotgun weight is easier to quantify, but the right weight depends on your shooting style, barrel length and gauge, and the loads you intend to fire. Excepting waterfowl guns intended for magnum loads, I like 12-bore double guns to scale about 7 pounds. Twenty-gauge models should weigh half a pound less. Part of that difference must come from the breech, because a 20-gauge is properly built on a smaller frame. In 28-gauge circles, the Ruger Red Label is much beloved because its frame is petite, as if it were designed around a shotshell, not as a down-sized 12-bore.

How much should you spend for an over/under? Well, gone are the days you could order a new Superposed for $315. You'll pay triple that to start. If you have $1,000, your options are limited, but E. Rizzini offers several from around $800. Between $1200 and $1800 you'll find a bonanza of field-grade models. The used-gun market offers more alternatives. A hunting gun that has few scars, appears tight and shows evidence of even rudimentary care can be a great buy. Competition guns are less attractive to me, because they get a lot more shooting. While well-made over/unders have a long life, I'd rather buy a gun that's hammered out a few hundred rounds than one that's fired many thousands. Avoid guns with marred screw heads or signs of hand tools at the breech juncture. Look for grip cracks behind the tang. Refinished wood or metal will affect resale value. If there's side-play in the hinge, or breech movement with the gun closed, take your money and run.

A new over/under won't make you an expert wingshooter, but its handling qualities should get you on target quicker than you can point your autoloader or pump. My next shotgun may be a Remington 332. It won't have quite the appeal of a stackbarrel owned by Jack O'Connor. But it will probably shoot just as well.

English side-by-sides are acknowledged as the best of upland guns. But this lovely Fausto Massi, an Italian over/under, shows top-end fit and finish. It points like a wish.

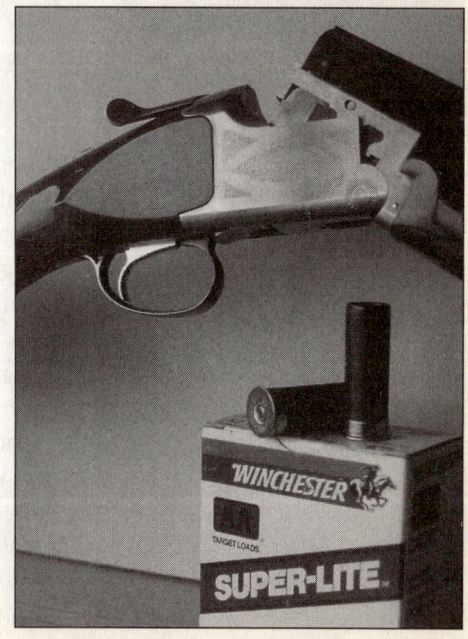

The best shotgun weight depends on the application and the ammunition, as well as your own idea of how a shotgun should feel. Light loads in a 7-pound 12-bore make a good upland combination.

Features Articles • 53

Hunting with Remington's New Short Action Ultra Mag
by Jim Zumbo

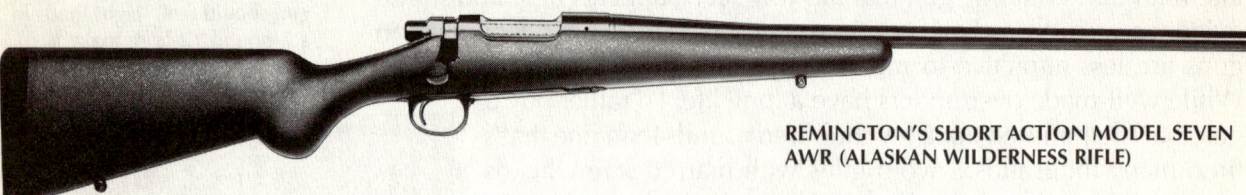

REMINGTON'S SHORT ACTION MODEL SEVEN AWR (ALASKAN WILDERNESS RIFLE)

Above: The author with British Columbia black bear taken with the .300 Remington Short Action Ultra Magnum.

Every now and then a gun has a special look, even though it's essentially a conventional model without frills, such as fancy checkering and engraving. That's how it was when I first hefted Remington's new Model Seven Short Action Ultra Mag in .300 caliber. I liked the way it felt, the way it handled, and I was eager to see how it shot. A couple of those shots, I hoped, would be directed to the vitals of a big game animal or two.

Homework at my community rifle range showed impressive performance from the short action, though I needed to battle typical and formidable Wyoming winds every time I shot it. Using 180-grain Nosler bullets, I was able to make very acceptable groups. Frankly, the gun was so new that the ammo provided by Remington was hand loaded. As luck would have it, I received a box of 180-grain Core-Lokts, which have been my favorite bullets over the years. These cartridges, howev-

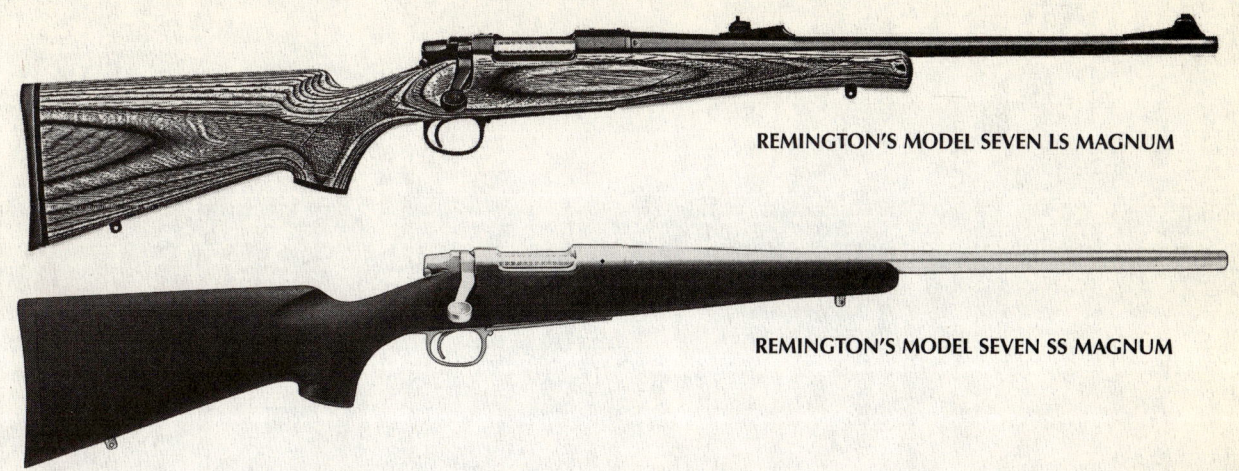

REMINGTON'S MODEL SEVEN LS MAGNUM

REMINGTON'S MODEL SEVEN SS MAGNUM

er, were only prototypes and would not be part of Remington's offerings. Instead, the company is producing 150 gr. PSP, Core-Lokt Ultras; 165 gr. PSP Core-Lokts; and 180 gr. Nosler Partitions.

The Short Action I hunted with comes from the Custom Shop, and is the Model Seven AWR (Alaskan Wilderness Rifle). It weighs 6 1/8 pounds soaking wet, sports a sweet little 22-inch barrel, and has a three-round magazine with hinged floor plate. The production models are the Model Seven LS Magnum, and the Model Seven SS Magnum. They weigh in at 7 1/8 pounds.

According to Remington's ballistic chart, the .300 S.A. Ultra Mag, when zeroed at 200 yards, has a drop of only 6.8 inches at 300 yards, and 19.7 inches at 400, when using 180-grain Nosler Partition bullets. Velocity with the same bullet at 200 yards is an impressive 2572 fps, and a whopping 2214 fps at 400 yards. Energy is also an eye-opener; 2642 foot pounds at 200 yards, and 1959 foot pounds at 400.

My first hunt with the Short Action was a black bear trip to British Columbia with my good outfitter pal, Darrell Collins. We'd be hunting bears north of Prince George, the most northerly large city in British Columbia. This trip was engineered by Remington Arms to specifically field test and evaluate some of their newer model firearms, including the Short Action. Linda Powell, Press Relations manager for Remington, was hosting the trip along with Greg Jones of Kahles Optics, who would provide scopes and binoculars. Besides Linda and Greg, six more people, including myself, rounded out our party.

I know some folks who aren't much into bear hunting. If they score on a hunt, they're not inclined to try it again. I'm most definitely not in that category. I've been on 50 plus black bear hunts, some self-guided, and some with outfitters, and I never get tired of hunting the bruins. I've never gotten over the thrill of seeing a bear, regardless of how many show themselves during a hunt. More than once I've been on hunts when I've honestly seen 20 different bears, and every one has sent a chill up my spine.

I also have some very definite opinions about firearms for bears, and

This moose fell on the spot after being struck by a 180 gran Nosler bullet fired from a .300 Remington Short Action Ultra Magnum.

I was anxious to try the new Remington. At the time of the hunt, the Short Action was yet to come off the production line. As I mentioned, Linda provided me with a gun fresh out of the custom shop, and I used the prototype 180-grain Core-Lokts.

British Columbia doesn't allow baiting, as do most other Canadian provinces. Spotting and stalking is the primary strategy, either from hiking, via pickup trucks or ATV's. Since Darrell's camp sits smack in the middle of prime bear territory, we didn't have to travel far to see a bear. In fact, several were spotted within a half-mile of our very comfortable tent camp.

Prior to hunting we sighted in to insure our firearms were dialed in. Mine was right on the money, zeroed at 100 yards, which is almost always my preference regardless of what I'm shooting.

Over the next three days I passed on several bears. Darrell explained that the late spring kept the bigger bruins in their dens, as well as inaccessible. Many of the logging roads we traveled were still blocked by snow, though we used a six-wheel ATV to negotiate some of the lower country. We frequently left the vehicles and hiked ridges and places where bears were apt to be feeding on green grass. As we walked, I noted how comfortable it was to carry the Short Action. The light weight of the Model Seven was most appealing, since practically all my big game hunting over the past 40 some years was done with a heavier rifle. I swear there's a dent in my right shoulder from carrying weighty firearms all those decades.

At one point Darrell spotted a bear 500 yards away, but it disappeared into a small patch of timber. I made a quick stalk for a closer look, and thought I saw the animal asleep under some trees. After a half hour, the form of a bear suddenly appeared, and the bruin walked along a log into the open. I rested the Remington on a stump and held for the crease just behind the shoulder. At the shot, the bear was hurled off the log, righted itself, and ran a few yards before collapsing.

The Short Action had done its job without a hitch. The bear never knew what hit him, and I learned later from Linda that this was the first bear ever to be taken with the .300 Short Action.

Later that summer, in mid-September and just a week after the terrorist attack, I hunted again with the Short Action, this time for a moose in Utah. I'd drawn a once in-a-lifetime tag, and foolishly decided to hunt alone. I had an option of hunting with an outfitter, but I wanted to do this my way. I promised myself I'd shoot a moose only if it was close to a road, for obvious reasons. If it wasn't real close to a road, it would at least be on the uphill side.

As soon as I stepped out of the pickup the first day, I loaded the Short Action with 180-grain Nosler Partition bullets, and wandered away from the road. I followed a mooseylooking willow bottom that virtually screamed moose. Fresh sign abounded, and I was drawn farther and farther away from the road, until I finally came to my senses.

This was dumb, I thought, and headed back toward the road. Though I could have cut a moose up in little pieces and readily transported it to the truck, the warm weather required that I get it out quickly. I've long ago learned that flies and heat are two major problems when hunting on hot days.

As I slowly eased through patches of willows, I carried the rifle at the ready so it could be shouldered quickly if I jumped a moose. I liked the way the Short Action was balanced, and the 22-inch barrel

Linda Powell, Senior Press Relations Manager for Remington, with her Colorado bull elk taken with a .300 Remington Short Action Ultra Magnum.

allowed me to slip and weave in the thick brush with no pesky hang-ups.

There were some dandy moose in the unit, and I'd been applying for the tag for about 20 years, but I was unnerved by the terrorist attack. I'd planned on camping, but instead stayed in a motel in a small town where I could watch the news on TV. I passed on some small bulls, but I wasn't really in the mood to make an extended hunt. For that reason, the 40-inch bull that stood on a slope on the uphill side of the road looked mighty good. Using a forked stick that I fished out of a beaver dam to rest my rifle on, I touched the trigger of the Short Action. Mr. Bullwinkle went down hard and renewed my respect for the rifle. I swore, after fielddressing the huge animal in the dark, that I'd never again do this solo. I reaffirmed this ironclad resolution the next day when I cut the moose into little pieces and hauled it out.

The .300 Short Action Ultra Mag performed perfectly, and I was ready for the next test, which would be for elk in Colorado. Though I hunt big-game extensively, I've always had a passion for elk. I live in northwest Wyoming where I can see the big, wonderful animals practically every day from my house. I've hunted every "elk state" in the west, and wrote six books on elk hunting. Curiously, of the 40-some elk I've taken, I never took one with a Remington rifle, any Remington. My first 19 bull elk were taken with my Winchester Model 70 in .30/06 caliber, and another dozen or so were taken with a 7mm Rem Mag Browning A-bolt. Marlins, Rugers, and other brands claimed elk for me as well, so I was looking forward to finally shooting an elk with a Remington and putting the Short Action to the test. Frankly, I wasn't worried. The lightweight, hard-hitting rifle that shoots the fat cartridges was receiving A-plus ratings from me.

The elk hunt would be hosted by Remington, with optics provided by Zeiss. Linda Powell was on the hunt, along with four writers, including me. This was Linda's first elk hunt ever, and she was looking forward to the trip, as we all were. We'd be hunting with Tenderfoot Outfitters. I'd hunted with them twice before, and I'd taken a bull on both hunts. Paul and Steve Pike, the former owners, had sold the business recently, but continued to guide occasionally for the new owners, Tom Evans and Mark Nichols. The Pike brothers and I had become close pals over the years since my first hunt with them, and I was anxious to get back in the wilderness camp where many memories were forged.

It was a typical wilderness elk hunt, with comfortable tents, good food, and excellent horse and guides. The weather wasn't cooperative however, in that the elk were "jungled up," because of the warm, balmy days. Though we rode out of camp every morning in the dark well before the first hint of gray in the eastern skies, the elk retreated into the timber before shooting light. The rut was basically over, eliminating the possibility of calling.

But the elk didn't win every day. On the third morning, Linda and Paul sat beneath a ridge covered with quaking aspens, and a herd of elk

Linda Powell, Senior Press Relations Manager for Remington Arms, poses with an antelope she took with one shot at 250 yards with her .300 Remington Short Action Ultra Magnum.

made the mistake of running by. A bull was in the group, and Linda put it down in a heap with one shot from her .300 Short Action Ultra Mag. I was a quarter mile away, and walked over when I heard the shot. She and Paul wore ear-to-ear grins when I showed up.

We had heard a shot about a half hour after Linda scored, and noted the time. This was critical, because we had a friendly pool among the hunters as to who would get the first elk. Linda not only won the pool, but she was the first hunter to ever score on an elk with the .300 Short Action.

I was unable to connect on that hunt, though I gave it everything I had. Plenty of elk were around, but, as I like to say, they were simply being elk –elusive, sneaky, and tough to locate in the immensely timbered world they live in.

Linda also had another first with the Short Action, a pronghorn antelope that she handily dropped with one shot at 250 yards.

Later that fall I went on to take a seven-point whitetail with the Short Action, and he too dropped in his tracks. I was again a happy camper with the .300.

As one who writes hunting articles and hunts literally more than 150 days a year, I shoot more than one rifle nowadays. It wasn't always that way; for most of my life I had "pet" rifles that I used almost exclusively. If the Short Action keeps up the quality of shooting I've seen so far, it might just be at the top of the rack for some time to come. For sure, it will accompany me on the three elk hunts I'm planning this fall. It's time to finally take an elk with a Remington, and the .300 Short Action is just the ticket.

Features Articles • 59

The Saboted Muzzle-Loaded Hunting Projectile
by Toby Bridges

Plastic saboted bullets, center, have become the most widely used muzzleloader hunting projectiles, replacing the soft lead round ball and bore-sized conical bullet.

The No. 209 shotshell primer ignited Knight D.I.S.C. Rifle is one of today's more advanced models, capable of exceptional accuracy with magnum charges of Pyrodex Pellets and saboted bullets.

Muzzleloader shooting has experienced something of an accelerated metamorphosis during the past several decades. No longer is muzzleloading simply driven by the desire to master old-fashioned front-loaded gun designs from the past. Instead, it has become an extremely performance driven hunting sport, and the rifles now favored by an entirely new following of muzzleloader fanciers are far different than the authentically styled reproductions of 150 to 200 year old originals that enjoyed popularity during the 1960s and 1970s.

Browse through the Blackpowder Arms listings of the catalog section found in this publication and you'll discover that the number of modern in-line ignition muzzleloading rifles or variations of those rifles now significantly outnumber the selection of traditionally styled muzzleloaders. The heart of each model or type is an ultra-modern ignition system that insures fast, positive and sure-fire combustion of the powder charge. Many of the more advanced models have even moved away from using the standard No. 11 percussion cap for ignition, turning to hotter winged musket caps or even still hotter No. 209 shotshell primers.

Likewise, the majority of the best selling models now incorporate modern "center-fire rifle" type stocks, plus other more modern features, such as safeties, fiber-optic sights, and on some enclosed break-open or bolt-action ignition systems. On nearly all, receivers come drilled and tapped for easy installation of telescopic sights. One look at any of these new wave muzzleloaders and it becomes readily apparent that these rifles have been built to deliver pinpoint accuracy. However, instead of loading and shooting traditional round ball or bore-sized lead conical projectiles from the past, today's muzzleloading hunter has turned to a projectile system that's just as modern as the muzzleloader he or she now packs into the deer woods. The muzzleloader hunting projectile of choice these days has become a modern jacketed or all-copper bullet that's loaded into the rifle with a tight-fitting plastic sabot.

Just 25 years ago, muzzleloaders with rifling which spun with a complete revolution in anything less than 48 inches was considered to have a fast rate of twist. Today, a 1 turn-in-48 inches rate of twist is considered slow. Muzzleloading rifle manufacturers have found that optimum accuracy with a plastic saboted bullet is best achieved with relatively shallow rifling having a rate of twist as fast as one turn-in-24 to 28 inches. And the bores of most modern in-line ignition rifles feature grooves that spiral at those stepped up rates for best accuracy with saboted projectiles.

The .50 caliber Knight rifles come with a turn-in-28 inches twist, Gonic Arms relies on a slightly faster turn-in-24 inches in both .45 and .50 caliber models, both Remington and Ruger feature rifling with a turn-in-28 inches in their .50 caliber in-line rifles, while the new .50 caliber Savage Model 10ML II comes with a snappy one turn-in-24 inch rate of twist. Some of the more recent "Super" .45 caliber in-line ignition muzzleloaders now feature rifling as fast as one turn-in-20 or 22 inches.

The sabot concept has been around for ages. In its simplest form, a sabot is almost anything that allows an under-sized projectile to be loaded and fired from a larger diameter bore. The sabot simply takes up the void between the smaller diameter projectile and larger bore. In fact, the cloth patch used to grip both a smaller diameter round ball and the grooves of a traditional muzzleloader bore is in essence a sabot. Saboted projectiles have been loaded and fired from cannon for hundreds of

Writer Toby Bridges with a dandy Missouri whitetail buck taken at 170 yards With a saboted .45 caliber handgun bullet from his Savage Model 10ML II muzzleloader. The buck dropped on the spot.

The sharp-pointed nose of the 180, 200 and 220-grain all-copper Barnes/Knight "Red Hot" bullets give this design a much better ballistic coefficient than blunt-nosed jacketed hollow-point handgun bullets, resulting in exceptional accuracy from some in-line rifles, plus better retention of downrange energy levels.

years. Saboted shotgun slugs have been around for more than 30 years. And about that many years ago, Remington introduced their Accelerator line of saboted center-fire rifle cartridges that allowed shooters to fire light .223" diameter "varmint bullets" from larger bore rifles like the .30/30 Winchester or .30/06 Springfield.

During the early 1980s, muzzleloading shooter Del Ramsey, of Harrison, Arkansas, began his search for a muzzle-loaded hunting projectile that would perform better on big game than simple pure-lead round ball and conical projectiles. Ramsey happened to own a small plastic injection molding company and quickly set out to design a plastic sabot, or cup, which would allow him to load and shoot modern jacketed pistol bullets out of .45, .50 and .54 caliber frontloading rifles. He established Muzzleload Magnum Products in 1984 and since has become the leading manufacturer of muzzleloader sabots. In addition to being marketed under the MMP brand name, a half-dozen other companies now also package and market his sabots, either alone or matched with an appropriate bullet.

While the design of the various sabots produced under contract by MMP for companies such as Knight, Hornady and Barnes may vary slightly from one company to another, the sabot configuration is basically the same. These are a cup-like arrangement, looking much like the shotcup for a very small-bore shotgun. The "cup" features four petals or sleeves that encompass the cylindrical portion of a bullet, while the base of the sabot features a slight cup that seals the bore when pushed down the barrel by the burning powder charge. The tight grip of the petals or sleeves on the bullet and the rifling of the bore transfer the spin of the rifling to the bullet. Almost at the instant the sabot and bullet leave the bore, the petals peel out and away from the bullet and the sabot falls back from the projectile. The bullet is then on its way to the target, without any other further influence from the sabot.

The author has found the 250-grain Hornady .452" XTP to be one of the most reliable, best performing muzzle-loading hunting projectiles he's every used on deer-sized game. Shown here with a Muzzleload Magnum Product high-pressure sabot.

Muzzleload Magnum Products currently offers nine different sabots, for rifles ranging in caliber from .36 up to .58. However, his best selling sabots are those designed to shoot .44 or .45 caliber bullets from .50 caliber muzzleloading big game rifles. And, this shouldn't come as any surprise since modern in-line ignition rifles of .50 caliber currently account for nearly 75-percent of all muzzleloaders sold.

Since the introduction of the MMP sabots, one size has remained the best selling – the company's green sabot that's designed to shoot bullets of .429-.430" diameter out of a .50 caliber bore. The second best selling version is a black sabot for loading and shooting .451-.452" projectiles from a fast twist .50 caliber barrel.

Ramsey attributes the popularity of the green .50 caliber sabot to the fact that when he first hit the market with his muzzleloader projectile system, there happened to be a much greater selection of .429-.430" bullets for the extremely popular .44 Remington Magnum handguns than there were for the venerable ol' .45 handguns. And it was handgun bullets for which the sabots had been designed. However, as a better selection of .451-.452" bullets continue to be developed for powerhouse handguns like the .454 Casull, the popularity of the black .50 caliber sabot is quickly closing on his green .50x.44 sabot.

Experienced in-line .50 caliber muzzleloading rifle shooters have long favored the black .50x.45 sabot over the green .50x.44 sabot for superior accuracy. More than a decade ago, I personally discovered that if I could get one of the modern in-line ignition rifles to shoot a 2-inch group at 100 yards with a green MMP sabot and .44 caliber bullets, I could usually get that same rifle to print honest 1 ?-inch or tighter groups by simply switching to the black sabot and a .45 caliber projectile. It became apparent to me and other veteran in-line rifle shooters that the best accuracy tended to come from a bullet and sabot combination that utilized a bullet diameter that was as close to the bore size of the rifle as possible.

When shooting just about any .429-.430" diameter bullet with a green sabot, you're apt to find these sabots lying on the ground 15 to 20 yards from the muzzle of the rifle. However, when shooting with the black sabot and slightly larger diameter .451-.452" bullets, these sabots will normally hit the ground 5 or more yards closer to the muzzle. Early on, my conclusion was that due to thinner petals or sleeves of the .50x.45 plastic sabots, they tended to peel away from the projectile more rapidly than the thicker and stiffer petals/sleeves of the .50x.44 green MMP sabots. Del Ramsey of Muzzleload Magnum Products agrees.

"Had the selection of .45 caliber bullets available today been around in the early 1980s, more than likely I would have never come out with the .44 green sabot," comments Ramsey.

Hornady, Nosler, Speer, Sierra, Barnes, Swift and a few other bullet makers now catalog an unbelievable selection of .44 and .45 caliber bullets, in weights ranging from as light as 180 grains all the way up to 325 grains. There are a number of bullets in the selection that are ideally suited for hunting any species of big game roaming the North American continent. Unfortunately, there are also a few choices that were never designed to be shot at the velocities produced by magnum powder charges in a muzzleloading rifle. The construction or design of some bullets simply won't perform well enough for use on big game.

Two of my long time favorite .45 caliber bullets for shooting out of a modern in-line muzzleloader have been the .452" diameter Hornady XTP jacketed hollow-point bullets in both 250 and 300 grains. I've shot each of these bullets out of a variety of .50 caliber rifles at velocities ranging from around 1,500 f.p.s. all the way up to more than 2,300

The non-expanding "Radially Dynamic" DEVEL bullet from Leved Cartridge Ltd. introduces totally new technology to the field of muzzleloader hunting projectiles.

Jacketed hollow-point bullets that feature exposed soft lead at the nose, such as this 260-grain .451" diameter Speer, perform well at velocities up to around 1,700 f.p.s. Higher velocities often result in erratic accuracy.

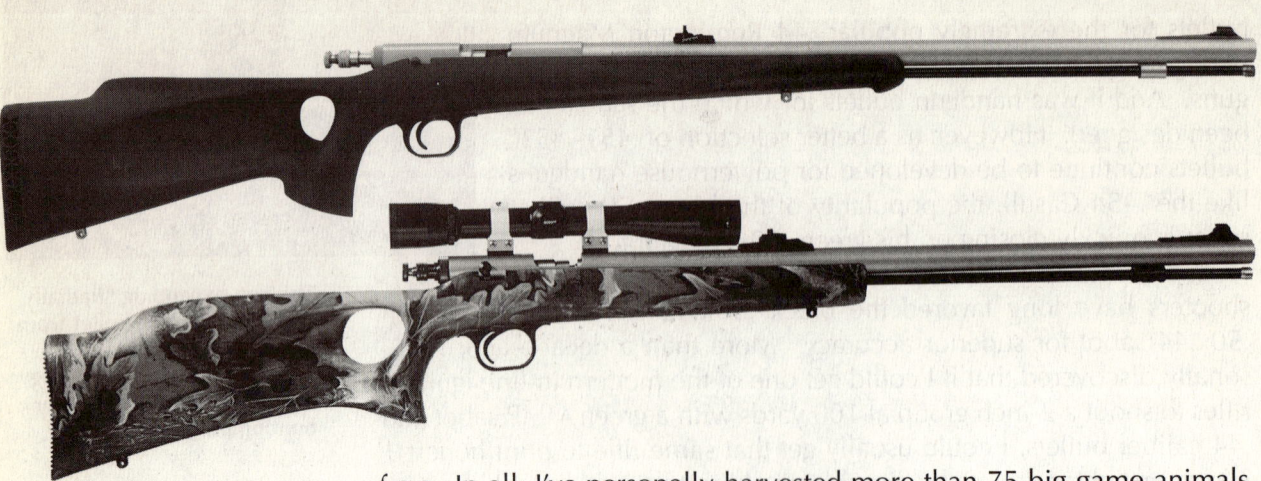

Top:
The Knight MK-85, shown with composite thumbhole stock, was the in-line ignition rifle that started the move to modern muzzleloading designs and the use of saboted hunting bullets.

Bottom:
Compared to many other in-line ignition rifles, the Knight Wolverine, shown with a composite thumbhole stock, features the same turn-in-28 inches rate of twist found in other Knight barrels and delivers the same superb accuracy with saboted bullets.

f.p.s. In all, I've personally harvested more than 75 big game animals with these two bullets, and I've never had to shoot anything twice!

During the 2001 muzzleloading season in North Carolina, I joined a group of nine other muzzleloading hunters to conduct performance tests with the Hornady 250 and 300 grain .452" XTP jacketed hollow-point bullets. Everyone in the camp was shooting the new Savage Model 10ML II "smokeless powder" muzzleloaders, loading and shooting various loads of Accurate Arms XMP-5744, IMR-4227 or Vihtavuori N110. Most of the loads being shot got the saboted 250-grain XTP out of the muzzle of the 24-inch barrels at around 2,300 f.p.s., and the heftier 300-grain version at around 2,250 f.p.s. These velocities translate into around 2,950 ft. lbs. of energy with the 250-grain loads and right at 3,375 ft. lbs. of knockdown power at the muzzle with the 300-grain Hornady bullet.

In all, our group harvested 42 whitetails during the six-day hunt. These deer were shot at ranges of 40 to 200 yards. A total of 31 of the deer were taken with the 250-grain bullet, 11 with the heavier 300 grain XTP. Special care was taken to try recovering every bullet that stayed inside these deer, and in the end we recovered 17 of the 250-grain slugs and only 2 of the 300-grain bullets.

While every deer shot went down to single hits, it was noted that all but one of the whitetails taken with the 300-grain XTP ran some distance before going down. The average was around 30 yards. On the other hand, most of the deer shot with the lighter 250-grain Hornady bullet practically dropped on the spot. Just four ran any distance after being hit, and all went less than 20 yards.

From this study, we concluded that the 250-grain XTP jacketed hollow-point was a better choice for deer-sized game than the heavier 300-grain version. Even though, with the powder charges being shot, the heavier bullet produced an average muzzle energy that was more than 400 ft. lbs. greater, the lighter bullet did a better job of putting the deer down cleanly. All but one of the hunters in camp were veteran muzzleloading hunters, and the general consensus was that the heavier bullet tended to punch on through, taking some of that added ener-

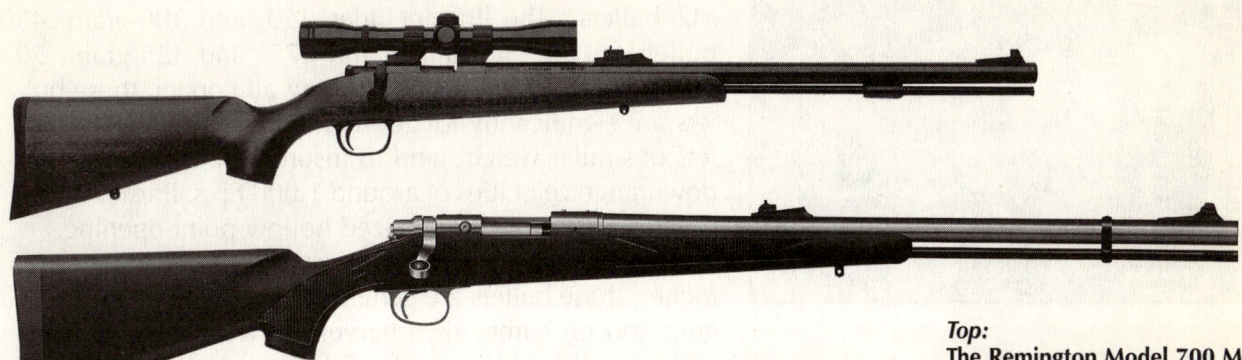

Top:
The Remington Model 700 ML "bolt-action" in-line muzzleloader has established a great reputation for outstanding accuracy with saboted bullets. The rifle features a turn-in-28 inches rate of rifling twist.

Bottom:
The Traditions Lightning has established a reputation for delivering affordable performance with saboted bullets. The turn-in-32 inches rate of twist performs best with the shorter bullet lengths.

gy with it. The lighter 250-grain bullet seemingly did a much better job of transferring most, if not all, of its energy to the target. Nicely expanded 250-grain bullets were recovered from roughly 55-percent of the deer shot with that bullet weight, while only about 20-percent of the deer taken with the 300-grain bullet produced a recovered slug.

During a Nebraska hunt later that fall, I took a nice ten-point whitetail buck at 214 yards with my scoped .50 caliber Savage Model 10ML II. I was shooting 45 grains of Vihtavuori N110 behind one of the 250-grain .45 Hornady XTPs, loaded with one of the more recent MMP "High-Pressure" black sabots. At the muzzle, the load develops a velocity of 2,397 f.p.s., with an astounding 3,175 ft. lbs. of energy. Out at the distance I took my buck, the bullet still drove home with close to 1,200 ft. lbs. of knockdown power. The near 250-pound live weight whitetail went just 20 feet before going down, and the recovered slug still weighed 246.2 grains.

Before going to the smokeless powder Model 10ML II for all of my hunting, I hunted often with a saboted 260-grain Speer .451" jacketed hollow-point bullet ahead of 90 to 110 grains of Pyrodex "RS/Select". At the muzzle of most in-line percussion hunting rifles, this load is good for 1,550 to 1,650 f.p.s., with 1,380 to 1,570 ft. lbs. of energy. The bullet was accurate, expanded well and accounted for a lot deer-sized game

The Savage Model 10ML II is the only muzzleloader designed to shoot modern smokeless powders. The rifle will consistently print saboted bullets inside of 1½-inches at a hundred yards shooting loads with a muzzle velocity of 2,300 f.p.s. and faster.

for me through the late 1980s and early 1990s. However, when I began to shoot and hunt with magnum 150-grain Pyrodex Pellet charges and early versions of the Savage smokeless powder muzzleloader, the bullet simply would not fly as true once velocities approached and surpassed 2,000 f.p.s.

During the mid to late 1990s, several bullet makers began to produce designs specifically for loading and shooting out of a muzzleloader with a plastic sabot. One of the more popular bullets of this type has been the Barnes all-copper Expander

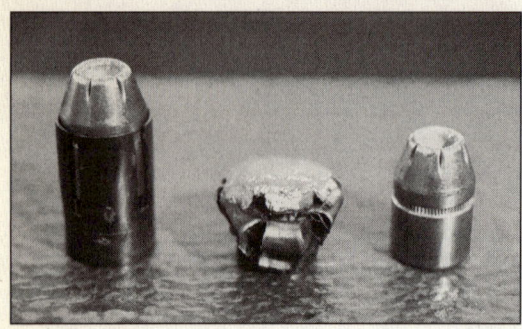

The fully mushroomed 250-grain .452" Hornady XTP shown here was recovered from a buck taken at about 100 yards. The deer dropped in its tracks.

Noted muzzleloading big game hunter Jim Shockey with a record book musk-ox, taken with a Knight D.I.S.C. rifle and saboted 300-grain bullet.

MZ bullets. The line includes 250- and 300-grain .45 bullets for the .50 caliber and 275- and 325-grain .50 bullets for .54 caliber rifles. Being all-copper, these bullets are significantly longer than jacketed lead-core bullets of similar weight, and to insure proper expansion at downrange velocities of around 1,000 f.p.s. Barnes incorporates a volcanic crater sized hollow-point opening.

Out of rifles with a rifling twist of one turn-in-24 to 28 inches, these bullets are generally very accurate and do a great job on game. I've harvested two mature bull elk with the 300-grain Expander MZ out of .50 caliber rifles, and neither went more than 50 yards. However, this bullet is so long that out of rifles with a turn-in-32 inches or slower rate of twist, they often do not stabilize and keyhole badly. The huge opening at the nose also seems to hinder accuracy when velocities exceed 1,900 f.p.s. Anyway, that's been my findings.

Knight Rifles has contracted with Barnes Bullets to produce several all-copper bullets for .50 caliber fast-twist barrels. Marketed as the Knight "Red Hot" bullets, the lineup includes the standard 250 and 300 grain Expander MZ designs, plus lighter 180, 200 and 220 grain bullets that feature a dramatically superior aerodynamic hollow-point nose. The better ballistic coefficients of these lighter all-copper Barnes bullets not only improve accuracy at higher muzzleloader velocities, the sharp spire-point design also give better retention of energy downrange.

Out of a .50 caliber Knight D.I.S.C. Rifle, I've found that a three 50-grain Clean Shot Pellet load will get one of the saboted 220 grain Red Hot bullets out of the muzzle at 2,231 f.p.s., with 2,431 ft. lbs. of energy. At 100 yards, the load consistently prints inside of 1 ?-inches. Stoking the Savage Model 10ML II with a 44.5 grain charge of Vihtavuori N110 and a 220-grain Red Hot bullet loaded with one of the MMP High-Pressure sabots, I can up muzzle velocity to 2,435 f.p.s. and muzzle energy to 2,893 ft. lbs. This bullet has a ballistic coefficient of around .217 (compared to just .147 for the 250-grain Hornady XTP). At the D.I.S.C. Rifle velocity, it would still hit with 1,652 ft. lbs. at 100 yards, and 1,142 ft. lbs. out at 200 yards. Thanks to the higher velocity produced by the Savage Model 10ML II and smokeless powder charge, the bullet has close to 1,900 ft. lbs. of remaining energy at 100 yards, and continues to drive home with nearly 1,400 ft. lbs. of punch at 200 yards.

Another new muzzleloading bullet design that's taking this old sport into the future is the DEVEL "Radially Dynamic" bullet from Leved Cartridge Ltd.

(Georgetown, TX). This is a non-expanding copper/tin composite bullet that features five deep flutes at the nose. The design relies on hydraulics for transferring energy to the game animal rather than expansion. It is one of the most accurate muzzleloading bullets I've ever shot, and I've taken several deer and a half-dozen or so wild hogs with the company's 175 grain saboted .45 bullet for the .50 caliber rifles. Leved Cartridge also offers a 130-grain .40 caliber design for shooting with a sabot in a .45 caliber bore.

Manufacturers have taken muzzleloading rifle development about as far as possible. Some now see the promise of improved muzzleloader performance in a new breed of "Super" or "Magnum" .45 caliber in-line rifle. Whether or not these replace the .50 caliber rifles as the favored choice of muzzleloading hunters will depend largely on future improvements to muzzleloader projectiles. Muzzleloading is now a performance driven game and the caliber or projectile that delivers that performance will lead the pack.

The all-copper Barnes Expander MZ bullets have been designed to expand at the velocities produced by most .50 or .54 caliber muzzleloading big game rifles.

Shooting a saboted 300-grain all-cooper Barnes Expander MZ pushed out the barrel by 100 grains of Pyrodex Select, Toby Bridges watched this near 900-pound bull elk go down after just a short 40-yard run.

Features Articles • 67

One Cartridge, Many Bullets
by Sam Fadala

Author shooting another 30-30, this one a Winchester Model 94. Handloading increases the versatility of the venerable 30-30 with a wide variety of different bullets. Ammo companies also offer a wide range of loads.

There is much to be said for choosing one, and only one, projectile for a given cartridge. I've never waltzed with the 30-'06 Springfield because there are so many more romantic rounds to dance with: the 7mm magnum class for all-around big game authority on one end, my ever-present "outdated" 30-30 on the other, along with myriad rounds smaller and larger. However, I can see choosing a 165-grain bullet for that grand old round and never looking back. It makes infinite good sense. A stout handload pushes that deadly projectile at 2,900 feet per second at the muzzle from the '06, a trace faster with certain maximum loads from a 24-inch barrel. The only problem with pure practicality in the fascinating world of shooting is boredom. No matter how successful the 30-'06 performed with that single missile, I would never load her up that way all the time for everything. I don't even do that with my 30-30.

In fact, the 30-30 is my favorite example of one cartridge, many bullets. I like the way the old round thrives, especially in light of the darts and barbs tossed at her by modern scribes. One of my favorite remarks comes from a recent loading manual. The author says the 30-30 hangs on because of "an irrational love for this marginally performing round." Well stated and he's right (almost). I can think of triple fistfuls of cartridges that outflank the little 30. But I feel a certain kinship with hunters of the late 19th and early 20th centuries when I shoot a Winchester 94 or Marlin 336 30-30. And one other little thing worth mentioning—it works. The little 30 works especially well with different bullets in either factory or home rolled fodder. My friend Shannon Thomas took his young son on an Arizona Coues deer hunt last season. The lad dropped a fine buck with one shot from a Thompson/Center rifle chambered for the "marginally performing" 30-30. The 125-grain Nosler bullet performed flawlessly, plenty strong for a diminutive southwestern whitetail. The 125-grain Sierra bullet in the 30-30 worked equally well for another friend, Paul Van Leuven, this time on mule deer and antelope in South Dakota. A year earlier I managed to collect a rather decent pronghorn with a 100-year old Savage levergun shooting the "outdated" 30-30 hand loaded with a modern 150-grain Winchester bullet.

Look at the gamut. The 30-30 can accurately shoot projectiles ranging all the way from 100-grains to 190-grains. Why would I want to saddle her with only one missile? Loaded down to something in the neighborhood of 1,700 to 1,800 feet per second muzzle velocity (fps mv), a 100-grain bullet turns the 30-30 into a decent small game/mountain bird (grouse, partridges, legal for rifle where I hunt in Wyoming) round where shots are generally taken at about 10 to 15 yards. Personal handloads with Reloader-15 powder in my 24-inch barrel Marlin 336-A are especially effective on big game. Loads include the deep-penetrating 170-grain Laser-Cast bullet at about 2,300-fps mv. I worked my ammunition up very carefully from well below maximum. They are, of course, safe in my Marlin 336-A, but will lock up less strong actions.

A 165-grain Nosler Ballistic-Tip bullet achieved a chronographed 2,427-fps mv with a maximum charge of Reloader-15 powder. Pointed bullets must never be lined up in a tubular magazine for safety reasons, plus the shapely Ballistic Tip is too long to work in the Marlin 336 action anyway. Therefore, this bullet is a single-loaded proposition. Another good one in my Marlin rifle is the 165-grain Swift A-Frame, which can be seated deeply enough in the case to feed in my 30-30. The rifle is carried with zero rounds in the chamber, two in the magazine, hammer eared back to promote the slick action to work even quicker. One of the two rounds is brought into battery when it's time to shoot. Now the lone cartridge in the magazine has no primer in front of it. So here are two 165-grain bullets with different upset patterns on game. No wonder I choose not to make my 30-30 a one-bullet cartridge. Now add the 190-grain Silvertip extracted from Winchester brand 303 Savage ammo, a good heavy bullet black timber load. This .308-inch bullet escapes the muzzle at 2,165 fps, Reloader-15 powder

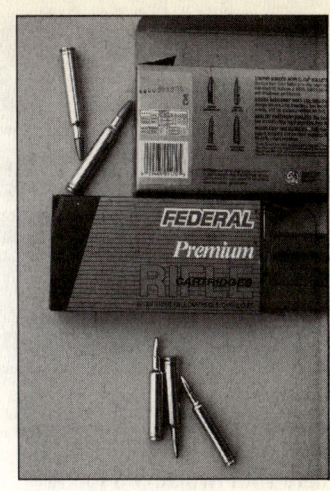

Bullet variation is so great because each design has a special purpose. Federal Premium ammunition is made with various bullet constructions to extend the versatility of each cartridge.

Author's Model 77 Ruger with Custom Morrison Precision barrel chambered for the wildcat 25-284 Winchester cartridge is treated to various bullets for various shooting

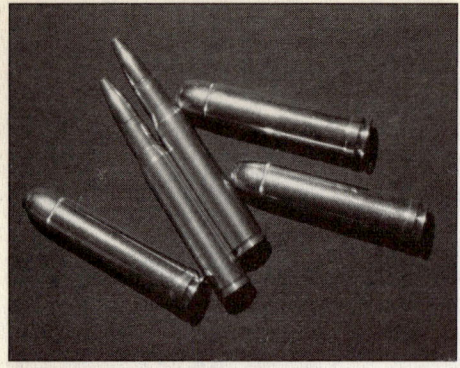

Each cartridge has its own niche. The 450 Marlin, shown here with two 30-'06 rounds for comparison, is intended for big game at medium ranges. Its heavy bullet is designed with a soft point to open up on impact.

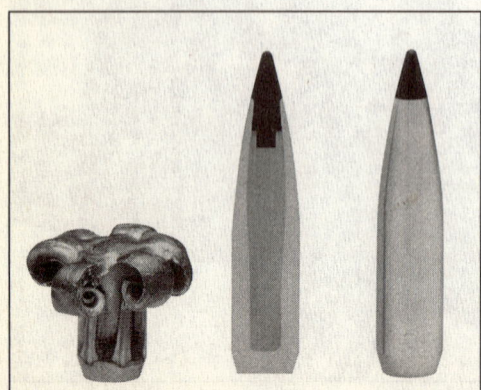

Typical of the rapid escalation in modern bullet design is this unique Swift Scirocco™ with bonded core. This one in 30-caliber can be loaded in a wide range of cartridges from 300 Savage to 30-378 Weatherby.

once again doing the work.

Choosing many different bullets for the 30-30 actually creates versatility in this centurion round. If it does that for the 30-30, what about the ever-successful 30-'06? Now the range of bullets grows. The lightweight 100-grain bullet on one end is joined by a 250-grain pill on the other. These bullets couldn't be more different, not only in the obvious weight department, but also structurally. A Speer 100-grain round nose soft-point, for example, is called the Plinker because it is. While it can be zipped downrange starting at over 3,400 fps with IMR-3031 powder, it can also be reduced to only 1,500 fps with a light charge of SR 4759. The Hornady 30-caliber 100-grain SJ (Short Jacket) is another fine bullet for gathering meat on the trail or popping beverage cans on a dirt bank, while a 125-grain Speer TNT hollow-point leaves the muzzle at high velocity for explosive effect on varmints.

It's easy to achieve over 3,000-fps mv with a 150-grain bullet in the '06 with H-380 and other powders. The 165-grain pill slams out at 2,900 fps mv with a dose of IMR-4350 or H-4350. The 30-'06 I worked most with, 24-inch barrel, clicked away at 2,812 fps mv with a 180-grain bullet, although 2,750 fps mv is more common with powders on the order of H-4831. In my tests a 200-grain bullet flew at close to 2,700-fps mv with H-414 or H-4831, the 220-grain taking off at 2,400-fps mv from a 24-inch barrel burning Reloader-22. Finally there's the Barnes 250-grain Original, called that because it is, going back a number of years. From the turn of the century '06 cartridge, this long, heavy missile cuts the air at 2,300-fps mv with a good dose of Reloader-22. If that bullet at close range in the Maine woods wouldn't end up on the offside of a moose I'd be surprised.

Bullet construction is always playing lead violin at the cartridge concert. Returning to the graybeard 30-30 I've found the 170-grain Laser-Cast to have strong penetration qualities in Sam's Bullet Box, a device I use for testing bullet upset. Of course this projectile has no jacket to shed. It's constructed of tough lead alloy, which tends to remain in one hunk rather than fragmenting. The Laser-Cast is a meat-saver, but will not turn to confetti in the boiler room for explosive type kills. Going for the shoulder region with this bullet makes sense. Cartridge case capacity dictates velocity potential. The 300 Weatherby Magnum drives the same 30-caliber bullets sent downrange by the 30-'06, only faster. Higher arrival velocities equate to greater impact energy, which in turn alters bullet performance. Staying with 30-caliber, what about the 300 WSM (Winchester Short Magnum)? This cartridge was generated from the theory that short and fat is better than long and slender for accuracy plus function in medium-length actions. Because bullets longer than 150-grains weight invade the powder chamber of this short round, the standard 300 Winchester Magnum gains slightly more velocity with 165s and heavier projectiles. But that's OK. The 300 WSM remains capable of jetting the 150-grain pill away at over 3,300-fps, a 180-grain pill over 3,000 fps mv. At the same time, this 30-caliber magnum can be tamed to 30-30 proportions for brush hunting whitetails shooting a 170-grain bullet at 2,300-fps mv with IMR-4759 powder.

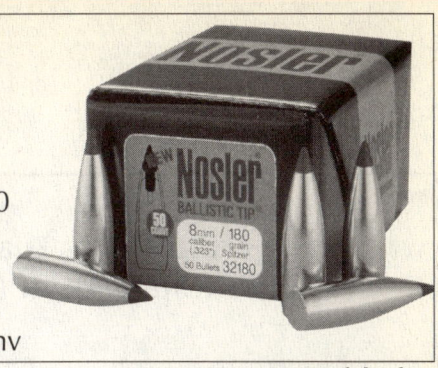

For many years one of the few bullets widely available in 8mm was 170-grains weight. Today, more bullets in caliber 8mm are offered, including this Nosler 180-grain. Rifles chambered for 8mm cartridges gained versatility through these new bullet weights and designs.

The wise husband or dad getting his wife or youngster started with a big game rifle never allows the newcomer to fire so much as one round of full-power ammunition during practice. Here is where one round, many bullets, comes to the fore again. Consider the excellent 7mm-08, my choice as an all-around big game cartridge for most ladies and young shooters getting. The cast bullet fan can make up a strong supply of 119-grain #287448 Lyman lead alloy bullets bumped out of the muzzle at only 1,400 fps with a light charge of Red Dot powder. The smaller shooter need not fire a single full-throttle shot from his or her 7mm-08, except in the field. This really works. On that deer, antelope, elk, whatever, noticeable recoil is nil. There's simply too much intent concentration for the shooter to worry about recoil. Instead of learning how to flinch from the pushback, or for that matter the noise, of the rifle, blast being another factor in trigger jerking, the hunter trained on low-power loads shoots high-power ammo with the same efficiency when the target is a big game animal.

Today, there are more bullet variations than ever, not only in weights per caliber, but also special constructions and designs. This Barnes XLC bullet is one of the company's special X configurations with solid copper construction.

The shooter interested in preparing loads with many different bullets for his favorite cartridge must thumb through the pages of loading manuals. The data are all there to be put into practice. A warning—never go with reduced loads that are not established through professional testing. Loading handbooks are worked up in laboratories under strict safety conditions, and it is possible for an underload to develop dangerous pressures. While this condition is not necessarily common, there are examples of slower-burning powders raising pressures when used in "half-charges." For example, one bullet company learned that reducing the normal charge of H-4831 in a 270 Winchester to only half its maximum produced not only high pressures, but also dangerous levels. In other words, stick to the data in the books. It's the safe and sane way to go.

My personal handloads for specific rifles always begin with printed information. Ideally, manuals reference a specific load to a specific rifle. But this is not always the case. The Hornady Handbook of Cartridge Reloading, Vo. 1, printed in 2000, shows different 45-70 Government loads based on three different rifle categories. On page 509, loads for the Springfield Trap Door are listed. This 1873 design is definitely not up to handling high pressures. In the same class Hornady includes

Sample Multi-Bullet Loads for Four Popular 30-Caliber Cartridges
Velocities Rounded off for Convenience

30-30 WINCHESTER

100-GRAIN HORNADY SJ (SHORT JACKET)
29.0-GRAINS H-322 • 2,100 FPS MV
Good small game load, also mountain grouse where allowed by law, as in Wyoming. Also good for plinking and training new shooters.

125-GRAIN SIERRA HPFN (HOLLOW POINT FLAT NOSE)
37.0-GRAINS W-748 • 2,650 FPS MV
This load has proved itself on smaller deer and antelope at ranges up to about 200 yards. Relatively light recoil.

150-GRAIN SPEER FP (FLAT POINT)
33.5-GRAINS AA2520 • 2,300 FPS MV
The late gunwriter, Warren Page, pointed out that the 30-30 with 150-grain bullet at medium velocity was a "balanced load" for deer. He was right. At modest ranges, one-shot kills are the norm with this bullet and load.

165-GRAIN BARNES XFN
31.0-GRAINS IMR-4895 • 2,100 FPS
Barnes shows this X-Bullet and load adequate for larger-than-deer game, including moose, in that company's loading manual. Expert hunters in Canada and Alaska have, of course, taken many moose with similar 30-30 ballistics, although there are certainly more adequate moose cartridges.

170-GRAIN SPEER FLAT POINT SOFT POINT
34.0-GRAINS W-748 • 2,100 FPS
While this load duplicates the velocity of the 150-grain bullet, the latter remains adequate for most deer hunting. For larger whitetails and mule deer, especially with shoulder shots, the heavier 170-grain bullet offers greater penetration.

308 WINCHESTER

100-GRAIN HORNADY SJ (SHORT JACKET)
16.0-GRAINS HERCO • 2,100 FPS MV
Same application as 30-30 load. This is a good short-range combination for getting the new shooter involved comfortably.

150-GRAIN SPEER BOAT-TAIL SPITZER SOFT POINT
49.0-GRAINS RELOADER 15 • 2,900 FPS MV
The 30-'06 earned a good reputation on deer and similar game with the same bullet at the same velocity in factory loads. In fact, most 30-'06 150-grain factory loads today leave the muzzle at about 2,900 fps.

165-GRAIN SIERRA BOAT-TAIL
46.0-GRAINS VHT N-150 • 2, 600 FPS MV
Good accuracy with more than sufficient power for deer-sized game, the 308 with 165-grain bullet.

170-GRAIN LASER-CAST
40.0-GRAINS IMR-4320 • 2,400 FPS MV
Simply turns the 308 Winchester into a 30-30+ for deer-sized game at medium distances.

190-GRAIN HORNADY BOAT-TAIL SOFT POINT
47.0-GRAINS W-760 • 2,400 FPS MV
This load proved itself on large antelope in Africa, USA game, too.

30-'06 SPRINGFIELD

110-GRAIN HORNADY V-MAX
58.0-GRAINS IMR-4064 • 3,400 FPS MV
While the 30-'06 cannot be considered a varmint cartridge, compared with rounds designed expressly for that use, such as the 22-250 Remington, this explosive bullet at high-velocity has a flat trajectory.

113-GRAIN LYMAN CAST BULLET NO. 311359
15.0-GRAINS UNIQUE • 2,000 FPS MV
This load turns the 30-'06 into a milder mannered rifle for practice. It's also useful for fur hunting during big game season, where the trapper goes loaded for deer, bear, or other with a few cast bullet loads in his pocket for furbearers.

125-grain Barnes XFB
56.0 BLC-2 • 3,200 FPS MV
This bullet has a ballistic coefficient of .351 and is more than adequate for long-range shooting in open country for prairie mule deer and antelope.

150-grain Sierra Spitzer Boat-Tail
61.0-grains Reloader 19 • 3,000 FPS MV
A standard for deer-size game even at the longer ranges. Shoots flat, with high remaining energy.

165-grain Speer Grand Slam
57.0-grains H-414 • 2,900 FPS MV
Admittedly, this bullet weight in the 30'06 is a great all-around performer, shooting about as flat as the 150-grain, but with more penetration potential, especially at the longer ranges. However, to use this one weight only in the 30-'06 is to restrict its versatility.

170-grain Laser-Cast
40.0-grains IMR-4064 • 2,400 FPS MV
Just like the same bullet in the 308, this load turns the 30-'06 into a strong 30-30 for deer-sized game at shorter ranges. The hardness of the bullet calls for shoulder shots.

180-grain Nosler Partition
60-0-grains Reloader 22 • 2,825 FPS MV
Out of a 24-inch barrel, this bullet and powder charge turn the 30-'06 into an all-around North American round, adequate for all but the unlikely charge of a grizzly. The partition design ensures good penetration.

200-grain Nosler Partition
57.5-grains Reloader 22 • 2,675 FPS MV
Another great combination for larger game is the 200-grain partition bullet with its high sectional density. Considering that the 30-'06, in its early stages, developed something like 2,750 fps mv with a 150-grain bullet, this load shows how far we have come with new bullets and powders.

250-grain Barnes Original
52.5-grains Reloader 22 • 2,300 FPS MV
When the 30-'06 is counted on for super penetration, this bullet can turn the trick at short to medium ranges.

300 Winchester Magnum

110-grain Hornady V-Max
81.0-grains H-4350 • 3,675 FPS MV
No cartridge that burns this much powder can be a pure pleasure to shoot on long-range varmints; however, the coyote hunter who happens to own a 300 Winchester Magnum, and who is interested in long-range shooting, will find this load workable.

151-grain Lyman Cast No. 311440
16.5-grains Green Dot • 1,750 FPS MV
Good load for practice, also useful for small game. Any and all of the larger magnum rounds produce quite a bit of recoil, muzzle blast, and noise. This load reduces all three.

165-grain Nosler Ballistic Tip
79.0-grains Reloader 22 • 3,300 FPS MV
There can be no question about flat shooting with this one. The sharp profile of the bullet hangs onto initial velocity well. This bullet reaches 300 yards doing 2,600 fps for more than a short ton of remaining energy.

180-grain Speer Grand Slam
81.0-grains H-1000 • 3,100 FPS MV
Depending upon the idiosyncrasies of individual rifles, this load can, and has, delivered a muzzle velocity of 3,165 fps. Obviously, this is what a 30-caliber magnum is all about.

250-grain Barnes Original
70.0-grains H-1000 • 2,550 FPS MV
There are many great bullets between the 180-grain and this heavyweight. However, this load moves the 300 Winchester Magnum into the bear-stopping realm with its high penetration potential.

NOTE: While all loads listed here were taken from standardized data found in printed manuals, the reader is cautioned to start low and work up in his or her individual rifles. Dimensions can vary in actual bore and chamber sizes. That is why certain loads in one rifle function perfectly, while the same load in another rifle may be too hot.

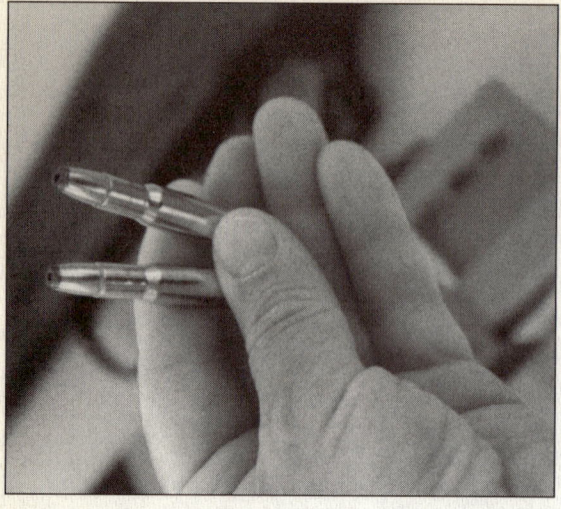

A good example of factory ammunition providing many different bullets for one cartridge is the 30-30 as loaded today, including lighter hollow-point bullets.

the H&R Shikari, 1886 Winchester, and Rolling Block rifles chambered for the 45-70 round. On page 511 loads are presented for the Marlin Model 1895 lever-action rifle chambered for the 45-70. On page 513 hotter recipes are supplied, but with this written caution: "WARNING. The following data is to be used in such actions as the Ruger #1, Browning 78, Wickliffe, and 45-70s chambered in the Siamese Mauser bolt action. This data has maximum charges that develop 50,000 c.u.p. [copper units of pressure] as tested in the Hornady Lab."

Meanwhile, it is not practical for companies building loading manuals to supply specific information for all rifles chambered for a given cartridge. Hornady, for example, tested the 30-30 in the Winchester Model 94 carbine. Recall that the Model 70 bolt-action Winchester was also chambered for the 30-30 at one time. Whenever a shooter experiments on his own he is on his own, even with a rather obvious situation, such as loads for a Model 70 30-30 with hotter-than-prescribed data. Therefore, the bell is rung once more, repeating the advice to stick with printed data from loading manuals presented by bullet and powder companies such as Sierra and Hodgdon's. These resource books hold a wealth of information for the shooter interested in loading many different bullets in one cartridge.

That's my take on handloading many different bullets for one cartridge, or for that matter looking into various factory ammo offered with different bullet choices. While there is no doubt that many rifle cartridges thrive on a specific projectile, such as the aforementioned 165-grain bullet in the 30-'06 Springfield cartridge, selecting different bullets for various rounds lifts their versatility to new heights. Also, different bullets in a single round change accuracy as well as application. One bullet, for whatever reason, may group closer than any other in a particular cartridge, while bullets of different construction perform uniquely in the field.

Gunmaker Mike Scherz specializes in rugged hunting rifles for all terrains. This is one of his Scouts chambered for the 450 Marlin cartridge, which enjoys a wide range of bullets in both cast and jacketed styles.

MANUFACTURER'S SHOWCASE

VERSATILE RACK COMPANY

Maximize the space in your safe with handgun racks from Versatile Rack Co. Made with a welded steel wire frame for years of dependable use, then vinyl-coated to protect the finish of your expensive handguns. Available in versions to hold either 4 or 6 handguns. Visit us online to see our complete line of quality products. Dealer inquiries welcome.

Web Site Address:
www.versatilegunrack.com
Or call us at: 323-588-0137

SITE-IN-CLEAN REST

Looking for a great value in a shooting rest?

MTM Case-Gard's Site-N-Clean is a rest so versatile, it makes sighting-in rifles, patterning shotguns, range cleaning, and even maintenance a breeze. The Site-N-Clean offers easy positioning using rubber padded shooting forks along with a handy, rear elevation dial. Available separately or as part of a Site-In-Clean Rest with Case combo, in which the rest rides inside a spacious, lockable range box. Shooters can carry the rest plus their shooting equipment in one handy, range-ready container.

MTM MOLDED PRODUCTS COMPANY
P.O. Box 13117, Dept. STB05 • Dayton, OH 45413
Tel: 937-890-7461 • www.mtmcase-gard.com

Grizzly Industrial, Inc.

MODEL G9977 WOOD MILL™
(WITH POWER FEED FOR TABLE)

FOR METALWORKING & WOODWORKING!

Specifications:
- Table size: 10" x 34"
- Table travel: 18 1/2" longitudinal & 10 3/4" cross
- Spindle taper: R-8
- Spindle travel: 3 1/2"
- Max. spindle to column: 18 1/2"
- Max. spindle to table: 19"
- 9 Speeds: 440-5000 RPM
- Motor: 1 1/2 HP, Single Phase
- Approx. ship. weight: 1350 lbs.

Includes:
- Way chip protectors
- Drawbar

The **G9977** is **$2,195.00** and is shipped in the lower 48 states for $200.00.
Please check current pricing before ordering!

3 LOCATIONS
Bellingham, WA / Muncy, PA / Springfield, MO

grizzly.com   Visit our Web site!
TEL: 1-800-523-4777 • FAX: 1-800-438-5901

MEDIA CODE **AD1307**

Think you own the best gun safe?
Or are you interested in owning the best?

AMERICAN SECURITY PRODUCTS (AMSEC) offers you Better service, Better construction, Better interiors and the Best safety and fire protection available. AMSEC, the world's best known provider of security safes, offers more than 50 years of engineering in every safe we make! Our Gun Safe catalog provides complete details on our entire product line—and the best warranty on the market! Want to update or purchase the Best gun safe in the industry? It's easy, just contact your local sporting goods and gun retailer. Or call **AMSEC** at (800) 421-6142.

MANUFACTURER'S SHOWCASE

FORREST INC. OFFERS RIFLE/PISTOL MAGAZINES

Whether you're looking for a few spare magazines for that obsolete 22 rifle or pistol, or wish to replace a 10-shot with the higher-capacity pre-ban original, all are available from FORREST INC. With one of the largest selections of magazines, they offer competitive pricing especially for dealers who buy in quantity.

FORREST INC. also stocks parts and accessories for the Colt 1911 45 Auto Pistol, the SKS and MAK-90 rifles, and many U.S. military rifles. One of their specialty parts is firing pins for obsolete weapons.

Call or write for more information and a FREE brochure, DEALERS WELCOME! HIGH CAPS OUR SPECIALTY!

FORREST INC.
P.O. Box 326, Lakeside, CA 92040
Tel: 619-561-5800 Fax: 1-888-GUNCLIP
Web: www.GUNMAGS.com

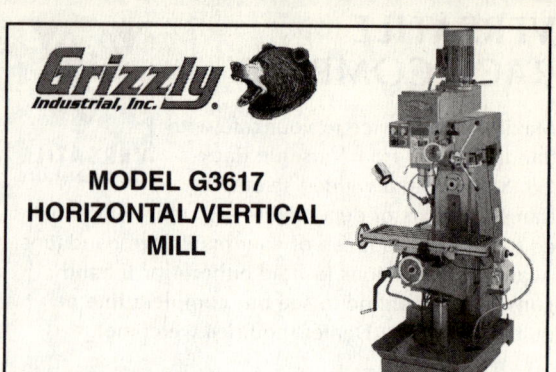

MODEL G3617 HORIZONTAL/VERTICAL MILL

Specifications:
- Table size: $9^{1}/_{2}$" x $39^{3}/_{8}$"
- Table travel: $17^{3}/_{4}$" longitudinal, 9" cross x $13^{3}/_{4}$" vertical
- Spindle taper: R-8
- Spindle travel: $5^{1}/_{4}$"
- Max. spindle to column: $25^{1}/_{8}$"
- Max. spindle to table: 16"
- Vertical spindle speeds: 270-2950 RPM
- Horizontal spindle speeds: 8, 72-1300 RPM
- Motor: 2 HP(vertical), $1^{1}/_{2}$ H.P.(horizontal), Single-Phase, 110/220V
- Table swivels side to side (not shown)
- Approx. ship. weight: 2137 lbs.

The **G3617** is **$2,995.00** and is shipped in the lower 48 states for $300.00. Please check current pricing before ordering!

3 LOCATIONS
Bellingham, WA / Muncy, PA / Springfield, MO

grizzly.com Visit our Web site!
TEL: 1-800-523-4777 • FAX: 1-800-438-5901

MEDIA CODE **AD1307**

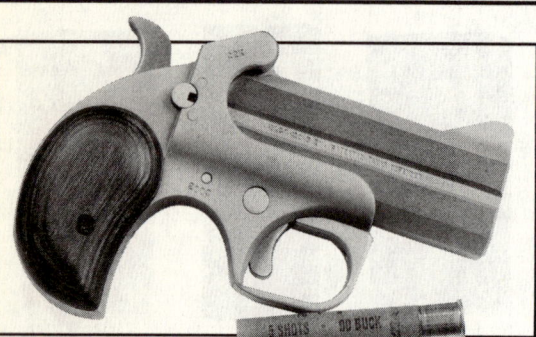

THE CENTURY 2000 DEFENDER "C2K" FROM BOND ARMS, INC.

The Century 200 Defender ("C2K") is the ultimate in self-defense. With its 3.5" double barrel, the C2K chambers the 3" .410 00 Buck Shot with five pellets. It also features a rebounding hammer, retracting firing pins, crossbolt safety, cammed locking lever, spring-loaded extractor and interchangeable barrels. Choice of caliber includes .410 with 3" chambers and .410/45LC with 2.5" chambers.

For further information, contact:

BOND ARMS, INC.
P.O. Box 1296 • Granbury, TX 76048
Tel: (817) 573-4445 • Fax: (817) 573-5636

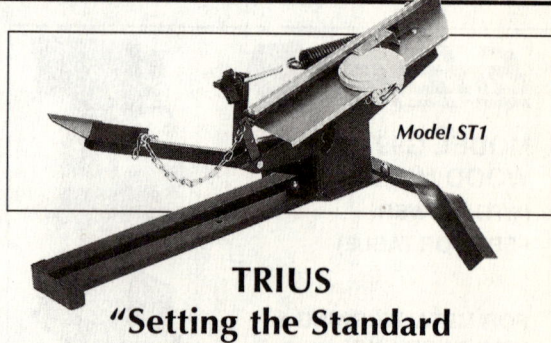

Model ST1

TRIUS "Setting the Standard for 45 Years"

The Trius 1-Step (shown) is almost effortless to use: (1) Set arm and place target on arm. (2) Step on pedal to put tension on arm and release target in one motion.

Birdshooter: quality at a budget price–now with high-angle retainer. **Model 92R:** the original "foot trap"
TrapMaster: sit-down comfort plus pivoting action.

Trius traps are adjustable without tools; feature lay-on loading: singles, doubles, plus piggy-back doubles–offer unparalleled variety.

TRIUS PRODUCTS INC.
P.O. Box 25, Cleves, OH 45002
Tel: 513-941-5682
Web Site: www.trius.com

MANUFACTURER'S SHOWCASE

GLASER SAFETY SLUG, INC.

For over 25 years Glaser has provided a state-of-the-art personal defense ammunition used by the law enforcement and civilian communities Available in two bullet styles, the Glaser Blue is offered in a full range of handgun calibers from 25ACP to 45 Colt (including the 9MM Makarov and 357 Sig) and four rifle calibers; .223, 308, 30-06 and 7.62x39. The Glaser Silver is available in all handgun calibers from 380ACP to 45 Colt. A complete brochure is available on the internet @ www.safetyslug.com or contact:

GLASER SAFETY SLUG, INC.
1311 Industry Road
Sturgis, South Dakota 57785
Tel: 800-221-3489
Fax: 605-347-5055

GARY REEDER Custom Guns

Montana Hunter

Gary Reeder Custom Guns offers its 45 Long Colt: the **MONTANA HUNTER**. This new 5-shot beauty comes in the barrel length of your choice in either hi polish or satin stainless finish. The **MONTANA HUNTER** features our "Gunfighter Grip" in laminated walnut, interchangeable front sight blades, and our soft satin Vapor-Honed finish with contrasting high polish on the small parts. For the serious handgun hunter, the MONTANA HUNTER is hard to beat.

GARY REEDER CUSTOM GUNS
Tel: 520-526-3313
Web site: www.reedercustomguns.com

Grizzly Industrial, Inc.

MODEL G9249 12" x 37" BELT DRIVE GAP BED LATHE

Specifications:
- Swing over bed: 12"
- Swing over gap: 18⁷⁄₈"
- Distance between centers: 37"
- Spindle size: D1-4 camlock
- Spindle nose taper: MT#5
- Spindle bore: 1⁷⁄₁₆"
- Speeds: 12
- Speed Range: 50-1200 RPM
- Tailstock barrel taper: MT#3
- Tailstock barrel travel: 3"
- Motor: 2 H.P., Single-Phase, 220V
- Approx. ship. weight: 790 lbs.

Includes:
- 6" 3-jaw chuck • 8" 4-jaw chuck
- 10" face plate • Steady rest
- Follow rest • Chip tray
- Heavy-duty stand • 4 way tool post
- Dual inch/metric dials

The **G9249** is **$1,895.00** and is shipped in the lower 48 states for $150.00.
Please check current pricing before ordering!

3 LOCATIONS
Bellingham, WA / Muncy, PA / Springfield, MO

grizzly.com   Visit our Web site!
TEL: 1-800-523-4777 • FAX: 1-800-438-5901

MEDIA CODE **AD1307**

NEW — AO LEVER SCOUT MOUNT

Scout Scope Mount for lever guns w/8" Weaver-style rail and cross slots on 1/2" centers. Mounts scope 1/8" lower than previously possible for Marlin 1895 Guide Gun, 1894 & 336. Positions intermediate eye relief scope forward for extremely fast reticle acquistion, facilitates both eyes wide open for better target acquistion, and allows use of AO Ghost-Ring Sights without scope. Simple installation, no gunsmithing required, uses existing rear dovetail and front two mounting holes on receiver. AO Sight Systems: makers of AO Express/Pro Express Sights. Price: Lever Scout™ Mount: $50.00

AO SIGHT SYSTEMS
2401 Ludelle Street • Fort Worth, TX 76105
Tel: 817-536-0136 • Fax: 800-734-7939
Toll-free: 888-744-4880 • Website: www.aosights.com

MANUFACTURER'S SHOWCASE

MODEL G4016
13½" x 40"
GEAR-HEAD LATHE WITH STAND

- Swing over bed: 13½"
- Swing over gap: 19"
- Distance between centers: 40"
- Spindle: Cam lock D1-4
- Spindle bore: 1 7/16"
- 8 Speeds: 78-2100 RPM
- Tailstock barrel taper: MT#3
- Tailstock barrel travel: 3½"
- Motor: 2 HP, Single Phase, 220V
- Approx. ship. weight: 1410 lbs.

Includes:
- 6" 3-jaw chuck • 8" 4-jaw chuck
- Steady rest • Follow rest
- 12" Face plate
- Tool Box
- 4-way turret tool post
- Two MT#3 dead centers
- Live center
- Stand, chip pan & splash guard
- Jog button & emergency stop

Specifications:

The **G4016** is **$2,695.00** and is shipped in the lower 48 states for $200.00. Please check current pricing before ordering!

3 LOCATIONS
Bellingham, WA / Muncy, PA / Springfield, MO

grizzly.com   Visit our Web site!
TEL: 1-800-523-4777 • FAX: 1-800-438-5901

MEDIA CODE **AD1307**

22nd Edition

Once again, this most recent 1,600+ page 22nd Edition of the *Blue Book of Gun Values* continues to be the firearms industry's primary source for both current information and up-to-date pricing.

$34.95
Plus $4 S/H = $38.95 Total

The *Blue Book of Gun Values* is now available online for downloading! Or you can order the new book at:

www.bluebookinc.com

Credit Card Orders Call: Dept: SB
800-877-4867
Blue Book Publications, Inc.
8009 34th Ave. So. Suite 175 • Minneapolis, MN 55425 U.S.A.
International: (952)854-5229 FAX: (952)853-1486 - Sorry No COD's

---

BENCH MASTER® RIFLE REST

The Bench Master Rifle Rest is a rugged, compact and highly adjustable rifle-shooting accessory—one that offers precision line-up and recoil reduction when sighting in a rifle, testing ammunition or shooting varmints. It features three course positions totaling 5.5", with 1.5" fine adjustment in each course position, plus leveling and shoulder height adjustments for maximum control and comfort. Because of its unique design, the Bench Master can easily double as a rifle vise for scope mounting, bore sighting and cleaning. It comes with a LIFETIME Warranty and a list price of only $124.95. For a free brochure, call or write:

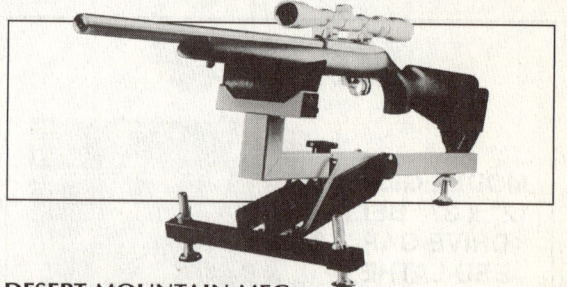

DESERT MOUNTAIN MFG.
2001 W. Fourth Plain • Vancouver, WA 98660
Tel: 360-693-5835 Fax: 360-693-7916

CNC Machined Trigger Guard

This is a complete CNC machined trigger guard eqipped with precision EDM parts. It features an internal pretravel adjustment that is set at the factory in order to greatly reduce pretravel. This new match trigger guard is CNC machined from a solid billet of high strength aircraft aluminum. The hammer is a precision ground 440C stainless steel. The sear and disconnector are EDM manufactured parts. The trigger is black anodized and equipped with an overtravel adjustment screw. The trigger is reset internally. An automatic bolt release and an extended magazine release are also included.

VOLQUARTSEN CUSTOM LTD.
24276 240th Street • P.O. Box 397 • Carroll, IA 51401
Telephone: 712-792-4238 Fax: 712-792-2542
E-mail: vcl@netins.net • Web Site: www.volquartsen.com

MANUFACTURER'S SHOWCASE

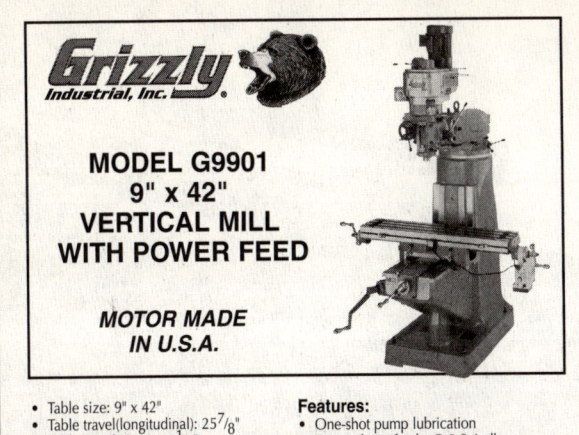

Grizzly Industrial, Inc.

**MODEL G9901
9" x 42"
VERTICAL MILL
WITH POWER FEED**

MOTOR MADE IN U.S.A.

- Table size: 9" x 42"
- Table travel(longitudinal): 25 7/8"
- Table travel(cross): 12 1/2"
- Max. dist. spindle to table: 18 1/4"
- Max. dist. spindle to column: 17 1/2"
- Speeds: 8
- Range of speeds: 78-2000 R.P.M.
- Motor: 2 HP, Single Phase
- Approx. ship. weight: 2400 lbs.

Features:
- One-shot pump lubrication
- Power down feed • R-8 Spindle
- Quill Feeds/Spindle Rev.: .0019", .0035", .0058"
- Auto stop w/ micro adjustable stop
- Longitudinal power feed
- Adjustable micrometer quill depth stop
- Hardened & ground table surface
- Chrome plated, precision ground quill

Specifications:

The **G9901** is **$3,495.00** and is shipped in the lower 48 states for $300.00.
Please check current pricing before ordering!

**3 LOCATIONS
Bellingham, WA / Muncy, PA / Springfield, MO**

grizzly.com Visit our Web site!
TEL: 1-800-523-4777 • FAX: 1-800-438-5901

MEDIA CODE AD1307

NEW FOR 2001!

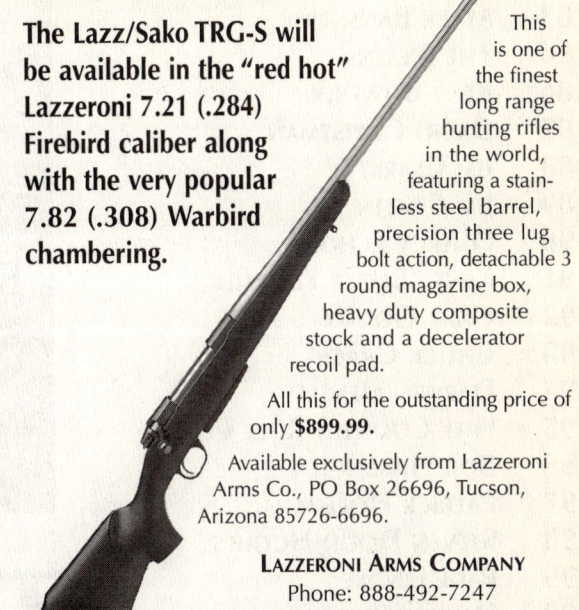

The Lazz/Sako TRG-S will be available in the "red hot" Lazzeroni 7.21 (.284) Firebird caliber along with the very popular 7.82 (.308) Warbird chambering.

This is one of the finest long range hunting rifles in the world, featuring a stainless steel barrel, precision three lug bolt action, detachable 3 round magazine box, heavy duty composite stock and a decelerator recoil pad.

All this for the outstanding price of only **$899.99**.

Available exclusively from Lazzeroni Arms Co., PO Box 26696, Tucson, Arizona 85726-6696.

LAZZERONI ARMS COMPANY
Phone: 888-492-7247
Fax: 520-624-4250
E-mail: arms@lazzeroni.com
Web Site: www.lazzeroni.com

African Hunter

GARY REEDER Custom Guns

Gary Reeder Custom Guns presents the ultimate in a full custom hunting handgun. The **AFRICAN HUNTER**, a 5-shot single action handgun, is available in either 475 Linebaugh or 500 Linebaugh. As soon as we get an order, each gun is built the way you want it. You can have it in the caliber of your choice and the barrel length of your choice.

You can also have it in high polish stainless or in our own satin Vapor-Honed finish. If desired, the **AFRICAN HUNTER** can be equipped with a muzzle brake at no extra charge.

GARY REEDER CUSTOM GUNS
Tel: 520-526-3313
Web site: www.reedercustomguns.com

SERIES S MODEL L

HARRIS ENGINEERING, INC.

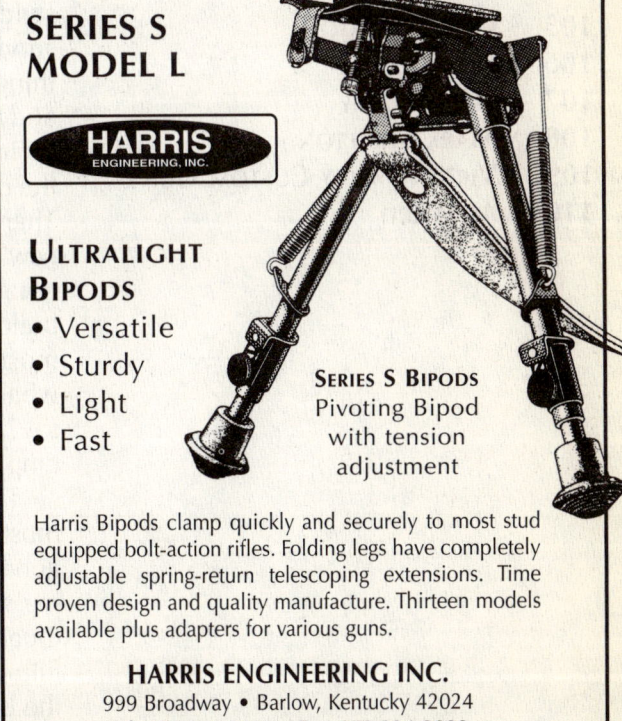

ULTRALIGHT BIPODS
- Versatile
- Sturdy
- Light
- Fast

SERIES S BIPODS
Pivoting Bipod with tension adjustment

Harris Bipods clamp quickly and securely to most stud equipped bolt-action rifles. Folding legs have completely adjustable spring-return telescoping extensions. Time proven design and quality manufacture. Thirteen models available plus adapters for various guns.

HARRIS ENGINEERING INC.
999 Broadway • Barlow, Kentucky 42024
Tel: 270-334-3633 • Fax: 270-334-3000

CUSTOM GUNMAKERS

81	AXTELL RIFLE COMPANY
82	LES BAER CUSTOM
83	MARK BANSNER
84	THE BIESENS
86	KENT BOWERLY
87	DAVID CHRISTMAN
88	JIM CLARK, JR
89	JIM COFFIN
90	D'ARCY ECHOLS
91	KENT "BUZZ" FLETCHER
92	GARY GOUDY
93	CHUCK GRACE
94	DARWIN HENSLEY
95	HILL COUNTRY RIFLE CO.
96	BOB HISSERICH
97	PATRICK HOLEHAN
98	STEVEN DODD HUGHES
99	PAUL LINDKE
100	DAVID MILLER
101	STEVE NELSON
102	DAVE NORIN
103	RAY RIGARIAN
104	TONY SCHUELKE
105	GENE SIMILLION
106	CHARLIE SISK
107	DALE STOREY
108	MARK STRATTON
109	VIRGIN VALLEY CUSTOM GUNS
110	AL WARD

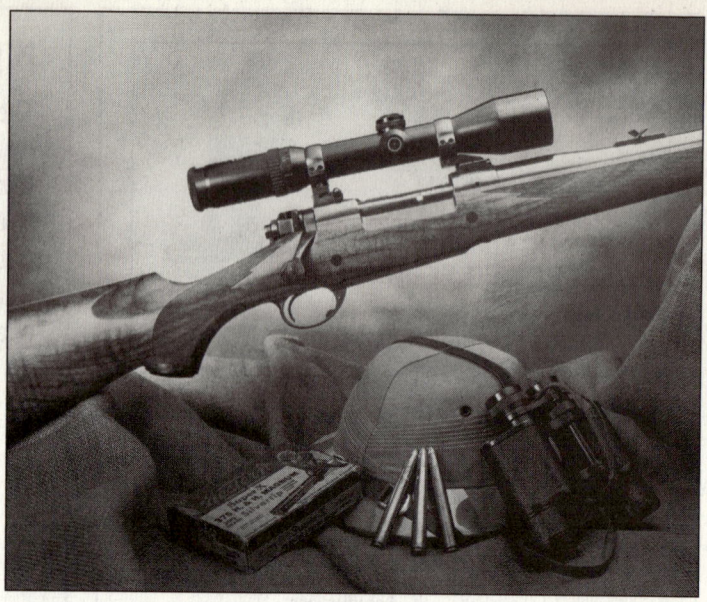

This section of Shooter's Bible features custom guns from the most prestigious American small shops. Mass production of interchangeable parts and the factory manufacture of small arms came about in the 19th century. Before that, all guns were essentially unique unto themselves, though basic mechanisms and styles were shared among many makers. The custom gun survives because connoisseurs of firearms want something better than can be had from factory assembly lines, and they're willing to pay for the hand labor.

In its true sense, "custom" means built-to-order, with the customer dictating the gun's features and dimensions. There are practical limits to custom orders, of course. Few shops will offer an action to the buyer's specifications. They are constrained by the costs of designing and building actions (as well as by patents and the fact that most of the best actions are already in production) to use what is already available from major arms suppliers. To say that a rifle is not really a custom rifle because it employs a Remington 700 action is being too severe.

The gunmakers featured in this section are some of the most competent craftsmen in the field. Indeed, there are gunmakers, stockers, metalsmiths and engravers practicing today whose work is the best of its kind ever seen. Quality standards (and prices) continue to climb. In future editions of Shooter's Bible, you'll continue to find the best of the best in custom guns.

Axtell Rifle Company
Sheridan, Montana

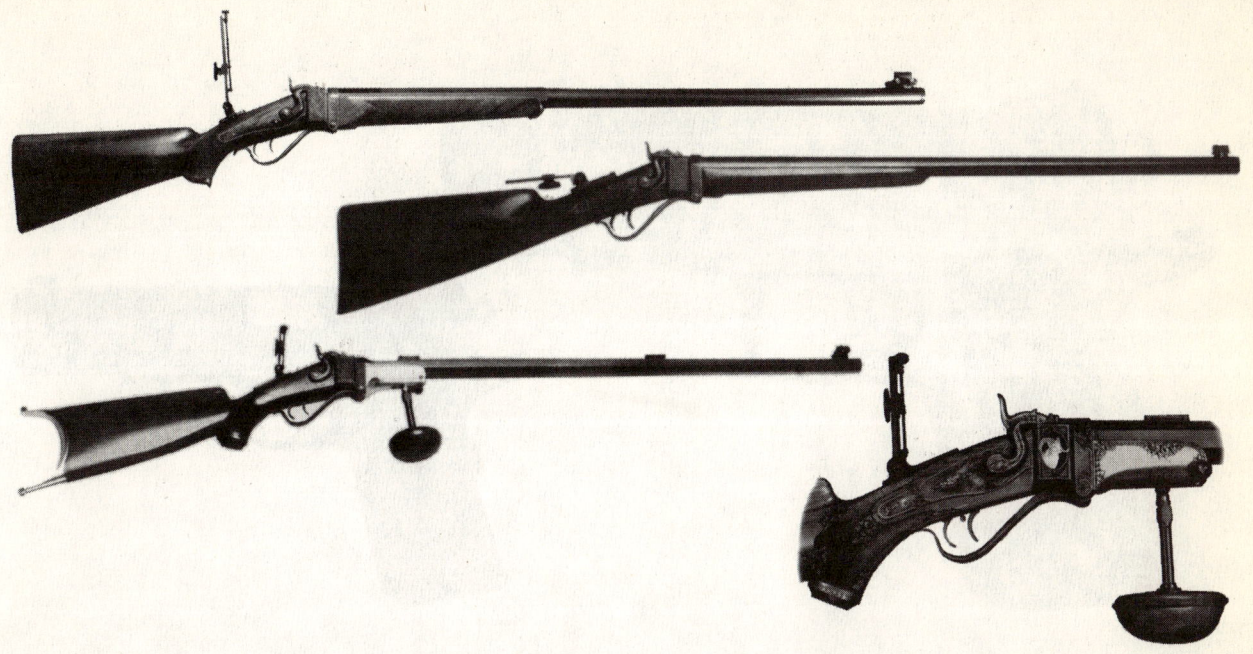

In 1973 Riflesmith, Incorporated began manufacturing exact replicas of the late 19th-century sights used on Sharps rifles, and others capable of long shooting. In 1989 the Axtell Rifle Company was formed to manufacture the New Model 1877 Sharps. Perhaps inevitably, the firm is located in southwest Montana, home to two other manufacturers producing Sharps rifles with the looks and feel of the originals. What's unusual about Axtell is that the company is run by a woman.

Carmen Axtell shrugs. "Anybody can make a rifle. You don't have to be a man." All doubts vanish with one look at any Sharps 1877 rifle from Axtell's Sheridan shop. Its artistry is remarkable not only for the authenticity of line, balance and mechanism, but for the meticulous care evident in the fitting and finishing of parts. The case coloring is exquisite, wood and metal finish, well, better than the original. "It's hard to make something less appealing than you can make it," says Carmen. "Even when you're trying very hard to be faithful to the original."

The original is not well known to casual gun enthusiasts, who for the most part are much more familiar with the 1874 Sharps rifles – the "buffalo guns" of book and film. Truth is, the Model 1877 is better. It evolved from a need for a more accurate long-range target rifle, about the time the famous Creedmoor Rifle Range was established on Long Island. The 1874 Sharps had proven its mettle in a match pitting Americans against the Irish. But shooters wanted faster lock time and a heavier barrel. The 1877 incorporated both.

"It's not a cheap rifle to produce," explains Carmen. "Our prices reflect cost more than profit. And you'll never be disappointed."

Axtell Rifle Company makes several variations of the 1877 Sharps: Custom Express, No. 1 Creedmoor, No. 2 Long Range, Lower Sporter, Lower Business, and Overbaugh Scheutzen. All 10 chamberings are original Sharps rounds, from the .45-70, .45-90 and .45-100 Express to the various 40- and 45-caliber cartridges only students of the period remember.

Axtell offers all manner of appropriate accoutrements, from tang sights (included on all models) to the palm rest on the Schuetzen version. A variety of tang and globe sights are listed for sale separately. Like the rifles, all ring true in looks and function, and show the highest level of craftsmanship.

The company has a catalog showing its various models. It's produced by Carmen Axtell. Who else?

Les Baer Custom
Hillsdale, Illinois

Pistol shooters know the Les Baer name well. The man and his firm have become the first stop for competitors seeking a superior .45 self-loading pistol. Baer's custom 1911-style .45s have not only turned up in the hands of many national pistol champions; they're the choice of people like Clint Smith, who runs a training facility for both police and civilian shooters. As committed to street-worthy guns as to National Match equipment, Les Baer offers the standard-size 1911 pistols, and more compact Comanche and Stinger versions. You can also buy the frames in steel, stainless steel and alloy form. Les Baer slides and barrels are available as well.

Other components include safeties, triggers, bushings, sights, magazines… the list is long.

The company markets custom-built autoloading "AR" series rifles and components, for tactical shooters, service rifle competitors and anyone who simply wants one of the best .223 rifles on the market. The NRA Match rifle has a 30-inch, hand-lapped fast-twist barrel, floating handguard, two-stage Jewell trigger, titanium striker and many other refinements. The Picatinny rail, available on other Baer .223s, accommodates both scope rings and a receiver sight. You can also find rifle components in the Baer catalog, from handstops and stocks to barrels, bolts and upper and lower receivers.

Mark Bansner
Adamstown, Pennsylvania

For more than 20 years now, Mark Bansner has been in the firearms business. He started with shotgun modifications. After establishing a solid reputation among turkey hunters who used his guns at long range, Mark gradually changed his focus to rifles. Now he specializes in sleek, lightweight bolt-action rifles, for which he furnishes his own synthetic stocks (produced under the name "High Tech"). Four employees help Mark ship about 120 custom-built rifles a year from his 3,000-square foot shop in Adamstown, Pennsylvania.

"We do no over-the-counter business," Mark explains. "While we have standard rifle configurations and options, each order is individual, and the customer can make his rifle truly personal." Though his rifles are each in fact one-of-a-kind, they cost much less than what many hunters would expect: between $2200 and $3700 for most.

Some things come standard in Mark's rifles: match-grade Lilja barrels, hand-lapped, are fitted to actions trued from centerline to ensure concentric chambering. Tuned or replacement triggers deliver a crisp, consistent pull, and the stocks of graphite, epoxy and fiberglass cloth are hand-bedded to cradle the metal securely and without imposing any stresses.

Bansner rifles are guaranteed to deliver fine accuracy. "We build hardware that shoots!" Mark emphasizes. "These rifles are for discriminating hunters who expect a high level of field performance. We – the people who build the rifles – are hunters too. I want my rifle to shoot a half-minute group, so that's what I offer prospective customers. A Bansner rifle will print half-minute 3-shot groups, or I'll make it right."

Shuffling through stacks of proof targets Mark has saved, even the most suspicious buyer has to be impressed. One-hole groups are common. These rifles do shoot well, even the 6-pound Sheep Hunter model. They look good too, with trim, functional lines and stock finishes that vary in color to taste. When ordered, speckling and spider-webbing is expertly applied. Stock-to-steel fit is skin-tight except on the barrel, which Mark provides in both fluted and conventional form. He even makes his own muzzle brakes. "They reduce recoil by up to 45 percent."

Mark got his first taste of big-bore shooting when he served in the military. Later honing his machining skills at gunsmithing school, he has since shared his expertise by conducting classes in armor for government agencies. Now he's very busy building rifles – but not too busy to take them afield on hunts. "Somebody has to test 'em," he grins.

CUSTOM GUNMAKERS

The Biesens
Napa, California

Many years ago, shooting a rifle match in Spokane, Washington, I met Al Biesen. Later I would visit his basement shop, where he fashioned custom rifles that defined custom rifles for a generation of shooters. The basement, its dark north end a repository of aging walnut blanks, was never neat. Gun parts and tools lay scattered below faded photos of Biesen rifles in the hands of hunters behind trophy game. The L-shaped workbench just inside the south entrance was small, the aisle facing it lined with guns and stacks of magazines. If you talked with Al, you had to do it on your feet while he worked. He liked to talk. For decades a sanctuary for people who dreamed of fine rifles, the shop was also a first stop for those able to buy them. Jack O'Connor visited here, and carried a pair of lightweight Biesen .270s on hunts all over the world. Al did not – does not – discriminate. He'll talk with you whether or not you'd buy a rifle. He talks of rifles and goose hunting and Parker doubles, but mostly of people he's known. Now 84, he's known quite a few. He's shared the basement and occasionally a hunt with legendary gun scribes – and he has clear opinions of them all!

Now throttling back on his gunmaking, Al has turned his shop over to son Roger, who makes no apology for incorporating his father's style in the new Biesen rifles. Roger's daughter, Paula, has even turned her hand to the business, as an engraver. She's good at it.

"No, I wasn't always wild about guns," she laughs. "Certainly not as a youngster. I had no interest in art either, let alone engraving." Then in junior high school she was mistakenly scheduled for a painting class. Her first watercolor wound up displayed at the Governor's office.

"After that I started drawing in earnest," she says. "I took more art classes and studied drafting. I looked toward a career in mechanical engineering." She allows that calculus almost scuttled her plan, but she persevered at a local college until redirected into a business program. Graduating in 1990, she experimented with the engraving tools in her father's shop.

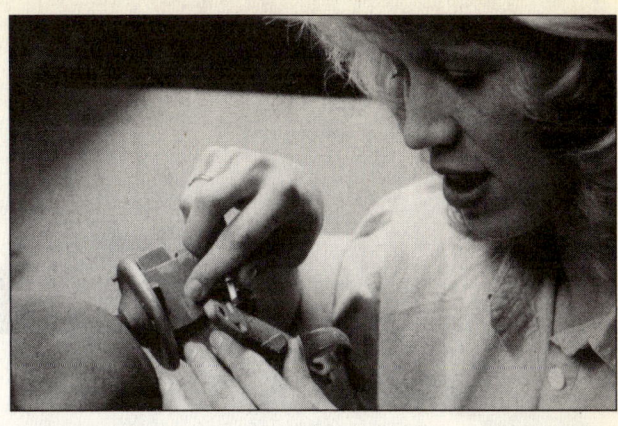

"Dad didn't force me into this. I got plenty of encouragement but no push. My idea was to cut what I painted – mostly animals." She grins. "It turned out that steel was less forgiving than my watercolor boards!"

Engraving took longer too. And Paula was up against stiff competition. "Grandpa would show me a Terry Wallace floorplate and tell me to try something like that! Sheesh! He might as well have suggested that I paint the shop ceiling like the Cistine Chapel's!"

But this pretty, vivacious blond had grit. She refined her talent on gold and German silver name plates, then started cutting grip caps and bottom metal. Meanwhile, she had been courted by David Malicki, a native of Napa, California. They married in 1992. David worked as a plumber in Spokane, while Paula began embellishing rifle furniture for her father's customers.

"It was difficult starting," she confides. "I didn't know if I could succeed. But Grandpa was patient, and eventually I lost my fear of ruining a rifle." Paula's work has appeared on rifles commissioned for auction by the National Rifle Association, the Rocky Mountain Elk Foundation and Safari Club International.

Paula makes initial cuts with a Gravermeister. She finishes with hand tools. But instead of a magnifying hood, Paula prefers a 15x microscope. "It helps me see detail better," she says. "And most of the parts I engrave are small and flat."

Lately Paula has been asked to engrave rifle barrels and receivers too. Her most daunting project was a rifle Al Biesen built for himself. "It's a Model 70 Winchester in .30-06," she tells me. "The wood was a gorgeous piece of French walnut that Grandpa salted away in 1968. It's a privilege to work on rifles like that; but there's also a lot of pressure to come up with something unique and very well executed. Grandpa could have gone to the best of engravers for that job."

Paula's modesty belies her clean rendering of detail and the lifelike appearance of the animals she scribes into steel. Her artistry shows in their facial expressions and musculature. "You learn tricks," she says, shrugging. "Like never setting an animal face-on so you have to duplicate details right and left. But just knowing what *not* to do isn't enough. Engraving game scenes is hard! Achieving fluid forms with a chisel is much tougher than with a brush. You're trying to fashion in steel an image of something that has color and depth and movement and temperature and living texture and a glint in the eye."

Paula works mostly at home, where her father checkers the gunstocks that still make a Biesen rifle one of the most coveted in the custom gun trade. "Home has fewer distractions than Grandpa's shop, mainly because it doesn't get the traffic. Customers are always stopping in to see Dad or Grandpa, and they talk a lot." She giggles. "Whoever said that women are talkative never spent time in that basement. It's been a rendezvous for gun bugs since Harry Truman was president."

Four years ago, just weeks before delivering her first baby, 29-year-old Paula Biesen was accepted as a member of the Custom Gunmakers Guild at the group's 1998 convention in Reno. Surely Paula Malicki will continue to be a working mother. As Al's rifles have visited the most distant game fields, and as Roger's craftsmanship continues to bring a shine to the eye of rifle enthusiasts, so Paula's work keeps the Biesen basement popular.

CUSTOM GUNMAKERS

Kent Bowerly
Redmond, Oregon

In 1958 Winchester announced its .338 Magnum, the Weatherby Mark V rifle was in its first year of production, and Kent Bowerly started work on a Springfield 03-A3, mating it to a Roberts semi-inletted stock. Friends liked the job Kent had done, and they offered to pay him for stockwork on their rifles. So began a hobby that would turn into a late career. During the 1960s, Kent studied under Al Biesen and Earl Milliron, both masters of the trade and living close by in the Pacific Northwest. He applied their techniques to classic hunting rifle stocks he shaped, fitted and finished.

"Mostly, I built handles for Winchester Model 70s," he says. "In those days, you could still get the early ones for a reasonable price, and a lot of hunters preferred them." He emphasizes that his stocks are of utilitarian design, though they carry the lines and detailing that sophisticated gun enthusiasts admire. "If a rifle won't shoot well in your hands, if it's not responsive, if it lacks the fine balance to point itself and put your eye behind the sight automatically, it's not stocked properly, no matter the quality of wood or workmanship."

Since his early retirement from the boat-building industry in 1985, Kent has been busy as a full-time stockmaker, working on both rifles and shotguns. He still likes the Model 70, but he's fitted walnut to Mausers as well, and the occasional Dakota 76 (a Model 70 look-alike). Kent has fashioned stocks for Ruger Number Ones, a rifle that adds variety to his workbench in Redmond, Oregon. Photographs of Bowerly rifles have appeared on Rifle magazine covers and in the Nikon sports optics catalog.

David Christman
Delhi, Louisiana

In Colville, Washington for 20 years, David Christman "came back home" to Louisiana after a downsizing at U.S. West. It may have been the move he needed, because now he's very pleased to divide his time between home, shop and church. His versatility shows in these photos. He's restocked Parker double shotguns and Stevens single-shot rifles, besides building the bolt-action rifles so popular with custom makers. David isn't limited to one component or operation. He does both wood and metal work, farming out only engraving.

"I suppose my favorite project is a bolt rifle on a Mauser 98 or Winchester 70 action. It should get a piece of English walnut, but Don Cantwell's high-grade Claro makes me almost as happy. Given the right parts and a little metal work, the Remington 700 can blossom into a handsome custom rifle too. Right now I'm finishing up a four-gun set on Searcy actions. Hard metal in those!"

David offers a full suite of restocking and refinishing services, including rust bluing, in the same shop that turns out complete custom shotguns and rifles.

Jim Clark, Jr.
Princeton, Louisiana

CUSTOM GUNMAKERS

Competitive pistol shooters know the Clark name well. In 1950 Jim Clark, Sr. became the fifth man to break the score of 2600 in bullseye competition, and he was the only civilian-trained man to do so. A decade later he became the fourth shooter to reach 2650. First president of the American Pistolsmiths Guild, Jim brought his match experience to the bench, where for many years he built handguns to outshoot the competition. In 1985 he received the Pistolsmith of the Year Award, and five years later the coveted Outstanding American Handgunner Award. Jim Clark, Sr. passed away two years ago, but his son has continued in the family tradition, not only serving shooters with first-class custom pistols but earning the accolades of fellow competitors. Jim, Jr. was named Pistolsmith of the Year in 2000, the year he won the Soldier of Fortune Sniper Match competition. He repeated that victory in 2001. He has topped the field in the Buckmasters World Pistol Championship and Kenneyathalon (both in 1997). Twice he has emerged as Steel Safari Champion, three times as Buckmasters World Rifle Champion, five times as Soldier of Fortune Champion.

While the Clark enterprise began as an "accurizing" service, Jim, Sr. making service and .22 pistols shoot better, the company has expanded to include revolvers, rifles and Clark's own aftermarket accessories. There's even a Clark tactical shotgun. Sights, mounts, triggers, safeties, magazines, grips, even the hardware to help install them – all are available from the Clark shop in Princeton, Louisiana. Conversion work remains a specialty. The Clark team has half a century of pistol know-how to draw from. If you shoot a pistol, and don't know Clark, it's about time you introduced yourself!

Jim Coffin
Corvallis, Oregon

CUSTOM GUNMAKERS

In 1954, Jim Coffin bought his first new rifle, a .30-06 Model 70 Winchester. "And a new Model 21 Winchester shotgun," he adds. "I'd bought other guns before, mainly Enfields. I guess I just wanted something nice for a change." During a 22-year career as a Marine pilot, Jim refined his interest in firearms, and was able to hunt near duty stations from Ontario to India. But it wasn't until after retirement that he began building his own custom rifles. In 1984 Jim became a member of the American Custom Gunmakers Guild.

"Mainly, I build hunting guns. I try hard to make my rifles handsome, and to show a superior level of craftsmanship. But these are not decorative pieces. They're built to shoot." Jim learned to checker and finish a stock before turning professional, reworking stocks to improve the way rifles felt in the hand. He knows that intrinsic rifle accuracy is of little account if the stock doesn't help the shooter aim and execute a shot.

He encourages customers to outline what they want; then he acts as advisor. Jim says he's fortunate to have attracted discriminating shooters – and to have made good friends in the trade. Like many of his colleagues, Jim specializes in fine gunstocks, subcontracting complex metalsmithing. He considers stockmaking an avocation, not a living. Jim's favorite rifles are built on 98 Mauser and Winchester Model 70 actions, though he'll work with other designs. He lives and works in the Willamette River town of Corvallis, Oregon.

"I spend a lot of time in the shop," he says. "You must if you're to learn enough to give customers the best work. Then, to apply what you've learned and reach the higher standards you set, you spend even more time at the bench." But Jim likes to hunt, and pulls himself away for a trip now and then. "One stocking job led to a moose hunt on Alaska's Copper River," he recalls. "A great trade!"

D'Arcy Echols
Providence, Utah

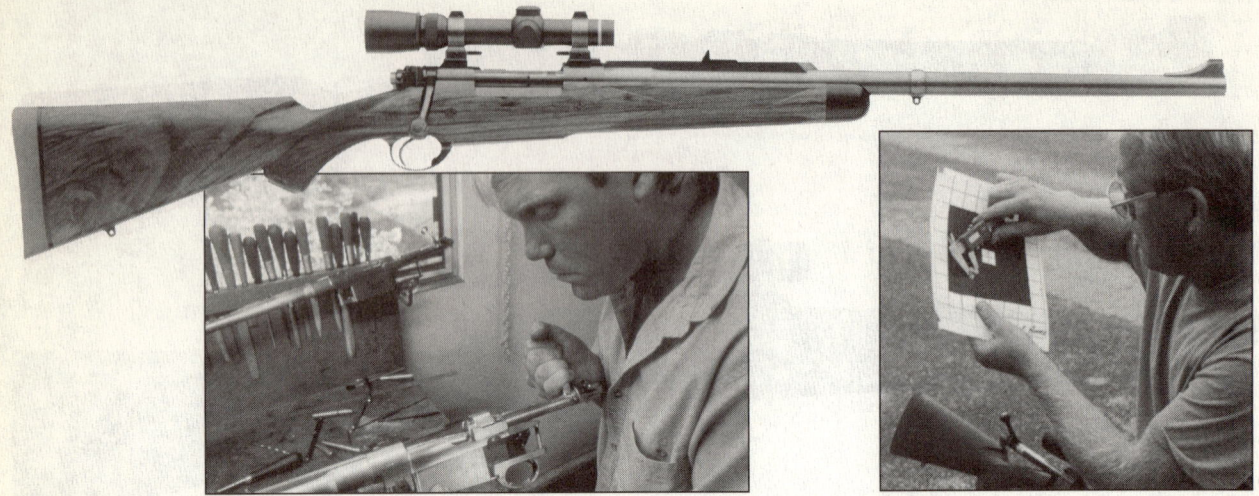

"It helps to have a sense of humor if you're a gunmaker," quips D'Arcy. "Crying drives the customers away." But D'Arcy relies neither on humor nor his quick wit to keep clients. His rifles do that. Trained as a gunmaker in Colorado, D'Arcy and his wife Rebecca, a veterinarian, make their home in Providence, Utah. There he has established himself as a riflemaker of the first order, with elegant bolt guns stocked in fine walnut. His eye for line and detail is matched by an uncanny ability to carry out the most intricate work in wood and metal. But D'Arcy avoids gingerbread. "I like to build rifles you'd hunt with," he says. "The profile of a great rifle must serve a purpose, not just attract attention on a rack." Rather than incorporate novel ideas for the sake of novelty, D'Arcy achieves superiority the hard way: with perfectly straight lines and a mating of wood to metal that looks impossibly tight. His checkering, remarkable for its symmetry and uniformity, adorns a grip and forend with sleek, clean, carefully engineered lines that all but grab your hands. Cast-off is standard, and D'Arcy's pantograph is set up to deliver the requisite difference in "bend" between toe and heel. The classic rifles from D'Arcy's shop point like fine English shotguns.

The problem is, they're very expensive.

When in 1997 a customer suggested that D'Arcy build a less costly rifle with a synthetic stock, the affable gunmaker asked "Why?" The answer: "So you can build more than eight rifles a year and sell them to real people." D'Arcy liked that reply, and got even more interested when the customer offered to help bankroll the operation. Since then, the Echols "Legend" rifle has given D'Arcy more customers "and headaches" than he had before. Built on new Winchester 70 Classic actions, mainly for belted magnum cartridges, the Legend wears a McMillan stock that D'Arcy designed in his shop. He overhauls the action, first modifying the magazine box to hold an extra cartridge. He lengthens the loading port and bores out scope base holes, tapping them for 8-40 screws. When fitting the Krieger cut-rifled barrel, he remachines then laps the lug seats and lugs, and squares up the receiver face and bolt face. He also repins the trigger and bolt stop and grinds the sear surface for a crisp, consistent 3 1/2-pound pull. After hand-bedding the matte-blued metal, D'Arcy shoots each rifle at least 40 times to break in the barrel and make sure the rifle meets his accuracy standards.

"I don't guarantee half-minute accuracy," he says, "but most of my Long-Range rifles in .300 Weatherby will deliver groups smaller than that." D'Arcy also builds a Dangerous Game rifle with a barrel-mounted sling swivel and action work to accommodate round-nose bullets. It's available with iron sights.

These days, D'Arcy is as busy baby-sitting his first-born daughter as he is making rifles. He's justifiably proud of both.

Kent "Buzz" Fletcher
Alamosa, Colorado

CUSTOM GUNMAKERS

The youngest of 10 children, Kent Fletcher longed for the day when he could accompany his six older brothers in the field. "Buzz" wanted to hunt deer. But his interest in rifles took a turn toward the custom gun trade when brother Phil steered him toward the writings of hunters who favored custom rifles, and the books by men who built them.

"I read from Kennedy and Dunlop, as well as from hunters like Francis Sell. The notion that I could build fine rifles suddenly had great appeal. It even seemed possible!" Buzz enrolled in gunsmithing school at Trinidad State Junior College, studying with the likes of Maurice Ottmar, Chuck Grace, Jim Turtin and others who later would establish themselves as premier gunmakers. After graduating in 1972, Buzz left for Austria, where he worked in a gunshop for a year. Then he returned to Colorado, setting up his own shop in Alamosa.

While Buzz has an American's affinity for the classic bolt-action sporting rifle, he's also an accomplished shotgun stocker. "The British got it right," he says. "And I've worked hard to understand the foundations of their designs. My quail guns have British line." Their weight and balance, and the cast, pitch and drop of the buttstock, result from painstaking study of the British game gun. Buzz also builds rifles after British patterns. Whatever the style, he strives to make a firearm handle like an extension of the shooter's body. "Fit is very important. If the gun doesn't point naturally, it's not acceptable."

Fletcher rifle and shotgun stocks are typically checkered 22 lines per inch. "My rifles and shotguns are for shooting, not for show," Buzz says, though he does cut some patterns at 24 lpi. He uses various fillers to get the stock surface he wants, but finishes only with Tung Oil. The details as well as the profiles of Buzz Fletcher's work reflect a desire to "get it right" every time.

Gary Goudy
Dayton, Washington

Now 37 years a stockmaker, Gary Goudy is known in the trade as one of the most talented and productive of his fraternity. "I'm 65 now, retired from the airline industry, but working as hard as ever on guns," he chuckles. "Hunting's expensive. I can't afford to quit!"

Not that he would if he could. Gary is a charter member of the American Custom Gunmakers Guild, and now its Vice President. His work belies a perfectionist's obsession, and a genuine affinity for fine guns and the best walnut. "I work mainly with California English," he says. "Or Bastogne. I've not had such good luck with European blanks." Unlike many of his colleagues, Gary buys most of his wood green, preferring to dry it himself. "Most blanks need a couple of years, but I like to give them four seasons before inletting." Gary is renowned not only for skin-tight wood-to-metal fit, but impossibly-detailed checkering that leaves ribbons the width of a pencil line and as even as a lightbeam.

My first custom rifle was stocked by Gary Goudy. The most recent big game rifle in my rack was, too.

"I like working on Model 70s," says Gary. "Because they're such good hunting rifles. But a 98 Mauser worked over by Hermann Waldron or Tom Burgess is every bit their equal. I've worked on shotguns from time to time – almost all of them side-by-sides. This year I have four to do, three more than usual!" He concedes that two of them are his own. "Dakotas. A 12 and a 20. They'll take a year to finish, but I'll have a couple of true exhibition-grade guns to show for the effort." Gary is also working on a Dakota takedown rifle for his own use. But he still hunts with the Winchester Model 70 Featherweight that he's been carrying for years. "It doesn't have one of my stocks," he laughs. "It shoots just fine in the factory wood, and I've been too busy to change it." Gary's taken all manner of North American big game with that rifle, and plans to take more.

"This year I'm headed into the River of No Return Wilderness in Idaho," he says. "It'll be a great trip for elk and mule deer. And I drew a Wyoming elk tag. Shot a big bull near home last year...."

Home, between hunts, is Dayton, Washington, where Gary keeps himself in top hunting shape and tends to his stockmaking in the shadow of the Blue Mountains.

Chuck Grace
Trinidad, Colorado

In 1971, Michigan native Chuck Grace traveled to Colorado for gunsmithing school – and stayed there. Since 1980, Chuck has been a full-time stockmaker, and in 1983 became a charter member of the American Custom Gunmakers Guild. His considerable talent was most recently shown on the ACGG's 16th annual fundraising project: a Winchester Model 70 rifle in 7x57. His rifles show sleek, open grips that make for fast handling. Clean, trim lines and expertly rendered forend tips are among Chuck's trademarks. This artisan also takes on rifle restoration and custom metal work in his Trinidad shop. Given their high quality, Grace rifles are affordable.

Darwin Hensley
Brightwood, Oregon

What was there to do on an Iowa farm during the 1940s? "Not much," says Darwin Hensley, who spent his childhood whittling. In 1952, when he was 10, Darwin moved with his family to town, but he spent summers on the farm, and he never gave up whittling. "When I did put that knife down, it was to pick up Grandpa's 1890 Winchester .22 pump. It kept me entertained, and put a little meat on the table. I still have that rifle."

After high school, Darwin earned B.A. and B.S. degrees and taught art for two years. He quit to earn more money in the field of marketing. "I stayed with that 25 years, raising a family." But Darwin still whittled, now on gunstocks. He also bought and sold high-grade firearms. In 1985 he gave up "real work" and became a full-time stockmaker. He doesn't regret it.

"I've been blessed with wonderful clients. I wake up every day eager to go to work. It's not the life for everyone, but there's nothing I'd rather do." Darwin's commitment to superior work is evident in the rifles he builds. They all show an artist's eye for line, and are notable for their trim profiling. "It's important that a rifle shoot and handle well; beyond that, its design should show a harmony of parts. I mean, the lines, components, engraving, checkering, fit and finish should work together to achieve an overall effect. It's wrong for one of the parts to draw attention from the whole."

Darwin takes care to fit each rifle stock to its owner. And he includes detailing so subtle that it's often visible only upon close inspection. The single-shot rifles shown here – a miniature Gibbs Farquharson in .17 Hornet, a miniature Jeffery Farquharson in 2R Lovell, and a miniature Alex Henry in .218 Bee – show the sleek, spare profiles that Darwin Hensley somehow turns into elegance. Metalwork on the first two (and on the featured bolt rifles) is by Steve Heilmann. The .218 Bee proves that Darwin is also an accomplished metalsmith. Engraving: Terry Wallace.

"I'll probably build rifles until I can't anymore," Darwin muses. "Or until my customers tire of my work." Little chance of that.

Hill Country Rifle Co.
New Braunfels, Texas

CUSTOM GUNMAKERS

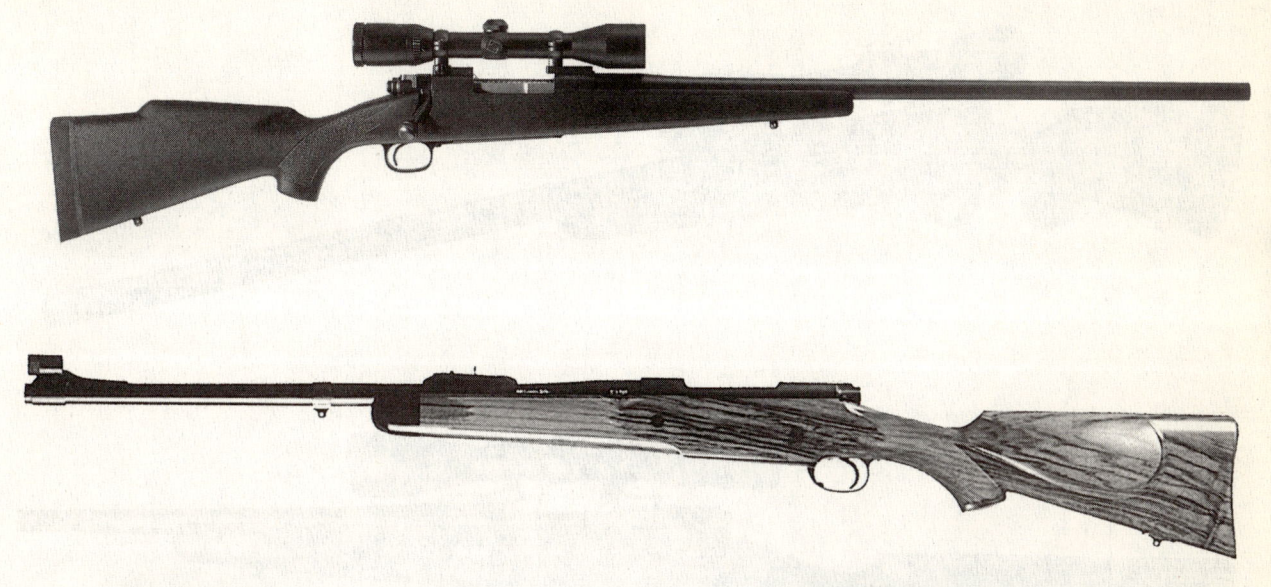

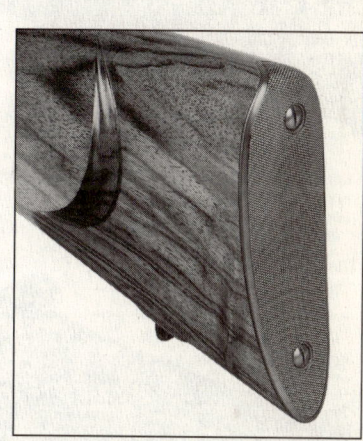

Hill Country Rifle Company specializes in high-quality custom rifles in both wood and synthetic stocks. Customers can choose a McMillan synthetic stock or French, English, or Turkish walnut. Claro and Bastogne walnut are also available upon request. Lilja, Hart, and Krieger barrels came standard on all rifles. Actions are pillar-bedded and barrels free-floated. For most calibers, a 3-shot 1/2" group at 100 yards is guaranteed.

Price: w/customer's action $1850

American Classic 375 H&H
- Winchester Model 70 Action
- Exhibition Grade English Walnut Stock
- Ebony Foroend Tip with Widow's Peak
- Lillja #6,Cm, 1:12 Twist 22' Barrel
- Sunny Hill Drop Box Bottom Metal
- Biesen Steel Butt Plate
- Fisher Skelton Grip Cap
- Talley European Rear Bridged Stud
- Contoured Cross Bolts
- Barrel Band Front Site
- Single Leaf Adjustable Rear Sight
- Custom Extended Extractor
- Custom Checkered Bolt Handle
- Custom Checkered Bolt Handle Release
- HCR Accurizing
- 1" Factory Ammo Guaranteed

Custom Gunmakers • 95

Bob Hisserich
Mesa, Arizona

CUSTOM GUNMAKERS

It's tough to build a rifle that looks as good as it shoots. Bob Hisserich might not get a nod from everyone on that – some gunmakers have the opposite problem as they try to make a handsome rifle shoot tight groups. "Accuracy is mainly a function of installing a good barrel on an action that's square with the barrel axis," Bob continues. "The bolt face must be true and the lugs made to bear evenly. Of course, the stock can't be allowed to interfere."

Bob is only 17 years into his career as a gunmaker, but his rifles and shotguns show a high level of craftsmanship and a good eye for line. He uses a Honig/Rodman stock duplicator (pantograph) capable of .0001 precision. His rifle stocks – laminates as well as traditional walnut versions – are all on classic patterns, though Bob also builds cross-over models for shooters with an off-side dominant eye. His wood-working talents appear on shotguns too. Bob works from a shop in Mesa, Arizona.

Patrick Holehan
Tucson, Arizona

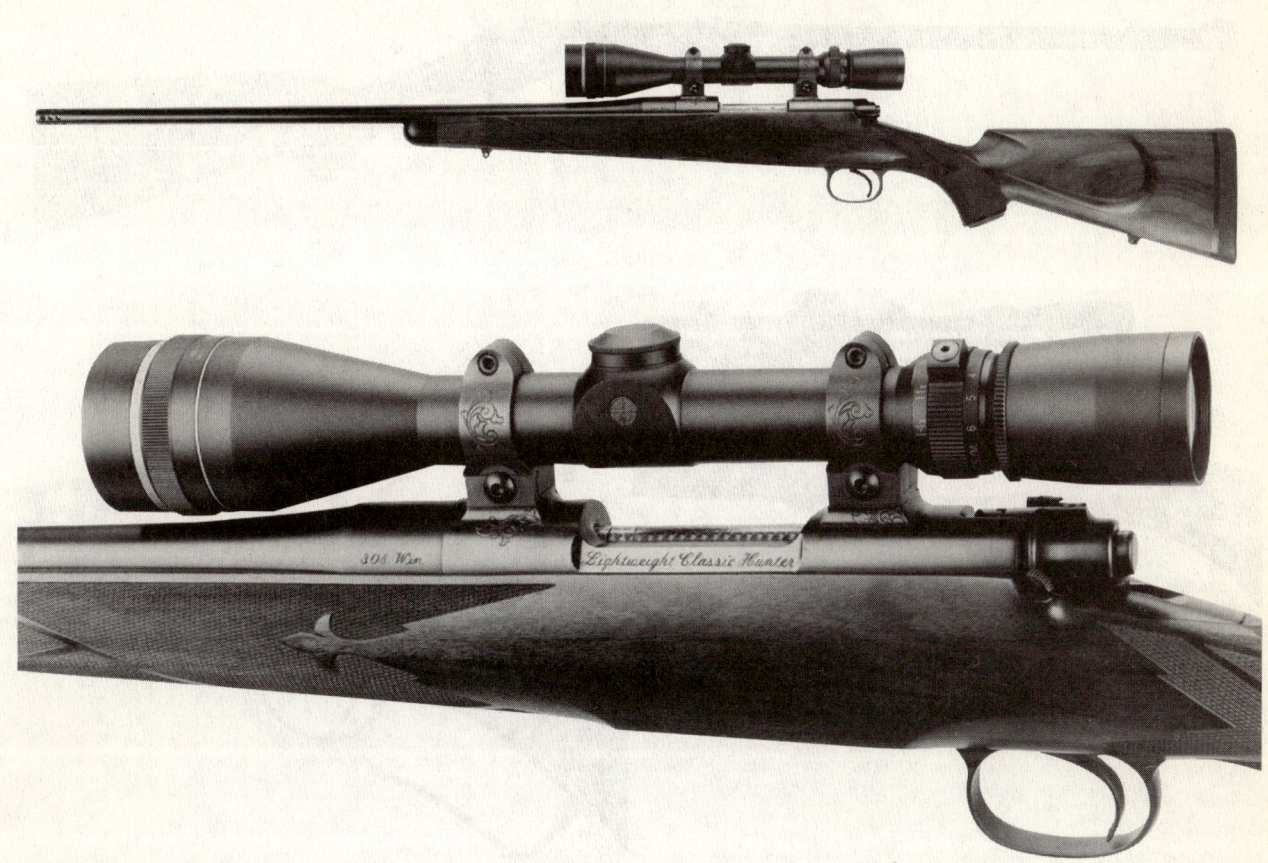

The 2002 Mule Deer Foundation annual fundraising auction in Reno included a custom rifle by a young man whose talents have quickly come to the attention of rifle connoisseurs. The MDF rifle has what maker Patrick Holehan calls his Arizona square bridge actions. "I start with Model 70 Winchester metal, then add the blocks, contouring them into the receiver. They're machined on top to accept quick-detachable scope rings." Pleasing to the eye, this Holehan touch is just one of many that make his rifles unique. "I hew to classic lines," says Pat. "But I also try hard to make my rifles distinctive. Of course, they must shoot well and function perfectly. I'm an avid hunter; my rifles are made for the field."

Named the "Hunter" series, Patrick's M70 bolt rifles include Long Range, Lightweight and Safari versions, with walnut or high-quality synthetic stocks pillar-bedded to the actions. Patrick trues barrel seating surfaces, laps the locking lugs and hones and polishes the feed ramp and bolt face. Customers can order from a long list of options; Patrick offers most standard and wildcat chamberings in cryogenically treated barrels. One of a small number of gunmakers who complete the entire rifle, stock and metal, in their own shops, Patrick admits he's not the fastest gunmaker around. "But you don't order a handmade rifle because you need a rifle right away. You order it because you want a rifle done just right."

Patrick takes the time to do rifles right in a Tucson shop "close to trophy-class Coues deer." His work is more affordable than those of established makers, but no less appealing to hunters who want better performance than is available from factory-built rifles. The sleek lines and careful detailing are bonuses.

Steven Dodd Hughes
Livingston, Montana

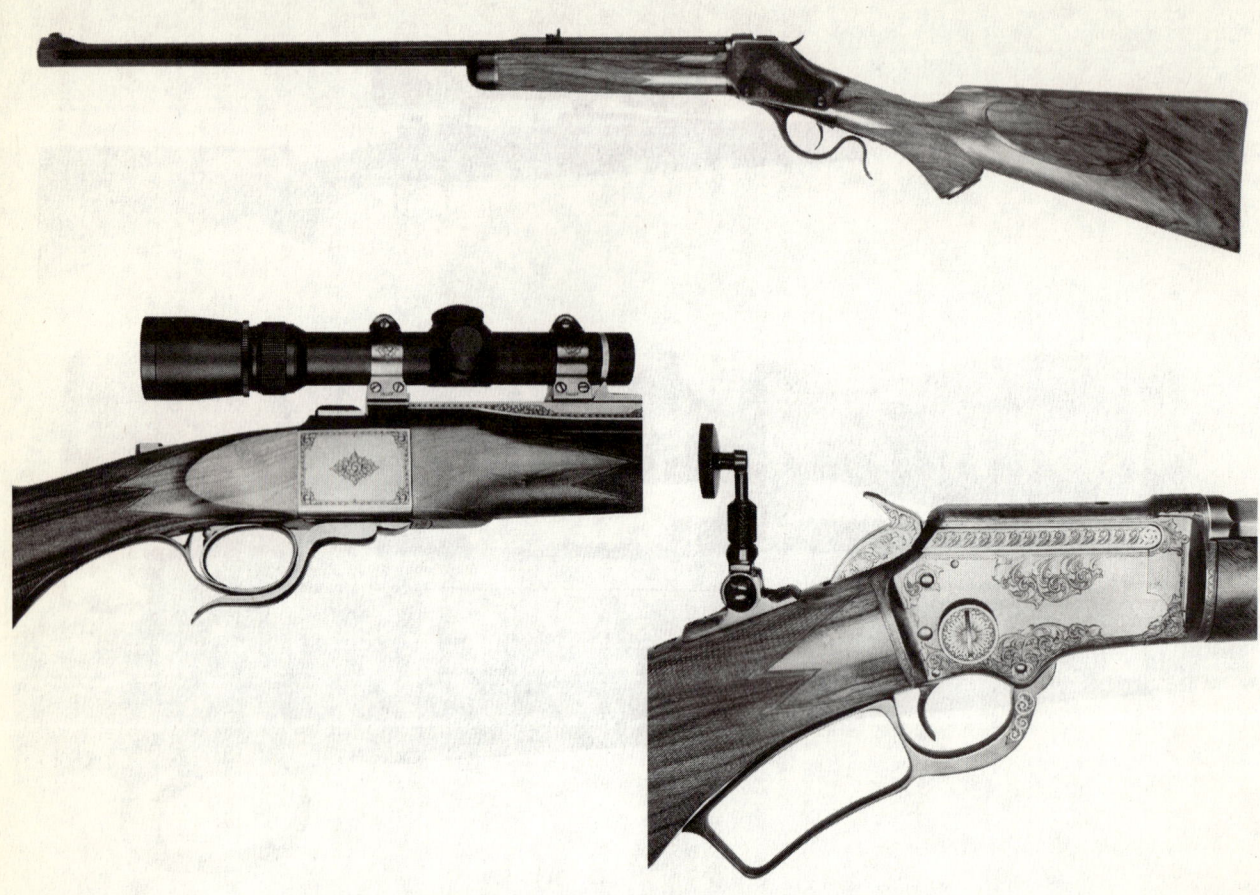

A renaissance stockmaker? Well, Steven Hughes has not only built exceptional firearms – lever-action and single-shot rifles as well as first-class double shotguns. He also writes a "Fine Gunmaking" column for Shooting Sportsman magazine. And he photographs guns with the skill of a pro. His gun photos have appeared on magazine covers as well as in books – you guessed it – that he has authored.

Multi-talented, Steven still considers himself a gunmaker. For a decade after starting his career in 1978, he focused on building muzzleloading firearms faithful to 18th and 19th century patterns. Now he works almost exclusively on cartridge guns, like the Marlin Model 39 rimfire lever rifle shown here with the Steven Hughes 1920s-pattern High Wall. William Gamradt, of Missoula, Montana, engraved the .280 Dakota Model 10 that Steven rebuilt with a new trigger and guard as well as an elegant stock.

"I leave the bolt rifles to the masses," jokes Steven, who points out that there are dozens of craftsmen building custom turnbolt guns for every one keen to tackle a single-shot. "I also like the old lever-actions. One of my favorite projects was an original Winchester 1873, refitted with new parts, many of which I made. I stocked it like one of the original 1-of-1,000 rifles. It came out nice."

So have his two books, "Fine Gunmaking: Double Shotguns" (Krause Publishing) and "Custom Rifles in Black and White" (Fandango Press). Steven is working on a third – between his gun projects and photography….

Steven Dodd Hughes began working on guns professionally in western Oregon, but now makes his home in Livingston, Montana.

Paul Lindke
Penn Valley, California

"I've been checkering stocks for about 40 years," says Paul Lindke, a modest reply to the often-asked question: "How do you make those diamonds all the same?" An active member of the American Custom Gunmakers Guild since 1995, Paul also does metal work. "My father was a tool and die maker," he explains. "So I guess that comes naturally." Beyond the mechanics of metal shaping and fitting, however, Paul also engraves. He's been at that for 16 years, practicing game scenes in high relief and Bolino styles, and inlaying precious metals. He cuts a variety of scroll patterns.

Though he's produced both rifles and shotguns, Paul is particularly fond of classic bolt rifles stocked in fine walnut – which he hand-cuts from the blank and finishes in oil. "I consider every project first-priority," he says. "Every rifle and shotgun gets my best efforts, no matter the level of embellishment or the finished cost."

"One of the best things about this industry is the relationships between craftsmen," muses Paul. "I routinely talk over products, procedures and new ideas with other riflemakers. And we all encourage young people just starting in the trade."

Paul works from his shop in Penn Valley, California.

David Miller
Tucson, Arizona

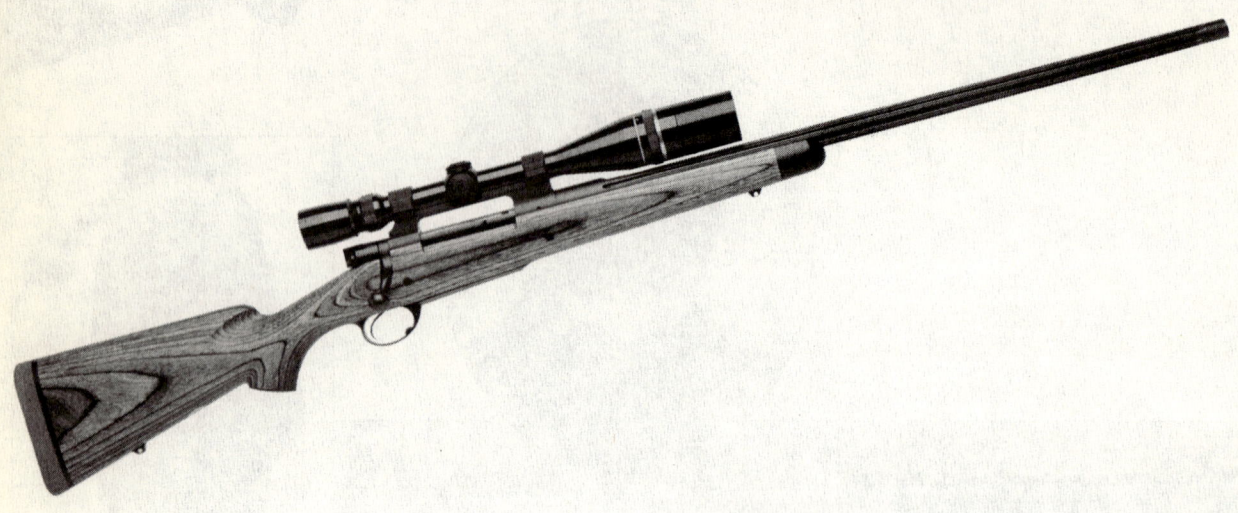

It's hard to tell by chatting with him whether David Miller would rather build rifles or use them. He's been doing both for most of his adult life. An institution at Safari Club International conventions, the David Miller booth not only serves as plush background to his custom rifles, but is long enough to display his collection of outstanding Coues deer bucks. Last year David spent 45 days in Mexico hunting Coues deer.

"It's something of an obsession," he shrugs. Then, chuckling: "It's not the worst vice a man can have."

David has been as successful building rifles as he has hunting Coues deer (he has more bucks in the records book than anyone else). A savvy marketer, David decided early on that rifles built to the highest standards and peddled to the wealthiest people would always sell. "I don't sell lots of them," he says. "But they're not production-class rifles. They can't be stamped out like cookies, and I don't sell 'em cheap."

Miller Classic rifles have earned the spotlight at several SCI conventions. The exquisite hand detailing of both wood and metal show his competence – and that of partner Curt Crum. In the custom gun industry, few partnerships survive long. This one has, to the benefit of both men.

Some years ago, David assembled a rifle for his own use, a .300 Weatherby on a Model 70 Winchester action, with a long fluted barrel and a laminated stock. The rifle wore a Leupold 6.5-20x scope in David's own bomb-proof mount. This outfit had the same clean lines as David's Classic rifle, but not the hand-checkering and expensive wood. As soon as other hunters heard of the project, they beat a path to Miller's Tucson shop. Now David and Curt offer their Marksman rifle at about half the price of a Classic.

"It's still not a cheap rifle," David says without apology. "We don't build cheap rifles. We build very accurate rifles that look good, for people who want the best there is."

Steve Nelson
Corvallis, Oregon

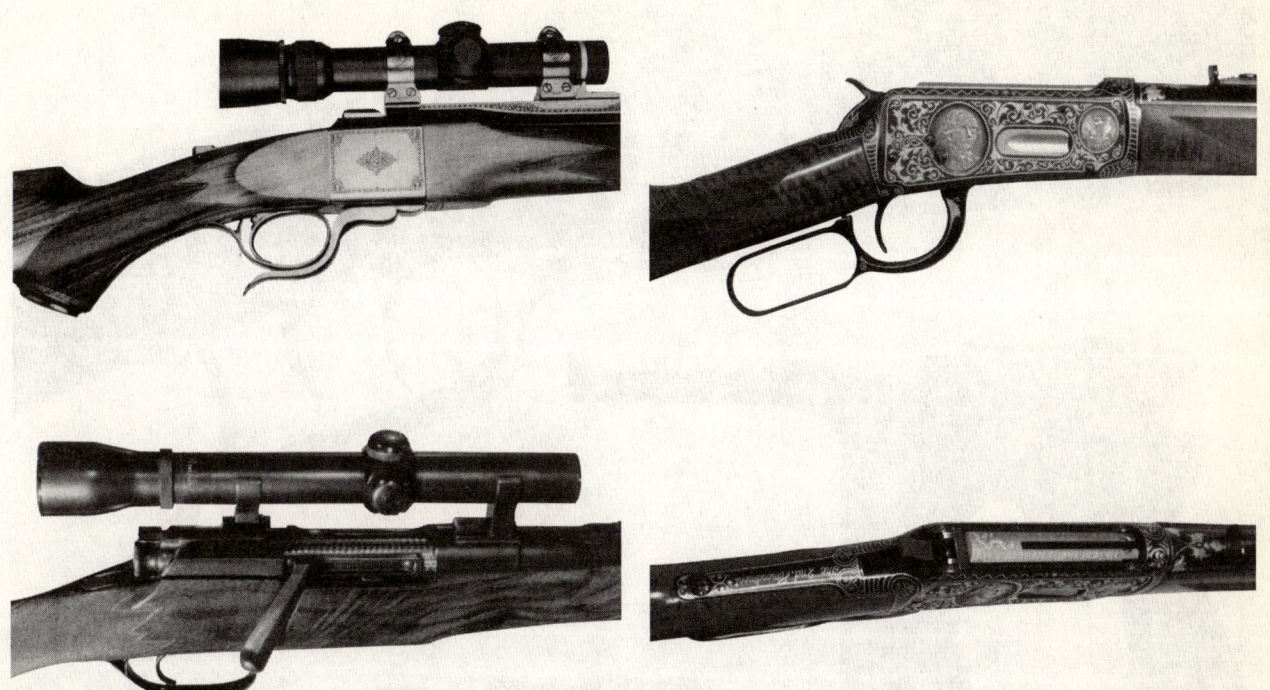

In 1974, Steve Nelson wanted a better rifle than he could afford. "So I figured I'd just build one," he recalls. "The result wasn't quite what I had in mind, but the process taught me a great deal. Enough, anyway, to prompt a followup. But before I bungled again, I signed up for one of Jerry Fisher's NRA summer seminars at Trinidad, Colorado. Then I attended the annual meeting of the American Custom Gunmakers Guild. What an eye-opener! I had no idea such flawless, sophisticated work was even possible. And I determined to come as close as I could to the craftsmanship presented there."

Steve eagerly accepted tips and encouragement from Al Lind, Mark Lee, Dale Goens and other luminaries in the custom gun trade. A decade later, after much hard work and steady progress as a gunmaker, he was accepted as a member of ACGG.

"Strictly defined, a custom firearm is one built for an individual. The rifle or shotgun has a stock fitted specifically for its owner, who also decides chambering, barrel dimensions, choke, sights, trigger and all the options that might make the product perform better or give the customer the look he or she wants. Of course, you can buy a custom rifle second-hand and shoot well with it even though it is no more built for your hands than is a factory rifle. And you can buy custom rifles from makers who insist on incorporating their own ideas, independent of your wishes. I like to think I'm a consultant as well as a gun-builder. My aim is to deliver a rifle that meets the client's needs specifically. I do all the work on a rifle or shotgun – wood and metal – except the engraving."

Steve appreciates the artistry of craftsmen who spare no effort to produce superior work and explore new ideas. He says the exhibitions of ACGG and the Firearms Engravers Guild of America not only showcase remarkable craftsmanship; they present a much different picture of firearms than is delivered by people who would restrict firearms ownership.

Dave Norin
Waukegan, Illinois

CUSTOM GUNMAKERS

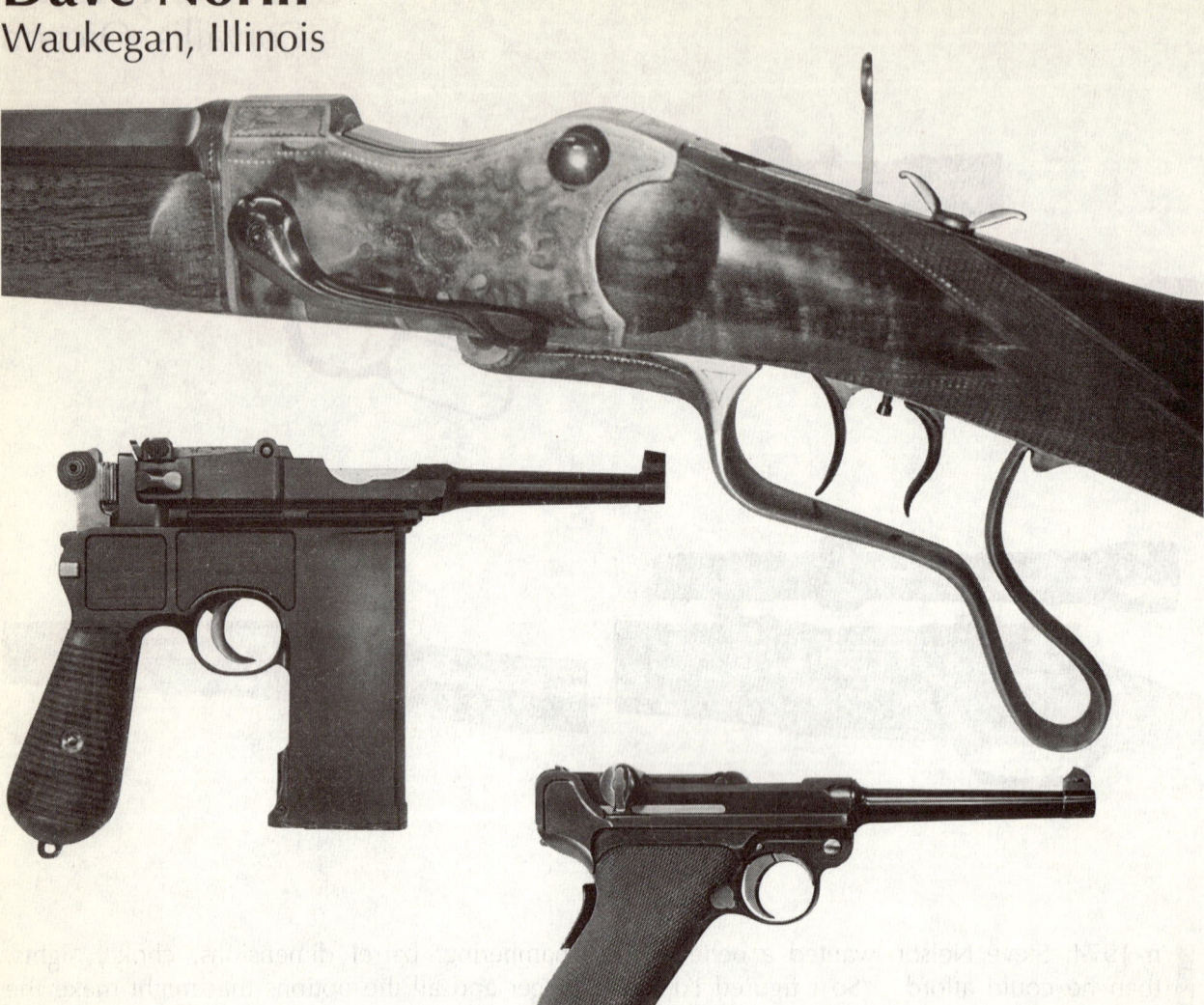

Graduating in 1972 from Trinidad State College in Colorado, Dave Norin joined a large fraternity in the gunmaking industry with that alma mater. But Dave has since distinguished himself by steering toward work less commonly done by custom gunmakers.

"I have a broad range of interests," he admits. "I collect pre-1945 self-loading pistols, Winchesters, any nice double I can afford…." A whitetail hunter first and an upland bird hunter second, Dave lives where both abound: in Waukegan, Illinois. He and his wife have four children and a grandchild. "Even without the shop and my hunting, I'd be busy!"

Dave's specialty these days is restoration of collector-quality firearms, and fine custom gunsmithing – like rebuilding a German 8x46R takedown target rifle and bringing an ultra-rare Farrow rifle back to life. He has restored Luger, Mauser and Mannlicher pistols, lever-action Winchester rifles "and of course the bolt-action rifles everybody else works on." But few other custom shops boast the suite of services available at the Norin digs: rust bluing, Niter bluing, color case hardening, stocking from blanks and vintage wood finishes. Dave's work shows an artist's attention to detail, and a faithfulness to original color and form that keeps his services in demand among sophisticated gun people.

"Oh, one more thing," says Dave. "I collect gun books. There's still a hole in the shelf for a 1952 Shooter's Bible…."

Ray Rigarian
Glendale, California

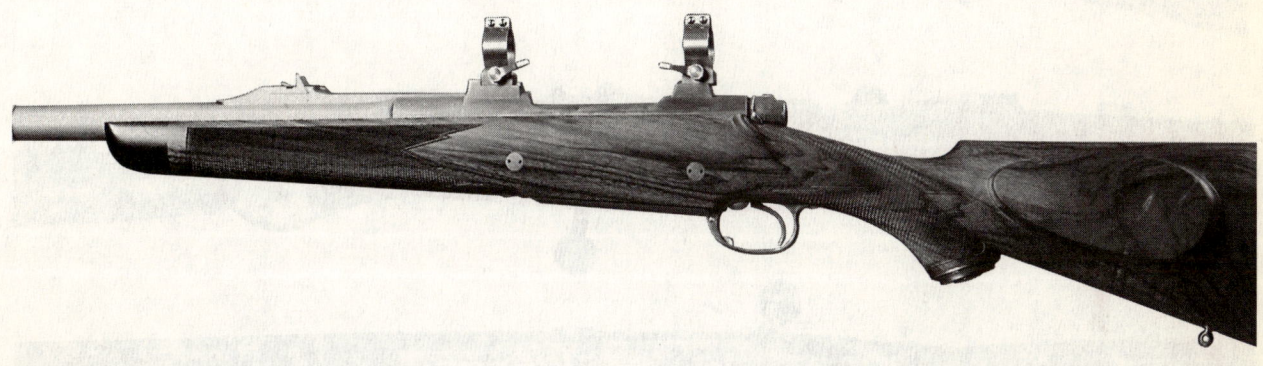

Not many custom gunmakers have Ray Rigarian's range of skills. A machinist in the aerospace industry before he began his career as a riflemaker, Ray does "almost all the work" in his benchrest and hunting rifles. "I machine my own sight and scope bases from bar stock, my own swivel bands too," he says. "Of course, I true up the bolt and receiver with the barrel shank, recutting threads when necessary and squaring the lug bearing surfaces."

Some components come from other sources: sights and his rifles' elegant Blackburn bottom metal, for example. He uses Talley scope rings. "Everything is carefully matched to the other components, and to the use the customer expects to make of his rifle." Ray likes the Model 70 Winchester for hunting rifles, because of its beefy extractor – "also the 98 Mauser, but it requires a lot of work to finish." His varmint rifles are commonly built on 700 Remingtons. "Long-range target and bench rifles typically get Stolle or Nishika actions. They're expensive but very precisely machined. Mostly, I use Krieger barrels for the big game rifles, Hart barrels on target guns." He sends the metal out for cold rust-bluing or a "special treatment that's more durable than Teflon and sticks better to the steel." Ray pillar-beds the actions to the stocks.

Ray's stocks show the same attention to detail and sensible line that he lavishes on metal. "I prefer to work on California English, but Circassian walnut is a close second choice. I buy dry blanks and will not start work on any with more than 8 percent moisture. My checkering is 22 or 24 lines per inch, because finer cuts are only a cosmetic touch. Function is much more important to me than showcasing my abilities in technical tours de force."

Ray emphasizes that reliability in the field matters to him because he is a hunter. "I'm just now planning an Ibex hunt in one of the republics south of Russia. It's an exciting way to test the rifles I build," he smiles. He might not have to travel *that* far.

Tony Schuelke
Glencoe, Minnesota

CUSTOM GUNMAKERS

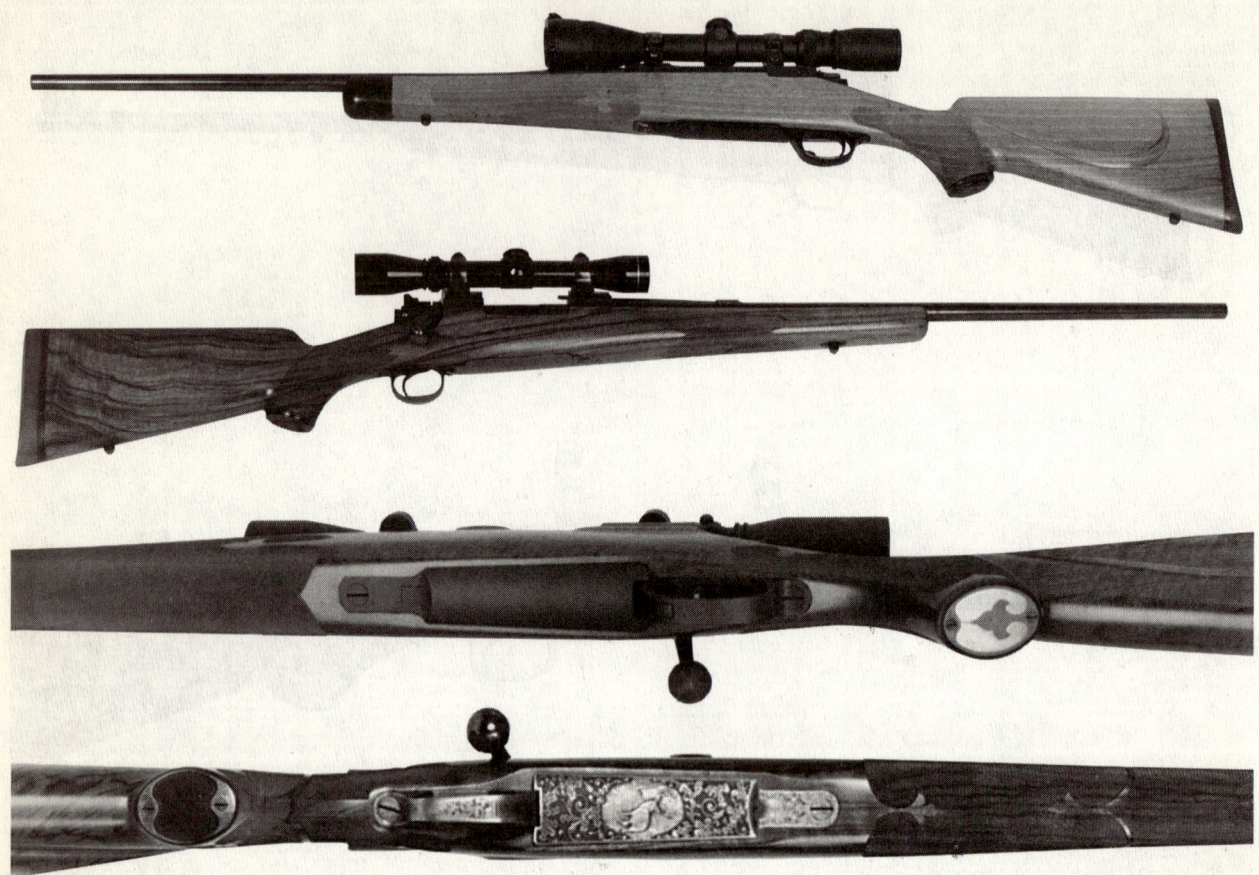

At age 16, Tony Schuelke stripped the stock on a Remington autoloading shotgun and tried to refinish the wood as Jack O'Connor had recommended in a book. Whether that effort encouraged him to continue or challenged him to do better, he can't say. But it became the first of many gun projects. Despite an early affinity for firearms, Tony didn't start building guns until very late in life. He worked as a certified auto mechanic, then ran a life insurance business. A stint in banking followed, then one in real estate. He's a machinist now, he says modestly. But that label is inadequate. Tony is a self-taught craftsman who tackles some of the toughest jobs in custom gunbuilding.

"I like working on side-by-side shotguns," he says. "About 70 percent of my projects are double-barrel smoothbores." He is an accomplished man with a file, checkering not only stocks but bolt handles, and fabricating skeleton grip caps.

While he doesn't imitate anyone, Tony takes every opportunity to study the work that he admires. He's constantly innovating. "If you're not a creative kind of a guy, there's not much interesting about building guns," he says.

Tony solicits the customer's ideas. He'd rather respond to them than recommend his own design. "Custom guns – especially side-by-sides – are more like art than implements. Customers have their own tastes, and they're paying the freight. So I listen." He adds that individuality can be important to gun people, and little details that have no bearing on performance often matter a great deal. Untested ideas intrigue him, though he says that a lot of what does make sense in gun design has already been tried – "at least on traditional double-barrel frames." Tony Schuelke's shop is in Glencoe, Minnesota, where he says winters "are just right for working on guns."

Gene Simillion
Gunnison, Colorado

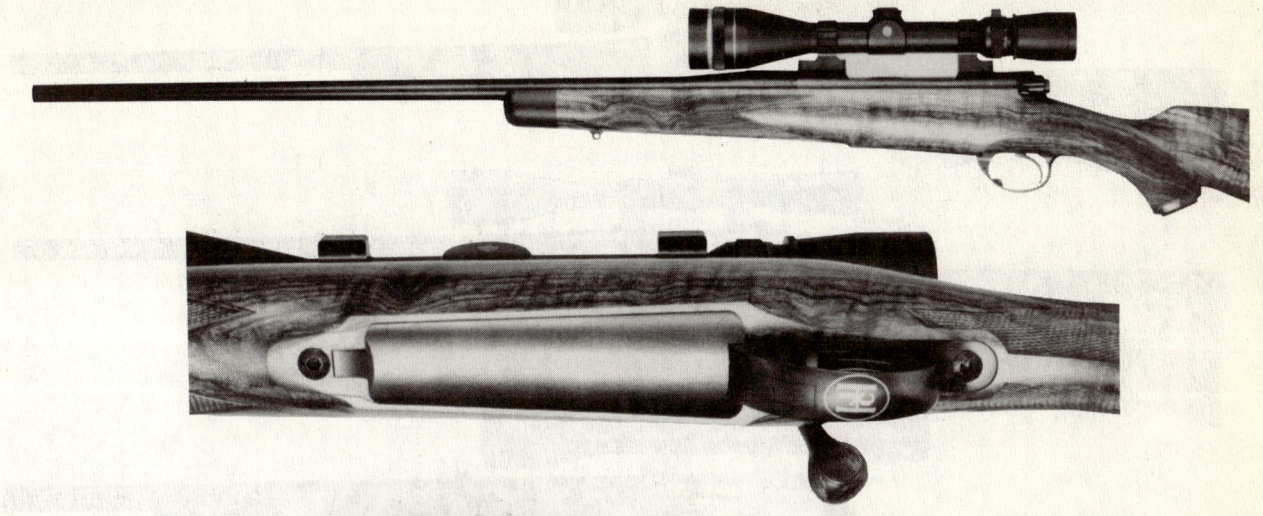

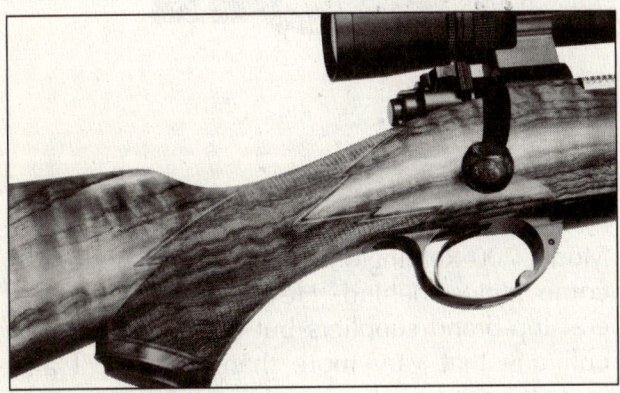

"I went to school 20 years ago to learn how to teach industrial arts," says Gene Simillion. "That wasn't smart. If you teach, you have to be in school during hunting season."

So Gene switched occupations. He worked for a year in Kalispell, Montana, under the tutelage of ace stockmaker Jerry Fisher. "Not very far down the road was Tom Burgess," grins Gene. "He's forgotten more about metalsmithing than most gunmakers will ever learn. I got the best education a young fellow could hope for." He also credits exposure to the work of D'Arcy Echols, Monte Mandarino and Don Klein.

A veteran rifle-builder now, Gene affirms that the classic bolt rifle is not only his favorite, but a product with timeless appeal. "It still sells, and the best of contemporary makers build them better than they've ever been built before." Gene's aim is to produce a rifle with "fine accuracy, flawless function and elegant beauty." He points out that the main difference between custom rifles and the best factory-built guns is in the detailing – "things like checkered bolt knobs and and screwless sling swivel studs" (both standard on Simillion rifles).

The Premier rifle is Gene's best, built to each customer's specifications. Gene prefers to work with new Model 70 Classic rifles but will substitute early Model 70s, Mauser 98s and Remington 700s. Gene installs his own scope bases. Magnums get a second recoil lug and a crossbolt in front of the magazine well. Quarter ribs and drop-box magazines are two of the options. The less costly Classic Hunter comes only on the new M70 action. It has fewer options and less detailing, but its cut-rifled barrel, hand-bedded to a checkered walnut stock, delivers the same level of performance.

When not hunting in the Mountain West or northern Canada, Gene works in his shop in Gunnison, Colorado.

Charlie Sisk
Crosby, Texas

Talking with customers may once have come hard to Charlie Sisk. Then again, he may have been talking since he was weaned. It's one of his strengths, keeping in close touch with the people who order his super-accurate rifles. But Charlie has other talents, refined since he built his first gun in a high-school machine shop. "It was a .257 Roberts on a 98 Mauser action. It's still in the rack." But the rack has filled up these days, mainly with synthetic-stocked bolt rifle. "I'd say they can all shoot half-inch, because I've managed half-inch groups," he grins. "But I have two-inch days."

Such candor endears Charlie to his customers, who are for the most part a pretty critical lot. Charlie's rifles don't wear handsome wood or engraving. They're meant to be shot. "Beauty is as beauty does – or somethin' like that," he drawls. Charlie works almost exclusively on bolt-action rifles but has lately tackled Marlin 1895 rifles in .45-70, smoothing up the action and installing a black leather cartridge band on the butt. He adds a Teflon finish to the metal, a soft black Decelerator pad to the stock, and a black Latigo sling. "A great gun for thick places." And handsome. In bolt rifles, Charlie prefers Model 700 Remingtons but says Winchester 70s come in close behind. He uses barrels from several top-brand suppliers but air-gauges them to cull any that vary more than .0001. "I also inspect each barrel with a bore-scope. And my chambering is done with match-grade live-pilot reamers to ensure concentricity." Charlie's standard rifle jobs include "blueprinting" the action to square up the bolt with the bore. He thinks most rifles will shoot about as well as they can shoot if the forend tip puts some pressure on the barrel. However, he will free-float barrels on request.

Bench accuracy isn't enough for hunters who must control lightweight rifles under field conditions. Charlie installs and adjusts aftermarket triggers (he likes Jewell and Timney), and he takes care that his synthetic stocks fit each client perfectly. Rifle balance and weight matter to Charlie, who prides himself in doing all the work personally. He makes his own muzzle brakes and commonly works up loads for his customers.

Charlie will talk to you anywhere, but his shop is in Crosby, Texas, 45 minutes northeast of Houston.

Dale A. Storey
Casper, Wyoming

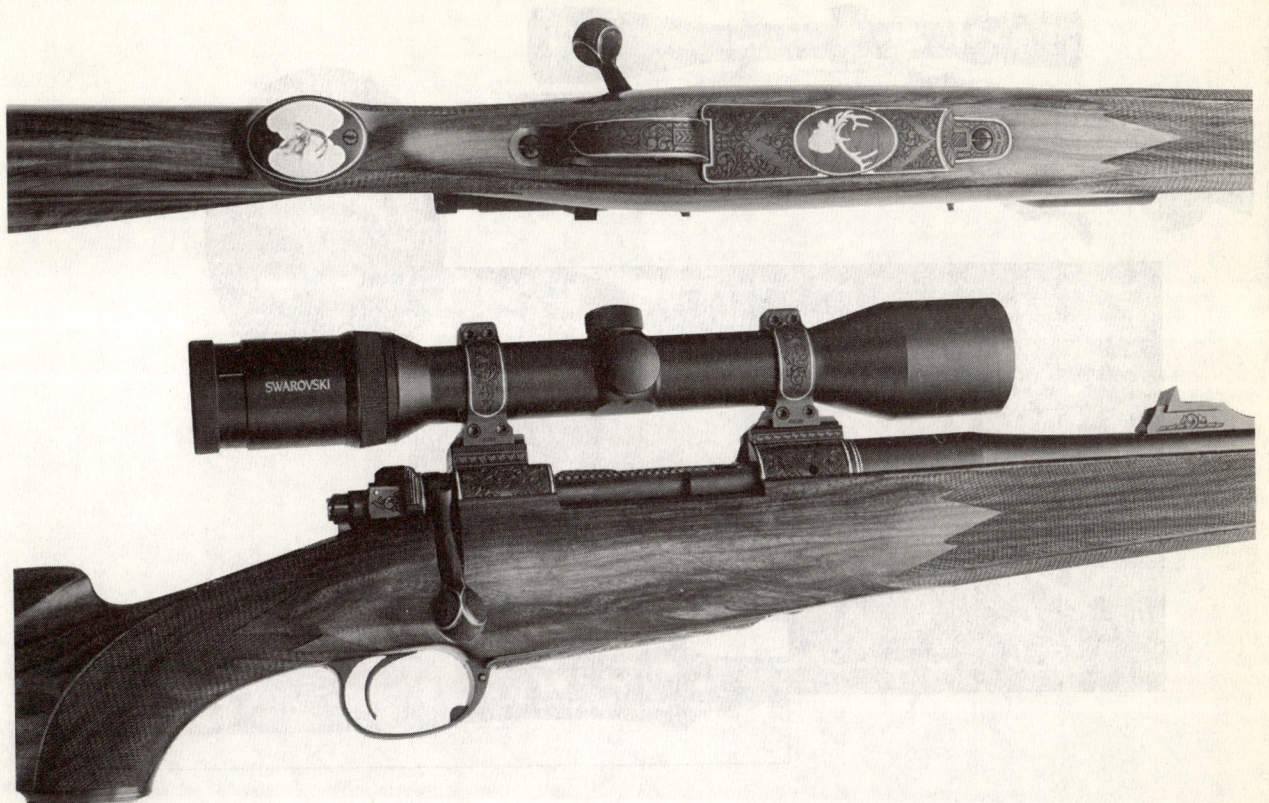

Dale Story is doing just what he thought he'd be doing decades ago. "In high school, I knew I wanted to be a gunbuilder," he laughs. "Prescient, eh?" He started working on guns soon after graduating from the Colorado School of Trades in 1962, but didn't commit to the craft full time until 1981. "Uncle Sam used my talents for awhile," he says. After military service and two degrees from Montana State University, Dale bankrolled his gunshop by teaching for 11 years at a high school and post-secondary schools. He has worked on a variety of rifles, from the black powder muzzleloaders that were his early love, to modern bolt guns.

For the most part, Dale builds modern hunting rifles, taking pains to give each the perfect balance he says is so crucial to good shooting. His economy of line emphasizes balance too. "No one thing should dominate a rifle, in form or function," he says. "A rifle should point quickly and shoot accurately from any hunting position." He concedes that high-quality parts are essential but adds that putting them together is what distinguishes an expert craftsman from a mere assembler. Dale says he can do "almost everything" in building a rifle, but he leaves the engraving and inlay work to others.

One of Dale's favorite rifle styles is the half-stock black powder pattern he followed on a recent project. The result: an exquisite rifle true in form and function to an original Alex Henry. It is most elegant, with engraving by Liz Dolbare. Dale traces his interest in muzzleloaders to mentor V.M. Starr, who taught him about their history and how they should be built. Starr was instrumental in bringing shotgun shooting to the annual black powder rendezvous at Friendship, Indiana.

Among Dale's latest projects are matched bolt rifles in .300 and .375 H&H Magnums. "I can't tell you what's next," he grins. "I expect to throttle back one of these days. But it's still fun to build rifles. And," he adds with a twinkle, "customers say I'm getting better at it." Dale Story brings his high school enthusiasm to the bench in Casper, Wyoming.

CUSTOM GUNMAKERS

Mark Stratton
Lynnwood, Washington

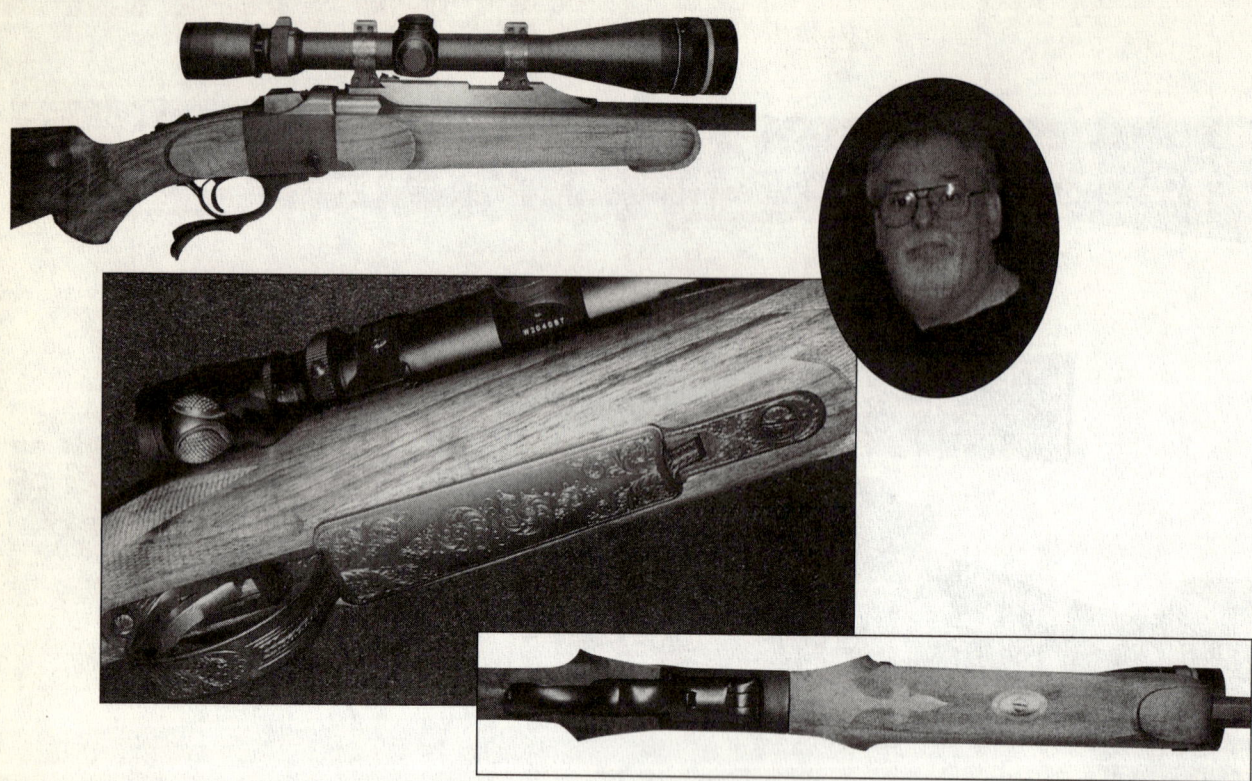

Sometime in 1971, after two years of gunsmithing school in Trinidad, Colorado, and a few days in a gunshop in his native southern California, Mark Stratton discovered that gun work paid only the small bills. He went to work as a machinist for an electronics firm but in his spare time started building rifles. He sold his first in 1974 to a friend – "for the cost of the parts." The next four years, a lot of his friends got good deals on custom rifles.

Then Mark moved to Seattle, to work for another electronics company. He continued his rifle-building off hours but lacked the confidence to abandon his "real" job. A decade later, at the 1988 American Custom Gunmakers Guild show in Reno, Mark saw the products of the country's finest craftsmen. He marveled. "I'd become pretty adept at metal work," he recalls. "But these fellows were way beyond me in the wood." Inspired, Mark set out to improve his stockmaking. In the meantime, though, he found that his moonlighting had taught him some techniques worth marketing.

"In 1991 a Guild member asked me about making an octagon barrel. I'd developed the tooling for making my octagon barrels years before, so decided to write it up. The article was very well received, and since then I've published 15 other technical tips. Later I was invited to write regularly for an industry magazine. I still do."

But even after his first writing on metal-smithing, Mark wasn't a member of ACGG. "I didn't think it appropriate when my work was still essentially a hobby." But in 1994 he started advertising his work. It brought kudos from buyers, and shortly thereafter Mark was asked to present a seminar on rifle-building at his alma mater in Trinidad. Full-time commitment to his hobby followed. In 2001, Mark joined the Guild. Each year he closes his Lynnwood, Washington, shop for a trip to Trinidad. He has also delivered seminars at other schools. "If there's anything more rewarding than rifle-building, it's sharing your techniques with others who love the craft," says Mark. As these photos show, he likes to work on Mauser rifles, but his talents have spun their magic on other rifles too.

Virgin Valley Guns
Hurricane, Utah

Just five years ago a group of investors committed their talents and resources to a custom gunshop. Steve Stratton, now point-man for the firm's eight employees, was among the founders. "We've grown fast," he says. "Partly because we're so versatile."

Indeed. Virgin Valley's craftsmen, working in wood and metal, turn out custom rifles on actions ranging from Martinis to the Nisika Bay. "We've built something of a reputation with the T/Cs," Steve tells me. "It still accounts for about half our business. The Encore has overtaken the Contender; three of every four Thompsons we build have Encore frames." Other single-shots, like the Ruger Number One, are also favored by Virgin Valley customers, partly because the firm specializes in wood stocks.

"We have our own sawmill," says Steve. "Much of our wood is American walnut bought on the stump, then cut and seasoned here. We live in a dry climate, so a blank can be ready for cutting in as little as a year." Virgin Valley also buys walnut from a California supplier and plans to offer its own (sub-contracted) fiberglass stocks for customers who value durability and stability over esthetic appeal. The company will also stock rifles in wood laminates.

While a few of its rifles go to target shooters, the overwhelming majority are built for big game hunters and varmint shooters. Virgin Valley machinists square up bolt faces and locking lugs as part of any rebarreling job. Complete tooling is on hand for "blue-printing" the popular Remington 700 action and a few others. A custom rifle normally includes a Shilen match-grade barrel, though Steve says "select" barrels are available on request, and the company also installs some Douglas barrels. "We prefer Jewell triggers for most of our work," he adds. But Canjar and Timney products are available too.

What's the most popular chambering at Virgin Valley? "Well, right now Winchester's .300 Short Magnum has brought us a lot of work. We've built quite a few Encores for cartridges derived from the WSM. The .17 Hornady Magnum Rimfire is another hot number." Both are new at this writing. "The beauty of the Encore is its versatility. We've chambered this rifle for the likes of the 7 STW, as well as for short rounds."

Virgin Valley Arms offers a suite of gunsmithing services, including scope mounting and zeroing, even load development.

Al Ward
Grass Valley, California

After 31 years working for a utility company, Al Ward retired to make stock-making a full-time job. "I'd been at it for 15 years, part-time," he says.

Time flies when you enjoy your work, and it's obvious that Al enjoys his. Specializing in stocking early Model 70 Winchesters, he also installs wood on other rifles and shotguns. He does little with metal. "My close relationships with other artisans – metalsmiths and engravers – allow me to give customers the best work of top specialists." He grins. "I have a passion for wood, particularly California English and Bastogne walnut." His store of blanks includes many he has cut and dried himself. Al Ward's stocks are of traditional line, with checkering to the customer's order. He has delivered hunting rifles "with no gingerbread", as well as ornate exhibition pieces. His oil finishes bring out the natural warmth and color contrast in the wood.

Al's Grass Valley, California shop also takes in custom service work, including stock refinishing and reshaping, pad installation and glass bedding.

RIFLES

AMERICAN HUNTING	112	LONE STAR	154
ANSCHUTZ	113	MAGNUM RESEARCH	155
AUTO-ORDNANCE	117	MARLIN	156
BERETTA	118	MERKEL	162
BLASER	121	MOSSBERG	162
ED BROWN	122	NAVY ARMS REPLICAS	163
BROWNING	124	NEW ENGLAND FIREARMS	166
BROWN PRECISION	127	NEW ULTRA LIGHT ARMS	167
CHRISTENSEN ARMS	129	PEDERSOLI REPLICAS	168
CIMARRON	130	PRAIRIE GUN WORKS	169
COLT	132	PURDEY	170
COOPER	133	REMINGTON	171
CZ	134	RIFLES, INC.	179
DAKOTA ARMS	137	ROGUE	180
EMF REPLICAS	139	ROSSI	181
EUROPEAN AMERICAN ARMORY	139	RUGER	182
HARRINGTON & RICHARDSON	140	SAKO	189
GIBBS	141	SAUER	194
HECKLER & KOCH	142	SAVAGE ARMS	195
HENRY	143	SPRINGFIELD	202
H-S PERCISION	144	SZECSEI & FUCHS	203
HOWA	146	TAYLOR'S	204
JARRETT	146	THOMPSON & CAMPBELL	205
JOHANNSEN	148	THOMPSON/CENTER	206
KBI/CHARLES DALY	149	TIKKA	207
KIMBER	150	UBERTI REPLICAS	209
KRIEGHOFF	151	WEATHERBY	210
L.A.R. GRIZZLY	151	WILD WEST GUNS	214
LAZZERONI	152	WINCHESTER	215

American Hunting Rifles

AHR BIG GAME RIFLE

AMERICAN HUNTING RIFLES

A few years ago, well-known firearms experimenter Ken Howell designed 12 rimless cases based on the .30-06 case. Well, not quite. The case looked like the '06 and had the same head dimensions, but it was 2.600 overall, or .106 longer than a .30-06 hull and .100 longer than a magnum case like the 7mm Remington or .338 Winchester. At 2.058, head-to-shoulder measure was .110 greater than on the .30-06; and the Howell hull had a .455 shoulder – bigger by .014.

The Howell necks accepted common bullets: .224, .243, .257, .264, .277, .284, .308, .323, .338, .358, .375 and .411. Ken established all shoulders at 25 degrees and kept the necks .375 in length (head-to-shoulder measure on formed cases thus varied slightly with caliber). The Stevensville, Montana gun enthusiast says he came up with these cartridges "for hunters who want more performance than they can get from a .30-06 but don't want the recoil or barrel-eating blast of a magnum."

There were eight larger cartridges too, on a rimless case best described as a medium-length magnum but named the Howell Express. Base-to-mouth, it was 2.75 inches long. The head miked .515, essentially the rim diameter of any belted magnum derived from the .375 H&H. Consequently, you could barrel any magnum action with a long magazine to a Howell Express – a .250, .270, .280, .300, .340, .350, .380 or .420. Shoulder angle for each was 25 degrees, neck length .375. The basic case measured .477 at the shoulder.

Ken and local entrepreneur Ed Plummer wanted to offer a new semi-custom rifles for these cartridges. Ed went first to Winchester for Model 70 actions. Nothing came of it. He then visited the Czech Republic, where he examined the CZ Model 550. It came in two action lengths and had other assets. Ed made a deal, then went to renowned Kalispell gunmaker Jerry Fisher for a stock design, engaging a Bitterroot valley craftsman to fit and finish the walnut. The result was a delightful rifle with a clean, slim look and excellent balance. Reshaping trigger and bolt handle improved function and appearance. Ed called his firm American Hunting Rifles.

When last I visited Ed, he was working on three new cartridges of his own design: a .450, .500 and .585 AHR.

If you like to load up with rounds the size of salt-shakers, you'll share Ed's enthusiasm for such artillery. The .500 AHR is an Ed Plummer original, similar in form to the potent .500 Jeffery but with a longer neck, 25-degree shoulder and full-diameter (not rebated) rim. Ballistically, it matches the Jeffery and the .505 Gibbs. Pressures are mild.

AHR rifles feature Mauser-type extractors, two-position thumb safeties, barrels from McGowan and Wilson (button rifled) and Lawrence (with cut rifling). Synthetic stocks are McMillans. Jim Weisner supplies replacement triggers and three-position safeties. Magnum rifles have integral dovetail scope bases.

"Our metal work is done right here in the Valley," says Ed. That includes truing the receiver and bolt face, lapping the lugs and ironing out the ribs on the CZ magazine boxes so they accept the AHR cases. A standard AHR bolt gun holds four in the magazine; magnum models hold three in a box not objectionably deep. Magnum rifles, incidentally, feature an additional recoil lug on the barrel and double cross-bolts at the magazine well. Instead of a forend swivel stud, magnums have a barrel-band stud.

You can buy a standard AHR rifle for $1495. This is a hunting rifle. Its beauty derives from economy of form and careful execution in detailing. Chambered for one of the medium-bore Howell rounds, it can't be far from an ideal North American big game rifle.

Two other AHR models, built on the double-square-bridge CZ 550 Magnum action, cost more. At $2995, the Safari 550 offers a medium-fancy quarter-sawn walnut stock cut to your specified length of pull, oil finished and capped with a black Decelerator pad. Checkering is 22 lines per inch in four panels. You can add custom options. Chambering: almost any common belted round, plus the .350 Rigby. The Safari 550 DGR (Dangerous Game Rifle) lists for $3495. A custom trigger and Weisner three-position safety are part of the package. So is an extra-fancy grade of walnut. Ordinarily bored for the likes of the .416 Rigby, .458 Lott, and .450 and .500 AHR, the DGR can be had in a host of standard and wildcat chamberings that require a long action and big bolt face. NECG supplies custom rear swivel studs for the Safari rifles, as well as fixed-and-folding rear open sights and barrel-band front sights. All are standard features. A quarter rib is available. Order the .500 AHR with the notion of launching 535-grain bullets, and you may want the optional muzzle brake.

Anschutz Rifles

MODEL 2013 SUPER MATCH

J.G. Anschutz began as a company in 1856, making pistols, rifles and shotguns. Since its rebirth following World War II, the firm has been best known for its fine rimfire target rifles. But there is also a line of bolt-action target pistols with the same features that have put Anschutz rifles in the winner's circle more often than any other rimfires in recent times.

Julius Gottfried Anschutz, son of a German gunsmith, founded J.G. Anschutz in 1856 to build pocket pistols, shotguns and rifles. In 1896 the firm moved out of its small workshop into a factory. Five years later Julius Anschutz died, and his sons, Fritz and Otto, assumed control of the business. By 1911 there were 200 people working at the Anschutz plant. When Otto died shortly after the first world war, Fritz and his sons, Rudolf and Max, continued to build the enterprise.

Growth came to an abrupt halt in 1945, when the factory was shut down pursuant to Germany's surrender in World War II. But five years later J.G. Anschutz GmbH was founded to make air pistols and repair firearms. Soon it turned to target rifles and even resumed manufacture of the Flobert-type guns that had been among the firm's original products. Anschutz target rifles began to build a reputation among the world's elite shooters, and the company grew to 250 employees.

In 1968 Dieter Anschutz, a fourth-generation member of the family, became chief executive, as the Anschutz name became more and more prominent in Olympic competition. In 1992 his son, Jochen, became company president. Jochen and Dieter now manage J.G. Anschutz together. An ultra-modern plant in Ulm, Germany, produces what has become recognized world-wide as the standard against which all rimfire target rifles and pistols are judged. Anschutz rifles captured all of the gold medals, and all but two of the silver medals in the Barcelona Olympic Games. The company's competition air rifles and pistols have done almost as well as the firearms.

MODEL 2013 "SUPER MATCH"

Since the 1960s, the Model 54 rimfire action has set the standard in competitive three-position and smallbore prone shooting. The current version, with a heavy, rectangular receiver, attaches to the stock with four action screws. This action is the heart of the Model 2013 Super Match Special — and of the 2013 Benchrest, the 2007, 2012, 1907, 1912, and 1913 rifles. It is also featured in the 1808 D-RT Running Target, 54.18 MS Metallic Silhouette and 1808 MS-R Silhouette rifles. Its fine trigger mechanism, close tolerances and extremely fast lock time make it a logical choice for competitive marksmen. Anschutz .22 rimfire barrels, noted for one-hole accuracy, complement the 54 action.

The 2013 Super Match is the latest and most sophisticated in a long line of Super Match rifles for freestyle shooting events. Available in both right- and left-hand versions, it comes with adjustable two-stage match trigger (with safety). The trigger-piece can be moved longitudinally and tilted up to 15 degrees. There's a forearm accessory rail with hand stop and palm rest fitted to the thumbhole stock. A fully adjustable cheekpiece complements a hook butt assembly adjustable for cant, pitch, length and drop. A host of accessories, including match sights and counter-weights is available.

Barrel length: 27.1 inches.
Rifle weight: 14.3 pounds.
Price: w/palm rest $2270
left-hand 2360

Anschutz Rifles

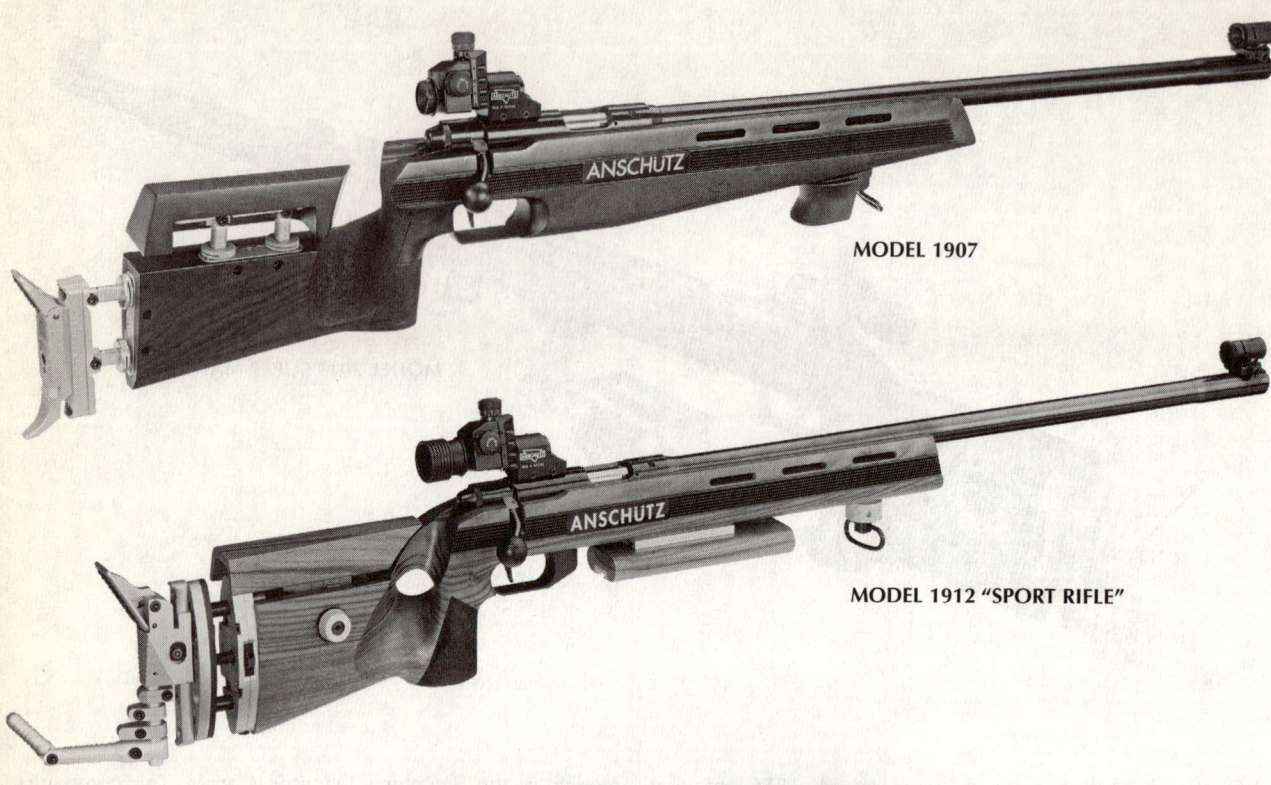

MODEL 1907

MODEL 1912 "SPORT RIFLE"

MODEL 2013 "BENCHREST" BR-50

Model 1907
Match 54 action in an economical rifle, with adjustable cheekpiece and butt assembly.
Barrel Length: 25.9 inches
Rifle Weight: 10.5 pounds
Price: $1375
   left-hand. 1475
   with 2213 metal stock. 1995

Model 1912 "Sport Rifle"
Match 54 action in a lightweight international-style rifle engineered to stay under the 6.5kg weight limit. The walnut stock has a forend raiser block, fully adjustable hook buttplate and cheekpiece, and forward hand stop and swivel.
Barrel Length: 25.9 inches.
Rifle Weight: 11.4 pounds.

Price: $1690
   left-hand. 1785

Model 2013 "Benchrest" BR-50
Barreled action: Compact connection between barreled action and stock, heavy rectangular receiver attached with 4 action screws. The precise machining of barrel and action, and the extremely short locktime, help you shoot more accurately. **Barrel:** Cylindrical match barrel **Stock:** Non-stained stock with wide, flat, forend, especially developed for benchrest shooting **Caliber:** .22 LR **Barrel length:** 50 cm/19.6" **Rifling:** 50 cm/16.6" **Total length:** 97 cm/38.1" **Weight appr.:** 4,7 kg/10.3 lbs **Version:** Single loader
Price: 1575

Anschutz Rifles

MODEL 54.18 MS R "SILHOUETTE"

MODEL 1827 "FORTNER"

MODEL 1903

MODEL 54.18 MS R "SILHOUETTE"
Designed expressly for metallic silhouette shooting, this rifle weighs only 8.1 pounds. The adjustable two-stage trigger is set at 4.4 ounces. The Match 54 action has been modified to accept a 5-shot magazine. A rubber buttpad is standard.
Barrel Length: 22.4 inches
Price: $1225
 w/thumbhole 1350

MODEL 1827 "FORTNER"
This rifle is built for biathlon competition, an Olympic event that combines skiing and marksmanship. Competitors must shoot twice at the 10-km point, four times at 20 km into the race and twice at a relay point of 7.5 km. Each station requires five shots prone and five standing. The Anschutz 1827 has a straight-pull repeating action to increase speed of fire. It weighs 8.8 pounds and is equipped with magazine holders. The walnut stock features adjustable cheekpiece and butt assembly. A special front sight hood protects the sight and bore from snow.
Barrel Length: 21.6 inches.
Price: $1850
 left-hand 1940

MODEL 1903
A competitive rifle for riflemen on a budget, the 1903 has a M64-type action with two-stage adjustable trigger. The hardwood stock features a forward accessory rail and an adjustable cheekpiece. The buttplate is vertically adjustable; length of pull can be changed by adding or deleting spacers.
Price: 690
 left-hand 730

Anschutz Rifles

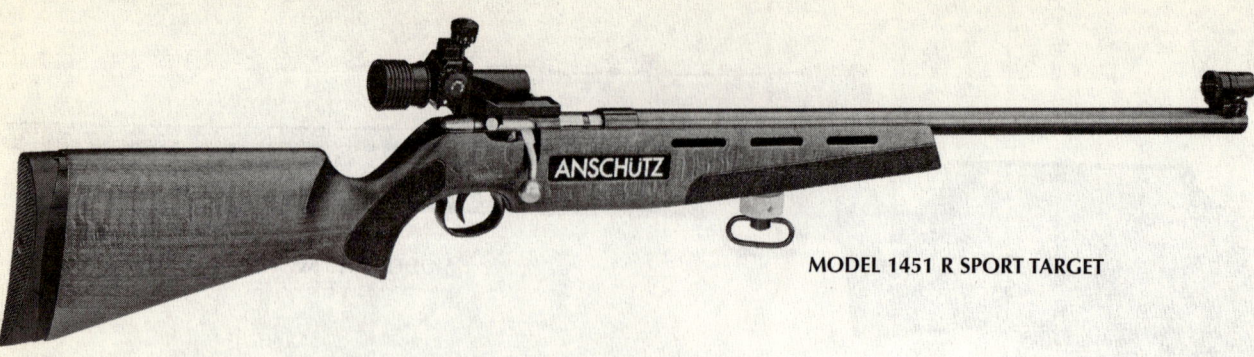

MODEL 1451 R SPORT TARGET

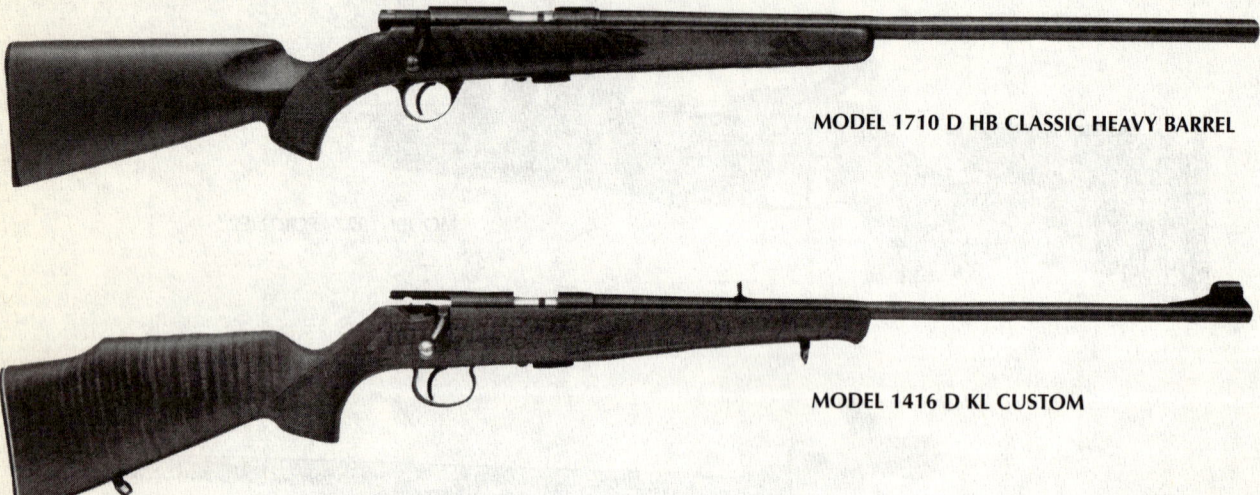

MODEL 1710 D HB CLASSIC HEAVY BARREL

MODEL 1416 D KL CUSTOM

Model 1451 Sporter Target Prisma
Action: bolt-action repeater **Stock:** target stock is vertically and horizontally adjustable at the butt plate, pistol grip and forearm are stippled **Barrel:** 22" heavy target barrel, grooved for front sight **Weight:** 6.3 lbs. **Caliber:** .22 LR **Magazine Capacity:** 10
Price: $449

Model 1700 Series Sporters
Both the Anschutz 1700 custom & classic series are bolt-action repeaters with a 54 sporter action and detachable magazine. Features include dual locking lugs, claw extractor, recessed bolt face and independent bolt release, wing safety, single stage trigger. Barrel is free floated, drilled and tapped with a target-crowned muzzle. Available with a Monte Carlo stock or Meister grade.

Prices: Custom Series
1710D MC stock 22LR 1116
   Meister Grade. 1298
1730D Sporting Rifle 22 Hornet 1244
   Meister Grade. 1425
1740D Sporting Rifle 222 Rem 1244
   Meister Grade. $1425
Classic Series
1710D Heavy Barrel 22LR 1030
   Meister Grade. 1211
1730D Sporting Rifle 22 Hornet 1159
   with heavy barrel 1159
   Meister Grade. 1340
1740D Sporting Rifle 222 Rem 1159

Model 1416 Series (Match 64 Action)
Action: bolt-action with cam cocking system and claw extractor **Stock:** Walnut with checkered grips, available in classic, Monte Carlo or Mannlicher **Sights:** folding rear sight is adjustable in height; as is the hooded sporting ramp front sight **Weight:** 5.5 lbs. (64 MPR is 9 lbs.) **Caliber:** .22LR or .22 WMR **Magazine Capacity:** 5 (.22 WMR has 4-shot).
Other features: 2-stage match trigger
Price:
1416 Walnut Classic. 671
1416 Walnut Monte Carlo 684
1416 Mannlicher 983
64 MPR 729

Auto-Ordnance
Semi-Automatic Rifles

THOMPSON MODEL M1 CARBINE

THOMPSON DELUXE MODEL 1927 A1

MODEL 1927 A1 COMMANDO

This veteran design became famous during the "Roaring Twenties" and World War II. These replicas are legal autoloaders, not machine guns.

THOMPSON MODEL M1 CARBINE
Specifications
Caliber: 45 ACP **Barrel Length:** 16.5"
Overall Length: 38" **Weight:** 11.5 lbs.
Sights: Blade front; fixed rear
Stock: Walnut stock and horizontal foregrip
Features: Side cocking lever; frame and receiver milled from solid steel
Price:.................................$925

THOMPSON DELUXE MODEL 1927 A1
Specifications
Caliber: 45 ACP
Barrel Length: 16.5"
Overall Length: 41" **Weight:** 13 lbs.
Sights: Blade front; open rear adjustable
Stock: Walnut stock; vertical foregrip
Also available:
THOMPSON 1927A1C LIGHTWEIGHT (45 Cal.). Same as the 1927 A1 model, but weighs only 9.5 lbs.
Price:.................................$950

MODEL 1927 A1 COMMANDO
Specifications
Caliber: 45 ACP
Barrel Length: 16.5"
Overall Length: 41"
Weight: 13 lbs.
Sights: Blade front; open rear (adjustable)
Finish: Black (stock and forend)
Price:.................................950

Beretta High-Grade Rifles

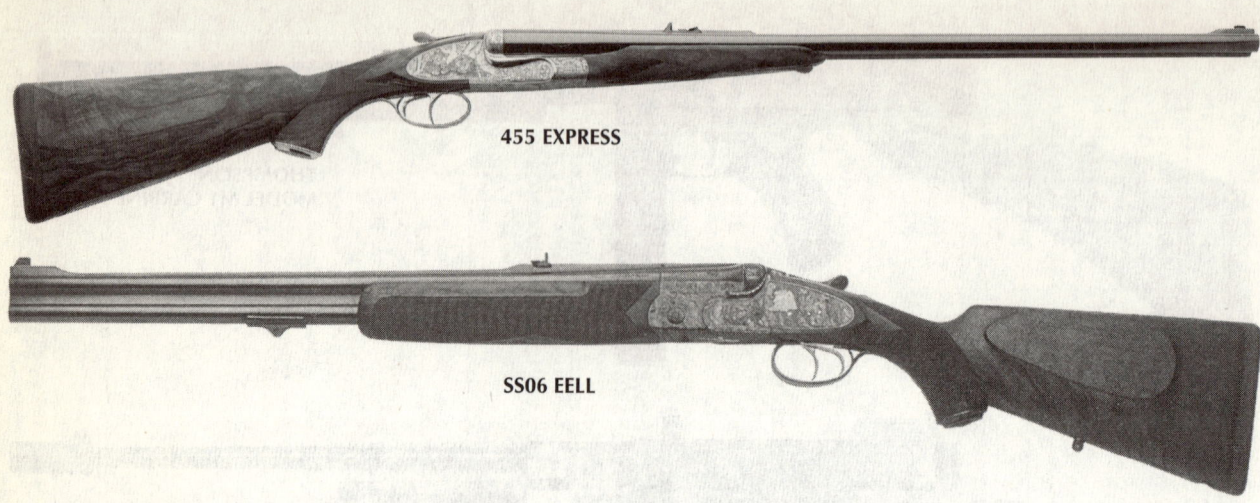

455 EXPRESS

SS06 EELL

PREMIUM GRADE EXPRESS RIFLE SPECIFICATIONS

Model	9.3x74R	.375 H&H Mag.	Caliber* .416 Rigby	.458 H&H Mag.	.470 N.E.	.500 N.E.	Barrel Length (cm/in)	Average Weight (Kg/Lbs)**
SS06	√	√		√			62/24	5.00/11.0
SS06 EELL	√	√		√			62/24	5.00/11.0
455		√	√	√	√	√	60/23 to 65/25	5.00/11.0
455 EELL		√	√	√	√	√	60/23 to 65/25	5.00/11.0

*SS06 EELL MODELS ARE AVAILABLE WITH INTERCHANGEABLE 12 GAUGE SHOTGUN BARRELS UPON REQUEST.
**WEIGHTS ARE APPROXIMATE, DEPENDENT ON WOOD DENSITY AND BARREL LENGTH.

Express Rifles

Double rifles require strong, precisely-fitted actions to handle large, high pressure cartridges. Barrels must be joined with absolute precision for optimum convergence. The SS06 and SS06EELL Over-and Under Express Rifles offer rifled barrels of special steel cold-hammered in three calibers: 9.3x74R, .375 H&H Mag. and .458 Win. Mag. An extra set of matching 12 gauge barrels is available. Hand-finished, hand-checkered stocks and forends are made from select walnut or walnut briar. A special trap door compartment for extra cartridges is fitted inside the stock, and a cavity under the pistol-grip cap holds a set of spare front sights. The SS-06 is finished with light engraving on the color case-hardened receiver. The SS06 EELL sports a receiver hand-engraved with game scenes, or a color case-hardened version with gold inlaid animals.

The 455 Side-by-Side Express Rifle action is made of special high-strength steel and forged with an elongated 60mm plate. This increases the distance between the hinge pin and the three-lug locking system to compensate for stress when shooting. To withstand the pressure of high-powered cartridges, the sealed receiver has reinforced sides, and the top tang extends fully up to the stock comb to strengthen attachment of the stock. An articulated front trigger and automatic blocking device eliminate the possibility of simultaneous discharge. The safety (automatic on request) provides for quick, reliable and positive on/off operation. The Boehler steel barrels are joined with a Demibloc chamber system.

SS06 Over-Under Express Rifle
Specifications
Calibers: 375 H&H, 458 Win. Mag., 9.3x94R
Barrel length: 24" (12 ga. matching interchangeable barrels available)
Weight: 11 lbs.
Sights: Blade front sight; V-notch rear sight w/folding leaf (claw mounts for Zeiss scope factory fitted and sighted-in at 100 meters)
Price: $39,500
Note: Model SS06 EELL
is also available in same calibers and features hand-engraved game scenes on the receiver or color case-hardened w/gold inlaid animals
Price: 42,500

455 Side-By-Side Express Rifle
Specifications
Calibers: 375 H&H, 416 Rigby, 458 Win. Mag., 470 N.E., 500 N.E.
Barrel length: 23" - 25"
Weight: 11 lbs.
Sights: Fixed front sight w/folding blade; V-notch rear sight
Price: 53,000
Note: Model 455 EELL
is also available (same price and calibers) featuring Bulino-style game scene engraving or intricate scroll work and walnut briar stock and forend.

Beretta Rifles

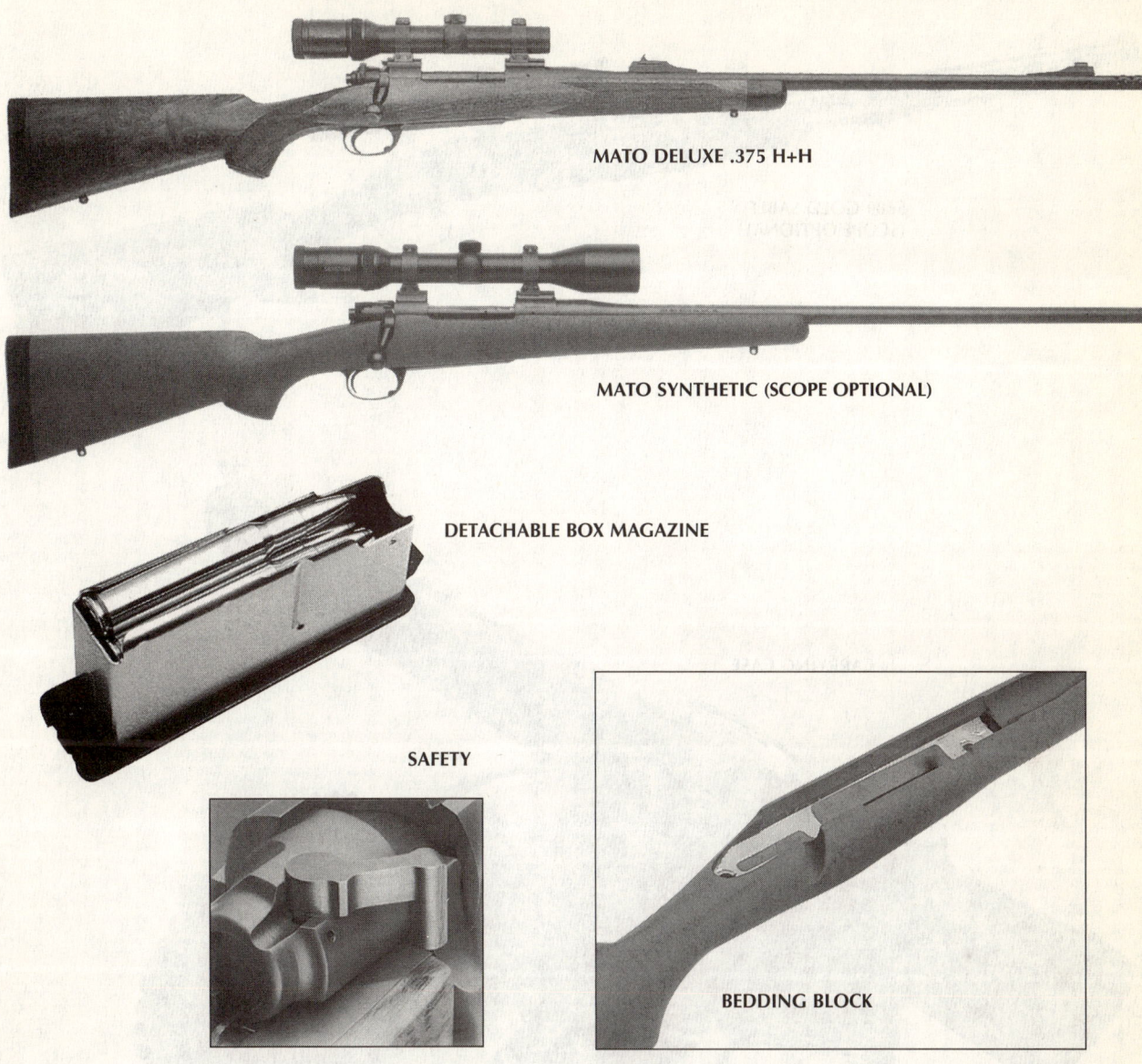

MATO DELUXE .375 H+H

MATO SYNTHETIC (SCOPE OPTIONAL)

DETACHABLE BOX MAGAZINE

SAFETY

BEDDING BLOCK

BERETTA MATO BOLT-ACTION RIFLE

Beretta's Mato was developed with help from Don Allen, whose Dakota rifles have the same clean, appealing lines. ("Mato", incidentally, is the Dakota Indian name for "bear.") This Beretta features controlled-round feed with a Mauser-style extractor that grabs cartridges from a detachable box magazine clipped to a hinged floorplate. The magazine can be top-loaded. A three-position safety allows cycling of the bolt while the striker is locked back. The Mato's sturdy trigger can be adjusted for weight of pull, sear engagement and overtravel. Receivers are machined from bar stock, and the 24-inch barrels are hammer-forged from top-grade chrome-moly steel. Stocks have high, straight combs for quick aim and a classic profile. On the walnut-stocked Deluxe model, wood with exceptional figure is available as an "X-Tra Wood" option. The Mato is also available with a synthetic stock of Kevlar, fiberglass and graphite. An action-length aluminum bedding block ensures rigidity and perfect fit. All stocks come standard with a solid recoil pad. The Mato in .375 features iron sights and a muzzle brake; its front swivel is on a barrel band. Engraving, fiber-optic sights, a set trigger and other options are available for this rifle, which comes in .270 Win., .280 Rem., 7mm Rem. Mag., .30-06 Sprg., .300 Win. Mag., .338 Win. Mag. and .375 H&H Mag. Weight: 8 pounds.

Price: Mato Synthetic $1117
   Mato Synthetic .375 1474
   Mato Deluxe 2470
   Mato Deluxe .375 2795

Beretta Rifles

S689 GOLD SABLE (SCOPE OPTIONAL)

CARRYING CASE

BERETTA SILVER SABLE II AND GOLD SABLE OVER/UNDER RIFLES

Built on Beretta's 20-gauge boxlock frame, these over/under rifles are chambered in .30-06, 9.3x74R and .444 Marlin. They feature double mechanical triggers for reliability. The front trigger is hinged for greater comfort. The 24" barrels are regulated with iron sights but can also be fitted with hook-type scope rings. Hand-finished walnut stocks feature a European-style cheekpiece, ventilated recoil pad and initial plate. The Silver Sable has a nickel-colored receiver engraved with game scenes; the Gold Sable has a scroll-engraved case-hardened receiver.

Weight: 7.7 lbs.
Price: Silver Sable II $3850
   Gold Sable 5750

Blaser Rifles

BLASER R93 PRESTIGE

BLASER R93 SYNTHETIC

LRS2 LONG RANGE RIFLE

LRS2 LONG RANGE RIFLE

Model R93 Bolt Action Series

The Blaser straight-pull action is the fastest bolt mechanism on the market. An expanding collar locks the bolt. A finely adjustable trigger and interchangeable barrel option are bonuses.

Specifications (Classic)
Calibers: (interchangeable) **Standard:** .25-06 Rem 6.5x55, 7x57, 7mm/08 Rem, 22-250, 243 Win., 270 Win., 30-06, 308 Win. **Magnum:** 257 Weatherby Mag., 7mm Rem. Mag., 300 Win. Mag., 300 Wby. Mag., 300 Rem U.M., 338 Win. Mag., 375 H&H, 416 Rem. Mag. **Barrel lengths:** 22" (Standard) and 26" (Magnum) Overall length: 40" (Standard) and 44" (Magnum) **Weight:** (w/scope mounts) 6.5 lbs. (Standard) and 7 lbs. (Magnum) **Safety:** Cocking slide **Stock:** Two-piece Custom and Deluxe Walnut recoil pad, hand-cut checkering (18 lines/inch, borderless) **Length of pull:** 13.75" All Blaser 93 rifles can be ordered left-handed at an additional $155.00.

Prices: Classic $2950
  LX 1990
  Synthetic 1695
  Attaché. 4150
  Luxus 3050
  Prestige 2100

Blaser K95

The Blaser K95 is a single-shot, break-action rifle available in two styles, the Luxus with hand engraving on the receiver, and the Prestige. Both lightweight models can be easily taken down and reassembled without any loss of zero. Select walnut stocks, point-pattern checkering.

Specifications
Calibers: Standard: .243 Win., .270 Win., 30-06 Sprg., 308 Win. **Magnum:** 7mm Rem., 300 Win., .300 Wby. **Barrel lengths:** 23.6" (Standard) and 25.6" (Magnum) **Overall length:** 40.16" (Standard) and 42.13" (Magnum) **Weight:** 5.5 lbs. (Standard) and 5.8 lbs. (Magnum)
Prices: Luxus $3395
  Prestige 2895

Blaser R93 Long Range Sporter 2

Features: straight-line bolt pull with a radial locking system; fully adjustable trigger; fore-and-aft-adjustable trigger blade; removable, adjustable comb; adjustable buttstock (for length); right- and left-hand adaptability by in-the-field replacement of the bolt assembly; heavy, fluted barrel; ambidextrous magazine release; gas nitrate steel treatment to provide a hard, rust-proof surface. The LRS2 has an improved stock and a new 5-shot in-line magazine. Accessories include a folding bipod, muzzle brake and hand rest. Available in .308 Win., .300 Win. Mag. and .338 Lapua. Mag.

Price: $2480
  .338 Lapua Mag 2840
Also available:
  Long Range Tactical. 3480
  .338 Lapua Mag 4350

Ed Brown Rifles
702 Tactical

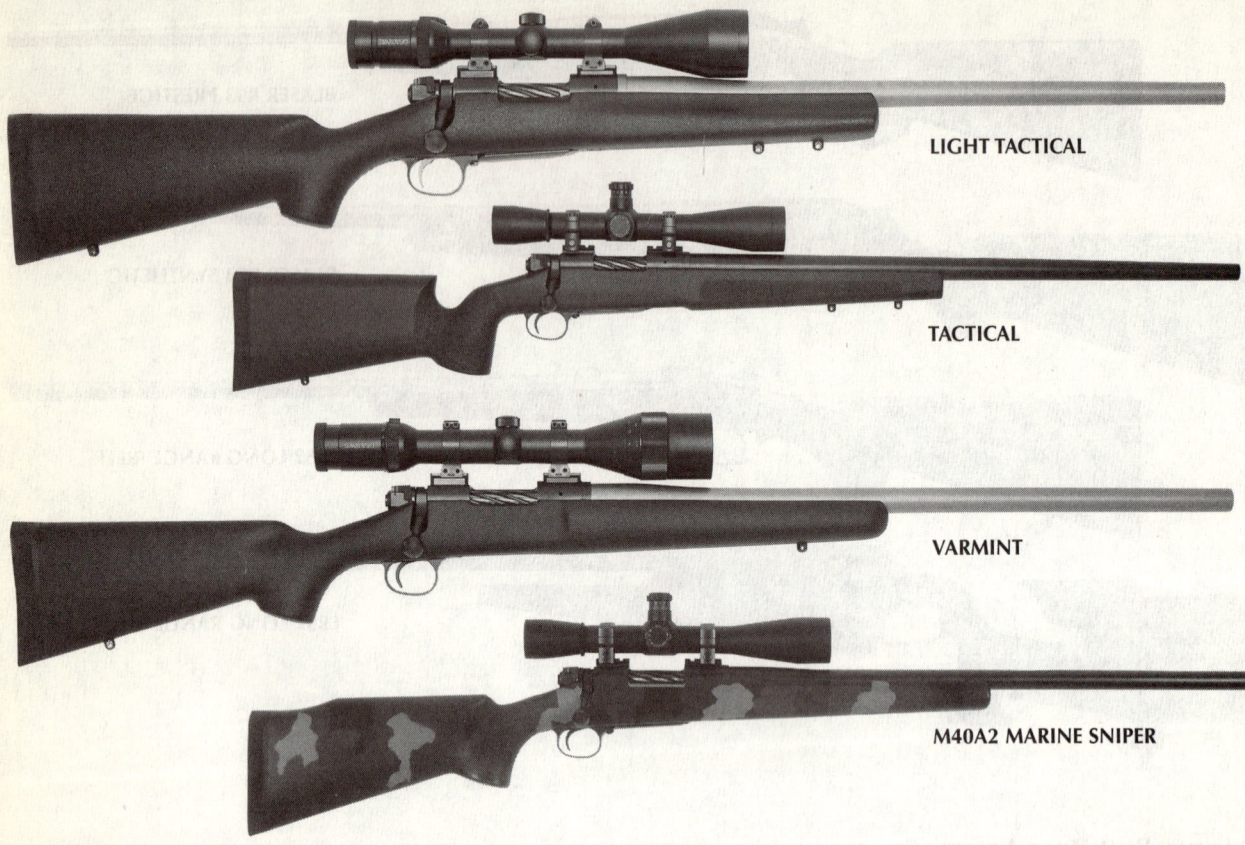

LIGHT TACTICAL

TACTICAL

VARMINT

M40A2 MARINE SNIPER

LIGHT TACTICAL
A compact, super accurate tactical weapon intended for military, law enforcement and security forces around the world. Makes a great compact varmint rifle too!
Specifications
Caliber: 223, and 308 **Barrel:** match grade hand lapped and precision chambered medium weight #5 contour 21" barrel **Weight:** approx. 8.75 lbs. **Stock:** hand bedded fiberglass with recoil pad **Sights:** Leupold Mark 4 30mm scope mounts utilizing heavy duty 8-40 screws **Features:** Brown Custom short repeater action, aluminum trigger guard and floor plate. Three position safety securely locks bolt closed **Options:** stock color, stainless steel barrel, different contour barrel, additional calibers, hinged steel floor plate.
Price: from................................$2800

TACTICAL
A heavy-barreled tactical rifle with prone stock. Built for the utmost in accuracy.
Specifications
Caliber: (308), 300 Win Mag. **Barrel:** match grade, hand lapped and precision chambered. Heavy weight #6 contour, 26"barrel **Weight:** approx. 12.25 lbs. **Stock:** hand bedded A-3 fiberglass tactical stock with recoil pad **Sights:** Leupold Mark 4 30mm scope mounts utilizing heavy duty 8-40 screws **Features:** Ed Brown Custom short or long repeater action, steel trigger guard and hinged floor plate. Action length depends on caliber. Three position safety securely locks bolt closed. **Options:** stock color, stainless steel barrel, different contour barrel, additional calibers
Price: from................................$2900

VARMINT
A custom varmint rifle with tactical rifle heritage.
Specifications
Caliber: 223, 22-250, 220 Swift, 243, 6mm Rem, 308 Win. **Barrel:** match grade, hand lapped and precision chambered. Medium weight #5 contour 26" or heavy weight #17 contour 24" barrel **Weight:** approx. 9 lbs. **Stock:** hand bedded fiberglass with recoil pad **Sights:** Talley scope mounts utilizing heavy duty 8-40 screws **Features:** Ed Brown Custom short single shot action with a steel trigger guard, fully adjustable trigger, and a three position safety **Options:** Stock color, stainless steel barrel, different contour barrel, additional calibers, 2 oz. trigger
Price: from................................2500

M40A2 MARINE SNIPER
Action: 702 bolt **Stock:** Hand-bedded McMillan GP fiberglass tactical stock with recoil pad in Woodland Camo molded in colors **Barrel:** 24" heavy, match grade **Sights:** Leupold Mark 4 30mm scope mounts **Weights:** 9.25lbs **Calibers:** .308 Win., .30/06 Springfield **Other features:** three position safety, steel trigger guard and hinged floor plate. Available in left hand.
Price: from 2900

Ed Brown Rifles
702 Hunting

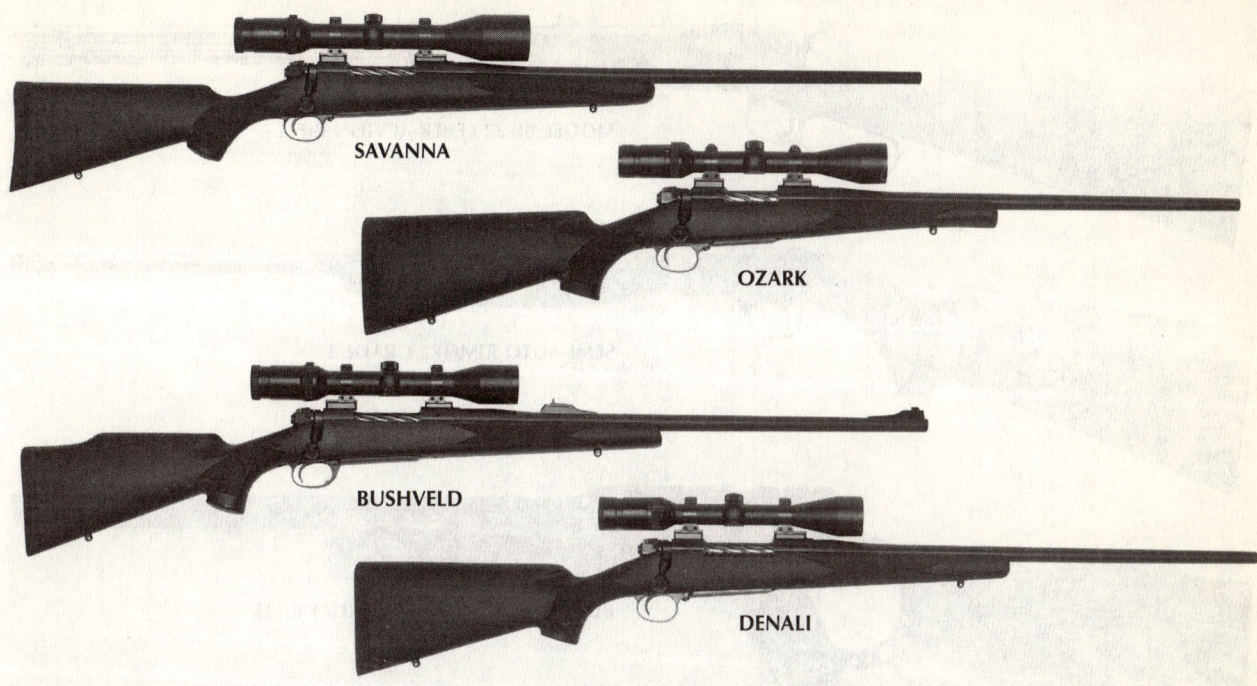

SAVANNA
An accurate hunting rifle with classic-style stock, in most popular chamberings.
Specifications
Long Action Calibers: 25/06, 270 Win., 280 Remington, 7mm Rem Magnum, 7STW, 30/06, 300 Win Magnum, 300 Wby, 338 Win. Mag. **Short Action Calibers:** same as Ozark plus 270 WSM, 7mm WSM, 300 WSM **Barrel:** match grade hand lapped and precision chambered. Light weight #3 contour in standard calibers 24" length, medium weight #4 on magnum calibers, 26" length **Weight:** approx. 7.5 lbs. **Stock:** fiberglass sporter with cheek piece, checkering and recoil pad **Sights:** Talley scope mounts utilizing heavy duty 8-40 screws **Features:** Ed Brown Custom action with machined steel trigger guard and hinged floor plate. Three position safety securely locks bolt closed. 3.700 magazine box length **Options:** stock color, stainless steel barrel, different contour barrel, additional calibers, detachable box magazine
Price: from.............................. $2800
(WSM cartridges $100 extra)

OZARK
A light-weight hunting rifle, made on a short action with a light stock and short barrel. A modern carbine.
Specifications
Caliber: 223, 243, 6mm, 260 Rem, 7mm/08, 308 **Barrel:** match grade hand lapped and precision chambered. Extra light weight #2 contour, 21" length **Weight:** approx. 6.5 lbs. **Stock:** light weight sporter fiberglass with checkering and recoil pad **Sights:** Talley scope mounts included utilizing heavy duty 8-40 screws **Features:** Ed Brown Custom short repeater action with a blind magazine and steel trigger guard. Three position safety securely locks bolt closed. 2.850 magazine box length **Options:** stock color, stainless steel barrel, different contour barrel, additional calibers, hinged steel floor plate, detachable box magazine
Price: from.............................. $2800

BUSHVELD
A dependable dangerous game rifle with iron sights and deep magazine.
Specifications
Caliber: 338 Win Mag., 375 H&H, 416 Rem Mag., 458 Win Mag **Barrel:** match grade hand lapped and precision chambered. Medium weight, or heavy weight depending on caliber 24" length **Weight:** approx. 8.5 lbs. **Stock:** hand bedded fiberglass stock with Monte Carlo style butt, cheek piece, and recoil pad **Sights:** scope mounts utilizing heavy duty 8-40 screws **Features:** Ed Brown Custom action, steel trigger guard and floor plate. Three position safety securely locks bolt closed **Options:** stock color, stainless steel barrel, different contour barrel, additional calibers, QD scope rings, iron sights, barrel mounted sling swivel
Price: from.............................. 2900

DENALI
A light-weight rifle designed for mountain hunting.
Action: 702 bolt action **Stock:** Fully glass-bedded McMillan fiberglass with cheek piece, checkering and recoil pad **Barrel:** 22" - 23", match grade and lapped **Sights:** Talley scope mounts included **Weight:** 6.75lbs. **Calibers:** Long action - .25/06, .270 Win., .280 Rem., .30/06, 7mm Rem Mag. Short action - .22-.250, .243, 6mm, .260 Rem., 7mm/08, .308, .270 WSM, 7mm WSM, .300 WSM
Price:.............................. 2800
(WSM cartridges $100 extra)

Browning Rimfire Rifles

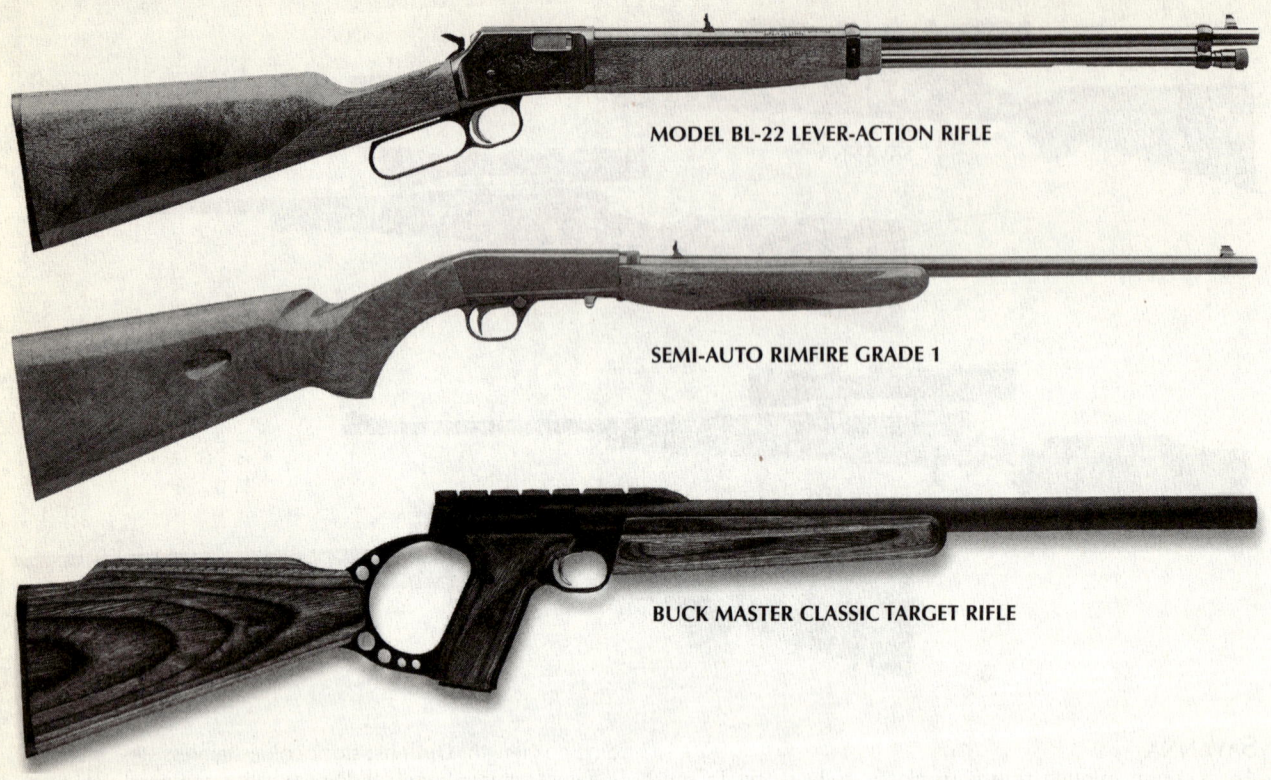

MODEL BL-22 LEVER-ACTION RIFLE

SEMI-AUTO RIMFIRE GRADE 1

BUCK MASTER CLASSIC TARGET RIFLE

RIMFIRE RIFLE SPECIFICATIONS

Model	Caliber	Barrel Length	Sight Radius	Overall Length	Average Weight	Price
Semi-Auto 22 Grade I	22 LR	19.25"	16.25"	37"	5 lbs. 3 oz.	$489.00
Semi-Auto 22 Grade VI*	22 LR	19.25"	16.25"	37"	5 lbs. 3 oz.	1,049.00
BL-22 Grade I	22 LR, Long, Short	20"	15.875"	36.75"	5 lbs.	423.00
BL-Grade II	22 LR, Long, Short	20"	15.875"	36.75"	5 lbs.	480.00

*Blued or Grayed.
BL-22 Lever-action .22 rifle, straight-grip walnut carbine stock, short-stroke action with trigger group in lever, open sights. Grade VI has checkering.

22 SEMI-AUTOMATIC RIMFIRE RIFLES GRADES I AND VI (SEE TABLE ABOVE FOR PRICES)
Specifications (See also table above)
Capacity: 11 cartridges in magazine, 1 chamber **Safety:** Cross-bolt type **Trigger:** Grade I is blued; Grade VI is gold colored **Sights:** Gold bead front, adjustable folding leaf ear; drilled and tapped for Browning scope mounts **Stock & Forearm:** Grade I, select walnut with checkering (18 lines/inch); Grade VI, high-grade walnut with checkering (22 lines/inch).

BUCK MARK RIFLE SERIES
Built on the same design as the proven Buck Mark pistol's straight blowback action. Offered in a Sporter model with a tapered barrel. Hi-Viz fiber optic sights and an integral rail scope mount. Also offered in a Target model with a heavy barrel with the same integral rail scope mount. All chambers are hand-reamed and muzzle crowns are recessed to protect them from damage that could deteriorate accuracy.
Barrel: 18"
Overall Length: 33 5/8"
Price:
   Sporter or Target........................$528

BUCK MARK CLASSIC TARGET
.22 rimfire with heavy bull barrel. Gray laminated stock and forearm. Integral rail scope mount 18" barrel.
Weight: 5lbs. 8oz.
Magazine holds 11 rounds.
Price..544

Browning Rifles

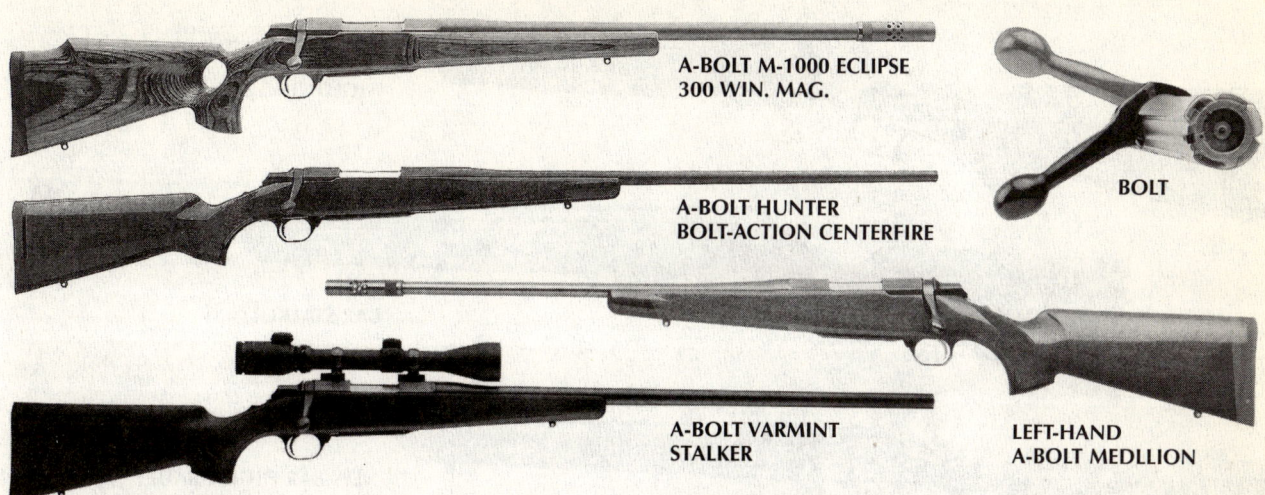

A-BOLT M-1000 ECLIPSE 300 WIN. MAG.

BOLT

A-BOLT HUNTER BOLT-ACTION CENTERFIRE

A-BOLT VARMINT STALKER

LEFT-HAND A-BOLT MEDLLION

A-Bolt Eclipse Models with Thumbhole Stock
The proven action and barrel of the A-Bolt are included in the A-Bolt Eclipse Series. The thumbhole stock itself is crafted from rugged gray/black, multi-laminated hardwood. The Eclipse is available in long and short action hunting models with standard A-Bolt barrel, and a short-action varmint version with a heavy barrel. All are BOSS equipped.

A-Bolt Hunter Bolt-Action Centerfire Rifles
Stock: A-Bolt stocks vary from the classic walnut on the Hunter model to the composite stock on the /stalker and laminated thumbhole on the Eclipse **Barrel:** The barrel is free floating and glass bedded at the recoil lug and rear of receiver. 26" in magnum calibers and 22" in standard and short action calibers. Micro Hunters have a 20" barrel, except 22 Hornet, .223 and .22-250. All rifles in the WSM family feature a 23" barrel. **Sights:** A-Bolt rifles feature drilled and tapped receivers for scope mounts. Open sights are included on .375 H&H. Weight: ranges from 6 lbs. 4 oz. for the Micro Hunters to 9 lbs. 13 oz. for the Eclipse M-1000. Caliber: all popular cartridges from 22 Hornet to .375 H&H, including the new WSM's in .270, 7mm, .300. **Magazine Capacity:** Standard Calibers: 4 in magazine; magnum calibers including WSM, 3. Capacity of 223 Rem. is 6 rounds. **Other features:** BOSS (Ballistic Optimizing Shooting System) is available on most models. The trigger is chrome plated and adjustable.

Prices: No Sights	$639
Magnum	665
Micro Hunter (shorter barrel and length of pull)	632

A-Bolt Medallion Series
Prices: Medallion no sights standard, BOSS	$832
Medallion standard, no sights	752
Medallion L.H., no sights, BOSS	861 - 888
Medallion L.H., no sights	781 - 808
Medallion Magnum no sights, BOSS	859
Medallion Magnum, no sights	779

A-Bolt Stalker Series
Prices: Stainless Stalker no sights, BOSS	$917 - 944
Stainless Stalker no sights	$837 - 864
Stainless Stalker L.H., no sights, BOSS	943 - 970
Stainless Stalker L.H., no sights	863 - 890
Composite Stalker, no sights, BOSS	738 - 765
Composite Stalker, no sights	658 - 685
Varmint Stalker, no sights (223 Rem, 22-250)	772
Eclipse Hunter, no sights, BOSS	$1048 - 1074
Eclipse M-1000, w/BOSS	1079

White Gold Medallion
Price:	$1750 - 1776
no sights	1077 - 1104
w/Boss	1157 - 1184

Winchester Short Magnum
in 270, 7mm, 300 **Features:** 23" barrel, 3-round detachable magazine, lightweight (6 lbs. 9 oz.)

Price: Hunter	$665
Composite Stalker	685
Medallion	779
Stainless Stalker	864
Classic Hunter	746

Left-Hand A-Bolt Medallion
Only a few popular bolt-action rifles have traditionally been built in left-hand versions. Browning joins a growing movement to accommodate lefties with its A-Bolt II, Boss is available.

Bolt
The short 60° bolt throw allows faster follow-up shots and also permits greater clearance between the bolt handle and scope. The flattened bolt knob itself is canted at a 30° angle to fit the hand more naturally.

Boss
(Ballistic OptimizingShooting System) is now optional on all A-Bolt models(except standard). BOSS adjusts barrel vibrations to allow a bullet toleave the rifle muzzle at the most advantageous

Browning Rifles

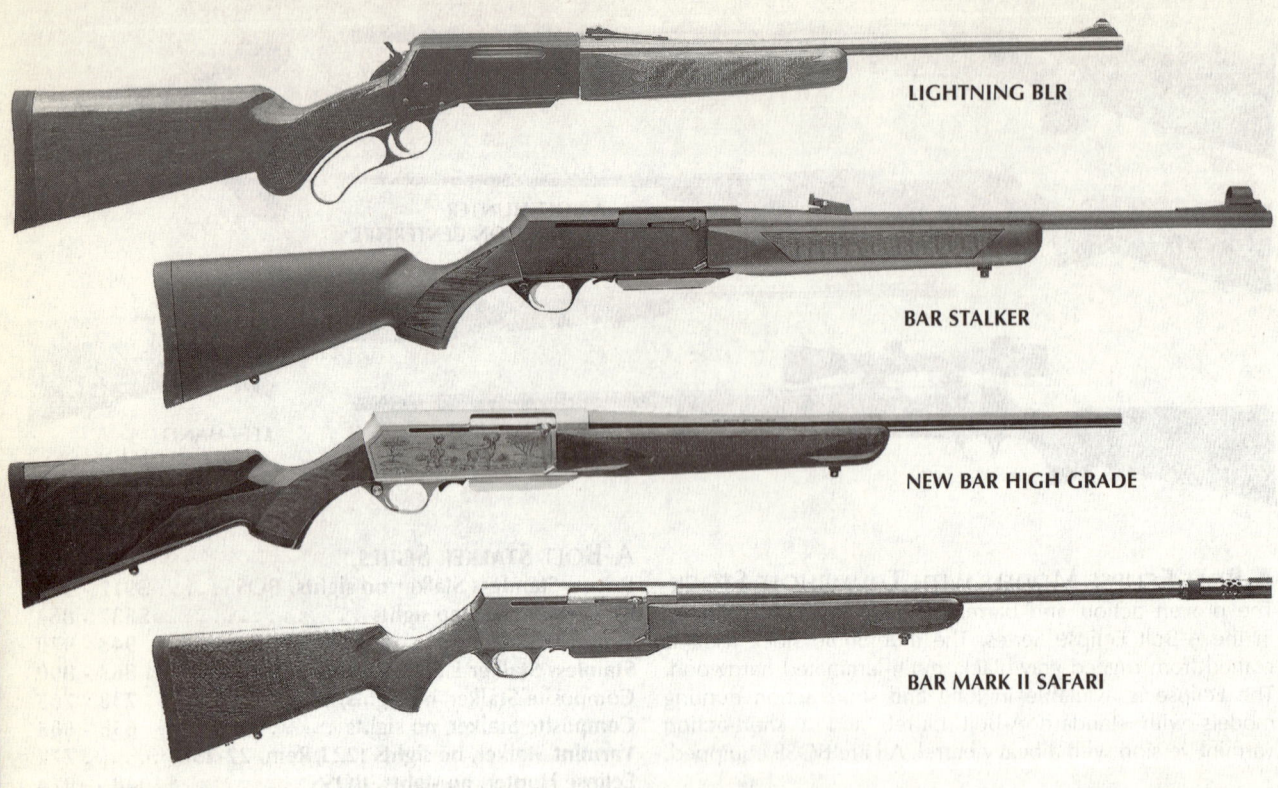

LIGHTNING BLR

BAR STALKER

NEW BAR HIGH GRADE

BAR MARK II SAFARI

LIGHTNING BLR
Specifications
Calibers: Long Action–270 Win., 30-06 Springfield, 7mm Rem. Mag., 300 Win. Mag. Short Action–22-250 Rem., 243 Win., 7mm-08 Rem., 308 Win. **Capacity:** 4 rounds; 3 in magnum calibers **Barrel Length:** Long Action–22" (24" magnum calibers) Short Action–20" **Overall Length:** Long Action–42 7/8" (44 7/8" magnum calibers) Short Action–39.5" **Approximate Weight:** Long Action–7 lbs. 4 oz. (7 lbs. 12 oz. magnum calibers) Short Action–6 lbs. 8 oz. **Sight Radius:** 17.75" (19.75" magnum calibers)
Prices: Short Action $681
    Long Action 721

BAR LIGHTWEIGHT STALKER SERIES
Composite, short action with open sights (243, 308, 270, 30-06)
Price: $809
    Composite, open sights
    (300 WSM, 7mm, 300, 338) 883
    Composite, Boss (Magnum) 944

BAR MARK II SAFARI, LIGHTWEIGHT & STALKER SEMIAUTOMATIC RIFLES
The BAR Mark II features an engraved receiver, a redesigned bolt release, new gas and buffeting systems, and a removable trigger assembly. Crossbolt safety with enlarged head; hinged floorplate, gold trigger; select walnut stock and forearm with cut-checkering and swivel studs; 13.75" length of pull; 2" drop at heel; 1 5/8" drop at comb. The New Lightweight model features alloy receiver and shortened barrel. Features high-grade, gloss walnut stock, gray receivers with engraved scenes (mule and whitetail deer on standard and elk and moose on Magnum).

BAR MARK II Specifications
Calibers: Standard–243 Win., 25-06, 270 Win., 308 Win.; Magnum–7mm Rem. Mag., 300 Win. Mag. 300 WSM, 338 Win. Mag.; Lightweight–243 Win., 270 Win., 30-06 Springfield; 308 Win. **Capacity:** 4 rounds; 3 in magnum Barrel Length: Standard–22"; Magnum–24"; Lightweight –20" **Overall Length:** Standard–43"; Magnum–45"; Lightweight–41" **Average Weight:** Standard–7 lbs. 6 oz.; Magnum–8 lbs. 6 oz.; Lightweight–7 lbs. 2 oz. **Sight Radius:** Standard–17.5"; Magnum–19.5"; Lightweight–15.5"
Prices: BAR Mark II Safari

Standard Calibers: No sights, BOSS $895
    Open sights, no BOSS 833
    No sights, no BOSS 815
Magnum Calibers: No sights, BOSS 970
    Open sights 909
    No sights, no BOSS 890
Bar Mark II Lightweight
    Open sights, no BOSS 833
    Open sights, no BOSS Magnum 909
BAR High Grade
Standard (270 Win or 30-06) 1,820
    Magnum (7mm Mag or 300 Win Mag) 1,876
BAR Mark II Acera
    No sights, 30-06 896
    w/BOSS 976
No sights, 300 Win. 930

Brown Precision Rifles

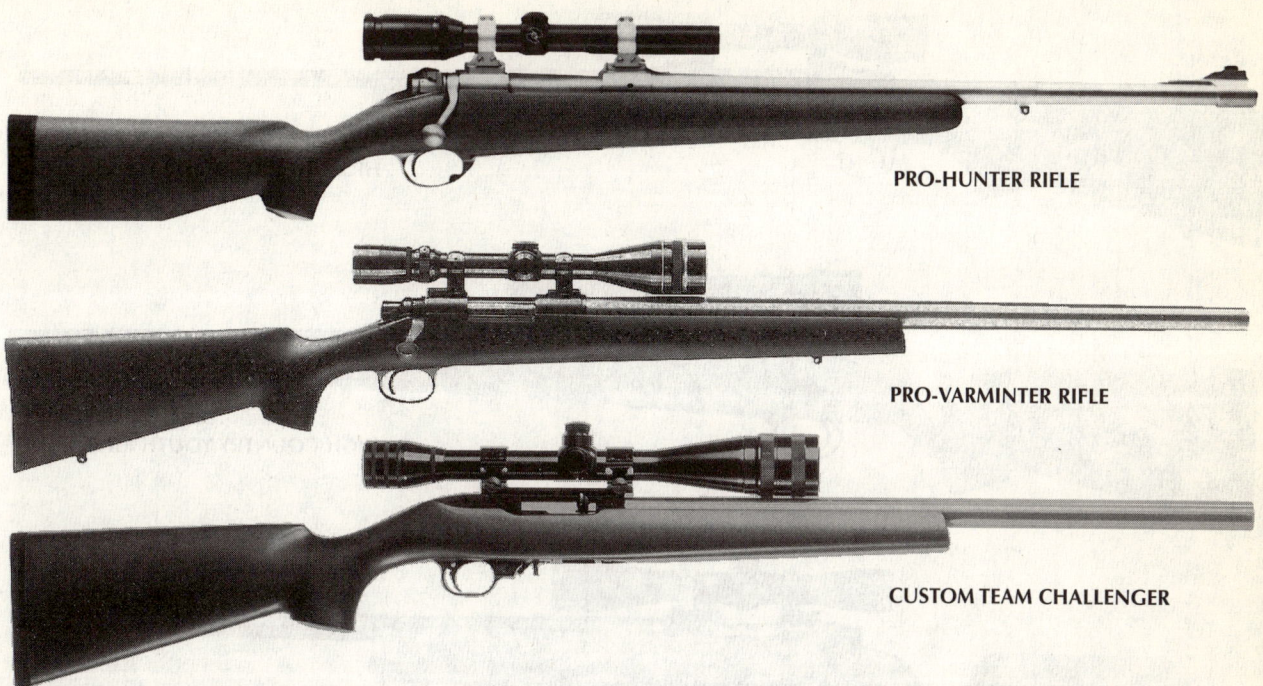

PRO-HUNTER RIFLE

PRO-VARMINTER RIFLE

CUSTOM TEAM CHALLENGER

CUSTOM TEAM CHALLENGER
Designed for the serious game hunter or guide, this custom version of Brown Precision's Pro-Hunter rifle begins as a Winchester Model 700 Super Grade action with controlled feed claw extractor. The trigger is tuned to crisp let-off at each customer's specified weight. A Shilen Match Grade stainless-steel barrel is custom crowned and hand fitted to the action.

The Pro-Hunter Elite features choice of express rear sight or custom Dave Talley removable peep sight and banded front ramp sight with European dovetail and replaceable brass bead. An optional flip-up white night sight is also available, as is a set of Dave Talley detachable T.N.T. scope mount rings and bases installed with Brown's Magnum Duty 8X40 screws.

All metal parts are finished in either matte electroless nickel or black Teflon. The barreled action is glass bedded to a custom Brown Precision Alaskan-configuration fiberglass stock, painted according to customer choice and fitted w/premium 1" buttpad and Dave Talley trapdoor grip cap. Weight ranges from 7 to 15 lbs., depending on barrel length, contour and options.

Optional equipment includes drop box magazine, KDF or Answer System muzzle brake, Mag-Na-Port, Zeiss, Swarovski or Leupold scope, Americase aluminum hard case.
Prices:
> Pro-Hunter $3495
> Left-hand Pro-Hunter 3695
> Pro-Hunter Elite 4495

CUSTOM TEAM CHALLENGER
The standard Pro-Varminter is buillt on the Remington 700 or Rremington 40X action (right or left hand) and features a hand-fitted Shilen Match Grade Heavy Benchrest stainless-steel barrel in bright or bead-blasted finish. The barreled action is custom-bedded in Brown Precision's Varmint Special Hunter Bench or 40X Benchrest-style custom fiberglass, Kevlar or graphite stock.

Options include metal finishes, muzzle brakes, target or varmint scopes, triggers, barrels, stock dimensions
Prices:
> Right-hand Model 700 . . . . $2495
> Left-hand Model 700. 2695
> Model 40-XB (inc. target trigger) 3195

CUSTOM TEAM CHALLENGER
This custom rifle was designed for use in the Chevy Trucks Sportsman's Team Challenge shooting event. It's also used in metallic silhouette competition, as well as in the field for small game and varmints. Custom built on the Ruger 10/22 semi-automatic rimfire action, which features an extended magazine release, a simplified bolt release and finely tuned trigger. This rifle is fitted with either a Brown Precision fiberglass or Kevlar stock with custom length of pull up to 15". The stock can be shortened at the butt and later relengthened and repainted to accommodate growing youth shooters. Stock color is also optional. To facilitate shooting with scopes, the lightweight stock has high-comb classic styling. The absence of a cheekpiece accommodates either right- or left-handed shooters, while the stock's flat-bottom, 1 3/4" forearm ensures maximum comfort in both offhand and rest shooting. Barrels are custom-length Shilen Match Grade .920" diameter straight or lightweight tapered.
Prices:
> Blued action/barrel 1395
> Blued action/stainless barrel 1495
> Silver action/stainless barrel 1595

Brown Precision Rifles

HIGH COUNTRY RIFLE

HIGH COUNTRY YOUTH RIFLE

TACTICAL ELITE RIFLE

HIGH COUNTRY RIFLE
High Country Rifle Standard Features: • Remington 700 ADL, BDL or Mountain Rifle standard caliber barreled action • Brown Precision Custom Fiberglass, Kevlar or Graphite stock in Classic configuration with QD sling swivels attached • Custom stock length of pull • Choice of standard recoil pads • Trigger tuned to a crisp pull (customer specifies weight) • Choice of stock finish colors: black, grey, brown or green • Weight: 5 lbs. and up depending on stock, barrel length and contour, caliber, options and customer's intended use.
Prices:
High Country Rifle . . . . from $2795
Custom High Country ES II . . . . from 3795

HIGH COUNTRY YOUTH RIFLE
This custom rifle has all the same features as the standard High Country rifle, but scaled down to fit the smaller shooter. Based on the Remington Model 7 or Model 700 barreled action, it is available in calibers 223, 243, 7mm-08, 6mm and 308. The rifle features a shortened fiberglass, Kevlar or graphite stock, which can be lengthened as the shooter grows, a new recoil pad installed and the stock refinished. Custom features/options include choice of actions, custom barrels, chamberings, muzzle brakes, metal finishes, scopes and accessories.

All Youth Rifles include a deluxe package of shooting, reloading and hunting accessories and information to increase a young shooter's interest.
Price: High Country Youth Rifle . . . . from $1435

TACTICAL ELITE RIFLE
Brown Precision's Tactical Elite is built on a Remington 700 action and features a bead-blasted Shilen Select Match Grade Heavy Benchrest Stainless Steel barrel custom-chambered for 223 Rem., 308 Win., 300 Win. Mag. (or any standard or wildcat caliber). A nonreflective custom black Teflon metal finish on all metal surfaces ensures smooth bolt operation and 100 percent weatherproofing. The barreled action is bedded in a target-style stock with high rollover comb/cheekpiece, vertical pistol grip and palmswell. The stock is an advanced, custom fiberglass/Kevlar/graphite composite for maximum durability and rigidity, painted in flat black (camouflage patterns are also available). QD sling swivel studs and swivels are standard.

Other standard features include: three-way adjustable buttplate/recoil pad assembly with length of pull, vertical and cant angle adjustments, custom barrel length and contour, and trigger tuned for a crisp pull to customer's specifications. Options include muzzle brakes, Leupold or Kahles police scopes, among others, and are priced accordingly.
Price: Tactical Elite Rifle 3195

Christensen Arms Rifles

CARBON CHALLENGER THUMBHOLE
CARBON ONE CUSTOM
CARBON ONE HUNTER RIFLE
CARBON TACTICAL
CARBON RANGER

Carbon Challenger Thumbhole
Action: Pump **Stock:** Synthetic or wood **Barrel:** Graphite with up to 20" long match-grade stainless barrel liner **Sights:** Fitted for scope mounts **Weight:** 3 to 4.5 lbs. **Chamberings:** 22 rimfire **Other Features:** Custom ultra-lightweight target and smallgame rimfire rifle, custom trigger, bedded with action free floating
Price: $999

Carbon One Custom Series
Action: Pump **Stock:** Synthetic or wood **Barrel:** Graphite with up to 28" match-grade stainless barrel liner, bedded with graphite barrel free floating **Sights:** Fitted for scope mounts **Weight:** 5.5 to 6.5 lbs. **Chamberings:** popular magnum calibers available **Other Features:** Custom trigger, head spaced minimum, accurized action
Price: 2950

Carbon Tactical Series
Action: Pump **Stock:** Synthetic or wood **Barrel:** Graphite with up to 28" match-grade stainless barrel liner, muzzle break option **Sights:** Fitted for scope mounts **Weight:** 5 to 8 lbs. **Chamberings:** All popular calibers **Other Features:** Tactical rifle, accurized action, custom trigger. Accuracy: 3 shots .5" or less at 100 yards
Price: . . . . P.O.R.

Carbon Ranger Series
Action: Pump **Stock:** Retractable **Barrel:** Up to 36" stainless barrel liner, chambered to minimum tolerances **Sights:** Scope mounts **Chamberings:** 50 caliber **Other Features:** Custom long range sniper rifle. E.D.M. precision machined Omni Wind Runner accurized action, custom trigger, 5 shots 8" at 1000 yards
Price: $4950
Single Shot: 3950

Carbon One Hunter Rifle Series
Action: Pump **Stock:** Synthetic **Barrel:** Graphite/epoxy barrel casing applied over factory grade steel, machined barrel **Sights:** Scope mounts **Weight:** 6.5 to 7.25 lbs. **Chamberings:** Factory action of your choice **Other Features:** Trigger: 3-3.5 lbs.
Price: 1499

Cimarron Firearms
Single-Shot Rifles

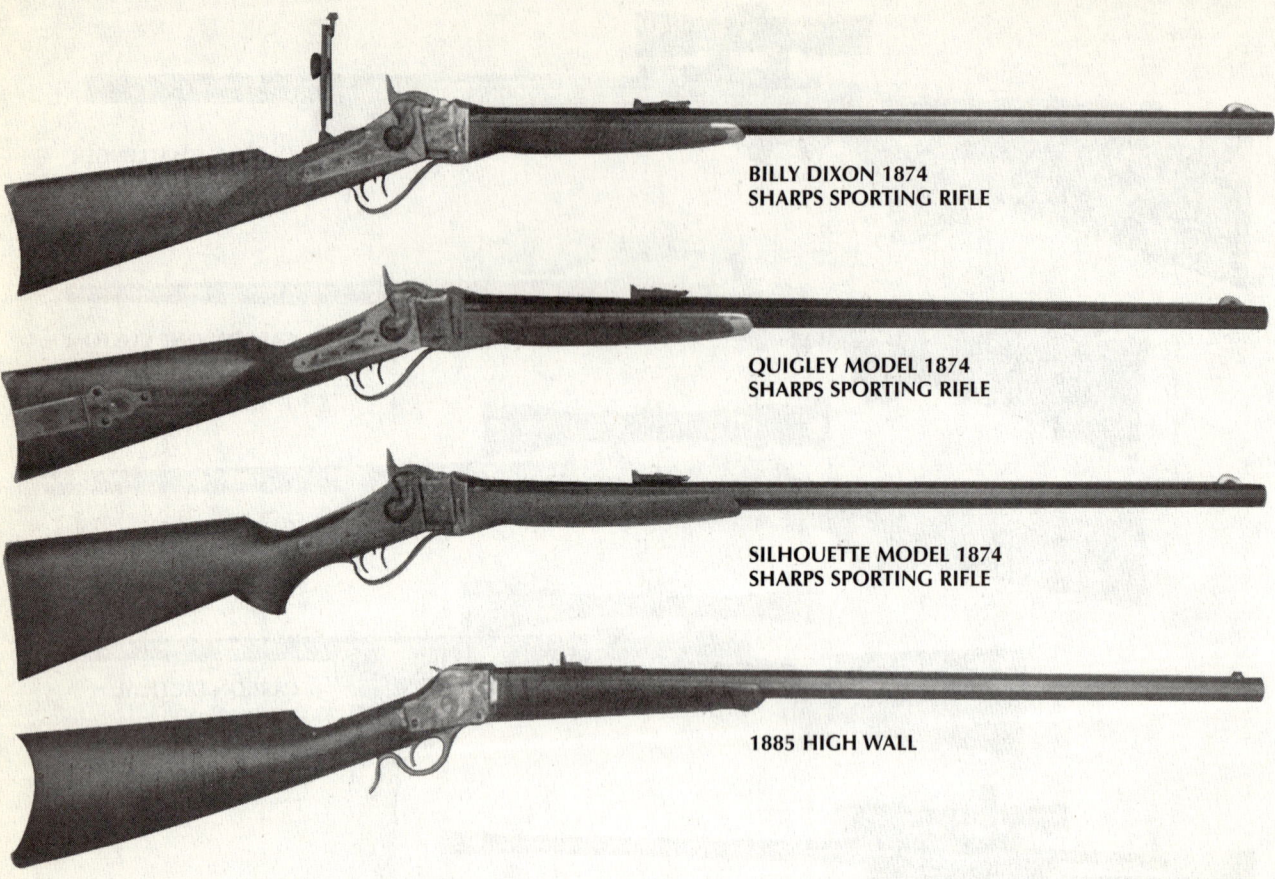

BILLY DIXON 1874 SHARPS SPORTING RIFLE

QUIGLEY MODEL 1874 SHARPS SPORTING RIFLE

SILHOUETTE MODEL 1874 SHARPS SPORTING RIFLE

1885 HIGH WALL

BILLY DIXON 1874 SHARPS SPORTING RIFLE
It was June 27, 1874 at Adobe Walls on the Canadian River in the Texas panhandle. Billy Dixon and 27 buffalo hunters were surrounded by more than 500 Kiowa and Comanche warriors. The Kiowa medicine man told the warriors that his medicine made them invisible to the bullets of the white eyes. When Dixon fired his Sharps sporting rifle and reportedly knocked a Kiowa from his horse at 1538 yards (7/8 mile) the Indians departed with haste. Billy Dixon was later awarded the Congressional Medal of Honor while acting as scout of the Army under Gen. Nelson Miles. He lived a long life as a Texas peace officer.
Barrel: 32" Octagon
Caliber: .45-.70
Prices:
Retail.................................$1295

QUIGLEY MODEL 1874 SHARPS SPORTING RIFLE
This single shot rifle is capable of the accuracy depicted in the epic film. The Cimarron Quigley model is a faithful reproduction of that long rifle from Down Under.
Barrel: 34" Octagon
Caliber: .45-70, .45-.120
Prices:
Retail:................................$1495

SILHOUETTE MODEL 1874 SHARPS SPORTING RIFLE
The Cimarron Model 1874 Sharps silhouette rifle was created for the shooter who demands a sound, accurate, basic Sharps. The pistol grip stock gives ultimate control for off hand shooting, while the shotgun style buttplate provides maximum comfort. The barrel features cut rifling, lapped and polished for maximum accuracy.
Barrel: 32" Octagon **Caliber:** .45-.70
Prices:
Retail.................................$1195

1885 HIGH WALL
The Winchester single shot hunting rifle was placed on the market in the early 1880's. It is regarded by many as the most reliable, strongest, most symmetrical and altogether best single shot rifle ever produced. It is doubtless stronger than the Sharps rifle, is better designed, made of better materials and is of better appearance than that famous arm. All these rifles proved very accurate and reliable. Regrettably, the Winchester single shot rifle is no longer available. Cimarron's rendition of this John Browning rifle is every bit as strong and accurate as the original.
Barrel: 30" **Octagon Caliber:** 45-70, 45-90, 40-65, 38-55
Prices:
Retail..................................$999

Cimarron Firearms

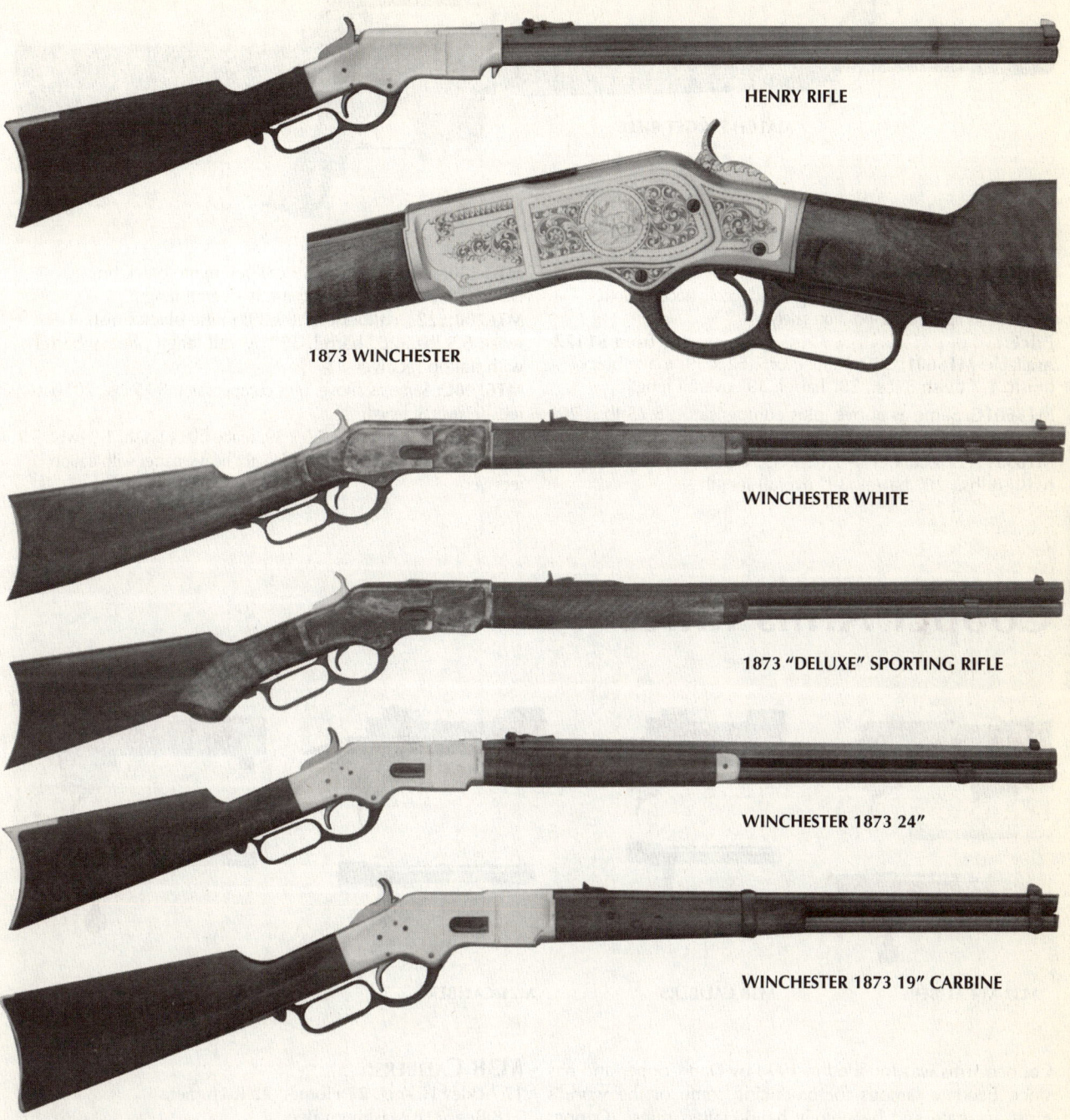

HENRY RIFLE

1873 WINCHESTER

WINCHESTER WHITE

1873 "DELUXE" SPORTING RIFLE

WINCHESTER 1873 24"

WINCHESTER 1873 19" CARBINE

HENRY RIFLE
Replicas of the most famous American rifles of the Old West.
Prices: 24", .44 W.C.F., .45 L.C. $1049

1873 WINCHESTER "1 of 1,000"
Price: . . . . special order

1873 "SPORTING" RIFLE
24" barrel, in 45 Colt, 44 WCF, 357/38 Special, 32-20, 44 Special, 38-40
Price: 949

1873 "DELUXE" SPORTING RIFLE
Price: 1089
Also available:
   1873 "Long Range" Rifle (30" barrel) 999
   Deluxe: 1149

WINCHESTER 1873
Prices: 24" 949
   19" carbine 949
   ($50 more for charcoal blue)

Rifles • 131

Colt Rifles

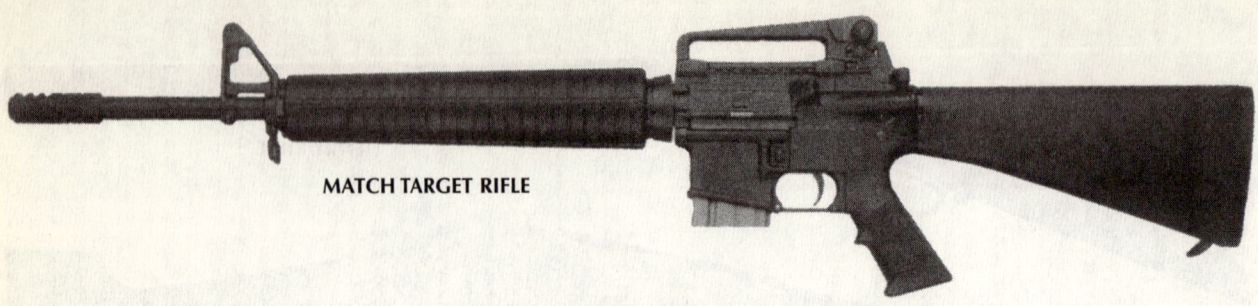

MATCH TARGET RIFLE

MATCH TARGET RIFLES
Features: Improved accuracy; suppressed recoil; accepts optics; ideal for competition; 2-position safety
Price: . . . . from $1172
Available: MT6601: .223 caliber; or 7.62 x 39, matte black finish, 1-7 twist, 8 lbs., 20" barrel, 39" overall length
MT6601C: Same as above, plus compensator; 8.75 lbs., 20" barrel, 39" overall length
MT6551: .223 caliber or 7.62 x 39; matte black finish, 1-7 twist; 8 lbs., 20" barrel, 39" overall length

MT 6530: .223 or 7.62 x 39 caliber, matte black finish, 1-7 twist, 6.7 lbs., 16.1" barrel, 34.5" overall length.
MT6700: .223 caliber or 7.6 x 39; matte black finish, 1-9 twist; 8.5 lbs., 20" barrel, 39" overall length; heavy barrel with flattop receiver
MT6700C: Same as above, plus compensator; 8.75 lbs., 20" barrel, 39" overall length
MT6731: .223 caliber or 7.6 x 39; matte black finish, 1-9 twist; 7.1 lbs., 16.1" barrel, 34.5" overall length; heavy barrel with flattop receiver

Cooper Arms Rifles

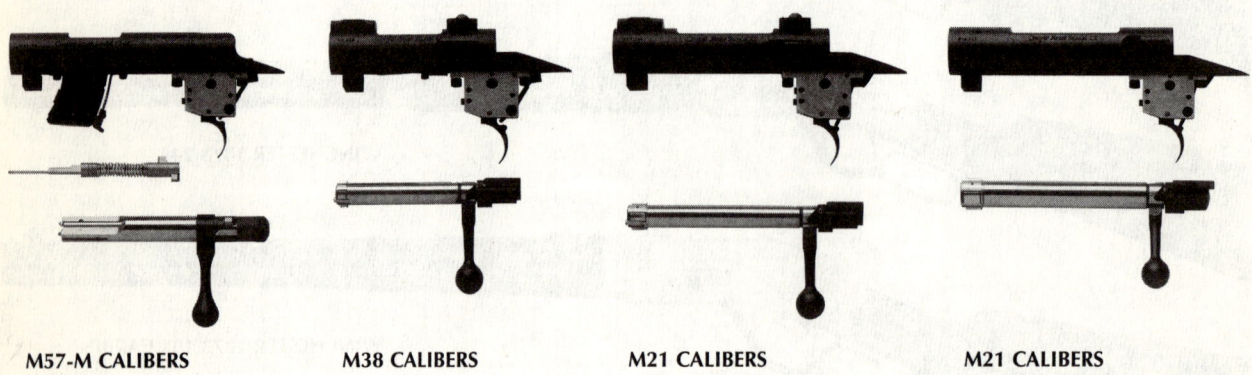

M57-M CALIBERS   M38 CALIBERS   M21 CALIBERS   M21 CALIBERS

Cooper Arms was founded in 1990 by Dan Cooper and has since become famous for producing some of the world's most accurate and beautifully hand-crafted rifles. Cooper Arms employs 20 artisans who produce a line of bolt-action single-shot centerfire and bolt-action repeating rimfire rifles. Cooper guarantees their accuracy to $^1/_2$ MOA. Rimfires are available in .22LR, .22WMR, and .17HMR. Centerfires are available in a variety of standard and wildcat cartridges. There are four action sizes available in any of six stock configurations. Cooper Arms offers varmint and traditional classic configurations.

M57-M CALIBERS:
22LR, 22WMR, 17HMR

M38 CALIBERS:
17 Ackley Hornet, 22 Hornet, 22 K-Hornet, 218 Bee, 218 Mashburn Bee

M21 CALIBERS:
17 Rem, 17 Mach IV, Tactical 29, 221 Fireball, 222 Rem Mag, 223, 223 AI, 22 PPC, 6 PPC

M22 CALIBERS:
22-250 Rem, 22-250 AI, 25-06 AI, 243 Win, 243 Win, 243 AI, 220 Swift, 257 Roberts, 257 AI, 7-08, 6mm Rem, 6x284, 22 BR, 6 BR, 308 Win, 20 Rem

Cooper Arms Rifles

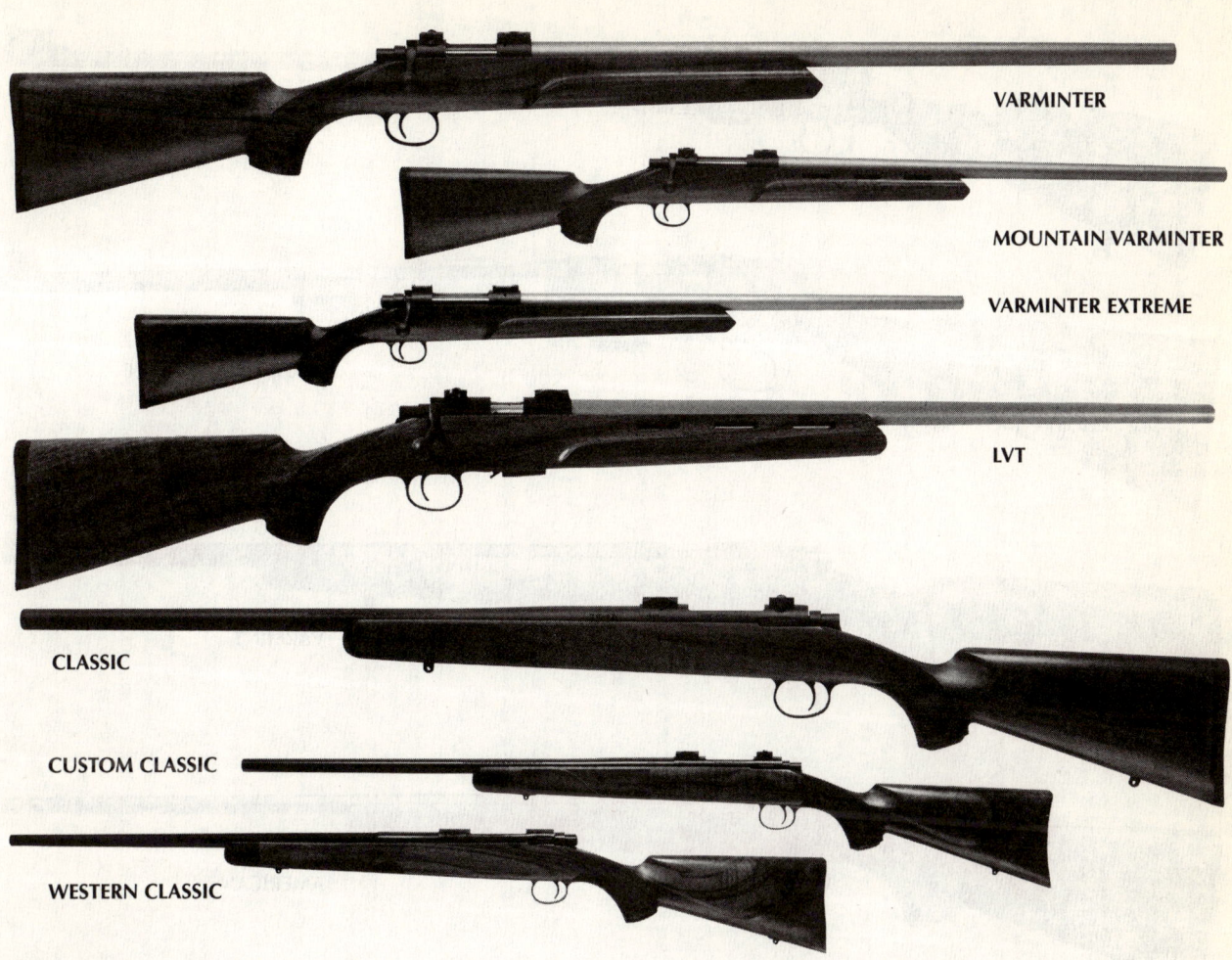

Varminter
Hand crafted AA Claro walnut stock, stainless steel match barrel, 3 front locking lug action. Available in M38, M21, and M22 with no options.
Price: ....$995 to 1199

Montana Varminter
Hand crafted AA select Claro walnut stock, cool vents, stainless steel match barrel, 3 front locking lug action. Available in M38, M21, and M22 with options.
Price.............................$1295 to 1495

Varminter Extreme
Hand crafted AAA select Claro walnut stock, stainless steel match barrel, 3 front locking lug action. Available in M38, M21, and M22 with options.
Price.............................$1795 to 1995

LVT
Hand crafted AA select Claro walnut stock, lightening vents, stainless steel match barrel, 3-rear locking lug bolt-action repeater. Available in M57-M only with options.
Price.............................$1295 to 1395

Classic
Hand crafted AA Claro walnut stock, wrap around checkering, 4140 match barrel. Available in all models and calibers, no options available.
Price.............................$1100 to 1295

Custom Classic
Hand crafted AAA Claro walnut stock, ebony tip, beaded sheek piece, wrap around checkering, 4140 match barrel. Available in all models and calibers, options available.
Price: ....$1895 to 2195

Western Classic
Hand crafted AAA select Claro walnut stock, ebony tip, beaded cheek piece, hand struck octagon barrel, case color metal work, 4140 match barrel. Available in all models and calibers, options available.
Price: ....$2495 to 2795

Model 7 Peregrine (not shown)
Single shot falling block Peregrine action, 4140 match barrel, hand crafted AAA Claro walnut stock, available in center fire calibers only, options available.
Price:.............................$1995 to 2795

CZ Rifles

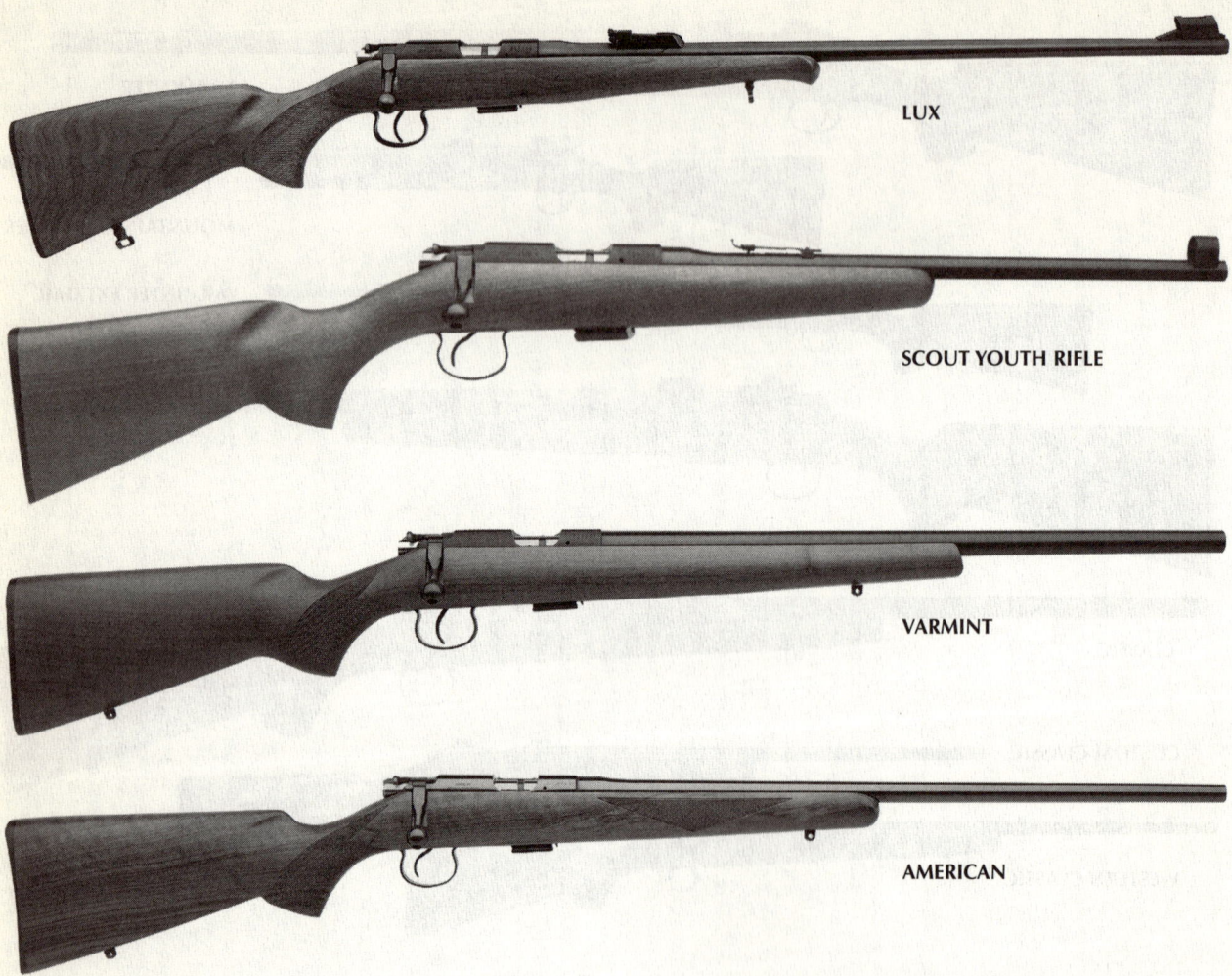

LUX

SCOUT YOUTH RIFLE

VARMINT

AMERICAN

The rimfire rifles produced by Ceska Zbrojovka Uhersky Brod are ranked among the best of their kind. Quality, long service life, accuracy and safety are the main virtues of these firearms. The CZ 452 rimfire rifles offer a compact design with a robust Mauser-type action and an adjustable pull. The rifles feature a tangent rear sight adjustable for elevation and windage. The receiver is factory milled for telescopic sight mounts. The CZ 452 rifles are supplied with a 5-shot magazine.

CZ 452 Lux
Specifications
Caliber: .22 LR (5/10 cartridges), .22 WMR (5 cartridges)
Overall length: 42.6" **Barrel Length:** 24.8" **Sight Radius:** 20.0" **Weight:** 7 lbs. **Sights** tangent rear sight: 25-200m
Prices:
  22 LR $368
  22 mag 394

CZ 452 Scout Youth Rifle
The CZ 452 Scout rifle is a compact rimfire rifle intended for young shooters. Due to its shortened dimensions, reduced weight and single round loading device it is a perfect first rifle for any boy or girl. 5 and 10 round magazines are available for the Scout rifle.
Specifications
Caliber: .22 LR **Magazine Capacity:** 5/10 cartridges **Overall length:** 32.8" **Barrel Length:** 16.2" **Weight:** 4.0 lbs.
Hammer forged barrel
Price: $191

CZ 452 Varmint
Caliber: .22 LR **Overall length:** 39" **Weight:** 7 lbs.
Price: 394

CZ 452 American
CZ 452 American - This quality rimfire rifle has been adapted to the requirements governing the USA. The barrel is 22 1/2" long, and is made without open sights. The top of the receiver is grooved for mounting a scope.
Specifications
Caliber: .22 LR, .22 WMR **Overall length:** 40" **Weight:** 6 lbs.
Prices:
  22 LR 368
22 mag 394

CZ Rifles

CZ550 FS

CZ 550 LUX

CZ 700 SNIPER M1

The CZ 550 series rifles represent a line of elegant, aesthetic and ergonomically designed firearms. The diversified range of CZ 550 rifles feature two-lug bolts with long claw extractors, and adjustable single-stage trigger and two-position thumb safety. Stocks are fitted with sling-swivels as standard, and quick release swivels can be fitted on request. The CZ 550 rifles come with a bead front sight and rear sight located so as not to interfere with even the biggest rifle scopes.

CZ 550 Lux
Specifications
Capacity: 5 cartridges, 4 cartridges
Caliber: 5 cartridges (.243 Win.; .270 Win, .308 Win.; 7x57, 7x64; 6.5x55 SE; 30-06 Sprg.; 9.3 x 62
Overall length: 44.7"
Barrel length: 23.6" **Weight:** 7.3 lbs.
Price: $566
  with detachable magazine 586
American 566
FS (full-stock) 663

CZ 550 Safari Magnum (not shown)
The CZ 550 Safari is a true "Magnum" length action, it has all the features of the CZ 550 line and one standing 2 folding express sights, a Turkish walnut Lux stock is standard. This model is intended for heavy or dangerous game. Calibers 375 H&H Mag., .416 Rigby, 458 Win Mag.
Price: $809
Also Available: CZ 550 Medium Magnum,
  .300 Win. Mag. and 7mm Rem. Mag. 650
  CZ 550 Varmint, 308 Win only 615
  CZ 550 Varmint laminated 706

CZ 700 Sniper M1
The CZ 700 Sniper M1 cal. .308 Win. is designed for tactical sniping and long-range hunting.
Features:
1) Match-grade barrel in 7.62 NATO (308)
2) Thumbhole laminated stock with adjustable butt and cheekpiece
3) Oversize, easy-to-reach bolt handle on low-throw bolt
4) Deep-well magazine 5) Bipod/swivel rail
Price: 2100

Rifles • 135

CZ Rifles

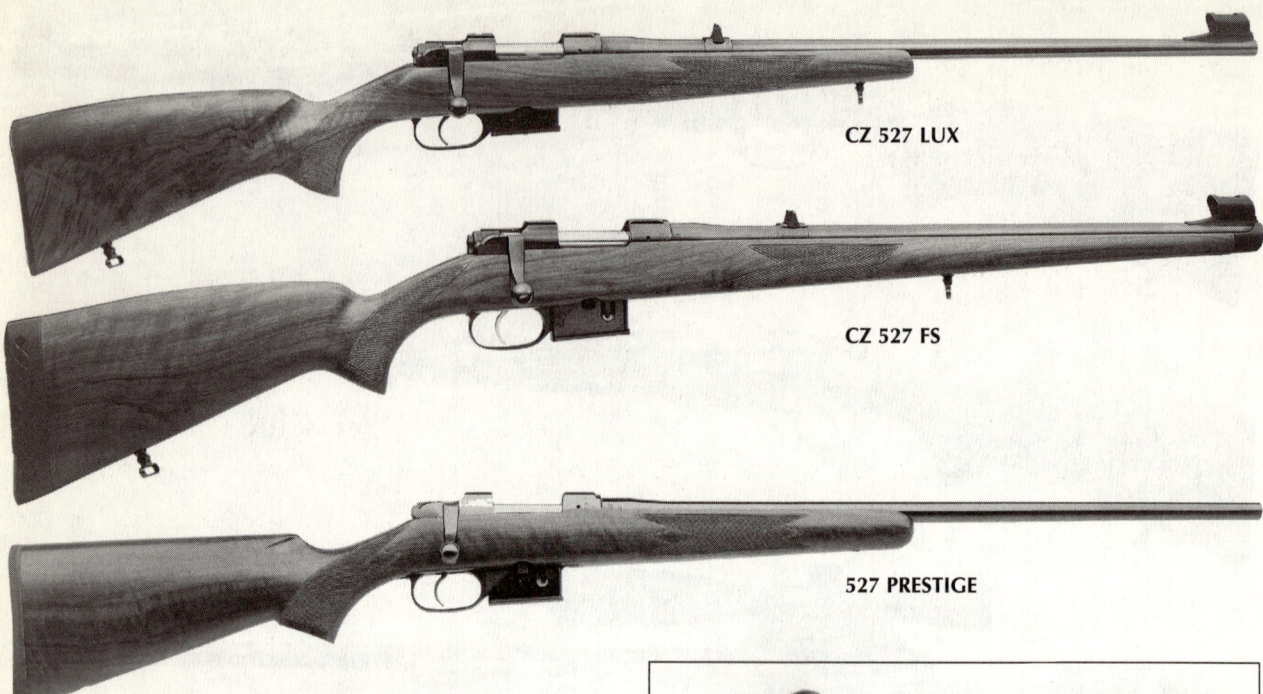

CZ 527 LUX

CZ 527 FS

527 PRESTIGE

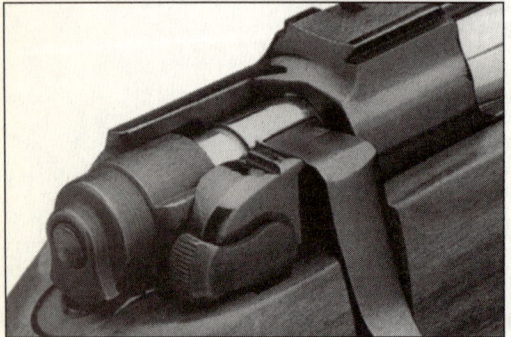

FINE MACHINING AND POLISHING ARE CZ TRADEMARKS

A SHORT-STROKE, LOW-LIFT BOLT AND DETACHABLE BOX MAGAZINE ARE DESIGNED FOR SMOOTH FEEDING.

The CZ 527 is a precision repeating rifle, designed for sport shooting and hunting. The trigger mechanism is a single set design adjustable for both pull and trigger travel. The safety is a two-position rotary lever which locks the trigger mechanism, while simultaneously locking the bolt closed. The top of the receiver has milled grooves to accommodate scope mounts. The stock's surface is finished in a semi-matte polyurethane lacquer.

CZ 527 Lux
CZ 527 Lux with Turkish walnut stock with cheekpiece
Specifications
Caliber: .22 Hornet, .222 Rem., .223 Rem. **Magazine Capacity:** 5 cartridges **Overall length:** 42.4"
Barrel length: 23.6" **Weight:** 6.2 lbs.
Price: $566
Also Available: CZ 527 Carbine, Caliber, .223 Rem . . 566

CZ 527 FS
CZ 527 FS - a classic Bavarian-style Mannlicher stock of turkish walnut, cheekpiece
Specifications
Caliber: .22 Hornet, .222 Rem., .223 Rem. **Magazine Capacity:** 5 cartridges
Overall length: 38.5" **Barrel length:** 20.5"
Weight: 6.0 lbs.
Price: 650

527 Prestige
Specifications
Caliber: .22 Hornet, .223 Rem. **Magazine Capacity:** 5 cartridges **Overall length:** 40.4" **Barrel length:** 21.9"
Weight: 6.2 lbs.
Price: 829

Dakota Arms

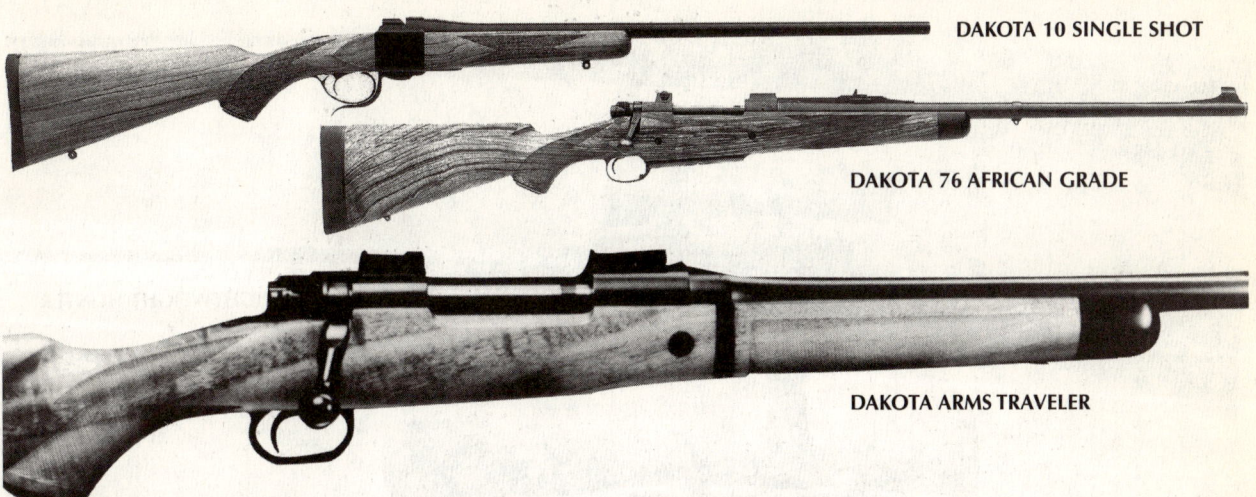

DAKOTA 10 SINGLE SHOT
DAKOTA 76 AFRICAN GRADE
DAKOTA ARMS TRAVELER

DAKOTA 10 SINGLE SHOT
Specifications
Calibers: Most rimmed/rimless commercially loaded types; New for 2002: 270 WSM, 7mm WSM and 300 WSM
Barrel Length: 23" **Overall Length:** 39.5" **Weight:** 6 lbs.
Features: Receiver and rear of breech block are solid steel without cuts or holes for maximum lug area (approx. 8 times more bearing area than most bolt rifles); crisp, clean trigger pull; removable trigger plate allows action to adapt to single-set triggers; straight-line coil-spring action and short hammer fall combine for fast lock time; smooth, quiet top tang safety blocks the striker forward of the main spring; strong, positive extractor and manual ejector adapted to rimmed/rimless cases. XX grade oil-finished English, Bastogne or Claro walnut stock.
Price: $3595
   Barreled Actions 2050
   Actions Only 1675
Also Available:
   Dakota 10 Magnum Single Shot 3595
   Barreled actions 2050
   Actions only 1675

DAKOTA 76 RIFLES
Specifications
Calibers: Safari Grade: from 257 Roberts to 458 Win Mag.
Classic Grade: from 220 Swift to 416 Rem. (inc. WSM)
African Grade: 404 Jeffery, 416 Dakota, 416 Rigby, 450 Dakota
Barrel Lengths: 21" or 23" (Classic); 23" only (Safari); 24" (African) **Weight:** 7.5 lbs. (Classic); 9.5 lbs. (African); 8.5 lbs. (Safari) **Safety:** Three-position striker-blocking safety allows bolt operation with safety on **Sights:** Ramp front sight; standing-leaf rear **Stock:** Choice of X grade oil-finished English, Bastogne or Claro walnut (Classic); choice of XXX grade oil-finished English or Bastogne walnut w/ebony forent tip (Safari)
Prices:
   Classic Grade $3595
   Safari Grade 4595
   African Grade $4995
   Barreled Actions: Classic Grade 2095
   Safari Grade 2450
   African Grade 2950
   Actions: Classic Grade 1850
   Safari Grade 1995
   African Grade 2500

DAKOTA ARMS TRAVELER
The Dakota Traveler rifle can be easily taken apart and carried in a small case or conventional suitcase, with the largest portion of the disassembled rifle being the barrel. Additional barrels in a wide range of calibers are available.

The Traveler is based on the long-proven Dakota 76 design, and is stocked in checkered walnut. It features threadless disassembly. There are no threads to wear or stretch, no interrupted cuts and no possibility of headspace increasing even after repeated assembly and disassembly. Because of the Traveler's rigid design, it can be quickly taken down without disturbing the scope and mounts, assuring consistent, repeatable accuracy.

Additional barrels/calibers can be fitted on the same action, providing true worldwide hunting capability. Three families of actions are available: standard length, including the .257 Roberts, .25-06, 7x57, .270, .280, .30-06, .338-06 and .35 Whelen; the 7mm Rem. Mag., .300 Win. Mag., .338 Win. Mag. 270 WSM, 7mmWSM, 300 WSM Mag., 416 Taylor and .458 Win. Mag.; and Dakota short magnums that include the proprietary 7mm, .300, .330 and .375 Dakota cartridges.
Prices:
   Classic 4495
   Safari 5495
   African 5995

NEW DAKOTA DOUBLE RIFLE
Available in most common calibers. Exhibition walnut, pistol grip, 25" barrel, round action, elective ejectors, recoil pad, Americase.
Price: $25,000

Dakota Arms

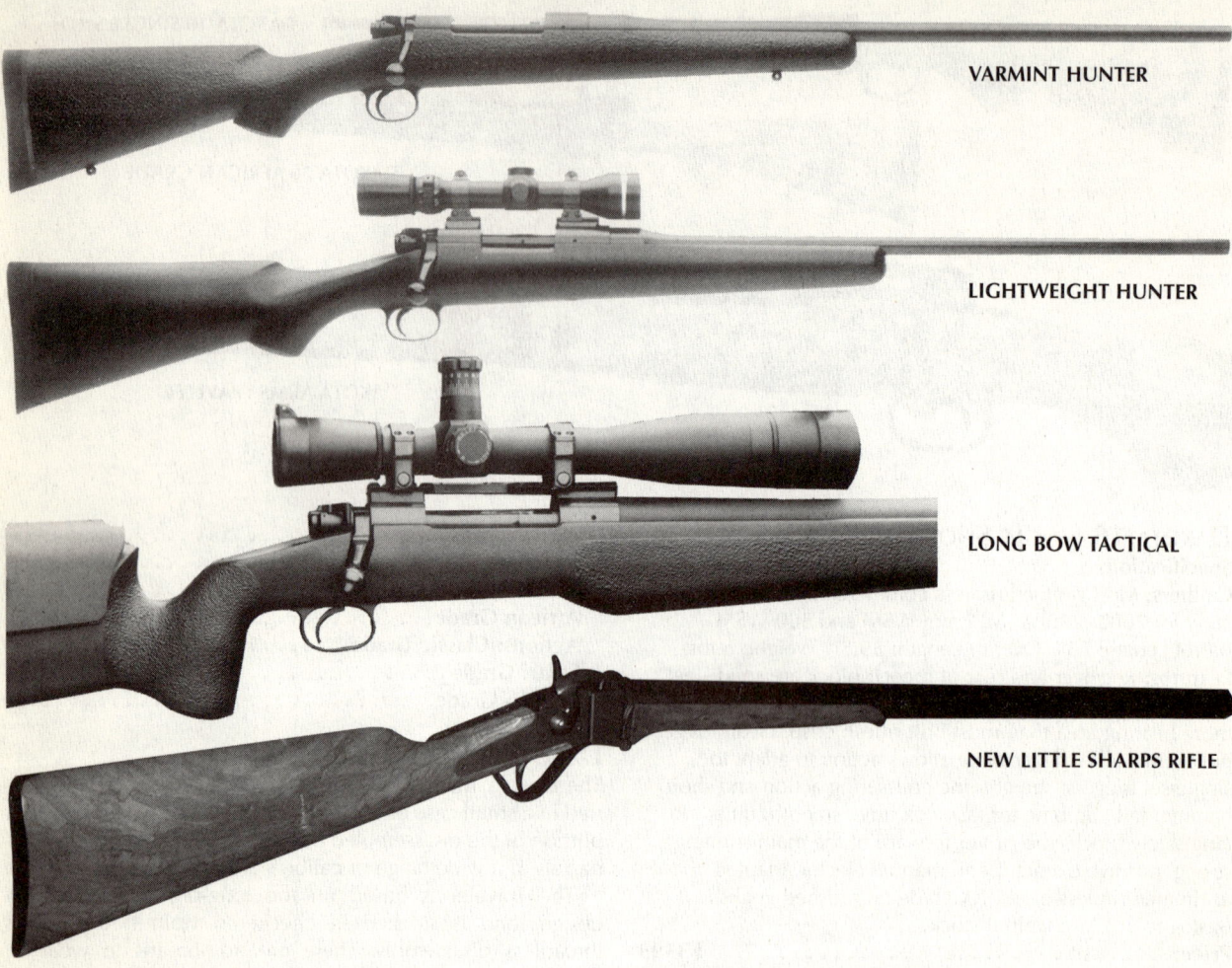

VARMINT HUNTER

LIGHTWEIGHT HUNTER

LONG BOW TACTICAL

NEW LITTLE SHARPS RIFLE

DAKOTA 97 VARMINT, LONG RANGE & LIGHTWEIGHT HUNTER RIFLES
Dakota Hunter Series Bolt Action Rifles (not shown)

97 Long Range Hunter
Fibergass stock, 2 sling swivel studs, 1" black recoil pad, 13 5/8 length of pull, overall weight 7.7 lbs., overall length 45" to 47", calibers 25-06 through 375 Dakota. RH only.
Price: $1995

97 Lightweight Hunter
Fibergass stock, 2 sling swivel studs, 1" black recoil pad, 12 5/8 length of pull, overall weight approximately 6-6 1/2 lbs., overall length 43", calibers 22-250 through 330, RH only.

97 Varmint Hunter
Walnut-stocked round short-action solid-bottom single shot, 24" chrome-moly barrel #4, adjustable trigger, 13 5/8 length of pull, 1/2" black pad, approximate weight 8 lbs, calibers 17 Rem through 22-250, RH only.
Prices:
97 w/semi-fancy wood stock. 2495
   action only 1000
   Barreled action 1300

LONG BOW TACTICAL E.R.
(ENGAGEMENT RIFLE)
Specifications
Caliber: 338 Lapua, 300 Dakota, 330 Dakota
Action: Blind magazine
Barrel Length: 28" stainless steel
Overall Length: 50"-51"
Length Of Pull: 12 7/8"-14 3/8"
Weight: 13.7 lbs. (w/o scope)
Stock: McMillan fiberglass (black or olive drab green); matte finish
Features: Adjustable cheekpiece; 3 sling swivel studs; bipod spike in forend; controlled round feeding; claw extraction system; one-piece optical rail; 3-position firing pin block safety; deployment kit; muzzlebrake
Price: $4250
   Action only 2500

NEW LITTLE SHARPS RIFLE
Falling block single shot, straight grip with walnut stock, 26" octagon barrel, steel buttplate, tang sight and front bead.
Price: 2900

EMF Replica Rifles

MODEL 1866 YELLOW BOY RIFLE & CARBINE
MODEL 1873 SPORTING RIFLE
"NEW GENERATION" 1874 SHARPS
HARTFORD 1892 LEVER ACTION RIFLE & CARBINE

1860 Henry Rifle (not shown)
Specifications
Calibers: 44-40 and 45 LC **Barrel length:** 24";
Overall length: 43.75" **Weight:** 9.25 lbs. Blued barrel, walnut stock, brass frame
Price: $900

Model 1866 Yellow Boy Rifle & Carbine
Specifications
Calibers: 45 Long Colt, 38 Special and 44-40. Blued barrel, walnut stock, brass frame.
Prices:
   Rifle 725
   Carbine 750

Model 1873 Sporting Rifle
Specifications
Calibers: 32/20, 357, 38/40, 44-40, 45 Long Colt **Barrel length:** 24" octagonal **Overall length:** 43.25" **Weight:** 8.16 lbs.
Features: Magazine tube in blued steel; frame is casehardened steel; stock and forend are walnut
Price 865
Also available:
   1873 Carbine, 20" barrel in 32/20, 357 or 45LC .. 865

"New Generation" 1874 Sharps
Created by Christian Sharps, this rifle played a major role in the Civil War and settling of the West. Caliber: 45/70. Barrel: 28" octagonal in blue, "white" or "brown patina." Double-set triggers, Schnabel Forearm, tang pre-drilled for sight.
Price: $800
   w/brown patina 825
   w/"white" finish 850
Also available:
   Target model 850
   Carbine 695

Hartford 1892 Lever Action Rifle & Carbine
Specifications
Caliber: 357 and 45 Long Colt. **Barrel Length:** 24" (Carbine: 20"). Octagonal or round barrel, blued. **Frame:** Blued, case-hardened, or stainless steel.
Prices:
   Rifle, blued frame 525
   Rifle, case-hardened 535
   Rifle, stainless 575
   Carbine, blued, round barrel 455
   Carbine, Case-hardened, round barrel .. 470
   Carbine, stainless, round barrel 520

European American Armory

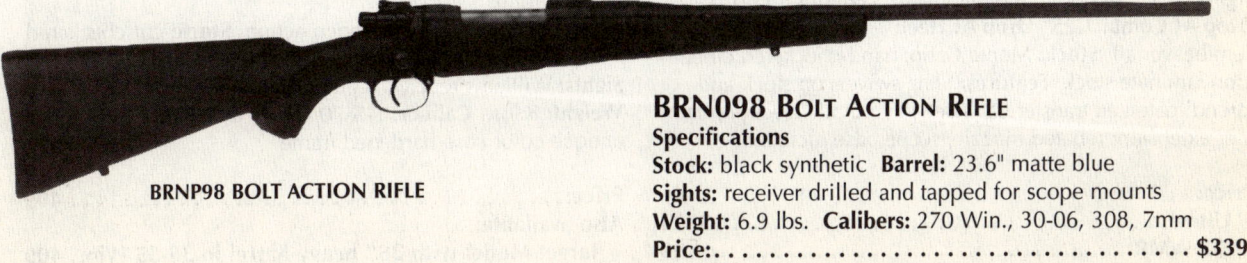

BRNP98 BOLT ACTION RIFLE

BRN098 Bolt Action Rifle
Specifications
Stock: black synthetic **Barrel:** 23.6" matte blue
Sights: receiver drilled and tapped for scope mounts
Weight: 6.9 lbs. **Calibers:** 270 Win., 30-06, 308, 7mm
Price: $339

Harrington & Richardson

ULTRA HUNTER

BUFFALO CLASSIC

ULTRA SINGLE-SHOT RIFLES
Specifications
Calibers: 22 WMR, 223 Rem. & 243 (Varmint), 25-06, 308 Win., 450 Marlin **Action:** Break-open; side lever release; positive ejection **Barrel Length:** 22" (308 Win.); 24" bull barrel (223 Rem., Varmint) 26" (25-06) **Weight:** 7 to 8 lbs. **Sights:** None (scope mount included) **Length Of Pull:** 14.25" **Drop At Comb:** 1.25" **Drop At Heel:** 1 1/8" **Forend:** Semibeavertail **Stock:** Monte Carlo; hand-checkered cinnamon laminate stock **Features:** Sling swivels on stock and forend; patented transfer bar safety; automatic ejection; hammer extension; rebated muzzle; scope base included.

Price:
Ultra $324
.22 WMR 189

Also available:
Ultra Comp in 30-06 and 270 Win. $366
Barrel Length: 24". **Weight:** 7-8 lbs. Camo laminate stock, muzzle brake scope base included

BUFFALO CLASSIC
Specifications
Action: single-shot, break-open action **Stock:** cut-checkered American black walnut with steel buttplate **Barrel:** 32" **Sights:** Williams receiver sight; Lyman target front sight **Weight:** 8 lbs. **Caliber:** .45-70 Govt. **Other features:** antique color case hardened frame

Price: 409
Also available:
Target Model with 28" heavy barrel in 38-55 Win. . 409

Gibbs Rifle Company

QUEST II EXTREME CARBINE
WEIGHT: 8 LBS.
BBL LENGTH: 20"
CALIBER: .308 WIN.

- CHROME VANADIUM 2A ACTION
- SEE THROUGH SCOPE MOUNT
- FRONT SIGHT PROTECTOR
- COMPENSATOR/FLASH-HIDER
- WEATHERPROOF ELECTROLESS NICKEL FINISH
- CORROSION RESISTANT BUTT TRAP
- HARDWOOD STOCK
- 12 ROUND MAGAZINE
- SURVIVAL KIT

M71/84 REFURBISHED

QUEST II EXTREME CARBINE
Gibbs Rifle Company's Sport Specialty rifles include the Quest II Extreme Carbine. The Quest II is made on a modern 2A Chrome Vanadium steel barreled action and is chambered for the popular, powerful .308 Winchester. The Quest II's electroless nickel finish protects against the elements and is fitted with a compensator/flash-hider that tames recoil and reduces muzzle jump. Pre-fitted see-through scope mount allows open sights to be used and accepts Weaver-based optics and accessories. The butt trap houses a survival kit with Brunton liquid-filled compass, waterproof matches, fire starter, snare wire, twine and fishing kit.
Price: $280

M71/84 REFURBISHED
Gibbs Rifle Company's newest addition to its line of historical re-makes is the arsenal reconditioned Mauser M71/84, the first bolt-action repeating rifle ever built by Paul and Wilhelm Mauser. The M71/84 was adopted by Germany in 1871 and upgraded to an 8-round tubular magazine repeater in 1884. It saw combat in the colonial wars of Africa and in World War I.

Gibbs has taken original M71/84 rifles with 100+ years of grime, use and wear, and carefully restored them to new condition using both original and reproduction parts. All barreled actions are completely original, with the exception of some small parts, and have been arsenal refinished using the same methods employed in their original manufacture. These barreled actions are then hand-fitted to 1-piece replica stocks that mirror the originals in every way, including all interior and exterior dimensions and inspection marks.

The Gibbs Arsenal Reconditioned M71/84 rifle are available for a limited time only.
Price: $300

Rifles • 141

Heckler & Koch Rifles

USC CARBINE BASE MODEL

SL8-1 RIFLE BASE MODEL

SLB 2000 K PREMIUM CALIBER .30-06

USC .45 ACP Autoloading Carbine
A combination of advanced polymers, ordnance steel and a simple blow-back action make this a reliable, lightweight autoloading rifle. An optional Picatinny rail mounts easily for attaching a scope or electronic sight. The rear sight is fully adjustable. A bolt catch holds the action open after the last round from the 10-shot polymer magazine. An oversize trigger guard and ambidextrous safety make shooting easier with gloves. The 16-inch hammer-forged barrel and skeleton polymer stock keep weight to only 6 pounds. Sling swivel holes and a rubber cheek rest and recoil pad are standard.
Price:. $1249

SL8-1 .223 Autoloading Rifle
Built largely of polymers around a steel frame, this gas-operated autoloader weighs only 8.5 lbs with a 21" free-floating barrel. The mechanism is based on the proven German G36 design. Field-stripping to three modular components can be done in seconds with the removal of two hex screws. The thumbhole stock includes an adjustable butt and hardpoints for mounting a forend rail. A removable, adjustable rear sight complements a Picatinny scope rail that can also be removed. The safety is ambidextrous; so is the bolt cocking lever. A 10-round detachable box magazine is of clear polymer.
Price:. $1649

SLB 2000 .30-06 Rifle
The SLB uses a proven gas operating system that is extremely robust. The same bolt system can handle a wide array of popular international hunting cartridges (.308, .30-06, 7x64mm, 9.3x62mm) when a barrel conversion is made. The exaggerated shape and angle of the pistol grip makes offhand shooting easier. Iron sights are included.
Price:. 1399

Henry Rimfire Rifles

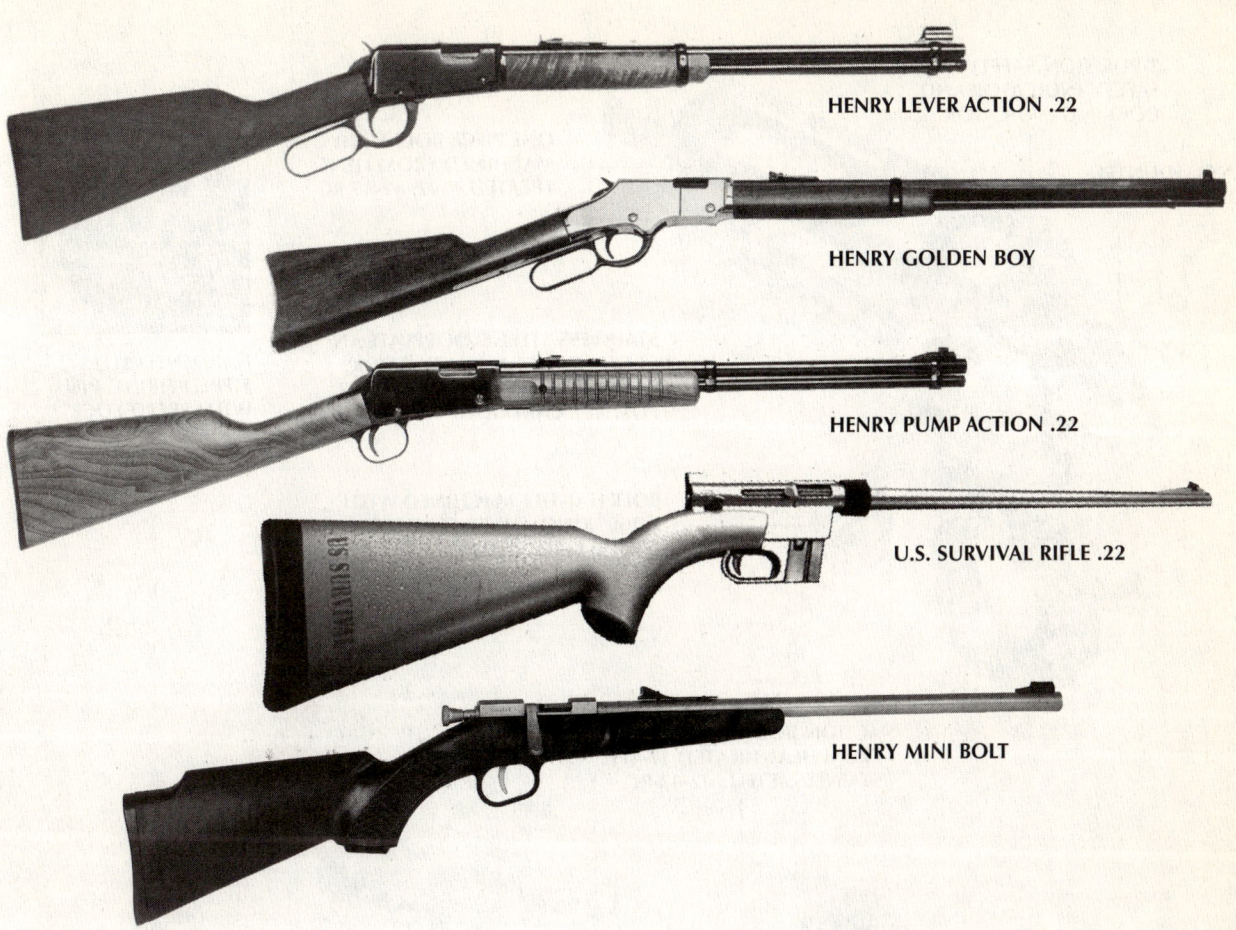

HENRY LEVER ACTION .22

HENRY GOLDEN BOY

HENRY PUMP ACTION .22

U.S. SURVIVAL RIFLE .22

HENRY MINI BOLT

HENRY LEVER ACTION .22
Specifications
Calibers: 22 S, L, LR **Capacity:** 15 rounds (22 LR); 17 rds. (22 L); 21 rds. (22 S) 11 rds (22 mag) **Barrel Length:** 18"
Overall Length: 36.5" **Weight:** 5.5 lbs. **Stock:** American Walnut **Sights:** Adjustable rear; hooded front
Features: Grooved receiver for scope mount
Price:
(also carbine and youth model) $249.95
.22 Magnum with deluxe checkered stock,
19" barrel 299.95
"Golden Boy" replica of Henry rifle 20"
octagon barrel 379.95

HENRY GOLDEN BOY
Specifications
Stock: American walnut, straight grip. **Barrel:** 20" octagon.
Sights: Open, U-notch rear, blade front **Weight:** 6.75 lbs.
Caliber: .22 S, L, LR **Magazine Capacity:** 16-22
Other features: Lever action, Brasslite receiver and brass butt plate
Price: $380

HENRY PUMP ACTION .22
Henry Repeating Arms expands its family of .22 rifles with the introduction of the Henry Pump Action .22. Made in America, this rifle features an American walnut stock, grooved receiver for a scope mount and adjustable rear sight.
Specifications
Capacity: 15-rounds .22 long rifle
Barrel Length: 18.25" Weight: 5.5 lbs.
Price: $249.95

U.S. SURVIVAL RIFLE .22
Specifications
Calibers: 22 long rifle **Capacity:** 9-shot
Barrel Length: 16.25" **Overall Length:** 35.25"
Sights: Adjustable rear sight **Features:** Barrel and action fit in floating waterproof stock; comes with two 8-round magazines, grooved receiver for scope.
Price: $165

HENRY MINI BOLT .22
Specifications
Stock: Synthetic, with pistol grip, wrap-around checkering and beavertail forearm **Barrel:** 16.25" Stainless
Sights: Williams Fire Sights, illuminated two green dot adjustable rear and contrasting red front sight
Weight: 3.25 lbs. **Caliber:** 22 magazine **Capacity:** Single shot **Other features:** Great first gun for beginners
Price: $170

H-S Precision Rifles

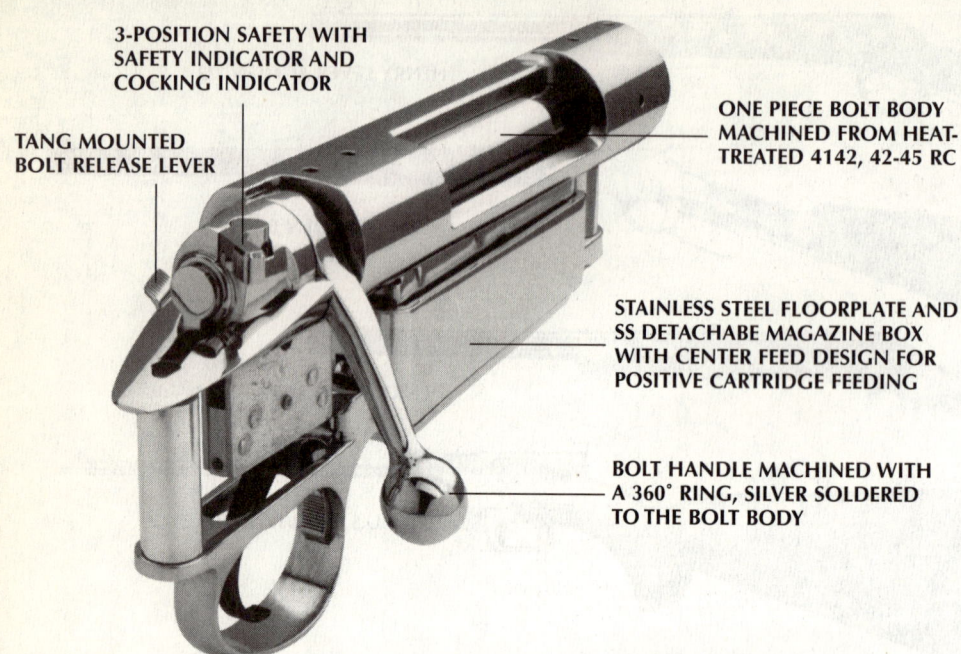
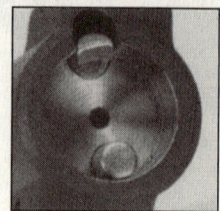
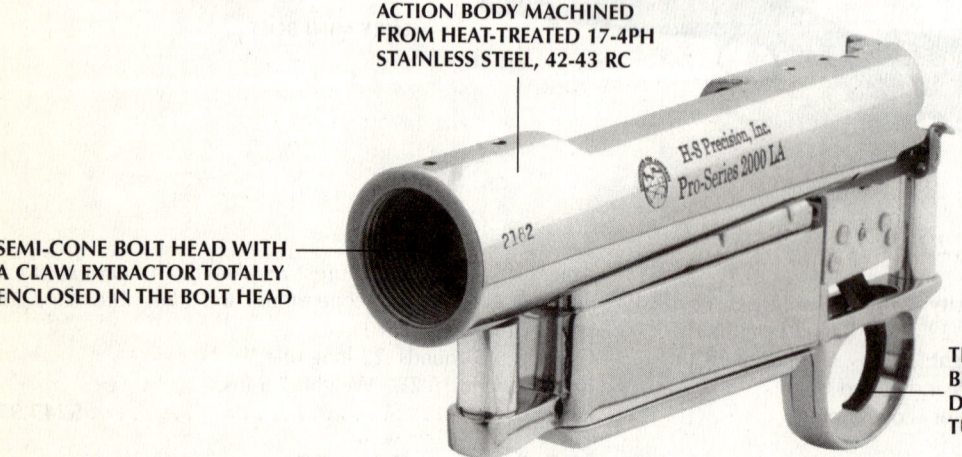

In 1978 Tom Houghton bought Atkinson Gun Company and combined it with H-S Engineering to form H-S Precision, Inc., in Prescott, Arizona. Two years later the firm began manufacturing test barrels for Winchester, and two years after that H-S began producing Fiberthane rifle stocks. In 1984 the company came up with an aluminum bedding block, now used on all its Pro-Series stocks, which appeared in 1985. They feature a blend of fiberglass, Kevlar and unidirectional carbon fiber. In 1988 H-S Precision developed a take-down rifle, receiving the patent two years later when the firm moved to Rapid City, South Dakota. There Tom Houghton and his crew updated both engineering and manufacturing with CAD and CNC technology. In 1994 the 15,000-square-foot facility grew with the addition of 10,000 square feet designated for stock production only. By this time H-S was manufacturing synthetic stocks for both Remington and Winchester. It was also building custom rifles with its own super-accurate cut-rifled barrels. Law enforcement agencies were steady patrons. In 1996 the plant expanded by another 25 percent; the next year the series 2000 single-shot pistol appeared, followed by series 2000 rifles on the company's own actions.

The H-S Precision Pro-Series 2000 action combines many of the best features of the Winchester Model 70 and Remington 700 rifles. Available in two lengths, it is the heart of several H-S Precision semi-custom rifles, including a take-down model. Rifles of 30 caliber and smaller are guaranteed to shoot 1/2-inch groups at 100 yards. Big-bore rifles are guaranteed to shoot into one minute of angle.

H-S Precision Rifles
Pro-Series 2000

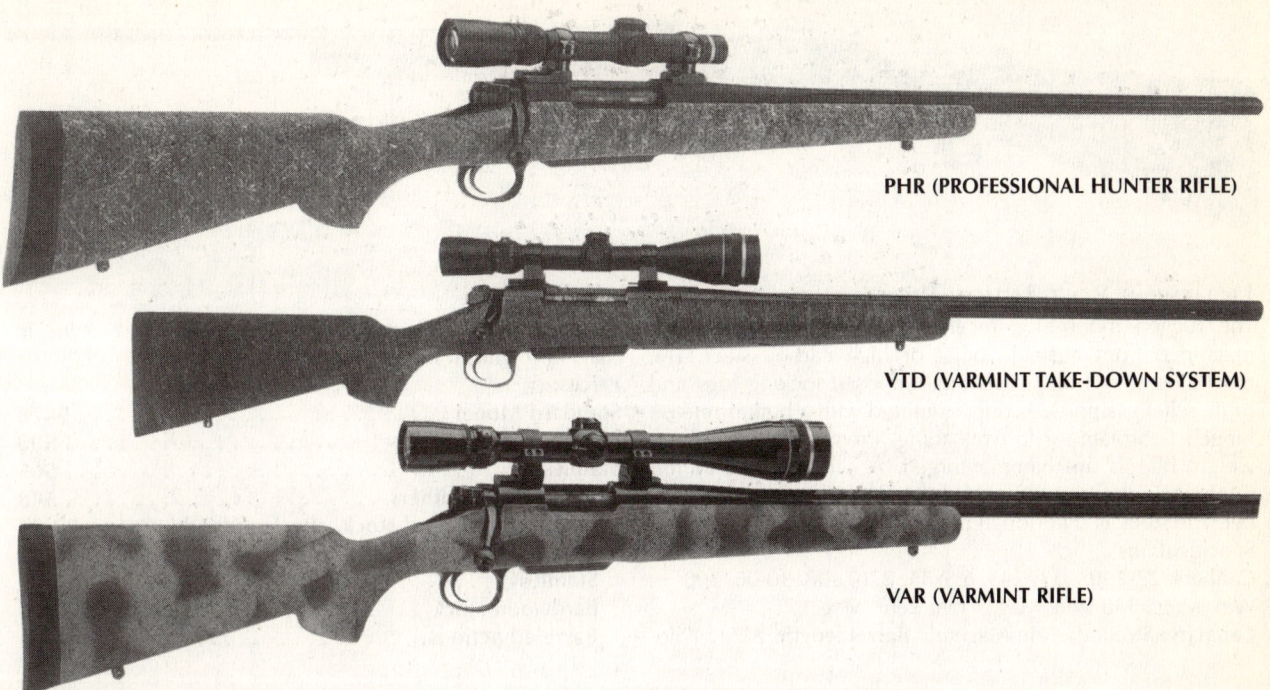

PHR (PROFESSIONAL HUNTER RIFLE)

VTD (VARMINT TAKE-DOWN SYSTEM)

VAR (VARMINT RIFLE)

PHR (PROFESSIONAL HUNTER RIFLE)
The Pro-Series 2000 PHR is a slightly heavier version of the Pro-Series 2000 SPR rifle. Because of the larger magnum calibers, available for the Pro-Series 2000 PHR, the increased weight is a necessity. The Pro-Series 2000 PHR is designed to handle the new "super magnums", such as the 300 Rem Ultra Mag or the 338 Lapua.

Features:
Pro-Series 2000 stainless steel action with detachable magazine, 3 rounds in the magazine box
Pro-Series 10X match grade stainless steel barrel, Fluted (except 416 Rigby), 24" or 26" magnum contour, Optional muzzle brake, built-in recoil reducer, choice of color, metal finish – Teflon® or
Pro-Series PFTE Matte Black, Weight – 7.75 - 8.25 pounds Calibers – all standard SAAMI calibers
Pro-Series synthetic stock with full length bedding block chassis system, sporter style

VTD (VARMINT TAKE-DOWN SYSTEM)
Pro Series 2000 Take-Down rifles are covered by the same 1/2 minute of angle accuracy and repeatability guarantee as all other Pro-Series 2000 rifles (3 shots at 100 yards). Pro-Series 2000 Take-down rifle systems are tested for accuracy and repeatability with factory match ammunition.

Features
Pro-Series 2000 stainless steel action, long or short
Pro-Series stainless steel floorplate with detachable magazine, 4 rounds in the magazine box, standard calibers, 3 rounds in the magazine box, magnum calibers
Pro-Series 10X match grade stainless steel barrel, Fluted, 23.5" varmint contour, Optional muzzle brake, PSV29B - long action, Choice of color, Metal finish – Teflon® or
Pro-Series PFTE Matte Black, Weight* – 8.50 - 9 pounds, Calibers: all standard SAAMI calibers, Options, Additional caliber capability by adding a second barrel
Pro-Series synthetic stock with full length bedding block chassis system, varmint style

VAR (VARMINT RIFLE) FEATURES
Pro-Series 2000 stainless steel action, long or short
Pro-Series stainless steel floorplate with detachable magazine, 4 rounds in the magazine box, standard calibers, 3 rounds in the magazine box, magnum calibers, 3 rounds in the magazine box, 338 Lapua
Pro-Series 10X match grade stainless steel barrel, heavy barrel, Fluted, 24" heavy contour, Optional muzzle brake
Pro-Series synthetic stock with full length bedding block chassis system, tactical style, PST25 - short action, fully adjustable length of pull and cheek piece, PST26 - long action, fully adjustable length of pull and cheek piece, Choice of color, Metal finish – Teflon® or
Pro-Series PFTE Matte Black, Weight* – 10.75 - 11.25 pounds, Calibers: all standard SAAMI calibers

Prices: Sporter, with 2000 action $1950
Sporter,
  with customer's M70 or M700 action 1520
Pro-Hunter, with 2000 action 2200
Varmint, with 2000 action 1975
Varmint,
  with customer's M70 or M700 action 1630
Pro-Hunter Take-Down,
  with 2000 action and one barrel 2600
Varmint Take-Down,
  with 2000 action and one barrel 2500
Left-hand models: . . . . Add $150 - 250

Howa Lightning Rifles

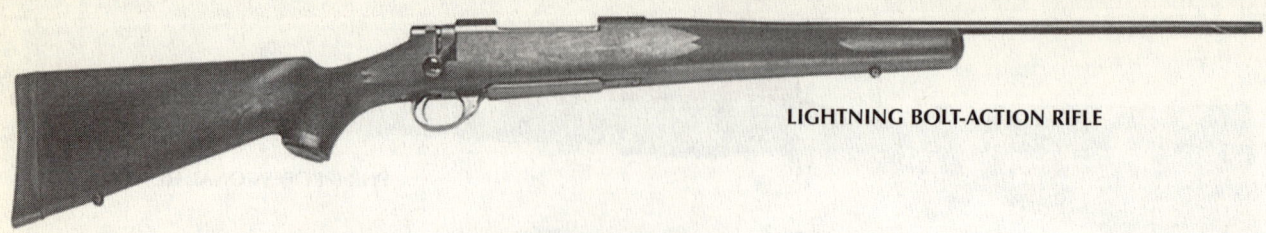

LIGHTNING BOLT-ACTION RIFLE

Lightning Bolt-Action Rifle

The rugged mono-bloc receivers on all Howa rifles are machined from a single billet of high carbon steel. The machined steel bolt boasts dual-opposed locking lugs and triple relief gas ports. Actions are fitted with a button-release hinged floorplate for fast reloading. Premium steel sporter-weight barrels are hammer-forged. A silent sliding thumb safety locks the trigger for safe loading or clearing the chamber. The stock is ultra-tough polymer.

Specifications
Calibers: 22-250, 223, 243, 6.5x55, 270, 308, 30-06, 300 Win. Mag., 338 Win. Mag., 7mm Rem. Mag.
Capacity: 5 rounds (3 in Magnum) **Barrel length:** 22" (24" in Magnum) **Overall length:** 42.5" **Weight:** 7.5 lbs. (7.7 lbs. in Magnum) **Finish:** Blue
Prices:
Standard Model $478
  In Magnum calibers 500
Stainless. 565
  In Magnum calibers 588
  Hunter (hardwood stock, checkered) add 22-24
Varmint (223, 22-250, 308 Win) 511
  Stainless. 612
  hardwood stock . . . . add 22-24
Barreled actions. 357-484

Jarrett Custom Rifles

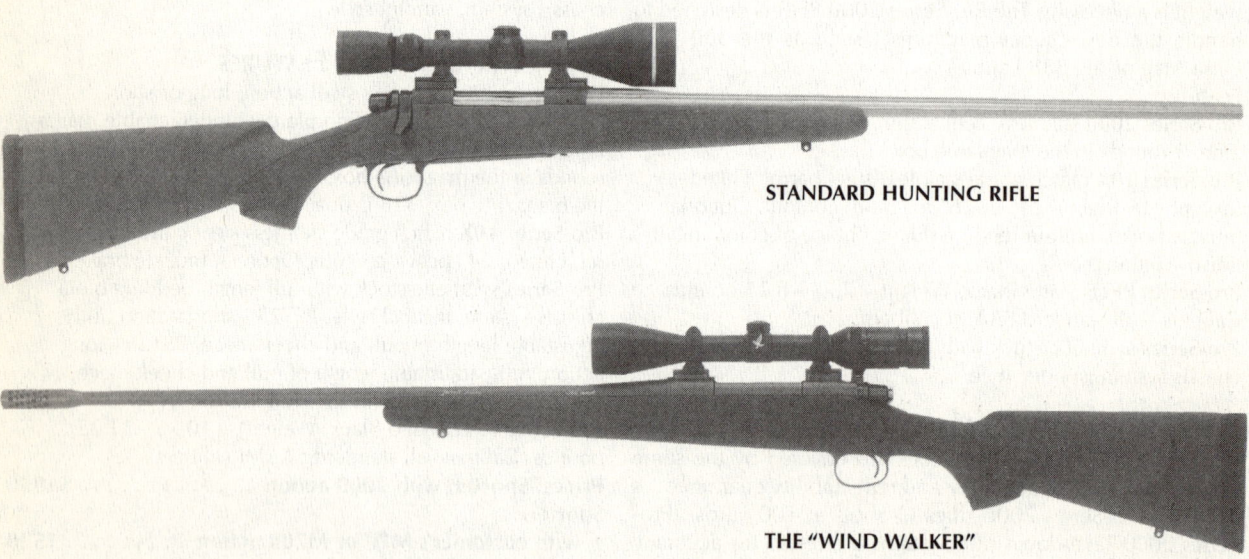

STANDARD HUNTING RIFLE

THE "WIND WALKER"

Standard Hunting Rifle

Jarrett's Standard Hunting Rifle incorporates a McMillan stock with Decelerator pad in choice of finishes. #4 match-grade barrel on Remington 700 or Winchester 70 action with Talley scope mounts. Case, sling load data and custom-loaded ammo included. Finished Weight: 8.5 lbs.
Price:. $3550

Wind Walker

Same specifications as the Standard model, but with a Kevlar stock and skeletonized Rem. 700 action for lighter weight (finished, with Swarovski 3-10x 42 A1 scope in Talley mounts, the Windwalker weighs 7.25 lbs.). Muzzle brake, case, sling, load data and custom-loaded ammo included.
Price:. $4395

Jarrett Custom Rifles

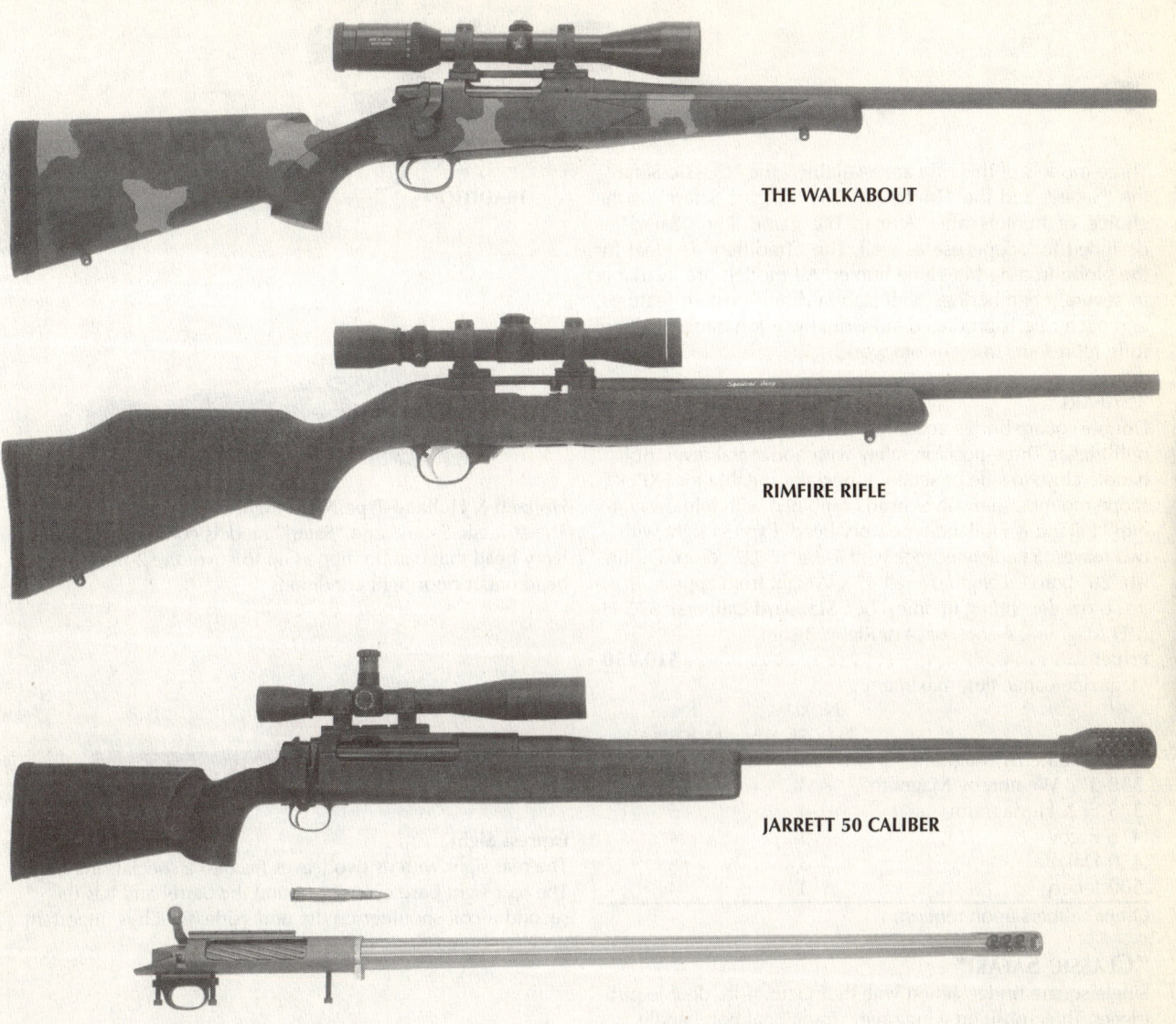

THE WALKABOUT

RIMFIRE RIFLE

JARRETT 50 CALIBER

THE WALKABOUT
The WalkAbout is a short, handy rifle built on a Remington 700 short action and chambered for your choice of standard or popular wildcat cartridges. The Jarrett barrel is 20" long; the stock is by McMillan and comes in a variety of finishes. At 7.5 pounds, finished, the WalkAbout includes Talley mounts and rings with the scope you specify. Case, sling, load data and 20 rounds of ammunition are also furnished.
Price:..................................$3550

RIMFIRE RIFLE
The Jarrett Rimfire Rifle is built on a Ruger 10/22 receiver. The 18-inch match-grade barrel is available in Target and hunting contours. Action work includes precise barrel fitting, a trigger job and a modified bolt lock. The stock is from Brown Precision, in your choice of finishes. Talley rings and bases, and an accuracy guarantee of 1/2 m.o.a. at 50 yards, are part of the package. This is a carefully built rimfire designed for one-hole groups.
Price:..................................$1800
  Target..................................1995

JARRETT 50 CALIBER
The Jarrett 50 is built on a McMillan receiver in either single-shot or magazine configuration. A match-grade KP barrel with compensator, a McMillan stock and military scope mounts bring rifle weight to 28 to 45 pounds depending on your choice of barrel contour and length (30" to 34"). Jarrett develops an accurate load and supplies 20 rounds of ammunition. Scope of choice: Leupold Ultra 24X.
Not shown: Jarrett special rifles made to order in Tactical, Bench Rest, Youth and Professional Hunter styles.
Price: (single shot)..........................6,700
  Repeater..................................6,950

Johannsen Express Rifles

TRADITION

Three models of this rifle are available - the "Classic Safari", the "Safari" and the "Tradition". The "Classic Safari", is the choice of hunters after African big game. The "Safari" is designed for scope use as well. The "Tradition" is ideal for the globe-trotting big-game hunter. All models are available in several chamberings with standard and custom features, and each rifle is produced individually. A Johannsen Express Rifle represents true custom work.

"Safari"
Double square bridge action without thumbcut. 4-lb. double-pull trigger. Three-position safety with horizontal lever. Bolt handle close to side of action. Especially suitable for EXPERT scope mount. 2-mm silver bead combined with fold-away 4-mm Holland & Holland-type ivory bead. Express sight with two leaves. Safari-style stock with 1-3/4"/2-1/2" drop. Oil finish. 26" barrel. Length overall 47". Weight from approx. 8 lbs. 6 oz. depending upon caliber. **Standard calibers:** .375 H & H Magnum, 4-shot, or .416 Rigby, 3-shot.
Price: $10,250

Magazine capacities, maximum:

Caliber	Normal Floorplate	Rigby Floorplate
.300 Weatherby Magnum	4	5
.338-378 Weatherby Magnum	3	4
.375 H & H Magnum	4	5
.416 Rigby	3	4
.450 Dakota	3	4
.500 Jeffery	3	4

Other calibers upon request.

"Classic Safari"
Single square bridge action with thumbcut. 4-lb. double-pull trigger. Three-position wing safety. Traditional bolt handle. 2-mm silver bead combined with a fold-away 4-mm Holland & Holland-type ivory bead. Express sight with two leaves. Safari-style stock with 1-3/4"/2-1/2" drop. Oil finish. 24" barrel. Length overall 45". Weight from approx. 8 lbs. 3 oz. depending upon caliber. **Standard calibers:** .375 H & H Magnum, 4-shot, or .416 Rigby. 3-shot.
Price: 9,500

"Tradition"
Double square bridge action without thumbcut. Adjustable-pull single-set trigger. Three-position safety with horizontal lever. Low bolt handle. Especially suitable for EXPERT scope mount. "Masterpiece" front sight base with 2.5-mm fluorescent bead. Express sight with two leaves. Stock with straight comb and 1-3/4"/2" drop. Oil finish. 26" barrel. Length overall 47". Weight from approx. 8 lbs. depending upon caliber. **Standard calibers:** .300 Weatherby Magnum, 4-shot, .375 H & H Magnum, 4-shot.
Price: 10,550

Holland & Holland-Type Night Sight
The "Classic Safari" and "Safari" models come with a 4-mm ivory bead that can be flipped up to cover the 2-mm silver bead under poor light conditions.

Express Sight
The rear sight with its two leaves fits into a special ring base. The rear sight base extends around the barrel and has the second recoil shoulder on the underside, which is important for large-bore rifles.

Wing Safety
The "Classic Safari" features a wing safety with "safe" and "fire" clearly indicated in gold.

Peep Sight
For precision sighting with open sights - or to compensate for less than perfect vision - the peep sight mounted on the cocking piece can be raised into position.

KBI/Charles Daly Rifles

FIELD GRADE MAUSER SS

SUPERIOR GRADE MINI-MAUSER

SUPERIOR GRADE SAFARI MAUSER

FIELD SS .22LR SEMI-AUTO

FIELD .22LR TRUE YOUTH BOLT ACTION

Field Grade Mauser Bolt Action
Specifications
Stock: Synthetic **Barrel:** Blue chrome-moly or stainless 22" (magnum: 24") **Calibers:** 22-250, 243, 25-06, 270, 308, 30-06, 7mm, 300 Win. Mag.
Prices: $449
   with stainless barrel 479
   Magnum calibers 479
   with stainless barrel 519

Superior Grade Mini-Mauser Bolt Action
Specifications
Stock: Walnut **Barrel:** 20" high-polish blue
Calibers: 22 Hornet, 223 Rem., 7.62x39, 223
Price: 529
   Left-hand model 559

Superior Grade Mauser
Same specs as Field Grade with walnut stock and high-polish blue
Price: $529
Magnums: 559

Superior Grade Safari
375 H & H, 458 Win. Mag.
Price: 729

Charles Daly 22 Caliber
Field Grade
Bolt-action 6-shot with 22 5/8" barrel or semi-automatic with 10-shot and 21" barrel
Price: 135
   with stainless barrel and hardwood stock: 159
Also available:
   True Youth, single-shot 155
   Youth, 6-shot 149
   Superior Grade 22 MRF 209
   Superior Grade 22 Hornet 369

Kimber Rifles
Kimber 22 Rifles

CLASSIC
SUPERAMERICA
HUNTER SILHOUETTE
SHORT VARMINT TARGET
MODEL 84M CLASSIC

Classic
The Classic features the Kimber 22 action with Mauser claw extractor, 2-position Model 70-type safety, an AA Claro walnut stock with hand-rubbed oil finish and 4-point checkering. The 22" match grade barrel has a scalloped barrel contour. Bead-blasted blue finish and 5-round magazine. Each Kimber is tested to shoot a 5-shot, 50-yard group measuring less than .400". Test targets are included.
Price: $1085

SuperAmerica
This is Kimber's finest rifle. It is similar to the Classic; the AAA Claro stock has full wrap-around checkering and ebony forend tip, cheekpiece and polished blue
Price: 1764
Also available:
Hunter: A Claro walnut stock, 2-point checkering . . . 678
Youth: Same specifications as the Hunter,
   w/ shorter barrel 746

HS
Similar to the Classic, the HS (Hunter Silhouette) is designed for NRA Rimfire Silhouette competition as well as varminting. It has a 24-inch medium heavy barrel with half fluting and walnut high comb Monte Carlo stock. Weight is 7 pounds.
Price: 813

SVT
The SVT (Short Varmint Target) has the Kimber 22 action finished in bead blasted blue, an 18-inch fluted stainless steel match grade bull barrel with satin finish, and a gray laminated wood high comb target stock. It is ideal for both target and varmint shooting.
Price: $949

84M
The Model 84M Classic features a lightweight Mauser action with full length claw extractor, two position Model 70-type safety, match grade trigger and five round magazine with sculpted steel floorplate and trigger guard. The 22-inch match grade barrel has a light sporter contour and match grade chamber. The A-grade premium Claro walnut stock has 20 LPI side panel checkering and a steel grip cap. Available in .243 Win, .260 Rem., 7 mm-08 Rem. and .308 Win. Weight is approximately 5 pounds, 10 ounces.
Price: 917
Varmint Model 7 lbs. 5 oz. in 22-250
   w/26" stainless fluted heavy sporter barrel 1001
Long Master Classic 7 lbs. 5 oz. in 308 win
   w/24" stainless fluted heavy sporter barrel 1001
Long Master VT 26" Stainless steel bull barrel,
   laminate high-comb
   target stock in 22-250., 10 lbs 1122

Krieghoff Double Rifles

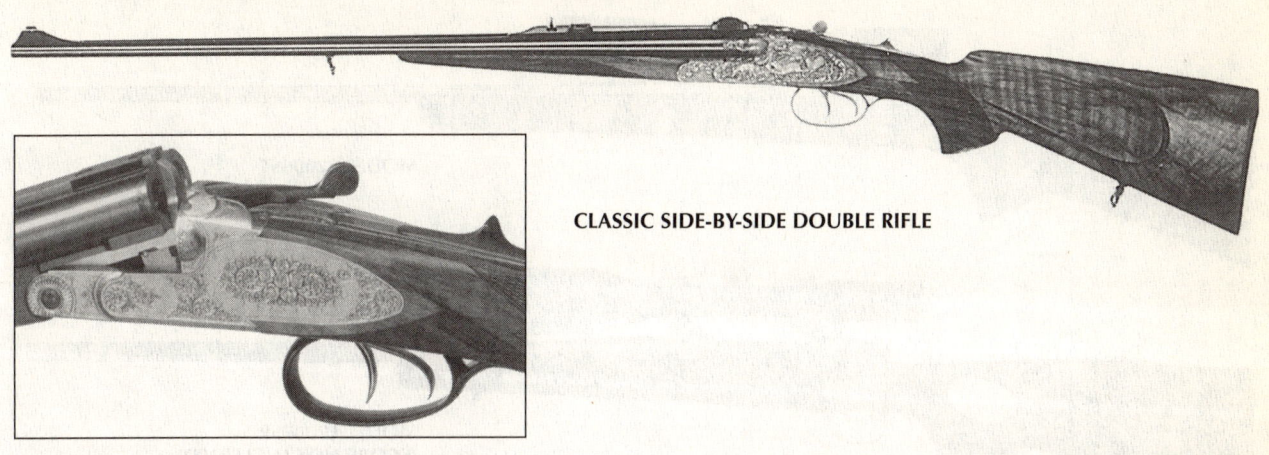

CLASSIC SIDE-BY-SIDE DOUBLE RIFLE

CLASSIC SIDE-BY-SIDE DOUBLE RIFLE
Krieghoff's Classic Side-by-Side offers many standard features, including: Schnable forearm...classic English-style stock with rounded cheekpiece...UAS anti-doubling device...1" quick-detachable sling swivels... Decelerator recoil pad...short opening angle for fast loading ...compact action with reinforced sidewalls...sliding, self-adjusting wedge for secure bolt...automatic hammer safety...horizontal firing-pins...Purdey-style barrel extension.
Specifications
Calibers: Standard—7x65R, 308 Win., 30-06, 30R Blaser, 8x57 JRS, 8X75 JRS, 9.3X74R; Magnum—375 H&H Flanged Mag. N.E., 375 H&H Mag., 416 Rigby, 458 Win. Mag., 470 N.E., 500 N.E. **Action:** Thumb-cocking break/action **Barrel length:** 23.5 **Trigger:** Double triggers with steel trigger guard **Weight:** 7.5 to 11 lbs. (depending on caliber and wood density) **Options:** 21.5" barrel; engraved sideplates

Prices: Standard	$7850
Interchangeable barrels (installed, w/extra forearm)	4500
Magnum	9450
Interchangeable barrels	5500

L.A.R. Grizzly Big Boar Rifle

BIG BOAR COMPETITOR

BIG BOAR COMPETITOR
Specifications
Caliber: 50 BMG **Capacity:** Single shot **Action:** Bolt action, bull pup, breechloading **Barrel length:** 36" **Overall length:** 45 1/2" **Weight:** 30.4 lbs. **Safety:** Bolt stop safety **Features:** All-steel construction; receiver made of 4140 alloy steel, heat-treated to 42 R/C; bolt made of 4340 alloy steel; low recoil (compares to a 12 ga. shotgun)

Prices:	$2570
Parkerized	2670
Nickel Frame	2820
Full Nickel	2920

Lazzeroni Rifles

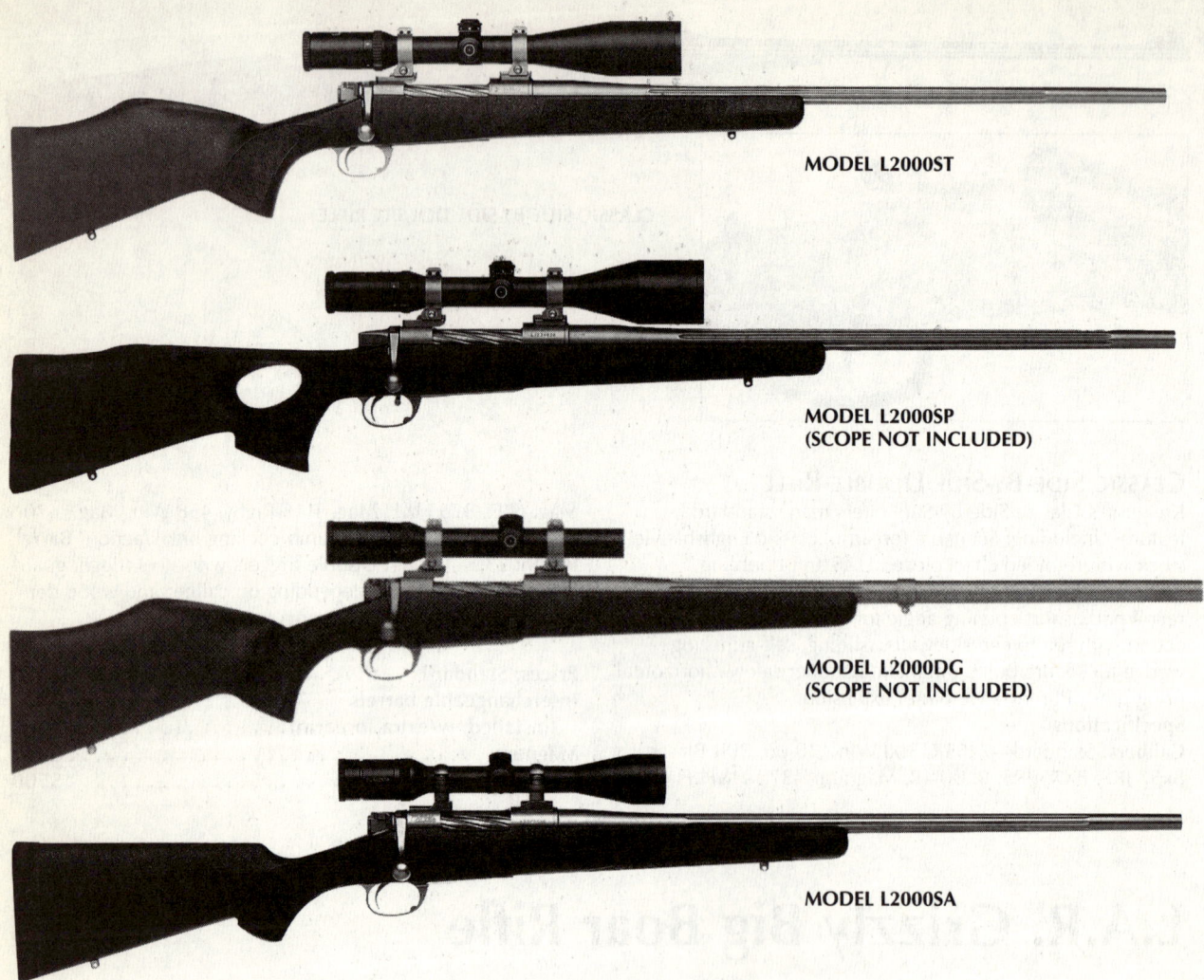

MODEL L2000ST

MODEL L2000SP
(SCOPE NOT INCLUDED)

MODEL L2000DG
(SCOPE NOT INCLUDED)

MODEL L2000SA

These state-of-the-art rifles feature 17R stainless steel receivers with two massive locking lugs, a match grade 416R stainless steel barrel, fully adjustable benchrest-style trigger, and a Lazzeroni-designed synthetic stock that is hand-bedded using aluminum pillar blocks. Included is a precision-machined floorplate/triggerguard assembly.

Model L2000ST
Specifications
Calibers: 6.53 (.257) Scramjet®; 7.21 (.284) FirebirdTM; 7.82 (.308) Warbird®; 8.59 (.338) Titan® **Capacity:** 4 rounds (one in chamber) **Barrel Length:** 27" **Overall Length:** 47.5"
Weight: 8.1 lbs. **Stock:** Lazzeroni fiberglass sporter; right or left hand available
Price: L2000ST **$4,999.00**

Model L2000SP
Specifications
Calibers: 6.53 (.257) Scramjet®; 7.21 (.284) FirebirdTM; 7.82 (.308) Warbird®; 8.59 (.338) Titan® **Capacity:** 4 rounds (one in chamber) **Barrel Length:** 25" **Overall Length:** 45.5"
Weight: 7.8 lbs. **Stock:** Lazzeroni fiberglass thumbhole; right hand only
Price: L2000SP **$4,999.00**

Model L2000DG
Specifications
Calibers: 6.53 (.257) Scramjet®; 7.21 (.284) FirebirdTM; 7.82 (.308) Warbird®; 8.59 (.338) Titan® **Capacity:** 4 rounds (one in chamber) **Barrel Length:** 25" **Overall Length:** 45.5"
Weight: 7.8 lbs. **Stock:** Lazzeroni fiberglass thumbhole; right hand only
Price: L2000DG **4,999.00**

Model L2000SA
Specifications
Calibers: 6.53 (.257) Scramjet®; 7.21 (.284) FirebirdTM; 7.82 (.308) Warbird®; 8.59 (.338) Titan® **Capacity:** 4 rounds (one in chamber) **Barrel Length:** 25" **Overall Length:** 45.5"
Weight: 7.8 lbs. **Stock:** Lazzeroni fiberglass thumbhole; right hand only
Price: L2000SA **4,999.00**

Lazzeroni Ballistics

Long Magnum Cartridges

CARTRIDGE	BULLET	VELOCITY in Feet per Second						ENERGY in Foot-Pounds						PATH OF BULLET Above or below line-of-sight of riflescopes mounted 2" above bore				
Cartridge	Weight Grains	Muzzle	100 Yards	200 Yards	300 Yards	400 Yards	500 Yards	Muzzle	100 Yards	200 Yards	300 Yards	400 Yards	500 Yards	100 Yards	200 Yards	300 Yards	400 Yards	500 Yards
6.53 (.257) SCRAMJET®	85	4000	3689	3399	3128	2874	2633	3021	2569	2181	1847	1559	1309	1.3	2.2	0.0	−5.7	−15.7
	100	3750	3501	3266	3044	2833	2631	3123	2722	2370	2058	1782	1537	1.6	2.4	0.0	−6.2	−16.7
	120	3550	3319	3101	2893	2694	2504	3219	2814	2456	2138	1854	1602	1.9	2.8	0.0	−6.9	−18.7
7.21 (.284) FIREBIRD™	120	3950	3698	3461	3237	3024	2821	4158	3645	3193	2792	2437	2121	1.3	2.1	0.0	−5.4	−14.7
	140	3750	3522	3306	3101	2905	2718	4372	3857	3399	2990	2625	2297	1.6	2.4	0.0	−6.0	−16.1
	160	3550	3351	3161	2979	2805	2637	4478	3990	3551	3155	2796	2471	1.9	2.7	0.0	−6.6	−17.6
7.82 (.308) WARBIRD®	130	3975	3697	3438	3193	2962	2742	4562	3948	3412	2944	2533	2172	1.3	2.1	0.0	−5.5	−15.1
	150	3775	3542	3323	3114	2915	2724	4747	4181	3679	3231	2831	2473	1.6	2.4	0.0	−6.0	−16.0
	180	3550	3352	3163	2983	2810	2643	5038	4493	4001	3558	3157	2794	1.9	2.7	0.0	−6.6	−17.6
	200	3350	3162	2983	2810	2644	2484	4985	4442	3952	3509	3106	2742	2.3	3.1	0.0	−7.5	−20.0
8.59 (.338) TITAN®	185	3550	3334	3129	2933	2746	2566	5178	4568	4023	3535	3098	2706	1.9	2.7	0.0	−6.8	−18.2
	200	3450	3230	3020	2820	2629	2445	5287	4633	4051	3533	3070	2656	2.1	2.9	0.0	−7.3	−19.7
	225	3300	3110	2927	2752	2584	2421	5442	4832	4282	3785	3336	2929	2.4	3.2	0.0	−7.8	−20.8
	250	3150	2977	2810	2649	2494	2344	5510	4920	4384	3896	3453	3050	2.7	3.5	0.0	−8.5	−22.6
10.57 (.416) METEOR®	300	3100	2888	2686	2493	2308	2131	6403	5559	4809	4143	3550	3026	3.0	3.9	0.0	−9.5	−25.6
	400	2800	2634	2474	2320	2171	2028	6965	6165	5440	4784	4190	3656	1.5	0.0	−7.2	−20.8	−41.9

Note: This table was calculated by computer using a standard modern technique to predict trajectories and recoil energies from the best available cartridge data. Figures shown are expected to be reasonably accurate; however, the shooter is cautioned that performance will vary because of variations in rifles, ammunition, atmospheric conditions and altitude. Velocities were determined using 27-inch barrels; shorter barrels will reduce velocity by 30 to 85 fps per inch of barrel removed. Trajectories were computed with the line-of-sight 2 inches above the bore centerline at 3000 ft. elevation. B.C.: Ballistic Coefficient supplied by the bullet manufacturers. An * in the ballistics chart indicates Lazzeroni factory-loaded ammunition.

Short Magnum Cartridges

CARTRIDGE	BULLET	VELOCITY in Feet per Second						ENERGY in Foot-Pounds						PATH OF BULLET Above or below line-of-sight of riflescopes mounted 2" above bore				
Cartridge	Weight Grains	Muzzle	100 Yards	200 Yards	300 Yards	400 Yards	500 Yards	Muzzle	100 Yards	200 Yards	300 Yards	400 Yards	500 Yards	100 Yards	200 Yards	300 Yards	400 Yards	500 Yards
6.17 (.243) SPITFIRE®	70	3812	3492	3195	2917	2656	2410	2259	1895	1587	1323	1097	903	1.7	2.6	0.0	−6.6	−18.2
	85	3618	3316	3036	2992	2523	2287	2471	2077	1740	1450	1202	987	2.0	2.9	0.0	−7.4	−20.3
	100	3419	3181	2957	2743	2539	2344	2596	2248	1942	1671	1432	1220	2.3	3.1	0.0	−7.7	−20.9
6.71 (.264) PHANTOM®	100	3514	3294	3086	2887	2697	2515	2742	2411	2115	1851	1616	1404	2.0	2.8	0.0	−7.0	−18.8
	120	3312	3117	2930	2751	2579	2414	2923	2589	2289	2018	1773	1553	2.4	3.2	0.0	−7.8	−20.9
	140	3109	2934	2767	2605	2450	2299	3005	2678	2381	2111	1866	1644	2.9	3.7	0.0	−8.8	−23.4
7.21 (.284) TOMAHAWK®	120	3563	3333	3115	2908	2710	2521	3383	2961	2587	2254	1958	1693	1.9	2.8	0.0	−6.9	−18.5
	140	3379	3170	2971	2781	2598	2423	3550	3125	2745	2405	2100	1826	2.3	3.1	0.0	−7.6	−20.4
	160	3152	2970	2796	2629	2467	2311	3530	3136	2779	2456	2163	1899	2.8	3.6	0.0	−8.6	−23.0
7.82 (.308) PATRIOT®	130	3571	3318	3080	2855	2640	2436	3681	3180	2740	2354	2013	1713	2.0	2.8	0.0	−7.1	−19.2
	150	3363	3152	2951	2759	2575	2398	3767	3310	2902	2536	2209	1916	2.3	3.2	0.0	−7.7	−20.7
	180	3184	3000	2825	2656	2493	2336	4052	3600	3191	2821	2485	2182	2.7	3.5	0.0	−8.5	−22.5
	200	3012	2838	2671	2510	2355	2205	3626	3221	2853	2519	2217	1943	3.1	4.0	0.0	−9.5	−25.3
8.59 (.338) GALAXY®	185	3201	3002	2811	2629	2454	2285	4210	3703	3248	2840	2474	2146	2.7	3.6	0.0	−8.6	−23.0
	225	2968	2786	2611	2443	2281	2125	4402	3899	3407	2983	2600	2257	3.3	4.2	0.0	−10.1	−26.8
	250	2761	2594	2433	2277	2128	1984	4232	3736	3287	2881	2515	2186	1.6	0.0	−7.4	−21.6	−43.5
10.57 (.416) MAVERICK®	300	2741	2542	2351	2169	1995	1830	5006	4306	3685	3136	2653	2232	1.7	0.0	−7.9	−23.4	−47.5
	400	2452	2302	2158	2019	1885	1758	5341	4710	4138	3622	3159	2747	2.3	0.0	−9.7	−28.0	−56.1

Note: This table was calculated by computer using a standard modern technique to predict trajectories and recoil energies from the best available cartridge data. Figures shown are expected to be reasonably accurate; however, the shooter is cautioned that performance will vary because of variations in rifles, ammunition, atmospheric conditions and altitude. Velocities were determined using 26-inch barrels; shorter barrels will reduce velocity by 30 to 85 pfs per inch of barrel removed. Trajectories were computed with the line-of-sight 2 inches above the bore centerline at 3000 ft. elevation. B.C.: Ballistic Coefficient supplied by the bullet manufacturers.

Lone Star Rifles

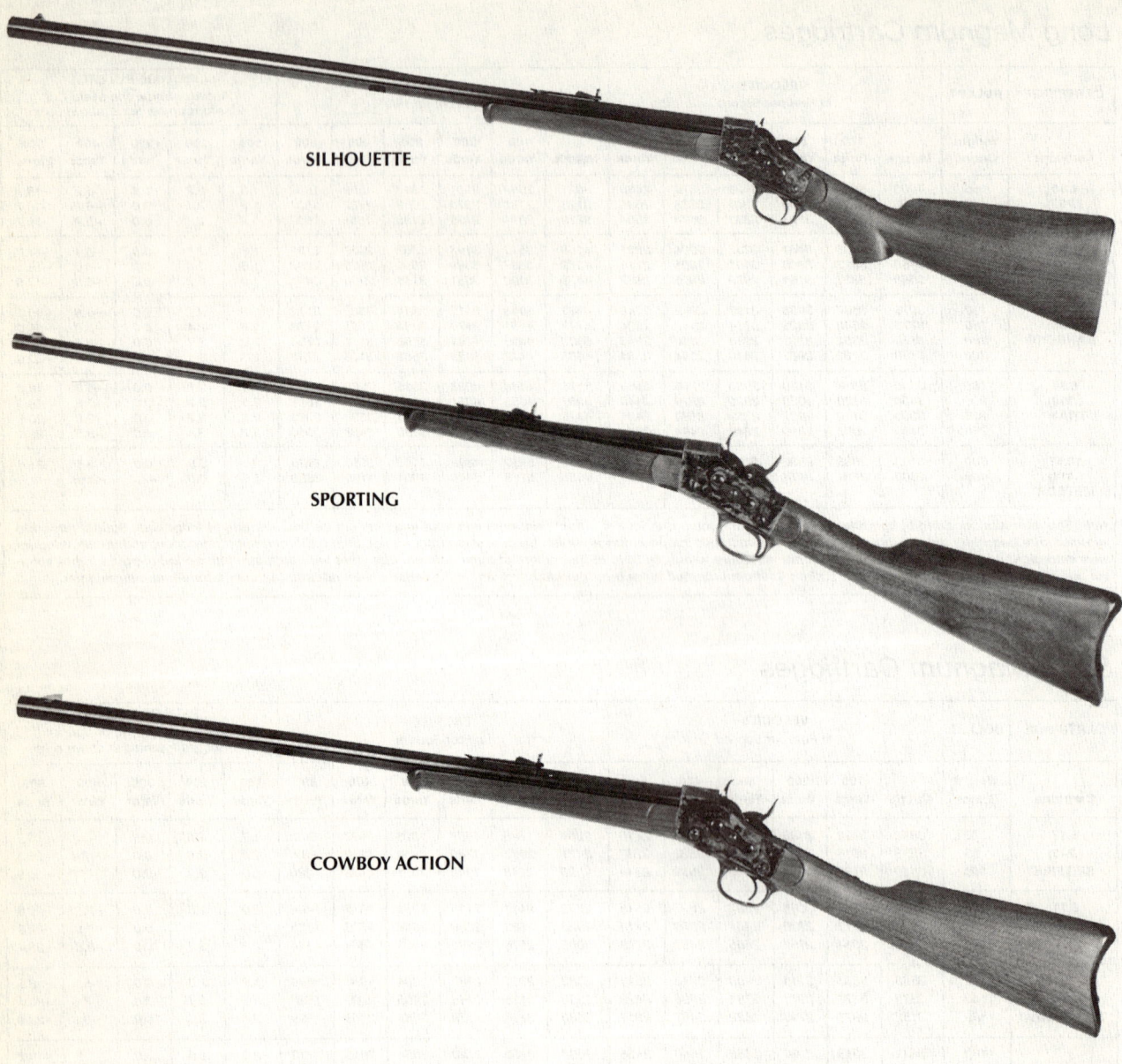

SILHOUETTE

SPORTING

COWBOY ACTION

Lone Star specializes in rolling block rifles, a design popularized by Remington after the Civil War. Some buffalo hunters used rolling blocks because, like the fabled Sharps, they could handle large, powerful cartridges. Lone Star builds commercial and custom rifles on actions manufactured in house. Styles available include:
- Black Powder Silhouette • Creedmoor • Sporting
- Deluxe Sporting • Buffalo Rifle • Custer Commemorative
- Gove Underlever • Cowboy Action

Standard rifles are available in three configurations and come with round barrels, single trigger, case-colored actions and straight-grained American walnut stocks. The match-grade barrels are the same as those used on custom models.

Chamberings for the standard rifles include:
- 32-40, 38-55, 40-65, 40-70, 45-70, 45-90, 45-110, 50-70, 50-90

Price: standard rifles **$1,495**

Custom rifles can be ordered with a host of options in various hunting and target configurations.
Chamberings include (but are not limited too):
- 32-40 • 38-55 • 40-65 • 40-70 • 45-70 • 45-90
- 45-110 • 50-70 • 50-90

Price: custom rifles . . . . **$1995 and up**

All Lone Star rifles are manufactured entirely in the United States.

Magnum Research

MOUNTAIN EAGLE SPORT BARREL

BARRACUDA STOCK STYLE

MAGNUM LITE RIMFIRE

MOUNTAIN EAGLE BOLT-ACTION RIFLE
Specifications
Calibers: 280 Rem., 30-06 Springfield, 7mm Mag., 300 Win. Mag., Capacity: 5-shot magazine (long action); 4-shot (Magnum action) **Action:** SAKO-built to MRI specifications
Barrel length: 24 or 26" **Overall length:** 44"
Weight: 7 lb. 13 oz. **Sights:** None **Stock:** Fiberglass composite **Length of pull:** 13 5/8"
Features: Adjustable trigger; high comb stock one-piece forged bolt; free-floating, match-grade, Krieger, benchrest barrel; recoil pad and sling swivel studs; Platform Bedding System for front lug; pillar-bedded rear guard screw; lengthened receiver ring; solid steel hinged floorplate
Price: $2295
Also available:
Varmint Edition. In 22/250 and 223 Rem.
  with stainless steel Krieger barrel (26") 2295
Mountain Eagle rifles are now available in a left-hand version, and with "Magnum Lite" carbon fiber barrels.

MAGNUM LITE RIMFIRE
The Magnum Research Magnum Lite 10/22 rifle is built on a Ruger action with rotary magazine and blowback, autoloading mechanism. The carbon-fiber barrel is 75 percent lighter than a comparable steel barrel but gives match-quality accuracy. An integral muzzle port reduces whip. Available in .22 Long Rifle and .22 WMR, the Magnum Lite comes with a Hogue composite stock of traditional design, or a Turner laminated "Barracuda" stock.
Price: w/"Barracuda" stock $799
  w/Hogue composite stock 599
  WMR Model w/"Barracuda" 999
  WMR Model w/Hogue 799

MAGNUM RESEARCH TACTICAL RIFLE
.308 Winchester or .300 Winchester Magnum
• MAGNUM LITE™ graphite barrel (26 inch) Unidirectional graphite composite
• Accurized Remington® 700 action
• H-S Precision™ tactical stock
Specifications
Weight: average 8.3 lbs.
Overall Length: adjustable
Adjustable Trigger: 2.5 to 5 lbs.
Height: adjustable comb
Price: 2400
Also Available:
  .223 Rem, 22-250 and 300 Win mag Short

Marlin .22 Rifles

MODEL 60
MODEL 60C
MODEL 70PSS "PAPOOSE"
MODEL 7000
MODEL 795SS

Model 60
Specifications
Caliber: 22 Long Rifle **Capacity:** 14-shot tubular magazine **Barrel Length:** 22" **Overall Length:** 40.5" **Weight:** 5.5 lbs. **Sights:** Ramp front sight with brass bead and Wide-Scan hood; adjustable open rear, receiver grooved for scope mount **Action:** Self-loading; side ejection; manual and automatic "last-shot" hold-open devices; receiver top has serrated, nonglare finish; crossbolt safety **Stock:** One-piece Maine birch Monte Carlo stock, press-checkered, with full pistol grip; Mar-Shield® finish
Price: $181
    Stainess 60SB 231
    Stainess, synthetic stock 60SSK 252
    Stainess, laminated stock 60SS 290
    New 60C with blued steel, camo stock 216

Model 70PSS "Papoose"
Specifications
Caliber: 22 Long Rifle **Capacity:** 7-shot clip **Barrel Length:** 16.25" **Overall Length:** 35.25" **Weight:** 3.25 lbs. **Action:** Self-loading; side ejection; manual bolt hold-open; crossbolt safety; stainless-steel breech bolt and barrel **Sights:** Screw adjustable open rear; ramp front; receiver grooved for scope mount **Stock:** Black fiberglass-filled synthetic with abbrev. forend, nickel-plated swivel studs
Price: $297

Model 7000
Specifications
Caliber: 22 LR **Capacity:** 10 shots **Action:** Self-loading; side ejection **Barrel Length:** 18" heavy target; recessed muzzle (16 grooves) **Overall Length:** 37" **Weight:** 5.25 lbs. **Stock:** Monte Carlo black fiberglass-filled synthetic **Sights:** No sights; receiver grooved for scope mount (1" scope ring mounts standard) **Features:** Manual bolt hold-open; crossbolt safety; steel charging handle
Price: 245
Also available: Model 795. Same as Model 7000 but w/screw-adjustable open rear sight w/brass bead; no scope mount **Weight:** 4.5 lbs. 173

Model 795 SS
Specifications
Caliber: .22 Long Rifle only **Capacity:** 10-shot **Action:** Automatic self-loading, side ejection **Stock:** Monte Carlo black fiberglass-filled synthetic **Barrel:** 18" stainless **Sights:** Adjustable semi-buckhorn folding rear, ramp front sight **Weight:** 4.5 lbs.
Price: 231

Marlin .22 Rifles

Model 25NC (shown) and 25N
A bolt-action, bottom-fed repeater, the 25N holds 7 .22 Long Rifle cartridges. The 22" Micro-Groove barrel ensures fine accuracy. Fitted with open sights, this rifle readily accepts a scope and can be ordered with one. The hardwood stock has a natural finish. Mossy Oak Break-Up camouflage distinguishes the 25NC stock. **Weight:** 5.5 lbs.
Price:
25N $205
  with scope 213
25NC 241

Model 25MN
Specifications
Caliber: 22 WMR (not interchangeable w/other 22 cartridges) **Capacity:** 7-shot clip magazine **Barrel Length:** 22" with Micro-Groove® rifling **Overall Length:** 41" **Weight:** 6 lbs. **Sights:** Adjustable open rear; ramp front sight; receiver grooved for scope mount **Stock:** One-piece walnut finished press-checkered Maine birch Monte Carlo w/full pistol grip; Mar-Shield® finish; swivel studs
Price: 235
  Model 25 MNC with camo stock 272

Model 81TS
Specifications
Caliber: 22 Short, Long or Long Rifle **Capacity:** Tubular magazine holds 25 Short, 19 Long, 17 Long Rifle cartridges **Barrel Length:** 22" w/Micro-Groove® rifling (16 grooves) **Overall Length:** 41" **Weight:** 6 lbs. **Sights:** Screw-adjustable open rear; ramp front **Stock:** Monte Carlo black fiberglass-filled synthetic w/swivel studs and molded-in checkering
Price: $207

Model 83TS
Specifications
Caliber: 22 WMR (not interchangeable with other 22 cartridges) **Capacity:** 12-shot tubular magazine **Action:** Bolt action; positive thumb safety; red cocking indicator **Barrel Length:** 22" with Micro-Groove® rifling (20 grooves) **Overall Length:** 41" **Weight:** 6 lbs. **Sights:** screw adjustable open rear; ramp front sight; receiver grooved for scope mount **Stock:** Monte Carlo black fiberglass synthetic stock; swivel studs
Price: 252
Also available
  Model 883 with walnut stock 328
  Model 883SS with laminate 2-tone stock and
  stainless steel barrel 348

Marlin 17V and 17VS
Marlin's launching pad for the new 17 Hornady Magnum Rimfire. Bolt-action with 22" heavy barrel. VS is stainless steel. Monte Carlo stock with full pistol grip. VS is laminated gray/black with rubber butt pad. Both have a 7-shot magazine capacity. **Weight:** V, 6 lbs. VS, 7 lbs.
Prices:
17V 263
17VS 392

Marlin .22 Rifles

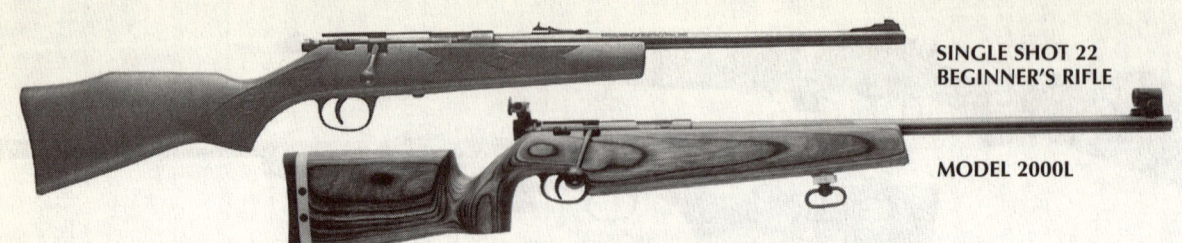

SINGLE SHOT 22 BEGINNER'S RIFLE

MODEL 2000L

MARLIN 15YN "LITTLE BUCKAROO™"
Specifications
Caliber: 22 Short, Long or Long Rifle **Capacity:** Single shot **Action:** Bolt action; easy-load feed throat; thumb safety; red cocking indicator **Barrel Length:** 16.25" (16 grooves) **Overall Length:** 33.25" **Weight:** 4.25 lbs. **Sights:** Adjustable open rear; ramp front sight **Stock:** One-piece walnut-finished press-checkered Maine birch Monte Carlo w/full pistol grip; tough Mar-Shield® finish
Price:. $204
  15 YS stainless 228

MODEL 2000L
Specifications
Caliber: 22 LR only **Capacity:** Single shot **Action:** Bolt action; thumb safety; patented two-stage target trigger; red cocking indicator **Barrel Length:** 22" heavy, selected Micro-Groove w/match chamber and recessed muzzle **Overall Length:** 41" **Weight:** 8 lbs. **Sights:** Fully adjustable target rear peep sight; hooded front sight w/10 aperture inserts **Stock:** Laminated black/grey w/ambidextrous pistol grip; butt plate adjustable for length of pull, height, angle; aluminum forearm
Price: $711

Marlin Lever-Action .22 Rifle

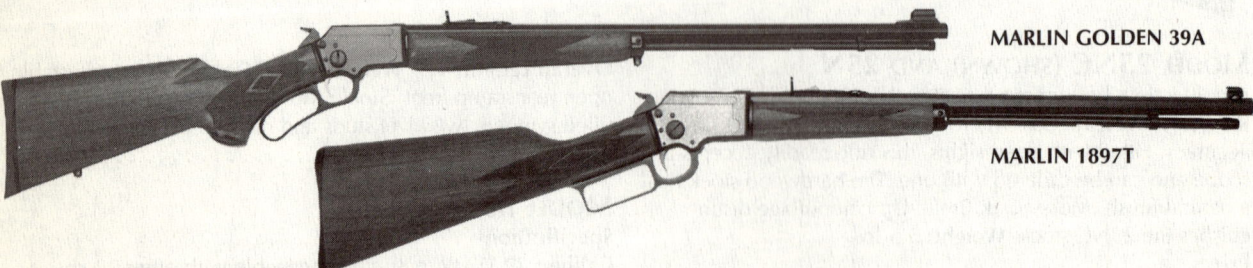

MARLIN GOLDEN 39A

MARLIN 1897T

MARLIN GOLDEN 39A
A premier-quality .22 rifle, the 39A features:
- **Solid Receiver Top.** You can mount a scope on your Marlin 39 by screwing on the machined scope adapter base provided. The screw-on base is a neater, more versatile method of mounting a scope on a 22 sporting rifle. The solid top receiver and scope adapter base provide a maximum in eye relief adjustment. The 39 receiver is clean, flat and sandblasted to prevent glare. Exclusive brass magazine tube
- **Micro-Groove® Barrel.** Marlin's famous rifling system of multi-grooving has consistently produced fine accuracy because the system grips the bullet more securely, minimizes distortion, and provides a better gas seal.
- And the Model 39 maximizes accuracy with the heaviest barrels available on any lever-action 22.

Specifications
Caliber: 22 Short, Long and Long Rifle **Capacity:** Tubular magazine holds 26 Short, 21 Long and 19 LR cartridges **Action:** Lever; solid top receiver; side ejection; one-step takedown; deeply blued metal surfaces; receiver top sandblasted to prevent glare; hammer block safety; rebounding hammer **Barrel:** 24" with Micro-Groove® rifling (16 grooves) **Overall Length:** 40" **Weight:** 6.5 lbs. **Sights:** Adjustable folding semi-buckhorn rear, ramp front sight with Wide-Scan™ hood; solid top receiver tapped for scope mount or receiver sight; scope adapter base; offset hammer spur for scope use—works right or left **Stock:** Two-piece cut-checkered American black walnut w/fluted comb; full pistol grip and forend; blued-steel forend cap; swivel studs; grip cap; Mar-Shield® finish; rubber buttpad
Price:. $540

MODEL 1897 T
Specifications :
Action: Lever action; solid top receiver; side ejection; deep blue **Stock:** American black walnut straight-grip with cut checkering; blued steel fore end cap; hard rubber butt plate **Sights:** Adjustable Marble semi-buckhorn rear; Marble carbine front sight with brass bead **Weight:** 6 lbs. **Capacity:** 21 short, 16 long, or 14 long rifle **Caliber:** 22 Short, long, or long rifle
Price:. 732

Marlin Centerfire Rifles

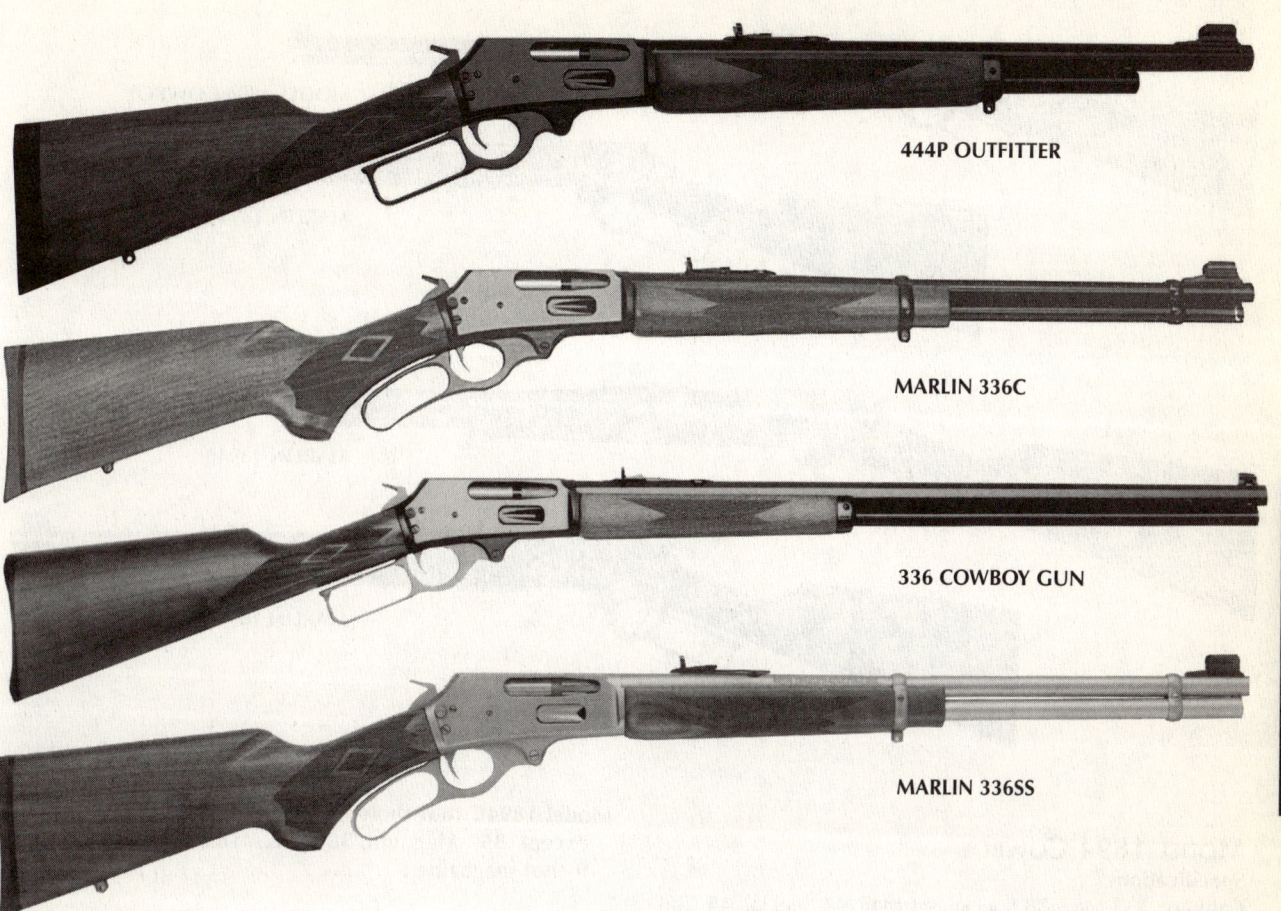

444P OUTFITTER

MARLIN 336C

336 COWBOY GUN

MARLIN 336SS

MARLIN 444P
The 444P "Outfitter" is chambered in .444 Marlin. It features 2/3-length magazines (5-shot capacity), straight-grip walnut stocks with cut checkering, recoil pad.
Length: 37" (barrel 18.5") **Weight:** 6.75 pounds
Price: (with sights) $631

MARLIN 336C
Specifications
Calibers: 30-30 Win., and 35 Rem. **Capacity:** 6-shot tubular magazine **Action:** Lever action w/hammer block safety; deeply blued metal surfaces; receiver top sandblasted to prevent glare **Barrel:** 20" Micro-Groove® barrel
Sights: Adjustable folding semi-buckhorn rear; ramp front sight w/brass bead and Wide-Scan™ hood; tapped for receiver sight and scope mount; offset hammer spur for scope use (works right or left) **Overall Length:** 38.5" **Weight:** 7 lbs. **Stock:** Checkered American black walnut pistol-grip stock w/fluted comb and Mar-Shield® finish; rubber rifle buttpad; swivel studs
Price: 518
Model 336 A, 30-30 only, birch stock 441
Model 336 CC, 30-30 only, camo stock. 491
Model 336 W, 30-30 only,
   walnut stock, gold-plated trigger 447

MARLIN 336
COWBOY GUN
Available in 30/30 and 38/55, this rifle has a 24-inch octagon barrel and 6-shot full-length magazine. The checkered, straight-grip walnut stock has a hard-rubber butt. Ballard-type rifling gives fine accuracy with cast bullets. Marble open sights add a traditional touch.
Length: 42-1/2 inches **Weight:** 7-1/2 pounds
Price: $719

MODEL 336SS
IN STAINLESS STEEL
WITH CUT CHECKERING
30/30 Win. Lever action; 6-shot tubular magazine; approx. wt. 7lbs.; 20" stainless steel Micro-Groove® barrel; hammer block safety; 38.5" o.a. length; genuine American black walnut checkered pistol grip stock with fluted comb and tough Mar-Shield® finish; rubber rifle butt pad; nickel-plated swivel studs; adjustable folding semi-buckhorn rear, ramp front sight with brass bead and removable Wide-Scan™ hood; tapped for receiver sight and scope mount; offset hammer spur for scope use – works right or left. Stainless steel receiver, barrel, lever, trigger guard plate, magazine tube and loading gate. Safety lock included.
Price: 627

Marlin Centerfire Rifles

MODEL 1894 COWBOY
MARLIN 1894
MARLIN 1894P
MARLIN 1894SS

Model 1894 Cowboy
Specifications
Calibers: 357 Mag./38 Special, 44 Mag./44 Special, 45 Colt
Action: Lever action w/squared finger lever
Capacity: 10-shot tubular magazine
Barrel Length: 24" tapered octagon (6 grooves)
Overall Length: 41.5" **Weight:** 7.5 lbs.
Sights: Adjustable semi-buckhorn rear; carbine front
Stock: Straight-grip American black walnut w/cut-checkering and hard rubber buttplate
Features: Mar-Shield™ finish; blued steel forend cap; side ejection; blued metal surfaces; hammer block safety
Price: $802
Also available:
1894 Cowboy Competition in .38 special
  with 20" barrel, 6 lbs. 965

Marlin 1894
Specifications
Calibers: 44 Rem. Mag./44 Special **Capacity:** 10-shot tubular magazine **Action:** Lever action w/square finger lever; hammer block safety **Barrel Length:** 20" w/deep-cut Ballard-type rifling **Sights:** Ramp front sight w/brass bead; adjustable semi-buckhorn folding rear and Wide-Scan™ hood; solid-top receiver tapped for scope mount or receiver sight
Overall Length: 37.5" **Weight:** 6 lbs.
Stock: Checkered American black walnut stock w/Mar-Shield® finish; blued steel forend cap; swivel studs
Price: $544
Also Available:

Model 1894C (not shown) similar to 1894
  except .357 Magnum, 38 Spec., 18.5" barrel,
  9-shot magazine 544

Model 1894P with Ported Barrel
44 Rem. Magnum/44 Special. Lever action; 8-shot tubular magazine; squared finger lever; 16.25" ported barrel with deep-cut Ballard-type rifling; hammer block safety; 33.75" o.a. length; approx. wt. 5.75 lbs.; adjustable semi-buckhorn folding rear, ramp front sight with brass bead and Wide-Scan™ hood; solid top receiver tapped for scope mount or receiver sight. Straight-grip genuine American black walnut checkered stock with tough Mar-Shield® finish; deeply blued metal surfaces; receiver top sandblasted to prevent glare; ventilated recoil pad; swivel studs; blued steel fore-end cap; offset hammer spur for scope use—works right or left. Safety lock included.
Price: 566
Also Available
  Model 1894 CP (357 Mag/38 Spec) 566

Marlin 1894SS
Specifications
Action: Lever Action; side ejection; stainless steel receiver, lever, trigger guard plate **Stock:** straight-grip American black walnut; cut checkering; rubber rifle butt pad; nickel-plated steel fore end cap; swivel studs **Barrel:** Stainless steel, 20"
Sights: Adjustable semi-buckhorn folding rear, ramp front with brass bead and Wide-Scan hood **Weight:** 6 lbs.
Caliber: 44 Rem. Mag., 44 S&W Special **Capacity:** 10-shot
Price: 665

Marlin Centerfire Rifles

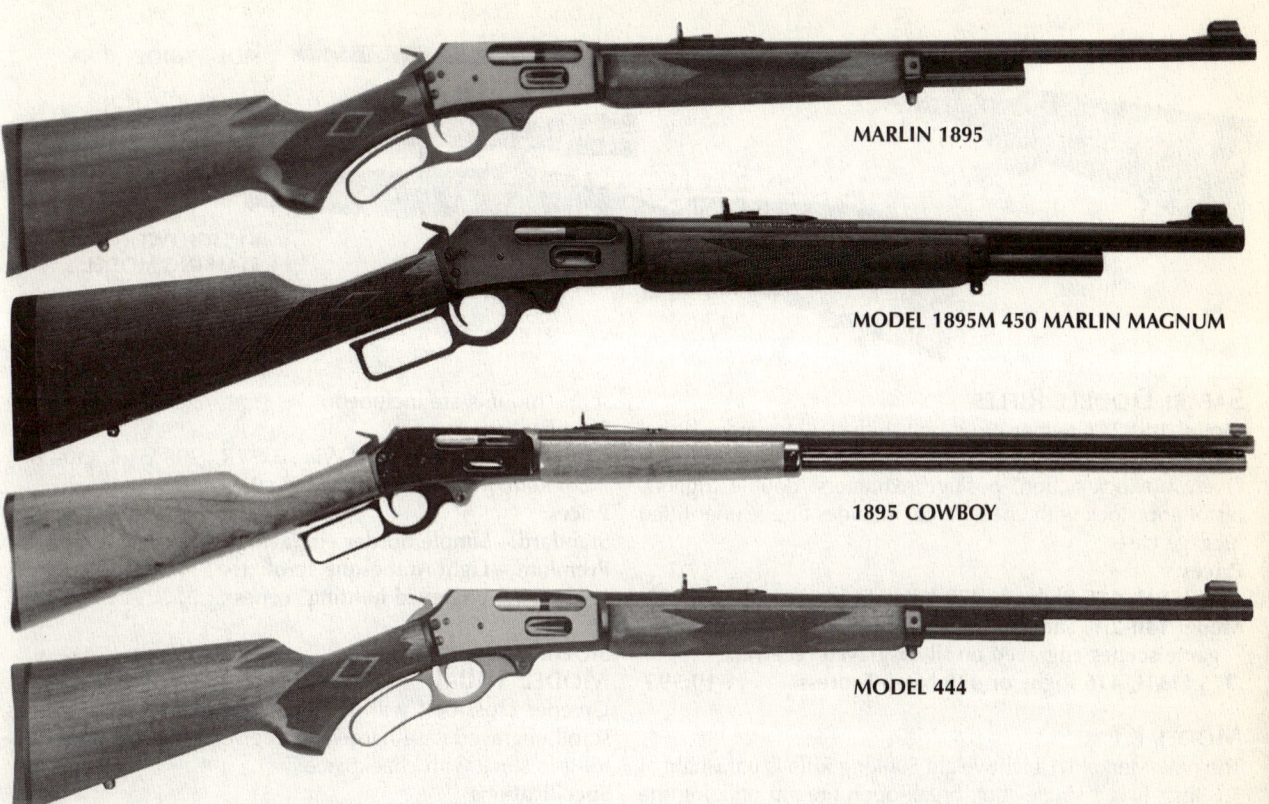

MARLIN 1895

MODEL 1895M 450 MARLIN MAGNUM

1895 COWBOY

MODEL 444

Marlin 1895
Specifications
Caliber: 45-70 Government **Capacity:** 4-shot tubular magazine **Action:** Lever action; hammer block safety; receiver top sandblasted to prevent glare **Barrel:** 22" w/deep-cut Ballard-type rifling **Sights:** Ramp front sight w/brass bead; adjustable semibuckhorn folding rear and Wide-Scan™ hood; receiver tapped for scope mount or receiver sight **Overall Length:** 40.5" **Weight:** 7.5 lbs. **Stock:** Checkered American black walnut pistol-grip stock w/rubber rifle buttpad and Mar-Shield® finish; swivel studs
Price: $618
Also available:
Model 1895G "Guide Gun" with Ported Barrel. Same caliber, capacity, action, sights. Stock has straight grip, ventilated recoil pad. Barrel Length: 18.5" Overall Length: 37" Weight: 6.75 lbs.
Price: 631
    Model 1895 GS in stainless steel 744

Model 1895M 450
Marlin Magnum
Chambered for new belted magnum cartridge. Lever action; 4-shot tubular magazine; 18.5" ported barrel with Ballard-type cut rifling; hammer block safety; 37" o.a. length; approx. wt. 6.75 lbs.; genuine American black walnut straight-grip stock with cut checkering; ventiliated recoil pad; tough Mar-Shield® finish; swivel studs; adjustable folding semi-buckhorn rear, ramp front sight with brass bead and Wide-Scan™ hood; receiver tapped for scope mount or receiver sight; offset hammer spur for scope use – works right or left; deeply blued metal surfaces; receiver top sandblasted to prevent glare. Safety lock included.
Price: $680

Model 1895 Cowboy
45-70 Government. 9-shot tubular magazine; squared finger lever; 26" tapered octagon barrel with deep-cut Ballard-type rifling; hammer block safety; 44.5" o.a. length; approx. wt. 8 lbs.; straight-grip genuine American black walnut stock with hard rubber butt plate and tough Mar-Shield® finish; blued steel fore-end cap; adjustable Marble semi-buckhorn rear, Marble carbine front sight; receiver tapped for scope mount or receiver sight; offset hammer spur for scope use – works right or left; deeply blued metal surfaces; receiver top sandblasted to prevent glare. Safety lock included.
Price: 802

Model 444
Specifications
Caliber: 444 Marlin **Capacity:** 5-shot tubular magazine **Barrel:** 22" w/deep-cut Ballard-type rifling **Overall Length:** 40.5" **Weight:** 7.5 lbs. **Stock:** Checkered American black walnut pistol grip stock with rubber rifle buttpad; swivel studs **Sights:** Ramp front sight with brass bead and Wide-Scan™ hood; adjustable semi-buckhorn folding rear; receiver tapped for scope mount or receiver sight
Price: 618

Merkel Rifles

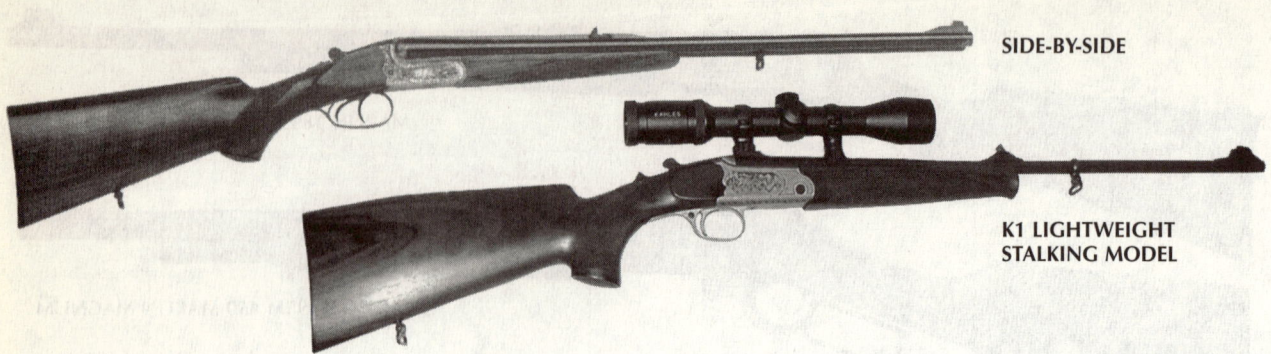

SIDE-BY-SIDE

K1 LIGHTWEIGHT STALKING MODEL

SAFARI DOUBLE RIFLES
Model 140-2, Greener cross bolt with double under barrel locking lugs, scroll engraved silver-grayed receiver, Anson & Deely boxlock action, positive extractors, double triggers, pistol grip stock with cheekpiece, includes fine leather fitted luggage case.
Prices:
.375 H&H, 416 Rigby or 470 Nitro Express $8,995
Model 140-2.1, Same as 140-1, but with fine African game scenes engraved on silver-grayed receiver.
.375 H&H, 416 Rigby or 470 Nitro Express 10,595

MODEL K1
The new Merkel K1 Lightweight Stalking Rifle is ultra-light at 5.6 lbs. It is a single-shot, break-open firearm utilizing the patented Franz Jager action. A cocking/uncocking slide provides a positive safety system. A selector lever offers the shooter a choice of three trigger weights. Quick detachable scope mounts are included.
Specifications
Calibers: .243 Win., .270 Win., 7x57R, .308 Win., .30-06, 7mm Rem. Mag., .300 Win. Mag., 9.3x74R
Prices:
Standard – Simple border engraving $3795
Premium – Light Arabesque scroll 4095
Jagd – Fine engraved hunting scenes 4395

SIDE-BY-SIDE RIFLES
MODEL 140-1
Greener cross-bolt with double-under barrel, locking lugs, scroll-engraved case-hardened receiver, double triggers, pistol-grip stock with cheekpiece
Specifications
Calibers: .308 Win., .30-06 Spr., 7x57R, 9.3x74R
Includes fitted luggage case
Price: 7795

Mossberg Rifles

SSI-ONE SPORTER

SSI-ONE VARMINT

MOSSBERG SSI-ONE SINGLE SHOT INTERCHANGEABLE RIFLE & SHOTGUN
The Mossberg SSI is a bold step into the competitive centerfire rifle market for the 80-year-old company. This hammerless single-shot with quick-change barrels offers a choice of six chamberings and is easy for left-handed shooters to use.
Specifications
Calibers, Gauge: .223 Rem., .22-250 Rem., .243 Win., .270 Win., .308 Rem., .30-06 Sprg., 12 Gauge rifled slug and smoothbore with Turkey choke tube, 3.5" chamber
Finish: Classic Satin finished stock & forend. Matte blue receiver & barrel **Length Overall:** 40" Sporter, Varmint, Slug
Barrel Length: 24" Sporter, Varmint, Slug **Action:** Lever-opening, break-action, top tang safety, selective ejector
Approx. Weight: 8 lbs. Sporter, Slug 10 lbs. Varmint
Sights: Barrel drilled and tapped for scope mounts (scope base included) **Stock:** Select Walnut
Price: $459
Also Available:
SSI-One Varmint 22-250 or 223 with bull barrel

Navy Arms Replica Rifles

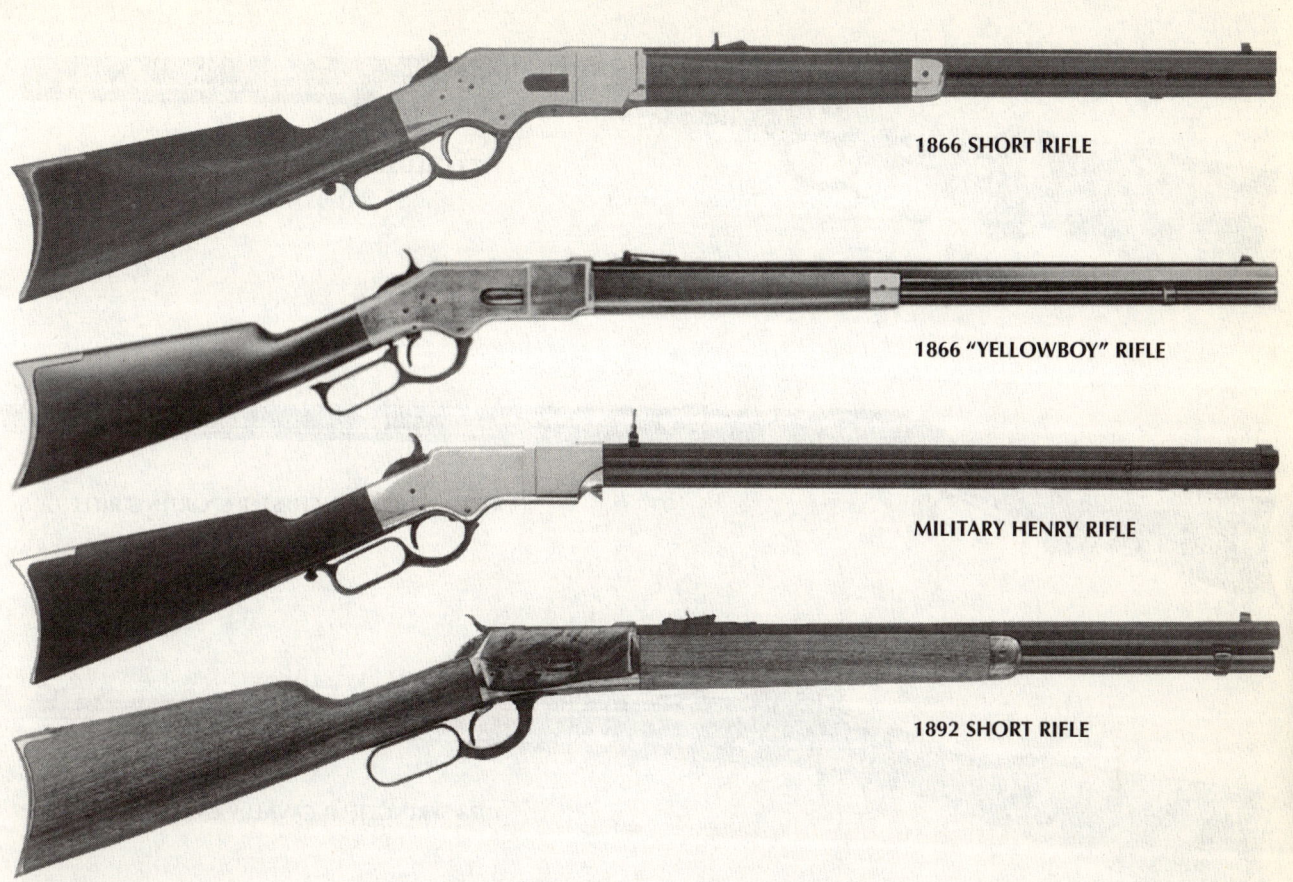

1866 SHORT RIFLE

1866 "YELLOWBOY" RIFLE

MILITARY HENRY RIFLE

1892 SHORT RIFLE

1866 SHORT RIFLE
Designed for the Cowboy Action Shooter, this model features a handy 20" octagon barrel with a semi-buckhorn rear sight.
Specifications
Caliber: .38 Special, .44-40 or .45 Colt **Barrel Length:** 20"
Weight: 7 lbs. 8 oz. **Overall Length:** 39.25"
Sights: Buckhorn rear, blade front
Price: $725

1866 "YELLOWBOY" RIFLE
The 1866 model was Oliver Winchester's improved version of the Henry rifle. Called the "Yellowboy" because of its polished brass receiver, it was popular with Indians, settlers and cattlemen alike.
Specifications
Caliber: 38 Special, 44-40, 45 Colt **Barrel Length:** 24" full octagon **Overall Length:** 42.5" **Weight:** 8.25 lbs.
Sights: Blade front; open ladder rear **Stock:** Walnut
Price: 725
   Carbine version w/19" barrel 715

MILITARY HENRY RIFLE
This accurate replica of "that damned Yankee rifle" – The Henry – gave troops unrivaled firepower in its day. Navy Arms redesigned the highly polished brass frame by specially reinforcing it to handle the demands of skirmishing and Cowboy Action Shooting. Authentic in every detail, including left-side sling swivel and buttplate trap.
Price: $955

1892 SHORT RIFLE
The Winchester 92 came with several barrel lengths. Two are available from Navy Arms. The "Short Rifle" is a replica of the "Texas Special" 92 Winchester that featured a 20" full octagonal barrel. Color casehardened or blued receiver and furniture.
Specifications
Calibers: 357 Mag., 44-40 or 45 Colt
Barrel Length: 24" octagon
Weight: 6.25 lbs. or 7 lbs.
Sights: Blade front; semi-buckhorn rear
Stock: American walnut
Price: 525
Also Available:
   Stainless Steel 565
   Stainless Carbine (20" barrel) 500

IRON FRAME HENRY
Specifications
Caliber: 44-40 or 45 Colt **Capacity:** 13 rounds
Barrel Length: 24" **Overall Length:** 43"
Weight: 9 lbs. **Stock:** Walnut
Finish: Blued or casehardened **Feature:** Steel frame
Price: 1005

Navy Arms Replica Rifles

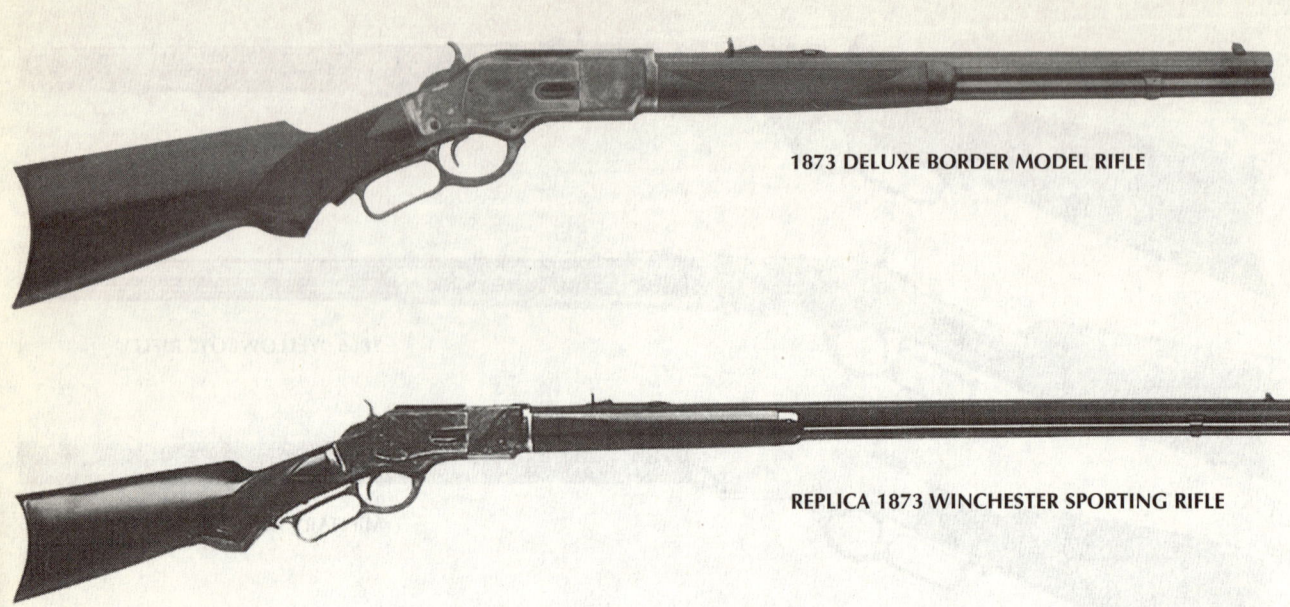

1873 DELUXE BORDER MODEL RIFLE

REPLICA 1873 WINCHESTER SPORTING RIFLE

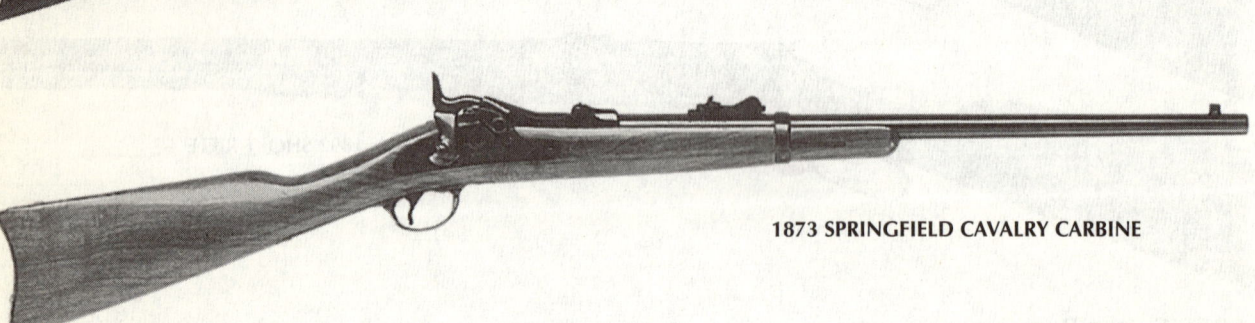

1873 SPRINGFIELD CAVALRY CARBINE

1873 DELUXE BORDER MODEL RIFLE
This deluxe version of the 1873 Border Model features a 20" octagonal barrel and a walnut stock with checkered pistol grip and forend.
Specifications
Caliber: 357 Mag., 44-40 or .45 Colt
Barrel Length: 20" **Overall Length:** 39.25"
Weight: 7 lbs. 6 oz. **Sights:** Blade front, buckhorn rear
Price:..................................... $995

REPLICA 1873 WINCHESTER RIFLE (NOT SHOWN)
Known as "The Gun That Won the West," the 1873 was the most popular lever-action rifle of its time. This fine replica features a casehardened receiver.
Specifications
Caliber: 357 Mag., 44-40 or 45 Colt
Barrel Length: 24" **Overall Length:** 43" **Weight:** 8.25 lbs.
Sights: Blade front; open ladder rear **Stock:** Walnut
Price:..................................... 875
Also available: 1873 Carbine
    (19" barrel) 855
1873 "Border Model" Rifle
    (20" Oct. barrel)........................ $875

REPLICA 1873 WINCHESTER SPORTING RIFLE
This replica of the elegant Winchester 1873 Sporting Rifle features a checkered pistol grip, buttstock, casehardened receiver and blued octagonal barrel.
Specifications
Caliber: 357 Mag., 44-40 or 45 Colt
Barrel Length: 24" **Overall Length:** 43 1/4"
Weight: 8 lbs. 4 oz. **Sights:** Blade front; buckhorn rear
Price: 24" Barrel........................... 995

1873 SPRINGFIELD CAVALRY CARBINE
A reproduction of the classic U.S. "Trapdoor" Springfield carbine used by the 7th Cavalry at The Battle of Little Big Horn.
Specifications
Caliber: 45-70 Government
Barrel Length: 22" **Overall Length:** 40.5"
Weight: 7 lbs. **Sights:** Blade front, military ladder rear
Stock: Walnut **Features:** Saddle bar with ring
Price:..................................... 930

Navy Arms Replica Rifles

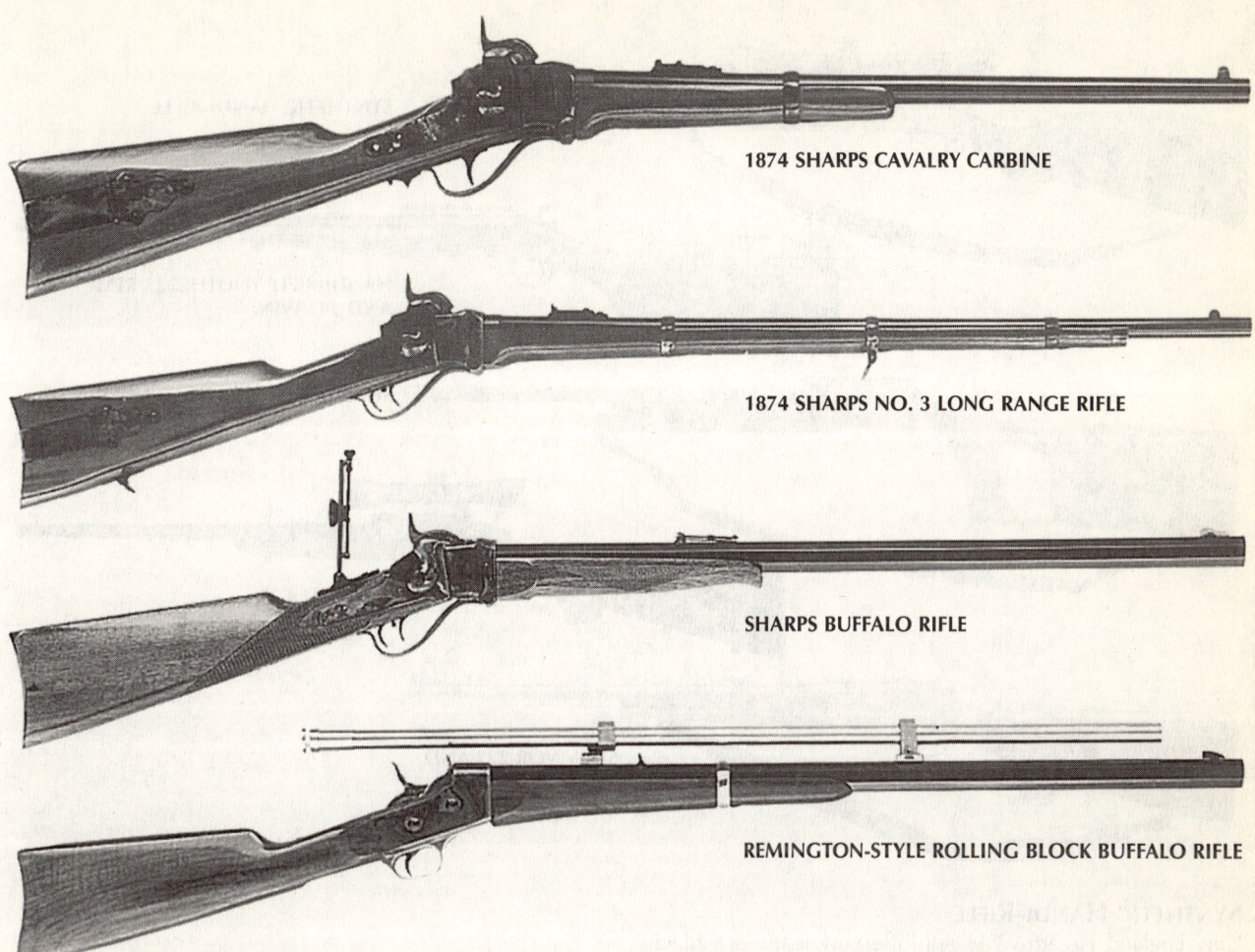

1874 SHARPS CAVALRY CARBINE

1874 SHARPS NO. 3 LONG RANGE RIFLE

SHARPS BUFFALO RIFLE

REMINGTON-STYLE ROLLING BLOCK BUFFALO RIFLE

1874 Sharps Cavalry Carbine
This cavalry carbine version of the Sharps rifle features a side bar and saddle ring.
Specifications
Caliber: 45-70 percussion **Barrel Length:** 22"
Overall Length: 39" **Weight:** 7 3/4 lbs. **Sights:** Blade front; military ladder rear **Stock:** Walnut
Price: $1000

1874 Sharps No. 3 Long Range Rifle
Originally designed for target work, the 1874 Sharps No.3 Long Range rifle was also popular with hunters in the 19th century.
Specifications
Caliber: 45-70 **Barrel Length:** 34" **Overall Length:** 51.2"
Weight: 10 lbs. 14 oz. **Stock:** Walnut
Features: Double-set triggers; casehardened receiver; patchbox and furniture, silver forend cap.
Price: 1860
Also available:
Plains Rifle (32" barrel) 1125

Sharps Buffalo Rifle
This deluxe version of the rifle that came to be known simply as "buffalo gun" was favored by market hunters on the Great Plains after the Civil War.
Specifications
Caliber: 45-70 **Barrel Length:** 28" octagonal
Overall Length: 46" **Weight:** 10 lbs. 10 oz. **Sights:** Blade front, ladder rear (tang sight optional w/set triggers only–$75
Stock: Walnut **Features:** Color casehardened receiver and furniture; double-set trigger
Price: $1160

Remington-Style Rolling Block Buffalo Rifle
This replica of the rifle used by buffalo hunters and plainsmen of the 1800s features a casehardened receiver, trigger guard and walnut stock and forend. The tang is drilled and tapped to accept the optional Creedmoor sight.
Specifications
Caliber: 45-70 **Barrel Length:** 26" or 30"; full octagon
Sights: Blade front, open notch rear **Stock:** Walnut stock and forend **Features:** Shown with optional 32.5" Model 1860 brass telescopic sight $210; Compact Model (18"): $200
Price: With casehardened steel 815
Creedmoor model w/globe front, folding tang sights, checkered pistol grip stock 995

New England Firearms Rifles

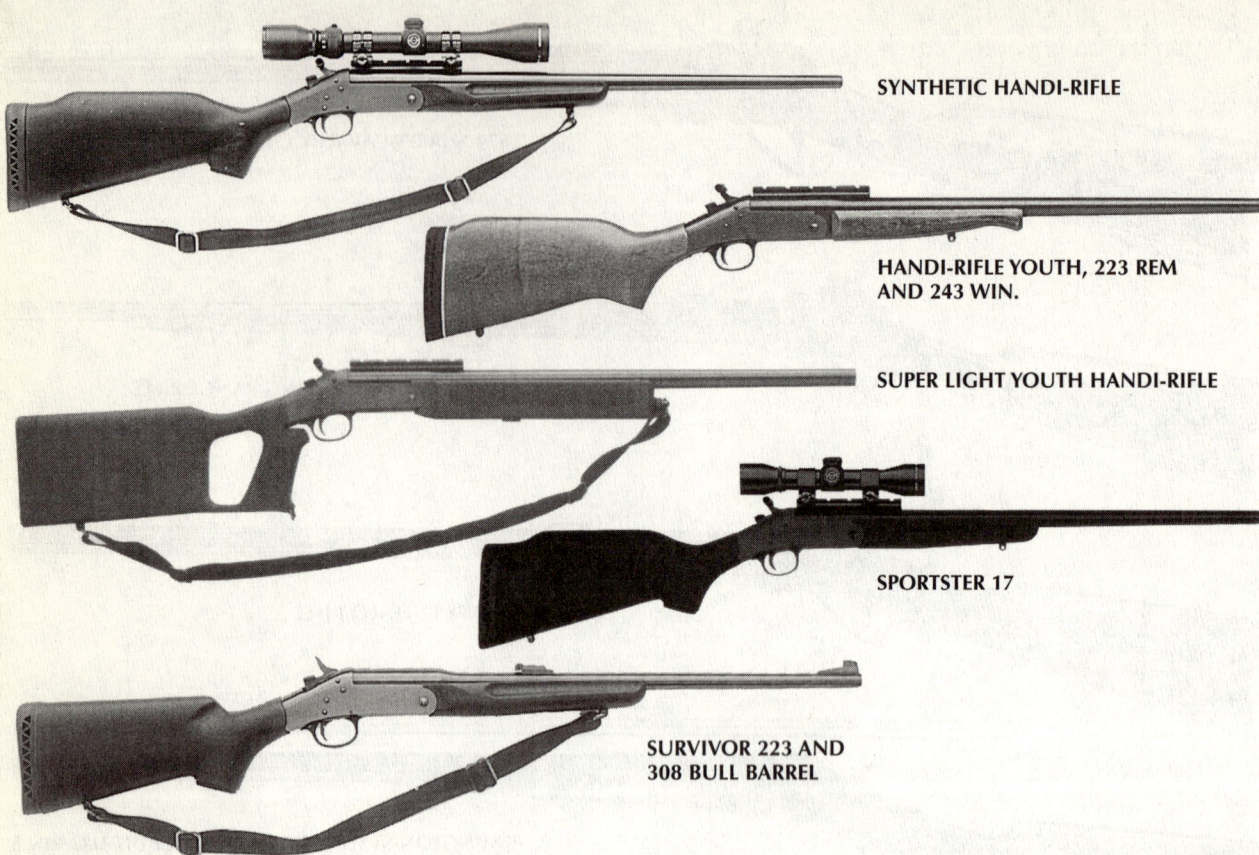

SYNTHETIC HANDI-RIFLE

HANDI-RIFLE YOUTH, 223 REM AND 243 WIN.

SUPER LIGHT YOUTH HANDI-RIFLE

SPORTSTER 17

SURVIVOR 223 AND 308 BULL BARREL

Synthetic Handi-Rifle
New England Firearms® Handi-Rifle now features a black Monte Carlo synthetic stock and forend. This version includes a factory-mounted scope base and an offset hammer extension to ease cocking when a scope is mounted. The rifles all include the patented NEF Transfer Bar System, which virtually eliminates the possibility of accidental discharge.
Specifications
Calibers: 22 Hornet, 223 Rem., 243 Win., 270 Win., 280 Rem., 30-30 Win., 30-06 Springfield; 44 Rem. Mag., 45-70 Gov't **Action:** Break-open; side lever release; automatic ejection **Barrel Length:** 22" (26" in 270 Win.) **Overall Length:** 38" (40" in 270 Win.) **Length Of Pull:** 14.25" Weight: 7 lbs. **Sights:** Ramp front; fully adjustable rear; tapped for scope mount **Stock:** High density polymer; black matte finish; sling swivels; recoil pad
Price: $274
Also available:
Handi-Rifle with hardwood stock in all chambering plus 308 Win., 7x57, 7x64, .357 Mag. with sights or scope base, depending on chambering and barrel style
Handi-Rifle Youth with hardwood stock, 223 Rem. and 243 Win. 264

Super Light Youth Handi-Rifle™
New England Firearms' youth version of its Superlight Handi-Rifle with lightweight synthetic stock and Super Light taper on the barrel. The matte black synthetic stock and forend feature a non-slip finish plus a sling, swivels and recoil pad.
Specifications
Caliber: 22 Hornet, 223 Rem & 243 Win. Action: Single shot; break-open; side lever release; automatic ejection Barrel Length: 20" Overall Length: 33" Drop At Heel: 1 1/8" Drop At Comb: 1 1/8" Length Of Pull: 11.75" Weight: 5 1/3 lbs. Sights: Ramp front; fully adjustable rear; tapped for scope mount Stock: High density polymer; black matte finish; sling swivels; recoil pad
Price: $274
Also available:
Super Light Handi-Rifle in adult configurations
   Sportster youth or adult in 22 LR and 22 WMR . . . 147
The Survivor is available in 223 and 308.
   Features include bull barrel, hollow synthetic stock, thumbscrew take down 227

Sportster 17 Magnum Rimfire
Specifications
Stock: Monte Carlo black matter synthetic, sling swiverl studs, recoil pad **Barrel:** 22" heavy varmint **Sights:** Scope mount rail **Weight:** 7 lbs. **Caliber:** .17 Hornady Magnum Rimfire (Hornady's new .17 Magnum Rimfire is the same length as a .22 Win. mag. cartridge, but generates 2,500 fps muzzle velocity)
Price: 160

New Ultra Light Arms

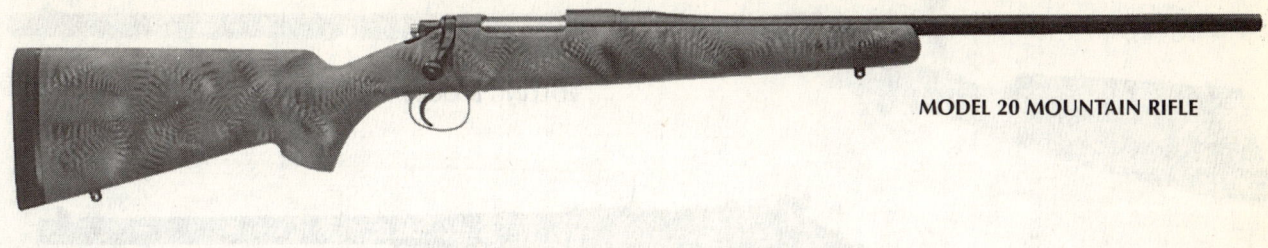

MODEL 20 MOUNTAIN RIFLE

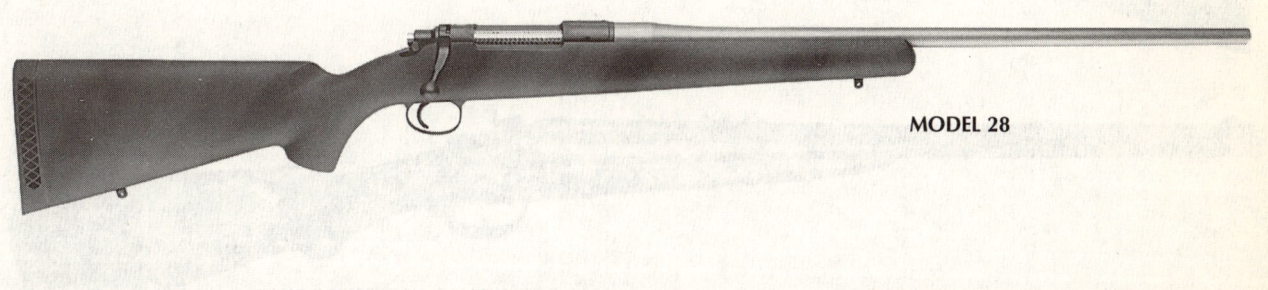

MODEL 28

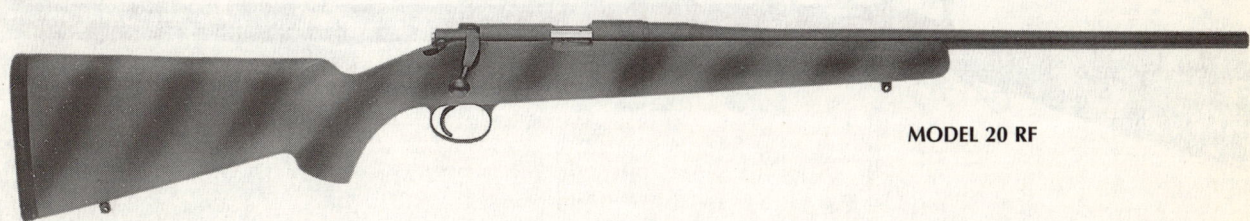

MODEL 20 RF

Model 20 Series
Specifications
Calibers (Short Action): 6mm Rem., 17 Rem., 22 Hornet, 222 Rem., 222 Rem. Mag., 22-250 Rem., 223 Rem., 243 Win., 250-3000 Savage, 257 Roberts, 257 Ackley, 7x57 Mauser, 7X57 Ackley, 7mm-08 Rem., 284 Win., 300 Savage, 308 Win., 358 Win. **Barrel Length:** 22" **Weight:** 4.75 lbs. **Safety:** Two-position safety allows bolt to open or lock with sear blocked **Stock:** Kevlar/Graphite composite; choice of 7 or more colors
Price: $2500
    Left Hand 2600

Also Available:
Model 24 Series (Long Action) in 270 Win., 30-06, 25-06, 280 Rem., 280 Ackley, 338-06, 35 Whelen Weight: 5.25 lbs.
Barrel Length: 22" 2600
    Same as above in Left-Hand Model 2700
Model 28 Series (Magnum Action) in 264 Win.,7mm Rem., 300 Win., 338 Win., 300 WSM, 270 WSM, 7mm WSM

Weight: 5.5 lbs. **Weight:** 5.4 lbs.
Barrel Length: 24" $2900
    Same as above in Left-Hand Model 3000
Model 40 Series (Magnum Action) in 300 Wby. and 416 Rigby Weight: 6.5 lbs. and up
Barrel Length: 24" 2900
    Same as above in Left-Hand Model 3000

Model 20 Series
Specifications
Caliber: 22 LR **Barrel Length:** 22" (Douglas Premium #1 Contour) **Weight:** 5.25 lbs. **Sights:** None (drilled and tapped for scope) **Stock:** Composite **Features:** Recoil pad; sling swivels; fully adjustable Timney trigger; 3-function safety; color options
Price:
Single Shot. 800
    Repeater. 850

Pedersoli Replica Rifles

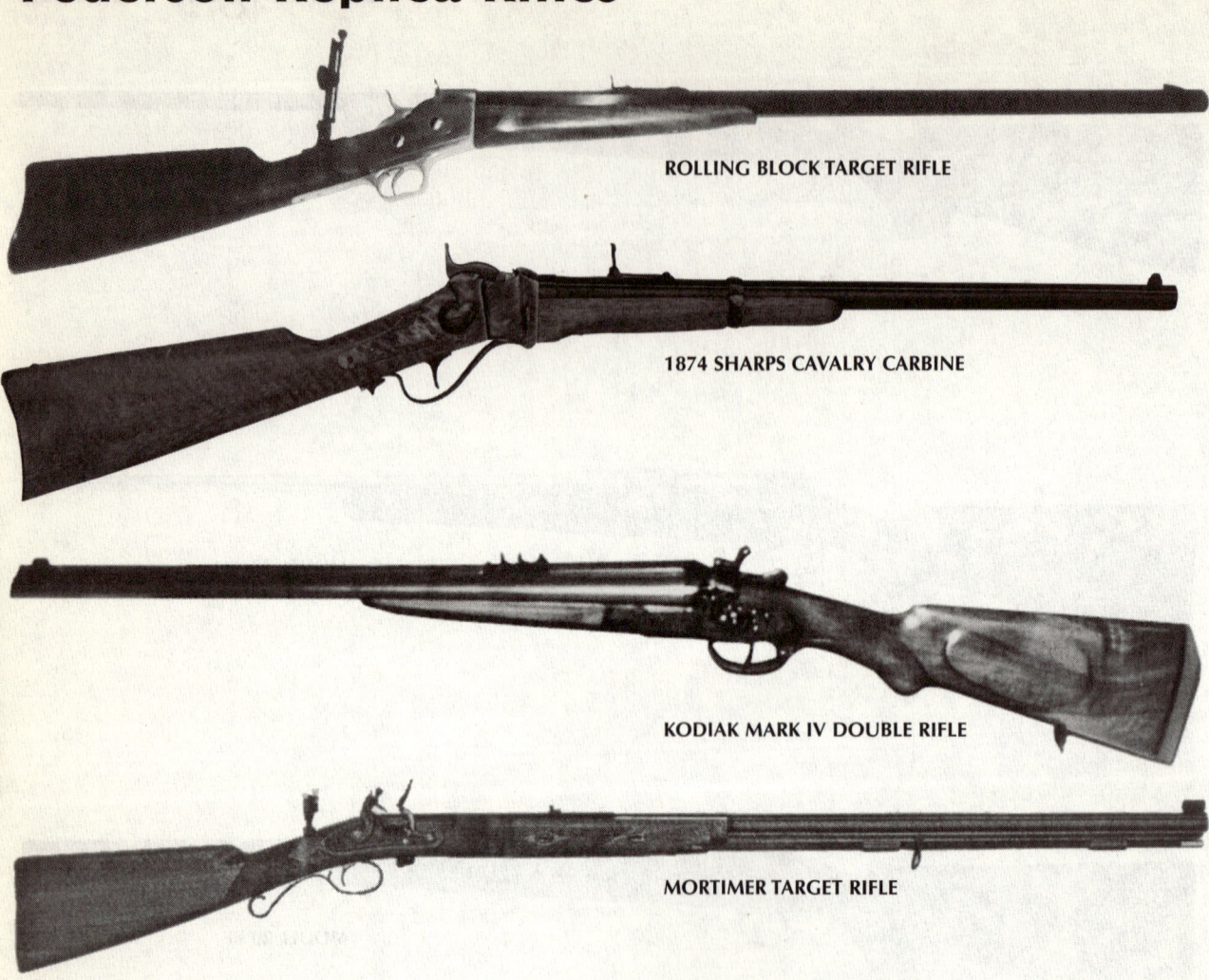

ROLLING BLOCK TARGET RIFLE

1874 SHARPS CAVALRY CARBINE

KODIAK MARK IV DOUBLE RIFLE

MORTIMER TARGET RIFLE

ROLLING BLOCK TARGET RIFLE
Specifications
Calibers: 5-70 and 357 **Barrel length:** 30" octagonal (blued)
Weight: 9 1/2 lbs. (45-70); 10 lbs. (357) **Sights:** Adjustable rear sight; tunnel modified front (all models designed for fitting of Creedmoor sight)
Prices: $875
Also available:
Buffalo, Big Game, Sporting, Baby Carbine,
  Custer, Long Range Creedmoor . . . . 775–$1150

SHARPS 1874 CAVALRY MODEL
Specifications
Caliber: .45/70 **Barrel length:** 22" round (6 grooves)
Overall length: 39" **Weight:** 8.4 lbs.
Price: 975
Also available:
Sharps 1874 Infantry Rifle (.45/70 set trigger,
  30" barrel) 1195
1874 Sharps Sporting Rifle .40/65 or 45/70 set
  triggers, 32" oct. barrel. 1095
1874 Sharps Long Range Rifle (.45/70, .45/90,
  .45/120, 34" half octagon barrel, target sights) . . 1495

KODIAK MARK IV DOUBLE RIFLE
Specifications
Calibers: 45-70, 9.3x74R, 8x57JSR **Barrel length:** 22" (24" 45-70) **Overall length:** 39" (40.5" 45-70)
Weight: 8.24 lbs. (9.7 lbs. 45/70)
Prices:
45-70. . . . . $3125
8x57, 9.3x74 3250
Also available: Kodiak Mark IV
  with interchangeable 20-gauge barrel 4375

MORTIMER TARGET RIFLE
Specifications
English-style European walnut stock with cheekpiece and hand checkering; color-case-hardened lock; 54 caliber, 7-groove barrel (octagon to round) 36" long.
Specifications
Overall length: 52" **Weight:** 8.8 pounds
Price: 1025

Prairie Gun Works

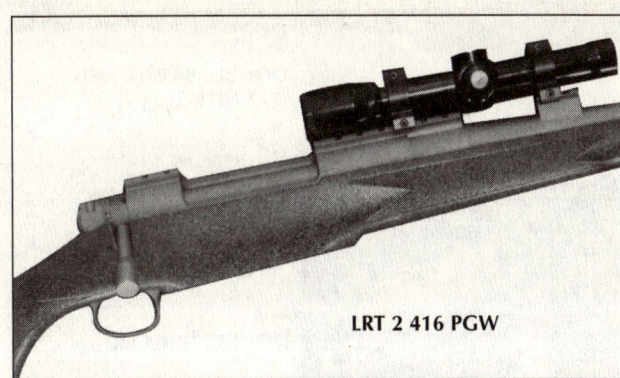

LRT 2 416 PGW

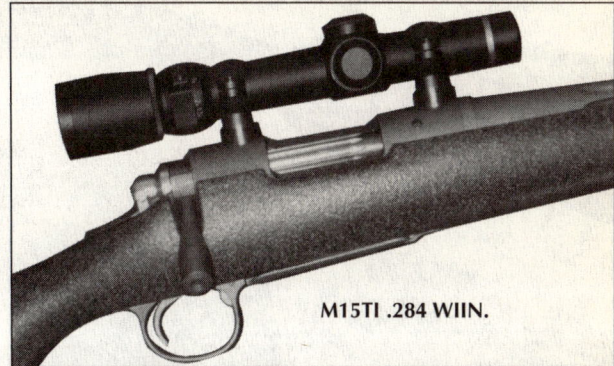

M15TI .284 WIIN.

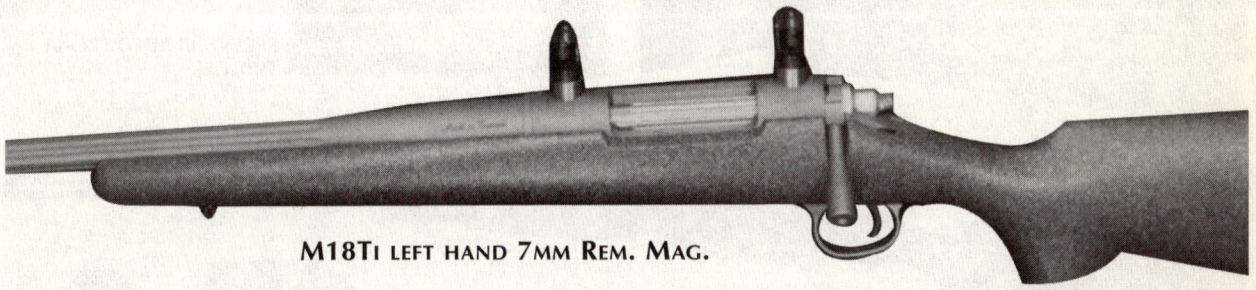

M18Ti LEFT HAND 7MM REM. MAG.

LRT-2 SERIES RIFLES
Dangerous game, long range target, and tactical versions are available in this series. The smallest rounds that this action is suitable for is the .378 and Rigby based magnums. These rifles are ideal for large calibers such as the .505 Gibbs (and PGW line of wildcats), and other large rounds like the .585 Nyati. A 4-shot magazine box is available on this rifle. The .408 Cheyenne (.416) is capable of firing a 400-grain bullet at over 3000-fps, making this the flattest shooting and hardest hitting .416 on the market. Stainless pillars and McMillan "Express" or Tactical stocks hold the recoil. These rifles are available with several different scope mount/sight options, plus muzzle brakes. Weights in this series range from 10 to 18 pounds.

M15 AND M18 SERIES RIFLES
Lightweight rifles based on Ti series of Titanium rifle actions. These rifles feature match grade stainless barrels, kevlar/glass stocks, Titanium scope bases, fully adjustable triggers, and customer supplied specifications, such as length of pull, barrel length, and twist. The M15Ti rifle (short) is suitable for cartridges up to the size of the .284 Win. and its wildcats. The M18Ti rifle (long) is suitable for cartridges up to the Remington "Ultramag" and its wildcats. These rifles can be built from 4.25 lbs. to 6.25 lbs.

Some of the unique features found on the Ti series rifles: cone breech, 1/4"-28 base/ring screw attachment, wire EDM lugways, one piece bolt, double plunger ejectors, Sako type extraction, left- or right-hand bolt/port configurations available, aluminum pillar bedding, removable muzzle brake with cap, barrel flutes X8.

Prices:

M15Ti Ultralight	from $2800
Mi8Ti Ultralight	from 2800
SS Series Big Game (same actions as Ti, but stainless)	from 2500
LRT-2	from 3800
LRT-3 (50 BMG target)	from 4200
Coyote & CoyotTi Benchrest	from 2500
Timberwolf Super Magnum Tactical	from 4000
M15 & M18 Varmint	from 2400
Coyote & CoyoTi Tactical Rifle Systems	from 3300

MODEL M-15 AND M-18Ti ULTRA LITE
(NOT SHOWN)
Specifications
Caliber: Most Short Action calibers **Action:** Remington 700 Short Action **Barrel length:** 22" Douglas Match Grade **Length of pull:** 13.5" **Weight:** 4.5-5.25 lbs. **Stock:** Fiberglass-Kevlar composite w/integral recoil lug; recoil pad installed **Finish:** Black or grey textured finish **Sights:** Custom aircraft-grade aluminum scope mounts **Features:** Trigger set and polished for 3 lb. pull; bolt fluted, hollowed and tapped w/Ultra Lite custom firing pin and bolt shroud

Also available:
Coyote and CoyoTi Benchrest: Integral scope mounts, coned breech, integral recoil lug, three locking lugs; BR system.
Timberwolf Super Magnum Tactical: Single shot or repeater for long-range shooting. Specifically disgned for the .338 Lapua and suitable for .408 Chevy-Tav and .416 PGW.
Coyote & Coyoti Tactical Rifle Systems: based on the Coyote and a little brother of the Timberwolf. Available in any of the McMillan tactical stocks.

Purdey
Double Barrel Rifles

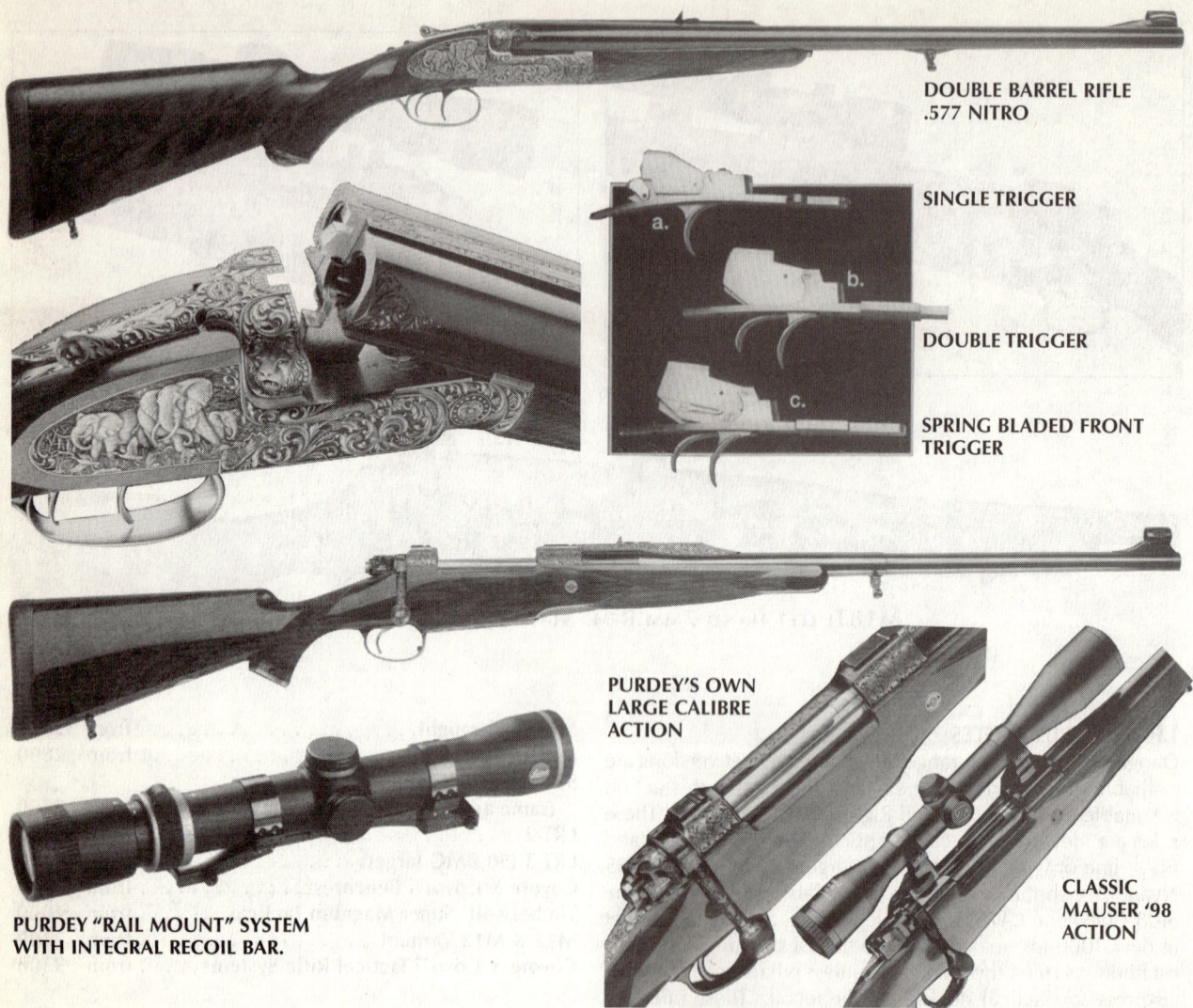

DOUBLE BARREL RIFLE .577 NITRO

SINGLE TRIGGER

DOUBLE TRIGGER

SPRING BLADED FRONT TRIGGER

PURDEY'S OWN LARGE CALIBRE ACTION

CLASSIC MAUSER '98 ACTION

PURDEY "RAIL MOUNT" SYSTEM WITH INTEGRAL RECOIL BAR.

Double Barrel Rifle .577 Nitro

The word "Express" was coined by James Purdey the younger to publicize his rifles. He likened their performance to a railway or "Express" train, which was heavy, travelled with great velocity and had a flat trajectory.

Purdey's double-barrel Express rifles are built to customer specifications on actions sized to each particular cartridge. Standard chamberings include .375 H&H Magnum and .470, .577 and .600 Nitro Express. The Purdey side-by-side action patented in 1880 is still made now with only very minor changes. The action mechanism, designed by Frederick Beesley, retains a portion of the energy in the mainsprings to facilitate the opening of the gun.

The over-under is derived from the Woodward, patented in 1913. The action blocks for all guns are cut from certified forgings, for consistency of grain throughout, and are so fitted to the barrels as to give an absolute joint.

The actioner then fits the fore-part, the locks, the strikers and the safety work before finally detonating the action.

A – Single trigger

The Purdey single trigger works both by inertia and mechanically. It is simple, effective and fast. The firing sequence is fixed, therefore no barrel selection is possible.

B & C – Double Triggers

The standard double triggers (B) can be augmented with an articulated front trigger (C). This device alleviates damage to the back of the trigger finger on discharge.

Purdey makes its own dedicated actions for bolt rifles in the following calibers: .375 H&H, .416/450 Rigby or other, .500 and .505 Gibbs.

The action length is suited to cartridge length in each caliber. Mauser Square Bridge and Mauser '98 actions are available.

Rail Mount System

This is Purdey's own system for big bolt rifles. It is very secure and facilitates fast on/off. Rings and mounts are all made with an integral recoil bar from a single piece of steel. This system is recommended for Purdey actions and Mauser Square Bridge actions.

Remington Bolt-Action Rifles

MODEL 700 BDL DM

MODEL 700 BDL SS CAMO

MODEL 700 BDL SS

Model 700 BDL DM

The Model 700 Remington bolt-action rifle first appeared in 1962. Since then it has become one of the most popular rifles of all time and is now available in myriad configurations and chamberings.

Model 700 BDL DM rifles feature the standard Remington BDL barrel contour, with 22" barrels on standard-caliber models and 24" barrels on magnum-caliber rifles. The detachable box magazine holds 4 standard rounds, 3 magnums. Chamberings include .270, 30-06, 7mm Rem. Mag., .300 Win. Mag. Stainless version comes in .25-06, .270, .280, 7mm-08, .30-06, 7mm Rem. Mag., .300 Win. Mag. All barrels have a hooded front sight and adjustable rear sight. Additional features include polished blued-metal finish, high-gloss, Monte Carlo-style walnut stock, white line spacers, 20 lines-per-inch checkering, recoil pad and swivel studs. All models feature fine-line engraving on receiver front rings, rear bridges, non-ejection receiver sides and floorplates.

**Prices: Model 700 BDL DM..................$728
Magnum..................................755
Stainless...........................775 - 801**

Model 700 BDL SS Camo

Special Edition Rocky Mountain Elk Foundation rifle. 7mm Remington Ultra Mag; Realtree Hardwoods Camo stock; 416 stainless barrel, bolt and receiver. Portion of proceeds donated to RMEF.
Price:..808

Model 700 BDL and BDL SS

This Model 700 features the Monte Carlo American walnut stock finished to a high gloss with fine-cut checkering. Also includes a hinged floorplate, sling swivel studs, hooded ramp front sight and adjustable rear sight. Also available in stainless synthetic version (Model 700 BDL SS) with stainless-steel barrel, receiver and bolt plus synthetic stock for maximum weather resistance.

Model 700 BDL custom deluxe
**Prices: In 222 Rem., 22-250 Rem., 223 Rem., 243 Win.,
.280, 25-06 Rem., 270 Win., 30-06, 7mm-08......$661
In 17 Rem., 7mm Rem. Mag., 300 Win. Mag.,
.338 Win. Mag..............................688
Ultra Mags (7mm, 300, 338, 375)..............701
Left Hand in 270 Win., 30-06..................688
Left Hand in 7mm Rem. Mag....................715
Left Hand Ultra Mags (7mm, 300, 338)..........728
Model BDL SS (Stainless Synthetic)
In 270 Win. 30-06...........................708
In 7357mm Rem. Mag.,
300 Win. Mag., .338 Win. Mag., .375 H&H Mag..735
In 7mm Rem Ultra Mag, .375 Rem Ultra Mag.,
.300 Rem. Ultra Mag., .338 Rem. Ultra Mag.....748**

MODEL 700 BDL SS DM

Barrel length: 25.5" (magnum contour barrel). Stainless synthetic detachable magazine.
**Price: 25-06, 270, 280, 30-06..................775
In 7mm Rem Mag., 300 Win Mag..............801**

Remington Bolt-Action Rifles

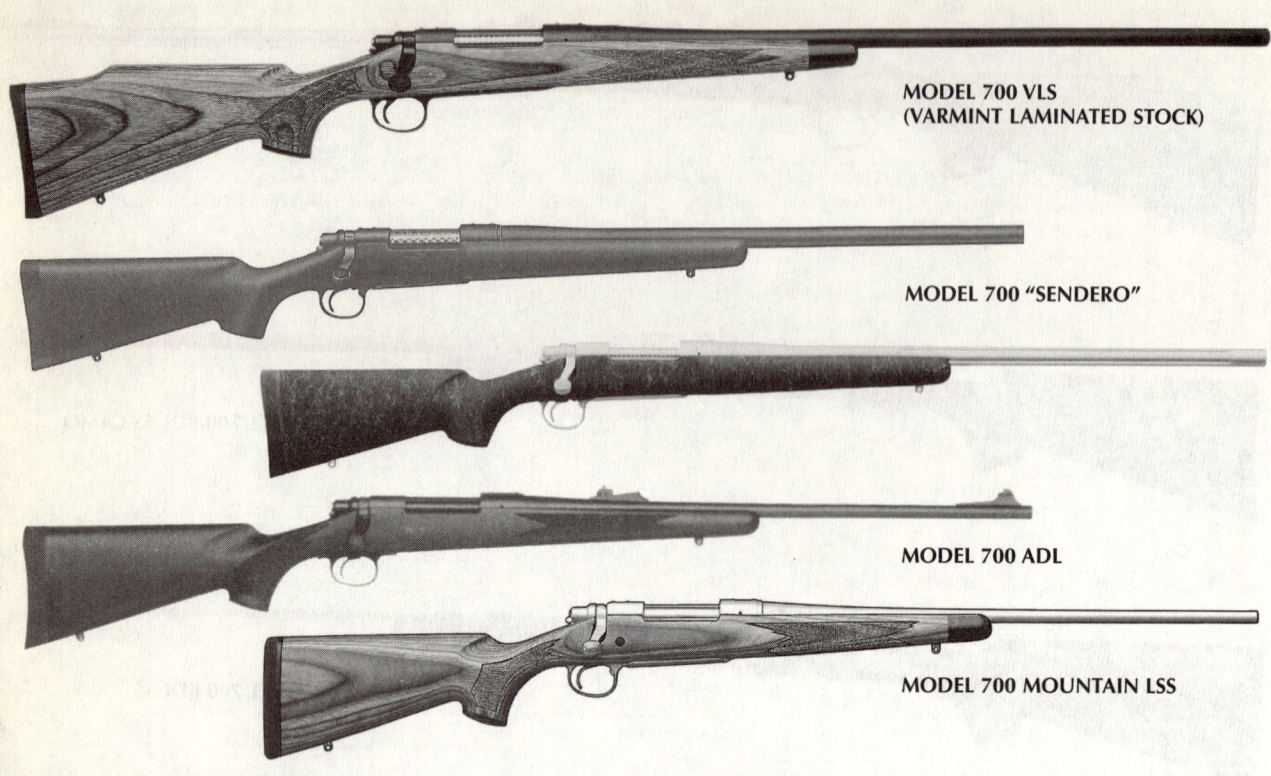

MODEL 700 VLS (VARMINT LAMINATED STOCK)

MODEL 700 "SENDERO"

MODEL 700 ADL

MODEL 700 MOUNTAIN LSS

MODEL 700 VLS (VARMINT LAMINATED STOCK)
The Model 700 VLS features a blued, heavy-contour varmint barrel, laminated synthetic stock, hinged magazine floorplate and sling swivel studs.
Barrel length: 26" **Overall Length:** 45.5" **Weight:** 9 lbs.
Length of pull: 13 3/8" **Drop at comb:** 1/2" **Drop at heel:** 3/8"
Chamberings: .223, .22-250, 6mm Rem., .243, .308
Price: $705
VS with synthetic stock in .223, .22-250, .308...... 788
Left hand, same calibers........................... 815
  VSSF w/26" fluted barrel in 22-250 Rem.,
  223 Rem., 220 Swift........................... 949

MODEL 700 "SENDERO"
Remington's Sendero rifle combines the accuracy features of the Model 700 Varmint Synthetic with long action and magnum calibers for long-range hunting. The 26-inch barrel has a heavy varmint profile and features a spherical concave crown. For additional specifications, see table on the following page.
Price: .25-06,...................................... 788
  Magnum: 7mm Rem. Mag., .300 Win. Mag....... 815

MODEL 700 SENDERO SF (STAINLESS FLUTED)
This version of the Model 700 Sendero features satin-finished stainless steel receiver and bolt and a 26-inch heavy stainless barrel with six longitudinal flutes designed to improve heat dissipation and reduce gun weight (8.5 lbs.). A spherical, concave crown protects the muzzle. Other features include a composite synthetic fiberglass stock, graphite reinforced by aramid fiber, and a full-length aluminum bedding block.
Chamberings: .25-06, 7mm Rem. Mag, 7STW, .300 Win. Mag., .300 Ultra Mag., .338 Ultra Mag., 7mm Rem Ultra Mag
Price: $949
  Magnum.. 976
  Ultra Magnum..................................... 989

MODEL 700 ADL
Synthetic model has a fiberglass-reinforced synthetic stock, positive checkering, straight comb, raised cheekpiece and black rubber recoil pad. Stock and blued metalwork have a non-reflective black matte finish. Also available in satin finished walnut stock w/cut checkering.
Price: ADL Synthetic............................... 484
  Magnum Synthetic............................... 511
  Youth (1" shorter)............................... 484
  ADL Deluxe...................................... 559
  Deluxe Magnum................................. 585

MODEL 700 LSS AND MOUNTAIN LSS
416 stainless steel barrel, bolt and receiver; gloss gray laminated hardwood stock. Mountain version has 22" mountain-contour barrel and satin-finished brown laminated stock
Price: LSS – 7mm Rem. Mag., .330 Win. Mag....... 803
  7mm, .300, .338, .375 Rem. Ultra Mag.......... 816
  (left hand versions: $843)
  LSS Mountain - .260, 7mm-08, .270, .30-06..... 776

Remington Bolt-Action Rifles

MODEL 700 CLASSIC
MODEL 700 MOUNTAIN DM
MODEL 710
MODEL SEVEN
MODEL SEVEN MAGNUM

MODEL 700 CLASSIC (221 REM FIREBALL)
Since Remington's series of Model 700 Classics began in 1981, the company has offered this model in a special chambering each year.

The Model 700 Classic features an American walnut, straight-combed stock without a cheekpiece for rapid mounting, better sight alignment and reduced felt recoil. A hinged magazine flloorplate, sling swivel studs and satin wood finish with cut-checkering are standard, along with 24" barrel. Receiver drilled/tapped for scope mounts.
Price:....................................$661

MODEL 700 MOUNTAIN DM (DETACHABLE MAGAZINE) RIFLE
The Remington Model 700 MTN DM rifle features the traditional mountain rifle-styled stock with a pistol grip pitched lower to position the wrist for a better grip. The cheekpiece is designed to align the eye for quick, accurate sighting. The American walnut stock has a handrubbed oil finish and comes with a brown recoil pad and deep-cut checkering. The Model 700 MTN DM also features a lean contoured 22" barrel that helps reduce total weight to 6.5 pounds (no sights). All metalwork features a glass bead-blasted, blued-metal finish. **Calibers:** 25-06 Rem., 260 Rem., 270 Win., 280 Rem., 7mm-08 Rem., and 30-06 Springfield.
Price:....................................728

MODEL 710
Features: New Model 710 bolt design employs three unique locking lugs that lock the bolt inside the barrel rather than the receiver. Proven Remington cylindrical receiver design features a unique new fiberglass-reinforced, self-lubricating nylon receiver insert, impregnated with both silicon and Teflon, for smooth, reliable bolt operation. Shorter 60° degree bolt throw (vs. 90° throw on competing rifles) delivers faster follow-up shots. 22" steel barrel is cold-forged and button-rifled with 6-groove, right-hand, 1-in-10 twist rifling. Additionally, the barrel is hydraulically pressed to the receiver for permanent attachment and bedded in the stock. Removable, dual-stack steel magazine box with center feed and four-round capacity. Dark-gray specially textured synthetic composite stock with raised cheekpiece black recoil pad and sling swivel studs. 42.5" overall length, 7 1/8 lbs. Exclusive, key-operated Remington Integrated Security System. Pre-mounted, bore-sighted 3-9x40 Bushnell Sharpshooter scope with high-grade rings and mounts. Initially offered in popular .270 Win. and .30-06 Sprg. calibers.
Price: with scope............................$425

MODEL SEVEN
The short-action Model Seven is built to the accuracy standards of the famous Model 700. Its tapered 20" barrel is free floating out to a single pressure point at the forend tip. A fully enclosed bolt and extractor system, ramp front and fully adjustable rear sights and sling swivel studs are standard. The Youth Model features a hardwood stock that is 1 inch shorter for easy control.
Prices:
Laminate LS 223,243,7mm-08, 308..............677
   Laminate/Stainless LSS 22-250,7mm-08.........770
   Youth (hardwood) 223,243, 260, 7mm-08........531
   Stainless Synthetic SS 223,243, 260,
   7mm-08, 308.............................703

MODEL SEEVEN MAGNUM
Chambered for the new 7mm and .300 Rem. Short-Action Ultra Mags. 22" barrel. Available in LS (laminated stock) and SS (stainless synthetic) versions.
Price: LS....................................743
   SS.......................................717

Remington Custom Rifles

MODEL SEVEN AWR

MODEL SEVEN MS

MODEL SEVEN CUSTOM KS

NO.1 ROLLING BLOCK MID-RANGE SPORTER

MODEL 40-XB

Model Seven AWR (Alaskan Wilderness Rifle)
22" 416 stainless steel barrel, Black composite stock. Offered in 7mm Rem. Ultra Mag., and .300 Rem. Ultra Mag.
Price:.....................................$1524

Model Seven MS (Mannlicher Style) Rifle
Full-length Mannlicher-style laminated wood stock. 20" carbon-steel barrel chambered in short-action calibers from .222 Rem. to .350 Rem. Mag.
Price:.......................................1312

Model Seven Custom KS
Price:.......................................1294

Rolling Block Mid-Range Sporter
American walnut stock; 30" barrel in .45-70 Government caliber.
Price:.......................................1429
   Silhouette w/heavy barrel:..................1537

Model 40-XB Target Rifle
Single-shot or repeater target rifle with 27.25" stainless heavy barrel in 16 calibers from .220 Swift to .300 Rem. Ultra Mag. Walnut, aramid fiber-reinforced or laminated thumbhook stock.

Remington Custom Rifles

MODEL 700 AFRICAN BIG GAME

MODEL 700 SAFARI

MODEL 700 ALASKAN WILDERNESS RIFLE (AWR)

MODEL 700 AFRICAN PLAINS RIFLE (APR)

MODEL 700 KS MOUNTAIN RIFLE

MODEL 700 ABG (AFRICAN BIG GAME)
Brown laminated stock, 26" blued satin carbon steel barrel and action in 375 Rem. Ultra Mag., 375 H&H Mag., 416 Rem. Mag., 458 Win. Mag.
Price: $1726

MODEL 700 CUSTOM SAFARI KS
Model 700TM Safari Grade bolt-action rifles provide big-game hunters with a choice of either wood or synthetic stock. Model 700 Safari Monte Carlo (with Monte Carlo comb and cheekpiece) and Model 700 Safari Classic (with straight-line classic comb and no cheekpiece) are the satin-finished wood-stock models. Both feature hand-cut checkering and two reinforcing crossbolts covered with rosewood plugs. The Monte Carlo model also has rosewood pistol-grip and forend caps. All models are fitted with sling swivel studs and 22" or 24" barrels. Synthetic stock has simulated wood-grain finish, reinforced with Aramid Fiber.
Calibers: 8mm Rem. Mag., 375 H&H Magnum, 416 Rem. Mag. and 458 Win. Mag. **Capacity:** 3 rounds. **Avg. Weight:** 9 lbs. **Overall Length:** 44.5" **Rate of Twist:** 10" (8mm Rem. Mag.); 12" (375 H&H Mag.); 14" (416 Rem. Mag., 458 Win. Mag.)
Price:
Custom KS Safari 1497
LH Custom KS Safari 1577
Custom KS Safari Stainless 1672

MODEL 700 ALASKAN WILDERNESS RIFLE (AWR)
This custom-built rifle has the same rate of twist and custom magnum barrel contour as the African Plains Rifle below, but features an aramid-fiber-reinforced composite stock.
Calibers: 7mm Rem. Mag., 7mm STW, 7mm Rem Ultra Mag., .300 Rem. Ultra Mag., 300 Win. Mag., 300 Wby. Mag., 338 Win. Mag., .338 Rem. Ultra Mag., 375 H&H Mag., 375 Rem Ultra Mag. **Capacity:** 3 shots **Barrel length:** 24" **Overall Length:** 44.5" **Weight:** 6 lbs. 12 oz.
Price: $1569

MODEL 700 AFRICAN PLAINS RIFLE (APR)
The custom-built Model 700 APR rifle has a laminated classic wood stock and the following specifications. **Calibers:** 7mm Rem. Mag., 7mm Rem Ultra Mag., 300 Win. Mag., 300 Wby. Mag., 300 Rem. Ultra Mag., 338 Win. Mag., 338 Rem Ultra Mag., 375 H&H Mag., 375 Rem Ultra Mag **Capacity:** 3 shots **Barrel length:** 26" **Overall Length:** 46.5" **Weight:** 7.75 lbs. **Rate Of Twist:** R.H. 1 turn in 9.25" (7mm Rem. Mag.); 10" (300 Win. Mag. and 338 Win. Mag., .338 Rem. Ultra Mag.); 12" (30 Wby. Mag. and 375 H&H Mag.)
Price: 1690

MODEL 700 KS MOUNTAIN RIFLE
Aramid fiber-reinforced fiberglass stock with stainless or carbon custom profile barrel in calibers from .270 Win. to .375 Rem. Ultra Mag.
Price: . . . . 1294 - 1477

MODEL 700 CUSTOM RIFLE (NOT SHOWN)
Built to personal specifications
Price: 2897

Remington Rifles

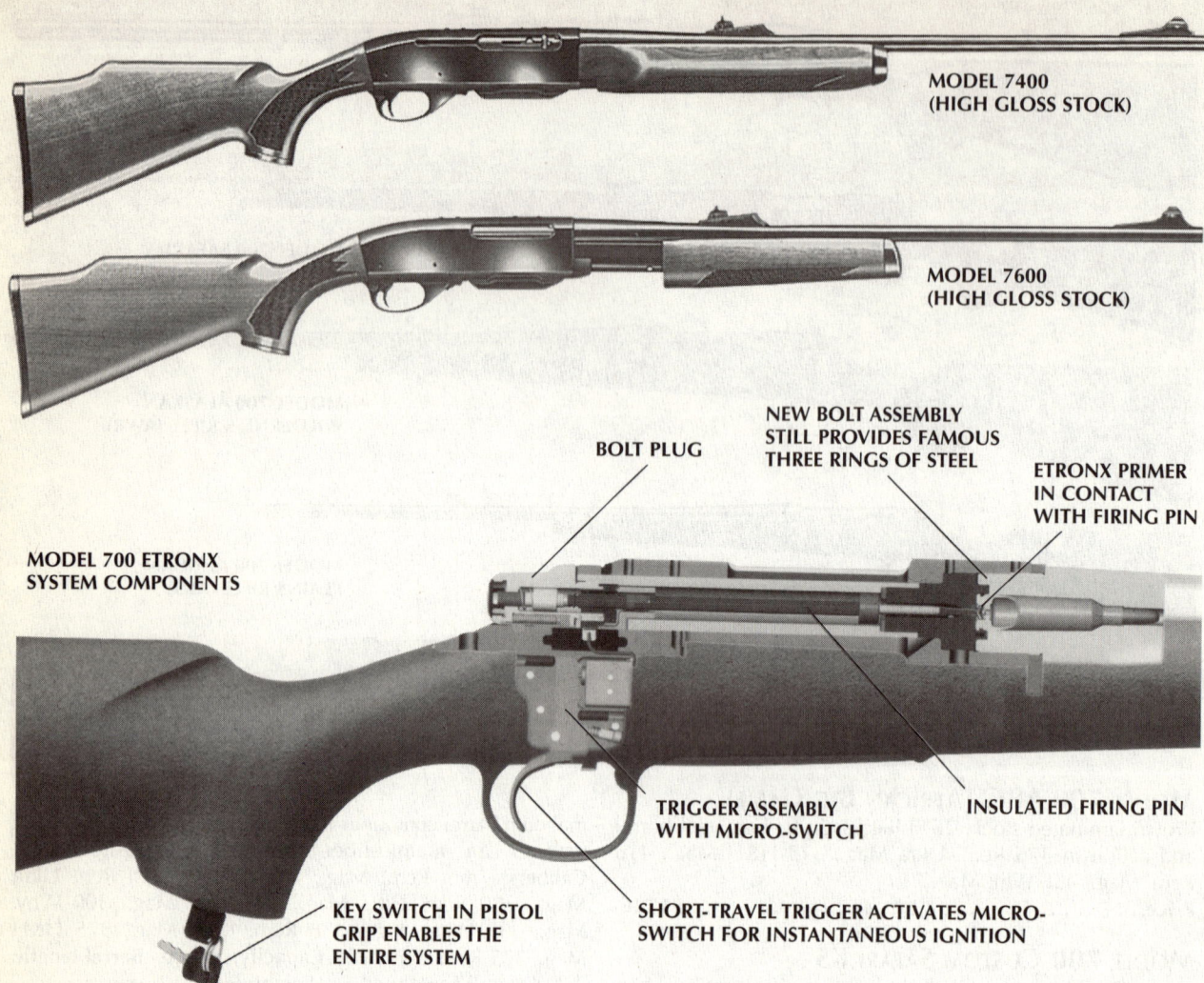

MODEL 7400 (HIGH GLOSS STOCK)

MODEL 7600 (HIGH GLOSS STOCK)

MODEL 700 ETRONX SYSTEM COMPONENTS

BOLT PLUG

NEW BOLT ASSEMBLY STILL PROVIDES FAMOUS THREE RINGS OF STEEL

ETRONX PRIMER IN CONTACT WITH FIRING PIN

TRIGGER ASSEMBLY WITH MICRO-SWITCH

INSULATED FIRING PIN

KEY SWITCH IN PISTOL GRIP ENABLES THE ENTIRE SYSTEM

SHORT-TRAVEL TRIGGER ACTIVATES MICRO-SWITCH FOR INSTANTANEOUS IGNITION

MODEL 7400 (HIGH GLOSS STOCK)
Calibers: 243 Win., 270 Win., 30-06, 30-06 Carbine, 308 Win. **Capacity:** 5 centerfire cartridges (4 in the magazine, 1 in the chamber); extra 4-shot magazine available **Action:** Gas-operated; receiver drilled and tapped for scope mounts **Barrel Lengths:** 22" (18.5" in 30-06 Carbine) **Weight:** 7.5 lbs. (7.25 lbs. in 30-06 Carbine) **Overall Length:** 42" **Sights:** Standard blade ramp front; sliding ramp rear **Stock:** Satin or high-gloss (270 Win. and 30-06 only) walnut stock and forend; curved pistol grip **Length Of Pull:** 13 $3/8$" **Drop At Heel:** 2.25" **Drop At Comb:** 1 $13/16$"
Price: $624
  Synthetic 520

MODEL 700 ETRONX SYSTEM COMPONENTS
The Model 7600 shares nearly the same specifications as the Model 7400 featured above, except the 7600 is pump action. **Drop At Heel:** $15/16$" **Drop At Comb:** $9/16$"
Price: 588
  Synthetic 484

REMINGTON 700 ETRONX
Remington's ground-breaking EtronX System is claimed to be the most significant advance in rifle and ammunition performance since the development of self-contained cartridges. For the first time, cased centerfire cartridges can be fired by a completely non-mechanical system that ignites primers by means of an electric pulse.

The electronic fire control has no moving parts other than the trigger – no sear to be released or firing pin to move and strike the primer. Instead, an internal electric circuit is completed when the trigger is pulled. This sends an electrical charge through the system to an electrically responsive primer, igniting it instantaneously. The result is the fastest lock time of any rifle on the market.

In outward appearance, the EtronX resembles a 700 VS SF, with its fluted 26" barrel. The EtronX is chambered in .220 Swift, .22-250 and .243.
Price: $1999

Remington Rimfire Rifles

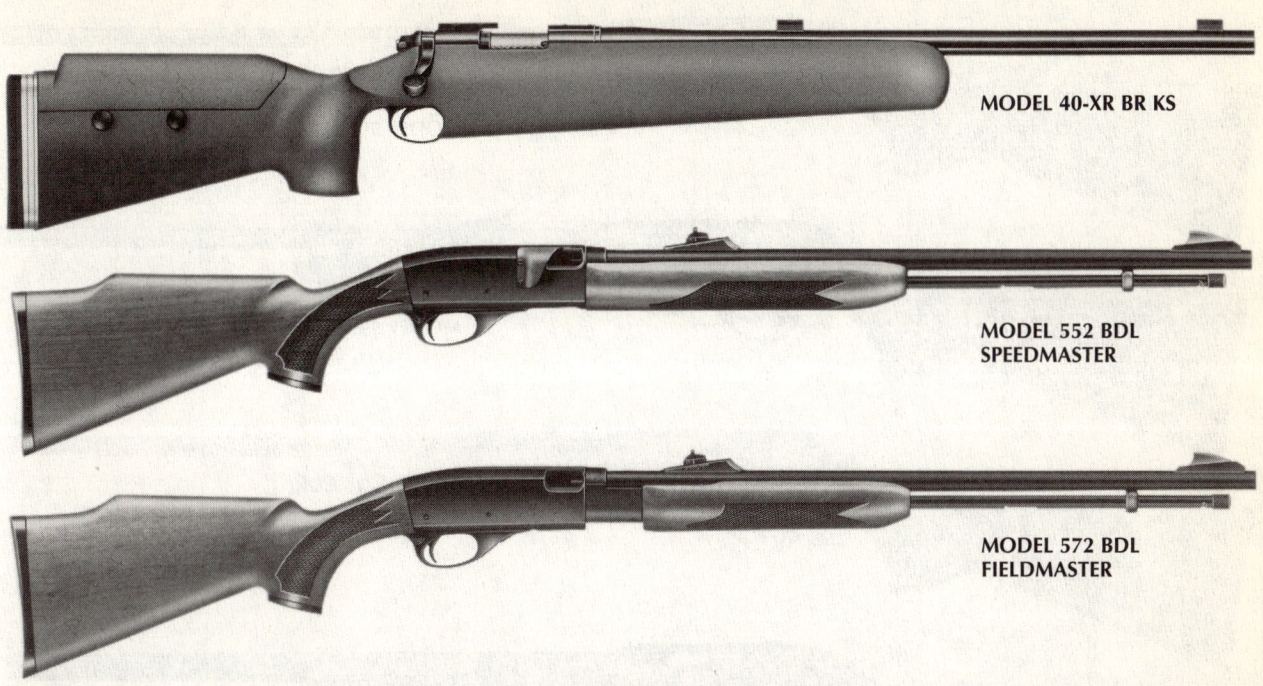

MODEL 40-XR BR KS

MODEL 552 BDL SPEEDMASTER

MODEL 572 BDL FIELDMASTER

MODEL 572/552 RIFLE DIMENSIONS/AVERAGE WEIGHTS

Model	Action Type	Mag./Clip Capacity	Barrel Length	Overall Length	Avg. Wt. (lbs.)	Order No.	Stock Mat'l	Stock Finish	BBL Mat'l	BBL Finish
552 BDL Deluxe Speedmaster	Autoloading (.22 S, L, LR)	15*	21"	40"	5 3/4	5594	American Walnut	Gloss	Carbon Steel	Polished Blue
572 BDL Deluxe Fieldmaster	Pump (.22 S, L, LR)	15*	21"	40"	5 1/2	5624	American Walnut	Gloss	Carbon Steel	Polished Blue

Nominal stock dimensions: (552/572): 13 5/8" length of pull, 1 3/8" drop at comb, 2 5/8" drop at heel. *17 .22 shorts.

MODEL 597 RIFLE DIMENSIONS/AVERAGE WEIGHTS

Model	Action Type	Barrel Length	Overall Length	Avg. Wt. (lbs.)	Order No.	Stock Mat'l	Stock Finish	BBL Mat'l	BBL Finish
597	Autoloading (.22 LR)	20"	40"	5 1/2	6550	Gray Synthetic	Matte	Carbon Steel	Satin Blue
597 LSS	Autoloading (.22 LR)	20"	40"	5 1/2	6556	Brown Laminated	Satin	416 Stainless	Satin Stainless
597 SS	Autoloading (.22 LR)	20"	40"	5 1/2	6565	Gray Synthetic	Matte	416 Stainless	Satin Stainless
597 MAGNUM	Autoloading (.22 WMR)	20"	40"	6	6560	Black Synthetic	Matte	Carbon Steel	Satin Blue
597 MAGNUM LS	Autoloading (.22 WMR)	20"	40"	6	6566	Gray Laminated	Satin	Carbon Steel	Satin Blue
*597 HB	Autoloading (.22 LR)	20"	40"	6	6579	Brown Laminated	Satin	Carbon Steel	Satin Blue
*597 HB MAGNUM	Autoloading (.22 WM)	20"	40"	6	6581	Brown Laminated	Satin	Carbon Steel	Satin Blue

Nominal stock dimensions: (597): 14" length of pull, 1 1/2" drop at comb, 2 1/4" drop at heel. *New For 2001

MODEL 40-XR BR KS
Model 40-XR BR with 22" stainless-steel barrel (heavy contour), 22 LR match chamber and bore dimensions. Receiver and barrel drilled and tapped for scope mounts (mounted on green, aramid fiber reinforced fiberglass benchrest stock. Adjustable trigger (2 oz. trigger optional).
Price: $1866

(Additional target rifles are available through Remington's Custom Shop: $1612 - $3333)

MODEL 552 BDL SPEEDMASTER
The rimfire semiautomatic 552 BDL Deluxe has adjustable sights and a high-capacity tube magazine. 21" barrel, walnut stock; shoots 22 short, long & long rifle.
Price: $385

MODEL 572 BDL FIELDMASTER
The pump-action 572 Fieldmaster has all the features of the 552 autoloader, including high-comb checkered stock, tube magazine, adjustable sights.
Price: 399

Remington Rimfire Rifles

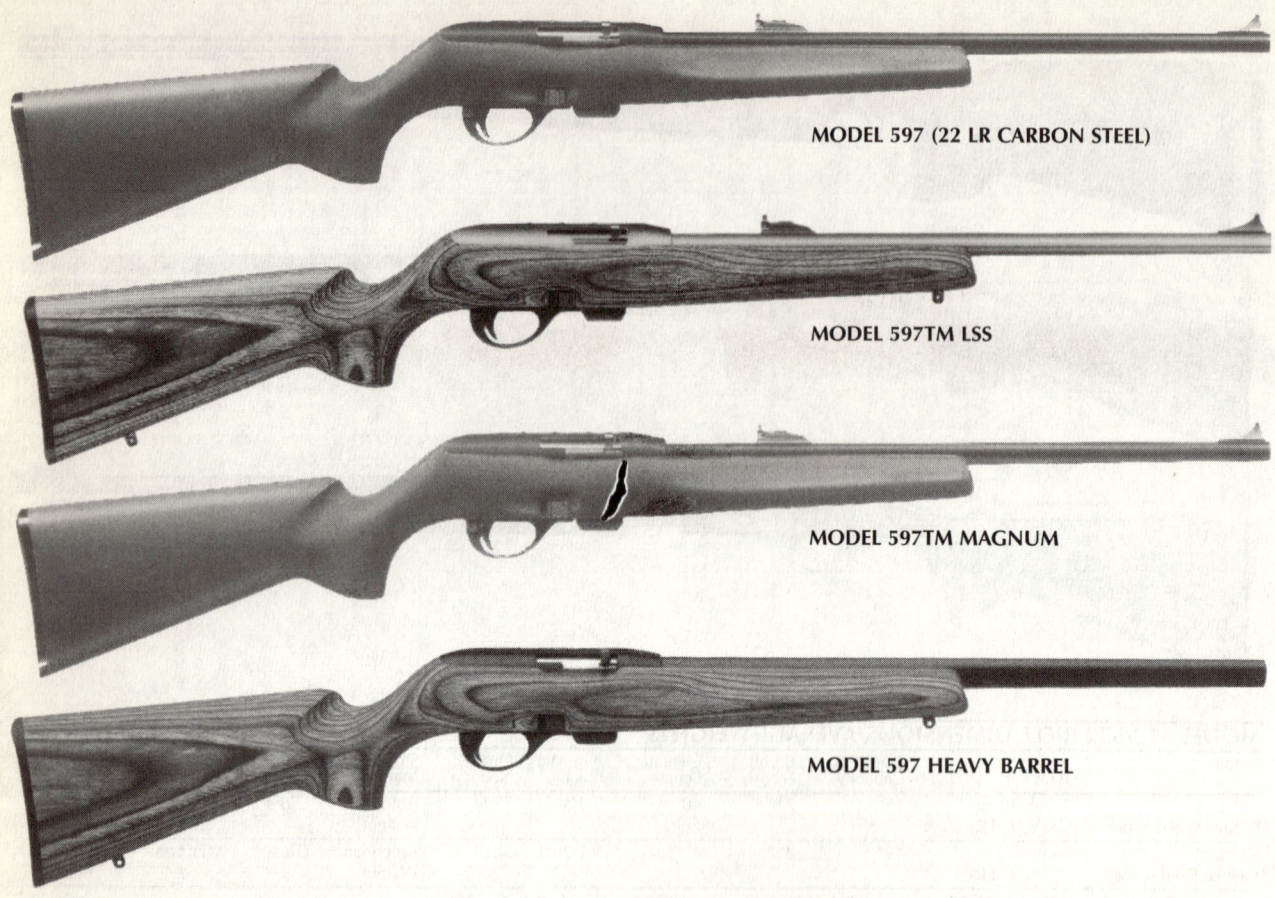

MODEL 597 (22 LR CARBON STEEL)
MODEL 597TM LSS
MODEL 597TM MAGNUM
MODEL 597 HEAVY BARREL

MODEL 597 SERIES
Remington's autoloading rimfire rifles–the Model 597TM Series–are available in 7 versions, offering a choice of carbon or stainless steel barreled actions, synthetic or laminated wood stocks, and chambering for either standard 22 Long Rifle or 22 Magnum ammo. All M597TM rifles feature beavertail-style forends rounded with finger grooves for hand-filling control. The top of the receiver blends into the pistol grip, creating a rimfire autoloader that points like a shotgun but aims like a rifle. Features include a bolt guidance system of twin steel rails for smooth bolt travel and functional reliability. The 20-inch barrels are free-floated for consistent accuracy with all types of rimfire ammunition. A new trigger design creates crisp let-off for autoloading rifles. Bolts on the 22 LR versions are nickel-plated. The magnum-version bolt has a special alloy steel to provide controlled, uniform function with magnum cartridges. All receivers are grooved for standard tip-off mounts and are also drilled and tapped for Weaver-type bases. Adjustable open sights and one-piece scope mount rails are standard, as are spare magazines.

MODEL 597 (22 LR CARBON STEEL)
The M597TM is chambered for 22 Long Rifle ammunition and matches Remington's carbon steel barrel with a strong, light-weight, alloy receiver. All metal has a non-reflective, matte black finish. The rifle is housed in a one-piece, dark gray synthetic stock.
Price:....................................$163
   w/stainless barrel............................217

MODEL 597 (22 LR CARBON STEEL)
The M597TM LSS (Laminated Stock Stainless) has a satin-finished stainless steel barrel and matching, gray-tone alloy receiver. Chambered for 22 LR cartridges. Its stock is of laminated wood in light and dark brown tones.
Price:....................................272

MODEL 597TM MAGNUM
Chambered for 22 Win. Mag. rimfire cartridges, the M597TM MAGNUM features a carbon steel barrel, alloy receiver and black synthetic stock.
Price:....................................321
   w/Laminated Stock............................377

MODEL 597 HEAVY BARREL
Model 597 HB 22LR and 22 Win Mag. Features heavy-contour barrel for vibration reduction and top accuracy. Satin finished blued carbon steel barrel and receiver. Features a brown laminated-wood stock.
Price: Model 597 HB 22 LR....................265
   22 Win Mag...............................399

Rifles, Inc.

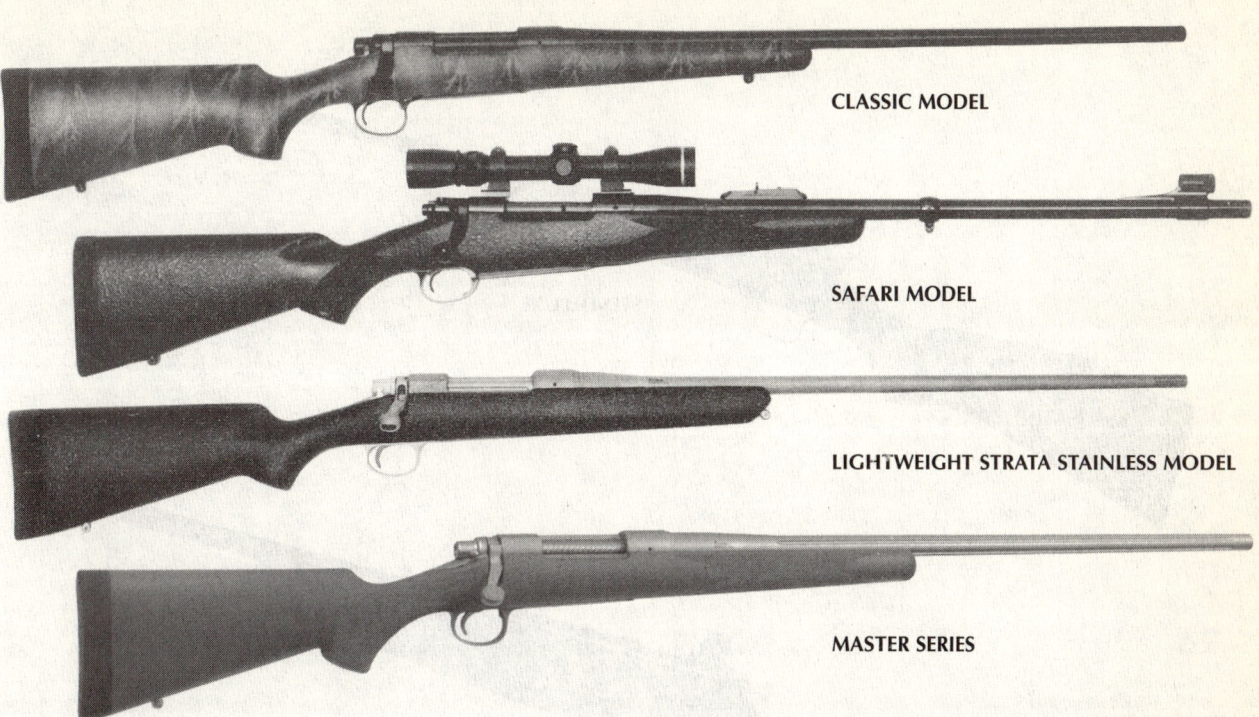

CLASSIC MODEL

SAFARI MODEL

LIGHTWEIGHT STRATA STAINLESS MODEL

MASTER SERIES

CLASSIC MODEL
Specifications
Calibers: Customized for varmint, target or hunter specifications, up to 375 H&H **Action:** Remington or Winchester stainless steel controlled-round feed with lapped bolt **Barrel Length:** 24"-26"; stainless-steel match grade, lapped **Weight:** 6.5 lbs. **Stock:** Pillar glass bedded; laminated fiberglass, finished with textured epoxy **Features:** Fine-tuned adjustable trigger; hinged floor-plate triggerguard
Price: $2500
   left hand. 2600
Also Available:
Signature Series, a long-range rifle on the stainless Remington 700 action, with 27-inch fluted stainless barrel, McMillan synthetic stock, 300 Rem. Ultra Mag only, 1/2 m.o.a, numbered and signed 2800
   Left-hand 2950

SAFARI MODEL
Specifications
Action: Winchester Model 70 controlled-round feed; hand lapped and honed bolt; drilled and tapped for 8X40 base screws **Barrel Length:** 23"-25"; stainless-steel match grade, lapped **Weight:** 9 lbs. **Muzzle Break:** Stainless Quiet Slimbrake **Metal Finish:** Matte stainless or black Teflon **Stock:** Pillar glass bedded; double reinforced laminated fiberglass/graphite; finished with textured epoxy **Features:** Fine-tuned adjustable trigger; hinged floor-plate **Options:** Drop box for additional round; express sights; barrel band; quarter ribs
Price: 3000
   w/Options 4100

LIGHTWEIGHT STRATA STAINLESS MODEL
Specifications
Calibers: Up to 375 H&H **Action:** Stainless Remington; fluted, tapped and handle-hollowed bolt; aluminum bolt shroud **Barrel Length:** 22"-24" depending on caliber; stainless-steel match grade **Weight:** 4.75 lbs. **Stock:** Pillar glass bedded; laminated Kevlar/Boron/Graphite, finished with textured epoxy **Features:** Matte stainless metal finish; aluminum blind or hinged floorplate trigger guard; custom Protektor pad
Price: $2850
   left hand. 2950

Also Available: LIGHTWEIGHT 70 in calibers up to 375 H&H. **Barrel Length:** 22" to 24" stainless steel match grade. **Weight:** 5.75 lbs. **Stock:** laminated Kevlar/Graphite/Boron finished with textured epoxy. Trigger is fine-tuned.
Price: 2750
   left hand. 2850

LIGHTWEIGHT TITANIUM STRATA (NOT SHOWN)
Action: Remington 700, lightened **Stock:** Hand-laminated **Barrel:** matchgrade stainless steel, matte finish **Weight:** 4.5 lbs. **Caliber:** Up to 300 Weatherby **Other features:** Spiral fluted bolt, handle lightened and lapped and fitted with hexagon bolt shroud; customer trigger
Price: 3850

MASTER SERIES
Specifications
Calibers: up to 300 Rem Ultra Mag. **Action:** Rem 700 **Barrel:** select match grade #5, 24-27" **Weight:** 7.75 lbs. **Stock:** Fiberglass
Price: 2950

Rogue Rifle Company

STD-DELUXE

TARGET MODEL

The Rogue River thrashes its way toward the Pacific in southwest Oregon, and that's where the Rogue Rifle Company got its start. It's in Lewiston, Idaho now, on the Snake River. But the company name doesn't register with most shooters; they've come to know these rifles by their product label: Chipmunk.

In the 1980s, when Chipmunks were still very new and the original owners promoted them through the Rocky Mountain Elk Foundation, as well as via retail outlets, the rifles seemed grossly overpriced. A single-shot .22 with the dimensions of a Red Ryder BB gun shouldn't cost $130! But for some people – youngsters – the Chipmunk became a best buy. No other factory rifle offered a stock proportioned for them. Functional, accurate and well-balanced, if by some standards crude, the rifles scaled less than 3 pounds. Chipmunks were novel enough to sell.

These mini-size .22s have improved over the years, and new versions have evolved. The Lewiston firm lists three this year: a Chipmunk sporting rifle in .17 HMR, a Target Model .22 and a .410 shotgun with the Chipmunk's now-classic look. Retail prices range from $194 to $279. Blued chrome-moly steel is still standard, but no longer are you limited to plain walnut stocks. Chipmunks come with figured walnut and with laminated stocks too. Camo finish is an option. So is the chambering in .22 WMR. The Target Model comes with a competition-style receiver sight and globe front. You can adjust its trigger down to 1 1/2 pounds.

The base-model Chipmunk rifle is 30 inches long with a 16-inch barrel button-rifled 1-in-16. Length of pull is 11 1/2 inches, or 2 inches shorter than that on most adult-size rimfire rifles. The Target Model (which, like the .410 shotgun, has an 18-inch barrel) features an extendable buttplate that also slides vertically, plus a front rail for a forend stop. Weight varies from 2 1/2 pounds for the standard version, to just over 3 pounds for the shotgun, to 5 pounds for the Target Model. All Chipmunks have manual-cocking actions, and all except the shotgun wear receiver-mounted rear sights.

The Rogue Rifle Company offers a variety of accessories for its Chipmunks, including cases, sling swivels, scopes. You can even buy a Chipmunk belt buckle.

Rossi Rifles

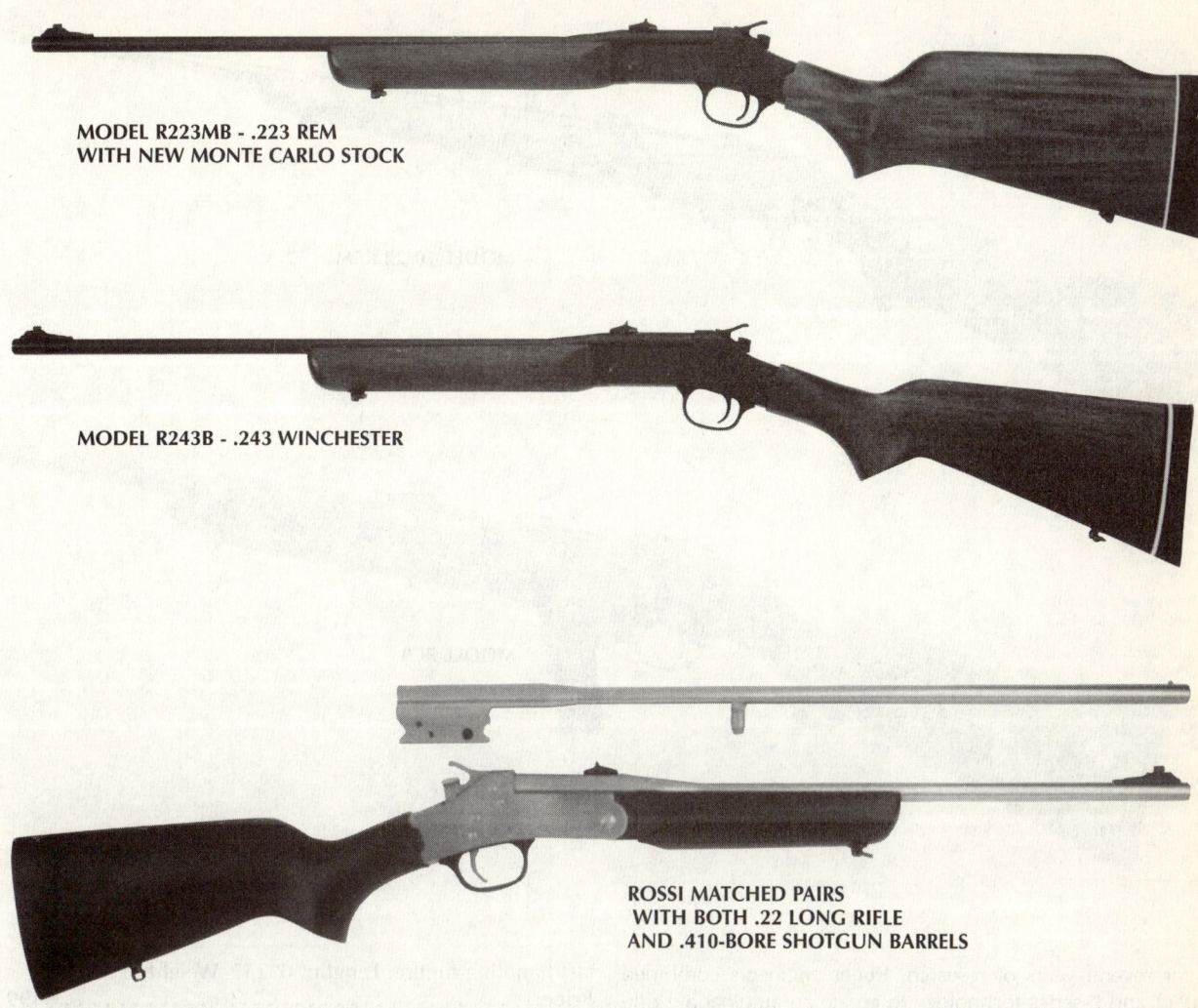

MODEL R223MB - .223 REM WITH NEW MONTE CARLO STOCK

MODEL R243B - .243 WINCHESTER

ROSSI MATCHED PAIRS WITH BOTH .22 LONG RIFLE AND .410-BORE SHOTGUN BARRELS

For 2002, Rossi introduces a line of single shot rifles in your favorite calibers. The Rossi single shot rifles feature hand-fitted wood stocks, Rossi's recoil pad, fully adjustable sights, sling swivels and an extra-wide positive-action extractor to ensure ejection of the spent case when you open the breech. These rifles are perfect for training first time shooters, as well as target shooting and hunting. Available in 22 LR, 22 Magnum, 357 Magnum, 223 Rem., 243 Win and 45/410.
Price:
22LR or 22 Mag, Blue w/natural wood $150
    Stainless w/black wood. 180
357 or 44 Rem Mag, Blue w/natural wood 160
    Stainless w/black wood. 190
223 Rem
    Blue w/natural wood 175
    Blue w/Monte Carlo stock. 180
243 Win Blue w/Monte Carlo stock 180
410/45 Colt Blue 170
    Stainless. 200
Also available:

Youth Model w/Monte Carlo stock $180

ROSSI MATCHED PAIR
Specifications
Calibers: .22 Long Rifle and .410 bore **Action Type:** break-open, single-shot **Finish:** stainless steel **Overall Length:** 32 1/4" (rifle), 35 3/4" (shotgun) **Barrel:** 18 1/2" (rifle), 22" (shotgun) **Rifling:** six-groove, 1:12" RH twist **Weight:** 4 lbs. **Sights:** square-post front adjustable for elevation, square-notch blade rear adjustable for windage (rifle); brass front bead (shotgun) **Trigger:** single-stage, non-adjustable 6 3/4 lbs. pull **Stock:** hardwood: length of pull, 12 1/2"; drop at heel, 1 1/2"; drop at comb, 1".
Price: Blued 140
    Stainless 170

Also available:
Centerfire Rifle/Shotgun Matched Pair - Full size configuration 12 or 20 gauge with 223 Rem or 243 Win
Price: 200

Ruger Carbines

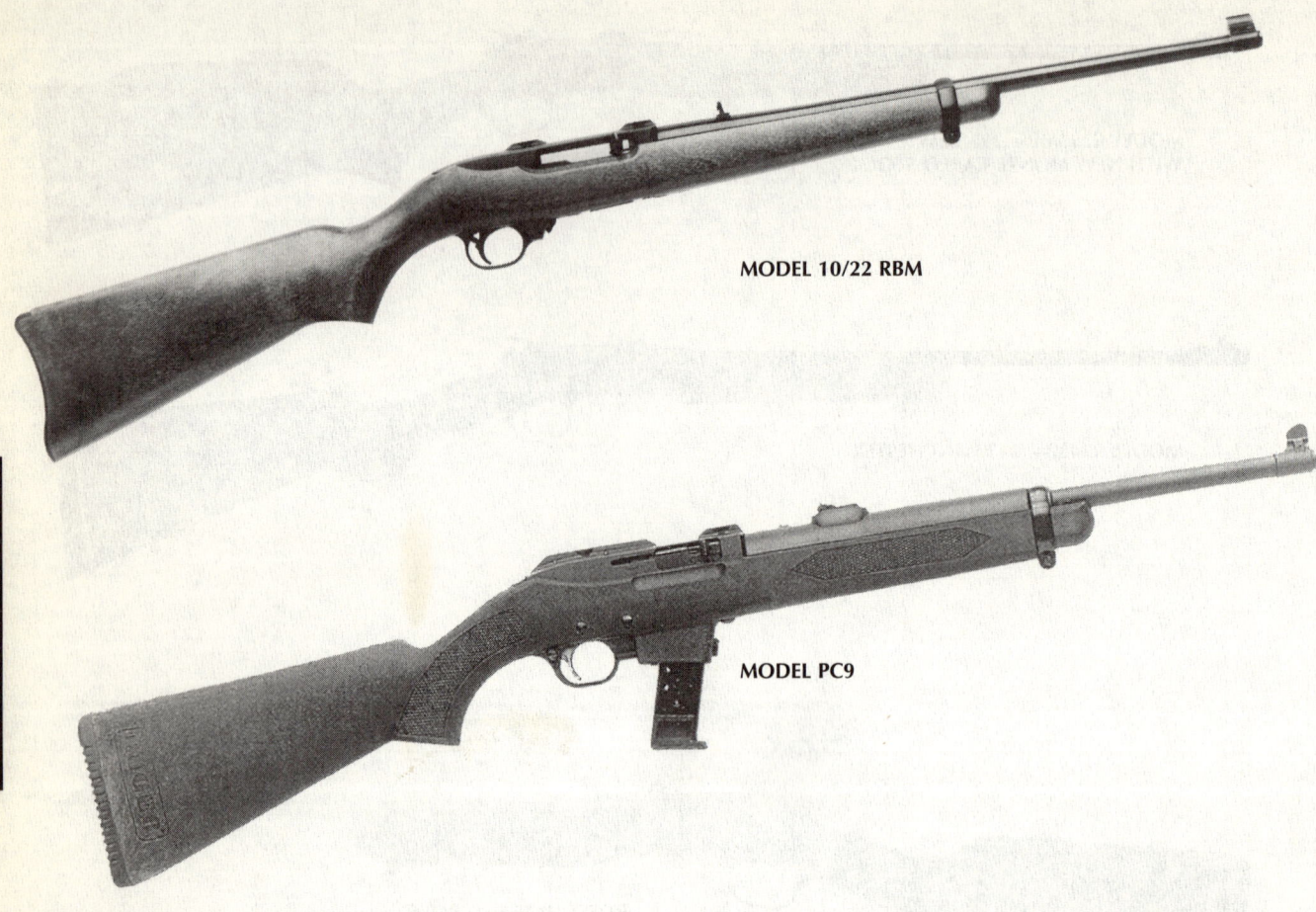

MODEL 10/22 RBM

MODEL PC9

After several years of research, Ruger engineers combined 10/22 and P-series technology to create an autoloading rifle that uses popular pistol cartridges and Ruger pistol magazines. This handy carbine meets the needs of personal defense, sporting use, law enforcement and security agencies. Advanced synthetics and precision investment-casting technologies allow for improved performance and substantially reduced costs. The Ruger Carbine has a chrome-moly steel barrel, receiver, slide and recoil springs, and features a checkered High Impact Synthetic stock with rubber buttplate. Adjustable open sights and patented integral scope mounts are standard. The Ruger Carbine also features a combination firing-pin block and slide lock. Trigger engagement is required for the firing pin to strike the primer. The slide locks to prevent chambering or ejection of a round if the riflle is struck on the buttpad. This safety system is backed up by a manual crossbolt safety located at the rear of the trigger guard. A slide stop locks the slide open for inspection and cleaning.

Ruger 10/22 Magnum

This .22 Magnum autoloader uses a heavy bolt in a blowback mechanism that feeds from the proven 10/22 rotary magazine. Integral scope bases augment open sights. The carbine-style walnut stock and 18.5" barrel make this a fast-handling rimfire. **Length:** 37.25" **Weight:** 6 lbs.
Price: $499

Model PC9 Autoloading Carbine
Specifications
Caliber: 9mm or 40 auto
Capacity: 10 rounds
Action: Mass impulse delayed blowback
Barrel Length: 16.25" **Overall Length:** 34 3/8"
Weight: 6 lbs. 4 oz. **Trigger Pull:** Approx. 6 lb.
Rifling: 6 grooves, 1 turn in 10" RH
Stock: High impact synthetic
Finish: Matte black oxide
Sights: Blade front, open rear plus provision for scope mounts (ghost ring version also available)
Sight Radius: 12.65"
Safety: Manual push-button crossbolt safety (locks trigger mechanism) and internal firing-pin block safety
Features: Bolt lock to prevent accidental unloading or chambering of a cartridge; steel barrel, receiver, slide and recoil spring unit w/black composite stock
Price: 605
  w/ghosted rings rear sight 628
All Ruger long guns come standard with cable lock & keys.

Ruger Carbines

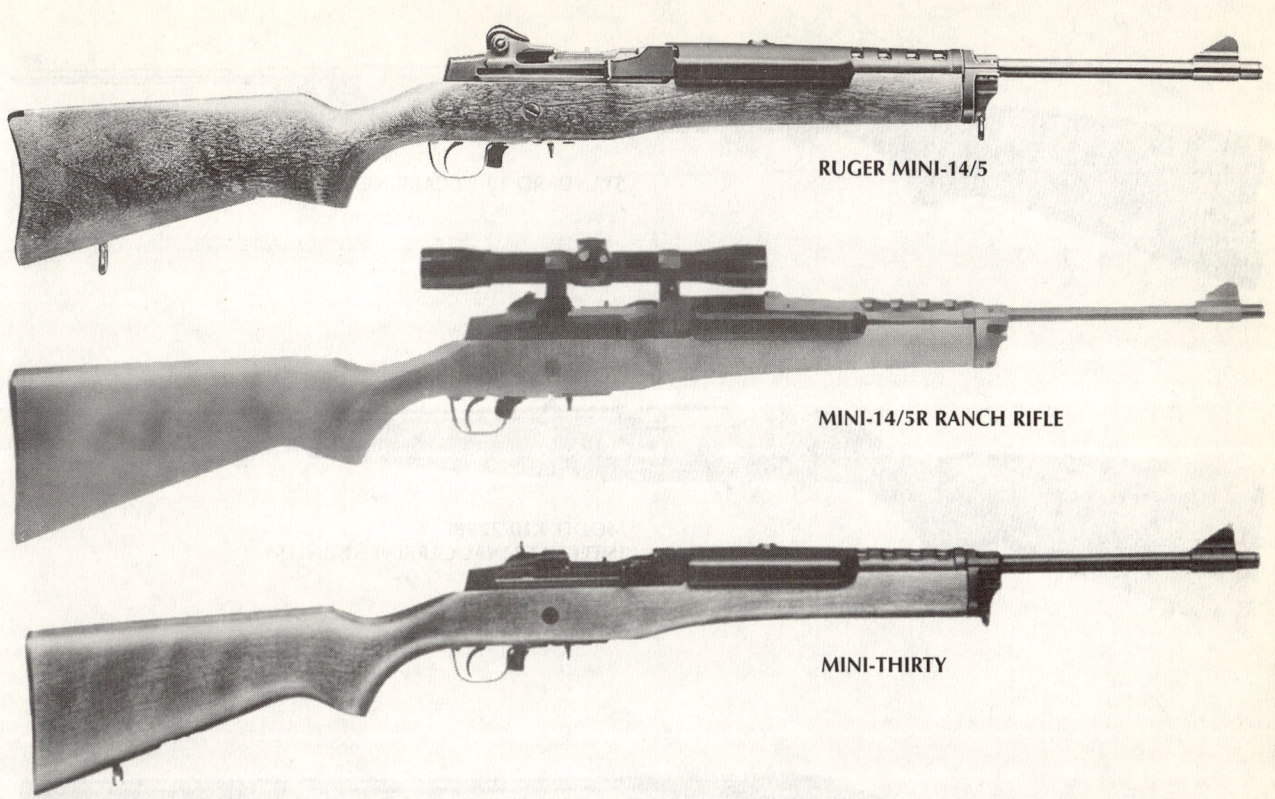

RUGER MINI-14/5

MINI-14/5R RANCH RIFLE

MINI-THIRTY

Ruger Mini-14/5
Mechanism: Gas-operated, autoloading. **Materials:** Heat-treated chrome molybdenum and other alloy steels as well as music wire coil springs are used throughout the mechanism to ensure reliability under field-operating conditions. **Safety:** The guard-mounted safety blocks both the hammer and sear. The slide can be cycled when the safety is on. **Firing pin:** The firing pin is retracted mechanically as the bolt unlocks. The rifle can only be fired when the bolt is safely locked. **Stock:** One-piece American hardwood reinforced with steel liner at stressed areas. Sling swivels standard. Handguard and forearm separated by air space from barrel to promote cooling under rapid-fire conditions. **Field stripping:** The Carbine can be field-stripped to its eight (8) basic sub-assemblies in a matter of seconds and without use of special tools.

Ruger Mini-14
Specifications
Caliber: 223 (5.56mm)
Barrel Length: 18.5"
Overall Length: 37 1/8" **Weight:** 6 lbs. 8 oz.
Magazine: 5-round, detachable box magazine
Sights: Rear adj. for windage/elevation.
Prices: Mini-14/5 Blued $636
K-Mini-14/5 Stainless 696
K-Mini-14/5P Stainless, synthetic 696
  (Scope not included)

Mini-14/5R Ranch Rifle
Specifications
Caliber: 223 (5.56mm) **Barrel Length:** 18.5"
Overall Length: 37 1/8" **Weight:** 6 lbs. 8 oz.
Magazine: 5-round detachable box magazine.
Sights: Fold-down rear sight; 1" scope rings (factory machined scope mount system available on all Ranch models)
Prices: Mini-14/5R Blued $675
K-Mini-14/5R Stainless 745
K-Mini-14/5RPS Stainless, Synthetic 745

Mini-Thirty
This modified version of the Ruger Ranch rifle is chambered for the 7.62 x 39mm Soviet service cartridge. Designed for use with telescopic sights, it features low, compact scope-mounting for greater accuracy and carrying case, and a buffer in the receiver. Sling swivels are standard.
Specifications
Caliber: 7.62 x 39mm **Barrel Length:** 18.5" **Overall Length:** 37 1/8" **Weight:** 6 lbs. 14 oz. (empty) **Magazine Capacity:** 5 shots **Rifling:** 6 grooves, R.H. twist, 1:10" **Finish:** Blued or stainless **Stock:** One-piece American hardwood w/steel liners in stressed areas **Sights:** Blade front; peep rear (factory machined scope mount system available on all Ranch models).
Prices: Blued 675
  Stainless Steel 745
Also Available: K-Mini-30P, 7.62x39mm, all-weather, matte stainless 745

Ruger Carbines

STANDARD 10/22 CARBINE

MODEL K10/22RBI INTERNATIONAL CARBINE STAINLESS

MODEL 10/22T TARGET

Introduced in 1964, Ruger's 10/22 is still a best-seller. It follows the Ruger design practice of building a firearm from integrated sub-assemblies. For example, the trigger housing assembly contains the entire ignition system, which employs a high-speed swinging hammer to ensure the shortest possible lock time. The barrel is assembled to the receiver by a unique dual-screw dovetail system that provides unusual rigidity and strength—and accounts, in part, for the exceptional accuracy of the 10/22.

Specifications
Mechanism: Blow-back, semiautomatic.
Caliber: 22 LR, high-speed or standard-velocity loads.
Magazine: 10-shot capacity, exclusive Ruger rotary design; fits flush into stock.
Barrel: 18.5", assembled to the receiver by dual-screw dovetail mounting for added strength and rigidity.
Overall Length: 37 1/4".
Weight: 5 lbs.
Sights: 1/16" brass bead front; single folding-leaf rear, adjustable for elevation; receiver drilled and tapped for scope blocks or tip-off mount adapter (included).
Trigger: curved finger surface, 3/8" wide.
Safety: sliding cross-button type; safety locks both sear and hammer and cannot be put in safe position unless gun is cocked.
Stocks: Birch, laminated, American walnut or synthetic.
Finish: blued or anodized or brushed satin.

Prices: Model 10/22 RB Standard $239
Model 10/22 DSP Deluxe
   (Hand-checkered American walnut). 299
Model K10/22 RB Stainless. 279
Model K10/22 RBI International Carbine
   w/full-length stock stainless. 299
10/22 RBI blue. 279
Model 10/22T TARGET (no sights) Hammer-
   forged 20" barrel, laminated target-style stock. . . . 425
   stainless 485
Model 10/22RPF "All Weather" synthetic stock 239
   stainless 279

Ruger Single-Shot Rifles

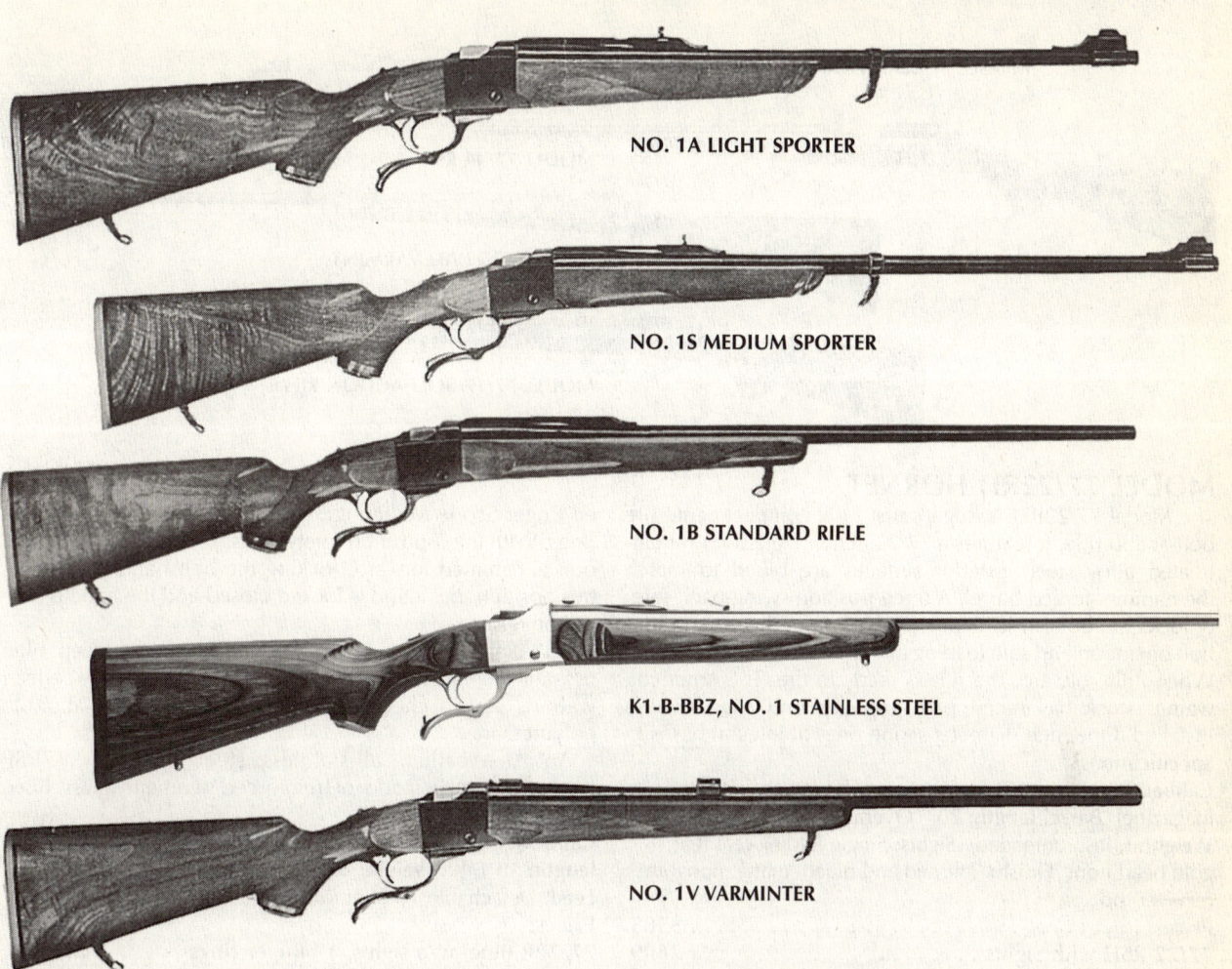

NO. 1A LIGHT SPORTER

NO. 1S MEDIUM SPORTER

NO. 1B STANDARD RIFLE

K1-B-BBZ, NO. 1 STAINLESS STEEL

NO. 1V VARMINTER

Ruger's Farquharson-style single-shot rifle first appeared in 1966. These illustrations show the variations currently offered in the Ruger No. 1 Single-Shot Rifle Series. Ruger No. 1 rifles have a Farquharson-type falling-block action and select American walnut stocks. Pistol grip and forearm are hand-checkered to a borderless design. All rifles come with Ruger 1" scope rings.

Price for any listed model is **$850**
  (except the No. 1 RSI International Model 865
Barreled Actions (blued only): 600

NO. 1A LIGHT SPORTER
Calibers: 243 Win., 270 Win., 30-06, 7x57mm. **Barrel Length:** 22". **Sights:** Adjustable folding-leaf rear sight mounted on quarter rib with ramp front sight base and dovetail-type gold bead front sight; open. **Weight:** 7 1/4 lbs.

NO. 1S MEDIUM SPORTER
Calibers: 218 Bee, 7mm Rem. Mag., 300 Win. Mag., 338 Win. Mag., 45-70. **Barrel Length:** 26" (22" in 45-70). **Sights:** (same as above). **Weight:** 8 lbs. (7 1/4 lbs. in 45-70). 45-70 available in stainless.

NO. 1B STANDARD RIFLE
Calibers: 218 Bee, 22 Hornet, 22-250, 220 Swift, 223, 243 Win., 6mm Rem., 25-06, 257 Roberts, 270 Win., 270 Wby. Mag., 7mm Rem. Mag., 280, 30-06, 300 Win. Mag., 300 Wby. Mag., .308 Win, 338 Win. Mag. **Barrel Length:** 26". **Sights:** Ruger 1" steel tip-off scope rings. **Weight:** 8 lbs.

K1-B-BBZ, NO. 1 STAINLESS STEEL
No. 1 Stainless Steel, K1-B-BBZ **Calibers:** 243 Win, 25-06, 7mm Rem Mag, 7mm STW, 30-06, 308 Win.
Price: $885

NO. 1V VARMINTER
Calibers: 22-250, 220 Swift, 223, 25-06, 6mm. **Barrel Length:** 24" (26" in 220 Swift). **Sights:** Ruger target scope blocks, heavy barrel and 1" tip-off scope rings. **Weight:** 9 lbs. **Stainless:** .22-250
Also available:
NO. 1H TROPICAL RIFLE (24" heavy barrel w/sights) in 375 H&H Mag., 458 Win. Mag., 416 Rigby and 416 Rem. Mag. .375 H&H, .416 Rigby available in stainless
NO 1. RSI INTERNATIONAL (20" lightweight barrel and full-length stock) in 243 Win., 270 Win., 30-06 and 7x57mm

Ruger Bolt-Action Rifles

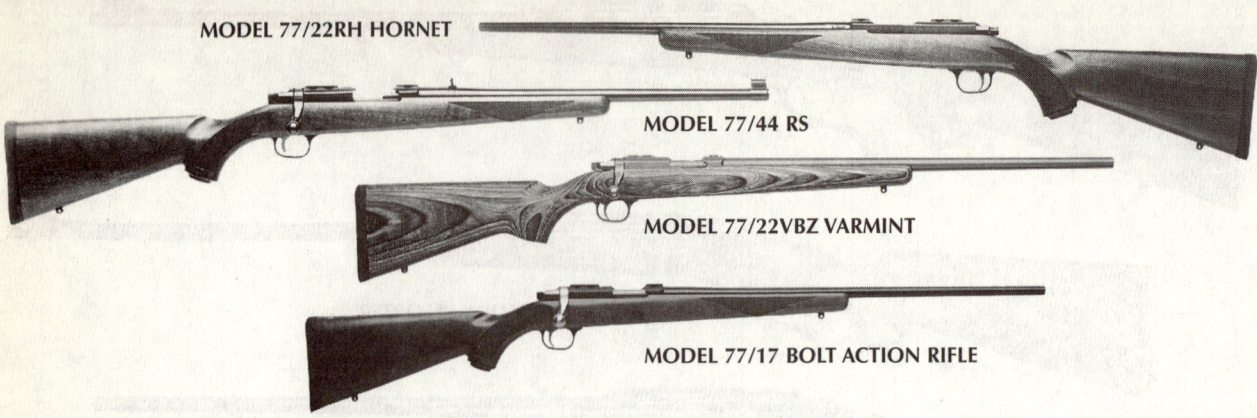

MODEL 77/22RH HORNET
The Model 77/22RH is Ruger's first truly compact centerfire bolt-action rifle. It features a 77/22 action crafted from heat-treated alloy steel. Exterior surfaces are blued to match the hammer-forged barrel. A three-position swing-back safety locks the bolt; in its center position firing is blocked, but bolt operation and safe loading and unloading are permitted. When fully forward, the rifle is ready to fire. The American walnut stock has recoil pad, grip cap and sling swivels installed. One-inch diameter scope rings fit integral bases.
Specifications
Caliber: 22 Hornet **Capacity:** 6 rounds (detachable rotary magazine) **Barrel length:** 20" **Overall length:** 39.25"
Weight: 6 lbs. (unloaded) **Sights:** Single folding-leaf rear; gold bead front **Finish:** Polished and blued, matte, nonglare receiver top
Prices: $585
77/22 RSH with Sights 609
without sights 625
Also available:
MODEL K77/22VHZ Varmint w/stainless-steel heavy barrel, laminated American hardwood stock.

MODEL 77/44 RS
Chambered in .44 Magnum, the new 77/44 is a short (18.5" barrel), lightweight (6 lbs.) deluxed grade carbine based on the same action used in the 77/22. Action features right-hand turning bolt with 90-degree bolt throw.
Specifications
Capacity: 4 rounds
Price:
blued 599
stainless (K77/44RSP) 599

MODEL 77/22 RIMFIRE RIFLE
The Ruger 22-caliber rimfire 77/22 bolt-action rifle has been built especially to function with the patented Ruger 10-Shot Rotary Magazine concept. The magazine throat, retaining lips and ramps that guide the cartridge into the chamber are solid alloy steel that resists bending.
The 77/22 weighs just under six pounds. Its heavy-duty receiver incorporates the integral scope bases of the patented Ruger Scope Mounting System with 1-inch Ruger scope rings. With the 3-position safety in its "lock" position, a dead bolt is cammed forward, locking the bolt handle down. In this position the action is locked closed and the handle cannot be raised.

All metal surfaces are finished in nonglare deep blue or satin stainless. Stock is select straight-grain American walnut, hand checkered and finished with durable polyurethane.

An All-Weather, all-stainless steel MODEL K77RSP features a stock made of reinforced synthetic glass fiber.
Specifications
Calibers: 22 LR and 22 Magnum. **Barrel length:** 20". **Overall length:** 39 1/4". **Weight:** 6 lbs. (w/o scope, magazine empty).
Feed: Detachable 10-Shot Ruger Rotary Magazine.
Prices:
77/22R Blue, w/o sights, 1" Ruger rings $565
77/22RM Blue, walnut stock, plain barrel,
no sights, 1" Ruger rings, 22 Mag. 565
77/22RS Blue, sights included, 1" Ruger rings 585
77/22RSM Blue, American walnut, iron sights 585
K77/22-RP Synthetic stock, stainless steel, plain
barrel with 1" Ruger rings. 565
K77/22-RMP Synthetic stock, stainless steel,
plain barrel, 1" Ruger rings. 565
K77/22-RSP Synthetic stock, stainless steel, gold
bead front sight, folding-leaf rear, Ruger 1"rings . . 585
K77/22RSMP Synthetic stock, metal sights,
stainless 585
Varmint Specifications: Barrel length: 24", **Overall Length:** 43.25", **Weight:** 6 7/8 lbs.
K77/22VBZ Varmint Laminated stock, scope
rings, heavy barrel, stainless 599

RUGER 77/17 BOLT ACTION RIFLE
Specifications
Stock: Checkered American walnut with butt pad, grip cap and sling swivel studs. **Barrel:** 22" with target crown.
Sights: scope rings included. **Weight:** 6.5 lbs. **Caliber:** 17 Hornady Magnum Rimfire (17HMR).
Magazine capacity: 9 rounds.
Price: 565

Ruger Bolt-Action Rifles
Mark II Series

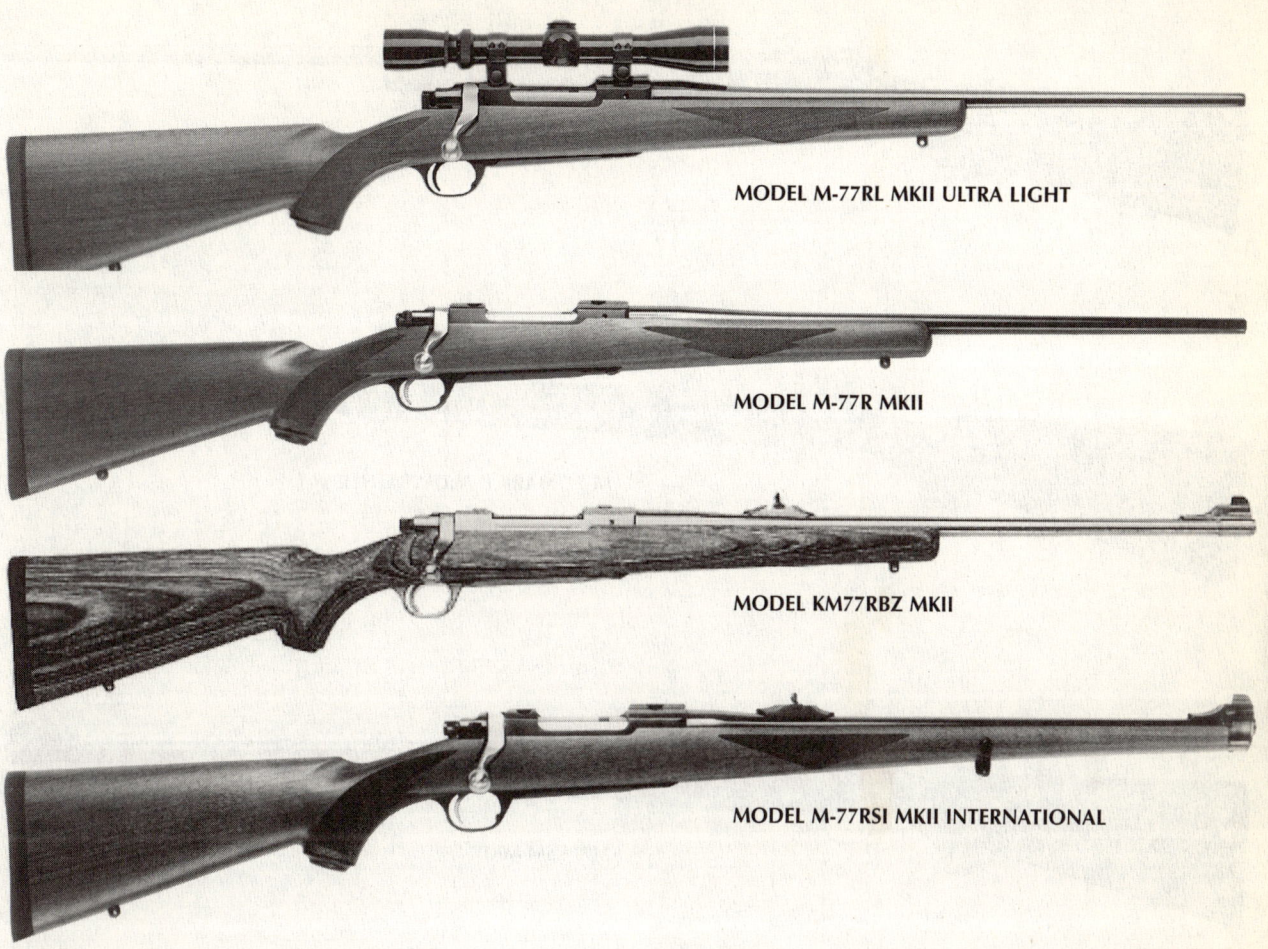

MODEL M-77RL MKII ULTRA LIGHT

MODEL M-77R MKII

MODEL KM77RBZ MKII

MODEL M-77RSI MKII INTERNATIONAL

Model M-77RL MKII Ultra Light
This big-game, bolt-action rifle encompasses the traditional features that have made the Ruger M-77 one of the most popular centerfire rifles in the world. It includes a sliding top tang safety, a one-piece bolt with Mauser-type extractor and diagonal front mounting system. American walnut stock is hand-checkered in a sharp diamond pattern. A rubber recoil pad, pistol-grip cap and studs for mounting quick detachable sling swivels are standard. Available in both long- and short-action versions, with Integral Base Receiver and 1" Ruger scope rings. **Calibers:** 223, 243, 257, 270, 30-06, 308. Barrel length: 20".
Weight: Approx. 6 lbs.
Price: $729

Model M-77R MKII
Integral Base Receiver, 1" scope rings. No sights.
Calibers: (Long action) 6mm Rem., 6.5x55mm, 7x57mm, 257 Roberts, 270, 280 Rem., 30-06 (all with 22" barrels); 220 Swift, 25/06, 7mm Rem. Mag. 7mm RSUM, 300 Win. Mag. .300 RSUM, .300 WSM, 338 Win. Mag. (all with 24" barrels); and (Short Stroke action), 22/250, 223, 243, 260 Rem., 308 (22" barrels). **Weight:** Approx. 7 lbs.
Price: 675

Also available: **M-77LR MKII Left Hand** (not shown).
Calibers: 270, 30-06, 7mm Rem. Mag., 300 Win. Mag
Price: $675

Model M-77RS MKII (not shown)
Integral Base Receiver, Ruger steel 1" rings, open sights.
Calibers: 243, 25-06, 270, 7mm Rem. Mag., 30-06, 300 Win. Mag., 308, 338 Win. Mag., 6mm (22" barrel) **Weight:** Approx. 7 lbs.
Price: 759

Model KM77RBZ MKII
Stainless steel, laminated stock, scope rings
Calibers: 223, 22-250, 243, 270, 280, 7mm Mag., 308, 30-06, 300 Win. Mag., 338 Win. Mag.
Price: KM77RSBZ 729
  With sights & rings (243 Win., 7mm Mag., 30/06, .300 Win. Mag., 338 Win Mag) 799

Model M-77RSI MKII International
International full-length stock, Integral Base Receiver, open sights, Ruger 1" steel rings. **Calibers:** 243, 270, 30-06, 308
Barrel Length: 18.5" **Weight:** Approx. 6 lbs.
Price: 769

Ruger Bolt-Action Rifles
Mark II Series (w/Three Position Safety/Fixed Ejectors)

MODEL M-77VT MK II HEAVY BARREL TARGET

M-77 MARK II ALL-WEATHER

M77RSM MKII

Model M-77VT MK II Heavy-Barrel Target
Features Mark II stainless-steel bolt action Target, gray matte finish, two-stage adjustable trigger. No sights.
Specifications
Calibers: 22-250, 220 Swift, 223, 243, 25-06 and 308.
Barrel Length: 26", hammer-forged, free-floating stainless steel.
Weight: 9 3/4 lbs.
Stock: Laminated American hardwood with flat forend.
Price: KM-77VT MKII $819

M-77 II Mark II All-Weather
KM77RFP MK II ALL-WEATHER
Receiver w/integral dovetails to accommodate Ruger 1" rings, no sights, stainless steel, full synthetic stock.
Calibers: 223, 22-50, 243, 25-06, 270, 280, 30-06, 7mm Rem. Mag., 7mm RSUM, 300 Win. Mag., 300 RSUM, 300 WSM, 308, 338 Win. Mag. 260 Rem.
Price 675
Model KM77RSFP
Receiver w/integral dovetails to accommodate Ruger 1" rings, metal sights, stainless steel, synthetic stock.
Calibers: 243, 270, 7mm Rem. Mag., 30-06, 300 Win. Mag., 338 Win. Mag.
Price: 729

Ruger 77 RSM Mk II Magnum Rifle
This "Bond Street"-quality African hunting rifle features a quarter rib machined from a single bar of steel; Circassian walnut stock with black forend tip; steel floorplate and latch; a Ruger Magnum trigger guard with floorplate latch designed flush with the contours of the trigger (to eliminate accidental dumping of cartridges); a three-position safety; express rear sight and front sight ramp with gold bead sight. Also available in Express Model (long action, no heavy barrel).
Specifications
Calibers: 375 H&H, 416 Rigby.
Capacity: 4 rounds (375 H&H) and 3 rounds (416 Rigby).
Barrel Length: 23"
Overall Length: 44"
Barrel Thread Diameter: 11/8"
Weight: 9 1/4 lbs. (375 H&H); 10 1/4 lbs. (416 Rigby), 9.75 lbs. (others)
Price: 375, 416. . . . . $1695
Also available:
Express Model, (long action) 270, 7mm, 30-06, 300 Win. Mag., 338 Win. Mag.
Price: Express 1625

Sako Rifles
Sako 75 Hunter

SAKO 75 VARMINT RIFLE

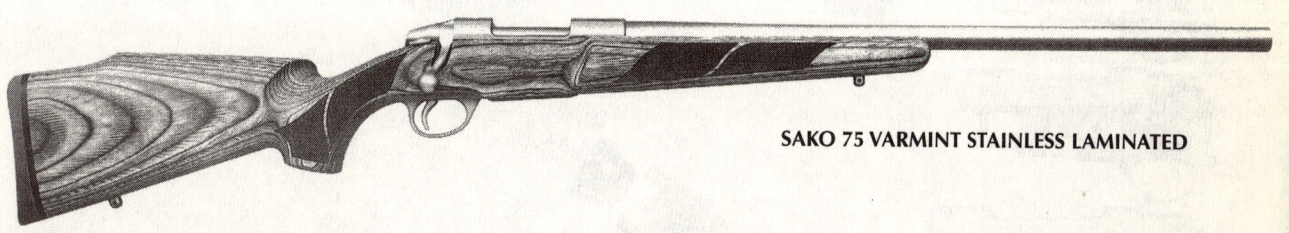

SAKO 75 VARMINT STAINLESS LAMINATED

Sako 75 Hunter
The Sako 75 Hunter is the first rifle to offer an action furnished with both a bolt with three locking lugs and a mechanical ejector. The traditional thumb safety has two positions. Cartridge removal or loading is done by pressing a separate bolt release button in front of the safety. No need to touch the safety to remove a cartridge and then disengage it by mistake under difficult or stressful conditions. The new cold hammer-forged barrel is manufactured in an advanced custom-built robotic cell. The Sako features a totally free-floating barrel. Instead of checkering, this all-stainless, all-weather model has soft rubbery grips molded in the stock to provide a firmer, more comfortable grip than with conventional synthetic stocks. The selected moisture stabilized high-grade walnut ensures quality and craftsmanship.

Other features include:
- Five bolt siding guides
- 70° Bolt Lift
- Totally free-floating cold hammer-forged barrel
- Positive safety system with separate bolt release button for safe unloading
- Detachable staggered 5-round magazine
- Five (5) action sizes for perfect cartridge match
- All-Stainless metal parts and All-Weather synthetic stock with special grips
- Selected moisture stabilized walnut stock with hand-crafted checkering
- Integral scope rails

Prices:
Sako 75 Hunter
22"barrel (17 Rem., 222 Rem., 223 Rem.,
   22-250 Rem., 243 Win., 7mm-08, 308 Win.,
   25-06 Rem., 270 Win., 280 Rem., 30-06) $1129
24" barrel (7mm Rem. Mag., 300 Win. Mag.,
   338 Win. Mag., 375 H&H Mag., 416 Rem. Mag) 1163
26" barrel (7mm STW, 7mm Wby. Mag., 300 Wby.
   Mag., 340 Wby. Mag., 300 Rem. Ultra Mag) . . . 1163
Sako 75 Stainless Synthetic
22" barrel (22-250 Rem., 243 Win., 308 Win.,
   7mm-08 25-06 Rem., 270 Win., 30-06). 1239
24" barrel (7mm Rem. Mag., 300 Win.
   Mag., 338 Win. Mag., 375 H&H Mag.) 1274
26" barrel (7mm STW, .300 Wby. Mag.,
   300 Rem Ultra Mag.) Hinged floor plate.

Sako 75 Varmint Rifle
The Sako 75 Varmint Rifle uses only the highest grade steel in the construction of the action, bolt, barrel and all internal parts. Sako cold hammer-forges heavyweight bar stock into one of the truest, most accurate barrels available. The 24" free-floated barrel is matched to the appropriate action size to eliminate excessive weight. The matte lacquered walnut stock features a beavertail forearm for additional stability and support when shooting from sandbags. The Sako 75 is the first and only rifle with three locking lugs and a mechanical ejector. Other Sako features include a one-piece forged bolt with five gliding surfaces, a detachable magazine, and a smooth 70 degree bolt lift.

Specifications
Calibers: 17 Rem., 222 Rem., 223 Rem., 22-250 Rem., 22 PPC, 6mm PPC
Price: 1337
Also Available: 75 Varmint Stainless Laminated
from 222 Rem. to 6mm PPC. 1448

Sako Rifles

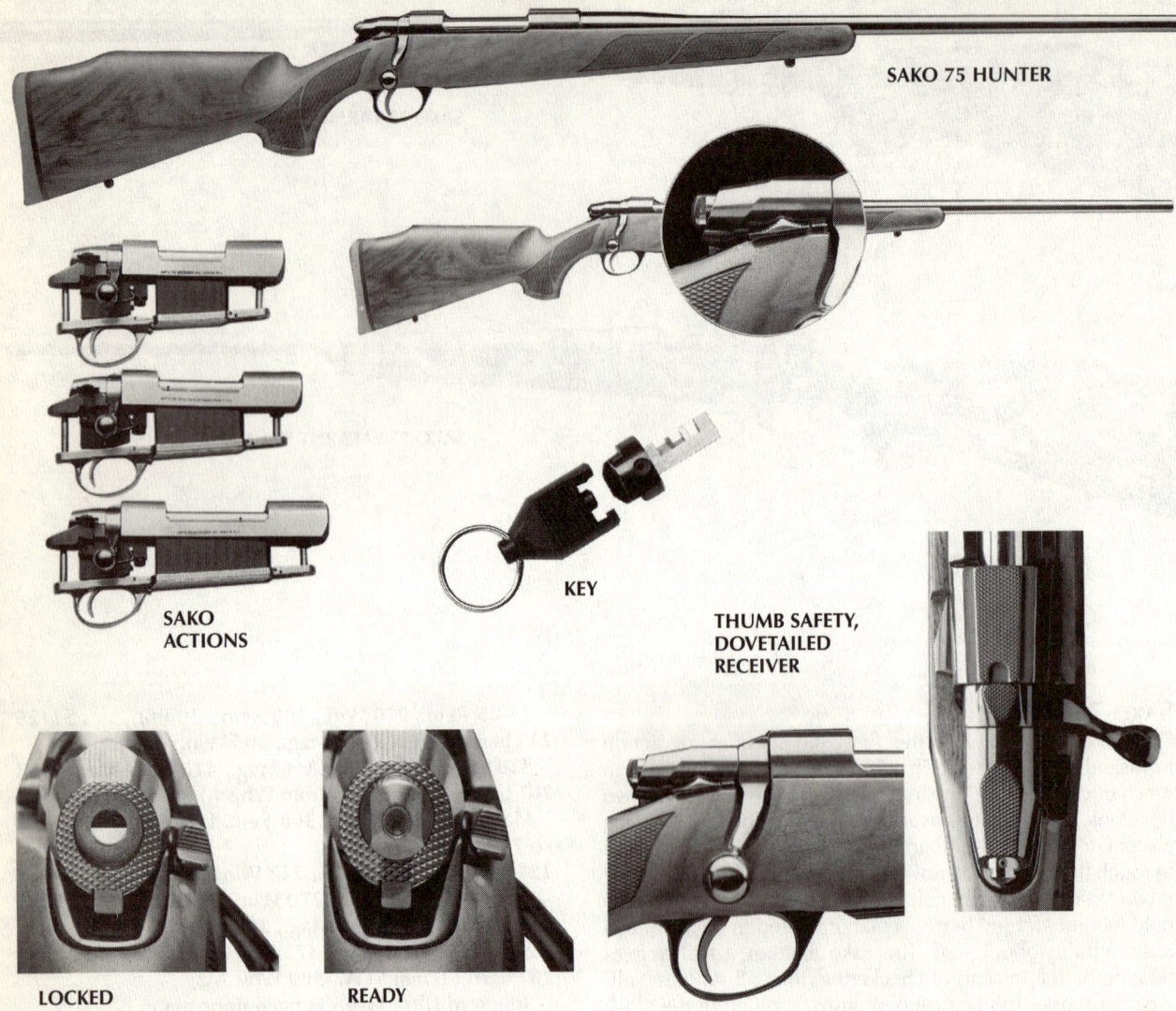

Sako 75 Actions

Sako 75 actions are renowned for their graceful lines, strength and reliability. Each of the four action sizes is manufactured for a specific range of calibers. The Sako 75 is the first to offer a bolt with three locking lugs and a mechanical ejector while maintaining a bolt lift of only 70°. Five guiding surfaces prevent the bolt from binding and provide ultra smooth-operation. The two-position thumb safety is located conveniently behind the bolt handle. A separate button in front of the safety allows the bolt to be opened while the safety is on. The detachable magazine can be loaded through the ejection port. Both carbon steel and stainless steel actions are available.

The three largest Sako actions now feature "key concept", a mechanism on the cocking piece that locks or unlocks the striker. You can thus render the 75 absolutely safe, disabling it with a turn of the key. Three keys are provided with each rifle, and others can be ordered by rifle serial number from the 7500 patterns. All Sako Model 75 rifles except those built on the smallest actions will soon come standard with the key concept lock.

"The key blends into the rifle contours when the lock is open and the gun is operational," explained Mr. Paul-Erik Tolvo, former president of Sako Ltd. "When the key is removed, the lock takes effect and the hunting rifle is completely safe and inoperative."

This revolutionary concept puts complete control of the safety and security of the rifle in the hands of its owner. "When the key is removed, there is no way to operate the gun, even accidentally. Any attempts to pick the lock will render the rifle unusable," said Mr. Tolvo. He also noted that the Sako 75 is considered the very best bolt action rifle in the industry. "The Sako 75 is the best hunting rifle in the world. It is only natural that we wanted to offer it with added security and safety for its owner and society in general. We believe this will become the new standard in gun safety."

Sako Rifles

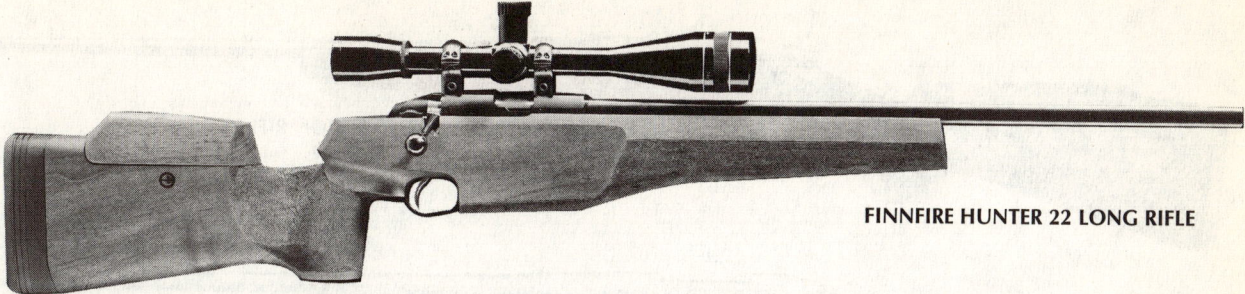

FINNFIRE HUNTER 22 LONG RIFLE

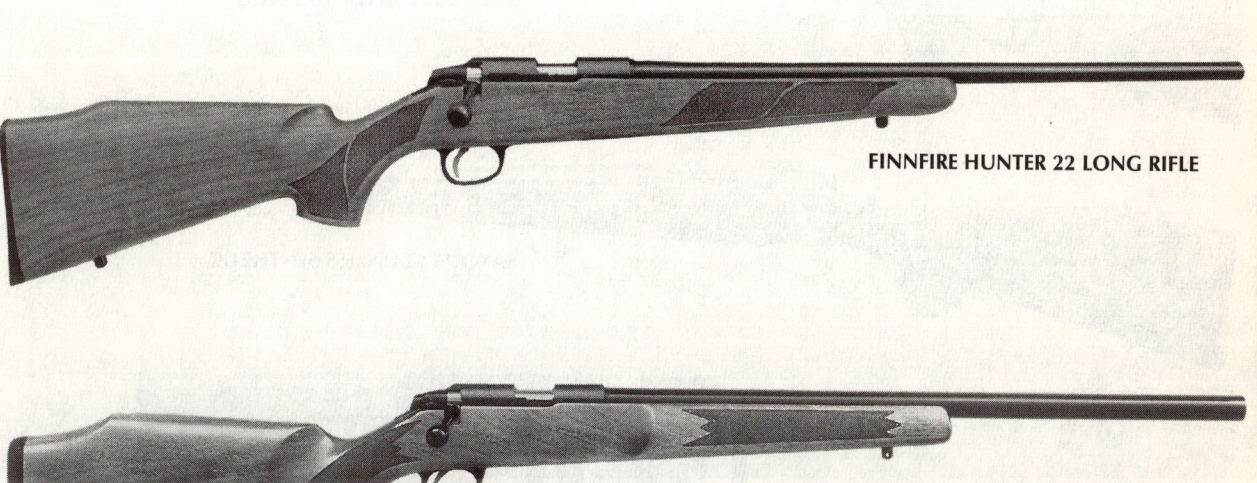

FINNFIRE HUNTER 22 LONG RIFLE

FINNFIRE VARMINT HEAVY BARREL

FINNFIRE SPORTER
The Sporter has a competition-style stock, adjustable cheekpiece and butt plate. The heavy barrel makes it an ideal gun when unerring accuracy is required. (scope and mount not included)

FINNFIRE 22 LR BOLT-ACTION RIFLE
Sako of Finland designed the .22 Finnfire to make it as similar to its "big brothers" as possible—just scaled down. The single-stage adjustable trigger is a carbon copy of the trigger found on the Model 75. The 22-inch barrel is cold-hammered to ensure superior accuracy.
Specifications
Overall length: 37 1/2" **Weight:** 5 1/4 lbs. (Hunter, Sporter) ; 7 1/2 lbs. (Varmint) **Rate of twist:** 16 1/2"
Other outstanding features include:
- European walnut stock with matte lacquer finish
- 50° bolt lift
- Free-floating barrel
- Integral 11mm dovetail for scope mounting
- Two-position safety that locks the bolt
- Cocking indicator
- Five- or 10-shot detachable magazine
- Available with open sights

Price:
Sporter	$951
Hunter	854
Varmint	896

SAKO 75 FINNLIGHT (NOT SHOWN)
The Sako 75 Finnlight is especially suited for long hunts. It offers pinpoint accuracy, excellent balance, uncompromising strength and reliability in a compact and attractive package.

Sako 75 Finnlight has been built to meet the same demanding requirements as other Sako 75 rifles. The free floating barrel is fluted for rigidity, lightness and faster cooling. Light synthetic stock with soft over-moulded rubber surfaces ensures good grip in all conditions. For a lightweight rifle, Sako 75 Finnlight has a broad caliber selection.

Prices:
Synthetic/Stainless (243 Win., 7mm-08 Rem., 308 Win., 25-06 Rem., 270 Win., 280 Rem., 30-06, 6.5x55) 1235
Magnums (7mm Rem. Mag., 300 Win. Mag.) 1260

Sako Rifles

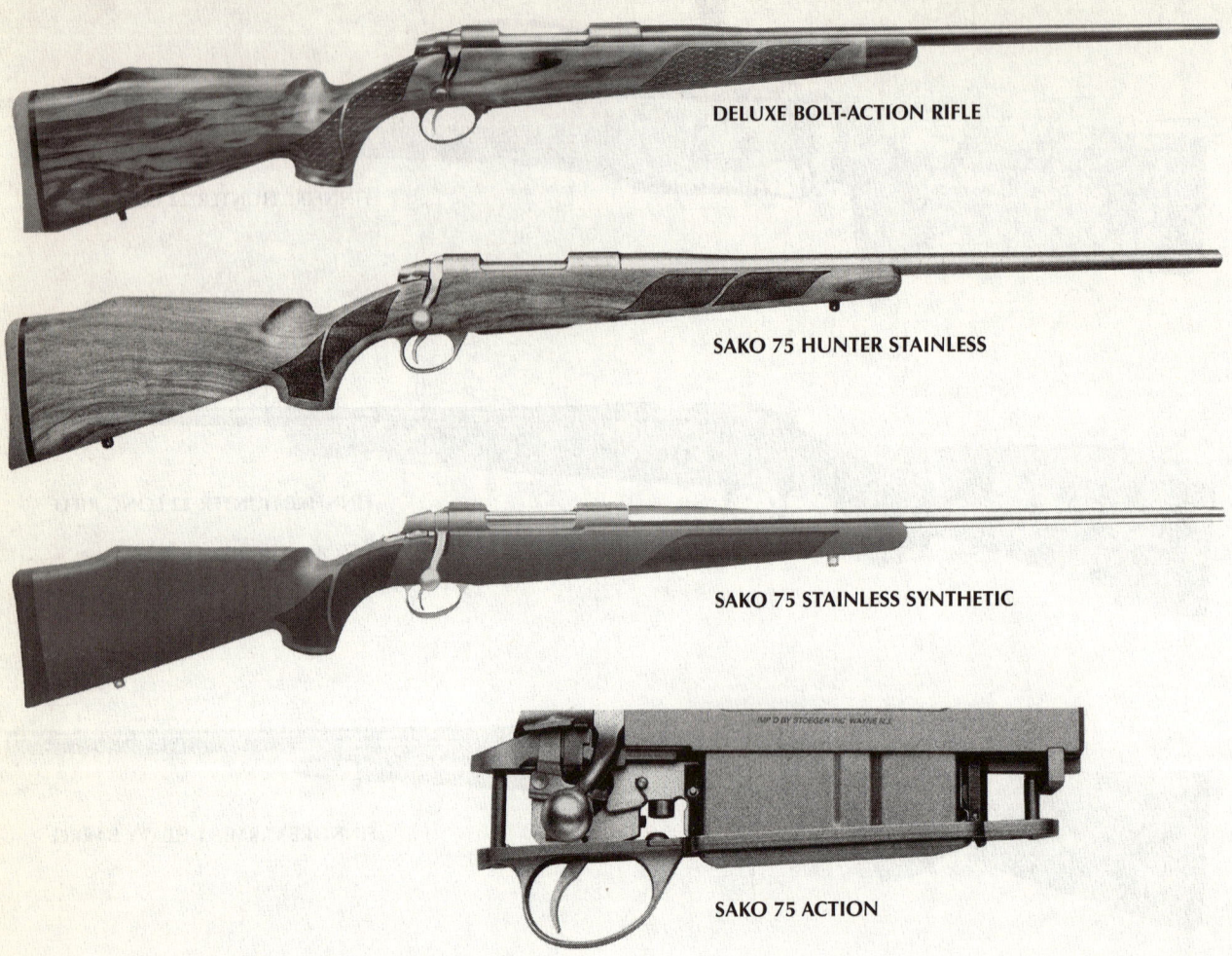

DELUXE BOLT-ACTION RIFLE

SAKO 75 HUNTER STAINLESS

SAKO 75 STAINLESS SYNTHETIC

SAKO 75 ACTION

SAKO 75 DELUXE BOLT-ACTION RIFLE
The fine-touch features you expect of the deluxe grade Sako are here:
1. Reliable safety system with a separate bolt release button.
2. First ever bolt with three locking lugs and a mechanical ejector. Five guiding surfaces prevent bolt binding and provide smooth operation. Four action sizes for perfect cartridge fit.
3. Totally free-floating cold hammer forged barrel for ultimate accuracy. Test with a slip of paper.
4. Sako Deluxe 75 Hunting Rifle has stainless steel lined staggered magazine with hinged floorplate and aluminum follower for faultless operation. Positive feeding angle is only 3-5 degrees.
5. Fancy grade, high-grained walnut. Old-world craftmanship Rosewood pistol grip cap with silver inlay.
6. Classic detail–Rosewood fore-end tip. The accuracy, reliability and superior field performance for which Sako is famous are still here too.

The scope mounting system on these Sakos are among the strongest in the world. Instead of using separate bases, a tapered dovetail is milled into the receiver, to which the scope rings are mounted. This sleek system has been proven over 20 years on the field. Sako Original Scope Mounts and Sako scope rings are available in low, medium and high in one-inch and 30mm.

Prices:
Action I in 17 Rem., 222 Rem. & 223 Rem. $1653
Action III in 22-250 Rem., 243 Win.,
   7mm-08 and 308 Win. 1653
Action IV in 25-06 Rem., 6.5x55 SE, 270 Win.,
   280 Rem., 30-06. 1653
Action V in 270 Wby. Mag., 7mm Rem. Mag.,
   7mm STW, 7mm Wby. Mag., 300 Win. Mag.,
   300 Wby. Mag., 338 Win. Mag., .340 Wby. Mag.,
   375 H&H Mag., 416 Rem. Mag. 1688

SAKO 75 HUNTER STAINLESS
Detachable box magazine, checkered walnut stock, standard and magnum chamberings.
Price:
23", .270 Win., 30-06. 1239
24" 7mm Rem. Mag., 300 Win. Mag.,
   338 Win. Mag. 1274
26" 7mm STW, 300 Wby. 1274

Sako Rifles

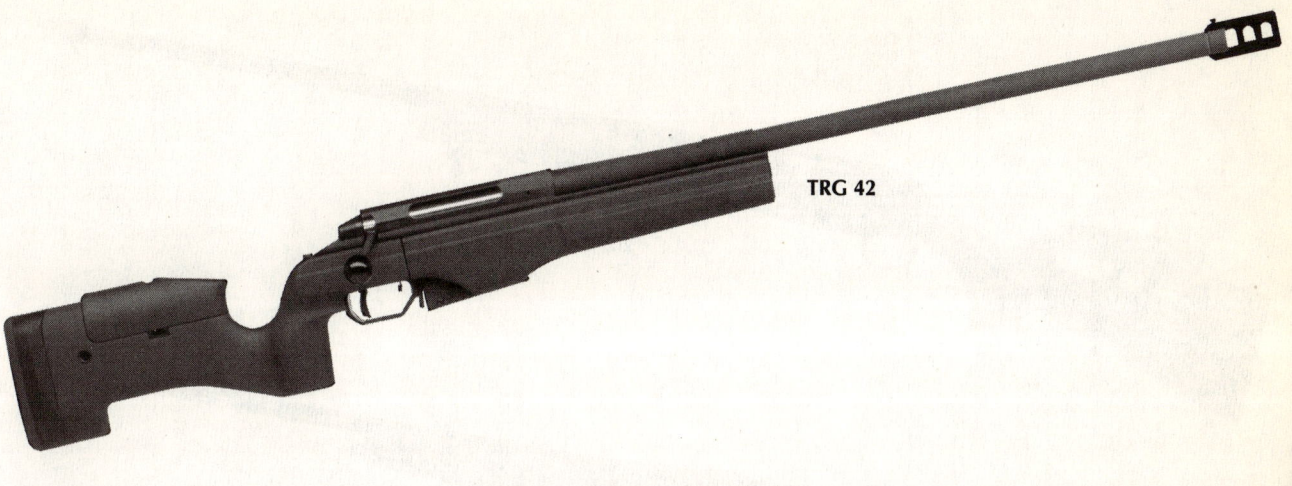
TRG 42

TRG S

Sako TRG 22/42

Sako TRG 22/42 rifles are designed for long-range competition. The TRG 22 in 308 Win. excels in 300-meter UIT standard competition rifle and serves the governments of several nations as their primary sniper rifle.

The TRG 42 in 300 Win. Mag and .338 Lapua Mag. is a true long-range competition rifle. It can also be equipped with implements for the tactical sniper.

Both TRG actions and special match grade barrels (chrome-moly or stainless) are cold hammer-forged. The sturdy bolt with three locking lugs feeds rounds reliably from the centerline of a detachable staggered magazine. The high-tech constructed aluminum-reinforced composite stock can be completely adjusted to match the individual preferences of all shooters. The target trigger is a fully adjustable 2-stage unit. Optilock quickmount allows any target scope to be positioned properly on the action.

Prices:
TRG-22 in 308 Win . . . . from $2484
TRG-42 in .338 Lapua or 300 Win Mag. . . . . . from 2829

Sako TRG-S

This sophisticated hunting rifle is designed around Sako's famed competition TRG rifle. Bolt is massive, with 3 symmetrical locking lugs and thus a short 60 degree bolt lift. Detachable magazine feeds reliably from centerline, straight to chamber. Stock is high-tech composite with integrated fiberglass reinforced skeleton for rigidity and accuracy.

Free floating cold hammer-forged barrel, adjustable trigger.
Specifications
Calibers: .338 Lapua Mag, 30-378 Wby. Mag
Price:. 882

Sauer Rifles

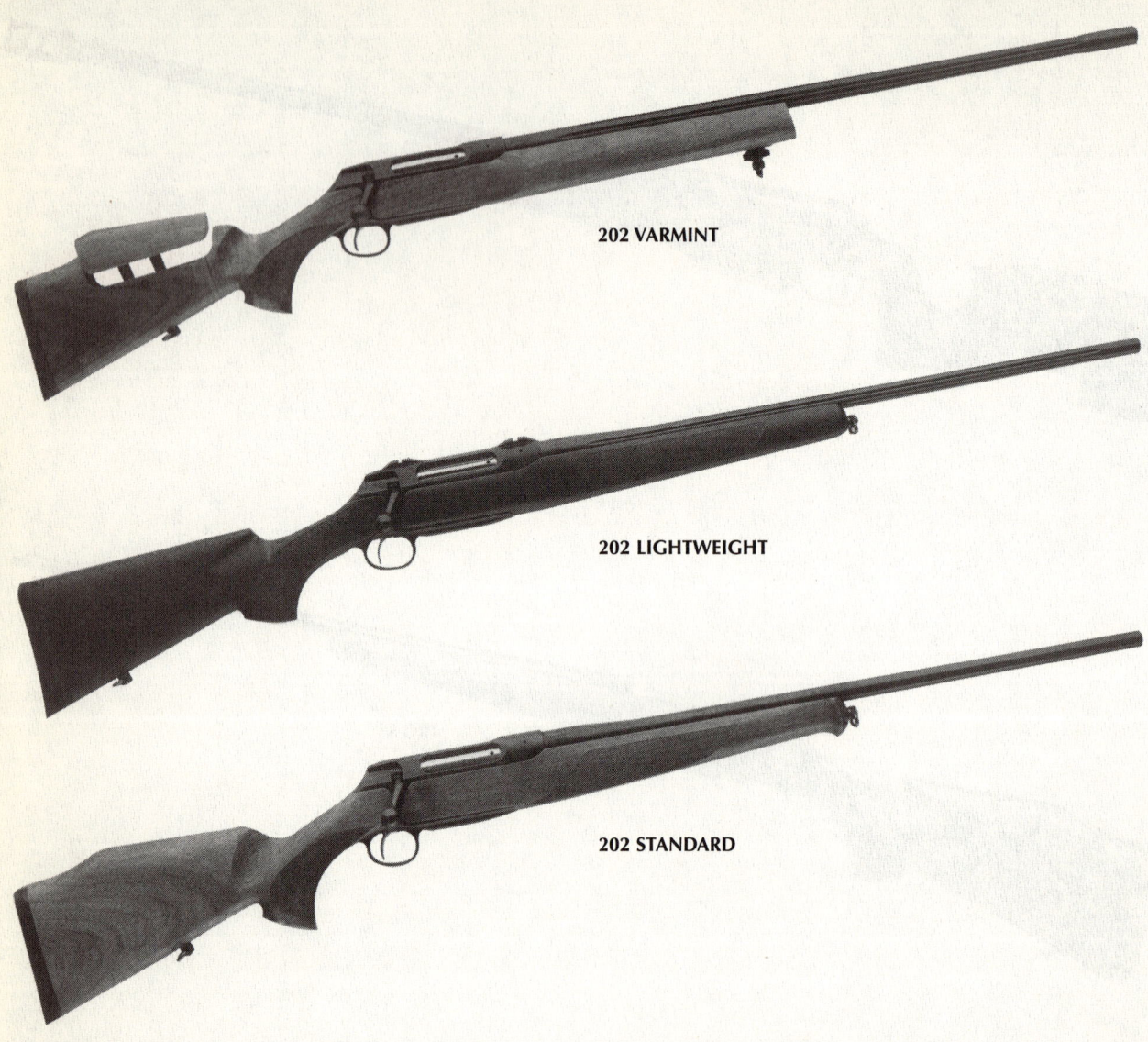

202 VARMINT

202 LIGHTWEIGHT

202 STANDARD

Model 202 Bolt Action
Specifications
Calibers: 25-06 Rem., 243 Win., 6.5x55, 270 Win., 308, 30-06 S'field;
Supreme Magnum calibers: 7mm Rem. Mag., 300 Win. Mag., 300 Wby. Mag., 375 Win.
Mag. Action: Bolt takedown
Capacity: 3 rounds
Barrel Length: 23.6"; 26" (Supreme Magnum)
Overall Length: 44.3"; 46" (Supreme Magnum)
Weight: 7.7 lbs.; 8.4 lbs. (Supreme Magnum)
Stock: Select American Claro walnut with high-gloss epoxy finish and rosewood forend and grip caps; Monte Carlo comb with cheekpiece; 22 line-per-inch diamond pattern, hand-cut checking

Sights: Drilled and tapped for sights and scope bases
Features: Adjustable two-stage trigger; polished and jeweled bolt; quick-change barrel; tapered bore; QD sling swivel studs; black rubber recoil pad; Wundhammer palm swell; dual release safety; six locking lugs on bolt head; removable box magazine; fully enclosed bolt face; three gas relief holes; firing-pin cocking indicator on bolt rear
Prices:
Standard synthetic $1259
   Standard walnut 1249
Also available: Lightweight. 1395
   Supreme w/walnut stock 1385
   SSG 3000 Tactical Rifle 2560
   Varminter 1495
   Left hand (30-06 w/walnut only) 1395

Savage Arms
Centerfire Rifles

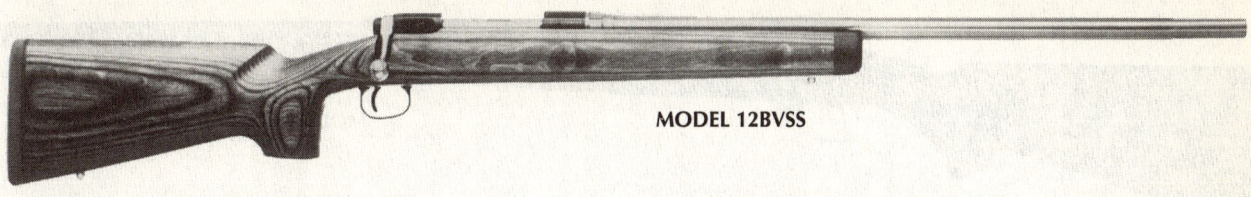

MODEL 12BVSS

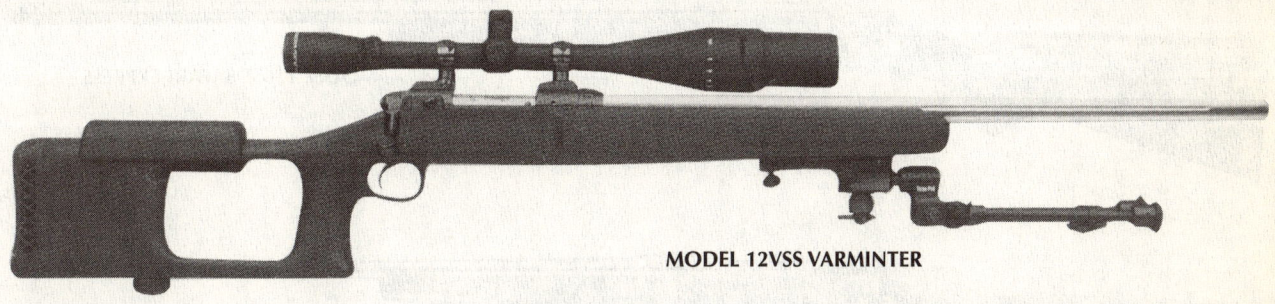

MODEL 12VSS VARMINTER

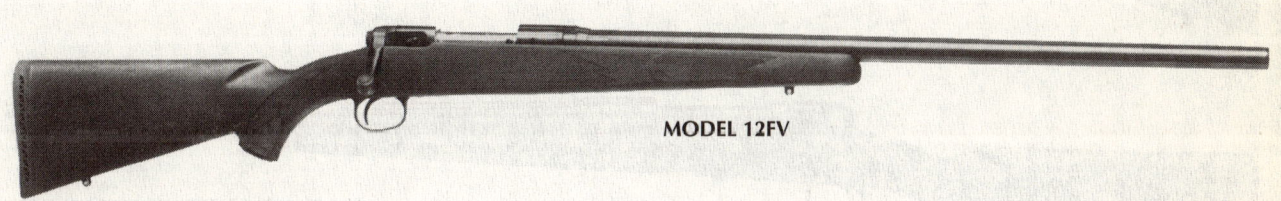

MODEL 12FV

Model 12BVSS Short Action Varmint
Specifications
Calibers: 223 Rem., 22-250 Rem., .243 Win, and 308 Win. and 22-250 Rem.
Capacity: 5 + 1
Barrel Length: 26" fluted heavy barrel
Overall Length: 46.75"
Magazine: Top loading internal
Weight: 9.5 lbs.
Sights: None. Drilled and tapped for scope mounts
Stock: Laminated hardwood with high comb, ambidextrous grip and ebony tip
Finish: Fluted stainless steel with recessed muzzle
Features: Short Action precision long range rifle with dual pillar bedding
Price:..................................$616
Also Available:
FVSS with black syntheticstock, 9 lbs............569

Model 12VSS-Short Action
Specifications
Calibers: .223 Rem., 22-250 Rem., 308 Win.
Overall Length: 45.75"
Weight: 11.25 lbs.
Sights: Drilled and tapped for scope mounts

Stock: Choate™ adjustable black synthetic stock.
Barrel: Heavy fluted stainless steel, recessed target muzzle, button rifled and free floating.
Magazine: Internal box with (4) round capacity
Features: Blue/Stainless steel bolt action, Sharp Shooter trigger, Choate™ stock. Scopes, rings, bases and bipod not included.
Price:..................................$900

Model 12FV Short Action Varmint
Specifications
Calibers: 223 Rem., 22-250 Rem., .243 Win,, 308 Win.
Capacity: 5
Barrel Length: 26"
Overall Length: 46.75"
Magazine: Top loading internal
Weight: 9 lbs.
Sights: None. Drilled and tapped for scope mounts
Stock: Durable black synthetic with scrolled checkering and dual pillars
Finish: Blued with recessed muzzle
Features: Short-action varmint rifle with 26" button rifled heavy barrel
Price:..................................481

Rifles • 195

Savage Arms

MODEL 10FP-LE1 - SHORT ACTION

MODEL 116SE SAFARI EXPRESS

MODEL 114U

MODEL 10FM SIERRA LIGHTWEIGHT

LE Series
The new LE (Law Enforcement) series is based upon a short .308-length action. It has a 20" or 26" heavy barrel and oversized bolt handle.
Price:................................... $511

Model 116SE Safari Express
Specifications
Calibers: .375 H&H, 300 Rem. Ultra Mag., 458 Win. Mag.
Capacity: 4 rounds (1 in chamber)
Barrel Length: 24" stainless steel w/AMB
Overall Length: 45.5" **Weight:** 8.5 lbs. **Sights:** 3-leaf express
Stock: Classic-style select-grade walnut w/cut checkering; ebony tip; stainless-steel crossbolts; internally vented recoil pad
Price:................................... 975

Model 114U
Specifications
Calibers: 270 Win., 30-06 Spfld (22" bbl.); 7mm STW, 7mm Rem. Mag., 300 Win. Mag. (24" bbl.) **Overall Length:** 43.5"
Weight: Approx. 7 lbs. **Rifling Twist:** 1 in 10" (270 Win., 30-6 Spfld., 300 Win. Mag.); 1 in 9.5" (7mm Rem. Mag.)
Features: High gloss American Walnut Stock with ebony tip; Custom checkering on the grip and forend; high luster blued finish on the barrel, receiver, and bolt handle; precision laser-etched Savage logo on bolt body; drilled and tapped for scope mounts
Price:................................... $532

Model 10FM Sierra Lightweight
Specifications
Calibers: 243, 7mm-08, 308
Capacity: 5 + 1 **Barrel Length:** 20"
Overall Length: 41.5" **Magazine:** Top loading internal
Weight: 6.25 lbs. **Sights:** None. Drilled and tapped for scope mount; bases included
Stock: Lightweight graphite/fiberglass filled composite stock with positive checkering
Finish: Blued
Features: Blue alloy steel barreled action
Price:................................... 476

Savage Arms Rifles

MODEL 11F SHORT ACTION HUNTER

MODEL 11G SHORT ACTION CLASSIC AMERICAN STYLE HUNTER

MODEL 10GY SHORT ACTION LADIES/YOUTH RIFLE

Model 11F Short Action Hunter
Specifications
Calibers: 223 Rem., 22-250 Rem., 243 Win., 7mm-08 Rem., .300 WSM and 308 Win. **Capacity:** 5 **Barrel Length:** 22" standard weight **Overall Length:** 42.75" **Magazine:** Top loading internal **Weight:** 6.75 lbs. **Sights:** Available in right/left hand. Drilled and tapped for scope mounts **Stock:** Durable black synthetic with scrolled checkering and dual pillars **Finish:** Blued
Features: Short Action with dual pillar bedded stock
Price:. **$442**

Model 11G Short Action Classic American Style Hunter
Specifications
Calibers: 223 Rem., 22-250 Rem., 243 Win., 7mm-08 Rem., 300WSM, 7mm RSUM, and 300 RSUM and 308 Win. **Capacity:** 5 **Barrel Length:** 22" **Overall Length:** 42.75" **Magazine:** Top loading internal **Weight:** 6.75 lbs. **Sights:** Available with or without (11GNS) Available in right/left hand. Drilled and tapped for scope mounts **Stock:** American-style walnut finished hardwood with fancy scrolled, diamond point checkering and black recoil pad **Finish:** Blued
Price:. **$418**

Model 10GY Short Action Ladies/Youth Rifle
Specifications
Calibers: 223 Rem., 243 Win. and 308 Win.
Capacity: 5
Barrel Length: 22" standard weight
Overall Length: 39.25"
Magazine: Top loading internal
Weight: 6.25 lbs.
Sights: None. Drilled and tapped for scope mounts
Stock: American style walnut finished hardwood with cut checkering
Finish: Blued
Price:. **418**

Rifles • 197

Savage Centerfire Rifles
Long Range And Scout Rifles

MODEL 112FVSS LONG ACTION

MODEL 112BVSS LONG ACTION

MODEL 10/110 LONG RANGE

SAVAGE "SCOUT" RIFLE-MODEL 10FCM

Model 112FVSS Long Action
Specifications
Calibers: 25-06 Rem., 30-06, 7mm Rem. Mag., 300 Win. Mag. **Capacity:** 4 + 1 **Barrel Length:** 26" fluted, stainless steel **Overall Length:** 47.5" **Weight:** 10.3 lbs. **Sights:** Graphite/fiberglass-filled composite w/positive checkering
Price: $569

Model 112BVSS Long Action
Specifications
Calibers: 25-06, 7mm Rem. Mag., 300 Win Mag., 30-06 Sprgfld., **Capacity:** 4 + 1 **Barrel Length:** 26" fluted heavy barrel, stainless steel **Overall Length:** 47.5" **Weight:** 10 lbs. (approx.) **Sights:** None; drilled and tapped **Stock:** Laminated hardwood w/high comb; ambidextrous grip
Price: 616

Model 10/110 Long Range
Specifications
Calibers: 25-06 Rem., 30-06 Spfd., 7mm Rem. Mag., 300 Win. Mag. **Capacity:** 5 rounds (1 in chamber) **Barrel Length:** 24" (w/recessed target-style muzzle) **Overall Length:** 45.5" **Weight:** 8.5 lbs.
Sights: None; drilled and tapped for scope mount; bases included **Features:** Black matte nonreflective finish on metal parts; bolt coated with titanium nitride; stock made of black graphite/fiberglass-filled composite with positive checkering; left-hand model available
Price: 110 FP $502
Also available:
10FP 223 Rem & 308 Win 502

Savage "Scout" Rifle-Model 10FCM
Ultra-light weight and extremely well balanced, the 10FCM Savage "Scout" is the ideal rifle for any outdoor situation. Weighing approximately 6 pounds and sporting a 20" barrel, this fast handling carbine is chambered in 7mm-08 and .308. Features: Detachable Box Magazine: Capacity four (4) plus one (1) in the chamber; Removabe Ghost Ring Rear Sight with Gold Bead Front Sight; One-piece Scope Mount for long eye relief scope; Large Ball Bolt Handle; Rifleman's Combo Shooting Sling/Carry Strap with Q.D. Swivel Set; "Dual Pillar Bedded" synthetic stock
Price: 559

Savage Centerfire Rifles
All-Weather 116 Rifles

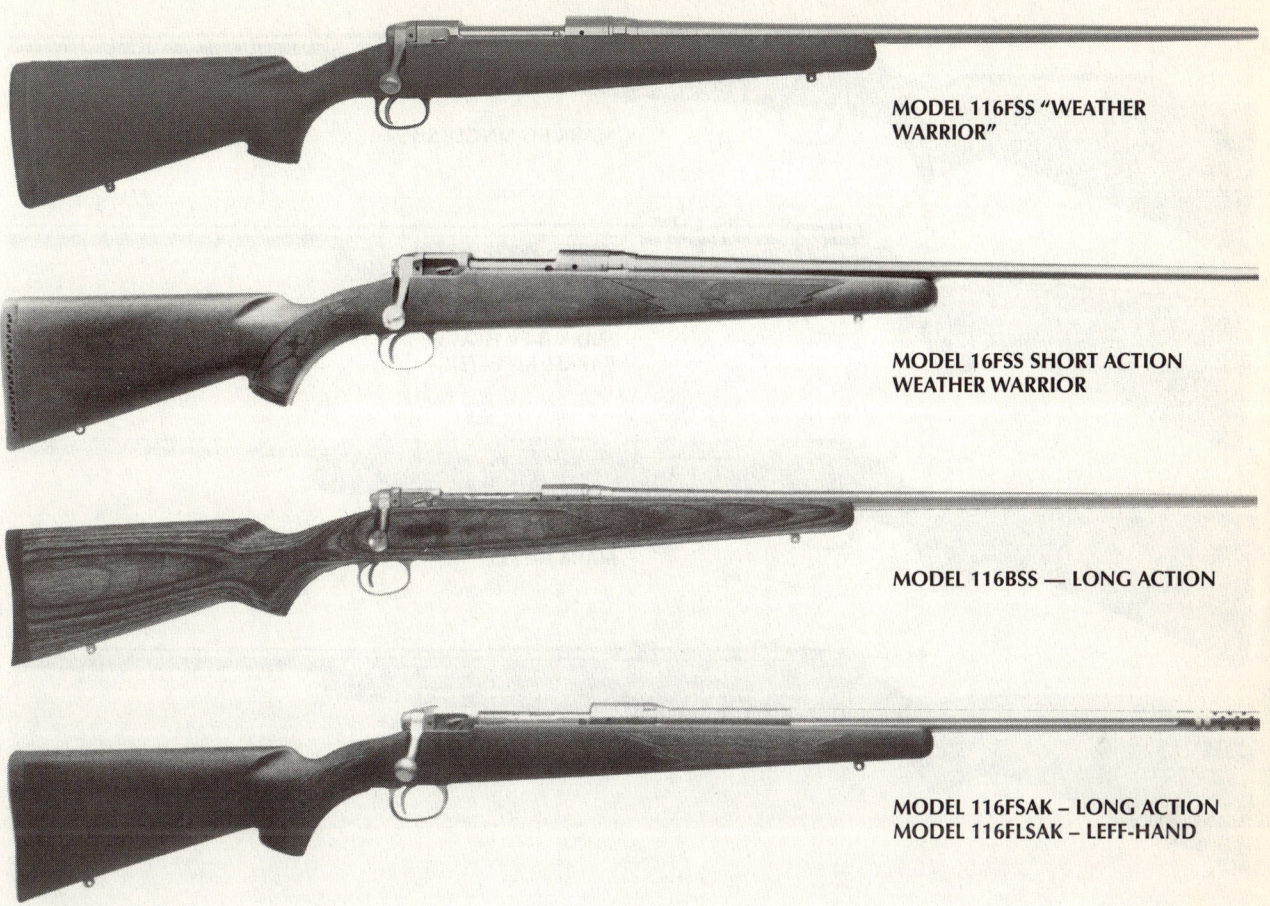

MODEL 116FSS "WEATHER WARRIOR"

MODEL 16FSS SHORT ACTION WEATHER WARRIOR

MODEL 116BSS — LONG ACTION

MODEL 116FSAK – LONG ACTION
MODEL 116FLSAK – LEFF-HAND

MODEL 116FSS "WEATHER WARRIOR"
Savage Arms combines the strength of a black graphite fiberglass polymer stock and the durability of a stainless-steel barrel and receiver in this bolt-action rifle. Major components are made from stainless steel, honed to a low refllective satin finish. Drilled and tapped for scope mounts. Left-hand model available.
Specifications
Calibers: 270 30-06, 7mm Rem. Mag., 300 Win. Mag., 338 Win. Mag., .375 H&H, 7mm STW, 7mm Rem Ultra Mag, 300 Rem Ultra Mag **Capacity:** 2-4 rounds **Barrel Length:** 22"-26" **Overall Length:** 45"-46.5" **Weight:** 6.5-7.75 lbs.
Price: $500

MODEL 16FSS SHORT ACTION WEATHER WARRIOR
Specifications
Calibers: 223, 243, 7mm-08, 308, 300 WSM, 7mm RSUM, 300 RSUM, 300 WSM 7mm RSUM, 300 RSUM **Capacity:** 5 **Barrel Length:** 22" **Overall Length:** 40.75" **Magazine:** Top loading internal **Weight:** 6 lbs. **Sights:** None. Drilled and tapped for scope mounts **Stock:** Durable black synthetic with scrolled checkering and dual pillars **Finish:** Stainless steel **Features:** Short action satin finished 400 series stainless steel barreled action
Price: $500

MODEL 116BSS WEATHER WARRIOR
Specifications
Calibers: 270 Win., 30-06, 7mm Rem. Mag., 300 Win Mag., 300 Rem Ultra Mag. **Barrel Length:** 24" or 26" **Weight:** 7 lbs to 7.75 lbs. **Features:** Laminate stock with cut checkering, stainless steel barrel.
Price: 644
Also available
   16BSS .300 WSM 644

MODEL 116FSAK
Specifications
Calibers: 270 Win., 30-06, 7mm, 300 Win Mag., 338 Win. Mag. .375 H&H, 7mm STW, 7mm Rem Ultra Mag, 300 Rem Ultra Mag. **Barrel Length:** 22" -26" **Weight:** 6.75 lbs to 7.75 lbs. **Features:** Synthetic stock, stainless barrel, adjustable muzzle brake. Left-hand available.

Price: 578

Savage Sporting Rifles
Rimfire Rifles

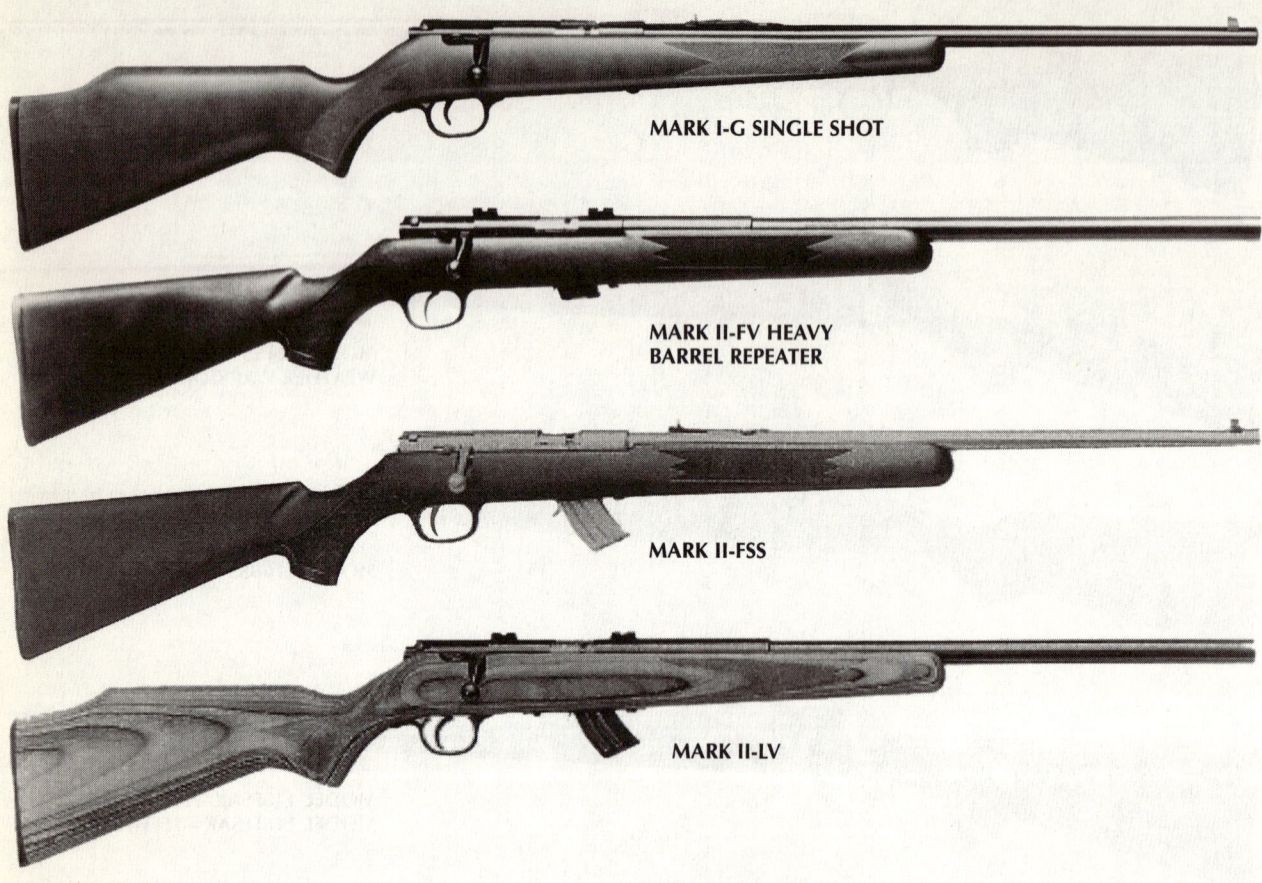

MARK I-G SINGLE SHOT
Specifications
Caliber: 22 Short, Long or LR
Single shot Action: Self-cocking bolt action, thumb-operated rotary safety **Barrel Length:** 20.75" **Overall Length:** 39.5"
Weight: 5.5 lbs. **Sights:** Open bead front; adjustable rear
Stock: One-piece, walnut-finish hardwood, Monte Carlo buttstock w/full pistol grip; checkered pistol grip and forend
Features: Receiver grooved for scope mounting
Price:.................................$135
Also available:
Mark I-G Youth (19" barrel)..................135
Mark I-LY (Youth with color laminate stock).......166
Mark I-Y Camo (Youth with Camo stock).........167

MARK II-FV HEAVY BARREL REPEATER
Specifications
Caliber: 22 LR **Capacity:** 5 rounds **Barrel Length:** 21" heavy weight **Overall Length:** 39.75" **Magazine:** 5 shot detachablle clip **Weight:** 6 lbs. **Sights:** None. Weaver-style bases included **Stock:** Black synthetic with positive checkering **Finish:** Blued free floated, button rifled with recessed targetstyle muzzle **Features:** Heavy barrel with synthetic stock in 22 LR
Price:.................................205
Alos available
Mark II FVXP (with scope)...................240

MARK II-FSS
Specifications
Caliber: 22 LR **Capacity:** 10 rounds **Barrel Length:** 21" (1 in 16" twist) **Overall Length:** 39.5" **Weight:** 5 lbs. **Stock:** Synthetic **Sights:** Bead front sight; adjustable open rear
Features: Stainless steel barrelled action
Price:.................................$179
Also available: Mark II-G w/one-piece walnut-finished Monte Carlo-style hardwood stock,
 blued steel bolt-action
 receiver, bead front sight...................148
Mark II-GY Ladies/Youth w/19" barrel (37" overall)
 Weight: 5 lbs..........................148
Mark II-GXP w/4x15mm scope (LH model avail.)...155
Mark II-F synthetic stock....................135
Mark II Camo............................167

MARK II-LV
Specifications
Caliber: 22 LR *Capacity:* 10 rounds *Barrel Length:* 21" heavy barrel (1 in 16" twist) *Overall Length:* 39.75" *Weight:* 6.5 lbs. *Stock:* Grey laminated hardwood stock; cut-checkered *Features:* Precision button rifled with recessed target-style muzzle; machined blued steel barreled action; dovetailed for scope mounting
Price:.................................235

Savage Sporting Rifles

MODEL 93G MAGNUM

MODEL 64FV SEMI-AUTOMATIC HEAVY BARREL

MODEL 30GM

MODEL III FXP3

MODEL 93G MAGNUM
Specifications
Caliber: 22 WMR **Capacity:** 5 rounds **Barrel Length:** 20.75"
Overall Length: 39.5" **Weight:** 5.75 lbs. **Sights:** Bead front; sporting rear with step elevator **Stock:** cut-checkered walnut stained hardwood. Left hand available
Price: $173

MODEL 64FV SEMI-AUTOMATIC HEAVY BARREL
Specifications
Caliber: 22 LR **Capacity:** 10 rounds **Barrel Length:** 21" heavy weight **Overall Length:** 40.75" **Magazine:** 10 shot detachable clip **Weight:** 6 lbs. **Sights:** None. Weaver-style bases included **Stock:** Black synthetic with positive checkering **Finish:** Blued, button rifled with recessed target style muzzle **Features:** Semiauto blue alloy steel barreled action
Price: 173
Also Available: Model 64F standard barrel
  with sights 5.5 lbs. 132
Model 64G standard barrel with sights 5.5 lbs.
  and hardwood stock 142

Model 64FVSS (stainless) $225
Model 64FSS (stainless) 171

30 G AND 30GM
Specifications
Walnut stock and forend with 21" octagonal barrel in 22 LR or 22 WMR (30GM).
Price: 214
  30GM 251

MODEL III FXP3
"Package" rifle with internal-box magazine (C version with detachable box), black synthetic stock, 22" barrel, sling, 3-9x32 scope.
Specifications
Calibers: 223 Rem, 22-250 Rem., 243 Win., 308 Win., 300 WSM 25-06 Rem., 270 Win., 30-06 Sprg., 7mm Rem. Mag., 300 Win. Mag., 338 Win. Mag 300 Rem Ultra Mag.
Capacity: 5 rounds (4 in Magnum) **Weight:** 6.5 lbs.
Price: 502

Springfield Rifles

MODEL M-6 SCOUT RIFLE/SHOTGUN COMBO FOLDING SURVIVAL GUN

M1A STANDARD

M1A-A1 SCOUT RIFLE

M1 GARAND

Model M-6 Scout Rifle/Shotgun Combo Folding Survival Gun
Specifications
Calibers: 22 LR/.410 and 22 Hornet/.410
Barrel Length: 18.25" (1:15" R.H. twist in 22 LR; 1:13" R.H. twist in 22 Hornet) **Overall Length:** 32" **Weight:** 4 lbs.
Sight Radius: 16 1/8" **Finish:** Parkerized or stainless steel
Features: .410 shotgun barrel (2.5" or 3" chamber) choked Full; drilled and tapped for scope mount with Weaver base; lockable plastic carry case
Price: $185
Stainless Steel 219

M1A Standard
Specifications
Calibers: 308 Win./7.62mm NATO **Action:** gas-operated, self-loading **Capacity:** 5- or 10-round box magazine
Barrel Length: 22" **Rifling:** 6 groove, RH twist, 1 turn in 11"
Overall Length: 44 1/3" **Weight:** 9.2 lbs.
Sights: Military square post front; military aperture rear, adjustable for windage and elevation **Sight Radius:** 26.75"
Prices:
Standard w/walnut stock 1448
Also available:
Basic M1A Rifle w/painted black fiberglass stock, caliber 308/7.62mm only 1319
M1A Scout Rifle w/scope mount and handguard, black fiberglass stock 1529
with walnut stock 1639
National Match (match-grade barrel and trigger) .. $1995
Super Match (heavy match barrel, special rod guide, heavy stock) 2449

M1A-A1 Scout Rifle
Specifications
Calibers: 308 Win./7.62mm **Action:** gas-operated, self-loading **Barrel Length:** 18" (w/o flash suppressor) **Overall Length:** 40.5" **Weight:** 9 lbs. (9.3 lbs. w/walnut stock)
Sights: Military square post-front, aperture rear with one MOA adjustments **Sight Radius:** 22.75"
Prices:
w/walnut stock 1639
w/black fiberglass stock 1529

M1 Garand
Built using the original USGI specs, the M1 Garand stands alone as a classic American combat rifle. The Garand features all-new receiver, barrel and stock, with all the remaining parts U.S. G.I. mil-spec. Chambered in .30-06 or .308 Win.
Specifications
Action: Gas operated, semi-automatic. **Stock:** American walnut **Barrel:** 24", 1-in-10" twist. **Weight:** 9.5 lbs.
Sights: front military square post, rear military aperture with MOA adjustments for windage and elevation.
Magazine capacity: 8 rounds.
Price: 1061

Szecsei & Fuchs Rifles

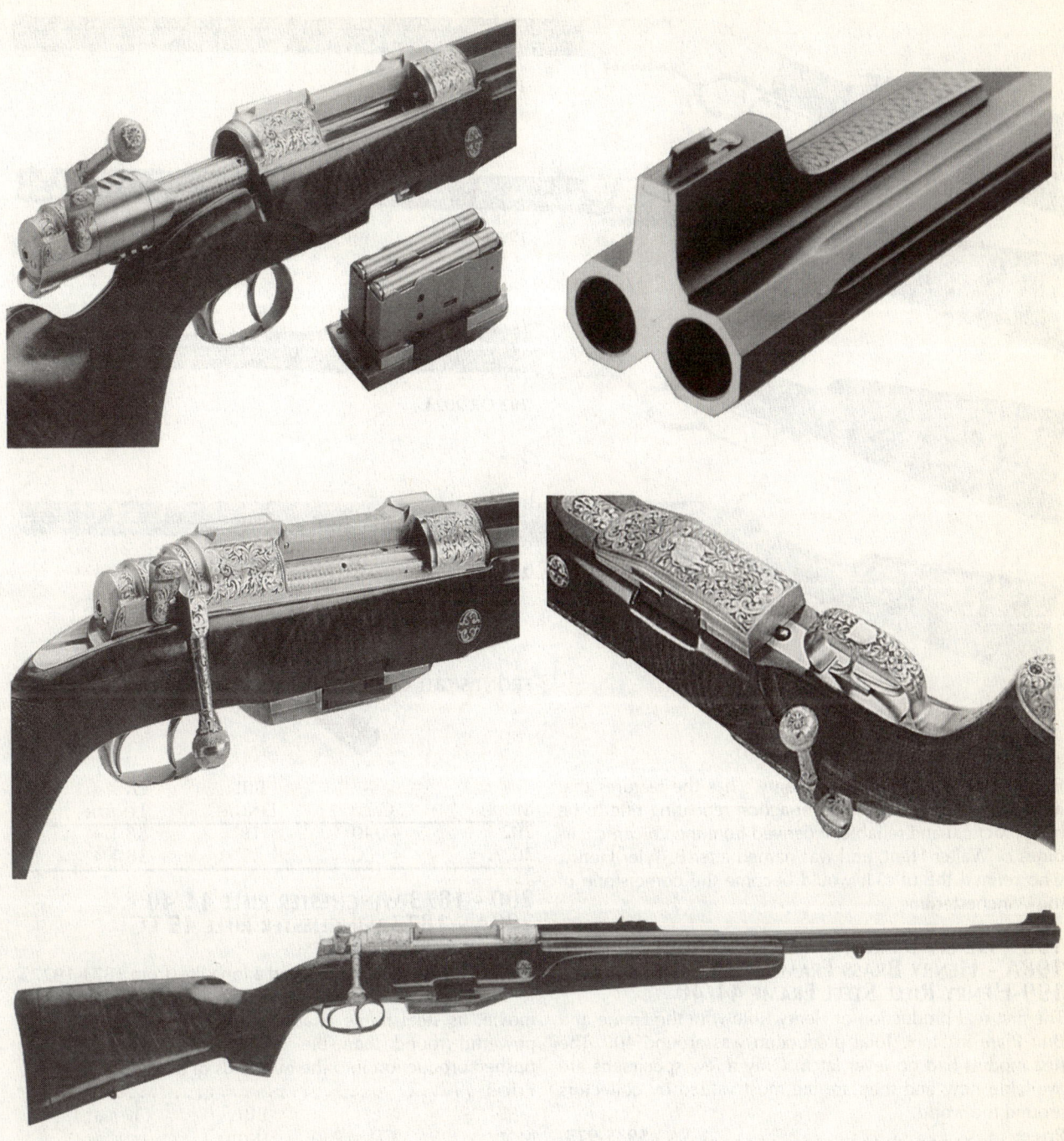

The Szecsei & Fuchs double-barrel bolt action rifle may be the only one of its kind. Built with great care and much handwork from the finest materials, it follows a design remarkable for its cleverness. And while the rifle is not light-weight, it can be aimed quickly and offers more large-caliber firepower than any competitor. The six-shot magazine feeds two rounds simultaneously, both of which can then be fired by two quick pulls of the trigger.

Specifications
Chamberings: .300 Win, 9.3 x 64, .358 Norma, .375 H&H, .404 Jeff, .416 Rem., .458 Win., .416 Rigby, .450 Rigby, .460 Short A-Square, .470 Capstick, .495 A-Square, .500 Jeffery
Weight: 14 lbs. with round barrels, 16 with octagon barrels.
Price: . . . . **Available on request**

Taylor's Rifles

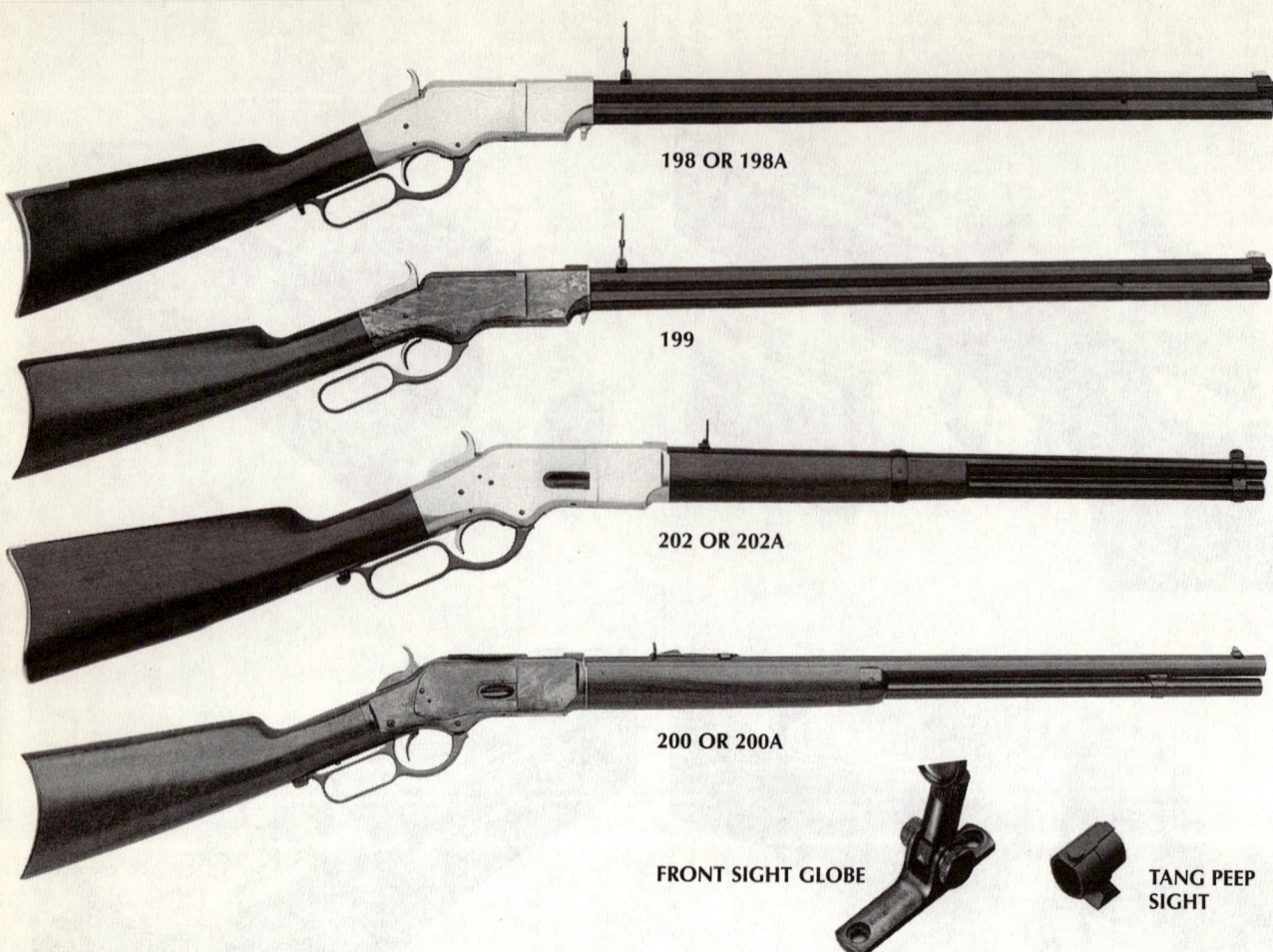

198 OR 198A

199

202 OR 202A

200 OR 200A

FRONT SIGHT GLOBE

TANG PEEP SIGHT

Faithful to the original, this "Henry", has the features that made its forebear the first lever-action repeating rifle to be both practical and reliable. It derived from the Volcanic carbines of Walter Hunt, and was named after B. Tyler Henry, who refined the rifle. It would become the cornerstone of the Winchester line.

198 - HENRY BRASS FRAME 44/40
198A - HENRY BRASS FRAME .45 LC
199 - HENRY RIFLE STEEL FRAME 44/40

The first real production of Henry Rifle with the Frame and Butt Plate in Steel. Total production was around 400. The first models had no lever latch. Only a few specimens are available now and they are the most valued by collectors around the world.
Price: $935-975

MODEL	CAL.	BBL. LENGTH	OVERALL LENGTH	MAGAZINE CAPACITY
198	44/40	24-1/4"	43-3/4"	13-9 shots
198A	45 LC	24-1/4"	43-3/4"	13-9 shots
199	44/40	24-1/4"	43-3/4"	13-9 shots

202 - 1866 YELLOWBOY CARBINE 44/40
202A - 1866 YELLOWBOY CARBINE .45 LC
1866 YELLOW CARBIN
Price: 735

MODEL	CAL.	BBL. LENGTH	OVERALL LENGTH
202	44/40	19"	38 1/4"
202A	45 LC	19"	38 1/4"

200 - 1873 WINCHESTER RIFLE 44/40
200A - 1873 WINCHESTER RIFLE 45 LC
1873 SPORTING RIFLE

The original Winchester 73 had a long life, from 1873-1927. It is probably the only gun to have given its name to a movie. Its steel frame enabled use of the .44/40, a more powerful round than the .44 Henry. Demand quickly pushed production into the hundreds of thousands.
Price: $895

MODEL	CAL.	BBL. LENGTH	OVERALL LENGTH
200	44/40	24 1/4"	43 1/4"
200A	45 LC	24 1/4"	43 1/4"

Prices:
5505-Front Sight Globe, Sight has a 3/8" dovetail. ... 22
5508-Tang Peep Sight 80
This tang sight is the famous target and hunting sight of the Old West. This sight has the precision adjustment for windage and elevation. Sight is blue finish and will fit original 1873 Winchester Rifles.

Thompson & Campbell Rifles

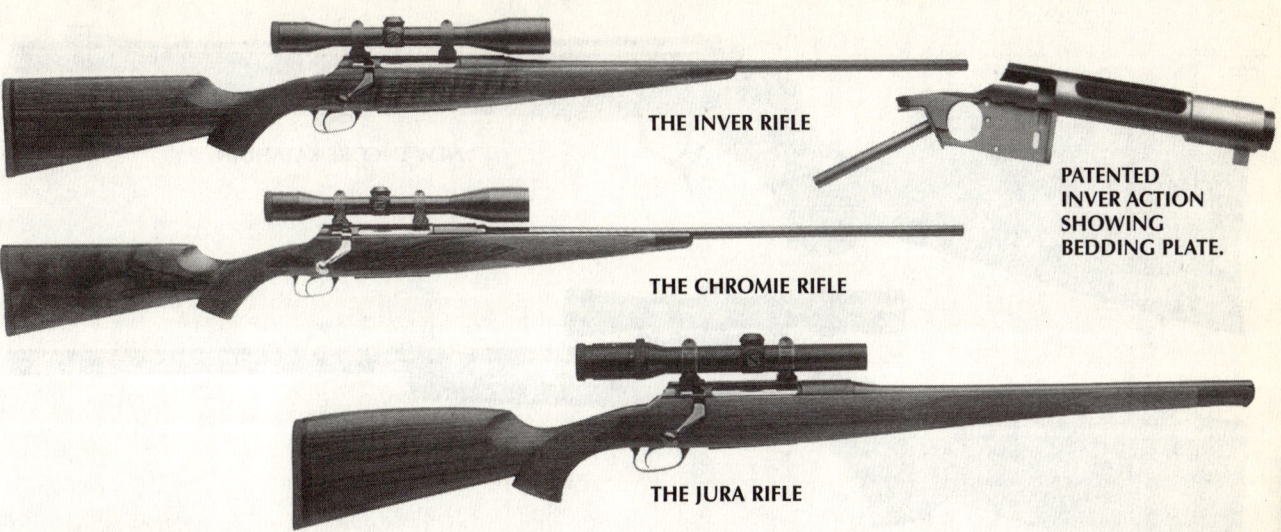

THE INVER RIFLE

THE CHROMIE RIFLE

THE JURA RIFLE

PATENTED INVER ACTION SHOWING BEDDING PLATE.

THE INVER RIFLE
The heart of this rifle is the patented Inver action, designed and developed by Thompson & Campbell. Machined from a single block of high-grade steel, it provides flawless functioning, mechanical simplicity and great strength. A conical triple-lugged bolt head enshrouds and supports the head of the chambered cartridge.

Designed primarily for use with a fine quality telescopic sight supplied on quick-detachable mounts, the Inver rifle also incorporates a unique system of open sights. A detachable foresight and flip-up backsight allow precision shooting with the same sighting axis as the scope, thus maintaining the firer's head position on the carefully-tailored stock. A two-stage trigger system is available as an option.

Specifications
Action: Patented front lock-in 3 lug bolt action
Magazine: Detachable 4 round box **Barrel length:** 22 inches
Safeties: Stalking safe on tang, wing safety on bolt; firing pin immobiliser on both **Trigger:** Single stage (two stage optional) **Telescopic Sight:** Best quality optics–owner's preferred choice can be fitted **Open Sights:** Flip-up rear aperture; Detachable post foresight **Stock:** Walnut, takedown capacity **Weight:** From 8 lbs **Calibers:** All popular sporting calibers **Other Features:** Flush-fitting pop-out sling swivel studs; fitted case
Price: . . . . Available on request

THE CROMIE RIFLE
The deluxe Cromie rifle is the flagship of the Thompson & Campbell range. The Cromie is stocked to the owner's personal fit and style with a stock of exhibition-grade walnut and supplied in a traditional leather carrying case. The action, receiver and detachable scope mounts are hand-engraved with gold inlays. The action and scope-mount steel are blued or colour case-hardened. The latter provides a marbled finish that is protective and wear-resistant. The Cromie model also comes with an octagonal barrel, a distinctive and traditional design feature of many fine old sporting rifles now revived by Thompson & Campbell.
Specifications
Action: Patented front locking 3 lug bolt action
Magazine: Detachable 4 round box **Barrel length:** 24 inches octagonal profile **Safeties:** Stalking safe on tang, wing safety on bolt; firing pin immobiliser on both **Trigger:** Single stage (two stage optional) **Telescopic Sight:** Best quality optics - owner's preferred choice can be fitted **Open Sights:** Optional **Stock:** Exhibition grade walnut; takedown capacity **Weight:** 8 lbs **Calibers:** All popular sporting calibers **Other Features:** Flush-fitting pop-out sling swivel studs; fitted case.
Price: . . . . Available on request

THE JURA RIFLE
Fully stocked, with the walnut running right up to the muzzle, the Jura is true to a long-established Continental tradition. Owing to its full length stock, the Jura is not a takedown rifle, and comes in a full-length carrying case. The 17-inch barrel gives the Jura a significantly shorter overall length than the other Thompson & Campbell models.

The Jura's short overall length makes it both fast-handling and easy to carry even in thick cover. When shooting from the confines of a high seat, and when climbing in and out, the Jura is particularly easy to use. Since much woodland and driven rifle shooting is done from a standing or sitting position, rather than prone as on the open hill, the Jura's stock dimensions, pistol grip contours, scope eye-relief and wide angle lens can be subtly but significantly regulated to provide the most comfortable and accurate fit for this kind of sport.
Specifications
Action: Patented front locking 3 lug bolt action
Magazine: Detachable 3- and 5-round box **Barrel length:** 17 inches **Safeties:** Stalking safety on tang, wing safety on bolt; firing pin immobiliser on both **Trigger:** Single stage (two stage optional) **Telescopic Sight:** Best quality optics - owner's preferred choice can be fitted **Open Sights:** Optional **Stock:** Walnut; not takedown **Weight:** from 7.5 lbs **Calibers:** All popular sporting calibers **Other Features:** Flush fitting pop out sling swivel studs; fitted case.
Price: . . . . Available on request

Thompson/Center Rifles

NEW ENCORE KATAHDIN

ENCORE HUNTER

T/C 22LR CLASSIC

ENCORE RIFLE

NEW Encore Katahdin Carbine
Single action, break open design in 444 Marlin, 450 Marlin and 45/70 Gov't. Heavy 18" barrel with integral Muzzle Tamer and adjustable fiber optic sights. Weight: 6 lbs. 10 oz. Composite Monte Carlo style stock with pistol grip and rubber butt pad. Molded in checkering.
Price: $606

Encore Hunter's Packages
308 Win (24" barrel) or 300 Win. Mag. (25" barrel) with blued steel and walnut stock. Comes with 3-9x40mm T/C scope in Weaver-style rings and bases. Includes lockable hardcase.
Price: 870

T/C 22LR Classic
Specifications
A blowback autoloading 22, the new Classic featues fiber optic sights, an 8-shot magazine, walnut stock and match-grade 22" barrel threaded to the receiver.
Price: 330

Encore Rifle
Specifications
Calibers: 22-250 Rem., 22 Hornet, .223 Rem., .243 Win., 25-06 Rem., .270 Win., .7mm-08 Rem., 7mm Rem. Mag., .308 Win., .30-06 Spfd., .300 Win. Mag., 45-70 Govt.
Action: Single-shot, break-open **Barrel lengths:** 24" and 26" heavy barrel (.22-250 Rem., 223 Rem., 25-06 Rem., 7mm Rem. Mag., and 300 Win. Mag. only) **Overall length:** 38 1/2" (24" barrel); 40 1/2" (26" barrel) **Weight:** 6 3/4 lbs. (24"); 7 1/2 lbs. (26") **Trigger:** Adjustable for overtravel
Safety: Automatic hammerblock w/bolt interlock
Stock: American walnut with Schnabel forend and Monte Carlo buttstock **Features:** Interchangeable barrels, sling swivel studs
Prices:
with composite walnut $614
with composite stock 588
45-70 Government 598
Composite walnut 624
SST 657
45-70 Govt. SST 668

Tikka Rifles

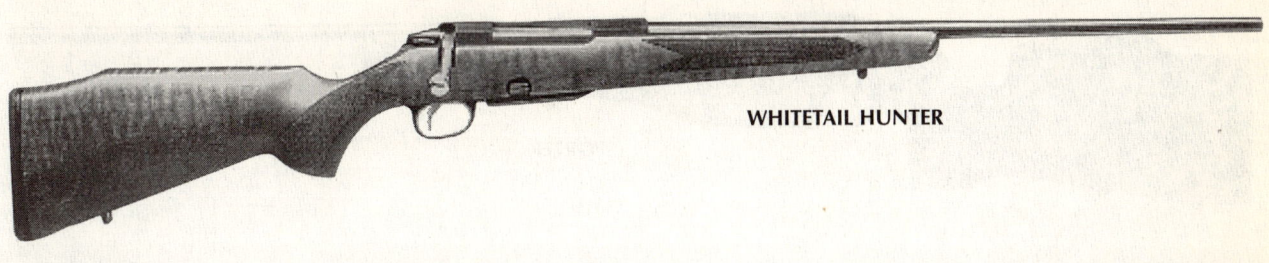
WHITETAIL HUNTER

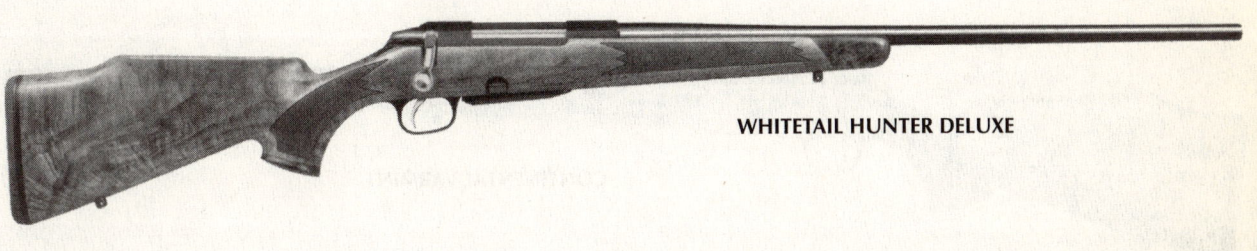
WHITETAIL HUNTER DELUXE

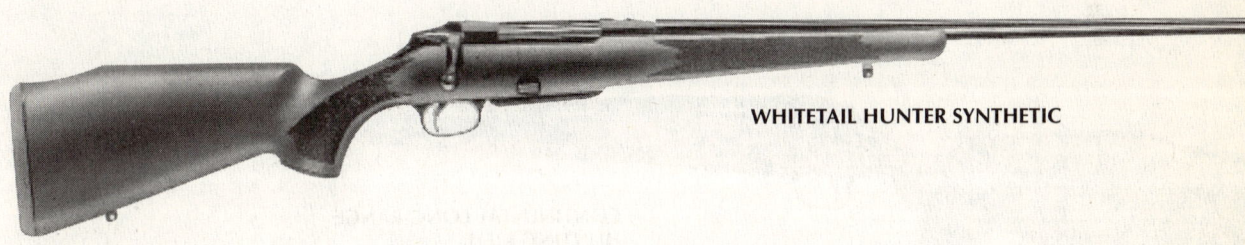
WHITETAIL HUNTER SYNTHETIC

WHITETAIL HUNTER
Specifications
Calibers: 22-250, 223, 243, 7mm-08, 308 (Medium); 25-06, 270, 6.5x55, 30-06 (Long); 7mm Mag., 300 Win. Mag., 338 Win. Mag. **Capacity:** 3 rounds (5 rounds optional); detachable magazine **Barrel Lengths:** 22.5" (24.5" Magnum) **Overall Length:** 42" (Medium); 42.5" (Long); 44.5" (Magnum) **Weight:** 7 lbs. (Medium); 7 1/4 lbs. (Long); 7.5 lbs. (Magnum) **Sights:** No sights; integral scope mount rails; drilled and tapped **Safety:** Locks trigger and bolt handle **Features:** Oversized trigger guard; short bolt throw; customized spacer system; walnut stock with palm swell and matte lacquer finish; cold hammer-forged barrel
Price:...$615
   Magnum..645
Also Available:
Left Hand 680
Left Hand Magnum 710
Whitetail Pro, identical to Hunter,
   with adjustable cheekpiece

WHITETAIL HUNTER DELUXE
Specifications
This Whitetail Hunter Deluxe has a select walnut stock, plus contrasting grip cap and forend tip and modified cheekrest.
Prices:
Standard Calibers............................$745
Magnums...775

WHITETAIL HUNTER SYNTHETIC
Specifications
Same specifications as the standard Whitetail Hunter, except with All-Weather synthetic stock.
Price:...615
   Magnum..645
Also available:
Whitetail Hunter Stainless Synthetic.
   Same specifications as above, except with
   stainless steel receiver, barrel and bolt.........680
In Magnum calibers 710

Tikka Rifles

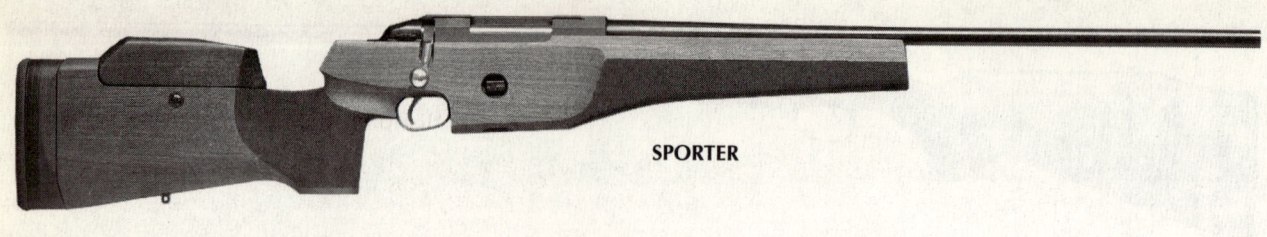

SPORTER

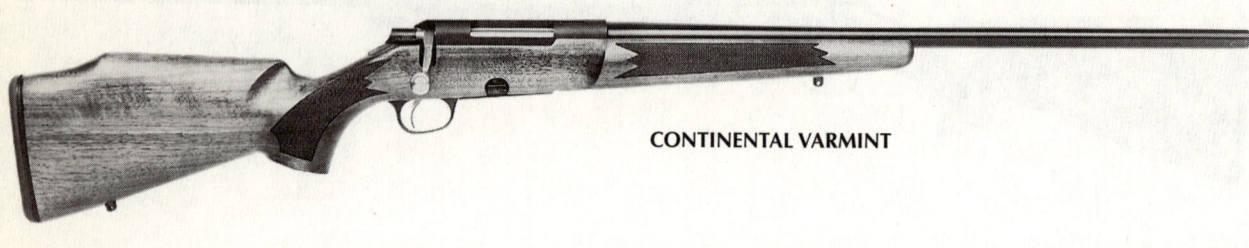

CONTINENTAL VARMINT

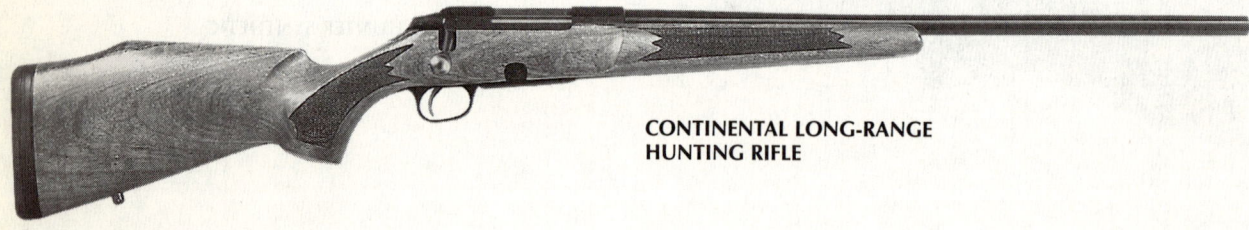

CONTINENTAL LONG-RANGE HUNTING RIFLE

Sporter
Specifications
Calibers: 223 Rem., 22-250 Rem., 308 Win.
Weight: 9 1/4 lbs.
Features: 2-lug bolt with 75° lift, straight-line feed, 5-shot magazine. Competition-style stock with adjustable butt and comb, hammer-forged barrel, integral scope rail, adjustable trigger.
Price: $950

Continental Varmint
Specifications
Calibers: 17 Rem., 22-250, 223, 308
Capacity: 5 rounds
Barrel Length: 26" **Overall Length:** 46"
Weight: 8 lbs. 10 oz.
Finish: Matte lacquer walnut stock w/palm swell
Features: Recoil pad spacer system; quick-release detachable magazine; beavertail forend; cold hammer-forged barrel; integral scope mount rails; adjustable trigger
Price: $720

Continental Long-Range Hunting Rifle
Specifications
Calibers: 25-06 Rem., 270 Win., 7mm Rem. Mag., 300 Win. Mag.
Capacity: 5 rounds in standard calibers, 4 rounds in magnum calibers
Barrel Length: 26" heavy barrel
Overall Length: 46.5"
Weight: 8 lbs. 12 oz.
Finish: Matte lacquer walnut stock w/palm swell
Features: Same as Continental Varmint model
Price: 720
   Magnum Calibers 750

Uberti Replicas

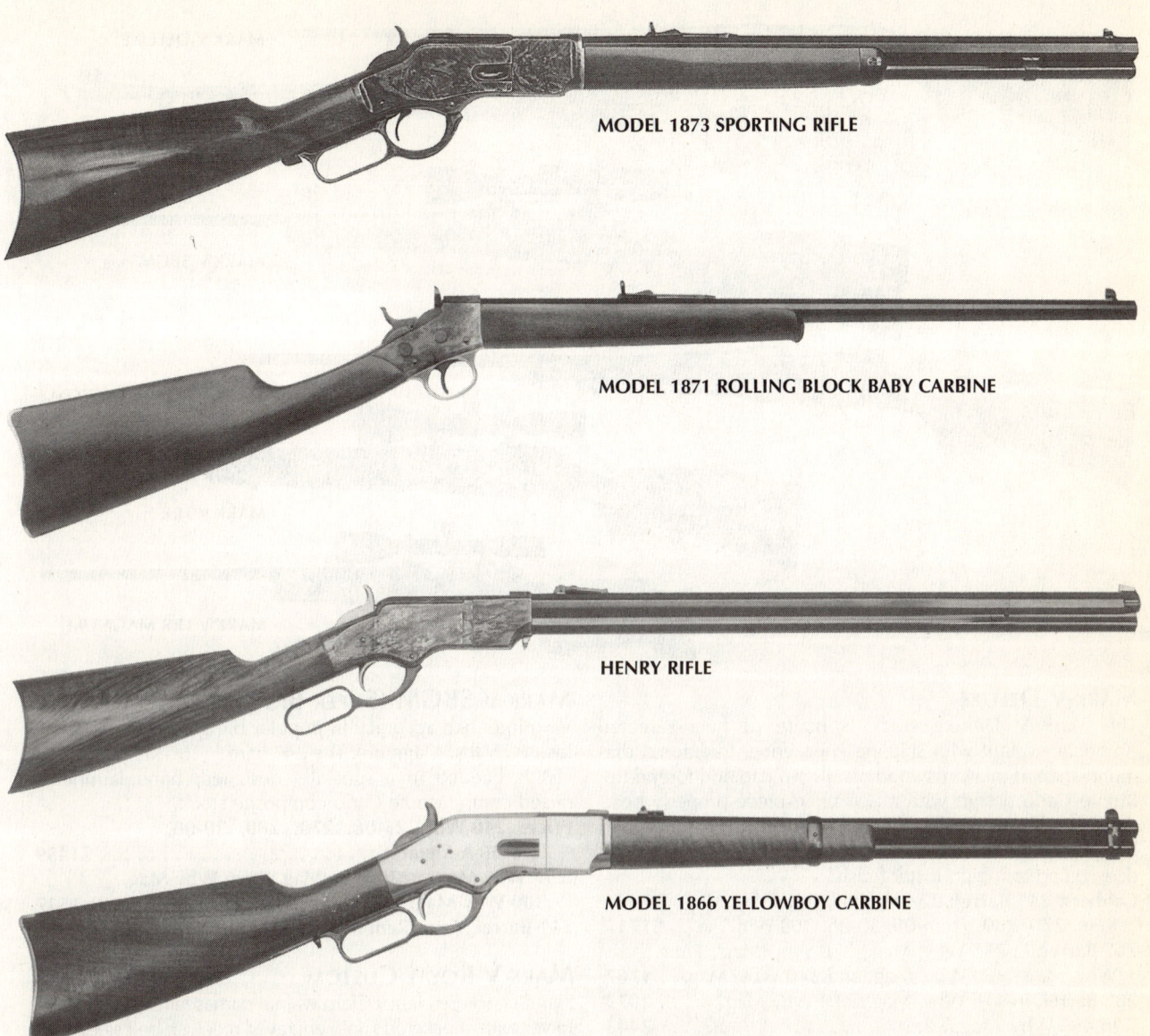

MODEL 1873 SPORTING RIFLE

MODEL 1871 ROLLING BLOCK BABY CARBINE

HENRY RIFLE

MODEL 1866 YELLOWBOY CARBINE

MODEL 1873 SPORTING RIFLE
Action: Model 1873 Sporting Rifle **Stock:** Hand checkered walnut; straight or pistol-grip **Barrel:** 20"; also available with 24.25" or 30" octagonal **Sights:** Open **Chamberings:** 32/20, 357 Magnum, 44-40 and 45 LC **Other Features:** Color case-hardened steel
Price: $973
  with pistol grip: 999
  with pistol grip and 30"barrel: 1050

MODEL 1871 ROLLING BLOCK BABY CARBINE
Action: Model 1871 Rolling Block Baby Carbine **Stock:** Walnut, straight grip **Barrel:** 22" **Sights:** Fully adjustable rear, ramp front **Weight:** 4.85 lbs. **Chamberings:** 22 LR, 22 Hornet, 22 Magnum, 357 Magnum **Other Features:** Color case-hardened steel
Price: 590

HENRY RIFLE
Action: Henry Rifle **Stock:** Varnished American walnut **Barrel:** 18.5", 22.25", 24.25" half-octagon, with tubular magazine **Sights:** Open **Weight:** 7.9, 9, 9.26 lbs. **Chamberings:** 44-40, 45 LC **Other Features:** Brass frame or steel
Price: Brass: $980
  Steel: 1050

MODEL 1866 YELLOWBOY CARBINE
Action: Model 1866 Yellowboy Carbine **Stock:** Walnut **Barrel:** 19" round, tapered **Sights:** Vertically adjustable rear; horizontally adjustable front **Weight:** 7.38 lbs. **Chamberings:** 22 LR, 22 Mag, 38 SP, 44-40, and 45 LC **Other Features:** Brass frame
Price: 760

Weatherby Mark V Rifles

MARK V DELUXE
MARK V DANGEROUS GAME RIFLE
MARK V SBGM
MARK V ROYAL CUSTOM
MARK V TRR
MARK V TRR MAGNUM

Mark V Deluxe
The Mark V Deluxe stock is made of hand-selected American walnut with skipline checkering, traditional diamond-shaped inlay, roswood pistol-grip cap and forend tip. Monte Carlo design with raised cheekpiece properly positions the shooter while reducing felt recoil. The action and hammer-forged barrel are hand-bedded for accuracy, then deep blued to a high-luster finish.
Calibers: 24" Barrel: 22-250, 243, 240 Wby. Mag., 25-06 Rem, 270, 280, 7mm-08, 30-06, 308 Win...... **$1715**
26" Barrel: In 257 Wby. Mag., 270 Wby. Mag., 7mm Wby. Mag., 300 Wby. Mag. and 340 Wby. Mag... **1767**
28" Barrel: In 416 Wby. Mag., 378 Wby Mag........ **2079**
In 460 Wby. Mag.............................. **2443**

New! Mark V Dangerous Game Rifle
The new Mark V Dangerous Game Rifle is designed specifically for the person who makes their living as a professional hunter or the hunter who is serious about their pursuit of dangerous game. It features a hand-laminated, black composite stock (Kevlar and fiberglass) with a CNC-machined aluminum bedding block, combined with a short bolt throw Mark V action and a 24" to 26" barrel. An adjustable ramp, shallow gold-filled "V" rear and barrel band hooded front sight with large gold bead provides for immediate sight alignment and target acquistion. A Pachmayr Decelerator recoil pad reduces felt recoil.
Prices:
Available in 300 Win, 300 Wby, 338 Win, 340 Wby, 375 H&H, 375 Wby, 416 Rem., 458 Win (24")... **2703**
378 Wby, 416 Wby, (26")................. **2853**
460 Wby (26")............................ **2935**

Mark V SBGM (Super Big Game Master)
Varminter-like accuracy in popular big game calibers. 5.75 lbs. (6.75 lbs. Magnum). The 24" barrel (26" Magnum models) is bedded in a specially designed, hand laminated, raised comb, Monte Carlo composite stock.
Price: .240 Wby, .25-06, .270, .280, .30-06,
.338-06 A-Square:.................... **$1459**
.257 Wby Mag., .270 Wby Mag, 7mm Wby Mag,
.300 Wby Mag:........................ **1517**
24" Barrel, 7mm Rem Mag and 300 Win Mag:..... **1517**

Mark V Royal Custom
Hand checkered fancy Claro walnut damascened bolt and follower with checkered knob, engraved receiver, bolt sleeve and floorplate of scroll pattern, encountered with selective 24kt gold and nickel plating. 26" barrel in .257 Wby, 270 Wby. Mag, 7mm Wby. Mag., 300 Wby. Mag and 340 Wby Mag.
Price:................................... **5399**

Mark V TRR (Threat Response Rifle)
The new tactical TRR Mark V action has a heavy, 22" hand-lapped matte black Krieger barrel and is available in .223 and .308 Rem. The magnum (.300 Win Mag and .300 Wby. Mag) has a 26" barrel
Price: 24" barrel:........................ **1018**
26" barrel:............................ **1569**

Mark V TRR Magnum Custom
All the performance features of the TRR, with the addition of an ergonomic, fully-adjustable, composite stock and 28" barrel.
Price:................................... **1725**

Weatherby Mark V Rifles

NEW! MARK V SPM

WEATHERBY SVM VARMINTMASTER BOLT-ACTION RIFLE

EUROMARK

SLS

ACCUMARK

Mark V SPM
The new SPM (Super Predator-Master) was designed specifically for the "on-the-move" varmint hunter calling in coyote, fox, bobcat or other large predators. Built on the Mark V action for standard cartridges, the SPM is a lightweight 6.25 lbs. and features a 24" Criterion "button-rifled" barrel by Krieger. The SPM features a specially-designed ultra lightweight hybrid composite Monte Carlo stock in tan with black spiderweb patterning. A CNC-machined aluminum bedding block provides a solid, stable platform for the action while a Pachmayr Decelerator pad reduces felt recoil. Available in .223, .22-250, 243, 7mm-08, 308
Price: $1459

Weatherby SVM Varmintmaster Bolt-Action Rifle
Weatherby's new SVM Varmintmaster has a short Mark V action and a 26" Krieger button-rifled barrel of stainless steel. A hand-laminated synthetic stock features an aluminum bedding block and wide, flat forend. Weight: 8.5 lbs.
**Price: 223, 22-250, 243, 7mm-08, 308
   (single-shot or repeater)** 1517

Mark V Euromark
The Euromark features a hand-rubbed oil finish and Monte Carlo stock of American walnut, plus custom grade, hand-cut checkering with an ebony pistol-grip cap and forend tip.
Prices:
**26" Barrel In Weatherby Magnum calibers
   257, 270, 7mm, 300 and 340** 1819

**28" Barrel In .378 Wby Mag. and
   416 Wby. Mag.** $2131
**24" Barrel In 7mm Rem. Mag., 300 Win. Mag.,
   338 Win. Mag. and 375 H&H Mag.** 1819
SLS (stainless laminate sporter). 1393

Mark V Accumark
This rifle features a specially-designed, hand-laminated raised-comb Monte Carlo synthetic stock. It also features a molded-in, CNC-machined aluminum bedding plate that stiffens the receiver area of the rifle when the barreled action is secured to the block, providing a stable and rigid platform for the action. A matte black gel coat finish is accented with faint grey "spider web" patterning. A cold hammer-forged, heavy contour, 26" (button-rifled 24" for standard calibers) 410 Series stainless steel free-floated barrel features longitudinal fluting, blackened in the grooves. Each trigger is fully adjustable with sear engagement preset at between 8 to .014 and a let-off weight of 4 lbs.
Prices:
**24" Barrel in 223 Rem, 22-250, 243, 25-06,
   270, 280 Rem, 7mm-08, 30-06, 308** 1455
**26" Barrel In 257, 270, 7mm, 7mm STW, 300, 340
   Magnum calibers, 7mm Rem Mag, 300 win Mag** . 1507
**28" Barrel In 30-378 Wby. and 338-378
   Magnum calibers.** 1724
Also available:
26" barrel, left hand 1559
28" barrel, left hand 1788

Weatherby Mark V Rifles

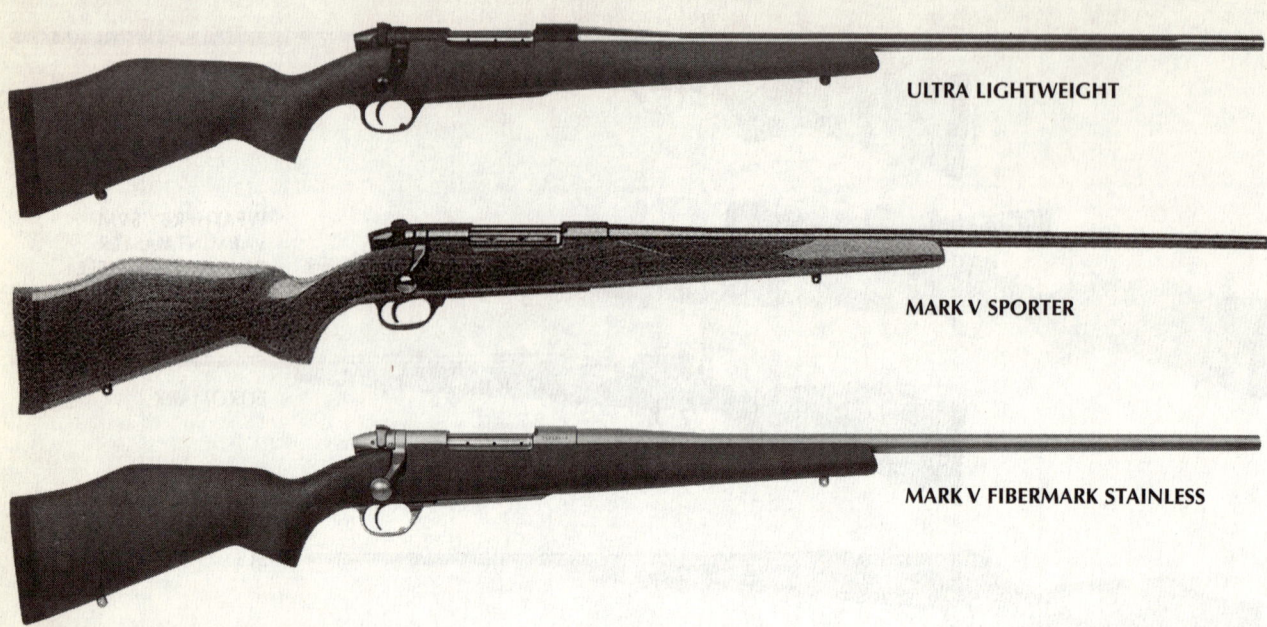

ULTRA LIGHTWEIGHT

MARK V SPORTER

MARK V FIBERMARK STAINLESS

Mark V Ultra Lightweight

The Mark V Ultra Lightweight provides everything a custom-built lightweight does at half the price. It tips the scales at 5.75 lbs. (6.75 lbs. on magnum models), making it an ideal choice for packing into mountainous terrain or for all-day hunts.

Based on the Mark V action, it features a chrome moly receiver, with weight-trimming alloy follower and floorplate. Deepened and widened flutes on the bolt reduce weight, along with a "skeletonized" bolt handle and bolt sleeve. Weight-reducing flutes are also employed on the 410 Series stainless steel 24" or 26" (depending on caliber) special-contour barrel, which features an accuracy-enhancing recessed field crown. Rounding out the Ultra Lightweight is a specially-designed, hand-laminated raised comb Monte Carlo stock. A Pachmayr Decelerator pad dissipates recoil. Ultra lightweight. Also available in a left-hand model. Overall length: 44" and 46". Weight: about 6 lbs.

Prices:
24" Barrel: 243, 240 Wby., 25-06, .270, 7mm-08,
  .280, .308, .30-06, 338-06 A Square $1459
24" Barrel: 7mm Rem, .300 Win 1517
26" Barrel: 257 Wby., 270 Wby., 7mm Rem.,
  7mm Wby, 300 Wby., .300 Win. 1517
Also Available: Left hand 1559

Mark V Sporter

Weatherby performance in an affordable wood stock design. The Claro walnut stock sports a satin urethane finish, fineline diamond point checkering and a Pachmayr Decelerator pad. All metalwork is bead blasted matte blued to a low lustre finish for a distinctive and functional look.

Prices:
26" Barrel: 257 Wby. Mag., 270 Wby. Mag., 7mm
  Wby. Mag., 300 Wby. Mag. and 340 Wby. Mag. . . 1143
24" Barrel: 7mm Rem. Mag., 300 Win. Mag.,
  338 Win. Mag. and 375 H&H Mag. $1143
24" Barrel: 22-250, 243, 240 wby, 25-06, 270, 280,
  Rem, 7mm-08, 30-06, 308. 1091
Also available:
Eurosport. Same specifications and prices but with hand-rubbed satin oil finish.

Fibermark Composite

The Weatherby Fibermark was first introduced in 1983, sporting the industry's first production rifle with a composite stock.

This Fibermark is set on a black hybrid composite stock of Kevlar and fiberglass. The Monte Carlo stock is pillar-bedded to reduce torque on the action and improve accuracy. Metalwork is bead-blasted matte blue. The rifle is available on both Magnum (26" barrels) or Standard (24" barrels) Mark V actions.

Fibermark Stainless

Similar to the new Fibermark, the Fibermark Stainless offers a black hybrid composite stock that is pillar-bedded to reduce action torque and improve accuracy—a feature not found on other production composites. All metalwork is 410 Series stainless steel, bead-blasted to a matte finish. Available in magnum or standard actions.

Prices: 1070
Magnum 1122
  30-378 Wby. 1347
  .416 Rem Mag 1122
Stainless. 1165
  Magnum 1217
  30-378 Wby. 1390

Weatherby Mark V Rifles

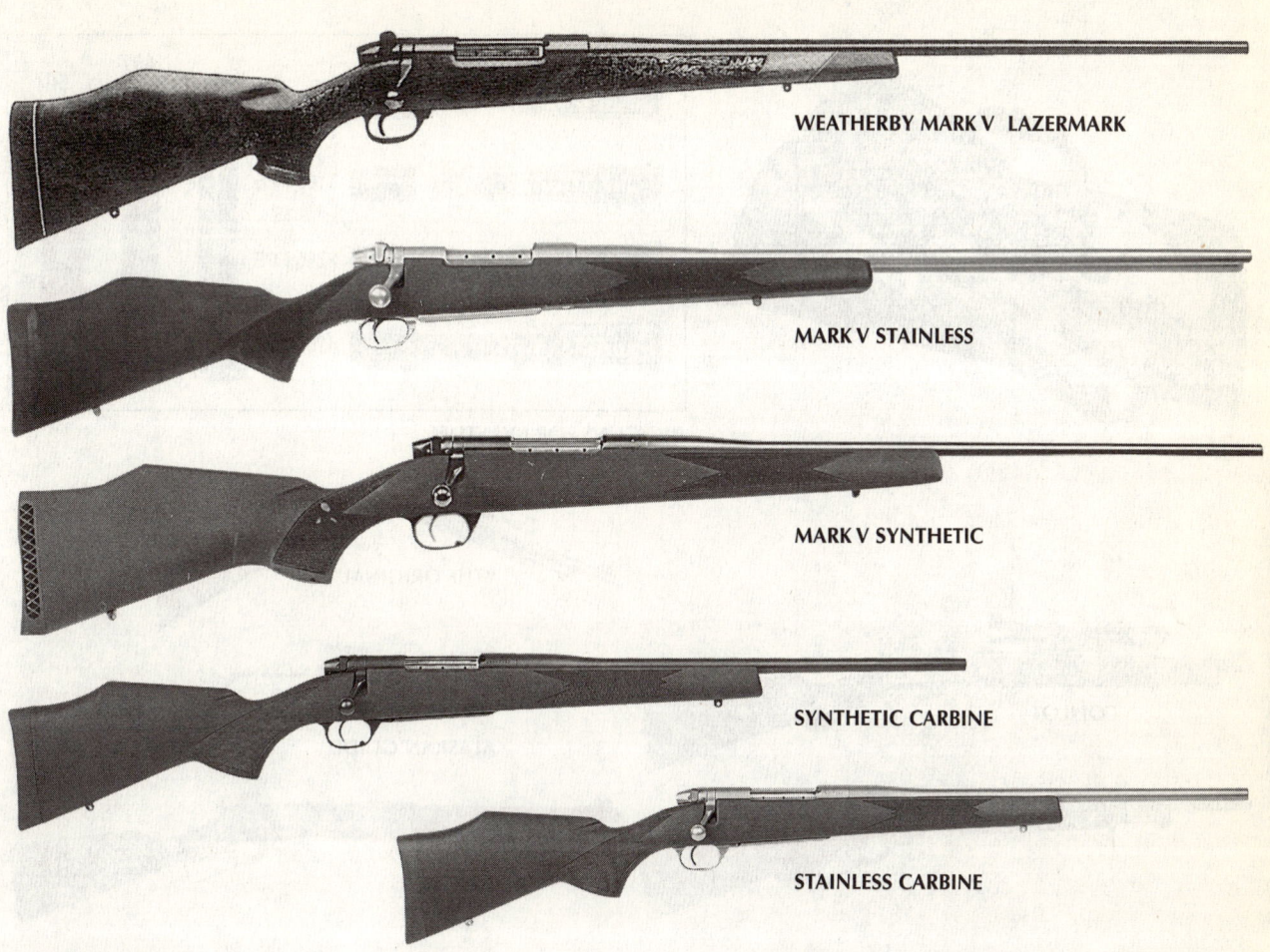

WEATHERBY MARK V LAZERMARK

MARK V STAINLESS

MARK V SYNTHETIC

SYNTHETIC CARBINE

STAINLESS CARBINE

Lazermark
A custom-carved walnut stock distinguishes this Weatherby. Traditional high-gloss finish.
Prices: 26" Barrel
In Weatherby Magnum calibers 257, 270, 7mm,
   300 and 340 . . . . $1923
28" Barrel, 378 Wby. Mag. + 416 Wby Mag. 2266
460 Wby. Mag. 2661

Mark V Magnum or Standard Lightweight Stainless
Features 400 Series stainless steel. The action is hand-bedded to a lightweight, injection-molded synthetic stock.
Prices: Mark V Stainless
24" Barrel, .22-250, .243, .240 Wby., 25-06,
   .270, .280, 7mm-08, .30-06, .308 1018
7mm Rem. Mag., 300 Win. Mag., 338 Win.
   Mag. and 375 H&H Mag. 1070
26" Barrel, Weatherby Magnum calibers 257,
   270, 7mm 300 and 340. 1070
28" Barrel, 30-378 Wby. Mag. 1237

Mark V Synthetic
Features an injection-molded synthetic stock with dual-tapered checkered forearm. Comes with custom floorplate release/trigger guard assembly and engraved flying "W" monogram.
Prices: Mark V Synthetic
24" Barrel: .22-250, .243, .240 Wby., .25-06,
   .270, 7mm-08, .280, .30-06, .308 . . . . $923
7mm Rem. Mag., 300 Win. Mag., 338 Win.
   Mag. and 375 H&H Mag. 975
26" Barrel, Weatherby Magnum calibers 257, 270,
   7mm, 7mm STW, 300 and 340 975
28" Barrel, 30-378 Wby. Mag., 338-378 Wby. 1151

Mark V Synthetic & Stainless Carbine
Synthetic. With a lightweight 20" barrel, this is a good choice for the tight confines of a treestand, high in the mountains, or as a working ranch rifle. All metalwork is bead-blasted matte blued, bedded to a raised comb, injection-molded synthetic stock. From buttstock to barrel, it tips the scales at just six pounds.
Stainless. Has all of the features of the Mark V Stainless and a lightweight 20" barrel.
Prices:
Carbine Model (20" in 243 Win., 7mm-08
   Rem., 308 Win.) 923
Stainless Carbine 1018

Wild West Guns
Custom Guns

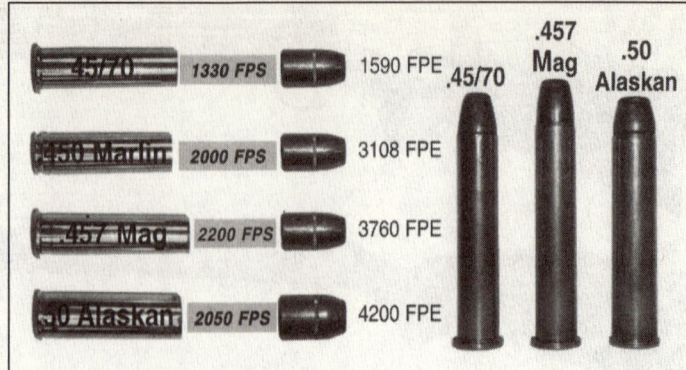

BIG GUNS FOR BIG STUFF

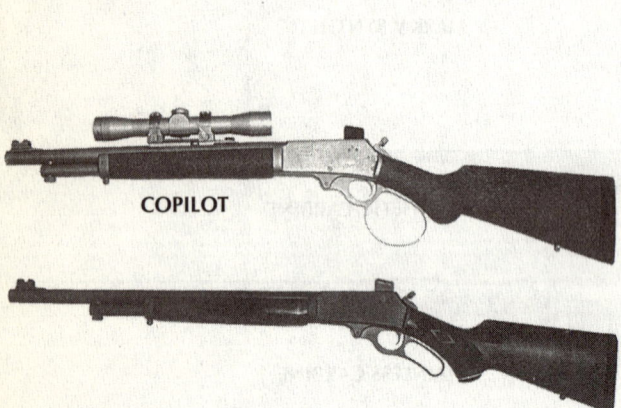

COPILOT

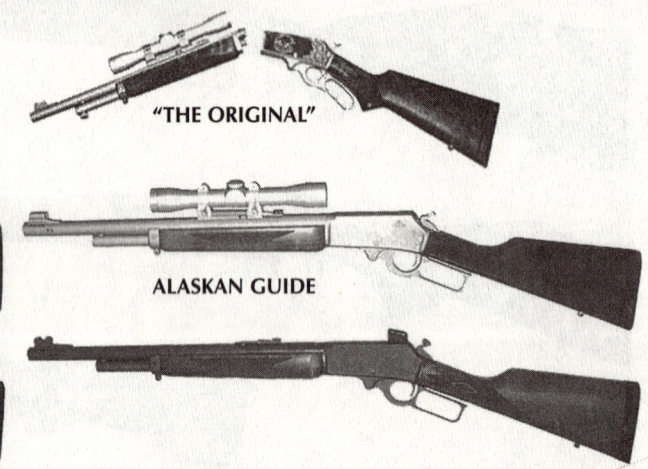

"THE ORIGINAL"

ALASKAN GUIDE

Copilot .457 Magnum
Wild West Gun's Alaskan CoPilot rifle, a big-bore take-down lever-action, has become renowned for its quality, reliability and compactness. Now, there's a new .457 Magnum, which uses a 350 grain bullet at 2200 fps to develop 3700 foot-pounds of muzzle energy.

Parkerized Copilot .50 Alaskan
Not only does the .50 Alaskan CoPilot fit in a compact carry case, it chambers a 50-caliber cartridge that fires 450-grain bullet at approximately 2050 fps with 4200 foot pounds of muzzle energy. The performance of this will impress anyone looking for serious knockdown power!

Alaskan Guide
For those who don't need the take-down feature, Wild West guns has a standard Marlin in .457 Magnum. This short quick-handling rifle will use standard 45/70 ammunition too. The .50 Alaskan chambered in the Alaskan Guide is capable of stopping any animal on earth. It offers peace of mind if you're hiking where dangerous animals can be encountered.

Alaskan CoPilot
Take-Down Rifle • WWG .457 Mag or .50 Alaskan caliber • wood stock cut to your length of pull • Take-Down Rifle Conversion • Trigger pull set at 3-4 pounds • Barrel cut & crowned 16 1/2", 18 1/2" or 20" • Vented magazine tube • Fiber-optic front sight with slotted hood • Carry case (padded canvas) • Action Tuned for reliability • Pachmayr Decelerator Pad • Parkerized finish • WWG recoil control porting system

Prices:
WWG .457 Mag - 45/70 Package $1799
On your 1895 Marlin 1449
.50 Alaskan Conversion, add: 200

Alaskan Guide
• WWG .457 Mag or .50 Alaskan Caliber • Trigger pull set at 3-4 pounds • Barrel length 18 1/2" only • Action tuned for reliability • Recoil Control Porting • Wood stock cut to your length of pull • fiber optic front sight with slotted hood • Vented magazine tube • WWG Ghose Ring rear sight • Straight-grip stock • Parkerized finish • Pachmayr Decelerator Pad

Prices:
WWG .457 Mag - 45/70 Package 1199
On your Marlin 1895G 849
.50 Alaskan Conversion, add: 200
    stainless steel, add 100

Winchester Bolt-Action Rifles
Model 70 WSM

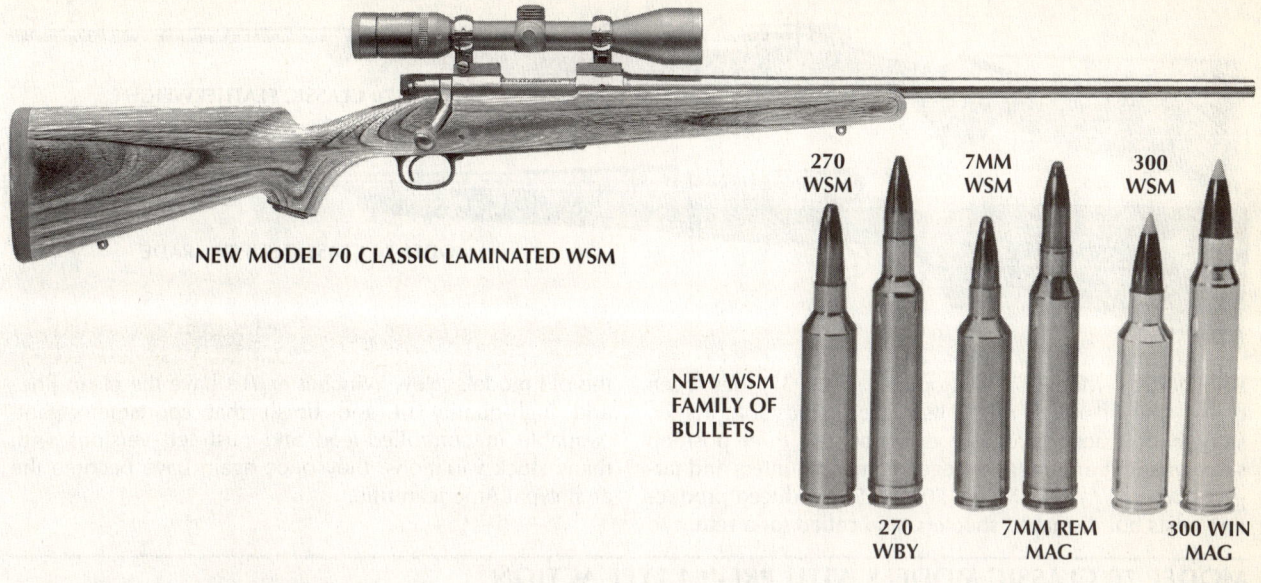

NEW MODEL 70 CLASSIC LAMINATED WSM

NEW WSM FAMILY OF BULLETS

270 WSM · 270 WBY · 7MM WSM · 7MM REM MAG · 300 WSM · 300 WIN MAG

Caliber	Bullet Weight (Grains)	Overall Cartridge Length (in.)	Muzzle Velocity (fps.)	Trajectory at 300 yds. (Zero 100 yds)	Muzzle Energy (ft. lbs.)
270 BALLISTICS COMPARISON					
270 WSM	130 grains	2.860"	3,275 fps	-8.9	3,096
270 Win.	130 grains	3.340"	3,050 fps	-10.8	2,685
270 Wby Mag.	130 grains	3.295"	3,200 fps	-9.5	2,955
7MM BALLISTICS COMPARISON					
7MM WSM	140 grains	2.860"	3,225 fps	-9.1	3,233
7MM Rem. Mag.	140 grains	3.290"	3,100 fps	-10.22	2,987
300 BALLISTICS COMPARISON					
300 WSM	180 grains	2.860"	2,970 fps	-11.7	3,526
300 Win. Mag.	180 grains	3.340"	2,960 fps	-11.9	3,503
300 H&H	180 grains	3.600"	2,880 fps	-12.7	3,316

All specifications approximate and subject to change depending on ammunition manufacturer, barrel length, specific load and conditions. For more ballistic details visit the Winchester Ammunition website at: www.winchester.com. Study the comparisons. You get much better ballistics in a smaller package with the new WSM Family.

Model 70 Classic Laminated WSM
Combines 300 WSM and a special laminated stock made for short action compactness and taming magnum recoil. Scope not included.

Model 70 Classic Featherweight WSM
The Featherweight WSM features a true short action receiver for compact proportions and a sporter-weight 24" barrel for accuracy. The walnut stock has the Featherweight configuration with Schnabel fore-end, checkering, jeweled bolt, knurled bolt handle and Classic style, claw extractor action.

Model 70 Classic New Stainless WSM
Sometimes the weather and conditions demand a stainless barrel and action, along with a rugged composite stock. They're often the situations in which you need a magnum caliber. The Stainless WSM has a slightly more compact short action combined with a compact stock and 24" sporter barrel for handling ease, all with the knockdown power previously reserved for much heavier, bulkier rifles.

Model 70 Classic Laminated WSM
With its special brown laminated stock, short magnum action and sporter-weight barrel, this is the most distinctive of all the WSM rifles. The laminated stock forms a solid platform for the action. The stock is fitted with a 1" deluxe recoil pad for your comfort. The 24" barrel provides extra compactness and a few ounces less weight. Blued receiver and barrel.

Model 70 Classic Coyote
Specially designed for hunters who need the carrying ease and pointability of a sporter-style rifle, combined with the long range accuracy of a varminter. Available now in all three new WSM calibers. Medium-heavy stainless steel 24" sporter barrel, rugged laminated stock with reverse taper fore-end. Ideal for larger varmints like coyotes and chucks and now for big game too. Stock made for a bi-pod, sticks or sandbags. Push feed bolt.

Winchester Bolt-Action Rifles

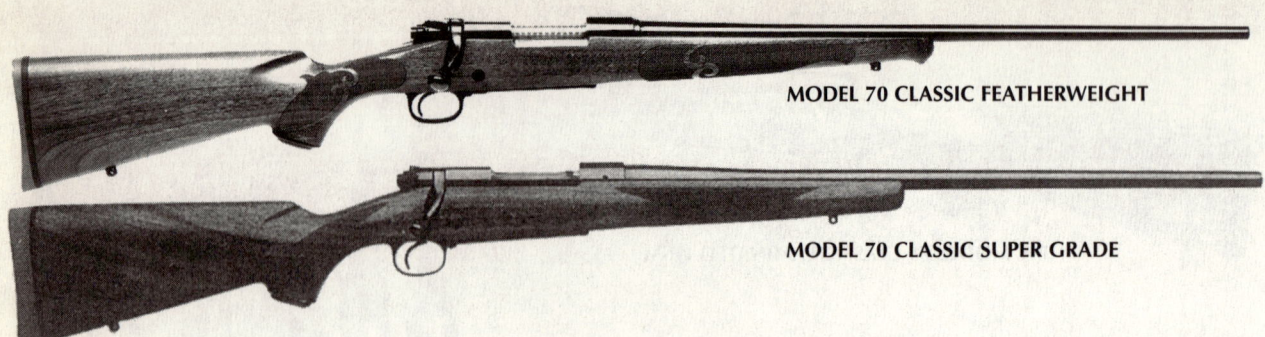

MODEL 70 CLASSIC FEATHERWEIGHT

MODEL 70 CLASSIC SUPER GRADE

Winchester's Model 70, introduced in 1937, has been called "the rifleman's rifle." Its rugged, adjustable trigger, smooth bolt action, Mauser extractor and three-position safety made it an American legend among hunters and target shooters. A "new Model 70" in 1964 reduced production costs but dismayed shooters who called for a return to the old model. Now Winchester 70s have the clean lines and high-quality fit and finish that sportsmen want. Available in controlled-feed and push-fed versions with many stock variations, they once again have become the archetypal American rifle.

MODEL 70 CLASSIC MODELS WITH PRE-'64 TYPE ACTION

Suggested Retail Right Handed	Left Handed	Caliber	Magazine Capacity*	Barrel Length	Nominal Overall Length	Nominal Length of Pull	Nominal Drop at Comb	Nominal Drop at Heel	Nominal Weight (Lbs.)	Rate of Twist 1 Turn In	Features
CLASSIC FEATHERWEIGHT (BLUED)											
$726	—	22-250 Rem.	5	22"	42"	13-1/2"	9/16"	7/8"	7	14"	Walnut Stock
726	—	243 Win.	5	22	42	13-1/2	9/16	7/8	7	10	Walnut Stock
726	—	6.5 x 55mm Swed.	5	22	42	13-1/2	9/16	7/8	7	8	Walnut Stock
726	—	308 Win.	5	22	42	13-1/2	9/16	7/8	7	12	Walnut Stock
726	—	7mm-08 Rem.	5	22	42	13-1/2	9/16	7/8	7	10	Walnut Stock
726	—	270 Win.	5	22	42-1/2	13-1/2	9/16	7/8	7-1/4	10	Walnut Stock
754	—	300 WSM	3	24	44	13-1/2	9/16	7/8	7-1/2	10	Walnut Stock
754	—	270 WSM	3	24	44	13-1/2	9/16	7/8	7-1/2	10	Walnut Stock
754	—	7MM WSM	3	24	44	13-1/2	9/16	7/8	7-1/2	9-1/2	Walnut Stock
726	—	30-06 Spfld.	5	22	42-1/2	13-1/2	9/16	7/8	7-1/4	10	Walnut Stock

Stainless Models available in 22-250, 243, 308, 270, 30-06.
*For additional capacity, add one round in chamber when ready to fire. Drops are measured from center line of bore. Rate of twist: RH.

SPECIFICATIONS & PRICES: MODEL 70 CLASSIC MODELS

Suggested Retail Right Handed	Left Handed	Caliber	Magazine Capacity*	Barrel Length	Nominal Overall Length	Nominal Length of Pull	Nominal Drop at Comb	Nominal Drop at Heel	Nominal Weight (Lbs.)	Rate of Twist 1 Turn In	Features
CLASSIC SAFARI EXPRESS											
$1103	$1140	375 H&H Mag.	3	24"	44-3/4"	13-3/4"	9/16"	1 5/16"	8-1/2	12"	Sights, Walnut Stock
1103	—	416 Rem. Mag.	3	24	44-3/4	13-3/4	9/16	1 5/16	8-1/2	14	Sights, Walnut Stock
1103	—	458 Win. Mag.	3	22	42-3/4	13-3/4	9/16	1 5/16	8-1/4	14	Sights, Walnut Stock
CLASSIC SUPER GRADE											
$995	—	25-06 Win.	5"	24"	44-3/4"	13-3/4"	9/16"	13/16"	7-3/4"	10"	Walnut Stock
995	—	270 Win.	5	24	44-3/4	13-3/4	9/16	13/16	7-3/4	10	Walnut Stock
995	—	30-06 Spfld.	5	24	44-3/4	13-3/4	9/16	13/16	7-3/4	10	Walnut Stock
1024	—	7mm Rem. Mag.	3	26	46-3/4	13-3/4	9/16	13/16	8	9-1/2	Walnut Stock
1024	—	300 Win. Mag.	3	26	46-3/4	13-3/4	9/16	13/16	8	10	Walnut Stock
1024	—	338 Win. Mag.	3	26	46-3/4	13-3/4	9/16	13/16	8	10	Walnut Stock
CLASSIC SPORTER LT (BLUED)											
$713	—	25-06 Rem.	5	24"	44-3/4"	13-3/4"	9/16"	13/16"	7-3/4	10"	Walnut Stock
713	$747	270 Win.	5	24	44-3/4	13-3/4	9/16	13/16	7-3/4	10	Walnut Stock
713	747	30-06 Spfld.	5	24	44-3/4	13-3/4	9/16	13/16	7-3/4	10	Walnut Stock
741	—	7mm STW	3	26	46-3/4	13-3/4	9/16	13/16	8	9-1/2	Walnut Stock
741	777	7mm Rem. Mag.	3	26	46-3/4	13-3/4	9/16	13/16	8	9-1/2	Walnut Stock
741	777	300 Win. Mag.	3	26	46-3/4	13-3/4	9/16	13/16	8	10	Walnut Stock
741	—	338 Win. Mag.	3	26	46-3/4	13-3/4	9/16	13/16	8	10	Walnut Stock
777	—	300 WSM	3	24	44-	13-3/4	9/16	13/16	7-3/4	10	Laminated Stock
777	—	270 WSM	3	24	44-	13-3/4	9/16	1-3/16	7-3/4	10	Laminated Stock
777	—	9MM WSM	3	24	44-	13-3/4	9/16	1-3/16	7-3/4	9-1/2	Laminated Stock

Winchester Bolt-Action Rifles

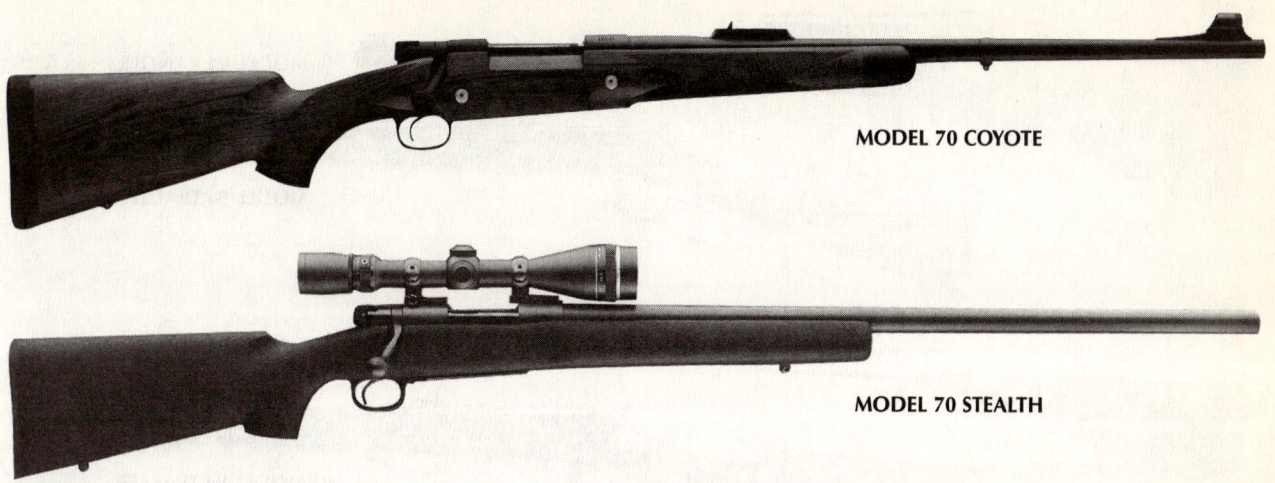

MODEL 70 COYOTE

MODEL 70 STEALTH

SPECIFICATIONS & PRICES: MODEL 70 CLASSIC MODELS (Cont.)

Suggested Retail Right Handed	Left Handed	Caliber	Magazine Capacity*	Barrel Length	Nominal Overall Length	Nominal Length of Pull	Nominal Drop at Comb	Nominal Drop at Heel	Nominal Weight (Lbs.)	Rate of Twist 1 Turn In	Features
CLASSIC STAINLESS (COMPOSITE)											
$785	—	270 Win.	5	24"	44-3/4"	13-3/4"	9/16"	13/16"	7-1/4	10"	Composite Stock
785	—	30-06 Spfld.	5	24	44-3/4	13-3/4	9/16	13/16	7-1/4	10	Composite Stock
813	—	7mm STW	3	26	46-3/4	13-3/4	9/16	13/16	7-1/2	9-1/2	Composite Stock
813	—	7mm Rem. Mag.	3	26	46-3/4	13-3/4	9/16	13/16	7-1/2	9-1/2	Composite Stock
813	—	300 Win. Mag.	3	26	46-3/4	13-3/4	9/16	13/16	7-1/2	10	Composite Stock
813	—	300 Ultra. Mag.	3	26	46-3/4	13-3/4	9/16	13/16	7-1/2	10	Composite Stock
813	—	300 WSM	3	24	44	13-3/4	9/16	13/16	7-1/4	10	Composite Stock
813	—	270 WSM	3	24	44	13-3/4	9/16	1-3/16	7-1/4	10	Composite Stock
813	—	7mm WSM	3	24	44	13-3/4	9/16	1-3/16	7-1/4	9-1/2	Composite Stock
813	—	338 Win. Mag.	3	26	46-3/4	13-3/4	9/16	13/16	7-1/2	10	Composite Stock
906	—	375 H&H Mag.	3	24	44-3/4	13-3/4	9/16	13/16	7-1/4	12	Sights, Composite Stock
CLASSIC COMPACT											
$726	—	243 Win.	4	20"	39-1/2"	13"	9/16"	3/4"	6-1/2	10"	Walnut Stock
726	—	308 Win.	4	20	39-1/2	13	9/16	3/4	6-1/2	12	Walnut Stock
726	—	7mm-08 Rem.	4	20	39-1/2	13	9/16	3/4	6-1/2	9-1/2	Walnut Stock

MODEL 70 PUSH FEED MODELS

Suggested Retail Right Handed	Left Handed	Caliber	Magazine Capacity*	Barrel Length	Nominal Overall Length	Nominal Length of Pull	Nominal Drop at Comb	Nominal Drop at Heel	Nominal Weight (Lbs.)	Rate of Twist 1 Turn In	Features
COYOTE											
$691	—	223 Rem.	6	24	44	13-1/2	5/8	3/4	9	9	Laminated Stock
691	—	22-250 Rem.	5	24	44	13-1/2	5/8	3/4	9	14	Laminated Stock
691	—	243 Win.	5	24	44	13-1/2	5/8	3/4	9	10	Laminated Stock
691	—	308 Win.	5	24	44	13-1/2	5/8	3/4	9	12	Laminated Stock
720	—	300 WSM	3	24	44	13-1/2	5/8	3/4	9	10	Laminated Stock
720	—	270 WSM	3	24	44	13-1/2	5/8	3/4	9	10	Laminated Stock
720	—	7mm WSM	3	24	44	13-1/2	5/8	3/4	9	9-1/2	Laminated Stock
STEALTH											
$785	—	223 Rem.	6	26	46	13-1/2	3/4	1/2	10-3/4	9	Accu Block
785	—	22-250 Rem.	5	26	46	13-1/2	3/4	1/2	10-3/4	14	Accu Block
785	—	308 Win.	5	26	46	13-1/2	3/4	1/2	10-3/4	12	Accu Block
BLACK SHADOW®											
$512	—	270 Win.	5	22"	42-3/4"	13-3/4"	9/16"	13/16"	7-1/4	10"	Composite Stock
512	—	30-06 Spfld.	5	22	42-3/4	13-3/4	9/16	13/16	7-1/4	10	Composite Stock
541	—	7mm Rem. Mag.	3	24	42-3/4	13-3/4	9/16	13/16	7-1/4	9-1/2	Composite Stock
541	—	300 Win. Mag.	3	22	42-3/4	13-3/4	9/16	13/16	7-1/4	10	Composite Stock

Rifles • 217

Winchester Rifles
Lever Action

MODEL 94 RANGER
MODEL 94 TRADITIONAL
MODEL 94 TRAILS END
MODEL 94 TRAPPER
MODEL 94 LEGACY

Model 94 Standard Walnut Rifle
The traditional choice for lever-action styling and craftsmanship. America's favorite deer rifle for half a century. Exposed-hammer lever action with angled ejection and crossbolt safety. American walnut stock and forearm have a protective stain finish with precise-cut wraparound checkering. It has a 20-inch barrel with hooded blade front sight and semibuckhorn rear sight.

Model 94 Traditional
Specifications
Calibers: 30-30 Win., 480 Ruger.
Prices:
30-30 Win $416
480 Ruger 458

Model 94 Traditional-CW (not shown)
Specifications
Calibers: 30-30 Win., 44 Rem. Mag., 480 Ruger. Capacity: 6 shot (30-30), 11 shot (44), 10 shot (480). Barrel Length: 20". Overall length: 38 1/8". Weight: 6.25 lbs. Checkered stock.
Prices:
30-30 Win $449
44 Rem Mag. 471
480 Ruger 518

Model 94 Trapper
The Trapper, with its short 16" barrel is suited for the cowboy action enthusiast or thick brush hunter. it features a saddle ring with hammer spur extension included. Available in 30-30 Win., 44 Rem. mag., 257 Mag., and 45 colt.
Prices:
30-30 . . . . $416
other calibers 439

Model 94 Ranger
Model 94 Ranger is an economical version of the Model 94. Also available: Ranger Compact in 30-30 Win. and 357 Mag.
Price: $363-384

Model 94 Trails End
Specifications
Calibers: 357 Mag., 44 Rem. Mag., 45 Colt. Capacity: 11 shot magazine. Barrel length: 20". Overall length: 38 1/8". Weight: 6.5 lbs. Standard loop or large loop.
Price: 453

Model 94 Legacy Standard Loop Lever
Specifications
Calibers: 30-30 Win., 357 Mag., 44 Rem. Mag., 45 Colt. Capacity: 6 shots (30-30 Win.); 11 shots (other calibers); add 1 shot for 24" barrel. Barrel length: 20" or 24". Overall length: 42 1/8" w/24" barrel. Weight: 6.75 lbs.
Price: 465

Model 94 Traditional Rifle
The traditionsl choice for lever-action styling and craftsmanship. America's favorite deer rifle for half a century. Exposed-hammer lever action with angled ejection and crossbolt safety. American walnut stock and forearm have a protective stain finish with precise-cut wraparound checkering. It has a 20-inch barrel with hooded blade front sight and semi-buckhorn rear sight.

Winchester Lever-Action
.22 Rifles

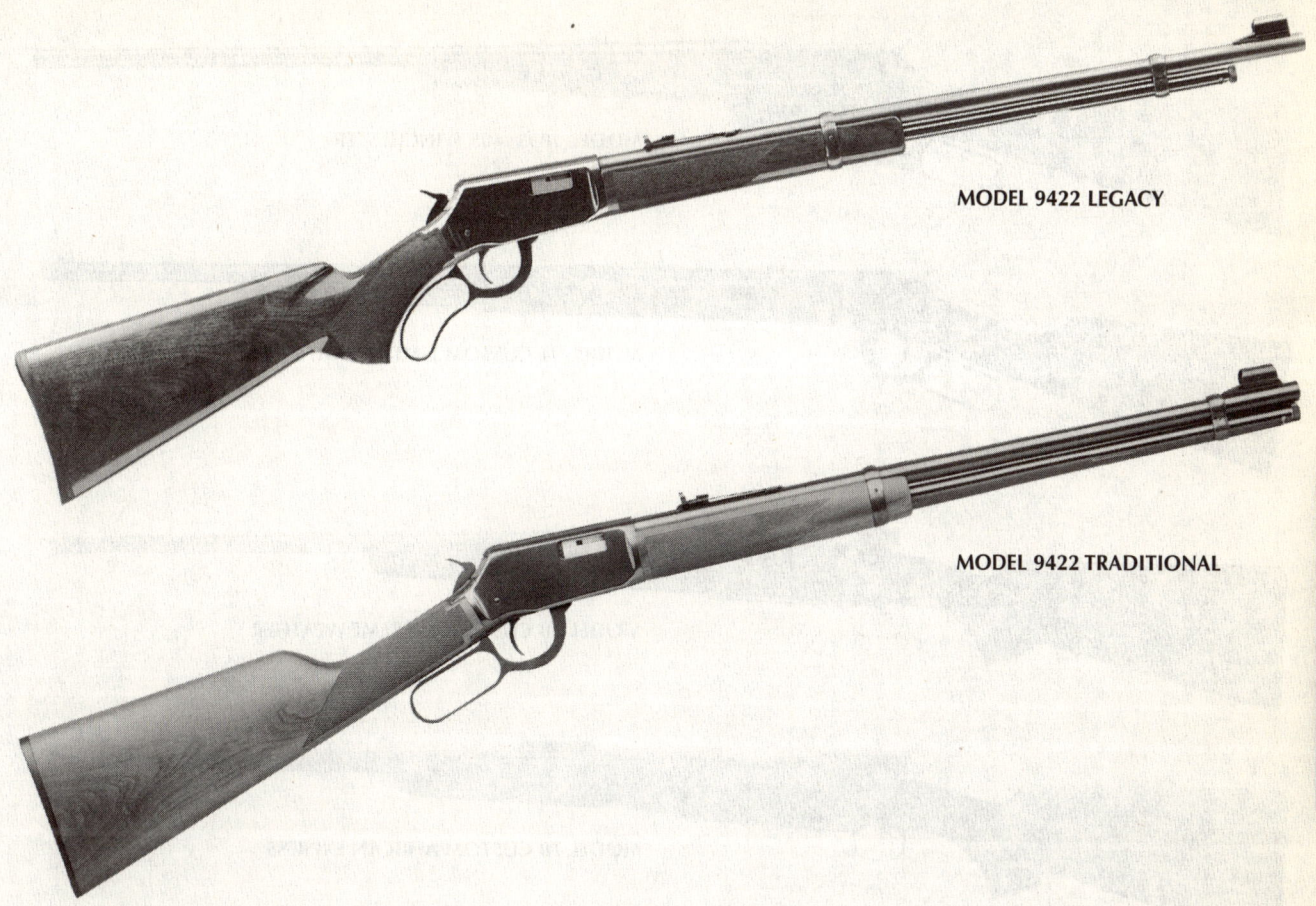

MODEL 9422 LEGACY

MODEL 9422 TRADITIONAL

The 9422 Series is based on an exposed-hammer, side-ejecting lever action noted for its smoothness and reliability. Checkered American walnut stocks and a rich blue add to the appearance. Open sights augment a receiver grooved for scope mounts.

Model 9422 Legacy
The Model 9422 Legacy has a semi-pistol grip stock, long forearm nose, and long 22 1/2" barrel. Styled after centerfire levers of a century ago, it features a cut checkered walnut stock and fore-end, adjustable sights. Hammer extension (for use with a scope) included.

Model 9422 Traditional
The Traditional features a straight grip walnut stock with cut checkering. Modeled after the famous Winchester 94, this rifle has become the standard of comparision for other 22 lever actions. Choose 22 LR or 22 WMR. Hammer extension (for use with a scope) included.

MODEL 9422 RIMFIRE RIFLES

Caliber	Magazine Capacity	Barrel Length	Nominal Overall Length	Nominal Length of Pull	Nominal Drop at Comb	Nominal Drop at Heel	Nominal Weight (Lbs.)	Rate of Twist 1 Turn In	U.S. Sugg. Retail
LEGACY									
22 Rimfire	15 LR	22-1/2"	39-1/8"	13-1/2"	1-1-8"	1-7/8"	6	16"	$484
22 WMR	11	22-1/2	39-1/8	13-1/2	1-1/8	1-7/8	6	16	505
TRADITIONAL									
22 Rimfire	15 LR	20-1/2"	37-1/8"	13-1/2"	1-1/8"	1-7/8"	6	16"	$452
22 WMR	11	20-1/2	37-1/8	13-1/2	1-1/8	1-7/8	6	16	472

Winchester Rifles
Historic and Custom

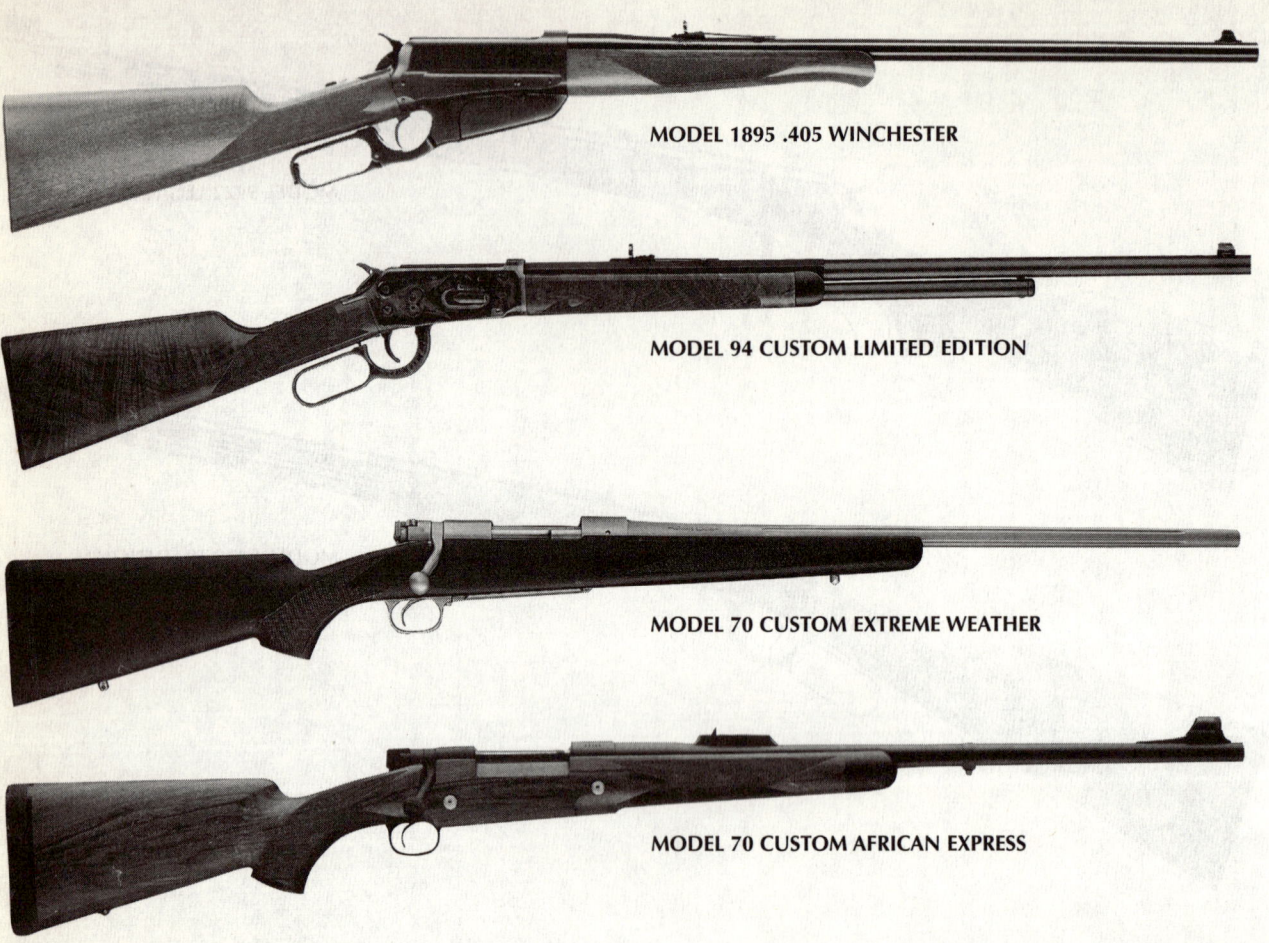

MODEL 1895 .405 WINCHESTER

MODEL 94 CUSTOM LIMITED EDITION

MODEL 70 CUSTOM EXTREME WEATHER

MODEL 70 CUSTOM AFRICAN EXPRESS

HISTORIC RIFLES

Model	Caliber	Magazine Capacity *	Barrel Length	Nominal Overall Length	Nominal Length of Pull	Nominal Drop at Comb	Nominal Drop at Heel	Nominal Weight (Lbs.)	Rate of Twist 1 Turn in	U.S. Sugg. Retail
MODEL 1895 GRADE I	.405 Win.	4	24"	42"	13-1/4"	2-7/8"	3-5/8"	8	10"	1,045
MODEL 1895 HIGH GRADE	.405 Win.	4	24"	42"	13-1/4"	2-7/8"	3-5/8"	8	10"	1,532

MODEL 1895 .405 WINCHESTER
This was the gun Teddy Roosevelt described as his "big medicine". He took three of them in .405 caliber on his historic African safari. High grades have engraved elk and whitetail scenes on a polished white receiver. Grade I is blued. (Small quantities available).

THE WINCHESTER CUSTOM SHOP
Select from either the Model 70 or Model 94 custom versions as your starting point. Then choose the specific embellishments you want. All custom Model 70's include match grade, cut-rifled barrels with squared, hand-honed actions. Most are available in stainless or blued, and right or left-handed, hand-fitted actions. All utilize the legendary Pre-'64 type action with controlled round feed in most (SAAMI) approved calibers, with specially tuned trigger systems. Approximately six additional steps, modifications and processes set every Winchester Custom Shop rifle apart. All are shipped in a hard case.

Price: . . . . P.O.R.

SHOTGUNS

AYA	222	Mossberg	252
Benelli	223	New England Arms /FAIR	254
Beretta	227	New England Firearms	255
Browning	232	Perazzi	257
Charles Daly	237	Purdey	259
Dakota	240	Remington	260
Fox	240	Renato Gamba	264
Flodman	241	B. Rizzini	265
Franchi	242	Rossi	266
Harrington & Richardson	244	Ruger	267
Heckler & Koch	245	Savage	268
Ithaca	246	SIG Arms	268
Kimber	247	SKB	269
Krieghoff	248	Stoeger	271
Marocchi	249	Weatherby	273
Merkel	250	Winchester	275

AYA Shotguns
Boxlock Shotguns

MODEL XXV BOXLOCK

Model XXV Boxlock
AYA boxlocks use the Anson & Deeley system with double locking lugs, incorporating detachable cross pin and separate plate to allow easy access to the firing mechanism. Barrels are chopper-lump, firing pins bushed. Other features: Automatic safety and ejectors and metal oval for engraving of initials, disc set strikers, replaceable hinge pin.

Specifications
Barrel lengths: 26", 27" and 28"
Weight: 5 to 7 pounds, depending on gauge.
Prices:
Model XXV Boxlock: 12 and 20 gauge only $2635
Model 4/53 Boxlock: 12, 16, 20, 28, .410 ga. 1995
Model 4 Deluxe Boxlock:
    Same gauges as above 2995

Sidelock Shotguns

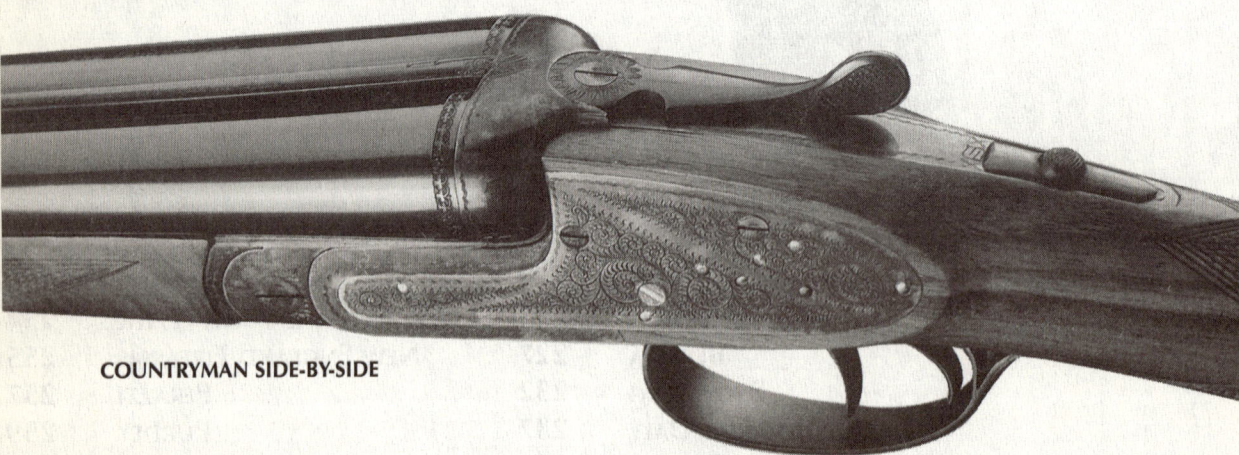

COUNTRYMAN SIDE-BY-SIDE

Countryman Side-By-Side
AYA sidelock shotguns are fitted with London Holland & Holland system sidelocks, double triggers with articulated front trigger, automatic safety and ejectors, cocking indicators, bushed firing pins, replaceable hinge pins and chopper lump barrels. Stocks are of figured walnut with hand-cut checkering and oil finish, complete with a metal oval on the buttstock for engraving of initials. Exhibition grade wood is available, as are many special options, including a true left-hand version. Available from Armes de Chasse (see Directory of Manufacturers and Suppliers).
Specifications
Barrell lengths: 26", 27", 28", 29" and 32".

Weight: 5 to 7 pounds, depending on gauge.
Prices:
Model 1: Sidelock in 12 and 20 ga. with special
    engraving and exhibition quality wood $7,170
Deluxe 8,295
Model 2: Sidelock in 12, 16, 20, 28 ga.
    and .410 bore 3,375
Model 53: Sidelock in 12, 16 and 20 ga.
    with 3 locking lugs and side clips 4,745
Model 56: Sidelock in 12 ga. only
    with 3 locking lugs and side clips 7,870
Model XXV/SL: Sidelock in 12 and 20 ga.
    only with Churchill-type rib 3,895

Benelli Shotguns

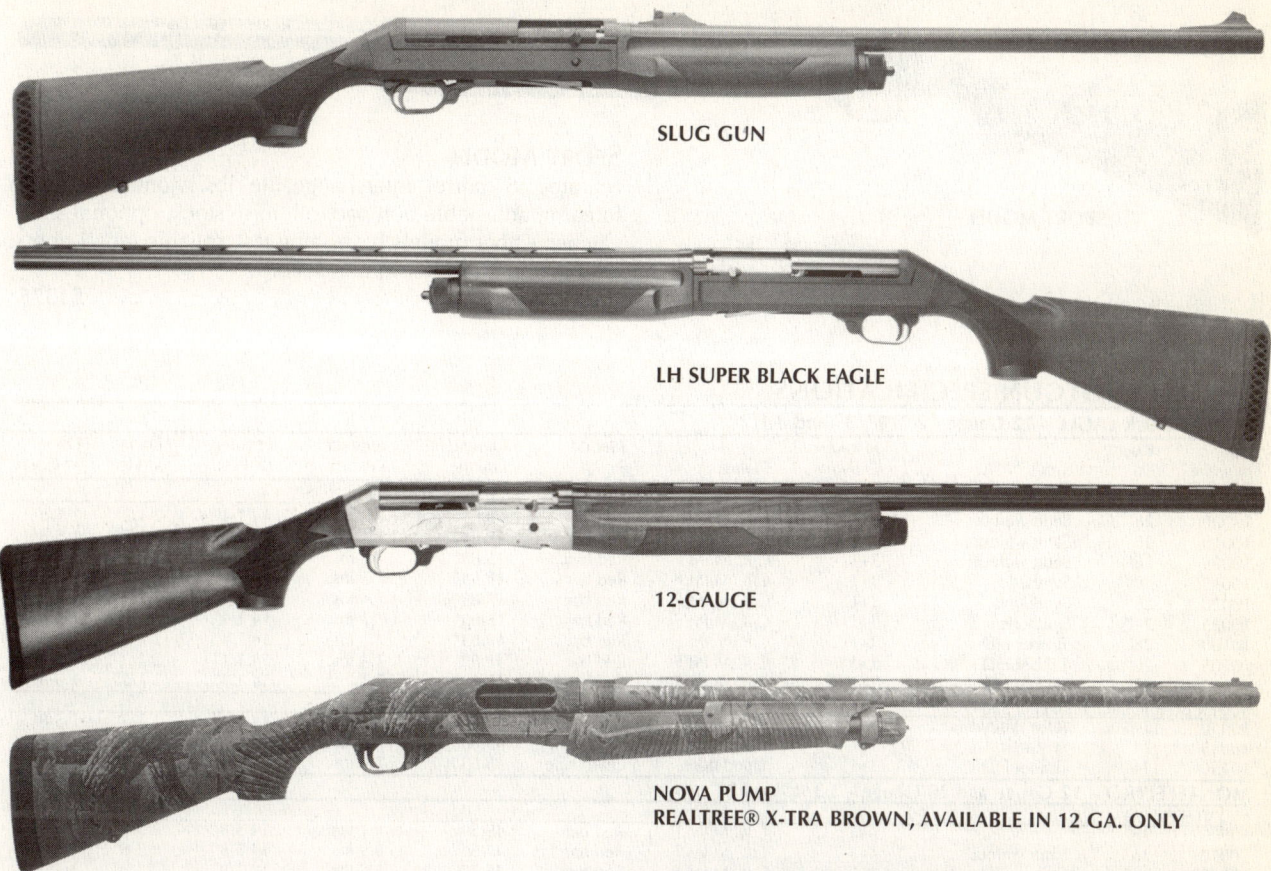

SLUG GUN

LH SUPER BLACK EAGLE

12-GAUGE

NOVA PUMP
REALTREE® X-TRA BROWN, AVAILABLE IN 12 GA. ONLY

SUPER BLACK EAGLE
(LEFT-HAND VENT RIB AND SLUG GUN SHOWN)
Benelli's Super Black Eagle shotgun fires, without adjustment, every type of 12 gauge shell currently available.
    It also features a specially strengthened steel upper receiver mated to the barrel to endure the toughest shotgunning with magnum loads. The alloy lower receiver keeps overall weight low. Comes w/a set of 5 choke tubes.
Specifications
Stock: Satin walnut (28") with drop adjustment kit; high-gloss walnut (26") with drop adjustment kit; or synthetic stock
Barrel length: 24", 26", 28"
Finish: Matte black finish on receiver, barrel and bolt (28"); blued finish on receiver and barrel (26") with bolt mirror polished (camo options available)
Features: Montefeltro rotating bolt with dual locking lugs. For additional specifications, see table on folllowing page.
Prices:
Wood Satin $1275
Synthetic 1260
Camo. 1360
In lefthand, synthetic 1310
LH Camo 1415
Rifled slug, wood 1335
    Synthetic 1320
    Camo. 1450

LEGACY (20- AND 12-GAUGE)
Features lower alloy receiver and upper steel receiver cover and interchangeable barrel with mid-point bead and red light-gathering bar front sight. Also Benelli's inertia recoil operating system; cartridge drop lever (to indicate hammer-cocked condition; set of 5 choke tubes for use with lead or steel shot); chambered round removable without emptying the magazine; handles all 2 3/4" and 3" shells within gauge with over 1 1/2 oz. of shot.
Price: $1390

NOVA PUMP (12- AND 20-GAUGE)
The world's first truly modern shotgun is the Benelli NOVA. A molded, steel reinforced glass/polymer matrix replaces the traditional stock and receiver. The bolt locks directly into the barrel and provides all the strength necessary for heavy 3.5" loads. The Nova's forend is finger-grooved for a sure grasp and extends over the receiver front to prevent pinching as it is pumped. A button in the bottom of the fore-arm activates a shell stop that allows the chambered shell to be removed without releasing the ammunition in the magazine.
Prices:
Synthetic 405
Camo. 470
Rifled Slug 575
Synthetic, 20 ga. 450
Timber HD Camo, 20 ga. 535

Shotguns • 223

Benelli Shotguns

SPORT MODEL

Sport Model
Features 28" barrel, interchangeable ribs, Montefeltro style forearm, adjustable butt pad, oil finish stock, optional shell catcher. Other models have same fast, reliable recoil-operated action but differ in dimensions.
Price: **$1375**

BENELLI SHOTGUN SPECIFICATIONS

SUPER BLACK EAGLE – 12 Gauge – 2 3/4", 3" and 3 1/2"

Item Number	Barrel Length	Stock	Magazine Capacity	Choke(s)	Type of Sights	Overall Length	Average Weight	Length of Pull	Drop at Heel	Drop at Comb
SUPER BLACK EAGLE										
10000	28"	Satin walnut	3+1	C,IC,M,IM,F	Red bar	49.63"	7.5 lbs.	14 1/4"	2 1/2"	1 5/8"
10010	26"	Satin walnut	3+1	C,IC,M,IM,F	Red bar	47.63"	7.4 lbs.	14 1/4"	2 1/2"	1 5/8"
10005	26"	Satin walnut	3+1	C,IC,M,IM,F	Red bar	45.63"	7.3 lbs.	14 1/4"	2 1/2"	1 5/8"
10015	28"	Synthetic	3+1	C,IC,M,IM,F	Red bar	49.63"	7.5 lbs.	14 1/4"	2 1/2"	1 5/8"
10020	26"	Synthetic	3+1	C,IC,M,IM,F	Red bar	47.63"	7.4 lbs.	14 1/4"	2 1/2"	1 5/8"
10025	24"	Synthetic	3+1	C,IC,M,IM,F	Red bar	45.63"	7.3 lbs.	14 1/4"	2 1/2"	1 5/8"
10100	28"	Timber HD	3+1	C,IC,M,IM,F	Red bar	49.63"	7.5 lbs.	14 1/4"	2 1/2"	1 5/8"
10105	26"	Timber HD	3+1	C,IC,M,IM,F	Red bar	47.63"	7.4 lbs.	14 1/4"	2 1/2"	1 5/8"
10110	24"	Timber HD	3+1	C,IC,M,IM,F	Red bar	45.63"	7.3 lbs.	14 1/4"	2 1/2"	1 5/8"
SUPER BLACK EAGLE RIFLED SLUG										
10030	24"	Satin Walnut	3+1	Rifled bore	Open rifle	45.63"	7.6 lbs.	14 1/4"	2 1/2"	1 5/8"
10035	24"	Synthetic	3+1	Rifled bore	Open rifle	45.63"	7.6 lbs.	14 1/4"	2 1/2"	1 5/8"
10130	24"	Timber HD	3+1	Rifled bore	Open rifle	45.63"	7.6 lbs.	14 1/4"	2 1/2"	1 5/8"
MONTEFELTRO – 12 Gauge and 20 Gauge – 2 3/4" and 3"										
MONTEFELTRO - 12 Gauge										
10800	28"	Satin walnut	4+1	C,IC,M,IM,F	Red bar	49.5"	7.1 lbs.	14 3/8"	2 3/8"	1 1/2"
10810	26"	Satin walnut	4+1	C,IC,M,IM,F	Red bar	47.5"	6.9 lbs.	14 3/8"	2 3/8"	1 1/2"
10820	24"	Satin walnut	4+1	C,IC,M,IM,F	Red bar	45.5"	6.8 lbs.	14 3/8"	2 3/8"	1 1/2"
MONTEFELTRO - 20 Gauge										
10830	26"	Satin walnut	4+1	C,IC,M,IM,F	Red bar	47.5"	5.6 lbs.	14 3/8"	2 3/8"	1 1/2"
10835	24"	Satin walnut	4+1	C,IC,M,IM,F	Red bar	45.5"	5.5 lbs.	14 3/8"	2 3/8"	1 1/2"
MONTEFELTRO SHORT STOCK - 20 Gauge										
10831	26"	Satin walnut	4+1	C,IC,M,IM,F	Red bar	45.6"	5.4 lbs.	12 1/2"	2 1/8"	1 1/2"
10836	24"	Satin walnut	4+1	C,IC,M,IM,F	Red bar	43.6"	5.3 lbs.	12 1/2"	2 1/8í	1 1/2"
LEGACY – 12 Gauge – 2 3/4" and 3"										
LEGACY - 12 Gauge										
10400	28"	Select Satin walnut	4+1	C,IC,M,IM,F	Red bar*	49.63"	7.5 lbs.	14 1/2"	2 1/4"	1 3/8"
10405	26"	Select Satin walnut	4+1	C,IC,M,IM,F	Red bar*	47.63"	7.4 lbs.	14 1/2"	2 1/4"	1 3/8"
LEGACY – 20 Gauge – 2 3/4" and 3"										
LEGACY - 20 Gauge										
10420	26"	Select Satin walnut	4+1	C,IC,M,IM,F	Red bar*	47.63"	6.0 lbs.	14 1/2"	2 1/4"	1 3/8"
10425	24"	Select Satin walnut	4+1	C,IC,M,IM,F	Red bar*	45.63"	5.8 lbs.	14 1/2"	2 1/4"	1 3/8"
SPORT – 12 Gauge – 2 3/4" and 3"										
SPORT - 12 Gauge										
10610	28"	Satin walnut	4+1	C,IC,M,IM,F	Red bar	49.63"	7.1 lbs.	14 3/8"	2 1/4"	1 3/8"
M1 FIELD – 12 Gauge – 2 3/4" and 3"										
11000	28"	Satin walnut	3+1	C,IC,M,IM,F	Red bar	49.5"	7.4 lbs.	14 3/8"	2 1/4"	1 3/8"
11010	26"	Satin walnut	3+1	C,IC,M,IM,F	Red bar	47.5"	7.3 lbs.	14 3/8"	2 1/4"	1 3/8"
11005	28"	Synthetic	3+1	C,IC,M,IM,F	Red bar	49.5"	7.4 lbs.	14 3/8"	2 1/4"	1 3/8"
11015	26"	Synthetic	3+1	C,IC,M,IM,F	Red bar	47.5"	7.3 lbs.	14 3/8"	2 1/4"	1 3/8"
11020	24"	Synthetic	3+1	C,IC,M,IM,F	Red bar	45.5"	7.2 lbs.	14 3/8"	2 1/4"	1 3/8"
11025	21"	Synthetic	3+1	C,IC,M,IM,F	Red bar	42.5"	7.0 lbs.	14 3/8"	2 1/4"	1 3/8"
11100	28"	Timber HD	3+1	C,IC,M,IM,F	Red bar	49.5"	7.4 lbs.	14 3/8"	2 1/4"	1 3/8"
11105	26"	Timber HD	3+1	C,IC,M,IM,F	Red bar	47.5"	7.3 lbs.	14 3/8"	2 1/4"	1 3/8"
11110	24"	Timber HD	3+1	C,IC,M,IM,F	Red bar	45.5"	7.2 lbs.	14 3/8"	2 1/4"	1 3/8"
11115	21"	Timber HD	3+1	C,IC,M,IM,F	Red bar	42.5"	7.0 lbs.	14 3/8"	2 1/4"	1 3/8"
M1 FIELD RIFLED SLUG										
11060	24"	Synthetic	3+1	Rifled bore	Open rifle	45.6"	7.6 lbs.	14 3/8"	2 1/4"	1 3/8"
11140	24"	Timber HD	3+1	Rifled bore	Open rifle	45.6"	7.6 lbs.	14 3/8"	2 1/4"	1 3/8"
M1 FIELD – 20 Gauge – 2 3/4" and 3"										
11090	26"	Synthetic	3+1	C,IC,M,IM,F	Red bar	47.3"	5.8 lbs.	14 3/8"	2 1/4"	1 3/8"
11092	24"	Synthetic	3+1	C,IC,M,IM,F	Red bar	45.3"	5.7 lbs.	14 3/8"	2 1/4"	1 3/8"
11094	26"	Timber HD	3+1	C,IC,M,IM,F	Red bar	47.3"	5.8 lbs.	14 3/8"	2 1/4"	1 3/8"
11096	24"	Timber HD	3+1	C,IC,M,IM,F	Red bar	45.3"	5.7 lbs.	14 3/8"	2 1/4"	1 3/8"

MEET THE FAMILY
THAT JUST GOT BIGGER
XTREMA 3.5

Beretta Introduces the A391 Xtrema 3.5

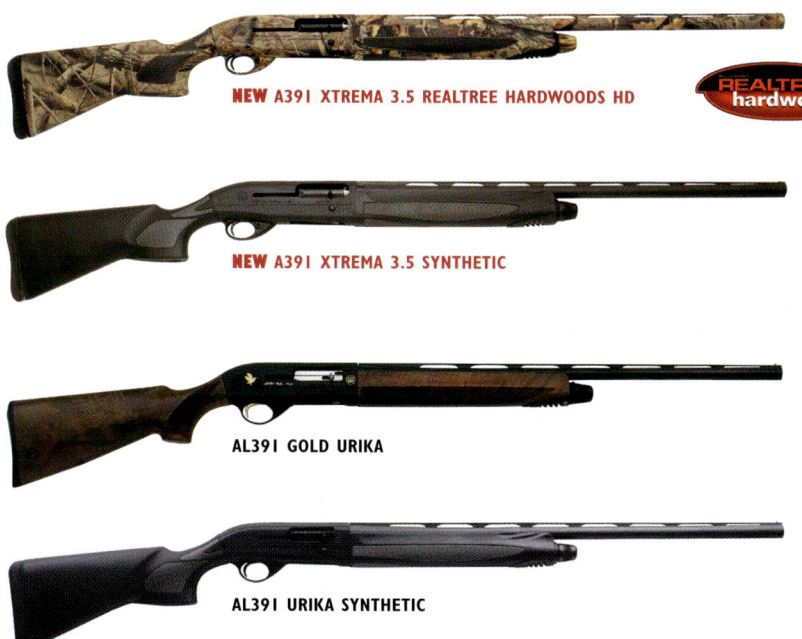

NEW A391 XTREMA 3.5 REALTREE HARDWOODS HD

NEW A391 XTREMA 3.5 SYNTHETIC

AL391 GOLD URIKA

AL391 URIKA SYNTHETIC

The latest and biggest step in the evolution of a revolutionary 391 series. No mere extension of its 3" forebears, the Xtrema is a totally new model built to excel with 3 1/2" ammunition, that complements and completes the Beretta 391 shotgun family.

The Xtrema combines a gas operating system with a rotating locking bolt. Recoil is minimized four ways: patented Gel-Tek recoil pad; overbored Optima-Bore barrel; spring-mass recoil reducer; and bolt-travel recoil absorber. In tests, the Xtrema reduced felt recoil by up to 20%.

The A391 Xtrema 3.5, the first 3 1/2" semi-automatic for the 21st century. Welcome to the family.

For a free Xtrema video ($3 S&H), or to find a Beretta dealer near you, call 1.800.528.7453.

WWW.BERETTAUSA.COM

Beretta U.S.A. Corp., 17601 Beretta Dr., Accokeek, MD 20607. For free product catalogs ($3 S&H) or for a free firearm lock ($4 S&H) call 1.800.528.7453.
All Beretta pistols come with a cable lock to aid in safe storage.

Benelli Shotguns

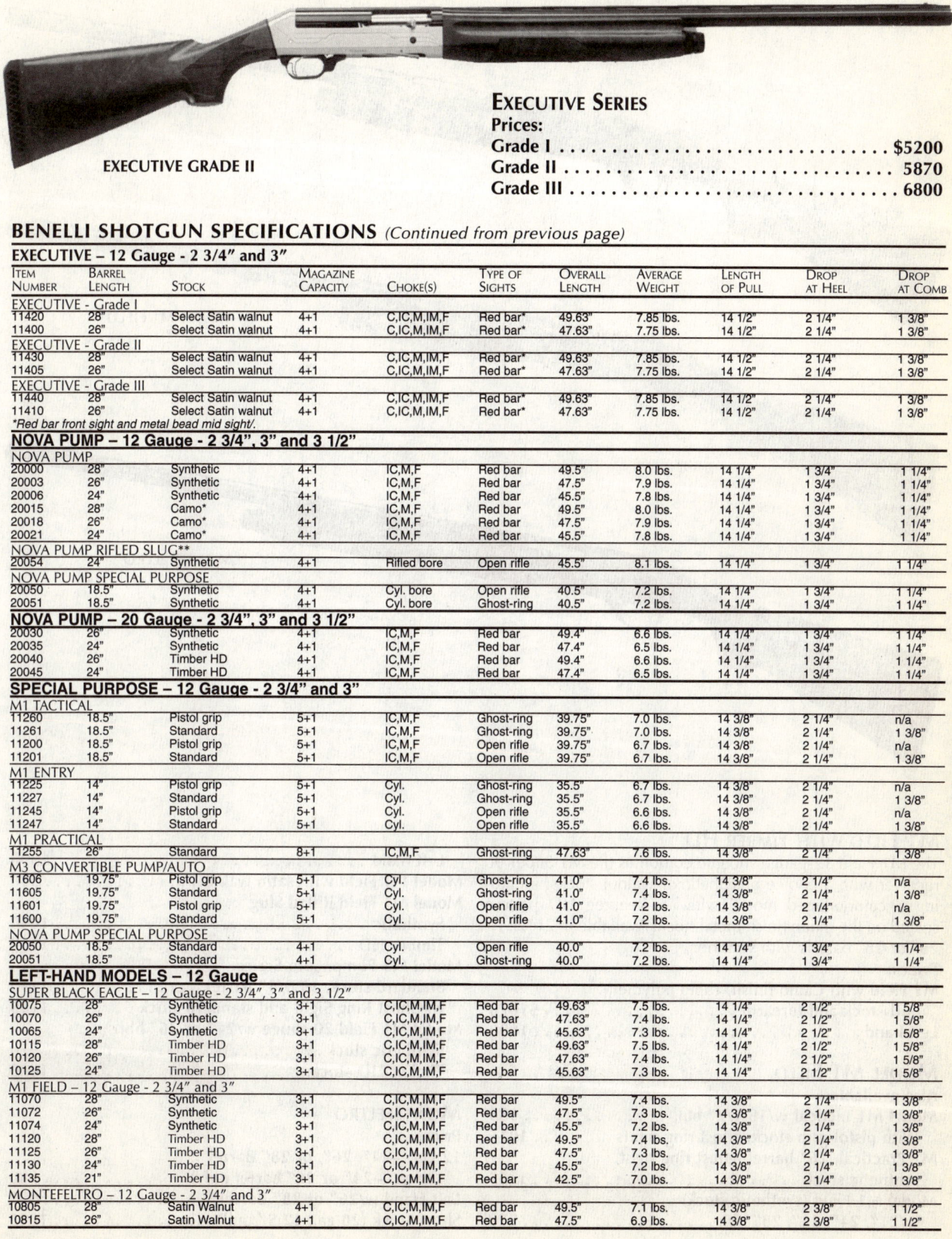

EXECUTIVE GRADE II

EXECUTIVE SERIES
Prices:
Grade I $5200
Grade II 5870
Grade III 6800

BENELLI SHOTGUN SPECIFICATIONS *(Continued from previous page)*

EXECUTIVE – 12 Gauge - 2 3/4" and 3"

Item Number	Barrel Length	Stock	Magazine Capacity	Choke(s)	Type of Sights	Overall Length	Average Weight	Length of Pull	Drop at Heel	Drop at Comb
EXECUTIVE - Grade I										
11420	28"	Select Satin walnut	4+1	C,IC,M,IM,F	Red bar*	49.63"	7.85 lbs.	14 1/2"	2 1/4"	1 3/8"
11400	26"	Select Satin walnut	4+1	C,IC,M,IM,F	Red bar*	47.63"	7.75 lbs.	14 1/2"	2 1/4"	1 3/8"
EXECUTIVE - Grade II										
11430	28"	Select Satin walnut	4+1	C,IC,M,IM,F	Red bar*	49.63"	7.85 lbs.	14 1/2"	2 1/4"	1 3/8"
11405	26"	Select Satin walnut	4+1	C,IC,M,IM,F	Red bar*	47.63"	7.75 lbs.	14 1/2"	2 1/4"	1 3/8"
EXECUTIVE - Grade III										
11440	28"	Select Satin walnut	4+1	C,IC,M,IM,F	Red bar*	49.63"	7.85 lbs.	14 1/2"	2 1/4"	1 3/8"
11410	26"	Select Satin walnut	4+1	C,IC,M,IM,F	Red bar*	47.63"	7.75 lbs.	14 1/2"	2 1/4"	1 3/8"

*Red bar front sight and metal bead mid sight/.

NOVA PUMP – 12 Gauge - 2 3/4", 3" and 3 1/2"

Item Number	Barrel Length	Stock	Magazine Capacity	Choke(s)	Type of Sights	Overall Length	Average Weight	Length of Pull	Drop at Heel	Drop at Comb
NOVA PUMP										
20000	28"	Synthetic	4+1	IC,M,F	Red bar	49.5"	8.0 lbs.	14 1/4"	1 3/4"	1 1/4"
20003	26"	Synthetic	4+1	IC,M,F	Red bar	47.5"	7.9 lbs.	14 1/4"	1 3/4"	1 1/4"
20006	24"	Synthetic	4+1	IC,M,F	Red bar	45.5"	7.8 lbs.	14 1/4"	1 3/4"	1 1/4"
20015	28"	Camo*	4+1	IC,M,F	Red bar	49.5"	8.0 lbs.	14 1/4"	1 3/4"	1 1/4"
20018	26"	Camo*	4+1	IC,M,F	Red bar	47.5"	7.9 lbs.	14 1/4"	1 3/4"	1 1/4"
20021	24"	Camo*	4+1	IC,M,F	Red bar	45.5"	7.8 lbs.	14 1/4"	1 3/4"	1 1/4"
NOVA PUMP RIFLED SLUG**										
20054	24"	Synthetic	4+1	Rifled bore	Open rifle	45.5"	8.1 lbs.	14 1/4"	1 3/4"	1 1/4"
NOVA PUMP SPECIAL PURPOSE										
20050	18.5"	Synthetic	4+1	Cyl. bore	Open rifle	40.5"	7.2 lbs.	14 1/4"	1 3/4"	1 1/4"
20051	18.5"	Synthetic	4+1	Cyl. bore	Ghost-ring	40.5"	7.2 lbs.	14 1/4"	1 3/4"	1 1/4"

NOVA PUMP – 20 Gauge - 2 3/4", 3" and 3 1/2"

Item Number	Barrel Length	Stock	Magazine Capacity	Choke(s)	Type of Sights	Overall Length	Average Weight	Length of Pull	Drop at Heel	Drop at Comb
20030	26"	Synthetic	4+1	IC,M,F	Red bar	49.4"	6.6 lbs.	14 1/4"	1 3/4"	1 1/4"
20035	24"	Synthetic	4+1	IC,M,F	Red bar	47.4"	6.5 lbs.	14 1/4"	1 3/4"	1 1/4"
20040	26"	Timber HD	4+1	IC,M,F	Red bar	49.4"	6.6 lbs.	14 1/4"	1 3/4"	1 1/4"
20045	24"	Timber HD	4+1	IC,M,F	Red bar	47.4"	6.5 lbs.	14 1/4"	1 3/4"	1 1/4"

SPECIAL PURPOSE – 12 Gauge - 2 3/4" and 3"

Item Number	Barrel Length	Stock	Magazine Capacity	Choke(s)	Type of Sights	Overall Length	Average Weight	Length of Pull	Drop at Heel	Drop at Comb
M1 TACTICAL										
11260	18.5"	Pistol grip	5+1	IC,M,F	Ghost-ring	39.75"	7.0 lbs.	14 3/8"	2 1/4"	n/a
11261	18.5"	Standard	5+1	IC,M,F	Ghost-ring	39.75"	7.0 lbs.	14 3/8"	2 1/4"	1 3/8"
11200	18.5"	Pistol grip	5+1	IC,M,F	Open rifle	39.75"	6.7 lbs.	14 3/8"	2 1/4"	n/a
11201	18.5"	Standard	5+1	IC,M,F	Open rifle	39.75"	6.7 lbs.	14 3/8"	2 1/4"	1 3/8"
M1 ENTRY										
11225	14"	Pistol grip	5+1	Cyl.	Ghost-ring	35.5"	6.7 lbs.	14 3/8"	2 1/4"	n/a
11227	14"	Standard	5+1	Cyl.	Ghost-ring	35.5"	6.7 lbs.	14 3/8"	2 1/4"	1 3/8"
11245	14"	Pistol grip	5+1	Cyl.	Open rifle	35.5"	6.6 lbs.	14 3/8"	2 1/4"	n/a
11247	14"	Standard	5+1	Cyl.	Open rifle	35.5"	6.6 lbs.	14 3/8"	2 1/4"	1 3/8"
M1 PRACTICAL										
11255	26"	Standard	8+1	IC,M,F	Ghost-ring	47.63"	7.6 lbs.	14 3/8"	2 1/4"	1 3/8"
M3 CONVERTIBLE PUMP/AUTO										
11606	19.75"	Pistol grip	5+1	Cyl.	Ghost-ring	41.0"	7.4 lbs.	14 3/8"	2 1/4"	n/a
11605	19.75"	Standard	5+1	Cyl.	Ghost-ring	41.0"	7.4 lbs.	14 3/8"	2 1/4"	1 3/8"
11601	19.75"	Pistol grip	5+1	Cyl.	Open rifle	41.0"	7.2 lbs.	14 3/8"	2 1/4"	n/a
11600	19.75"	Standard	5+1	Cyl.	Open rifle	41.0"	7.2 lbs.	14 3/8"	2 1/4"	1 3/8"
NOVA PUMP SPECIAL PURPOSE										
20050	18.5"	Standard	4+1	Cyl.	Open rifle	40.0"	7.2 lbs.	14 1/4"	1 3/4"	1 1/4"
20051	18.5"	Standard	4+1	Cyl.	Ghost-ring	40.0"	7.2 lbs.	14 1/4"	1 3/4"	1 1/4"

LEFT-HAND MODELS – 12 Gauge

Item Number	Barrel Length	Stock	Magazine Capacity	Choke(s)	Type of Sights	Overall Length	Average Weight	Length of Pull	Drop at Heel	Drop at Comb
SUPER BLACK EAGLE – 12 Gauge - 2 3/4", 3" and 3 1/2"										
10075	28"	Synthetic	3+1	C,IC,M,IM,F	Red bar	49.63"	7.5 lbs.	14 1/4"	2 1/2"	1 5/8"
10070	26"	Synthetic	3+1	C,IC,M,IM,F	Red bar	47.63"	7.4 lbs.	14 1/4"	2 1/2"	1 5/8"
10065	24"	Synthetic	3+1	C,IC,M,IM,F	Red bar	45.63"	7.3 lbs.	14 1/4"	2 1/2"	1 5/8"
10115	28"	Timber HD	3+1	C,IC,M,IM,F	Red bar	49.63"	7.5 lbs.	14 1/4"	2 1/2"	1 5/8"
10120	26"	Timber HD	3+1	C,IC,M,IM,F	Red bar	47.63"	7.4 lbs.	14 1/4"	2 1/2"	1 5/8"
10125	24"	Timber HD	3+1	C,IC,M,IM,F	Red bar	45.63"	7.3 lbs.	14 1/4"	2 1/2"	1 5/8"
M1 FIELD – 12 Gauge - 2 3/4" and 3"										
11070	28"	Synthetic	3+1	C,IC,M,IM,F	Red bar	49.5"	7.4 lbs.	14 3/8"	2 1/4"	1 3/8"
11072	26"	Synthetic	3+1	C,IC,M,IM,F	Red bar	47.5"	7.3 lbs.	14 3/8"	2 1/4"	1 3/8"
11074	24"	Synthetic	3+1	C,IC,M,IM,F	Red bar	45.5"	7.2 lbs.	14 3/8"	2 1/4"	1 3/8"
11120	28"	Timber HD	3+1	C,IC,M,IM,F	Red bar	49.5"	7.4 lbs.	14 3/8"	2 1/4"	1 3/8"
11125	26"	Timber HD	3+1	C,IC,M,IM,F	Red bar	47.5"	7.3 lbs.	14 3/8"	2 1/4"	1 3/8"
11130	24"	Timber HD	3+1	C,IC,M,IM,F	Red bar	45.5"	7.2 lbs.	14 3/8"	2 1/4"	1 3/8"
11135	21"	Timber HD	3+1	C,IC,M,IM,F	Red bar	42.5"	7.0 lbs.	14 3/8"	2 1/4"	1 3/8"
MONTEFELTRO – 12 Gauge - 2 3/4" and 3"										
10805	28"	Satin Walnut	4+1	C,IC,M,IM,F	Red bar	49.5"	7.1 lbs.	14 3/8"	2 3/8"	1 1/2"
10815	26"	Satin Walnut	4+1	C,IC,M,IM,F	Red bar	47.5"	6.9 lbs.	14 3/8"	2 3/8"	1 1/2"

Shotguns • 225

Benelli Shotguns
Model M1 Series

M1 FIELD FIELD TIMBER HD

MODEL M1 FIELD

MONTEFELTRO

M1 Field with Timber HD™
The M1 Field 12-gauge shotgun combines the M1 Super 90 receiver with a choice of sythetic or walnut stocks, including a camouflaged model with an Realtree HD pattern sealed on the matte finish metal stock. Available in 21", 24", 26" or 28" barrels with vent rib.

Prices:
M1 Field with Camo finish, camo polymer
   butt-stock and forearm $1070
Left-hand 1090

Model M1 Field
Also available:
Model M1 Tactical w/18 1/2" bbl. 935
   With pistol-grip stock, ghost ring sights 1015
M1 Practical, 26" barrel, ghost ring sight,
   synthetic stock 1255
Model M1 Field (synthetic stock)
   w/21", 24", 26", 28" bbl. 970

Left hand $990
Model M1 Field with satin walnut 980
Model M1 Field Rifled Slug
   Synthetic 1040
   Timber HD 1150
Model M3 Pump/Auto Series
   Standard stock, 19 3/4" barrel. 1110
   w/Ghost Ring Sight and standard stock 1155
Model M1 Field 20 gauge w/24" or 26" bbl.
   Synthetic stock 970
   Timber HD stock. 1070

Montefeltro
Prices:
12 Ga.—24", 26", or 28" Barrel
   (20 ga.—24" or 26" barrel only) 980
Left Hand w/26" or 28" Barrel. 995
Short Stock (20 ga., 12.5" pull). 1015

Beretta Shotguns

SERIES 682 GOLD E COMPETITION TRAP OVER/UNDER

MODEL 682 GOLD E TRAP W/ADJUSTABLE STOCK

MODEL 682 GOLD E COMPETITION SKEET O/U

MODEL 682 GOLD E SPORTING

A391 XTREMA 3.5

Model 682 Trap
These 12 gauge Model 682 Trap guns feature adjustable gold-plated, single-selective sliding trigger; low-profile improved boxlock action; manual safety w/barrel selector; 2.75" chambers; auto ejector; competition recoil pad buttplate; hand-checkered walnut stock.
Specifications
Weight: Approx. 8 lbs.
Barrel Lengths/Chokes: 30 Imp. Mod./Full (Black); 30" or 32" Mobilchoke® (Black); Top Single 32" or 34" Mobilchoke®; **Combo:** 30" or 32" Mobilchoke® (Top), 30" IM/F (Top), 32" Mobilchoke® (Mono), 30" or 32" Mobilchoke® ported
Prices:
Model 682 Gold E trap
 w/Adjustable Stock $4320
 Combo Top 5305

Model 682 Skeet
This 12-gauge skeet gun sports a hand-checkered premium walnut stock w/silver oval for initials, forged and hardened receiver w/Greyston finish, manual safety with trigger selector, auto ejector, silver inlaid on trigger guard.
Specifications
Action: Low-profile hard chrome-plated boxlock
Trigger: Single adjustable sliding trigger
Barrels: 28" or 30" blued barrels with 2.75" chambers
Stock dimensions: Length of pull 14.75"; drop at comb 1 3/8"; drop at heel 2.25" **Sights:** fluorescent front and metal middle bead **Weight:** Approx. 7.5 lbs.
Price: (incl. fitted case) 4320

Model 682 Sporting
These competition-stye sporting clays guns feature 28" or 30" barrels with four flush-mounted screw-in choke tubes (Full, Modified, Improved Cylinder and Skeet), plus hand-checkered stock and forend of fine walnut, 2.75" or 3" chambers and adjustable trigger. Model 682 Gold features Greystone finish, an ultra-durable finish in gunmetal grey w/gold accents; also available in 32" barrel. Model 686 Silver Pigeon Sporting has coin silver receiver with scroll engraving.
Prices:
682 Gold E Sporting $3850
686 Silver Pigeon Sporting 1931

A391 Xtrema 3.5
For 2002, Beretta is releasing the A391 Xtrema 3.5, designed to handle 3.5 ammunition. The action of the Xtrema features a unique gas system. The Xtrema is the first shotgun to incorporate a gas system with a rotating locking bolt. This minimizes barrel movement caused by powerful loads and improves accuracy.
Specifications
Gauge: 12. **Weight:** 7.8 lbs.
Safety: Cross-bolt.
Stock: Synthetic with rubber inlays.
 Sights: Metal front bead.
Prices:
Xtrema Synthetic 1129
Xtrema Camo 1241

Beretta Shotguns

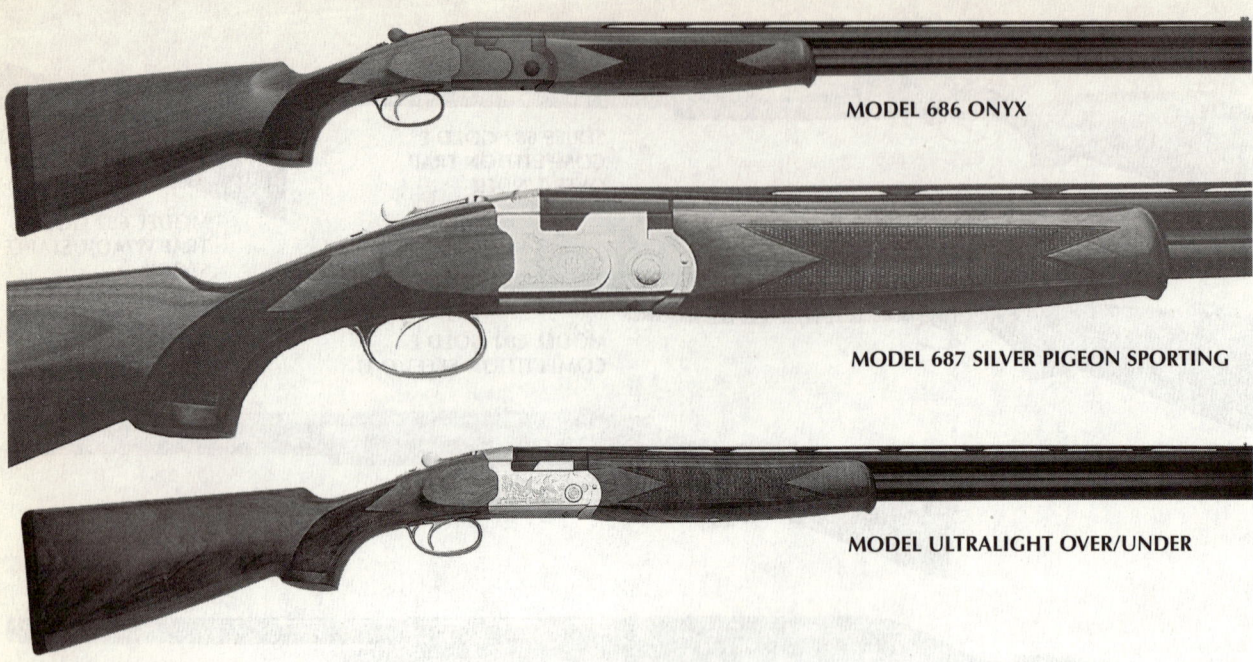

MODEL 686 ONYX

MODEL 687 SILVER PIGEON SPORTING

MODEL ULTRALIGHT OVER/UNDER

Model 686 Onyx
Specifications
Gauges: 12, 20 **Chambers:** 3" and 3.5" **Barrel Lengths:** 26"" and 28" **Chokes:** Mobilchoke® screw-in system
Weight: 6 lbs. 12 oz. (12 ga.); 6.2 lbs. (20 ga.)
Stock: American walnut with recoil pad (English stock available)
Features: Automatic ejectors; matte black finish on barrels and receiver to reduce glare
Price:..$1583
Model 686 Onyx Sporting.......................1639
w/X-Tra Wood...................................1778
Onyx Waterfowler 3.5...........................1648

Model 687 Silver Pigeon Sporting
This boxlock over/under features enhanced engraving pattern, schnabel forend and an electroless nickel finished receiver.
Chamber: 3" Mobilchoke® screw-in tube system
Gauges: 12 & 20
Prices:
Model 687 Silver Pigeon Sporting Combo........3151
Model 687 Silver Pigeon II, 12 or 20.............2196
Model 687 Silver Pigeon II Sporting, 12 ga. only...2196

Model 687EELL Diamond Pigeon (not shown)
Model 687EELL Combo (20 and 28 ga.)
In 12, 20 or 28 ga., this model features the Mobilchoke® engraved choke system, a special premium walnut stock and silver receiver with engraved sideplate.
Prices:
Model 687 EELL Diamond Pigeon................5630
Model 687EELL Combo (20 and 28 ga.).........6279

Also available:
Model 687EELL Diamond Pigeon Skeet.........$4984
  w/adjustable stock............................6050
Diamond Pigeon Sporting (12 ga.).............5741

Model 687EL Gold Pigeon (not shown)
Features game-scene engraving on receiver with gold highlights. Available in 12, 20 gauge (28 ga. and .410 in small frame).
Specifications
Barrels/Chokes: 26" and 28" with Mobilchoke®
Action: Low-profile improved boxlock
Weight: 6.8 lbs. (12 ga.)
Trigger: Single selective with manual safety
Extractors: Auto ejectors
Prices:
Model 687EL (12, 20, 26" or 28" bbl.)...........4099
Model 687EL Small Frame (28 ga./.410).........4273
Model 687ELGR II Sporting (12 ga. and 28 ga.)...4595
  w/deep relief sideplate engraving.............4554
Model 687EL Gold Pigeon II (sideplate engraving)..4513
Model 687EL Gold Pigeon II Sporting Combo.....5244

Model Ultralight Over/Under
Specifications
Barrel: 12 ga, 26" or 28"
Stock: Select walnut
Features: Nickel finish receiver w/game scene engraving; black rubber recoil pad; single selective trigger
Price:...1931
Also available:
Ultralight Deluxe w/matte electroless nickel finish receiver w/gold game scene engraving; walnut stock and forend; light aluminum alloy receiver reinforced w/titanium breech plate
Price:...2323

Beretta Shotguns

DT10 TRIDENT SKEET – ADJUSTABLE STOCK

Four major developments set the Beretta DT10 Trident competition over-and-unders apart from other competition shotguns: 1) A new internal barrel configuration (Optima-Bore), available on some models, improves shot distribution. 2) The new Optima-Choke competition choke-tubes. Longer and slimmer, with an internal profile to make patterns uniform. 3) Specific point of impact. While the models for Olympic Trap, Skeet and Sporting Clays have a common central point of impact, the models designed for American Trap deliver a high point of impact. 4) Correct distribution of mass. This gives the gun a center of mass coaxial with the first (bottom) barrel, eliminating muzzle rise and affording faster target acquisition on the second shot.

The DT10 Trident X-Trap Combo allows the shooter to maintain a steady, unaltered sighting plane and point of impact with both barrels. The initials "DT" in DT10 are an abbreviation of "Detachable Trigger". The trigger position can be adjusted with the screwdriver provided. Top lever design is based on the needs of the top shooters. The gun is simpler to use for left-handers. The safety is shaped to provide the best hold and smoothest working movement. Lightning-fast lock times and an ultra-crisp trigger pull are provided by "V" shaped mainsprings. Trident available in 12 gauge with barrel length ranging from 28" to 34".

Prices:
Trident Trap, Adjustable stock	$8500
Trident Trap, Combo Top Single	10,790
Trident Trap, Bottom Single Combo	11,040
Trident Skeet	8030
Trident Sporting	7850
Trident Trap, Top Single, Adjustable stock	8500

WHITEWING

Practical and functional, the Whitewing is distinguished by a polished finish of the receiver, top lever, trigger plate and trigger guard. The top and hinges have a matte, anti-glare finish, while the trigger is gold-plated. The side panels are lightly engraved with hunting scenes.

The polished blued barrels feature an open side rib design that not only allows more rapid cooling, but also makes for even quicker handling. Special sling swivels can be installed on request. The stock dimensions and fore-end are customized for hunting to afford pointability and balance.

Prices:
Whitewing (12 or 20 ga.)	$1298
Blackwing (12 or 20 ga.)	1398

S686 SILVER PIGEON
BERETTA'S CLASSIC OVER-AND-UNDER

Rich scroll work on the receiver and an elegant nickel finish set the Silver Pigeon apart, as do its superior performances. The stock's fine-cut checkering and the Schnabel fore-end complements the Silver Pigeon's stylish appearance. The Silver Pigeon Combo set includes interchangeable barrels in 20 and 28 gauges, while the High Gloss version features ultra-polished enhancements on the receiver, stock and fore-end. The X-Tra Wood model boasts beautifully grained walnut wood finish.

Produced in 12, 20 and 28 gauge models, the Silver Pigeon features Beretta's exclusive universal chamber, which allows the Silver Pigeon to accommodate all 3" Magnum cartridges (excluding 28 gauge) and improves performance when using 2 3/4" cartridges.

Prices:
Silver Pigeon	1817
w/ X-tra wood	2022
Silver Pigeon (2 barrel set)	2587
Silver Pigeon Trap Top Mono	1869
686 Silver Pigeon S.	1917
686 Silver Pigeon S Combo	2634

Also available:
686E Sporting (12 or 20 ga.)
Features: enhanced styling, carrying case, accessories, 5 choke tubes
Price: 2008

Beretta Shotguns

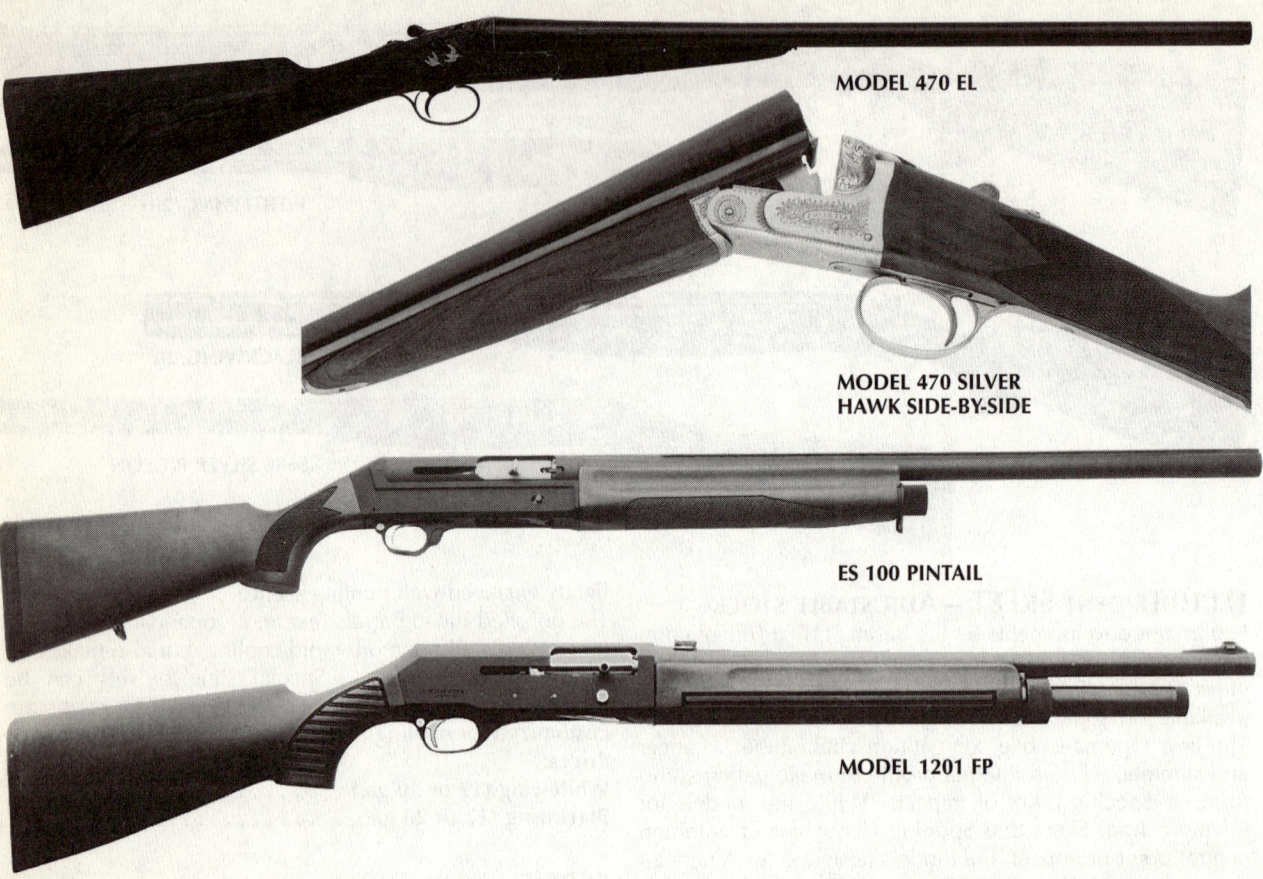

MODEL 470 EL

MODEL 470 SILVER HAWK SIDE-BY-SIDE

ES 100 PINTAIL

MODEL 1201 FP

Model 470 EL
Features color case hardened side plates with gold-filled game scene engraving. Optima choke available in 12 ga. only.
Price: (12 and 20 ga.) $5980

Model 470 Silver Hawk Side-By-Side
Specifications
Gauge: 12 and 20 **Chamber:** 3"
Action: Low profile, improved box lock
Choke: IC/IM, M/F **Barrel Length:** 26" and 28"
Weight: 6.5 lbs. (12 ga.); 5.9 lbs. (20 ga.)
Sights: Metal front bead
Stock: Select walnut, checkered
Features: Silver satin chrome finish on receiver, trigger guard, forend iron, top lever, trigger, trigger plate and safety/select lever; hand-chased scroll, engraving on receiver, top lever, forend iron and triggerguard; gold inlaid hawk's head on top lever.
Prices:
12 ga. 2596
20 ga. 2726

ES 100 Pintail
This 12-gauge semiautomatic shotgun with short-recoil operation is available with 24" or 26" barrels and Mobilchoke®. Finish is nonreflective matte on alll exposed wood and metal surfaces; receiver is aluminum alloy.

Specifications
Barrel Lengths: 24", 26", 28"; 24" Slug
Weight: 7.3 lbs. Stock: Checkered selected hardwood or camo Sights: Bead front
Price: $725
Camo 766
Also Available:
Pintail Rifled Slug Combo featuring fully rifed barrel w/1 in 24" and 28" twist. Upper receiver and barrel permanently joined as one unit.
Price: 932

Model 1201 FP
This all-weather semiautomatic shotgun features an adjustable polymer stock and forend with recoil pad. Lightweight, it sports a unique weather-resistant matte black finish to reduce glare, resist corrosion and aid in heat dispersion; short recoil action for light and heavy loads, tritium sights.
Specifications
Gauge: 12 **Chamber:** 3" **Capacity:** 6 rounds
Choke: Cylinder (fixed) **Barrel Length:** 18"
Weight: 6.3 lbs. **Sights:** Blade Front; adjustable rear
Price: 890

Beretta Shotguns
Semiautomatics for Hunting and Competition

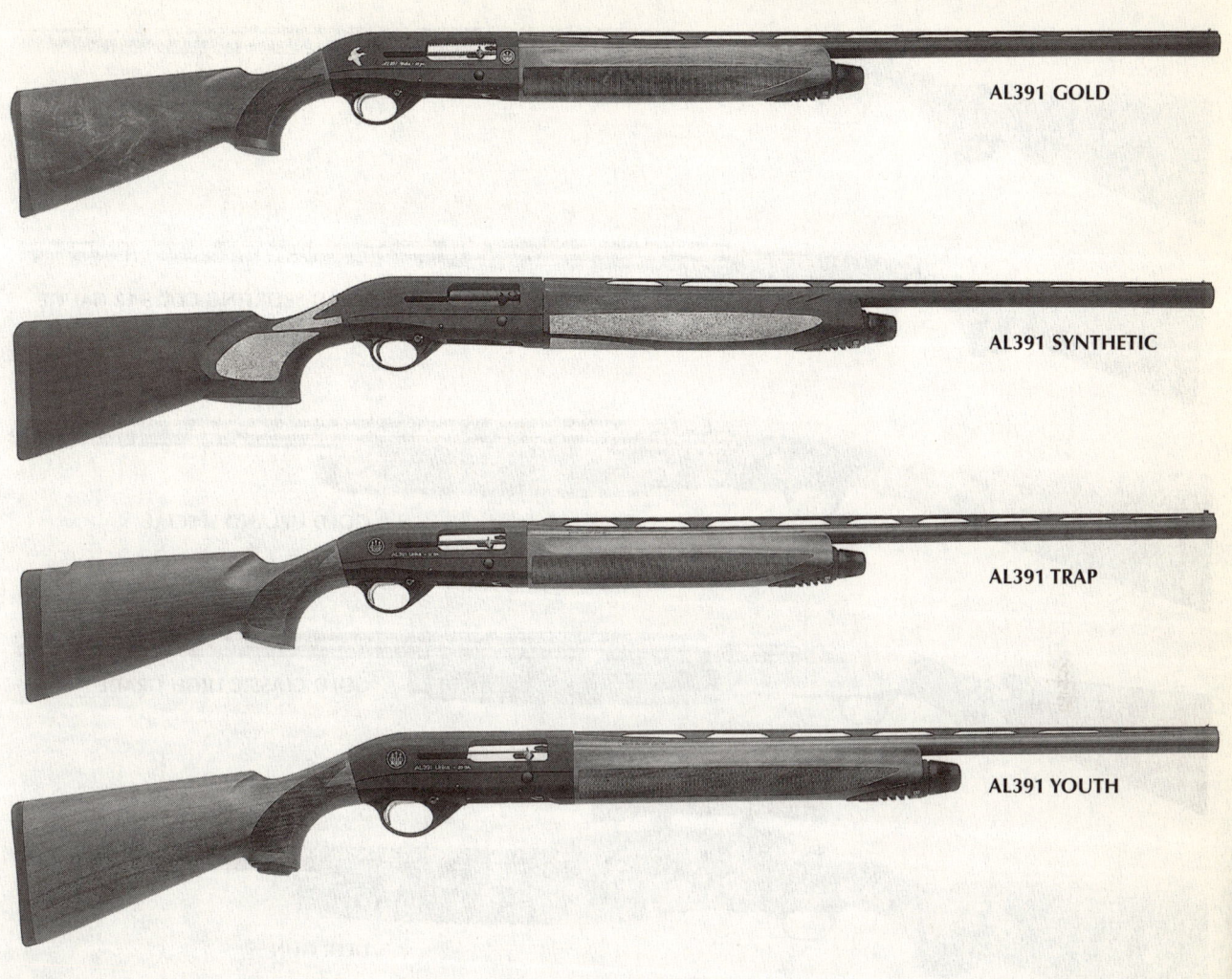

AL391 GOLD

AL391 SYNTHETIC

AL391 TRAP

AL391 YOUTH

Beretta Urika AL391
AUTOLOADING SHOTGUN

The Beretta AL391 features a self-compensating gas valve that ensures reliable functioning with a wide range of factory loads, from skeet to heavy waterfowl charges. The valve is housed in a cylinder that stays with the barrel to permit quick and easy removal of the barrel. A gas valve flange on the front of the forend deflects gas away from the shooter. The gas system is compact, keeping forend bulk to a minimum. Recoil has been reduced by a small device at the rear of the receiver that cushions bolt thrust, and a spring and polymer ring inside the forend cap. Beretta considered details when designing this gun, equipping the forend cap with a magnet so the sling swivel does not fall off during disassembly. Both synthetic and walnut stocks adjust for drop and cast via shims. The receiver is of lightweight alloy to limit weight (the lightest 12-bore weighs only 6.6 lbs.) Camouflage versions of the AL391 are available with Advantage, Wetlands and Realtree Hardwoods patterns. Special-purpose configura-tions make this shotgun suitable for all clay-target games, and there's a youth model with smaller dimensions. All AL 391s, 12- and 20-gauge, are chambered for 2 3/4- and 3-inch shells and come with barrel lengths from 24" to 30". The guns come in a molded lockable case with five interchangeable chokes and wrenches, stock shims and two recoil pads, plus gun oil.

Prices:
Urika AL391	**$984**
Synthetic	984
Camouflage	1090
Gold (black receiver)	1213
Gold Lightwt.	1254
Youth	984
Sporting	1027
Gold Sporting (black receiver)	1254
Gold Sporting (silver receiver)	1296
Trap	1027
Gold Trap (black receiver)	1254
Parallel Target	1027

Browning Shotguns

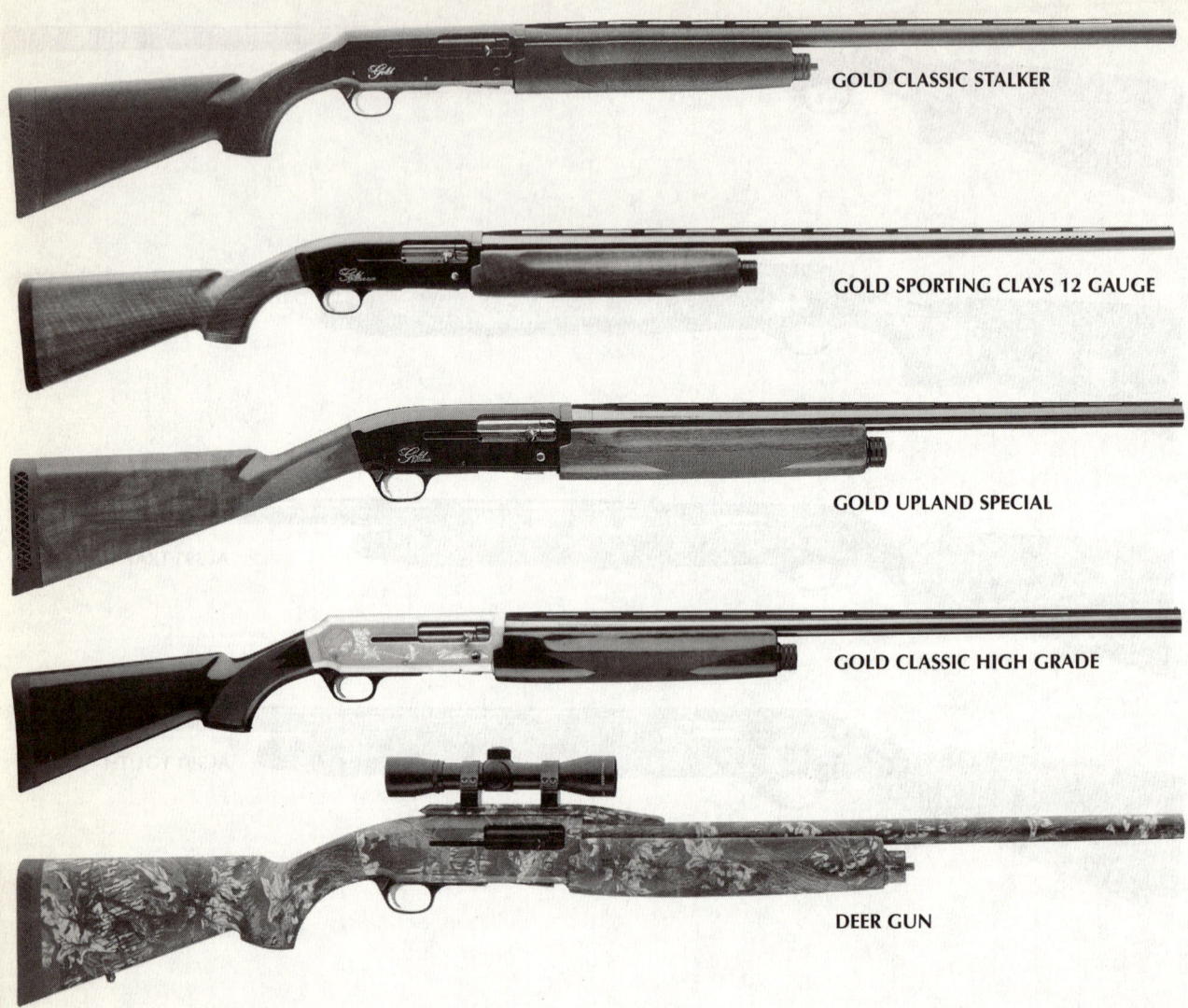

GOLD CLASSIC STALKER

GOLD SPORTING CLAYS 12 GAUGE

GOLD UPLAND SPECIAL

GOLD CLASSIC HIGH GRADE

DEER GUN

Browning Gold

Browning Gold Shotguns have been called the most versatile autoloaders on the market, with a unique gas metering system that shoots light 2.75" shells or heavy loads from 3.5" hulls. An assortment of barrels, stocks and sights adapts this shotgun to all upland game, waterfowl and deer hunting situations. There's also a 10-gauge version. The gun's quick pointing qualities and reliability have already made it a favorite of hunters and clay target shooters–a fitting heir to the now-discontinued Browning Auto 5.

Prices:

Gold Hunter 12 or 20 ga., 3" chamber	$894
3.5" chamber	1038
Gold Rifled Deer Hunter 20 ga.	987
Gold Stalker 12 ga., 3"	856
3.5"	1002
Gold Rifled Deer Stalker	948
Gold Mossy Oak 12 ga., 3"	967
3.5"	1146
Gold Rifled Deer Break-Up	1046
Gold Sporting Clays	965
Gold GC Sporting Clays	1490
Gold Ladies Sporting Clays	902
Gold Fusion 12 & 20 ga.	985
Gold Upland Special 12 & 20 ga., 24" bbl., 20 ga. 26" bbl.	894
Gold Classic High Grade 20ga.	1716
Gold Turkey Stalker	744

SPECIFICATIONS GOLD LIGHT 10 BREAKUP ($1255) & STALKER ($1184)

Chamber	Barrel Length	Overall Length	Average Weight	Chokes
3.5	28"	50"	9 lbs. 10 oz.	Standard Invector
3.5	26"	48"	9 lbs. 7 oz.	Standard Invector

Browning Shotguns

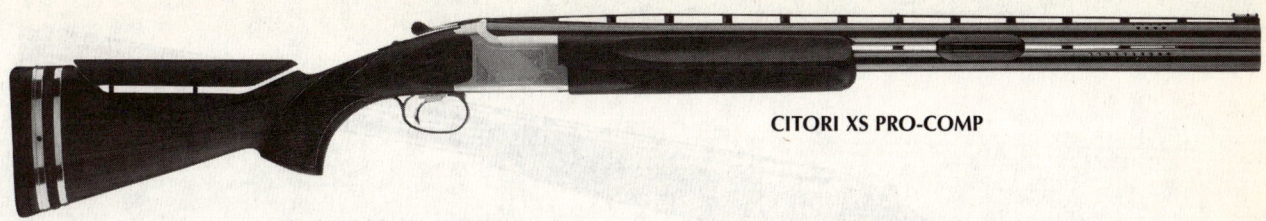
CITORI XS PRO-COMP

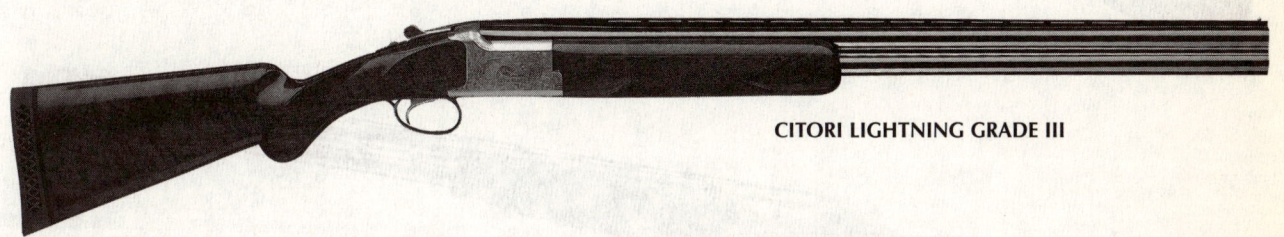
CITORI LIGHTNING GRADE III

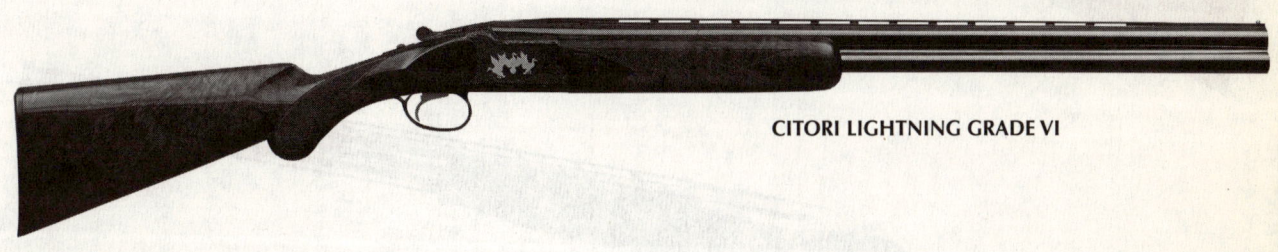
CITORI LIGHTNING GRADE VI

Citori XS Pro-Comp
The ultimate shotgun for competition shooters. Ported barrels, adjustable comb, beavertail forearm, GraCoil recoil reduction system, right-hand palm swell, Triple Trigger™ System.
Specifications
Gauge: 12 **Barrel:** 28", 30"
Price: $3,796

Citori Lightning Grade III
Delicate scroll engraving encompasses the grayed receiver on all major surfaces including the trigger guard and tang screws. 12 gauge models illustrate pheasants on the right and mallards on the left side of the receiver. 20, 28 gauge and .410 bore models highlight quail and grouse.

Prices:
12 or 20 ga. 2,346
28 or 410 ga. 2,621

Citori Lightning Grade VI
Deep relief engraving garnishes the entire receiver, trigger guard, top tang, takedown lever and bracket. Bird depictions are crafted in 24 karat gold with a unique gold plating and engraving process. The left side depicts two flushing ringnecks. The right side displays three mallard drakes rising out of the cattails. Available with either a distinctive grayed or deeply blued receiver.
Prices:
12 or 20 ga. 3,615
28 or .410 ga. 3,893

Browning Shotguns

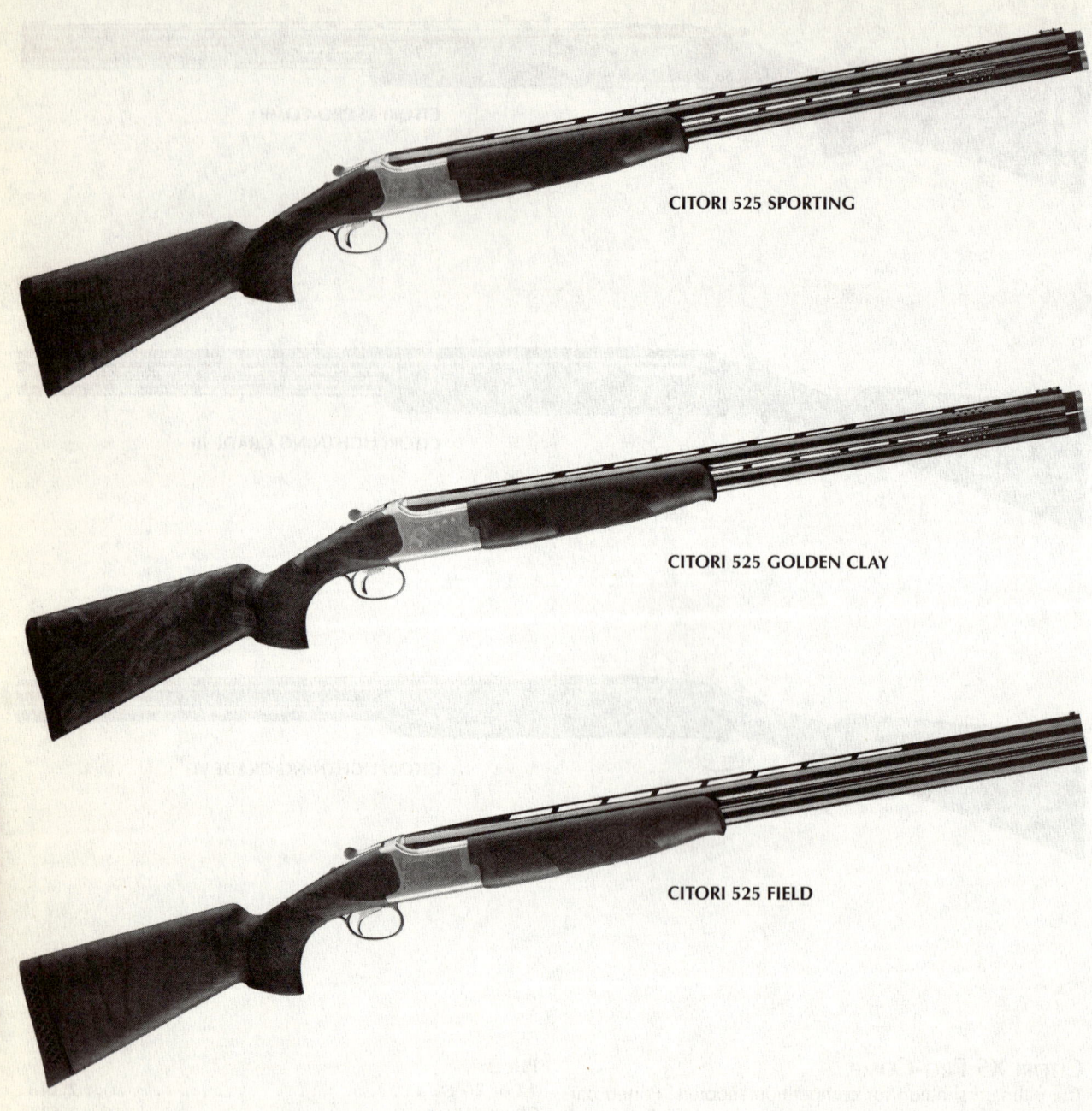

CITORI 525 SPORTING

CITORI 525 GOLDEN CLAY

CITORI 525 FIELD

NEW CITORI 525
Browning has added a new line to the popular Citori model. The Citori 525 features a new stock design with a more pronounced pistol grip, European comb and a Euro checkering pattern. The floated, tapered and ventilated top and side ribs have forward-angled posts. The slimline barrels reduce weight and improve balance. Citori 525 sporting guns come with Midas-Grade extended choke tubes.

Prices:
Citori 525 Sporting, 12 and 20 gauge
 with 28" or 30" barrels, 2-3/4" chamber $2493
Citori 525 Golden Clays, 12 and 20 gauge
 with 28" or 30" barrels, 2-3/4" chamber with
 high-grade walnut stock and gold inlays 3993
Citori 525 Field, 12 and 20 gauge with
 26" or 28" barrels. 3" chamber 1777

Browning Shotguns

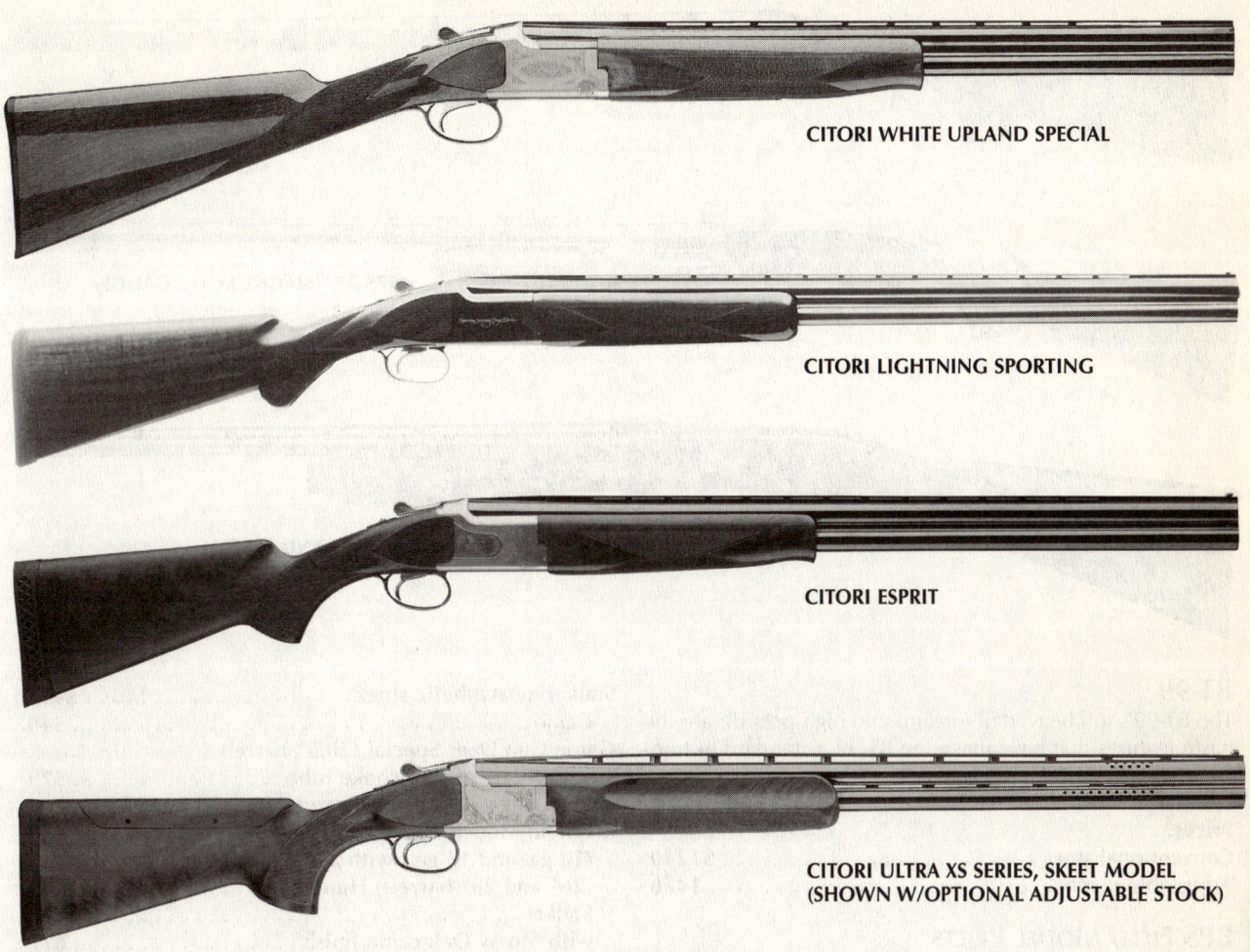

CITORI WHITE UPLAND SPECIAL

CITORI LIGHTNING SPORTING

CITORI ESPRIT

**CITORI ULTRA XS SERIES, SKEET MODEL
(SHOWN W/OPTIONAL ADJUSTABLE STOCK)**

Citori White Upland Special
Has a shorter, straight-grip stock Schnabel forend and 24" barrel, 12 or 20 ga., 2 3/4". Like all Citoris, the White Upland has backbored barrels and automatic ejectors.
Price: $1583

Nitex Feather XS Series (Not Shown)
Sporting clays shotguns with alloy receivers incorporating steel breech face.
Prices:
12, 20 ga. 2311
28, .410 ga. 2385

Citori Lightning Sporting
Many of these lively over/under shotguns are available with ported barrels, adjustable combs, the option of high or low ribs.
Prices:
Lightning Sporting
   Grade I, high rib, ported bbl., 3" 1770
   Grade I, low rib 1691

Citori Esprit
12 gauge, 28" barrel. Features removable decorative side plates, Schnabel forearm, satin finish and high-grade walnut stock and forearm.
Price $2453

Ultra XT Trap Models
Prices:
12 Gauge, Silver Nitride Receiver,
   Ported Barrels, Grade I 2083
   w/adjustable comb 2333

Ultra XS Skeet Models
Prices:
12 & 20 Gauge, Silver Nitride, Ported Barrels
   Grade I. 2227
   w/adjustable comb 2451

Shotguns • 235

Browning Shotguns

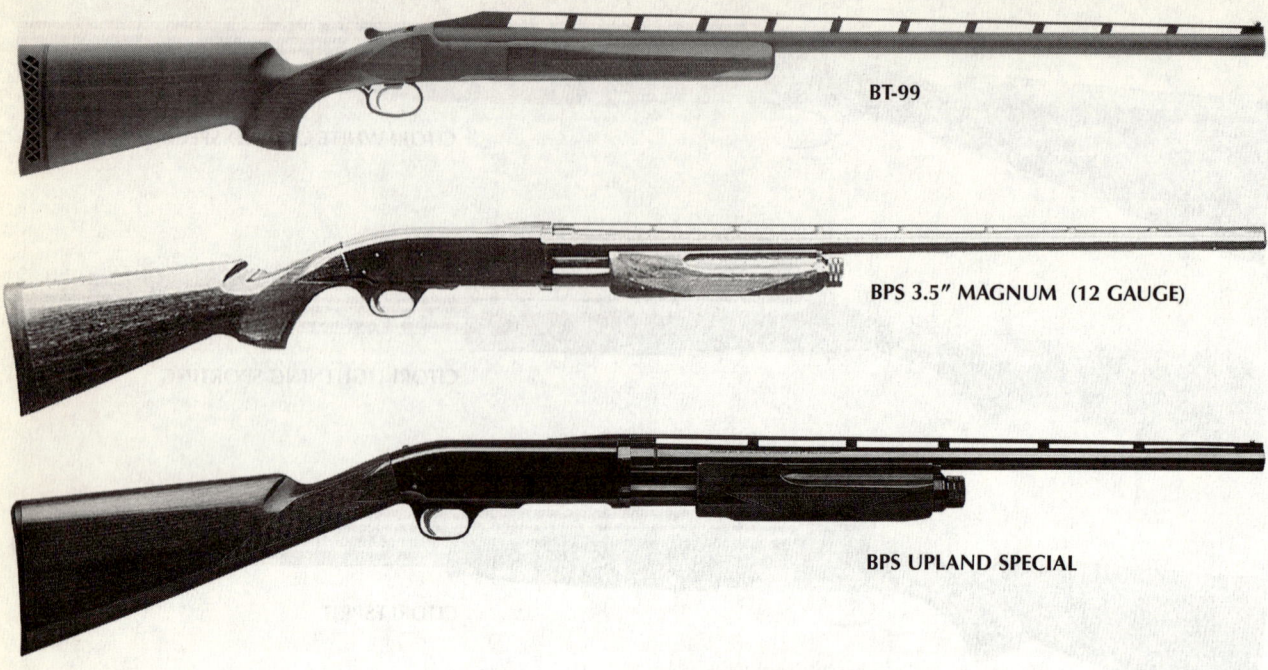

BT-99
BPS 3.5" MAGNUM (12 GAUGE)
BPS UPLAND SPECIAL

BT-99
The BT-99's full beavertail forearm and high-post rib are the basic features that have made the BT-99 a standard in trapshooting. Choice of a conventional stock version or with an adjustable comb.
Prices:
Conventional stock..........................$1240
Adjustable comb..............................1478

BPS Field Model Prices
Prices:
Hunter 3" chamber 26", 28", 30" barrels..........473
Stalker, w/synthetic stock.....................$457
Camo...540
Game Gun Deer Special (20.5" barrel)
  with 5" rifled slug choke tube................579
Small Gauge Field (28 gauge or 410, 28" or 26")...505
Magnum Models Hunting & Stalker Grades
  (10 ga. and 12 ga.) with 3.5" Mag. chamber
  (26" and 28" barrels) Hunter..................552
  Stalker.......................................537
  with Mossy Oak camo finish....................617
Upland special (12 or 20 ga.)...................473
Micro (20 ga.)..................................473

BPS SPECIFICATIONS

Gauge	Model	Chamber	Capacity[2]	Barrel Length	Overall Length	Average Weight	Chokes Available[1]
10 Mag	Hunter & Stalker	3.5"	4	30, 28, 26, 24"	46-52"	9.25-9.5 lbs.	Invector
12, 3.5" Mag	Hunter	3.5"	4	30, 28, 26, 24"	45-51"	7.5-8.5 lbs.	Invector-Plus
12, 3.5" Mag	Stalker	3.5"	4	30, 28, 26, 24"	45-51"	7.5-8.5 lbs.	Invector-Plus
12	Hunter & Stalker	3"	4	30"	50.75"	7 lbs. 12 oz.	Invector-Plus
12	Hunter & Stalker	3"	4	28"	48.75"	7 lbs. 11 oz.	Invector-Plus
12	Hunter & Stalker	3"	4	26"	46.75"	7 lbs. 10 oz.	Invector-Plus
12	Standard Buck Special	3"	4	24"	44.75"	7 lbs. 10 oz.	Slug/Buckshot
12	Upland Special	3"	4	22"	42.5"	7 lbs. 8 oz.	Invector-Plus
12	Hunter & Stalker	3"	4	22"	42.5"	7 lbs. 7 oz.	Invector-Plus
12	Game Gun Turkey Special	3"	4	20.5"	40 7/8"	7 lbs. 7 oz.	Invector
12	Game Gun Deer Special/Rifled	3"	4	20.5"	40 7/8"	7 lbs. 7 oz.	Fully Rifled Barrel
12	Game Gun Deer Special/Smooth	3"	4	20.5"	40 7/8"	7 lbs. 7 oz.	Special Inv./Rifled
12	Game Gun Cantilever Mount	3"	4	20.5"	40 7/8"	7 lbs. 9 oz.	Fully Rifled
20	Hunter	3"	4	28"	48.75"	7 lbs. 1 oz.	Invector-Plus
20	Hunter	3"	4	26"	46.75"	7 lbs.	Invector-Plus
20	Micro	3"	4	22"	41.75"	6 lbs. 11 oz.	Invector-Plus
20	Upland Special	3"	4	22"	42.75"	6 lbs. 12 oz.	Invector-Plus
28	Hunter	2.75"	4	28"	48.75"	7 lbs. 1 oz.	Invector
28	Hunter	2.75"	4	26"	46.75"	7 lbs.	Invector
.410	Hunter	3"	4	26"	46.75"	6 lbs. 13 oz.	

Charles Daly Shotguns
Imported by K.B.I. Inc.

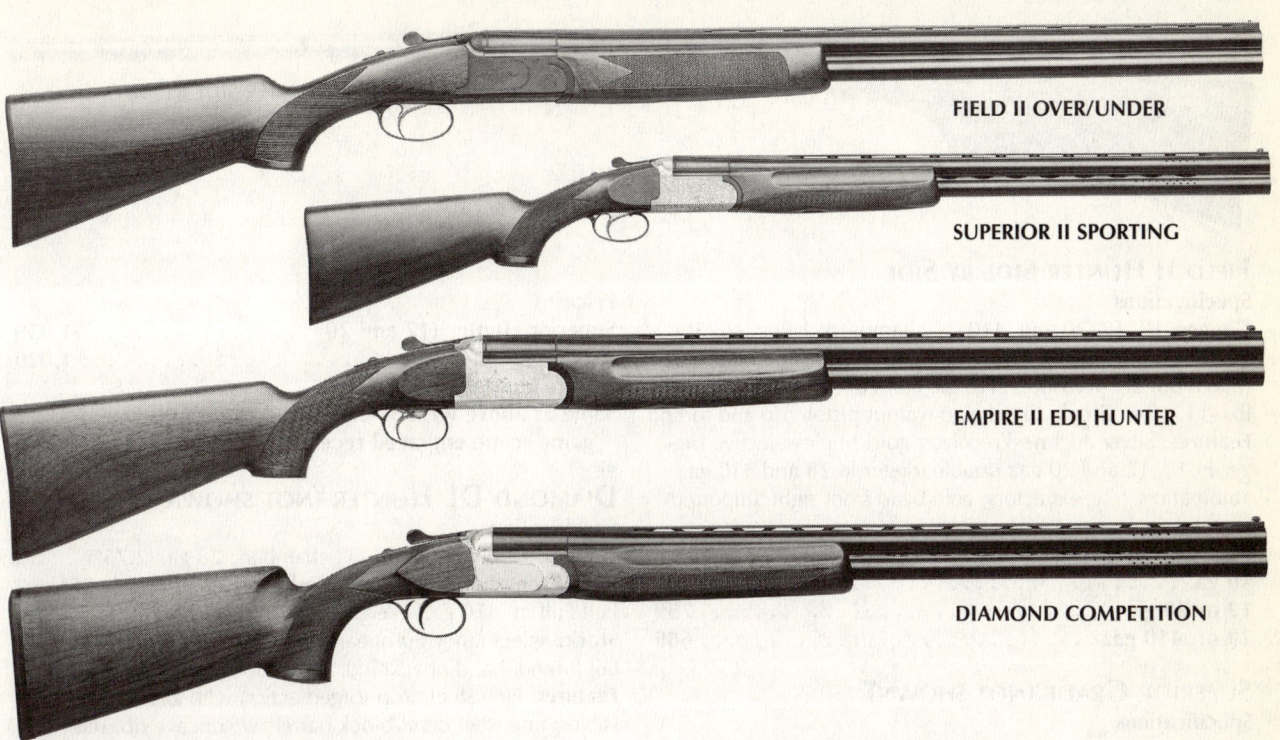

FIELD II OVER/UNDER
SUPERIOR II SPORTING
EMPIRE II EDL HUNTER
DIAMOND COMPETITION

FIELD II HUNTER OVER/UNDER
Specifications
Gauges: 12, 16, 20, 28 and .410 (3" chambers); 28 ga. (2.75") **Barrel Lengths/Chokes:** 28" Mod./Full; 26" IC/Mod.; .410 ga. **Full/Full Weight:** Approx. 7 lb.
Stock: Checkered walnut pistol-grip and forend
Features: Blued engraved receiver; chrome-moly steel barrels, gold single-selective trigger, automatic safety, extractors, gold bead front sight
Prices:
Field II Hunter - 12, 16 or 20 ga. $789
   28 ga. 849
   .410 ga. 895
Field II Hunter - Ultra-Light MC 12 or 20 ga. 899
Field II Hunter AE-MC. Same as Field Hunter but w/5 choke tubes (12 and 20 ga. only). 999
Superior II Hunter AE. Gold single-selective trigger, gold bead front sight, silver engraved receiver.
   28 ga. 1,109
   .410 ga. 1,155
Superior II Hunter AE-MC. Same as above in 12 and 20 ga. w/5 choke tubes 1,199

SUPERIOR II SPORTING
Specifications
Gauges: 12 (3" chambers)
Barrel Lengths/Chokes: 28" & 30" with multi-choke (5 tubes)
Weight: Approx. 7 lb.
Stock: Checkered walnut pistol-grip buttstock w/semi-beavertail forend
Features: Silver engraved receiver, ported chrome-moly steel barrels, gold single-selective trigger, automatic safety, auto-ejectors, red bead front sight
Prices:
Superior II Sporting 1279
Superior II Trap-MC. Same as above
   (2.75" chamber) 30" bbl. only. 1325

EMPIRE II EDL HUNTER
Specifications
Gauges: 12, 20, .410 ga. (3" chambers); 28 ga. (2.75")
Barrel Lengths/Chokes: 26" & 28"–5 multi-choke tubes in 12 & 20 ga.; 26" IC/M in 28 ga.; 26" Full/Full in .410 ga.
Weight: Approx. 7 lb. **Sights:** Red bead front; metal bead center
Stock: Checkered walnut pistol-grip buttstock w/semi-beavertail forend **Features:** Silver engraved receiver, full sideplate, chrome-moly steel barrels, gold single-selective trigger, automatic safety, auto-ejector, recoil pad
Prices:
Empire II EDL Hunter 12 or 20 ga. 1619
   28 ga. 1579
   .410 ga. 1629
Empire II Sporting. 12 only, w/30" and 28" ported barrels, no metal bead center sight 1519
Empire II Trap-MC. 12 ga. w/30" bbl. (unported) metal bead center sight, recoil pad 1559

DIAMOND COMPETITION
Prices:
Diamond Sporting MC-5 12 only, 28" or 30" bbl. . . . 5849
Diamond Trap AE 6699
Diamond Trap Mono AE-MC 6619

Charles Daly Shotguns
Imported by K.B.I. Inc.

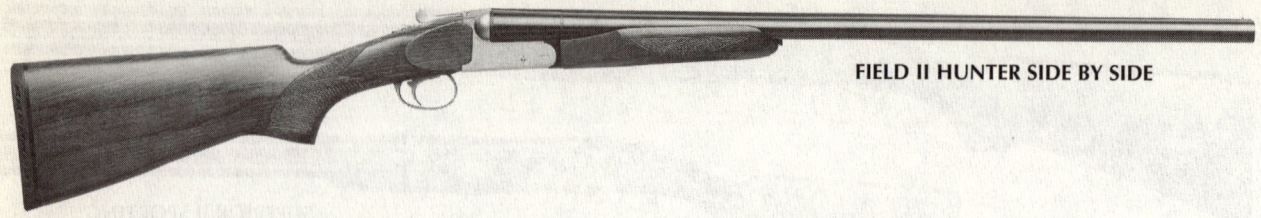

FIELD II HUNTER SIDE BY SIDE

FIELD II HUNTER SIDE BY SIDE
Specifications
Gauges: 10, 12, 20 and .410 (3" chambers); 28 ga. (2.75")
Barrel Lengths/Chokes: 32" Mod./Mod.; 30" Mod./Full; 28" Mod./Full; 26" IC/Mod.; .410 ga. Full/Full **Weight:** Approx. 6 lbs.-11.4 lbs. **Stock:** Checkered walnut pistol-grip and forend
Features: Silver engraved receiver; gold single-selective trigger in 10, 12 and 20 ga.; double trigger in 28 and 410 ga.; automatic safety, extractors, gold bead front sight. Imported from Spain
Prices:
10 ga. $789
12 or 20 ga. 759
28 or .410 ga. 689

SUPERIOR GRADE (NOT SHOWN)
Specifications
Gauges: 12 and 20; 3" chambers **Barrel Lengths/Chokes:** 28" Mod./Full; 26" IC/Mod. **Weight:** Approx. 7 lb. Stock: Checkered walnut pistol-grip buttstock and splinter forend
Features: Silver engraved receiver, chrome-lined steel barrels, gold single trigger, automatic safety, extractors, gold bead front sight

Prices:
Superior Hunter (12 and 20) $1,059
28 gauge or 410. 1,029
Empire Hunter
Same as above w/hand-checkered stock auto ejectors, game scene engraved receiver 1,349

DIAMOND DL HUNTER (NOT SHOWN)
Specifications
Gauges: 12, 20, .410 ga. (3" chambers; 28 ga. (2.75")
Barrel Lengths/Chokes: 28" Mod./Full; 26" IC/Mod.; 26" Full/Full in .410 ga. **Weight:** Approx. 5-7 lbs.
Stock: Select fancy European walnut, English-styled, beavertail forend, hand-checkered, hand-rubbed oil finish
Features: Fine steel drop-forged action with gas escape valves; fine steel demi-block barrels w/concave rib; selective auto ejectors, hand-detachable double safety sidelocks w/hand-engraved rose and scrollwork; front-hinged trigger, casehardened receiver. Imported from Spain.
Prices:
Diamond DL 6,999
28 or .410 ga. 6,999

Rifle/Shotgun Combination Guns

SUPERIOR COMBINATION

COUNTRY SQUIRE OVER/UNDER .410
Barrels: 26" Chrome Moly steel **Stock:** Oil-finished 20 LPI hand-checkered European with recoil pad. Color case hardened receiver; gold-plated triggers. **Sights:** Williams receiver sight; Lyman target front sight
Price: . . . . A.O.R.
Also available:
Country Squire Side-by-Side .410 . . . . A.O.R.

SUPERIOR COMBINATION
Specifications
Gauge/Calibers: 12/22 Hornet, 223 Rem., 30-06 Sprgfld.
Barrel Length/Choke: 23.5", shotgun choke IC
Weight: Approx. 7.5 lbs.
Stock: Checkered walnut pistol-grip buttstock and semi-beavertail forend
Features: Silver engraved receiver forged and milled from a solid block of high-strength steel; chrome-moly steel barrels, double trigger, extractors, sling swivels, gold bead front sight
Prices:
Superior Combination $1359
Empire Combination.
Same as above w/deluxe walnut European-style comb/cheekpiece, slim forend. 1799

Charles Daly Shotguns
Semi-Auto Shotguns

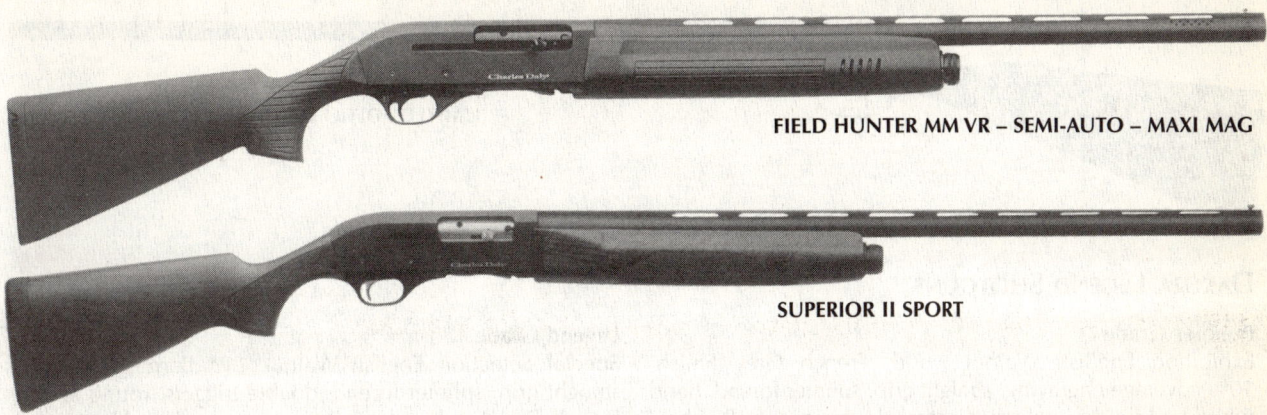

FIELD HUNTER MM VR – SEMI-AUTO – MAXI MAG

SUPERIOR II SPORT

Field Hunter MM VR
Specifications
Field Grade-20, 28 and 12 gauge
Barrel lengths/chokes: 22"/ CYL, 24"/MC-3, 26"/MC-3, 28"/MC-3, 30"/MC-3.
Features: walnut, synthetic or camo stock.

Prices:
synthetic stock $399
28 ga. 449
camo stock 489
Also Available:

Field Grade Maxi-Mag 3.5", 12 ga.
synthetic. $579
camo 679

Superior II Grade
Features: hand checkered Turkish Walnut stock. Sporting model has a wide 10mm rib and ported barrel and Monte Carlo stock.

Prices:
Hunter (12, 20 & 28 ga.) 589
Sport (12 ga. only) 559
Trap (12 ga. only) 569

Pump Shotguns

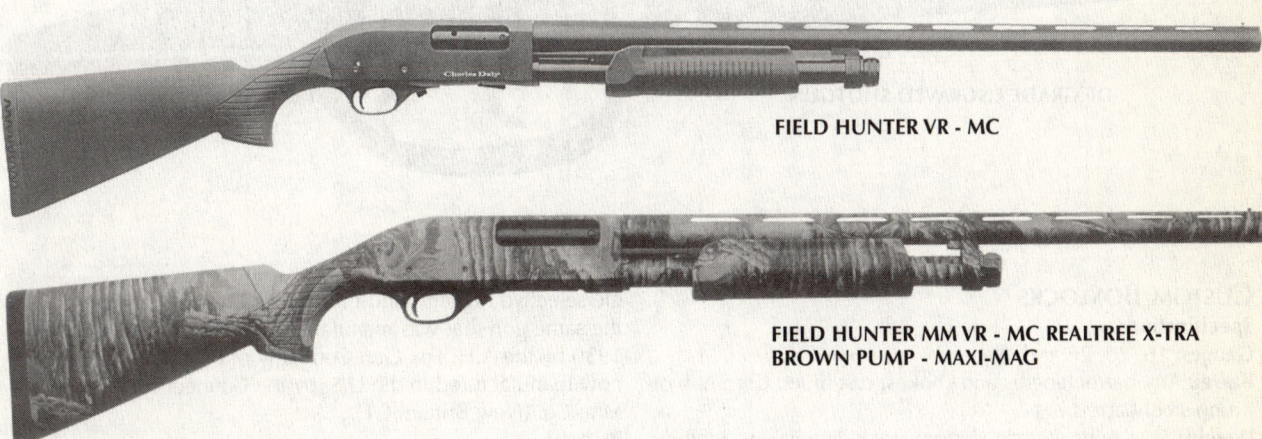

FIELD HUNTER VR - MC

FIELD HUNTER MM VR - MC REALTREE X-TRA BROWN PUMP - MAXI-MAG

Field Hunter VR-MC and MM VR-MC
Specifications
Field Grade-12 and 20 ga.
Prices:
synthetic stock 12 ga. $269
camo 12 ga. 359

synthetic 20 ga. $269
camo 20 ga. 359
Also Available:
Maxi-Mag 3.5"
12 ga. synthetic 329
12 ga. camo 429

Dakota Arms Inc.

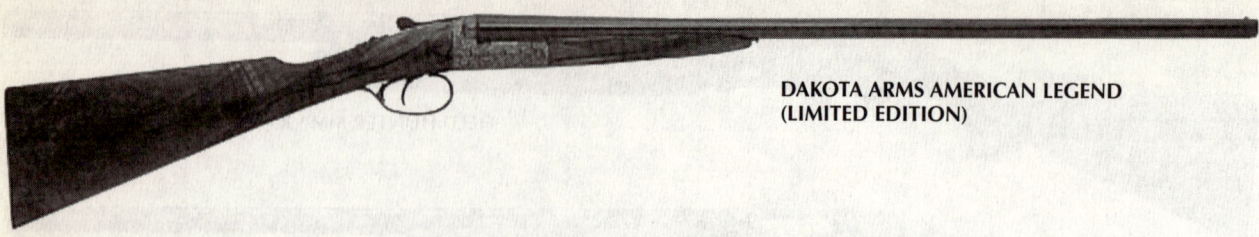

DAKOTA ARMS AMERICAN LEGEND (LIMITED EDITION)

Dakota Legend Shotguns

Premier Grade
Exhibition Engllish Walnut wood, French Grey Finish, 50% coverage engraving, straight grip, splinter forend, hand rubbed oil finish, boxlock, ejectors double trigger, 27" barrels, game rib with gold bead, selective ejectors, choice of chokes, and Americase.
Price: (12 or 20 ga) **$13,950**
add 10% for 28 or 410 ga.

Legend Grade
Special Selection English Walnut, 27" barrel, game rib, straight grip, splinter forend, double triggers, round aciton, French Grey finish, selective ejectors, checkered butt, stock oval, full coverage scroll engraving, choice of chokes, gold bead, oak and leather case.
Price: (12 or 20 ga) **$18,000**
add 10% for 28 or 410 ga.

Fox Shotguns

DE GRADE ENGRAVED SHOTGUN

Custom Boxlocks

Specifications
Gauges: 16, 20, 28 and .410
Barrel: Any barrel lengths and chokes; rust blued Chromox or Krupp steel barrels
Weight: 5 /to 6/lbs. **Stock:** Custom stock dimensions, including cast; hand-checkered Turkish Circassian walnut stock and forend with hand-rubbed oil finish; straight grip, full pistol grip (with cap), or semi-pistol grip; splinter, Schnabel or beavertail forend; traditional pad, hard rubber plate, checkered, or skeleton butt
Features: Boxlock action with automatic ejectors; scalloped, rebated and color casehardened receiver; double or Fox single selective trigger; hand-finished and hand-engraved. This is the same gun that was manufactured between 1905 and 1930 by the A.H. Fox Gun Company of Philadelphia, PA, now manufactured in the U.S. by the Connecticut Shotgun Mfg. Co. (New Britain, CT).

Prices:*
CE Grade **$11,000**
XE Grade **12,500**
DE Grade **15,000**
FE Grade **20,000**
Exhibition Grade **30,000**

*Grades differ in engraving and inlay, grade of wood and amount of hand finishing needed.

Flodman Shotguns

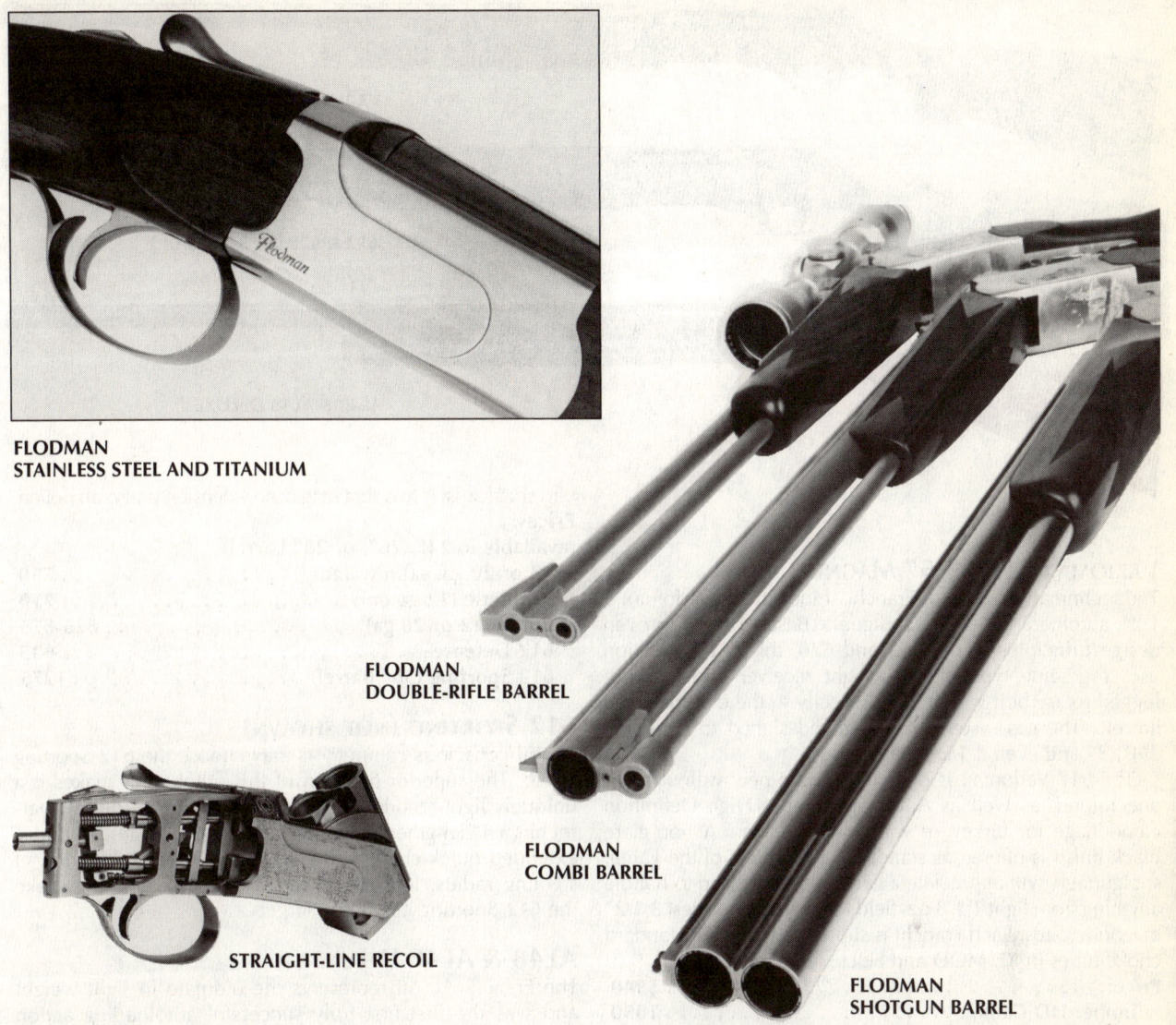

FLODMAN
STAINLESS STEEL AND TITANIUM

FLODMAN
DOUBLE-RIFLE BARREL

FLODMAN
COMBI BARREL

STRAIGHT-LINE RECOIL

FLODMAN
SHOTGUN BARREL

Flodman Guns and Rifles

Flodman Guns is a family business and part of the Skullman Enterprise AB Group (est 1978).

The company's founder, Sixten Skullman, was originally an airplane mechanic and previously built racing engines. In 1992 Skullman Enterprises AB took over Flodman Guns.

In 1993 Flodman Guns began manufacturing combi and double-barreled shotguns. At the time they offered the option of titanium barrels.

Exquisite walnut wood is a standard fitting on the Flodman, which is self-opening. In contrast to other over-and-under weapons, the barrels are not used to break the weapon. When the mechanism is cocked with the top lever, the barrels fall in place under their own weight. The system's opening angle is larger for quick reloading.

During manufacture it is tested under gas pressure three times greater than a standard cartridge.

Flodman shotgun barrels are of ss2377, a stainless steel. Barrels are available in titanium (grade 5) from Sandvik Steel (www.sandvik.com) giving superiority in relation to strength/weight.

Flodman has changeable chokes, but it may be ordered with fixed chokes.

The ejector mechanism is released by the cartridge expansion on firing for dry firing without ejector movement.

No hammer, rather a primed firing pin that moves perpendicularly, the shortest way to the detonator. This gives an action (lock) time of approximately 2 thousandths of a second from pulling the trigger to detonating the cartridge.

If you need to change a firing pin or firing spring, it takes approximately 1 minute with the accompanying tool.

Flodman is delivered with automatic safety, which can easily be changed to manual.

Prices: . . . . **P.O.R.**

Franchi Shotguns

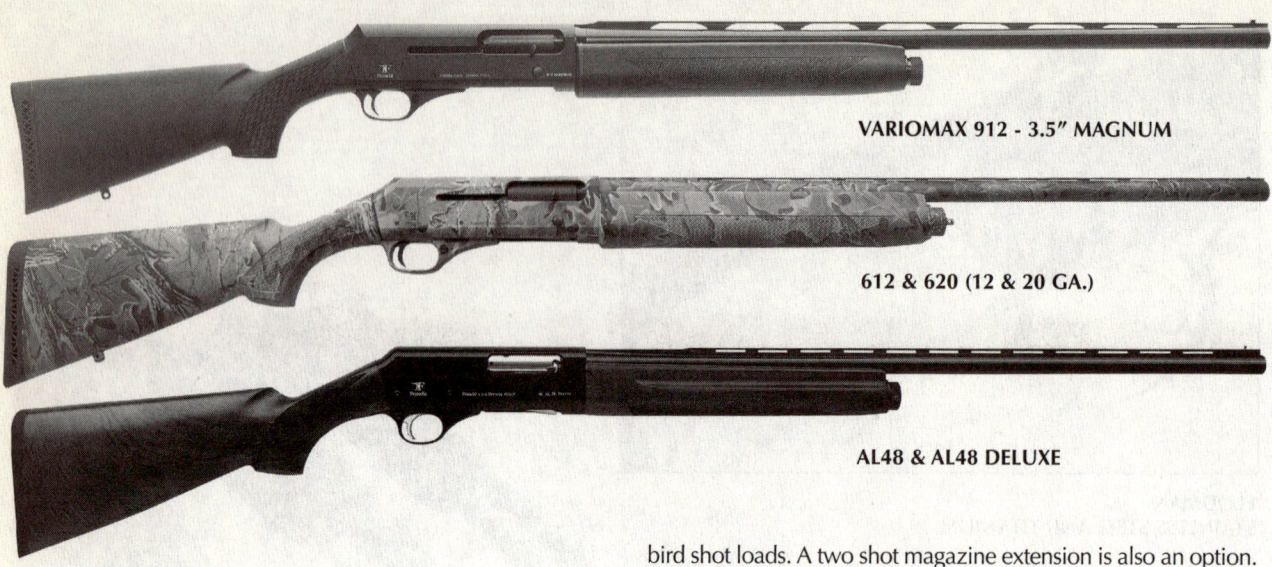

VARIOMAX 912 - 3.5" MAGNUM

612 & 620 (12 & 20 GA.)

AL48 & AL48 DELUXE

VARIOMAX 912 - 3.5" MAGNUM
The technical prowess of Franchi shines in the Variomax 3 1/2" autoloading 12 ga. shotgun. Based on the proven design principles of the 612 and 620, this 3 1/2" version uses the same type of lightweight receiver and a multi-lugged rotary bolt which locks directly to the chrome-lined barrel. The gas system has been redesigned to handle 2 3/4", 3" and even 3 1/2" shells.

The 912 Variomax is offered with the new walnut stock and forend, as well as Advantage Timber High Definition camouflage for turkey or waterfowl hunters. A non-glare black finish is offered as standard. Regardless of the game, shotgunners will appreciate a gas system designed to handle anything from light 1 1/8 oz. field loads to the heaviest 3 1/2" magnum loads. Each Franchi is supplied with three standard choke tubes in IC, MOD and FULL.

Price:	$940
Timber HD Camo	1050
Walnut	1000

612 & 620 (12 & 20 GA.)
Autoloading shotguns have undergone a great deal of refinement since their inception, and Franchi has moved the arena of development to the next level of sophistication with the 612 and 620 gas-operated shotguns.

A strong and lightweight receiver houses a multi-lugged rotary bolt which locks directly to the barrel. The included three choke tubes, IC, MOD and FULL, can handle virtually any game a true shotgunner may pursue.

The 612 and 620 use a patented dual safety system which blocks the sear and removes tension from the hammer spring if the bolt is out of battery.

For the traditionalist, walnut stocks and forends are available, but black synthetic is offered as well. The Advantage Timber High Definition 612 and 620 are also available in full Advantage camouflage. There is even a defense model of the 612 which has an 18 1/2" barrel with a true CYL bore. It can handle 3" slugs to light bird shot loads. A two shot magazine extension is also an option.

Prices:
(available in 24", 26", or 28" barrel)

12 or 20 ga. satin walnut	750
Synthetic (12 ga only)	710
Camo (12 or 20 ga)	825-875
612 Defense	635
612 Sporting (30" barrel)	1275

612 SPORTING (NOT SHOWN)
Recoil-conscious competitors may choose the 612 Sporting Auto. The superior function of this autoloader makes it a uniquely light-recoiling competition shotgun. The 30" barrel has a 4" lengthened forcing cone, is ported, and includes extended quick-change choke tubes. This combination of sighting radius, low recoil and excellent patterning make the 612 Sporting deadly on targets.

AL48 & AL48 DELUXE
The Franchi AL 48 represents the ultimate in light weight and was the first first truly successful autoloading action refinement of John Browning's long recoil design for autoloaders. Today, the Franchi AL 48 continues to prove just how strong and reliable the long recoil design can be.

A standard field grade is available in 20 and 28 ga., and a Deluxe grade is available in 20 and 28 ga. All models include a steel-shot-proofed, chrome-lined barrel. The entire AL 48 series features a ventilated rib and IC and MOD choke tubes for added versatility. The field grade AL 48 has a walnut stock and forend, as well as a matte finish on metal surfaces to minimize reflected light. The Deluxe grade includes a higher-grade walnut stock and forend, plus a high-polish finish on most metal surfaces. New for 2002 is a straight-gripped English stock. this deluxe speedster will make a great addition to any upland hunter's collection.

Prices:

AL48, 20 ga	715
28 ga	825
AL48 Deluxe, 20 ga	940
28 ga	990

Franchi Shotguns

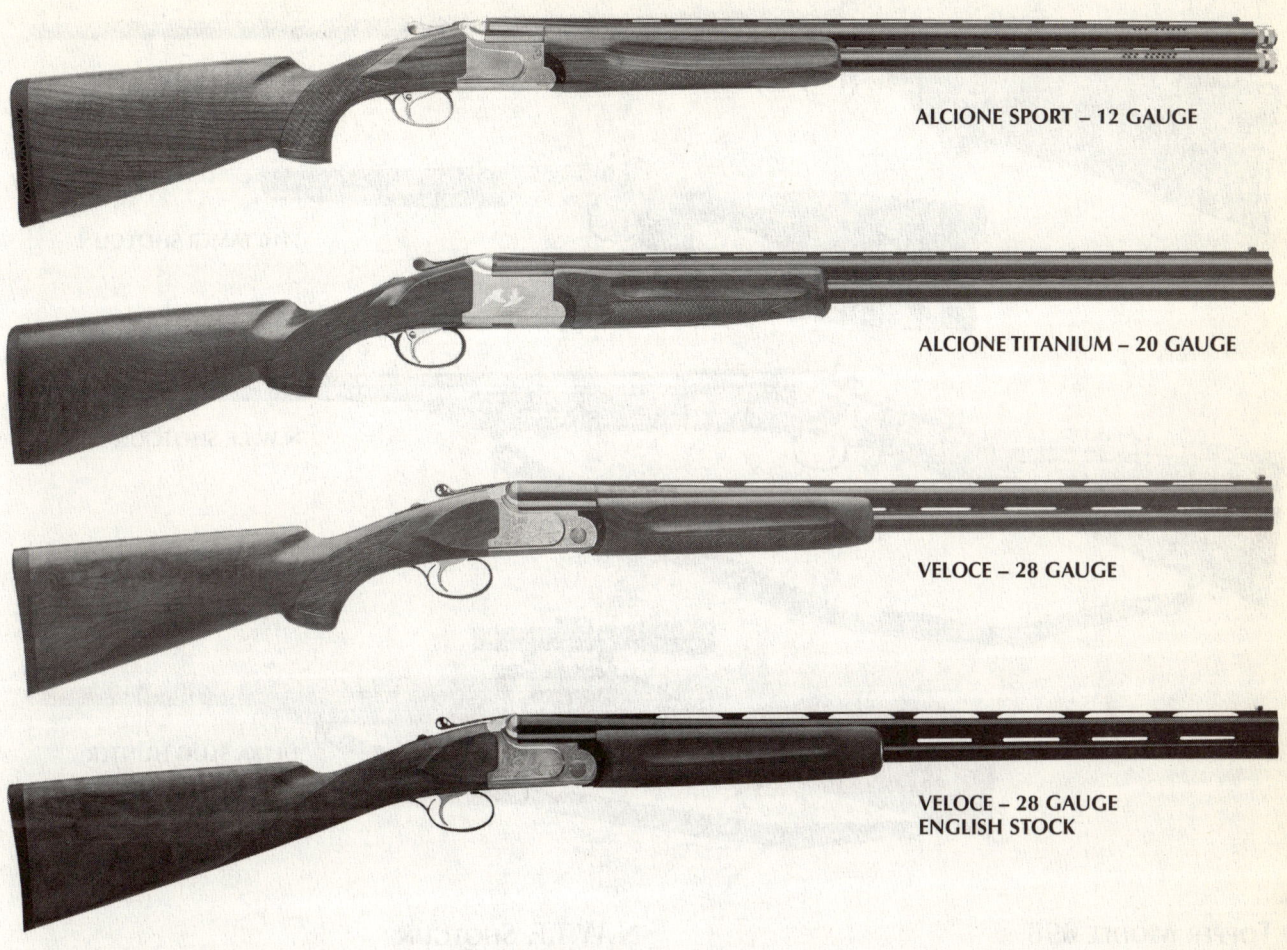

ALCIONE SPORT – 12 GAUGE

ALCIONE TITANIUM – 20 GAUGE

VELOCE – 28 GAUGE

VELOCE – 28 GAUGE ENGLISH STOCK

ALCIONE SPORT

The Alcione Sport over-under is available in 12 ga. with 30" ported barrels and extended knurled choke tubes. It is chambered for 2 3/4" target loads. A 10mm-wide rib quickly pulls the eye to targets and builds scores. A manual safety complements mechanical triggers, which do not require recoil from the first barrel to fire the second barrel.

The Alcione Sport and SX have removable receiver sideplates. The stock and forend are shaped from high-grade walnut and have special dimensions for the serious competitor. The Alcione Sport and Field offer left-handed stock dimensions.

The Alcione SX has a high-grade walnut stock with fine checkering. The receivers are highly polished and feature delicate etchings. Unique to the Alcione product line is the ability to interchange barrels without the need for fitting. Simply swap any barrel set (12 or 20 gauge) onto any other frames and forend. No gunsmithing is required.

Price:
Alcione Field $1275
Left Hand. 1275
Alcione SX 1800
Alcione SL Sport. 1650
Alcione Titanium (12 or 20 ga) 1425

VELOCE

The lightweight Veloce is available in 20 ga. and 28 ga. only, and is built on its own aluminum alloy scaled-down frame. This mechanism allows the receiver to be quite shallow, adding to the balance and feel. A steel insert in the breech face adds further strength. The Veloce features engraved sideplates with gold-embellished game scenes. The trigger is mechanical for added reliability. The barrel selector doubles as a safety. Stocks and forends are beautifully-figured walnut and expertly checkered. The stock features a straight English or round pistol grip for natural pointing and the forend has a fluted design. The barrels have 3" chambers in 20 ga. and 2 3/4" chambers in 28 ga. All are chrome-lined for increased durability. A set of choke tubes in CYL, IC and MOD is included. The monoblock is jeweled for both a pleasing appearance and added resistance to wear. "Veloce" means "fast" in Italian, and at only 5 1-2 pounds, this fast-swinging speedster is the perfect companion for a long day's hunt.

Prices:
Veloce, 20 ga. $1425
Veloce, 28 ga. 1500

Harrington & Richardson
Single-Barrel Shotguns

TOPPER MODEL 098

.410 TAMER SHOTGUN

N.W.T.F. SHOTGUN

ULTRA SLUG HUNTER

Topper Model 098
Specifications
Gauges: 12, 20 and .410 (3" chamber); 16 and 28 ga. (2.75" chamber) **Barrel Lengths:** 26" and 28" **Weight:** 5 to 6 lbs.
Action: Break-open; side lever release; automatic ejection
Stock: Full pistol grip; American hardwood; black finish with white buttplate spacer **Length Of Pull:** 14.5"
Price: $140
Also Available:
Topper Deluxe - Model 098 12 ga. 28"
   mod screw in choke 3.5" 164
Topper Junior Classic 20, 28, and .410, 22" barrel,
   hand checkered American black walnut stock
   and 12.5" pull. 180

.410 Tamer Shotgun
This .410 snake gun features single-shot action, transfer-bar safety and high-impact synthetic stock and forend. Stock has a thumbhole design that sports a full pistol grip and a recessed open side, containing a holder for storing ammo. Forend is modified beavertail configuration. Other features include a matte, electroless nickel finish.
Weight: 5-6 lbs. **Barrel Length:** 20" (3" chamber)
Choke: Full
Price: 157

N.W.T.F. Shotgun
Specifications
12 gauge with NWTF engraved frame; hand checkered; camo laminate stock and forend, 24" barrel with 3.5" chamber and full choke.
Price: $212
Also Available:
NWTF Youth 20 ga., 22" barrel, 3" chamber
   and Modified choke 203

Ultra Slug Hunter
Features: 12 or 20 gauge, 3" chamber, fully rifled, 24" barrel, heavy slug barrel (1:35" twist); Monte Carlo stock and forend of American hardwood w/dark walnut stain; matte black receiver; transfer-bar system; scope rail, swivels and sling; ventilated recoil pad.
Price: 249
Also available:
Ultra Youth Slug Hunter.
   Features 12-gauge barrel blank underbored to 20 gauge
   and shortened to 22"; factory-mounted Weaver-style
   scope base; reduced Monte Carlo stock of American
   hardwood with dark walnut stain; vent recoil pad, sling
   swivels and black nylon sling. 249
Slug Hunter Deluxe.
   Features hand checkered camo laminate wood. . . . 306

Heckler & Koch Shotguns
Fabarm Series

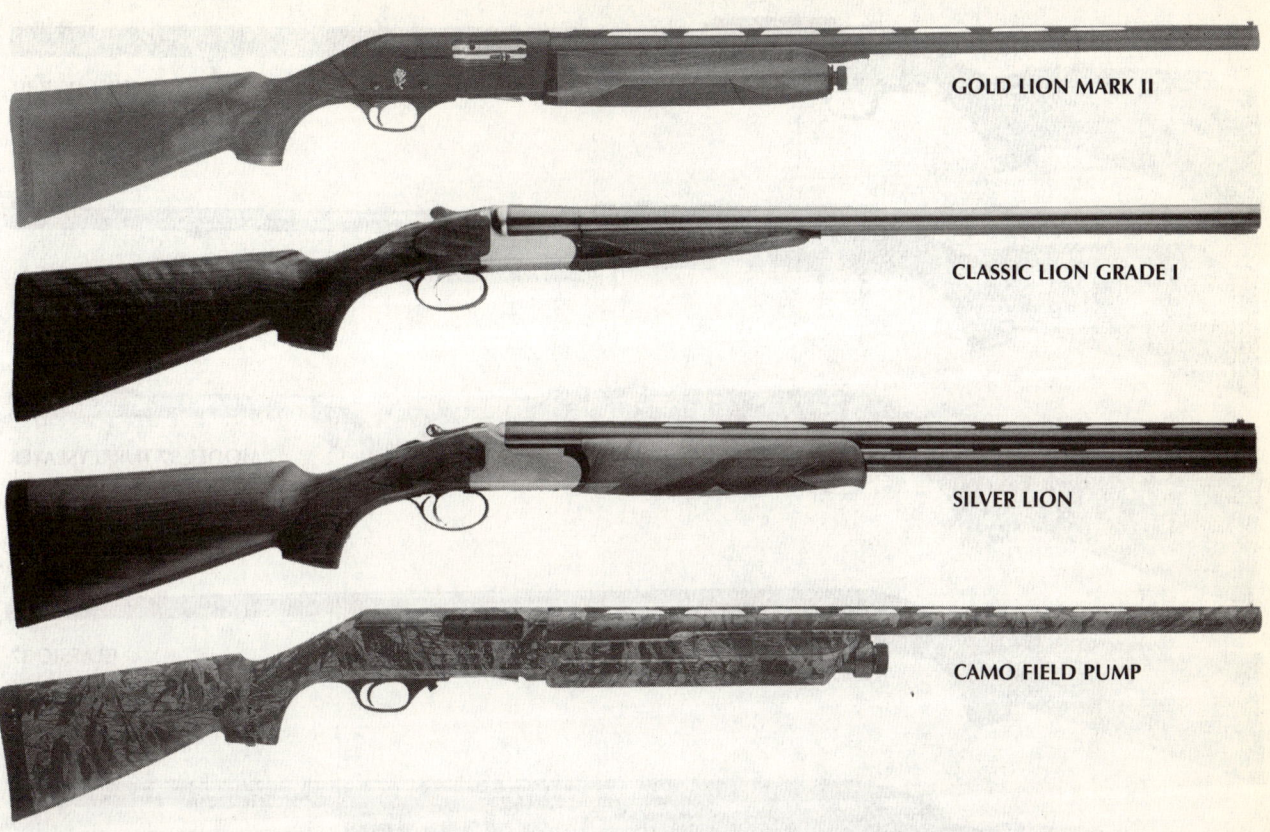

GOLD LION MARK II

CLASSIC LION GRADE I

SILVER LION

CAMO FIELD PUMP

HECKLER & KOCH FABARMS SHOTGUNS
Heckler & Koch shotguns have features for top ballistic performance and durability, plus fine handling qualities. Double guns are built on milled steel or alloy monoblocs, with single selective triggers, interchangeable chokes, hand-checkered walnut stocks. They're chambered for 3" shells (turkey and waterfowl models for 3.5-inch magnums). Autoloaders are gas-operated with no parts in the buttstock. They have fixed ejectors and shim-adjustable buttstocks. Camouflage models are available. Pump guns have synthetic stocks, double action bars and Picatinny rails for scopes. Weights vary on all models, depending on gauge and barrel length. Youth and special-purpose shotguns are part of the line.

FABARM'S TRIBORE BARREL SYSTEM
The ported TriBore Barrel System consists of three distinct internal bore profiles. It offers the advantages of back-boring, but with even less recoil. The first or "overbore" region is just in front of the chamber and forcing cone. Its .7401 diameter reduces pressure and kick. A second bore, or "first choke", is in the middle of the barrel and gradually takes inside diameter to .7244 (cylinder bore), allowing the shot to attain its maximum velocity. The third bore consists of standard choking, followed by a cylinder area at the muzzle, allowing charge to exit with no disruption, improving downrange pellet distribution.

GOLD LION MARK II SEMIAUTOMATIC
Prices:
Gold Lion Mark II Semiautomatics 12 ga. $849
Camo Lion 12 ga. 849
Sporting Clays Extra 1249
Gold Lion Mark II 12 Gauge with 28" barrel
 (26- and 24" models also available)

CLASSIC LION GRADE I
Prices:
Classic Lion Grade II S/S 12 ga. 2249
Grade I S/S 1499
Classic Lion Elite S/S 1599

SILVER LION
Prices:
Max Lion O/U 12&20 ga. 1899
Max Lion Paradox O/U 12&20 ga. 1199
Silver Lion O/U 12&20 ga. 1299
Ultra Camo Mag Lion O/U 12 ga. 1229
Silver Lion Cub 12 + 20 ga/26" barrel. 1299
Sporting Clays O/U 1749

MODEL FP6 PUMP ACTION
Prices: FP6 Pump Action 12 ga. $499
FP6 Camo Field Pump 12 ga. w/28" barrel 469
FP6 Field Pump 399

Ithaca Shotguns

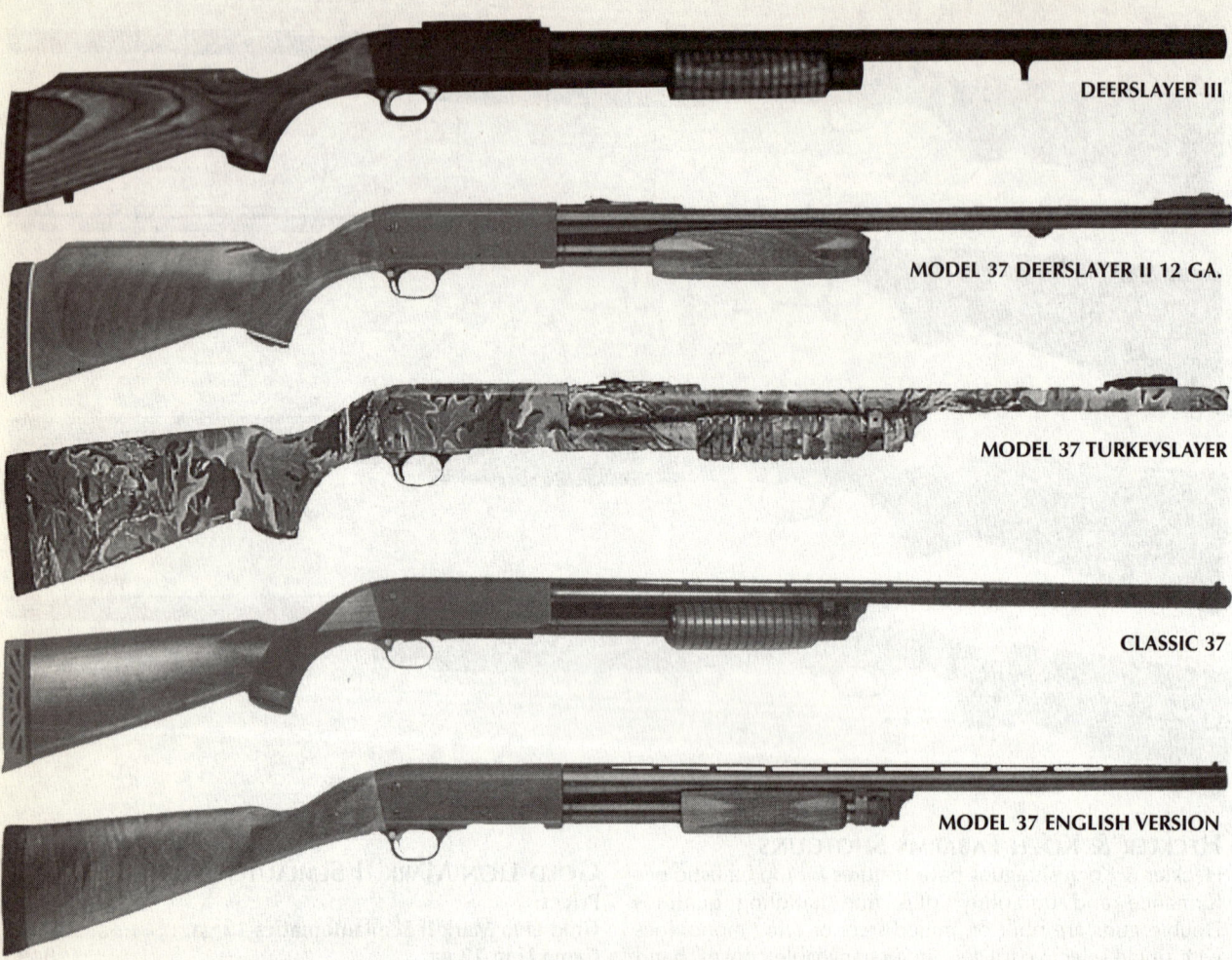

Deerslayer III
Pump-action 12 gauge. 26" heavy-wall barrel permanently attached to the receiver. The barrel is fully rifled and free-floated. Trigger and sear set are hand-filed and stoned for creep-free operation. Matte blue for lower visibility in the field. The stock is of Monte Carlo design, laminated for durability and strength. Receiver is fitted with a Weaver-style scope base.
Price: $900

Model 37 Deerslayer II 12 Ga.
Specifications
Gauges: 12, 16 or 20 (3" chamber) **Barrel Lengths:** 20" or 25" **Choke:** Rifled bore; or smooth bore **Weight:** 7 lbs.
Stock: Monte Carlo cut-checkered walnut stock and forend
Price: 633
Also Available:
 Deerslayer Rifled Deluxe (12 or 20). 582

Model 37 Turkeyslayer
Specifications
Gauge: 12, 20 and 20 Youth **Barrel Lengths:** 22" (3" chamber) with Turkey Tightshot choke tube **Weight:** 7 lbs.

Features: Available in RealTree Hardwoods 20/200 and Advantage Timber camo
Price: 654

Classic 37
Specifications
Gauges: 12, 16, 20 **Barrel Lengths:** 28", 26", 24"
Weight: 7 lbs. Checkered corncob ringtail forearm, sunburst recoil pad, American walnut stock, screw-in choke tubes, vent rib
Price: $510
 Ultralight (16 or 20 ga. only). 824

Model 37 English Version
Specifications
Gauge: 12, 16, 20 (3" chamber)
Barrel Lengths: 24", 26" and 28"
Weight: 7 lbs. with slim, checkered straight-grip stock
Price: 803
Also Available:
Ithaca 37 Classic Trap and Sporting Clays shotguns with special stocks and Briley choke tubes.
 Adjustable stocks optional. 1185

Kimber

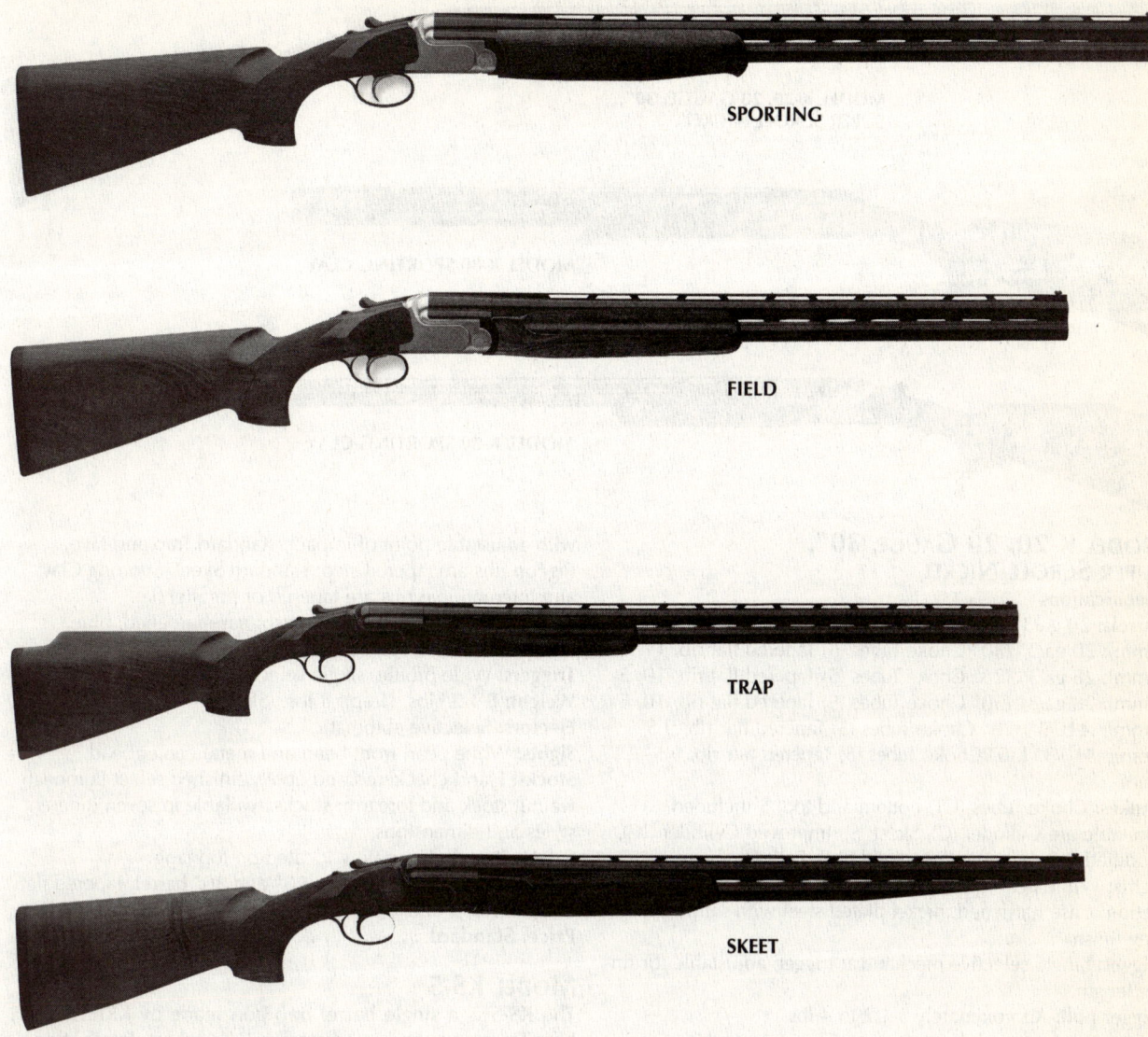

SPORTING

FIELD

TRAP

SKEET

KIMBER AUGUSTA SHOTGUNS
Augusta shotguns are based on a Boss-type action like that found on the world's best over-and-under competition and field shotguns. 12 gauge only with back-bored barrels, coil spring trigger, automatic ejectors, adjustable trigger, Hi-Viz sight, ventilated rib and barrel. Sporting, Trap, Skeet and Field models are available. Dimensions and features can be customized to meet the needs of any shooter. Imported from Italy
Prices: . . . . from $4500

SPORTING
The Augusta Sporting is a world class sporting clays shotgun. Standard features include .736 backbored barrels with long forcing cones and single select trigger.

FIELD
Augusta Field shotguns have similar features to the Sporting model. Options include English stock, beavertail forend, exhibition walnut and engraving.

TRAP
Augusta Trap shotguns are similar to the sporting model. Options include custom dimensions and barrel lengths, and engraved side plates.

SKEET
Augusta Skeet shotguns are similar to the Trap model. A full suite of options allows each shotgun to be perfectly fitted to any shooter.

Krieghoff Shotguns

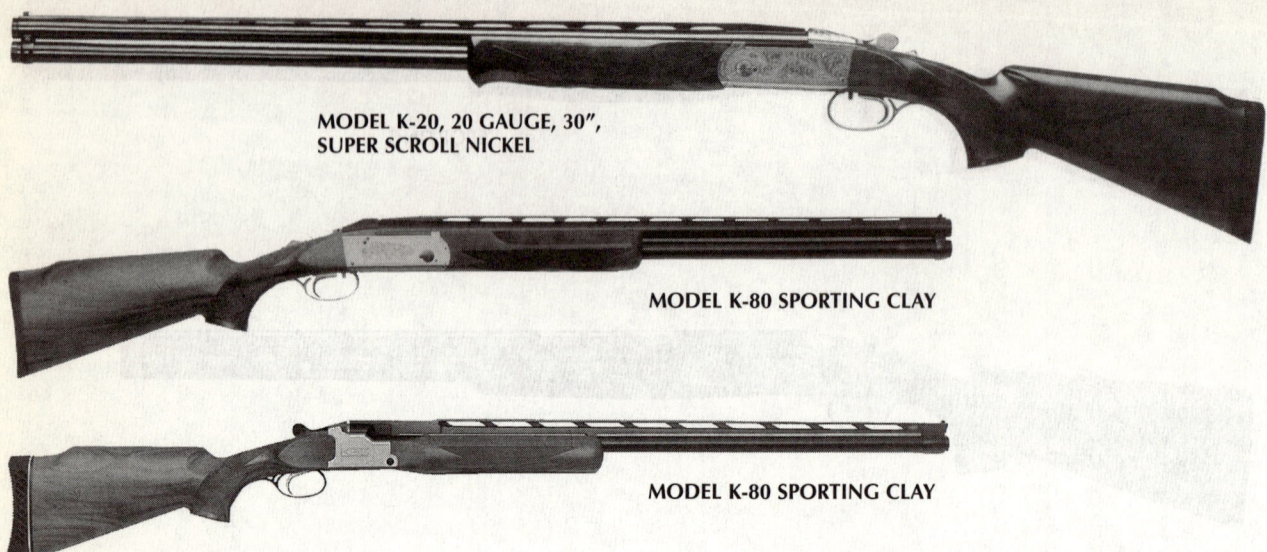

MODEL K-20, 20 GAUGE, 30", SUPER SCROLL NICKEL

MODEL K-80 SPORTING CLAY

MODEL K-80 SPORTING CLAY

Model K-20, 20 Gauge, 30", Super Scroll Nickel
Specifications
Barrels: 20 ga/3" (28" Choke Tubes (5) Tapered flat rib, 11-7, 5 mm); 20 ga/3" (30" Choke Tubes (5) Tapered flat rib, 11-7, 5 mm); 28 ga/3" (28" Choke Tubes (5) Tapered flat rib, 10, 5-7 mm); 28 ga/3" (30" Choke Tubes (5) Tapered flat rib, 10, 5-7 mm); .410/3" (28" Choke Tubes (5) Tapered flar rib, 9,5-6mm); .410/3" (30" Choke Tubes (5) Tapered flar rib, 9,5-6mm)
Chokes: Choke Tubes (CT) bottom and top, 5 included. Available are Cylinder (C), Skeet (S), Improved Cylinder (IC), Modified (M), Improved Modified (IM), Full (F).
Sights: White pearl front bead and metal center bead
Action: Case hardened, nickel plated steel with satin grey finish
Trigger: Single selective mechanical trigger, adjustable for finger length.
Trigger pull: Approximately 3-1/2 to 4 lbs.
Safety: Top tang push button safety. Can be locked in "off" position.
Stocks: Hand-checkered select European walnut with satin epoxy finish.
Standard stocks are: # 3 Sporting/International Skeet. #9 Skeet/Field.
Forearm Standard: # VII Schnabel.
Grade: Standard is classic scroll engraving, similar to the K-80.
Weight: Approximately 7 1/4 lbs.
Case: All K-20 sporting guns come in a fitted aluminum case holding one, two or three sets of barrels.
Prices: . . . . **Price on request**

Model K-80 Trap, Skeet, Sporting Clay and Live Bird
Specifications
Barrels: Made of Boehler steel; free-floating bottom barrel with adjustable point of impact; standard Trap and Live Pigeon ribs are tapered step; standard Skeet, Sporting Clay and International ribs are tapered or parallel flat.
Receivers: Hard satin-nickel finish; casehardened; blue finish available as special order
Triggers: Wide profile, single selective, position adjustable.
Weight: 8 1/2" lbs. (Trap); 8 lbs. (Skeet)
Ejectors: Selective automatic
Sights: White pearl front bead and metal center bead
Stocks: Hand-checkered and epoxy-finished select European walnut stock and forearm; stocks available in seven different styles and dimensions
Safety: Push button safety located on top tang.
Also available: Skeet Special 28" and 30" barrel; tapered flat or 8mm rib; 5 choke tubes.
Price: Standard . . . . **Price on request**

Model KS-5
The KS-5 is a single barrel trap gun made by KRIEGHOFF, Ulm/Germany, and marketed by Krieghoff International. Standard specifications include: 12 gauge, 2 3/4" chamber, ventilated tapered step rip, and a casehardened receiver (satin gray finished in electroless nickel). The KS-5 features an adjustable point of impact from 50/50 to 70/30 by means of different optional fronthangers. Screw-in chokes and factory adjustable comb stocks are available options. An adjustable rib (AR) and comb stock (ADJ) are standard features.

The KS-5 is available with pull trigger or optional factory release trigger, adjustable externally for poundage. The KS-5 can be converted to release by the installation of the release parts. To assure consistency and proper functioning, release triggers are installed only by Krieghoff International. Release parts are not available separately. These shotguns are available in Standard grade only. Engraved models can be special ordered.

Prices: . . . . **Price on request**

Marocchi Shotguns

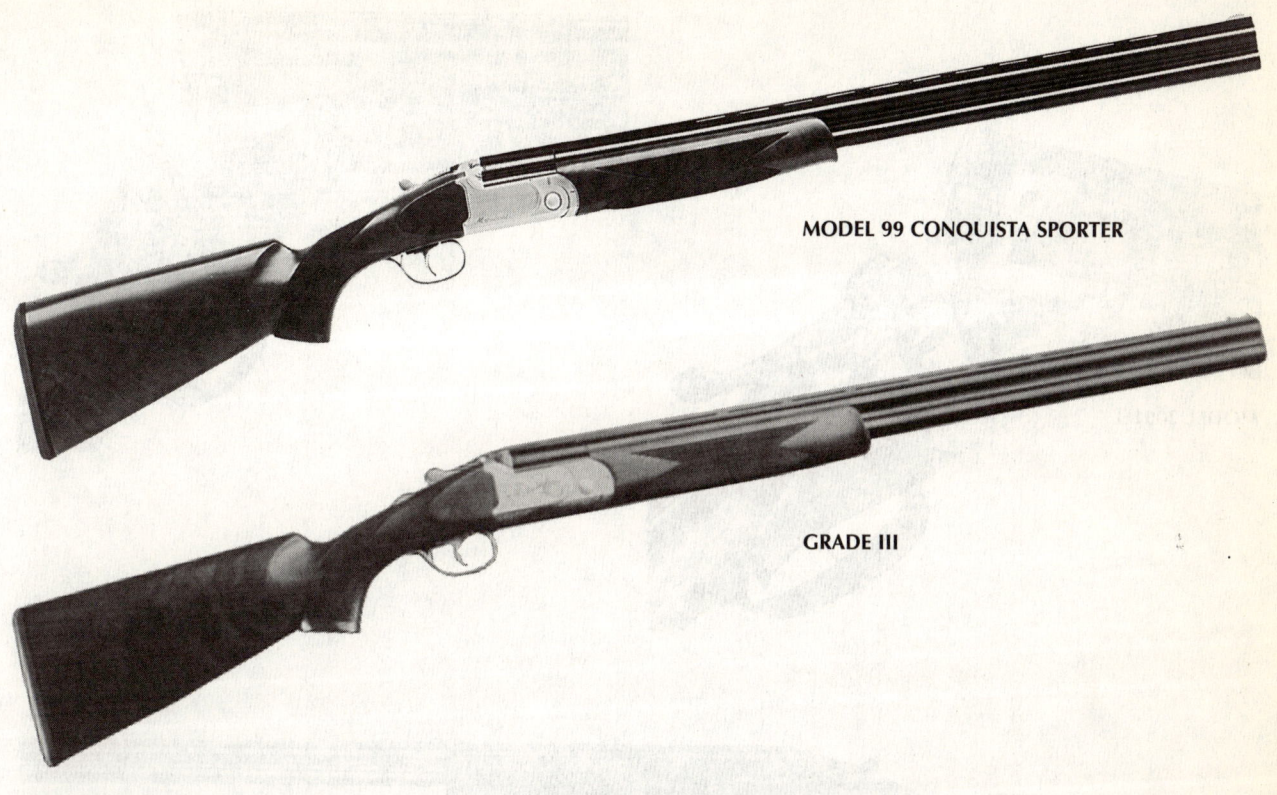

MODEL 99 CONQUISTA SPORTER

GRADE III

Conquista Sporting Clays

Marocchi shotguns feature concave ventilated ribs. Classic middle rib on barrels fitted with chokes. Boxlock action has replaceable hingepins, adjustable selective trigger and automatic ejectors. Magnum Field model is bored for 3" shells. Classic Doubles are 3" guns with back-bored, ported barrels. All Marocchi shotguns have checkered walnut stocks. Classic and automatic extractors/ejectors.

Prices:
Conquista Sporter Grade I $1490
Model 99 Sporter, Skeet, Trap, Double Trap
  and Electrocibles
  Grade I 2350
  Grade II 2870-3025
  Grade III 3275-3450

SPECIFICATIONS MAROCCHI SHOTGUNS

	TRAP	DOUBLE TRAP	SKEET	SPORTER	ELECTROCIBLES
BARRELS					
Gauge	12	12	12	12	12
Chamber	2 3/4"	2 3/4"	2 3/4"	2 3/4"	2 3/4"
Barrel Length	29 3/4"/ 30"/ 32"	29 1/2",30",32"	28"	28"/ 30"/ 32"	28 3/8"/ 30"
Chokes	Imp. Mod/Full	Contre/Full	SK/SK	Contre Choke	Contre Choke
TRIGGER					
Calibration	3-4 lbs.	3-4 lbs.	3-4 lbs.	3 1/2 - 4 1/2 lbs.	3 1/2 - 4 1/2 lbs.
STOCK	Pistol grip	Pistol grip	Pistol grip	Pistol grip	Pistol grip
Drop at comb	1 1/4"	1 1/4"	1 1/4"	1 1/4"	1 1/4"
Drop at heel	1 3/4"	1 3/4"	2"	2"	1 3/4"
Length	14 3/4"	14 3/4"	14 1/2"	14 3/4"	14 3/4"
Cast at heel	1/8"	1/8"	1/16"	1/8"	1/8"
FOREND	Bevertail	Bevertail	Bevertail	Bevertail	Bevertail
Approx Total Weight	8 lbs.	8 lbs.	7 3/4 lbs.	7 1/2 - 7 3/4 lbs.	7 1/2 - 7 3/4 lbs.

Merkel Shotguns
Over/Under Shotguns

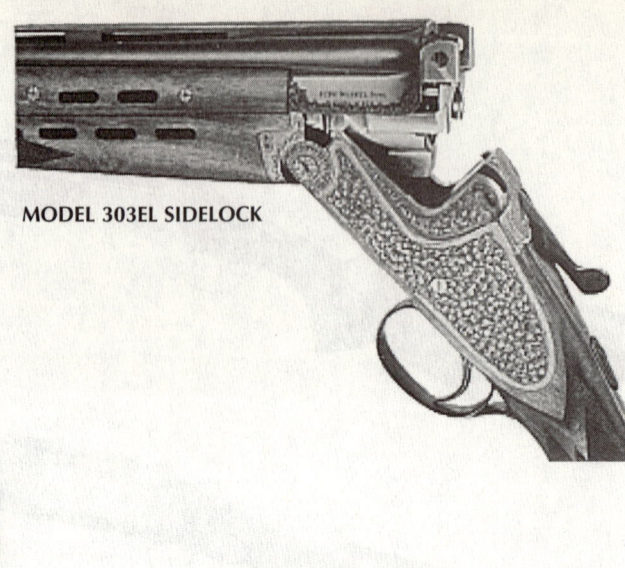

MODEL 303EL SIDELOCK

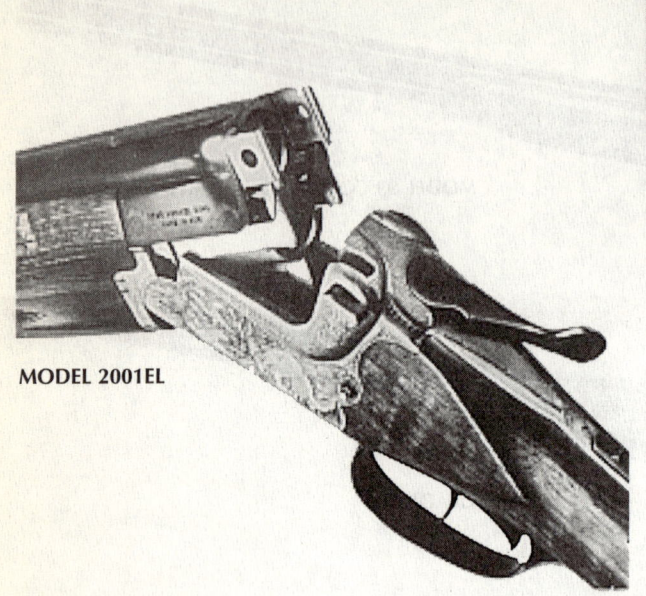

MODEL 2001EL

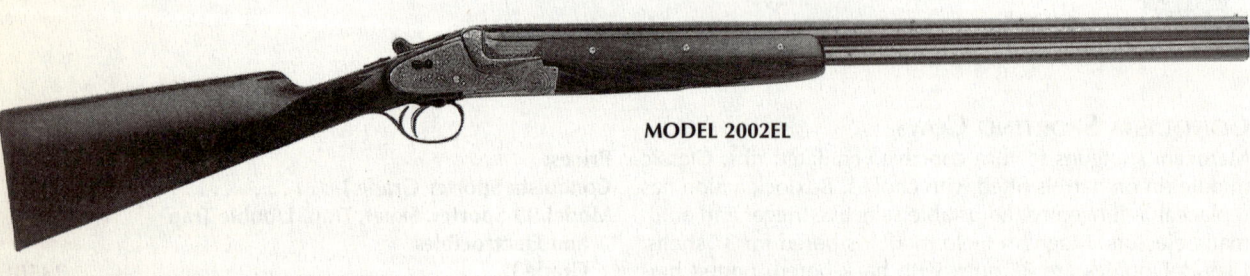

MODEL 2002EL

MERKEL OVER/UNDER SHOTGUN

Merkel over-and-unders were the first hunting guns with barrels arranged one above the other, and they have since rivaled side-by-sides in popularity.
- Available in 12, 16 and 20 gauge (28 ga. in Model 201E with 26 3/4" barrel)
- Lightweight (6.4 to 7.28 lbs.)
- The high, narrow forend protects the shooter's hand from the barrel in hot or cold climates
- The forend is narrow and therefore lies snugly in the hand to permit easy and positive swinging
- The slim barrel line provides an unobstructed field of view and thus permits rapid aiming and shooting
- The over-and-under barrel arrangement gives straight-line recoil, eliminating the torque and lateral deflection of side-by-sides

Specifications
Gauges: 12, 20, 28
Barrel Lengths: 26.75" and 28"
Weight: 6.4 to 7.28 lbs.

Stock: English or pistol grip in European walnut
Features: All models include three-piece forearm, automatic ejectors, Kersten double crossbolt lock, Blitz action and single selective or double triggers.
Prices:
Model 2001EL
  12, 20, 28 . . . . $7295
  2001EL Sporter 7295
Model 2000EL Kersten double cross-bolt lock; scroll engraved silver-grey receiver; modified Anson & Deeley box action; ejectors; single or double triggers, luxury grade wood; pistol grip or English-style stock.
  12 ga., 20 ga. 28 ga. 5795
  2000EL Sporter 5795
Model 2002EL Same features as Model 2000EL but with hunting scenes w/arabesque engraving
  12 ga. 28"; 20 ga. and 28 ga., 26.75" 10,995
Sidelocks
Model 303EL Double trigger, auto ejectors, straight or pistol grip. 12, 20, 28. 19,995

Merkel Shotguns
Side-by-Side shotguns

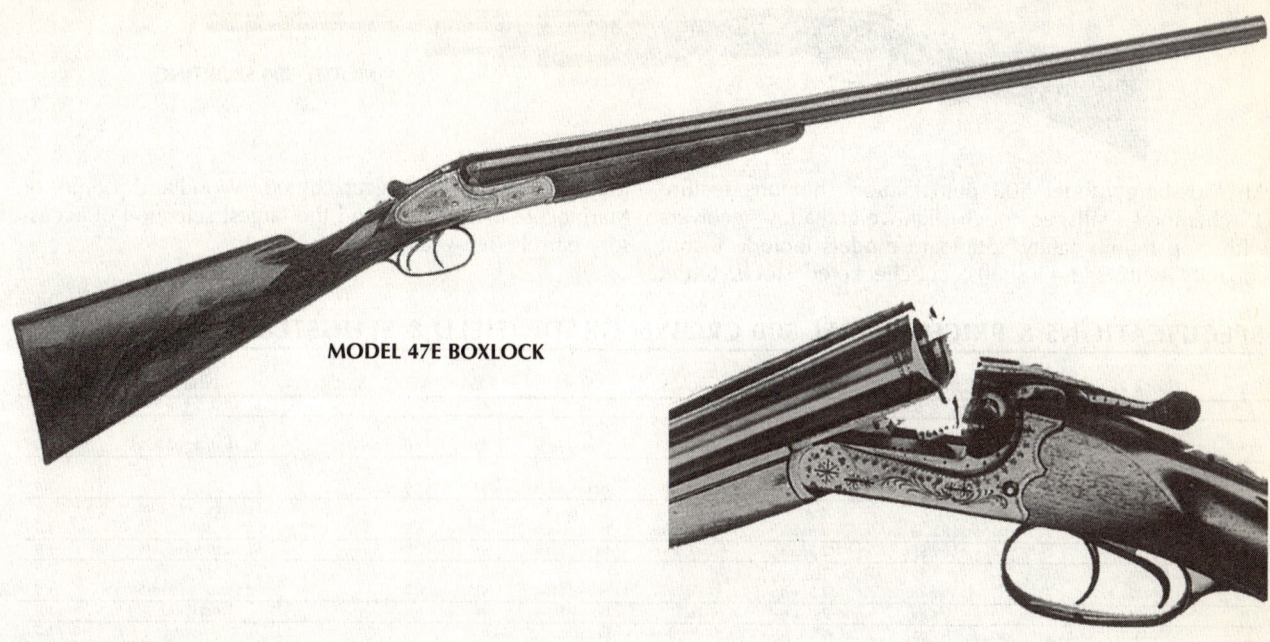

MODEL 47E BOXLOCK

MODEL 47E
Greener crossbolt with double under barrel locking lugs, scroll engraved casehardened receiver, Anson and Deely box-lock action, Holland & Holland ejectors, single selective or double triggers, pistol grip or English-style stock, includes fitted luggage case
12 ga. 28" IC/MOD, MOD/FULL $3295
20 ga. 26 3/4" or 28" IC/MOD, MOD/FULL 3295

MODEL 147E
Greener crossbolt with double under barrel locking lugs, fine engraved hunting scenes on silver-grayed receiver, Anson and Deely boxlock grip or English-style stock, includes fitted luggage case
12 ga. 28" IC/MOD, MOD/FULL 3995
20 ga. 26 3/4" or 28" IC/MOD, MOD/FULL 3995

MODEL 147EL
Greener crossbolt with double under barrel locking lugs, fine engraved hunting scenes on silver-grayed receiver, receiver, Luxury Grade Wood, Anson and Deely boxlock action, Holland & Holland ejectors, single selective or double triggers, pistol grip or English-style stock, includes fitted luggage case
12 ga. 28" IC/MOD, MOD/FULL 4995
20 ga. 26 3/4" or 28" IC/MOD, MOD/FULL 4995

MODEL 280EL
Greener crossbolt with double under barrel locking lugs, fine hunting scenes on silver-grayed receiver, Anson and Deely boxlock action, Holland & Holland ejectors, double triggers, luxury grade wood, English-style stock, includes fitted luggage case.
28 ga. 28" IC/MOD 5795

MODEL 360EL
Greener crossbolt with double under barrel locking lugs, fine hunting scenes on silver-grayed receiver, Anson and Deely boxlock action, Holland & Holland ejectors, double triggers, luxury grade wood, English-style stock, includes fitted luggage case
410 ga. 28', MOD/FULL $5795

MODEL 280/360EL TWO BBL SET
Greener cross bolt with double under barrel locking lugs, fine hunting scenes on silver-grayed receiver, Anson and Deely boxlock action, Holland & Holland ejectors, double triggers, luxury grade wood, English-style stock, includes fitted luggage case
Price:
28 ga. 28", IC/MOD; extra barrels - 410 ga. 28"
   MOD/FULL, ... 8295
Also Available:
S models with Holland & Holland
   sidelock actions . . . . from 5995
147SS model with detachable locks 8995
247 SL and 447 SL models with Arabesque engraving
   (sidelock) 247SL 7995
447SL 9995

CUSTOM STOCKING
(Stock dimensions to customers specs.)
Price: 1795

LEFT HAND STOCKING
(Standard stock dimensions, 4mm cast on)
Price: 895

Mossberg Shotguns
Model 500 Sporting

MODEL 500 SPORTING

All Mossberg Model 500 pump-action shotguns feature 3" chambers, Milspec tough, lightweight alloy receivers with "top thumb safety." Standard models include 6-shot capacity with 2 3/4" shells, cut-checkered stock, Quiet Carry forend, gold trigger, blued, Woodland Camo or Marinecote metal finish and the largest selection of accessory barrels. Ten-year limited warranty.

SPECIFICATIONS & PRICES MODEL 500 CROWN GRADE (FIELD & SLUGSTER)

Ga.	Stock #	Barrel Length	Barrel Type	Sights	Chokes	Stock	Length O/A	Wt.	Q.D. Studs	Notes	Prices
12	50120	28"	Vent rib, ported	2 Beads	Accu-Choke	Honey Satin	48"	7.2		IC, Mod. & Full Tubes	$307
12	Bantam 52132	24"	Vent rib, ported	2 Bead	Accu-Set	Honey Satin	43"	7.0		IC, Mod. & Full Tubes	307
12	Slug 50045	24"	Slugster, ported	Rifle	CYL Bore	Honey Satin	44"	7.0			307
20	Bantam 54132	22"	Vent Rib, ported	2 Beads	Accu-Choke	Honey Satin	42"	6.9		Mod. Tube Only, Bantam Stock	307
20	50136	26"	Vent Rib	2 Beads	Accu-Choke	Honey Satin	46"	7.0		IC, Mod. & Full Tubes	307
.410	Bantam 50112	24"	Vent Rib	2 Beads	Full	Honey Satin	43"	6.8		Fixed Choke, Bantam Stock	307
.410	50104	24"	Vent Rib	2 Beads	Full	Honey Satin	44"	6.8		Fixed Choke	307
12	56045-0	24"	Ported	Adj. Rifle	Cylinder Bore	Blk. Synthetic	44 1/2"	7.25		Parkerized	307
12	56420-5	28"	Vent rib, ported	Twin Bead	Accu-Set	Blk. Synthetic	48 1/2"	7.5		Parkerized	307
12	56436-6	26"	Vent rib	Twin Bead	Accu-Set	Blk. Synthetic	45 1/4"	7		Parkerized	307
12	52193-2	28"	Vent rib, ported	Twin Bead	Accu-Set	Synthetic	48 1/4"	7.5		Woodlands Camo	382
12	52195-6	24"	Vent rib, ported	FO Turkey	xx-Full	Synthetic	44 1/4"	7.25		Woodlands Camo	395
12	58235-3	22"	Vent rib	FO Turkey	x-Full	Wood	40 3/4"	6.5		Woodlands Camo	395
12	54232	24"	Trophy Slugster™ Ported	Scope Mount	Rifled Bore	Honey Satin	44"	7.3	Y	Dual-Comb™ Stock	406
12	54244	24"	Slugster, ported	Rifle	Rifled Bore	Honey Satin	44"	7.0	Y		375
12	54844	24"	Slugster, ported	Rifle	Rifled Bore	Honey Satin	44"	7.0	Y		406
20	54233	24"	Trophy Slugster™ Ported	Scope Mount	Rifled Bore	Honey Satin	44"	s6.9	Y	Dual-Comb™ Stock	406
20	Bantam 58252	24"	Slugster	Rifle	Rifled Bore	Honey Satin	44"	s6.9	Y	Bantam Stock	375

SPECIFICATIONS MODEL 500 COMBOS

Ga.	Stock #	Barrel Length	Barrel Type	Sights	Chokes	Stock	Length O/A	Wt.	Q.D. Studs	Notes	Prices
12	54243	28" / 24"	Vent rib, ported / Trophy Slugster™ ported	2 Beads / Scope Mount	Accu-Choke / Rifled Bore	Honey Satin	48"	7.2	Y	IC, Mod. & Full Tubes / Dual-Comb™ Stock	$410
12	54264	24"	Vent rib, ported / Slugster, ported	2 Beads / Rifle	Accu-Choke / Rifled Bore	Honey Satin	48"	7.2	Y	IC, Mod. & Full Tubes	398
12	50/583	28"	Vent rib, ported	Twin bead	Accu-Set	Honey Satin	47 1/2"	7.5		Blue	369
12		24"	Ported	Adj. Rifle	Cylinder Bore	Honey Satin	47 1/2"	7.5		Blue	398
20	54282	26" / 24"	Vent Rib / Slugster, ported	2 Beads / Rifle	Accu-Choke / Rifled Bore	Honey Satin	46"	7.0	Y	IC, Mod. & Full Tubes	398
12	54169	28" / 18.5"	Vent rib, ported / Plain	2 Beads / Bead	Accu-Choke / Cyl. Bore	Honey Satin	48"	7.2		IC, Mod. & Full Tube Pistol Grip Kit	366
20	54188	22" / 24"	Vent Rib / Slugster, ported	2 Beads / Rifle	Accu-Choke / Rifled Bore	Honey Satin	42"	7.0		IC, Mod. & Full Tubes Bantam Stock & Forearm	398

SPECIFICATIONS 500/590 MARINER & 500 SPECIAL PURPOSE

Gauge	Barrel Length	Sight	Stock #	Finish	Stock	Capacity	Overall Length	Weight	Notes	Price
MODEL 500/590 MARINER™ (CYLINDER BORE BARRELS)										
12	18.5"	Bead	50273	Marinecote™	Synthetic	6	38.5"	6.8	Includes Pistol Grip	$482
12	20"	Bead	50299	Marinecote™	Synthetic	9	40"	7.0	Includes Pistol Grip	499
MODEL 500 SPECIAL PURPOSE (CYLINDER BORE BARRELS) PERSUADER/CRUISER										
12	18.5"	Bead	50411	Blue	Synthetic	6	38.5"	6.8	Includes Pistol Grip	$342
12	18.5"	Bead	50440	Blue	Pistol Grip	6	28"	5.6	Includes Heat Shield	347
20	18.5"	Bead	50452	Blue	Synthetic	6	38.5"	6.8	Includes Pistol Grip	342
20	18.5"	Bead	50450	Blue	Pistol Grip	6	28"	5.6		335
.410	18.5"	Bead	50455	Blue	Pistol Grip	6	28"	5.3		335
12	20"	Bead	50579	Blue	Synthetic	8	40"	7.0	Includes Pistol Grip	342
12	20"	Bead	50580	Blue	Pistol Grip	8	40"	7.0		347
MODEL 500 HS .410 HOME SECURITY										
410	18.5"	Bead	50359	Blue	Blk Synthetic	6	37.25"	5.5	Spreader Choke	$345

Mossberg Shotguns
Model 835 Ulti-Mag Pump Shotguns

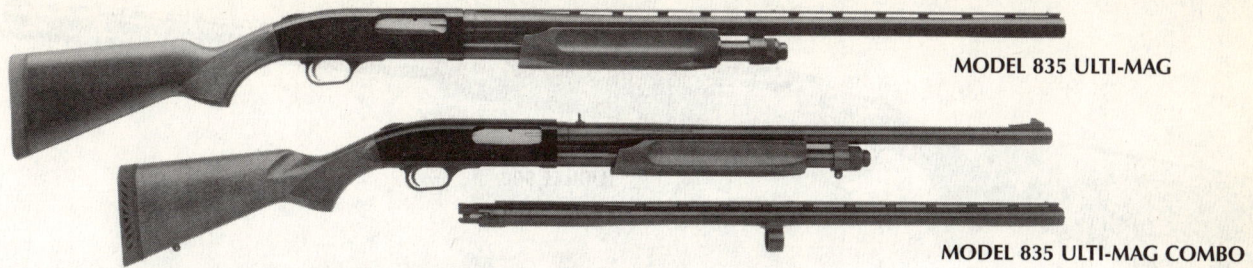

MODEL 835 ULTI-MAG

MODEL 835 ULTI-MAG COMBO

SPECIFICATIONS AND PRICES MODEL 835 ULTI-MAG (12 GAUGE, 6 SHOT)

GA	Stock No.	Barrel Length	Type	Sights	Choke	Finish	Stock	O.A. Length	W.	Studs	Notes	Price

CAMO

GA	Stock No.	Barrel Length	Type	Choke	Finish	Stock	Price
12	62447	24"	Vent Rib, Ported, Fiber Optic Sights	Ulti-Full Only	Advantage Timber	Synthetic	$541.00
12	62234	24"	Vent Rib, Ported, Fiber Optic Sights	Ulti-Full Only	R.T. Hardwoods	Synthetic	541.00
12	68143-8	24"	Combo, Vent Rib, Ported	Ulti-Full Only	Woodlands	Dual Comb®	540.00
		24"	Integral Scope Base, Ported	Fully Rifled Bore	Woodlands		
12	62445-9	28"	Vent Rib, Ported	Hunter Set	M.O. Shadow Grass	Synthetic	500.00
12	68231-2	24"	Vent Rib, Ported, Fiber Optic Sights	Ulti-Full Only	Woodlands	Synthetic	437.00
12	68235-0	28"	Vent Rib, Ported	Mod Only	Woodlands	Synthetic	419.00
12	68243-5	24"	Combo, VR, Ported, Fiber Optic Sights	Ulti-Full Only	Woodlands	Synthetic	590.00
12		24"	Fiber Optic Rifle Sights, Ported	Fully Rifled Bore	Woodlands		

MODEL 835® SPECIAL HUNTER™

| 12 | 66720-3 | 28" | Vent Rib, Ported | Mod Only | Parkerized | Synthetic (Black) | $382.00 |
| 12 | 61120 | 28" | Vent Rib, Ported | Mod Only | Blue | H.S. Finish | $382.00 |

Mossberg's Model 835 Ulti-Mag

Mossberg's Model 835 Ulti-Mag pump action shotgun has a 3.5" 12-gauge chamber but can also handle standard 2.75" and 3" shells. Field barrels are over-bored and ported for optimum patterns, reduced muzzle-jump and felt recoil reduction. Cut-checkered Honey Satin-finished stocks, Quiet Carry™ forearms and gold triggers are standard. Camo models are drilled and tapped for scope and feature detachable swivels and sling. All models include a Cablelock™ and 10-year limited warranty.

Model 695 Bolt Action

**MOSSBERG MODEL 695 BOLT ACTION
(SCOPE NOT INCLUDED)**

SPECIFICATIONS

Gauge	Model No.	Barrel Length	Barrel Type	Sights	Finish	Stock	Choke	Price
12	59001	22"	Rifled Ported	Iron	Matte	Black Synthetic	Cyl. Bore	$345.00
12	59802	22"	Rifled Ported	Fiber Optic	Matte	Synthetic	Cyl. Bore	367.00

The 3-inch chambered 12-gauge Model 695 bolt-action shot-gun features a 22-inch rifled barrel and rugged syntheti stock. This combination delivers the fast handling and fine balance of a classic sporting rifle. Every Model 695 comes with a two-round detachable magazine and Weaver-style scope bases to give hunters the advantage of today's specialized optics.

Mossberg's fully rifled slug barrels are specially "ported" to help soften the recoil and reduce muzzle jump. Non-rotating dual claw extractors ensure reliable ejection and feeding. Ten-year limited warranty. New fiber-optic sights speed your aim. Also available with Woodland Camo stock.

Shotguns • 253

New England Arms/FAIR
(Fabrica Armi Di Isidoro Rizzini)

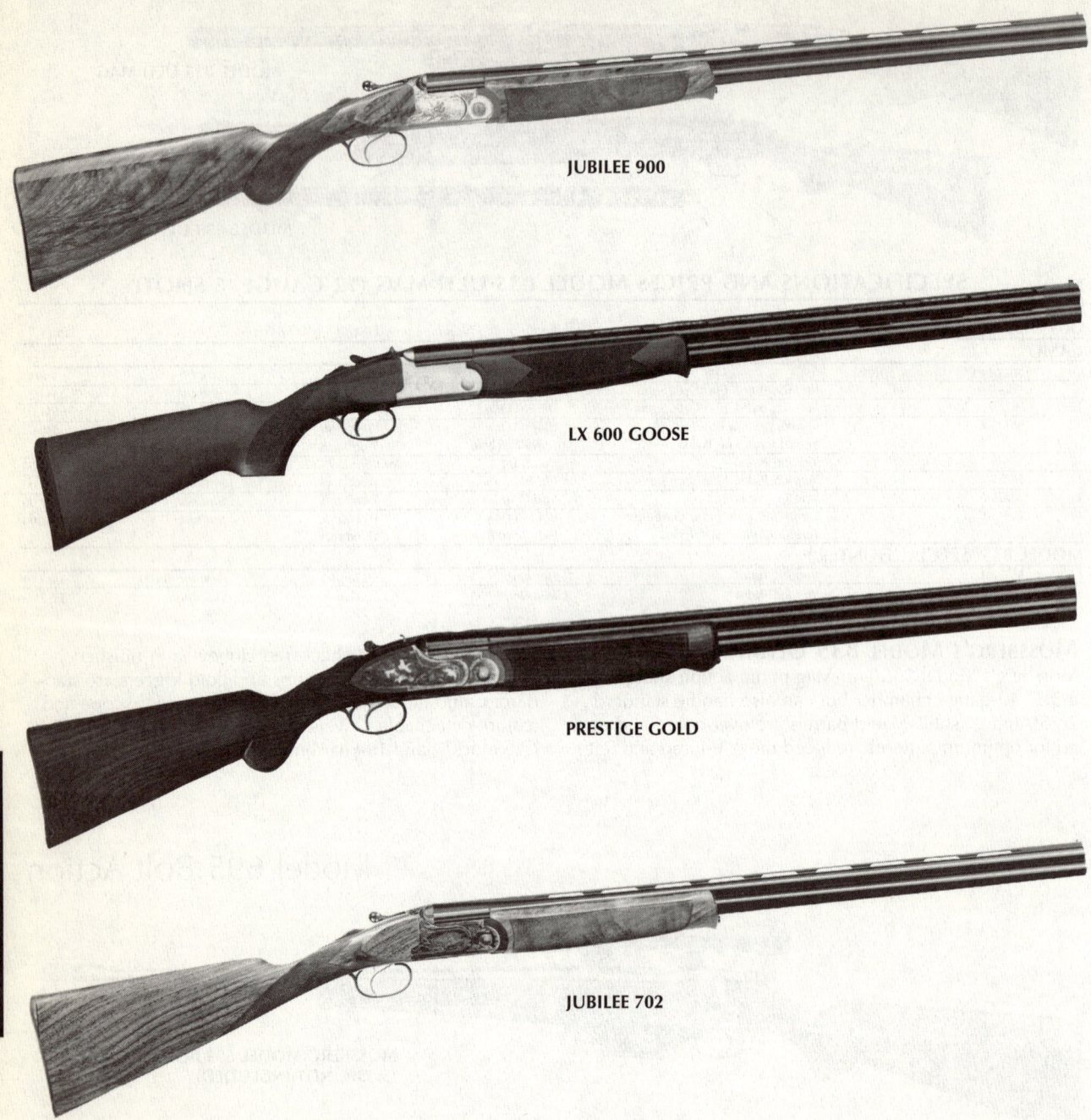

JUBILEE 900

LX 600 GOOSE

PRESTIGE GOLD

JUBILEE 702

New England Arms/FAIR (Fabrica Armi di Isidoro Rizzini) shotguns: Boxlock, fullly chrome-lined monoblock barrels with vent ribs, choke tubes standard on 12, 16, 20, 28 gauge guns (fixed chokes on .410), hand-checkered Turkish walnut, single selective triggers, automatic safety and ejectors, straight or semi-pistol grip, custom options available.
Prices:.............................**price on request**

New England Firearms

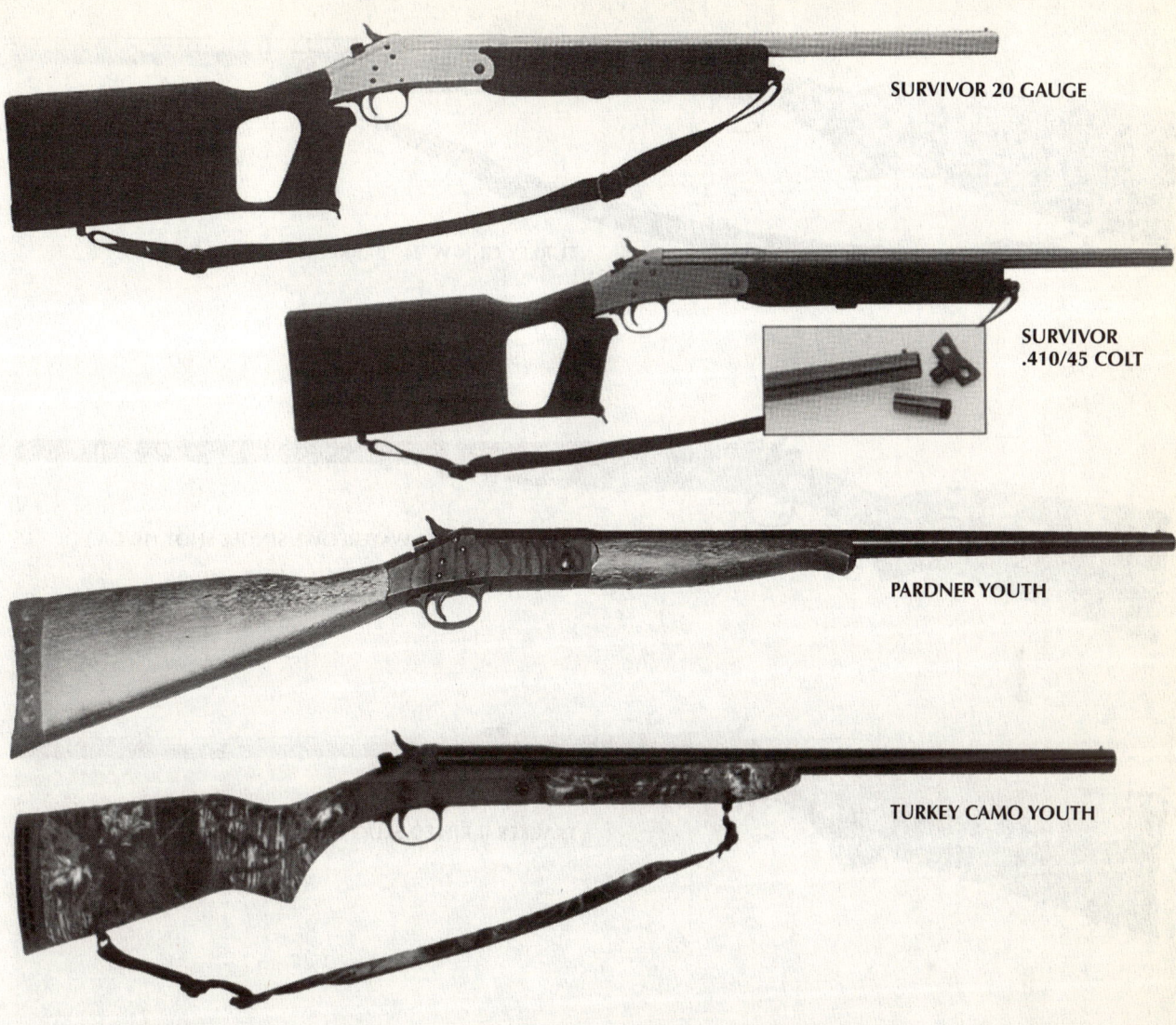

SURVIVOR 20 GAUGE

SURVIVOR .410/45 COLT

PARDNER YOUTH

TURKEY CAMO YOUTH

Survivor Series

This series of survival arms is available in 12 and 20 ga. with either a blued or electroless nickel finish. All shotguns feature the New England Firearms action with a patented transfer bar and high-impact, synthetic stock and forend. The stock is of modified thumbhole design with a full and secure pistol grip. The buttplate is attached at one end with a large thumbscrew for access to a large storage compartment holding a wide variety of survival gear or extra ammunition. The forend, which has a hollow cavity for storing three rounds of ammunition, is accessible by removing a thumbscrew (also used for takedown).

Specifications
Action: Break open, side-lever release, automatic ejection
Gauge: 12, 20, .41/45 Colt (Combo)
Barrel Length: 22″ (20″ combo)
Choke: Modified
Chamber: 3″ (Combo also available w/2.5″ chamber)
Overall Length: 36″   **Weight:** 6 lbs.   **Sights:** Bead
Stock: High-density polymer, black matte finish, sling swivels

Prices: Blued finish.............................$157
Nickel finish....................................183
.41/45 Colt Combo, blued.....................199
   Nickel..216

Pardner Single-Barrel Shotguns
Specifications
Gauges: 12, 16, 20, 28 and .410 **Barrel Lengths:** 22″ (Youth); 26″ (20, 28, .410); 28″ (12 and 16 ga.), 32″ (12 ga.) **Chokes:** Full (alll gauges, except 28); Modified (12, 20 and 28 ga.)
Chamber: 2.75″ (16 and 28 ga.); 3″ (all others)
Price:...128
   w/32″ barrel................................143
Also available:
Pardner Youth. With 22″ barrel in gauges 12, 20, 28 and .410..................................136
Turkey Camo Youth. 20 gauge, 3″, fixed full choke....................................183

Shotguns • 255

New England Firearms

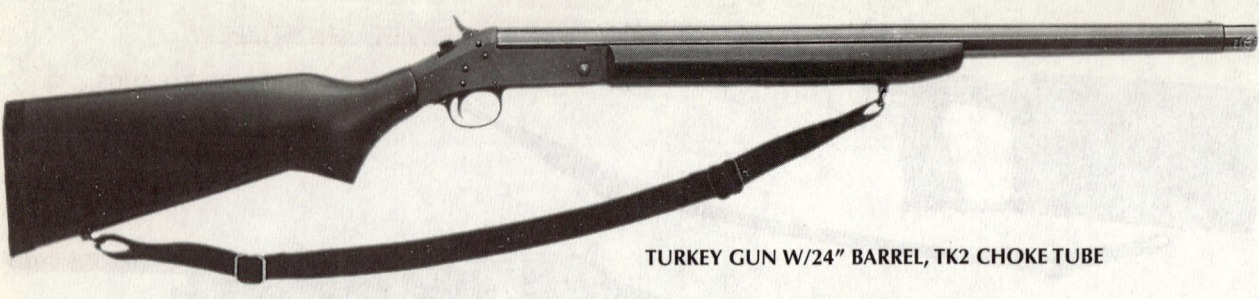

TURKEY GUN W/24" BARREL, TK2 CHOKE TUBE

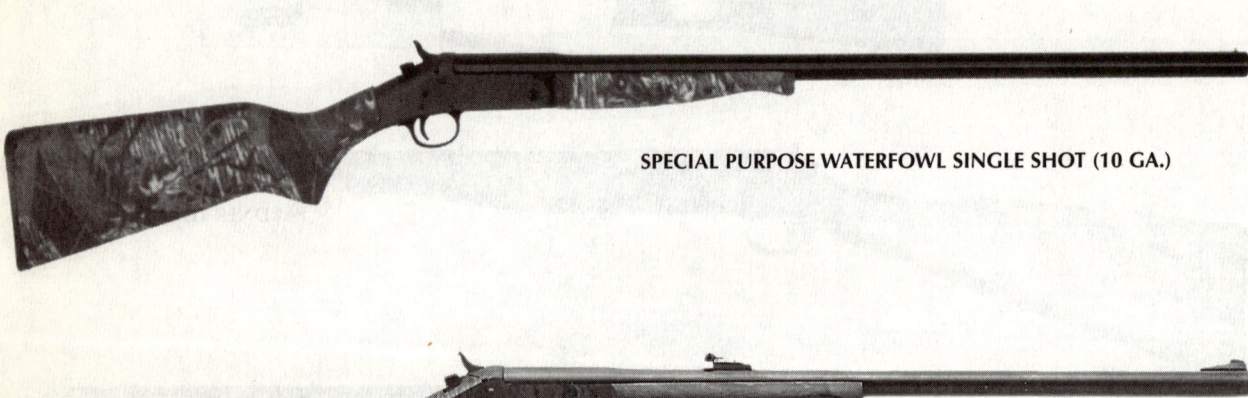

SPECIAL PURPOSE WATERFOWL SINGLE SHOT (10 GA.)

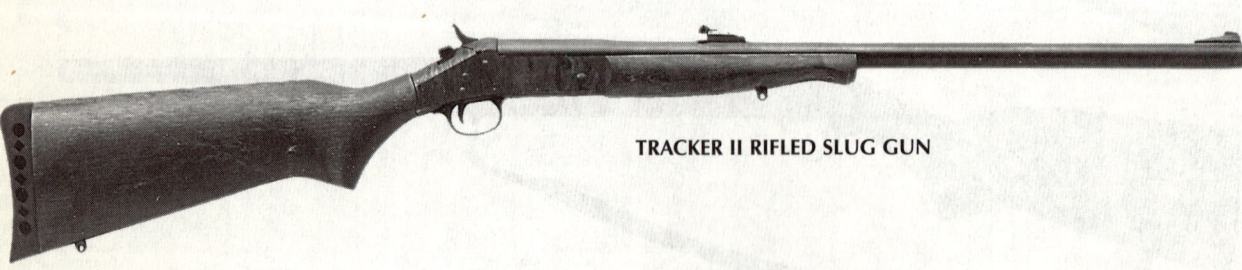

TRACKER II RIFLED SLUG GUN

TURKEY GUN
Specifications
Gauge: 12 (3.5" chamber) **Choke:** Full
Barrel Length: 24" **Overall Length:** 44"
Weight: 9.5 lbs. **Sights:** Bead sights
Stock: American hardwood; walnut or camo finish; full pistol grip; ventilated recoil pad.
Length Of Pull: 14.5"
Price:
   with full choke, camo paint, swivels & sling $183
   with screw-in choke, black finish. 175
Also Available:
Turkey Gun. With 24" 10 ga., screw in, choke,
   black matte finish, swivels and sling 243
   with camo paint 268

SPECIAL PURPOSE
WATERFOWL SINGLE SHOT (10 AND 12 GA.)
This sporting shotgun features a 32" barrel, (48" overall), Modified choke, camo paint finish, swivels and sling.
Weight: 9.5 lbs.
Price: 10 ga.. . . . . $263
Also Available:
with 28" barrel, walnut finish stock 208
12 ga. Camo 161

TRACKER II RIFLED SLUG GUN
Specifications
Gauges: 12 and 20 (3" chamber)
Choke: Rifled bore **Barrel Length:** 24"
Overall Length: 40"
Weight: 6 lbs.
Sights: Adjustable rifle sights
Length Of Pull: 14.5"
Stock: American hardwood; walnut or camo finish; full pistol grip; recoil pad; sling swivel studs
Price:. 180

BENELLI

SUPER BLACK EAGLE

The Original 3½″ Magnum.

The world's first auto designed to tame the recoil of the potent 12-gauge 3½″ shell: the Super Black Eagle. The Benelli inertia system enables this auto to handle a full range of ammunition from 2¾″ target loads to the thumping 3½″ magnums.

With its modest weight and superb balance it is truly a universal auto for all types of shooting and hunting... one gun for all occasions.

Think Safety!

For a free catalog write to:

Benelli U.S.A. Corporation
17603 Indian Head Highway
Accokeek, MD 20607

Tel: 301-283-6981
Fax: 301-283-6988

High-tech simplicity
Cycling is faster due to a reduced moving mass of parts • No complicated linkages or o-rings to malfunction • Better gun balance without heavy weights and pistons in the forend • Rotating bolt head features oversized lugs for solid, steel-to-steel lock-up with the barrel extension • Stays cleaner due to the hard-chrome locking head which prevents powder residue build-up on the bolt assembly • Fouling and gases are expelled out the barrel, not through the operating system, therefore, the action remains cleaner and more reliable in wet and cold weather conditions.

BENELLI INERTIA SYSTEM™

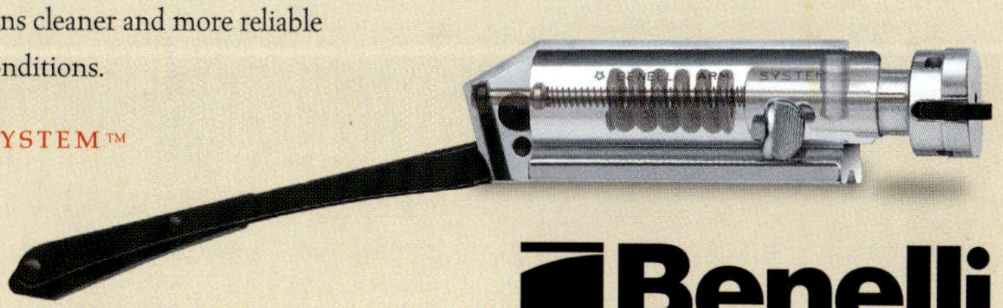

Performance Worth the Price

WWW.BENELLIUSA.COM

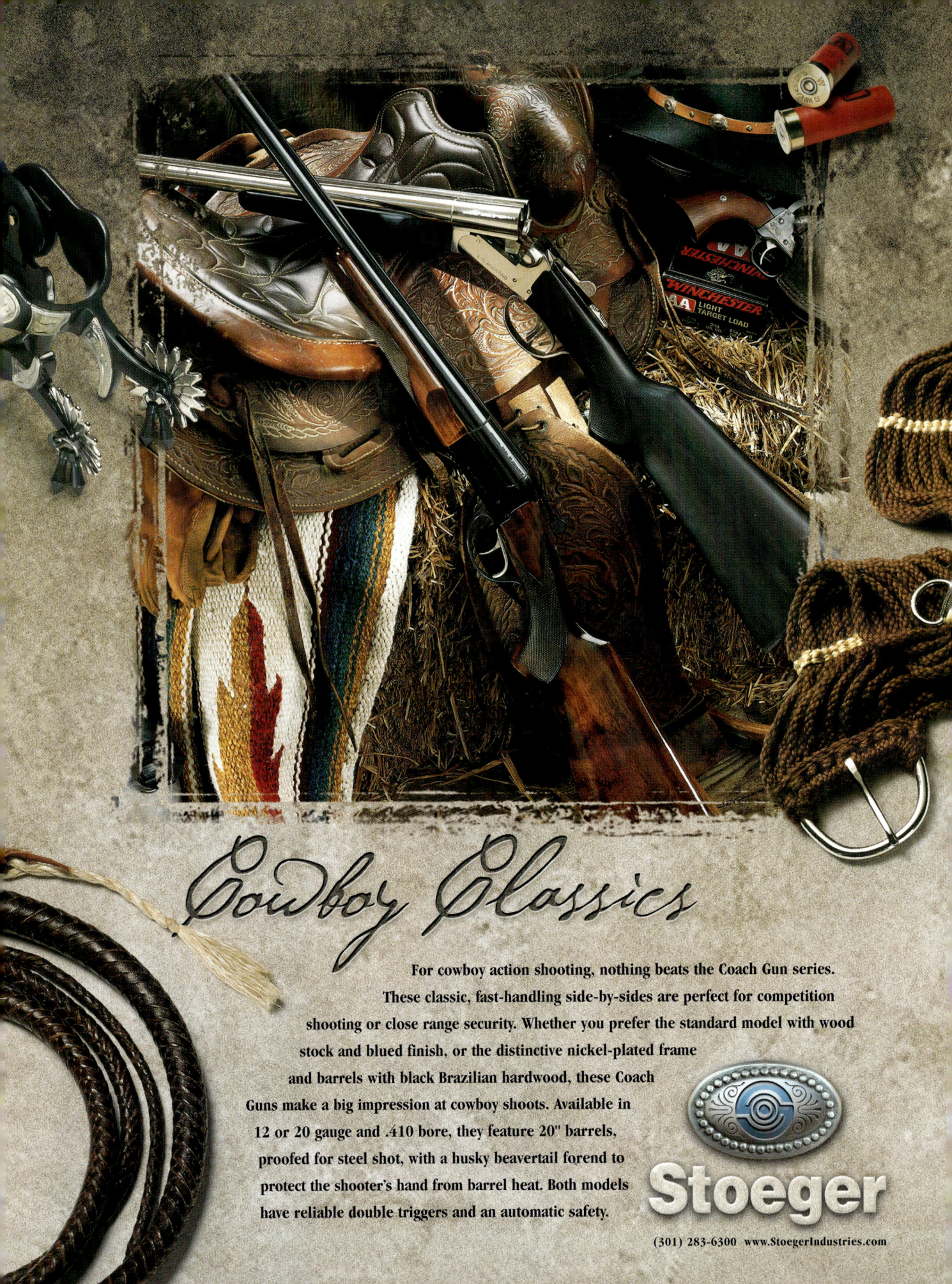

Perazzi Shotguns
Over/Under Game Models

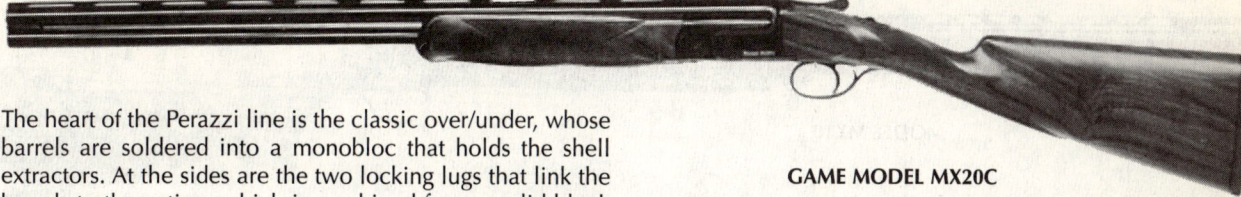

GAME MODEL MX20C

The heart of the Perazzi line is the classic over/under, whose barrels are soldered into a monobloc that holds the shell extractors. At the sides are the two locking lugs that link the barrels to the action, which is machined from a solid block of forged steel. Barrels come with flat, step or raised ventilated rib. The finely checkered walnut forend is available with Schnabel, beavertail or English styling, and the walnut stock can be of standard, Monte Carlo, Skeet or English design. Double or single nonselective or selective triggers. Sideplates and receiver are hand engraved.

GAME MODELS MX8, MX12, MX16, MX20, MX8/20, MX28 & MX410
Specifications
Gauges: 12, 20, 28 & .410
Chambers: 2.75"; also available in 3"
Barrel Lengths: 26" and 27.5"
Weight: 6 lbs. 6 oz. to 7 lbs. 4 oz.
Trigger Group: Nondetachable with coil springs and selective trigger
Stock: Interchangeable and custom; Schnabel forend

Prices:
Standard Grade..................$9930 - $18,020
SC3 Grade......................15,300 - 24,270
SCO Grade......................26,000 - 35,080
SCO Gold Grades ....29,370 - 38,350

ASCO SIDEPLATE ENGRAVING (APPLICABLE TO MX8 AND MX12 MODELS OF ANY VERSION)

American Trap Single Barrel Models

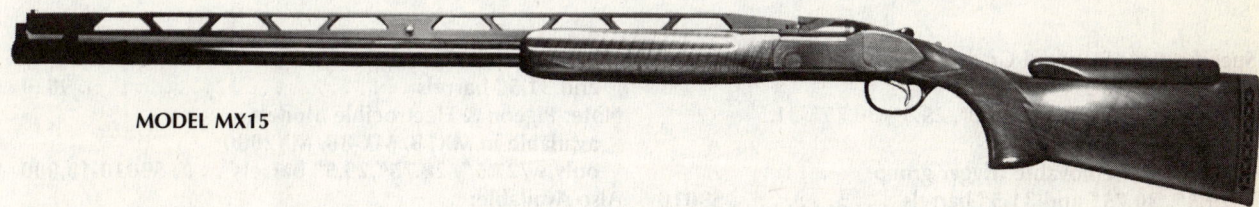

MODEL MX15

AMERICAN TRAP SINGLE-BARREL MODELS MX15, MX15L & MX2000
Specifications
Gauge: 12
Chamber: 2.75"
Barrel Lengths: 32" and 34"
Weight: 8 lbs. 6 oz.
Choke: Full

Trigger Group: Detachable and interchangeable with coil springs
Stock: Interchangeable and custom made
Forend: Beavertail
Prices:
MX15...$7670
MX15L..9270
MX2000...8830

Shotguns • 257

Perazzi Shotguns
Competition Over/Under Shotguns

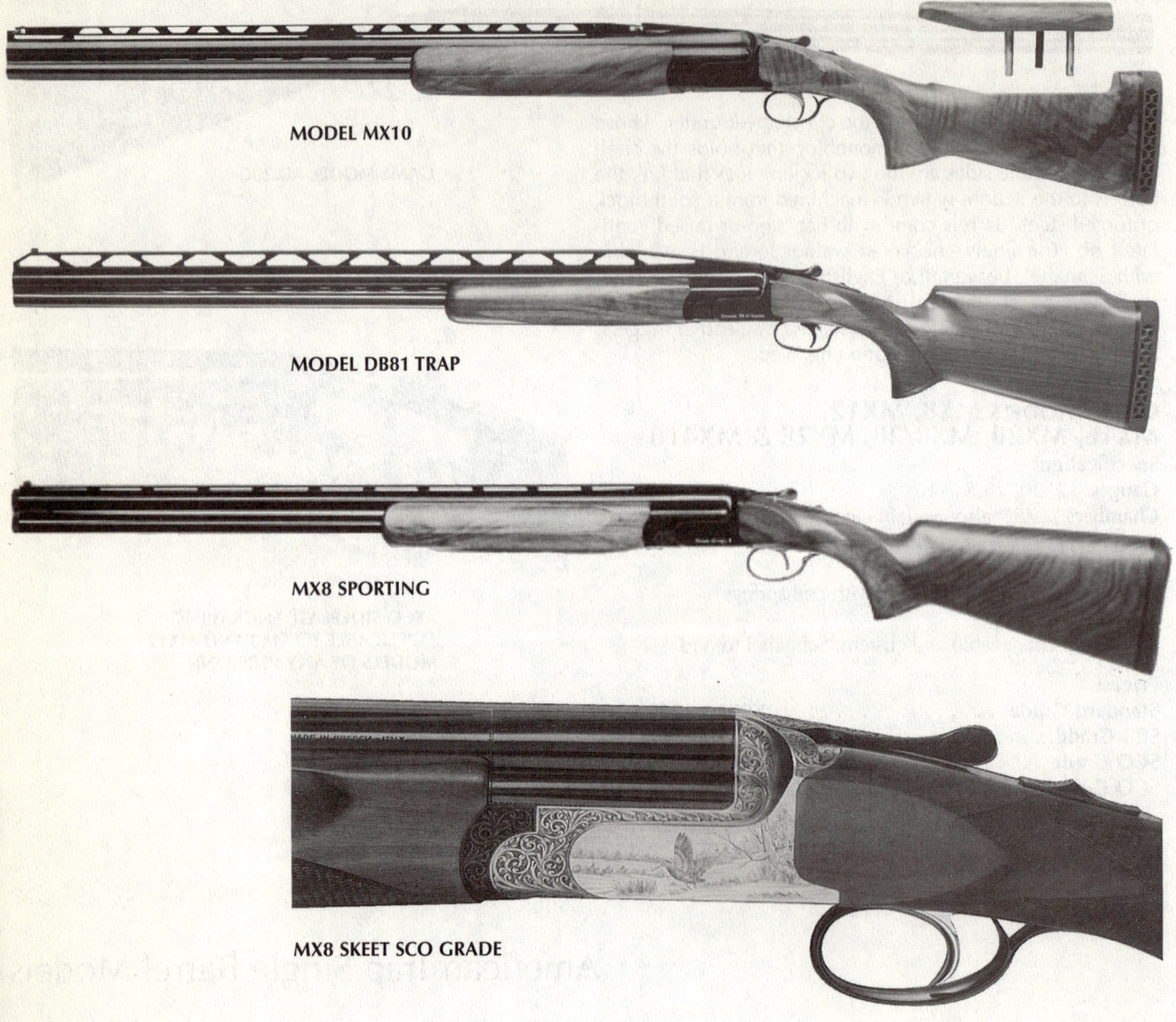

MODEL MX10

MODEL DB81 TRAP

MX8 SPORTING

MX8 SKEET SCO GRADE

Specifications Standard Grade
Gauges: 12 and 20
Barrel Lengths: 27.5", 28 3/8", 29.5", 30.75", 31.5"
Prices:
MX8 12 ga., removable trigger group
  29.5", 30.75" and 31.5" barrels $9010
MX10 12 & 20 ga., w/adj. stock and rib 29.5",
  30.75" and 31.5" bbl. 14,980
MX8/20 20 ga. removable trigger group
  26.75", 27.5", 28 3/8", 29.5", 30.75"
  and 31.5" barrels 9010
MX8 Sporting 12 ga. w/external selector
  and 5 chokes; 27.5", 28 3/8", 29.5",
  and 31.5" barrels 9980
MX8 Classic 12 ga. 11,380
MX2000 12 ga.. 9930

DB81 w/adjustable trigger 29.5",
  and 31.5" barrels 9820
Note: Pigeon & Electrocible Models
  available in MX1B, MX-8B, MX2000
  only w/27.5", 28.75", 29.5" barrels $9010-18,000
Also Available:
SC3 Grade (Models MX8, MX820,
  MX8C, MX1B, MX8B) $15,300-16,470
SCO Grade (same models as
  SC3 Grade) 26,000-27,230
SCO Gold Grade
  (same models as above) 29,370-30,540
SCO Grade Sideplates
  (same models as above) 39,880-41,100
SCO GOLD Grade Sideplates
  (same models above) 46,350-47,530

Purdey Shotguns
Side by Side Game Gun

Purdey easy opening action:
All side-by-side guns are built on the easy opening system invented by Frederick Beesley when he was working for Purdey. This system is incorporated in guns built from 1880 onwards.
Dedicated action sizes – Important to the overall weight and proportion of the gun is the action size. Purdey offers dedicated action sizes for each of the bores 10, 12, 20, 28 & .410 in square bar, round bar and ultra bar shapes.
Extra barrels – Purdey's can supply an extra pair of barrels of a different gauge for their guns, such as 28 gauge on a 20 gauge, and .410 on a 28 gauge. These guns are made with a single forend for both bores.
Chopper Lump Barrels – All Purdey barrels, both SxS and O/U, are of chopper lump construction.
Each individual tube is hand filled and then "struck up" using striking files. This gives the tube the correct Purdey profile with wall thickness tollerance of 1". Dependant on the final weight of the gun wall thicknesses are recommended at, and made to, .032".
Once polished the individual tubes are jointed (joined at the breech) using silver solder. The loop iron is similarly fixed. Once together, the rough chokes can be cut and the internal bores finished using a traditional lead lapping technique.
Ribs – always designed to provide the sighting profile the shooter seeks - are hand-filed to suit the barrel contour exactly, and then soft-soldered (using tin) to the barrels, using pine resin as the fluxing agent. Pine resin provides extra water resistance to the surfaces enclosed by the ribs.

Over/Under Gun

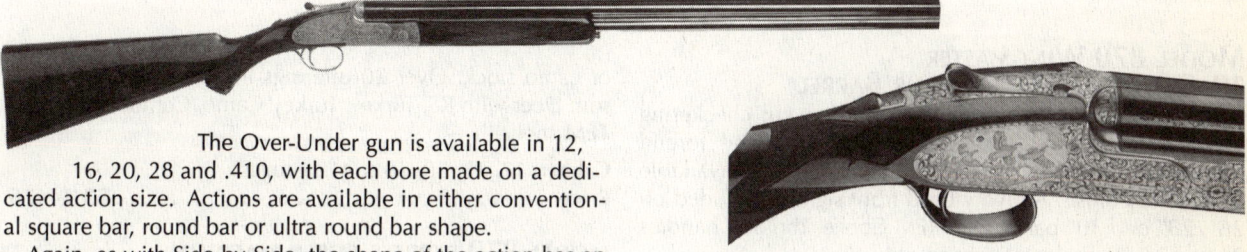

The Over-Under gun is available in 12, 16, 20, 28 and .410, with each bore made on a dedicated action size. Actions are available in either conventional square bar, round bar or ultra round bar shape.
Again, as with Side-by-Side, the shape of the action has an effect on the weight of the gun.
Firing sequence – Conventionally, the Purdey over-under will shoot the lower barrel first, but can be made to shoot the top barrel first if required. All prices on request.
The standard for regulating and patterning the shooting of a gun is the percentage of the shot charge, which is evenly concentrated in a circle of 30" diameter at a range of 40 yards. (Purdey choke restrictions 1/1000 inch.)

THE CHOKE SECTION

THE PERCENTAGES OF CHOKE	
Cylinder	45%
Improved Cylinder	50%
1/4 Choke	55%
1/2 Choke	60%
3/4 or Modified Choke	65%
Choke	70%
Full Choke	75%
Skeet (2)	45%
Skeet (1)	40%

12 Bore 2.75" 1.25 oz No.6	
FULL CHOKE	.038 - .040
CHOKE	.035
.75 (MOD)	.022
.5 CHOKE	.016-.017
.25 CHOKE	.010-.01
IMP CYL	7-8
CYL	3
SKEET	Open Bore

20 Bore 2.75"	
FULL CHOKE	.038 - .040
CHOKE	.030
.75 (MOD)	.018-.019
.5 CHOKE	.012-.013
.25 CHOKE	7-8
IMP CYL	6
CYL	3
SKEET	Open Bore

12 Bore 2.5" 1 oz. No. 6	
FULL CHOKE	.038 - .040
CHOKE	.030
.75 (MOD)	.018-.019
.5 CHOKE	.012-.013
.25 CHOKE	6-7
IMP CYL	3
CYL	2

28 Bore 2.75"	
FULL CHOKE	.026
CHOKE	.020
.75 (MOD)	.018
.5 CHOKE	.015
.25 CHOKE	.011
IMP CYL	7
CYL	3
SKEET	Open

Remington Shotguns

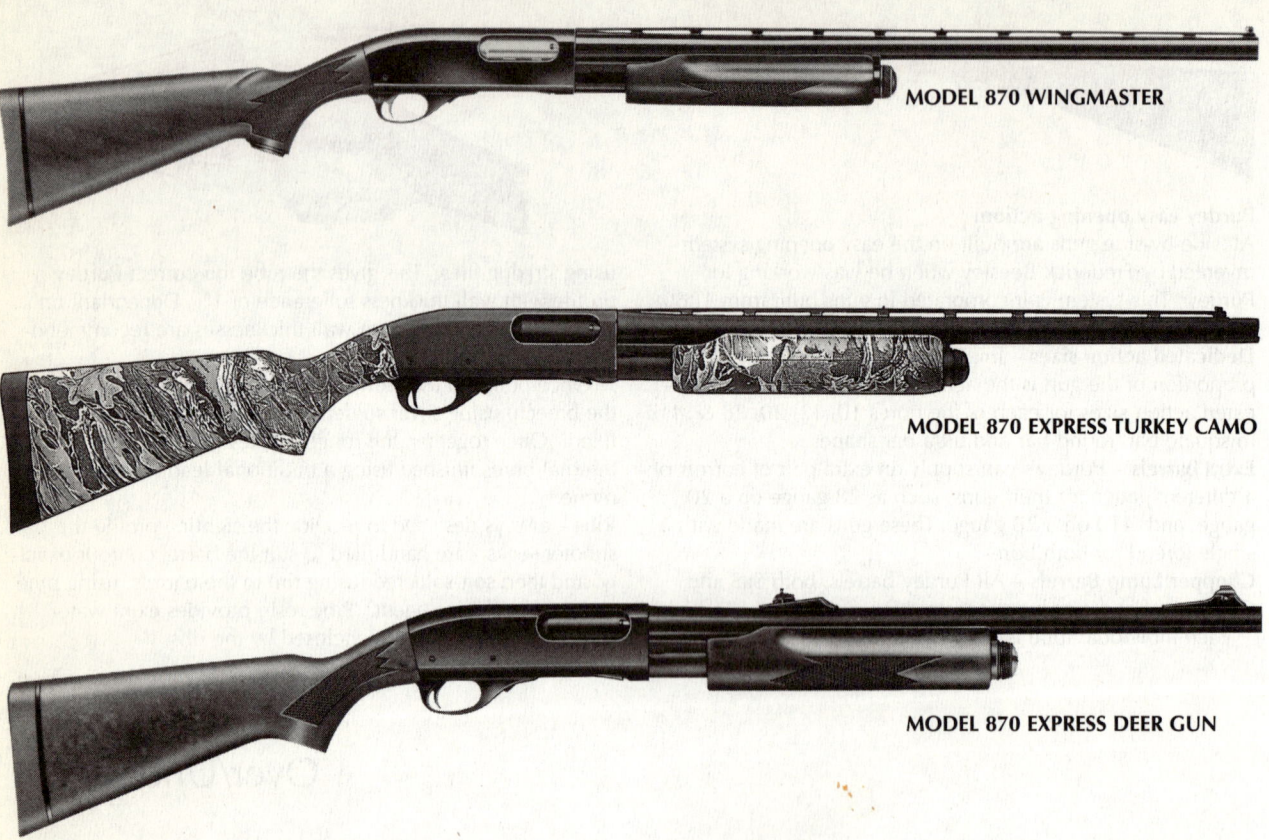

MODEL 870 WINGMASTER

MODEL 870 EXPRESS TURKEY CAMO

MODEL 870 EXPRESS DEER GUN

Model 870 Wingmaster
12 Gauge, Light Contour Barrel

This restyled 870 "Wingmaster" pump has cut checkering on its satin-finished American walnut stock and forend for confident handling, even in wet weather. Also available in Hi-Gloss finish. An ivory bead front sight is included on 26", 28" and 30" barrel with REM Choke. The 870 handles 3" and 2 1/2" shells interchangeably.

Specifications
Overall length: 46.5" (26" barrel), 48.5" (28" barrel), 50.5" (30" barrel).
Weight: 7.25 lbs. (w/26" barrel).
Price: $579
   Super magnum (3 1/2") 659
Also available:
Model 870 Wingmaster. 20 Ga. 3" chamber. Lightweight (6.5 lbs.), American walnut stock and forend.
   Price:
   20 or 16 ga. $579
   28 ga. 659
   410 ga. 605
Wingmaster Classic Trap (12 ga, 30" barrel, 2.75", Monte Carlo stock) 784

Model 870 Express

Same durability and reliability as 80 Wingmaster at a more ecomonical price. Flat-finished hardwood, black synthetic or camo stock. Over 20 offerings including left hand verison, Deer with RS, Turkey, Turkey Camo, Combo, Youth and TEM shoke.
Caliber: 12, 16, 20, 28 & 410 gauges
Price: $319-476

Model 870 Express Super Magnum (not shown)

For those who seek the power and range of 12 gauge 3.5" magnum shotshells, the Model 870 Express Super Magnum represents a good value. In addition to having the strength and reliability of the Model 870 Wingmaster, this model has the added versatility of handling 12 ga. 2 3/4" to 3 1/2" loads. The existing breech bolt and receiver have been designed to accommodate the big shells. Also available is a Turkey Camo shotgun with a 23" vent rib and 3 1/2" chamber with a synthetic stock and forend, plus checkering and vented recoil pad. Fully camouflaged with Real Tree Advantage. Remington also offers Synthetic and wood or Combo models

Prices:
Model 870 Express Super Magnum 376
   Turkey Camo 500
   Synthetic Model (26" vent rib) 376
**Combo 20" fully rifled deer barrel and 26" vent rib
   w/wood stock and forend, vented recoil pad** 523

Remington Shotguns

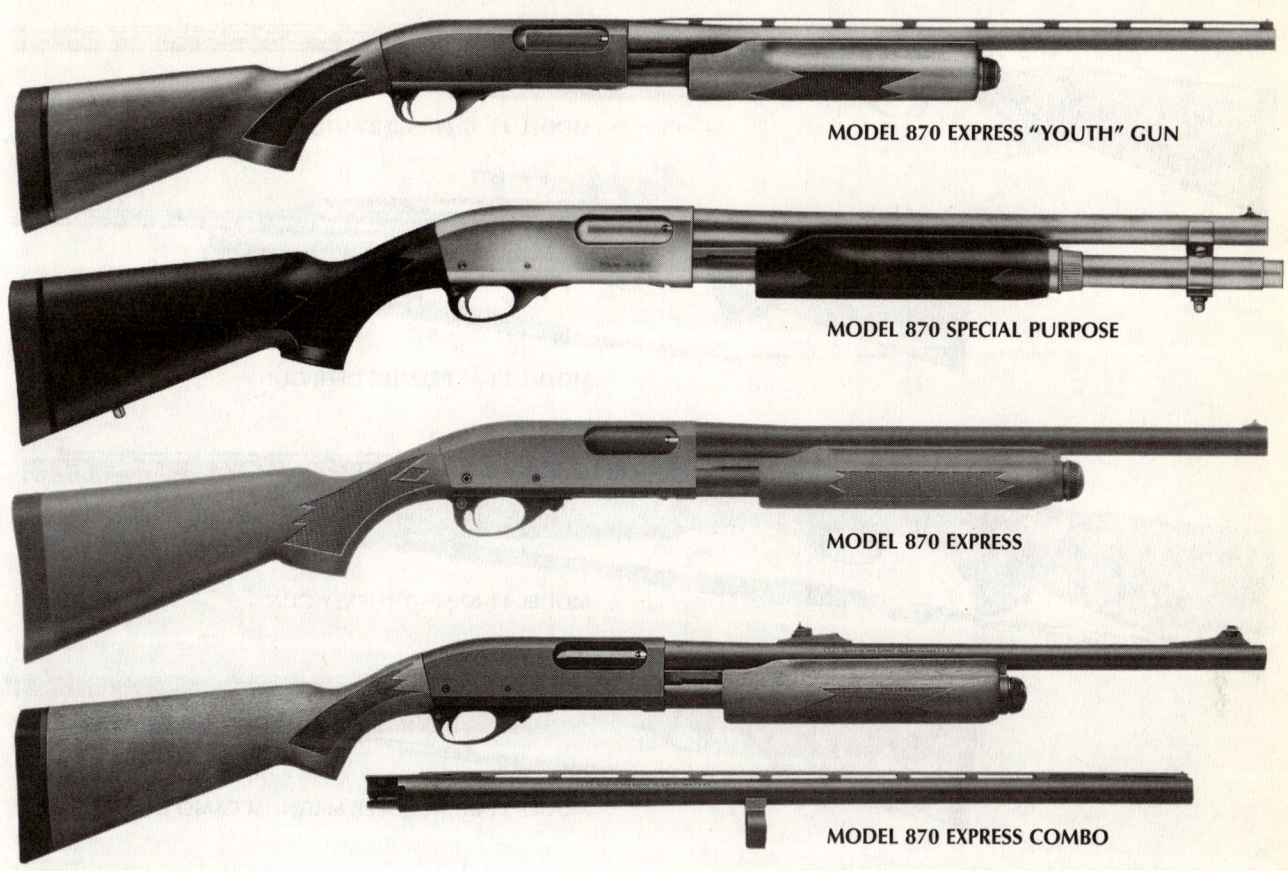

MODEL 870 EXPRESS "YOUTH" GUN

MODEL 870 SPECIAL PURPOSE

MODEL 870 EXPRESS

MODEL 870 EXPRESS COMBO

MODEL 870 EXPRESS "YOUTH" GUN
Designed for youngsters and small adults. It's a 20-gauge lightweight with a 1-inch shorter stock and 21-inch barrel. Complete with REM Choke and ventilated rib barrel, it is also available with a 20" fully rifled, rifle-sighted deer barrel.
Specifications
Barrel length: 21"   **Stock Dimensions:** Length of pull 12.5" (including recoil pad); drop at heel; 2.5" drop at comb 1 5/8"
Overall length: 39" (40.5" w/deer barrel)
Average weight: 6 lbs.
Choke: REM Choke-Mod. (vent-rib version).
Prices:
20-Gauge Lightweight $332
w/Deer Barrel (20" RS) 365
w/Real Tree Advantage camo stock and forend,
   21" VT barrel 399

MODEL 870 SECIAL PURPOSE MARINE MAGNUM
Remington's Model 870 Special Purpose Marine Magnum is a versatile, multipurpose security gun featuring a rugged synthetic stock and extensive, electroless nickel plating on all metal parts. This shotgun utilizes a standard 12-gauge Model 870 receiver with a 7-round magazine extension tube and an 18" cylinder barrel (38.5" overall) with bead front sight. The receiver, magazine extension and barrel are protected (inside and out) with heavy-duty, corrosion-resistant nickel plating. The synthetic stock and forend reduce the effects of moisture. The gun is supplied with a black rubber recoil pad, sling swivel studs, and positive checkering on both pistol grip and forend.
Weight: 7.5 lbs.
Price: $555

MODEL 870 EXPRESS SYNTHETIC
This 12-gauge pump-action shotgun features an 18" plain barrel with Cylinder choke and front bead sight. The synthetic stock and forend have a textured black, nonreflective finish and positive checkering.
Price: 319

MODEL 870 EXPRESS COMBO
The Model 870 Express in 12 and 20 gauge offers all the features of the standard Model 870, including twin-action bars, quick-change 26" or 28" barrels, REM Choke and vent rib plus low-luster, checkered hardwood stock and no-shine finish on barrel and receiver. The Model 870 Combo is packaged with an extra 20" deer barrel, fitted with rifle sights. The 3-inch chamber handles all 2 3/4" and 3" shells.
Weight: 7.5 lbs.
Price: 443
   with Fully rifled barrel with rifle sights 476

Remington Shotguns

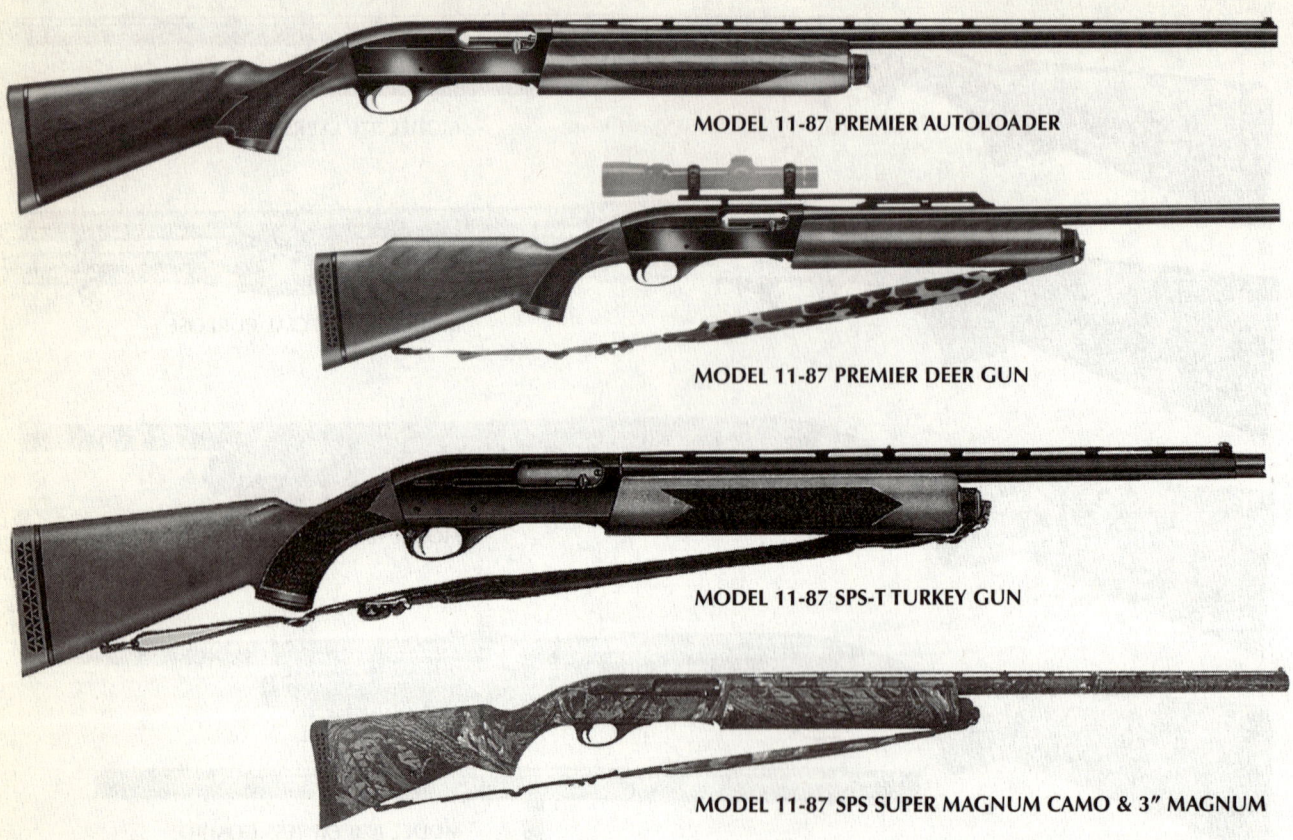

MODEL 11-87 PREMIER AUTOLOADER

MODEL 11-87 PREMIER DEER GUN

MODEL 11-87 SPS-T TURKEY GUN

MODEL 11-87 SPS SUPER MAGNUM CAMO & 3" MAGNUM

MODEL 11-87 PREMIER AUTOLOADER
Remington's redesigned 12-gauge Model 11-87 Premier Autoloader features new, light-contour barrels that reduce both barrel weight and overall weight, embellished receiver. The shotgun has a standard 3-inch chamber and handles all 12-gauge shells interchangeably— from 2 3/4" field loads to 3" Magnums. The gun's interchangeable REM choke system includes Improved Cylinder, Modified and Full chokes. Select American walnut stocks with fine-line, cut-checkering in satin or high gloss finish are standard. Right-hand models are available in 26", 28" and 30" barrels (left-hand models are 28" only).
Prices:
Light Contour Barrel........................$765
Left Hand, 28" Barrel........................819
Also available:
Model 11-87 3 1/2" Super Magnum............852
Model 11-87 upland Special 12 or 20 ga.
 23"/straight grip English style stock...........765

MODEL 11-87 SPS SPECIAL PURPOSE DEER GUN
Features the same finish as other SP models plus a padded, camo-style carrying sling of Cordura nylon with QD sling swivels. Barrel is 21" (41" overall) with rifle sights and rifled and IC choke (handles all 2 3/4" and 3" rifled slug and buckshot loads as well as high-velocity field and magnum loads (does not function with light 2 3/4" field loads).
Weight: 8.5 lbs. with black synthetic stock

Price:.......................................$799
Also Available:
Premier Model with Fully Rifled Barrel
 and cantilevered mount 845
w/ SP wood, 21" RS barrel.....................745

MODEL 11-87 SPST TURKEY GUN
3" Chamber, All-Black Synthetic Stock, Turkey Super Full Choke Tube, 21" Barrel
Price:
 w/Turkey Glo Rifle Sights 897
 w/Cantilever Mount 907
 w/REM choke 879

MODEL 11-87 SPS SUPER MAGNUM CAMO & 3" MAGNUM
Fully camouflaged, Mossy Oak Break-up camo stock, 28" barrel. Includes sling & swivels.
Price: 3 1/2" 935
Also Available:
SPS-T (Turkey gun with rifle sights, REM choke,
 23" barrel) 935
SP Wood (3 1/2", 26" or 28" barrel)............852
SPS Synthetic (3 1/2", 26" or 28" barrel) 852
SP Wood (3", 26" or 28" barrel)................765
SPS Synthetic (3", 26" or 28" barrel) 765
SPS Camo (3", 26" VT barrel)..................879

Remington Shotguns
Autoloading Shotguns

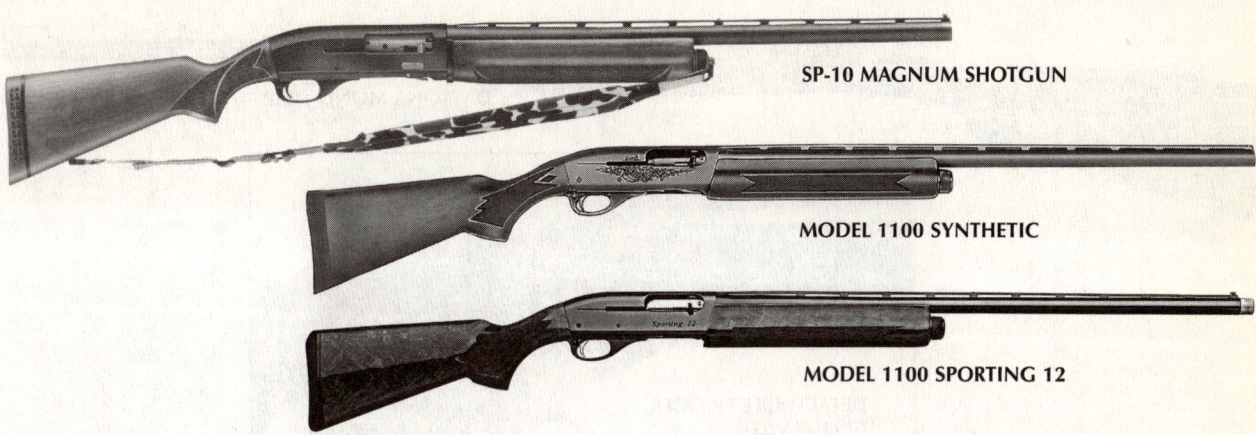

SP-10 MAGNUM SHOTGUN

MODEL 1100 SYNTHETIC

MODEL 1100 SPORTING 12

SP-10 MAGNUM SHOTGUN
Remington's SP-10 Magnum is the only gas-operated semi-automatic 10-gauge shotgun made today. This autoloader features a vented, noncorrosive, stainless-steel gas system, in which the cylinder moves—not the piston. This reduces felt recoil energy by spreading the recoil over a longer time. The receiver is machined from solid steel for integral strength. The SP-10 has a 3/8" vent rib with mid and front sights for a better sight plane. The American walnut stock and forend have a protective, low-gloss satin finish for reduced glare, and deep-cut checkering. The receiver and barrel have a matte finish, and the stainless-steel breech bolt features a non-reflective finish. The SP-10 also has a brown vented recoil pad and a padded camo sling of Cordura nylon.

Barrel lengths/choke: 26" or 30"/REM Choke.
Overall length: 51.5" (30" barrel) and 47.5" (26" barrel).
Weight: 11 lbs. (30" barrel) and 10.75 lbs. (26" barrel).
Price: $1292
Also available:
SP in Mossy Oak Camo 26" 1412
Synthetic 26" 1292

MODEL 1100 SYNTHETIC
Prices:
12 ga. 28" barrel $549
20 ga. 26" barrel/light contour 549
12 ga. Cantilever deer – RS with 21" barrel. $629
20 ga. Light contour deer with 21" barrel/
 REM choke 538
Youth Version:
20 ga. 21" barrel/light contour with REM choke 549
Youth turkey 20 ga. 21" VT,
 Realtree Advantage camo 612

MODEL 1100 SYNTHETIC
The Remington Model 1100 Synthetic is a 5-shot gas-operated autoloader with a gas-metering system designed to reduce recoil. This design enables the shooter to use 23/4" standard velocity "Express" and 23/4" Magnum loads without gun adjustments. Barrels, within gauge and versions, are interchangeable. All 12- and 20-gauge versions have modified REM choke and black synthetic stock.

MODEL 1100 TARGET SHOTGUNS
Target autoloaders with light-contour vent-rib barrels. Sporting Clay and Trap versions in 12 ga. Semi-fancy American walnut stock and fore end, gloss finish. Gold-plated trigger. Sporting clays version also available in 20 ga. with 28" VT and in 28 ga. with 25" VT barrel.
Prices:
Trap $895
Sporting Clay 868

Over/Under Shotguns

MODEL 332 O/U

MODEL 332 IDEAL O/U 12-GAUGE
12 GA. IN 26", 28", OR 30" vent rib, light-contour barrel. REM choke. Classic field gun patterned after the famous Model 32. Dark satin American walnut stock and fore end. Blue metal with a "Pointer" roll engraving.
Price: $1532

Renato Gamba

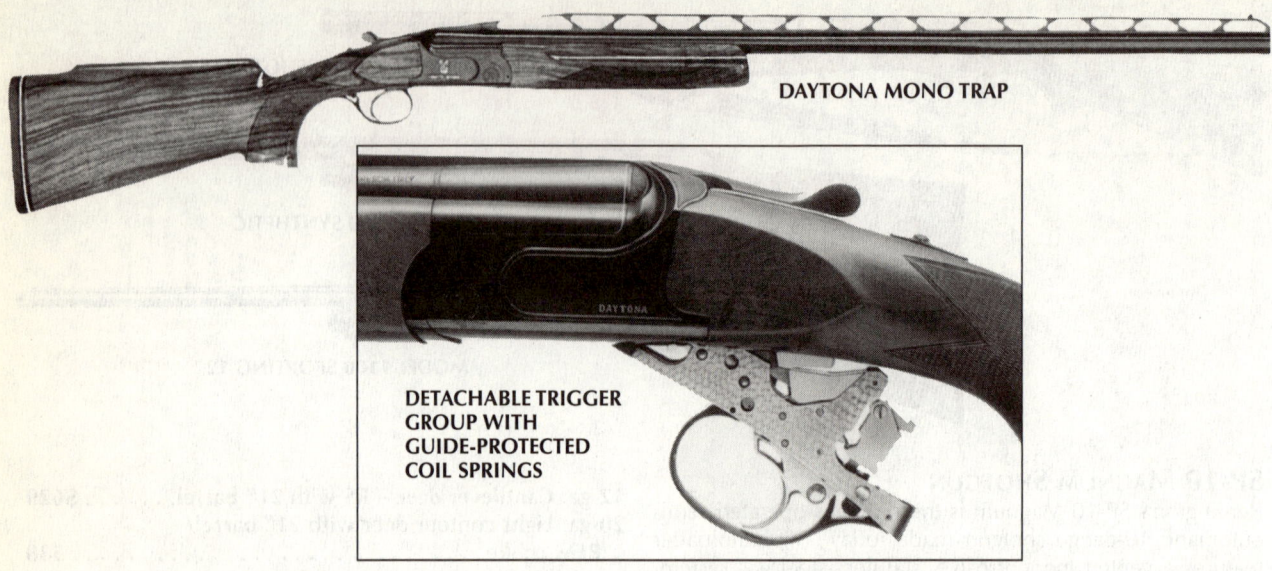

DAYTONA MONO TRAP

DETACHABLE TRIGGER GROUP WITH GUIDE-PROTECTED COIL SPRINGS

	TRAP	DOUBLE TRAP	SKEET	SPORTING CLAYS	HUNTING	MONO TRAP
GAUGE	12 - 20					
BARRELS	HEAT TREATED SPECIAL CHROME-NICKEL-MOLYBDENUM STEEL					
CHANBER	MM 70 (2"3/4) • MM 79 (3") ON REQUEST					
BARRELS LENGTH	CM. 76 - CM.81 30" - 32"	CM. 76 30"	CM. 68-71 26"3/4 - 28"	CM. 71-74 CM 76 - CM.81 28"- 29"- 30"- 32"	CM. 68- CM. 71 26"3/4 - 28"	CM. 81- CM. 86 32" - 34"
CHOKES	IMP. MOD/ FULL-MAC/FULL	IMP. CIL./FULL	SK/SK	MOD./FULL	IMP. CIT./IMP.MOD. MOD./FULL	FULL
INTERCH. CHOKES	5 SCREW-IN CHOKE TUBES SET AVAILABLE ON REQUEST					

THE DAYTONA SHOTGUN

The Daytona shotgun is available in several styles oriented specifically to American Trap, International Trap, American Skeet, International Skeet, and Sporting Clays. The Daytona SL, (the side plate model), and the Daytona SLHH, (the side lock model), are the top of the Daytona line.

The wood: The Gamba Daytona model shotgun carries selected walnut for both the fore end and stock, while the Daytona SLHH is produced with a higher grade root walnut stock featuring even more pronounced figure. The stock itself incorporates a palm swell for superior grip and very fine checkering to enhance the competitor's hand contact with the firearm. The finish is satin hand rubbed oil, with other types available on request.

Engraving: On request, customized engraving can be done. The engraved Daytona gun, to the smallest detail, is guaranteed to meet the most discriminating shooter's scrutiny. Gamba uses only the finest craftsmen to execute the works shown on custom designs provided by the customer.

THE DAYTONA FIREARM SYSTEM

The action: The action of the Daytona is milled from a massive block of forged Ni-Cr-Mo steel. The receiver features the most streamlined frame ever manufactured, in that the barrels ride lower and deliver the best angle for straight line recoil.

The Boss Locking System: The Gamba solid steel locking bolt is located precisely where recoil forces transfer their energy, giving the Daytona the legendary longevity that shotgunners have long expected form the Gamba line.

The barrels: the Daytona's barrels are chrome lined, then assembled into a monoblock; they feature an antiglare rib of extruded steel, and are supplied with or without choke tubes on customer request.

The trigger group: The trigger group is detachable and is removable without the use of tools. The frame that contains the hammers, sears and springs is milled from a single block of special steel and jeweled for oil retention. On special order, an adjustable trigger may be produced with one inch of movement that can accomodate shooters with exceptionally large or small hands. Internally, the hammer springs are constructed from coils that are contained in steel sleeves placed directly behind the hammers. With the fail safe capsule surrounding the springs, a competitor lives with the assurance that the shotgun will fire even if breakage occurs.

Prices: Hunter o/u . . . . from $1390
Le Maus o/u . . . . from 1580
Concorde o/u . . . . from 6100
Daytona 2K o/u . . . . from 7600

B. Rizzini Shotguns

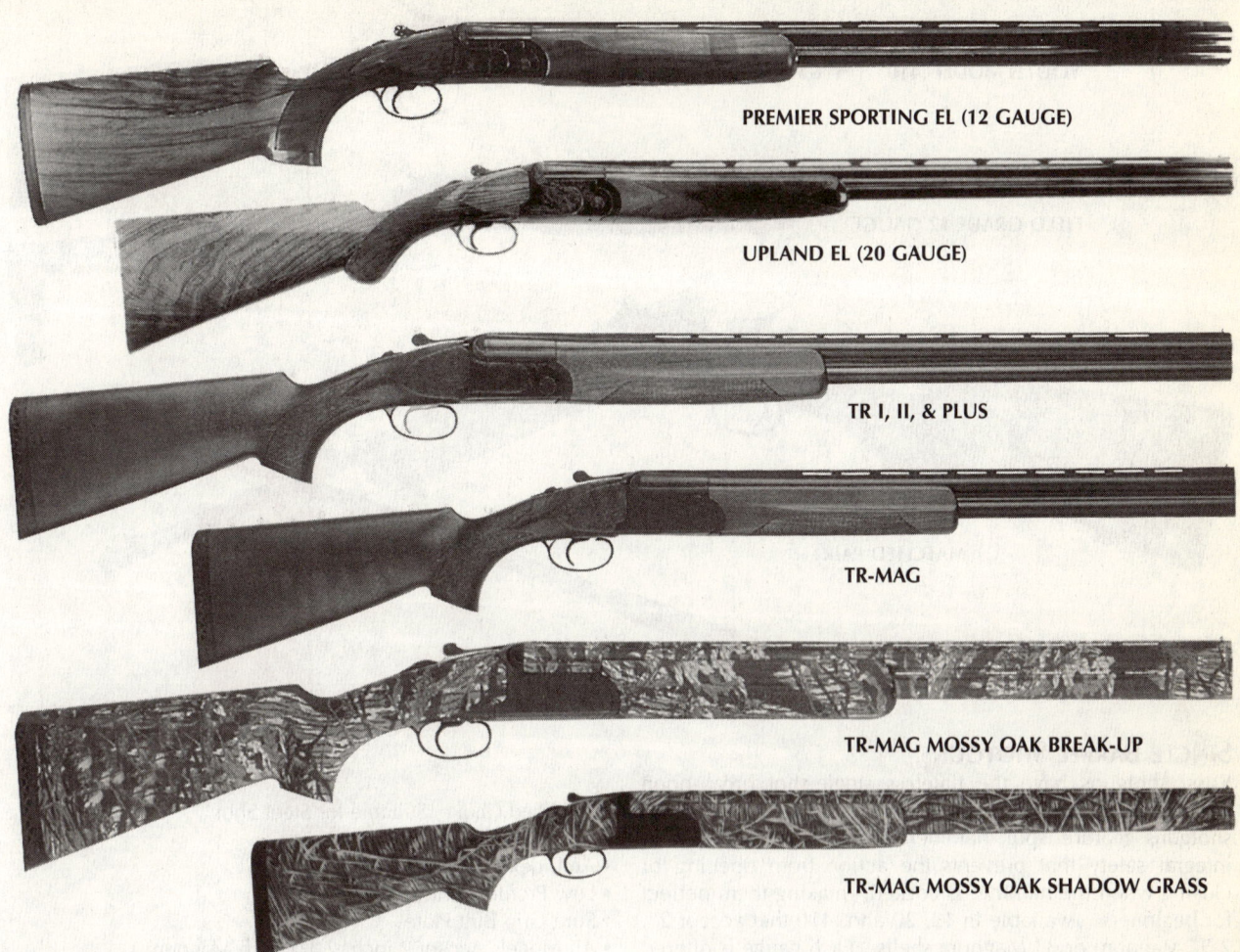

PREMIER SPORTING EL (12 GAUGE)

UPLAND EL (20 GAUGE)

TR I, II, & PLUS

TR-MAG

TR-MAG MOSSY OAK BREAK-UP

TR-MAG MOSSY OAK SHADOW GRASS

Rizzini Sporting and Upland EL

Rizzini builds a well-finished boxlock ejector over/under that is available in all gauges and in many different configurations.

The Artemis and Premier are production guns built to standard specifications. The EL models, which include the Upland EL, the Sporting EL and the High Grades, feature higher grade wood, checkering and hand finishing.

Field guns are available with case-colored or coin-finish actions with straight grips or round knob semi-pistol grips. Also available are multi-gauge field sets with .410, 28 or 20 gauge barrels in any combination. These sets are available in EL or High Grade level guns. On custom orders, stock dimensions, chokes and barrel length may be specified. Screw-in chokes are available on 12 and 20 gauge guns.

Sporting guns, in 12 and 20 gauge only, feature heavier weight and a target-style rib, stock and forearm. The Sporting models are available in three versions: Premier Sporting, Sporting EL and S790EL.

High Grade models, with or without sideplates, come in four engraving styles, including game scenes and gold inlays.

Prices: Sporting El (12 gauge) $3,600.00
  Upland El (20 gauge) 2,800.00
  S790 EMEL High Grade 7,800.00
  Artemis El High Grade 12,650.00

Emilio Rizzini Over/Unders

The TR-I, TR-I Plus, and TR-II Emilio Rizzini boxlocks have walnut stocks, 3" chambers (except the 28 & 16 gauge models: 2 3/4" chamber) and ventilated ribs. The TR-1 has a fixed choke and extractors, the new TR-I-Plus two choke tubes and extractors, and the TR-II three choke tubes (IC/M/F) and auto ejectors. The TR-MAG series has 3" magnum chambers, choke tubes, extractors (All 10GA, & 12GA.WF) or ejectors (12GA. MOB & 12 GA. MOS) and a ventilated 7mm top rib in three handsome models: The standard matte blue finish with walnut stock, Mossy Oak Break-up camouflage pattern, and Mossy Oak Shadow Grass camouflage pattern. **Weight:** 6.75-7.5 lbs. (10 ga., 9.75 lbs.)
Barrel Length: 24-28"
Prices: TR-I (fixed chokes) $687.00
  TR-I Plus (choke tubes) 748.00
  TR-II 12, 16 ga. 879.00
  TR-II 20, 28, .410. . . . . 924.00
  TR-MAG 12 ga. 764.00
  12 ga. camo 942.00
  10 ga. camo 1,132.00

Rossi Shotguns

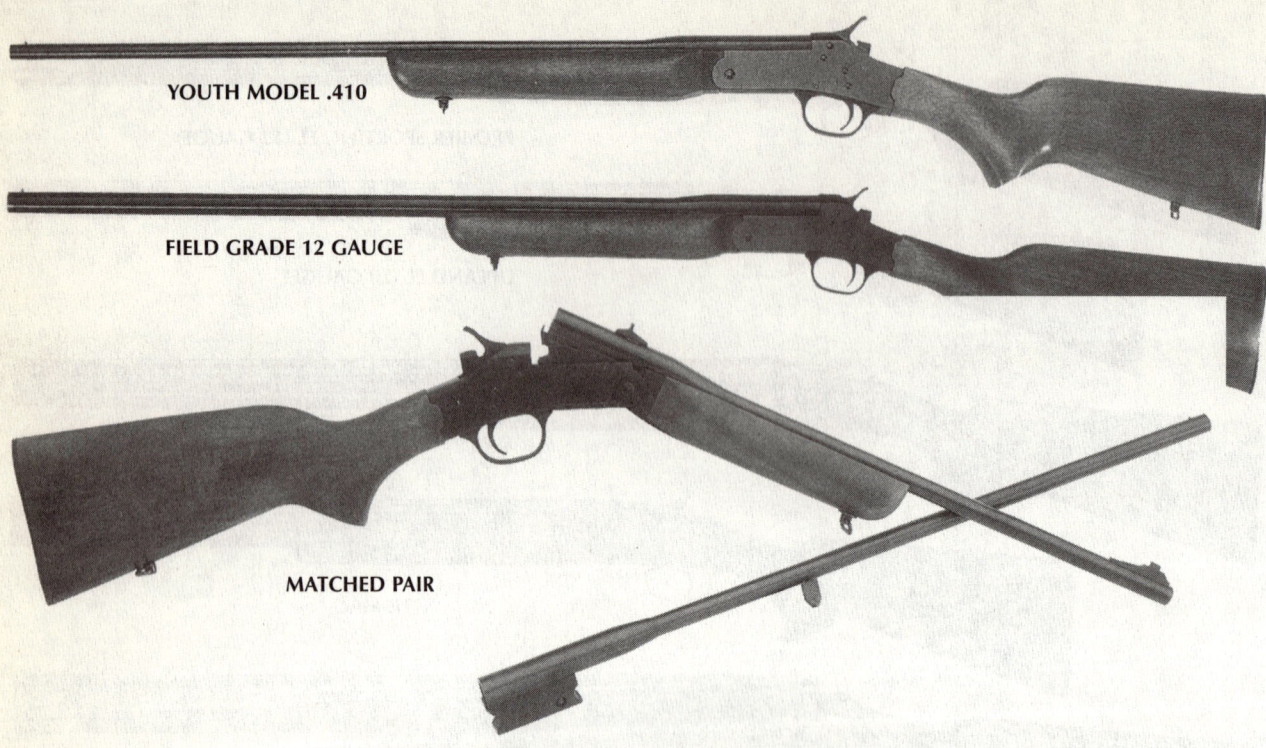

YOUTH MODEL .410

FIELD GRADE 12 GAUGE

MATCHED PAIR

Single Barrel Shotguns

Rossi shotguns have the timeless single-shot break-open breech design updated with modern safety features. These shotguns feature spur hammer, transfer bar action and integral safety that prevents the action from opening or closing when the hammer is cocked, making them perfect for beginners. Available in 12, 20 and .410 that accept 2", 2.5" Magnum or 3" Magnum shells. Each gauge is offered in a lighter youth model scaled down to fit young shooters. Shotguns feature brass bead front sight, straight stock with pistol grip, oil finished hardwood and sling swivels.

All Rossi Shotguns Feature:
- Brass Bead Front Sight
- Satin, Oil Finished Exotic Hardwoods
- Straight Stock with Pistol Grip
- Modified Choke, Suitable for Steel Shot
- Sling Swivels Installed
- Ambidextrous Operation
- Low Profile Serrated Hammer
- Sure Grip Butt Plate
- All Models Accept 2 inch, 2 1/2 inch Magnum and 3 inch Magnum Shells

Matched Pair

Rossi's Matched Pair is a single-shot break-open shotgun in a choice of .410, 20 gauge or 12 gauge, plus a completely interchangeable barrel chambered for .22 Long Rifle. The rifle barrel features fully adjustable sights. This makes the Matched Pair ideal (and economical) for the younger shooter.

Barrel Length	Finish	Weight	Length	Stocks/Grips	Description	Price
FIELD GRADE SHOTGUNS						
28'	blue	5.25 lbs.	43 1/4"	wood	S12 12 Gauge 28" Modified Choke or Full	$101
28"	blue	5.25 lbs.	43 1/4"	wood	S20 20 Gauge 28" Modified Choke or Full	101
28"	blue	4 lbs.	43 1/4"	wood	S41 .410 28" Modified Choke or Full	101
YOUTH MODEL SHOTGUNS						
22"	blue	5 lbs.	35 1/2"	wood	S20 20 Gauge 22" Modified Choke Youth Model	101
22"	blue	3.75 lbs.	35 1/2"	wood	S41 .410 22" Modified Choke Youth Model	101
MATCHED PAIR COMBO GUNS						
28"/23"	blue	TBA	TBA	wood	Matched Pair 12 Gauge/.22 Mag., Adjustable Sights	140
28"/23"	blue	TBA	TBA	wood	Matched Pair 12 Gauge/.22LR, Adjustable Sights	140
22"/18.5"	blue	TBA	TBA	wood	Matched Pair 20 Gauge/.22LR, Adjustable Sights	140
22"/18.5"	blue	TBA	TBA	wood	Matched Pair .410/.22LR, Adjustable Sights	140
22"/18.5"	stainless	TBA	TBA	wood	Matched Pair .410/.22LR, Adjustable Sights	170

Ruger Shotguns

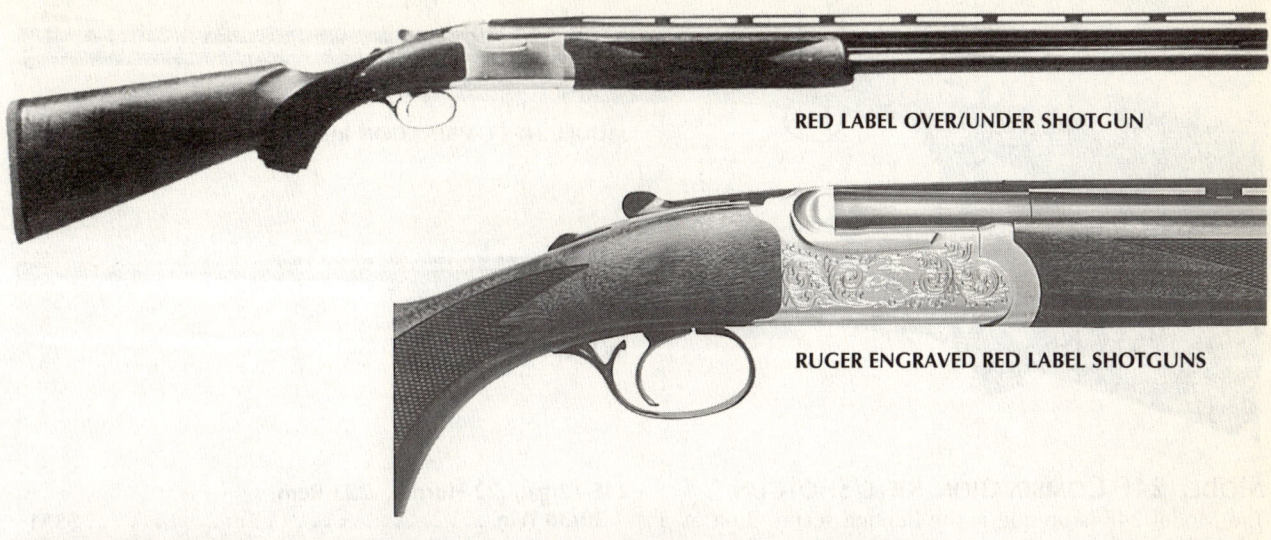

RED LABEL OVER/UNDER SHOTGUN

RUGER ENGRAVED RED LABEL SHOTGUNS

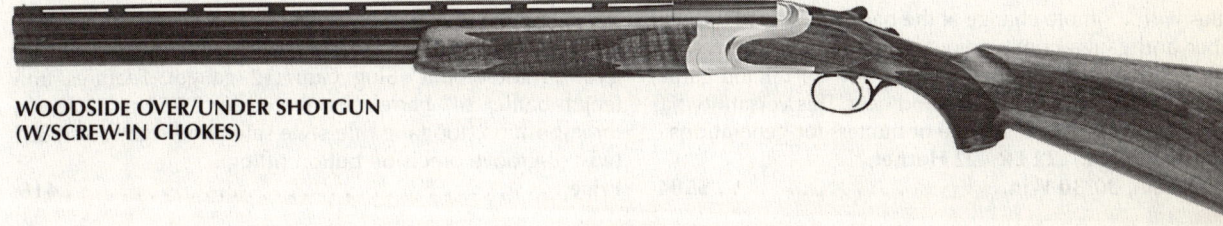

WOODSIDE OVER/UNDER SHOTGUN
(W/SCREW-IN CHOKES)

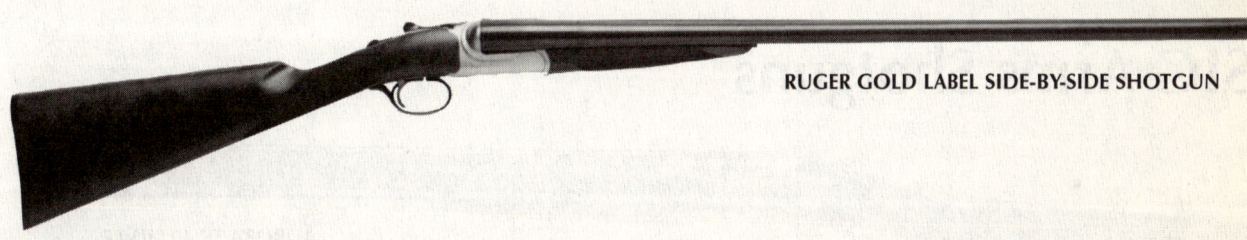

RUGER GOLD LABEL SIDE-BY-SIDE SHOTGUN

Ruger Red Label Over/Under Shotguns
Price:
12, 20, 28 ga. pistol or straight grip,
  26" – 28" barrel $1489
12 or 20 ga., 30" barrel 1545

Engraved Red Label
12 ga. all-weather synthetic stock,
  26" or 28" barrel 1650
12 ga., 30" barrel 1725
12, 20, 28 ga. w/ walnut stock, 26"– 28" barrel ... 1650
12 ga. w/ walnut stock, 30" barrel 1725

All-Weather Red Label
12 ga., 26" or 28" barrel 1489
12 ga., 30" barrel 1545

Ruger Woodside
12 ga., 26", 28", or 30" barrel, pistol
  or straight grip 1889

Ruger Trap Model
12 ga., 34" barrel and 2 3/4" chamber $2850

Ruger Gold Label Side-by-Side Shotgun
New for 2002!
Gauge: 12 gauge
Action: Round frame, box-lock, side-by-side
Stock: High-quality American walnut, straight or pistol grip, checkered 22 lines per inch. Splinter fore end, Anson push-rod release.
Weight: 6.5 lbs.
Barrel: 28" blued with skeet choke tubes
Sights: Gold bead front; full-length rib w/ serrated top surface
Chokes: Five interchangeable screw-in choke tubes
Finish: Polished stainless steel frame
Price: 1950

Savage Shotguns

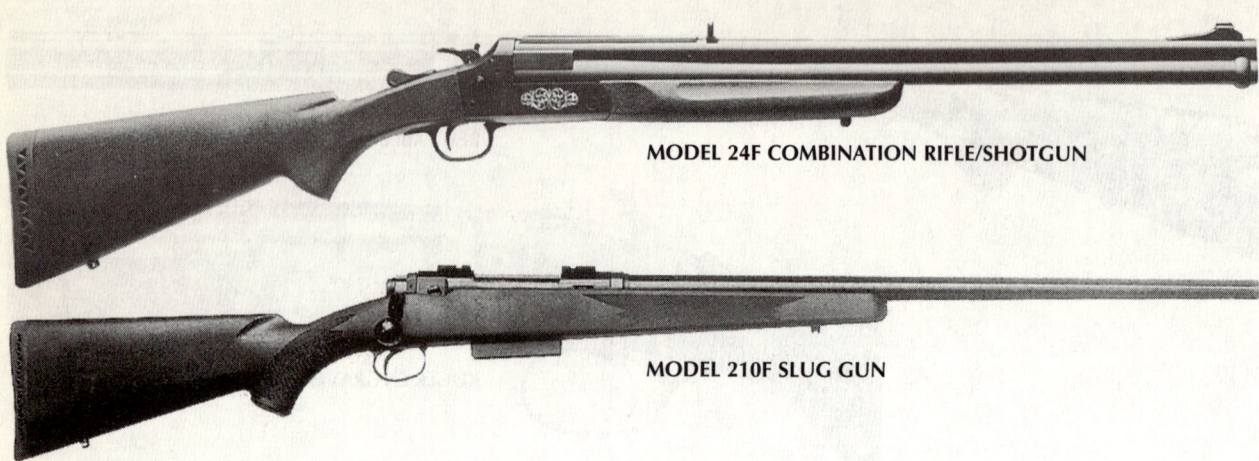

MODEL 24F COMBINATION RIFLE/SHOTGUN

MODEL 210F SLUG GUN

MODEL 24F COMBINATION RIFLE/SHOTGUN
The Model 24F is unique in the hunting scene. Built as a true combination gun, it combines rifle and shotgun capabilities with a simple change of the barrel selector. Different caliber and gauge combinations are available. The various 24F combination rifle/shotguns outfit you for upland game, turkeys, waterfowl, small game and deer. This versatility has made the Savage 24F a favorite of hunters for generations.
**Price: 24F-20 ga., .22 LR, .22 Hornet,
.223 Rem, 30/30 Win. $504**

24F-12 ga., .22 Hornet, .223 Rem,
30/30 Win. $531

MODEL 210F SLUG GUN
210F "Master Shot" Slug Gun (12 gauge). Features full-length baffle; 24" barrel chambered for 2.75" or 3" shells; three-position, top tang rifle-style safety; no sights; 1 in 35" twist (8-groove precision button rifling).
Price: 416

SIG Arms Shotguns

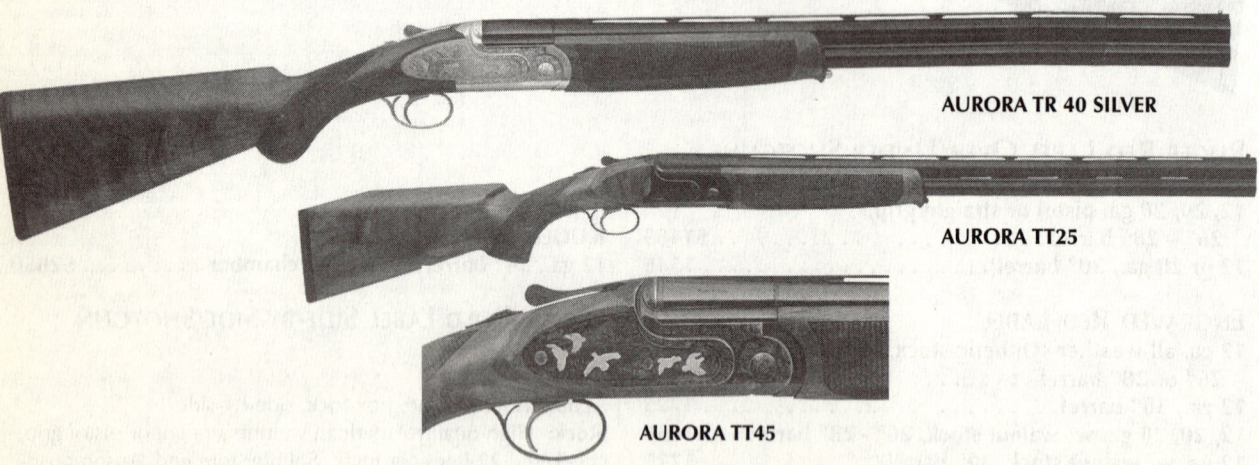

AURORA TR 40 SILVER

AURORA TT25

AURORA TT45

SIGARMS AURORA SHOTGUNS
The Aurora family of field and competition over-and-unders are available in a wide range of receiver styles. Competition TT25 models include Seminole choke tubes, specialty dimensioned stocks with palm swells and more. TT25s are available in 12 and 20 Gauge. TR Series field guns feature polished blued barrels and Prince of Wales pistol grips on oiled select walnut stocks. TR field models are available in 12, 20 and 28 Gauge and .410.
**Price: Aurora $1865
TT25: 1995
TT45: 2795
TR Series: . . . . from 1865 to 2675**

SKB Shotguns

MODEL 385 SIDE-BY-SIDE

MODEL 505

MODEL 385 SIDE-BY-SIDE
The Model 385 features silver nitride receiver with engraved scroll and game scene design; solid boxlock action w/double locking lugs; single selective trigger; selective automatic ejectors; automatic safety; sculpted American walnut stock; pistol or English straight grip; semi-beavertail forend; stock and forend finished w/18-line fine checkering; standard series choke tube system; solid rib w/flat matte finish and metal front bead. For additional specifications, see table below.
Price:.................................$2049
Field Set..............................2929

Also available:
Model 485 Series. Features engraved upland game scene; semi-fancy American walnut stock and beavertail forend; raised vent rib with flat matte finish.
Price:.................................$2769

MODEL 505
Prices:
Field...................................1189
Sporting Clays.........................1299
Sporting Clays, Ported................1429

NEW FOR 2002 85TSS TARGET SUPER SPORT
Prices:
Sporting Clay in 12, 20, 28...........1949
Sporting Clay in 410...................1999
with/adjustable comb..................2129
410 w/adjustable comb.................2179
Also available: Skeet or Trap Models

SPECIFICATIONS MODEL 385 & 485

FIELD MODELS

GAUGE	CHAMBER	BARREL LENGTH	OVERALL LENGTH	INTER CHOKE	SIGHTS✓	RIB WIDTH	STOCK	AVERAGE WEIGHT* 385	485
12	3"	28"	44 1/2"	STND-A	MFB	5/16"	PISTOL	7 lb. 3 oz.	7 lb. 1 oz.
12	3"	28"	44 1/2"	STND-A	MFB	5/16"	ENGLISH	7 lb. 1 oz.	7 lb. 5 oz.
12	3"	26"	42 1/2"	STND-A	MFB	5/16"	PISTOL	7 lb. 1 oz.	7 lb. 5 oz.
12	3"	26"	42 1/2"	STND-A	MFB	5/16"	ENGLISH	7 lb. 0 oz.	7 lb. 4 oz.
20	3"	26"	42 1/2"	STND-B	MFB	5/16"	PISTOL	6 lb. 10 oz.	6 lb. 14 oz.
20	3"	26"	42 1/2"	STND-B	MFB	5/16"	ENGLISH	6 lb. 10 oz.	6 lb. 14 oz.
28	2 3/4"	26"	42 1/2"	STND-B	MFB	5/16"	PISTOL	6 lb. 13 oz.	7 lb. 2 oz.
28	2 3/4"	26"	42 1/2"	STND-B	MFB	5/16"	ENGLISH	6 lb. 13 oz.	7 lb. 2 oz.

2 BARREL FIELD SETS

GAUGE	CHAMBER	BARREL LENGTH	OVERALL LENGTH	INTER CHOKE	SIGHTS✓	RIB WIDTH	STOCK	AVERAGE WEIGHT*
20	3"	26"	42 1/2"	STND-B	MFB	5/16"	PISTOL	6 lb. 10 oz.
28	2 3/4"	26"	42 1/2"	STND-B	MFB	5/16"	PISTOL	6 lb. 13 oz.
20	3"	26"	42 1/2"	STND-B	MFB	5/16"	ENGLISH	6 lb. 10 oz.
28	2 3/4"	26"	42 1/2"	STND-B	MFB	5/16"	ENGLISH	6 lb. 13 oz.

*Weights may vary due to wood density. Specifications may vary. *INTER-CHOKE SYSTEMS: COMP - Competition series includes Mod., Full, Imp. Cyl. STND-A - Standard series includes Mod., Full, Imp. Cyl. STND-B- Standard series includes Imp. Cyl., Mod. Skeet <u>STOCK DIMENSIONS:</u> Length of Pull - 14 1/8" Drop at Comb - 1 1/2" Drop at Heel - 2 3/4" ✓MFB-Metal Front Bead

505 FIELD OVER AND UNDERS

GAUGE	CHAMBER	BARREL LENGTH	OVERALL LENGTH	INTER CHOKE	SIGHTS✓	RIB WIDTH	AVERAGE WEIGHT*
12	3"	28"	45 3/8"	STND-A	MFB	3/8"	7 lb. 12 oz.
12	3"	26"	45 3/8"	STND-B	MFB	3/8"	7 lb. 11 oz.
20	3"	26" or 28"	45 3/8"	STND-B	MFB	3/8"	6 lb. 10 oz. (6 lb. 11 oz.)

505 SPORTING CLAYS

GAUGE	CHAMBER	BARREL LENGTH	OVERALL LENGTH	INTER CHOKE	SIGHTS	RIB WIDTH	AVERAGE WEIGHT* 505
12	3"	30"	47 3/8"	STND-B	CP/WFB	15/32" CH/STP	8 lb. 5 oz.
12	3"	28"	45 3/8"	STND-B	CP/WFB	15/32" CH/STP	8 lb. 1 oz.

*Weights may vary due to wood density. Specifications may vary. *INTER-CHOKE SYSTEMS: STND-A-Standard series includes Full, Mod, Imp. Cyl. STND-B-Standard series includes Imp. Cyl., Mod, Skeet <u>STOCK DIMENSIONS:</u> Length of Pull-14 1/8" Drop at Comb-1 1/2" Drop at heel-2 3/16" **MFB-Metal Front Bead**

SKB Shotguns
Model 585 and 785 Series

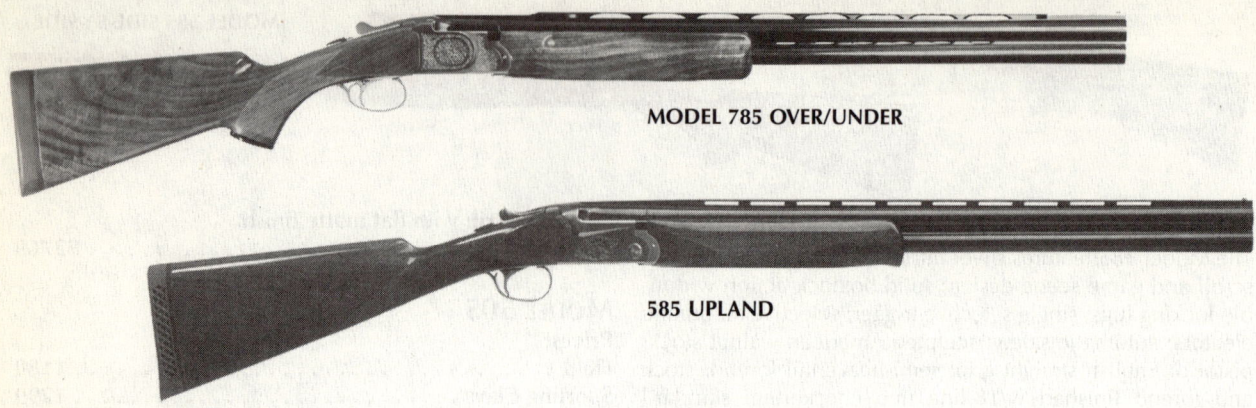

MODEL 785 OVER/UNDER

585 UPLAND

Model 785 Over/Under
The SKB 785 Series features chrome-lined chambers and bores, lengthened forcing cones, chrome-plated ejectors and competition choke tube system.

Prices
Field (12 & 20 ga.)	$2119
28 or .410 ga.	2199
Two-Barrel Field Set (12 & 20 ga.)	3079
20/28 ga. or 28/.410 ga	3179
Skeet (12 or 20 ga.)	2199
28 or .410 ga.	2239
2-Bbl. Set	4439
Sporting Clays (12 or 20 ga.)	2269
28 gauge	2349
2-Barrel Set (12 or 20 ga.)	3249
Trap (Monte Carlo or Std.)	2199
2-Barrel Trap Combo	3079

585 Upland
Prices MODEL 585 OVER/UNDER
Field (12 & 20 ga.)	$1499
28 or .410 ga.	1569
Youth/Ladies (12 & 20 ga.)	1499
Upland (12 & 20 ga.)	1499
28 ga.	1569
Field Set (12 & 20 ga.)	2399
20/28 + 28/410	2469
Sporting Clays (28" to 32" barrel)	
12 + 20 ga.	1679
28 ga.	1729
Sporting Clay Set	2419
Skeet (12 + 20 ga.)	1619
28 + .410 ga.	1679
Skeet set	3779
Trap (12 + 20 ga.)	1619
Combo	2419

Gauge	Barrel√ Length	Overall Length	Inter Choke	Sights√	785 Rib Width	585 Rib Width	Average Weight* 785	585
TRAP MODELS – STANDARD OR MONTE CARLO								
12	30"	47 3/8"	COMP-A	CP/WFB	15/32" CH/STP	3/8" STP	8 lb. 15 oz.	8 lb. 7 oz.
12	32"	49 3/8:	COMP-A	CP/WFB	15/32" CH/STP	3/8" STP	9 lb. 1 oz.	8 lb. 10 oz.
TRAP COMBOS – STANDARD OR MONTE CARLO								
12	O/U-30"	47 3/8"	COMP.	CP/WFB	15/32" CH/STP	3/8" STP	8 lb. 15 oz.	8 lb. 6 oz.
12	S/O-32"	49 3/8"	COMP.	CP/WFB	15/32" CH/STP	3/8" STP	9 lb. 0 oz.	8 lb. 6 oz.
12	O/U-30"	47 3/8"	COMP.	CP/WFB	15/32" CH/STP	3/8"STP	9 lb. 0 oz.	8 lb. 4 oz.
12	S/O-34"	51 3/8"	COMP.	CP/WFB	15/32" CH/STP	3/8"STP	9 lb. 1 oz.	8 lb. 6 oz.
12	O/U-32"	49 3/8"	COMP.	CP/WFB	15/32" CH/STP	3/8" STP	9 lb. 0 oz.	8 lb. 7 oz.
12	S/O-34"	51 3/8"	COMP.	CP/WFB	15/32" CH/STP	3/8" STP	9 lb. 1 oz.	8 lb. 8 oz.
YOUTH & LADIES								
12	28"	44 1/2"	COMP.	MFB		3/8"		7 lb. 11 oz.
12	26"	42 1/2"	COMP.	MFB		3/8"		7 lb. 9 oz.
20	26"	42 1/2"	STND-B	MFB		3/8"		6 lb. 7 oz.
SKEET MODELS								
12	30"	47 1/4"	COMP.	CP/WFB		3/8"	8 lb. 9 oz.	8 lb. 1 oz.
12	28"	45 1/4"	COMP.	CP/WFB		3/8"	8 lb. 6 oz.	7 lb. 12 oz.
20	28"	45 1/4"	STND.	CP/WFB		5/16"	7 lb. 2 oz.	6 lb. 15 oz.
28	28"	45 1/4"	STND.	CP/WFB		5/16"	7 lb. 5 oz.	6 lb. 15 oz.
410	28"	45 1/4"	SK/SK	CP/WFB		5/16"	7 lb. 5 oz.	7 lb. 0 oz.

*Weights may vary due to wood density. Specifications may vary. *INTER-CHOKE SYSTEMS: COMP. - Competition series includes 2 -SKI/SCI, 1-Mod/SCIV STND - Standard series includes Skeet, Skeet and Imp. Cyl. NOTE: 785's Are Equipped with Step-Up Style Ribs STOCK DIMENSIONS: Length of Pull - 14 1/8" Drop at Comb - 1 1/2" Drop at Heel - 2 3/16" √CP/WFB - Center Post/White Front Bead

Stoeger Shotguns
Side-by-Sides

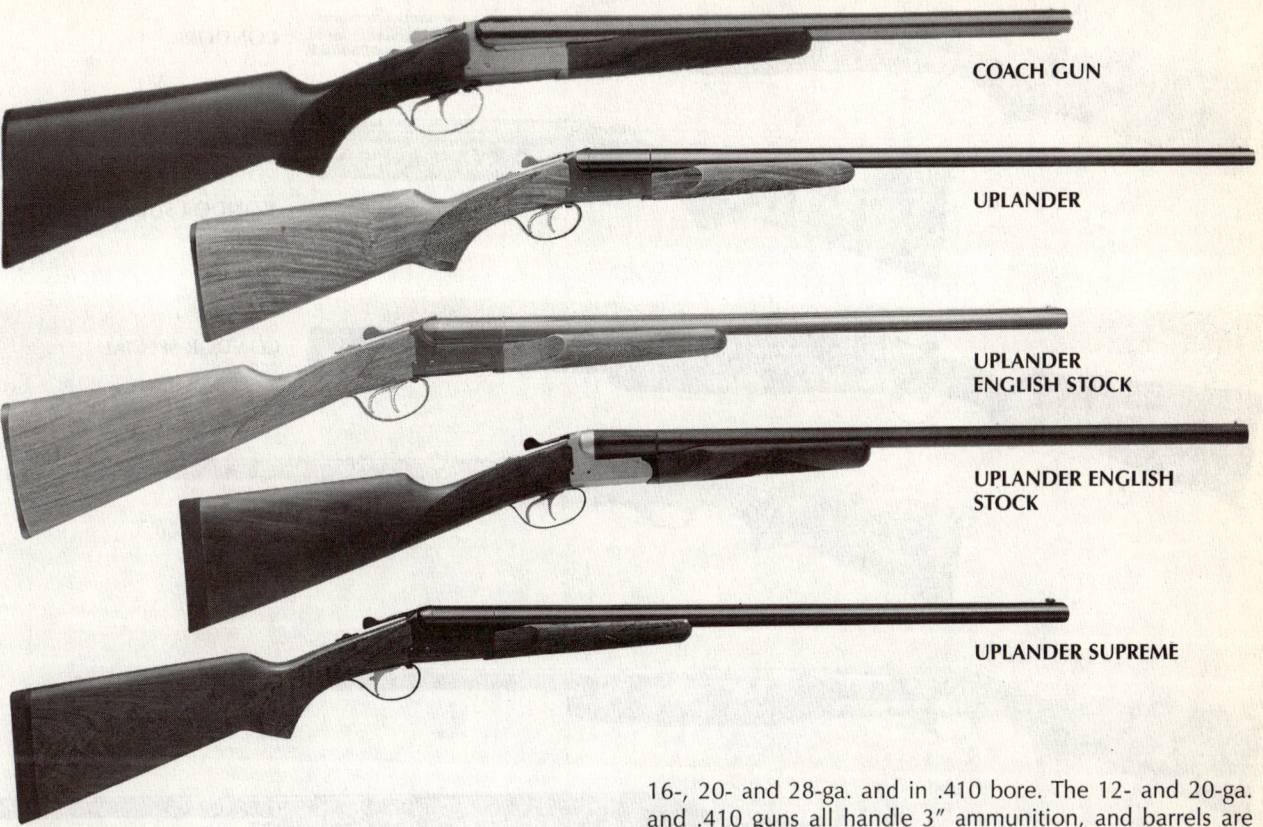

COACH GUN

UPLANDER

UPLANDER ENGLISH STOCK

UPLANDER ENGLISH STOCK

UPLANDER SUPREME

COACH GUN

The Stoeger Coach Gun sports a 20-inch barrel. Two massive underlugs provide a super-safe, vise-tight locking system for lasting strength and durability. The mechanical extraction of spent shells and double-trigger mechanism assures reliability. The automatic safety is actuated whenever the action is opened, whether or not the gun has been fired. The polish and blue is deep and rich, and the solid sighting rib is matte-finished for glare-free sighting. Chrome-moly steel barrels with micro-polished bores give dense, consistent patterns. Nickel finish and matte nickel finish are now available. The classic stock and forend are of durable hardwood, oil-finished, hand-rubbed and hand-checkered.

Improved Cylinder/Modified choking and its short barrel make the Coach gun the ideal choice for hunting in close quarters, security and police work. 3-inch chambers.

Prices:
In 12 and 20 Gauge or .410 Bore............ $310
Nickel 365
Silverado 365
Silverado w/ English stock 365

UPLANDER

American hunters have trusted the reliable side-by-side shotgun for more than 100 years, and the Stoeger Uplander carries on the tradition of sturdy double-trigger arms a hunter can count on. The safety is reset automatically anytime the gun is opened. The Uplander is available in 12-, 16-, 20- and 28-ga. and in .410 bore. The 12- and 20-ga. and .410 guns all handle 3" ammunition, and barrels are proofed for steel shot. The 12- and 20-ga. models are available with recessed interchangeable choke tubes.

Prices:
In 12, 16, 20, 28 and .410 Gauge $325
In 12, 20 w/Choke Tubes 345
Also available with English stock and in 20 ga
  w/choke tubes and in .410 w/fixed modified
  chokes 325 (.410) 345

UPLANDER SUPREME

The Supreme is a refinement of the Uplander, with a single selective trigger, automatic ejectors, interchangeable choke tubes and a cut-checkered American walnut stock. Gold trigger, red front and middle beads and a soft rubber recoil pad round out the features of a gun that offers an unusual combination of features and low price. It is available only in 12- and 20-ga.

Price: $435
Uplander Short Stock
  20 ga. & .410 with 24" stock 325

SINGLE BARREL SHOTGUNS

Completely redesigned for 2002! The Stoeger Single Barrel Shotgun features include a transfer bar and cross-bolt safety, screw-in chokes on 12 and 20 ga, and a break-open design operated by the trigger guard. Available in 12, 20 and 410 ga.

Price: $109
Youth model with English stock, 20 or 410 ga. 109

Stoeger Shotguns

CONDOR

CONDOR SUPREME DELUXE

CONDOR SPECIAL

MODEL 2000

MODEL 2000 DELUXE

MODEL 2000 ADVANTAGE

Condor
The Stoeger Condor brings the advantages of the over-under to the shotgunner on a budget. Features include a single trigger and mechanical extractors. Recessed choke tubes (improved cylinder and modified) give the Condor flexibility. Both 12-ga. and 20-ga. versions handle 3" ammunition and steel shot. Stock and fore-end are made from Brazilian hardwood and have a hand-rubbed oil finish.
Price: $390

Condor Supreme Deluxe
The Supreme Deluxe Condor features a cut-checkered American walnut stock with soft rubber recoil pad and high-luster bluing on the barrels. The stepped ventilated rib is fitted with red front and center beads. A single selective trigger and automatic ejectors distinguish this shotgun from the standard model.
Price: 490

NEW Condor Special
The Condor Special offers all the features of the field-grade Condor, plus a matte nickel receiver and a rubbed-oil finish.
Price: 12 and 20 ga. 430

Model 2000
Stoeger Model 2000 shotguns offer an unusual combination of efficient design and old-world craftsmanship.

The heart of the gun is an inertia-recoil operating system that offers great reliability. There's no gas system to clean; the vital parts are all inside the receiver.

All guns are fitted with ventilated ribs and eye-catching white bar front sights for fast target acquisition. Ventilated rubber recoil pads help dampen the already mild recoil.

While the Model 2000 has a checkered American walnut stock and matte finished receiver, the Model 2000 Deluxe adds high grade American walnut to a floral-etched receiver with gold-colored trigger. A vent rib gives the 2000 Deluxe an immediately recognizable profile.

New for 2002, The Model 2000 is also available with a black synthetic or camo stock.

The Model 2000 is available in 12 gauge with 2.75" and 3" chambers and set of fine screw-in chokes. **Barrel length:** 24", 26", 28", 30"
Price: $499
 Deluxe (26" or 28" barrel only) 620
 Synthtic 480
Advantage Timber HD Camo 550

Weatherby Shotguns

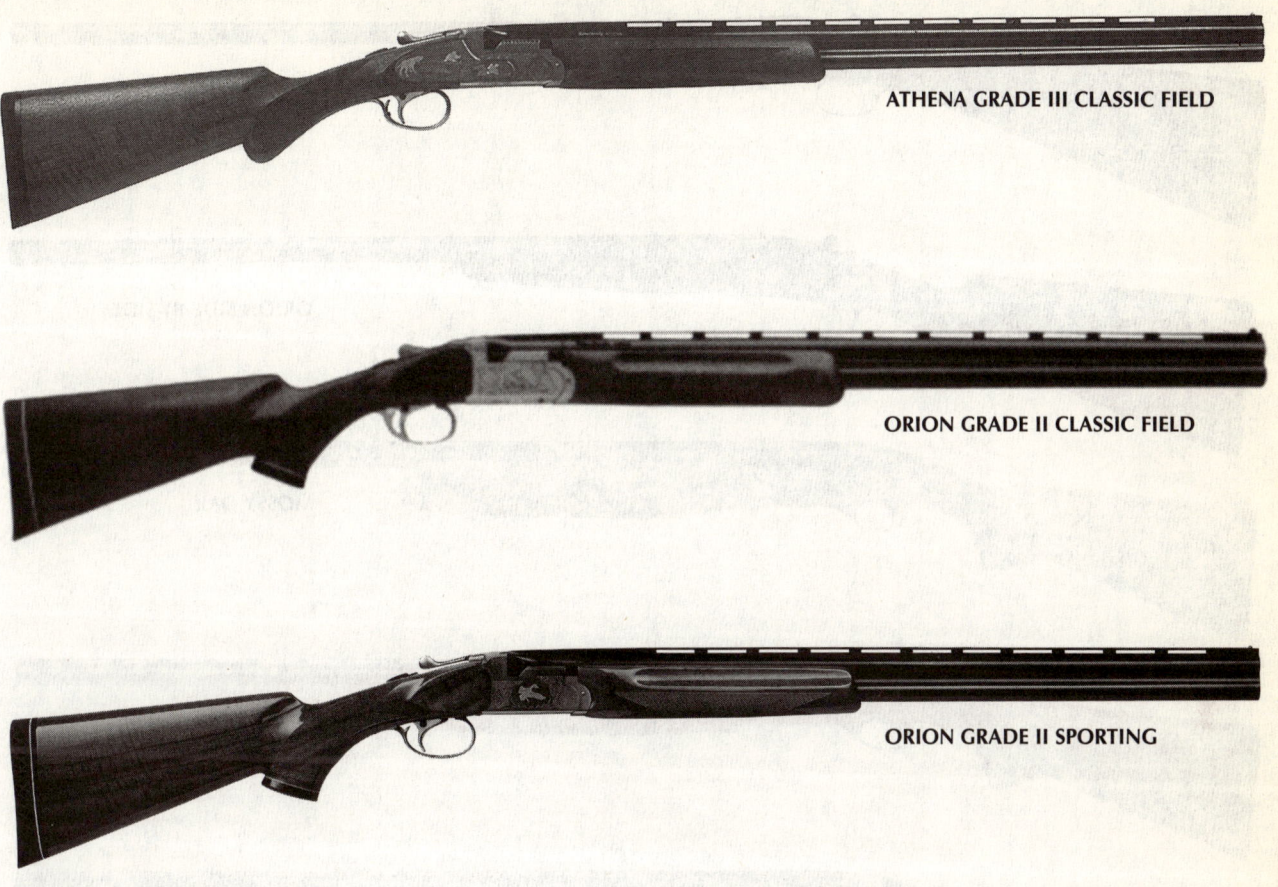

ATHENA GRADE III CLASSIC FIELD

ORION GRADE II CLASSIC FIELD

ORION GRADE II SPORTING

ATENA GRADES III, IV, V
The Athena features a boxlock action and sidelock-type plates with fine floral engraving. The hinge pivots are made of high-strength steel alloy. The locking system employs the Greener crossbolt design. The single selective trigger is mechanically operated, allowing the second barrel to be fired on a subsequent trigger pull, even after a misfire. The selector lever enables you to fire the lower barrel or upper barrel first.

The breech block is hand-fitted to the receiver. Every Athena is equipped with a matted, ventilated rib and bead front sight. Ejectors are fully automatic. The safety is a slide type located on the upper tang atop the pistol grip. Each stock is carved from Claro walnut, with fine-line hand-checkering and oil finish. (Athena II has high-luster finish.)
Grade III, 12, 20, 28 ga.
Grade IV + V, 12 or 20 ga.
Prices:
Athena Grade III $2131
Athena Grade IV 2549
Athena Grade V 2977

ORION GRADES I, II & III OVER/UNDERS
For greater versatility, the Orion incorporates the integral multichoke (IMC) system. Available in Extra-full, Full, Modified, Improved Modified, Improved Cylinder and Skeet, the choke tubes fit flush with the muzzle. Three tubes are furnished with each gun. The precision hand-fitted monobloc and receiver are machined from high-strength steel with a highly polished finish. Pistol grip stock and forearm are carved of Claro walnut with hand-checkered diamond inlay pattern and high-gloss finish. Chrome-moly steel barrels and the receiver are deeply blued. The Orion also features selective automatic ejectors, single selective trigger, front bead sight and ventilated rib.
Weight: 12 ga. Field, 7 1/2 lbs.; 20 ga. Field,
  7 1/2 lbs.; Trap, 8 lbs.
Prices:
Upland (12 or 20 ga.) $1274
Grade I (12 or 20 Gauge) 1539
Grade II (12, 20, 28 ga.) 1559
Sporting Clays (12 ga.)
  Sporting and Field Sporting 1753
  Super Sporting 2019
Grade III
  IMC Multi-Choke, Field, 12 or 20 Gauge 1917
  Classic Field 1917
  English Field 1998

Weatherby Shotguns

ATHENA SIDE-BY-SIDE

ORION SIDE-BY-SIDE

MOSSY OAK

FIELD

SHADOW GRASS

ATHENA
Specifications
Gauge: 12 or 20 ga., 3" chamber
Stock: Hand-rubbed Turkish walnut stock with fine 22 LPI checkering. Long tang triggerguard with traditional straight grip and splintered forearm.
Other features: Color case-hardened receiver and false sideplates with intricate rose and scrollengraving.
Price:.................................$1549

ORION
Similar to the Athena, with 18 LPI checkering and a half-round pistol grip and semi-beavertail forearm. Available in 12, 20, 28, and .410 with 26" and 28" barrels.
Price:.................................1099

WEATHERBY SAS SEMI-AUTOMATIC SHOTGUN
Weatherby's SAS autoloader is available in 12 gauge with 26-28- and 30-inch vent rib barrels. To allow a wide range of shot patterns, it comes with the Weatherby Integral Multi-Choke (IMC) system, including five interchangeable Briley stainless steel screw-in choke tubes: skeet, improved cylinder, modified, improved modified and full. The self-compensating gas mechanism accommodates light and heavy loads, including 3" magnums. A magazine cutoff makes load changes a snap. The Claro walnut stock is carefully checkered and satin-finished. Synthetic stocks come in black, "Mossy Oak Break-Up" and "Shadow Grass".
Weight: 6.8 to 7.8 lbs.
Prices:
Field..................................$799
Synthetic.............................749
Camo patterns.........................849
Sporting Clays........................899

Winchester Shotguns

NEW SUPER X2 UNIVERSAL HUNTER

NEW SUPER X2 PRACTICAL MK II

SUPER X2 SPORTING CLAYS 3"

SUPER X2 TURKEY 3.5"

SUPER X2 SPORTING CLAYS 3"
The SX2 Sporting is a hard-working, specialized shotgun with the extra features competitors need, like a specially designed adjustable sporting buttstock and a full selection of sporting choke tubes. Its two supplied gas pistons cover the full range of factory sporting ammo at its extremes with exceptional reliability.

SUPER X2 TURKEY 3.5"
The Super X2 Magnum 3 1/2" Turkey version has all the handling advantages of the Super X2 design. Like a 24" barrel combined with the short receiver. The back-bored barrel fitted with an extra-full extended choke tube offers extreme pattern density. And the standard 3-dot TRUGLO® fiber optic sights offer an advantage, with more precise shot placement in early morning low-light conditions. And the gas-operated action reduces the kick of recoil.

SUPER X2 SHOTGUNS

Item Number	Gauge	Barrel Length & Type	Chamber	Choke(s)	Overall Length	Nominal Length Of Pull	Nominal Drop At Comb	Nominal Drop At Heel	Nominal Weight (Lbs.)	Suggested Retail
3-1/2" MAGNUM										
Universal Hunter (Composite Stock, Mossy Oak Break-Up)										
511028266 **NEW**	12	26	3-1/2 Mag.	Invector+XF	47"	14-1/4	1-3/4	2	7.75	$1116
3-1/2" Magnum Greenhead (Soft Touch, Composite Stock)										
511029246 **NEW**	12	28"	3-1/2" Mag.	Invector+(3)	49"	14-1/4"	1-3/4"	2"	8	1116
3-1/2" Magnum (Black Composite Stock)										
511001250	12	26"	3-1/2" Mag.	Invector+(3)	47"	14-1/4"	1-3/4"	2"	7.75	936
511001246	12	28"	3-1/2" Mag.	Invector+(3)	49"	14-1/4"	1-3/4"	2"	8	936
3-1/2" NWTF Turkey (Black Composite Stock)										
511022257	12	24"	3-1/2" Mag	Invector+XF	45"	14-1/4"	1-3/4"	2"	7.5	1018
3-1/2" NWTF Turkey (Composite Stock, Mossy Oak Break-Up)										
511021257	12	24"	3-1/2" Mag	Invector+XF	45"	14-1/4"	1-3/4"	2"	7.5	1101
3-1/2" Camo Waterfowl (Composite Stock, Mossy Oak Shadow Grass)										
511003246	12	28"	3-1/2" Mag	Invector+(3)	49"	14-1/4"	1-3/4"	2"	8	1080
3" MODELS										
3" Magnum Practical MK II (Black Composite Stock, 8 round Magazine)										
511015355 **NEW**	12	22"	3" Mag.	Cyl Std Inv	43"	14-1/4"	1-3/4"	2"	8	1065
3" Sporting Clays (Walnut Stock)										
511006446	12	28"	3" Mag.	Invector+(SC)	49"	14-3/8"	1-3/4"	2"	8	921
511006445	12	30"	3" Mag.	Invector+(SC)	51	14-3/8"	1-3/4"	2"	8.25	921
3" Magnum Field (Walnut Stock)										
511004350	12	26"	3" Mag.	Invector+(3)	47"	14-1/4"	1-3/4"	2"	7.25	819
511004346	12	28"	3" Mag.	Invector+(3)	49	14-1/4"	1-3/4"	2	7.5	819
3" Magnum (Black Composite Stock)										
511001350	12	26"	3" Mag.	Invector+(3)	47"	14-1/4"	1-3/4"	2"	7.75	819
511001346	12	28"	3" Mag.	Invector+(3)	49"	14-1/4	1-3/4	2"	8	819
3" Magnum Rifled Deer with Cantilever (Black Composite Stock)										
511030340 **NEW**	12	22"	3" Mag.	Rifled Barrel	43"	14-1/4"	1-3/4"	2"	7.25	862

SHOTGUNS

Winchester Shotguns

NEW MODEL 1300 UNIVERSAL HUNTER

MODEL 1300 RANGER
12 GAUGE DEER COMBO

MODEL 1300 RANGER LADIES/YOUTH
PUMP-ACTION SHOTGUN

MODEL 1300 SHOTGUNS

Item Number	Ga.	Barrel Length & Type	Chamber	Chokes	Overall Length	Nominal Length of Pull	Nominal Drop at Comb	Nominal Drop at Heel	Nominal Weight (Lbs)	U.S. Sugg. Retail
SPORTING/FIELD MODELS										
Sporting/Field (Walnut Stock)										
512906369 NEW	12	28"VR	3" Mag.	W5W	49"	14"	1-1/2"	2-1/2"	7.5	$426
Compact Sporting/Field (Walnut Stock)										
512905367 NEW	12	24"VR	3" Mag.	W5W	44"	13"	1-1/2"	2-3/8"	7.5	426
FIELD MODELS										
Upland Special Field (Walnut Stock)										
512050352	12	24"VR	3" Mag.	W3	45"	14"	1-1/2"	2-1/2"	6.75	405
512050641	20	24"VR	3" Mag.	W3	45"	14"	1-1/2"	2-1/2"	6.75	405
Walnut Field										
512034329	12	28"VR	3" Mag	W3	49"	14"	1-1/2"	2-1/2"	7.375	405
512034330	12	26"VR	3" Mag	W3	47"	14"	1-1/2"	2-1/2"	7.125	405
Black Shadow® (Composite Stock)										
512041303	12	28"VR	3" Mag	W1M	49"	13-3/4"	1-1/2"	2-1/2"	7.25	343
512041307	12	26"VR	3" Mag	W1M	47"	13-3/4"	1-1/2"	2-1/2"	7	343
512041607	20	26"VR	3" Mag	W1M	47"	13-3/4"	1-1/2"	2-1/2"	6.875	343
RANGER MODELS										
Ranger® (Hardwood Stock)										
512035239	12	28"VR	3"Mag	W3	49"	14"	1-1/2"	2-1/2"	7.375	357
512035629	20	28"VR	3"Mag	W3	49"	14"	1-1/2"	2-1/2"	7.125	357
Ranger® Compact (Hardwood Stock)										
512036352	12	24"VR	3"Mag	W3	44"	13"	1-1/2"	2-3/8"	7	356
512036631	20	24"VR	3"Mag	W3	42"	13"	1-1/2"	2-3/8"	6.625	356
TURKEY & UNIVERSAL HUNTER MODELS										
Universal Hunter (Composite, Mossy Oak® Break-Up)™										
512904366 NEW	12	26"VR	3"Mag	HDXF,W3	47"	13-3/4"	1-1/2"	2-1/2"	7	550
NWTF Buck & Tom (Composite, Mossy Oak® Break-Up)™										
512903365 NEW	12	22"Smooth	3"Mag	RS/HDXF	43"	14"	1-1/2"	2-1/2"	6.75	525
NWTF Short Turkey (Composite, Mossy Oak® Break-Up)™										
512902342 NEW	12	18"	3"Mag	WXLX	40"	14"	1-1/2"	2-1/2"	6.5	489
DEER MODELS										
Deer Black Shadow® (Composite Stock)										
512040320	12	22"Smooth	3"Mag	W1C	43"	14"	1-1/2"	2-1/2"	6.75	341
512040315	12	22"Rifled	3"Mag	Rifled Barrel	42-3/4"	14"	1-1/2"	2-1/2"	6.75	366
512040615	20	22"Rifled	3"Mag	Rifled Barrel	42-3/4"	14"	1-1/2"	2-1/2"	6.5	366
Deer Black Shadow® Cantilever (Composite Stock)										
512040340	12	22"Rifled	3"Mag	Rifled Barrel	42-3/4"	14"	1-1/2"	2-3/4"	7	409
Deer Black Shadow® Combo (Composite Stock)										
512042326	12	22"Rifled	3"Mag	Rifled Barrel	42-3/4"	14"	1-1/2"	2-1/2"	6.75	442
	12	28"VR	3"Mag	W3	49"	14"	1-1/2"	2-1/2"	7.375	
Deer Ranger® Compact (Hardwood Stock)										
512036615	20	22"Rifled	3"Mag	Rifled Barrel	42-3/4"	13"	1-1/2"	2-1/2"	6.625	377

Winchester Shotguns

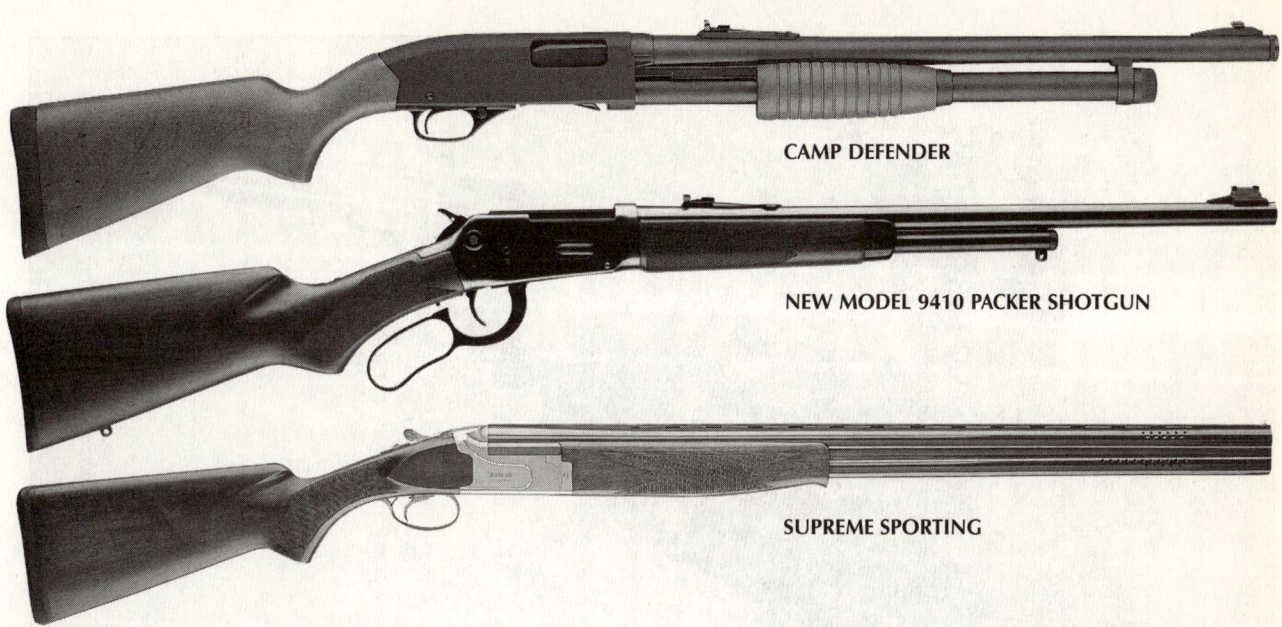

CAMP DEFENDER

NEW MODEL 9410 PACKER SHOTGUN

SUPREME SPORTING

Model 1300 Camp Defender
The new Camp Defender is a multi-purpose camp gun for the occasional grouse around camp, family protection, or even as a quick handling slug gun at the end of a deer drive. Features a rugged, dark-stained hardwood stock. Fitted with fully adjustable open sights. Eight shot total capacity 22" barrel. Interchangeable WinChoke system for versatile buckshot, birdshot or slug performance.

Lever Action New Model 9410 Shotgun
At first glance it looks like a Model 94 rifle. But it's a shotgun inside: fitted with a smoothbore 24" barrel and chambered to handle all current factory 2-1/2" .410 bore shotgun loads, including Foster-type rifled slugs. With a variety of shotshells and slugs available today, the Model 9410 may be the most versatile combination gun ever. The unique sight system features an easy-to-align TRUGLO front sight combined with a modified shallow "V" adjustable rear sight. The rear sight offers a clearer field of view for fast, shotgun-style shooting. The walnut straight-grip stock and traditional forearm ensures fast handling and pointability. The tubular magazine provides 9 shots at the ready.

Price: **$553**
Also Available:
New 9410 Packer Shotgun w/ 20" barrel **574**

Winchester Supreme O/U Shotgun
Tapered locking lugs between the barrels reduce the bulk of this over/under without sacrificing strength. Back-bored barrels with Invector Plus chokes ensure uniform patterns. Chromed chambers, vent rib, checkered walnut stock are standard. Choose from Field or Sporting Models, both with barrel selector on the safety. Field Model is bored for 3" shells; sporting model has a competition trigger, ported barrels.

Prices:
Field **1383**
Sporting **1551**

SPECIFICATIONS MODEL 1300 DEFENDER

Suggested Retail	Gauge	Barrel Length & Type	Chamber	Shotshell Capacity*	Choke	Overall Length	Nominal Length of Pull	Nominal Drop at Comb	Nominal Drop at Heel	Nominal Weight (Lbs.)	Features
SYNTHETIC PISTOL GRIP, 8 SHOT											
$333	12	18	3" Mag.	8	Cyl.	29-1/8	—	—	—	5-1/2	Studs, MBF
SYNTHETIC STOCK, 8 SHOT											
$333	12	18	3" MAG.	8	Cyl..	39-1/2	14	1-1/2	2-1/2	6-3/8	Studs, Truglo
333	20	18	3" MAG.	8	Cyl.	39-1/2	14	1-1/2	2-1/2	6-1/4	Studs, Truglo
COASTAL MARINE SYNTHETIC STOCK, NICKEL PLATE, TRUGLO SIGHTS											
$518	12	18	3" Mag.	7	Cyl.	39-1/2	14	1-1/2	2-1/2	6-1/2	Studs, MBF
CAMP DEFENDER											
$380	12	22	3" Mag.	8	W/C.	42-3/4	14	1-1/2	2-1/2	6-7/8	Studs, Rifle Sights

Model 1300 Feature Abbreviations: MBF=Metal bead front, Rifle=Rifle type front and rear sights. Rifle sights=Adjustable rear sight and ramp style front sight. SB=Scope Bases Included. B&R=Scope, Bases and Rings included. D&T=Drilled and tapped to accept scope bases. Studs=Buttstock and magazine cap sling studs provided VR=Ventilated rib. W3W=WinChoke, Extra Full, Full and Modified Tubes. W3=WinChoke, Full, Modified and Improved Cylinder Tubes. Cyl.=Non-WinChoke, choked Cylinder Bore. WIM=Modified Tube. WIC=Cylinder Choke Tube. WF=Full Choke Tube. WXF=Extra Full Choke Tube. Smooth=Non-Rifled Bore.

HANDGUNS

279	American Derringer	308	Israel Arms & Firearms International
279	Auto-Ordnance		
280	Beretta	309	Kahr
285	Bersa	309	KBI
285	Bond Arms	310	Kel-Tec
286	Ed Brown	311	Kimber
287	Browning	313	Llama
288	Charles Daly	314	Magnum Research
289	Cimarron	315	MOA
290	Colt	316	Navy Arms Replicas
292	CZ	317	North American Arms
294	Downsizer	318	Para-Ordnance
294	EMF/Dakota	320	Rossi
295	Entreprise	321	Ruger
296	European American Armory	328	Safari Arms
298	FireStorm	329	Savage Arms
299	Freedom Arms	330	SIG Arms
300	Glock	332	Smith & Wesson
302	Hämmerli	342	Springfield
303	Heckler & Koch	343	Taurus
305	Heritage	348	Thompson/Center
305	High Standard	349	Uberti Replicas
307	Hi-Point Firearms	350	Walther
308	H-S Precision	350	Wildey

American Derringer Pistols

MODEL 4 STAINLESS STEEL DOUBLE DERRINGER
Specifications
Calibers: 45 Colt and 3" .410 **Capacity:** 2 shots
Barrel Length: 4.1" **Overall Length:** 6" **Weight:** 16.5 oz.
Finish: Satin or high-polish stainless steel
Price: $450
Also available:
In 357 Mag. 435
   357 Maximum 440
In 45-70, both barrels 585
In 44 Mag. w/oversized grips 540
   45 Colt 435
   45 Automatic 440
Model M-4 Alaskan Survival
   in 45-70/45-.410, 45-70/45 Colt 500
Lady Derringer (Stainless Steel Double)
38 Special 385
32 Mag. 400
357 Mag. 430
45 Colt, 45/410 460

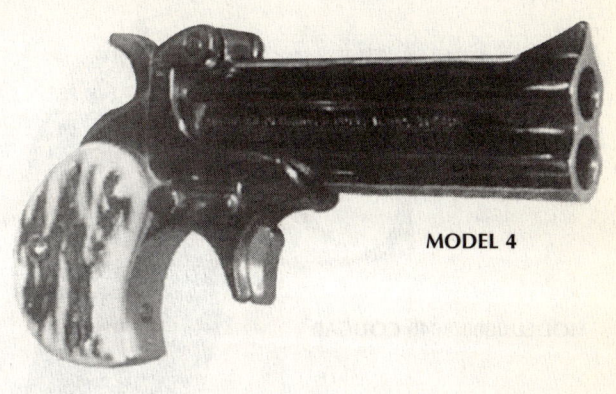

MODEL 4

Auto-Ordnance Pistols

AUTO-ORDNANCE 1911A1 "STANDARD"
Specifications
Model T1911
Caliber: .45 ACP
Barrel: 5"
Length: 8.5" overall
Weight: 39 oz.
Sights: Blade front, rear drift adj. for windage
Grip: Brown checkered plastic with medallion
Mag. Capacity: 7-shot
Price: $511
Also available:
Mid size "standard" with 4.25" barrel. 511
WWII Parkerized version 515

AUTO-ORDNANCE 1911A1 "DELUXE"
Specifications
Model 1911WGS
Caliber: .45 ACP
Barrel: 5"
Length: 8.5" overall
Weight: 39 oz.
Sights: Hi-profile 3 white dot system
Grip: Black textured, rubber wrap-around with medallion
Mag. Capacity: 7-shot
Prices: 525

T1911

1911WGS

• All models have a one year warranty

Beretta Pistols
Compact Frame Cougar Pistols

MODEL 8000/8040 COUGAR

MODEL 8040 MINI-COUGAR

COUGAR SERIES
Beretta's 8000/8040/8045 Cougar Series semiautomatics use a proven locked-breech system with a rotating barrel. This design makes the pistol compact and easy to conceal chamberings: 9mm, 40 cal. and 45 ACP cal. ammunition. When the pistol is fired, the initial thrust of recoil energy is partially absorbed as it pushes slide and barrel back, with the barrel rotating by cam action against a tooth on the rigid central block. When the barrel has turned 30 degrees, the locking lugs on the barrel clear the locking recesses, freeing the slide to continue rearward. The recoil spring absorbs the remaining recoil energy as the slide extracts and ejects the spent casing, rotates the hammer, and then reverses direction to chamber the next round. The Cougar reduces felt recoil by channeling part of the recoil energy into barrel rotation and by partially absorbing the barrel and slide recoil shock through the central block before it is transferred to the frame.

MODEL 8000/8040 COUGAR
Specifications
Calibers: 9mm, 40 S&W, 45 ACP
Capacity: 10 rounds (8 rounds in 45 ACP)
Action: Double/Single or Double Action only
Barrel length: 3.6"
Overall length: 7"
Weight: 32.6 oz.
Overall height: 5.5"
Sight radius: 5.2"
Sights: Front and rear sights dovetailed to slide
Finish: Bruniton/Plastic
Features: Firing-pin block; chrome-lined barrel; short recoil, rotating barrel; anodized aluminum alloy frame
Prices:
Double or Single action (9mm and 40 cal.) $709
Double action only (45 ACP) 739
Double or Single action (45 ACP) 764
Also Available:
  8357 Cougar F, 357 Sig Double or Single Action . . . 709

MODEL 8000/8040/8045 MINI-COUGAR
Specifications
Caliber: 9mm and 40 S&W, 45 ACP
Capacity: 8 rounds
Action: Double/Single or Double Action only
Barrel length: 3.6"
Weight: 27.6 oz. (9mm); 27.4 oz. (40 S&W)
Features: One inch shorter in the grip than the standard Cougar
Prices:
Double or Single actions (9mm & 40 cal.) 709
Double action only (45 ACP) 739
Double or single action (45 ACP) 739

Beretta Pistols

Beretta Elite Pistols

The Elite pistols were developed to meet the specific requirements of action shooting, personal defense, and law enforcement agencies. Elite pistols feature the recontoured slide and removable front sight of the Brigadier. The barrel is stainless steel, and slightly shorter (4.7") for compactness. The beveled magazine well facilitates rapid reloading while the rubber magazine base protects the magazine if it is dropped. Front and rear side serrations provide a sure grip for fast, easy racking of the slide, and the skeletonized hammer reduces lock time. The lanyard loop has no ring. Beretta Elite models are available only in the G configuration. The G models differ from FS models in that the hammer drop lever does not function as a traditional safety. When the lever is released, after having been activated to lower the hammer, it automatically returns to the ready-to-fire position. The Elite II has stainless slide and barrel, front and backstrap checkering, low profile Novak sights.

92G, 96G ELITE

Prices:
92G Elite (9mm)............................$812
96G Elite (40 S+W)...........................812
92G Elite II (9mm)............................912
96G Elite II (40 S+W)..........................912

Beretta 9000s Series

The new compact Beretta 9000S pistols are distinguished by their light weight and potent calibers (9mm and .40 S & W), making them comfortable and practical carry guns. The high magazine capacity (12 rounds in 9 mm, 10 rounds in .40 S & W) makes the 9000S pistols ideally suited for personal defense and the law enforcement profession.

The frame is manufactured with a fiberglass reinforced techno-polymer incorporating two special steel alloy rail inserts that guarantee perfect slide-to-frame fit and the optimal tilt barrel movement during the locking and unlocking phases. The innovative locking system consists of a unique tilt-barrel, open-slide design. The two strong barrel locking lugs engage the slide directly.

9000S TYPE F

The grips are made of a high-tech soft polymer, overmolded onto the frame. This durable and wear-resistant material absorbs vibrations and ensures a firm grip even in adverse weather conditions.

All 9000S models feature an automatic firing pin block that prevents the gun from firing in case of inadvertent drops or strikes against hard surfaces. It is deactivated only when the trigger is pulled back.

The type F models come in double or single action, while the type D is only available in double action.

Prices:
9000S Type D, 9mm or 40 S&W................551
9000S Type F, 9mm or 40 S&W.................551

Beretta Pistols
Small Frame Pistols

MODEL 3032 TOMCAT

MODEL 21 BOBCAT

MODEL 950 JETFIRE

BERETTA U22 NEOS

Model 3032 Tomcat
Specifications
Caliber: 32 Auto
Capacity: 7-shot magazine
Barrel length: 2.45"
Overall length: 4.9"
Weight: 14 1/2 oz.
Sights: Blade front, drift-adjustable rear
Features: Double or single action, thumb safety, tip-up barrel for direct loading/unloading, blued or matte finish
Prices:
Matte/Plastic $340
Blued/Plastic 370
Stainless/Plastic 418
Titanium/Plastic 572
Titanium (AO sight system) 412

Model 21 Bobcat DA Semiautomatic
A safe, dependable, accurate small-bore pistol in 22 LR or 25 Auto. Easy to load with its unique barrel tip-up system.
Specifications
Caliber: 22 LR or 25 ACP
Magazine capacity: 7 rounds (22 LR); 8 rounds (25 ACP)
Overall length: 4.9"
Barrel length: 2.4"
Weight: 11.5 oz. (25 ACP); 11.8 oz. (22 LR)
Sights: Blade front: V-notch rear
Safety: Thumb-operated
Grips: Plastic or Walnut
Frame: Forged aluminum
Prices:
Matte/Plastic 252
Blued/Plastic 285
Stainless/Plastic 307

Model 950 Jetfire
Single-Action Semiautomatic
Specifications
Calibers: 25 ACP
Barrel length: 2.4"
Overall length: 4.7"
Overall height: 3.4"
Safety: External, thumb-operated
Magazine capacity: 8 rounds
Sights: Blade front; V-notch rear
Weight: 9.9 oz.
Frame: Forged aluminum.
Prices:
Matte/Plastic 226
Stainless/Plastic 267

Beretta U22 Neos
Specifications
Caliber: 22LR. **Action:** Single. **Barrel length:** 4.5" and 6".
Sights: Target/plastic. **Grip:** Removable grips, colored rubber inserts available.
Price: 256
Inox: 299

Beretta Pistols
Medium Frame Cheetah Pistols

Model 84 Cheetah
This pistol is pocket sized with a large magazine capacity. The first shot (with hammer down, chamber loaded) can be fired by a double-action pull on the trigger without cocking the hammer manually.

The pistol also features a positive thumb safety (designed for both right- and left-handed operation), quick takedown (by means of special takedown button) and a conveniently located magazine release. Black plastic grips. Wood grips extra.

Specifications
Caliber: 380 Auto (9mm Short).
Magazine capacity: 10 rounds.
Barrel length: 3.8". (approx.)
Overall length: 6.8". (approx.)
Weight: 23.3 oz. (approx.).
Sights: Fixed front; rear dovetailed to slide.
Height overall: 4.85" (approx.).
Prices:
Bruniton/Plastic............................$589

MODEL 84 CHEETAH

Model 85 Cheetah (not shown)
Some basic specifications as the model 84 Cheetah, except has a single line 8-round magazine, ambidextrous safety.
Prices:
Bruniton/Plastic.............................545
Nickel/Wood................................609
Also available:
Model 87 in 22 LR.
   Capacity: 7 rounds. Straight blow-back open slide design. Width: 1.3". Barrel length: 3.8"
   Overall length: 6.8". Overall height: 4.7"
   Weight: 20.1 oz. Finish: Blued with wood.......589

Model 86 Cheetah
Specifications
Caliber: 380 Auto (9mm Short).
Barrel length: 4.4". **Overall length:** 7.3"
Capacity: 8 rounds. **Weight:** 23.3 oz.
Sight radius: 4.9". **Overall height:** 4.8"
Overall width: 1.4". **Grip:** Walnut
Features: Same as other Medium Frame, straight blow-back models, plus the safety and convenience of a tip-up barrel (rounds can be loaded directly into chamber without operating the slide).
Price:
Bruniton/Wood Grips........................591

MODEL 86 CHEETAH

Model 87 Target
Specifications
Caliber: 22 LR. **Capacity:** 10 rounds.
Barrel length: 5.9" **Overall length:** 8.9"
Weight: 40.9 oz. **Finish:** Blued with plastic
Price:.....................................669

MODEL 87 TARGET

Beretta Pistols
Large Frame 92/96 Series Pistols

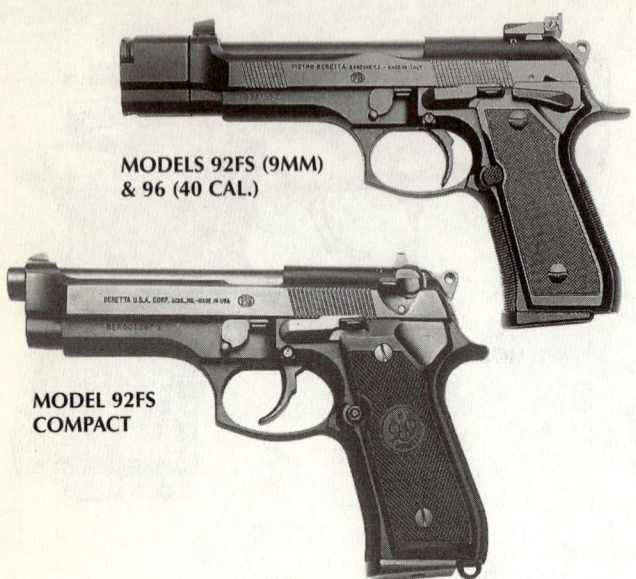

MODELS 92FS (9MM) & 96 (40 CAL.)

MODEL 92FS COMPACT

MODEL 96 COMBAT

MODEL 92/96 VERTEC

Models 92FS (9mm) & 96 (40 Cal.)
Specifications
Calibers: 9mm and 40 cal. **Capacity:** 10 rounds Action: Double/Single **Barrel length:** 4.9" Overall length: 8.5" **Weight:** 34.4 oz. Overall height: 5.4" **Overall width:** 1.5" **Sights:** Integral front; windage adjustable rear; 3-dot or tritium night sights **Grips:** Wood or plastic **Finish:** Bruniton (also available in blued, stainless, silver or gold)
Features: Chrome-lined bore; visible firing-pin block; open slide design; safety drop catch (half-cock); combat trigger guard; external hammer; reversible magazine release Model Brigadier (9mm and 40 cal.) same as above, but with a heavier slide. Barrel length: 4.3". Overall length: 7.8". Weight: 35.3 oz.
Model 92 Compact L Type M (9mm)
Barrel length: 4.3" Overall length: 7.8" Weight: 30.9 oz.

Model 96 Combat
Specifications
Calibers: 40 S&W Capacity: 11 rounds **Action:** Single action only (Combat); single/double (Stock) **Barrel length:** 5.9" **Overall length:** 9.5" **Weight:** 40 oz. **Sights:** 3 interchangeable front sights (Stock)
Features: Rubber magazine bumpers; replaceable accurizing barrel bushings; checkered grips; machine-checkered front and backstraps; fitted ABS cases; Brigadier slide; extended frame-mounted safety; competition-tuned trigger and adjustable rear target set and tool set
Prices:
Model 96 Brigadier (heavy slide and removable
  front sight, 35 oz.) $731
Model 96 Brigadier Stainless. 771
Model 96 Compact (32 oz.) 676
Model 96 Compact Stainless. 734

Model 92FS Compact and Compact Type M
Specifications
Same features as the proven 92FS, but in a more compact overall size and weight. **Overall length:** 7.8" **Barrel length:** 4.3" **Overall width:** 1.4" **Overall height:** 5.3" **Sight radius:** 5.8" **Weight:** 32.0 oz. Compact, 30.9 oz. Type M (unloaded). A contoured magazine bottom improves hand support and control. The Compact 92FS features a double column magazine, while the Compact Type M features a single-column magazine for a thinner grip (1.28" instead of 1.39") and reduced weight.
Prices:
Model 92 Compact. $676
Model 92 Compact Stainless. 734
Model 92FS Plastic w/3-Dot sights 676
Model 92FS Stainless w/3-dot sights 734
Model 96 w/3-dot sights. 676
Model 96 Stainless 734
Model 92FS Brigadier. 731
Model 92FS Brigadier Stainless. 771
Model 92 Type M 676
Model 92 Type M Stainless 721
Model 92 Black Stainless 734
Model 96 Black Stainless 734
Model 92 Millenium Limited Edition 1357
  (1 of 2000 steel frame, carbon fiber grips & interchangeable sights)

Model 92/96 Vertec
The new vertical grip design, short reach trigger and thin, dual-textured grip panels assures maximum control. An accessory rail is built into the frame to attach white light and laser devices.
Specifications
Barrel length: 4.7". **Weight:** 32.2 oz. **Magazine capacity:** 10. **Calibers:** 9mm and 40 S&W.
Prices:
Vertec 712
Vertec Inox: 762

Bersa Pistols

Thunder 380
Specifications
Caliber: 380 ACP
Capacity: 7 rounds
Action: Double
Barrel length: 3.5"
Overall length: 6 5/8"
Weight: 23 oz.
Sights: Notched-bar dovetailed rear; blade integral with slide front
Safety: Manual firing pin
Grips: Black polymer
Finish: Blue, satin nickel.
Prices:
Matte $257
Satin Nickel 274
9-Shot Deluxe 292

THUNDER 380 LITE

Bond Arms

450 Bond Super Defender
Specifications
Barrel Length: 3"
Weight: 21 oz.
Length: 5"
Features: Custom grip, crossbolt safety, interchangeable barrels, retracting firing pin, rebounding hammer, stainless steel, blade front sight
Prices:
Super Defender $359
Century 2000 Defender 379
Texas Defender 359
Cowboy Defender 359
Additional Barrels 129-149

450 BOND SUPER DEFENDER

CENTURY 2000 DEFENDER

Handguns • 285

Ed Brown Pistols

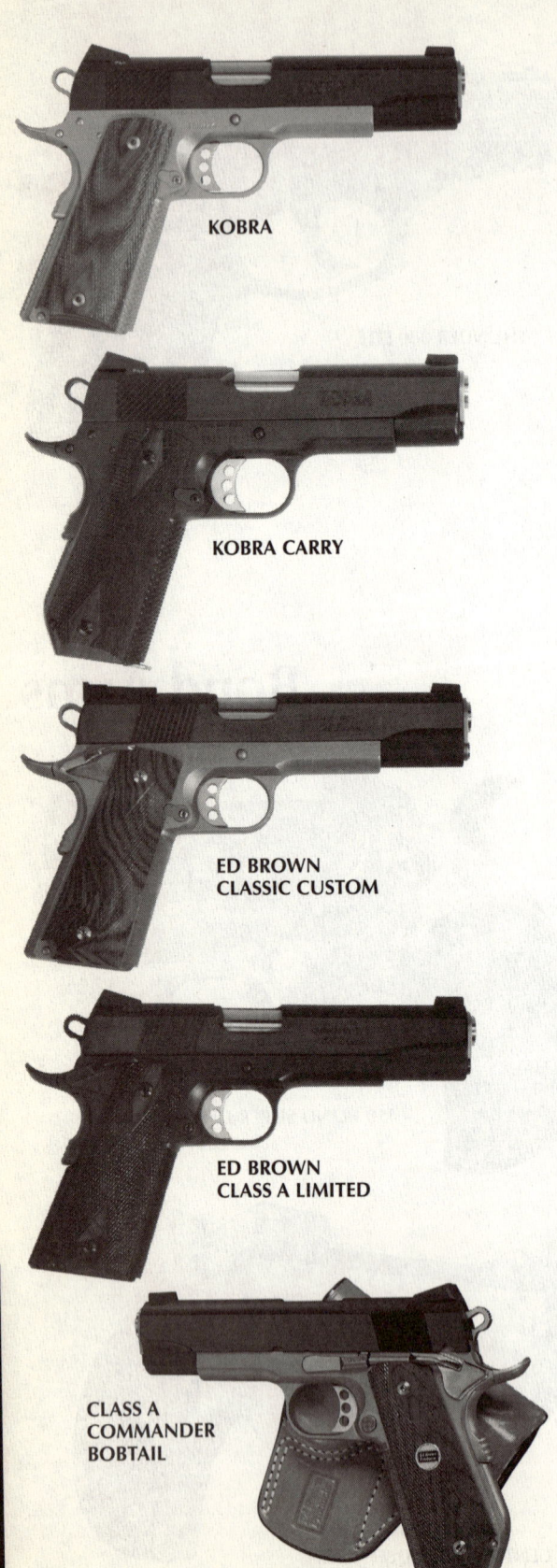

KOBRA

KOBRA CARRY

ED BROWN CLASSIC CUSTOM

ED BROWN CLASS A LIMITED

CLASS A COMMANDER BOBTAIL

KOBRA
Specifications
Caliber: .45 ACP
Barrel: 5" **Weight:** 39 oz.
Grips: Hogue exotic wood
Sights: Ramp-style front, rear fixed Novak Low-mount night sights
Features: Snakeskin treatment on the frame, mainspring housing and slide. Single action, M1911 style. Beavertail grip, low-gloss finish and 7-round magazine.
Price: $1795

KOBRA CARRY
Same specifications as Kobra, with a 4.25" barrel and weight of 34 oz. Stainless steel optional on both Kobra and Kobra Carry
Price: 1995

CLASSIC CUSTOM
Specifications
Caliber: .45 ACP
Barrel: 5" **Weight:** 39 oz.
Grips: Hogue exotic wood
Sights: Modified Ramp or post front, rear fully-adjustable Bo-Mar
Features: Single action, M1911 style, completely built to the customer's order. Extensive hand-polishing to 1200-grit finish. Top is flattened and finely grooved, two-piece guide rod, oversize mag release, ambidextrous safety, "Memory Groove" beavertail grip safety, 3 LPI checkered forestrap, 7-shot magazine, carrying case. Stainless steel optional.
Price: 2895

CLASS A LIMITED
A versatile handgun with nearly limitless options.
Specifications
Caliber: .45 ACP, .400 Cor-Bon, 10mm, .40 S&W, .357 Sig, .38 Super, 9x23, 9mm Luger
Barrel: 5" or 4.25"
Weight: 34 - 39 oz.
Features: All options of Ed Brown handguns available to customize this handgun.
Price: . . . . From 2250

COMMANDER BOBTAIL
Specifications
Caliber: .45 ACP, .400 Cor-Bon, .40 S&W, .357 Sig, .38 Super, 9mm Luger
Barrel: 4.25"
Weight: 34 oz.
Grips: Hogue exotic wood
Sights: Any style front, rear fixed Novak Low-mount, optional night sights
Features: Bobtail butt, beavertail grip safety, checkered forestrap, matte finishing, 7-shop magazine; handmade to customer's order. Stainless steel frame or slide optional.

Price: . . . . From 2300

Browning Pistols
Buck Mark 22 LR Series

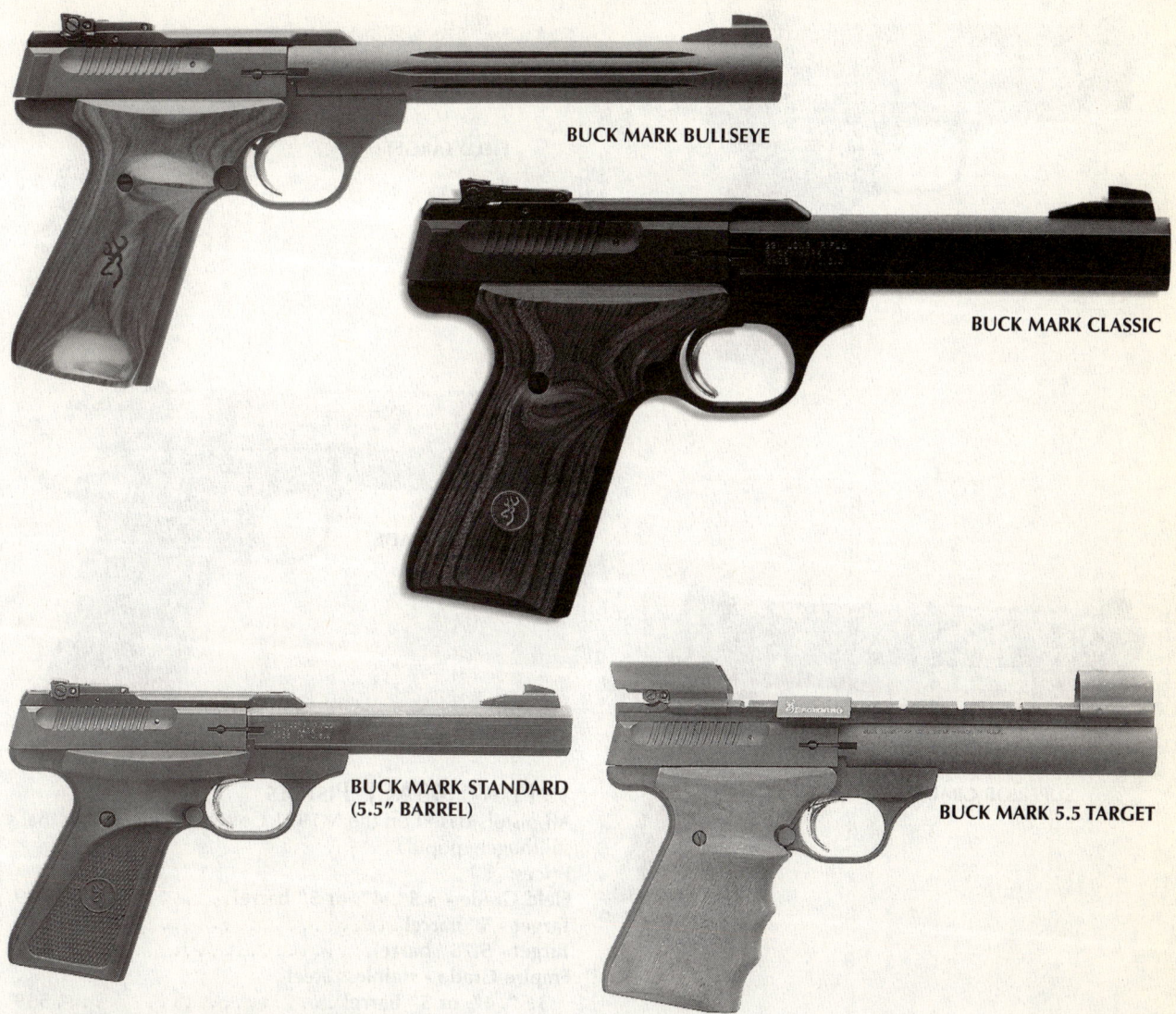

BUCK MARK BULLSEYE

BUCK MARK CLASSIC

BUCK MARK STANDARD (5.5" BARREL)

BUCK MARK 5.5 TARGET

BUCK MARK SPECIFICATIONS

Buck Mark Models	Mag. Cap.	Barrel Length	Overall Length	Weight	Overall Height	Sight Radius	Grips	Price
Standard	10	5.5"	9.5"	36 oz.	5 3/8"	8"	Molded Composite, Ambidextrous	$292
Micro Standard	10	4"	8"	32 oz.	5 3/8"	9 9/16"	Molded Composite, Ambidextrous	292
Nickel	10	5.5"	9.5"	36 oz.	5 3/8"	8"	Molded Composite, Ambidextrous	345
Micro Nickel	10	4"	8"	32 oz.	5 3/8"	9 9/16"	Molded Composite, Ambidextrous	345
Plus Nickel	10	5.5"	9.5"	36 oz.	5 3/8"	8"	Laminated Hardwood	391
Plus	10	5.5"	9.5"	36 oz.	5 3/8"	8"	Laminated Hardwood	357
Camper Nickel	10	5.5"	9.5"	34 oz.	5 3/8"	8"	Composite	293
Camper	10	5.5"	9.5"	34 oz.	5 3/8"	8"	Composite	263
Challenge	10	5.5"	9.5"	25 oz.	5 3/8"	8"	Walnut	326
NEW Classic Plus with Rosewood Grips	10	5.5"	9.5"	34 oz.	5 3/8"	8"	Laminated Hardwood	357
Bullseye, Standard	10	7.25"	11 5/16"	36 oz.	5 3/8"	9 7/8"	Molded Composite, Ambidextrous	428
Bullseye, Target	10	7.25"	11 5/16"	36 oz.	5 3/8"	9 7/8"	Contoured Rosewood or Wraparound fingergroove	552
5.5 Field	10	5.5"	9 5/8"	35.5 oz.	5 5/16"	8.25"	Contoured Walnut or Wraparound fingergroove	468
5.5 Target	10	5.5"	9 5/8"	35.5 oz.	5 5/16"	8.25"	Contoured Walnut or Wraparound fingergroove	468
Extra Magazine								26

Micro 4"-barrel models available for all standard Buck Marks and Challenge. Same price as 5.5".
Finishes are matte blue w/polished barrel flats or nickel plated slide and barrel. Pro Target rear sight and 1/8" wide front sight standard.

Charles Daly Pistols

FIELD GRADE

FIELD TARGET

EMPIRE GRADE

SUPERIOR GRADE

1911 A-1 45ACP Pistols
All pistols based on the M1911 Colt, a proven design that's still hugely popular.

Prices:
Field Grade - 3.5", 4", or 5" barrel $499
Target - 5" barrel 599
Target - 5.75" barrel. 679
Empire Grade - stainless steel
   3.5", 4", or 5" barrel 599
Target - stainless. 699
Superior Grade – Two-Tone, 5" barrel 549
Carry Comp (not shown)
   Blue, 3.5" or 4" barrel 619
   Stainless steel 719

Daly Double Action
Specifications
Caliber: .45 or .40 S&W
Barrel: Full size or ultra-compact (shown, with 3 5/8" barrel)
Capacity: 10
Grips: black or two-tone in full size; yellow, fuschia, olive, two-tone or black in combat

Prices:
Compact in 45 or 40 S+W 519
Two-tone (45 only) 559
OD green or yellow/blue (45 only) 529
Fuchsia/Chrome (45 only) 549
Full size 519
2-Tone (45 only) 559

DDA CS YELLOW

Cimarron Firearms

The Cimarron Firearms Co. has an impressive line of 19th-century replica revolvers and rifles. They are high-quality firearms, faithfully crafted to show the form, fit and function of the originals. They're ideal for Cowboy Action shooting. Take a look if you want the feel of another century between your hands.

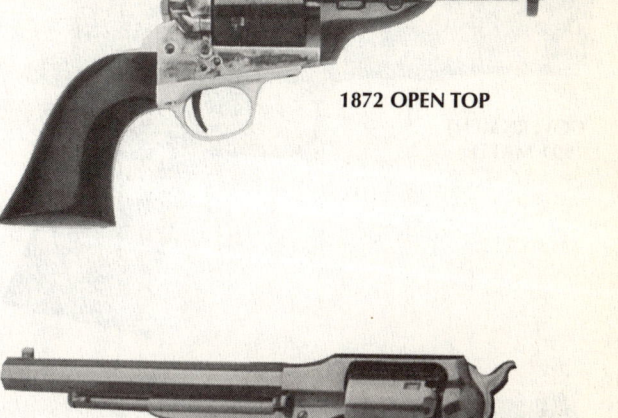
1872 OPEN TOP

1872 Open Top
The 1872 Open Top was the first cartridge firing six shooter manufactured by Colt and the forerunner of the famous 1873 Colt Model 'P' or Peacemaker. The Colt 1872 Open Top was manufactured at the same time as the percussion conversion models. The Cimarron Firearms Co. Open Top revolver is manufactured from the ground up, utilizing high quality modern gun steel. It is made much stronger than the original and other Open Top replicas made from percussion parts.

Specifications
Barrels: 5 1/2" & 7 1/2" **Calibers:** .38 Colt & S&W Special, .44 Colt & Russian, .45 S&W Schofield **Grips:** Walnut, Early Navy style brass or Later steel Army style. **Finish:** Blue, charcoal blue, nickel, or original finish
Price $489
Also Available: 1858 Army .44 249

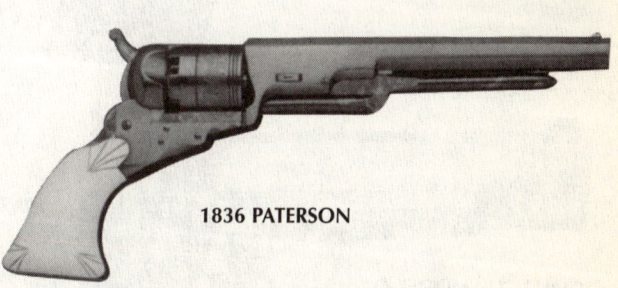
1858 ARMY .44

1836 Paterson
The 1836 Paterson in 36-caliber, was produced shortly before the factory shut down in 1942.
Price: 399

Model 'P' Jr
The Cimarron Model 'P' Jr. (MPJ) is styled after–but 20% smaller than–the famous 1873 Colt Peacemaker. The MPJ features a down-sized traditional style Colt grip instead of the bird's head grip found on the Cimarron Lightning SA model. The MPJ features Cimarron's exclusive Cowboy Comp action and is manufactured to Cimarron's superior level of fit, finish and function. Shoulder rigs and holsters are now available for the Lightning SA and Model 'P' Jr.

1836 PATERSON

Specifications
Barrels: 3 1/2" & 4 3/4"
Calibers: .38 Special
Finish: Blue with case hardened frame
Price:
Retail: 389

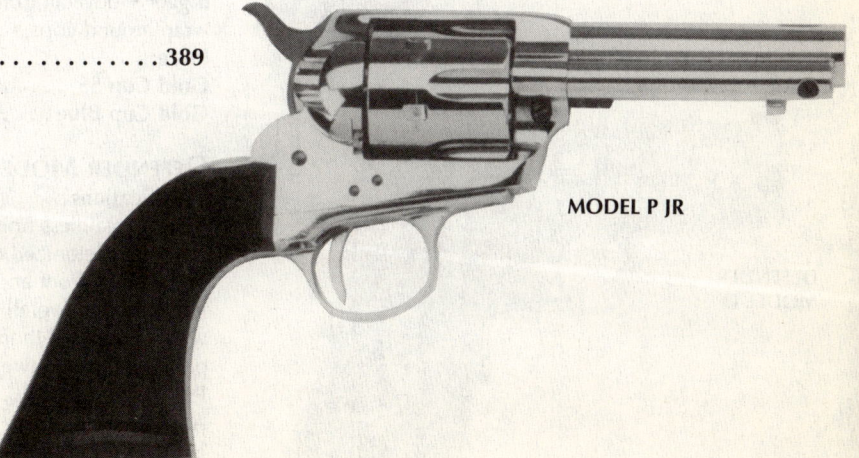
MODEL P JR

Handguns • 289

Colt M1911 Pistols
Model O Series 1991 and XSE

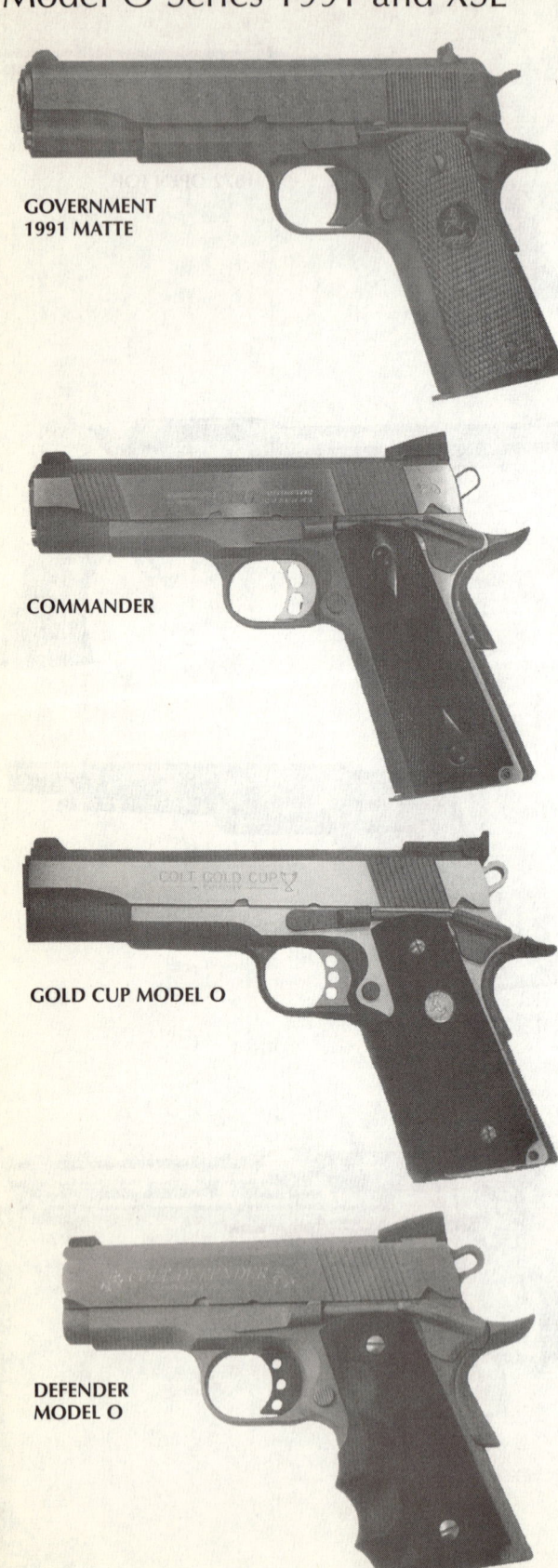

GOVERNMENT 1991 MATTE

COMMANDER

GOLD CUP MODEL O

DEFENDER MODEL O

1991 Series
Specifications
Single-action, .45 ACP • checkered rubber composite grips • smooth, composite trigger • fixed sights • beveled mag well • standard thumb safety and service style grip safety • 7+1 capacity. All "O" models shipped with two magazines.
Prices:
Blue 5" Barrel, rosewood grips $699
Stainless 5" Barrel 800
Also available:
Commander Stainless, matte stainless finish, stainless frame & slide, 4.25" barrel length, 7.75" overall length
Commander, matte black finish, carbon steel frame & slide, 4.25" barrel length, 7.75" overall length, Rosewood grips

XS E Series
Specifications
Single-action, .45 ACP • stainless brushed finish • front and rear slide serrations • checkered, double diamond, rosewood grips • extended ambidextrous thumb safeties • upswept beavertail with palm swell • three dot dovetail front and rear sights • adjustable 2-cut aluminum trigger • elongated slot hammer
Price: 950
Also available:
Government blue, 5" barrel length, 8+1 capacity
Commander, 4.25" barrel length, 8+1 capacity
Lightweight Commander, 4.25" barrel length, 8+1 capacity

Gold Cup Model O Pistols
Specifications
Stainless steel frame • stainless round top slide • brushed stainless finish on both frame and slide • 5" barrel length and 8.5" overall length • .45 caliber • 8+1 round capacity • Enhanced elongated slot hammer • adjustable aluminum trigger • dovetail front sight • Bomar-style rear sight • black wrap around grips • 39 ounce overall weight • single action
Price:
Gold Cup SS 1116
Gold Cup Blue 1050

Defender Model O Pistols
Specifications
Brushed stainless finish • wrap around rubber finger groove grips • skeletonized composite trigger • single action • three dot dovetail front and rear sights • .45 caliber • 3" barrel length, 6.75" overall length • 7+1 capacity • beveled mag well • extended thumb safety and upswept beavertail with palm swell • lightweight • enhanced tolerances
Price: 45 cal. 842
Also available:
  Defender Plus 876

Colt Revolvers

ANACONDA

COWBOY SINGLE ACTION REVOLVER

PYTHON ELITE

Cowboy Single Action Revolver
Specifications
Blue color case finish • first generation grips • .45 Colt caliber • 5.5" barrel length, 11" overall length • 6 round capacity • transfer bar safety • enhanced tolerances
Price: Model CB1850 .... $670
Also available: Traditional Single Action Army Revolvers
P1640/50, 357. barrel: 4.75"/5.5"
P1840, blue color case finish, .45 Colt, 4.75" barrel length, 10.25" overall length
P1841, nickel finish, .45 Colt, 4.75" barrel length, 10.25" overall length
P1850, blue color case finish, .45 Colt, 5.5" barrel length, 11" overall length
P1856, nickel finish, .45 Colt, 5.5" barrel length, 11" overall length
P1940, blue color case finish, .44-.40 caliber, 4.75" barrel length, 10.25" overall length
P1941, nickel finish, .44-.40 caliber, 4.75" barrel length, 10.25" overall length
P1950, blue color case finish, .44-.40 caliber, 5.5" barrel length, 11" overall length
P1956, nickel finish, .44-.40 caliber, 5.5" barrel length, 11" overall length
Price: 1530

Anaconda
Specifications:
Caliber: .44 Magnum
Capacity: 6 rounds
Grips: Rubber combat
Barrel: 4", 6", 8", stainless
Sights: Adjustable rear with repeatable clicks. Drilled and tapped for scope mounts.
Weight: 4" barrel, 47 oz. 6" barrel, 53 oz. 8" barrel: 59 oz.
Prices:
4" and 6" $1000
8" ported 1050

Python Elite
Specifications:
Caliber: .357 Magnum
Capacity: 6 rounds
Grips: wood
Barrel: 4", 6", stainless or blue
Sights: Adjustable sight red ramp front
Weight: 4" barrel, 47 oz. 6" barrel, 43.5 oz.
Price: 1150

CZ Pistols

CZ 75 B

CZ 75 STANDARD IPSC

CZ 75 CHAMPION

CZ 75 COMPACT

CZ 75
The CZ 75 pistol is a product of Ceska Zbrojovka, Uhersky Brod. The CZ 75 B is the basis of the all-steel, semi-automatic, double action pistols of the CZ 75 pistol family.

CZ 75 B
The characteristic features of all CZ75 versions are the following: large capacity double-column magazine; comfortable grip in either hand; good results at instinctive shooting (without aiming); low trigger pull weight; high accuracy of fire; long service life; high reliability even with various brands of ammunition; the slide stays open after the last cartridge has been fired; the sights are outfitted with a three-dot illuminating system for better aiming in poor visibility conditions; suitable for competitive combat action shooting.

Versions differ in the caliber, size, weight, magazine capacity, trigger mechanism operation, safety elements, surface finish, grip panel types.

Specifications
Caliber: 9 mm Luger, .40 S&W
Magazine capacity: 10 cartridges **Overall length:** 8.1"
Barrel length: 4.7" **Height:** 5.4" **Weight:** 2.2 lbs.
Trigger mechanism: SA/DA **Safety elements:** Manual safety, safety stop on the hammer, firing pin safety
Price: 9mm $480
40 S&W 494

CZ 75 CHAMPION
Specifications
Caliber/Magazine capacity: 9 mm Luger / 10, 40 S&W / 10
Length: 9.5" **Barrel Length:** 4.5" **Height:** 5.6"
Weight: 2.2 lbs. **Mode of operation:** SA
Safety elements: Manual safety, safety stop on the hammer
Price: 1551

CZ 75 STANDARD IPSC
Specifications
Caliber/Magazine capacity: .40 S&W/10 **Length:** 8.9"
Barrel Length: 5.4" **Height:** 5.9" **Weight:** 2.8 lbs.
Mode of operation: SA **Safety elements:** Manual safety, safety stop on the hammer
Price: 1086

CZ 75 COMPACT
Specifications
Frame: Steel **Caliber:** 9mm Luger
Magazine Capacity: 10 cartridges
Overall Length: 7.3" **Barrel Length:** 3.9" **Height:** 5.0"
Weight: 2.0 lbs. **Trigger Mechanism:** SA/DA
Safety elements: Manual safety, safety stop on the hammer, firing pin safety
Price: 508

CZ Pistols

CZ Kadet Pistol .22 cal.
Specifications
Caliber: .22 LR **Barrel length:** 4.9"
Magazine capacity: 10 cartridges **Weight:** 2.4 lbs
Overall Length: 8.1" **Barrel Length:** 4.9"
Price: $477

CZ Kadet .22 cal. Conversion Kit
(NOT SHOWN)
The CZ 75 Kadet conversion kit is a separate accessory for the CZ 75/85 pistol series, allowing the use of .22 LR calibre cartridges. The Kadet adapter has its own sights, adjustable for elevation and windage, so there's no loss of zero when slides are switched.
Specifications
Caliber: .22 LR **Magazine capacity:** 10 cartridges
Overall length: 8.1" **Barrel length:** 4.9" **Weight:** 1.1 lbs.
Empty magazine weight: 0.3 lbs.
Price: Adapter Kit 282

CZ 85 Combat
Specifications
Caliber: 9mm Luger **Magazine Capacity:** 10 cartridges
Overall Length: 8.1" **Barrel Length:** 4.7" **Height:** 5.4"
Weight: 2.2 lbs. **Trigger Mechanism:** SA/DA
Safety elements: Manual safety, safety stop on the hammer
Price: 586

CZ 97 B
Specifications
Caliber/Magazine capacity: .45 Auto / 10
Length: 8.3" **Barrel Length:** 4.8" **Height:** 5.9"
Weight: 2.6 lbs. **Mode of operation:** SA/DA
Safety elements: Manual safety, safety stop on the hammer, firing pin safety, loaded chamber indicator
Price: 625

CZ 83
Specifications
Caliber: 7,65 mm Browning; 9mm Makarov, 9mm Browning
Magazine Capacity: 10 **Length:** 6.8"; 6.8"
Barrel Length: 3.8"; 3.8" **Height:** 5.0"; 5.0"
Weight: 1.7 lbs.; 1.8 lbs. **Mode of operation:** SA/DA; SA/DA **Safety elements:** Manual safety, automatic safety
Price: 397

CZ 100
Specifications
Caliber/Magazine capacity: 9mm Luger/10; .40 S&W/10
Length: 180 mm (7.1") **Barrel Length:** 98 mm (3.9")
Height: 130 mm (5.1") **Weight:** 665 g 1.5 lbs.)
Mode of operation: SA/DA **Safety elements:** firing pin block, loaded chamber indicator, cocking indication button, decocking lever
Price: 424

CZ 75 KADET

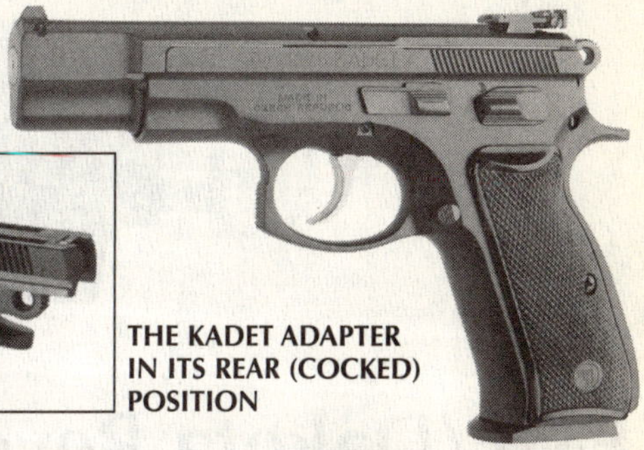

THE KADET ADAPTER IN ITS REAR (COCKED) POSITION

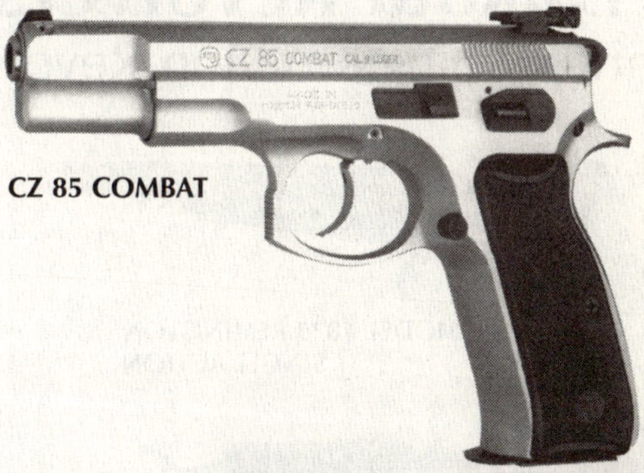

CZ 85 COMBAT

CZ 97B

CZ 83

CZ 100

Downsizer Pistols

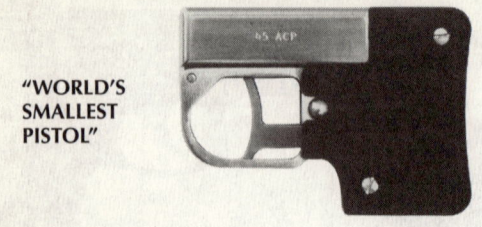

"WORLD'S SMALLEST PISTOL"

MODEL WSP "WORLD'S SMALLEST PISTOL"
Specifications
Action: Single-shot, double-action only Caliber: 45 ACP, 357 Mag. Barrel length: 2.1", tip-up barrel Overall length: 3.25" Weight: 11 oz. Height: 2.25" Width: 0.9" Materials: Stainless steel; CNC machined from solid bar stock
Price:. $499

EMF/Dakota Revolvers
EMF Hartford Single-Action Revolvers

MODEL 1875 REMINGTON SINGLE ACTION

HARTFORD PINKERTON

MODEL 1890 REMINGTON POLICE

1873 DAKOTA SINGLE ACTION WITH 5.5" BARREL

1873 HARTFORD "BUNTLINE"

1st and 2nd generations models available. Parts are interchangeable with the original Colts. Forged steel frames, case hardened, steel backstrap & trigger guard. Original blue finish, walnut grips. Barrel lengths: 4.75", 5.5", 7.5", 12" buntline.

MODEL 1875 REMINGTON SINGLE ACTION
Engraved; case hardened frame
Prices: Blued $590
Nickel 790

HARTFORD PINKERTON
Specifications
Caliber: 45 LC, 357 Magnum
Barrel length: 4". Bird's-head grip with ejector tube.
Price:. 450

MODEL 1890 REMINGTON POLICE
Specifications
Calibers: 44-40, 45 Long Colt and 357 Magnum.
Barrel length: 5.75".
Finish: Blued or nickel Features:
Original design (1891-1894) with lanyard ring in buttstock; case hardened frame; walnut grips
Price:. 590
  Nickel 790

1873 DAKOTA SINGLE ACTION
Specifications
Calibers: 357 Mag., 44-40, 45 Long Colt. Barrel lengths: 4.75", 5.5" and 7.5". Finish: Blued, case hardened frame.
Grips: One-piece walnut. Features: Classic Colt design, set screw for cylinder pin release; black nickel backstrap and trigger design
Price:. 350
  Buntline (.45 L.C., 12") 525

1873 HARTFORD "BUNTLINE"
Specifications
Caliber: 45 LC Barrel Length: 12"
Features: Steel backstrap & trigger
Price:. 525

Entréprise Arms Pistols

Tactical P325 Plus
Specifications
Caliber: .45 ACP, 10 round magazine.
Barrel: 3.25". **Weight:** 37 oz. **Length:** 7.25" overall.
Stocks: Black Ergo Ultra Slim, double diamond checkered grip panels. **Sights:** Tactical2 Ghost Ring sight or Novak Lo-mount sight. Features: Same as the Elite series, plus extended ambidextrous thumb safety, front & rear cocking serrations, full length guide rod, barrel throated & frame ramp polished, tuned match extractor, fitted barrel & bushing, stainless steel firing pin, serrated ramp front sight, slide lapped to frame, dehorned and trigger set at a crisp 4.5 pounds.
Price:....................................$1049
P425 (4.25" barrel) 980
P500 (5" barrel).............................980

TACTICAL P325 PLUS

Elite P425 (and P500, P325)
Specifications
Caliber: .45 ACP, 10 round magazine.
Barrel: 4.25" (5" P500, 3.25" P325) **Weight:** 38 oz. (40 oz. P500, 36 oz. P325) **Length:** 7.75" overall
Stocks: Black Ergo Ultra Slim, double diamond checkered grip panels.
Sights: 3-dot fixed sights (dovetail-cut front sight).
Features: Reinforced dustcover, lowered & flared ejection port, squared trigger guard, adjustable match trigger, bolstered front strap, high grip cut, hardened steel magazine release, high ride beavertail grip safety, steel flat mainspring housing (checkered 20 LPI), checkered slide release, extended thumb lock, EDM skeletonized match hammer & sear, match grade disconnector with polished contact points and Wolff springs throughout.
Price:.......................................740

ELITE P425

Boxer P500
Specifications
Caliber: .45 ACP, .40 S&W. **Barrel:** 5". **Weight:** 44 oz. **Length:** 7.25" overall. **Stocks:** Black Ergo Ultra Slim, double diamond checkered grip panels. **Sights:** Adjustable rear sight with dovetail partridge front sight. **Features:** Same as the Elite model, plus machined slide parallel rails with polished breech face & barrel channel, front & rear cocking serrations, lowered & flared ejection port, full length stainless steel one piece guide rod with plug, National match barrel 5" Government length, match bushing, stainless steel firing pin, match extractor, oversized firing pin stop, fitted barrel & bushing, slide lapped to frame, barrel throated & ramp polished, and trigger set at a crisp 4.5 pounds.
Prices:
45ACP...................................1399

BOXER P500

European American Armory

WITNESS

WITNESS P COMPACT

WITNESS-PS

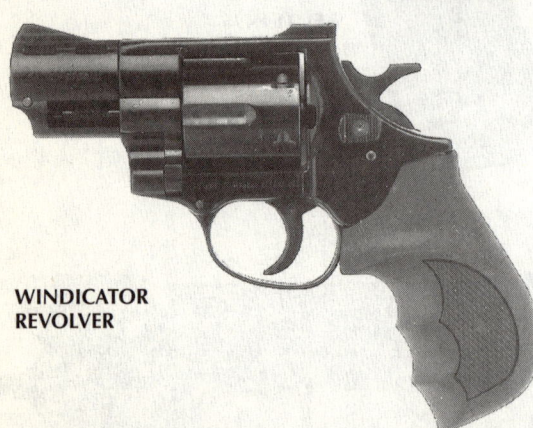
WINDICATOR REVOLVER

WITNESS COMPACT

Witness Double-Action Pistols
Specifications
Calibers: 9mm, 38 Super, 40 S&W, 10mm, and 45 ACP
Capacity: 10 rounds, (45 ACP) **Barrel length:** 4.5"
Overall length: 8.1" **Weight:** 33 oz.
Finish: Blued or Wonder Finish
Sights: 3-dot; windage adj. rear **Grips:** Black rubber
Prices:
Blue $449
Wonder Finish 459
Polymer/Blue 429

Witness Compact
Specifications
Calibers: 9mm, 40 S&W, 38 Super, 10mm, 45 ACP
Capacity: 10 rounds; (45 ACP)
Barrel length: 3 5/8"
Overall length: 7.3"
Weight: 29 oz.
Finish: Hard chrome
Prices:
Steel/Blue 449
  Wonder 459
Polymer/Blue 429
  Wonder 449
Polymer/Blue/Ported 459
Polymer/Wonder/Ported 479

Windicator Revolver
Specifications
Calibers: 38 Special, 357 Mag. **Capacity:** 6 rounds
Action: Single/Double action **Barrel length:** 2" or 4"
Sights: Fixed (No-Snag) or windage adj. **Finish:** Blued only
Features: Swing-out cylinder; black rubber grips; hammer block safety

Prices:
38 Special w/2" barrel 249
38 Special w/4" barrel 259
357 Magnum w/2" barrel 259
357 Magnum w/4" barrel 279

European American Armory

BIG BORE BOUNTY HUNTER SINGLE ACTION

SMALL BORE BOUNTY HUNTER

MODEL IZH35 TARGET PISTOL

BIG BORE BOUNTY HUNTER SINGLE ACTION
Specifications
Calibers: 357 Mag., 45 Long Colt and 44 Mag.
Capacity: 6 rounds **Barrel length:** 4.5" or 7.5"
Sights: Fixed **Weight:** 37 oz. (4.5") and 42 oz. (7.5")
Finish: Blued, color casehardened or nickel
Features: Transfer-bar safety, 3 position hammer; hammer-forged barrel; walnut grips (polymer grips optional)
Prices:
Blued or color casehardened receiver **$379**
Nickel 399
Also available:

In 22 LR/WMR (4.75" or 6.75" barrel)
with blue finish. **$269**
Nickel 299

MODEL IZH35 TARGET PISTOL
The IZH35 Target Pistol is available in .22 LR. Standard features include a machined steel receiver, 6" forged target-grade barrel, adjustable trigger assembly, fully-adjustable right-hand walnut trigger grip, integral grip safety, manual slide hold-open, fully-adjustable rear sight, and a detachable scope mount.
Price:. 539

FireStorm Pistols

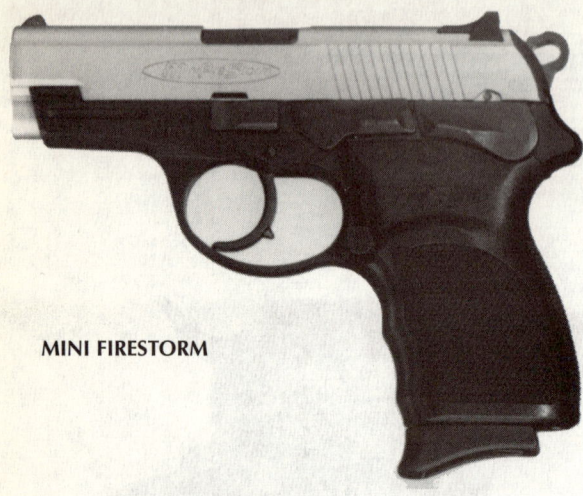

MINI FIRESTORM

Mini Firestorm
Specifications:
Caliber: 9mm or 40 S&W
Action: double action, semi automatic
Sights: adjustable target sight
Barrel length: 3.5"
Weight: 24.5 oz
Grips: polymer grips
Finish: matte
Magazine capacity: 10 shot
Price:...$367
   Duotone..375
   Nickel..392
Also available: 45 caliber (7 shot)
Price:...375
   Duotone..388
   Nickel..400

FIRESTORM 45 GOVERNMENT AND COMPACT

Firestorm 45 Government and Compact
Specifications:
Caliber: 45 ACP **Action:** double, semi-automatic
Sights: 3-Dot combat
Barrel length: 5 1/8" (4.25" compact)
Weight: 36 oz. (34 oz. compact)
Grips: Rubber
Finish: matte, duo-tone
Magazine capacity: 7 shot
Price: matte...315
   Duotone..325

Firestorm 380
Specifications:
Caliber: 380
Action: double action, semi-automatic
Sights: 3-Dot Combat
Barrel length: 3.5"
Weight: 23 oz.
Grips: rubber
Finish: matte, duotone
Magazine capacity: 7 shot
Price: matte...249
   Duotone..274
Also available in 22 LR

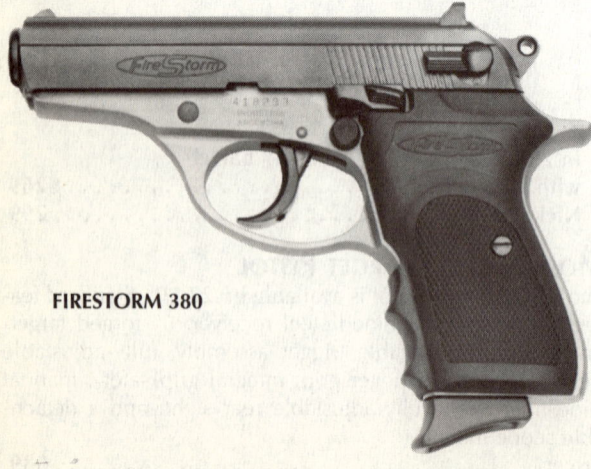

FIRESTORM 380

Freedom Arms Revolvers

Model 83 Rimfire
Specifications
Caliber: 22 LR (optional 22 Magnum cylinder)
Barrel Lengths: 5.13", 7.5" (Varmint Class) and 10" (Silhouette Class) **Sights:** Silhouette competition sights Silhouette Class); adjustable rear express sight; removable front express blade; front sight hood **Grips:** Black micarta (Silhouette Class); black and green laminated hardwood (Varmint Class) **Finish:** Stainless steel **Features:** Dual firing pin; lightened hammer; pre-set trigger stop; accepts all sights and/or scope mounts
Prices:
Silhouette Class (10" barrel) $1879
Varmint Class (5.13" & 7.5" barrels) 1828

MODEL 83 RIMFIRE
SILHOUETTE CLASS 10" BARREL

Model 97 Premier Grade
Specifications
Caliber: 357 Magnum, 45 Colt, 41 Magnum
Capacity: 6 shots (357) 5 shots (45 and 41)
Action: Single Action **Barrel Lengths:** 4.25", 5.5" and 7.5"
Sights: Removable front blade; adjustable rear
Grips: Impregnated hardwood or optional black micarta
Price: Adjustable Sight 1668

MODEL 97 PREMIER GRADE

Model 83 Silhouette/Competition
(NOT SHOWN)
Specifications
Calibers: 357 Magnum, 41 Rem. Mag. and 44 Rem. Mag.
Barrel Lengths: 9" (357 Mag.) and 10" (41 Rem. Mag., 44 Rem. Mag.) **Sights:** Silhouette competition **Grips:** Pachmayr
Trigger: Pre-set stop; trigger over travel screw
Finish: Field Grade
Price: 1635

Model 83 Premier & Field Grades
Specifications
Calibers: 454 Casull, 41 Rem. Mag., 44 Rem. Mag., .475 Linebaugh, 50 AE, 357 Mag. **Action:** Single action
Capacity: 5 rounds **Barrel Lengths:** 4.75", 6", 7.5", 10"
Overall Length: 14" (w/7.5" barrel)
Weight: 3 lbs. 2 oz. (w/7.5" barrel)
Safety: Patented sliding bar
Sights: Notched rear; blade front (optional adjustable rear and replaceable front blade)
Grips: Impregnated hardwood (Premier Grade) or rubber Pachmayr (Field Grade)
Finish: Brushed stainless (Premier Grade); Matte Finish (Field)
Features: ISGW silhouette, Millett competition and express sights are optional; SSK T'SOB 3-ring or 2-ring Leupold scope mount optional; optional cylinder in 454 Casull, 45 ACP, 45 Win. Mag. ($343.00)

MODEL 83 454 CASULL FIELD GRADE

Prices:
Model 83 Premier Grade
  With adjustable sights (50A, 475L, 454C) 2058
  357, 41 and 44 Magnums w/adjustable sights . . . 1976
Model 83 Field Grade
  .454C, 475L, 50 AE, adj. sights 1591
  .357, 41, 44 adj. sights 1527

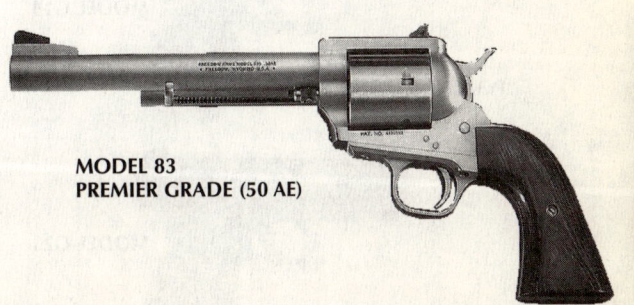

MODEL 83 PREMIER GRADE (50 AE)

Glock Pistols

FULL SIZE

Model G17
Specifications
Barrel Length: 4.49 in. Weight: 22.04 oz.
Mag Cap: 10/17 Overall Height: 5.43"
Overall Length: 7.32" Caliber: 9x19
Also Available:
G17L with 6" barrel

Model G22
Specifications
Barrel Length: 4.49 in. Weight: 22.92 oz.
Mag Cap: 10/15 Overall Height: 5.43"
Overall Length: 7.32" Caliber: 40

Model G31
Specifications
Barrel Length: 4.49 in. Weight: 22.28 oz.
Mag Cap: 10/15 Overall Height: 5.43"
Overall Length: 7.32"
Caliber: 357

Model G20
Specifications
Barrel Length: 4.60 in. Weight: 26.28 oz.
Mag Cap: 10/13 Overall Height: 5.47"
Overall Length: 7.59"
Caliber: 10mm Auto

Model G21
Specifications
Barrel Length: 4.60 in. Weight: 26.28 oz.
Mag Cap: 10/13 Overall Height: 5.47"
Overall Length: 7.59"
Caliber: 45 Auto

COMPACT

Model G19
Specifications
Barrel Length: 4.02 in. Weight: 20.99 oz.
Mag Cap: 10/15 Overall Height: 5.00"
Overall Length: 6.85" Caliber: 9x19

Model G23
Specifications
Barrel Length: 4.02 in. Weight: 21.16 oz.
Mag Cap: 10/13 Overall Height: 5.00"
Overall Length: 6.85" Caliber: .40

Prices on request.

Glock Pistols

COMPACT

Model G32
Specifications
Barrel Length: 4.02 in. Weight: 21.16 oz.
Mag Cap: 10/13 Overall Height: 5.00"
Overall Length: 6.85" Caliber: 357

Model G29
Specifications
Barrel Length: 3.78 in. Weight: 24.69 oz.
Mag Cap: 10 Overall Height: 4.45"
Overall Length: 6.77" Caliber: 10mm

Model G30
Specifications
Barrel Length: 3.78 in. Weight: 23.99 oz.
Mag Cap: 10(9) Overall Height: 4.76"
Overall Length: 6.77" Caliber: 45 Auto

SUB COMPACT

Model G26
Specifications
Barrel Length: 3.46 in. Weight: 19.75 oz.
Mag Cap: 10 Overall Height: 4.17"
Overall Length: 6.29" Caliber: 9x19

Model G27
Specifications
Barrel Length: 3.46 in. Weight: 19.75 oz.
Mag Cap: 9 Overall Height: 4.17"
Overall Length: 6.29" Caliber: .40

Model G33
Specifications
Barrel Length: 3.46 in. Weight: 19.75 oz.
Mag Cap: 9 Overall Height: 4.17"
Overall Length: 6.29" Caliber: 357

Model G34
Specifications
Barrel Length: 5.32 in. Weight: 22.92 oz.
Mag Cap: 10/17 Overall Height: 5.43"
Overall Length: 8.15" Caliber: 9x19

Model G35
Specifications
Barrel Length: 5.32 in. Weight: 24.52 oz.
Mag Cap: 10/15 Overall Height: 5.43"
Overall Length: 8.15" Caliber: 40

Model G36 (NOT SHOWN)
45 Auto

Prices on request.

PORTED BARREL
MODEL G32
MODEL G29
MODEL G30
MODEL G26
MODEL G27
MODEL G33
9X19
MODEL G34
.40
MODEL G35

Hämmerli USA Pistols

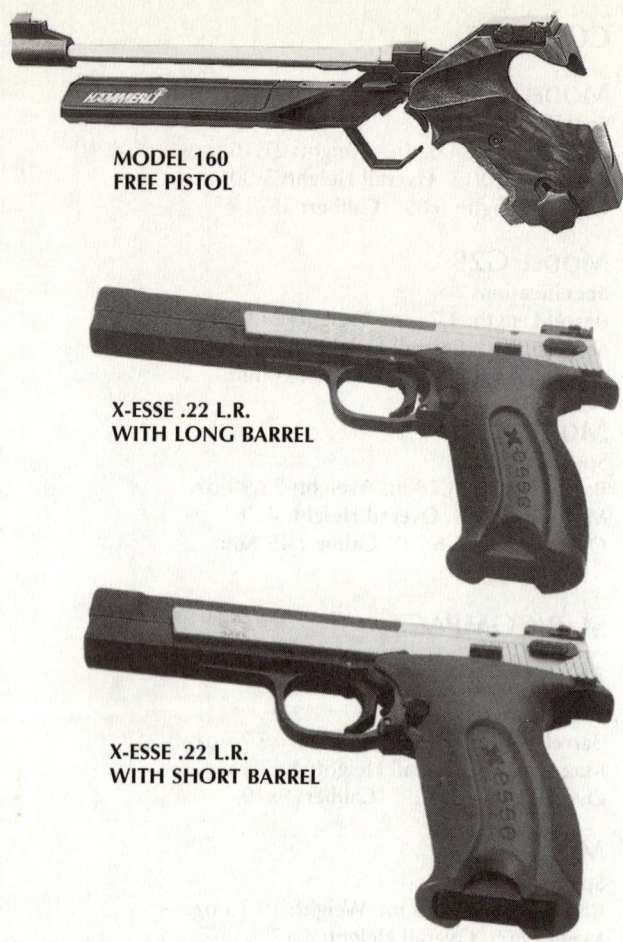

Model 160 Free Pistol
Specifications
Caliber: 22 LR
Barrel Length: 11.3"
Overall Length: 17.5"
Height: 5.7" **Weight:** 45 oz.
Trigger Action: Infinitely variable set trigger weight; cocking lever located on left of receiver; trigger length variable along weapon axis
Locking Action: Martini-type locking action w/side-mounted locking lever **Barrel:** Free-floating, cold-swagged precision barrel w/low axis relative to the hand **Ignition:** Horizontal firing pin (hammerless) in line w/barrel axis; firing pin travel 0.15" **Grips:** Selected walnut w/adj. hand rest for direct arm to barrel extension
Price **$2189**
  with electronic trigger. **2410**

Model FP10 Free Pistol
The Hammerli model FP 10 Free Pistol is designed for advanced competitors who know how to take advantage of this advanced pistol's many adjustments and very high level of accuracy. Features: Trigger tongue adjustable for length and rotates around its own vertical axis. Rear sight adjusts for width of notch; interchangeable front sight posts; integrated compensator in front ramp.
Price . . . . **on request**

Hammerli SP20 New Face
The HAMMERLI SP 20 target pistol has a front-end magazine, match trigger and synthetic stock.
Specifications
Caliber: 22 LR/.32 S&W LWC
Barrel Length: 4.58"
Magazine Capacity: 5/6 (22LR/32S&W)
Sights: Integral front sight with 3 different widths.
Available in blue, anthracite or black.

X-ESSE Sport Pistol
The all-steel, high precision 22LR pistol comes equipped with a "Hi-Grip" in a new anatomical shape and an adjustable support.
Specifications
Sights: Integral front sight with 3 widths
Magazine: 10 round **Grips:** Available in red, black or yellow

Heckler & Koch Pistols

Model HK USP 9 &40 Universal Self-Loading Pistol
Specifications
Calibers: 9mm and 40 S&W   **Capacity:** 10 + 1
Operating System: Short recoil, modified Browning action
Barrel Length: 4.25"   **Overall Length:** 7.64"
Weight: 28 oz. (40 S&W); 26 oz. (9mm)
Height: 5.35"   **Sights:** Adjustable 3-dot
Grips: Polymer receiver and integral grips
Prices:
9mm & 40 S&W $766
Also available:
HK USP45 Tactical Pistol
  w/cleaning kit & case 1124

Model USP45 Universal Self-Loading Pistol
Specifications
Caliber: 45 ACP   **Capacity:** 10 rounds
Action: DA/SA or DAO   **Barrel Length:** 4.41"
Overall Length: 7.87"   **Height:** 5.55"
Weight: 30 oz.   **Grips:** Polymer frame & integral grips
Prices: 827

HK USP Compact Universal Self-Loading Pistol
Specifications
Calibers: 9mm, 40 S&W, .357 Sig and 45 ACP
Capacity: 10 rounds
Operating System: Short recoil, modified Browning action
Barrel Length: 3.58"   **Overall Length:** 6.81"
Weight: 28 oz. (40 S&W); 26 oz. (9mm)   **Height:** 5"
Sights: Adjustable 3-dot
Grips: Polymer frame and integral grips
Prices:
9mm, 40 S+W, and .357 Sig 786
Also available:
  Stainless (9mm and 40 S+W) 878-909
  45 ACP 857
  45 ACP, stainless 909

USP Compact LEM
Specifications
Action: Double-action self-loading
Grips: Full-hand grip frame with choice of extended or flush-fitting magazine floorplates.
Barrel: 3.58", blued   **Sights:** 3-dot
Weight: 1.53 lbs.   **Caliber:** .40 S&W magazine
Capacity: 10
Other features: the Law Enforcement modification was developed especially for the U.S. government
Price: 821

MODEL HK USP45 TACTICAL PISTOL

MODEL HK USP45 UNIVERSAL SELF-LOADING PISTOL

HK USP45 COMPACT UNIVERSAL SELF-LOADING PISTOL

USP COMPACT LEM

Heckler & Koch Pistols

HK USP EXPERT

HK USP45 Expert
Specifications
Caliber: 45 ACP or 40 S+W
Capacity: 10 rounds
Operating System: Short recoil, modified Browning action
Barrel Length: 6.02″
Overall Length: 9.45″
Weight: 39 oz.
Height: 5.90″
Sights: Adjustable 3-dot
Grips & Stock: Polymer frame and integral grips
Prices:
Blued $1533

Mark 23 Special Operations Pistol (SOCOM)
Specifications
Caliber: 45 ACP
Capacity: 10 rounds
Operating System: Short recoil, modified Browning action
Barrel Length: 5.87″
Overall Length: 9.65″
Height: 5.9″
Weight: 42 oz.
Sights: 3-dot
Grips: Polymer frame & integral grips
Price: 2444

MARK 23 SPECIAL OPERATIONS PISTOL (SOCOM)

Model P7M8
Specifications
Caliber: 9mmX19 (Luger)
Capacity: 8 rounds
Barrel Length: 4.13″
Overall Length: 6.73″
Weight: 28 oz.
Sight Radius: 5.83″
Sights: Adjustable rear
Grips: Plastic
Finish: Blue or nickel
Operating System: Recoil-operated; retarded inertia slide
Price: 1472

MODEL P7M8

Heritage Manufacturing

ROUGH RIDER 3.5" NICKEL W/BIRD'S HEAD GRIP

ROUGH RIDER SA

These single-action revolvers are patterned after the Colt Single-Action Army.
Specifications
Caliber: 22 LR or 22 LR/22 WMR **Capacity:** 6 rounds
Weight: 31 to 38 oz. **Barrel Lengths:** 4.75", 6.5", 9" (regular grip); 3.75", 4.75" (Bird's-Head grip)
Sights: Blade front, adjustable sight or Red Dot reflex
Grips: Exotic hardwood **Finish:** Blue or nickel
Features: Rotating hammer block safety; brass accent screws
Prices:
22 LR (4.75", 6.5" bbl.) blued, regular grip $108
22 LR/22 WMR W/blued finish, regular grip:
  4.75" & 6.5" barrels 119
  9" barrel 122
W/satin finish, regular grip:
  4.75" & 6.5" barrels $150
W/blued finish, bird's-head grip:
  3.75" & 4.75" barrels 119
W/satin finish: bird's-head grip:
  4.75" barrels 150
W/blued finish, adjustable sights 9" barrels. 146
W/satin finish, adjustable sights (6.5") 176
also available: Mother of Pearl grips . . . . add 18
W/steel frame/blue (3.75", 4.75", 6.5" barrels). 150
W/steel frame/nickel (6.5" barrel) 200
W/steel frame/blue (9" barrel) 154
W/steel frame/blue/adj. sights
  (4.75", 6.5", 9" barrel) 176

High Standard Pistols

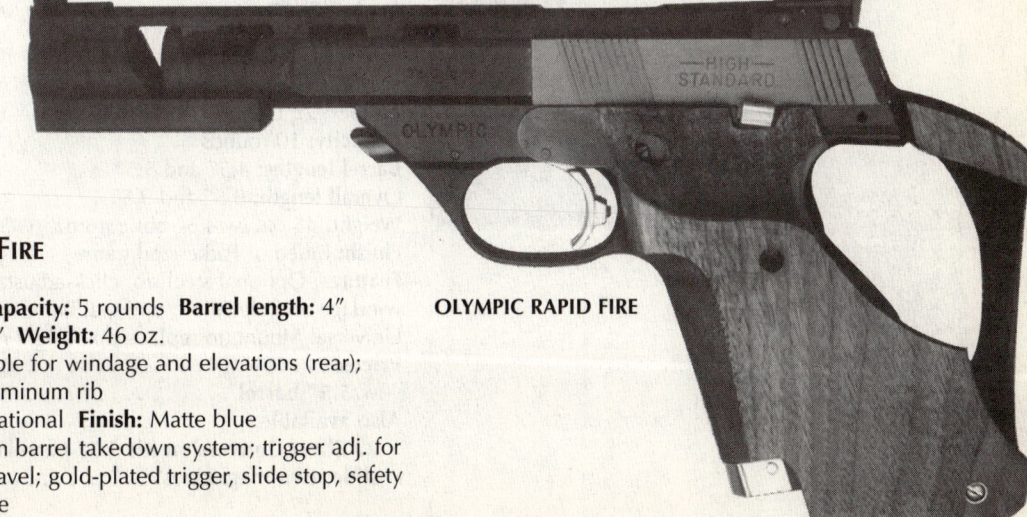

OLYMPIC RAPID FIRE

OLYMPIC RAPID FIRE
Specifications
Caliber: 22 Short **Capacity:** 5 rounds **Barrel length:** 4"
Overall length: 11.5" **Weight:** 46 oz.
Sights: Click-adjustable for windage and elevations (rear); mounted on vent aluminum rib
Grips: Special International **Finish:** Matte blue
Features: Push-button barrel takedown system; trigger adj. for weight of pull and travel; gold-plated trigger, slide stop, safety and magazine release
Price: $1027

High Standard Pistols

SUPERMATIC CITATION MS

OLYMPIC

TROPHY

VICTOR 22 LR

SUPERMATIC CITATION
Specifications
Caliber: 22 LR **Capacity:** 10 rounds
Barrel length: 5.5" **Overall length:** 9.5"
Weight: 44 oz. **Finish:** Blued or Parkerized
Features: Optional Universal Mount to replace open-sight rib (deduct $30.00)
Price:...................................$490
Also available:
Supermatic Citation MS. Similar to Citation above, except 10" barrel (14" overall), 54 oz. weight, checkered right-hand thumbrest and matte blue finish........................... 696
Trophy/Citation 22 Short Conversion Kit (incl. barrel w/sight, slide, 2 magazines)......... 317

OLYMPIC MILITARY
Specifications
Caliber: 22 LR **Capacity:** 10 rounds
Barrel length: 5.5" **Overall length:** 9.5"
Weight: 44 oz. **Finish:** Matte frame
Features: Fully adjustable rear sight; non-adjustable trigger
Price:....................................... 625

SUPERMATIC TROPHY
Specifications
Caliber: 22 LR **Capacity:** 10 rounds
Actions: Recoil-operated semiautomatic
Barrel length: 5.5" bull or 7.25" fluted
Overall length: 9.5 (w/5.5" bbl.) and 11.25" (w/7.25" bbl.)
Weight: 44 oz. (w/5.5" bbl.) and 46 oz. (w/7.25" bbl.)
Sights: Click-adjustable rear for windage/elevation; undercut ramp front **Grips:** Checkered American walnut with right-hand thumbrest (left-hand optional)
Features: Gold-plated trigger; slide lock lever; push-button takedown system; magazine release
Prices:
5.5" Barrel................................. 603
7.25" Barrel............................... 689

VICTOR 22 LR
Specifications
Caliber: 22 LR
Capacity: 10 rounds
Barrel lengths: 4.5" and 5.5"
Overall length: 8.5" and 9.5"
Weight: 45 oz. (w/4.5" bbl.); 46 oz. (w/5.5" bbl.)
Finish: Blued or Parkerized frame
Features: Optional steel rib; click-adjustable sights for windage and elevation; optional barrel weights and Universal Mount (to replace open-sight rib)
Prices:.................................... 564
   w/5.5" barrel............................ 625
Also available:
   22 Short Conversion Kit 5.5" barrel w/vent rib, slide, two magazines........................ 317

Hi-Point Firearms
Semi-Automatic Handguns

9MM COMPACT POLYMER

9MM COMP GUN

MODEL 380 COMP

380 POLYMER

Hi-Point Firearms offer reliability and accuracy at an affordable price. Hi-Point handguns are sized to feel good in your hand and provide exceptional recoil control. All models feature sleek lines and a scratch-resistant, non-glare military black finish with high-impact grips. New 3-dot sights.

9MM COMPACT POLYMER
Specifications
Caliber: 9mm parabellum
Capacity: 8 shot mag
Action: Single action
Barrel Length: 3.5" alloy steel barrel
Sights: Low-profile 3 dot adj. sights
Safety: Quick on-off thumb safety
Overall Length: 6.75"
Frame: Polymer frame
Price:. $137

9MM COMP GUN
Specifications
Hi-Point Firearms has introduced a 9mm Comp Gun featuring a 4" barrel, adjustable sights, magazine disconnect safety, muzzle compensator, last round hold-open feature. 10 rounds. Also available with a laser sight mounted to the compensator
Prices:. $169
  With laser and mount. 219

MODEL 380 COMP
Specifications
Hi-Point Firearms' 380 Comp Gun features a 4" barrel, adjustable sights, 2 magazines (10 round and 8 round). The 380 Comp Pistol is also available with a Laser Sight mounted to the compensator.
Price:. 125
  w/laser sights. 190

MODEL 380 POLYMER
Model 380 Polymer similar to 9mm but with 3.5" alloy steel barrel, 29 oz.
Price:. 100
Also available:
  Caliber: .45 ACP **Action:** semi-automatic
  Capacity: 7 shot **Barrel length:** 4.5"
  Sights: 3 dot adjustable sights 169
  Caliber: 40 S&W **Action:** semi-automatic
  Capacity: 8 shot **Barrel length:** 4.5"
  Sights: 3 dot adjustable sights 169

H-S Precision Pistols

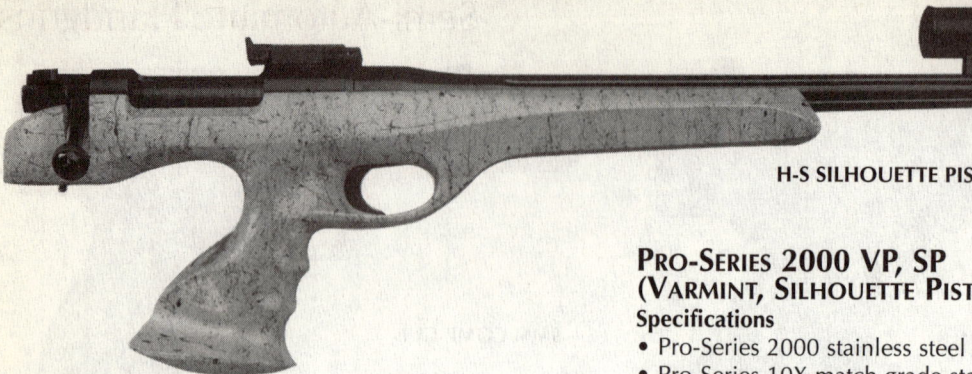

H-S SILHOUETTE PISTOL

H-S Precision

H-S Precision single-shot pistols employ a right-handle bolt, with handle engineered so the bolt head is over the well of the grip for good balance. As on the Series 2000 rifles, triggers are fully adjustable and can be set from 2.5 to 3.5 pounds pull. These super-accurate pistols are held to the same accuracy standards as Pro-Series rifles. They're available in many chamberings, in both varmint and silhouette versions. The silhouette pistol has a titanium safety shroud and a lighter barrel that is drilled and tapped for sights. It meets IHMSA competition weight requirements.
Price: (either version) **$1350**

Pro-Series 2000 VP, SP (Varmint, Silhouette Pistols)
Specifications
- Pro-Series 2000 stainless steel pistol action, single shot
- Pro-Series 10X match grade stainless steel barrel
  - Fluted (except 35 Rem, Silhouette style)
  - Sporter contour, silhouette model
  - Heavy contour, varmint model
- Pro-Series synthetic stock, center grip with bedding block chassis system
  - Choice of color
  - Metal finish – Teflon® or Pro-Series PFTE Matte Black
- Weight
  - 5 pounds, silhouette
  - 5.25 - 5.50 pounds, varmint
- Calibers – 17 Rem, 6mm PPC, 223 Rem, 22-250 Rem, 243 Win, 257 Roberts, 260 Rem, 35 Rem, 308 Winc, 7mm-08 Rem, 7mm BR

Israel Arms & Firearms International

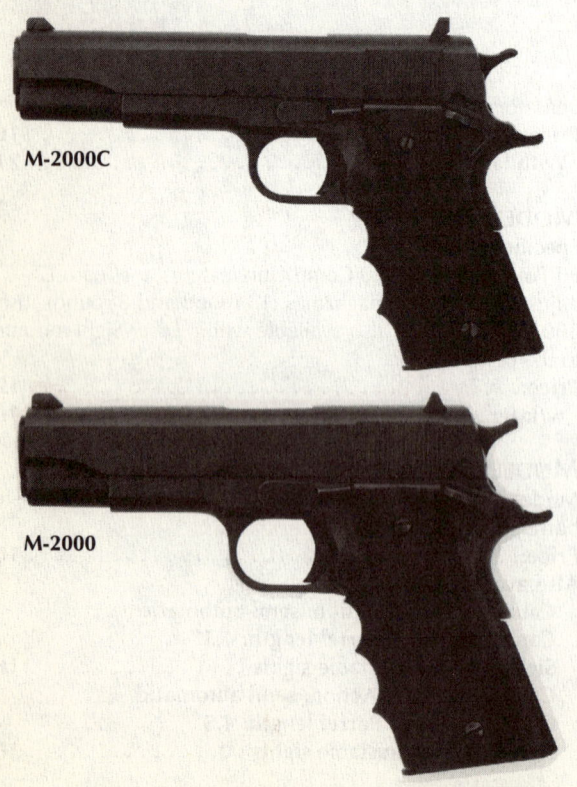

M-2000C

M-2000

M-2000C
Compact .45 U.S. Army Model, ACP, complete frame & slide Parkerized
Specifications
Barrel Length: 4.25"
Overall Length: 6" **Height:** 5.25"
Mag. Capacity: 8 round
Weight unloaded: 36 oz.
Features: GI grip safety; fixed sights; plastic grips; beveled feed ramp barrel
Price: **$465**

M-2000
1911 Gov. .45 ACP, Complete Frame & Slide, 4140 Steel, Blue Parkerized
Specifications
Barrel Length: 5"
Overall Length: 8.5" **Height:** 5.25"
Capacity: 8 **Weight unloaded:** 36 oz.
Features: Beveled feed ramp barrel; grip safety; GI, fixed sights; plastic grips
Price: **465**

Kahr Arms Pistols

P40
Specifications
Caliber: .40 S&W
Capacity: 6+1
Barrel: 3.5", 1-16 RH twist
Overall length: 6.1"
Height: 4.5"
Weight: 18.7 oz.
Prices:
P40 .... $599
K40 580
K40, Stainless. 638
KS40, Stainless covert. 594
K40 Elite, stainless 694

P9
Specifications
Caliber: 9x19
Capacity: 7+1
Barrel: 3.5", 1-10 RH twist
Overall length: 6.0"
Height: 4.5"
Weight: 17.7 oz.
Prices:
K9 Elite, stainless 694
MK9 Elite 98, stainless 694
MK9 Elite 2000, black 694
MK9, stainless 638
P9 (black or stainless). 599
K9 (black or stainless) 580
PM9, black frame, stainless slide. 622

P40

P9

KBI Pistols

FEG Model PJK-9HP (Hi-power)
Specifications
Caliber: 9mm Luger Parabellum
Magazine capacity: 10 rounds
Action: Single **Barrel Length:** 4.75"
Overall Length: 8"
Weight: 21 oz.
Grips: Hand-checkered walnut
Safety: Thumb safety
Sights: 3-dot system **Finish:** Blue
Features: One 10-round magazine, cleaning rod
Price: $299

FEG MODEL PJK-9HP

Kel-Tec

P-32 CALIBER .32 AUTO

P-11 CALIBER 9MM LUGER

SUB RIFLE 2000 CALIBERS 9MM & 40 S&W

SUB RIFLE 2000 (READY TO FIRE)

P-32 Caliber .32 Auto
The P-32 is designed for maximum concealability. It is lighter and flatter than any other self-loading gun. This has been achieved by using a locked breech combined with the composite structure of the successful P-11 and P-40 pistols. The firing mechanism is slide-assisted double-action only, employing an internal hammer block. Trigger pull is 6 lbs. The P-32 can shoot any configuration, including hot European or emerging +P cartridges. All edges are rounded, sights are integrated, and the slide stop internal for a snag-free deployment.

Specifications
Caliber: .32 AUTO, 7.65x17 **Weight unloaded:** 6.6 oz., 186 g **Loaded magazine:** 2.8 oz., 81g **Length:** 5.07″, 129mm **Height:** 3.52″, 89mm **Width:** .75″, 19 mm **Barrel length:** 2.68″, 68mm **Muzzle energy:** 200 ftlbs, 270 J **Capacity:** 7+1 rounds
Prices:
P-32 (not shown), 6.6 oz, 7+1 round capacity blue . $300
Parkerized 340
Chromed 355

P-11 Caliber 9mm Luger
The P-11 is a semi-automatic, locked breech pistol, chambered for the 9mm Luger cartridge. The firing mechanism is double-action only.

Specifications
Caliber: 9mm Luger, 9x19 **Weight unloaded:** 14.4 oz., 408g **Loaded magazine:** 5.6 oz., 159g **Length:** 5.85″, 148mm **Height:** 4.3″, 109mm **Width:** 1.05″, 26 mm **Barrel length:** 3.1″, 79mm **Muzzle energy ftlbs:** 400 ftlbs, 540 J **Capacity:** 10+1 rounds **Trigger Pull:** 9 lbs, 40N
Prices:
P11, blue $314
Parkerized 355
Chromed 368

Sub Rifle 2000 Calibers 9mm & 40 S&W
The SUB RIFLE 2000 is a self-loading carbine for pistol cartridges. Different versions of the SUB-2000 will accept most modern handgun magazines, e.g. S&W, Glock or Beretta. By rotating the barrel upwards and back, the SUB-2000 can be reduced to a size of 16″ x 7″ to facilitate secure storage. The SUB-2000 also features an internal keyed deployment lock.

Specifications
Weight unloaded: 4 lbs., 1.8 kg **Length open:** 30″, 762mm **Length closed:** 16″, 406mm **Barrel length:** 16.1″, 409 mm **Practical range:** 150 yd, 150 m **Safeties:** recessed push-bolt. Lock-back operating handle, keyed deployment lock.
Price:
Sub-Rifle 2000 383

Kimber Pistols

Custom II and Custom Target II

The first Kimber 1911 shipped in 1996. Kimber has since become the world's largest producer of 1911-style pistols. A custom-quality pistol with a production price, the base Kimber has a 5" match-grade barrel, weighs 38 oz. and is 8.7" in overall length. .45 ACP, .40 S&W, and .38 Super versions are available.

Prices:
Custom II	$730
Custom stainless II	832
Custom stainless II in 40 S&W	945
Royal II (rosewood grips)	886
Custom Target II (not shown)	837
Stainless Target II	945
Stainless Target II in 38 super	974

CUSTOM II & CUSTOM TARGET II

Gold Match II

Specifications
Features: Hand-fitted stainless steel barrel, match grade trigger, hand checkered rosewood grips.
Barrel length: 5"
Weight: 38 oz.
Overall length: 8.7"
Caliber: 45 ACP
Prices:
Gold Match II	1168
Stainless II	1315
Stainless II in 40 S&W	1345

STAINLESS GOLD MATCH II

Compact II & Pro Carry II

These compact pistols are good choices for concealed carry and defense.
Specifications
Barrel: 4" **Overall length:** 7.7"
Weight: 34 oz. (compact) and 28 oz. (PRO CARRY)
Caliber: 45 ACP, or 38 super
Prices:
Compact II (45 ACP only)	870
Pro Carry II (not shown) (45 ACP)	773
Pro Carry Stainless (45 ACP)	845
Pro Carry HD II	879
Pro Carry HD II in 38 super	917

COMPACT II & PRO CARRY II

Ultra Carry II

Specifications
Caliber: 45 ACP and 40 S&W **Barrel:** 3"
Weight: 25 oz. **Overall length:** 6.8"
Prices:
Ultra Carry II 45 ACP	767
Stainless II	841
Stainless II in 40 S&W	884

STAINLESS ULTRA CARRY II

Kimber Pistols

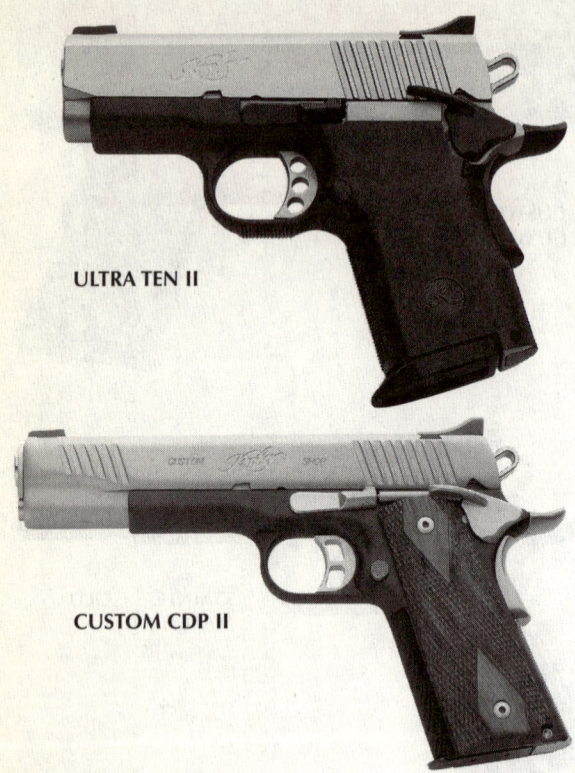

ULTRA TEN II

CUSTOM CDP II

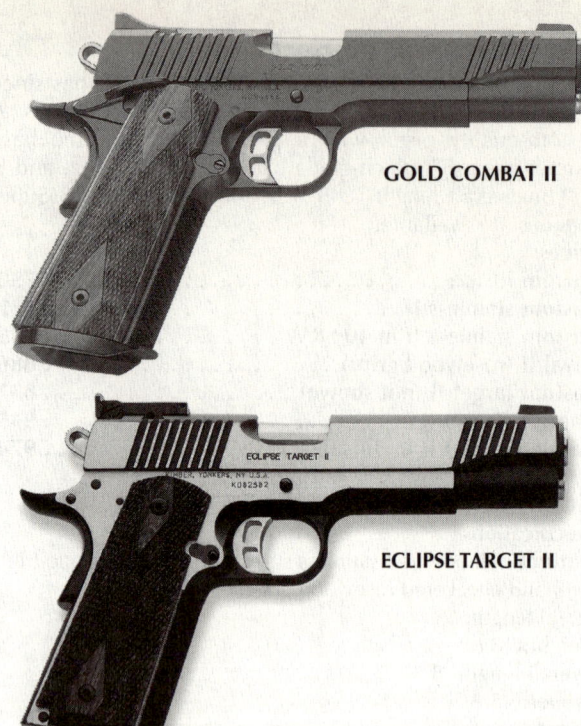

GOLD COMBAT II

ECLIPSE TARGET II

TEN II HIGH CAPACITY
All-new American-made polymer frame with 10-round double-stack magazine. Frame dimensions are almost identical to standard 1911. Available in all sizes. 14-round magazines still available where legal.
Specifications
Caliber: .45 ACP
Barrel Length: 3: (Ultra Ten II), 4" (Pro Carry Ten II), and 5" (Stainless Ten II and Gold Match Ten II)
Weight: 24 oz. – 34 oz.
Prices:
Ultra Ten II $850
ProCarry Ten II. 828
Stainless Ten II 812
Gold Match Ten II 1118

CUSTOM SHOP PISTOLS
The Gold Combat II has most of the features of the Gold Match II and includes many Custom Shop features like a stainless steel match grade barrel and chamber, 30 LPI front strap checkering, extended beveled magazine well, stainless steel match grade barrel bushing, special bordered and hand-checkered double diamond rosewood grips, extended ambidextrous thumb safety, match grade Premium Aluminum Trigger, Meprolight Tritium three dot (green) night sights and special Custom Shop markings.
Specifications
Caliber: 45 ACP **Barrel length:** 5"
Weight: 38 oz. **Overall length:** 8.7"
Prices:
Gold Combat II 1681

Stainless II $1623
Also Available: Super Match II 1926
LTP II. 2036

CDP II SERIES
The Custom Defense Package pistols feature a lightweight aluminum frame and stainless steel slide. Edges and corners have been rounded and grips are checkered rosewood.
Specifications
Caliber: 45 ACP & 40 S&W
Weight: 25-38 oz.
Overall length: 6.8-8.7"
Prices:
Ultra CDP II(3" barrel). 1084
Compact CDP II (4" barrel) 1084
Custom CDP II (5" barrel) 1084
Pro CDP II. 1084
Ultra CDP II. 1120

ECLIPSE II
The new Eclipse II series is available in .45 ACP. the stainless steel forging is finished in matte black oxide, with all flat surfaces brush-polished; 3-dot Meprolight night sights are standard. Front straps have 30-LPI checkering. The Eclipse Pro Target II has a 4" barrel; the Eclipse Target is 5".
Prices:
Eclipse Custom II 1071
Eclipse Target II 1153
Eclipse Ultra II 1052
Eclipse Pro II 1052
Eclipse Pro Target II 1153

Llama Pistols

MICROMAX .380 MATTE FINISH
- High impact polymer grips
- Mini combat hammer
- Extended slide release
- Mini beavertail grip safety
- Extended manual safety
- 3-dot sight system
- Matte, duo-tone, satin chrome finishers
- Available in 32 ACP and 380 caliber (8 rounds)

Prices:
Matte. $282
Satin chrome 299

MINIMAX .45 SATIN CHROME FINISH
- Extended beavertail grip
- Skeletonized combat hammer
- Upgraded new steel design
- 3-dot sight system
- Rubber grips
- Extended slide release
- Cone-style barrel system for easy take-down and increased accuracy
- Matte, satin chrome & duo-tone finishes
- Shortened barrel and grip frame
- Flared ejection port
- Available in .45 ACP, .40 S&W & 9mm
- LIFETIME SERVICE CONTRACT

Prices:
Matte. 325
Satin chrome 342
Duo-tone. 334
Also available: Sub compact . . . . 342 - 359

MAX-I 45 GOVERNMENT DUO-TONE FINISH
- 3-dot sight system
- Anatomically designed rubber grip system
- Precision machined from high-strength steel
- Ultra-smooth serrated trigger
- Extended slide release
- Serrated grip frame
- Skeletonized combat hammer
- Extended manual safety
- Non-glare matte blue, satin chrome & duo-tone finishes
- Beaver tail grip safety
- LIFETIME SERVICE CONTRACT

Caliber: 45 auto
Price:. 395

MINIMAX .45 SATIN CHROME FINISH

MICROMAX .380 MATTE FINISH

MAX-I 45 GOVERNMENT DOU-TONE FINISH

Magnum Research Handguns

MARK XIX COMPONENT SYSTEM

DESERT EAGLE PISTOL MARK XIX .50 MAGNUM TITANIUM FINISH

BABY EAGLE RS

BABY EAGLE

Mark XIX Component System

The Desert Eagle Pistol Mark XIX Component System is based on a single platform that transforms into six different pistols, each with a 6-inch or 10-inch barrel. Changing calibers is a simple matter of switching barrels and magazines. (Converting to or from .357 Magnum also involves changing the bolt.)

All six barrels, including the optional 10-inch barrels, have a 7/8" dovetailed design with cross slots to accommodate scope rings; no other scope mounts are required. The .50 A.E.'s new 10-inch barrel will fit existing .50s, as well as the new Mark XIX platform.

The pistol's gas operation, polygonal rifling, low recoil and safety features remain the same, as do the Mark VII adjustable trigger, slide release and safety levers.

Specifications
Calibers: 357 Magnum, 44 Magnum and 50 A.E.
Capacity: 9 rounds (357 Mag.); 8 rounds (44 Mag.); 7 rounds (50 A.E.) **Barrel Lengths:** 6" and 10" **Overall Length:** 10.74" (w/6" bbl.); 14.75" (w/10" bbl.) **Weight:** 4 lbs. 6.5 oz. (w/6" bbl.); 4 lbs. 15 oz. (w/10" bbl.) (empty) **Height:** 6.25"
Width: 1.25" **Finish:** Standard black and new Titanium nitride
Prices:
with 6" barrel $1199
with 10" barrel 1299
Titanium finish, 6" (50AE only) 1699
Chrome or nickel, 6" 1424
Polished blue with gold, 6" 1649
NEW: Also available:
   440 Cor-Bon Magnum, 6" 1389
   440 Cor-Bon Magnum, 10" 1429

Baby Eagle RS

The Baby Eagle RS in 9mm offers a frame-mounted safety and a shorter barrel than the standard Baby Eagle Pistol. The RS is available in standard black, matte hard chrome or brushed hard chrome (as shown). A polymer-frame version is also available. These autoloading pistols are available in 9mm, .40 S+W and .45 ACP.
Price: Baby Eagle 499

Magnum Research Handguns

"Single-Action Hunting Revolver"

Magnum Research, Inc., manufacturers the Desert Eagle autoloading pistol, but also makes the BFR (biggest finest revolver). Manufactured in the United States, it is available in two models, both built to close tolerances, entirely of stainless steel. The long-cylindered model fires big-bore calibers .45/70, .444 Marlin, and .45 Long Colt/.410. The short cylinder model is available in .454 Casull, .45 Long Colt + P, and .22 Hornet.

Barrel length options of 6.5, 7.5, and 10 inches, depending on chambering.

Price:	$999
Accessories	
Hogue Wood Grips Pau Ferro	75
Leupold mount/rings	49
Cordura hip hoister	30
Millett sights, rear adjustable, white outline	39

Standard equipment sights have fixed orange front ramp and rear sight adjustable for windage and elevation.

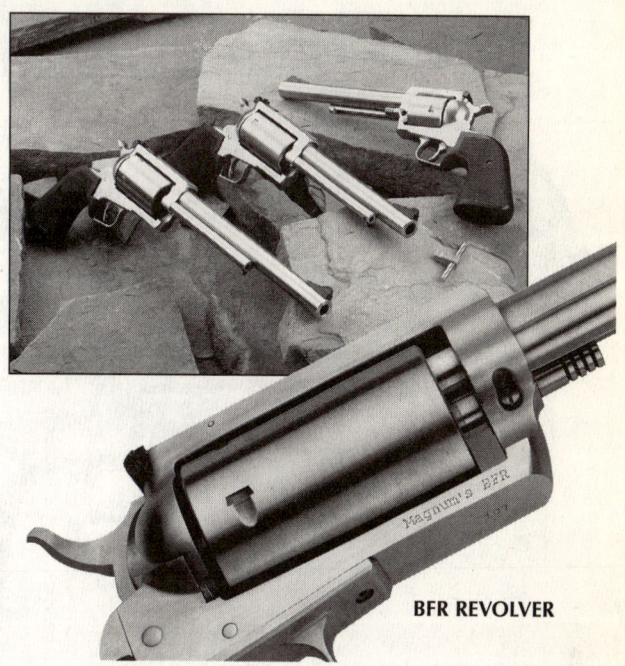

BFR REVOLVER

MOA Maximum Pistols

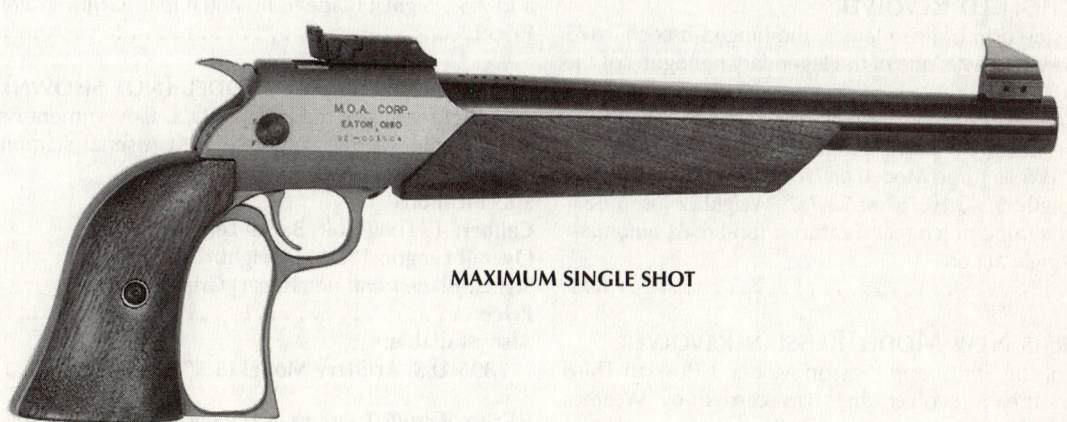

MAXIMUM SINGLE SHOT

Maximum

This single-shot pistol with its unique falling-block action performs like a finely tuned rifle. The single-piece receiver of stainless steel is mated to a Douglas barrel for optimum accuracy and strength.

Specifications
Calibers: 22 Hornet to 375 H&H
Barrel Lengths: 8.5", 10.5" and 14"
Weight: 3 lbs. 8 oz. (8.5" bbl.); 3 lbs. 13 oz. (10.5" bbl.); 4 lbs. 3 oz. (14" bbl.)

Prices:	
Stainless receiver, blued barrel	$799
Stainless receiver and barrel	883
Extra barrels (blue)	254
Stainless	317
Muzzle brake	125

Navy Arms Replicas

1873 SINGLE ACTION ARMY REVOLVER

1875 SCHOFIELD CAVALRY MODEL REVOLVER

NEW MODEL RUSSIAN REVOLVER

1873 SINGLE ACTION ARMY REVOLVER
The quintessential sidearm of the American West. One of the most popular revolvers of all time, manufactured 1873-1940. This superb replica of the Colt Single Action Army features color case hardened frame and hammer, and a blued steel barrel, cylinder, trigger guard and backstrap. Available in the same barrel lengths as the originals: 4-3/4", 5-1/2", 7-1/2". Chambered for .45 Colt, .44-40 and .357 Magnum
Price: $395

1875 SCHOFIELD REVOLVER
A favorite side arm of Jesse James, the hinged-breech 1875 Schofield revolver was one of the legendary handguns of the Old West.
Specifications
Caliber: 44-40, 45 LC **Barrel Lengths:** 3.5" (Hide Out Model), 5" (Wells Fargo Model) or 7" (U.S. Cavalry Model)
Overall Length: 9.5", 10.75" or 12.75" **Weight:** 2 lbs. 5 oz.
Sights: Blade front; notch rear **Features:** Top-break, automatic ejector single action
Price: 695

NAVY ARMS NEW MODEL RUSSIAN REVOLVER
A replica of the Smith and Wesson Model 3 Russian Third Model top break revolver that was carried by Western Lawman Pat Garrett.
Specifications
Caliber: .44 Russian **Barrel Lengths:** 6.5"
Overall Length: 12" **Weight:** 2 lbs. 8 oz.
Sights: Blade front; notch rear Grips: Walnut
Price: 745

BISLEY MODEL SINGLE ACTION REVOLVER (NOT SHOWN)
Introduced in 1894, Colt's "Bisley Model" was named after the Bisley shooting range in England. Most of these revolvers were sold in the United States and were popular sidearms in the American West at the turn of the century. This replica features the unique Bisley grip style, low-profile spur hammer, blued barrel and color casehardened frame.
Specifications
Calibers: 44-40 or 45 Long Colt **Barrel Lengths:** 4.75", 5.5" and 7.5" **Sights:** Blade front, notch rear **Grips:** Walnut
Price: $415

1873 U.S. CAVALRY MODEL (NOT SHOWN)
An exact replica of the original U.S. Government issue Colt Single-Action Army, complete with Arsenal stampings and inspector's cartouche.
Specifications
Caliber: 45 Long Colt **Barrel Length:** 7.5"
Overall Length: 13.25" **Weight:** 2 lbs. 7 oz.
Sights: Blade front; notch rear **Grips:** Walnut
Price: 465
Also available:
1895 U.S. Artillery Model (5.5" barrel) 465

"FLAT TOP" TARGET MODEL SA REVOLVER (NOT SHOWN)
A fine replica of Colt's rare "Flat Top" Single Action Army revolver used for target shooting.
Specifications
Caliber: 45 Long Colt **Barrel Length:** 7.5"
Overall Length: 12.75" **Weight:** 2 lbs. 7 oz.
Sights: Spring-loaded German silver Partridge front, adjustable notch ear. **Grips:** Walnut. **Finish:** Blue
Price: 435

North American Arms

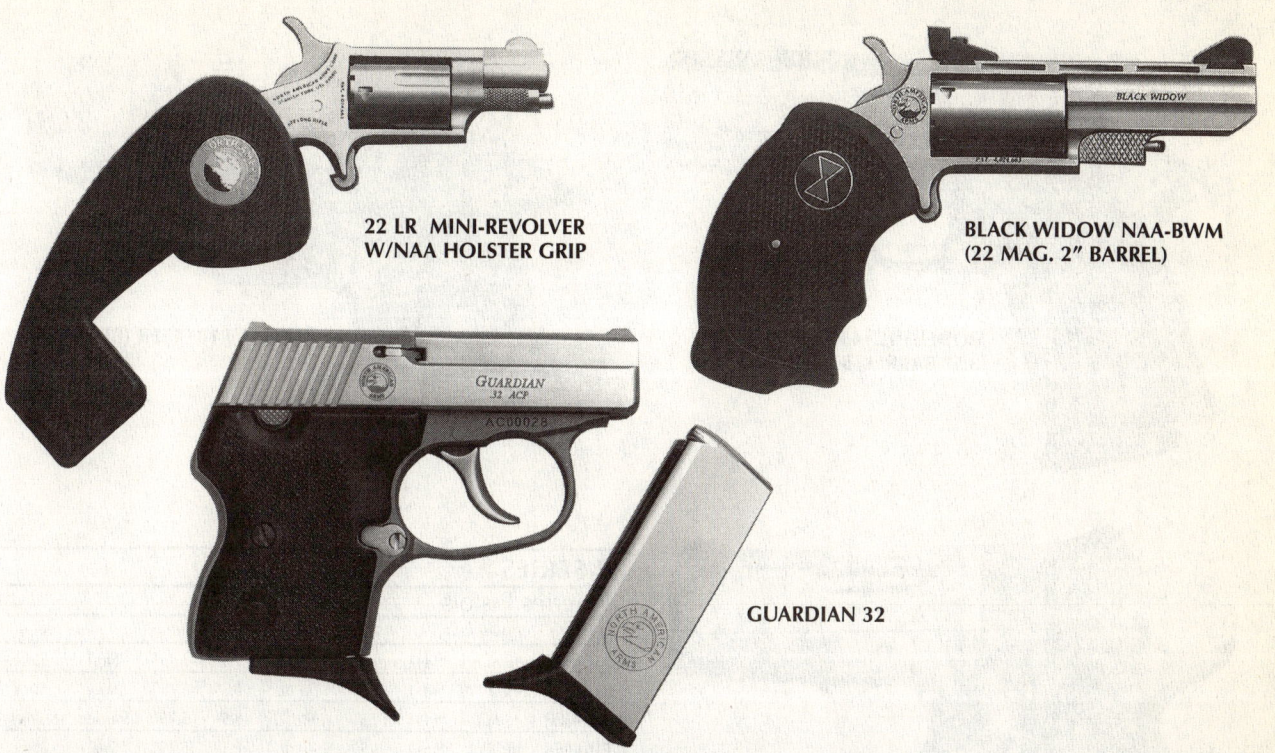

22 LR MINI-REVOLVER W/NAA HOLSTER GRIP

BLACK WIDOW NAA-BWM (22 MAG. 2" BARREL)

GUARDIAN 32

Mini-Revolvers
Specifications (See also table below)
Calibers: 22 Short (1 1/8" bbl. only), 22 LR and 22 Magnum
Capacity: 5-shot cylinder **Grips:** Laminated rosewood
Safety: Half-cock safety **Sights:** Blade front (integral w/barrel); fixed, notched rear **Material:** Stainless steel
Finish: Matte with brushed sides

Mini-Master Series
Specifications
Calibers: 22 LR and 22 Magnum **Rifling:** 8 land and grooves, 1:12 R.H. twist **Grips:** Oversized black rubber
Sights: Front integral with barrel; rear Millett adjustable white outlined (elelvation only) or low-profile fixed

Prices:
Mini-Master NAA-MMT-M $304
  w/Fixed sight 286
Mini-Master NAA Black Widow
  Adjustable sight 274
  Fixed sight 256

Guardian 32
Stainless steel autoloading pistol; double action; fixed sights; 6-shot magazine in .32 ACP
Price: 408
Also available:
NAA Guardian .380 .380/9mm Kurz **Features:** 6 shot, fixed sights **Barrel length:** 2.5" **Height:** 3.5" **Total length:** 4.75"
Price: 449

SPECIFICATIONS: MINI-REVOLVERS & MINI-MASTER SERIES

Model	Weight	Barrel Length	Overall Length	Overall Height	Overall Width	Price
NAA-MMT-M	10.7 oz.	4"	7 3/4"	3 7/8"	7/8"	$304
NAA-MMT-L	10.7 oz.	4"	7 3/4"	3 7/8"	7/8"	304
*NAA-BW-M	8.8 oz.	2"	5 7/8"	3 7/8"	7/8"	256
*NAA-BW-L	8.8 oz.	2"	5 7/8"	3 7/8"	7/8"	256
NAA-22LR**	4.5 oz.	1 1/8"	4 1/4"	2 3/8"	13/16"	186
NAA-22LLR**	4.6 oz.	1 5/8"	4 3/4"	2 3/8"	13/16"	186
*NAA-22MS	5.9 oz.	1 1/8"	5"	2 7/8"	7/8"	205
*NAA-22M	6.2 oz.	1 5/8"	5 3/8"	2 7/8"	7/8"	205
NAA-22S	4 oz.	1 1/8"	3 5/8"	2 3/8"	13/16"	205

*Available with Conversion Cylinder chambered for 22 Long Rifle ($245.00) **Available with holster grip ($240.00)

Para-Ordnance Pistols

MODEL P12•45 ACP
(3.5" BARREL, STAINLESS)

MODEL P10•45ER (BLACK)

MODEL P10•45 LIMITED

P-Series Pistols

Built on the proven M1911-A1 single-action autoloading pistol, the Para-Ordnance P-series was developed beginning in 1988. The P14.45 appeared in 1990 as one of the first high-capacity autoloaders of this type. Uninterrupted slide rails, beefier slide stop, contoured feed ramp and ejection port, combat hammer, 3-dot sights, beveled magazine well and polymer magazine are all standard.

Specifications
Magazine Capacity: 10+1 in compact models to 18+1 in full-size.

P-SERIES
Prices:
P-Series Steel $795
P-Series Stainless 865
P-Series Alloy 765

Para-Ordnance "Limited"

Para-Ordnance "Limited" pistols feature adjustable sights, competition hammer, front slide serrations, match-grade barrel, ambidextrous safety, full-length recoil guide.
Prices:
Steel 949
Stainless. 999
Alloy 945

P-SERIES
P-Series Pistols

Model	Caliber	Rounds	Barrel	Weight	Length	Height	Receiver	Finish
P14-45ER	.45 ACP	*14+1	5"	40 oz.	8.5"	5.75"	Steel	Black
P14-45RR	.45 ACP	*14+1	5"	31 oz.	8.5"	5.75"	Alloy	Black
P14-45SR	.45 ACP	*14+1	5"	40 oz.	8.5"	5.75"	Stainless	Stainless
P16-40ER	.40 S&W	*16+1	5"	40 oz.	8.5"	5.75"	Steel	Black
P16-40SR	.40 S&W	*16+1	5"	40 oz.	8.5"	5.75"	Stainless	Stainless
P18-9SR	9mm	*18+1	5"	40 oz.	8.5"	5.75"	Stainless	Stainless
P13-45ER	.45 ACP	*13+1	4.25"	36 oz.	7.75"	5.25"	Steel	Black
P13-45RR	.45 ACP	*13+1	4.25"	28 oz.	7.75"	5.25"	Alloy	Black
P13-45SR	.45 ACP	*13+1	4.25"	36 oz.	7.75"	5.25"	Stainless	Stainless
P12-45ER	.45 ACP	*12+1	3.5"	34 oz.	7.13"	5"	Steel	Black
P12-45RR	.45 ACP	*12+1	3.5"	26 oz.	7.13"	5"	Alloy	Black
P12-45SR	.45 ACP	*12+1	3.5"	34 oz.	7.13"	5"	Stainless	Stainless
P10-45ER	.45 ACP	*10+1	3"	31 oz.	8.5"	5.75"	Steel	Black
P10-45RR	.45 ACP	*10+1	3"	24 oz.	8.5"	5.75"	Alloy	Black
P10-45SR	.45 ACP	*10+1	3"	31 oz.	8.5"	5.75"	Stainless	Stainless
P10-40ER	.40 S&W	*10+1	3"	31 oz.	8.5"	5.75"	Steel	Black
P10-40RR	.40 S&W	*10+1	3"	24 oz.	8.5"	5.75"	Alloy	Stainless
P10-40SR	.40 S&W	*10+1	3"	31 oz.	8.5"	5.75"	Stainless	Stainless
P10-9RR	9mm	*10+1	3"	24 oz.	8.5"	5.75"	Alloy	Black

LIMITED P-SERIES
P-Series Limited Pistols

Model	Caliber	Rounds	Barrel	Weight	Length	Height	Receiver	Finish
S14-45ER	.45 ACP	*14+1	5"	40 oz.	8.5"	5.75"	Steel	Black
S14-45SR	.45 ACP	*14+1	5"	40 oz.	8.5"	5.75"	Stainless	Stainless
S16-40ER	.40 S&W	*16+1	5"	40 oz.	8.5"	5.75"	Steel	Black
S16-40SR	.40 S&W	*16+1	5"	40 oz.	8.5"	5.75"	Stainless	Stainless
S13-45ER	.45 ACP	*13+1	4.25"	36 oz.	7.75"	5.25"	Steel	Black
S13-45RR	.45 ACP	*13+1	4.25"	28 oz.	7.75"	5.25"	Alloy	Black
S13-45SR	.45 ACP	*13+1	4.25"	36 oz.	7.75"	5.25"	Stainless	Stainless
S12-45ER	.45 ACP	*12+1	3.5"	34 oz.	7.13"	5"	Steel	Black
S12-45RR	.45 ACP	*12+1	3.5"	26 oz.	7.13"	5"	Alloy	Black
S12-45SR	.45 ACP	*12+1	3.5"	34 oz.	7.13"	5"	Stainless	Stainless
S10-45ER	.45 ACP	*10+1	3"	31 oz.	6.5"	4.5"	Steel	Black
S10-45RR	.45 ACP	*10+1	3"	24 oz.	6.5"	4.5"	Alloy	Black
S10-45SR	.45 ACP	*10+1	3"	31 oz.	6.5"	4.5"	Stainless	Stainless

Para-Ordnance Pistols

Para-Ordnance LDA
The Para-Ordnance LDA pistol is a double-action carbon-steel gun in .45ACP, .40 S+W and 9mm.
Specifications
Capacity: 14+1, 16+1, and 18+1, respectively
Barrel: 5″
Weight: 40 oz.
Prices:
LDA Series $825
   Stainless 899
Limited LDA Series 975
   Stainless 1049

LDA

LDA SERIES
LDA Lightning Double-Action Pistols

Model	Caliber	Rounds	Barrel	Weight	Length	Height	Receiver	Finish
D14-45ER	.45 ACP	*14+1	5″	40 oz.	8.5″	5.75″	Steel	Black
D14-45SR	.45 ACP	*14+1	5″	40 oz.	8.5″	5.75″	Stainless	Stainless
D16-40ER	.40 S&W	*16+1	5″	40 oz.	8.5″	5.75″	Steel	Black
D16-40SR	.40 S&W	*16+1	5″	40 oz.	8.5″	5.75″	Stainless	Stainless
D18-9ER	9mm	*18+1	5″	40 oz.	8.5″	5.75″	Steel	Black
D18-9SR	9mm	*18+1	5″	40 oz.	8.5″	5.75″	Stainless	Stainless
L12-45ER	.45 ACP	*12+1	3.5″	34 oz.	7.13″	5″	Steel	Black
L12-45SR	.45 ACP	*12+1	3.5″	34 oz.	7.13″	5″	Stainless	Stainless
L14-40ER	.40 S&W	*14+1	3.5″	34 oz.	7.13″	5″	Steel	Black
L14-40SR	.40 S&W	*14+1	3.5″	34 oz.	7.13″	5″	Stainless	Stainless

LIMITED LDA SERIES
LDA Lightning Double-Action "Limited Series" Pistols

Model	Caliber	Rounds	Barrel	Weight	Length	Height	Receiver	Finish
T14-45ER	.45 ACP	*14+1	5″	40 oz.	8.5″	5.75″	Steel	Black
T14-45SR	.45 ACP	*14+1	5″	40 oz.	8.5″	5.75″	Stainless	Stainless
T16-40ER	.40 S&W	*16+1	5″	40 oz.	8.5″	5.75″	Steel	Black
T16-40SR	.40 S&W	*16+1	5″	40 oz.	8.5″	5.75″	Stainless	Stainless
T18-9ER	9mm	*18+1	5″	40 oz.	8.5″	5.75″	Steel	Black
T18-9SR	9mm	*18+1	5″	40 oz.	8.5″	5.75″	Stainless	Stainless

LDA SINGLE STACK SERIES
LDA Single-Stack Series Pistols

Model	Caliber	Barrel	Weight	Length	Height	Receiver	Finish	Order No.
CARRY	.45 ACP	3″	30 oz.	6.5″	4.75″	Stainless	Stainless	C645S
COMPANION	.45 ACP	3.5″	32 oz.	7.13″	5″	Stainless	Stainless	C745S

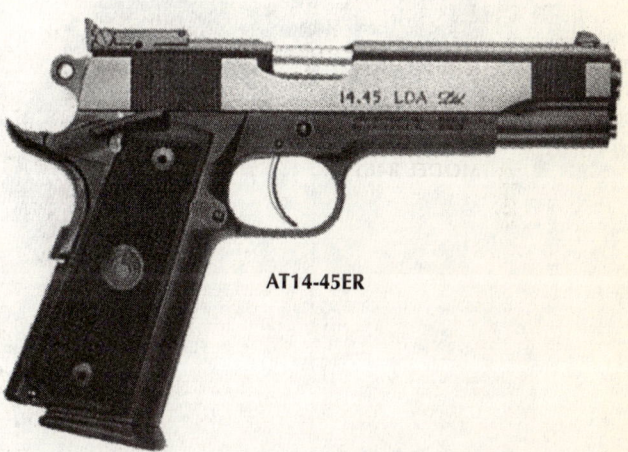
AT14-45ER

PARA CARRY
C6.45 LDA

Rossi Revolvers

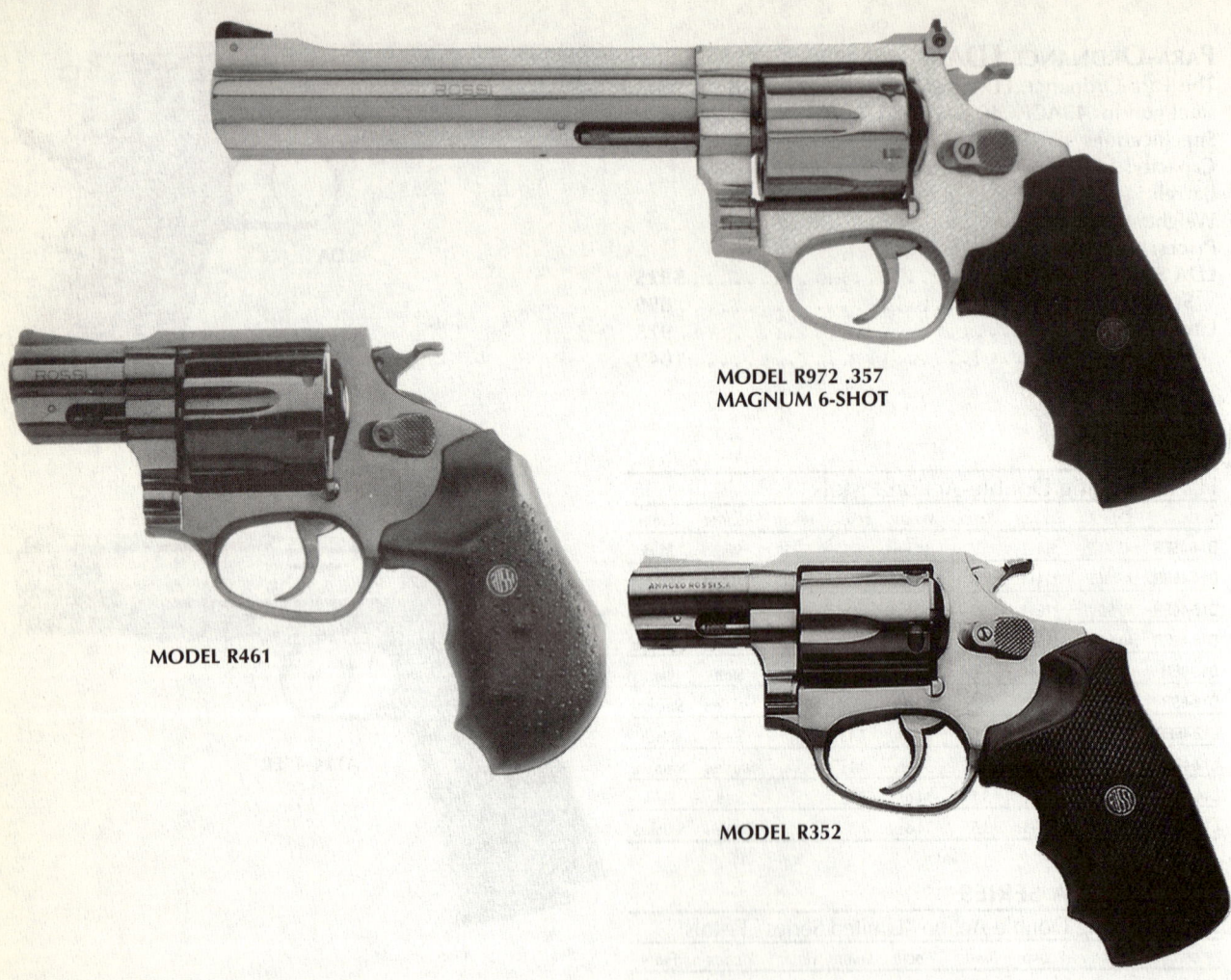

MODEL R972 .357 MAGNUM 6-SHOT

MODEL R461

MODEL R352

Model R972 .357 Magnum 6-Shot

For 2002, Rossi introduces new revolvers with longer barrels. These three new handguns are of the same quality and reliability that has been part of the Rossi name for the last century. In .357 Magnum, Rossi has two offerings - Model 971, with 4-inch chrome-moly barrel and Model 972, featuring a stainless steel 6 inch barrel model. There is also the Model 851, a .38 Special in blue steel with a 4 inch barrel and 6 round capacity. Like their shorter barreled companions, these revolvers are rated for factory-new +P ammunition and have a lifetime repair policy, as well as the patented Taurus Security System. All three feature adjustable rear sights and red inserts on the front sight for easier aim.

Model R462
Specifications
Caliber: 357 Magnum **Capacity:** 6 rounds
Barrel Length: 2" heavy **Overall Length:** 6.5"
Weight: 26 oz. **Height:** 5"
Grips: Rubber **Finish:** Stainless
Features: Fully enclosed ejector rod; serrated ramp front sight

Price: $345
Also available:
   Model R461 with matte blued finish 298
   Model R462 with stainless steel. 345
   Model R971 (with 4" barrel) 345
   Model R972 (with 6" stainless barrel) 391

Model R352
Specifications
Caliber: 38 Special
Capacity: 5 rounds, swing-out cylinder
Barrel Lengths: 2"
Overall Length: 6.5" (2" barrel)
Weight: 24 oz. (2")
Sights: Ramp front, square-notched rear adjustable for windage
Grips: Rubber (2" barrel only)
Finish: Stainless steel
Price: 345
Also available:
   Model R351 (not shown) w/matte blue finish 298
   Model R851 (.38 Special w/4" barrel) 298

Ruger Revolvers

Blued Steel Redhawk Revolver
The popular Ruger Redhawk® double-action revolver is available in an alloy steel model with blued finish or high-gloss standard steel in 44 Magnum caliber. Constructed of hardened chrome-moly and other alloy steels, this Redhawk is satin polished to a high luster and finished in a rich blue.
Specifications
Capacity: 6 rounds

Caliber	Barrel Length	Overall Length	Approx. Weight (Ounces)	Price
RUGER BLUED REDHAWK REVOLVER				
44 Mag.	5.5"	11"	49	$585
44 Mag.	7.5"	13"	54	585
44 Mag.*	7.5"	13"	54	625

*Scope model, with Integral Scope Mounts, 1" Ruger Scope rings.

REDHAWK REVOLVER

Stainless Redhawk Double-Action Revolver

Caliber	Barrel Length	Overall Length	Approx. Weight (Ounces)	Price
RUGER STAINLESS REDHAWK REVOLVER				
44 Mag.	5.5"	11"	49	$645
44 Mag.	7.5"	13"	54	645
44 Mag.*	7.5"	13"	54	685
45 LC	5.5"	11"	49	645
45 LC	7.5"	13"	54	645
45 LC*	7.5"	13"	54	685

*Scope model, with Integral Scope Mounts, 1" Stainless Steel Ruger Scope rings.

STAINLESS REDHAWK MODEL KRH-44

Super Redhawk Stainless Double-Action Revolver
The Super Redhawk double-action revolver in stainless steel features a heavy extended frame with 7.5" and 9.5" barrels. Cushioned grip panels w/wood inserts provide comfortable, nonslip hold. Comes with case and lock, integral scope mounts and 1" stainless steel Ruger scope rings.
Specifications
Caliber: 44 Magnum, 454 Casull, 480 Ruger
Barrel Lengths: 7.5" and 9.5" **Overall Length:** 13" w/7.5" bbl.; 15" w/9.5" bbl. **Weight (empty):** 53 oz. (7.5" bbl.); 58 oz. (9.5" bbl.) **Sight radius:** 9.5" (7.5" bbl.); 11.25" (9.5" bbl.)
Finish: Stainless steel Casull & 480 Ruger has Target gray finish; satin polished

Prices: 7.5" barrel $685
   9.5" barrel 685
KSRH-7454 (7.5" barrel) .454 Casull. 775
KSRH-9454 (9.5" barrel) .454 Casull. 775
KSRH-7480 (7.5" barrel) 480 Ruger 775
KSRH-9480 (9.5" barrel) 480 Ruger 775

All Ruger revolvers come with transfer-bar mechanism for safety, plus a high-impact case & gunlock.

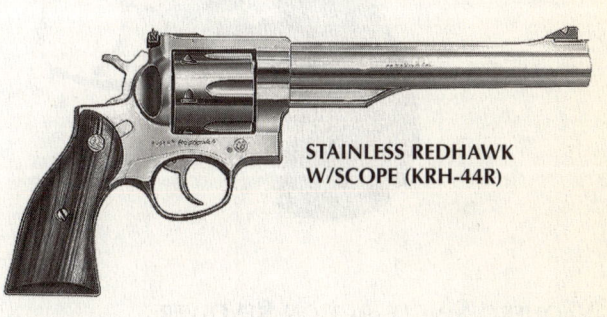
STAINLESS REDHAWK W/SCOPE (KRH-44R)

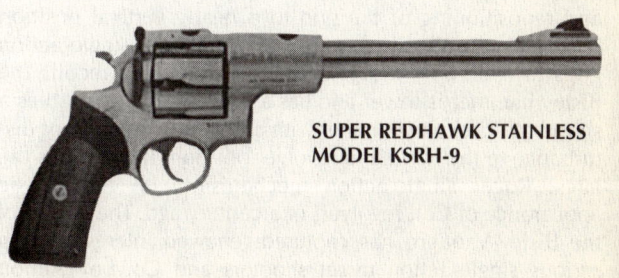
SUPER REDHAWK STAINLESS MODEL KSRH-9

Ruger Revolvers

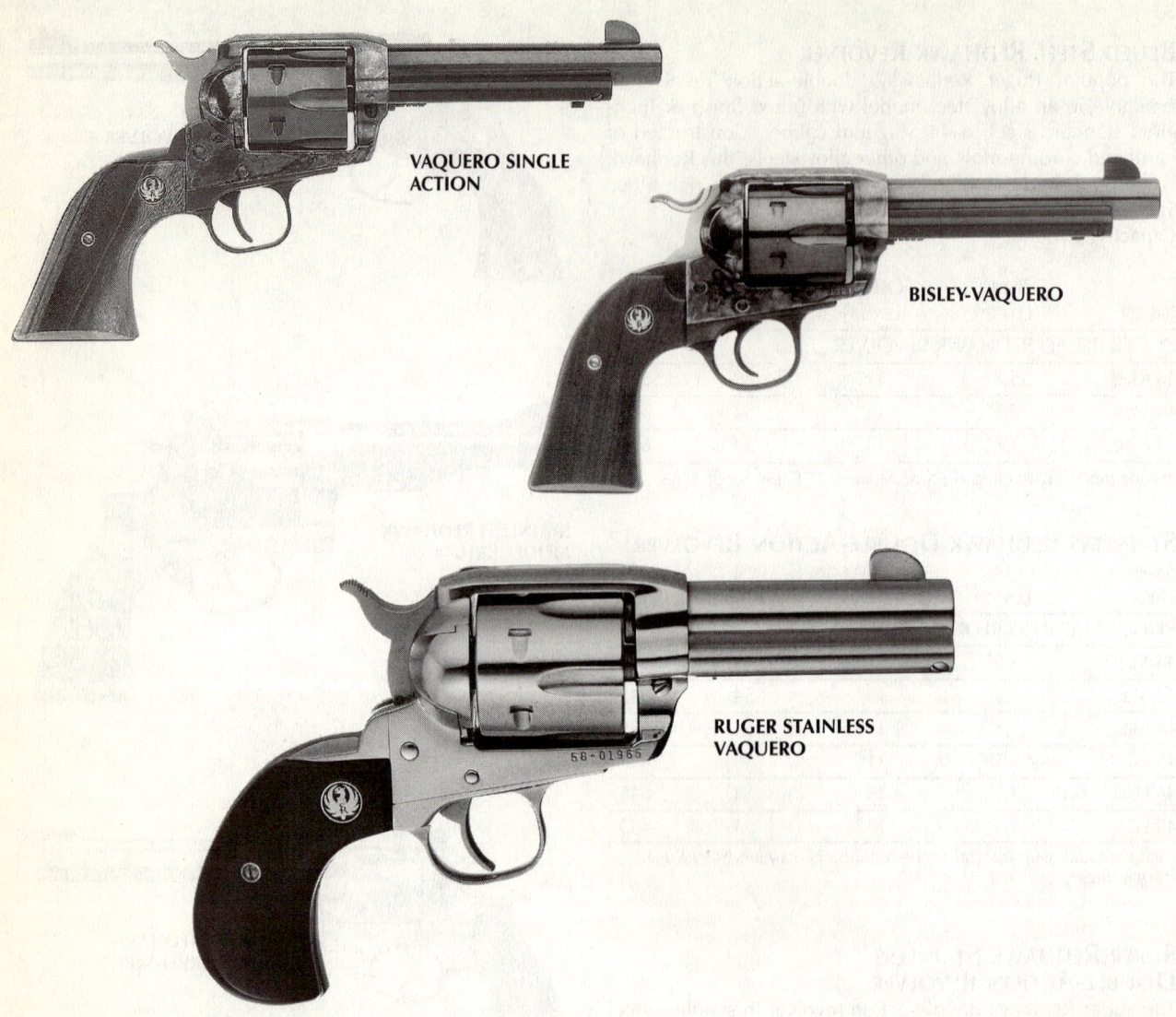

VAQUERO SINGLE ACTION

BISLEY-VAQUERO

RUGER STAINLESS VAQUERO

VAQUERO SINGLE-ACTION REVOLVER

Ruger's Vaquero single-action revolver is a sturdier rendition of the classic Colt SAA. The original Bisley single-action design was developed in the 1890s for England's famous target shooting matches held at Bisley Common. Modification and repositioning of the grip to a nearly vertical position reduced a tendency of some standard-frame single-action grips to "ride-up" in the shooter's hand during recoil. The Bisley hammer is lower and has a wide spur. This enables a shooter to cock the hammer with a minimum amount of disturbance to the hand and revolver position. It combines the latest Ruger single-action mechanism with the classic appearance of Colt revolvers of a century ago. The design of the Bisley-Vaquero has captured renewed interest among serious single-action target shooters and Cowboy Action Shooters alike. As with the Vaquero, the new Ruger Bisley-Vaquero is based on the Ruger New Model Blackhawk, single-action revolver, in production since 1973.

Specifications
Calibers: .44 Magnum, .45 Long Colt, 44-40, and .357 Magnum
Capacity: 6 rounds
Barrel Length: 4 5/8"-7.5"
Safety: Transfer bar and loading gate interlock
Sights: Blade front; notch rear; fixed
Sights Radius: 6.5"
Grips: Smooth rosewood with inletted Ruger medallion
Finish: Blued "color case finish" on frame; polished and blued barrel and cylinder
Features: Instruction manual, high impact case and gunlock; heat treated Chrome-moly steel frame, barrel and grip (blued version); 400 stainless steel
Price: $535-576
Bisley w/stainless 555
(Simulated ivory grips. . . . . $41-44 additional)

Ruger Revolvers

New Model Super Blackhawk Single-Action Revolver

Specifications
Caliber: 44 Magnum; interchangeable with 44 Special
Barrel Lengths: 4 5/8", 5.5", 7.5", 10.5" **Overall Length:** 13 3/8" (7.5" barrel) **Weight:** 45 oz. (4 5/8" bbl.), 46 oz. (5.5" bbl.), 48 oz. (7.5" bbl.) and 51 oz. (10.5" bbl.)
Frame: Chrome molybdenum steel or stainless steel
Springs: Music wire springs throughout **Sights:** Partridge style, ramp front matted blade 18" wide; rear sight click-adjustable for windage and elevation
Grip Frame: Chrome molybdenum or stainless steel, enlarged and contoured to minimize recoil effect
Trigger: Wide spur, low contour, sharply serrated for convenient cocking with minimum disturbance of grip
Finish: Polished and blued or brushed satin stainless steel
Prices:
KS45N, 5.5" bbl., brushed or satin stainless steel. . . $535
KS458N, 4 5/8" bbl.,
 brushed or high-gloss stainless. 535
KS47N, 7.5" bbl., brushed or high-gloss stainless. . . . 535
KS411N, 10.5" bull bbl., stainless steel 545
S45N, 5.5" bbl., blued 519
S458N, 4 5/8" bbl., blued 519
S47N, 7.5" bbl., blued 519
S411N, 10.5" bull bbl., blued 529

NEW SUPER MODEL BLACKHAWK SINGLE-ACTION REVOLVER

New Model Super Blackhawk Hunter

Single-action revolver in .44 Magnum. 400 series stainless steel with 7.5" barrel. Satin finish, smooth black laminated wood grips. 6-shot. 52 oz. 1" scope rings and gun lock standard.
Price: 639

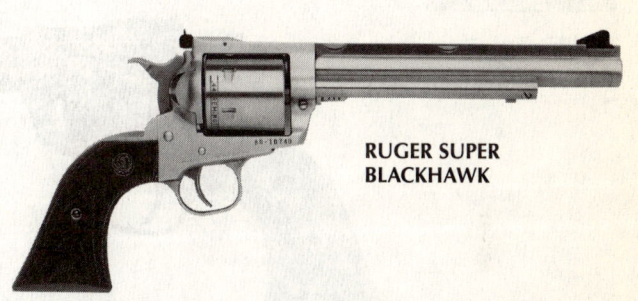

RUGER SUPER BLACKHAWK

New Model Blackhawk Revolver Stainless Steel

The Blackhawk has long been the workhorse of Ruger's single-action line. Extremely strong, it easily handles loads that would have jeopardized revolvers a century ago. Adjustable sights make it accurate. In .30 Carbine, .357, .41 Mag and .45 LC stainless or blued. Transfer bar safety, barrels 4.5" to 7.5".
Price: 435-530

NEW MODEL BLACKHAWK REVOLVER

New Ruger New Model Single-Six Revolver

In 32 H&R caliber with 4 5/8" barrel length and black micarta "Bird's Head' grips. Instruction manual, high-imact case, gun lock standard.
Price: 576

NEW MODEL SINGLE-SIX REVOLVER STAINLESS STEEL

Ruger Revolvers

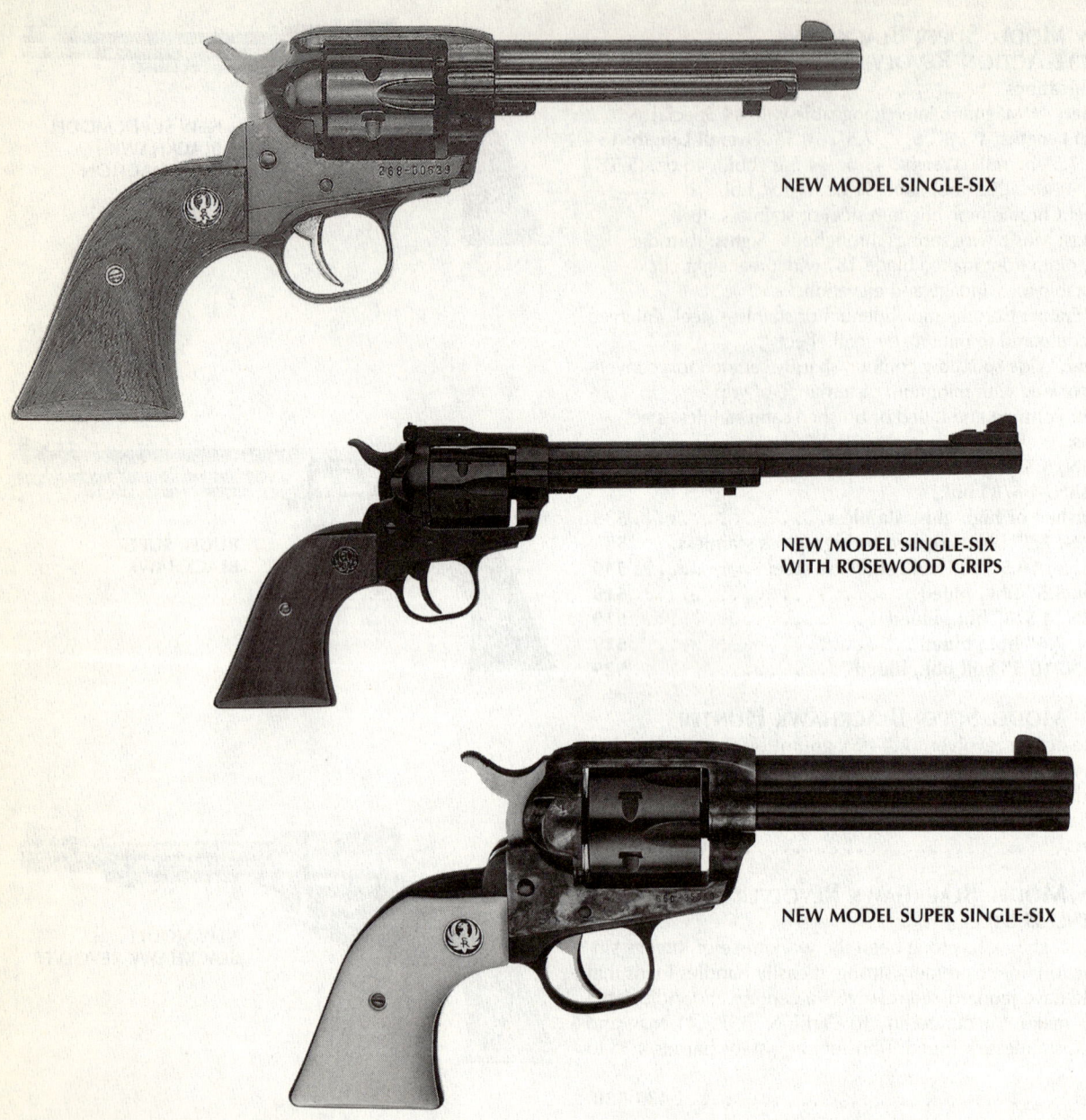

NEW MODEL SINGLE-SIX

NEW MODEL SINGLE-SIX WITH ROSEWOOD GRIPS

NEW MODEL SUPER SINGLE-SIX

NEW MODEL SINGLE-SIX AND NEW MODEL SUPER SINGLE SIX

Specifications
Caliber: 22 LR (fitted with 22 WMR cylinder)
Barrel Lengths: 4 5/8", 5.5", 6.5", 9.5"; stainless steel model in 5.5" and 6.5" lengths only
Weight (approx.): 33 oz. (with 5.5" barrel); 38 oz. (with 9.5" barrel)
Sights: Partridge-type ramp front sight; rear sight click adjustable for elevation and windage; protected by integral frame ribs. Adjustable sight model available with 4 5/8", 5.5", 6.5", or 9.5" barrel.

Finish: Blue or stainless steel
Features: 32 H&R offered with rosewood or "Bird's Head" grips and in stainless steel finish or color case.
Prices:
Blue Fixed sight $379
    Blue adjustable sight 389
Stainless steel
    (convertible 5.5" and 6.5" barrels only) 469
Also available:
New Model Single six in 32 H&R Mag. 576
All Ruger revolvers come with transfer-bar mechanism for safety, plus a high impact case and gunlock.

Ruger Pistols and Revolvers

GP-100 & SP101 DOUBLE-ACTION REVOLVERS
SP 101 REVOLVERS

In 1971 Ruger announced the Security Six, Police Service Six and Speed Six double-action revolvers that allowed quick dismantling without tools and handled the most powerful factory loads available. The improved G-P 100 followed in 1985, the SP101 in 1988. Cushioned grips soak up recoil and maintain hand position. Oversize frames bottle high-pressure loads. The cylinder is locked into firing position front and rear to ensure proper alignment.
All Ruger revolvers come with transfer-bar mechanism for safety, plus a lockable box and padlock.

SP101 REVOLVERS
Specifications
Calibers: .22LR, .32 Mag., .38+P, .357
Barrel: 2.25" to 4" Stainless; 5 or 6 shots in cylinder, 25 to 34 oz.
Price: $482

GP100 REVOLVERS
.357 Magnum in stainless steel or blue. 3", 4" or 6" barrels; 6 shots; 36 to 46 oz.
Price: . . . . 499 -539
Also available:
38 Spl. in stainless steel, 4" barrel $529

MARK IIs
Blowback .22 pistols in standard, target, government and bull-barrel configurations, stainless or blued, adjustable sights.
Prices:
Standard, blued or stainless 289-379
Bull Barrel 275-445
Target Models 349-529

MODEL SP101
SPURLESS DA

GP-100 357 MAGNUM
6" HEAVY BARREL

MARK II 22/45
W/ZYTEL FRAME

22/45 TARGET
MODEL P-512

RUGER MARK II

Handguns • 325

Ruger Revolvers

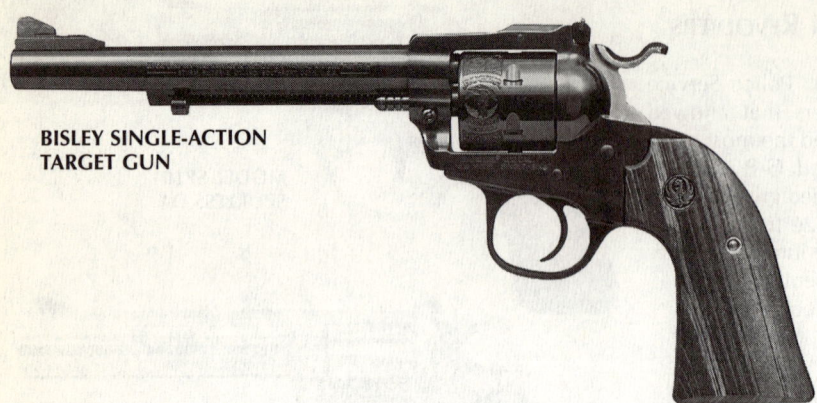

BISLEY SINGLE-ACTION TARGET GUN

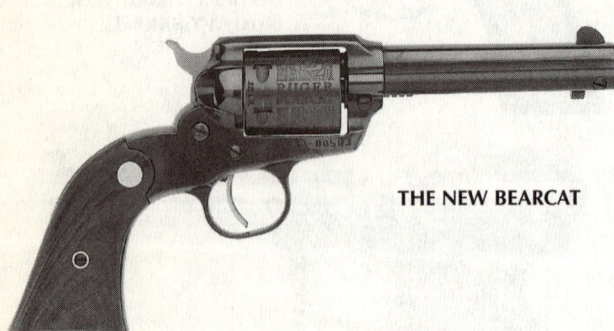

THE NEW BEARCAT

BISLEY SINGLE-ACTION TARGET GUN
The Bisley single-action was originally used at the British National Riflle Association matches held in Bisley, England, in the 1890s. Today's Ruger Bisleys are offered in two frame sizes, chambered from 22 LR to 45 Long Colt. These revolvers are the target-model versions of the Ruger single-action line.

Special Features: Unfluted cylinder roll-marked with classic foliate engraving pattern; hammer is low with smoothly curved, deeply checkered wide spur positioned for easy cocking.

Prices:
22 LR. $422
357 Mag., 44 Mag., 45 Long Colt 535

BISLEY SPECIFICATIONS

Caliber	Barrel Length	Overall Length	Sights	Approx. Wt. (Oz.)
22 LR	6.5"	11.5"	Adj.	41
357 Mag.	7.5"	13"	Adj.	48
44 Mag.	7.5"	13"	Adj.	48
45 LC	7.5"	13"	Adj.	48

*Dovetail rear sight adjustable for windage only.

THE SBC-4 NEW BEARCAT
Originally manufactured between 1958 and 1973, the 22-rimfire single-action Bearcat features an all-steel precision investment-cast frame and patented transfer-bar mechanism. The New Bearcat also has walnut grips with the Ruger medallion.

Specifications
Caliber: 22 LR Capacity: 6 shots
Barrel Length: 4" Grips: rosewood
Finish: Blued chrome-moly steel

Price:
Blued. 379
Stainless Steel 429

All Ruger revolvers come with transfer-bar mechanism for safety, plus a high impact case and gunlock.

Ruger P-Series Pistols

Model P95
Ruger's first centerfire pistols were introduced in 1985. Now available in a wide range of models in 9mm, 40 Auto and .45 ACP, the P-series pistols feature 3-dot sights and grips that hug the hand. Polymer-frame models offer a 4-oz. weight savings. Decock-Only pistols can be fired after decocking with a double-action pull of the trigger. Double-Action-Only models feature a spurless hammer. Ambidextrous grip, safety and decocking lever make the P-series pistols suitable for quick firing from either hand. An integral firing pin block prevents discharge unless the trigger is pulled and held rearward. P-series pistols come with a lockable case, spare magazine and magazine loading tool.

Ruger P-Series Pistols
Specifications
Caliber: 9mm, .40 auto, .45 ACP
Finish: blue or stainless steel **Capacity:** 9mm and .40 auto: 10 rounds, .45 ACP: 8 rounds
Weight: 30.5 to 34 oz.
Prices:
P89 and P90, 9 mm
   blue $475
   stainless 525
45 ACP
   blue 525
   stainless 565
P93 and P94, 9 mm and 40 auto
   blue 495
   stainless 575
P95, 9 mm
   blue 425
   stainless 475
P97, 45 ACP
   blue 460
   stainless 495

MODEL KP95D

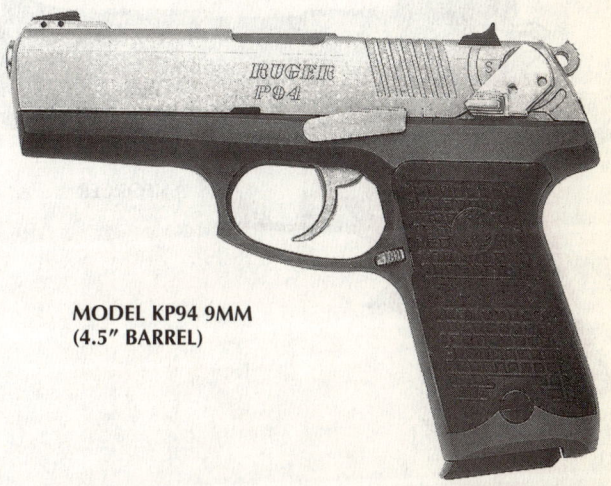

MODEL KP94 9MM
(4.5" BARREL)

MODEL P89D

Safari Arms Pistols

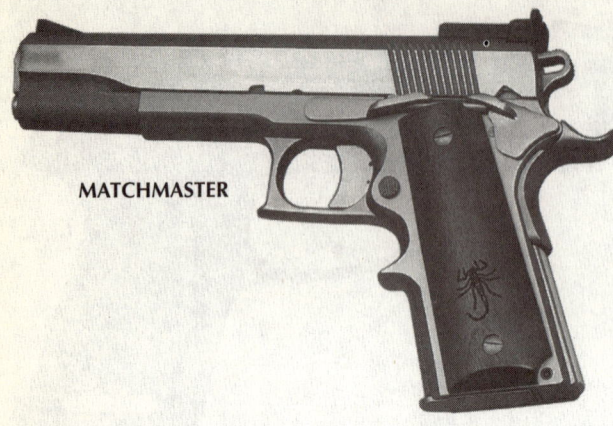

MATCHMASTER

MATCHMASTER
Specifications
Caliber: 45 ACP
Capacity: 7 rounds
Barrel length: 5" or 6"
Overall length: 8.75" or 9.75"
Weight: 40.3 oz. (44 oz. for 6" barrel)
Finish: Stainless steel or black Parkerized carbon steel
Features: Extended safety & slide stop; wide beavertail grip safety; LPA fully adjustable rear sight; full-length recoil spring guide; squared trigger guide & finger-groove front strap frame; laser-etched walnut grips
Prices:
5" Barrel $595
6" Barrel 645

ENFORCER

ENFORCER
Specifications
Caliber: 45 ACP
Capacity: 6 rounds
Barrel length: 4" conical
Overall length: 7.3"
Height: 4 7/8"
Weight: 36 oz.
Sight radius: 5.75"
Finish: Stainless steel or matte black Parkerized carbon steel
Features: Beavertail grip safety; extended thumb safety and slide release; smooth walnut stock w/laser-etched Black Widow logo
Price: 625

COHORT
Specifications
Caliber: 45 ACP
Capacity: 7 rounds
Barrel length: 4" conical
Overall length: 7.3"
Height: 5.5"
Weight: 38 oz.
Sights: Ramped blade front, LPA adjustable rear
Finish: Stainless steel or black Parkerized carbon steel
Features: Beavertail grip safety; extended thumb safety and slide release; rounded trigger guard, checkered nut stock
Price: 649

COHORT

Savage Arms Pistols

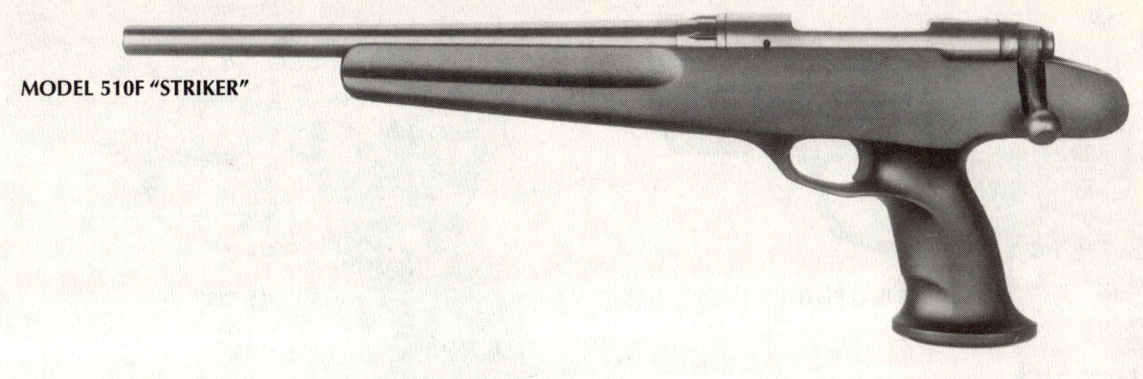

MODEL 510F "STRIKER"

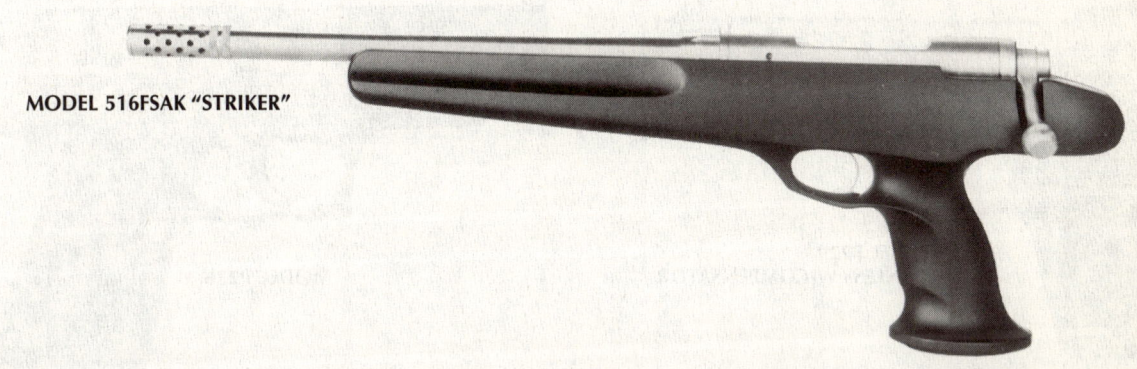

MODEL 516FSAK "STRIKER"

MODEL 516FSAK CAMO

Model 510F Striker
Specifications
Calibers: .223, 243, 7mm-08, 308
Capacity: 2 + 1 **Barrel Length:** 14" **Overall Length:** 22.5"
Weight: Approx. 5 lbs. **Sights:** None. Drilled and tapped for scope mounts **Stock:** Mid-grip, ambidextrous composite, with grooved forend and dual pillar bedding
Finish: Blued alloy steel **Features:** Bolt-action hunting handgun with left hand bolt and right hand ejection.
Price: $440
Also Available:
Sport Striker Model 501F 22 LR 216
Model 502F 22 WMR 238
Model 510FXP (with scope) 258

Model 516FSAK Striker
Specifications
Calibers: 243, 7-08, 308
Barrel Length: 14" **Overall Length:** 22.5"
Magazine: Top loading internal, 2+1 capacity
Sights: None. Drilled and tapped for scope mounts
Stock: Mid-grip, ambidextrous composite, with grooved forend and dual pillar bedding
Finish: Stainless steel
Features: Bolt-action hunting handgun with left-hand bolt and right-hand ejection. Adjustable muzzle brake.
Price: $531
Also available:
516 FSAK Camo in 300 WSM 588

SIG Arms Pistols

SIG PRO PISTOL

MODEL P239

MODEL P229
STAINLESS W/COMPENSATOR

MODEL P226

SIG PRO PISTOLS
The Sig Pro is among the most advanced of polymer-frame pistols, with a slide machined from solid stainless steel, integral fire control unit for easy conversion from SA/DA to double-action-only, integral accessory rail to mount a tactical light or laser sight, and Sig Pro's unique four-point safety system. The lightweight, maintenance-free, virtually indestructible polymer frame is engineered for quick pointing.

Specifications
Calibers: 9mm, .357 SIG, 40 S&W **Capacity:** 10 rounds
Barrel Length: 3.9" **Overall Length:** 7.4"
Weight: 28-30 oz. **Finishes:** Nitron or Two-Tone
Prices: $602
   w/"Siglite" night sights 661
Two-Tone 627
   w/"Siglite" night sights 681

MODEL P239
Specifications
Calibers: 357 SIG, 9mm, 40 S&W
Capacity: 7 rounds (8 in 9mm) **Barrel Length:** 3.6"
Overall Length: 6.6" **Height:** 5.2"
Width: 1.2" **Weight (empty):** 27.4 oz.
Finish: Nitron Stainless Steel, Two-Tone
Prices:
Nitron 636
   w/"Siglite" night sights 738

Two-Tone $682
   "Siglite" night sights 784

MODEL P229
Specifications
Caliber: 357 SIG, 40 S&W **Capacity:** 10 rounds **Action:** DA/SA **Barrel Length:** 3.9" **Overall Length:** 7.1" **Height:** 5.4" **Width:** 1.5" **Finish:** Nitron
Prices:
Nitron 851
   Nitron w/"Siglite" night sights. 953
   Two-Tone 897
   Two-Tone w/"Siglite" night sights 994

MODEL P226
Specifications
Calibers: 357 SIG, 9mm and 40 S&W
Capacity: 10 rounds **Action:** DA/SA or DA only
Barrel Length: 4.4" **Overall Length:** 7.7"
Weight (empty): 26.5 oz.; 30.1 oz. in 357 SIG
Height: 5.5" **Finish:** Nitron or Two-tone
Prices:
Nitron 851
   w/"Siglite" night sight. 953
Two-Tone. 897
   w/"Siglite" night sights 994

SIG Arms Pistols

Model P232
Specifications
Calibers: 9mm Short (380 ACP) **Action:** DA/SA or DAO
Capacity: 7 rounds (380 ACP) **Barrel Length:** 3.6"
OverallLength: 6.6" **Weight (empty):** 16.2 oz. **Height:** 4.7"
Width: 1.2" **Safety:** Automatic firing-pin lock
Finish: Blued or stainless steel
Prices: Blued finish...........................$518
Stainless steel................................559
Stainless w/"Siglite" night sight 600
Blued w/"Siglite" night sight...................559

Model P229
Specifications
Calibers: 9mm, 357 and 40 S&W **Capacity:** 10 rounds
Action: DA/SA or DA only **Barrel Length:** 3.8" **Overall
Length:** 7.1" **Weight (empty):** 27.5 oz. **Height:** 5.4"
Width: 1.5" **Finish:** Blackened stainless steel
Features: Stainless steel slide; automatic firing-pin lock; wood grips (optional); aluminum alloy frame
Prices: Model P229 851
w/"Siglite" night sight 953
w/Nickel slide................................897
w/Nickel slide/"Siglite" night sight.............994

SIG P210 Sport Series
The P210 Sport Series of handguns is the flagship of the SIGARMS handgun line. Originally manufactured in Switzerland in 1949, the single-action semi-auto gained a worldwide reputation for outstanding accuracy, and durability. SIGARMS now offers four P210 models in 9mm Parabellum.
- All 210 models are built on an alloy heavy frame.
- All models come with one 8 round magazine and a magazine loader

Prices:
The 210-8-9 is the top of the line with figured wood grip plates, adjustable target sights and a lateral magazine catch.. 4289
The 210-6-9 also offers adjustable target sights, wood grip plates and a target grade trigger action 2089
The 210-5-9 has a target trigger, wood grip plates, adjustable target sights and extended barrel of 5.85" with compensator....................2325
The 210-2-9 is the 9mm Parabellum Swiss Army Service model now with wood grip plates and standard sights. 1680

Technical Specifications

	P210-8	P210-6	P210-5	P210-2
Caliber	9mm	9mm	9mm	9mm
Length, overall	8.5"	8.5"	9.6"	8.5"
Height, overall	5.4"	5.4"	5.4"	5.4"
Width, overall	1.3"	1.3"	1.3"	1.3"
Barrel Length	4.8"	4.8"	5.9"	4.8"

SIG Trailside PL 22 Pistol
With an integral frame and barrel, and Hammerli engineering, the new SIG Trailside pistol might be more at home on

MODEL P232

P210-8-9

TRAILSIDE COMPETITION

MODEL P229

the target range, punching out the X-ring. But the standard models with 4.5" and 6" barrels are slim and easy to pack. At 28 and 30 ounces, they're nearly half a pound lighter than the Competition model, which features a hand-filling adjustable grip, modular counterweights and adjustable target sights. All guns feature an adjustable trigger and a top rail for scope mounts. The PL 22 Target model has target sights but a slender profile. Its laminated grips differ from the rubber composite grips of the trail model. The proven blow-back action feeds cartridges from a 10-round magazine.
Prices:
Standard 4.5" barrel.........................$449
Target 4.5" barrel............................529
Target 6" barrel..............................549
Competition 6" barrel........................699

Smith & Wesson Pistols
Full-Size Double-Action Pistols

MODEL 5900 SERIES
Specifications
Caliber: 9mm Parabellum **Capacity:** 15 rounds
Barrel Length: 4" **Overall Length:** 7.5"
Weight (empty): 29 oz. (Models 5903, 5943); 38.3 oz. (Model 5906, 5946); 38 oz. (Model 5906 w/adj. sight)
Sights: Front, post w/white dot; fixed rear, adj. for windage only w/2 white dots.
Adjustable sights and night sights available.
Finish: satin stainless (Models 5903 and 5943 have stainless/alloy construction)
Prices:
Model 5903	$841
Model 5906 Satin stainless	904
With fixed sights	863
With Tritium night sight	995
With safety trigger	882
Model 5946 Double action only	863
Model 5943 Double action only	844

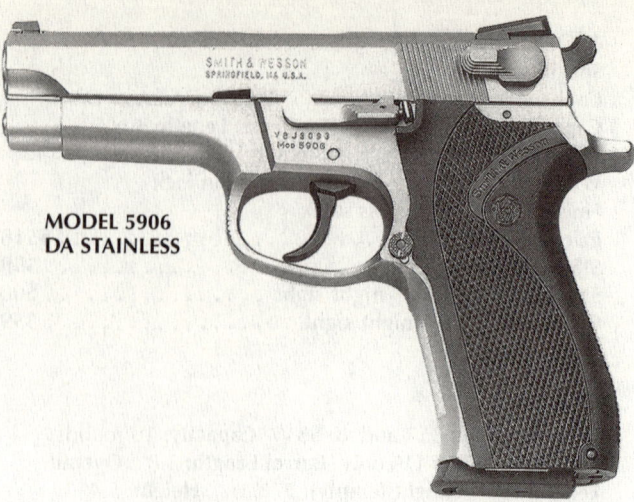

MODEL 5906 DA STAINLESS

MODEL 410, 910, 457
Specifications
Caliber: 40 S&W, 9mm Parabellum, .45 ACP
Capacity: 10 rounds+1 (7+1, .45)
Barrel Length: 4" (3.75", 45 ACP)
Overall Length: 7.5" **Weight:** 28.5 oz.
Sights: 3-dot sights **Grips:** Straight backstrap
Features: Right-hand slide-mounted manual safety; decocking lever; aluminum alloy frame; blue carbon steel slide; nonreflective matte blued finish; beveled edge slide
Prices:
410	591
With HiViz front sight	612
910	535

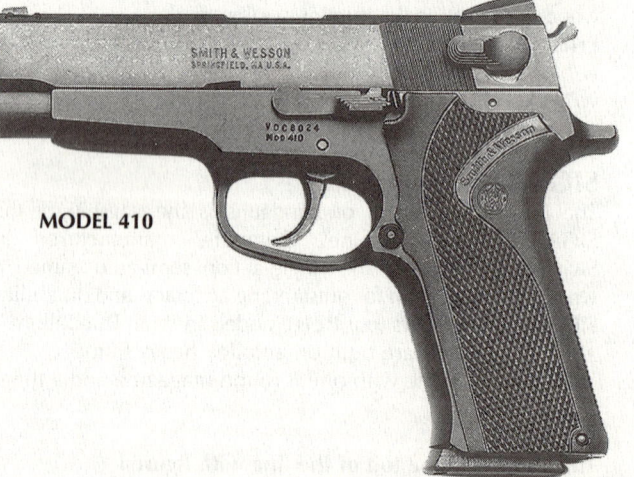

MODEL 410

MODEL 4000, 4500 SERIES
Specifications
Caliber: 40 S&W, 45 ACP
Capacity: 10 rounds, +1 (8 rounds + 1, .45)
Barrel Length: 4" (4.25", .45)
Overall Length: 7.5"
Weight: 28.5 oz. (.40 alloy), 30.5 oz. (.45 alloy), 37.8 oz. (.40 stainless), 39.1 oz. (.45 stainless)
Sights: Post w/white dot front; fixed w/white 2-dot rear, adjustable and night sights available
Grips: Straight backstrap
Finish: Stainless steel
Prices:
Model 4006 with fixed sights	907
Same as above with adj. sights	944
with fixed night sight	1040
With safety trigger	927
Model 4043 DA only (28 oz.)	886
Model 4046 Fixed sights, DA only (39.5 oz.)	907
Double action only, fixed Tritium night sight	1040
Model 4566 w/4.25" bbl., fixed sights	942
Model 4586 DA only, 4.25" bbl., 39.5 oz., fixed 2-dot rear sight, white dot front	942

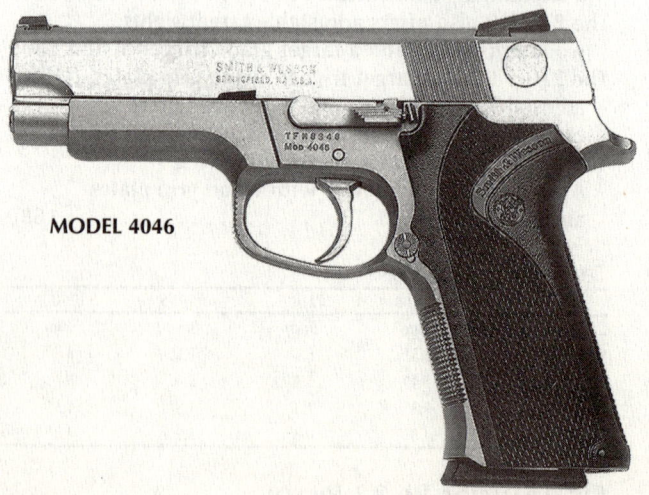

MODEL 4046

Smith & Wesson Pistols
Compact and Sigma Series Double-Action Pistols

MODEL 3913 LADYSMITH
Specifications
Caliber: 9mm Parabellum (traditional double-action)
Capacity: 8 rounds
Barrel Length: 3.5"
Overall Length: 6 7/8"
Weight (empty): 24.8 oz.
Sights: Front sight: white dot, Rear sight: Novak Lo Mount Carry 2-Dot
Finish: Satin stainless
Price: $782

MODEL 3913 LADYSMITH

SIGMA SERIES SW40E & VE
Smith & Wesson's Polymer-frame Sigma Series pistols combine traditional craftmanship and the latest technology to allow the guns to be assembled without the usual "fitting" process required for other handguns.
Prices:
Fixed night sights 657
Fixed sight blue or stainless 447
Night sight blue or stainless 494
Fixed sights, safety trigger 466

SW99
Specifications
Calibers: 9mm, 40 S+W
Capacity: 6 rounds
Barrel Length: 4", 4 1/8"
Overall Length: 7 1/8", 7 1/4"
Weight: 25 oz.
Sights: adjustable rear
Finish: Blue
Features: Lightweight polymer frame, stainless slide + barrel
Price: 629
   with safety trigger 648
   with night sights 744

MODEL SW-99

SIGMA SERIES MODEL SW9VE FULL SIZE DA

Smith & Wesson Pistols
Rimfire Single-Action Pistols

MODEL NO. 41

MODEL 22A SPORT

Model No. 41
Specifications
Caliber: 22 LR
Magazine Capacity: 12 rounds **Barrel Lengths:** 5.5" and 7"
Weight: 41 oz. (5.5" barrel) **Overall Length:** 10.5" (7" bbl.)
Sights: Front, 1/8" Partridge undercut; rear, S&W micrometer click sight adjustable for windage and elevation
Grips: Hardwood target **Finish:** S&W Bright blue
Trigger: .365" width; S&W grooving, adj. trigger stop
Features: Carbon steel slide and frame
Price: $958

Model 22A Sport
Specifications
Caliber: 22 LR **Capacity:** 10 rounds
Action: Single **Barrel Lengths:** 4", 5.5" (standard or bull barrel and 7")
Overall Length: 8" (4"), 9.5" (5.5"), 11" (7")
Grips: Two-piece polymer (4"); 2-piece Soft Touch (5.5" and 7")
Weight: 28 oz. (4"), 32 oz. (5.5"), 33 oz. (7")
Sights: Patridge front, adjustable rear **Finish:** Blue
Features: Single slide external safety
Prices:
4" $264
5.5" 292
5.5" Bull Barrel 367
5.5" Bull/Synthetic, HiViz sights 387
7" 331
Also available: in stainless steel (5.5" and 7" only)
Prices:
5.5" Standard 358
5.5" Bull Barrel 434
7" Standard 395
5.5" Bull/Synthetic, HiViz sights 453

Smith & Wesson Pistols
TSW Tactical Series Autoloaders

Model 3913TSW (Double Action)
Model 3953TSW (Double Action Only)
Specifications
Frame: Compact
Caliber: 9mm
Capacity: 8 Rounds + 1
Barrel Length: 3.5"
Front Sight: White Dot
Rear Sight: Novak Lo Mount Carry 2-Dot
Grips: Rubber, Straight Backstrap
Weight: 24.8 oz.
Overall Length: 6 3/4"
Material: Aluminum Alloy/Stainless Steel
Finish: Satin Stainless
Price:....................................$760

MODEL 3953TSW

Model 4013TSW (Double Action)
Model 4053TSW (Double Action Only)
Specifications
Frame: Compact **Caliber:** .40 S&W
Capacity: 9 rounds + 1 **Barrel Length:** 3.5"
Front Sight: White Dot
Rear Sight: Novak Lo Mount Carry 2-Dot
External Safety: Ambidextrous
Grips: Rubber, Curved Backstrap
Weight: 26.8 oz. **Overall Length:** 6 3/4"
Material: Aluminum Alloy/Stainless Steel
Finish: Satin Stainless
Price:....................................886

MODEL 4013TSW

Traditional DA Model 4513TSW
(Double Action)
Traditional DA Model 4553TSW
(Double Action Only)
Specifications
Frame: Compact **Caliber:** .45 ACP
Capacity: 7 Rounds + 1 **Barrel Length:** 3.75"
Front Sight: White Dot
Rear Sight: Novak Lo Mount Carry 2-Dot
Grips: Rubber, Straight Backstrap **Weight:** 28.6 oz.
Overall Length: 7 3/4"
Material: Aluminum Alloy/Stainless Steel
Finish: Satin Stainless
Price:....................................924
   Model 4553...........................924

Also available: Full-size TSW pistols with 4" barrels (4.25", .45)
Capacity: 10+1 (9mm and .40), 8+1 (.45)
Length: 7.5" (9mm and 40), 7 7/8" (.45)
Weight: 28.5 oz. (9mm and .40), 30.5 oz. (.45)
Sights: Same as compact series, but adjustable and night sights available.

MODEL 4513TSW

Smith & Wesson Revolvers
Small Frame

**MODEL 60LS LADYSMITH
38 S&W SPECIAL**

**MODEL 37
CHIEFS SPECIAL AIRWEIGHT
38 S&W SPECIAL**

MODEL 60

LADYSMITH HANDGUNS
MODEL 36-LS AND MODEL 60-LS
Specifications
Calibers: 38 S&W Special (357 Magnum 60-LS)
Capacity: 5 shots **Barrel Lengths:** 1 7/8" (2 1/8", 3")
Overall Length: 6 5/16" (6 9/16", 7.5") **Weight:** 20 oz. (22.5 oz., 24 oz.) **Sights:** Serrated ramp front (black pinned ramp in 357 Mag.); fixed notch rear
Grips: Contoured laminated rosewood, round butt
Finish: Glossy deep blue (36) or stainless (60)
Features: Both models come with soft-side LadySmith carry case
Prices:
Model 36-LS. $518
Model 60-LS 566

MODEL 37
CHIEFS SPECIAL AIRWEIGHT
Specifications
Caliber: 38 S&W Special **Capacity:** 5 shots
Barrel Length: 1 7/8" **Overall Length:** 6 5/16"
Weight: 11.9 oz.
Sights: Serrated ramp front; fixed, square-notch rear
Grips: Uncle Mike's Boot
Finish: S&W blued carbon steel
Features: .312" smooth combat-style trigger; .240" service hammer
Prices:
Model 37 Chiefs Special Airweight:
   Same as Model 36, except finish is blue or
   nickel aluminum alloy. 523
Model 637 Chiefs Special Airweight:
   Stainless finish., Weight: 13.5 oz.. 548

MODEL 60
38 CHIEFS SPECIAL, STAINLESS
Specifications
Calibers: .357 Mag. **Capacity:** 5 shots
Barrel Lengths: 2 1/8" (357 Mag.); 3" full lug (38 S&W Spec.)
Overall Length: 6 5/16" (2 1/8" bbl.)); 7.5" (3" bbl.)
Weight: 23.5 oz. (2 1/8" barrel); 24 oz. (3" full lug barrel)
Sights: Micrometer click rear, adj. for windage and elevation; pinned black front (3" full lug model only); standard sights as on Model 36
Grips: Uncle Mike's Combat **Finish:** Satin stainless
Features: .312" smooth combat-style trigger
Prices:
2 1/8" Barrel. 541
3" Barrel.. 574

Smith & Wesson Revolvers
Small Frame

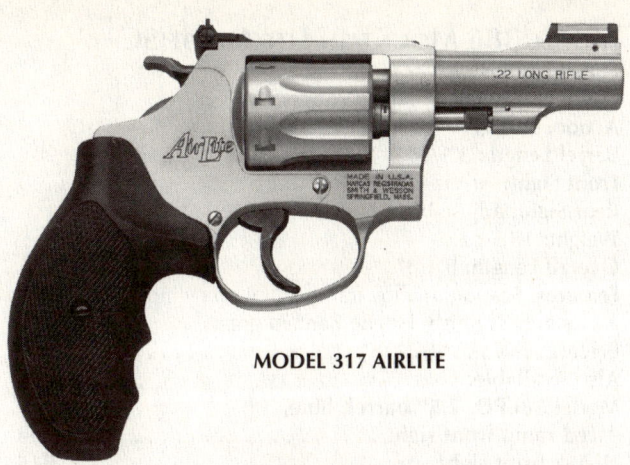

MODEL 317 AIRLITE

MODEL 442 38 SPECIAL

MODEL 640

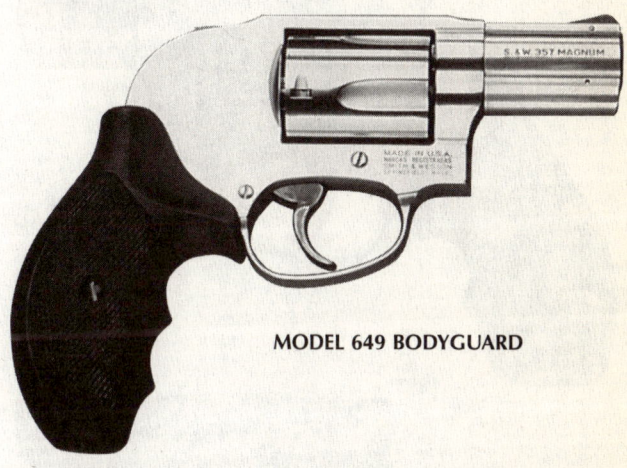

MODEL 649 BODYGUARD

MODEL 317 AIRLITE
Specifications
Caliber: 22 LR **Action:** Single or double action **Capacity:** 8 rounds **Barrel Length:** 1 7/8" and 3" **Overall Length:** 6 3/16" **Weight:** 9.9 oz. (10.5 oz. w/rubber grip) **Finish:** Clear Cote **Sights:** Serrated ramp front; fixed notch rear
Prices:
1 7/8" barrel w/synthetic grips.................$550
3" barrel w/HiViz front sight 600

MODEL 317 LADYSMITH
Specifications
Same as Model 317 Airlite with round butt grip, fixed sights and Dymondwood grip.
Price:..596

38 CENTENNIAL "AIRWEIGHT" MODEL 442
Specifications
Caliber: 38 S&W Special **Capacity:** 5 rounds
Barrel Length: 1 7/8" **Overall Length:** 6 5/16"
Weight: 15 oz. **Sights:** Serrated ramp front; fixed, square-notch rear **Finish:** Matte blue
Price:..547
Also available: Model 642 Centennial Airweight Stainless steel, synthetic round butt grip, double-action only........................571

LadySmith Model (satin stainless) $597

MODEL 640 CENTENNIAL
Specifications
Calibers: 357 Magnum and 38 S&W Special
Action: Double action only **Capacity:** 5 rounds
Barrel Length: 2 1/8" **Overall Length:** 6 3/4"
Sights: Pinned black ramp front; fixed, square-notch rear
Features: Fully concealed hammer; smooth hardwood service stock; satin stainless steel finish; round-butt synthetic grips
Price:..599

MODEL 649 BODYGUARD
Specifications
Caliber: 38 S&W Special/357 S&W Mag.
Capacity: 5 rounds
Barrel Length: 2 1/8"
Overall Length: 6 5/16"
Weight: 20 oz.
Sights: Black pinned ramp front; fixed, square-notch rear
Grips: Uncle Mike's Combat
Finish: Satin stainless
Price:..594

Smith & Wesson Revolvers
Small Frame

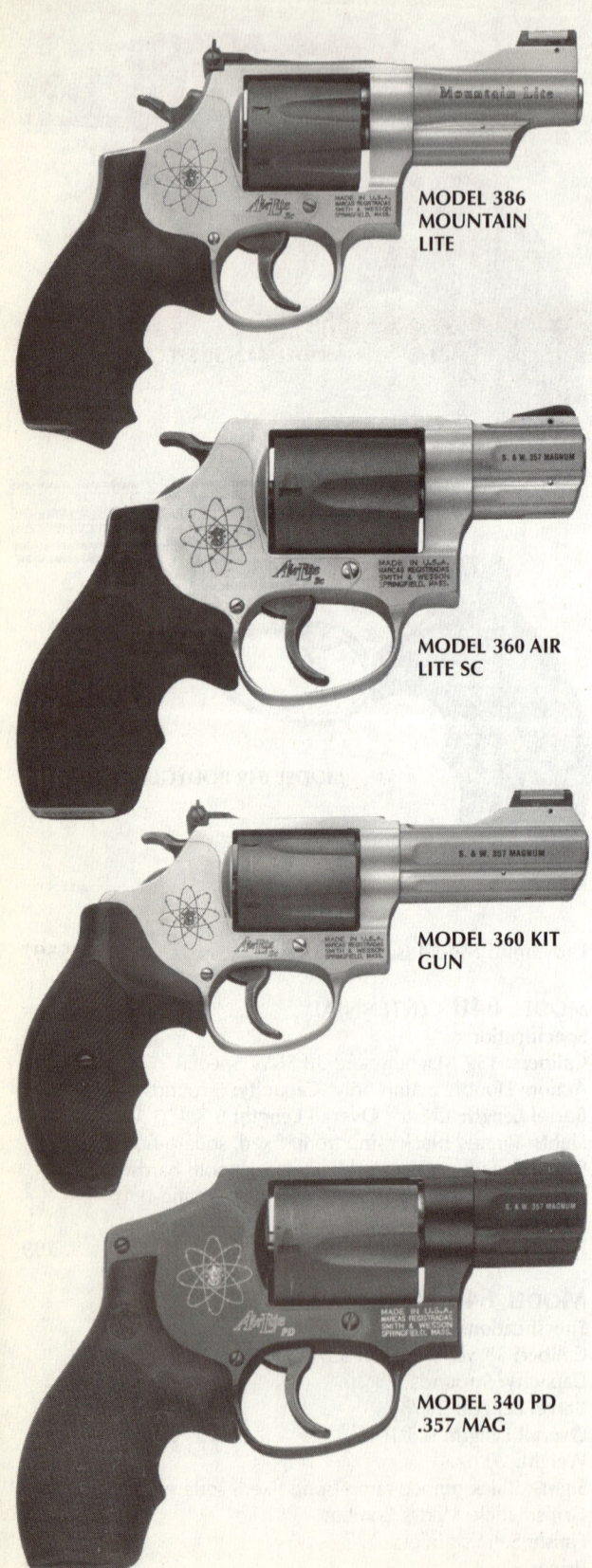

MODEL 386 MOUNTAIN LITE

MODEL 360 AIR LITE SC

MODEL 360 KIT GUN

MODEL 340 PD .357 MAG

Model 386 Mountain Lite Airlite SC
Specifications
Calibers: 357 Mag., .38 S+W Special
Action: SA/DA
Barrel Length: 3 1/8"
Front Sight: Hi-Viz Green Dot
Rear Sight: adjustable V-Notch
Weight: 18.5 oz.
Overall Length: 8 1/8"
Features: Scandium alloy frame, titanium cylinder, matte grey stainless finish, Hogue Bantam grips
Price:...$799
Also Available:
Model 386PD, 2.5" barrel, blue,
　red ramp front sight........................794
Hi-Viz front sight............................815

Model 360 Airlite SC
Specifications
Calibers: 357 Mag., .38 S+W Special
Action: DA/SA
Barrel Length: 1 7/8"
Front Sight: Black, serrated ramp
Rear Sight: fixed notch
Weight: 12 oz.
Overall Length: 6 5/16"
Features: Scandium alloy frame, titanium cylinder, matte grey stainless, Hogue grips
Price:...$745
　with red ramp front sight...................767
　with Hi-Viz front sight.....................781
Also Available:
Model 360 Kit Gun, w/3 1/8" barrel, HiViz
　orange dot sight..........................788

Model 340 Airlite SC
Specifications
Calibers: 357 Mag., .38 S+W Special
Action: SA/DA
Barrel Length: 1 7/8"
Front Sight: Black, serrated ramp
Rear Sight: fixed notch
Weight: 12 oz.
Overall Length: 6 5/16"
Features: Scandium alloy frame, titanium cylinder, matte grey stainless finish, Hogue grips
Price:...763
Also Available:
Model 340PD, Personal Defense
　with red front ramp.........................785
　with Hi-Viz front sight.....................799

Smith & Wesson Revolvers
Medium Frame

Model 617
Specifications
Caliber: 22 Long Rifle **Capacity:** 10 shots
Barrel Length: 4", 6" or 8 3/8" **Overall Length:** 9 1/8" (4" barrel); 11 1/8" (6" barrel); 13.5" (8 3/8" barrel)
Weight (loaded): 42 oz. with 4" barrel; 48 oz. with 6" barrel; 54 oz. with 8 3/8" barrel **Sights:** Front pinned Partridge; rear, S&W micrometer, click sight adjustable for windage and elevation **Grips:** Hogue rubber, square butt
Finish: Satin stainless **Features:** Target hammer and trigger; drilled and tapped for scope
Prices: 4" Barrel........................$644
  6" Bbl.................................625
  8 3/8" Barrel.........................679
Also available: 10-shot w/6" barrel..............669

MODEL 617 (6-SHOT, 6" BARREL SHOWN)

Model 10, 38 Military & Police
Specifications
Caliber: 38 S&W Special **Capacity:** 6 shots
Barrel Length: 4" heavy barrel **Overall Length:** 9.25"
Weight: 33.5 oz.
Sights: Front, fixed 1/8" serrated ramp; square-notch rear
Grips: Uncle Mike's Combat **Finish:** S&W blue
Price:..................................496

MODEL 10 HEAVY BARREL

Model 64, 38 Military & Police Stainless
Specifications
Caliber: 38 S&W Special **Capacity:** 6 shots
Barrel Length: 4" heavy barrel, square butt; 2" regular barrel, round butt **Overall Length:** 9.25" w/4" bbl., 6 7/8" w/2" barrel **Weight:** 28 oz. w/2" barrel; 33.5 oz. w/4" barrel **Sights:** Fixed, 1/8" serrated ramp front; square-notch rear **Grips:** Uncle Mike's Combat
Finish: Satin stainless
Prices:
2" Bbl..................................522
3 or 4" Bbl.............................532

MODEL 64

Model 65 (Heavy Barrel) 357 Military & Police
Specifications
K-frame .357 Magnum or 38 S+W Special with stainless steel frame and 4" barrel; 6 shots; fixed sights.
Price:..................................531
Also available: Model 65 LadySmith
Same specifications as Model 65, but with 3" barrel only (weighs 32 oz.) and rosewood laminate stock; satin stainless finish, smooth combat wood grips.
Price:..................................584

MODEL 65

Smith & Wesson Revolvers
Medium Frame

Model 686
Specifications
Calibers: 357 Mag, 38 S+W Special
Capacity: 6 shots
Barrel Lengths: 2.5", 4", 6", 8 3/8"
All models have stainless steel finish, combat or target stock and/or trigger; adjustable sights optional.
Prices:
2.5" Barrel $608
4" Barrel 632
6" Barrel 638
8 3/8" Barrel 663
Also Available:
  Model 686 Powerport, 6" barrel 681

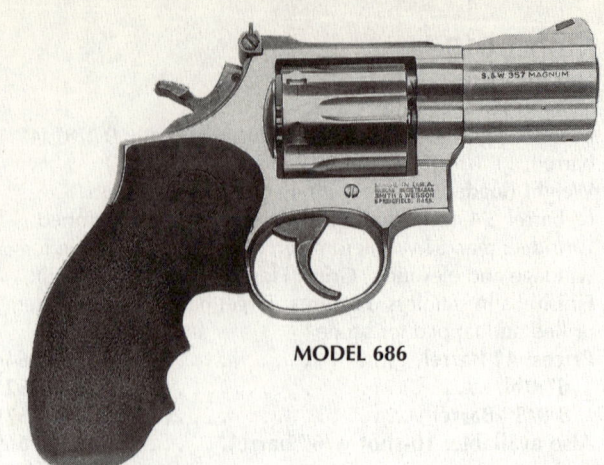
MODEL 686

Model 686 Plus Distinguished Combat Magnum
Specifications
Capacity: 7 rounds
Barrel Lengths: 2.5", 4" or 6" full lug.
Overall Length: 7.5" – 11 15/16" **Weight:** 34.5 oz. – 45 oz.
Prices:
2.5" bbl. 631
4" Barrel 653
6" Barrel 663

MODEL 686 PLUS

Model 66 357 Combat Magnum
Specifications
Caliber: 357 Magnum, 38 S+W Special
Capacity: 6 shots **Barrel Lengths:** 4" or 6" with square butt; 2.5" with round butt
Overall Length: 7.5" w/2.5" bbl.; 9.5" w/4" bbl.; 11 3/8" w/6" bbl. **Weight:** 30.5 oz. w/2.5" bbl.; 36 oz. w/4" bbl.; 39 oz. w/6" bbl. **Sights:** Front, 1/8"; rear, S&W Red Ramp on ramp base, S&W Micrometer Click, adjustable for windage and elevation
Grips: Uncle Mike's Combat
Trigger: .312" Smooth Combat
Finish: Satin stainless
Prices:
2.5" Bbl. 590
4" Bbl. 579
6" Bbl 608

MODEL 66

Model 696
Specifications
Caliber: 44 S&W Special
Capacity: 5 rounds
Action: Single or double action
Barrel Length: 3" **Overall Length:** 8 3/16" **Weight:** 48 oz.
Sights: Red ramp front; adjustable white outline rear **Grips:** Hogue rubber
Finish: Satin stainless
Features: .500" target hammer; .400" smooth combat trigger
Price: 620

MODEL 696

Smith & Wesson Revolvers
Large Frame Stainless

MODEL 629
Specifications
Calibers: 44 Magnum, 44 S&W Special **Capacity:** 6 shots
Barrel Lengths: 4", 6", 8 3/8" **Overall Length:** 9 5/8", 11 3/8", 13 7/8" **Weight (empty):** 44 oz. (4" bbl.); 47 oz. (6" bbl.); 54 oz. (8 3/8" bbl.) **Sights:** S&W Red Ramp front; white outline rear w/S&W Micrometer Click, adjustable for windage and elevation; drilled and tapped **Grips:** Hogue rubber **Finish:** Satin stainless steel **Features:** Combat trigger, target hammer
Prices: 4" Bbl. $717
6" Bbl. 739
8 3/8" Bbl. 756

MODEL 629

MODEL 629 CLASSIC
Specifications
Calibers: 44 Magnum, 44 S&W Special **Capacity:** 6 rounds
Barrel Lengths: 5", 6.5", 8 3/8" (all full lug) **Overall Length:** 10.5", 12", 13 7/8" **Weight:** 51 oz. (5" bbl.); 52 oz. (6.5" bbl.); 54 oz. (8 3/8" bbl.) **Grips:** Hogue rubber
Prices:
5" & 6.5" Bbl. 768
8 3/8" Bbl. 793
Also available:
Model 629 classic dx. Same features as the Model 629 Classic above, plus interchangeable front sights, wood grips. With 6.5" barrel. 986
With 8 3/8" barrel 1018
Model 629 powerport w/6.5" barrel (12" overall length), weighs 52 oz. Partridge front sight, adjustable black blade rear sight 768

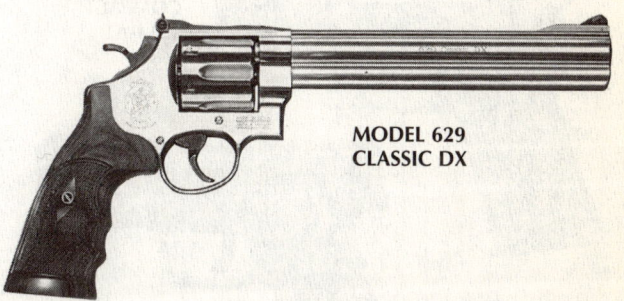

MODEL 629 CLASSIC DX

MODEL 625
Specifications
Caliber: 45 ACP **Capacity:** 6 shots **Barrel Length:** 4" or 5" full lug barrel **Overall Length:** 10 3/8" **Weight (empty):** 45 oz. **Sights:** Front, Partridge on ramp base; S&W Micrometer Click rear, adjustable for windage and elevation **Grips:** Hogue rubber, round butt **Finish:** Satin stainless
Price: 745

MODEL 657
Specifications
Calibers: 41 Magnum **Capacity:** 6 shots **Barrel Length:** 7.5" **Overall Length:** 11 3/8" **Weight (empty):** 52 oz. **Sights:** Front, pinned ramp on ramp base; black blade rear, adjustable for windage and elevation; drilled and tapped **Grips:** Hogue rubber **Finish:** Satin stainless steel
Price: 706

MODEL 657 .41 MAGNUM

MODEL 610 CLASSIC
Specifications
Calibers: 10mm **Frame:** N-Large **Capacity:** 6 rounds
Barrel Length: 4" **Overall Length:** 10.5" **Weight:** 50 oz.
Sights: Interchangeable front; micrometer click adj. black blade **Grips:** Hogue rubber **Finish:** Stainless steel
Feature: Unfluted cylinder
Price: 785

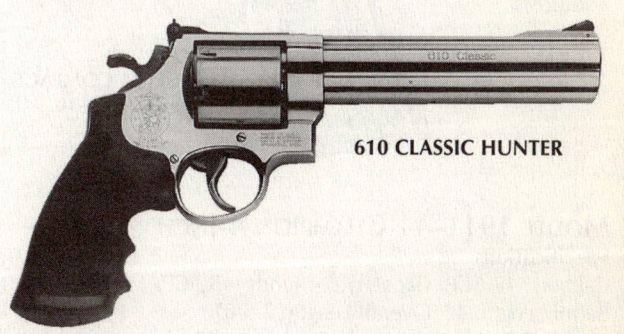

610 CLASSIC HUNTER

Springfield Pistols
Model 1911-A1 Pistols

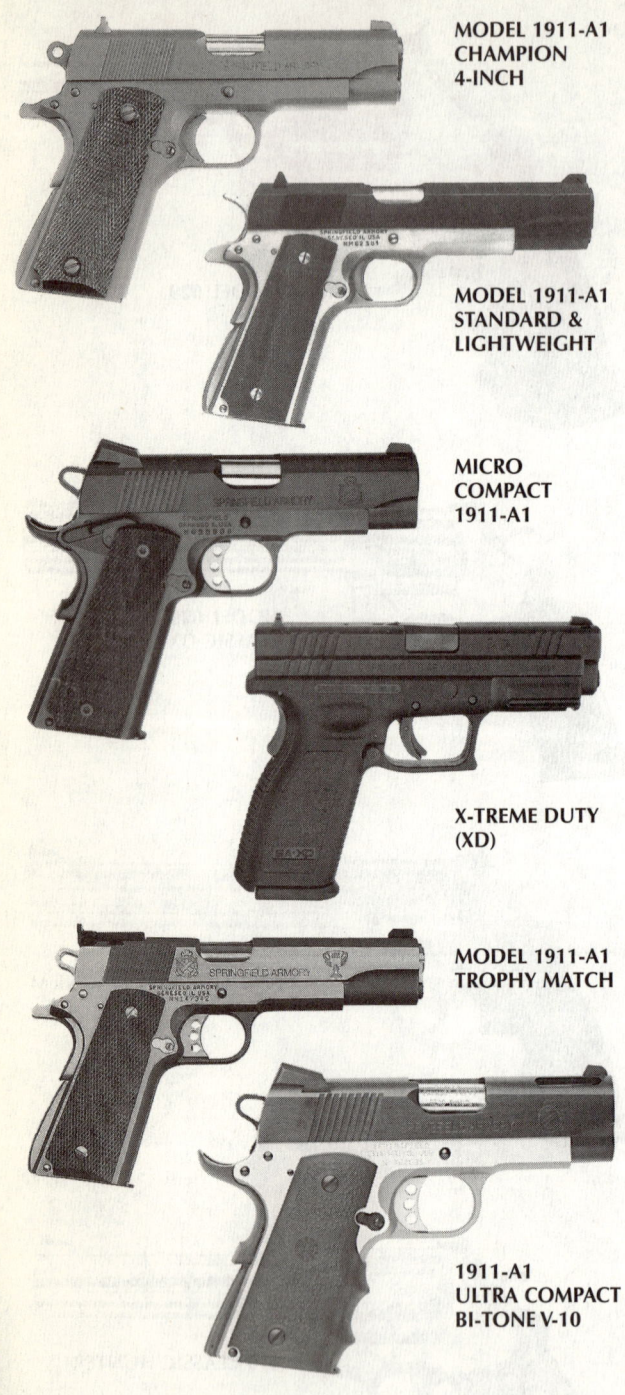

MODEL 1911-A1 CHAMPION 4-INCH

MODEL 1911-A1 STANDARD & LIGHTWEIGHT

MICRO COMPACT 1911-A1

X-TREME DUTY (XD)

MODEL 1911-A1 TROPHY MATCH

1911-A1 ULTRA COMPACT BI-TONE V-10

Stainless w/night sights. $870
Also available: compact 4" 45ACP

Model 1911-A1 Standard & Lightweight
Specifications
Calibers: 45 ACP/9mm **Capacity:** 7 rounds (45 ACP), 9 rounds/ 9mm **Barrel Length:** 5" **Overall Length:** 8 5/8" **Weight:** 38.5 oz. (31.5 oz. Lightweight) **Features:** Cocobolo grips
Prices: 45 ACP Blued 824
45 ACP Stainless. 828
45 ACP Stainless Steel V-12 (ported) 878
45 ACP Lightweight Matte with night sights. 877
45 Parkerized w/night sights. 799
40 S&W, stainless steel 860
9mm Stainless 837
High-capacity (10 rounds, 45 ACP) Parkerized 807

Micro Compact 1911-A1
Specifications
Barrel: 3" **Grips:** Slimline Cocobolo **Sights:** Novak
Weight: 24 oz. **Caliber:** 45 ACP
Price: 1060

X-Treme Duty (XD)
Specifications:
Action: Short recoil, single action
Stock: straight-grip American black walnut; cut checkering; rubber rifle butt pad; nickel-plated steel fore end cap; swivel studs **Barrel:** 4" **Sights:** Dovetail front and rear
Weight: 22.8 oz. **Caliber:** 9mm, .49 S&W, .357 Sig.
Capacity: 10-shot
Price: 489

Model 1911-A1 Trophy Match
Specifications
Calibers: 45 ACP or 40S&W **Capacity:** 7 rounds **Barrel Length:** 5" **Overall Length:** 8 5/8" **Weight:** 40 oz. **Trigger Pull:** 4-5.5 lbs. **Sights:** Fully adjustable target sights **Sight Radius:** 6.75" **Finish:** Blued or stainless **Features:** Match grade barrel; Videcki speed trigger; serrated front strap & top of slide
Prices: Blued 45 ACP 1148
Stainless 45 ACP. 1219
40 S&W, Blued. 1226

1911-A1 Ultra Compact Bi-Tone V-10
Specifications
Caliber: 45 ACP and 9mm **Capacity:** 6 rounds
Barrel Length: 3.5" **Overall Length:** 7.75" **Weight:** 34.8 oz.
Sights: Novak sights **Sight Radius:** 5.25"
Trigger Pull: 5-6.5 lbs. **Finish:** Bi-Tone or Parkerized
Prices:
Parkerized with night sights 817
Bi-Tone V-10 (Ported) 853
High-capacity (10 rounds, 45 ACP), Parkerized 909
Stainless. 884
9mm, lightweight, stainless. 870

Model 1911-A1 Champion 4-Inch
Specifications
Calibers: 45 ACP Capacity: 7 rounds (45 ACP)
Barrel Length: 4" Overall Length: 7 5/8"
Trigger Pull: 5-6.5 lbs. Sight Radius: 5.25"
Weight: 34 oz. Finish: Parkerized, Blued, Stainless
Prices:
Parkerized w/night sights $856

Taurus Pistols
Small and Medium Frame

Model PT 22
Specifications
Caliber: 22 LR **Action:** Semiautomatic (DA only)
Capacity: 8 shots **Barrel Length:** 2.75" **Overall Length:** 5.25" **Weight:** 12.3 oz. **Sights:** Fixed **Safety:** Manual
Grips: Rosewood grip panels or wood grips **Finish:** Blue, nickel, duotone or gold trimmed
Prices:
Blue, Nickel or DuoTone w/rosewood $215
w/wood grips. 190
Gold Trim 230

Model PT-25
Specifications
Caliber: 25 ACP **Capacity:** 9 rounds **Action:** Double action semiauto **Barrel Length:** 2.75" **Overall Length:** 5.25"
Weight: 12.3 oz. **Finish:** Blue, stainless steel, duotone or gold trimmed **Sights:** Fixed **Features:** Rosewood or wood grip panels; tip-up barrel; push button magazine release
Prices:
Blue, Nickel or DuoTone 215
w/wood grips. 190
Blue w/Gold Trim. 230

Model PT-938 Compact (not shown)
Specifications
Caliber: 380 ACP **Capacity:** 10 rounds
Action: Double action semiauto
Barrel Length: 3" **Overall Length:** 6.75"
Weight: 27 oz. **Finish:** Blue or stainless steel
Sights: Fixed **Grips:** Checkered rubber grips
Prices:
Blue. 500
Stainless. 530

PT 911 Compact (not shown)
Specifications
Caliber: 9mm **Capacity:** 10 rounds
Action: Double action semiauto **Barrel Length:** 4"
Overall Length: 7" **Weight:** 28.2 oz.
Safeties: Manual, ambidextrous hammer drop; intercept notch; firing pin block; chamber load indicator
Grips: Santoprene II **Sights:** Fixed 3-dot combat
Finish: Blue or stainless **Features:** Floating firing pin
Prices:
Blue. 525
Stainless. 535
Also available:
PT-111 9mm Millennium.
    Barrel Length: 3 1/8" Sights: Fixed 3-dot
    Capacity: 10 rounds, polymer frame 425
    Stainless. 435

MODEL PT 22

MODEL PT-25

MODEL PT 111 MILLENNIUM

Taurus Pistols
Medium and Large Frame

MODEL PT-92

MODEL PT-945

MODEL PT 99 STAINLESS

PT-145

Model PT-92
Specifications
Caliber: 9mm Parabellum **Action:** Semiautomatic double action **Capacity:** 15 + 1 **Hammer:** Exposed **Barrel Length:** 5" **Overall Length:** 8.5" **Height:** 5.39" **Width:** 1.45" **Weight:** 34 oz. **Rifling:** R.H., 6 grooves **Sights:** Front, fixed; rear adjustable **Finish:** Blue or stainless steel
Prices:
Blue..$575
Stainless..595
Also available:
Model PT-99 Same specifications as Model PT 92, but has micrometer click-adjustable rear sight.
Blue..595
Stainless..610

Model PT-945
Specifications
Caliber: 45 ACP **Capacity:** 8 shots **Action:** Semiauto-matic double **Barrel Length:** 4.25" **Overall Length:** 7.48" **Weight:** 29.5 oz. **Sights:** Drift-adjustable front and rear; 3-dot combat **Grips:** Checkered rubber or rosewood **Finish:** Blue or stainless
Prices:
Blue..560
Blue & gold w/rosewood......................610
Stainless..$580
Stainless & gold w/rosewood................625
w/factory porting (blue).......................600
w/factory porting (stainless).................620

Model PT-940 (not shown)
Specifications
Caliber: 40 S&W **Action:** Semiautomatic double **Capacity:** 10 rounds **Barrel Length:** 4" **Overall Length:** 7" **Weight:** 28.2 oz. **Grips:** Rubber, rosewood, or mother of pearl **Sights:** Low-profile 3-dot combat **Finish:** Blue or stainless **Features:** Factory porting standard
Prices:
Blue w/rubber grips.............................525
Stainless w/rubber grips......................535

Model PT-145
The Taurus Millennium PT-145 is available in .45 ACP caliber, carries a full 10+1 rounds in a double-stack magazine and features a manual safety. The PT-145 is also available with night sights.
Prices:
Blue..490
Stainless..500
Blue w/night sights.............................560
Stainless w/night sights.......................575

Taurus Revolvers

TAURUS PROTECTOR

RAGING BULL

MODEL 460 TRACKER

STELLAR TRACKER

RAGING BEE

TAURUS PROTECTOR – NEW FOR 2002
Specifications
Caliber: .357 Mag. **Barrel:** 2" **Weight:** 17 – 24.5 oz.
Stocks: Rubber **Sights:** Fixed sights
Features: Concealed S/A – D/A Action Design – Shrouded cockable hammer, available in Blued, Matte Stainless, Shadow Gray Total Titanium and Stainless UltraLight (38 only), 5-shot
Prices: .... $375 - $563

TAURUS RAGING BULL MODEL 416 – NEW FOR 2002
Specifications
Caliber: .41 Magnum **Barrel:** 6 1/2" **Weight:** 61.9 oz.
Stocks: Rubber **Sights:** Adjustable
Features: Vent-Rib, Ported, Double-Action, Matte Stainless, integral key lock, 6-shot
Price: 630

TAURUS MODEL 30C RAGING THIRTY – NEW FOR 2002
Specifications
Caliber: .30 Carbine **Barrel:** 10" **Weight:** 72.3 oz.
Stocks: Rubber **Sights:** Adjustable
Features: Double-Action, Vent-Rib, Matte Stainless, comes with (5) "Stellar" Full-Moon Clips, integral key lock. 8-shot
Price: 898

TAURUS MODEL 455 "STELLAR TRACKER" – NEW FOR 2002
Specifications
Caliber: .45 ACP **Barrel:** 2", 4", or 6"
Weight: 28/33/38.4 oz. **Stocks:** Rubber
Sights: Adjustable
Features: Double-Action, Matte Stainless, comes with (5) "Stellar" Full-Moon Clips, integral key lock. 5-shot
Price: $525

TAURUS MODEL 460 "TRACKER" – NEW FOR 2002
Specifications
Caliber: .45 Colt **Barrel:** 4" or 6" **Weight:** 33/38.4 oz.
Stocks: Rubber **Sights:** Adjustable
Features: Double-Action, Vent-Rib, Matte Stainless, comes with (5) "Stellar" Full-Moon Clips, integral key lock. 5-shot
Price: 525

TAURUS MODEL 218 RAGING BEE – NEW FOR 2002
Specifications
Caliber: .218 Bee **Barrel:** 10" **Weight:** 74.9 oz.
Stocks: Rubber **Sights:** Adjustable
Features: Adjustable action, Vent-Rib, Matte Stainless, integral key lock, 8-shot
Price: 898

TAURUS MODEL 217 TARGET 'SILHOUETTE' – NEW FOR 2002
Specifications
Caliber: .218 Bee **Barrel:** 12" **Weight:** 52.3 oz.
Stocks: Rubber **Sights:** Adjustable rear
Features: Double action, Vent-Rib, Matte Stainless, adjustable mainspring and trigger stop, integral key lock, 7-shot
Price: 461

Taurus Revolvers

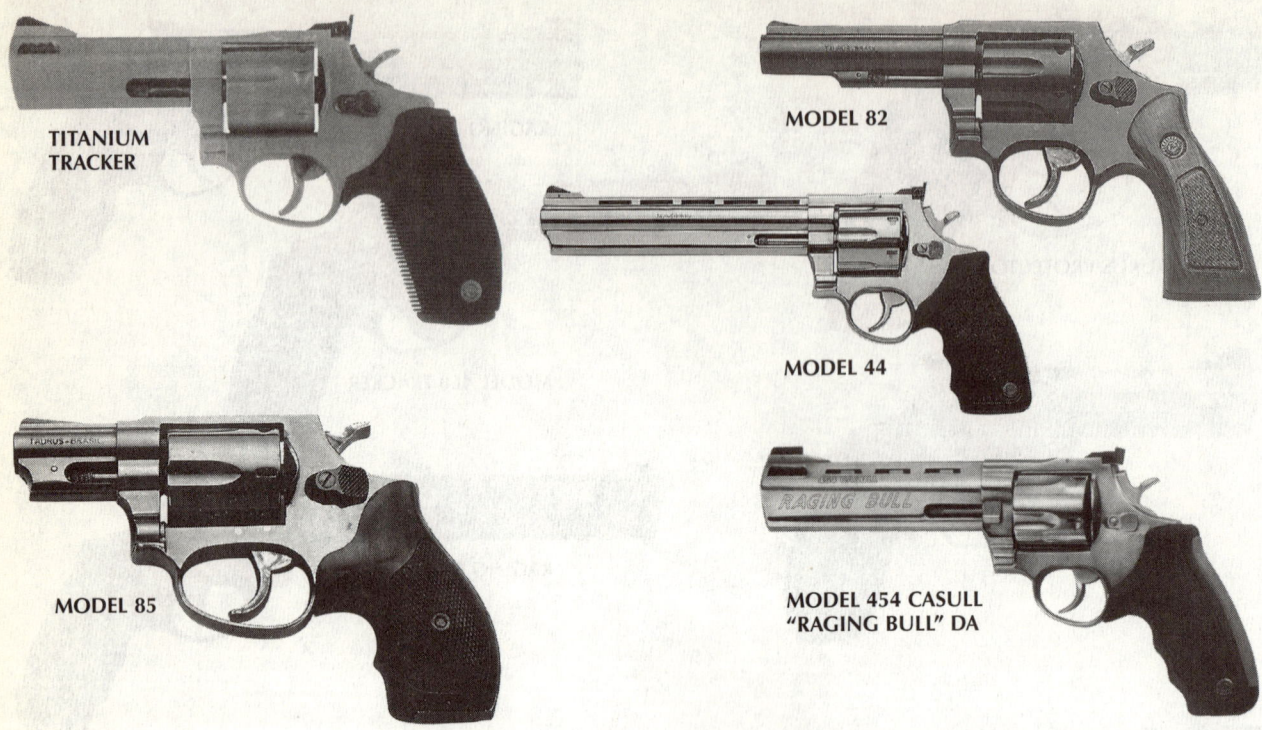

TITANIUM TRACKER

MODEL 82

MODEL 44

MODEL 85

MODEL 454 CASULL "RAGING BULL" DA

Model 44
Specifications
Caliber: 44 Mag. **Capacity:** 6 rounds **Barrel Lengths:** 4" (solid rib ported); 6.5" and 8 3/8" (vent. rib) **Weight:** 44 oz. (4"); 52 oz. (6.5"); 57 oz. (8 3/8") **Sights:** adjustable **Grips:** Rubber **Finish:** Blue or stainless steel
Prices:
4" barrel blue, ported solid rib $500
   stainless steel, ported solid rib 565
6.5" and 8 3/8" blue, ported vent. rib 525
   stainless steel, ported vent. rib 575

Model 454 Casull "Raging Bull" DA
Specifications
Caliber: 454 Casull **Capacity:** 5 rounds **Barrel Length:** 6.5" or 8.375" w/integral vent rib **Overall Length:** 12" (6.5" barrel); 14" (8.375" barrel) **Weight:** 53 oz. (6.5" barrel); 62.75 oz. (8.375" barrel) **Sights:** adjustable **Finish:** Polished stainless steel or bright blue steel **Grips:** Soft black rubber
Features: Ported barrel
Prices:
Blue ported $785
Stainless 855

Model 82
Specifications
Caliber: 38 Special **Capacity:** 6 shot **Action:** Double **Barrel Length:** 4" heavy barrel **Weight:** 34 oz. (4" barrel) **Sights:** Notched rear; serrated ramp front **Grips:** rubber **Finish:** Blue or stainless
Prices:
Blue $325
Stainless 375

Titanium Tracker
The Tracker family is designed for handgun hunting and personal protection. Now available in Total Titanium™, the Tracker features a Ribber Grip™ and extended ejector rod. The Tracker family is available in 4 inch 5-shot .41 Magnum and 4 and 6 inch 7-shot .357 Magnums. All have fully adjustable sights and come in lockable hard plastic cases.
Prices:
.357 4" or 6" 690
.41 Mag 4" 690

Model 85
Specifications
Caliber: 38 Special & 32 H&R Mag. **Capacity:** 5 shot **Action:** Double **Barrel Length:** 2" and 3" **Weight:** 21 oz. (2" barrel) **Sights:** Fixed sights **Grips:** Rubber, rosewood, or mother of pearl **Finish:** Blue or stainless steel
Prices:
Blue w/rubber 345
Stainless w/rubber 395
Also available:
Model 85CH. Same as Model 85, except has concealed hammer and 2" barrel only.
Model 85UL w/2" barrel only and optional porting . . 375
Stainless 425
Models 85CHB2C/85B2C w/2" barrel, blue finish,
   ported barrels $360
Stainless 405

Taurus Revolvers

Model 94
Specifications
Caliber: 22 LR **Number Of Shots:** 9 **Action:** Double **Barrel Lengths:** 2", 4", and 5" heavy, solid rib **Weight:** 25 oz (w/4" barrel) **Sights:** Serrated ramp front; rear micro-meter click adjustable for windage and elevation **Grips:** Brazilian hardwood (4", 5") **Finish:** Blue or stainless steel
Prices:
Blue..$325
Stainless Steel................................ 375
Also available:
Model 941 in 22 Magnum, 8-shot capacity; 2", 4", 5"
 barrel lengths available; ejector shroud. In blue... 345
 In stainless steel............................ 395

Model 608 Double Action
Specifications
Caliber: 357 Magnum **Capacity:** 8 shots **Barrel Lengths:** 4" (heavy solid rib); 6.5" and 8 3/8" (ejector shroud) **Weight:** 51.5 oz. (6.5" barrel) **Grips:** Santoprene I **Sights:** Serrated ramp front w/red insert; micrometer click adjustable **Finish:** Blue or stainless **Features:** Compensated barrel; transfer bar safety; concealed hammer
Prices:
4" Blue.. 445
4" Stainless..................................... 510
6.5", 8 3/8" Blue................................ 465
6.5", 8 3/8" Stainless........................... 525

Model 445 Double Action
Specifications
Caliber: 44 Special **Capacity:** 5 shots **Barrel Length:** 2" **Weight:** 28.25 oz. **Grips:** rubber **Sights:** Serrated ramp front; notched rear **Finish:** Blue or stainless **Features:** Optional porting; heavy solid rib barrel
Prices:
Blue.. 345
Stainless....................................... 395
NEW Ultralite, ported, walnut combat grip........ 500
NEW Titanium, blue, ported, walnut combat grip... 600
Also available:
Model 445CH. Same specifications as Model 445
 but features concealed hammer

Model 605
Specifications
Caliber: .357 Magnum **Capacity:** 5 shot **Barrel Length:** 2" or 2.25" **Weight:** 24.5 oz. **Sights:** Notched rear; serrated ramp front **Grips:** Rubber **Safety:** Transfer bar **Finish:** Blue or stainless **Features:** Optional porting ($19 add'l.)
Prices:
Blue.. 345
Stainless....................................... 395
Also available:
Model 605CH w/concealed hammer and
 ported barrel, blue............................ 360
 stainless...................................... 405

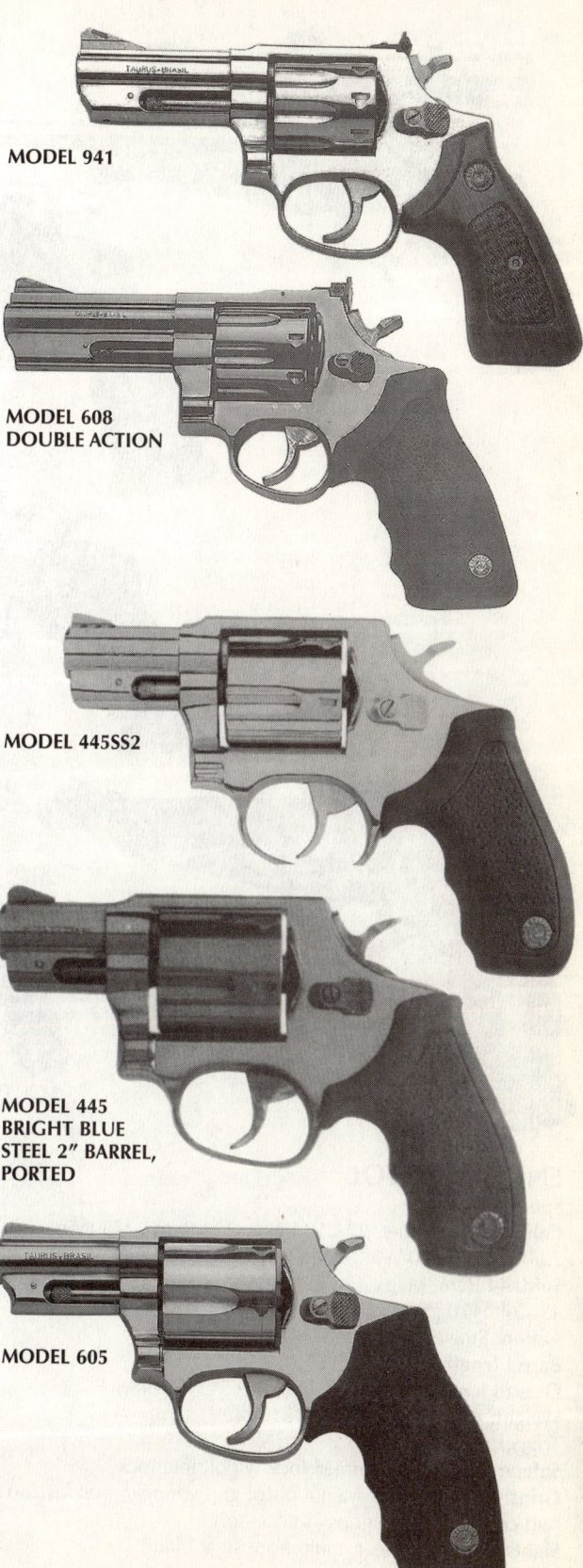

MODEL 941

MODEL 608 DOUBLE ACTION

MODEL 445SS2

MODEL 445 BRIGHT BLUE STEEL 2" BARREL, PORTED

MODEL 605

Thompson/Center Pistols

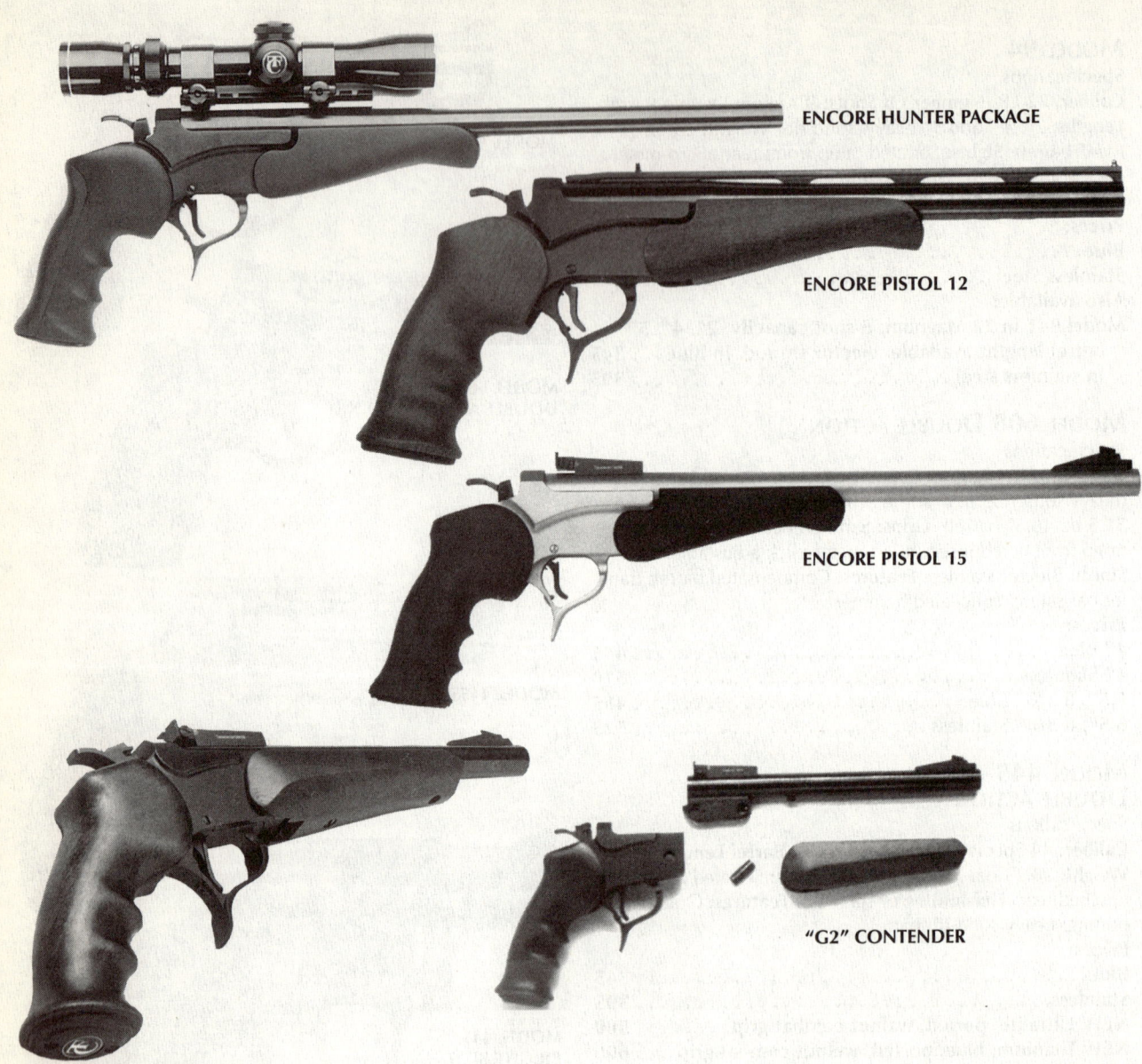

ENCORE HUNTER PACKAGE

ENCORE PISTOL 12

ENCORE PISTOL 15

"G2" CONTENDER

ENCORE PISTOL
Specifications
Calibers: 22 Hornet, 22-250 Rem., 223 Rem., 243 Win., 25/06 Rem., 270 Win., 7mm-08 Rem., 308 Win., 30-06 Spfd. 44 Rem. Mag., 454 Casull, 480 Ruger, 45-70 Gov't, 45 Colt/.410 ga.
Action: Single break-open
Barrel lengths: 12" and 15"
Overall length: 16.5" (12" bbl.); 19.5" (15" bbl.)
Weight: 4.25, 12"; 4.5 lbs. (15" bbl.)
Trigger: Adjustable
Safety: Automatic hammerblock w/bolt interlock
Grips: Ambidextrous walnut pistol grip w/finger grooves and butt cap; composite grips as accessory.
Sights: Adjustable rear; ramp front sight blade

Prices:
Interchangeable barrels 12"..............$250-274
15"......................................258-292
Blued..............................275-321 SST
  drilled and tapped for T/C scope mounts

Prices:
12" Blued..................................554-577
15" barrel Blued...........................562-595
SST..610-656
Also available:
Encore Hunter Package in 22-250 Rem., 270 Win., 308 Win. Barrel length: 15" Features: Weaver-style base and rings, 2.5-7X Recoil Proof pistol scope; blued frame and barrel; black composite grip and forend; soft carry case; no iron sights.................817

Uberti Replicas

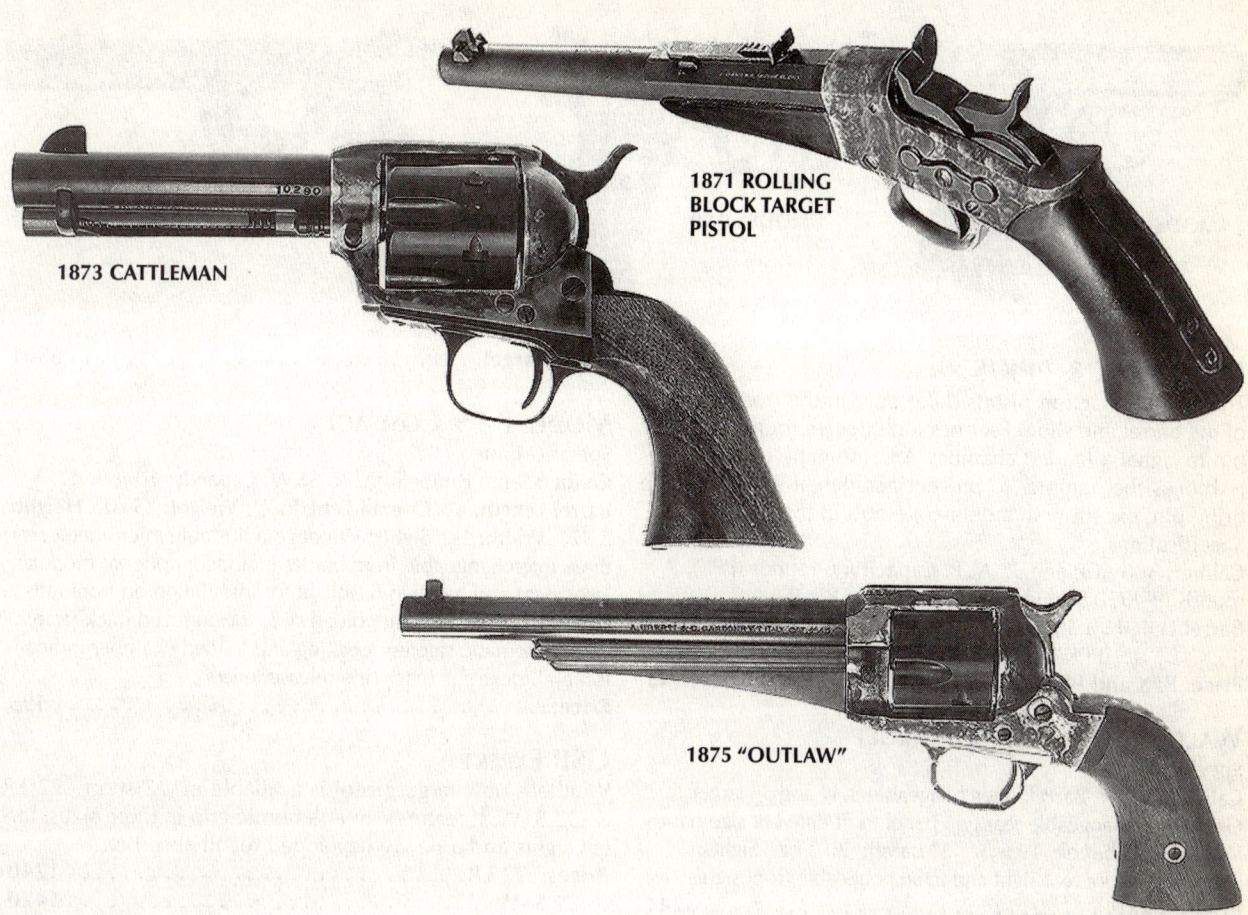

1873 CATTLEMAN
1871 ROLLING BLOCK TARGET PISTOL
1875 "OUTLAW"

1871 ROLLING BLOCK TARGET PISTOL
Specifications
Calibers: 22 LR, 22 Magnum, 22 Hornet and 357 Mag.
Capacity: Single shot **Barrel Length:** 9.5" (half-octagon/half-round or full round Navy Style)
Overall Length: 14" **Weight:** 2.75 lbs.
Sights: Fully adjustable rear; ramp front or open sight on Navy-Style barrel
Grip and forend: Walnut **Trigger guard:** Brass
Frame: Color case-hardened steel
Price: $410

DRAGOON REVOLVERS (NOT SHOWN)
Specifications
Calibers: .44 **Capcity:** 6 shots **Barrel Length:** 7.5"
Frame: color-case **Grips:** walnut **Weight:** 4 lbs.
Prices:
First Model 315
Second Model 315
Third Model 315

1873 CATTLEMAN S.A.
Specifications
Calibers: 357 Magnum, 38/40, 44 Sp., 44-40, 45 L.C.
Capacity: 6 shots **Barrel Lengths:** 4.75", 5.5", 7.5" round, tapered; 18" (Buntline) **Overall Length:** 10.75" w/5.5" barrel
Weight: 2.42 lbs. **Grip:** One-piece walnut **Frame:** Color case-hardened steel; also available in charcoal blue or nickel
Price: $410-435
Also available:
45 L.C./45 ACP Convertible 485

WALKER REVOLVER (NOT SHOWN)
Specifications
Calibers: .44 **Capcity:** 6 shots **Barrel Length:** 9"
Frame: color-case **Grips:** walnut **Weight:** 4.4 lbs. This is the most massive revolver of the "Old West" era; named after a Texas Ranger who carried it.
Price: 330

1875 "OUTLAW"
Specifications
Calibers: 357 Magnum, 44-40, 45 ACP, 45 Long Colt
Capacity: 6 shots **Barrel Lengths:** 5.5", 7.5" round, tapered
Overall Length: 13.75" **Weight:** 2.75 lbs.
Grips: Two-piece walnut **Finish:** Color case-hardened steel
Price: 483
45 L.C./45 ACP "Outlaw" Convertible 499
1890 Police (not shown) 483
45 L.C./45 ACP Police Convertible 499

Handguns • 349

Walther Pistols

MODEL PPK/S   MODEL P 99   GSP EXPERT .32

MODEL PPK & PPK/S
These double-action pistols differ only in the overall length of the barrel and slide. Features include live round indicator pin to signal a loaded chamber. An automatic internal safety blocks the hammer to prevent accidental striking of the firing pin, except with a deliberate pull of the trigger.
Specifications
Caliber: 380 ACP and 32 ACP **Capacity:** 6 rounds (PPK), 7 rounds (PPK/S), 8 rounds (PPK/S in 32 ACP only)
Barrel Length: 3.35" **Overall Length:** 6.25" **Weight:** 21 oz. (PPK); 23 oz. (PPK/S) **Finish:** Walther blue or stainless steel
Price: PPK and PPKS $543

WALTHER P22 AND P22 TARGET
Specifications
Caliber: .22 LR **Barrel:** Interchangeable 3.4" and 5" target
Grips: Interchangeable rear grip panel to fit different-size hands
Weight: 3.4" barrel: 19.6 oz. 5" barrel: 20.3 oz. **Sights:** Adjustable 2-dot rear sight and interchangeable front sights
Prices: P22 241
P22 Target $301

MODEL P 99 COMPACT
Specifications
Caliber: 9mm Parabellum, 40 S&W **Capacity:** 10 rounds
Barrel Length: 4" **Overall Length:** 7" **Weight:** 25 oz. **Height:** 5.37" **Width:** 1.2" **Sights:** Windage-adjustable micrometer rear; three interchangeable front blades included; optional modular laser sight and halogen flashlight for installation on front rails
Features: Polymer frame; blued slide; customized back-strap; three automatic safeties; cocking and loaded chamber indicator; ambidextrous magazine release levers
Price: 595

GSP EXPERT
Walther's new target pistol is available in .22 short, .22 LR & .32 S+W. It features an ergonomic grip in three sizes, target sights and a newly developed recoil absorber.
Prices: .22 LR 1240
.32 S+W 1420

Wildey Pistols

WILDEY SURVIVOR, GUARDSMAN & HUNTER
These gas-operated pistols are designed to meet the needs of hunters who want to use handguns for big game.
Specifications
Calibers: 45 & 475 Wildey Magnums and 45 Win. Mag.
Capacity: 7 shots **Barrel lengths:** 5", 6", 7", 8", 10", 12", 14" **Overall length:** 11" with 7" barrel **Weight:** 64 oz. with 5" barrel **Height:** 6"
SURVIVOR AND GUARDSMAN IN 45 WIN. MAG.
Prices: 5", 6" or 7" barrels $1386
8" or 10" barrels 1409
12" barrel 1492
14" barrel 1895
SURVIVOR MODEL IN WILDEY MAGS.
Prices: 8" or 10" barrels 1409
12" barrel 1493
14" barrel 1895
HUNTER MODEL IN 45 WIN. MAG.
Prices: 5", 6" or 7" barrels 1619
8" or 10" barrels 1643
12" barrel 1728
14" barrel 2115
HUNTER MODEL IN WILDEY MAGS.
Prices: 8" or 10" barrels 1642
12" barrel 1728
14" barrel 2115
Also available:
Interchangeable barrel extension assemblies
5" to 14" barrel . . . . 560 to 1148

BLACKPOWDER

Austin & Halleck	352	Markesbery	373
Cabela	353	Navy Arms	375
Colt	354	Pedersoli	380
CVA	356	Remington	381
Dixie	360	Ruger	382
EMF Hartford	364	Savage	383
Euroarms of America	365	Shiloh Sharps	383
Gonic Arms	368	Thompson/Center	384
Knight	369	Traditions	386
Lenartz	371	Winchester	389
Lyman	372	Uberti	390

Austin & Halleck Rifles

MODEL 320 REALTREE-HARDWOODS CAMO

MODEL 420 LR CLASSIC

MODEL 420 LR MONTE CARLO

MOUNTAIN RIFLE

Bolt-Action In-Line Rifle
Specifications
Caliber: 50 **Action:** In-line percussion (removable weather shroud) **Barrel Length:** 26" (1:28"); 8 lands & grooves; octagon to .75" tapered round **Overall length:** 47.5" **Weight:** 7 7/8 lbs. **Length of pull:** 13.5" **Stock:** Select grade tiger-striped curly maple (Classic model has filled-grain luster finish w/pistol grip cap; Monte Carlo has filled-grain high-gloss finish) **Features:** Match grade target triggers w/trigger block safety; 1" recoil pad; scope not included

Prices:
Model 420 LR Monte Carlo & Classic Standard	**$512**
Stainless Steel Standard	539
Fancy Standard	579
Fancy Stainless Steel	606
Hand Select	714
Hand Select Stainless Steel	741
Exhibition Grade	1179
Exhibition Grade Stainless Steel	1235

Model 320 LR BLU w/Synthetic Stock	$399
Model 320 LR S/S	444
Model 320 Blue/Camo	437-444
Model 320 SS/Camo	469-476

Mountain Rifle
Specifications
Caliber: 50 percussion or flintlock **Barrel length:** 32" (1:66 roundball or 1:28 bullet twist); 1" octagonal; rust brown finish **Overall length:** 49" **Weight:** 7.5 lbs. **Stock:** Select grade tiger-striped curly maple; filled-grain luster finish **Sights:** Fixed buckhorn rear; silver blade brass bead front **Features:** Double throw adjustable set triggers

Price: Std. percussion	529
Hand Select percussion	714
Fancy Percussion	639
Std. flint	583
Hand select flint	741
Fancy flint	667

Cabela's Rifles
Custom Hunting

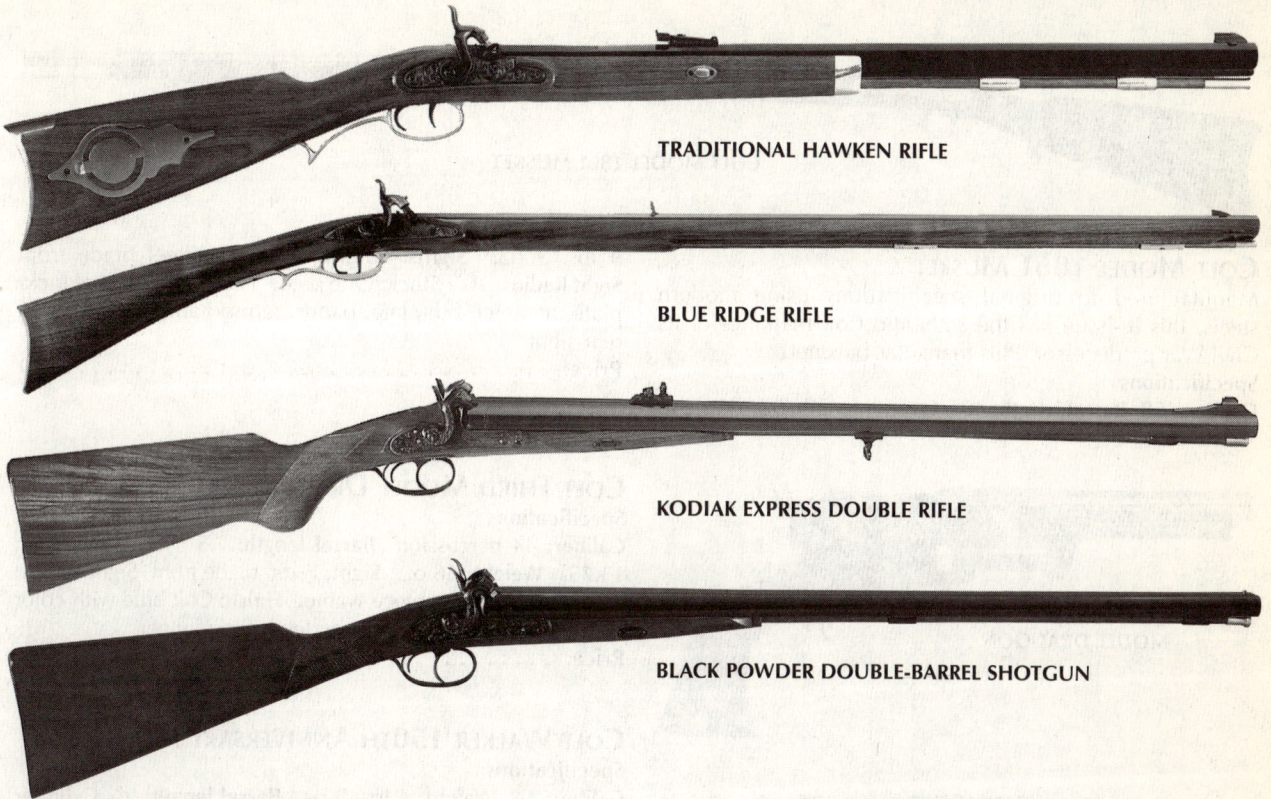

TRADITIONAL HAWKEN RIFLE

BLUE RIDGE RIFLE

KODIAK EXPRESS DOUBLE RIFLE

BLACK POWDER DOUBLE-BARREL SHOTGUN

Traditional Hawken Rifle

Cabela's Traditional Hawken is available in 50 or 54 caliber. It features fully adjustable sights, top-grade walnut stock with brass trigger guard, curved buttplate, forend cap, ferrules and ramrod fittings. Adjustable set triggers are standard. Percussion available in right- or left-hand versions.
Barrel: 24" octagon with 1-in-48 twist. **Weight:** 9 lbs.
Prices: Percussion, right-hand $190
    Percussion, left-hand 200
    Flintlock, right-hand 225

Blue Ridge Rifle

From the era of the American long rifle (1760-1840) comes the design for this faithful reproduction "squirrel rifle" Precision-rifled 39" browned octagonal barrel with 1-in-48" twist delivers exceptional precision with patched round balls. Its 8 lands and grooves will handle conical bullets surprisingly well. Locks are color case-hardened. Adjustable double-set, double-phase triggers. Buttplate and trigger guard are polished brass.

Percussion	Cal.	Overall Length	Barrel Length	Wt. Lbs.	Groove & Lands	Gun Only Price	Kit Price
	.32 or .36 Cal	55"	39"	7 3/4	7	$380	$420
	.50 Cal	55"	39"	7 1/4	8	$380	$420
Flintlock							
	.32 or .36 Cal	55"	39"	7 3/4	7	$400	$440
	.45 or .50 Cal	55"	39"	7 1/4	8	$400	$440

Kodiak Express Double Rifle

Early explorers of Africa and Asia had to rely on large-bore "express" rifles. This handsome sidelock replica features oil-finished, hand-checkered European walnut stock with case hardened steel buttplate, ramp-mounted, adjustable folding double rear sights, ramp front sight. Its drilled and tapped for a folding tang sight. Color-case hardened lock, blued top tang and trigger guard are all polished and engraved. **Calibers:** 50, 54, 58, 72 **Barrels:** 28" with 1:48" twist (regulated at 75 yards); blued. **Overall Length:** 45.25" **Weight:** 9.3 lbs.
Price: . . . . $650 to 680

Black Powder Double-Barrel Shotgun

These shotguns feature chrome-lined barrels for use with steel shot and screw-in choke tubes for greater flexibility. the 10 and 12 gauge models come with X-FULL, MOD and I.C. tubes. Go from doves to turkey in seconds by changing chokes and charges. Deep bluing, engraved locks and checkered American walnut stocks. **Barrel lengths:** 30" in 10 ga., 28.5" in 12 ga., 27.5" in 20 ga. **Weight:** 10 and 12 ga.: 7 lbs.; 20 ga.: 6.5 lbs. A Cabela's exclusive from Davide Pedersoli.
Price: . . . . 430 to 500

Colt Blackpowder Arms
Signature Series

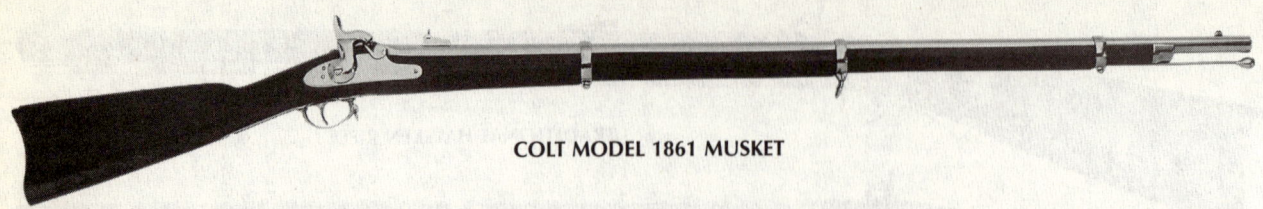
COLT MODEL 1861 MUSKET

Colt Model 1861 Musket
Manufactured to original specifications using modern steels, this re-issue has the authentic Colt markings of its Civil War predecessor. Plus triangular bayonet.
Specifications
Caliber: .58 **Barrel length:** 40" **Overall length:** 56" **Weight:** 9 lbs. 3 oz. **Sights:** Folding leaf rear; steel blade front **Sight Radius:** 36" **Stock:** One piece **Finish:** Bright steel lockplate, hammer, buttplate, bands, ramrod and nipple; blued rear sight
Price: $800

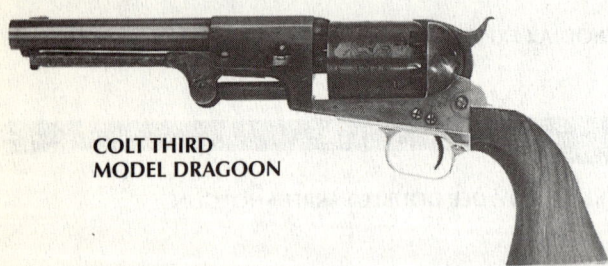
COLT THIRD MODEL DRAGOON

Colt Third Model Dragoon
Specifications
Caliber: 44 percussion **Barrel length:** 7.5" **Overall length:** 13.75" **Weight:** 66 oz. **Sight:** Fixed blade front **Sight radius:** 10.75" **Stock:** One-piece walnut **Finish:** Colt blue with color case-hardened frame; hammer, lever and plunger
Price: 500

Colt Walker 150th Anniversary Model
Specifications
Caliber: 44 **Weight:** 4 lbs. 9 oz. **Barrel length:** 9" **Cylinder length:** 2 7/16" **Finish:** Color case-hardened frame and hammer; smooth wooden grips **Features:** Colt's Signature Series 150th anniversary re-issue carries the identical markings as the original 1847 Walker. "U.S. 1847" appears above the barrel wedge, exactly as on the Walkers produced for service in the Mexican War. The cylinder has a battle scene depicting 15 Texas Rangers defeating a Comanche war party using the first revolver invented by Sam Colt. This Limited Edition features original A Company No. 1 markings embellished in gold. Serial numbers begin with #221, a continuation of A Company numbers.
Price: 700
    Standard 1847 Walker 500

COLT WALKER 150TH ANNIVERSARY MODEL

COLT 1849 POCKET REVOLVER

Colt 1849 Pocket Revolver
Specifications
Caliber: 31 **Barrel length:** 4" **Overall length:** 9.5" **Weight:** 24 oz. **Stock:** One-piece walnut **Finish:** Colt blue and color case-hardened frame
Price: 430

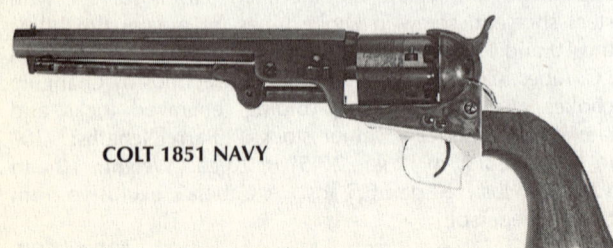
COLT 1851 NAVY

Colt 1851 Navy
Specifications
Caliber: 36 **Barrel length:** 7.5" **Overall length:** 13 1/8" **Weight:** 40.5 oz. (empty) **Sights:** Fixed blade front **Sight radius:** 10" **Stock:** Oiled American walnut **Finish:** Colt blue and color case-hardened frame
Price: 450

Colt Blackpowder Arms
Signature Series

Colt 1860 Army
A continuation in production of the famous cap-and-ball revolver used by the U.S. Cavalry with color case hardened frame, hammer and loading lever. Blued backstrap and brass trigger guard, roll-engraved cylinder and one-piece walnut grips
Specifications
Caliber: 44 **Barrel length:** 8" **Overall length:** 13.75" **Weight:** 42 oz. **Sights:** Fixed blade front **Sight radius:** 10.5" **Stock:** One-piece walnut **Finish:** Colt blue with color case hardened frame; hammer, lever and plunger
Price:.................................. $450

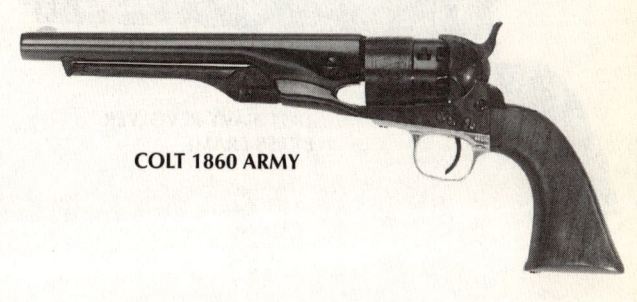
COLT 1860 ARMY

Colt Model 1860 Army Fluted Cylinder
The first Army revolvers shipped from Hartford were known as the "Cavalry Model"—with fluted cylinder, color case hardened frame, hammer, loading lever and plunger. Features blued barrel, backstrap and cylinder; brass trigger guard, fluted cylinder, one-piece walnut grip and a 4-screw frame (cut for optional shoulder stock)
Specifications
Caliber: 44 percussion **Barrel length:** 8" **Overall length:** 13.75" **Weight:** 42 oz. **Sight:** Fixed blade front **Sight radius:** 10.5" **Stock:** One piece walnut **Finish:** Colt blue with color case hardened frame; hammer, lever and plunger
Price:.................................. 450

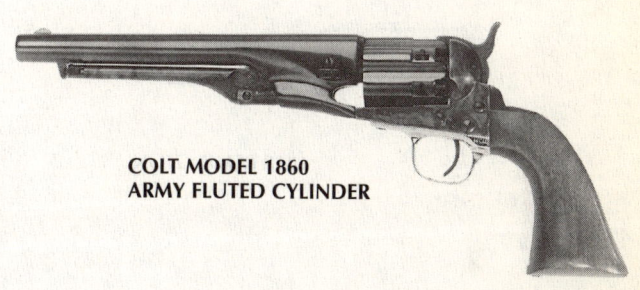
COLT MODEL 1860 ARMY FLUTED CYLINDER

Colt 1861 Navy
A personal favorite of George Armstrong Custer, who carried a pair of them during the Civil War. Loading lever and plunger; blued barrel, cylinder backstrap and trigger guard; roll-engraved cylinder; one-piece walnut grip.
Specifications
Caliber: 36 percussion **Barrel length:** 7.5" **Overall length:** 13 1/8" **Weight:** 42 oz. **Sight:** Fixed blade front **Sight radius:** 10" **Stock:** One-piece walnut **Finish:** Colt blue with color case hardened frame; hammer, lever and plunger
Price:.................................. 450

COLT 1861 NAVY

Trapper Model 1862 Pocket Police
The first re-issue of the rare and highly desirable Pocket Police "Trapper Model." The Trapper's 3.5" barrel without attached loading lever makes it an ideal backup gun, as well as a welcome addition to any gun collection. Color case-hardened frame and hammer; silver-plated backstrap and trigger guard; blued semi-fluted cylinder and barrel; one-piece walnut grip. Separate 4 5/8" brass ramrod.
Specifications
Caliber: 36 **Barrel length:** 3.5" **Overall length:** 8.5" **Weight:** 20 oz. **Sight:** Fixed blade front **Sight radius:** 6" **Stock:** One-piece walnut **Finish:** Colt blue with color case hardened frame and hammer
Price:.................................. 430

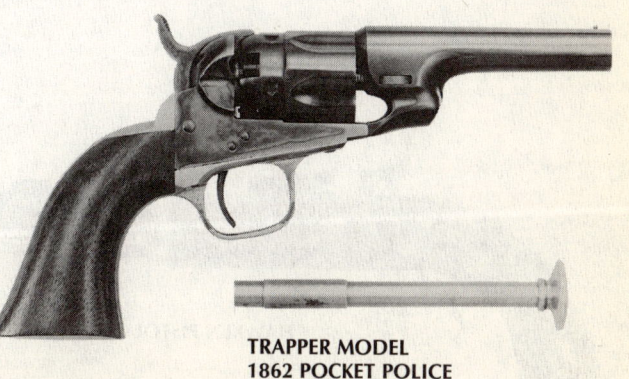
TRAPPER MODEL 1862 POCKET POLICE

CVA Revolvers/Pistols

BLACK POWDER

1851 NAVY REVOLVER BRASS FRAME

1851 NAVY REVOLVER BRASS FRAME
Specifications
Caliber: 44
Barrel length: 7.5" octagonal; hinged-style loading lever
Overall length: 13"
Weight: 44 oz.
Cylinder: 6-shot, engraved
Sights: Post front; hammer notch rear
Grip: One-piece walnut
Finish: Solid brass frame, trigger guard and backstrap; blued barrel and cylinder; color case hardened loading lever and hammer
Price: $144

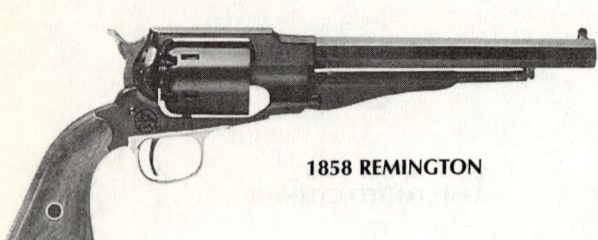

1858 REMINGTON

1858 REMINGTON
Specifications
Caliber: 44
Cylinder: 6-shot, engraved
Barrel length: 7.5" octagonal
Overall length: 13"
Weight: 38 oz.
Sights: Blade front; adjustable target
Grip: Two-piece walnut
Price: Brass Frame 160

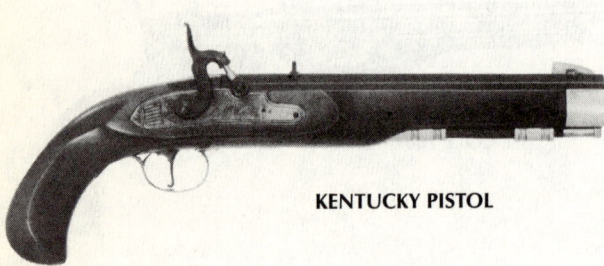

KENTUCKY PISTOL

KENTUCKY PISTOL
Specifications
Caliber: 50 percussion
Barrel: 9.75", rifled, octagonal
Overall length: 15.5" **Weight:** 40 oz.
Finish: Blued barrel, brass hardware
Sights: Brass blade front; fixed open rear
Stock: Select hardwood
Ignition: Engraved, color case hardened percussion lock, screw adjustable sear engagement
Accessories: Brass-tipped, hardwood ramrod; stainless-steel nipple or flash hole liner
Prices:
　Finished 168
　Percussion Kit 120

HAWKEN PISTOL

HAWKEN PISTOL
Specifications
Caliber: 50 percussion
Barrel length: 9.75", octagonal
Overall length: 16.5"
Weight: 50 oz.
Trigger: Early-style brass
Sights: Beaded steel blade front; fully adjustable rear (click adj. screw settings lock into position)
Stock: Select hardwood
Finish: Solid brass wedge plate, nose cap, ramrod thimbles, trigger guard and grip cap
Prices:
　Finished 168
　Kit 128

CVA Rifles/Shotguns

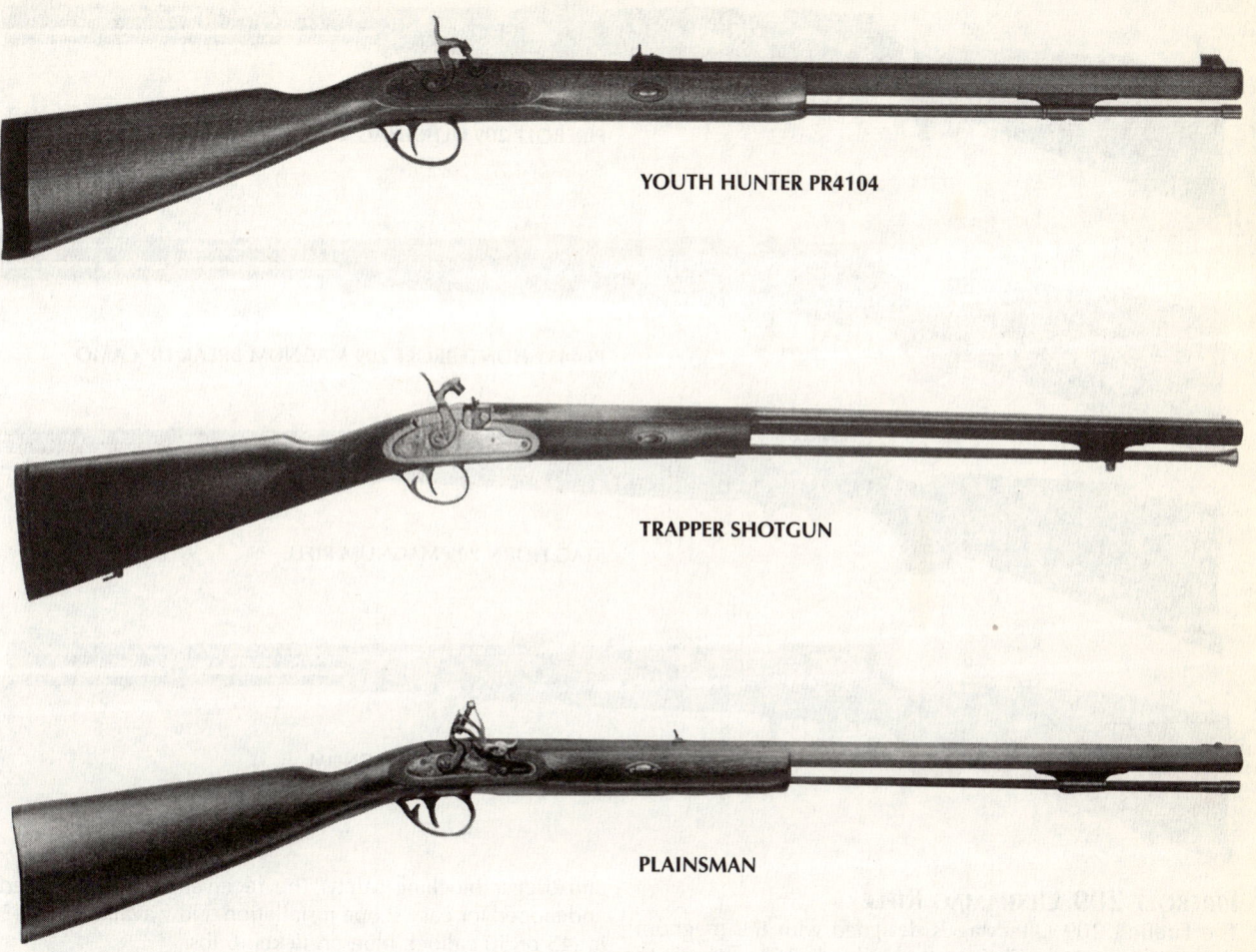

YOUTH HUNTER PR4104

TRAPPER SHOTGUN

PLAINSMAN

YOUTH HUNTER PR4104
The Youth Hunter rifle was custom made for the smaller shooter. It has a 24" octagonal barrel and a shortened hardwood stock. CVA's patented breech plug/bolster system ensures consistent ignition. A 1:48" twist deep-groove rifled barrel ensures accuracy with round ball or conical bullets. This rifle is also great for the petite lady. It is fully equipped with a Williams adjustable rear sight, oversized trigger guard and synthetic ramrod. All Youth Hunter rifles are backed by CVA's lifetime mechanical warranty and include complete shooting instructions.
Specifications
Calibers: .50 **Barrel:** 24" **Blued Twist:** 1:48 **Stock:** Hardwood
Weight: 5 lbs. **Length:** 38"
Price:..$136

TRAPPER SHOTGUN
The new chrome-lined barrel of the Trapper gives you the option to shoot either lead or steel shot. The light weight English-style hardwood stock allows for quick target pick-up and follow through. The engraved color case hardened lock contains an authentic V-type main spring. The barrel has a brass bead front sight, hook style breech and snail type bolster for convenient and easy cleaning. Includes CVA's lifetime mechanical warranty and complete instructions.
Specifications: Model PS419M
Gauge: 12 **Barrel:** 28" Blued **Choke:** Fixed Modified
Ramrod: Synthetic **Weight:** 6 lbs.
Price:..$288

PLAINSMAN
Specifications
Caliber: 50 Barrel: 26" blued barrel with patented breech plug system Sights: Fully adjustable
Price:..180

CVA Rifles

FIREBOLT 209 ULTRAMAG RIFLE

PR4451 HUNTERBOLT 209 MAGNUM BREAK-UP CAMO

STAG HORN 209 MAGNUM RIFLE

PR4478 ECLIPSE 209 MAGNUM

FIREBOLT 209 ULTRAMAG RIFLE
The FireBolt 209 UltraMag is designed with the magnum shooter in mind. The matted blued 26" one-piece MonoBlock barrel ensures a complete powder burn. Six precision machined flutes increase barrel stability while reducing weight. Like all the rifles in the FireBolt series, this gun is equipped with a stainless steel quick-release bolt, #209 ignition, and a Bullet Guiding Muzzle. Other features include Illuminator fiber optic sights, FiberGrip rubber-coated stock, ventilated recoil pad, and sling swivel studs. The receiver is factory drilled and tapped for easy scope installation. Includes synthetic ramrod, cleaning jag, breech plug/nipple wrench, and #209 capper/decapper. Now available in .45 or .50 Caliber. 7 lbs total weight.

Price: FiberGrip/Blued $260
  FiberGrip/Nickel. 280
  Camo/Blued 300
  Camo/Nickel 320

HUNTERBOLT 209 MAGNUM RIFLE
The Hunterbolt 209 Magnum is equipped with the same quick-release bolt design found on the FireBolt series. The #209 ignition provides unsurpassed reliability, even in the toughest hunting conditions, while the 24" one-piece MonoBlock barrel offers legendary accuracy. "Bullet Guiding Muzzle," Illuminator fiber optic sights, ventilated recoil pad synthetic black or camo stock, sling swivel studs, and trigger blocking safety. The receiver is factory drilled and tapped for easy scope installation. Now available in .45 in .45 or 50 caliber, blue or nickel, 6 lbs.

Price: Black/Blue $200
  Black/Nickel 220
  Camo/Blue 230
  Camo/Nickel 250

STAG HORN 209 MAGNUM RIFLE
The Stag Horn 209 Magnum has a one-piece MonoBlock barrel design. The Stag Horn will now handle a 3-pellet load (150 grain equivalent). It features the reliable #209 ignition, Illuminator Solar Sights, ventilated recoil pad, manual notch safety, stainless steel bolt, oversized trigger guard, and synthetic stock. The 24" blued barrel has a 1:28" twist. 6 lbs. total weight.

Price: 45 or 50 caliber 130

ECLIPSE 209 MAGNUM
Specifications
Barrel: 24" barrel, 1:28 twist, blued finish **Calibers:** 45 and 50 **Stock:** Synthetic black or camo in Mossy Oak Break-Up, Trebark Bigwoods or Advantage Timber **Weight:** 6 lbs. **Sights:** Fiber optic sights **Other Features:** Ventilated recoil pad, 209 ignition, stainless steel breech plug and lifetime warranty.

Price: Synthetic 160
  Camo 190

CVA Rifles
Caplock Rifles

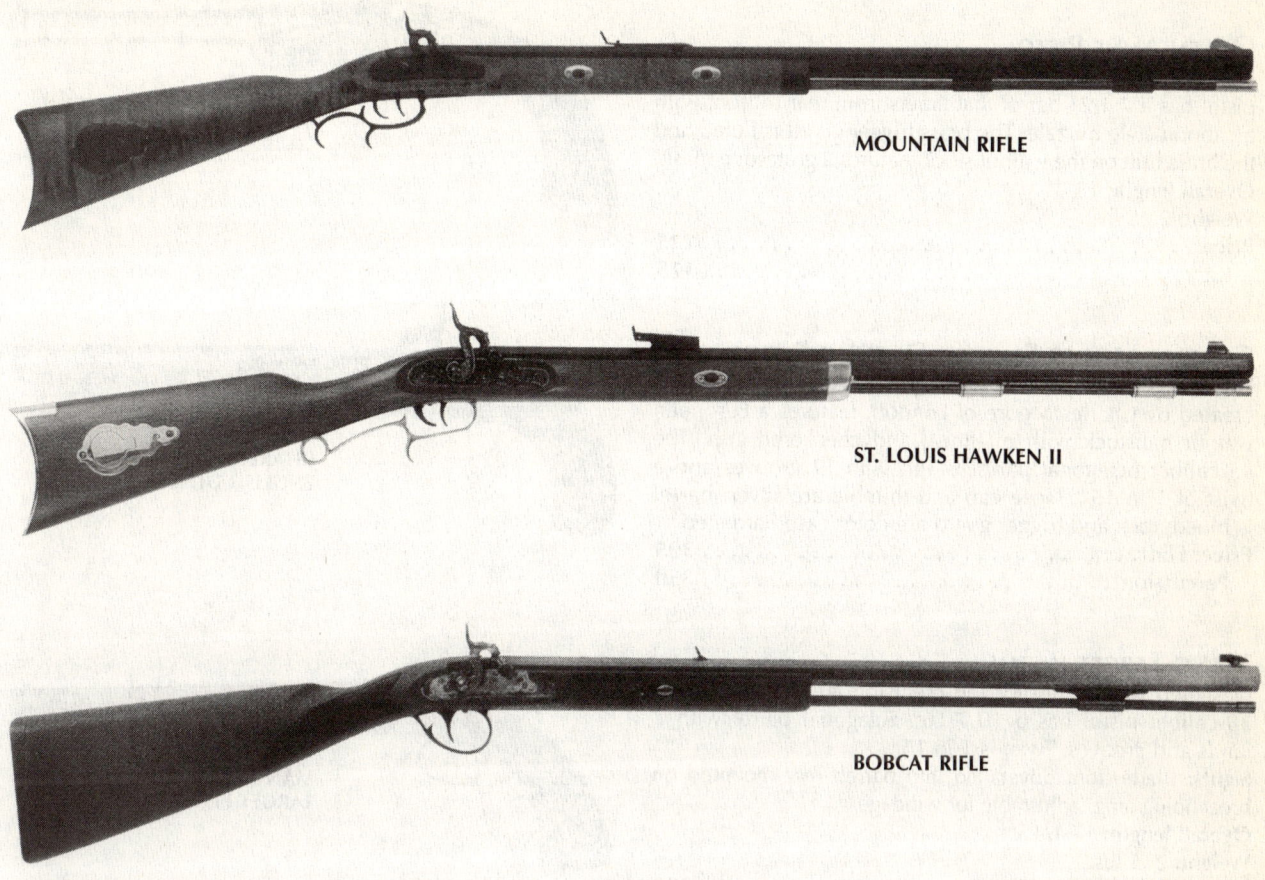

MOUNTAIN RIFLE

ST. LOUIS HAWKEN II

BOBCAT RIFLE

Mountain Rifle

The CVA Mountain Rifle helped launch the rebirth of black-powder hunting and shooting in the early 1970's. This 50 caliber gun authentically replicates the no-nonsense rifles of the mountain men who first explored the American West. Featuring all browned steel hardware, fine figured American hard maple stock, buckhorn rear sight, German silver wedge plates and blade front sight, this rifle offers custom quality and true traditional appeal. Designed to shoot patched round balls, the 32" browned steel barrel has 1 in 66" rifling and is extremely accurate. Made in the USA and limited to a production run of only 500 guns, the CVA Mountain Rifle is intended for the collector as well as the hunter.
Weight: 9 lbs
Price:. $400
Also available: MOUNTAIN HUNTER RIFLE w/ hardwood stock, blued. 1:48" twist barrel
  Price: 260

St. Louis Hawken II
Specifications
Caliber: 50 or 54 percussion
Barrel: 28" blued, 1:48" twist
Stock: UltraGrain Finish hardwood
Weight: 8 lbs.
Other Features: Double set triggers, solid brass butt plate, patch box, trigger guard
Price:. $230
  Left hand:. 275

Bobcat Rifle

The Bobcat Rifle is a basic muzzleloader that delivers value without compromising performance, now with a choice of hardwood or synthetic stock. The blued octagonal barrel is the same barrel used on CVA's top-of-the-line hunting rifles. Accuracy with sabots, conical bullets, and round balls is assured by CVA's deep groove rifling. The rifle has fixed sights and a wooden ramrod.
Specifications
Caliber: 50
Barrel: 26" blued barrel, 1:48" twist
Sights: Adjustable sights included
Weight: 6 lbs.
Price: 50 cal. Bobcat Percussion 105
  50 cal. Bobcat Percussion wood stock. 128

Dixie Pistols

QUEEN ANNE PISTOL
Named for the Queen of England (1702-1714), this flintlock pistol has a 7 1/2" barrel that tapers from rear to front with a cannon-style muzzle. The brass trigger guard is fluted and the brass butt on the walnut stock features a grotesque mask.
Overall length: 13".
Weight: 2.25 lbs.
Price:...$225
    Kit...175

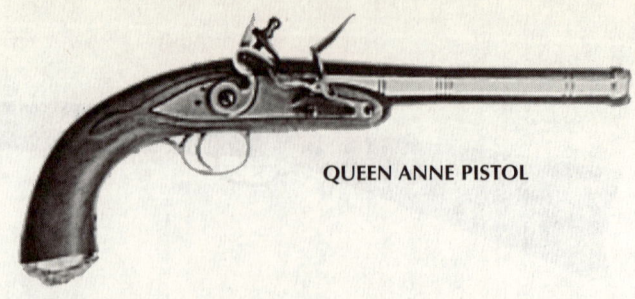
QUEEN ANNE PISTOL

CHARLES MOORE ENGLISH DUELING PISTOL
This reproduction of an English percussion dueling pistol, created by Charles Moore of London, features a European walnut halfstock with oil finish and checkered grip. The 45-caliber octagonal barrel is 11" with 12 grooves and a twist of 1 in 15". Nose cap and thimble are silver; barrel is blued; lock and trigger guard are color case hardened.
Price: Flint..395
    Percussion..350

CHARLES MOORE ENGLISH DUELING PISTOL

MANG TARGET PISTOL
Designed specifically for the precision target shooter, this 38-caliber pistol has a 10 7/16" octagonal barrel with 7 lands and grooves. Twist is 1 in 15".
Sights: Blade front dovetailed into barrel; rear mounted on breechplug tang, adjustable for windage.
Overall length: 17 1/4".
Weight: 2 .5 lbs.
Price:...825

MANG IN GRAZ TARGET PISTOL

LePAGE PERCUSSION DUELING PISTOL
This 45-caliber percussion pistol features a blued 10" octagonal barrel with 12 lands and grooves; a brass-bladed front sight with open rear sight dovetailed into the barrel; polished silver-plated trigger guard and butt cap. Right side of barrel is stamped "LePage á Paris." Double-set riggers are single screw adjustable.
Overall length: 16".
Weight: 2.5 lbs.
Price:...395

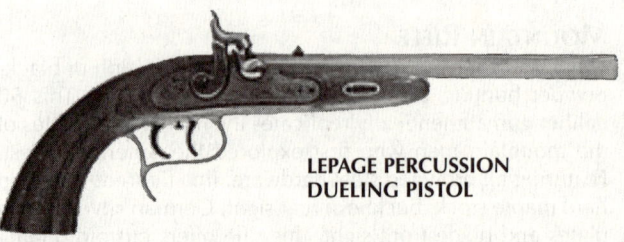
LEPAGE PERCUSSION DUELING PISTOL

SCREW BARREL (FOLDING TRIGGER) PISTOL
This little gun, only 6 1/2" overall, has a unique loading system that eliminates the need for a ramrod. The barrel is loosened with a barrel key, then unscrewed from the frame by hand. A .445 round ball is seated atop 10 grains FFFg and the barrel is then screwed back into place. The .245X32 nipple uses #11 percussion caps. The pistol also features a sheath trigger that folds into the frame, then drops down for firing when the hammer is cocked. Color case hardened frame, trigger and center-mounted hammer.
Price:...127
    Kit...95

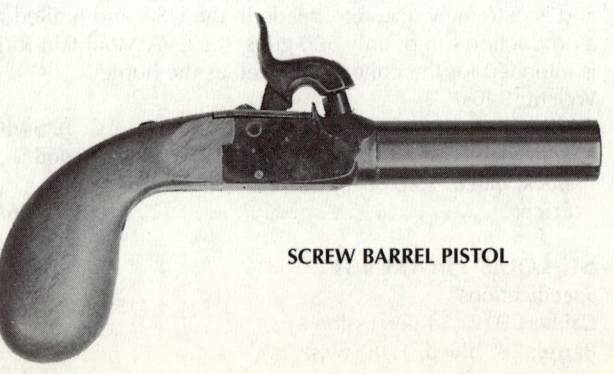
SCREW BARREL PISTOL

Dixie Rifles

SHARPS MODEL 1859 CARBINE
1874 SHARPS SILHOUETTE MODEL
SHARPS NEW MODEL 1859 MILITARY RIFLE
EARLY AMERICAN JAEGER RIFLE
1874 SHARPS LIGHTWEIGHT HUNTER RIFLE

SHARPS MODEL 1859 CARBINE
About 115,000 Sharps New Model 1859 carbines and its variants were made during the Civil War. Characterized by durability and accuracy, they became a favorite of cavalrymen on both sides. This true-to-life replica is made in Italy by Davide Pedersoli & Co.
Specifications
Caliber: 54 **Barrel length:** 22" (1 in 48" twist); blued, round barrel has 7-groove rifling **Overall length:** 37 1/2" **Weight:** 7 3/4 lbs. **Sights:** Blade front; adjustable rear **Stock:** Oil-finished walnut **Features:** Barrel band, hammer, receiver, saddle bar and ring all color case-hardened
Price:.................................. $775

SHARPS NEW MODEL 1859 MILITARY RIFLE
Initially used by the First Connecticut Volunteers, this rifle is associated mostly with the 1st U.S. (Berdan's) Sharpshooters. There were 6,689 made, with most going to the Sharpshooters (2,000) and the U.S. Navy (2,780). Replica is made in Italy by Davide Pedersoli & Co.
Specifications
Caliber: 54 **Barrel length:** 30" (1 in 48" twist) **Overall length:** 45 1/2" **Weight:** 9 lbs. **Sights:** Blade front; rear sight adjustable for elevations and windage **Features:** Buttstock and forend of straight-grained oil finished walnut; three barrel bands, receiver, hammer, nose cap, lever, patchbox cover and butt are all color case-hardened; sling swivels attached to middle band and butt
Price:.................................. 925

1874 SHARPS LIGHTWEIGHT HUNTER RIFLE
This Sharps rifle in .45-70 Government has a 30" octagon barrel with blued matte finish (1:18" twist). It also features an adjustable ladder rear sight and blade front, making it ideal for blackpowder hunters. The tang is drilled and threaded for tang sights. The oil-finished military-style buttstock has a blued metal buttplate. Double-set triggers. Color case hardened receiver and hammer. **Overall length:** 49 1/2". **Weight:** 10 lbs.
Price:.................................. $995

1874 SHARPS SILHOUETTE MODEL
This rifle in .40-65 and .45-70 has a shotgun-style buttstock with pistol grip and metal buttplate. The 30-inch tapered octagon barrel is blued and has a 1 in 18" twist. The receiver, hammer, lever and buttplate are color case-hardened. Ladder-type hunting rear and blade front sights are standard. Four screw holes are in the tang (two with 10 x 28 threads, two with metric threads) for attaching tang sights. Double set triggers are standard. **Weight:** 10 lbs. 3 oz. without target sights. **Overall length:** 47 1/2". Also available in .45-70
Price:.................................. 995

EARLY AMERICAN JAEGER RIFLE
This rifle is patterned after the original Jaeger that was popular in central Europe at the end of the 17th century. The .54 caliber has a browned octagon barrel and full stock with sliding wooden patchbox on the butt. Sights are fixed blade front and notch rear. **Overall length:** 43 1/2" **Weight:** 8.25 lbs.
Prices: Flint.................................. 695
   Percussion.................................. 695

HAWKEN RIFLE (NOT SHOWN)
The favorite of American frontiersman in the mid-1800s. This replica has a blued barrel 15/16" across the flats and 30" in length with a twist of 1 in 64". Stock is of walnut with a steel crescent buttplate, halfstock with brass nosecap. Double-set triggers, front-action lock and adjustable rear sight. Ramrod is equipped with jag. **Overall length:** 46 1/2". **Weight:** about 8 lbs., depending on the caliber; shipping weight is 10 lbs. Available in either finished gun or kit. **Calibers:** 45, 50 and 54.
Price:.................................. 250
   Kit.................................. 205

Dixie Rifles

KODIAK MARK IV
.45-.70 DOUBLE BARREL RIFLE

1873 TRAPDOOR CARBINE

1873 TRAPDOOR SPRINGFIELD

PENNSYLVANIA RIFLE

Kodiak Mark IV .45-70 Double Barrel Rifle
Patterned after a classic, limited edition 19th century Colt double rifle, the Kodiak Mark IV has been designed for hunters and collectors. The 24-inch browned barrels are semi-regulated and topped with a triple-leaf sight marked for 100, 200 and 300 yards. Locks, receiver, trigger guard and hammers are case-hardened. The two-piece stock is checkered European walnut with slug swirels. The buttstock has a cheekpiece and a solid, red rubber pad.
Weight: 10 lbs. **Overall length:** 40".
Price: $2495

1873 Springfield Rifle and Carbine
Developed from the Allin Conversion of Springfield muskets from the Civil War, 1873 Springfield "Trapdoors" finished the "winning of the West." Adopted in 1873 and immediately issued to troops on the frontier, the Trapdoor was the last single-shot, blackpowder rifle of the U.S. military, (it was later supplanted by the .30-.40 Krag-Jorgensen bolt rifle).
Rifle or Carbine
Caliber: 45-70 **Barrel length:** 32.5" (22" carbine) round. 1-22 twist; 3 groove rifling; all furniture blued; sling swivels; open sights; ladder style elevation rear adjustable. **Overall length:** 52" (41" carbine) **Weight:** 8.5 lbs. Walnut stock
Price: 895
Officer's Model
Caliber: 45-70. **Barrel length:** 26" round. 1-18 twist; 6 groove rifling; pewter ramrod tip and nosecap; case-hardened hammer and lock; walnut stock; checkered wrist and forearm; single set trigger; fully adjustable tang sight. **Overall length:** 45" **Weight:** 8 lbs.
Price: $995

Pennsylvania Rifle
A lightweight at just 8 pounds, this rifle has a 41 1/2" blued barrel fitted with an open buckhorn rear sight and front blade. The walnut one-piece stock is stained to contrast with the polished brass buttplate, toe plate, patch-box, sideplate, trigger guard, thimbles and nose cap. Featuring double-set triggers, the rifle can be fired by pulling only the front trigger, which has a normal pull of 4 to 5 pounds; or the rear trigger can first be pulled to set a spring-loaded mechanism that greatly reduces the amount of pull needed on the front trigger Land diameter is .450; recommended ball size is .445. **Overall length:** 51 1/2".
Prices: Percussion or Flintlock 525
Kit (Flint or Perc.) 435

Waadtlander Rifle (not shown)
This authentic re-creation of a Swiss muzzloading target rifle features a heavy octagonal barrel (31") that has 7 lands and grooves. **Caliber:** 45. Rate of twist is 1 turn in 48". Double-set triggers are multi-lever type and are easily removable for adjustment. Sights are post front and tang-mounted Swiss-type diopter rear. Walnut stock, color case hardened hardware, classic buttplate and curved trigger guard complete this reproduction. The original was made between 1839 and 1860 by Marc Bristlen, Morges, Switzerland.
Price: 1495

Dixie Rifles/Muskets

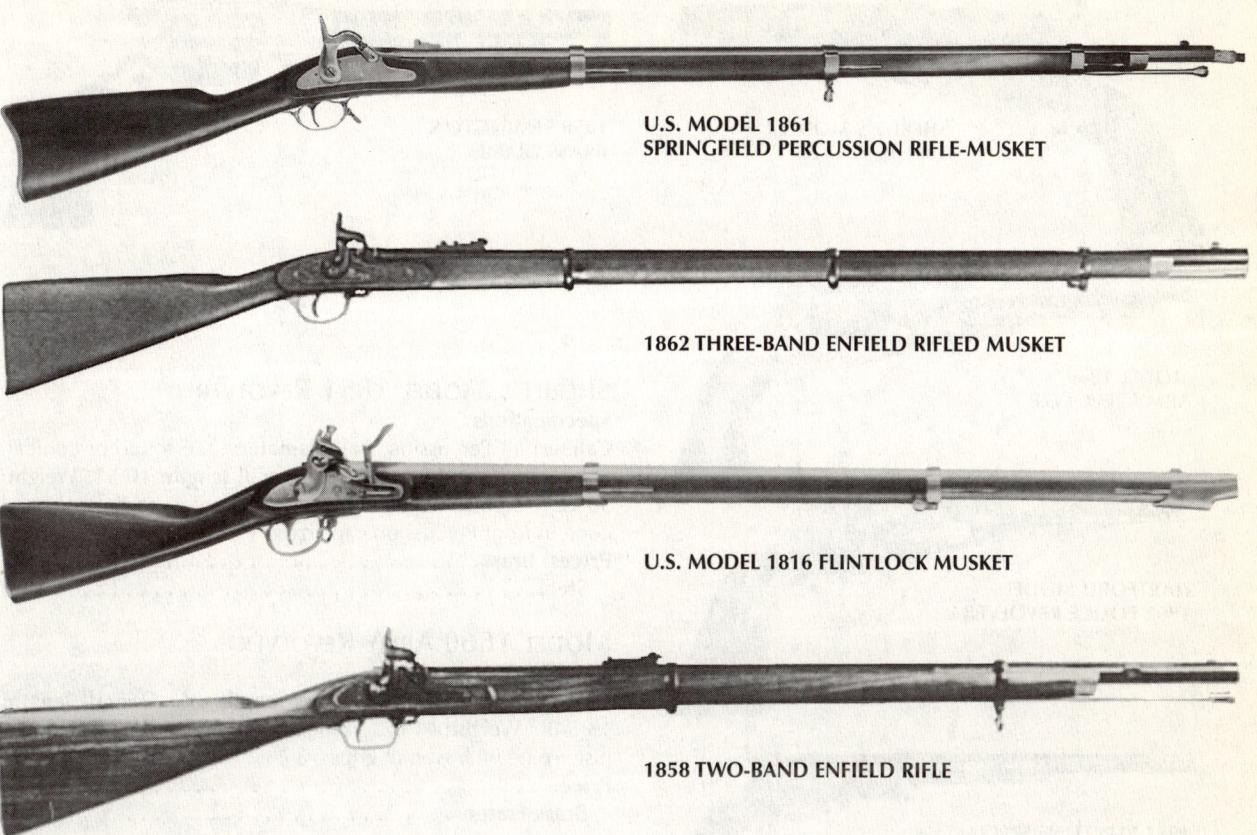

U.S. MODEL 1861 SPRINGFIELD PERCUSSION RIFLE-MUSKET

1862 THREE-BAND ENFIELD RIFLED MUSKET

U.S. MODEL 1816 FLINTLOCK MUSKET

1858 TWO-BAND ENFIELD RIFLE

U.S. MODEL 1861
SPRINGFIELD PERCUSSION RIFLE-MUSKET
An exact re-creation of an original rifle produced by Springfield National Armory, Dixie's Model 1861 Springfield 58-caliber rifle features a 40" round, tapered barrel with three barrel bands. Sling swivels are attached to the trigger guard bow and middle barrel band. The ramrod has a trumpet-shaped head with swell; sights are standard military rear and bayonet-attachment lug front. The percussion lock is marked "1861" on the rear of the lockplate with an eagle motif and "U.S. Springfield" in front of the hammer. "U.S." is stamped on top of buttplate. All furniture is "National Armory Bright." **Overall length:** 55 13/16". **Weight:** 8 lbs.
Prices: $595
  Kit 525

1862 THREE-BAND ENFIELD RIFLED MUSKET
The 1861 Enfield was widely used during the Civil War in its original version. This rifle follows the lines of the original almost exactly. The 58-caliber musket features a 39-inch barrel and walnut stock. Three steel barrel bands and the barrel itself are blued; the lockplate and hammer are case colored, and the remainder of the furniture is highly polished brass. The lock is marked, "London Armory Co."
Weight: 10.5 lbs. **Overall length:** 55".
Prices: 495
  Kit 425

U.S. MODEL 1816 FLINTLOCK MUSKET
The U.S. Model 1816 Flintlock Musket was made by Harpers Ferry and Springfield Arsenal from 1816 until 1864. More were produced than any other U.S. flintlock musket and after conversion to percussion it saw service in the Civil War. It has a 69-caliber, 42" smoothbore barrel held by three barrel bands with springs. All metal parts are finished in "National Armory Bright." The lockplate has a brass pan and is marked "Harpers Ferry" vertically behind the hammer, with an American eagle placed in front of the hammer. The bayonet lug is on top of the barrel and the steel ramrod has a button-shaped head. Sling swivels are mounted on trigger guard and middle barrel band. **Overall length:** 56.5". **Weight:** 9.75 lbs.
Price: $775

1858 TWO-BAND ENFIELD RIFLE
This 33-inch barrel version of the British Enfield is an exact copy of similar rifles used during the Civil War. The 58-caliber rifle sports a European walnut stock, deep blue-black finish on the barrel, bands, breech-plug tang and bayonet mount. The percussion lock is case hardened, and the rest of the furniture is brightly polished brass.
Price: 475

EMF Hartford Revolvers

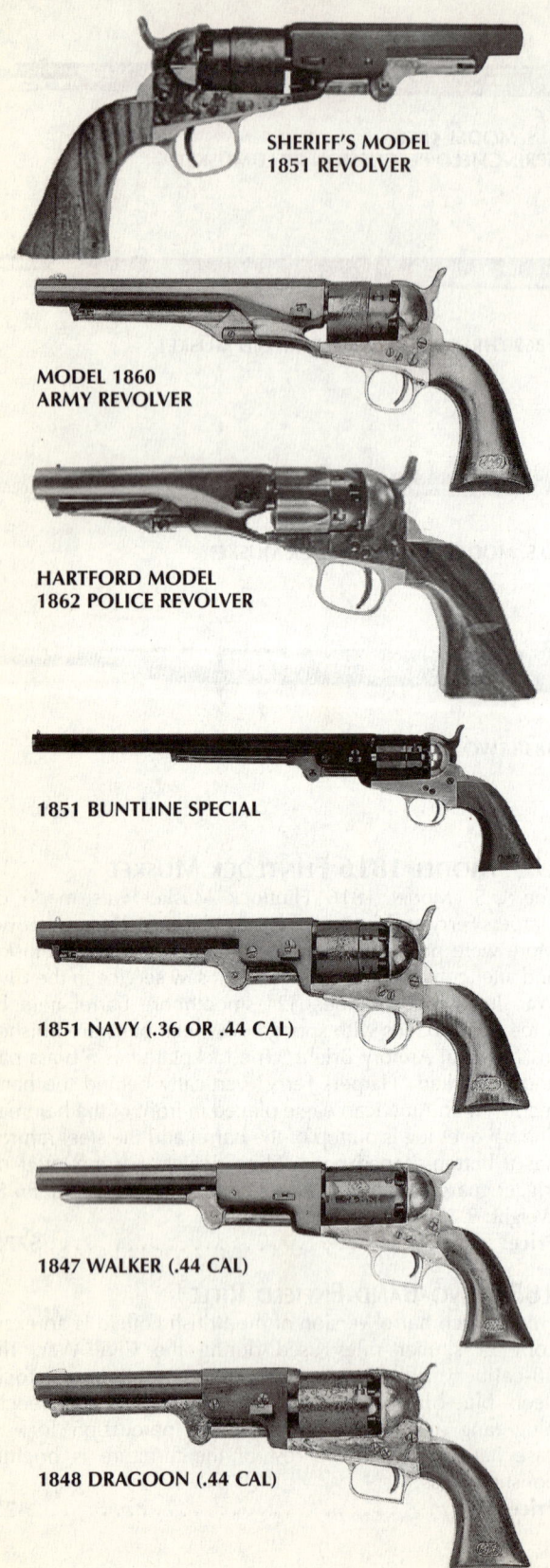

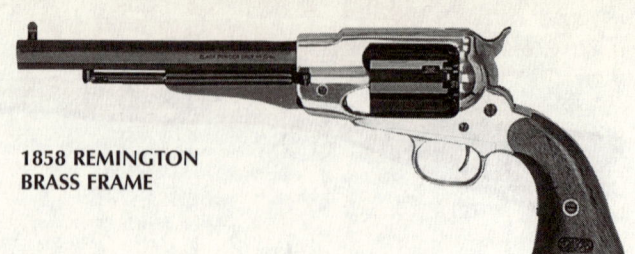

SHERIFF'S MODEL 1851 REVOLVER

1858 REMINGTON BRASS FRAME

MODEL 1860 ARMY REVOLVER

HARTFORD MODEL 1862 POLICE REVOLVER

1851 BUNTLINE SPECIAL

1851 NAVY (.36 OR .44 CAL)

1847 WALKER (.44 CAL)

1848 DRAGOON (.44 CAL)

SHERIFF'S MODEL 1851 REVOLVER
Specifications
Caliber: 44 Percussion **Ball diameter:** .376 round or conical, pure lead **Barrel length:** 5" **Overall length:** 10.5" **Weight:** 39 oz. **Sights:** V-notch groove in hammer (rear); truncated cone in front Percussion cap size: #11
Prices: Brass $115
    Steel 150

MODEL 1860 ARMY REVOLVER
Specifications
Caliber: 44 Percussion **Barrel length:** 8" **Overall length:** 13 5/8" **Weight:** 41 oz. **Frame:** Case hardened **Finish:** High-luster blue with walnut grips
Price: 170
    Brass Frame 125

HARTFORD MODEL 1862 POLICE REVOLVER
Specifications
Caliber: 36 Percussion **Capacity:** 5-shot **Barrel length:** 5.5"
Prices: Steel 200

1851 BUNTLINE SPECIAL
Specifications
Caliber: 44 **Barrel length:** 12" (blued) **Finish:** brass frame
Price: 150

1858 REMINGTON BRASS FRAME
Specifications
Caliber: 44 **Barrel length:** 8" (blued) brass frame
Price: Brass frame 140
    Case-hardened steel frame 170

1851 NAVY (.36 OR .44 CAL)
Price: 150
    Brass frame .44 115

1847 WALKER (.44 CAL)
Price: 250

1848 DRAGOON
Specifications
Caliber: 44 **Barrel length:** 7.5" (blued) **Finish:** case-hardened frame
Price: 240

Euroarms of America

BLACK POWDER

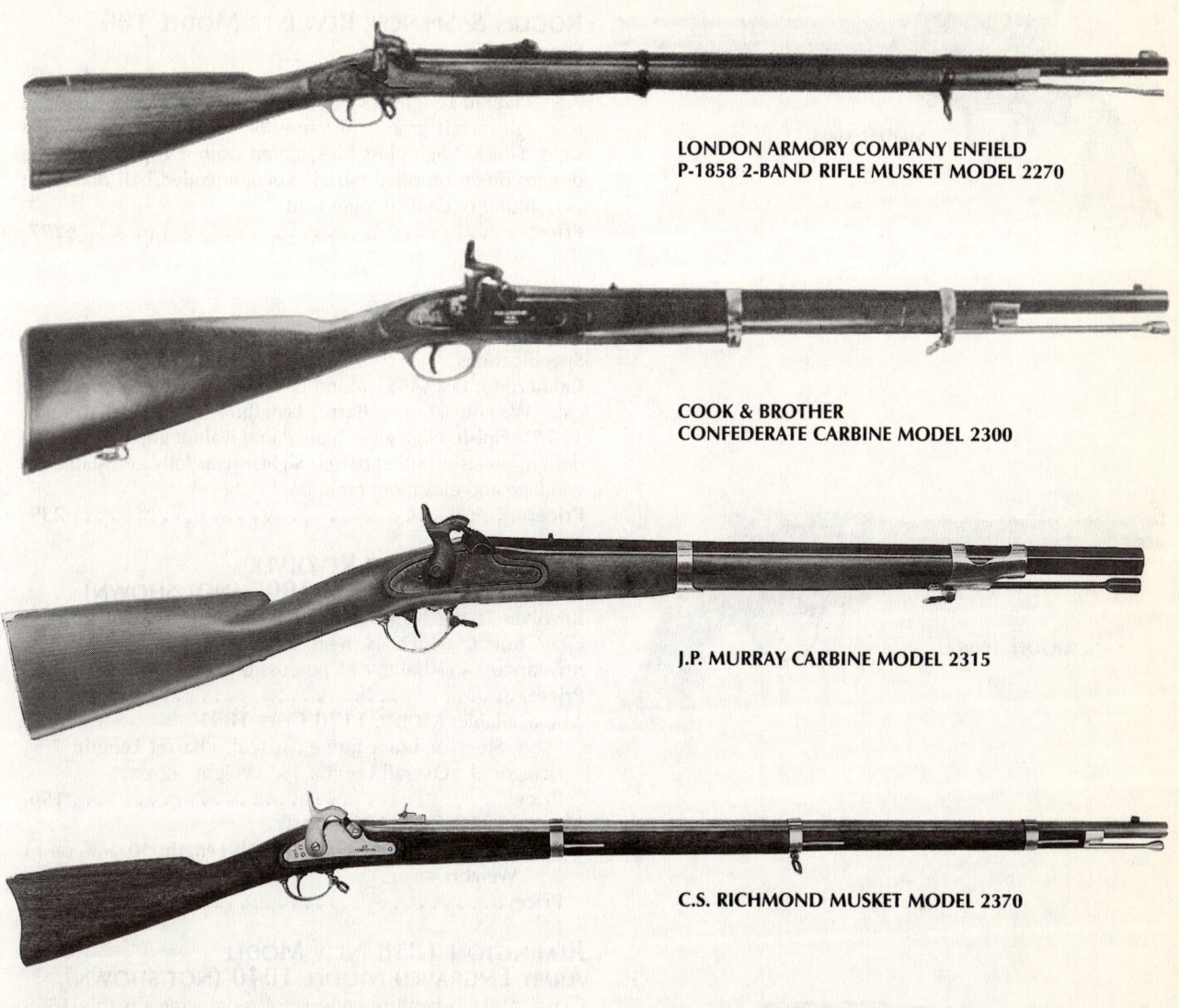

LONDON ARMORY COMPANY ENFIELD
P-1858 2-BAND RIFLE MUSKET MODEL 2270

COOK & BROTHER
CONFEDERATE CARBINE MODEL 2300

J.P. MURRAY CARBINE MODEL 2315

C.S. RICHMOND MUSKET MODEL 2370

LONDON ARMORY COMPANY ENFIELD P-1858 2-BAND RIFLE MUSKET MODEL 2270
Specifications
Caliber: 58 percussion **Barrel Length:** 33" **Weight:** 8.5 to 8.75 lbs., depending on wood density **Stock:** One-piece walnut; polished "bright" brass buttplate, trigger guard and nose cap; blued barrel and bands **Sights:** Inverted 'V' front sight; Enfield folding ladder rear **Ramrod:** Steel
Price: $470

COOK & BROTHER CONFEDERATE CARBINE MODEL 2300
Classic re-creation of the rare 1861, New Orleans-made Artillery Carbine.
Specifications
Caliber: 58 percussion **Barrel Length:** 24" **Sights:** Fixed blade front and adjustable dovetailed rear **Ramrod:** Steel **Finish:** Barrel is antique brown; buttplate, trigger guard, barrel bands, sling swivels and nose cap are polished brass; stock is walnut **Recommended ball sizes:** .575 r.b., .577 Minie and .580 maxi; uses musket caps
Price: $447
Also available: MODEL 2301 COOK & BROTHER FIELD with 33" barrel 480

J.P. MURRAY CARBINE MODEL 2315
Replica of an extremely rare CSA Cavalry Carbine based on an 1841 design of parts and lock.
Specifications
Caliber: 58 percussion **Barrel Length:** 23" **Features:** Brass barrel bands and buttplate; oversized trigger guard; sling swivels
Price: 453

C.S. RICHMOND MUSKET MODEL 2370
Specifications
Caliber: 58 percussion **Barrel Length:** 40"
Price: 530

Euroarms of America

MODEL 1005

ROGERS & SPENCER REVOLVER MODEL 1005
Specifications
Caliber: 44 Percussion; #11 percussion cap **Barrel Length:** 7.5" **Overall Length:** 13.75" **Weight:** 47 oz. **Sights:** Integral rear sight notch groove in frame; brass truncated cone front sight **Finish:** High gloss blue; flared walnut grip; solid frame design; precision-rifled barrel **Recommended ball diameter:** .451 round or conical, pure lead
Price: $227

ROGERS & SPENCER ARMY REVOLVER MODEL 1006 (TARGET)
Specifications
Caliber: 44; takes .451 round or conical balls; #11 percussion cap **Weight:** 47 oz. **Barrel Length:** 7.5" **Overall Length:** 13.75" **Finish:** High gloss blue; flared walnut grip; solid frame design; precision-rifled barrel **Sights:** Rear fully adjustable for windage and elevation; ramp front sight
Price: 239

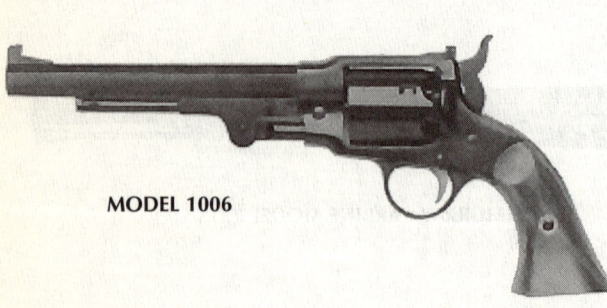

MODEL 1006

ROGERS & SPENCER REVOLVER LONDON GRAY MODEL 1007 (NOT SHOWN)
Revolver is the same as Model 1005, except for London Gray finish, which is heat treated and buffed for rust resistance; .451 balls, #11 percussion caps
Price: 245

Also available: MODEL 1120 COLT 1851
Navy Steel or brass frame. 36 cal. **Barrel Length:** 7.5" octagonal. **Overall Length:** 13" **Weight:** 42 oz.
Price: 156

MODEL 1210 COLT 1860 ARMY
Steel frame. 44 percussion **Overall Length:** 10 5/8" or 13 5/8" **Weight:** 41 oz.
Price: 177

REMINGTON 1858 NEW MODEL ARMY ENGRAVED MODEL 1040 (NOT SHOWN)
Classical 19th-century style scroll engraving on this 1858 Remington New Model revolver.
Specifications
Caliber: 44 Percussion; #11 cap **Barrel Length:** 8" **Overall Length:** 14.75" **Weight:** 41 oz. **Sights:** Integral rear sight notch groove in frame; blade front sight **Recommended ball diameter:** .451 round or conical, pure lead
Price: 275

MODEL 1010 (36 CAL. W/6.5" BARREL)

REMINGTON 1858 NEW MODEL ARMY REVOLVER MODEL 1020
This model features blued steel frame, brass trigger guard and 8" 44-caliber barrel
Specifications
Weight: 40 oz. **Overall Length:** 14.75" **Finish:** Deep luster blue rifled barrel; polished walnut stock; brass trigger guard.
Price: 200
Also available: MODEL 1010 Same as Model 1020, except w/6.5" barrel and in 36 caliber: 200

Euroarms of America

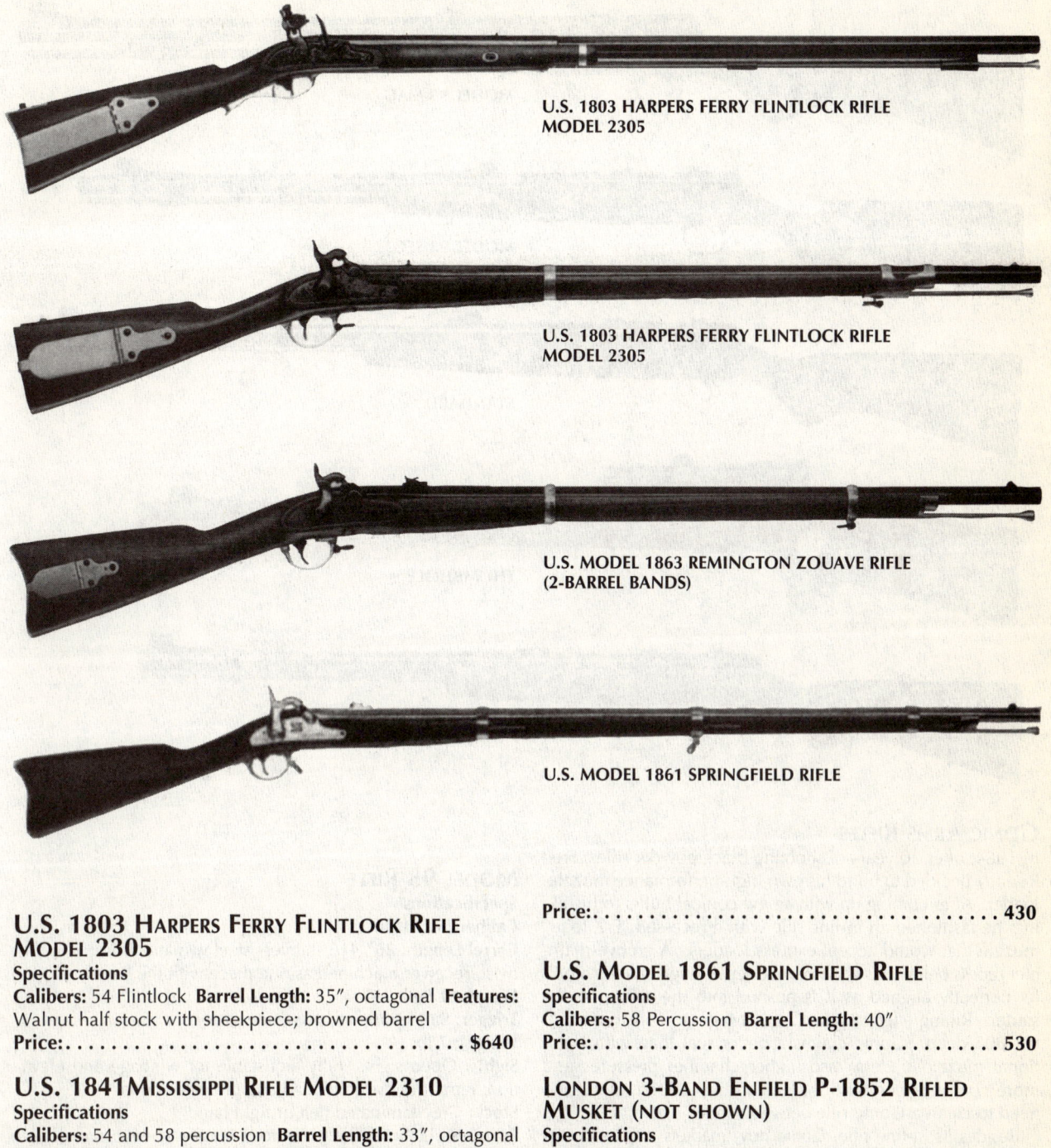

U.S. 1803 HARPERS FERRY FLINTLOCK RIFLE MODEL 2305

U.S. 1803 HARPERS FERRY FLINTLOCK RIFLE MODEL 2305

U.S. MODEL 1863 REMINGTON ZOUAVE RIFLE (2-BARREL BANDS)

U.S. MODEL 1861 SPRINGFIELD RIFLE

U.S. 1803 HARPERS FERRY FLINTLOCK RIFLE MODEL 2305
Specifications
Calibers: 54 Flintlock **Barrel Length:** 35", octagonal **Features:** Walnut half stock with sheekpiece; browned barrel
Price:..$640

U.S. 1841 MISSISSIPPI RIFLE MODEL 2310
Specifications
Calibers: 54 and 58 percussion **Barrel Length:** 33", octagonal **Features:** Walnut stock; brass barrel bands and buttplate; swing swivels
Price:..500

U.S. MODEL 1863 REMINGTON ZOUAVE RIFLE (2-BARREL BANDS)
Specifications
Calibers: 58 percussion **Barrel Length:** 33", octagonal **Weight:** 9.5 **Sights:** U.S. Millitary 3-leaf rear; blade front
Price:..430

U.S. MODEL 1861 SPRINGFIELD RIFLE
Specifications
Calibers: 58 Percussion **Barrel Length:** 40"
Price:..530

LONDON 3-BAND ENFIELD P-1852 RIFLED MUSKET (NOT SHOWN)
Specifications
Calibers: 58 percussion **Barrel Length:** 54" **Weight:** 9.5 pounds **Sights:** ladder rear, blade front
Price:..480

LONDON ENFIELD P-1861 (NOT SHOWN)
Specifications
Calibers: 58 percussion **Weight:** 7.5 pounds **Sights:** millitary leaf rear, blade front
Price:..415

Gonic Arms
Model 93 Rifle Series

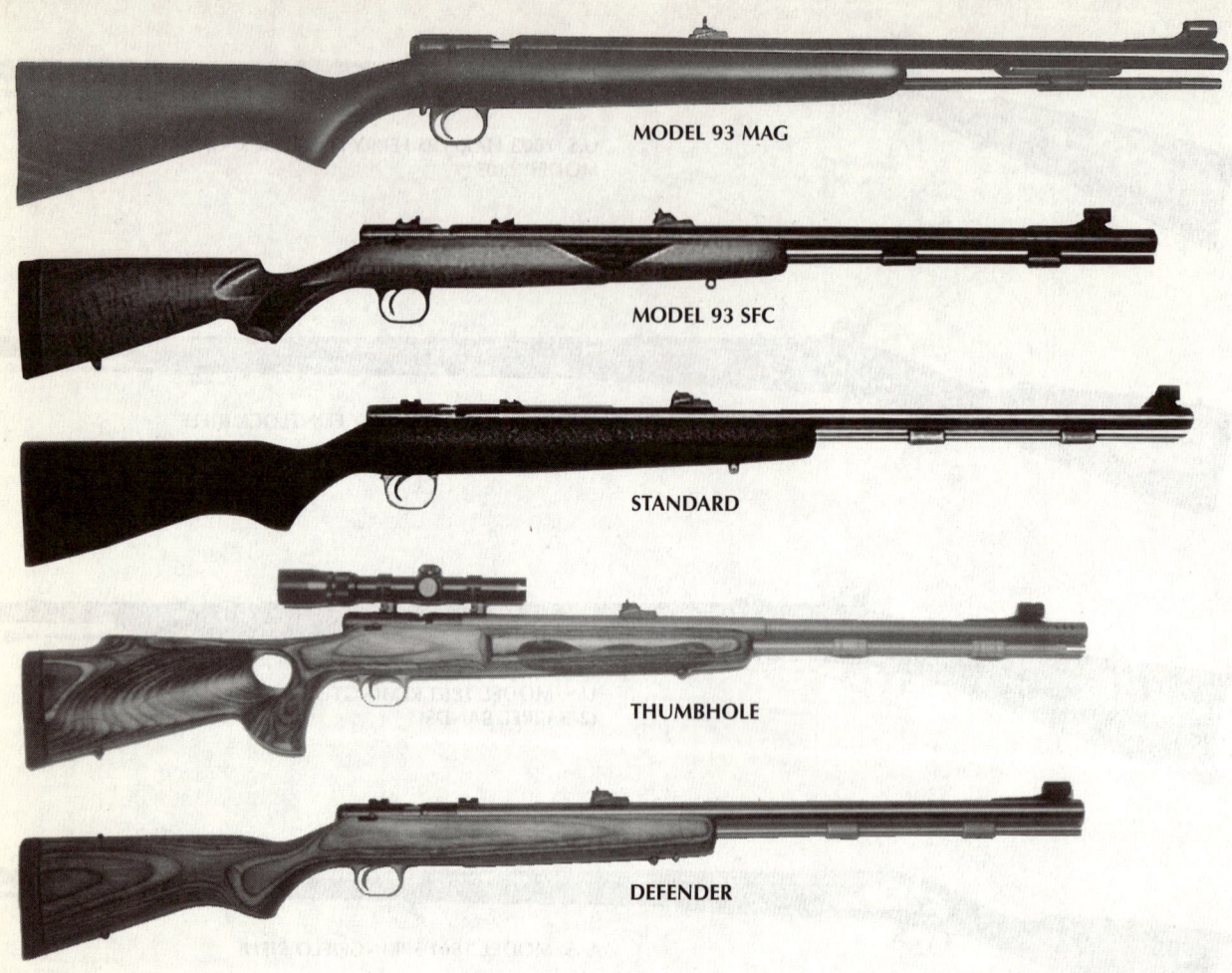

MODEL 93 MAG
MODEL 93 SFC
STANDARD
THUMBHOLE
DEFENDER

Gonic Arms Rifles

In 1984, after 20 years of shooting black powder rifles, Fred Rodney decided to build his own high-performance muzzleloader. After coming up with a new conical bullet to his liking, he fashioned an in-line rifle with a recessed "E-Z load" muzzle that would accept express loaders. A groove-diameter recess below this chamber is deep enough to keep a bullet perfectly aligned as it is pushed into the rifling by the starter. Rifling engraves the Gonic Magnum Penetrator bullet .005 deep. Gonic claims a better seal than with traditional muzzle-loaders, also higher chamber pressures and more complete combustion. According to Fred, there's no need to clean a Gonic rifle between shots.

Besides its in-line rifle, Gonic now markets a "Model 90" muzzleloading barrel that can be fitted to Thompson/Center Contender frames. There's also a custom Contender with a free-floating barrel lug that keeps forend pressure uniform and concentric. Gonic offers centerfire and rimfire as well as muzzleloading Model 90 guns with 16-inch barrels for $602. A stainless 50-caliber muzzleloading M90 costs $628. Carbine versions, with walnut and laminated thumbhole stocks and 18- or 24-inch barrels, list for $935 to $1,000, depending on model. They're available in chrome moly or stainless steel.

Model 93 Rifle
Specifications
Caliber: 50 Magnum
Barrel Length: 26" 416 stainless steel w/matte finish; 1-in-24" twist, receiver machined as one piece with the barrel.
Length of Pull: 14"
Trigger: Single, adjustable w/side safety
Weight: 7 lbs.
Sights: Open sights, fully adjustable for windage and elevation; ramp front w/gold bead and protector hood.
Stock: Grey laminated (left or right hand)
Features: Unbreakable ram rod; classic cheekpiece; three-point pillar bedding system; 1" decelerator recoil pad; sling swivel studs; E-Z-Load Muzzle System w/muzzle brake aluminum ram rod.
Price:. $999
Also Available:
Model 93 Thumhole Rifle w/same specification and features as above, but w/thumbhole Monte Carlo rollover cheekpeice, beavertail forend and palm swell grip
Price: Stainless (50 mag. only) 2700

Knight Muzzleloaders

TK2000 MUZZLELOADING SHOTGUN, NOW AVAILABLE IN ADVANTAGE TIMBER HD

THE WOLVERINE 209

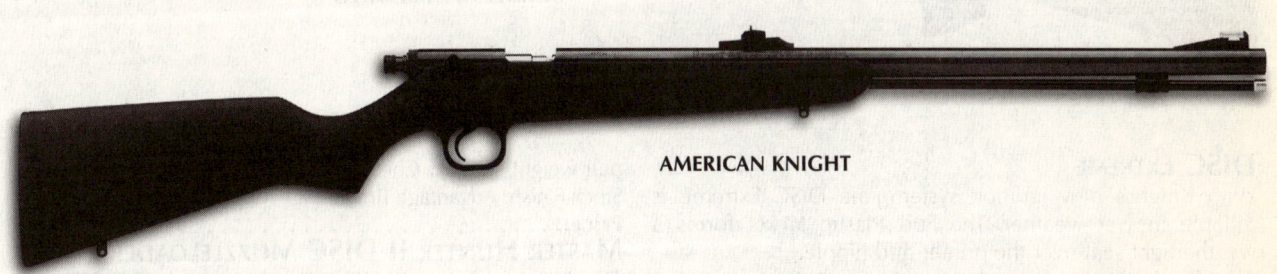

AMERICAN KNIGHT

Knight TK2000 Shotgun
The Knight TK2000 has large shotgun primer for sure-fire results; screw-in choke tubes add versatility
Specifications
Gauge: 12 **Barrel:** 26", blued, Advantage Timber HD, **Overall length:** 45" **Weight:** 7 lbs., 9 oz. **Sight:** Fully adjustable metallic Tru-Glo Fiber Optics **Trigger:** Adjustable (Creep and pull weight) **Stock:** Recoil pad, sling swivel studs **Stock Finish:** Black, Advantage Timber HD **Choke:** Screw-in tubes, xfull, MOD, MC
Prices: Blue/Black Composite $350
  Camo Stock/Barrel 400

The Wolverine 209
The Wolverine 209 uses Knight's new Full Plastic Jacket ignition system, making it reliable even in wet or cold weather.

Specifications
Caliber: 50 **Barrel:** 22", blued or stainless with 1:28" twist **Sights:** Metallic Tru-Glo fiber optic sights **Weight:** 7 lbs. **Stock:** Checkered composite recoil pad, sling swivel studs; available in black composite, black thumbhole, Mossy Oak Break-up or Advantage Timber camo
Price: $336

American Knight
Specifications
Caliber: .50 **Barrel Finish:** Blued **Barrel Length:** 22", 1:28" twist **Overall Length:** 41" **Weight:** 6 lbs., 3 oz. **Sight:** Fully adjustable Fiber-Lite rear, fiber optic front bead **Trigger:** Non-adjustable **Stock:** Full dimension hollow composite stock black with sling studs (14" length of pull)
Price: Blued only 200

Knight Muzzleloaders

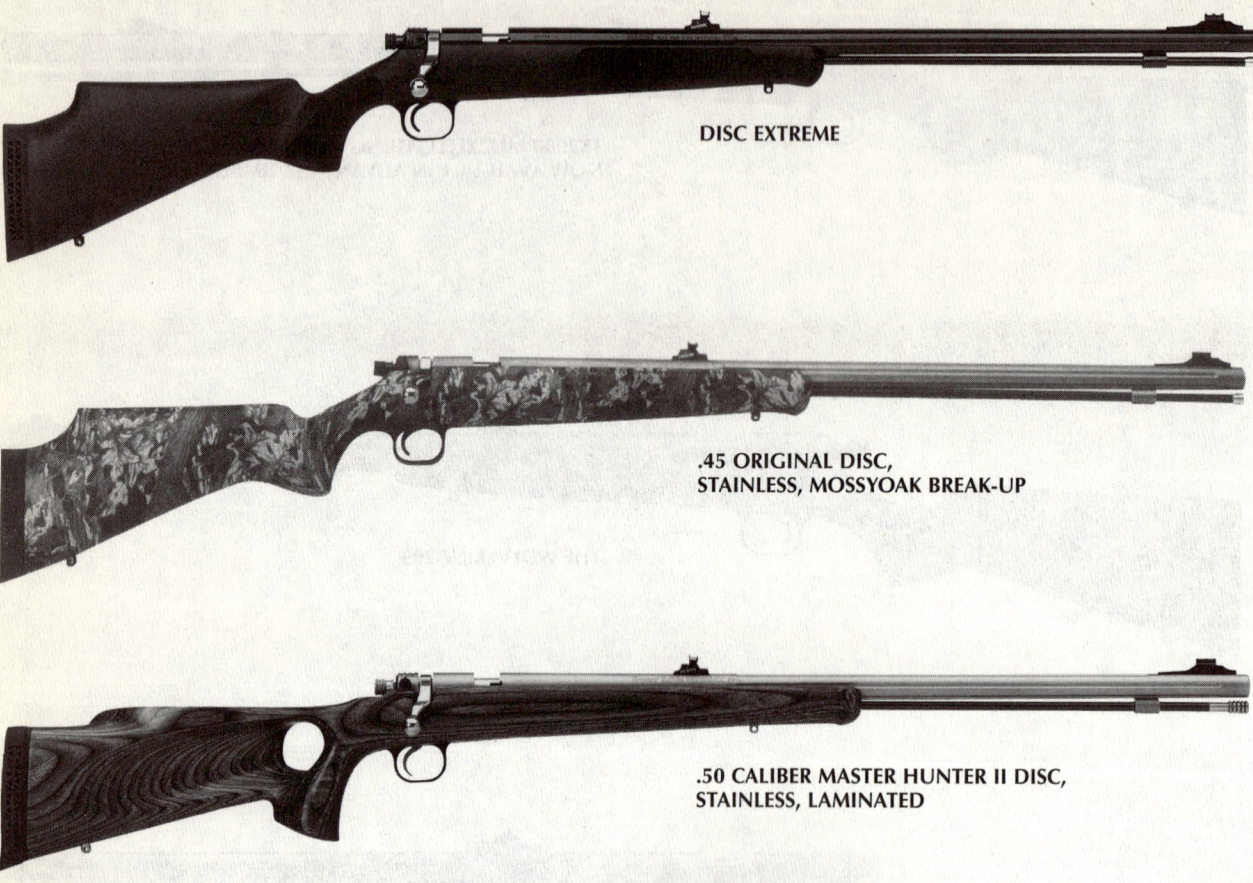

DISC EXTREME

.45 ORIGINAL DISC, STAINLESS, MOSSYOAK BREAK-UP

.50 CALIBER MASTER HUNTER II DISC, STAINLESS, LAMINATED

DISC Extreme
With Knight's new ignition system, the DISC Extreme is reliable in wet weather. The Full Plastic Jacket forms a weathertight seal over the primer and nipple.
Specifications
Caliber: 45 and 50 **Barrel:** 26" blued or stainless barrel with 1:28" twist **Weight:** 7 lbs., 5 oz. **Stocks:** Walnut or black composite thumbhole **Sights:** Fully adjustable metallic Tru-Glo fiber optic sights
Price: $550

Knight Original DISC
The .45 caliber Original DISC is Knight's latest in-line muzzleloader. It features a precisely-rifled Green Mountain Barrel air-gauged to exact tolerances with a 1:20" twist. The Knight .45 Original DISC outperforms other muzzleloaders as it: 1. Launches bullets up to 2,600 feet per second. 2. Connects at 100 yards with a whopping 1,353 foot pounds of energy. 3. At 200 yards, the bullet drops only 7.29 inches! As on all Knight Rifles, the .45 Original DISC includes a patented double-safety system.
Specifications
Caliber: .45 or .50 **Barrel Finish:** Blued or stainless **Barrel Length:** 24" or 26" **Weight:** 8 lbs., 3 oz. **Sight:** Fully adjustable metallic Tru-Glo Fiber Optics **Trigger:** Adjustable (Creep and pull weight) **Stock:** Checkered, recoil pad, sling swivel studs; Stock Finish: Advantage Timber HD, Mossy Oak break-up, black
Price: 550

Master Hunter II DISC Muzzleloader
The Master Hunter II DISC Green Mountain 26" barrel, features a fluted stainless air-gauged to exact tolerances with a 1:28" twist (1:30 twist in .45 caliber) providing the optimum projectile spin for highest accuracy. Two stocks are included with this premium model. A laminated stock with a comfortable thumbhole grip is complemented by a second stock made from a black, solid composite in the same thumbhole grip design.
Specifications
Caliber: .45 or .50 **Barrel Finish:** Fluted stainless **Barrel Length:** 26" **Overall Length:** 45" **Weight:** 7 lbs., 7 oz. **Sight:** Fully adjustable metallic Tru-Glo Fiber Optics **Trigger:** Adjustable for creep and letoff **Stock Finish:** Laminated thumbhole w/recoil pad, sling swivel studs (14.5" length of pull); black composite shipped with rifle
Price: $1100
Also Available: Knight .50 DISC
  Price: Blue/Black composite 460
  Blue/camo 510
  Stainless/Black composite 530
  Stainless/camo 580

Lenartz Muzzleloading

MODEL RDI-50 SHOWN WITH OPTIONAL SCOPE

LYMAN TRADE RIFLE

DEERSTALKER RIFLE

RDI-50
The Rdi-50 is a new 50-caliber muzzleloader by Lenartz Muzzleloading Inc. The Rdi-50 features a Radial Drop Ignition System (Rdi), which allows the shooter to drop a 209 shot shell primer into the Rdi Nipple cradle, close the cover and shoot. To remove the 209 shot shell primers, open the Rdi cover and the primer drops into your hand. Uses a 209 Shot Shell Primer and 3-50 grain Pyrodex Pellets with Black Beauty Sabots and a 300 gr. jacketed bullet at over 1900 ft/sec.
Specifications
Manufacturer: Lenartz Muzzleloading Inc., 8001 Whitneyville Rd, Alto, MI 49302 **Mechanism type:** Inline Muzzleloader using 209 Shot Shell Primers **Caliber:** .50 **Stock:** Walnut (with or without Comb.) **Barrel:** 26.5 inches with a 1-turn-in-28 inch rifling. **Trigger:** Adjustable made by Bold. **Sights:** Williams gun sights, with receiver drilled and tapped for scope mounts. **LMI Conversion Kit:** converts to primitive ignition and #11 Percussion Cap.
Price on request

Lyman Trade Rifle
The Lyman Trade Rifle features a 28-inch octagonal barrel, rifled 1 turn in 48 inches, designed to fire both patched round balls and popular conical bullets. Polished brass furniture with blued finish on steel parts; walnut stock; hook breech; single spring-loaded trigger; coil-spring percussion lock; fixed steel sights; adjustable rear sight for elevation also included. Steel barrel rib and ramrod ferrule.
Caliber: 50 and 54 percussion and flint. **Overall Length:** 45"
Price: Percussion **$315**
   Flintlock 340

Deerstalker Stainless
Lyman's Deerstalker rifle incorporates • high comb for quick sighting • nonglare hardware • 24" octagonal barrel • case hardened sideplate • Q.D. sling swivels • Lyman sight package (37MA beaded front, fully adjustable fold-down 16A rear) • walnut stock with black recoil pad• single trigger. Left-hand models available (same price). **Calibers:** 50 and 54, flintlock or percussion. **Weight:** 7.5 lbs.
Price: Percussion **$305**
   Left-Hand 330
   Flintlock 350
   Left Hand 360
Deerstalker Stainless. Features all stainless steel parts, plus walnut stock, recoil pad, Delrin ramrod, Lyman front and rear hunting sights.
Price: 395

Lyman Muzzleloaders
Custom Hunting

BLACK POWDER

GREAT PLAINS RIFLE

GREAT PLAINS HUNTER

THE PLAINS PISTOL

THE GREAT PLAINS RIFLE
The Great Plains Rifle has a 32-inch deep-grooved barrel and 1 in 66" twist to shoot patched round balls; blued steel furniture, including the thick steel wedge plates and toe plate; correct lock and hammer styling with coil spring dependability; a walnut stock w/o patchbox. A Hawken-style trigger guard protects double-set triggers. Steel front sight complements an authentic buckhorn adjustable rear sight. Fixed primitive rear sight also included.
Calibers: 50 and 54.
Price: Percussion **$470**
   Kit 360
   Flintlock. 495
   Kit 385
   Left-Hand Model Percussion 475
   Left-Hand Model Flintlock. 500
Also available: GREAT PLAINS HUNTER.
   Same features as standard rifle, but with 1 in 32" twist and shallow rifling groove for shooting modern sabots and black powder hunting bullets.
Price: Percussion **$455**
   Flintlock. 450

THE PLAINS PISTOL
Lyman Plains Pistol recreates the trapper's pistol of the mid-1800's while incorporating the best of modern steels and technology.
  The stained walnut stock complements blackened iron furniture, polished brass trigger guard and ramrod tips. The hooked patent breech takes down quickly and easily for cleaning. Just like the originals, the thimble is recessed into the rib and a detachable belt hook provides an alternative to a holster. A spring-loaded trigger and fast 1 in 30" twist make it accurate. **Caliber:** 50, 54
Price:. 245
   Kit 190

Markesbery Muzzle Loaders

BLACK BEAR

BROWN BEAR

GRIZZLY BEAR

MARKESBERY'S BLACK BEAR, GRIZZLY BEAR AND BROWN BEAR RIFLES

Markesbery's Black Bear, Grizzly Bear and Brown Bear rifles are made of eight cast, polished molded parts, coupled with an all-cast receiver and trigger guard. Pillow mount system with interchangeable barrels in 36, 45, .50 and 54 calibers. All rifles are constructed with Markesbery's **Magnum Hammer In-Line Ignition System**, the 400 SRP (small rifle primer) system, or optional No. 11 cap and nipple. This system, along with a 1-26" twist button precision 24" rifle barrel, is available in either 4140 or stainless steel models. All models have a double safety system with half cock and cross bolt hammer safeties. Marble adjustable sights with double adjustment features, hammer thumb rest and rubber recoil pad are standard.

The Black Bear features a two-piece, handcrafted hardwood walnut, black laminate and green laminate pistol grip stock. **Weight:** 6.5 lbs. **Overall Length:** 38.5". The Brown and Grizzly Bear models offer custom-checkered Monte Carlo (Grizzly Bear two-piece or Brown Bear one-piece) thumbhole stocks. **Overall Length:** 38.5" **Weight:** 6.5 lbs. (Brown Bear is 6.75 lbs.). Both models are available in black composite, crotch walnut, Mossy Oak Break-up, XTRA-Grey and Real Tree Advantage camo stock patterns. **Metal finishes:** blued, matte and stainless steel. All models have a solid aluminum ram rod with brass jag and bullet starter.

Price: BLACK BEAR (two-piece pistol grip stock)
(depending on stock) $537-574
BROWN BEAR
Features one-piece, Monte Carlo thumbhole stock
Price: (depending on stock) 659-703
Also available: POLAR BEAR SERIES
w/one-piece Monte Carlo pistol grip stock.
Price: (depending on stock) 539-574
GRIZZLY BEAR
Features twp-piece, Monte Carlo thumbhole stock
Price: (depending on stock) 643-640

Markesbery Muzzle Loaders

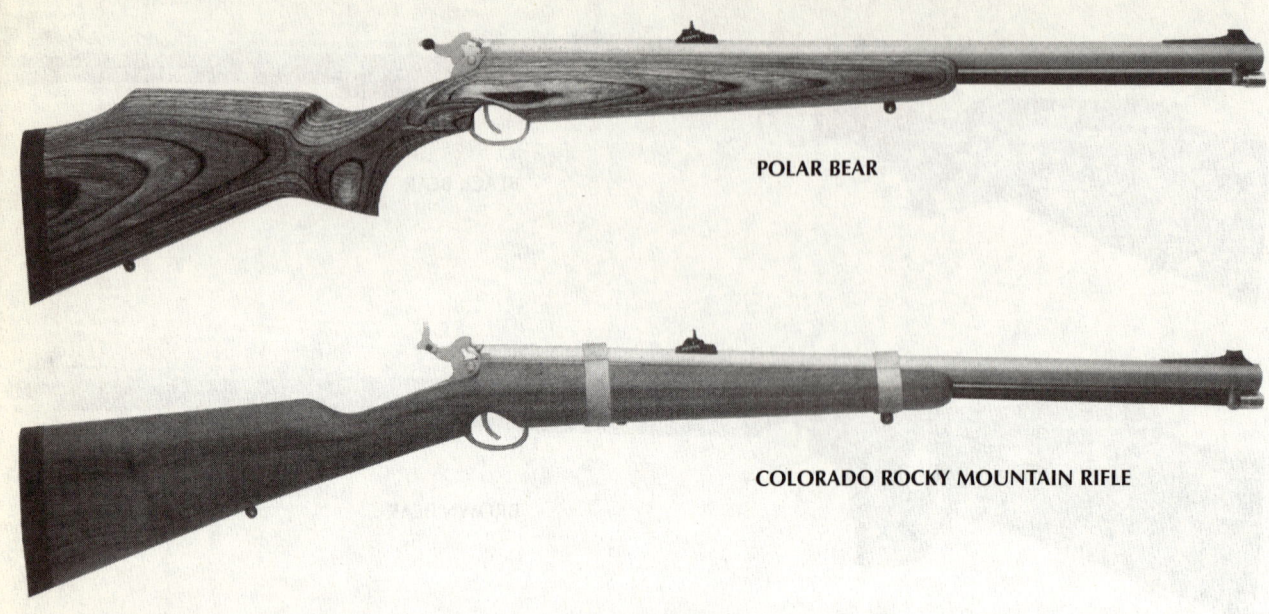

POLAR BEAR

COLORADO ROCKY MOUNTAIN RIFLE

KM Polar Bear™ Rifle Series
The Polar Bear has Markesbery's standard features, plus a one-piece pistol-grip stock of solid hardwood or laminated wood construction in black or green.

KM Polar Bear™ Rifle Series
(One piece Monte Carlo pistol grip stock)

Model	Barrel Length	Twist	Caliber	Suggested Retail
KMPB-B-Walnut Finish	24"	1-26"	36, 45, 50, 54	$540
KMPB-B-Black	24"	1-26"	36, 45, 50, 54	537
KMPB-B-Black Laminate	24"	1-26"	36, 45, 50, 54	542
KMPB-B-Green Laminate	24"	1-26"	36, 45, 50, 54	542
KMPB-B-Camo	24"	1-26"	36, 45, 50, 54	561
KMPB-SS-Walnut	24"	1-26"	36, 45, 50, 54	557
KMPB-SS-Black	24"	1-26"	36, 45, 50, 54	557
KMPB-SS-Black Laminate	24"	1-26"	36, 45, 50, 54	571
KMPB-SS-Green Laminate	24"	1-26"	36, 45, 50, 54	571
KMPB-SS-Camo	24"	1-26"	36, 45, 50, 54	574

KM Colorado Rocky Mountain™ Rifle Series
(One piece straight grip stock)

Model	Barrel Length	Twist	Caliber	Suggested Retail
KM-CRM-B-Walnut Finish	24"	1-26"	36, 45, 50, 54	$546
KM-CRM-B-Black Laminate	24"	1-26"	36, 45, 50, 54	549
KM-CRM-B-Green Laminate	24"	1-26"	36, 45, 50, 54	549
KM-CRM-SS-Walnut Finish	24"	1-26"	36, 45, 50, 54	564
KM-CRM-SS-Black Laminate	24"	1-26"	36, 45, 50, 54	567
KM-CRM-SS-Green Laminate	24"	1-26"	36, 45, 50, 54	567

KM Colorado Rocky Mountain™ Rifle
This traditional-style muzzleloader features a walnut stock with barrel bands and straight grip. The pronounced hammer spur is reminiscent of the style used by frontiersmen in the 1800s. A No. 11 cap mechanism comes standard, but the company's Magnum Ignition System can be installed.

Navy Arms Revolvers

Colt 1847 Walker
The 1847 Walker replica comes in 44 caliber with a 9-inch barrel. **Weight:** 4 lbs. 8 oz. **Features include:** rolled cylinder scene blued and case hardened finish and brass guard. Proof tested.
Price:. $295

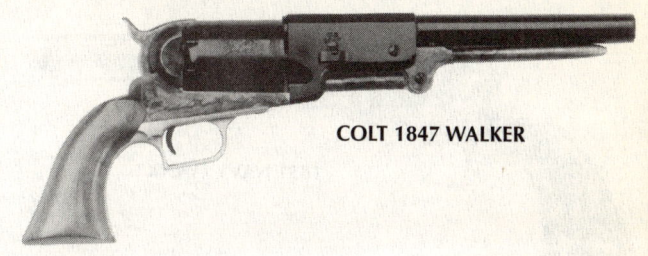
COLT 1847 WALKER

Le Mat Revolvers
Once the official sidearm of many Confederate cavalry officers, this 9-shot 44-caliber revolver with central single-shot barrel of 65 caliber gave the cavalryman great firepower.
Barrel Length: 7 5/8"
Overall Length: 14"
Weight: 3 lbs. 7 oz.
Price:
  Cavalry Model 665
  Navy Model 665
  Army Model 665
  LeMat Holster. 46

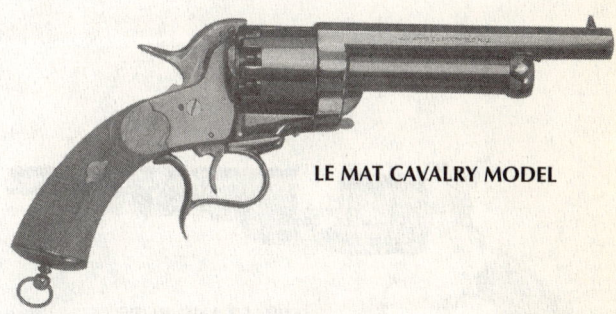
LE MAT CAVALRY MODEL

LE MAT NAVY MODEL

1862 New Model Police
This is the last gun manufactured by the Colt plant in the percussion era. It encompassed all the modifications of each gun, starting from the early Paterson, to the 1861 Navy. It was favored by the New York Police Dept. for many years. Fluted-cylinder, 36 caliber, 5 shot. This replica features brass trigger guard and backstrap. Case hardened frame, loading lever and hammer.
Barrel Length: 5.5"
Price:. 315

1862 NEW MODEL POLICE

Rogers & Spencer Revolver
This revolver features a 6-shot cylinder, octagonal barrel, hinged-type loading lever assembly, two-piece walnut grips, blued finish and case hardened hammer and lever.
Caliber: 44
Barrel Length: 7.5"
Overall Length: 13.75"
Weight: 3 lbs.
Price:. 260

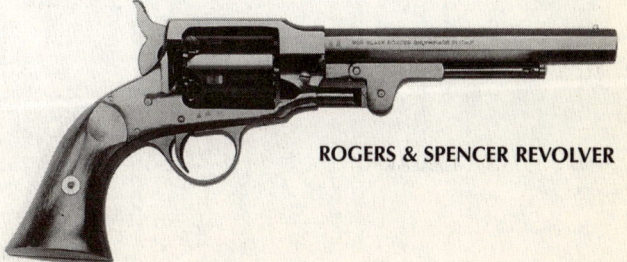
ROGERS & SPENCER REVOLVER

Black Powder • 375

Navy Arms Revolvers
Custom Hunting

1851 NAVY "YANK"

1851 Navy "Yank"
A favorite of "Wild Bill" Hickok, the 1851 Navy was originally manufactured by Colt from 1850 through 1876. This model was the most popular of the Union revolvers, mostly because it was lighter and easier to handle than the Dragoon.
Barrel Length: 7.5"
Overall Length: 14"
Weight: 2 lbs., 12 oz.
Rec. Ball Diam.: .375 R.B. (.451 in 44 cal)
Calibers: 36 and 44
Capacity: 6 shot
Features: Steel frame, octagonal barrel, cylinder roll-engraved with naval battle scene; backstrap and trigger guard are polished brass.
Price: 1851 Navy "Yank" $165
   Optional Shoulder Stock 115

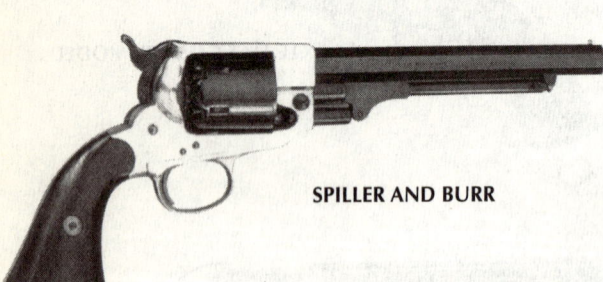

SPILLER AND BURR

Spiller And Burr
To ensure production, the Confederate government purchased the company that made this important Civil War revolver. This faithful replica has highly polished brass frame, blued cylinder and octagonal barrel. 36 caliber.
Price: 155

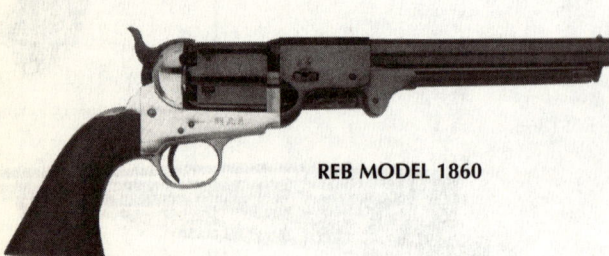

REB MODEL 1860

REB Model 1860
A modern replica of the confederate Griswold & Gunnison percussion Army revolver. Rendered with a polished brass frame and a rifled steel barrel finished in a high-luster blue with genuine walnut grips. All Army Model 60s are completely proof-tested by the Italian government to the most exacting standards.
Calibers: 36 and 44.
Barrel Length: 7.25"
Overall Length: 13"
Weight: 2 lbs. 10 oz.-11 oz.
Features: Brass frame, backstrap and trigger guard, round barrel.
Price: 120

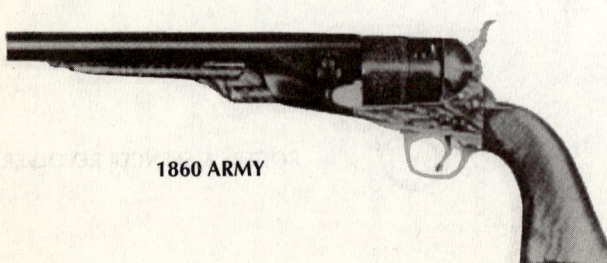

1860 ARMY

1860 Army
The 1860 Army satisfied the Union Army's need for a more powerful .44-caliber revolver. The cylinder on this replica is roll engraved with a polished brass trigger guard and steel strap cut for shoulder stock. The frame, loading level and hammer are finished in high-luster color case hardening. Walnut grips.
Weight: 2 lbs. 9 oz.
Barrel Length: 8"
Overall Length: 13 5/8"
Caliber: 44.
Finish: Brass trigger guard, steel backstrap, round barrel, creeping lever, rebated cylinder, engraved Navy scene.
Price: 185
   Optional Shoulder Stock 125

Navy Arms Handguns

1805 HARPERS FERRY FLINTLOCK PISTOL
Of all the early American martial pistols, Harpers Ferry is one of the best known and was carried by both the Army and the Navy. Navy Arms Company has authentically reproduced the Harpers Ferry to the finest detail, providing a well-balanced and well-made pistol.
Weight: 2 lbs. 9 oz.
Barrel Length: 10"
Overall Length: 16"
Caliber: 58
Finish: Walnut stock; case-hardened lock; brass-mounted browned barrel.
Price:. $325
    Single Cased Set 345

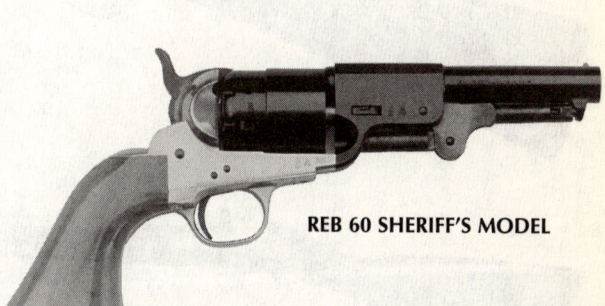

1805 HARPERS FERRY FLINTLOCK PISTOL

REB 60 SHERIFF'S MODEL
A compact version of the Reb Model 60 Revolver. The Sheriff's model version became popular because the shortened barrel was fast out of the leather. This is actually the original snub nose, the predecessor of the detective specials or "belly" guns designed for quick-draw use.
Calibers: 36 and 44
Price:. 120

REB 60 SHERIFF'S MODEL

1858 NEW MODEL ARMY REMINGTON-STYLE REVOLVER
This rugged, dependable, battle-proven veteran with its top strap and rugged frame was considered the Magnum of Civil War revolvers, ideally suited for heavy 44 charges. Blued finish.

Caliber: 44.
Barrel Length: 8"
Overall Length: 14.25"
Weight: 2 lbs. 8 oz.
Price: New Model Army Revolver 180
Also available: Brass Frame 135
    Stainless. 285

1858 NEW MODEL ARMY

Navy Arms Rifles

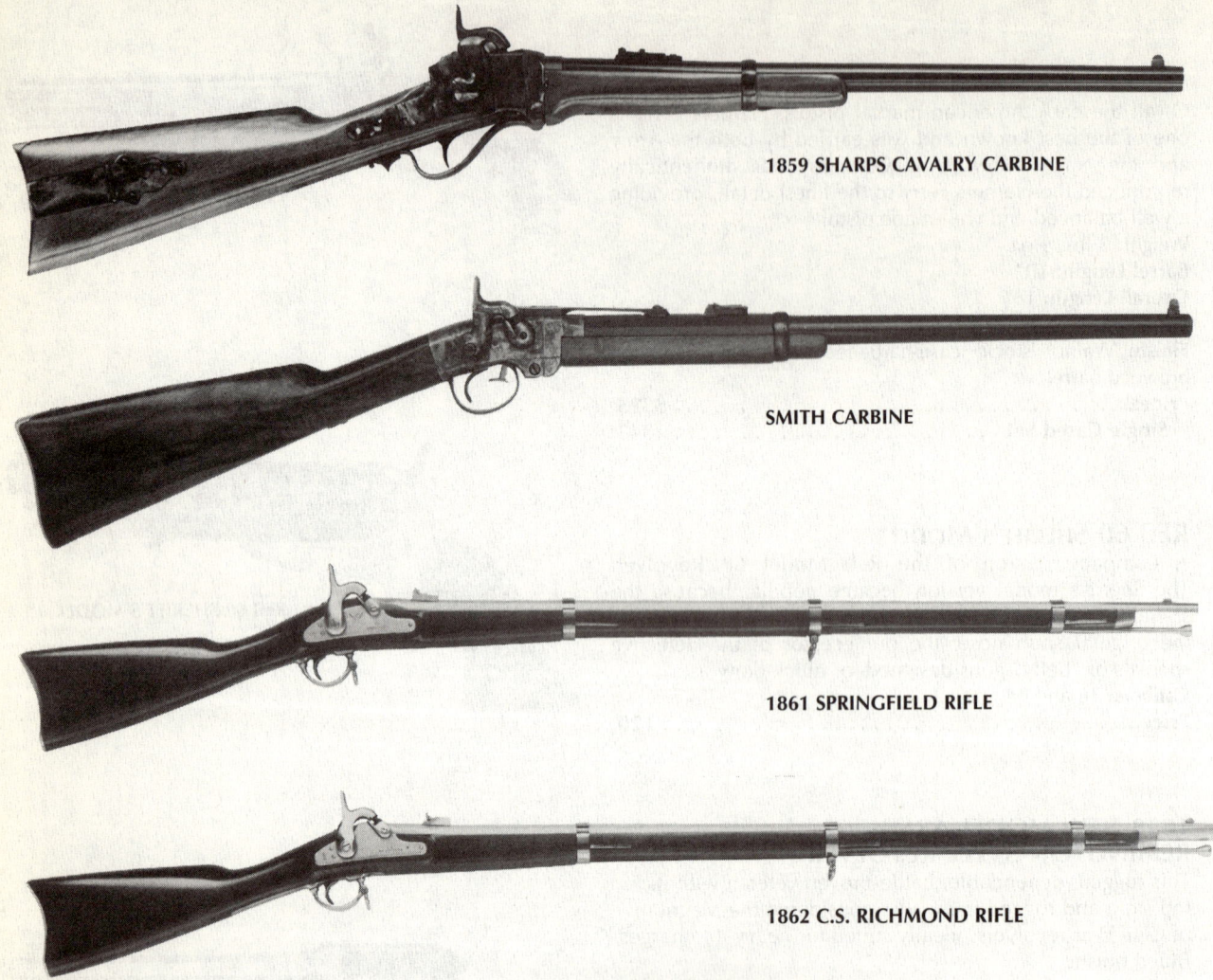

1859 SHARPS CAVALRY CARBINE

SMITH CARBINE

1861 SPRINGFIELD RIFLE

1862 C.S. RICHMOND RIFLE

1859 Sharps Cavalry Carbine
This percussion version of the Sharps is a copy of the popular breechloading Cavalry Carbine of the Civil War. It features a patchbox and bar and saddle ring on the left side of the stock. **Caliber:** 54 **Barrel Length:** 22" **Overall Length:** 39" **Weight:** 7.75 lbs. **Sights:** Blade front; military ladder rear. **Stock:** Walnut
Price: $1000
Also available:
   1859 Sharps Infantry Rifle (54 cal.) 1100

Smith Carbine
The Smith Carbine was considered one of the finest breechloading carbines of the Civil War period. The hinged breech action allowed fast reloading for cavalry units. Available in either the Cavalry Model (with saddle ring and bar) or Artillery Model (with sling swivels). **Caliber:** 50 **Barrel Length:** 21.5" **Overall Length:** 39" **Weight:** 7.75 lbs. **Sights:** Blass blade front; folding ladder rear **Stock:** American walnut
Price: 635

1861 Springfield Rifle
One of the most popular Union rifles of the Civil War, the 1861 model featured the 1855-style hammer. The lockplate on this replica is marked "1861, U.S. Springfield." **Caliber:** 58 **Barrel Length:** 40" **Overall Length:** 56" **Weight:** 10 lbs. **Finish:** Walnut stock with polished metal lock and stock fitting.
Price: $590

1863 C.S. Richmond Rifle
This model was manufactured by the Confederacy at the Richmond Armory utilizing 1855 Rifle Musket parts captured from the Harpers Ferry Arsenal. This replica features the unusual 1855 lockplate, stamped "1862 C.S. Richmond, V.A." **Caliber:** 58 **Barrel Length:** 40" **Overall Length:** 56" **Weight:** 10 lbs. **Finish:** Walnut stock with polished metal lock and stock fittings.
Price: 590

Navy Arms Rifles/Muskets

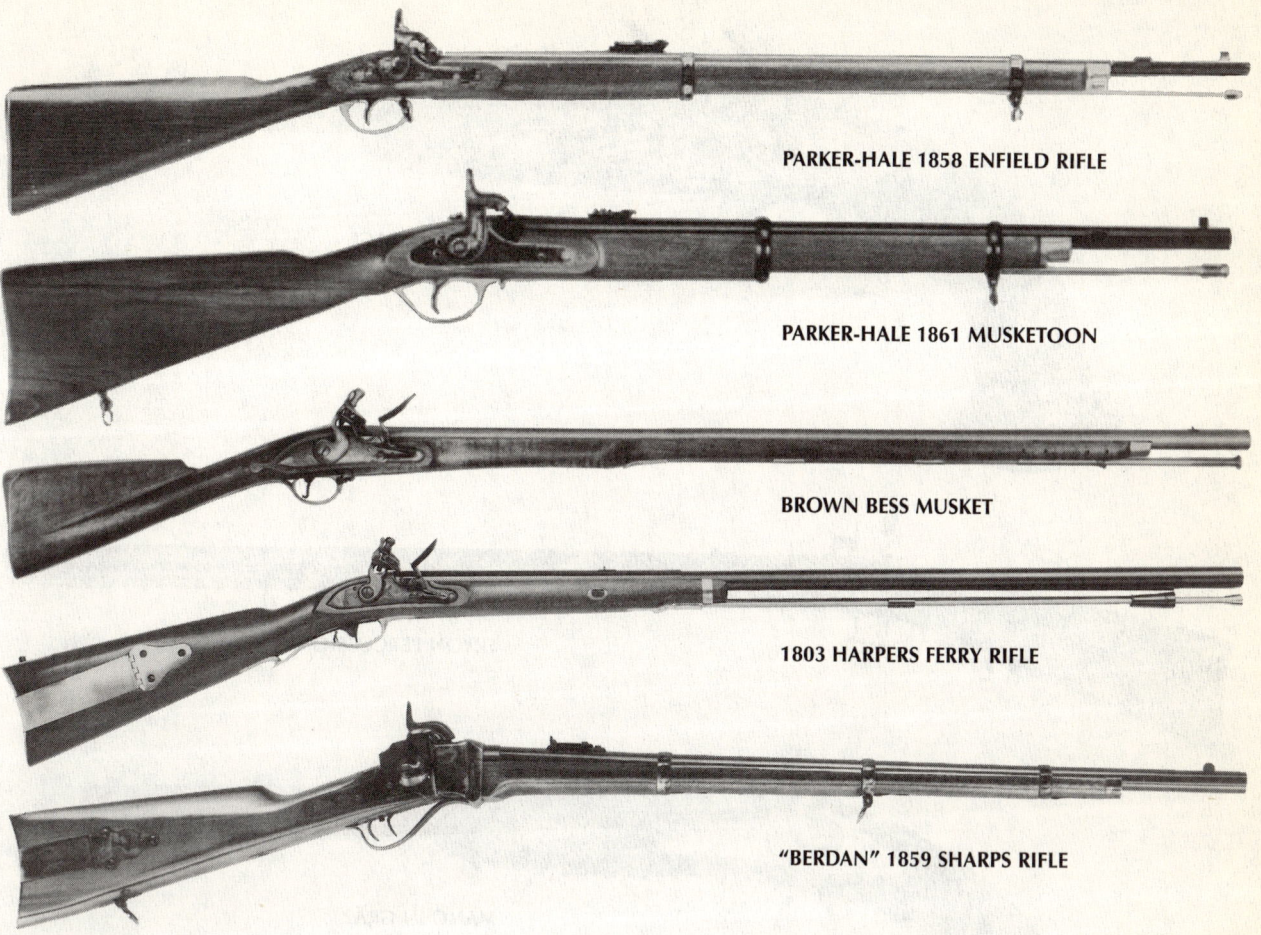

PARKER-HALE 1858 ENFIELD RIFLE

PARKER-HALE 1861 MUSKETOON

BROWN BESS MUSKET

1803 HARPERS FERRY RIFLE

"BERDAN" 1859 SHARPS RIFLE

Parker-Hale 1858 Enfield Rifle
In the late 1850s the British Admiralty, after extensive experiments, settled on a pattern rifle with a 5-groove barrel of heavy construction, with sights available to 1,100 yards. It was designated the Naval rifle, Pattern 1858. **Caliber:** 58 **Barrel Length:** 33"" **Weight:** 9 lbs. 10 oz. **Overall Length:** 48.5" **Sights:** Fixed front; graduated rear. **Stock:** Seasoned walnut w/solid brass furniture.
Price: $600

Parker-Hale 1861 Musketoon
The 1861 Enfield Musketoon was the favorite long arm of the Confederate Cavalry. **Caliber:** 58 **Barrel Length:** 24" **Weight:** 7 lbs. 8 oz. **Overall Length:** 40.25" **Sights:** Fixed front; graduated rear. **Stock:** Seasoned walnut with solid brass furniture.
Price: 515

Brown Bess Musket
Used extensively in the French and Indian War, the Brown Bess Musket proved itself in the American Revolution as well. This fine replica of the "Second Model" is marked "Grice" on the lockplate. **Caliber:** 75 **Barrel Length:** 42" **Overall Length:** 59" **Weight:** 9.5 lbs. **Sights:** Lug front **Stock:** Walnut
Price: 895

Also available: **Brown Bess Carbine**
Caliber: 75 **Barrel Length:** 30" **Overall Length:** 47" **Weight:** 7.75 lbs.
Price: $895

1803 Harpers Ferry Rifle
This 1803 Harpers Ferry rifle was carried by Lewis and Clark on their expedition to explore the Northwest Territory. This replica of the first rifled U.S. Martial flintlock features a browned barrel, case hardened lock and a brass patchbox. **Caliber:** 54 **Barrel Length:** 35" **Overall Length:** 50.5" **Weight:** 8.5 lbs.
Price: 675

"Berdan" 1859 Sharps Rifle
A replica of the Union sniper rifle used by Col. Hiram Berdan's First and Second U.S. Sharpshooters Regiments during the Civil War. **Caliber:** 54 **Barrel Length:** 30" **Overall Length:** 46.75" **Weight:** 8 lbs. 8 oz. **Sights:** Military-style ladder rear; blade front **Stock:** Walnut **Features:** Double-set trigger, case hardened receiver; patchbox and furniture.
Price: 1165

Pedersoli

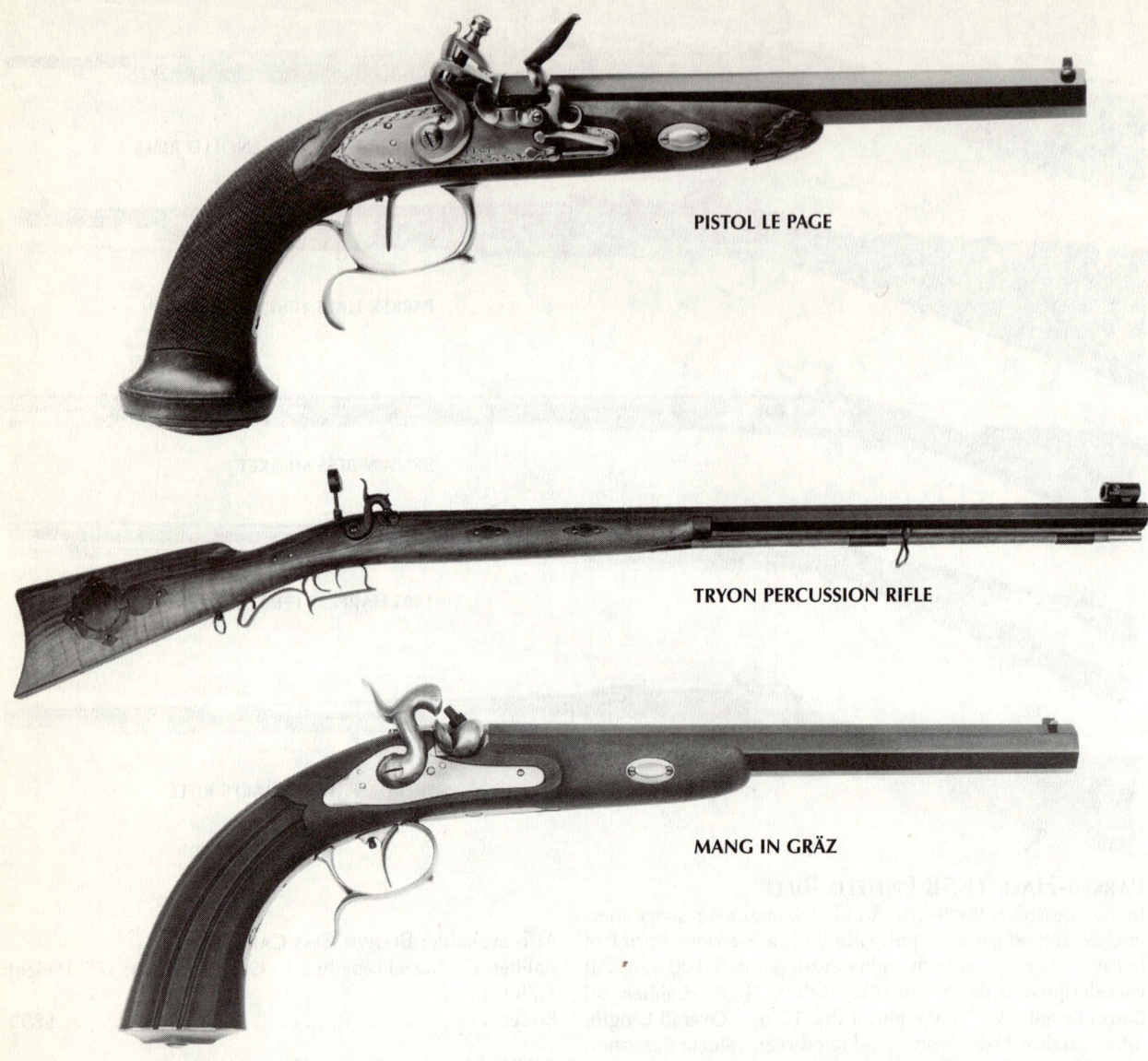

PISTOL LE PAGE

TRYON PERCUSSION RIFLE

MANG IN GRÄZ

PEDERSOLI "PISTOL LE PAGE"
INTERNATIONAL FLINTLOCK TARGET PISTOL
Specifications
Caliber: .44 or 45 (also in .44 smoothbore)
Barrel Length: 10.5"
Twist: 1-in-18" twist
Trigger: Single set
Weight: 2.5 lbs.
Stock: Walnut
Prices: $750
   Percussion model in 36, 38 or 44 caliber 595

PEDERSOLI TRYON PERCUSSION RIFLE
Specifications
Caliber: 45, 50 and 54
Barrel Length: 32"
Twist: 1-in-48" twist (1-in-66" twist for .54 bore)
Weight: 9.5 lbs.
Also available: Creedmoor version with fast-twist barrel (1-in-21, 451 caliber) and target sights (shown).
Prices: Standard $650
   Creedmoor 925

PEDERSOLI "MANG IN GRÄZ"
PERCUSSION PISTOL
Specifications
Caliber: 38 or 44
Barrel Length: 11"
Twist: 1-in-15" (38) or 1-in-18" (44) twist
Weight: 2.5 lbs.
Stock: Walnut
Prices: 1025

Remington Black Powder Rifles

MODEL 700 ML

MODEL 700 MLS STAINLESS

MODEL 700 ML AND MLS IN-LINE MUZZLELOADING RIFLES

Remington began building flintlock muzzleloaders in 1816. These two in-line muzzleloading rifles have the same cocking action and trigger mechanism as the original versions. The difference comes from a modified bolt and ignition system. The Model 700 ML has a traditionally blued carbon-steel barreled action. On the Model 700 MLS the barrel, receiver and bolt are made of 416 stainless steel with a non-reflective, satin finish. Each is set in a fiberglass-reinforced synthetic stock fitted with a Magnum-style recoil pad. One end of the solid aluminum ramrod is recessed into the forend and the outer end is secured by a barrel band. Instead of an open chamber, the breech is closed by a stainless-steel plug and nipple. In the internal structure of the modified bolt, the firing pin is replaced by a cylindrical rod that is cocked by normal bolt lift. It is released by pulling the trigger to strike a #11 percussion cap seated on the nipple. Lock time is 3.0 milli-seconds. Barrels are rifled with a 1 in 28" twist. The barrels are fitted with standard adjustable iron sights; receivers are drilled and tapped for short-action scope mount. Now all are equipped with 3-way ignition systems – use 209 shotshell primers, musket caps or No. 11 percussion caps, simply by changing nipples.

Specifications:
Barrel length: 24"on Model 700 ML (26" Magnum) **Twist:** 1-28" **Overall Length:** 44.5" **Weight:** 7.75 lbs. **Length Of Pull:** 13 3/8" **Drop At Comb:** .5" **Drop At Heel:** 3/8"

Prices:
   Model ML (.50 cal.) $415
   Model MLS Stainless (.50 + .45 cal.) 533
Also available: MLS 50 Caliber

Ruger Rifles/Revolvers

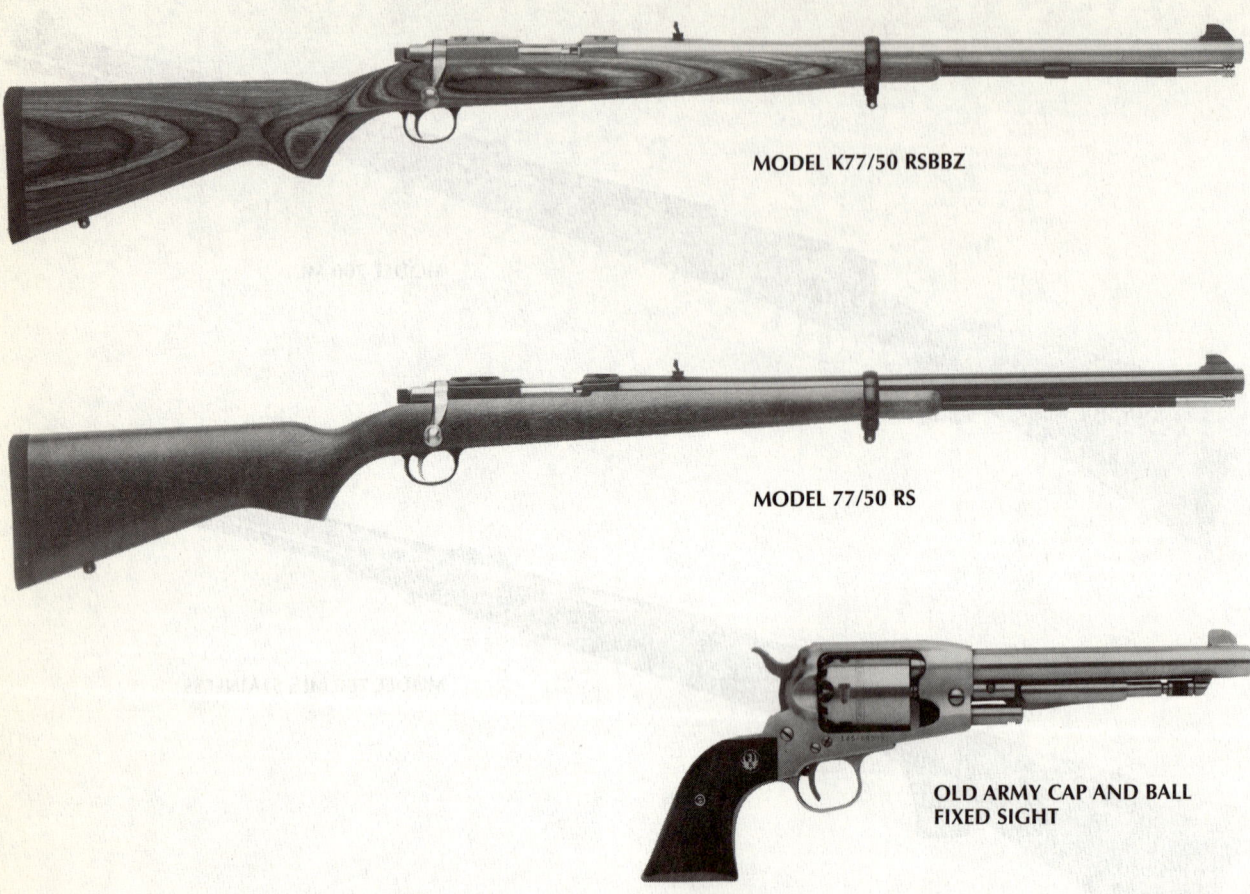

MODEL K77/50 RSBBZ

MODEL 77/50 RS

OLD ARMY CAP AND BALL FIXED SIGHT

MODEL K77/50 RSBBZ STAINLESS STEEL BLACK LAMINATED STOCK BLACK POWDER RIFLE
Specifications
Caliber: .50 **Action:** Bolt action In-line muzzle loader **Finish:** Non-glare matte stainless steel finish **Barrel Length:** 22" 400 series stainless steel **Overall Length:** 41.5" **Rifling:** 8 grooves, right hand twist (1-turn-in-28") **Safety:** Three-position wing safety **Sights:** Single folding leaf rear; gold bead front; rear receiver drilled and tapped for peep sights **Stock:** Black/gray laminated American hardwood w/rubber buttpad; studs for sling swivels **Length Of Pull:** 13.75" **Drop At Comb:** 11/16" **Drop At heel:** 15/16" **Weight (approx.):** 6.5 lbs. (unloaded) **Features:** Operator's manual, set of 1" stainless steel scope range; standard breech plug wrench; bolt disassemble tool; cleaning tube; right hand 90° turn bolt
Price: $601
Also available: MODEL 77/50 RS. Same specifications as above, except finish is matte blue and stock is American Hardwood w/rubber buttpad.
Price: 434
MODEL 77/50 RSO.
Same specifications as above, except for following: **Drop at Comb:** 25/32" **Drop At Heel:** 29/32" **Stock:** Straight gripped, checkered American black walnut stock, w/curved buttplate
Price: 555
K77/50 RSP All-weather, stainless, synthetic stock
Price: 580

OLD ARMY CAP AND BALL
This Old Army cap-and-ball revolver is reminiscent of the Civil War era martial revolvers and those used by the early frontiersmen in the 1800s. This Ruger model comes in both blued and stainless-steel finishes and features modern materials, technology and design throughout, including steel music-wire coil springs. Fixed or adjustable sights.
Specifications
Caliber: 45 (.443" bore; .45" groove)
Barrel Length: 7.5"
Weight: 2 7/8 lbs.
Rifling: 6 grooves, R.H. twist (1:16")
Sights: Fixed, ramp front; topstrap channel rear
Percussion cap nipples: Stainless steel (#10 or #11)
Price: Blued 499
  Stainless Steel 535

Savage Rifles

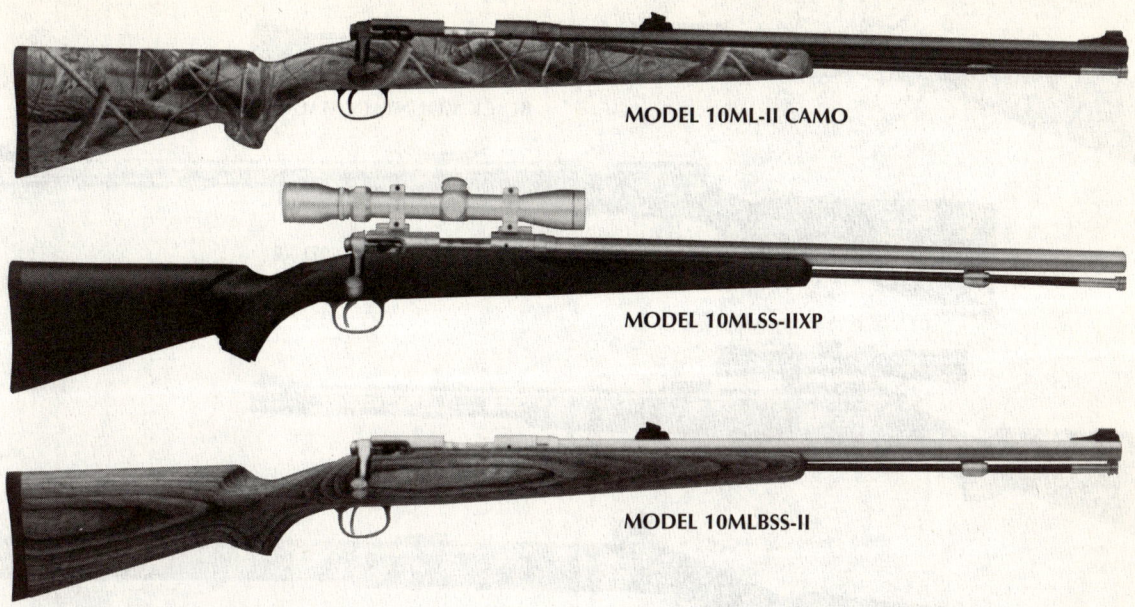

MODEL 10ML-II CAMO

MODEL 10MLSS-IIXP

MODEL 10MLBSS-II

Savage Muzzleloaders

The bolt-action Model 10ML-II gives you the choice of black powder or Pyrodex. It is the only 50 caliber muzzleloading big game rifle capable of producing velocities exceeding 2300 f.p.s., delivering more than 3,000 ft. lbs. of knock-down power. The Model 10ML-II now offers several stock options -- black synthetic, Realtree Hardwoods HD camo synthetic or brown laminate. Blued or stainless 24" barrel, No. 209 primer ignition, drilled and tapped receiver and adjustable fiber-optic sights.

Price:	$478
stainless	533
Camo/blue	512
Camo/Stainless	$567
Laminate	602

Shiloh Sharps
Model 1874

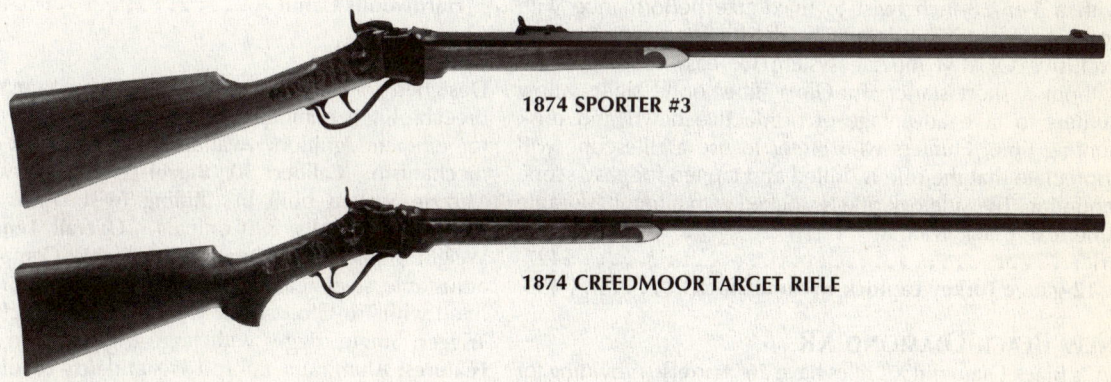

1874 SPORTER #3

1874 CREEDMOOR TARGET RIFLE

Shiloh Black Powder Rifles
Sharps Model 1874

Shiloh Sharps has a large selection of rifle styles and calibers from which to choose. Each gun is made to your custom specifications. Options include: standard, semi-fancy or extra-fancy wood, pistol or straight grip, 26" to 34" barrel, color case-hardened finish, or antique or French gray finish with engraving. Metallic black powder cartridges only.
Prices vary with options.

Thompson/Center Rifles

BLACK MOUNTAIN MAGNUM

NEW BLACK DIAMOND XR

NEW OMEGA 50

FIRE STORM

BLACK MOUNTAIN MAGNUM

The 50-caliber Black Mountain Magnum™ is designed to handle magnum loads of up to 150 grains of FFg black powder or the Pyrodex equivalent volume (up to three 50-grain Pyrodex pellets). Shooting a Mag Express Sabot with 240-grain XTP bullet, a 150-grain load produces a muzzle velocity of 2203 feed per second. The Black Mountain Magnum™ has a musket cap nipple, the hottest ignition available in a traditional-style muzzleloader. Standard nipples with #11 or #11 Magnum percussion caps can also be used. The blued, 26-inch barrel is button rifled with a 1-in-28-inch twist to maximize performance with conical projectiles. It is equipped with Thompson/Center's exclusive QLA™ muzzle system for easy loading, even without a short starter. Tru-Glo™ fiber optic sights allow hunters to take advantage of productive dawn and dusk hunting time. Hunters who prefer to use a riflescope will appreciate that the rifle is drilled and tapped for easy scope mounting. The sidelock rifle is stocked with a tough, durable American Black Walnut.

Price: $427
   12-gauge Turkey caplock w/camo stock 453

NEW BLACK DIAMOND XR

T/C's Black Diamond XR rifles have 26" barrels, providing for optimum burning of magnum charges. Available in 50 or 45 caliber. Adjustable Fiber Optic sights. **Weight:** 6lbs. 12 oz.

Price: Blue/Composite stock in 50 cal. 331
   Stainless/Composite in 50 cal. 377
   Stainless/Camo in 50 cal. 429
   Blue/Composite in 45 cal. 346
   Stainless/Composite in 45 cal. 392

NEW OMEGA 50

Specifications:
Caliber: 50 caliber. **Ignition:** 209 shotgun primer (closed swinging block breech action). **Barrel:** 28" twist for sabots and conical bullets. **Weight:** 7 lbs. **Sights:** click adjustable steel rear with Tru-Glo inserts; steel ramp front sight. **Stock:** composite or laminated. Blued or stainless.

Price: Blue/black composite stock $406
   Stainless/black composite stock. 465
   Stainless/gray laminated wood stock. 480
   Stainless/composite stock in Realtree
   Hardwoods Camo 517

FIRE STORM

Designed for Pyrodex pellets, the Fire Storm's removable breech plug is conical, directing flame to the pellet's center for efficient ignition. Available with caplock or flintlock mechanism. **Caliber:** 50 **Barrel Length:** 26"-with QLA™ Muzzle System built in **Rifling Twist:** 1 in 48" for use with Round Balls & Conicals **Overall Length:** 41.75" **Weight:** 7 lbs. (approximate) **Rifle Sights:** Competition click adjustable steel rear sight and ramp style front sights are fitted with Tru-Glo™ Fiber Optics **Stock:** Black Composite **Trigger:** Single trigger with large trigger guard bow. **Extra Features:** Aluminum ramrod is standard **Loading:** The Fire Storm™ can accept magnum charges of up to 150 grains of FFG Black Powder or Pyrodex® equivalent (or 3 Pyrodex 50 caliber, 50 grain Pellets).

Price: 407
   Stainless steel 460

Thompson/Center Rifles
Custom Hunting

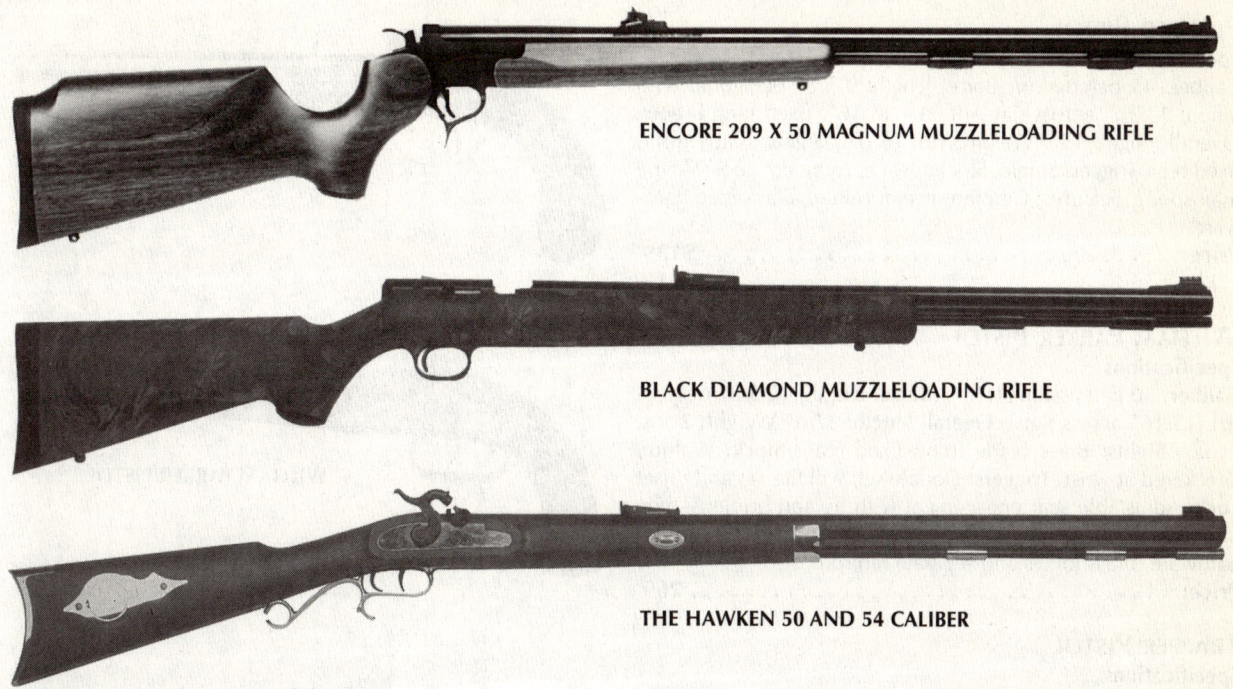

ENCORE 209 x 50 MAGNUM MUZZLELOADING RIFLE

BLACK DIAMOND MUZZLELOADING RIFLE

THE HAWKEN 50 AND 54 CALIBER

ENCORE 209 X 50 MAGNUM MUZZLELOADING RIFLE
Specifications
Caliber: .50 **Action:** Break-open action muzzleloader **Ignition:** 209 shotgun primer **Barrel Length:** 26" with QLA Muzzle System **Twist:** 1 in 28" **Overall Length:** 40.5" **Weight:** 7 lbs. **Sights:** Tru-Glo adjustable rear fiber optic sight; ramp-style fiber optic front sight **Safety:** Automatic hammerblock w/ bolt interlock **Finish:** Blued **Stock:** American walnut with schnabel forend and Monte Carlo buttstock **Features:** Barrel interchangeable with Encore rifles; equipped with sling swivel studs; accepts magnum charges of up to 150 grains of black powder or Pyrodex equivalent (or three 50-grain Pyrodex Pellets).

Price: Blued/Walnut	$622
Blued with hardwood camo stock	647
Stainless/composite	672
Blue/Composite	596
Stainless/Camo	724

Also available: ENCORE 209 x45 45 caliber. 26" barrel
Blue/walnut stock	637
Stainless/composite stock	687

BLACK DIAMOND MUZZLELOADING RIFLE
Specifications
Caliber: .50 **Ignition:** In-line ignition using Flame Thrower musket cap nipple or No. 11 nipple **Barrel:** Free-floated, 22.5" barrel with QLA **Twist:** 1 in 18" **Overall Length:** 41.5" **Weight:** 6 lbs. 9 oz. **Safety:** Patented sliding thumb safety **Sights:** Tru-Glo Fiber Optic adjustable rear sight; Fiber Optic ramp-style front sight **Stock:** Black Rynite stock with molded-in checkering and pistol grip cap **Loading:** Accepts magnum charges of up to 150 grains of black powder or Pyrodex equivalent, or three 50-grain Pyrodex Pellets **Features:** Removable universal breech plug; Aluminum ram rod; sling swivel studs; rubber recoil pad; musket nipple wrench, 5-pack or T/C Mag Express Sabots, and No. 11 nipple standard

Prices: Blued w/walnut stock	$386
Blued w/Rynite Stock	317
Blued with hardwoods camo stock	368
Stainless	363

Also Available: BLACK DIAMOND PREMIUM PACK (includes T-Handle Short Starter, 10 Mag Express Sabots, rifle powder measure, In-line U-View Capper, Super Jag, ball and bullet puller, 2 Quick Shots, breech plug wrench, Hunter's Field Pouch, Lube-N-Clean Kit, Gorilla Grease).

Prices: Blued	339
Stainless	398

THE HAWKEN 50 AND 54 CALIBER
Similar to the famous Rocky Mountain rifles made during the early 1800s, the Hawken has an octagon barrel. Button-rifled for ultimate precision, the Hawken is available in 45-, 50- or 54-caliber percussion or 50- caliber flintlock. It features a hooked breech, double-set triggers, first-grade American walnut stock, adjustable hunting sights, solid brass trim and color casehardened lock. Beautifully decorated; comes equipped with T/C's QLA™ Muzzle System. **Weight:** Approx. 8.5 lbs.

Prices: Hawken Caplock 50 or 54 caliber	529
Hawken Flintlock 50 caliber	5553

Also Available: CLELAND MATCH HAWKEN CAPLOCK,
40 caliber, blued, walnut stock	715

Traditions Pistols

PIONEER PISTOL
Specifications
Caliber: 45 percussion Barrel length: 9 5/8" octagonal with tenon; 13/16" across flats, rifled 1 in 16", fixed tang breech Overall length: 15" Weight: 1lb. 15 oz. Sights: Blade front; fixed rear Trigger: Single Stock: Beech, rounded Lock: V-type mainspring Features: German silver furniture; blackened hardware
Price: $139
 Kit 119

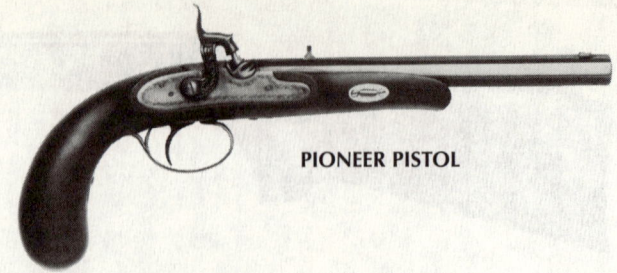
PIONEER PISTOL

WILLIAM PARKER PISTOL
Specifications
Caliber: 50 percussion (1:20") Barrel length: 10 3/8" octagonal (15/16" across flats) Overall length: 17.5" Weight: 2 lbs. 5 oz. Sights: Brass blade front; fixed rear Stock: Walnut, checkered at wrist Triggers: Double set; will fire set and unset Lock: Adjustable sear engagement with fly and bridle; V-type mainspring Features: Brass percussion cap guard; polished hardware, brass inlays and separate ramrod
Price: 269

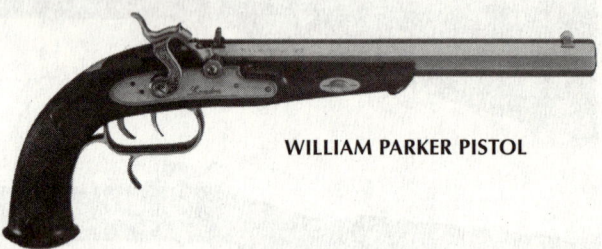
WILLIAM PARKER PISTOL

TRAPPER PISTOL
Specifications
Caliber: 50 percussion or flintlock (1:20") Barrel length: 9 3/4"; octagonal (7/8" across flats) with tenon Overall length: 15.5" Weight: 2 lbs. 14 oz. Stock: Beech Lock: Adjustable sear engagement with fly and bridle Triggers: Double set, will fire set and unset Sights: Primitive-style adjustable rear; brass blade front Furniture: Solid brass; blued steel on assembled pistol
Price: Percussion 189
 Percussion Kit 149
 Flintlock 209

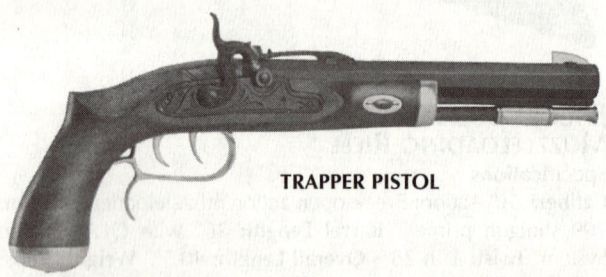
TRAPPER PISTOL

BUCKHUNTER PRO-IN-LINE PISTOLS
Specifications
Calibers: 50 Percussion Barrel length: 9.5" or 12.5" Overall length: 14.25" (17.75") Weight: 3.2 oz. (3.4 oz.) Trigger: Single Sights: Fold-down adjustable rear; beaded blade front Stock: Walnut or All-Weather Features: Blued or C-Nickel furniture; PVC ramrod; drilled and tapped for scope mounting; coil mainspring; thumb safety
Price: 9 5" barrel 229
 12 5" barrel 239
 w/All-Weather Stock 239
 14.75" fluted nickel w/muzzle brake 284
Also available: 45 percussion AW stock, 14.75" fluted nickel w/muzzle brake 289

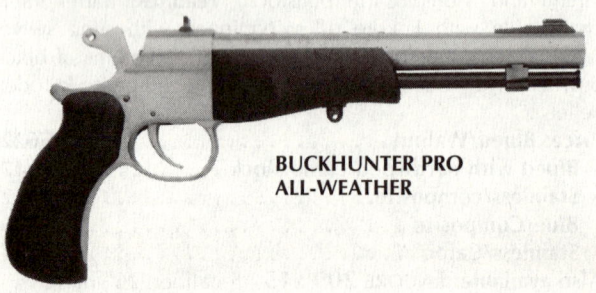
BUCKHUNTER PRO ALL-WEATHER

KENTUCKY PISTOL
Specifications
Caliber: 50 Percussion (1:20") Barrel length: 10" octagon (7/8" flats) Overall length: 15" Weight: 2 lbs. 8 oz. Trigger: Single Sights: Fixed rear; blade front Stock: Beechwood Features: Brass furniture; wood ramrod; kit available
Price: 139
 Kit 109

KENTUCKY PISTOL

Traditions Rifles
Deerhunter Rifles

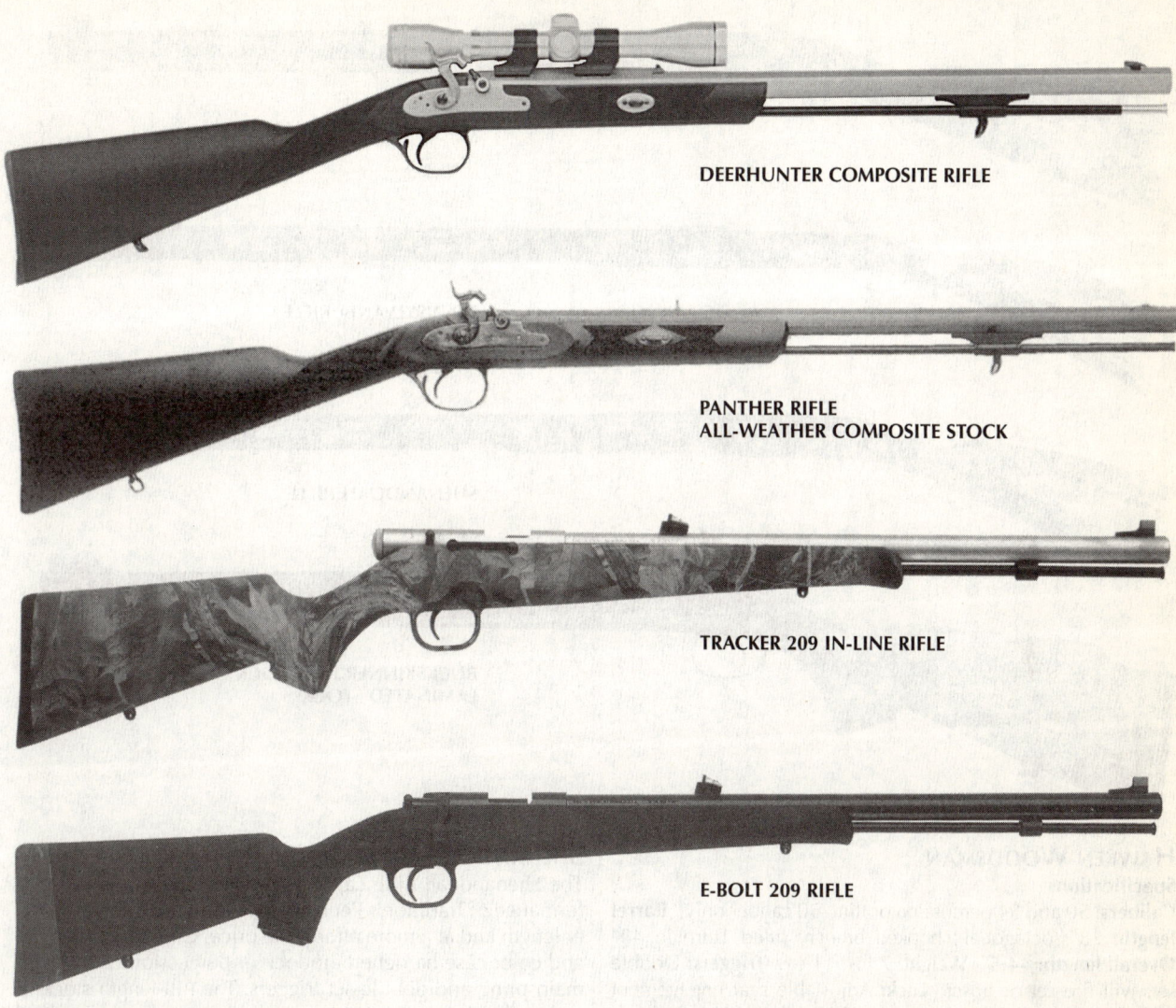

DEERHUNTER COMPOSITE RIFLE

PANTHER RIFLE
ALL-WEATHER COMPOSITE STOCK

TRACKER 209 IN-LINE RIFLE

E-BOLT 209 RIFLE

DEERHUNTER COMPOSITE RIFLE
Specifications
Calibers: 32, 50 and 54 percussion or flintlock **Barrel length:** 24" octagonal **Rifling twist:** 1:48" (flint or percussion) **Overall length:** 40" **Weight:** 6 lbs. (6 lbs. 3 oz. in Small Game rifle) **Trigger:** Single **Sights:** Fixed rear; blade front **Features:** PVC ramrod; blackened furniture; inletted wedge plates
Prices: Percussion w/blued barrel............$139 - 179
   Percussion w/nickel barrel 159
   Flintlock w/nickel barrel......................189
   Flintlock w/select hardwood stock.............189
   Flintlock w/camo 219

PANTHER RIFLE ALL-WEATHER COMPOSITE STOCK
An economy version of the Deerhunter, the Panther comes with 24" 50 or 53-caliber barrel and fixed blade sights.
Price:...119

TRACKER 209 IN-LINE RIFLE
Specifications
Features: 209 Primer Ignition system gives hot, reliable powder ignition; adjustable rear glow fiber front. **Caliber:** 50 or 45 **Barrel:** 22" blued or nickel (1-in-28" twist 1-in-20" twist/45 cal.) **Length:** 41" **Stock:** synthetic with checkering or camo
Prices: Synthetic w/blued stock..................$119
   Synthetic w/nickel stock 129
   Camo w/nickel stock.......................179

E-BOLT 209 RIFLE
Specifications
Caliber: 50 or 45 **Barrel:** 22" blued or nickel (1-in-28" twist 1-in-20" twist/45 cal.) **Length:** 41" **Stock:** synthetic with checkering or camo **Sights:** Adjustable rear glow fiber front
Prices: Synthetic w/blued barrel.................169
   Synthetic w/nickel barrel 179
   Camo w/blued barrel 219
   Camo w/nickel barrel 229

Traditions Rifles

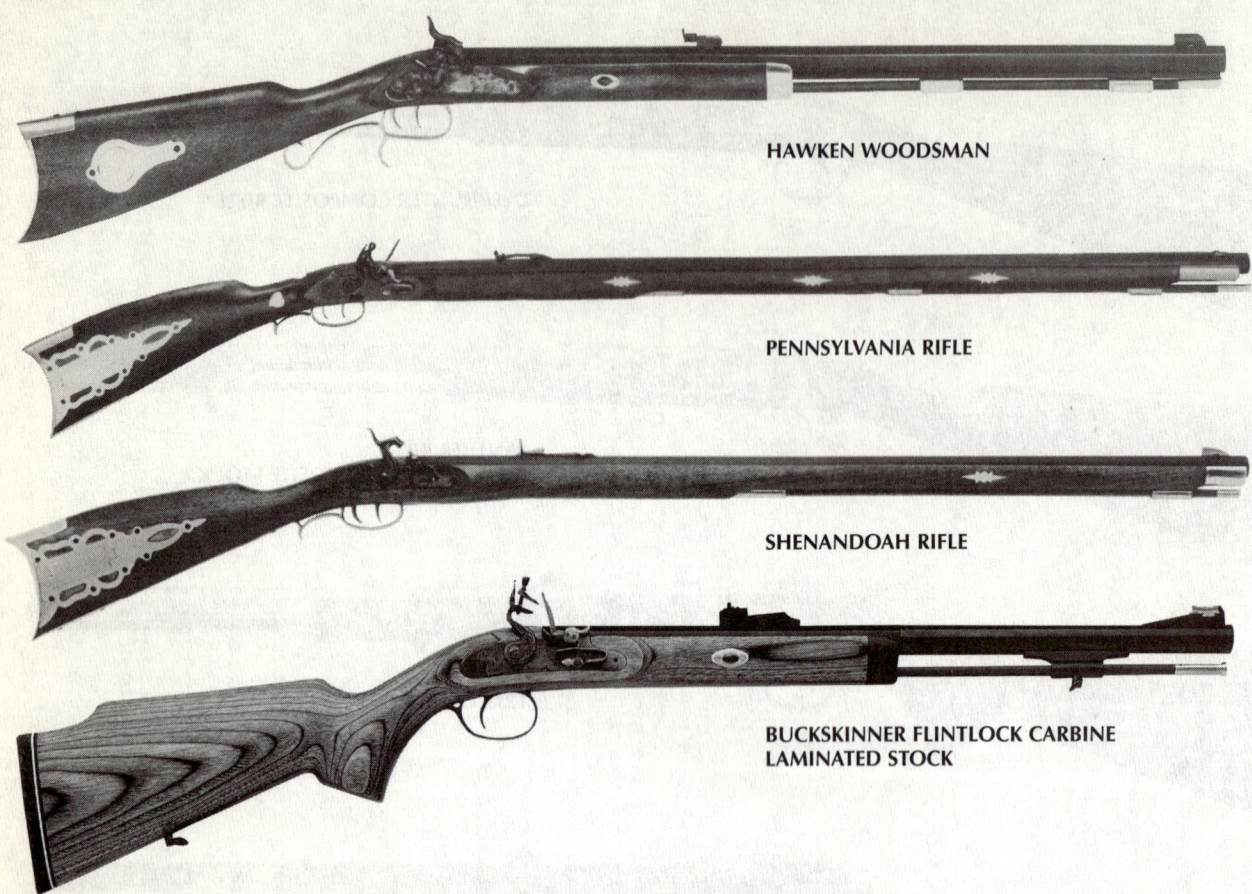

HAWKEN WOODSMAN

PENNSYLVANIA RIFLE

SHENANDOAH RIFLE

BUCKSKINNER FLINTLOCK CARBINE LAMINATED STOCK

HAWKEN WOODSMAN
Specifications
Calibers: 50 and 54 percussion or flint (50 caliber only) **Barrel length:** 28" (octagonal); hooked breech; rifled 1 turn in 48" **Overall length:** 44.5" **Weight:** 7 lbs. 11 oz. **Triggers:** Double set; will fire set or unset **Lock:** Adjustable sear engagement with fly and bridle **Stock:** Beech **Sights:** Beaded blade front; hunting-style rear, fully screw adjustable for windage and elevation **Furniture:** Solid brass, blued steel or blackened (50 cal. only); unbreakable ramrod
Prices: Percussion............................$239
   Flint...................................269
   Percussion, left-hand..................249

PENNSYLVANIA RIFLE
Specifications
Caliber: 50 **Barrel length:** 40 1/4"; octagonal (7/8" across flats) with 3 pins; rifled 1 turn in 66" **Overall length:** 57" **Weight:** 8 lbs. 8 oz. **Lock:** Adjustable sear engagement with fly and bridle **Stock:** Walnut, beavertail style **Triggers:** Double set; will fire set and unset **Sights:** Primitive-style adjustable rear; brass blade front **Furniture:** Solid brass, blued steel
Prices: Percussion............................479
   Flintlock..............................489

SHENANDOAH RIFLE
The Shenandoah Rifle captures the frontier styling and performance of Tradition's Pennsylvania Rifle in a slightly shorter length and at a more affordable price. Choice of engraved and color case hardened flintlock or percussion with V-type mainspring and double-set triggers. The full-length stock in walnut finish is accented by a solid brass curved buttplate, inletted patch box, nose cap, thimbles, trigger guard and decorative furniture.
Specifications
Caliber: 50 (1:66") flint or percussion **Barrel length:** 33.5" octagon **Overall length:** 49.5" **Weight:** 7 lbs. 3 oz. **Sights:** Buckhorn rear, blade front **Stock:** Beech
Prices: Percussion............................$369
   Flintlock..............................389
Also available: 36 caliber Percussion............389
   36 caliber Flintlock....................399

BUCKSKINNER CARBINE
Specifications
Caliber: 50 flintlock **Barrel length:** 21": octagonal-to-round with tenon; 1:48" twist (flintlock) **Overall length:** 37.5" **Weight:** 6 lbs. **Sights:** Hunting-style fiber optic, beaded blade **Trigger:** Single **Features:** Blackened furniture: German silver ornamentation; sling swivels; unbreakable ramrod

Prices: Flintlock............................229

Traditions Rifles
Lightning Bolt-Action Rifles

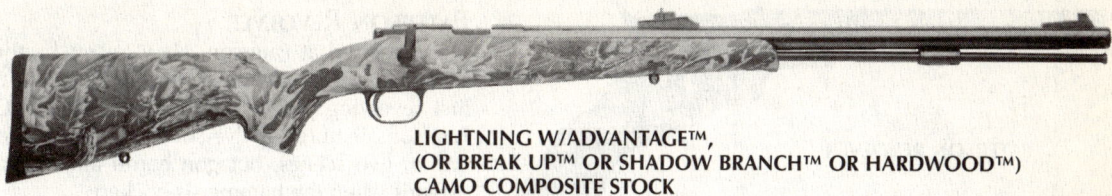

LIGHTNING W/ADVANTAGE™, (OR BREAK UP™ OR SHADOW BRANCH™ OR HARDWOOD™) CAMO COMPOSITE STOCK

Lightning Bolt-Action Rifles

Traditions' Lightning Bolt rifles include models with blued, chemical-nickel and stainless steel metal. Stock finishes include Advantage Timber (All-Weather Composite), Camo, Break-up and Spider Web. All models come with rugged synthetic ramrods, adjustable triggers, adjustable hunting sights, drilled and tapped barrels and field-removable stainless breech plugs. LFS (lightning fire system) allows use of #11 cap, musket cap on interchanable nipples provided.

Lightning Mag Bolt-Action Rifles

Model Number	Stock	Caliber	Barrel	Sights	Ramrod	Overall Length	Weight	Retail
R610029	AW Synthetic	.50p	24" Blued	Adj. Fiber Optic	Aluminum	43"	7 lb. 2 oz.	$199
R61003954	High Definition Advantage Timber	.50p	24" Blued	Adj. Fiber Optic	Aluminum	43"	7 lb. 2 oz.	229
R611029	AW Synthetic	.50p	24" C-Nickel	Adj. Fiber Optic	Aluminum	43"	7 lb. 10 oz.	219
R6170295	Break Up/AW Synthetic	.50p	24" Fluted Stainless/Muzzle Brake	Adj. Fiber Optic	Aluminum	45"	7 lb. 10 oz.	359
R618029	AW Synthetic	.50p	24" Stainless	Adj. Fiber Optic	Aluminum	43"	7 lb. 10 oz.	279
R6180295	Break Up/AW Synthetic	.50p	24" Stainless	Adj. Fiber Optic	Aluminum	45"	7 lb. 10 oz.	309

Lightning Lightweight Mag Bolt-Action Rifles with the "Lightning Fire Magnum System" and Fiber Optic Sights

Model Number	Stock	Caliber	Barrel	Sights	Ramrod	Overall Length	Weight	Retail
R630023	AW Synthetic/Spider Web	.50p	21" Fluted Blued	Adj. Fiber Optic	Aluminum	40"	6 lb. 5 oz.	$219
R631023	AW Synthetic/Spider Web	.50p	21" Fluted C-Nickel	Adj. Fiber Optic	Aluminum	40"	6 lb. 5 oz.	229

Lightning 45 Long Distance Bolt-Action Rifles

Model Number	Stock	Caliber	Barrel	Rate of Twist	Sights	Ramrod	Overall Length	Weight	Retail
R65050950	AW Synthetic/Check	.45p/.50p	26" Fluted Blued	1 in 20"	Adj. Fiber Optic	Aluminum	45"	7 lb. 0 oz.	$239
R65150950	AW Synthetic/Check	.45p/.50p	26" Fluted C-Nickel	1 in 20"	Adj. Fiber Optic	Aluminium	45"	7 lb. 2 oz.	249
R65150954	High Definition Advantage Timber	.45p	26" Fluted C-Nickel	1 in 20"	Adj. Fiber Optic	Aluminum	45"	7 lb. 2 oz.	299
R65050955	AW Synthetic/Breakup	.45p	26" Fluted Blued	1 in 26"	Adj. Fiber Optic	Aluminum	45"	7 lb. 0 oz.	279

All composite stocks are checkered. All Lightning 45 LD Bolt-Action Rifles are Drilled & Tapped for scope mounting. All Lightning Bolt-Action Rifles have Cheek-pieces. AW-All Weather

Winchester Muzzleloader Rifles

WINCHESTER MODEL X-150

Winchester Model X-150

New for 2002, Winchester Muzzleloading introduces the Model X-150 bolt-action magnum. Available in both 50 and 45 caliber. Winchester Muzzleloading's patented 209 breech plug ignition system endures reliable ignition. The bolt assembly is constructed of high-polish stainless steel for strength and corrosion resistance. The fluted 26" barrel features a 1:28" twist. The solid composite stock is equipped with a ventilated recoil pad and carrying strap. Weight: 8lbs. 3 oz. Metal-encased fiber-optic sights are standard. Stock available in black fleck, gray fleck, High definition Advantage Timber or Hardwoods Camo.

Price: Blue/gray fleck $390
Blue/Camo 435
Stainless/black fleck 465
Stainless/camo 510

Black Powder • 389

Uberti Revolvers

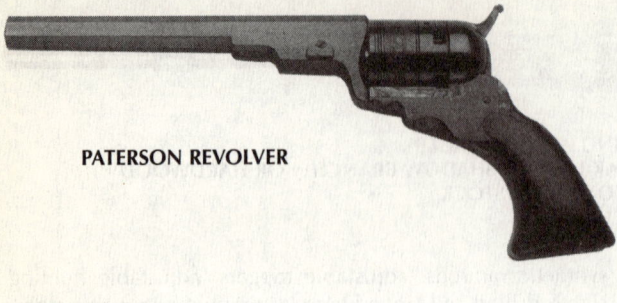

PATERSON REVOLVER

Paterson Revolver
Manufactured at Paterson, New Jersey, by the Patent Arms Manufacturing Company from 1836 to 1842, these were the first revolving pistols designed by Samuel Colt. All early Patersons featured a five-shot cylinder, roll-engraved with one or two scenes, octagon barrel and folding trigger that extends when the hammer is cocked.
Specifications
Caliber: 36 **Capacity:** 5 shots (engraved cylinder)
Barrel Length: 7.5" octagonal
Overall Length: 11.5"
Weight: 2.552 lbs.
Frame: Color casehardened steel
Grip: One-piece walnut
Price: $375
 w/Lever 415

1858 REMINGTON
NEW ARMY TARGET MODEL

1858 Remington New Army 44 Revolver
Prices: 8" barrel, open sights 260
 With stainless steel and open sights 350
 Target Model w/black finish 295
 Target Model w/stainless steel 389

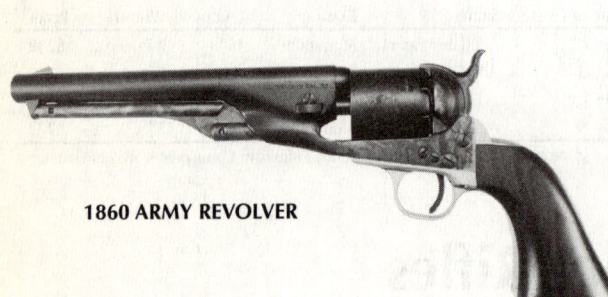

1860 ARMY REVOLVER

1860 Army Revolver
Specifications
Caliber: 44
Barrel length: 8" (round, tapered)
Overall length: 13 3/4"
Weight: 2.65 lbs.
Frame: One-piece, color case hardened steel
Trigger guard: Brass
Cylinder: 6 shots (engraved)
Grip: One-piece walnut
Price: 265
Also available:
 1860 Army Fluted 270

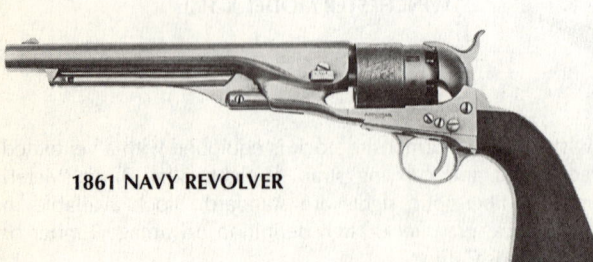

1861 NAVY REVOLVER

1861 Navy Revolver
Specifications
Caliber: 36
Capacity: 6 shots
Barrel length: 7 1/2"
Overall length: 13"
Weight: 2.75 lbs.
Grip: One-piece walnut
Frame: Color case hardened steel
Prices: 1861 Navy Civic 250
 Model 1851 (not shown) 250

SIGHTS & SCOPES

Aimpoint	392	Redfield	420
AO Sight Systems	393	Schmidt & Bender	422
BSA	395	Sightron	425
Burris	397	Simmons	427
Bushnell	401	Swarovski	431
Docter Sports Optics	406	Swift	433
Kahles	407	Tasco	435
Laseraim Technologies Inc.	408	Trijicon	438
Leupold	409	Weaver	439
Nikon	415	Williams	442
Pentax	418	Zeiss	446

Aimpoint Sights

AIMPOINT 7000S SIGHT

COMP M2 AND COMP ML2

SERIES 3000 UNIVERSAL

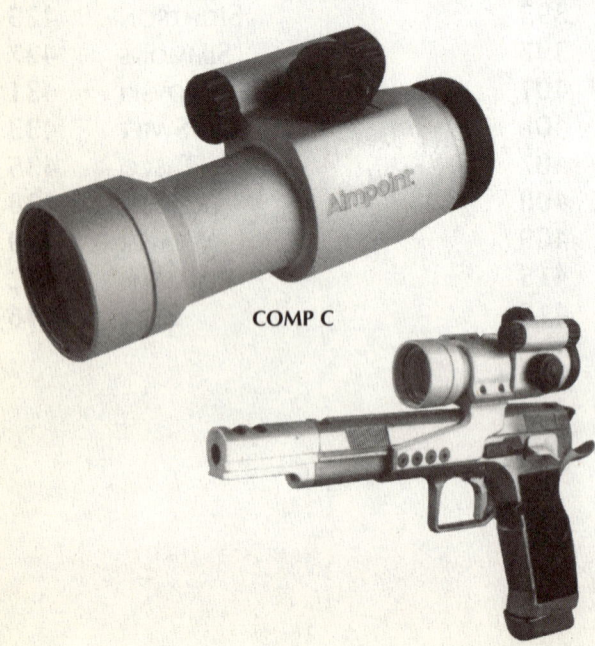

COMP C

AIMPOINT 7000S SIGHT
SPECIFICATIONS
System: Parallax free
Optical: Anti-reflex coated lenses
Adjustment: 1 click = 1/2 inch at 100 yards
Length: 6.3" **Weight:** 7.4 oz. **Objective diameter:** 36mm
Mounting system: 30mm rings **Magnification:** 1X
Material: Anodized aluminum; black finish
Diameter of dot: Red dot, 4 MOA
Price:...$298
Also Available:
7000L (length: 7.9")..........................298
7000S 2X (fixed 2X)..........................378
7000L 2X (fixed2X)..........................378

AIMPOINT COMP C2X
SPECIFICATIONS
System: Parallax free **Optical:** Anti-reflex coated lens
Adjustment: 1 click = 1/2" at 100 yards **Length:** 4.7"
Weight: 6.5 oz.
Objective diameter: 36 mm
Diameter of dot: 2 MOA
Mounting system: 30mm ring
Magnification: 2X fixed
Material: Anodized aluminum; black finish
Price:
  Comp ML2...............................368
  Comp M2................................410
  Comp M2 2X.............................521
  Comp ML2 2X............................467

SERIES 3000 UNIVERSAL
SPECIFICATIONS
System: 100% parallax free
Weight: 6 oz.
Length: 6.25"
Magnification: 1X
Scope attachment: 3X
Eye relief: Unlimited
Battery choices: 2X Mercury SP 675 1X Lithium or DL 1/3N
Material: Anodized aluminum, black finish
Mounting: 1" Rings (Medium or High)
Price: Black................................232

AIMPOINT COMP C
SPECIFICATIONS
System: 100% Parallax free
Optics: Anti-reflex coated lenses
Eye relief: Unlimited **Batteries:** 3V Lithium
Adjustment: 1 click = 1/2-inch at 100 yards
Length: 4 3/4" **Weight:** 6.5 oz.
Objective diameter: 36mm
Dot diameter: 4 MOA
Mounting system: 30mm ring **Magnification:** 1X
Material: Black or stainless finish
Price:................................324
Also Available: heavy-duty, hard anodized, graphite gray, submersible to 80'.....................411

AO Sight Systems

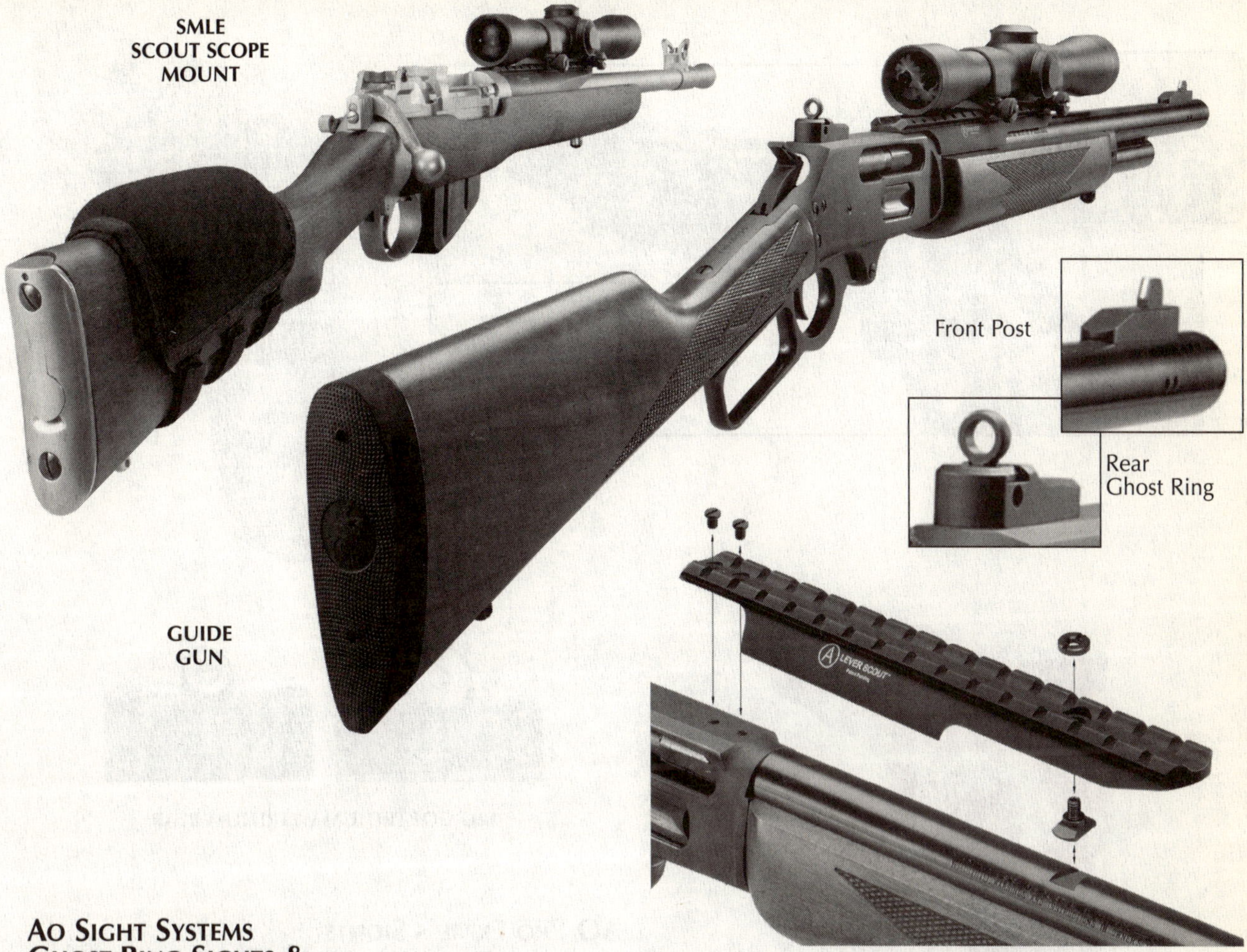

SMLE SCOUT SCOPE MOUNT

GUIDE GUN

Front Post

Rear Ghost Ring

MOUNT INSTALLATION

AO SIGHT SYSTEMS GHOST-RING SIGHTS & NEW LEVER SCOUT MOUNTS
• Scout Scope Mount with 8" long Weaver-style rail and cross slots on 1/2" Centers • Scope mounts 1/8" lower than previously possible on Marlin Lever Guns • Drop-in installation, no gunsmithing required • Installs using existing rear dovetail & front two screw holes on receiver • Allows fast target acquisition with both eyes open—better peripheral vision • Affords use of Ghost-Ring Sights with Scope dismounted • Recoil tested for even the stout 45/70 and .450 Loads • Available for Marlin Lever Models: 1895 Guide Series, new .450, .444P, the 336, and 1894.
Price: $50
New AO Lever Scout Mount for
 Win 94. 55

AO GHOST-RING HUNTING SIGHTS
• Fully adjustable for windage & elevation • Available for most rifles, including blackpowder • Minimum gunsmithing for most installations; matches most existing mounting holes • Compact design, CNC machined from steel and heat treated • Perfect for low light hunting conditions and brush/timer hunting, offers minimal target obstruction.
Price: AO Ghost-Ring Hunting Sight Set 90

SMLE SCOUT SCOPE MOUNTS
• Offers Scout Scope Mount with 7" long Weaver style rail
• Requires no machining of barrel to fit—no drilling or tapping
• Tapered counter bore for snug fit of SMLE Barrels
• Circular Mount is final filled with Brownells Acraglass
Price:
SMLE Scout Mount $60

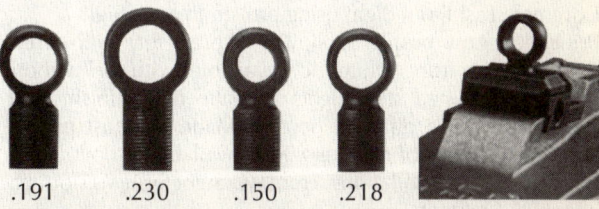

.191   .230   .150   .218

GHOST RING SIGHTS FOR RIFLES AND CARBINES
Price: rear 60
 front. 30

AO Sight Systems

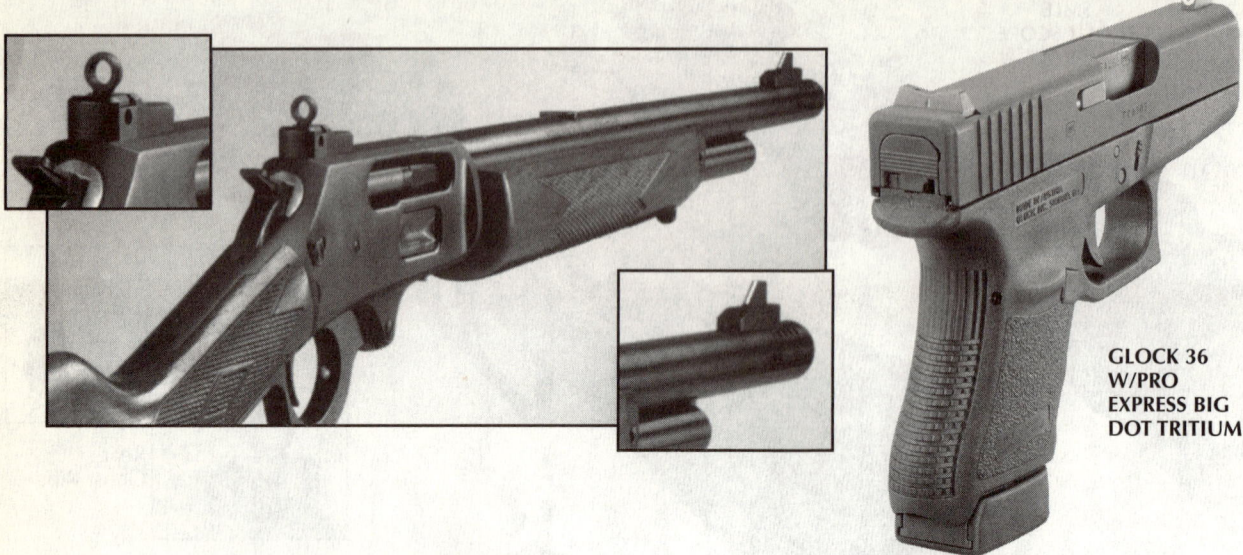

GLOCK 36 W/PRO EXPRESS BIG DOT TRITIUM

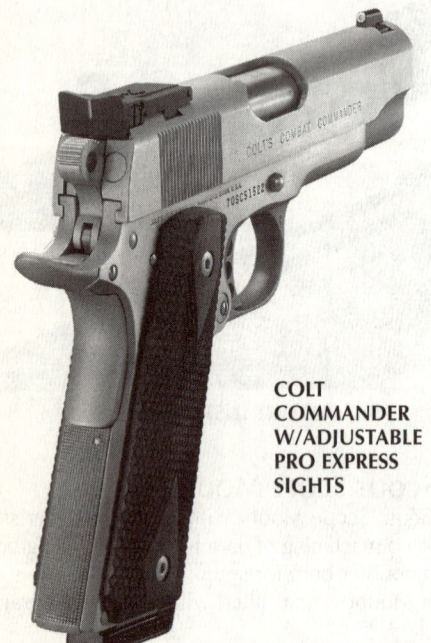

COLT COMMANDER W/ADJUSTABLE PRO EXPRESS SIGHTS

BIG DOT TRITIUM W/TRITIUM REAR

AO Pro Express Sights
Uses proven Express Sight Principle with Big Dot Tritium or Standard Dot Tritium Front Sight incorporating a vertical Tritium Bar within the Rear Express Sight. Enhanced low light sight acquisition with speed of Express Sight Principle. Rear sights available in double set-screw style for easier installation. From AO Sight Systems (formerly Ashley Outdoors).
**Prices: Pro Express Big Dot Tritium $120
Pro Express Standard Dot Tritium 120**

AO Express Sights
Extremely Fast Front Sight using proven Express Sight Principles. Low profile Shallow V Express rear with white vertical line, front white dot available with or without Tritium. Machined steel sights in matte black finish. Rear sight available in different heights. Made for most pistols, and limited styles of revolvers. Rear available in double set-screw for most installations. From AO Sight Systems (formerly Ashley Outdoors).
**Prices: Standard Dot Set. $60
Big Dot Set 60
Big Dot Tritium Set 90
Standard Dot Tritium Set 90**

AO Adjustable Express Sight Sets
Incorporates Adjustable Rear Express Sight with a white stripe rear, or Pro Express Rear with a Vertical Tritium Bar, fits Bomar style cut, LPA style cut, or a Kimber Target cut rear sight. Affords same Express Sight principles as fixed sight models. From AO Sight Systems (formerly Ashley Outdoors).
**Prices:
Adjustable Express w/White Stripe Rear and
  Big Dot Front or Standard Dot Front 120
Adjustable Express w/White Stripe Rear and
  Big Dot Tritium or Standard Dot Tritium Front 150
Adjustable Pro Express w/Tritium Rear and Big
  Dot Tritium or Standard Dot Tritium Front 150**

BSA Scopes

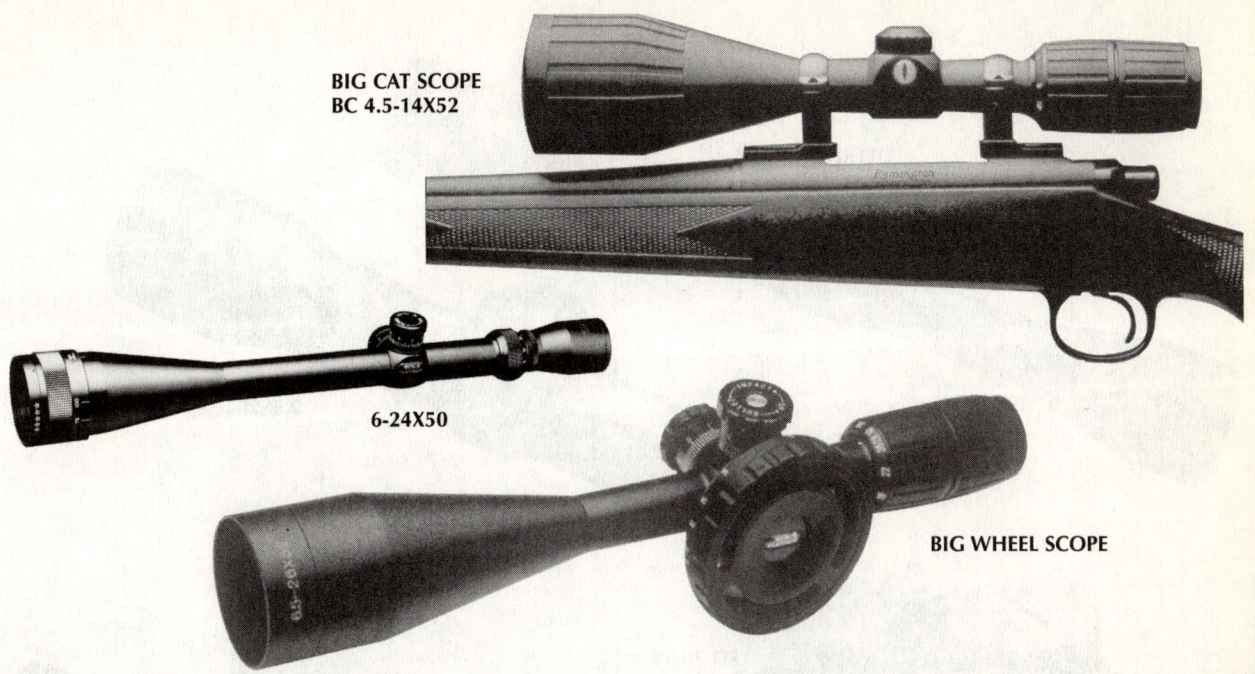

BIG CAT SCOPE
BC 4.5-14X52

6-24X50

BIG WHEEL SCOPE

BSA Scopes
The BSA name once reserved for superior rifles and motorcycles is now appearing on rifle scopes. The Catseye line, with multi-coated objective and ocular lenses and a European-style reticle for shooting in dim light, includes two new looks for 2001. The PowerBright has the features of a BSA Catseye plus a PowerBright reticle that lights up bright red against dark backgrounds. The Big Cat has all the features wanted in a hunting scope: long eye relief, fully multicoated, very bright three piece objective lens.

Prices: Catseye
1.5-4x32	$92
3-10x44	152
3.5-10x50	172
4-16x50 AO	192
6-24x50 AO	223

Bigcat
2-7x42	190
3.5-10x42	220
4.5-14x52 AO	250
1.5-4.5x42	220
3-9x42	250
3.5-10x42	270

Catseye Plus
1.5-4.5x32	122
3-10x44	172
3.5-10x50	192

BSA Catseye CE 6-24x50
SPECIFICATIONS
Magnification: 6x-24x **Objective Lens Diameter:** 50mm
Exit Pupil Range: 8.3-2.0 **Field of View at 100 yd:** 16'-3'
Optimum Eye Relief: 4.5" **Length/Weight:** 16"/23 oz.
Price: $223

Big Cat Scope BC 4.5-14x52
The Big Cat is an all new scope design, with a longer eye relief, finger adjustable windage, and elevation knobs. A three-piece objective lens system for sharper resolution, better color, and less distortion. And for extra brightness, the lenses are 14-layer, fully multi-coated. It is very compact and finished in Shadow Black. There are six BigCat models, 3 with large 30mm tubes.

BSA Platinum Target Scopes
BSA Platinum target scopes are fitted with finger-adjustable windage and elevation dials that move point of impact in 1/8-minute clicks. BSA's Big Wheel is for long distance shooting when parallax adjustments are extremely critical. It has a convenient sidewheel for extra-sensitive focusing. Actually the side wheel is two wheels in one. The larger outer wheel is best for off-hand or prone shooting, and the smaller wheel for benchrest. You just snap off the outer wheel to use the smaller focusing wheel. These new scopes are more compact than older models and have three-piece objective lens systems for sharper resolution, better color and less distortion.

SPECIFICATIONS
For **PT 6.5-26x52** • **Magnification:** 6.5x-26x **Objective lens Diameter:** 52mm **F.O.V. @ 100 yds:** 15'-3.5' **Eye Relief:** 4" **Weight:** 30 oz. **Tube:** 1"

Prices: PT 6-24x44 AO	222
PT 8-32x44 AO	242
PT 6.5-26x42 AO	300
PT 8.5-34x42 AO	330
PT 6.5-26x52 AO	330
PT 8.5-34x52 AO	400

BSA Scopes

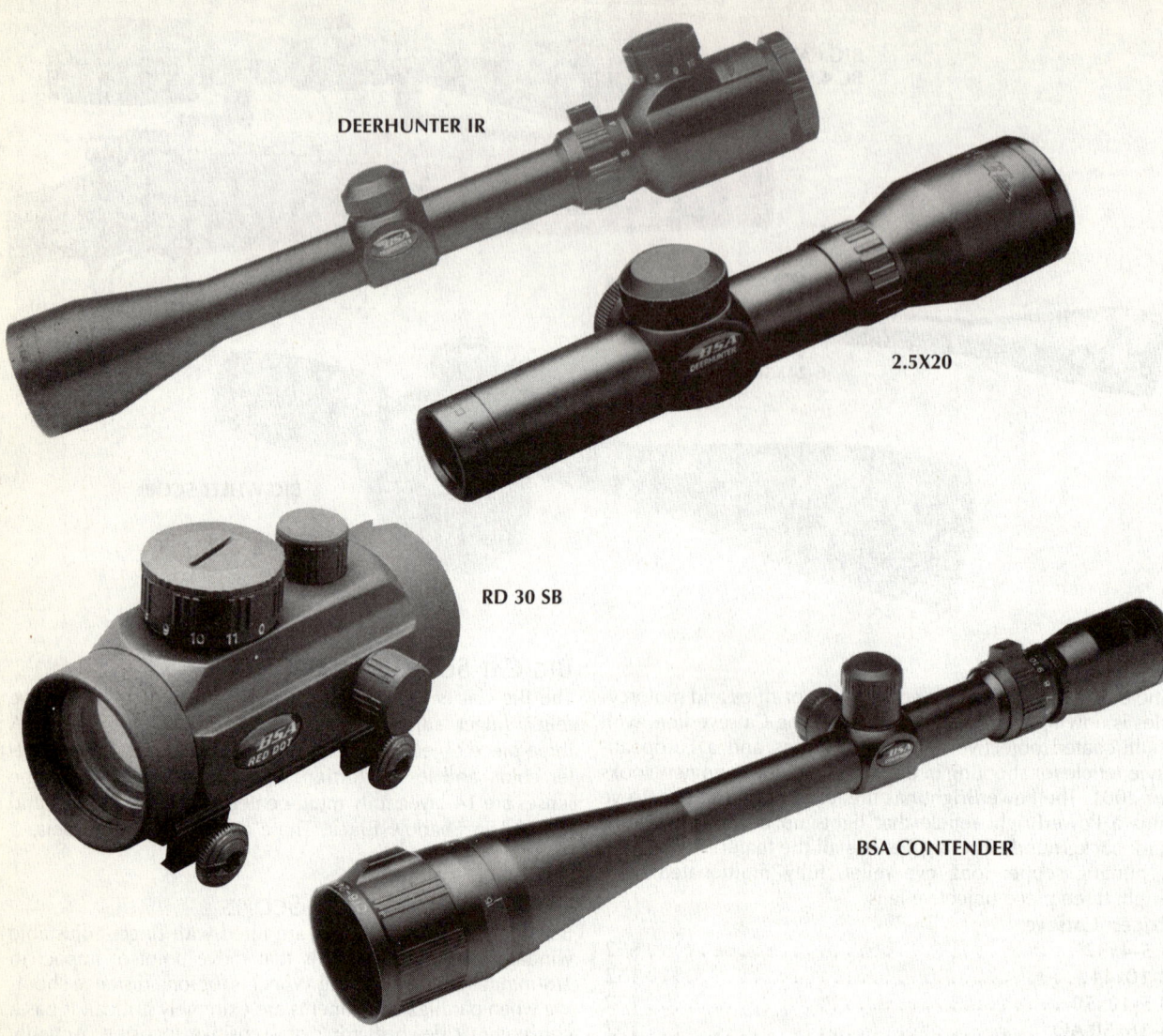

DEERHUNTER IR

2.5X20

RD 30 SB

BSA CONTENDER

BSA Deerhunter 3-9x40 Illuminated Reticle
SPECIFICATIONS
Magnification: 3x-9x **Objective Lens Diameter:** 40mm
Exit Pupil Range: 13.3-4.4 **Field of View at 100 yd:** 26'
Eye Relief: 4.5" **Weight:** 13 oz.
Price:.................................$130

BSA Deer Hunter scopes, from a 2.5x20 (shown) to a 3-9x50 offer value for the big game hunter on a budget.
Prices: from............................60 to 130

Red Dot Scope
Prices: RD30 (30mm black matte or silver).........60
RD30SB (30mm shadow black)................70
RD42 (42mm black matte)....................80
RD42SB (42mm shadow black)...............90
RD50SB (50mm shadow black)..............110

BSA Deerhunter DH 2.5x20
SPECIFICATIONS
Magnification: 2.5x Objective Lens Diameter: 20mm
Exit Pupil Range: 8 Field of View at 100 yd: 72'
Optimum Eye Relief: 6" Length/Weight: 7.5"/7.5 oz.
Price:.....................................$60

BSA Contender CT 6-24x40 TS
SPECIFICATIONS
Magnification: 6x-24x **Objective Lens Diameter:** 40mm
Exit Pupil Range: 6.7-1.7 **Field of View at 100 yd:** 16'-4'
Optimum Eye Relief: 3" **Length/Weight:** 15.5"/20 oz.
Price:......................................150
Also Available: 3-12x40.........................213
4-16x40......................................132
8-32x40......................................172
3-12x50......................................132
4-16x50......................................152
6-24x50......................................172
8-32x50......................................192

Burris Scopes
Black Diamond Riflescopes

BLACK DIAMOND T-PLATE

MODEL 3X-12X-50MM

New Black Diamond™ T-Plate Scopes
The popularity of Black Diamond scopes and T-Plate lens coating technology on Mr. T riflescopes created a significant number of requests to apply T-Plate to Black Diamond riflescopes. Available in 2.5x-10x and 4x-16x, these scopes are essentially the same as the Mr. T offering, except Black Diamonds are built on a foundation of 6061-T6 Aluminum instead of Titanium.

4x-16x Black Diamond
The Burris Black Diamond is designed for long-range big game rifles and dual-purpose big game/varmint rifles, it has a 50mm objective and Burris' best optics. It is available with the trajectory-compensating Ballistic Mil-Dot reticle. The heavy 30mm tube is notable for its ruggedness.

Burris's Black Diamond line includes three models of a 30mm main tube 3-12X50mm with various finishes, reticles, and adjustment knobs. These riflescopes have easy-to-grip rubber-armored parallax-adjust rings, an adjustable and resettable adjustment dial, and an internal focusing eyepiece.

SPECIFICATIONS
Models: 3-12X50mm/4-16x50/6-24x50/8-32x50
Field of View (feet @ 100yds.): 34'-12'/18-6
Optimum eye relief: 3.5"-4.0"/3.5-4
Exit Pupil: 13.7mm-4.2mm/7.6-2.1
Click adjust value (@ 100 yds.): .25"/.125
Max. internal adj. (@ 100 yds.): 100"/52
Clear objective diameter: 50mm/50mm
Ocular end diameter: 42mm/42mm
Weight: 25 oz./25 oz.
Length: 13.8"/16.2"
Reticles available: Plex, Mil-Dot, Ballistic MDot, and Fine Plex

4X-16X BLACK DIAMOND

BALLISTIC MIL-DOT

1X XER SCOUT

2.75X SCOUT

Scout Scopes
...for hunters who need a 7- to 14-inch eye relief for mounting in front of the ejection port; allows you to shoot with both eyes open. The 15-foot field of view and 2.75X magnification are ideal for brush guns and shotgunners. Rugged, reliable and fog proof.

Burris Speeddot 135
1x35mm pistol and shotgun sight. Electronic red dot reticle, 3 moa or 11 moa

BURRIS SPEEDDOT 135

Sights & Scopes • 397

Burris Riflescopes

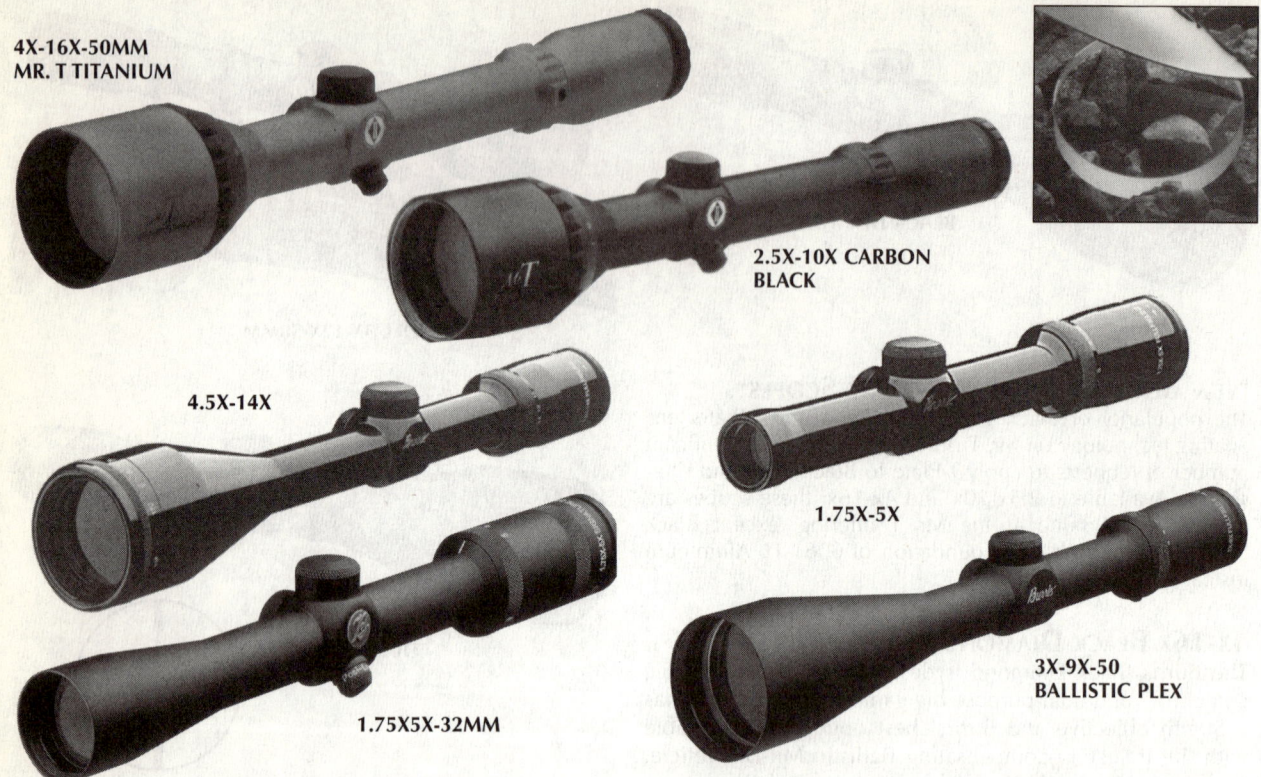

4X-16X-50MM MR. T TITANIUM

2.5X-10X CARBON BLACK

4.5X-14X

1.75X-5X

1.75X5X-32MM

3X-9X-50 BALLISTIC PLEX

Burris "Mr T" Titanium Black • Diamond Scopes

Substantially stronger than aluminum, and much lighter than steel, Mr. T is one scope worthy of the description 'tough'. Beyond the whole scope tube and eyepiece being made of solid titanium, each scope is coated with a nitride harder than carbide or hard chrome—such as titanium nitride, aluminum titanium nitride, or chrome nitride, depending on the color. These nitrides are molecularly bonded to the titanium through high intensity physical vapor deposition for maximum adhesion that will not blister, flake, or chip. The result is an ultra-hard (up to 85 Rockwell C), abrasion resistant surface. Also available in Autumn Gold.

New 1.75X-5X-32mm Signature™ Safari

A whole new optic system was designed to integrate a host of features into the ultimate riflescope for heavy brush country, for heavy recoiling dangerous game rifles, and for magnum slug shotguns. The new 1.75X-5X Signature Safari™ provides 3/4" additional eye relief to save your brow while shooting from awkward positions. The 32mm objective allows for ultra-flexibility in eye position. The eyepiece and power ring are combined into a single sturdy unit that makes changing magnifications faster. The Post and Crosshair reticle is the fastest and most instinctive reticle pattern available. Because of its size, shape, ruggedness, and lighter weight, the 1.75X-5X also makes a great scope for all the new short magnum rifles.

T-Plated Lenses

The toughness of this scope doesn't end with the metal work. The scratch-proof T-Plate coating applied to the objective and eyepiece lenses is remarkable. These lenses do not come with the warning of other "scratch-resistant" coatings about removing all dust before cleaning. T-plated lenses do not require a "soft clean lens cloth". Just knock the mud off the lens and wipe it clean with a dirty shirt tail. Ordinary dirt, dust, and grit won't touch it. This coating technology is prohibitively expensive for ordinary scopes. Mr. T is a premium - quality sight for discriminating hunters.

Burris Fullfield II Variable Scopes

The Fullfield II is now much more forgiving for eye positioning both fore and aft, and left and right. Burris has shaved roughly four ounces of weight on each model without effecting durability or optical performance. In fact, several areas are even stronger and more precisely fitted than before. Overall, the Fullfield is about one inch shorter than its predecessor for a more compact look and feel. Like the Fullfield, and unlike other scopes, Fullfield II eyepieces are sealed with special quad seals rather than old-tech O-rings. And the eyepiece is now part of the power ring. To change magnification, simply turn the entire eyepiece. A European-style adjustable eyepiece is easy to use and requires no locking mechanism. For 2002, Burris has added a 3X-9X-50mm to their Fullfield II line, as well as a fixed 6X for traditionalists, and a 6X-32mm HBRII for benchrest shooters.
Also available: 3.5-10x50, 4.5X-14X and 6.5-20x50

Burris Scopes
Signature Series

8X-32X SIGNATURE

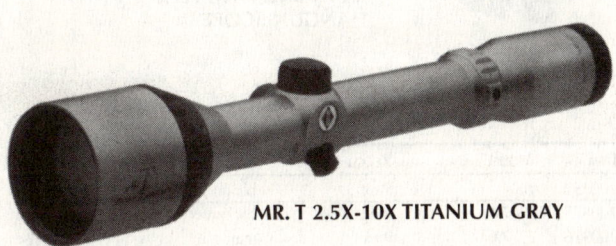
MR. T 2.5X-10X TITANIUM GRAY

MR. T 2.5X-10X CARBON BLACK

All models in the Signature Series have **Hi-Lume** (multi-coated) lenses for maximum light transmission. Many models also feature **Posi-Lock** to prevent recoil shift and protect against loss of zero from rough hunting use. It allows the shooter to lock the internal optics of the scope in position after the rifle has been sighted in.

NEW SIGNATURE SERIES SCOPES

Item	Model	Reticle	Finish	Features	List
200510	6X	Plex	blk		$442
200511	6X	Plex	mat		462
200700	1.5X-6X	Plex	blk		518
200701	1.5X-6X	Plex	mat		538
200706	1.5X-6X	Plex	mat	Posi-Lock	588
200711	1.5X-6X	Electro-Dot	mat		647
200550	2X-8X	Plex	blk		580
200554	2X-8X	Plex	mat	Posi-Lock	648
200600	3X-9X	Plex	blk		611
200601	3X-9X	Plex	mat		631
200597	3X-9X	Plex	blk	Posi-Lock	660
200598	3X-9X	Plexmat		Posi-Lock	680
200580	3X-9X	Electro-Dot	blk		721
200581	3X-9X	Electro-Dot	mat		741
200590	3X-9X	Electro-Dot	blk	Posi-Lock	771
200591	3X-9X	Electro-Dot	mat	Posi-Lock	791
200574	3X-9X-50mm	Plex	blk		645
200607	2.5X-10X	Plex	blk	PA	647
200631	2.5X-10X	Plex	mat	Posi-Lock/PA	728
200614	3X-12X	Plex	blk	Posi-Lock/PA	704
200707	1.75X-5X-Safari	Taper Plex	mat	-	$601
200708	1.75X-5X-Safari	Taper Plex	mat	Posi-Lock	649
200709	1.75X-5X-Safari	Post Crosshair	mat	Posi-Lock	667
200603	3X-9X	Ballistic Plex	mat	-	640
200817	6X-24X	Plex	blk	Target/PA	757
200750	4X-16X	Plex	blk	PA	738
200751	4X-16X	Plex	mat	PA	757
200767	4X-16X	Ballistic MDot	mat	PA	887
200756	4X-16X	Plex	mat	Posi-Lock/PA	810
200765	4X-16X	Electro-Dot	mat	PA	861
200766	4X-16X	Electro-Dot	mat	Posi-Lock/PA	914
200800	6X-24X	Plex	blk	PA	757
200804	6X-24X	Plex	mat	PA	776

Item	Model	Reticle	Finish	Features	List
200803	6X-24X	Fine Plex	blk	Target/PA	$795
200806	6X-24X	Fine Plex	mat	Target/PA	814
200811	6X-24X	Fine Plex	nic	Target/PA	823
200816	6X-24X	Ballistic MDot	mat	Target/PA	947
200813	6X-24X	Plex	mat	Posi-Lock/PA	831
200850	8X-32X	Fine Plex	blk	Target/PA	814
200860	8X-32X	Fine Plex	mat	Target/PA	833
200866	8X-32X	Fine Plex	nic	Target/PA	842
200861	8X-32X	Ballistic MDot	mat	Target/PA	965

MR. T BLACK DIAMOND TITANIUM SCOPES (30mm)

200920	2.5X-10X-50mm	Plex	titanium gray		$1,786
200922	2.5X-10X-50mm	Mil-Dot	carbon black	Target	1,786
200923	2.5X-10X-50mm	Plex	carbon black	Posi-Lock	1,875
200924	2.5X-10X-50mm	Plex	autumn gold		1,786

NEW MR. T BLACK DIAMOND

200928	4X-16X-50mm	Plex	titanium gray	PA	$1,875
200956	4X-16X-50mm	Ballistic MDot	titanium gray	PA	1,964

NEW BLACK DIAMOND T-PLATES SCOPES (30mm)

200912	2.5X-10X-55mm	Plex	mat	PA	$1,165
200956	4X-16X-50mm	Ballistic MDot	mat	PA	1,351

BLACK DIAMOND SCOPES (30mm)

200906	6X-50mm	Plex	mat		$745
200900	3X-12X-50mm	Plex	mat	PA	960
200901	3X-12X-50mm	Plex	mat	Posi-Lock/PA	1,031
200911	3X-12X-50mm	Mil-Dot	mat	Target/PA	1,123
200950	4X-16X-50mm	Plex	mat	PA	933
200951	4X-16X-50mm	Ballistic Dot	mat	PA	1,084
200952	4X-16X-50mm	Plex	mat	Posi-Lock/PA	1,000
200953	4X-16X-50mm	Ballistic Dot	mat	Posi-Lock/PA	1,155
200930	6X-24X-50mm	Fine Plex	mat	Target/PA	1,041
200931	6X-24X-50mm	Mil-Dot	mat	Target/PA	1,202
200932	6X-24X-50mm	Ballistic MDot	mat	Target/PA	1,202
200940	8X-32X-50mm	Fine Plex	mat	Target/PA	1,091
200941	8X-32X-50mm	Ballistic MDot	mat	Target/PA	1,272

ELECTRO-DOT SCOPES

200167	3X-9X Fullfield II	Electro-Dot	mat		$506
200711	1.5X-6X Signature	Electro-Dot	mat		647
200712	1.5X-6X Signature	Electro-Dot	mat	Posi-Lock	697
200581	3X-9X Signature	Electro-Dot	mat		741
200590	3X-9X Signature	Electro-Dot	blk	Posi-Lock	771
200591	3X-9X Signature	Electro-Dot	mat	Posi-Lock	791
200765	4X-16X Signature	Electro-Dot	mat	PA	861
200766	4X-16X Signature	Electro-Dot	mat	Posi-Lock/PA	914

Burris Scopes

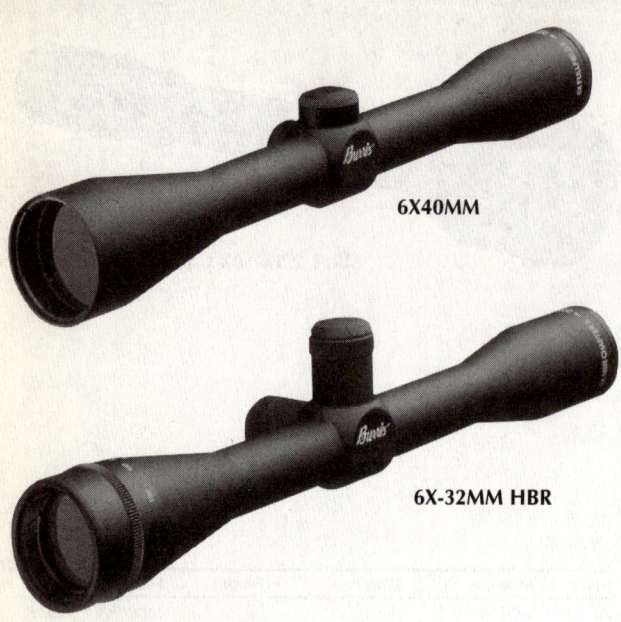

6X40MM

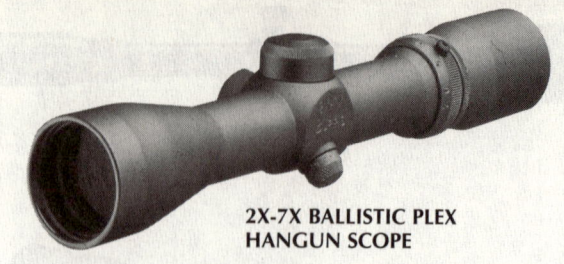

2X-7X BALLISTIC PLEX HANGUN SCOPE

6X-32MM HBR

Fullfield II™ Scopes
Fixed Power with Hi-Lume Lenses

FULLFIELD II SCOPES

Item	Model	Reticle	Finish	Features	List
200052	6X-40mm	Plex	mat	-	$379
200055	6X-32mm HBRII	Fine Plex	mat	Target/PA	488
200056	6X-32mm HBRII	.375 Dot	mat	Target/PA	527
200153	3X-9X-50mm	Plex	mat	-	472
200154	3X-9X-50mm	Ballistic Plex	mat	-	481
200086	1.75-5X	Plex	blk		$392
200087	1.75-5X	Plex	mat		412
200160	3X-9X-40mm	Plex	blk		392
200161	3X-9X-40mm	Plex	mat		392
200162	3X-9X-40mm	Ballistic Plex	mat		401
200163	3X-9X-40mm	Plex	nic		422
200167	3X-9X-40mm	Electro-Dot	mat		506
200170	3.5X-10X-50mm	Plex	blk		531
200171	3.5X-10X-50mm	Plex	mat		550
200172	3.5X-10X-50mm	Ballistic Plex	mat		559
200180	4.5X-14X	Plex	blk	PA	572
200181	4.5X-14X	Plex	mat	PA	572
200182	4.5X-14X	Fine Plex	mat	PA	591
200183	4.5X-14X-42mm	Ballistic Plex	mat	PA	591
200190	6.5X-20X-50mm	Fine Plex	blk	PA	644
200191	6.5X-20X-50mm	Fine Plex	mat	PA	661
200192	6.5X-20X-50mm	Fine Plex	mat	Target/PA	701
200193	6.5X-20X-50mm	Ballistic MDot	mat	PA	792

FULLFIELD SCOPES

200413	2.5X shotgun	Plex	mat		$308
200014	4X	Plex	mat		348
200054	6X	Plex	mat		379
200103	6X-18X	Fine Plex	blk	PA	543
200109	6X-18X	Fine Plex	mat	PA	562
200104	6X-18X	Fine Plex	blk	Target/PA	580

COMPACT SCOPES

200424	1X XER	Plex	mat		$319
200310	4X	Plex	blk		298
200311	4X	Plex	mat		319

Item	Model	Reticle	Finish	Features	List
200352	6X	Plex	blk	PA	$359
200375	2X-7X	Plex	blk		404
200376	2X-7X	Plex	mat		424
200387	3X-9X	Plex	mat		434
200388	3X-9X	Plex	nic		445
200384	3X-9X	Plex	mat	PA	443
200390	4X-12X	Plex	blk	PA	520
200395	4X-12X	Plex	mat	PA	527
200393	4X-12X	Fine Plex	blk	Target/PA	559
200394	4X-12X	Fine Plex	mat	Target/PA	578

RIMFIRE/AIRGUN SCOPES

200352	6X	Plex	blk	PA	$359
200384	3X-9X	Plex	mat	PA	443
200390	4X-12X	Plex	blk	PA	520
200395	4X-12X	Plex	mat	PA	527
200393	4X-12X	Fine Plex	blk	Target/PA	559
200394	4X-12X	Fine Plex	mat	Target/PA	578
200858	8X-32X	Plex	blk	Target/PA	835
200859	8X-32X	Fine Plex	mat	Target/PA	854

HANDGUN SCOPES

200299	2X-7X	Ballistic Plex	mat	Posi-Lock	$520
200309	3X-12X	Ballistic Plex	mat	PA	577
200424	1X XER	Plex	mat		$319
200220	2X	Plex	blk		281
200218	2X	Plex	mat		275
200229	2X	Plex	nic		301
200228	2X	Plex	mat	Posi-Lock	330
200235	4X	Plex	blk		333
200263	10X Target/PA	Plex	blk	Target	507
200214	1.5X-4X	Plex	nic		404
200207	1.5X-4X	Plex	mat	Posi-Lock	442
200213	1.5X-4X	Plex	nic	Posi-Lock	443
200290	2X-7X	Plex	blk		451
200291	2X-7X	Plex	mat		461
200293	2X-7X	Plex	blk	PA	499
200298	2X-7X	Plex	nic		472
200294	2X-7X	Plex	blk	Posi-Lock	492
200297	2X-7X	Plex	nic	Posi-Lock	513
200288	3X-9X	Plex	blk	Posi-Lock/PA	540
200306	3X-12X	Plex	blk	PA	550
200307	3X-12X	Plex	mat	PA	560
200308	3X-12X	Plex	blk	PA	569
200305	3X-12X	Fine Plex	blk	Target/PA	561
200303	3X-12X	Plex	mat	Posi-Lock	599

SPEEDDOT 135 SIGHTS

300200	1X-35mm	3 MOA Dot	mat	$291
300201	1X-35mm	11 MOA Dot	mat	291

SCOUT SCOPES

200424	1X XER	Plex	mat	$319
200269	2.75X	Heavy Plex	mat	342

Bushnell Riflescopes

ELITE 3200 — 5X-15X

ELITE 3200 RIFLESCOPES WITH RAINGUARD

Model	Special Feature	Actual Magnification	Obj. Lens Aperature (mm)	Field of View @ 100yds (ft.)	Weight (oz)	Length	Eye Relief (in.)	Exit Pupil (mm)	Click Value @ 100yds (in.)	Adjust Range @ 100yds (in.)	Selection	Suggested Retail
32-1040	Mil Dot Reticle, Target Turrets	10x	40	11	15.5	11.7	3.5	4	.25	100		$320
32-2632M	Handgun (32-2632S Silver Finish)	2x-6x	32	10-4	10	9	20	16-5.3	.25	50	Constant 20" eye relief at all powers w/max. recoil resistance	445
32-2732M	Matte Finish	2x-7x	32	44.6-12.7	12	11.6	3	12.2-4.6	.25	50	Compact variable for close-in brush or med. range shooting. Excellent for shotguns	304
32-3940G	(32-3940M Matte Finish, 32-3940S Silver Finish)	3x-9x	40	33.8-11.5	13	12.6	3.3	13.3-4.4	.25	50	For the full range of hunting. From varmint to big game. Tops in versatility.	320
32-3943	Matte, 3-2-1 low light reticle	3x-9x	40	33.8-11.5	13	12.6	3.3	13.3-4.4	.25	50	All types of hunting	320
32-3944M	Fast-Focus Eyepiece	3x-9x	40	33.8-11.5	13	12.6	3.3	13.3-4.4	.25	50	For the full range of hunting. From varmint to big game. Tops in versatility.	320
32-3945M	Fast-Focus Eyepiece	3x-9x	50	31.5-10-5	19	15.7	3.3	16-5.6	.25	50	All purpose variable with extra brightness.	383
32-3950M	Matte	3x-9x	50	31.5-10-5	19	15.7	3.3	16-5.6	.25	50	All purpose variable with extra brightness.	383
32-3955E	European Reticle Matte Finish	3x-9x	50	31.5-10.5	22	15.6	3.3	16-5.6	.36	70	Large exit pupil and 30mm tube for max. brightness.	641
32-3953	Matte, 3-2-1 low light reticle	3x-9x	50	31.5-10.5	19	15.7	3.3	16-5.6	.25	50	All purpose, extra bright	383
32-4124A	Adjustable Objective	4x-12x	40	26.9-9	15	13.2	3.3	10-3.33	.25	50	Medium to long-range variable makes a superb choice for varmint or big game	470
32-5154M	Matte adj. objective sunshade	5x-15x	40	21-7	19	14.5	4.3	9-2.7	.25	50	Long range, big game	502
32-5155M	Adjustable Objective	5x-15x	50	21-7	19	15.9	3.4	10-3.3	.25	40	Large objective for brightness	529

ELITE 4200 — 2.5-10X40

ELITE 4200

ELITE™ 4200 RIFLESCOPES WITH RAINGUARD™

Model	Special Feature	Actual Magnification	Obj. Lens Aperature (mm)	Field of View @ 100yds (ft.)	Weight (oz)	Length	Eye Relief (in.)	Exit Pupil (mm)	Click Value @ 100yds (in.)	Adjust Range @ 100yds (in.)	Selection	Suggested Retail
42-1636M	Matte Finish	1.5x-6x	36	61.8-16.1	15.4	12.8	3	14.6-6	.25	60	Compact wide angle for close-in & brush hunting. Max. brightness. Excel. for shotguns	$609
42-2104G	(42-2104M Matte Finish, 42-2104S Silver Finish)	2.5x-10x	40	41.5-10.8	16	13.5	3	15.6-4	.25	50	All purpose hunting scope w/4x zoom range for close-in brush & long range shooting	643
42-2105M	Matte Finish	2.5x-10x	50	40-10.8	18	14.3	3.5	15-2.5	.25	50	Ideal hunting and all purpose	764
42-2151M	Illum 1 Dot Reticle	2.5x-10x	50	40-10.8	18	14.3	3.5	15-2.5	.25	50	Ideal hunting and all purpose	799
42-4164M	Matte Adjustable Obj Sunshade	4x-16x	40	26-7	18.6	14.4	3.5	10-25	.25	40		646
42-4165M	Matte Finish	4x-16x	50	26-7.2	22	15.6	3	12.5-3.1	.25	50	The ultimate varmint, airgun and precision shooting scope. Parallax focus from 10 meter to infinity.	835
42-6244M	Adjustable Objective, Sunshade Matte	6x-24x	40	18-4.5	20.2	16.9	3	6.7-1.7	.125	26	Varmint, target & silhouette long range shooting and airgun. Parallax focus adjust. for pinpoint accuracy. Parallax focus from 10 meter to infinity.	730
42-6243A	Adjustable Objective and 1/4" MOA dot reticle	6-24x	40	18-4.5	20.2	16.9	3	6.7-1.7	.125	26	Varmint, target and silhouette long range shooting and airgun. Parallax focus adjust for pinpoint accuracy. Parallax focus from 10 meter to infinity.	730
42-6242M	Matte w/Mil Dot	6x-24x	40	18-6	20.2	16.9	3	6.7-1.7	.125	26	Long range varmint or target	753
42-8324M	Matte finish, adj. objective sunshade	8x-32x	40	14-3.75	22	18	4-3.5	5-1.25	.125	20	Long range varmint, bench	803

Sights & Scopes • 401

Bushnell Riflescopes

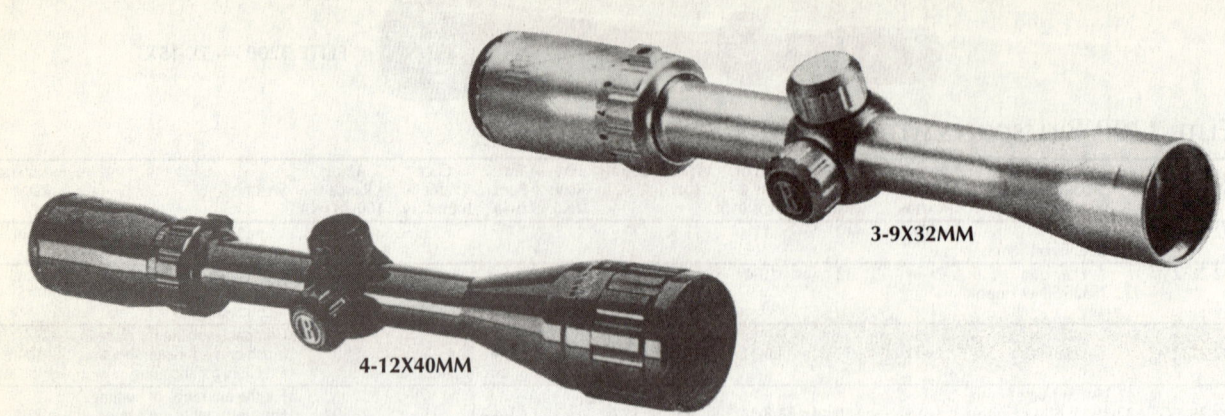

3-9X32MM

4-12X40MM

SPORTSMAN RIFLESCOPES

Sportsman Riflescopes have multi-coated optics, plus a long list of standard features, including a fast-focus eyepiece and 1/4 M.O.A. fingertip windage and elevation adjustments. The easy-grip power change ring makes changing magnifications fast and easy. The rigid one-piece 1" tube is waterproof, fogproof and shockproof.

3-9x32mm: Gloss, 72-1393; Silver, 72-1393S; Matte, 72-

BUSHNELL SPORTSMAN® RIFLESCOPES

Model	Finish	Features/Selection	Actual Magnification	Obj. Lens Aperture (mm)	Field of View Ft@100 yds	Weight (oz)	Length (in)	Eye Relief (in)	Exit Pupil (mm)	Click Value In@100yds	Adj. Range In@100yds	Price
72-0004	G	Adjustable Objective. Rings. General Purpose for Air Rifle and Rimfire Range Focus and Target Adjustments. 10yd-Infinity.	4x	32	29.5	13.7	11.9	3	8	.25	90	$99
72-0038		For High-Velocity Break Barrel Airguns. 50 Feet Parallax Setting	3x-9x	32	37 14	13.5	12	3.5	10.6-3.6	.25	100	80
72-0039	G	Adjustable Objective. Rings. Air Rifle, Rimfire with Range Focus Adjustments 10yd-Infinity.	3x-9x	32	13.1	163	12.2	3	3.6-11	.25	100	117
72-0130	M	Red Dot Sight. 6 M.O.A. Dot. Ideal for Handgun, Shotgun and Competitive Shooting.	1x	23	60	4.9	5.5	Unlimited	2.3@1x	.5	50	85
720-0412	G	Adjustable Objective. Long Range.	4x-12x	40	8.5 25.8	14.6	13.75	3	10-3.3	.25	90	142
72-1393 72-1393S 72-1398	G S M	All-Purpose Variable	3x-9x	32	14 41	13.5	12	3	10-3.6	.25	100	69
72-1403	M	General Purpose	4x	32	29	11	11.7	3	8	.25	110	58
72-1416	G	3/4"Tube with Rings. Airgun/ .22 Scope. Coated Optics	4x	15	17	3.6	10.7	3.5	3.8	Friction	60	12
72-1545	M	Shotgun/Muzzle Loader. Low Power Variable Ideal for Close-In or Medium-Range Shooting.	1.5x-4.5x	21	24 69	11.7	10.1	3	10-3.6	.25	210	87
72-1548	M	Circle-X Reticle. Turkey Hunting Shotgun Slugs and Muzzle Loading.	1.5x-4.5x	32	19.3 46.2	13.5	11.7	3	7.1-123	.25	100	105
72-3720	G	3/4" Tube with Rings. Airgun/ .22 Scope. Coated Optics	3x-7x	20	11 23	5.7	11.3	2.6	6.7-2.9	Friction	50	37
72-3940 72-3940M	G M	Excellent for Use at Any Range.	3x-9x	40	12 37	15	13	3.5	13-4.4	.25	100	96
72-3943	M	3-2-1 Low-Light Reticle. Improved Crosshair Visibility for Low-Light Shooting.	3x-9x	40	12 37	15	13	3.5	13-4.4	.25	100	96

Bushnell Riflescopes

3X-9X (40MM) TROPHY® WIDE ANGLE RIFLESCOPE

Bushnell Trophy® Riflescopes

Model	Special Feature	Actual Magnification	Obj. Lens Aperature (mm)	Field of View @ 100yds (ft.)	Weight (oz)	Length	Eye Relief (in.)	Exit Pupil (mm)	Click Value @ 100yds (in.)	Adjust Range @ 100yds (in.)	Selection	Suggested Retail
73-0131	Red Dot Sight 6 M.O.A. Dot	1x	28	68	6	5.5	-	28	.5	50	Ideal for handgun, shotgun, competitive	$103
73-0134	Red Dot Sight w/ 4 Dial in Reticles	1x	28	68	6	5.5	Unlimited	28	.5	50	Handgun and Shotgun	137
73-1500	Wide Angle	1.75x-5x	32	68-23	12.3	10.8	3.5	18.3-1.75x	.25	120	Shotgun, black powder or centerfire. Close-in brush hunting.	178
73-3940	Wide angle (73-3940S Silver)	3x-9x	40	42/14-14/5	13.2	11.7	3	13.3-4.44	.25	60	All purpose variable, excellent for use from close to long range. Circular view provides a definite advantage over "TV screen" type scopes for running game uphill or down.	160
73-3942	Long mounting length designed for long-action rifles	3x-9x	42	42-14	13.8	12	3	14-4.7	.25	40	7" mounting length.	165
73-3946	All Purpose Mil Dot Reticle	3x-9x	40	42	13.2	11.7	3.4	13.3	.25	60		171
73-3949	Wide angle with Circle-x™ Reticle	3x-9x	40	42-14	13.2	11.7	3	13.3-4.4	.25	60	Matte finish, Ideal low light reticle.	171
73-3948	Matte finish Wide Angle	3x-9x	40	42-14	13.2	11.7	3	13.3-4.4	.25	60	Ideal for game running uphill or down	160
73-4124	Wide angle, adjustable objective (73-4124M Matte)	4x-12x	40	32-11	16.1	12.6	3	10-3.3	.25	60	Medium to long range variable for varmint and big game. Range focus adjustment. Excellent air riflescope.	301
73-6184	Semi-turret target adjustments, adjustable objective	6x-18x	40	17.3-6	17.9	14.8	3	6.6-2.2	.125	40	Long-range varmint centerfire or short range air rifle target precision accuracy.	379

TROPHY® HANDGUN SCOPES

Model	Special Feature	Actual Magnification	Obj. Lens Aperature (mm)	Field of View @ 100yds (ft.)	Weight (oz)	Length	Eye Relief (in.)	Exit Pupil (mm)	Click Value @ 100yds (in.)	Adjust Range @ 100yds (in.)	Selection	Suggested Retail
73-0232S	(73-0232S Silver)	2x	32	20	7.7	8.7	9	16	.25	90	Designed for target and short to med. range hunting. Magnum recoil resistant.	219
73-2632	(73-2632S Silver)	2x-6x	32	11-4	10.9	9.1	18	16-5.3	.25	50	18 inches of eye relief at all powers	288

TROPHY® SHOTGUN/HANDGUN SCOPES

Model	Special Feature	Actual Magnification	Obj. Lens Aperature (mm)	Field of View @ 100yds (ft.)	Weight (oz)	Length	Eye Relief (in.)	Exit Pupil (mm)	Click Value @ 100yds (in.)	Adjust Range @ 100yds (in.)	Selection	Suggested Retail
73-1421	Brush Scope/Turkey with Circle-x™ Reticle	1.75x-4x	32	73-30	10.9	10.8	3.5	18-8	.25	120	Ideal for turkey hunting, slug guns or blackpowder guns. Matte finish.	172

TROPHY® AIR RIFLESCOPES

Model	Special Feature	Actual Magnification	Obj. Lens Aperature (mm)	Field of View @ 100yds (ft.)	Weight (oz)	Length	Eye Relief (in.)	Exit Pupil (mm)	Click Value @ 100yds (in.)	Adjust Range @ 100yds (in.)	Selection	Suggested Retail
73-4124	Wide angle, adjustable objective (73-4124M Matte)	4x-12x	40	32-11	16.1	12.6	3	10-3.3	.25	60	Medium to long range variable for varmint and big game. Range focus adjustment. Excellent air riflescope.	301
73-6184	Semi-turret target adjustments, adjustable objective	6x-18x	40	17-6	17.9	14.8	3	6.6-2.2	.125	40	Long-range varmint centerfire or short range air rifle target precision accuracy.	379

Sights & Scopes

Bushnell Riflescopes

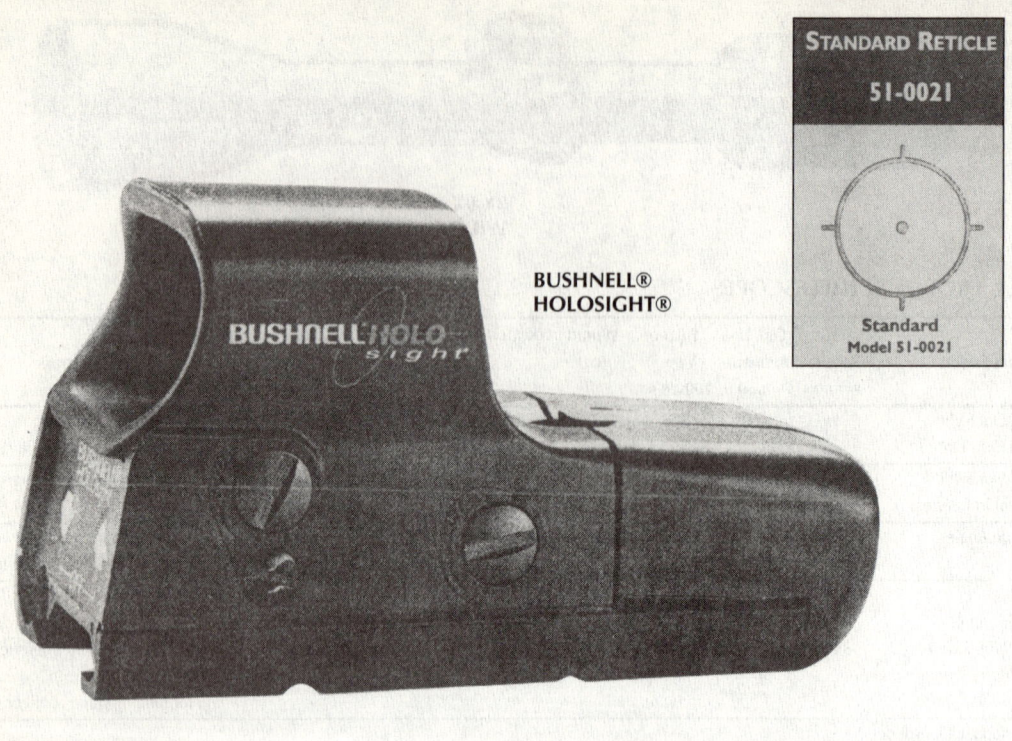

BUSHNELL®
HOLOSIGHT®

Bushnell® HOLOsight®

The BUSHNELL® HOLOsight® is the world's fastest sight. Advanced holographic technology lets you zero in on your target as quickly as you raise your firearm. Unlike conventional sights, HOLOsight® projects the appearance of an illuminated crosshair 50 yards in front of your gun, yet no forward light is projected. Sight from any distance behind the gun - without taking both eyes off the target. Offers unlimited field of view and eye relief. Shockproof, waterproof and fogproof. Half the length and weight of conventional scopes. Fits easily on handguns, shotguns and rifles with a standard Weaver® style mount. Uses 2 common N batteries.

Bushnell Holosight® Specifications

Optics	Magnification @ 100 yds	Field of View ft @ 100 yds	Weight (oz/g)	Length (in/mm)	Eye Relief (in/mm)	Batteries	Windage Click value in @100 yds mm@ 100m	Elevation Click Value in @100 yds mm@ 100m	Brightness adjustment settings
Holographic	1x	Unlimited	6.4/181	4.125/104.8	1/2" to 10 ft. 13 to 3045 mm	2 Type N 1.5 Volt	.25 M.O.A./ 7mm @100m	.5 M.O.A./ 14mm@100m	20 levels

Model	Reticle	Description			Uses				
HOLOsight®									
51-0021	Standard	2-Dimensional 65 M.O.A. ring with one M.O.A. dot and tick marks.			General all-purpose handguns, rifles, slug guns, and wing shooting				$445

Bushnell Riflescopes

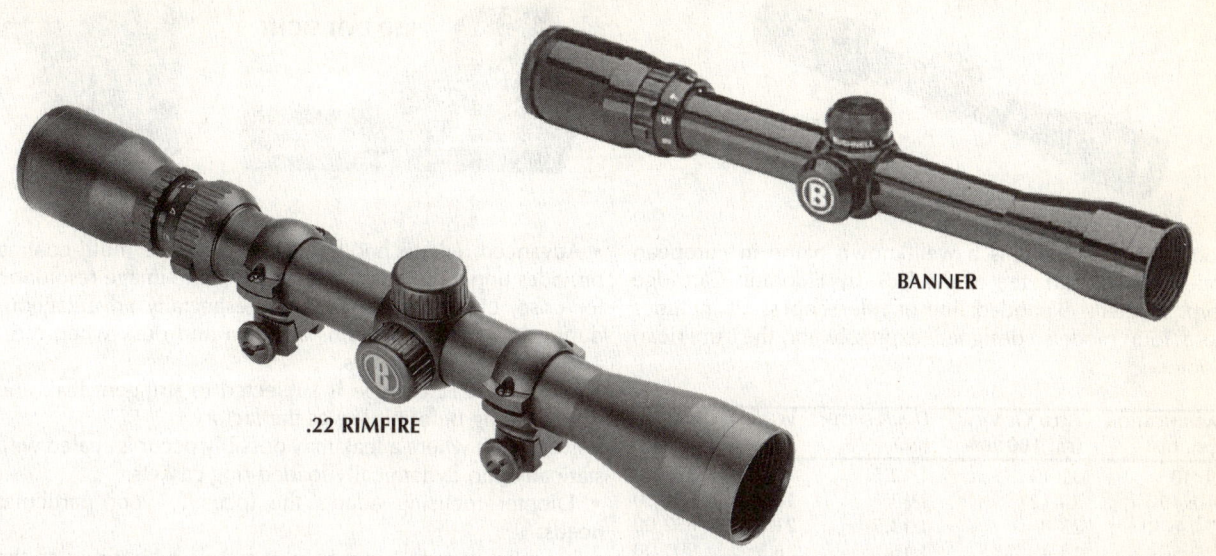

.22 RIMFIRE

BANNER

.22 RIMFIRE
Bushnell .22 Rimfire scopes are designed specifically for .22 Rimfire rifles, with 50-yard parallax setting. Includes rings, fully coated optics for low-light shooting and easy-grip power change ring. One-piece 1" tube is waterproof and fogproof. 1/4 M.O.A. fingertip windage and elevation adjustments.

BANNER
Banner Dusk & Dawn riflescopes feature DDB multi-coated lenses to maximize dusk and dawn brightness for clarity in low and full light. A fast-focus eyepiece and wide-angle field of view focus on and follow game easily. One-piece tube for durability under all conditions. Features 1/4" M.O.A. fingertip resettable windage and elevation adjustments. An easy-grip power change ring allows fast and easy zoom changes. Fully waterproof, fogproof and shockproof.

.22 RIMFIRE

MODEL	SPECIAL FEATURES	ACTUAL MAGNIFICATION	OBJ. LENS APERATURE (MM)	FIELD OF VIEW FT @ 100YDS/M	WEIGHT (OZ/G)	LENGTH (IN/MM)	EYE RELIEF (IN/MM)	EYE PUPIL (MM)	CLICK VALUE IN @ 100YDS MM @ 100M	ADJUST RANGE IN @ 100 YDS M@ 100M	SELECTION	SUGGESTED RETAIL
76-2239	Multix Reticle w/ rings	3x-9x	32	40	11.2	11.75	3	10.6-3.6	.25	40		$62
76-2243	Multix Reticle w/ rings	4	32	30	10	11.5	3	8	.25	40		53

BUSHNELL BANNER RIFLESCOPES

MODEL	SPECIAL FEATURES	ACTUAL MAGNIFICATION	OBJ. LENS APERATURE (MM)	FIELD OF VIEW FT @ 100YDS/M	WEIGHT (OZ/G)	LENGTH (IN/MM)	EYE RELIEF (IN/MM)	EYE PUPIL (MM)	CLICK VALUE IN @ 100YDS MM @ 100M	ADJUST RANGE IN @ 100 YDS M@ 100M	SELECTION	SUGGESTED RETAIL
71-0432	Shotgun/.22 scope Circle-x reticle, matte finish	4x	32	31.5	11.1	11.3	3.5	8	.25	50	Ideal for .22S/shotgun	$103
71-1432	Circle-x reticle Matte finish	1x-4x	32	78.5-24.9	12.2	10.5	3.8	16.9	.25	50	Ideal for .22S/shotgun	124
71-1545	Wide Angle	1.5x-4.5x	32	67-23	10.5	10.5	3.5	17-7	.25	60	Ideal Shotgun and median to short range scope.	117
71-4228	Compact .22 w/rings	4x	20	26.5	10	11.75	3.5	5	.25	60	small game and varmints	82
71-3944	Black powder scope w/extended eye relief and Circle-x@ reticle	3x-9x	40	36-13	12.5	11.5	4	13-4.4	.25	60	Specifically designed for black powder and shotguns	126
71-3948	Ideal scope for multi purpose guns	3x-9x	40	40-74	13	12	3	13.3-4.4	.25	60	General purpose	121
71-3950	Large objective for extra brightness in low light	3x-9x	50	31-10	19	16	3	16-5.6	.25	50	Low light conditions	187
71-3951	Matte finish low light reticle	3x-9x	50	26-12	19	16	3.5	16-5.6	.25	50	Good for low-light	187
71-4124	Adjustable objective	4x-12x	40	29-11	15	12	3	10-3.3	.25	60	Ideal scope for long-range shooting.	158
71-6185	Adjustable objective	6x-18x	50	17-6	18	16	3	8.3-2.8	.25	40	Long range varmint and target scope.	210

Docter Sports Optics

3-10 X 40MM

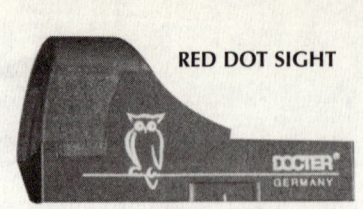

RED DOT SIGHT

Docter Sports Optics is a well-known name in European optics that is marketed in the U.S. by Eldorado Cartridge Corp. Docter's expanded line of rifle scopes. It includes these four models, designed expressly for the American shooter.

Magnification x obj. dia.	Field Of View (ft., 100 yds)	Dia./Length (in.)	Weight (oz.)	Price
3-9x40	31-13	1/12.5	17	$378.00
3-10x40	34-12	1/13	18.5	626.00
4.5-14x40	23-8	1/13.5	21.5	652.00
8-25x50	13-4	1/16	26.5	901.00

Some of Docter Optic 30mm scopes feature aspherical lenses, as do the company's binoculars. All Docter scopes offer these advantages:

RIFLE SCOPE SPECIFICATIONS
• High strength, one-piece tube construction of aircraft-grade aluminum eliminates weak screw-together joints that can leak or break, won't rust or corrode in adverse weather.
• Precise click-stop adjustments of 1/4" at 100 yards for windage and elevation. Wide range of adjustment (50") makes it easier to compensate for mounting errors. Excellent repeatability.
• Advanced lens technology and high grade multi-coating provides unparalled light transmission and image resolution for crisp, clear sighting picture - especially advantageous during low light conditions at dawn and dusk when most animal movement occurs.
• Every DOCTER scope is subjected to stringent leak and shock testing before it leaves the factory.
• Every joint where a leak may possibly occur is sealed with statically and dynamically loaded ring gaskets.
• Diopter focusing adapts the focus to your particular needs.
• Eye relief of over 3 inches, plus a wide rubber ring on the eye-piece protects the shooter from half-moon cuts, even with heavy calibers.

Doctor Red Dot Sight
A red dot sight is now available from Docter Sports Optics. Weighing just one ounce, it is not much bulkier than a standard rear sight, yet it offers the advantage of a single sighting plane. A red dot appears to project itself on the target—there's nothing to line up. You can shoot more quickly than with any other type of sight. Coated, high-quality lenses ensure a clear sight picture. There is no battery switch; batteries last up to five years without rest. Available in 3.5 or 7 M.D.A.

ONE-INCH TUBE SCOPES				
Description	Magnification	Objective Lens Dia.	Color	Reticle
3-9 x 40 Variable	3x to 9x	40 mm	Matte Black	Plex
3-9 x 40 Variable	3x to 9x	40 mm	Matte Black	German #4
3-10 x 40 Variable	3x to 10x	40 mm	Matte Black	Plex
3-10 x 40 Variable	3x to 10x	40 mm	Matte Black	German #4
4.5-14 x 40 Variable	4.5x to 14x	40 mm	Matte Black	Plex
4.5-14 x 40 Variable	4.5x to 14x	40 mm	Matte Black	Dot
8-25 x 50 Variable	8x to 25x	50 mm	Matte Black	Dot
8-25 x 50 Variable	8x to 25x	50 mm	Matte Black	Plex
30 mm TUBE SCOPES				
1.5-6 x 42 Variable	1.5x to 6x	42 mm	Matte Black	Plex
1.5-6 x 42 Variable	1.5x to 6x	42 mm	Matte Black	German #4
1.5-6 x 42 Var., Aspherical Lens	1.5x to 6x	42 mm	Matte Black	Plex
1.5-6 x 42 Var., Aspherical Lens	1.5x to 6x	42 mm	Matte Black	German #4
2.5-10 x 48 Variable	2.5x to 10x	48 mm	Matte Black	Plex
2.5-10 x 48 Variable	2.5x to 10x	48 mm	Matte Black	German #4
2.5-10 x 48 Var., Aspherical Lens	2.5x to 10x	48 mm	Matte Black	Plex
2.5-10 x 48 Var., Aspherical Lens	2.5x to 10x	48 mm	Matte Black	German #4
3-12 x 56 Variable	3x to 12x	56 mm	Matte Black	Plex
3-12 x 56 Variable	3x to 12x	56 mm	Matte Black	German #4
3-12 x 56 Var., Aspherical Lens	3x to 12x	56 mm	Matte Black	Plex
3-12 x 56 Var., Aspherical Lens	3x to 12x	56 mm	Matte Black	German #4

Kahles Riflescopes

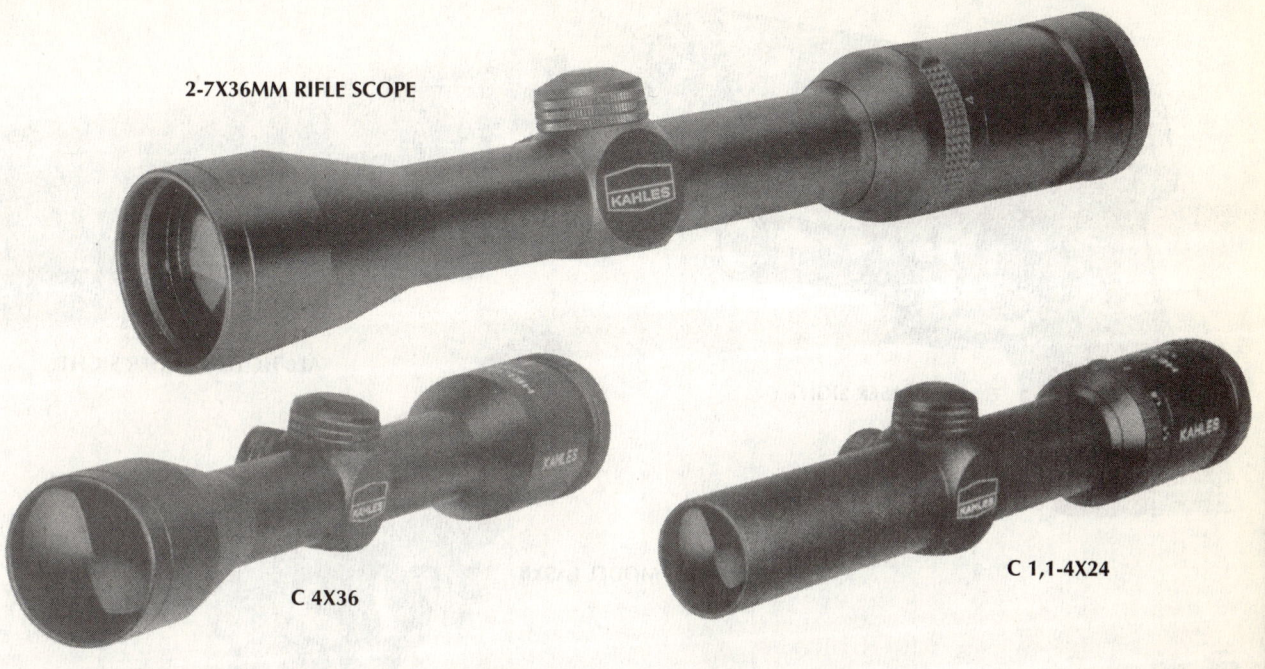

2-7X36MM RIFLE SCOPE

C 4X36

C 1,1-4X24

AMERICAN HUNTER
Kahles rifle scopes with a 1" main tube are compact and lightweight with excellent optical performance. One piece construction, generous eye relief, hard anodized, scratch resistant finish, shockproof and fogproof.

The AH's reticle is mounted in the second image focal plane, thus ensuring that the reticle's size in high magnification is minimized. Accurate aiming is enhanced at long distances.

Prices:
AH 2-7x36 (4A) $532
AH 2-7x36 (Plex) 532
AH 2-7x36RF (Rimfire) 4A 532
AH 2-7x36RF (Rimfire) Plex 532
AH 3-9x42 (4A) 621
AH 3-9x42 (Plex) 621
AH 3-9x42 (TDS) 665
AH 3.5-10x50 (4A) 665
AH 3.5-10x50 (Plex) 665

COMPACT
Kahles AMV-multi-coatings transmit up to 99.5% per air-to-glass surface. This ensures optimum use of incident light, especially in low light level conditions or at twilight.

Kahles rifle scopes are rugged, shockproof, waterproof and fogproof. Nitrogen purged several times to assure the absolute elimination of any moisture. 30mm tube.

Prices: C 1.1-4x24 (4A or 7A) 722
C 1.5-6x42 (4A or 7A) 832
C 2.5-10x50 (7A or Plex) 999
C 3-12x56 (7A, Plex or 4A) 1110
C 4x36 (1" tube, 4A or 7A) 555
C 6x42 (1" tube, 4A or 7A) 694
C 8x50 (1" tube, 4A or 7A) 749

4A   7A   Plex   TDS

4 NK   Plex N

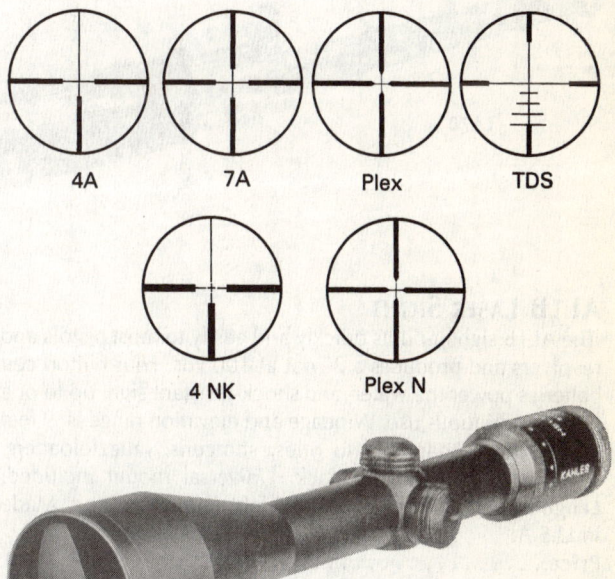

CB 3-12X56

ILLUMINATED
Bright reticle is adjustable for illumination, 30mm tube (1" tube on 8x50). Optimum illumination. Minimized straylight. Battery life - 110 hours.

Prices: CB 1.5-6x42 (4NK or PlexN) $1249
CB 2.5-10x50 (4NK or PlexN) 1353
CB 3-12x56 (PlexN or 4NK) 1471
K 8x50 (4N or PlexN) 1110

Laseraim Technologies Inc.

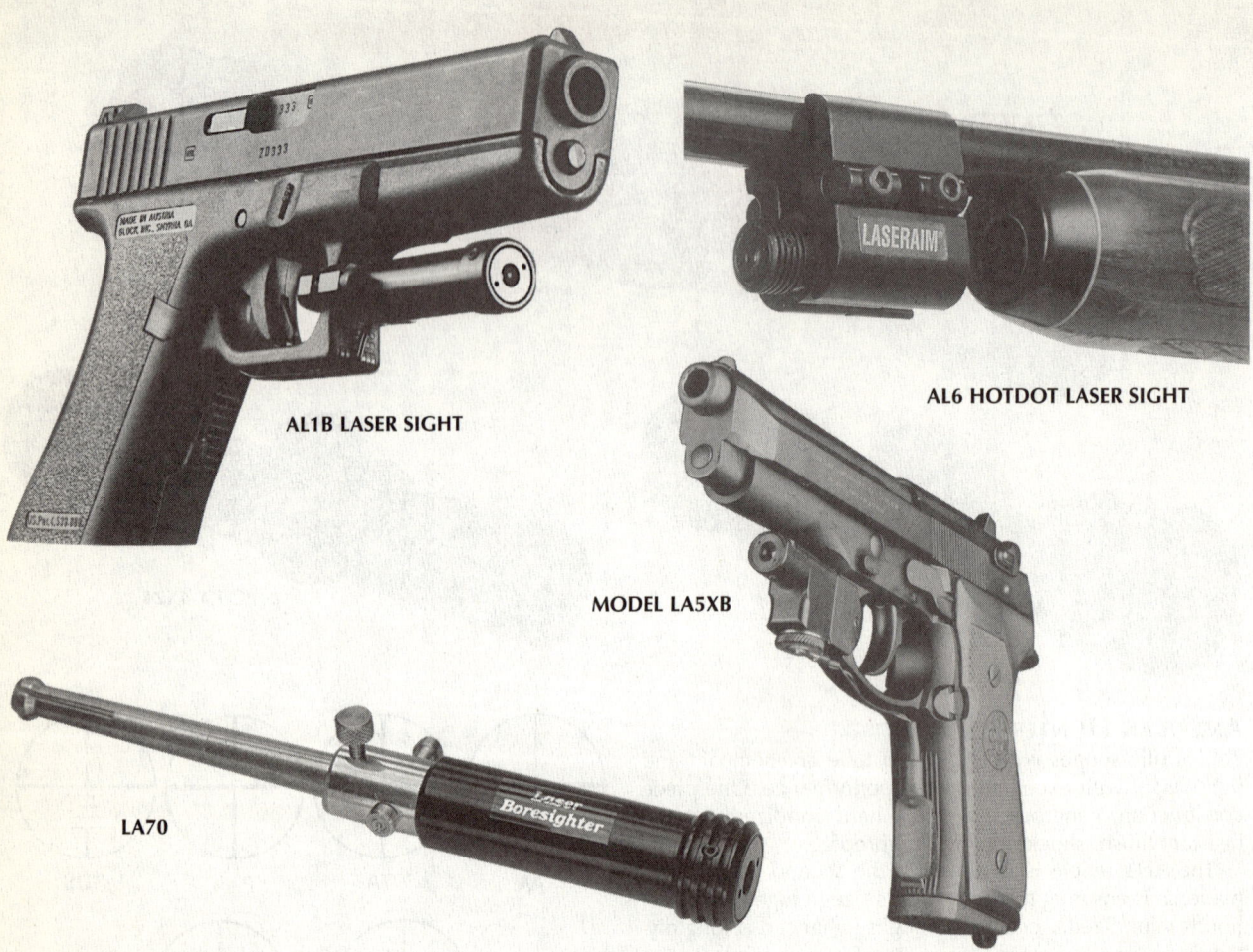

AL1B LASER SIGHT

AL6 HOTDOT LASER SIGHT

MODEL LA5XB

LA70

AL1B Laser Sight
The AL1B sight mounts quickly and easily to most pistols and revolvers and produces a 2" dot at 100 yds. Four button cell batteries power the water- and shock-resistant sight up to one hour's continuous use. Windage and elevation range is 9 feet at 25 yards. Adaptable to rifles, shotguns, muzzleloaders, and bows. Available in black. Universal mount included.
Length: 2.75" **Diameter:** 5/8" **Weight (approx.):** 2 oz. Made in U.S.A.
Price:..$99

LA70 Shotless Laser Bore Sighter™
The LA70 Shotless Laser Bore Sighter™ makes sighting in easier and quicker. To check the center of the bore, simply rotate the laser on axis of the gun bore. The LA70 is equipped with a rotational Laseraim™ with constant ON switch and six arbors fitting calibers 22 thru 45, 12-gauge shotguns and muzzleloaders (50 and 54 cal.). **Length:** 8" (w/laser and arbor).
Price:..169

AR15 Custom Laser Sight (not shown)
The AR15 laser sight is custom designed to fit all AR15/M16 rifles equipped with triangular front sight post. Laser provides three hours of continuous battery life with convenient replaceable battery. Machined from aircraft grade aluminum.
Weight: 3 oz. **Length:** 2"
Price:..$199

AL6 Hotdot Laser Sight
Ten times brighter than many other laser sights, this laser produces a 2-inch dot at 100 yards. The remote pressure switch provides operation for up to 2 hours of continuous power. The laser features Laseraim's unique 3-way micro-lock windage and elevation adjustment. Fits Laseraim mounts with no gunsmithing required and is suitable for handguns, rifles, shotguns, muzzle loaders, and bows. Uses convenient replaceable watch batteries.
Price: AL6 Hotdot laser sight...............99

Model LA5XB
Hotdot Mighty Sight
Up to 10 times brighter than other laser sights, Laseraim's Hotdot Lasersights include a rechargeable NICad battery and in-field charger. Produce a 2" dot at 100 yards with a 500-yard range. **Length:** 2". **Diameter:** .75". Can be used with handguns, rifles, shotguns and bows. Fit all Laseraim mounts. Available in black or satin.
Price:..139

Leupold Riflescopes
Vari-X III Line

The Vari-X III scopes feature a power-changing system that is similar to the sophisticated lens systems in today's finest cameras. Improvements include an extremely accurate internal control system and a sharp sight picture. All lenses are coated with Multicoat 4. Reticles are the same apparent size throughout the power range and stay centered during elevation/windage adjustments. Eyepieces are adjustable and fog-free. Reticles include German #1, German #1 European, German #4, Post and Duplex, and Leupold Dot.

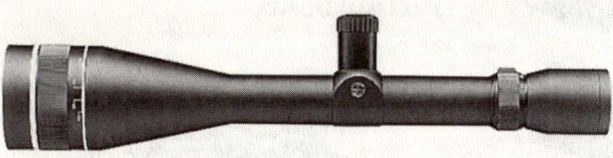

VARI-X III 6.5-20X50MM VARMINT

**VARI-X III
1.75-6X32MM E (EXTENDED VERSION)**

VARI-X III 1.5-5X20MM
This selection of hunting powers is for ranges varying from very short to those at which big game is normally taken. The field at 1.5X lets you get on a fast-moving animal quickly. With magnification at 5X, medium and big game can be hunted around the world at all but the longest ranges.
Duplex or Heavy Duplex, Gloss	$664
In black matte finish	686
German #4 (Gloss)	718
German #1 or #4 (Matte)	739

Also available:
VARI-X III 1.75-6X32mm. Matte finish	714
German Reticles	768

VARI-X III 2.5-8X36MM
This is an excellent range of powers for almost any kind of big game hunting. The top magnification provides enough resolution for varmint shooting.
Duplex	709
In matte or silver finish	734
Mil Dot (Matte)	868
German #4 (Matte)	788
Duplex or Post (Gloss)	780

VARI-X III 3.5-10X40MM
The extra power range makes these scopes the optimum choice for year-around big game and varmint hunting. The adjustable objective model, with its precise focusing at any range beyond 50 yards, also is an excellent choice for some forms of target shooting.
Duplex	730
With matte or silver finish	755
Leupold Dot, German #4	784
German #4 or #1 (Matte)	809

VARI-X III 3.5-10X50MM
The hunting scope is designed specifically for low-light situations. The 3.5X10-50mm scope, featuring lenses coated with Multicoat 4, is ideal for twilight hunting because of its efficient light transmission. The new scope delivers an exit pupil that transmits all the light the human eye can handle in typical low-light circumstances, even at the highest magnification.
Duplex or Heavy Duplex	$829
With matte or silver finish	854
#4 German (Gloss)	882
Matte or Silver (Dot or German #4)	907

VARI-X III 4.5-14X40MM (Adj. Objective)
This model has enough range to double as a hunting scope and as a varmint scope.
Duplex, Fine or Heavy Duplex	816
With matte finish	841
German #1 or #4	870
Matte	894
Same as above with 50mm adj. obj., Duplex, Fine or Heavy Duplex; matte finish only	939
German #1 or #4	993

VARI-X III 6.5-20X40MM (Adj. Objective)
This scope has a wide range of power settings, and can be used for any kind of big-game hunting where higher magnifications are useful. Side-focus adjustment allows shooters to eliminate parallax while in shooting position without taking their eyes off the target.
Gloss finish (duplex)	861
Leupold Dot	914
With matte or silver finish	886

Also available:
6.5-20x50mm Adj. Obj. w/duplex matte finish	984
6.5-20x50mm Adj. Obj. w/Mil Dot matte finish	1118
w/Leupold Dot or German #4	1038

VARI-X III 6.5-20X40MM E.F.R. Target
For those situations, such as air rifle or rimfire silhouette, where normal adjustable objective ranges are simply too distant, Leupold offers the EFR (Extended Focus Rifle) model of the 6.5-20. With this model, parallax distances as close as 10 meters can be set.
Fine Duplex (Matte)	957
Target Dot (Matte)	1011

Leupold Scopes
VX II Line

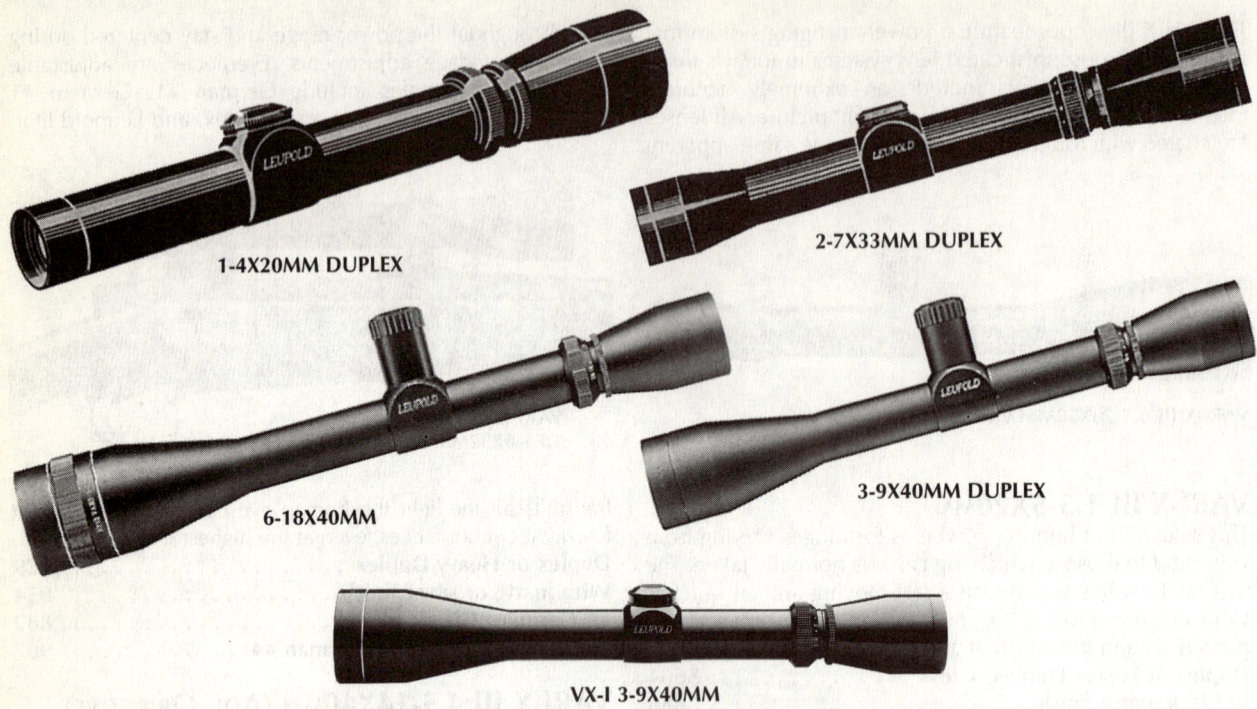

1-4X20MM DUPLEX
2-7X33MM DUPLEX
6-18X40MM
3-9X40MM DUPLEX
VX-I 3-9X40MM

The VX II line offers magnesium fluoride-coated lenses for improved light transmission, 1/4 M.O.A. click, a locking eyepiece for reliable ocular adjustment, and a sealed, nitrogen-filled interior for fog-free reliability. Many models are available with Dot, CPC, German #1, German #4, and Post & Duplex reticles in addition to Duplex.

VX II 1-4X20MM DUPLEX
This scope, the smallest of Leupold's VARI-X II line, is noted for its large field of view: 70 feet at 100 yards.
Matte finish only(Duplex) $425
CPC 479

VX II 2-7X33MM DUPLEX
A compact scope, no larger than the Leupold M8-4X, offering a wide range of power. It can be set at 2X for close ranges in heavy cover or zoomed to maximum power for shooting or identifying game at longer ranges.
VX II 2-7x 33 Shotgun (Duplex) matte 463
Leupold Dot 516

VX II 3-9X50MM
This LOV scope delivers a 5.5mm exit pupil for low-light visibility: Gloss (Duplex) 570
Matte finish (Leupold Dot or Duplex) 570
German reticles (Matte) 623

VX II 3-9X40MM DUPLEX
A wide selection of powers offers the right combination of field of view and magnification to fit most hunting conditions. Many hunters use the 3X or 4X setting most of the time, cranking up to 9X for positive identification of game or for extremely long shots. The adjustable objective eliminates parallax and permits precise focusing on any object from less than 50 yards to infinity for extra-sharp definition.
Gloss finish $468
In matte, silver (Duplex) 468
Matte (CPC, Leupold Dot, German) 521

VX II 4-12X40MM
(ADJ. OBJECTIVE)
The ideal answer for big game and varmint hunters alike. At 12.25 inches, the 4X12 is virtually the same length as Vari-X II 3X9. New fixed objective has same long eye relief and is factory-set to be free of parallax at 150 yds.
Matte or silver finish (Leupold Dot) 659
3/4 Mil. Dot (Gloss) German 4, Post, or Duplex 713

VX II 6-18X40MM ADJ. OBJ. TARGET
Features target-style click adjustments, fully coated lenses, adj. objective for parallax-free shooting from 50 yards to infinity.
In matte. 704
Leupold Dot 757
Dot w/Target knobs 811
Duplex w/Target knobs 757

NEW VX-I SERIES
A tough, gloss black finish and Duplex reticle. Leupold's high quality at an affordable price. Available in 2-7x33, 3-9x40 and 4-12x40mm
from 199

Leupold Scopes

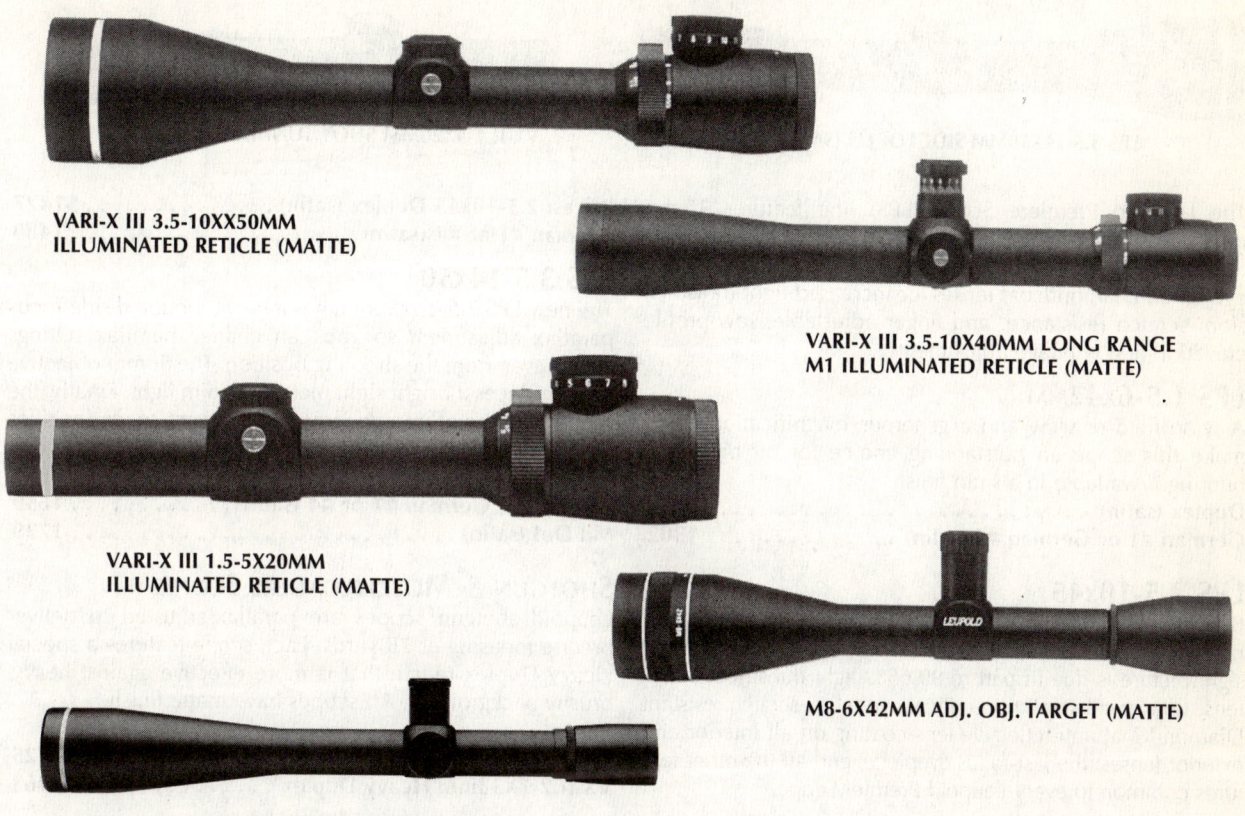

VARI-X III 3.5-10XX50MM
ILLUMINATED RETICLE (MATTE)

VARI-X III 3.5-10X40MM LONG RANGE
M1 ILLUMINATED RETICLE (MATTE)

VARI-X III 1.5-5X20MM
ILLUMINATED RETICLE (MATTE)

M8-6X42MM ADJ. OBJ. TARGET (MATTE)

COMPETITION SERIES 45X45MM

Illuminated Reticle

Leupold's Illuminated Reticle Scope helps hunters and target shooters take aim in poor light.

All Leupold Illuminated Reticle Scopes feature the Vari-X III system with Multicoat 4 lenses, and audible and tactile click adjustments. They are waterproof and fogproof. An 11-position intensity setting dial allows reticle brightness to be adjusted for dim and bright conditions. A 3-volt lithium cell supplies the power to keep the reticle evenly and constantly lit.

For big game hunters, the Leupold Vari-X III 1.5-5x20mm Illuminated Reticle Scope, with either an Illuminated Duplex or Illuminated German #4 reticle, offers lightning fast target acquisition. For more general hunting and sporting applications, the Vari-X III 4.5-14x50mm Adjustable Objective and the new Vari-X III 3.5-10x50 models offer extra-big objective lenses for conditions when you must use high magnification in low light. Both models are available in a matte finish with a choice of Illuminated Duplex, Illuminated German #4, or Illuminated Mil. Dot reticles.

The Leupold VX III 3.5-10x40mm Long Range M1 Illuminated Reticle and VX III 3.5-10x40mm Long Range M3 Illuminated Reticle models are good choices for military, law enforcement, and other tactical applications. Both models are available in a matte finish and feature side focus parallax adjusment dials and a 30mm maintube, with either the Illuminated Duplex or Illuminated Mil. Dot reticle.

Price: 1.5-5x20.............................$912
3.5-10x50 1034
4.5-14x50 1116
3.5-10x40 M1+M3 1548

Leupold 6 x 42 AO Target Scope

The Leupold M8 6x42mm Adjustable Objective Target Scope offers all the features needed by hunters and benchrest shooters. Both the elevation and windage dials of this scope feature 1/4 minute of angle, target-style click adjustments. An adjustable objective dial offers the ability to correct parallax from a distance of 50 yards to infinity.
Price: Matte w/Duplex........................ 661
Matte w/Mil Dot 795

Competition Series Scopes

Leupold's new Competition series includes the 35x45mm, 40x45mm and 45x45mm. Shooters get a bright, crisp sight picture with outstanding contrast, at extremely high magnification. The side-focus parallax adjustment knob allows you to adjust your scope to be parallax-free at distances from 40 yards to infinity. Available in matte finish with target dot or target crosshair reticle.
Price 1605

Sights & Scopes • 411

Leupold Scopes
Leupold Premier Scopes (LPS)

LPS 3.5-14X50MM SIDE FOCUS (SATIN FINISH)

VX-II 1-4X20MM SHOTGUN/MUZZLELOADER

The Leupold Premiere Scope (LPS) line features 30mm tubes, fast-focus eyepieces, armored power selector dials that can be read from the shooting position, 4-inch constant eye relief, Diamondcoat lenses for increased light transmission, scratch resistance, and finger adjustable, low-profile elevation and windage adjustments.

LPS 1.5-6x42mm
A wide field of view and a generous magnification range make this scope an outstanding choice for all big game hunting. Available in a satin finish.
Duplex (satin) $1248
German #1 or German #4 (satin) 1302

LPS 2.5-10x45
Big game hunters in particluar will enjoy the mid-range magnification of the new LPS 2.5-10x45mm. It's unusually bright sight picture is due in part to 99.65% light transmission per lens surface; constant, non-critical eye relief; scratch resistant DiamondCoat anti-reflective lens coating on all interior and exterior lenses; the fast-focus eyepiece; and all the other features common to every Leupold Premier Scope.
Prices: 2.5-10x45 Duplex (satin) $1427
German #1 or #4 (satin) 1480

LPS 3.5-14x50
The new LPS 3.5-14x50mm has a turret-mounted side-focus parallax adjustment so you can change parallax settings easily, even from the shooting position. The 50mm objective lens produces a bright sight picture, in dim light. Finally, the long maintube allows generous ring mount space for rifles with long actions.
Prices: Duplex (satin) 1605
Target Dot, German #1 or #4 (satin) 1659
Mil Dot (satin) 1739

Shotgun & Muzzleloaders Scopes
Leupold shotgun scopes are parallax-adjusted to deliver precise focusing at 75 yards. Each scope features a special Heavy Duplex reticle that is more effective against heavy, brushy backgrounds. All scopes have matte finish.
Prices:
VX II 1-4X20mm Model Heavy Duplex 425
VX II 2-7X33mm Heavy Duplex 463

Compact Scopes

M8 - 2.5X20MM COMPACT

M8 4X28 COMPACT RF SPECIAL

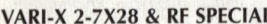
VARI-X 2-7X28 & RF SPECIAL

VARI-X 3-9X33 COMPACT

M8 2.5-20mm Compact
This small scope presents the shooter with an enormous field of view for fast target acquisition. It also features generous elevation and windage adjustment. Standard models are parallax adjusted to 100 yards. The Turkey Ranger model, with a special Post & Duplex reticle designed to subtend 9 inches from the post to crosswire at 40 yards, is parallax adjusted to 40 yards. Offered in a matte finish.
Duplex or Heavy Duplex (matte) $330
Turkey Ranger (matte) 384
M8 4x28mm Compact Rimfire Special
  Fine Duplex (gloss) 400

Vari-X 2-7x28mm Compact
  Duplex (gloss) $500
Vari-X 2-7x28mm Compact Rimfire Special
  Fine Duplex (gloss) 500
Vari-X 3-9x33mm Compact Duplex
  (matte, silver) 543

Vari-X 3-9x33mm Compact E.F.R.
With an adjustable objective capable of correcting parallax as close as 10 meters, this scope is perfectly suited to .22 rimfire silhouette and air rifle shooting.
Duplex (gloss) 584

Leupold Scopes
Tactical Scopes

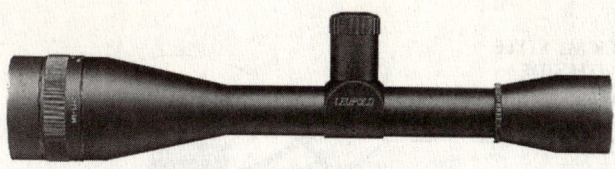

6X42MM AO TACTICAL SCOPE

The Leupold 6x42mm features 1/4-minute target-style adjustments for precise corrections in the field. Adjustment travel for windage or elevation is 76 inches. The exact 6X magnification, and adjustable objective make it an excellent choice for Hunter Benchrest Competitions. Leupold's exclusive Multicoat 4 lens coating is applied to all air-to-glass surfaces to provide the 6X42mm maximum light transmission.
Length: 12"
Weight: 11.5 ounces

Two reticles styles: classic Duplex or a 3/4-minute Military Dot. Black matte finish.
Matte finish $661
With 3/4-minute Military Dot.................... 795
Mark 4 MI 10x40 (Matte)/Mark 4 MI 16x40 (Matte)
Mark 4 MI 10x40 (Matte) • M3 10x40 with BDC
  Duplex 1925
  Mil Dot 2059
VX II 3-9x40 (Matte)
  Duplex 561
  Mil Dot 693
Vari-X III 3.5-10x40 (Matte)
  Duplex 834
  Mil Dot 968
Vari-X III 4.5-14x40 AO (Matte)
  Duplex 920
  Mil Dot 1054

Fixed Power Scopes

M8-2.5x28MM
For all the shooters wirldwide who are rediscovering the classic lever-action rifle, the M8-2.5x28mm IER Scout is the ideal choice. Designed specifically for lever-action and scout-style rifles, it offers 9 to 17 inches of eye relief (IER stands for "Intermediate Eye Relief"). The Scout is mounted on the barrel, in front of the receiver.
Matte finish (Duplex) $427
Matte or silver (Duplex) 427

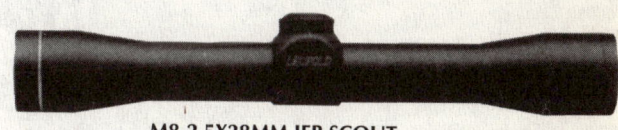
M8-2.5X28MM IER SCOUT

M8-4X
The 4X delivers a widely used magnification and a generous field of view **(Gloss)** 413-466
In black matte finish (Duplex) 438

M8-4X33

M8-6X
The 6X extends the range for big-game hunting and doubles in some cases as a varmint scope **(Gloss)** 438-491

M8-6X36

M8-6X42MM
Large 42mm objective lens features a 7mm exit pupil for increased light-gathering capability. Recommended for varmint shooting at night.
Duplex or Heavy Duplex 545
In matte finish 570

M8-6X42MM

M8-12X40MM STANDARD (ADJ. OBJ.)
Outstanding optical qualities, resolution and magnification make the 12X a natural for the varmint shooter. Adjustable objective is standard for parallax-free focusing.
Fine Duplex 609
Leupold Dot................................. 662

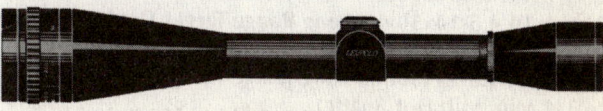
M8-12X40MM STANDARD

Leupold Scopes
Long-Range Models

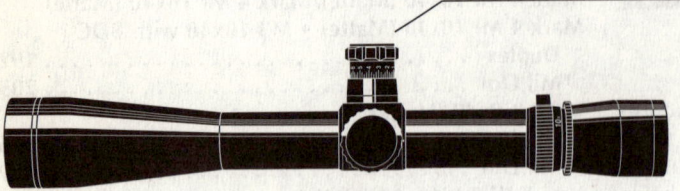

1/4 MINUTE CLICK M1 STYLE ADJUSTMENTS WITH SIDE FOCUS PARALLAX

VARI-X® III 3.5-10X40MM LONG RANGE M1

MARK 4 CQ/T 1-3X14MM

VARI-X III 3.5-10x40MM LONG RANGE TACTICAL M1
This scope combines the bold 1/4 minute of angle target dial design of the Leupold Mark 4 M1 scopes with the 30 mm maintube and side parallax dial of a long range scope to produce a low-profile, close-mounted tactical scope of remarkable versatility for hunters as well as snipers. Available in an all-matte (including the Leupold Golden Ring) finish.
Duplex (matte)..........................$1200
3/4 Min. Mil. Dot (matte)...................1343

VARI-X III 4.5-14x50MM LONG RANGE TACTICAL
With the increasing popularity of long range shooting, special scopes have been developed to accommodate the additional adjustment necessary to success in this discipline. The 4.5-14x50mm Long Range models with their 30mm maintubes, target style adjustment knobs, and side mounted parallax dials offer the shooter everything necessary to achieve success at great distances.
Vari-X III 4.5-14x50mm Long Range Target Duplex or Fine Duplex (matte)..........................1130
Vari-X III 4.5-14x50mm Long Range Tactical 3/4 Min. Mil. Dot (matte)...................1264

VARI-X III 6.5-20x50MM LONG RANGE TARGET
Designed with a 30mm maintube to provide additional elevation and windage adjustment, and featuring target style adjustment dials and a side-mounted parallax dial, this scope offers the long range shooter impressive magnification and convenient adjustment mechanisms.
Fine Duplex (matte, silver)...................$1218
Target Dot (matte,silver).....................1271
3/4 Min. Mil. Dot (matte)....................1352

VARI-X III 8.5-25x50MM LONG RANGE TARGET
With a 30mm maintube to provide additional elevation and windage adjustment, target style adjustment dials, and a side mounted parallax dial, this scope offers the long range shooter impressive magnification and convenient adjustment mechanisms.
Fine Duplex (matte).........................1316
Target Dot (matte)..........................1370

NEW MARK 4 CQ/T
The Leupold Mark 4 CQ/T 1-3x14mm is a revolutionary optical sight for tactical firearms. It combines the strengths of a red dot sight and variable-power riflescopes. Ten illumination settings match any light conditions; two low-intensity settings work with night-vision devices.
Price.....................................1248

Nikon Monarch Scopes

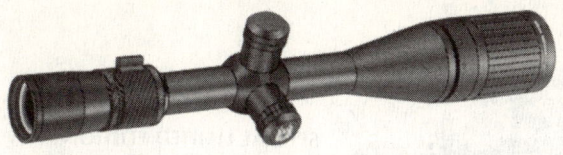

6.5-20X44 AO

2-7X32

1.5-4X20

TITANIUM SCOPE
3.3-10X44
5.5-16.5X44

Rifle Scopes
Model 6500 4x40 Lustre	$351
Model 6505 4x40 Matte	371
Model 6506 6x42 Lustre	371
Model 6508 6x42 Matte	391
Model 6510 2-7x32 Lustre	447
Model 6515 2-7x32 Matte	467
Model 6520 3-9x40 Lustre	451
Model 6525 3-9x40 Matte	471
Model 6528 3-9x40 Silver Matte	491
Model 6530 3.5-10x50 Lustre	665
Model 6535 3.5-10x50 Matte	685
Model 6537 3.3-10x44AO Lustre	579
Model 6539 3.3-10x44AO Matte	599
Model 6540 4-12x40 AO Lustre	573
Model 6545 4-12x40 AO Matte	593
Model 6580 5.5-16.5x44 AO Black Lustre	623
Model 6585 5.5-16.5x44 AO Black Matte	$643
Model 6550 6.5-20x44 AO Lustre	705
Model 6555 6.5-20x44 AO Matte	725
Model 6570 6.5-20x44 HV	705
Model 6575 6.5-20x44 HV	725
Model 6630 3.3-10x44 AO	899
Model 6680 5.5-16.5x44 AO	939

Handgun and Shotgun Scopes
Model 6560 2x20 EER Black Lustre	269
Model 6562 2x20 EER Matte	279
Model 6565 2x20 EER Silver	289
Model 6590 1.5-4.5x20 Shotgun Black Matte	385
Model 6595 1.5-4.5x20 Sabot/Slug Black Matte	385

Also Available:
Illuminated Scopes
3.5-10x50 (Nikoplex or Mildot)	865
6.5-20x44 (Nikoplex or Mildot)	981

MONARCH™ UCC RIFLESCOPE SPECIFICATIONS

Model	4x40	1.5-4.5x20	2-7x32	3-9x40	3.5-10x50	4-12x40AO	5.5-16.5x44AO	6.5-20x44AO	2x20EER
Lustre	6500	N/A	6510	6520	6530	6540	6580	6550/6556	6560
Matte	6505	6595	6515	6525	6535	6545	6585	6555/6558	6562
Silver	N/A	N/A	N/A	6528	N/A	N/A	N/A	N/A	6565
Actual Magnification	4x	1.5x-4.5x	2x-7x	3x-9x	3.5x-10x	4x-12x	5.5x-16.5x	6.5x-19.46x	1.75x
Objective Diameter	40mm	20mm	32mm	40mm	50mm	40mm	44mm	44mm	20mm
Exit Pupil (mm)	10	13.3-4.4	16-4.6	13.3-4.4	14.3-5	10-3.3	8-2.7	6.7-2.2	11.4
Eye Relief (in)	3.5	3.7-3.5	3.9-3.6	3.6-3.5	3.9-3.8	3.6-3.4	3.2-3.0	3.5-3.1	26.4-10.5
FOV @ 100 yds (ft)	26.9	50.3-16.7*	44.5-12.7	33.8-11.3	25.5-8.9	25.6-8.5	19.1-6.4	16.1-5.4	22
Tube Diameter	1 in.	1 in.	1 in.	1 in.	1 in.	1 in.	1 in.	1 in.	1 in.
Objective Tube(mm/in)	47.3-1.86	25.4/1	39.3-1.5	47.3-1.86	57.3-2.2	53.1-2.09	54-2.13	54-2.13	25, 4/1
Eyepiece O.D. (mm)	38	38	38	38	38	38	38	38	38
Length (in)	11.7	10	11.1	12.3	13.7	13.7	13.4	14.6	8.1
Weight (oz)	11.2	9.3	11.2	12.6	15.5	16.9	18.4	20.1	6.6
Adjustment Gradation	1/4 MOA	1/4 MOA	1/4 MOA	1/4 MOA	1/4 MOA	1/4 MOA	1/4 MOA	1/8 MOA	1/4 MOA
Max Internal Adjustment	120 MOA	120 MOA	70 MOA	55 MOA	45 MOA	45 MOA	40 MOA	38 MOA	120 MOA
Parallax Setting (yds)	100	75	100	100	100	50 to ∞	50 to ∞	50 to ∞	100

*FOV @ 75 yds (ft)   *FOV @ 50 yds (ft)

Nikon Buckmaster Scopes

SPECIAL LIMITED EDITION 3-9X40

4.5-14

Teamed with Buckmasters, Nikon has produced a limited edition riflescope line. Built to withstand the toughest hunting conditions, the scopes integrate shockproof, fogproof and waterproof construction, plus numerous other features seldom found on riflescopes in this price range. Nikon's Brightvue™ anti-reflective system of high-quality, multicoated lenses provides over 93% anti-reflection capability for high levels of light transmission and optical clarity required for dawn-to-dusk big game hunting. These riflescopes are parallax-adjusted at 100 yards and have durable matte finishes that reduce glare while afield. They also feature positive steel-to-brass, quarter-minute-click windage and elevation adjustments for instant, repeatable accuracy and a Nikoplex® reticle for quick target acquisition.

Prices:
Model 6465 1x20........................$241
Model 6405 4x40.........................249
Model 6425 3-9x40 Black Matte...........303
Model 6415 3-9x40 Silver................325
Model 6435 3-9x50.......................463
Model 6450 4.5-14x40 AO Blck Matte......431
Model 6455 4.5-14x40 AO Silver..........451

BUCKMASTERS SCOPES

Model	1x20	4x40	3-9x40	3-9x50	4.5-14x40AO
Matte	6465	6405	6425	6435	6450
Silver	N/A	N/A	6415	N/A	6455
Actual Magnification	1x	4x	3.3-8.5x	3.3-8.5x	4.5-13.5x
Objective Diameter	20mm	40mm	40mm	50mm	40mm
Exit Pupil (mm)	20	10	12.1-4.7	15.1-5.9	8.9-2.9
Eye Relief (in)	4.3-13.0	3.5	3.5-3.4	3.5-3.4	3.6-3.4
FOV @ 100 yds (ft)	52.5	30.6	33.9-12.9	33.9-12.9	22.5-7.5
Tube Diameter	1 in.	1 in.	1 in.	1 in.	1 in.
Objective Tube (mm/in)	27/1.06	47.3/1.86	47.3/1.86	58.7/2.3	53/2.1
Eyepiece O.D. (mm)	37	42.5	42.5	42.5	38
Length (in)	8.8	12.7	12.7	12.9	14.8
Weight (oz)	9.2	11.8	13.4	18.2	18.7
Adjustment Gradation	1/4: 1 click	1/4: 1 click	1/4: 1 click	1/4: 1 click	
Max Internal Adjustment	50	80	80	70	40
Parallax Setting (yds)	75	100	100	100	50 to ∞

Nikon Scopes

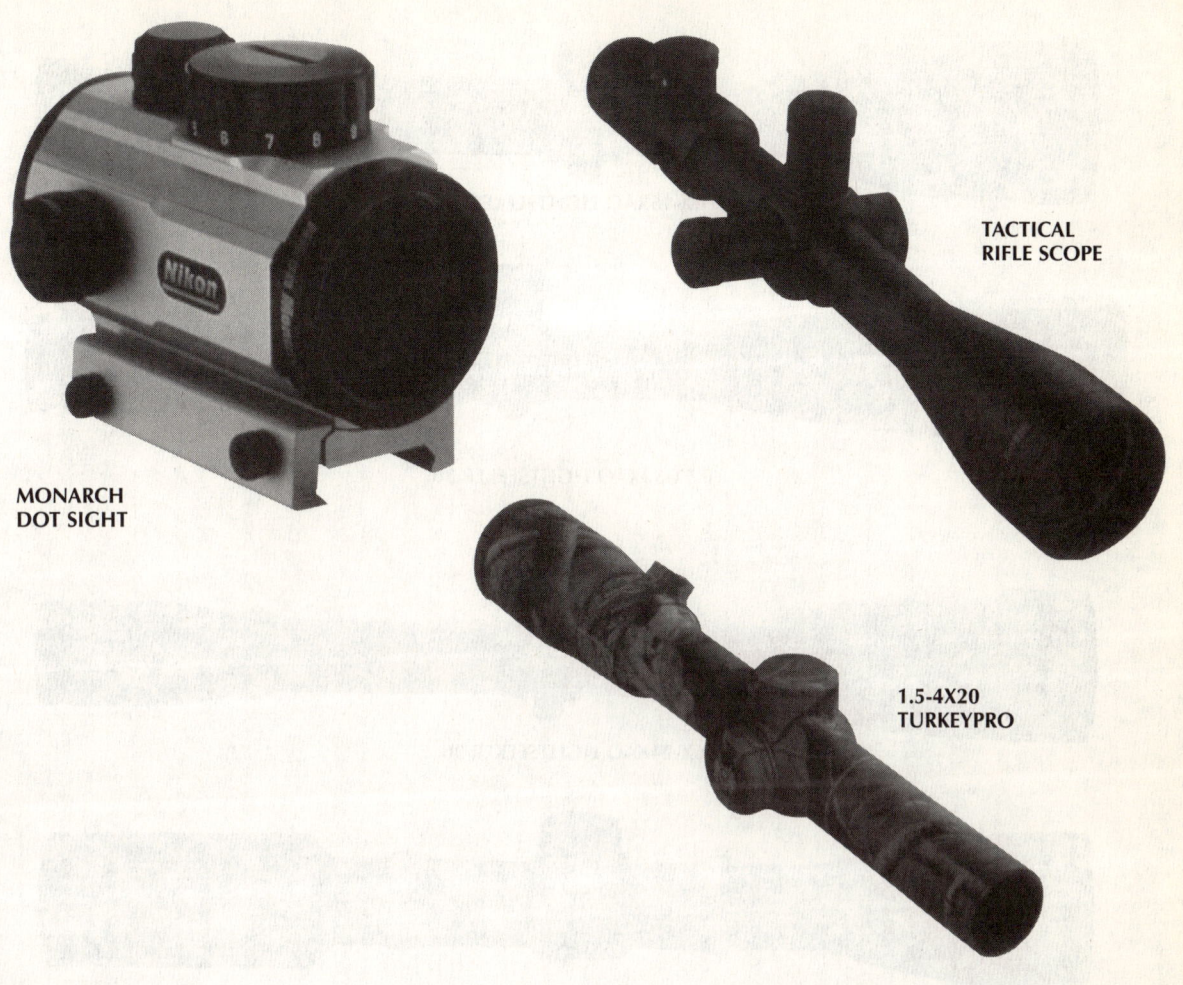

MONARCH DOT SIGHT

TACTICAL RIFLE SCOPE

1.5-4X20 TURKEYPRO

NEW FOR 2002
TACTICAL RIFLESCOPE
Nikon's Tactical Riflescopes are available in 2.5-10x44 and 4-16x50. The 2.5-10x44 features a choice of reticles: Nikoplex, Mildot, and Dual Illuminated Mildot. The 4-16 is offered with Nikoplex or Mildot. Both are equipped with turret mounted parallax adjustment knobs, have a tough, black-anodized matte finish and have easy-to-grip windage and elevation knobs for accurate field adjustments.
Prices:
Tactical 2.5-10x44 (Nikoplex or Mildot) $1361
With Illuminated Mildot 1561
Tactical 4-16x50 (Mildot or Nikoplex) 1461

MONARCH DOT SIGHT
The new Monarch Dot Sights are fully waterproof, fogproof and shockproof. Objective and ocular lenses are 30mm diameter and are fully multicoated. The Dot sights have zero magnification, providing unlimited eye relief and a 47.2' field of view at 100 yards, perfect for close up, fast shots. Brightness is controlled by a lithium battery. The standard Monarch Dot Sight is available in silver and black and has a 6 MOA dot. It is also available in Realtree camouflage.
Price Standard $401
VSD 461
VSD in camo 491

1.5-4.5x20 TURKEYPRO
The 1.5-4x20 Monarch TurkeyPro is now available in Realtree Hardwoods camo. It is parallax-free at 50 yards for great shotgun shooting.
Price: 415

2.5-8x28 EER HANDGUN SCOPE
Nikon's 2.5-8x28 EER (Extended Eye Relief) is a highly flexible variable handgun scope that should find favor with a wide assortment of hunters, varminters and competitors. It has a wide field of view at low power, but a twist of the power ring instantly supplies 8x magnification for long range shots.
Price: Matte 425
Silver 445

Pentax Scopes

4X-16XAO LIGHTSEEKER 30

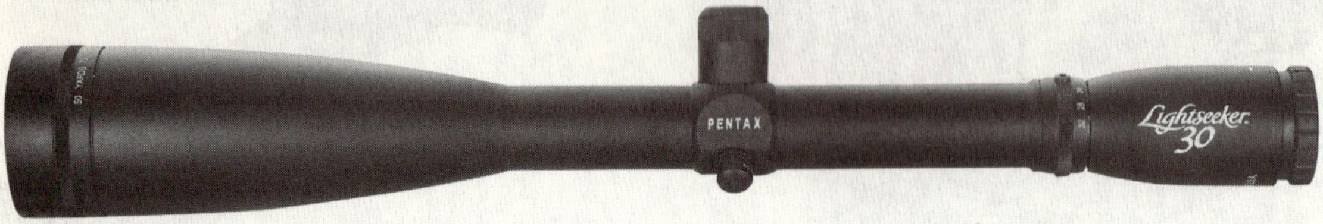

8.5X-32XAO LIGHTSEEKER 30

6X-24XAO LIGHTSEEKER 30

WHITETAILS UNLIMITED

PENTAX LIGHTSEEKER SERIES
Features:
- **Scratch-resistant outer tube.** Under ordinary wear and tear, the outer tube is almost impossible to scratch.
- High Quality cam zoom tube. No plastics are used. The tube is made of a bearing-type brass with precision machined cam slots. The zoom control screws are precision-ground to 1/2 of one thousandth tolerance.
- **Leak Prevention.** Power rings are sealed on a separate precision-machined seal tube. The scopes are then filled with nitrogen and double-sealed with heavy-duty "O" rings, making them leak-proof and fog-proof.
- **Optics.** Fully multi-coated, Lightseekers' optics are among the best in the industry, giving you a bright, sharp picture even in poor light.

THE LIGHTSEEKER-30 has the same features as the Lightseeker II, but with a 30mm tube.

The purchase of every Pentax Whitetails Unlimited rifle or shotgun scope includes a free one-year membership in Whitetails Unlimited, and a portion of the purchase price goes to the organization to support its conservation efforts.

PENTAX CORPORATION expands its extensive line of scopes by adding a Ballistic Plex reticle option to two of its Whitetail Unlimited models. Ballistic Plex reticles are available on the 3X-9X and 6.5X-20X Whitetails Unlimited Scopes.

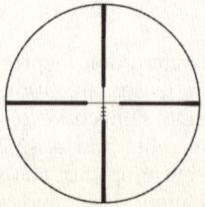

THE BALLISTIC PLEX RETICLE is a copyrighted design on the lower vertical crosshair that compensates for bullet drop. The Ballistic Plex reticle is set to provide dead-on aiming from 100 yards to 500 yards for many of the most common hunting cartridges.

Pentax Rifle Scopes

2.5 LIGHTSEEKER SG PLUS MOSSY OAK® BREAK-UP SCOPE

1.75X-6X LIGHTSEEKER

LIGHTSEEKER RIFLESCOPE AND WHITETAILS UNLIMITED

	Tube Diameter (in)	Objective Diameter (mm)	Eyepiece Diameter (mm)	Exit Pupil (mm)	Eye Relief (in)	Field of View (ft@100 yd)	Adjustment Graduation (in@100 yd)	Maximum Adjustment (in@100 yd)	Length (in)	Weight (oz)	Reticle	Price
RIFLE SCOPES												
Lightseeker 1.75X - 6X	1	35	39	15.3-5	3.5-4.0	71-20	1/2	110	10.75	13	P, TW	$526-546
Lightseeker 2X - 8X	1	39	39	11.0-4.0	3.5-4.0	53-17	1/3	80	11.7	14	P	594
Lightseeker 3X - 9X	1	43	39	12.0-5.0	3.5-4.0	36-14	1/4	50	12.7	15	P, MD	594-628
Lightseeker 3X - 9X	1	50	39	16.1-5.6	3.5-4.0	35-12	1/4	50	13.0	19	TW	718
Lightseeker 2.5X - 10X	1	50	39	16.3-4.6	4.2-4.7	35-10	1/4	100	14.1	23	TW	818
Lightseeker 2.5X SG Plus	1	25	39	7.0	3.5-4.0	55	1/2	60	10.0	9	DW	350-364
LIGHTSEEKER-30												
4X-16X AO	30mm	50	42	12-3.1	3.3-3.8	27-7.5	1/4	74	15.2	23	TW, MD	$888-988
6X-24X AO	30mm	50	42	7.6-2.1	3.2-3.7	18-5	1/8	52	16.9	27	MD, FP	928-1028
8.5X-32X AO	30mm	50	42	6.2-1.7	3.0-3.5	14-4	1/8	39	18.0	27	MD, FP	968-1068
WHITETAILS UNLIMITED												
2X-5X WTU	1	20	39	11.1-4.2	3.1-3.8	65-23	1/2	70	10.7	10	TW	$418
3X-9X WTU	1	40	39	12.9-4.7	3.1-3.8	31-13	1/4	50	12.4	13	TW	318-458
3.7X-11X WTU	1	42	39	13-5.1	3.1-3.8	28-11	1/4	50	13.1	15	TW	558
4.5X-14X WTU	1	50	39	9.1-3.1	3.1-3.8	25-9	1/4	40	14.1	15	TW	698
6.5X-20X WTU	1	50	39	7.6-2.6	3.1-3.6	17-6	1/4	30	14.6	19	BP	738
3X-9X WTU	1	50	39	16.0-5.3	3.1-3.8	32-13	1/4	50	13.2	17	BP	498

Scopes are available in high gloss black, matte black, or camouflage, depending on model.
P=Penta-Plex, FP=Fine-Plex, DW=Deepwoods Plex, MD=Mil-Dot, CP=Comp-Plex, TW=Twilight Plex

Redfield Scopes

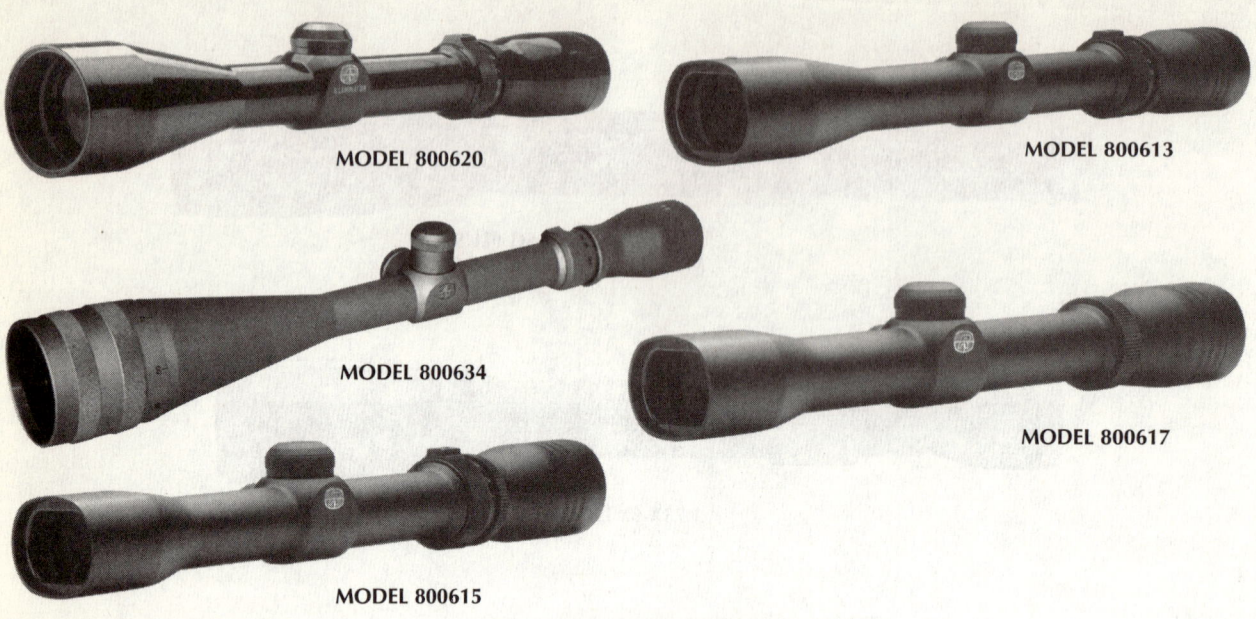

MODEL 800620
MODEL 800613
MODEL 800634
MODEL 800617
MODEL 800615

ILLUMINATOR
Illuminator is Redfield's best scope - made for the hardest of the hardcore hunters. Its large objective lens transmits maximum contrast and target definition to the eye, giving an edge in the uncertain light of dawn and dust. Crank up the magnification and Illuminator holds zero. The 3-9 variable with a 42mm objective lens comes in gloss, matte or brushed silver finish. The 3-10 variable with 50mm objective lens is available in gloss or matte black.

WIDEFIELD
Widefield's field of view is 30% wider than that of conventional scopes - over 40 feet at 100 yards on two models. It helps scan more area to detect the flick of an ear, or to pick the best shooting lane on running game. It's also designed to mount low on the receiver, a quicker sight picture when mounting the rifle. Choose a 2-7 power, 3-9 power or a fixed 4 power, in gloss or matte finish.

REDFIELD ILLUMINATOR

Model	Magnification Object Lens Dia-mm	Finish	Exit Pupil Range in Variable MM	Field of View in Feet @ 100 yds	Optimum Eye Relief Inches	Overall Length Inches	Weight Ounces	Reticle	Price
800619	3-9x42	Black matte	13-4.6	31x24-12.1x9.6	3.25-3.13	12.63	14.9	Truplex TV	$669
800620	3-9x42	Black polished	13-4.6	31x24-12.1x9.6	3.25-3.13	12.63	14.9	Truplex TV	669
800621	3-9x42	Silver matte	13-4.6	31x24-12.1x9.6	3.25-3.13	12.63	14.9	Truplex TV	675
800622	3-10x50	Black matte	12-5	34.5x24.5-11.3x8.7	3.125-3	14.75	1 lb 2.1 oz.	Truplex TV	752
800623	3-10x50	Black polished	12-5	34.5x24.5-11.3x8.7	3.125-3	14.75	1 lb 2.1 oz.	Truplex TV	752
800634	6-20x50 AO	Silver Matte	8.3-2.5	20.5-6.3	3.125-3.25	16	24	MX Dot	806
800635	6-20x50 AO	Black Matte	8.3-2.5	20.5-6.3	3.125-3.25	16	24	MX Dot	795
800636	6-20x50 AO	Black Matte	8.3-2.5	20.5-6.3	3.125-3.25	16	24	CH Dot	795
800637	6-20x50 AO	Black Polished	8.3-2.5	20.5-6.3	3.125-3.25	16	24	MX Dot	806

REDFIELD WIDEFIELD

Model	Magnification Object Lens Dia-mm	Finish	Exit Pupil Range in Variable MM	Field of View in Feet @ 100 yds	Optimum Eye Relief Inches	Overall Length Inches	Weight Ounces	Reticle	Price
800612	3-9x27x36	Black gloss	12x10-4x3	42.5x33-14.3x10.9	3.25-3	12.38	15	Truplex TV Oval	$443
800613	3-9x27x36	Black matte	12x10-4x3	42.5x33-14.3x10.9	3.25-3	12.38	15	Truplex TV Oval	443
800614	2-7x22x30	Black gloss	9x75x11.75-3.1x4	43.27x57.78-13.53x18.34	3.75-2.88	11.5	13.7	Truplex TV Oval	412
800615	2-7x22x30	Black matte	9x75x11.75-3.1x4	43.27x57.78-13.53x18.34	3.75-2.88	11.5	13.7	Truplex TV Oval	412
800616	4x22x30	Black gloss	5.3x7.4	29.75x35.95	2.88	11.38	12.4	Truplex TV Oval	360
800617	4x22x30	Black matte	5.3x7.4	29.75x35.95	2.88	11.38	12.4	Truplex TV Oval	360

Redfield Scopes

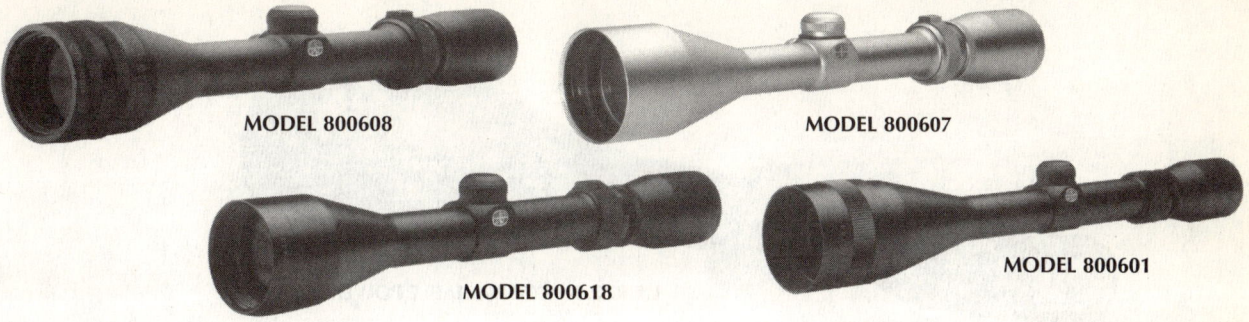

MODEL 800608
MODEL 800607
MODEL 800618
MODEL 800601

Golden Five Star
The Golden Five Star is purely practical. Its fully multi-coated optics give bright, clear sight pictures. The 3-9 power comes with 40 or 50mm objective lenses. A 40mm objective is standard on the 4-12 and 6-18 power.

Tracker
The Tracker is designed for the value-conscious hunter who wants a rugged Redfield scope at a modest price. Each Tracker is built from strong, lightweight aircraft aluminum and fine optical glass for maximum performance and clear bright images. The popular 3-9 power gives you a choice of 40 or 50m objective lens. Each scope has a black matte finish and is covered by the Redfield limited lifetime warranty.

Redfield Golden Five Star

Model	Magnification Object Lens Dia-mm	Finish	Exit Pupil Range In Variable MM	Field of View in Feet @ 100 yds	Optimum Eye Relief Inches	Overall Length Inches	Weight Ounces	Reticle	Price
800602	3-9x40	Black matte	13.3-4.4	34-11.3	3-2.88	12.75	13.5	Truplex	$309
800603	3-9x40	Black gloss	13.3-4.4	34-11.3	3-2.88	12.75	13.5	Truplex	309
800604	3-9x40	Silver matte	13.3-4.4	34-11.3	3-2.88	12.75	13.5	Truplex	319
800605	3-9x50	Black matte	11.85-5.1	36.7-12.66	3.63-3.38	13.13	1 lb. 2.7 oz.	Truplex	381
800606	3-9x50	Black gloss	11.85-5.1	36.7-12.66	3.63-3.38	13.13	1 lb. 2.7 oz.	Truplex	381
800607	3-9x50	Silver matte	11.85-5.1	36.7-12.66	3.63-3.38	13.13	1 lb. 2.7 oz.	Truplex	386
800608	4-12x40	Black matte	10.3-3.3	27-9.1	3-2.88	12.63	16	Truplex	443
800609	4-12x40	Black gloss	10.3-3.3	27-9.1	3-2.88	12.63	16	Truplex	443
800610	6-18x40	Black matte	6.6-2.22	17.8-6.1	3-2.88	13.5	16.3	Truplex	484
800611	6-18x40	Black gloss	6.6-2.22	17.8-6.1	3-2.88	13.5	16.3	Truplex	484

Redfield Tracker

Model	Magnification Object Lens Dia-mm	Finish	Exit Pupil Range In Variable MM	Field of View in Feet @ 100 yds	Optimum Eye Relief Inches	Overall Length Inches	Weight Ounces	Reticle	Price
800631	3-9x40	Black matte	13.3-4.5	35-11.3	3.25-3.13	12.75	13.5	Truplex	$216
800632	3-9x40	Black matte	15.8-6.3	35-11.75	3.25-3	13	1 lb. 2.5 oz.	Truplex	237
800618	3-12x44	Black matte	5.5-3.0	33-8.7	3-2.75	12.38	13.5	Truplex	268
800601	3-12x44	Black matte	5.5-2.7	26.2-7.42	3-2.625	14.375	16	Truplex	299

REDFIELD ESD MODEL 800624

Redfield ESD (Electronic Sighting Device)

Model	Objective	Description	Finish	Overall Length (Inches)	Weight (oz.)	Price
800624	28mm	Vari-Dot 4,8,12 &16 MOA	Black Matte	5.5	6.5	$395
800625	28mm	Vari-Dot 4,8,12 &16 MOA	Silver	5.5	6.5	400
800626	28mm	Multi-Reticle/16MOA Peep Plex/10 MOA DOT 3 MOA Center DOT/Standard Crosshair	Black Matte	5.5	6.5	388
800627	28mm	Multi-Reticle/16MOA Peep Plex/10 MOA DOT 3 MOA Center DOT/Standard Crosshair	Silver	5.5	6.5	395
800629	28mm	Compact ESD	Black Matte	4.25/5.5	5.25/5.6	286
800630	28mm	Compact ESD	Silver	4.25/5.5	5.2/5.6	291

Schmidt & Bender Rifle Scopes

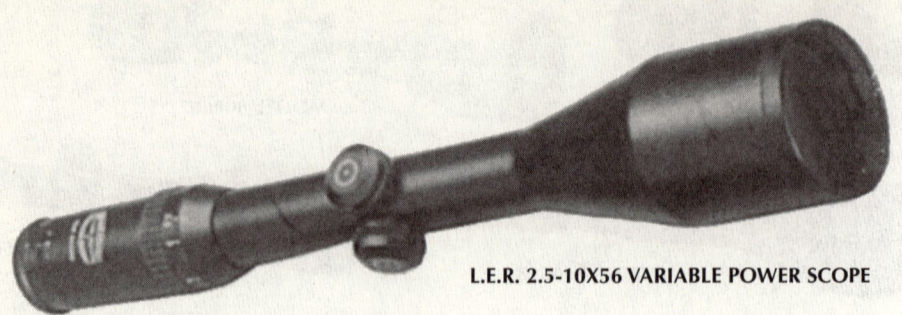

L.E.R. 2.5-10X56 VARIABLE POWER SCOPE

L.E.R. 2.5-10X56 VARIABLE POWER SCOPE
Price:.................................... $1390
Also available:
1.25-4X20 Variable Power Scope 995
1.5-6X42 Variable Power Scope................ 1125
3-12X42 Variable Power Scope 1290
3-12X50 Variable Power Scope 1360
4-16X50 Variable Power Scope 1595
Note: All variable power scopes have glass reticles and aluminum tubes.

Also available:
4X36 FIXED POWER SCOPE
1" Steel Tube w/o Mounting Rail. $760
6X42 Fixed Power Scope
Steel Tube w/o Mounting Rail 835
8X56 Fixed Power Scope
Steel Tube w/o Mounting Rail 960
10X42 Fixed Power Scope
Steel Tube w/o Mounting Rail 955

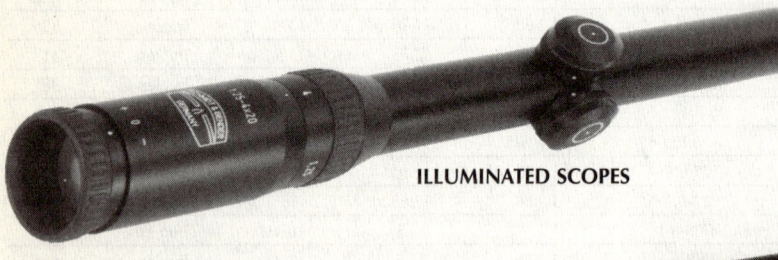

ILLUMINATED SCOPES

VARMINT

ILLUMINATED SCOPES
This 1.25-4x is designed for use on magnum rifles and for quick shots at dangerous game. Long eye relief, and a wide field of view (31.5 yards at 200 yards) speed your aim. The Flash Dot reticle shows up bright against the target at the center of the crosswire.
Magnification: 1.25-4X
Objective lens diameter: 12.7-20mm
Field of view at 100m: 32m-10m; at 100 yards: 96'-16'
Objective housing diameter: 30mm
Scope tube diameter: 30mm
Twilight factor: 3,7-8,9 **Lenses:** hard multi-coating
Click value 1 click @100 meters: 15mm; @100 yards: .540"
Price:.................................... 1480
Also available:
Illuminated reticles
1.5-6x42 1525
3-12x50................................... 1640
2.5-10x56................................. 1725
Zenith Series (not shown)
3-12x50................................... 1560
2.5-10x56 Illuminated 1810

Designed for long-range target shooters and varmint hunters, Schmidt & Bender 4-16X50 "Varmint" riflescope features a precise parallax adjustment located in a third turret on the left side of the scope, making setting adjustments quick and convenient. The fine crosshairs of Reticle No. 6 and 8 cover only 1.5mm at 100 meters (.053" at 100 yards) throughout the entire magnification range.
Magnification: 4-16X
Objective lens diameter: 50mm
Field of view at 100m: 7.5-2.5m; at 100 yards: 22.5'-7.5'
Objective housing diameter: 57mm
Scope tube diameter: 30mm
Twilight factor: 14-28
Lenses: Hard multi-coating
Click value 1 click @100 meters: 10mm; @100 yards: .360"
Price:.................................... 1595

Schmidt & Bender
Police/Marksman II

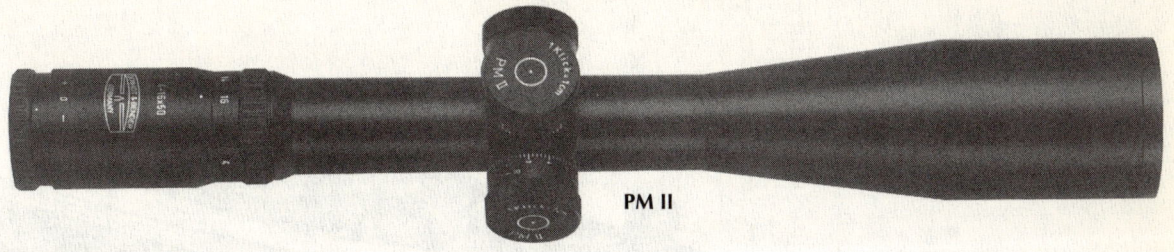

Specifications

	10 x 42	3-12 x 50	3-12 x 50 W/PARALLAX ADJ.	3-12 x 50 ILLLUMINATED	4-16 x 50 W/PARALLAX ADJ.
Price	$1085	1555	1785	1905	1870
Magnification	10x	3-12x	3-12x	3-12x	4-16x
Field of View	4m	11.1-4.2m	11.1-4.2m	11.1-4.2m	7.5-2.5 m
(100m/100yd)	12'	33.3-12.6'	33.3-12.6'	33.3-12.6'	22.5-7.5'
Objective Diameter	42mm	50mm	50mm	50mm	5mm
Exit Pupil	4.2mm	14.3-4.3mm	14.3-4.3mm	14.3-4.3mm	12.5-3.1mm
(mm/inches)	.165"	.563-.169"	.563-.169"	.563-.169"	.492"-.122"
Twilight Factor	20.5	11.4-24.5	11.4-24.5	11.4-24.5	14-28
Eye Relief	95mm	995mm	95mm	95mm	95mm
(mm/inches)	3.74"	3.74"	3.74"	3.74"	3.74"
Middle Tube Diameter	30mm	34mm	34mm	34mm	34mm
Weight	520g	7600g	810g	780g	880g
(gram/lb., oz.)	1 lb. 2 oz.	1 lb. 2.5 oz.	1 lb. 12.5 oz.	1 lb. 11.5 oz.	1 lb. 15 oz.
Adj. Range @	*270 cm/97"	200 cm/72"	200 cm/72"	200 cm/72"	185 cm/67"
(100m/100 yd)	**250 cm/990"	180 cm/64.8"	180 cm/64.8"	180 cm/64.8"	170 cm/61.2"
	***130 cm/46.8"	130 cm/46.8"	130 cm/46.8"	130 cm/46.8"	130 cm/46.8"

*Using the very ends of the elevation adjustment will reduce the windage adjustment range **Sighting-in adjustment range without restriction of windage ***With adjustment knob locked in place

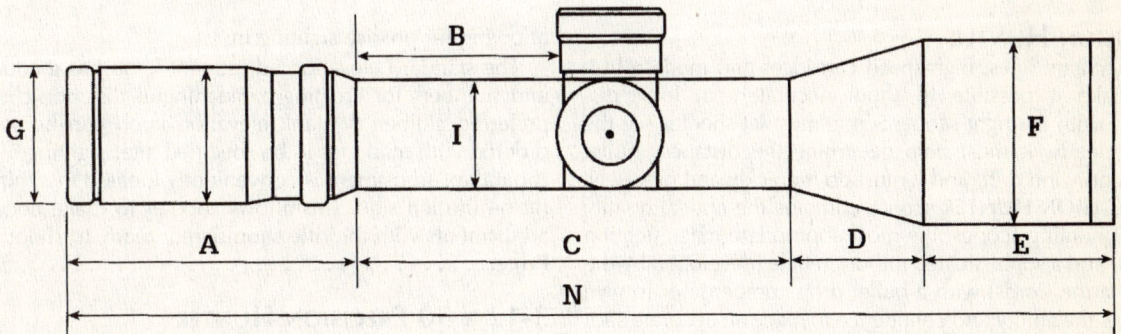

Dimensions

Model	A	B	C	D	E	F	G	I	N
10x42	98mm	56mm	139mm	55mm	54mm	50mm	43mm	30mm	346mm
	3.858"	2.204"	5.472"	2.165"	2.126"	1.969"	1.693"		13.622"
3-12x50	101.3mm	68.3mm	145.4mm	43.5mm	64.8mm	57mm	43mm	34mm	355mm
	3.988"	2.689"	6.076"	1.713"	3.354"	2.244"	1.693"		13.976"
4-16x50	101.3mm	68.3mm	145.4mm	85.2mm	75.5mm	57mm	43mm	34mm	405.7mm
	3.988"	2.689"	6.076"	1.713"	3.354"	2.244"	1.693"		15.972"

Schmidt & Bender
Scopes For Long Range Shooting

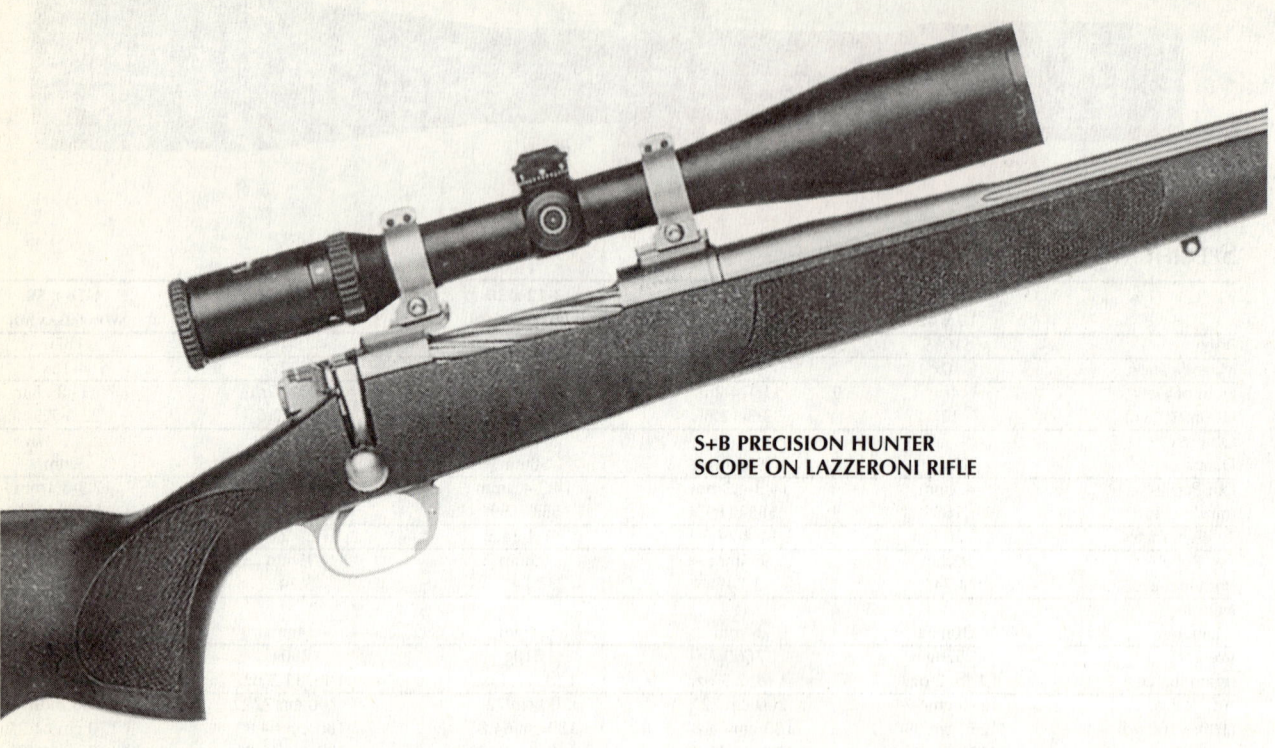

S+B PRECISION HUNTER SCOPE ON LAZZERONI RIFLE

PRECISION HUNTER

Very accurate rifles, high-speed cartridges and modern bullets make it possible to shoot accurately at long distances...with the right scope. Scope must let shooter see the target clearly. It must help determine the distance, bullet drop, and wind drift, and it must do it quickly and precisely.

PRECISION HUNTER scopes combine the optical quality of S&B hunting scopes, the most appropriate magnification ranges, and a sophisticated mil-dot reticle (developed by the U.S. Marine Corps) with a bullet drop compensator to give shooters the ability and confidence to place an accurate shot at up to 500 yards. Three different models are available:

4-16 x 50 PRECISION HUNTER SCOPE WITH PARALLAX ADJUSTMENT

Set on 4 power, the mil-dot reticle with fine crosshairs and four posts allows quick target acquisition.

Turned up to 16 power, the mil-dots become visible and can be used for range, trajectory and windage calculations. The top-mounted bullet drop compensator has 5mm (1/5") clicks, permitting quick adjustments up to 500 yards. The windage adjustment also has 5mm (1/5") clicks, allowing for precise sighting in.

The standard elevation adjustment knob has graduations and numbers for creating a meaningful distance chart for preferred caliber. A blank elevation knob can be special-ordered with markings to be specified after sighting in rifle. A parallax adjustment is conveniently located in a third turret on the left side. This allows shooter to make necessary adjustments with the rifle shouldered, ready to shoot.
Price: $1555

3-12 x 50 PRECISION HUNTER
Identical to the 4-16 x 50 with mil-dot reticle but 1cm (2/5") clicks and no parallax adjustment. It is factory-adjusted to be parallax free at 200 meters.
Price: 1285

2.5-10 x 56 PRECISION HUNTER
Identical to the 3-12 x 50, but with 1 cm (2/5") clicks for windage and elevation adjustment and with our Reticle No. 9, which makes it suitable for dangerous game.
Price: 1325

Sightron Scopes

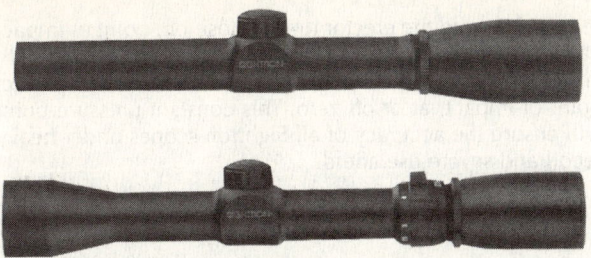

SIGHTRON SHOTGUN SCOPES

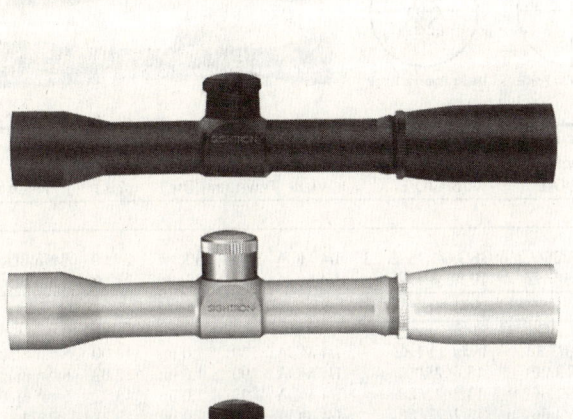

SIGHTRON PISTOL SCOPES

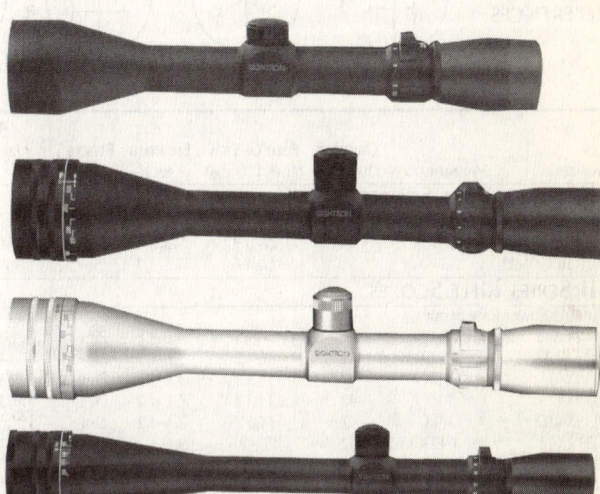

SIGHTRON BENCHREST SCOPES

SIGHTRON HUNTING SCOPES

SIGHTRON SERIES III 3.5-10x44
WITH SIDE-MOUNTED ("SADDLE")
PARALLAX ADJUSTMENT

Sightron's scope line offers nearly 40 models in fixed and variable power at modest prices. The SII series features 1-inch alloy tubes; the SIII series has 30 mm aluminum tubes, multicoated lenses, and "saddle" mounted parallax adjustments. Most target and competition scopes feature 1/8-minute clicks. Sightron offers stainless finish and a broad choice of reticles including the mil dot.

Prices:
SIII 3.5-10x44 mil dot	$697
SIII 1.5-6x50 plex	580
SII shotgun 2.5-7x32	243
SII shotgun 2.5x20	195
SII pistol 1x28	213
SII pistol 2x28	213

SII hunting scopes:
3-9x42	275
3-9x42 dot	324
3-9x50	340
1.5-6x42	288
2.5-8x42	262
3-12x42	312
3-12x50	343
3.5-10x42	$325
3.5-10x50	342
4.5-14x42	372
4.5-14x50	366
6.5-25x50	510

SII target scopes:
4-16x42	372
4-16x42 dot	412
6-24x42	394
6-24x42 dot	435

SII competition scopes:
3-9x42 mil dot	324
3-12x42 mil dot	331
4-16x42 mil dot	439
6-24x42 mil dot	463
24x44 Dot AO	342
6x42 AO	342
10-40x42	564
36x42	467

SII compact scopes:
4x32	206
2.5-10x32	261
2.5-7x32	243
6x42	225
12x42 Dot	366

Sightron Scopes

In conventional scopes a curved erector tube surface contacts the flat surface of the adjustment peg. This contact is only complete at zero adjustment. As the adjustments press the erector tube in any direction, the contact becomes imperfect, causing the reticle to drift from the optical center. In many cases, since the point of contact is less than what is required to hold the erector tube in position, point of impact can shift. Sightron has developed a new erector tube with an integral ring. ExacTrack will keep constant and perfect point-of-impact, at or off zero. This constant pressure point will ensure the accuracy of all Sightron scopes under heavy recoil and severe use afield.

Sightron Compact Scopes

RETICLE DIMENSION REFERENCES

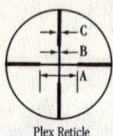 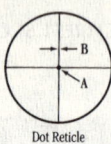 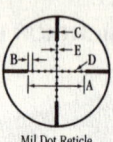 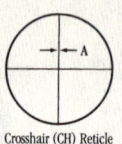 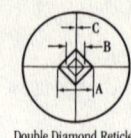 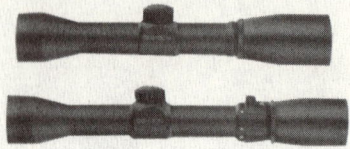

Plex Reticle | Dot Reticle | Mil Dot Reticle | Crosshair (CH) Reticle | Double Diamond Reticle

Item Number	Magnification	Objective Dia. (mm)	Field of View (ft @ 100 yds)	Eye Relief (in.)	Reticle Type	Reticle Subtensions (in. @ 100 yds) Min. Power A/B/C/D/E	Max. Power A/B/C/D/E	Click Value	Windage/Elevation Travel (in.)	Tube (Dia.)	Weight (oz.)	Finish
SIII Series Rifle Scopes												
30mm Side Saddle Rifle Scopes												
SIII3.510X44MD	3.5-10X	44	28-9.2	3.5	Mil-Dot	102.6/10.26/3.25/2.2/.69	36/3.6/1.15/.8/.23	1/4 MOA	80	30mm	24.60	Satin Black
SIII1.56X50MD	1.5-6X	50	64-17	4.3-3.7	Plex	79.0/1.33/5.32	19.8/.33/1.32	1/4 MOA	70	30mm	21.00	Satin Black
SII Series Rifle Scopes												
Variable Power Rifle Scopes												
SII1.56X42	1.5-6X	42	50-15	4.0-3.8	Plex	79.0/1.33/5.32	19.8/.33/1.32	1/4 MOA	70	1.0 in.	14.00	Satin Black
SII2.58X42	2.5-8X	42	36-12	3.6-4.2	Plex	48.0/.80/3.20	15.0/.25/1.0	1/4 MOA	90	1.0 in.	12.82	Satin Black
SII39X42	3-9X	42	34-12	3.6-4.2	Plex	39.9/.66/2.66	13.2/.22/.88	1/4 MOA	95	1.0 in.	13.22	Satin Black
SII39X42ST	3-9X	42	34-12	3.6-4.2	Plex	39.9/.66/2.66	13.2/.22/.88	1/4 MOA	95	1.0 in.	13.22	Stainless
SII39X42D	3-9X	42	34-12	3.6-4.2	Dot	4/.66	1.3/.22	1/4 MOA	95	1.0 in.	13.22	Satin Black
SII312X42	3-12X	42	32-9	3.6-4.2	Plex	39.9/.66/2.66	9.9/.16/.66	1/4 MOA	80	1.0 in.	12.99	Satin Black
SII3.510X42	3.5-10X	42	32-11	3.6	Plex	34.2/.57/2.28	12.0/.20/.80	1/4 MOA	60	1.0 in.	13.80	Satin Black
SII4.514X42	4.5-14X	42	22-7.9	3.6	Plex	26.4/.44/1.76	8.5/.14/.56	1/4 MOA	50	1.0 in.	16.07	Satin Black
SII39X50	3-9X	50	34-12	4.2-3.6	Plex	39.9/.66/2.66	13.2/.22/.88	1/4 MOA	*	1.0 in.	15.40	Satin Black
SII312X50	3-12X	50	34-8.5	4.5-3.7	Plex	39.9/.66/2.66	9.9/.16/.66	1/4 MOA	*	1.0 in.	16.30	Satin Black
SII3.510X50	3.5-10X	50	30-10	4.0-3.4	Plex	34.2/.57/2.28	12.0/.20/.80	1/4 MOA	50	1.0 in.	15.10	Satin Black
SII4.514X50	4.5-14X	50	23-8	3.9-3.25	Plex	26.4/.44/1.76	8.4/.14/.56	1/4 MOA	60	1.0 in.	15.20	Satin Black
SII6.525X50	6.5-25X	50	15-4.2	3.8-3.3	Plex	18.5/.3/1.2	4.8/0.1/.3	1/4 MOA	40	1.0 in.	20.70	Satin Black
Variable Power Target Scopes												
SII416X42	4-16X	42	26-7	3.6	Plex	30/.50/2.0	7.5/.125/.50	1/8 MOA	56	1.0 in.	16.00	Satin Black
SII416X42ST	4-16X	42	26-7	3.6	Plex	30/.50/2.0	7.5/.125/.50	1/8 MOA	56	1.0 in.	16.00	Stainless
SII416X42D	4-16X	42	26-7	3.6	Dot	1.7/.10	.425/.025	1/8 MOA	56	1.0 in.	16.00	Satin Black
SII416X42DST	4-16X	42	26-7	3.6	Dot	1.7/.10	.425/.025	1/8 MOA	56	1.0 in.	16.00	Stainless
SII624X42	6-24X	42	15.7-4.4	3.6	Plex	19.8/.33/1.32	4.8/.08/.32	1/8 MOA	40	1.0 in.	18.70	Satin Black
SII624X42ST	6-24X	42	15.7-4.4	3.6	Plex	19.8/.33/1.32	4.8/.08/.32	1/8 MOA	40	1.0 in.	18.70	Stainless
SII624X42D	6-24X	42	15.7-4.4	3.6	Dot	1.12/.066	.27/.016	1/8 MOA	40	1.0 in.	18.70	Satin Black
SII624X42DST	6-24X	42	15.7-4.4	3.6	Dot	1.12/.066	.27/.016	1/8 MOA	40	1.0 in.	18.70	Stainless
Competition/Tactical Scopes												
SII39X42MD	3-9X	42	34-14	3.6-4.2	Mil-Dot	150/15/10/4/1	50/5/3.3/1.3/.3	1/4 MOA	95	1.0 in.	13.22	Satin Black
SII312X42MD	3-12X	42	32-9	3.6-4.2	Mil-Dot	144/14/4.7/3.1/.7	36/3.6/1.2/.79/.1	1/4 MOA	80	1.0 in.	12.99	Satin Black
SII416X42MD	4-16X	42	26-7	3.6	Mil-Dot	144/14/4.7/3.1/.6	36/3.6/1.2/.79/.1	1/8 MOA	56	1.0 in.	16.00	Satin Black
SII416X42MDST	4-16X	42	26-7	3.6	Mil-Dot	144/14/4.7/3.1/.6	36/3.6/1.2/.79/.1	1/8 MOA	56	1.0 in.	16.00	Stainless
SII624X42MD	6-24X	42	15.7-4.4	3.6	Mil-Dot	144/14/4.7/3.1/.4	36/3.6/1.2/.79/.1	1/8 MOA	40	1.0 in.	18.70	Satin Black
SII624X42MDST	6-24X	42	15.7-4.4	3.6	Mil-Dot	144/14/4.7/3.1/.4	36/3.6/1.2/.79/.1	1/8 MOA	40	1.0 in.	18.70	Stainless
SII24X44D	24X	44	4.4	4.33	Dot		.27/.016	1/8 MOA	60	1.0 in.	15.87	Satin Black
SII6X42HBRD	6X	42	20	4.00	Dot		.375/.070	1/8 MOA	100	1.0 in.	16.00	Satin Black
SII6X42HBR	6X	42	20	4.00	CH		.33	1/8 MOA	100	1.0 in.	16.00	Satin Black
Compact Rifle Scopes												
SII4X32	4X	32	25	4.52	Plex		30/.50/2.0	1/4 MOA	120	1.0 in.	9.80	Satin Black
SII2.57X32	2.5-7X	32	41-11.8	3.8-3.2	Plex	48/.80/3.20	17.2/.29/1.2	1/4 MOA	120	1.0 in.	11.60	Satin Black
SII2.510X32	2.5-10X	32	41-10.5	3.8-3.5	Plex	48/.80/3.20	12/.20/.80	1/4 MOA	120	1.0 in.	10.93	Satin Black
SII6X42	6X	42	20	3.60	Plex		19.8/.33/1.32	1/4 MOA	100	1.0 in.	12.69	Satin Black
Shotgun Scopes												
SII2.5X20SG	2.5X	20	41	4.33	Plex		48.0/.80/3.20	1/4 MOA	160	1.0 in.	9.00	Satin Black
SII2.57X32SG	2.5-7X	32	41-11.8	3.8-3.2	DD	48/24/.60	17/8.5/.26	1/4 MOA	120	1.0 in.	11.60	Satin Black
Pistol Scopes												
SII1X28P	1X	28	30	9-24	Plex		120.0/2.0/8.0	1/8 MOA	60	1.0 in.	9.30	Satin Black
SII1X28PST	1X	28	30	9-24	Plex		120.0/2.0/8.0	1/8 MOA	60	1.0 in.	9.30	Stainless
SII2X28P	2X	28	15	9-24	Plex		60.0/1.0/4.0	1/8 MOA	60	1.0 in.	9.30	Satin Black

*Specifications not available at press time

Simmons Scopes
Aetec

AETEC MODEL 800865

MODEL 2100/2101/2102
2.8-10X44 WA **Length:** 11.9" **Weight:** 15.5 oz. **Reticle:** Truplex
Price: $216
    Model 2104 3.8-12x44mm AO 237

MODEL 800865/800866
Illuminated Reticle, black matte
Prices: Model 800865 (2.8-10x44) 230
        Model 800866 (3.8-12x44) 260

44 Mag Riflescopes

MODEL M1050DM

3.8-12X44mm **Length:** 13.08" **Weight:** 16.75 oz.
Price: $227

MODEL M1045 (BLACK MATTE)
4-12X44mm **Length:** 13.2" **Weight:** 18.25 oz.
Price: 196

MODEL M1044 (BLACK MATTE)
3-10X44mm **Length:** 12.75" **Weight:** 15.5 oz.
Price: $165

MODEL M1047 (BLACK MATTE)
6.5-20X44mm **Length:** 12.8" **Weight:** 19.5 oz.
Price: 206
Also available:

MODEL M1050DM
44 DIAMOND MG (BLACK MATTE)
RANGE-CALCULATING SMART RETICLE
(BLACK MATTE)

MODEL M1048
6.5-20X44 Target Turrets
Black Matte (1/8" MOA)..................... 237

44 Mag Riflescopes

PROHUNTER SE MODEL 807729

PRO 50 MODEL 8800

MODEL 7710
3-9X40mm Wide Angle Riflescope
Length: 12.6"
Weight: 13.5 oz.
Features: Truplex reticle; silver matte finish
Price: $134
(Same in black matte or black polish, Models 7711 and 7712) Also available:
Model 7700 2-7X32 Black Matte................ 113
Model 7716 4-12X40 Black Matte AO............ 154
Model 7721 6-18X40 AO Black Matte............ 165
Model 7740 6X40 Black Matte.................. 113

MODEL PRO50
Pro 50's have all the features of the Prohunter models, only with a 50mm lens.
Prices:

Model 8800 4-12x50mm, AO Black Matte........ $201
Model 8810 6-18x50mm, AO Black Matte......... 215
Model 8830 2.5-10x50mm, Black Matte.......... 175

NEW MODEL PROHUNTER SE
Sleek new design, one-piece body tube construction, Sure-grip power adjustments, Coated optics, 1/4 MOA windage and elevation adjustments, waterproof, fogproof and shockproof.
Prices:
Model 807719 2-7x32 Black Matte............... 90
Model 807723 3-9x40 Black Matte............... 99
Model 807724 4x32 Black Matte................. 70
Model 807730 4-12x40 AO Black Matte.......... 120
Model 807726 4-12x50 AO Black Matte.......... 153
Model 807727 6-18x40 AO Black Matte.......... 120
Model 807728 6-18x50 AO Black Matte.......... 138
Model 807729 3.5-10x50 AO Black Matte........ 150

Sights & Scopes • 427

Simmons Scopes

1022T Rimfire Target Scope
Magnification: 3-9X32mm WA/AO **Finish:** Black matte
Features: Adjustable for windage and elevation; adjustable objective lens, target knobs
Price: $162
Also available:
1022 4X32 black matte w/22 rings 68
1031 4X28 22 Mag Mini black matte w/22 rings 75
1032 4X28 22 Mag Mini silver matte w/22 rings 77
1033 4X32 silver matte w/22 rings 71
1037 3-9X32 silver matte w/22 rings 81
1039 3-9X32 black matte w/22 rings 79

1022T RIMFIRE TARGET SCOPE

Black Powder Scopes

MODEL BP2732M

Model BP2732M
Magnification: 2-7X32 **Finish:** Black matte
Field of view: 57.7'-16.6' 100 yards **Eye relief:** 3"
Reticle: Truplex **Length:** 11.6" **Weight:** 12.4 oz.
Price: $132

Also available: Models BP400M/400S
4X20 Black Matte or Silver Matte, Long Body
Field of view: 28' **Eye relief:** 5.0" **Length:** 10.25"
Weight: 8.7 oz. **Reticle:** Truplex
Price: $46
Model BPO420M/420S
4x20 Octagon, black or silver 111

Shotgun Scopes

MODEL 7790D

Models 21004/7790D
Magnification: 4X32 **Finish:** Black matte
Field of view: 16' (Model 21004); 17' (Model 7790D) **Eye relief:** 5.5" **Reticle:** Truplex (Model 21004); ProDiamond (Model 7790D) **Length:** 8.5" (8.8" Model 21004)
Weight: 8.75 oz. (9.1 oz. Model 7790D)
Prices:
Model 21004 . . . . $81
Model 7790D 111

Also available:
Model 21005 2.5X20 Black matte
  (Truplex reticle) $60
Model 7789D 2X32 Black matte
  (ProDiamond reticle) 101
Model 7791D 1.5-5X20 WA Black matte
  (ProDiamond reticle) 132
Model 77920 1.5-5X32 Camo Pro Diamond . . . . . P.O.R.

Simmons Scopes
8-Point

**SIMMONS 8 POINT
4X32 BLACK**

The Simmons 8-Point series is aimed at the entry level or budget-minded shooter who needs a reliable scope at an affordable price. The 8-Point family includes seven scopes in popular configurations: 3-9x32mm, 3-9x40mm, 3-9x50mm, 4x32mm, 4-12x40mm AO, and 4x32 mm shotgun. All versions are offered in black matte finish, and the 3-9x40mm is also available in silver. Fully coated lenses enhance light transmission for low-light viewing and reduce reflections. Simmons' popular Truplex reticle is standard. Windage and elevation are adjusted in 1/4-MOA increments. The new 8-Point scopes are shockproof, waterproof, and fogproof.

8-Point Scope
4-12x40mm AO
Magnification: 4-12X
Field of View: 29 - 10 ft. at 100 yards
Eye Relief: 3 inches at 4X and 2 7/8 inches at 12X
Length: 13.5 inches
Weight: 15.75 oz.
Reticle: Duplex
Finish: Black Matte
Price: $93

8-point Scope
4x32mm
Magnification: 4X
Field of View: 28.75 ft. at 100 yards
Eye Relief: 3 inches
Length: 11.625 inches
Weight: 14.25 oz.
Reticle: Duplex
Finish: Black Matte
Price: 31

8-Point Scope
3-9x32 mm
Magnification: 3-9X
Field of View: 37.5 - 13 ft. at 100 yards
Eye Relief: 3 inches at 3X and 2 7/8 inches at 9X
Length: 11.875 inches
Weight: 11.5 oz.
Reticle: Duplex
Finish: Black Matte
Price: $41

8-Point Scope
3-9x40mm
Magnification: 3-9X
Field of View: 37 - 13 ft. at 100 yards
Eye Relief: 3 inches at 3X and 2 7/8 inches at 9X
Length: 12.25 inches
Weight: 12.25 oz.
Reticle: Duplex
Finish: Black Matte or Silver
Price: Black Matte 46
Silver 51

8-Point Scope
3-9x50mm
Magnification: 3-9X
Field of View: 32 - 11.75 ft. at 100 yards
Eye Relief: 3 inches at 3X and 2 7/8 inches at 9X
Length: 13 inches
Weight: 15.25 oz.
Reticle: Duplex
Finish: Black Matte
Price: 67

Simmons Scopes
Whitetail Expedition

SIMMONS 3-9X42MM WHITETAIL EXPEDITION SCOPE

Simmons introduced aspherical lenses to shooters with the AETEC series of riflescopes. Now, Simmons offers aspherical lenses in the Whitetail Expedition series. Because aspherical lenses eliminate minor aberrations found in regular spherical lens systems, these scopes produce a sharp, crisp view all the way to the edges of the lens. Field of view is 30% greater than that of other scopes of comparable magnification and objective lens size. All lens surfaces of the new Whitetail Expedition scopes, inside and out, are fully-multicoated for maximum edge-to-edge brightness and reflection reduction. The scopes have a Truplex reticle, the most versatile and popular in the marketplace, and are shockproof, waterproof, and fogproof. Configurations available in the Whitetail Expedition series are: 1.5-6x32mm WA, 3-9x42mm WA, 4-12x42mm WA, and 6-18x42mm WA. The two higher-range scopes have adjustable objective lenses for precision shooting at any range. Adjustments for windage and elevation are 1/4-MOA increments.

WHITETAIL EXPEDITION 1.5-6X32MM
Magnification: 1.5-6X **Field of View:** 72 - 19 ft. at 100 yards **Eye Relief:** 3 inches **Length:** 11.16 inches **Weight:** 15 oz. **Reticle:** Duplex **Finish:** Black Matte
Price:..$268

WHITETAIL EXPEDITION 3-9X42MM
Magnification: 3-9X **Field of View:** 40 - 13.5 ft. at 100 yards **Eye Relief:** 3 inches **Length:** 13.2 inches **Weight:** 17.5 oz. **Reticle:** Duplex **Finish:** Black Matte
Price:..278

WHITETAIL EXPEDITION 4-12X42MM
Magnification: 4-12X **Field of View:** 29 - 9.6 ft. at 100 yards **Eye Relief:** 3 inches **Length:** 13.46 inches **Weight:** 21.25 oz. **Reticle:** Duplex **Finish:** Black Matte
Price:..309

WHITETAIL EXPEDITION 6-18X42MM
Magnification: 6-18X **Field of View:** 18.3 - 6.5 ft. at 100 yards **Eye Relief:** 3 inches **Length:** 15.35 inches **Weight:** 22.5 oz. **Reticle:** Duplex **Finish:** Black Matte
Price:..330

Prohunter Handgun Scopes

MODEL 7732 (2X)   MODEL 7738 (4X)

MODEL #7732/7733 (SILVER MATTE)
SPECIFICATIONS
Magnification: 2X **Field Of View:** 22' **Eye Relief:** 9-17" **Length:** 8.75" **Weight:** 7 oz. **Reticle:** Truplex **Finish:** Black matte
Price:..$129

MODEL #7738/7739 (SILVER MATTE)
SPECIFICATIONS
Magnification: 4X **Field Of View:** 15' **Eye Relief:** 11.8-17.6" **Length:** 9" **Weight:** 8 oz. **Reticle:** Truplex **Finish:** Black matte
Price:..139

Swarovski Scopes

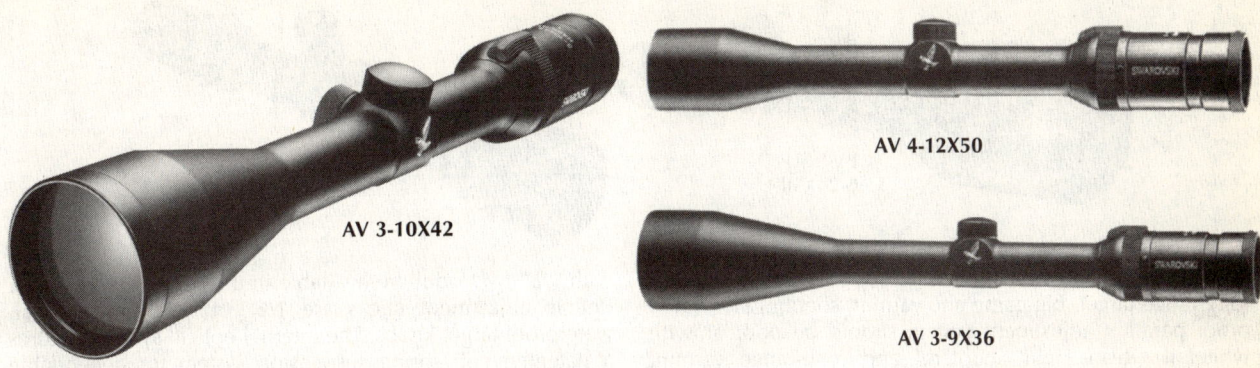

AV 3-10X42

AV 4-12X50

AV 3-9X36

SWAROVSKI AV-SERIES LIGHTWEIGHT 1-INCH SCOPES

Developed for American hunters, the AV scopes feature constant-size reticles, lightweight alloy tubes and satin finish. Totally waterproof even with caps removed, these scopes have fully multi-coated lenses and the quality that has made Swarovski famous.

Prices:
AV 3-10 x 42 (4A, Plex) $821
AV 4-12 x 50 (4A, Plex) 843
AV 3-9 x 36 (4A, Plex) 743
AV 6-18x50P (4A, Plex) 888
AV 6-18x50 (TDS) 938

AV RETICLES AVAILABLE:

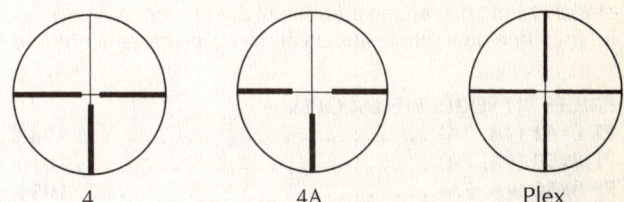

4   4A   Plex

AV 6-18x50

Swarovski's new 6-18x50 incorporates a parallax adjustment ring that insures parallax free accuracy from 50 yds to beyond 500. The objective bell, 1" tube, turret housing and ocular bell are machined out of one solid piece of alloy bar stock for strength, weight and waterproof integrity.
Price: 888

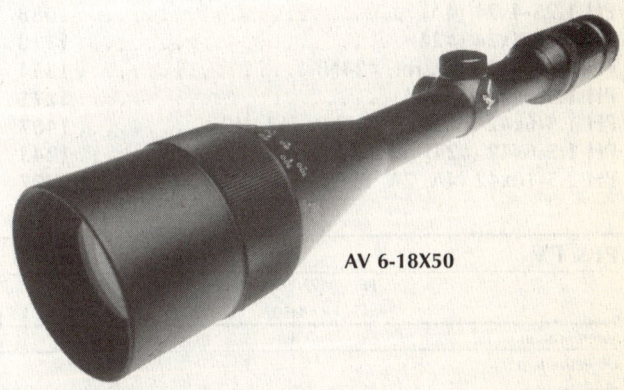

AV 6-18X50

	AV 3-9x36	AV 3-10x42	AV 4-12x50	AV 6-18x50
Magnification	3-9x	3.3-10x	4-12x	6-18x
Objective lens diameter: mm	36	42	50	50
in	1.42	1.55	1.97	1.97
Exit pupil, diameter: mm	12-4	12.6-4.2	12.5-4.2	8.3-2.8
Eye relief: in	3.5	3.5	3.5	3.5
Field of view, real: m/100m	13-4.5	11-3.9	9.7-3.3	17.4-6.5
ft/100yds	39-13.5	33-11.7	29.1-9.9	17.4-6.5
Diopter compensation (dpt)	± 2.6	±2.5	±2.5	±2.5
Transission (%)	94	94	94	92
Twilight factor (DIN 58388)	9-18	9-21	11-25	17-30
Impact Point correction per click: in/100yds	0.25	0.25	0.25	0.25
Max. elevation/windage adjustment range: ft/100yds	4.8	4.2	3.6	3.9
Length, approx: in	11.8	12.44	13.5	14.85
Weight, approx (oz.): L	11.6	12.7	13.9	20.3
LS	–	13.6	15.2	–

L=light alloy • LS=light alloy with rail

Swarovski Scopes

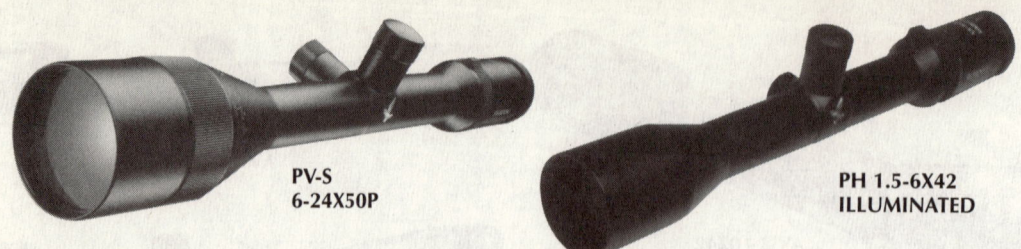

PV-S 6-24X50P

PH 1.5-6X42 ILLUMINATED

Swarovski's 6-24X50mm "PH" riflescope was developed for long-range target, big-game and varmint shooting. Its waterproof parallax adjustment system should be popular with whitetail "Bean Field Shooters" and long-range varmint hunters looking for a choice of higher powers in a premium rifle scope and still deliver accuracy. The scope will also appeal to many bench rest shooters who compete in certain classes where power and adjustment are limited. A non-magnifying, fine plex reticle and an all-new fine crosshair reticle with 1/8" MOA dot are available in the 6-24X50mm scope. Reticle adjustment clicks are 1/6" (minute) by external, waterproof target knobs. The internal optical system features a patented coil spring suspension system for dependable accuracy and positive reticle adjustment. The objective bell, 30mm middle tube, turret housing and ocular bell are machined from one solid bar of aluminum.

Price: **$1687**

PRICES PH SERIES RIFLESCOPES

PF 6x42 (4A, 7A)	$988
PF 8x50 (4A, 7A)	1010
PF 8x56 (4A, 7A)	1054
PH8x56 (Illum. ret. PLEXN)	1421
PH 1.25-4x24 (4A)	1088
PH 1.25-4x24 (#24)	1110
PH 1.25-4x24 (Ill. ret. #24N)	1354
PH 1.5-6x42 (4A, 7A)	1221
PH 1.5-6x42 (Illum. ret. #24N, 4A-1K)	1487
PH 1.5-6x42 (#24)	1243
PH 2.5-10x42 (4A, 7A, PLEX)	1377
illum reticle (4NK)	1666
PH 2.5-10x56 (4A, 7A)	1410
w/illum reticle (4NK, PLEXN)	1754
PH 3-12x50 (4A, 7A, PLEX)	1421
TDS reticle	1532
w/illum reticle (4NK, PLEXN)	1754
PH 6-24x50 (4A, PLEX) with low turret	1610
PH 6-24x50 (low turrets, TDS)	1665
PH 4-16x50 (4A, PLEX)	1477
PH 4-16x50 (TDS)	1532

PF & PV

	PF 6x42	PF/PF-N 8x50	PF/PF-N 8x56	PV/PV-1 1.25-4x24	PV 1.5-6x42	PV/PV-N 2.5-10x42	PV/PV-N 2.5-10x56	PV/PV-N 3-12x50	PV 4-16x50P	PV 6-24x50P	PV-S 6-24x50P
Magnification	6x	8x	8x	1.25-4x	1.5-6x	2.5-10x	2.5-10x	3-12x	4-16x	6-24x	6-24x
Objective lens diameter: mm	42	50	56	17-24	20-42	33-42	33-56	39-50	50	50	50
in	1.65	1.97	2.20	0.67-0.94	0.79-1.65	1.3-1.65	1.3-2.20	1.54-1.97	1.97	1.97	1.97
Exit pupil, diameter: mm	7	6.25	7	12.5-6	13.1-7	13.1-4.2	13.1-5.6	13.1-4.2	12.5-3.1	8.3-2.1	8.3-2.1
Eye relief: in	3.15	3.15	3.15	3.15	3.15	3.15	3.15	3.15	3.15	3.15	3.15
Field of view, real: m/100m	7	5.2	5	32.8-10.4	21.8-7	13.2-4.2	13.2-4.1	11-3.5	9.1-2.6	6.2-1.8	6.2-1.8
ft/100yds	21	15.6	15.6	98.4-31.2	65.4-21	39.6-12.6	39.6-12.3	33-10.5	27.3-7.8	18.6-5.4	18.6-5.4
Diopter compensation (dpt)	+2. -3	+2. -3	+2. -3	+2. -3	+2. -3	+2. -3	+2. -3	+2. -3	+2. -3	+2. -3	+2. -3
Transission (%)	94	94/92	93/91	93/91	93	94/92	93/91	94/92	90	90	90
Twilight factor (DIN 58388)	16	20	21	4-10	4-16	7-21	7-24	9-25	11-28	17-35	17-35
Impact Point correction per click: in/100yds	0.36	0.36	0.36	0.54	0.36	0.36	0.36	0.36	0.18	0.18	0.17
Max. elevation/windage adjustment range: ft/100yds	3.9	3.3	3.9	9.9	6.6	3.9	3.9	3.3	E:5.4/W:3	E:3.6/W:2.1	E:3.6/W:2.1
Length, approx: in	12.83	13.94	13.27	10.63	12.99	13.23	13.62	14.33	14.21	15.43	15.43
Weight, approx (oz.): L	12.0	14.8	15.9	12.7	16.2	15.2	18.0	16.9	22.2	23.6	24.5
LS	13.4	15.9	16.9	13.8	17.5	16.4	19.0	18.3	—	—	—

L=light alloy • LS=light alloy with rail

Swift Scopes

Swift Instruments, Inc., a prominent name in the optics industry since 1926, has four new scopes in its line: three rifle scopes that offer faster focusing with the Swift Speed Focus feature and one new shock resistant pistol scope. All four are waterproof, shock-tested and have multi-coated lenses for a bright image from dawn to dusk without glare.

Model 672M
Swift Premier Rifle Scope
6-18X, 50mm - WA - Multi-Coated - Waterproof - SPEED FOCUS
A great scope for varmint, silhouette and target shooters. The Speed Focus feature presents optimum focusing ability at any power setting. Multi-coated lenses with an adjustable objective to correct parallax. New longer tube body allows more eye relief adjustment in long action firearms. Black matte finish.
Price:..$260

Model 673M
Swift Premier Rifle Scope
Featuring a 30mm tube for a brighter image at dawn or dusk 2.5-10X, 50 - Wide Angle - Waterproof - Multi-Coated - SPEED FOCUS
This scope with a 30mm tube and a 50mm objective lens is brighter than other scopes under poor light condition. It has an extremely wide field. The objective adjustment allows accurate shooting from close up to distant ranges. Elevation and windage adjustments, full saddle hard anodized 30mm tube.
Price:..295

Model 676S
Swift Premier Rifle Scope
4-12X, 40 - WA - Waterproof -
Multi-Coated - Speed Focus
With a parallax adjustment from 10 yards to infinity, this scope is highly adaptable and excellent for use as a varmint scope or on gas powered air rifles. Elevation and windage adjustments are mounted full saddle on the hard anodized 1-inch tube. Speed Focus adjustment brings shooters on target easily. The objectives are multi-coated; Quadraplex reticle is standard. Available in regular (676), matte (676M), and silver finish (676S).
Price:..$190
Gloss...180
Matte...185

Model 679M Swift Pistol Scope
1.25-4X, 28mm - 8.2 oz.
An extremely versatile full saddle scope with excellent eye relief of 23 inches at 1.25x, 15 inches at 4x. This ruggedly made scope is shock resistant and waterproof. It has 7 magenta coated lens elements and weighs only 8.2 ounces. Matte finished.
Price:..250
Also available: Pistol scopes 4x32, 2x20
Price:..130

New for 2002
Swift Instruments add three new illuminated reticle rifle scopes to their line. All are waterproof, shock tested and have multi-coated lenses that provide a bright, sharp, glare-free image from dawn to dusk. Add to this variable-intensity red crosshairs in the center of the reticle that adjusts to make getting on target easier in low light conditions.
Model 680M 3-9x40
Model 681M 1.5-6x40
Model 682M 4-12x50
Prices:..P.O.R.

Swift Rifle & Pistol Scopes

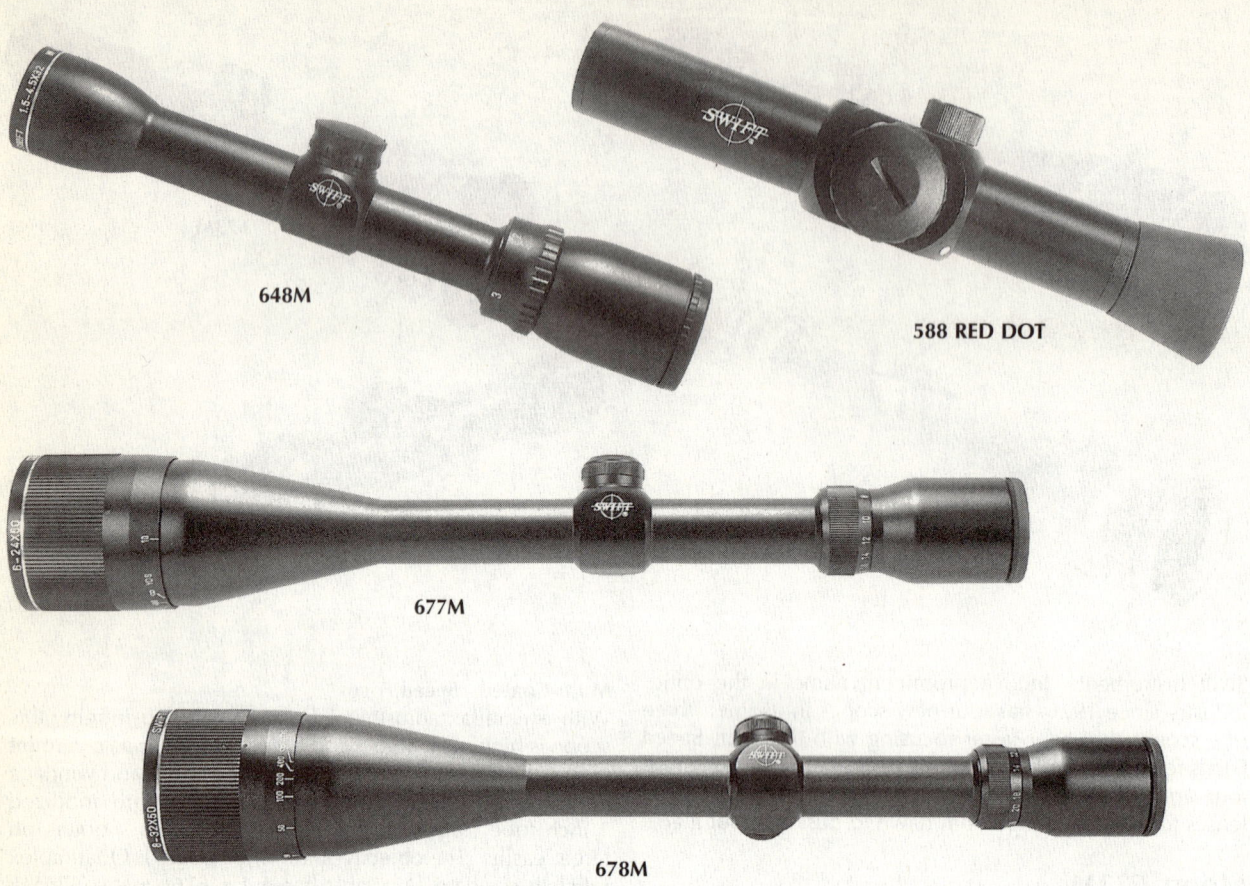

MODEL 648M SWIFT PREMIER
1.5-4.5x, 32MM - WA-WATERPROOF-MULTI-COATED-SPEED FOCUS
Considered to be the most versatile scope in the Premier line, the 1.5-45x is ideal on shotguns and black powder rifles. Eye relief ranges from 3.05 to 3.27. Crosshair and circle reticle make this riflescope easy to focus on target, and ideal for turkey hunting. Black matte finish. **Price** $180

MODEL 677M SWIFT PREMIER
6-24x, 50MM - WA - WATERPROOF - MULTI-COATED - SPEED FOCUS
With a magnification range of 6 to 24 power and a 50mm objective lens with sunshade, this scope is the one to use when you're after really tight groups. Elevation and windage adjustments are mounted full saddle on the hand anodized 1-inch tube. The objective may be adjusted for parallax. This is a fine scope for long-range big game hunting and varminting.   **Price** 280

MODEL 678M SWIFT PREMIER
8-32x, 50MM - WATERPROOF - MULTI-COATED - SPEED FOCUS
With an ample field of view of 13 feet at 100 yards and eye relief of 3.13 inches, this scope can be used for bench rest shooting and long range hunting. It is very effective on prairie dogs. Parallax adjustment adds versatility. Elevation and windage adjustments are mounted full saddle on the hard anodized 1-inch tube. Equipped with sunshade.
Price $290

MODEL 588 RED DOT SCOPE
1x, 21MM - FOG-PROOF - FULLY COATED
Under any light conditions this Aerolite red dot electronic sight can be rapidly aligned for pinpoint accuracy. It has a field of view of 39 feet at 100 yards and unlimited eye relief. It is free of parallax from 5 meters to infinity. Body length is 6 1/4" to 7 1/8" with the rubber eyecup. Weighs only 5 ounces. These characteristics make it especially suitable for handgun shooting, shotguns and bows. CR-2032: 3-volt button battery is included. **Price** 100
Also Available: Red Dot Fire Fly 1x30
Price. 220-240

Tasco Scopes

PROPOINT 1X25

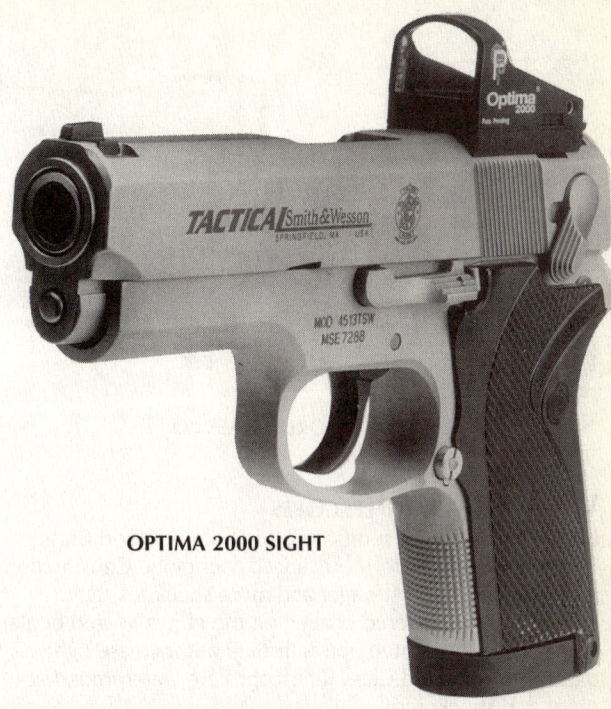

OPTIMA 2000 SIGHT

Optima 2000
What makes this ProPoint so revolutionary is that, unlike previous ProPoints, it does not have a tube. Smaller (only 1 1/2") and lighter (only 1/2 oz.) than any other sighting device, it is also extremely durable and rugged. After thousands of test rounds, it held its point of aim and its one-piece, dovetailed-style slide mount remained immovable. Its red dot was always on, with no time lost turning it on. While used primarily on pistols, the Optima 2000 can also be mounted on shotguns or slug guns. Optima 2000 is available with a bright, in-focus 3.5 or 7 M.O.A. dot on the same plane as iron sights for fast target acquisition.

Price: $199

Propoint Red Dot Sighting Device
Propoint Red Dot Sights have been the choice for competitive shooters, turkey hunters and slug gun enthusiasts for years. Built to last, the Propoint features solid construction, flawless tracking and a rheostat-controlled illuminated red dot. Included accessories: rings to fit standard 5/8" bases, extension tubes, polarizing filter and one lithium battery.

Propoint Scopes

Model	Power	Objective Diameter	Finish	Reticle	Field of View @ 100 Yds.	Eye Relief	Tube Diam.	Scope Length	Scope Weight	Prices
PDP2	1X	25mm	Black Matte	5 M.O.A. Dot	40'	Unlimited	30mm	5"	5.5 oz.	$129
PDP3	1X	25mm	Black Matte	5 M.O.A. Dot	52'	Unlimited	30mm	5"	5.5 oz.	149
PDP3ST	1X	25mm	Stainless	10 M.O.A. Dot	52'	Unlimited	30mm	5"	5.5 oz.	149
PDP3CMP	1X	30mm	Black Matte	10 M.O.A. Dot	68'	Unlimited	33mm	4.75"	5.4 oz.	169
PDP5CMP	1X	45mm	Black Matte	4,8,12,16 M.O.A. Dot	82'	Unlimited	47mm	4"	8 oz.	209
Red Dot Sights										
BKRD30	1X	30mm	Black Matte AWF	Illum. Red Dot	57"	Unlimited	38mm	3.75"	6 oz.	$44
BKRD25	1X	25mm	Black Matte	Illum. Red Dot	40"	Unlimited	30mm	5.25"	4.7 oz.	76
BKRD30/22	1X	30mm	Black Matte AWF	Illum. Red Dot	57"	Unlimited	38mm	3.75"	6 oz.	44
BKRD42	1X	42mm	Black Matte AWF	Illum. Red Dot	62"	Unlimited	47mm	3.75"	6.7 oz.	60

Tasco Scopes

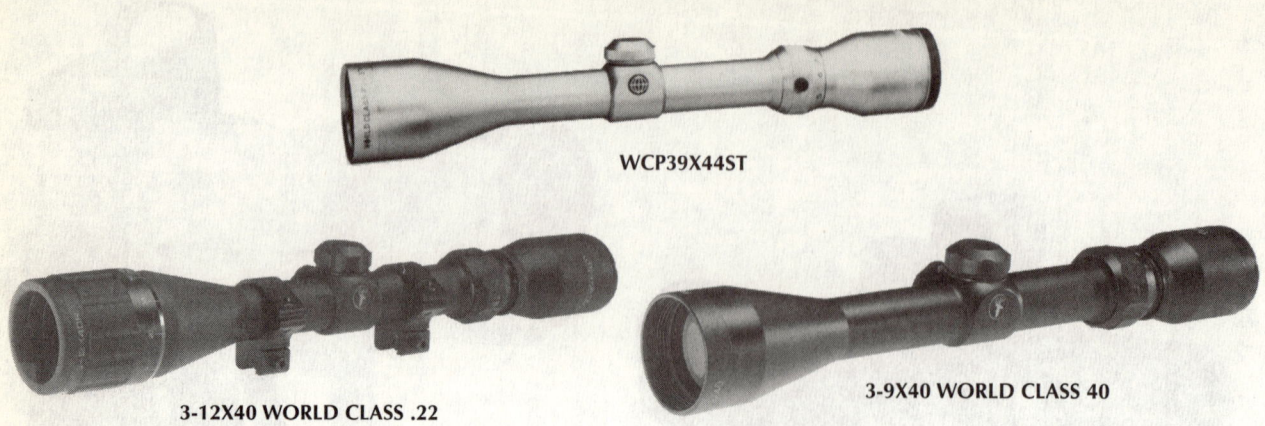

WCP39X44ST

3-12X40 WORLD CLASS .22

3-9X40 WORLD CLASS 40

WORLD CLASS RIFLESCOPES
Long a favorite with sportsmen, wide-angle World Class Riflescopes now have 1" Advanced Monotube Construction to make them even stronger and more shock resistant. SuperCon multi-layered coating on the objective and ocular lenses and fully-coated optics throughout increase light transmission. World Class Riflescopes are waterproof, fogproof and shockproof.

TITAN RIFLESCOPES
The Titan riflescope is big on superior performance and quality, with solid 30mm Monotube construction for strength and durability. Features include a wider field of view and more light gathering than 1" scopes. The scope is multi-coated, has finger adjustable windage and elevation controls and a fast-focus eyebell. Available with a 30/30 or German-style 4A reticle, the Titan is waterproof, fogproof and shockproof.

Model	Power	Objective Diameter	Finish	Reticle	F.O.V. @ 100 Yd.s	Eye Relief	Tube Diameter	Length	Weight	Prices
WORLD CLASS PLUS RIFLESCOPES										
DWCP39X44	3X-9X	44mm	Black Matte	30/30	39'-14'	3.5"	1"	12.75"	15.8 oz.	$178
WCP39X44ST	3X-9X	44mm	Stainless Steel	30/30	39'-14'	3.5"	1"	12.75"	15.8 oz.	188
DWCP3.510X50	3.5X-10X	50mm	Black Matte	30/30	30'-10.5'	3.75"	1"	13"	17.1 oz.	198
WORLD CLASS RIFLESCOPES										
DWC39X40N	3x-9x	40mm	Black Matte	30/30	41'-15'	3"	1"	12.75"	13 oz.	$99
DWC39X40TV	3x-9x	40mm	Black Matte	30/30 TV	41'-15'	3"	1"	12.75"	13 oz.	99
DWC39X40IT	3x-9x	40mm	Black Matte	30/30IT	41'-51'	3.5"	1"	12.75"	15.3 oz.	139
DWC39X40MIR	3x-9x	40mm	Black Matte	MIR	41'-51	3.5	1"	13"	15.3 oz.	149
WA39X40N	3x-9x	40mm	Black Gloss	30/30	41'-15'	3"	1"	12.75"	13 oz.	99
WA39X40STN	3x-9x	40mm	Stainless	30/30	41'-15'	3"	1"	12.75"	13 oz.	99
WORLD CLASS 50										
DWC39X50N	3x-9x	50mm	Black Matte	30/30	41'-13'	3"	1"	12.5"	15.8 oz.	$119
DWC520X50	5x-20x	50mm	Black Matte	30/30	16'-3'	3"	1"	16"	20 oz.	188
WORLD CLASS COMPACT										
DWC28X32	2x-8x	32mm	AWF/Black Matte	30/30	50'-17'	4"	1"	10.5"	12.5 oz.	$109
DWC4X32	4x	32mm	AWF/Black Matte	30/30	25'	5"	1"	10"	10.5 oz.	95
WORLD CLASS .22										
DWC28X32R	2x-8x	32mm	AWF/Black Matte	30/30	55'-14'	2.75"	1"	10.5"	12.5 oz.	$109
DWC312X40R	3x-12x	40mm	AWF/Black Matte	30/30	26'-7'	3"	1"	13.75"	17.5 oz.	119
TITAN RIFLESCOPES										
T1.254.4x26N4A	1.25x-4x	26mm	Black Matte	4A	77.5'-22'	3.25"	30mm	10.5"	15.2 oz.	$318
Tl.56x42N	1.5x-6x	42mm	Black Matte	30/30	59'-20"	3.5"	30mm	12"	16.4 oz.	337
Tl.56x42N4A	1.5x-6x	42mm	Black Matte	4A	59'-20'	3.5"	30mm	12"	16.4 oz.	347
T412x56IR	4x-12x	56mm	Black Matte	30/3ID	23'-13"	3.25"	30mm	13.25"	12.2 oz.	670
T39x42N	3x-9x	42mm	Black Matte	30/30	37'-13'	3.5"	30mm	12.5"	16.8 oz.	337
T39x42N4A	3x-9x	42mm	Black Matte	4A	37'-13'	3.5"	30mm	12.5"	16.8 oz.	347
T312x52N	3x-12x	52mm	Black Matte	30/30	27'-10'	4.5"	30mm	14"	20.7 oz.	397
T312x52N4A	3x-12x	52mm	Black Matte	4A	27'-10'	4.5"	30mm	14"	20.7 oz.	407
TAC840x56	8x-40x	56mm	Black Matte	Mil-Dot	13'-2.6'	3"	30mm	18.5"	32 oz.	745

Tasco Riflescopes

VARMINT/TACTICAL SCOPES
Long range shooting is easier with Tasco's True Mil-Dot system. SuperCon multi-layered lens coatings and fully coated optics throughout provide clear resolution. With extra large 42mm objectives, this line of Varmint riflescopes transmit more light than standard 40mm scopes.

NEW FOR 2002
Tasco's new LER (Long Eye Relief) combines a lightweight, compact scope with illuminated technology (IT) to make these riflescopes perfect for rifles, shotgun, black powder, slug and brush. Available in fixed 4 power and variable 1.5 to 6 power.

EXP 3-9X42/54
The Tasco EXP features an oval objective lens. This new technology allows low profile mounting with standard or low rings without sacrificing light transmission.

MAG IV RIFLESCOPES
The large 40mm objective of MAG IV riflescopes delivers a full four times magnification with more zooming range than most variable scopes. In addition, a focusing objective provides valuable parallax correction. MAG IV scopes feature 1/4-minute windage/elevation click stops and black matte finish. The result is a line of scopes that provide superior light transmission and clarity even at high magnifications. Waterproof, fogproof and shockproof.

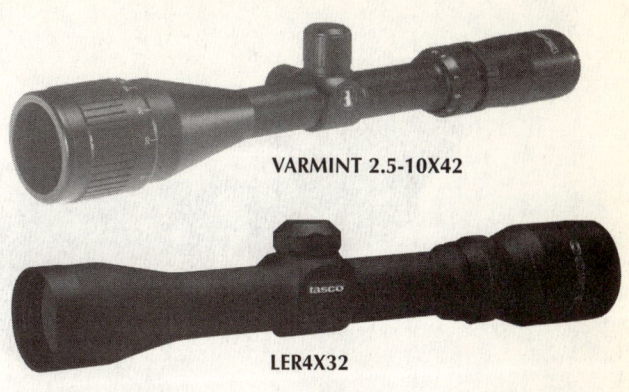

VARMINT 2.5-10X42

LER4X32

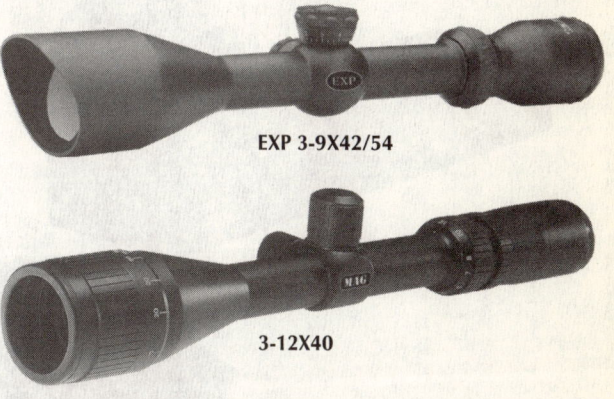

EXP 3-9X42/54

3-12X40

Model No.	Power	Objective Dia.	Finish	Reticle	F.O.V. @100 Yds.	Eye Relief	Tube Diameter	Length	Weight	Price
VARMINT/TACTICAL										
VAR2.510X42M	2.5X-10X	42mm	Black Matte	30/30	35'-9'	3"	1"	14"	19.1 oz.	$99
VAR624X42M	6X-24X	42mm	Black Matte	30/30	13'-3.7'	2.75"	1"	16"	19.6 oz.	119
VAR624X42MIR	6X-24X	42mm	Black Matte	MIR	13'-3.7'	3"	1"	16"	19.6 oz.	198
VAR832X42M	8X-32X	42mm	Black Matte	True Mil-Dot	11'-3.5'	3.25"	1"	17"	20 oz.	139
EXP										
H1.55X32/44	1.5X-5X	oval 32/44mm	AWF/Black Matte	30/30 wide view oval	62'-22'	5"	1"	13"	17 oz.	$169
H39X42/54	3X-9X	oval 42/54mm	AWF/Black Matte	30/30 wide view oval	41'-15'	3"	1"	13.5"	19.3 oz.	199
MAG IV RIFLESCOPES										
MAG624X40	6X-24X	40mm	Black Matte	30/30	17'-4'	3"	1"	16"	19.1 oz.	$143
MAG416X40ST	4X-16X	40mm	Stainless	30/30	26'-7'	3"	1"	15.25"	18.6 oz.	129
PRONGHORN										
PH4X32	4X	32mm	Black Gloss	30/30	32'	3"	1"	12"	12.5 oz.	$36
PH39X32	3X-9X	32mm	Black Gloss	30/30	39'-13'	3"	1"	12"	11 oz.	46
PH39X40	3X-9X	40mm	Black Gloss	30/30	39'-13'	3"	1"	13"	12.1 oz.	56
RIMFIRE										
RF4X15*	4X	15mm	Black Gloss	Crosshair	22.5'	2.5"	3/4"	11"	4 oz.	$8
RF4X20WA*	4X	20mm	Black Matte	30/30	23'	2.5"	3/4"	10.5"	3.8 oz.	12
RF37X20*	3X-7X	20mm	Black Gloss	30/30TV	24'-11'	2.5"	3/4"	11.5"	5.7 oz.	24
EZ01*	1X	20mm	Black Matte	Red Dot	35'	Unlimited	1"	4.75"	2.5 oz.	22
RIMFIRE MAG										
MAG4X32	4X	32mm	Black Matte	30/30	27'	3"	1"	12.25"	12.1 oz.	$48
MAG4X32ST	4X	32mm	Stainless	30/30	27'	3"	1"	12.25"	12.1 oz.	50
MAG39X32	3X-9X	32mm	Black Matte	30/30	35.5'-11.5'	3"	1"	12.75"	11.3 oz.	62
MAG39X32ST	3X-9X	32mm	Stainless	30/30	35.5'-11.5'	3"	1"	12.75"	11.3 oz.	64
LER (LONG EYE RELIEF)										
LER4X32	4X	32mm	Black Matte	30/30	18.75'	6"	1"	10.25	10 oz.	$100
LER4X32IT	4X	32mm	Black Matte	30/30 IT	18.75'	6"	1"	10.5"	12.1 oz.	119
LER1.56X32	1.5X-6X	32mm	Black Matte	30/30	44'-15'	4"	1"	12"	12.3 oz.	109
LER1.56X32IT	1.5X-6X	32mm	Black Matte	30/30 IT	44'-15'	4"	1"	12"	14.4 oz.	129

*Includes rings

Trijicon Sights & Scopes
Fiber-Optic

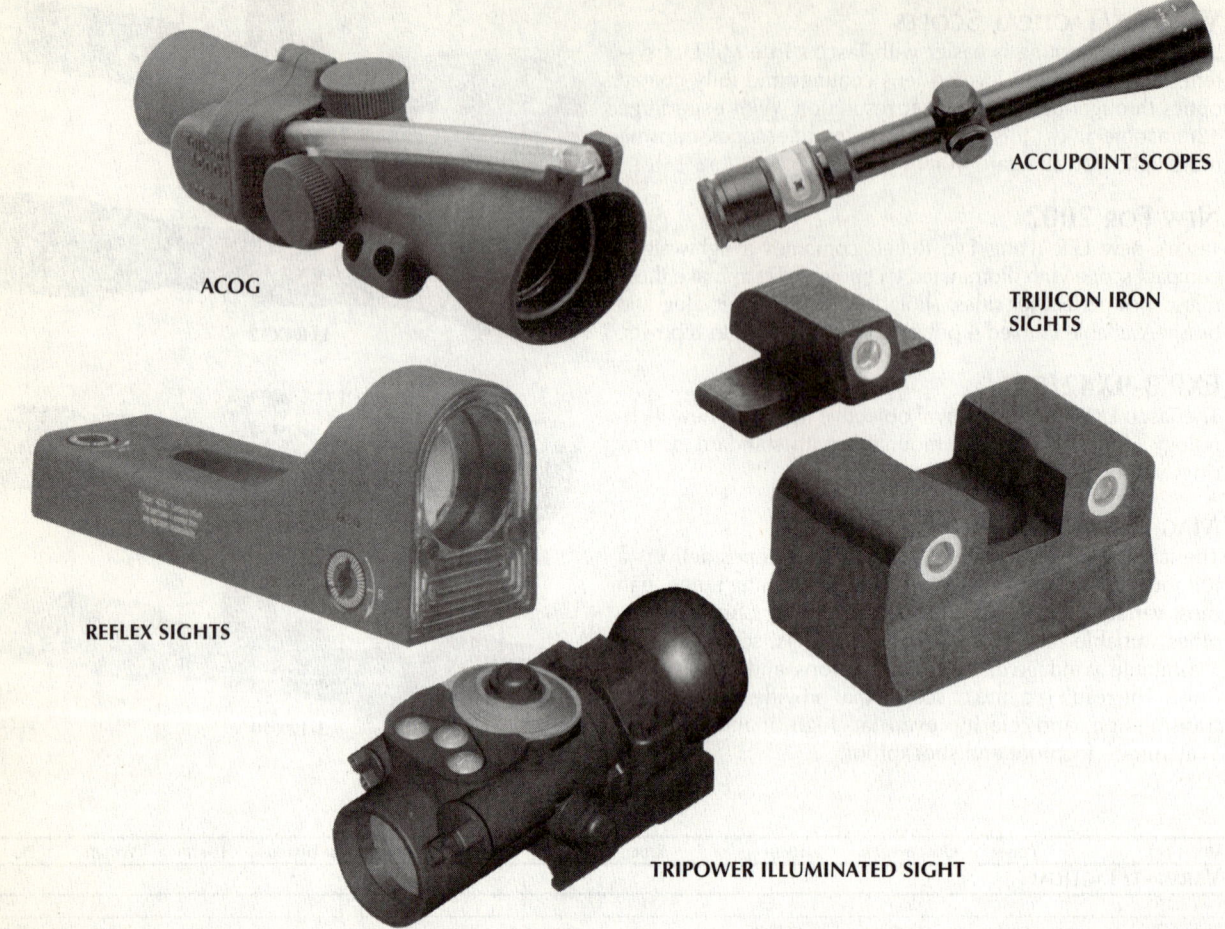

ACOG
ACCUPOINT SCOPES
TRIJICON IRON SIGHTS
REFLEX SIGHTS
TRIPOWER ILLUMINATED SIGHT

ACOG
The ACOGs are internally-adjustable, compact telescopic sights with tritium illuminated reticle patterns for use in low light or at night. Many models are dual-illuminated, featureing fiber optics which collect ambient light for maximum brightness in day-time shooting. The ACOGs combine traditional, precise distance marksmanship with close-in aiming speed.
Prices: .... $950 to 1672
Compact ACOG 895

ACCUPOINT SCOPES
AccuPoint's dual-illuminated aiming point offers a major advancement over crosshairs that can disappear due to lack of contrast when aiming at a dark animal, or in low-light conditions. Reticle illumination is supplied by advanced fiber optics or, in low-light conditions, by a self-contained tritium lamp.
Prices: 3-9x40, red or amber triangle 720
1.2-4x24, red or amber triangle 700

REFLEX SIGHTS
The dual-illuminated, Trijicon Reflex sight gives shooters next-generation technology for super-fast, any-light aiming-without batteries.

Developed for the military for use in both-eyes-open Close Quarters Battle (CQB) situations, the Reflex sight features an amber aiming dot that is illuminated both by light from the target area and from a tritium lamp.
Price: .... $350 to 599

TRIJICON IRON SIGHTS
Trijicon self-luminous iron sights are proven to give shooters greater night fire accuracy-with the same speed as instinctive shooting. That's why, along with their 12-year limited warranty, Trijicon Bright & Tough night sights are the first choice of major handgun manufacturers and standard issue with hundreds of municipal and county departments, numerous state and police departments and several Federal agencies.

TRIPOWER ILLUMINATED SIGHT
The new TriPower features a red chevron-shaped reticle illuminated by three lighting sources: an integrated fiber optic system, a Tritium-Illuminated reticle and on-call battery backup. The TriPower has a 30mm tube, coated lenses, and is sealed for underwater use up to 100 feet. The TriPower is 5 inches long and weighs 6 oz.
Price: 550

Weaver Scopes
T-Series

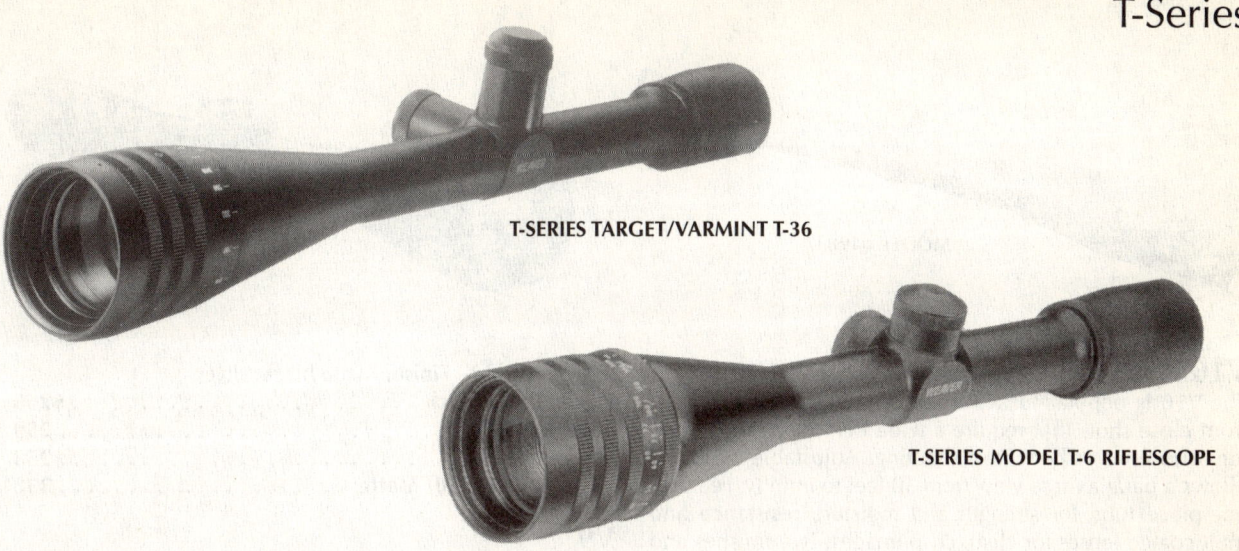

T-SERIES TARGET/VARMINT T-36

T-SERIES MODEL T-6 RIFLESCOPE

T-SERIES TARGET/VARMINT T-36
T-Series Target/Varmint Scopes - These fixed-power scopes feature Weaver's patented Micro-Trac adjustment system utilizing a dual-spring, four-bearing contact design that allows independent movement of windage and elevation. Optics are fully multi-coated, delivering premium image clarity in virtually all light conditions. Adjustable objective lens allows for zero parallax from 50' to infinity. Choice of fine crosshair or dot reticles. Scopes come with sunshade, extra pair of oversize benchrest adjustment knobs, and screw-in metal lens caps.
Model: T-36 **Magnification/Objective:** 36X40mm **Field Of View:** 3.0' **Eye Relief:** 3.0" **Length:** 15.1" **Weight:** 16.7 oz. **Reticle:** 1/8 MOA Dot, Fine Crosshair **Finish:** Matte black or silver
Price:...................................$794

T-SERIES MODEL T-6 RIFLESCOPE
Weaver's T-6 competition 6x scope is only 12.7 inches long and weighs less than 15 ounces. All optical surfaces are fully multi-coated for maximum clarity and light transmission. The T-6 features Weaver's Micro-Trac precision adjustments in 1/8-minute clicks to ensure parallel tracking. The protected target-style turrets are a low-profile configuration combining ease of adjustment with weight reduction. A 40mm adjustable objective permits parallax correction from 50 feet to infinity without shifting the point of impact. A special AO lock ring eliminates bell vibration or shift. The T-6 comes with screw-in metal lens caps and features a competition matte black finish.
Reticles: dot, Fine Crosshair
Price: 6x40 Satin Black......................$425

WEAVER TACTICAL SCOPES (NOT SHOWN)
These tactical scopes have a first-plane reticle, meaning the crosshair measurement maintains the same size relative to the size of the target at any power. The range-calculating reticle of the Tactical scope is etched into the glass in front of the adjustment housing.

At the center of the reticle is a small diamond that covers one inch outside. Marks beyond the diamond on the crosspieces can be used to bracket a target and determine range. Tactical scopes have 1/8-minute-of-angle windage and elevation adjustments with target-style knobs. The knobs also offer a "guaranteed zero" feature that allows the shooter to move the reticle for a specific shooting need, then return the scope to zero without sighting in again. An adjustable objective lens is also included on the 4.5-14x44mm scope for precise parallax-free adjustments.

All air-to-glass lens surfaces are fully multi-coated, and the scopes are waterproof to 10,000 feet and to 120 degrees with 100% humidity. Weaver's Tactical scopes are offered in black matte finish.
Price:.....................................716

SPECIFICATIONS

Magnification X Obj. Diam. (mm)	Exit Pupil (mm)	FOV (Ft. @ 100 Yds.)	Eye Relief (In.)	Overall Length (In.)	Weight (Oz.)	Reticle
3-9x40	13.3-4.4	33-14.5	4.17-3.02	12.5	17.0	Diamond
4.5-14x44	10-3	22-9.4	4.1-2.8	15.2	20.6	Diamond

Weaver Scopes

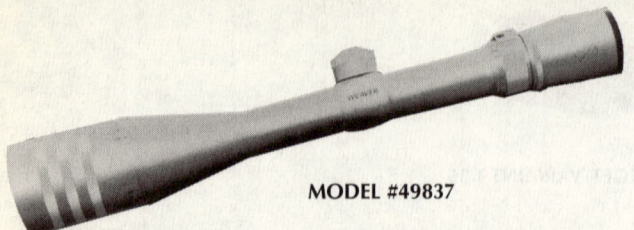

MODEL #49837

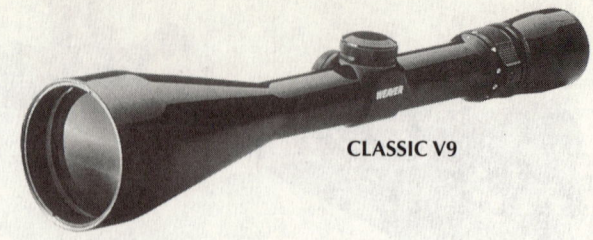

CLASSIC V9

V16 RIFLESCOPES
The V16 is popular for a variety of shooting applications, from close shots that require a wide field of view to long-range varmint or benchrest shooting. Adjustable objective allows a parallax-free view from 30 feet to infinity. Features one-piece tube for strength and moisture resistance and multicoated lenses for clear, crisp images. Two finishes and three reticle options.
Magnification/Objective: 4-16X42mm **Field Of View:** 26.8'-6.8' **Eye Relief:** 3.1" **Length:** 13.9" **Weight:** 16.5 oz.
Reticle: Choice of Dual-X, 1/4 MOA Dot, or Fine Crosshair **Finish:** Matte black
Price: $425
V24 6-24x42 (not shown) black matte 495

V10 (NOT SHOWN)
Magnification/Objective: 2-10X38mm **Field Of View:** 38.5-9.5 **Eye Relief:** 3.5" **Length:** 12.2" **Weight:** 11.2 oz.
Reticle: Dual-X **Finish:** Matte black, silver
Price: Matte black $259
Silver. 259
In gloss black. 253
V10x50 (2-10x50) Matte 358

V9
Magnification/Objective: 3-9x38 **Field Of View:** 34-11' **Eye Relief:** 3.5" **Length:** 12" **Weight:** 11 oz. **Finish:** Matte black, gloss
Price: Matte black 242
Gloss. 228
V9XX50 (3-9x50) Matte 310

V3 (NOT SHOWN)
Magnification/Objective: 1-3x20 **Field Of View:** 100x34 **Eye Relief:** 3.5" **Length:** 9" **Weight:** 9 oz. **Finish:** Matte black
Price: Matte black 228

CLASSIC HANDGUN 1.5-4X20

CLASSIC RIMFIRE RV7

WEAVER CLASSIC HANDGUN SCOPES
Fixed-power scopes include 2x28 and 4x28 scopes in gloss black or silver. Variables in 1.5-4x20 and 2.5-8x28 come with a gloss black finish. The 2.5-8x28 is also available in black matte. One-piece tubes, fully multi-coated lenses and generous eye relief (4-29") make these scopes top performers on hunting handguns.
Prices: 2x28. $209 (220 in silver)
4x28 . . . . 227 (231 in silver)
1.5-4x20 279
2.5-8x28 291
2.5-8x28 matte 296

CLASSIC RIMFIRE RV7
Lenses are multi-coated for bright, clear low-light performance and the one-piece tube design is shockproof and waterproof.
Prices:
2.5-7x28 Rimfire Matte $172
2.5-7x28 Rimfire Silver. 173

RIMFIRE SCOPE RV4 (NOT SHOWN)
This fixed 4x scope is ideal for a variety of shooting applications. It's durable, light-weight and waterproof.
Prices:
Rimfire Matte Black 4x28. 149

Weaver Scopes

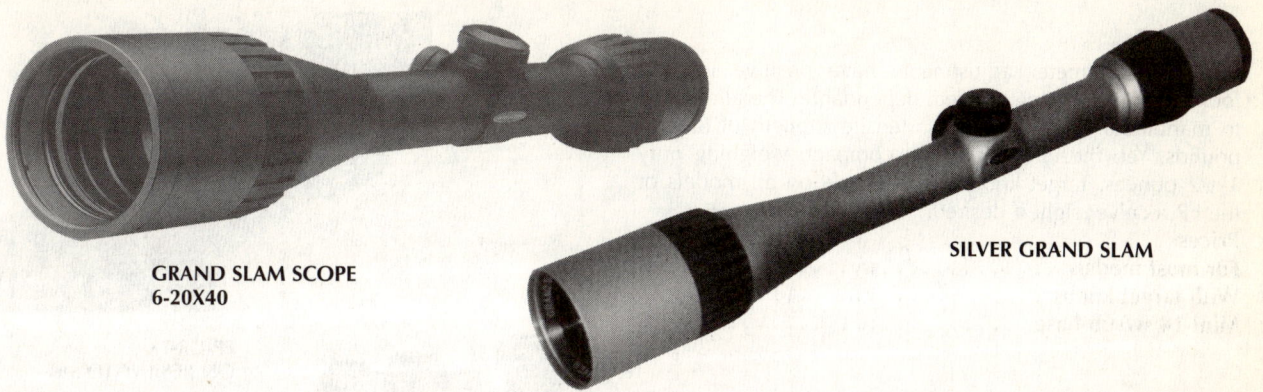

GRAND SLAM SCOPE 6-20X40

SILVER GRAND SLAM

Weaver Grand Slam Scopes

Among the advanced features of the Grand Slam series are a "sure-grip" power ring and AO adjustment that let you easily adjust the variable scopes, even while wearing heavy gloves, and an offset parallax indicator so you can remain in shooting position while adjusting the scope. Grand Slam scopes feature camera-quality, fully multi-coated lenses that ensure sharp, bright viewing. For quick focusing, the eyepiece has a fast-focus adjustment ring. Simply rotate the ring until the reticle becomes sharp.

Grand Slam scopes' solid, one-piece construction makes them not only rugged and reliable, but resistant to moisture and humidity. Configurations include: 4.75x40mm, a fixed-power scope with sufficient magnification for longer shots, yet a wide field of view for finding running game close in; 1.5-5x32mm, the ideal scope for short-range rifles and fast target acquisition in brushy country; 3.5-10x40mm, the traditional choice of big-game hunters for short- or long-range shooting; 3.5-10x50mm, which provides the brightest view in low-light situations; 4.5-14x40mm AO, possibly the most versatile Grand Slam scope, with a low range suitable for stand hunting and high enough magnification for target shooting or varmint hunting; and 6-20x40mm AO, two target/varminter models.

Windage and elevation knobs have target-type finger adjustments so 1/4-MOA adjustments can be made by gripping the rim of the knob between the thumb and index finger. The Grand Slam scopes are also equipped with Micro-Trac, Weaver's patented four-point adjustment system.

All Grand Slam scopes are offered with a plex reticle (except the 6-20x model, which is offered with a choice of Weaver's Varminter reticle or fine crosshairs with a dot). The scopes have a non-glare black matte or silver and black finish, featuring the new green and gold oval Weaver logo medallion on the scope saddle and green ring inside the objective lens hood.

Price: 6-20x40 AO $500
4.5-14x40 AO 500
3.5-10x50 460
3-10x40 380
1.5-5x32 430
4.75x40 360

CLASSIC 2.5 2.5X20MM

Weaver Classic K Series

The K2.5, K4 and K6 have a long history in America's game fields. New logos distinguish these versatile hunting scopes at a glance. Reasonably priced and great values, K scopes–including the target model, KT-15–have one-piece tubes and bright optics.

Prices: KT-15 (15x40 gloss) $364
K6 (gloss) 192
K6 (matte) 202
K4 (gloss) 180
K4 (matte) 189
K2.5 (2.5x20 gloss) 172

Williams Sights
FP Series

Internal micrometer adjustments have positive internal locks. The FP is strong, rugged, dependable. The alloy used to manufacture this sight has a tensile strength of 85,000 pounds. Yet, the FP is light and compact, weighing only 1-1/2 ounces. Target knobs are available on all models of the FP receiver sight if desired.

Prices:
For most models. $66
With target knobs 77
Mini 14 w/sub-base 71

FP-GR-TK ON REMINGTO 581

FP-AG-TK ON BEEMAN AIR RIFLE

FP-KNIGHT-TK SILVER ON MK-85

FP-94 SE SHOWN ON WINCHESTER 94 SIDE EJECT

FP MINI-14-TK WITH SUB-BASE

FP Receiver Sight Options

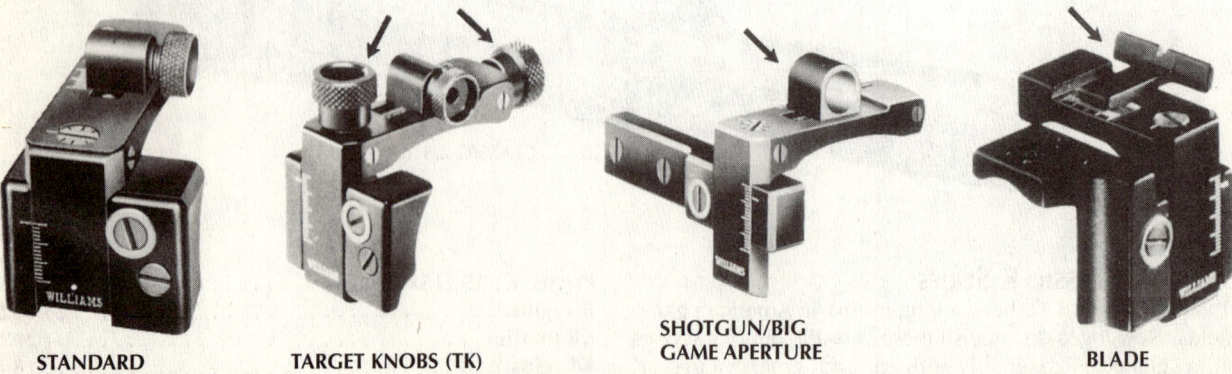

STANDARD   **TARGET KNOBS (TK)**   **SHOTGUN/BIG GAME APERTURE**   **BLADE**

Williams Sights
Open Sights

WGOS Series
- Made from high tensile strength aluminum. Will not rust.
- All parts milled - no stampings.
- Streamlined and lightweight with tough anodized finish.
- Dovetailed windage and elevation - Easy to adjust, positive locks.
- Interchangeable blades available in four heights and four styles.

Price: $18-25

Blades are sold separately, except "U" blades are available installed on WGOS octagon T/C and CVA.
Price:. 7

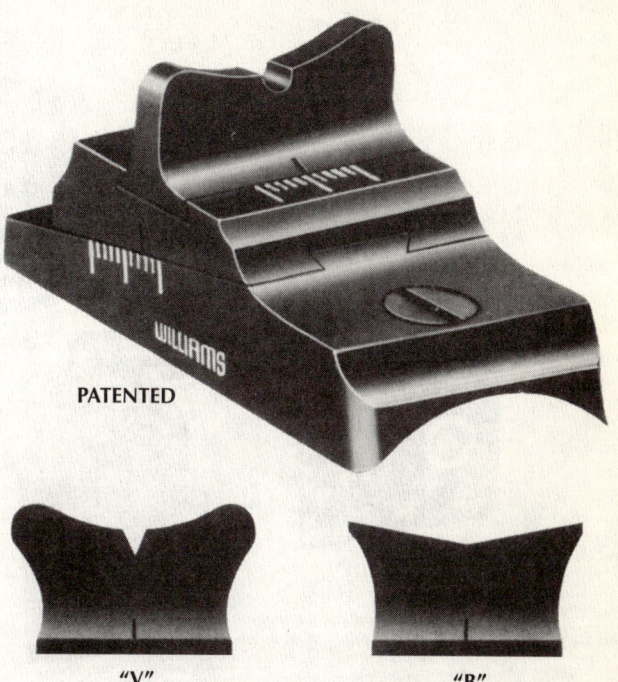

PATENTED

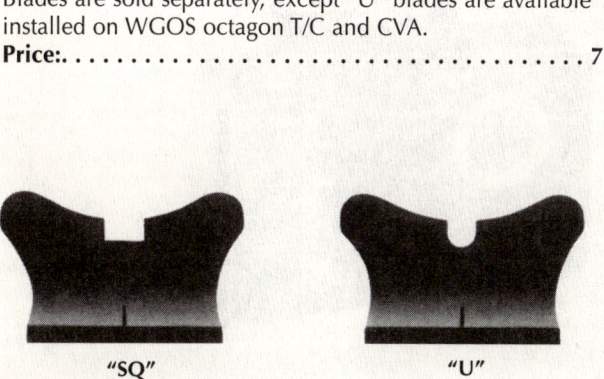

"SQ" "U" "V" "B"

Receiver Sights

WGRS-CVA ON CVA APOLLLO

"GHOST RING" SHOTGUN APERTURE AVAILABLE FOR WGRS RECEIVER SIGHTS. SOLD SEPARATELY.

FIRE SIGHTS

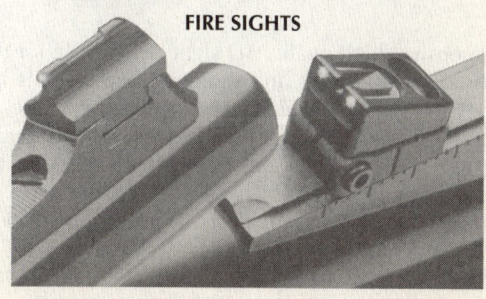

WGRS Series
- Compact Low Profile
- Lightweight, Strong, Rustproof
- Positive Windage and Elevation Locks

In most cases these sights utilize dovetail or existing screws on top of the receiver for installation. They are made from an aluminum alloy that is stronger than many steels. Light. Rustproof. Williams quality throughout.
Price: most models. $33

Fire Sights
Williams has introduced new "Fire Sights". These sights are machined from aircraft-strength aluminum and steel. This sight is lightweight, durable and brightens in low-light situations.
Prices:
Pistol Fire Sight Sets. 43
Shotgun Fire Sight Sets . . . . 27 to 37
Muzzleloader Fire Sight Sets . . . . 27 to 50
Rifle Fire Sight Sets . . . . 26 to 36
Peep Sets . . . . 40 to 77
Rifle Beads. 16
Vent Rib Shotgun Fire Sight Set. 40

Williams
5D Series

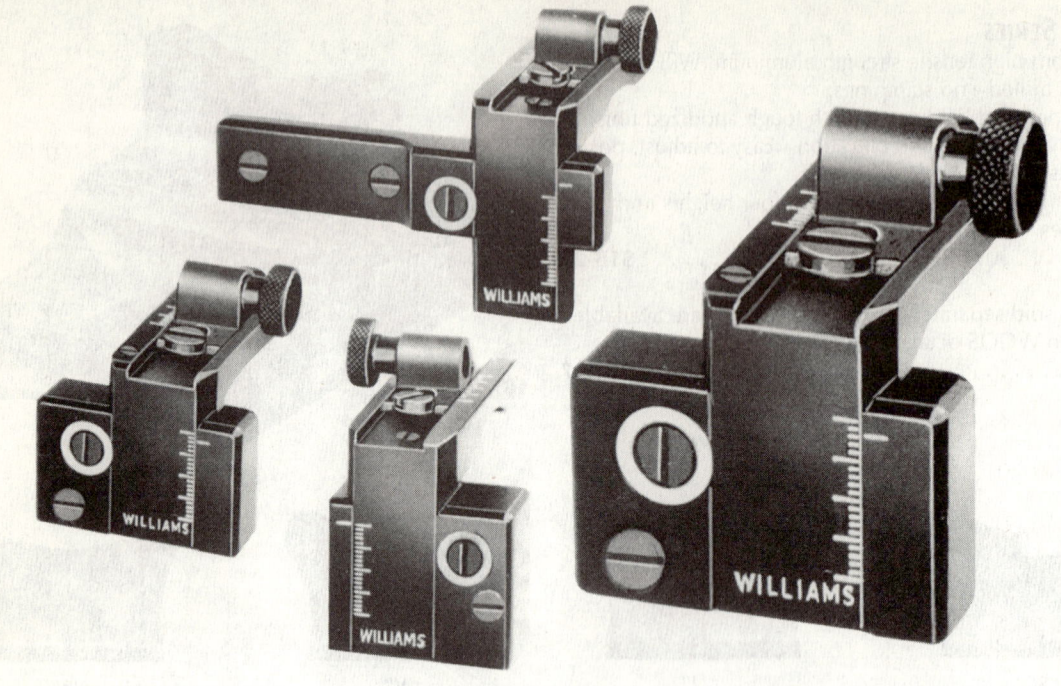

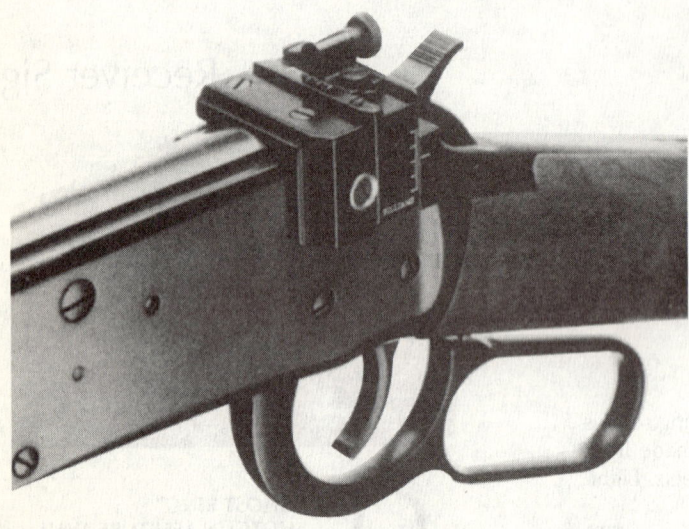

5D SERIES
- FOR BIG GAME RIFLES, 22'S, SHOTGUNS
- POSITIVE WINDAGE AND ELEVATION LOCKS
- LIGHTWEIGHT, STRONG, ACCURATE
- WILLIAMS QUALITY THROUGHOUT - RUSTPROOF

The inexpensive, high quality 5D sight is available for most of the more popular rifles and shotguns. These sights have the same strength, lightweight, and neat appearance, but without the micrometer adjustments. Designed for rugged hunting use, the 5D sights are dependable and accurate. Positive locks. Clear unobstructed vision. No knobs or side plates to blot out shooter's field of vision. Wherever possible, the manufacturers' mounting screw holes in the receivers of the guns have been utilized for easy installation. The upper staff of the Williams 5D sight is readily detachable. Just loosen one screw. The angular bushing locks this upper staff. A set screw is provided as a stop screw so that the sight will return to absolute zero after reattaching. The Williams 5D sight is made of one of the highest grade alloys obtainable. Laboratory tests show that the material used has a tensile strength approximately 25% greater than mild steels.
Price: Most 5D models $35

Williams
Target FP Series

TARGET - FP (HIGH)

TARGET - FP ANSCHUTZ

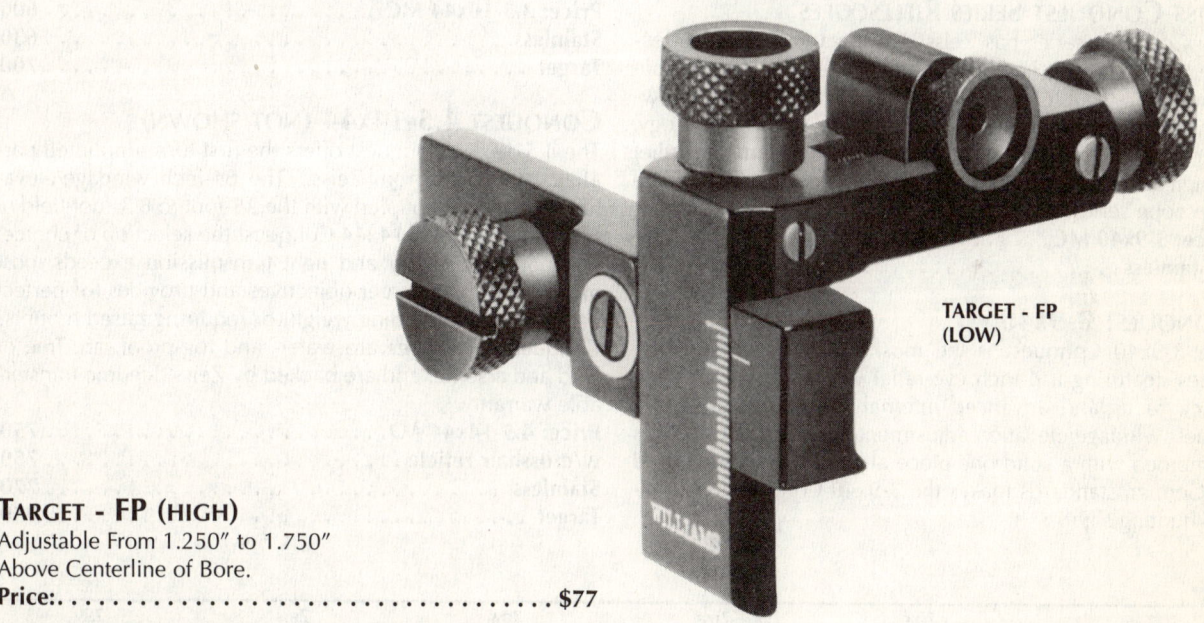

TARGET - FP (LOW)

TARGET - FP (HIGH)
Adjustable From 1.250" to 1.750"
Above Centerline of Bore.
Price:..$77

TARGET FP-ANSCHUTZ
Designed to fit many of the Anschutz Lightweight .22 Cal. Target and Sporter Models. No Drilling and Tapping required.
Price:..74

TARGET - FP (LOW)
Adjustable From .750" to 1.250"
Above Centerline of Bore.
Price:..77

Zeiss Scopes

CONQUEST 3-9X40

CONQUEST 3.5-10X44
STAINLESS STEEL FINISH

NEW FOR 2002!
CONQUEST 6.5-20X50 MC (NOT SHOWN)
The latest addition to the Conquest line of riflescopes is the 6.5-20X50. Developed for the American long-range shooter, this riflescope is ideal for big game hunting, varmint shooting or competition at great distances. Equipped with a turret-mounted parallax adjustment, the new 6.5-20X50 eliminates the need for the shooter to take his eye off the target. The external target turret knobs have no caps to lose and make it easier to view the windage and elevation. The riflescope does not require high mounts, allowing for a compact rifle profile and low line of sight.
Reticle: Z Plex or Fine Crosshair **Eye Relief:** 3.5"
F.O.V.: 17.6'-5.8' at 100 yds. **Weight:** 21.5 oz.
Price: Matte Black $950
Stainless 970

ZEISS CONQUEST SERIES RIFLESCOPES
The Conquest series has Zeiss' proprietary MC anti-reflective coating and is backed by a Lifetime Transferable Warranty. Couple this with Zeiss' world renowned low-light performance, new arsenic/lead-free glass technology, precision engineering, quick focus and constant eye relief design and you have one of the world's highest performance riflescope series.
Price: 3-9x40 MC 500
Stainless 530

CONQUEST 3-9x40
The 3-9x40 Conquest is the most versatile scope in the series, featuring a 4-inch eye-relief with unique European quick focus and advanced internal design, enabling the widest windage/elevation adjustment to 64 inches. All this combined with a solid one-piece alloy body manufactured to German standards makes the 3-9x40 Conquest a practical hunting sight.

CONQUEST 3-9x40S (NOT SHOWN)
The 3-9x40S Conquest is designed to support sportsmen who demand a shotgun, airgun, or muzzleloader scope with heavy reticle. The 3-9x40S has the same glass and coating as the 3-9, with a safe 4-inch eye relief, etched glass reticle and one-piece alloy tube.
Price: 3-9x40S $500
w/turkey reticle 500

CONQUEST 3.5-10x44
The 3.5-10x44 Conquest, designed to replace Zeiss' Diavari C 3-9x36, is superior in design and has all the standard Conquest features. Additionally, the 3.5-10x44 Conquest offers a 22-percent larger objective and a 66-inch windage/elevation adjustment. Combine these features with a weight of just 14 oz., the 3.5-10x44 Conquest makes it suitable for general big game hunting.
Price: 3.5-10x44 MC 600
Stainless. 630
Target 700

CONQUEST 4.5-14x44 (NOT SHOWN)
The 4.5-14x44 Conquest offers the first turret-mounted parallax adjustment from Zeiss. The 64-inch windage/elevation adjustment coupled with the 25-foot to 8.3-foot field of view made the 4.5-14x44 Conquest the selection of choice. The objective clarity and light transmission exceeds most models that have larger objectives and provides for perfect balance without adding weight or requiring raised mounts. Conquest riflescopes are water- and fog-proof, are free of lead and arsenic, and are backed by Zeiss' lifetime transferable warranty.
Price: 4.5-14x44 AO. 750
w/crosshair reticle 750
Stainless. 770
Target 850

SPECIFICATIONS	ZEISS CONQUEST 3-9x40	ZEISS CONQUEST 3-9x40S	ZEISS CONQUEST 3.5-10x44	ZEISS CONQUEST 4.5-14x44	ZEISS CONQUEST 6.5-20x50AO
Magnification	3-9x	3-9x	3.5-10x	4.5-14X	6.5-20X
Objective	40	40	44	44	50
Tube diameter	1"	1"	1"	1"	1"
Field of View (ft.@100yards)	11.01'-34'	11.01'-34'	11.61'-35.1'	8.31'-24.99'	17.6'-5.8'
Parallax (yards)	100	50	100	30-Infinity	50-Infinity
Exit Pupil (mm)	13.3-4.4	13.3-4.4	12.57-4.4	9.7-3.14	7.7-2.5
Eye Relief	4"	4"	3.5"	3.5"	3.5"
Length	13.15"	13.15"	12.7"	13.86"	15.6"
Weight	15 oz.	15 oz.	15.8 oz.	17.5 oz.	21.5 oz.
MOA	1/4	1/4	1/4	1/4	1/4

Zeiss Scopes

Diavari VM/V 3-9x42 T*

Over the years, the 3-9x power range has proven its staying power. It is still the favorite power range of North American hunters. The 42 mm objective, coupled with the Zeiss T* coating, extends the hunting day. Whether the quarry is elk, Dall sheep or Boone and Crockett white-tail, the VM/V Diavari 3-9 x 42T* offers top quality and the right magnification.

POWER	3-9x
EFFECTIVE OBJECTIVE DIAMETER (MM)	30-42
EXIT PUPIL DIAMETER (MM)	10-4.7
TWILIGHT FACTOR	8.5-18.4
FIELD OF VIEW AT 100 YARDS (FEET)	36-12.9
MINIMUM SQUARE ADJUSTMENT RANGE AT 100 YARDS (INCH)	49.7
EYE RELIEF (INCH)	3.74
CENTER TUBE DIAMETER (INCH)	1
OBJECTIVE BELL DIAMETER (INCH)	1.89
LENGTH (INCH)	13.3
WEIGHT (OUNCES)	15.2
PARALLAX FREE (YARDS)	109.4
PRICE:	$1250

Diavari VM/V 5-15x42 T*

Precise windage and elevation adjustments make the Diavari VM/V 5 - 15 x 42 T* the perfect companion for a target or varmint rifle. The rugged adjustment system provides fast, accurate and repeatable adjustments. By aligning the optical and mechanical axes, Zeiss ensures full range of adjustment.

POWER	5-15x
EFFECTIVE OBJECTIVE DIAMETER (MM)	42-42
EXIT PUPIL DIAMETER (MM)	8.4-2.8
TWILIGHT FACTOR	14.1-25.1
FIELD OF VIEW AT 100 YARDS (FEET)	23.7-7.8
MINIMUM SQUARE ADJUSTMENT RANGE AT 100 YARDS (INCH)	30
EYE RELIEF (INCH)	3.74
CENTER TUBE DIAMETER (INCH)	1
OBJECTIVE BELL DIAMETER (INCH)	1.89
LENGTH (INCH)	13.3
WEIGHT (OUNCES)	14
PARALLAX FREE (YARDS)	109.4
PRICE:	$1500

Diavari VM/V 3-12x56 T*

In the quiet haze of dawn or the fleeting light of sunset, a riflescope is put to the ultimate test. Under these conditions, the Diavari VM/V 3-12x56 T* excels. The patented Zeiss T* anti-reflection coating is designed to transmit the optimum percentage of light throughout the spectral range to take full advantage of your eye's sensitivity. Weighing in at 13.5 ounces, the VM/V 3-12x56 T* won't slow you down.

POWER	3-12x
EFFECTIVE OBJECTIVE DIAMETER (MM)	44.0-56
EXIT PUPIL DIAMETER (MM)	14.7-4.7
TWILIGHT FACTOR	8.5-25.9
FIELD OF VIEW AT 100 YARDS (FEET)	37.5-10.4
MINIMUM SQUARE ADJUSTMENT RANGE AT 100 YARDS (INCH)	36.7
EYE RELIEF (INCH)	3.54
CENTER TUBE DIAMETER (INCH)	1.18
OBJECTIVE BELL DIAMETER (INCH)	2.44
LENGTH (INCH)	13.54
WEIGHT (OUNCES)	17.8/16.8
PARALLAX FREE (YARDS)	109.4
PRICE:	$1600
W/ILLUMINATED RETICLE	2050

Zeiss Scopes
Zeiss Premuim Sports Optics

1.1-4 X 24 T*

DIAVARI 1.1-4 X 24 T* VM/V
- Compact riflescope with 108 ft. field of view at 1.1 power
- Extremely lightweight - ideal for safari rifles
- With illuminated varipoint reticle for fast target acquisition clearly visible also in critical lighting conditions
- Especially designed for running shots and hunting in heavy brush
- Available with bullet drop compensator
- Eye relief: 3.74 in.

Price: $1800

1.5-6 X 42 T*

DIAVARI 1.5-6 X 42 T* VM/V
- Excellent choice for white-tail or moose hunter
- Compact and easy to handle
- Lightest scope of its class
- 72 ft. field of view - largest field of view in premium class
- Easy-grip adjustment knob
- Available with bullet drop compensator
- Eye relief: 3.54 in.

Price: 1350
   w/Varipoint, reticle 1850
   w/Varipoint 54 reticle 1900

2.5-10 X 50 T*

DIAVARI 2.5-10 X 50 T* VM/V
- High powered riflescope with superior twilight performance
- Light, compact with a wide field of view
- Available with an illuminated reticle
- Easy-grip adjustment knob
- Excellent choice for world-wide all-round hunting
- Available with bullet drop compensator
- Eye relief: 3.54 in.

Price: $1550
   w/illuminated reticle 2000

Also Available (not shown)
DIAVARI 3-12X56 ZM/Z
Magnification: 3.12 **Tube Diameter:** 30mm **Eye Relief:** 3.2"
Field of view: 27.6' - 9.9' **Length:** 15.3" **Weight:** 27oz.
Price: Black matte 1100
    Stainless 1150
    w/illuminated reticle 1500

AMMUNITION

BLACK HILLS	450
FEDERAL	451
FIOCCHI	453
HORNADY	456
KNYOCH	457
MAGTECH	458
PMC	458
REMINGTON	460
ROTWELL BRENNEKE	462
RWS CENTERFIRE	463
WINCHESTER	465
Z-HAT	466

Black Hills Ammunition

Black Hills, aptly named for its South Dakota base of operations, offers an expanding line of factory-new and remanufactured ammunition for handguns and rifles. The Cowboy Action Line includes loads for the .32 H+R, .357 Magnum, .38-40, .44-40, .45 Colt, .32-20, .44 Colt, .44 Spl., .45 Schofield, .38 Spl, .38 Long Colt, .44 Russian, .45-70. Modern handgun ammunition, from .40 S+W to .44 Magnum, features a variety of bullet types. Black Hills rifle cartridges include the popular .223, .308, 6.5-284, .300 Win. Mag, and the potent long-range tactical round, the .338 Lapua. There's also specialty ammo, with frangible or moly-coated bullets. New for 2002 is Black Hills Gold ammunition, hunting rounds available in 243 Win, 270 Win, 308 Win, 30-06, and 300 Win Mag.

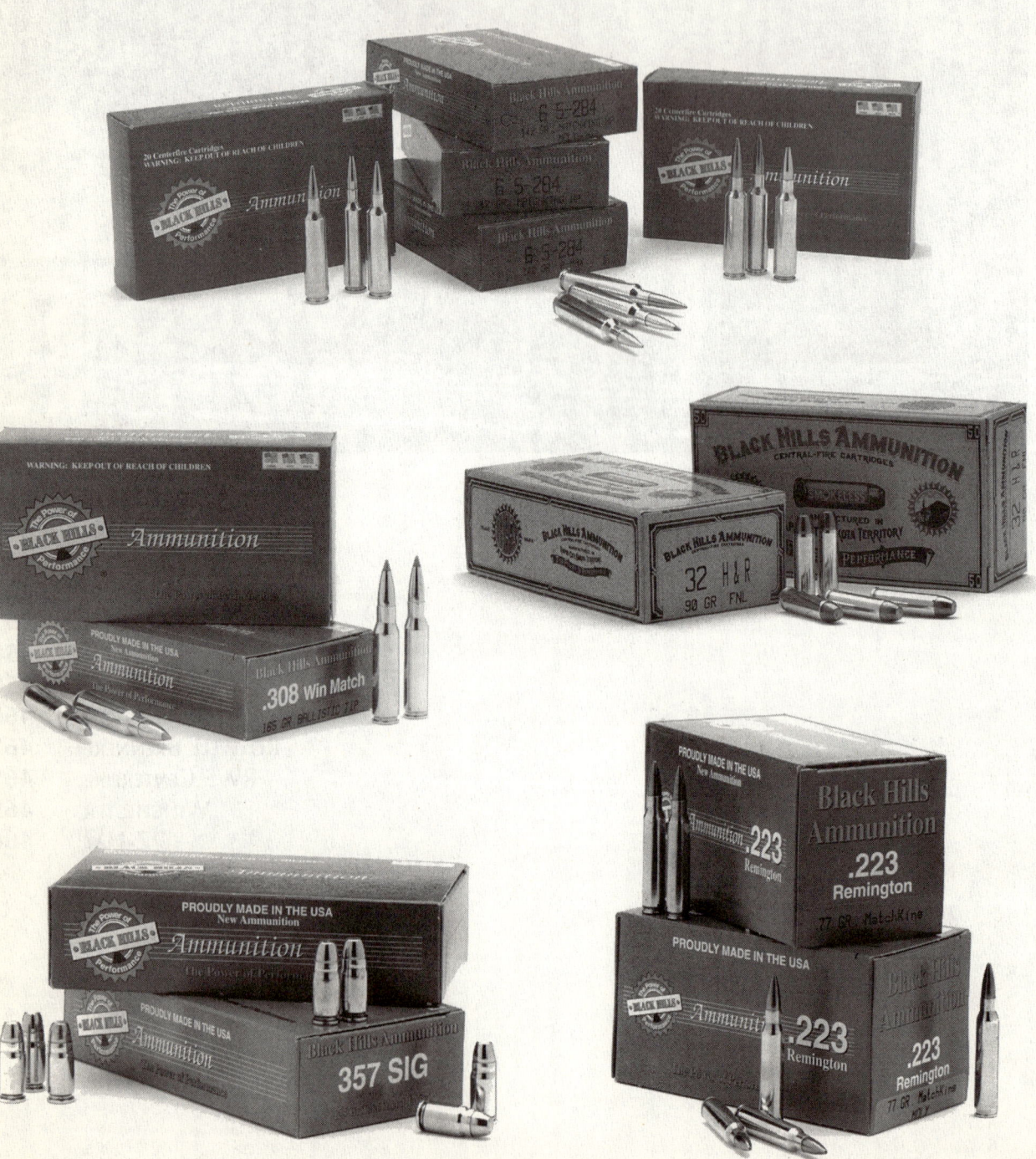

Federal Ammunition

Federal's 2002 line-up includes ammunition and components for big game and wildfowl hunters and personal defense. Some examples:

PREMIUM PISTOL EXPANDING FULL METAL JACKET

Premium Grand Slam Turkey Load
Features & Benefits
- High velocity provides increased downrange pellet energy and deep penetration
- Copper-plated extra hard shot for tight patterns
- Granulated plastic shot buffer cushions the shot for dense, uniform patterns
- Triple-Plus wad column provides positive gas sealing for uniform ballistics
- High base hull with high output 209A primer for consistant reliable ignition
- Portion of the proceeds from the sales go to the National Wild Turkey Federation

Classic Steel - Heavy High Velocity
Features & Benefits
- Increased shot payload with more downrange energy
- High velocity so it is quicker to target
- Three watertight seals at crimp, wad and primer
- High density shot cup prevents pellets from contacting bore surface
- High output 209A Primer provides consistent ballistic performance at all temperatures
- New box design
- Water resistant packaging

Premium Pistol Expanding Full Metal Jacket
Features & Benefits
- No hollowpoint to fill and block expansion, insuring consistent expansion through barriers
- Internally skived jacket gives consistent, symmetrical expansion with a large diameter
- Rubber front core performs well under a wide range of operating velocities and temperatures
- Works well in short barreled and standard barrel length handguns
- Low flash propellant for low light tactical use
- Reliable feed and function in semi-auto and automatic firearms

Premium Rifle 300 Win. Short Magnum
Features & Benefits
- Designed for short action rifles
- Beltless high capacity case provides ballistics equal to the longer 300 Win Magnum
- Available with Trophy Bonded Bear Claw or Speer Grand Slam bullets

-Trophy Bonded Bear Claw features:
- 100% fusion bonded jacket and core
- 95% weight return
- Reliable expansion from 25 yards to extreme ranges
- Better penetration through bone and muscle with no fragmentation

-Speer Grand Slam features:
- Exclusive hot core process insures reliable expansion and penetration
- Excellent retained weight and flat trajectory

American Eagle Pistol
Features & Benefits
- Gives price conscious customers top value for their money
- Federal brass for easy reloading
- Made in USA
- Quality components with reliable performance

Federal Centerfire Rifle Ammunition

TROPHY BONDED BEAR CLAW®
This legendary Jack Carter design is ideal for medium to large dangerous game and is loaded exclusivly by Federal. The jacket and core are 100% fusion-bonded for reliable bullet expansion from 25 yards to extreme ranges. The bullet retains 95% of its weight, assuring deep penetration. The bullet jacket features a hard solid copper base tapering to a soft, copper nose section for controlled expansion.

TROPHY BONDED SLEDGEHAMMER®
Use it on the largest, most dangerous game in the world. This Jack Carter design maximizes stopping power and your confidence. It's a bonded bronze solid with a flat nose that minimizes deflection off bone and muscle for a deep, straight wound channel.

SIERRA® GAMEKING® BOAT-TAIL
Long ranges are its specialty. With varying calibers, it's an excellent choice for everything from varmints to big game animals. The GameKings's tapered, boat-tail design provides extremely flat trajectories. The design also gives it a higher downrange velocity, so there's more energy at the point of impact. Reduced wind drift makes it a good choice for long-range shots.

BARNES® XLC™ COATED X-BULLET™
Recommended for medium to large game. A solid copper bullet provides reliable four-petal expansion and 100% weight retention for deep penetration. The outer heat-cured, dry film coating prevents copper-fouling in your barrel, reduces bore friction and won't rub off on your hands.

WOODLEIGH® WELDCORE
Safari hunters have long respected this bonded Australian bullet for its superb accuracy and excellent stopping power. Its special heavy jacket provides 80-85% weight retention. These bullets are favored for large or dangerous game.

NOSLER® PARTITION®
This Nosler design is a proven choice for medium to large game animals. A partioned copper jacket allows the front half of the bullet to mushroom, while the rear core remains intact, driving forward for deep penetration and stopping power.

NOSLER® BALLISTIC TIP®
With proven fast, flat-shooting wind-defying performance, it's specially designed for long-range shots at varmints, predators and small to medium game. A color-coded polycarbonate tip provides easy identification, prevents deformation in the magazine and drives back on impact for expansion and immediate energy transfer.

SPEER® GRAND SLAM®
An excellent all-around choice for medium to large game. When hunting both woods and clearings, you need a bullet that handles any situation. The Speer Grand Slam features a slim profile, yet thicker metal on the jacket's shank and internal flutes at the bullet's tip. This gives you flat shooting capability, a tip that mushrooms perfectly on impact and a bullet that stays in one piece.

SPEER® AFRICAN GRAND SLAM®
For big, dangerous game, you need a bullet that penetrates deep without excessive expansion. That's precisely the nature of our African Grand Slam bullet. A massive solid gilding metal jacket helps the bullet maintain its length and weight, while a "stop shoulder" prevents tip rollback. The Hot-Cor is firmly held by multi-lock serrations which help lock the core to the jacket.

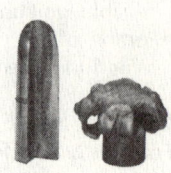

SPEER® AFRICAN GRAND SLAM® SOLID
The African Grand Slam features a Tungsten-Carbide core to keep the weight up without making the bullet too long. A flat tip ensures stability and straight line penetration.

SPEER® TNT®
Varmint hunters require two things from a bullet: tight groups and quick expansion. The Speer TNT gives you both. For rapid expansion, TNT jackets are fluted more than 90% of their length and have a dead-soft lead core.

Fiocchi Ammunition

Known for its shotshells and .22 rimfire ammunition, Fiocchi also markets centerfire pistol and rifle cartridges. This Italian firm has been in business since 1876.

Fiocchi Target Loads offer you many choices to suit the shell to your game: Standard 1 1/8-ounce loads for everything from registered trap and skeet to sporting clays. One-ounce loads that deliver superior performance with less recoil than a comparable 1 1/8-ounce load. Also, a 7/8-ounce training load for new or recoil sensitive shooters. Fiocchi lilac-colored hulls are fully reloadable.

Stock #		Gauge	Shell Length	Dram. Equiv.	Muzzle Velocity	Shot Oz.	Shot Sizes	Rds./Box	Shot Type
Steel (Waterfowl Loads)									
1235ST	Speed Steel	12	3 1/2"	Max.	1460	1 3/8	T BBB BB 1	25	Treated Steel
1235SH	Heavy Steel	12	3 1/2"	Max.	1300	1 9/16	T BBB BB 1	25	Treated Steel
123ST	Speed Steel	12	3"	Max.	1475	1 1/8	BBB BB 1 2 3 4	25	Treated Steel
123S	Steel	12	3"	Max.	1320	1 1/4	T BBB BB 1 2 3 4	25	Treated Steel
123SH	Heavy Steel	12	3"	Max.	1350	1 3/8	BB 1 2 3 4	25	Treated Steel
12S78	Training Load	12	2 3/4"	Max.	1440	7/8	7	25	Treated Steel
12S1OZ	Upland Steel	12	2 3/4"	Max.	1400	1	4 6 7	25	Treated Steel
12S118	Steel	12	2 3/4"	Max.	1375	1 1/8	BB 1 2 3 4 6	25	Treated Steel
12S114	Heavy Steel	12	2 3/4"	Max.	1275	1 1/4	BB 1 2 3 4	25	Treated Steel
20S	Upland Steel	20	2 3/4"	Max.	1470	3/4	3 4 6 7	25	Treated Steel
203ST	Speed Steel	20	3"	Max.	1500	7/8	2 3 4	25	Treated Steel
Field Loads (Upland Game Loads)									
12HF	Heavy Field	12	2 3/4"	3 1/4	1225	1 1/4	6 7-1/2 8 9	25	Lead
12FLD	Field Load	12	2 3/4"	3 1/4	1255	1 1/8	6 7-1/2 8 9	25	Lead
16FLD	Field Load	16	2 3/4"	2 3/4	1185	1 1/8	6 7-1/2 8	25	Lead
20FLD	Field Load	20	2 3/4"	2 1/2	1165	1	6 7-1/2 8 9	25	Lead
Dove Loads									
12MS3	Multi-Sport	12	2 3/4"	3	1250	1	7-1/2 8 9	25	Lead
12GT1	Game & Target	12	2 3/4"	3 1/4	1290	1	6 7-1/2 8 9	25	Lead
12GT118	Game & Target	12	2 3/4"	3	1200	1 1/8	7-1/2 8	25	Lead
16GT	Game & Target	16	2 3/4"	2 1/2	1165	1	6 7-1/2 8 9	25	Lead
20GT	Game & Target	20	2 3/4"	2 1/2	1210	7/8	6 7-1/2 8 9	25	Lead
28GT	Game & Target	28	2 3/4"	2	1200	3/4	8 9	25	Lead
410GT	Game & Target	410	2 1/2"	Max	1200	1/2	8 9	25	Lead
Target Loads									
12TL	Target Light	12	2 3/4"	2 3/4	1150	1	7-1/2 8 8-1/2 9	25	Hi-Antimony Lead
12TH	Target Heavy	12	2 3/4"	3	1200	1	7-1/2 8 8-1/2	25	Hi-Antimony Lead
12TX	Little Rhino	12	2 3/4"	HDCP	1250	1	7-1/2 8 8-1/2	25	Hi-Antimony Lead
12CRSR	Crusher	12	2 3/4"	Max	1300	1	7-1/2 8 8-1/2 9	25	Hi-Antimony Lead
12LITE	Lite	12	2 3/4"	2 7/8	1165	1 1/8	7-1/2 8 9	25	Hi-Antimony Lead
12VIPL	VIP Light	12	2 3/4"	2 3/4	1150	1 1/8	7-1/2 8 9	25	Hi-Antimony Lead
12VIPH	VIP Heavy	12	2 3/4"	3	1200	1 1/8	7-1/2 8 9	25	Hi-Antimony Lead
12WRNO	White Rhino	12	2 3/4"	HDCP	1250	1 1/8	7-1/2 8 8-1/2 9	25	Hi-Antimony Lead
1278OZ	Training Load	12	2 3/4"	3	1200	7/8	7-1/2 8	25	Hi-Antimony Lead
12IN24	International	12	2 3/4"	Max	1350	24 grams	7-1/2 8 8-1/2	25	Hi-Antimony Lead
Sub-Gauge									
20VIP	VIP	20	2 3/4"	2 1/2	1200	7/8	7-1/2 8 9	25	Hi-Antimony Lead
28GT	Game & Target	28	2 3/4"	2	1200	3/4	8 9	25	Lead
28HV	High Velocity	28	2 3/4"	2 1/4	1285	3/4	6 7-1/2 8 9	25	Lead
410GT	Game & Target	410	2 1/2"	Max	1200	1/2	8 9	25	Lead
High Velocity									
12HV	High Velocity	12	2 3/4"	3 3/4	1330	1 1/4	4 5 6 7-1/2 8 9	25	Lead
16HV	High Velocity	16	2 3/4"	3 1/8	1300	1 1/8	4 6 7-1/2 8	25	Lead
20HV	High Velocity	20	2 3/4"	2 3/4	1220	1	4 5 6 7-1/2 8 9	25	Lead
28HV	High Velocity	28	2 3/4"	2 1/4	1285	3/4	6 7-1/2 8 9	25	Lead
410HV	High Velocity	410	3"	Max	1140	11/16	6 7-1/2 8 9	25	Lead

Fiocchi Ammunition

Shotshell Application Guide

Game	Lead Shot Size	Steel Shot Size	Recommended Loads
Geese	NA	T-BBB-BB-1	Heavy Steel, Speed Steel
Ducks	NA	BB-1-2-3-4-6	Heavy Steel, Speed Steel, Upland Steel
Pheasant	4-5-6	3-4-5-6	Golden Pheasant, HV, Speed Steel, Upland Steel, HVN
Turkey	4-5-6	4-5	Turkey Tunder, HV, HVN
Grouse/Partridge	5-6-7 1/2-8	4-6-7	Field Loads, Upland Steel, HV, HVN, HFN
Quail	7 1/2-8-9	7	Field Loads, HV, Upland Steel, HVN, HFN
Dove/Pigeon	6-7 1/2-8-9	6-7	Field Loads, GT, Dove, HV, HFN, HVN
Rabbit/Squirrel	4-5-6-7 1/2	6-7	Field Loads, HV, GT, Upland Steel, HFN, HVN
Deer/Boar	00-Slug	NA	12HV00BK, 12 Gauge Slug, 20 Gauge Slug
Trap	7 1/2-8-8 1/2	6-7	TL, TH, TX, VIP, LITE, WRNO, MS, TRAPH, TRAPL
Skeet	8-8 1/2-9	7	TL, TH, TX, VIP, LITE, WRNO, MS
Sporting Clays	7 1/2-8-8 1/2-9	7	TL, TH, TX, TIP, LITE, WRNO, MS
Steel Target			Upland Steel, Training Load

Shot Pellet Sizes

Size #	9	8-1/2	8	7-1/2	6	5	4	3	2	1	BB	BBB	T	#4	00
Dia. In.	.08	.085	.09	.095	.11	.12	.13	.14	.15	.16	.18	.19	.20	.24	.33
Dia. MM	2.03	2.16	2.29	2.41	279	3.05	3.30	3.56	3.81	4.06	4.57	4.83	5.08	6.10	8.38

Number of Lead Pellets in Various Loads

Lead Pellets	9	8-1/2	8	7-1/2	6	5	4
1 oz.		585	480	409	345	232	172	136
1 1/8 oz.	658	540	460	388	251	194	153
1 1/4 oz.	731	600	511	431	276	215	170
1 3/8 oz.	804	660	562	474	307	237	187
1 3/4 oz.	-	-	-	-	395	304	239

Number of Steel Pellets in Various Loads

Steel Pellets	7	6	4	3	2	1	BB	BBB	T
3/4 oz.	315	237	143	115	-	-	-	-	-
7/8 oz.	365	-	167	134	109	-	-	-	-
1 oz.	420	316	191	-	-	-	-	-	-
1 1/8 oz.	-	355	215	172	140	115	81	68	-
1 1/4 oz.	-	-	239	191	151	128	90	-	-
1 3/8 oz.	-	-	262	210	171	141	99	84	73
1 9/16 oz.	-	-	-	-	161	113	95	83	

Note: When comparing steel shot to lead shot, increase shot size by two to get similar downrange results (i.e. Lead #4 to Steel #2). Check your shotgun and choke manufacturer for steel shot compatibility.

Fiocchi Ammunition

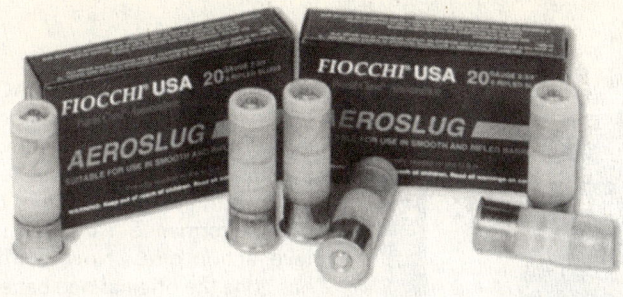
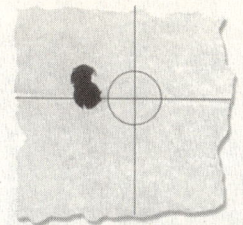

SLUGS
Fiocchi's Slugs in both 12 and 20 gauge feature an attached wad profiled to provide in-flight stability and increased accuracy.

The three-shot group here measures .450 inches; it was fired at 50 yds. from a bench rest with a Mossberg 500 Crown Grade 24" fully rifled barrel and 4 power scope.

Stock #	Gauge	Shell Length	Dram. Equiv.	Muzzle Velocity	Pellet Ct.	Shot Sizes	Rds. Box	Shot Type
BUCKSHOT								
12HV4BK Buckshot	12	2 3/4"	Max	1325	27 pell.	4 Buck	10	Hi-Antimony Nicke-Plated
12HV00BK Buckshot	12	2 3/4"	Max	1300	9 pell.	00 Buck	10	Hi-Antimony Nickel-Plated
12LE00BK Reduced Recoil*	12	2 3/4"	Max	1150	9 pell.	00 Buck	10	Hi-Antimony Nickel-Plated

Stock #	Gauge	Shell Length	MM	Dram. Equiv.	Muzzle Velocity	Shot Oz.	Shot Sizes	Rds. Box	Shot Type
SLUGS									
12TS1 Trophy Slug	12	2 3/4"	70	Max	1560	1	Rifled Slug	5	Lead w/attached Wad
20TS78 Trophy Slug	20	2 3/4"	70	Max	1650	7/8	Rifled Slug	5	Lead w/attached Wad

Stock #	Gauge	Shell Length	Dram. Equiv.	Muzzle Velocity	Shot Oz.	Shot Sizes	Rds. Box	Shot Type
NICKEL PLATED HUNTING LOADS								
12HFN Live Bird Pigeon	12	2 3/4"	3 1/4	1225	1 1/4	7-1/2 8	25	Nickel-Plated Lead
12HVN High Velocity Nickel	12	2 3/4"	3 3/4	1330	1 1/4	4 5 6 7-1/2 8 9	25	Nickel-Plated Lead
12GP Golden Pheasant	12	2 3/4"	Max	1250	1 3/8	4 5 6	25	Nickel-Plated Lead
203GP Golden Pheasant 20	20	3"	Max	1200	1 1/4	4 5 6	25	Nickel-Plated Lead
12TT Turkey Thunder	12	2 3/4"	Max	1250	1 3/8	4 5 6	10	Nickel-Plated Lead
123TT Turkey Thunder	12	3	Max	1150	1 3/4	4 5 6	10	Nickel-Plated Lead
FITASC								
12HFN Live Bird Pigeon/FITASC	12	2 3/4"	3 1/4	1225	1 1/4	7-1/2 8	25	Nickel-Plated Lead
12HFN Heavy Field	12	2 3/4"	3 1/4	1225	1 1/4	7-1/2 8	25	Lead
INTERCEPTOR SPREADER								
12CPTR Interceptor	12	2 3/4"	Max	1300	1	7-1/2 8 8-1/2 9	25	Lead
SPORTING CLAYS POWER SPREADERS								
12SSCH Power Spreader	12	2 3/4"	3	1200	1 1/8	7-1/2 8 8-1/2 9	25	Lead
12SSCX Power Spreader	12	2 3/4"	Max	1250	1 1/8	8 8-1/2 9	25	Lead
SPORTING TARGET LOAD								
12S78 Steel Target Load	12	2 3/4"	Max	1440	7/8	7	25	Steel
12S1OZ Steel Target Load	12	2 3/4"	Max	1400	1	6 7	25	Steel
20S Steel Target Load	20	2 3/4"	Max	1490	3/4	6 7	25	Steel
ULTRA LOW RECOIL LOADS								
1278OZ Trainer	12	2 3/4"	Lite	1200	7/8	7-1/2 8	25	Hi-Antimony Lead
MULTI-SPORT LOADS-GAME & TARGET								
12MS3 Multi-Sport	12	2 3/4"	3	1250	1	7-1/2 8 9	25	Lead
12GT Game & Target	12	2 3/4"	3 1/4	1290	1	6 7-1/2 8 9	25	Lead
12GT118 Game & Target	12	2 3/4"	3	1200	1 1/8	7-1/2 8	25	Lead
LOW RECOIL TRAP LOADS								
12TRAPL Low-Recoil Trap Light	12	2 3/4"	2 3/4	1140	1 1/8	7-1/2 8	25	Hi-Antimony Lead
12TRAPH Low-Recoil Trap Heavy	12	2 3/4"	3	1185	1 1/8	7-1/2 8	25	Hi-Antimony Lead

Hornady
New for 2002

.444 Marlin Light Mag
When the .444 Marlin was born as a joint project between Marlin and Remington, shooters quickly fell in love with the combination of a high-performance cartridge in a lever-action rifle. Now, Hornady has gone the original one better by loading the .444 Marlin with the high-performance 265-grain bullet that has been a staple of the line since 1964.

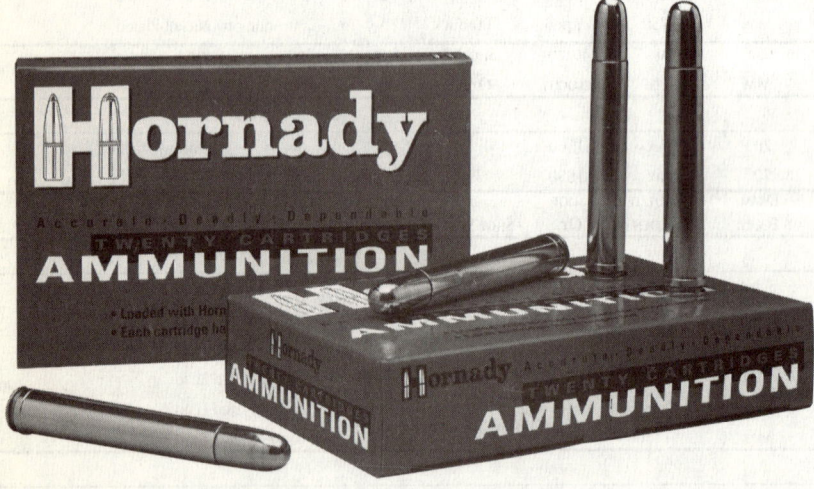

.458 Lott
Developed by Jack Lott and long a favorite of custom rifle builders and African hunters, the .458 Lott has suffered from one shortcoming – a steady supply of commercially-loaded ammunition.

All that has changed with the introduction of Hornady's .458 Lott cartridge, built from brass to bullet by Hornady.

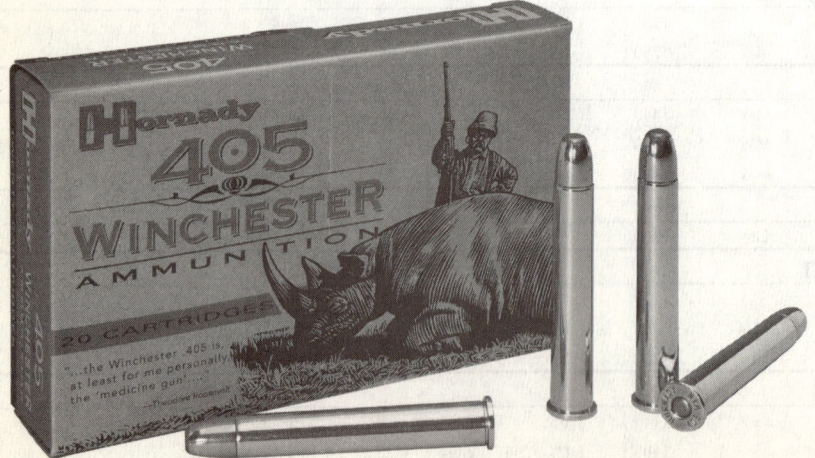

Hornady .405 Winchester
Hornady has brought the old warhorse favored by Teddy Roosevelt into the 21st century by designing a high-performance cartridge that delivers amazing power and accuracy from the .405 Winchester. In fact, this new .405 Winchester cartridge with a 300-grain FP bullet from Hornady lets this icon of American shooting take its place next to even the latest large-caliber guns.

Knyoch
Nitro-Express-Sporting Ammunition

FOR SPORTING RIFLES

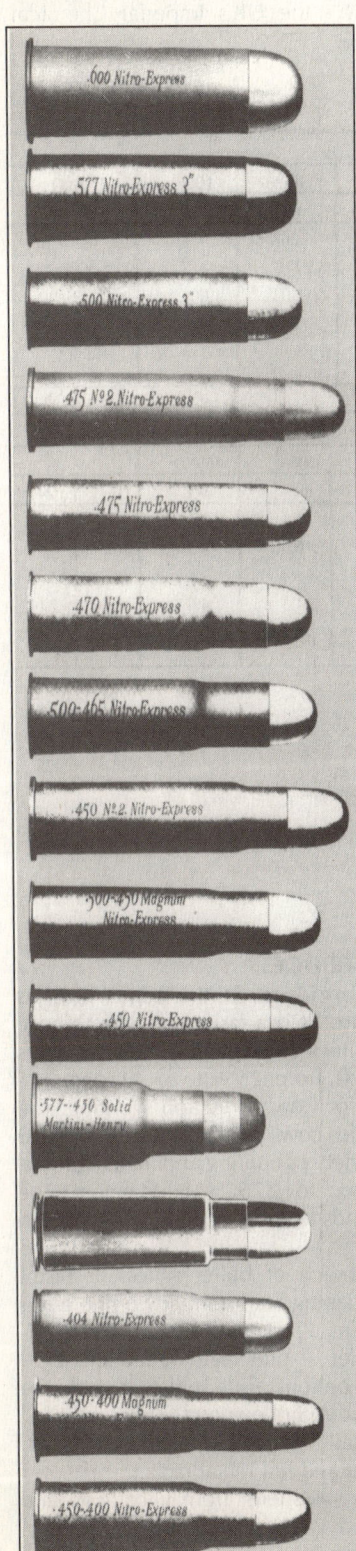

.600 NE
900 gr Solid or SN

.577 NE 3"
750 gr Solid or SN

.500 NE 3"
570 gr Solid or SN

.475 No. 2 NE
480 gr Solid or SN for
Jeffery Rifles: 500 gr
Solid or SN

.475 NE
480 gr Solid or SN

.470 NE
500 gr Solid or SN

.500/.465 NE
480 gr Solid or SN

.450 No. 2 NE
480 gr Solid or SN

.500/.450
Magnum NE
480 gr Solid or SN

.450 NE
480 gr Solid or SN

.577/.450 MH
480 gr Solid Lead

.416 Rigby
410 gr Solid or SN

.404 Rimless NE
400 gr Solid or SN

.450/.400
Magnum NE
400 gr Solid or SN

.450/.440 NE
400 gr Solid or SN

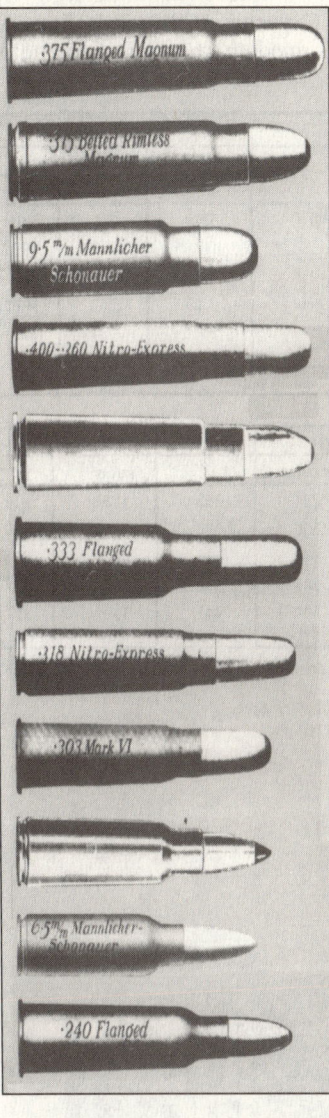

.375 Flanged Magnum
300, 270 or 235 gr
Solid or SN

.375 Belted Magnum
300, 270 or 235 gr
Solid or SN

9.5 mm Mannlicher
Schonauer 270 gr Solid or SN

.400/.360 NE for Purdey
Rifles: 300 gr for
Westley Richards: 314
gr. Solid or SN

.350 Rigby Magnum
225 gr or 250 gr, Solid or SN

.333 Jeffrey Flanged NE
300 gr Solid or SN

.318 Rimless NE
250 gr Solid or SN
180 gr SN

.303 British
215 gr Solid or SN

.275 Rigby Rimless
140 gr SN

6.5 m/m Mannlicher
Schonauer 160 gr SN

.240 H&H Flanged
100 gr SN

ADDITIONAL PROPRIETARY CALIBERS AVAILABLE:

.700 NE
1000 gr Solid

.500 Jeffery
535 gr Solid or SN

.450 Rigby Rimless Magnum
480 gr Solid or SN

.400 - 3" Purdey
230 gr SN

.505 Gibbs Magnum
525 gr Solid or SN

.425 Westley Richards
Magnum
410 gr Solid or SN

.300 H&H Flanged Magnum
220 gr Solid or SN

Magtech Ammunition

Magtech Ammunition Co. imports and distributes high-quality rifle and pistol cartridges manufactured by Companhia Brasileira de Cartuchos (CBC). This firm, in business since 1926, has a modern factory in Sao Paulo, Brazil. Before 1976, it was owned and managed by Remington Arms and ICI - the UK's Imperial Chemical Company.

Symbol	Caliber	Bullet			Velocity						
		Style	Weight		Muzzle		50M	50YD	100M	100YD	
			G	GR	M/S	FPS	M/S	FPS	M/S	FPS	
GG380A	.380 Auto+P JHP		5.5	85	330	1,082	303	999	282	936	
GG40A	.40 S&W	JHP	10.0	155	367	1,025	338	1,118	317	1,502	
GG45A	.45 Auto+P JHP		12.0	185	350	1,148	323	1,066	303	1,005	
GG38A	.38 SPL+P JHP		8.10	125	310*	1,017*	295	971	282	931	
GG9MA	9mm Luger+P	JHP	7.45	115	380	1,246	344	1,137	318	1,056	

Symbol	Energy						Mid-Range Trajectory				Barrel	
	Muzzle		50M	50YD	100M	100YD	50M	50YD	100M	100YD		
	J	FT/LBS	J	FT/LBS	J	FT/LBS	CM	INCH	CM	INCH	CM	IN
GG380A	300	221	252	188	219	166	3.1	1.0	13.3	4.3	9.5	3-3/4
GG40A	677	500	596	430	523	381	2.5	0.8	10.9	3.5	10.2	4
GG45A	735	540	626	467	551	415	2.7	0.9	11.8	3.8	12.7	5
GG38A	389	287	352	262	322	241	3.4	1.1	14.3	4.6	10.2	4
GG9MA	538	397	441	330	377	285	2.4	0.8	10.5	3.4	10.2	4

* Velocity obtained from 10.2 cm (4") vented test barrel. Abbrevation: JHP JACKETED HOLLOW POINT

PMC

PMC RIFLE CARTRIDGES

Precision Made Cartridges

PMC (Precision Made Cartridges) is the same firm as Eldorado Cartridge Company. It is a fast-growing enterprise whose product line continues to expand. The firm offers more than 50 handgun loads, from .25 Auto to .44 Magnum, including five specifically for Cowboy Action shooting. The centerfire rifle stable includes cowboy action loads in .30-30 and .45-70, plus a wide variety of hunting and match ammunition from .222 Remington to .375 H&H Magnum. The selection of .22 rimfire rounds features hunting, plinking and match loads.

PMC offers a broad choice of bullet styles. In pistol ammo, there's the quick-opening Starfire hollowpoint, a traditional jacketed hollowpoint, a jacketed softpoint and a full-metal-jacket (hardball) bullet — plus lead wadcutter, semi-wadcutter and round-nose options. Rifle bullets include the Barnes X-Bullet, .30-30 Starfire hollowpoint, Sierra boat-tail hollowpoint, Sierra boat-tail softpoint, pointed softpoint, softpoint, flat-nose softpoint and full metal jacket.

PMC also manufactures shotshells, from light dove and quail and target loads to heavy steel-shot loads for geese. PMC also has a rural Nevada plant that offers test-firing opportunities out the back door.

PMC

CENTERFIRE RIFLE AMMUNITION

FIELD AND TARGET

LESS LETHAL RUBBER FIN BATON

LESS LETHAL RUBBER BUCK SHOT

PMC Gold Line Now Features The Barnes XLC Coated X-Bullet

New for 2002, premier-performance PMC Gold Line rifle cartridges will feature the Barnes SLC Coated X-Bullet. The solid-copper X-Bullet has a reputation for deep penetration and reliable expansion. The exclusive blue XLC coating is a high-tech, dry-film lubricant that will decrease the friction within the rifle bore. The barrel stays cooler and copper fouling is reduced.

PMC Field & Target Shotshells

The new PMC Field & Target shell combines the dense patterning and target-smashing performance of a PMC Clay Target shell with the solid penetration necessary for taking lighter upland birds and small game. It's the perfect all-purpose load for shooters who wish to use the same load for clay targets and wing shooting. Features include clean-burning powder to keep your shotgun functioning smoothly, high antimony, chilled lead shot to give good penetration, reliable ignition primers and a tough, reloadable ribbed plastic hull.

PMC Less-Lethal Shotshells

PMC introduces a new shotshell line for law enforcement and home defense. The rubber projectiles discourage home intruders when lethal force may not be desirable.

Fin-stabilized Rubber Baton

The rubber projectile in this shell utilizes canted fins and a bore-riding band, both of which contribute to stable flight and enhanced accuracy. It will produce groups of 2-4 inches at 20 yards. Available in 12 gauge only.

000 Rubber Buckshot

Low-energy shell loaded with twelve 3/8th-inch rubber balls. Available in 12 gauge only.

Remington Ammunition
New Ammunition

Premier® Hevi-Shot Magnum Turkey Loads

If you're passionate about turkey hunting, new Premier Hevi-Shot is the load for you. This load won all event classes at the 2001 National Wild Turkey Federation Annual Turkey Shoot. It routinely achieves patterns in excess of 90%. Shot material alloy of tungsten, nickel and iron features a 10% higher density than lead, which yields denser patterns and higher energy - a lead improvement. A superior product for serious turkey hunters.

Premier® Hevi-Shot® High Velocity Magnum Turkey Buffered Loads

Index/ EDI No.	Gauge	Shell Length	Powder Dr. Eq.	Velocity (ft./sec.@3 ft.)	Ounces Of Shot	Shot Sizes
PRHSHV12M	12	3"	Max	1300	1 1/2	4, 5, 6
PRHSHV1235M	12	3 1/2"	Max	1300	1 3/4	4, 5, 6

Premier® Hevi-Shot® Magnum Turkey Buffered Loads

PRHS12SM	12	2 3/4"	Max	1250	1 3/8	4, 5, 6
PRHS12HM	12	3"	Max	1225	1 5/8	4, 5, 6
PRHS1235M	12	3 1/2"	Max	1225	1 7/8	4, 5, 6

Premier® Hevi-Shot Nitro Magnum Waterfowl Loads

Hunters who have longed for the "good old days" of lead shot now have a non-toxic shot that's not just a lead alternative, it's a lead improvement. Introducing Remington Premier Hevi-Shot Nitro Magnums, the most dramatic performance increase ever in waterfowl shotshells. Manufactured of a tungsten-nickel-iron alloy, Hevi-Shot is 10% denser than lead and an amazing 54% denser than steel. Shooting an equal payload and shot size, Hevi-Shot pellets have 25% more energy at 50 yards than steel pellets have at 30 yards. This allows you to drop down three shot sizes to maintain pattern energy and dramatically increase on-game pellet count. The resulting Hevi-Shot patterning, with full chokes, yields an average of 88% efficiency.

Density Comparison

Density Of Steel	7.8
Density Of Lead	10.9
Density Of Hevi-Shot	12.0

Premier® Hevi-Shot® Nitro Magnum Waterfowl Loads

Index/ EDI No.	Gauge	Shell Length	Powder Dr. Eq.	Velocity (ft./sec.@3 ft.)	Ounces Of Shot	Shot Sizes
PRHSN10M	10	3 1/2"	Magnum	1300	1 3/4	2, 4
PRHSN12SM	12	2 3/4"	Magnum	1325	1 1/4	4, 6, 7 1/2
PRHSN12HM	12	3"	Magnum	1300	1 1/2	2, 4, 6
PRHSN1235	12	3 1/2"	Magnum	1300	1 3/4	2, 4, 6
PRHSN20M	20	3"	Magnum	1300	1 1/8	4, 6

Remington Ammunition

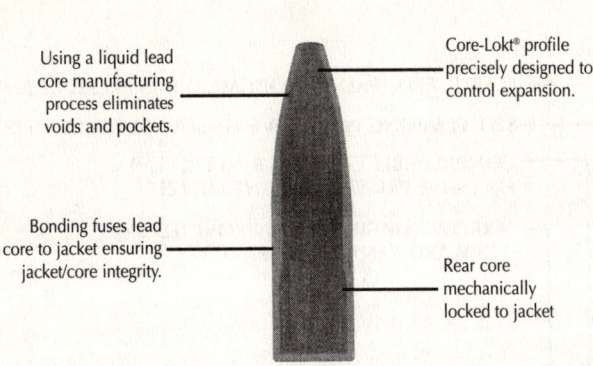

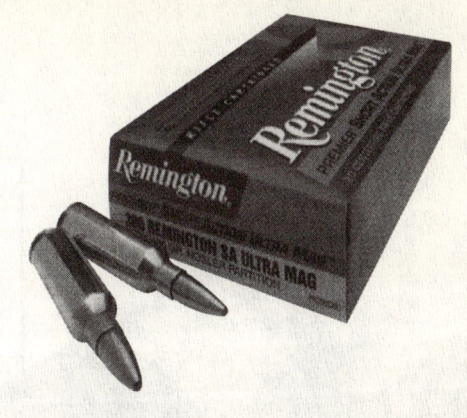

Premier Short-Action Ultra Mag

Long-action magnum performance is now available in a short-action configuration. The new Premier SA Ultra Mag cartridges feature a state-of-the-art design. The SA Ultra Mag cartridge headspaces off the shoulder of the case, rather than a belt, promoting more precise bore alignment and therefore improved accuracy. Furthermore, the highly efficient case design duplicates or exceeds belted magnum ballistics with less powder, which in turn means less felt recoil. Finally, the entire package achieves greater downrange velocity and energy than traditional 300 Win Mag and 7mm Remington Mag calibers. For 2002, SA Ultra Mag ammo will be available to match Remington's Model Seven Magnum rifles in two popular calibers: 300 Remington SA Ultra Mag and 7mm Remington SA Ultra Mag.

Premier® Short Action Ultra Mag™

Caliber	Index/EDI No.	Bullet Weight	Bullet Type
7mm Rem. SA UM	PR7SM1	140	PSP Core-Lokt® Ultra
7mm Rem. SA UM	PR7SM2	150	PSP Core-Lokt®
7mm Rem. SA UM	PR7SM3	160	Nosler® Partition®
300 Rem. SA UM	PR300SM1	150	PSP Core-Lokt® Ultra
300 Rem. SA UM	PR300SM2	165	PSP Core-Lokt®
300 Rem. SA UM	PR300SM3	180	Nosler® Partition®

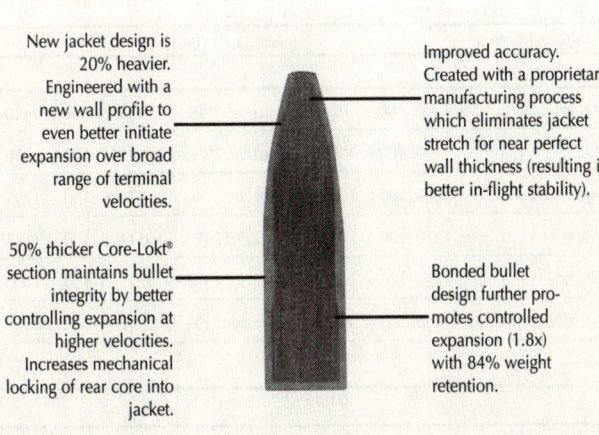

Premier Core-Lokt Ultra

For 2002, Remington introduces the Premier Core-Lokt Ultra. The bonded bullet retains up to 90% of its original weight with maximum penetration and energy transfer. Featuring a progressively-tapered jacket design, the Core-Lokt Ultra bullet initiates and controls expansion up to 1.8X. The unique design of the bullet, combined with the bonded lead core, provides the hunter with a Premier bullet that yields unmatched performance from 50 yards to 500 yards and all yardages in between.

Premier® Core-Lokt® Ultra

Caliber	Index/EDI No.	Bullet Weight	Bullet Type
270 Win	PRC270WB	140	Core-Lokt® Ultra PSP
7mm Remington Mag	PRC7MMRA	140	Core-Lokt® Ultra PSP
30-06 Springfield	PRC3006C	180	Core-Lokt® Ultra PSP
300 Win Mag	PRC300WC	180	Core-Lokt® Ultra PSP
308 Winchester	PRC308WC	180	Core-Lokt® Ultra PSP

Rotwell Brenneke Cartridges

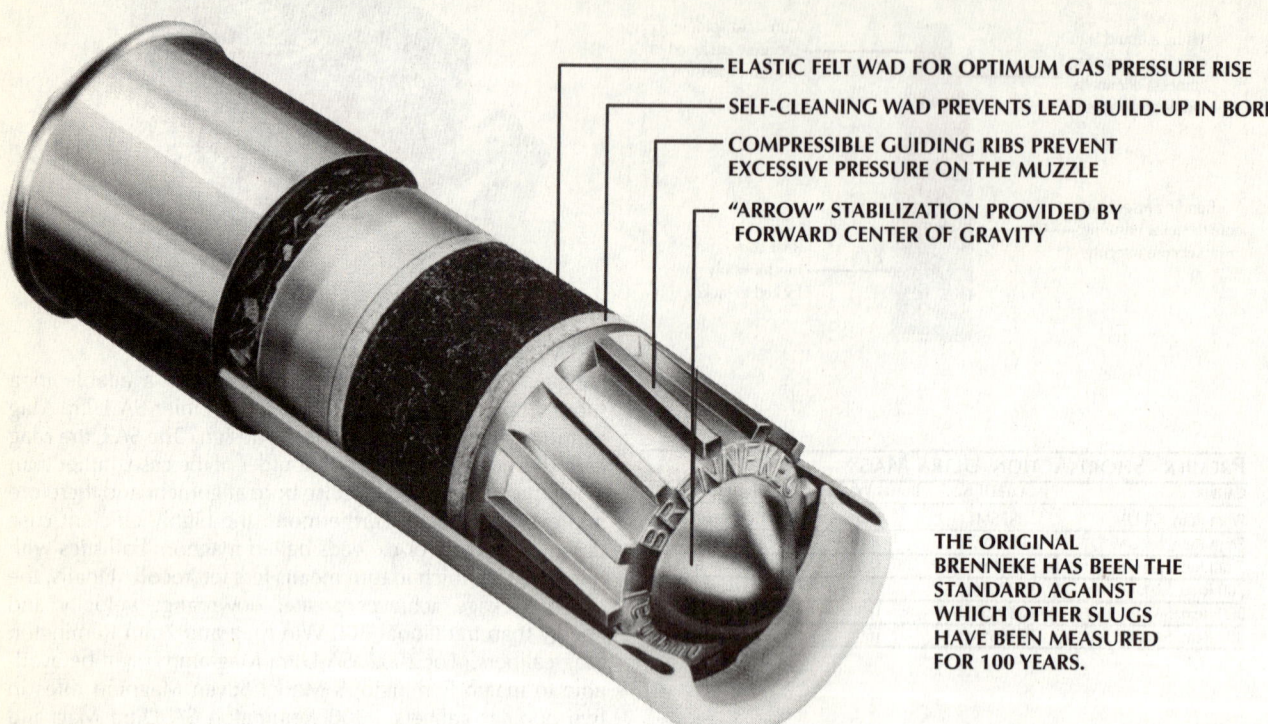

- ELASTIC FELT WAD FOR OPTIMUM GAS PRESSURE RISE
- SELF-CLEANING WAD PREVENTS LEAD BUILD-UP IN BORE
- COMPRESSIBLE GUIDING RIBS PREVENT EXCESSIVE PRESSURE ON THE MUZZLE
- "ARROW" STABILIZATION PROVIDED BY FORWARD CENTER OF GRAVITY

THE ORIGINAL BRENNEKE HAS BEEN THE STANDARD AGAINST WHICH OTHER SLUGS HAVE BEEN MEASURED FOR 100 YEARS.

Specifications

Brenneke Load	Size	Barrel	Slug Weight	Velocity (ft./sec.)	Energy (ft./lbs.)
12 Gauge					
Super Magnum	3"	Rifled only	1-3/8 oz.	Muzzle: 1476, 50 y: 1200, 100 y: 1025	Muzzle: 2902, 50 y: 1915, 100 y: 1410
Magnum	3"	Rifled or smooth	1-3/8 oz.	Muzzle: 1476, 50 y: 1200, 100 y: 1025	Muzzle: 2902, 50 y: 1915, 100 y: 1410
Heavy Field Short Magnum	2-3/4"	Rifled or smooth	1-1/4 oz.	Muzzle: 1476, 50 y: 1200, 100 y: 1030	Muzzle: 2540, 50 y: 1675, 100 y: 1235
Field Short Magnum	2-3/4"	Smooth only	1-1/8 oz.	Muzzle: 1510, 50 y: 1220, 100 y: 1040	Muzzle: 2480, 50 y: 1625, 100 y: 1181
High Velocity	2-3/4"	Smooth only	1 oz.	Muzzle: 1560, 50 y: 1255, 100 y: 1060	Muzzle: 2375, 50 y: 1545, 100 y: 1100
Low Recoil	2-3/4"	Smooth only	1 oz.	Muzzle: 1150, 50 y: 1000, 100 y: 905	Muzzle: 1290, 50 y: 980, 100 y: 805
Buckshot	2-3/4"	Smooth	1 oz. (9 pellets)	–	–
16 Gauge					
Field Short Magnum	2-3/4"	Smooth only	1 oz.	Muzzle: 1510, 50 y: 1220, 100 y: 1040	Muzzle: 2100, 50 y: 1375, 100 y: 1000
20 Gauge					
Magnum	3"	Rifled or smooth	1 oz.	Muzzle: 1476, 50 y: 1200, 100 y: 1025	Muzzle: 2130, 50 y: 1400, 100 y: 1035
Field Short Magnum	2-3/4"	Smooth only	7/8 oz.	Muzzle: 1510, 50 y: 1220, 100 y: 1040	Muzzle: 1870, 50 y: 1225, 100 y: 890
.410 Gauge					
Magnum	3"	Smooth only	1/4 oz.	Muzzle: 1510, 50 y: 1220, 100 y: 1040	Muzzle: 556, 50 y: 365, 100 y: 265

RWS Centerfire Cartridges
Bullets and Ballistics for Norma

Vulkan
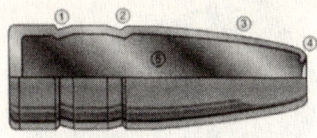
Vulkan bullets are strengthened by the folded jacket at the front. The folds protect the tip from deformation. The bullet penetrates before expansion starts. Subsequently, mushrooming to double the original diameter follows rapidly. 1. Reinforced rear jacket with lead core lock. 2. Crimping groove for secure seating in the case. 3. Thin forward jacket with internal notches. 4. Jacket folded into the lead core. 5. Antimony hardened lead core.

Soft Point
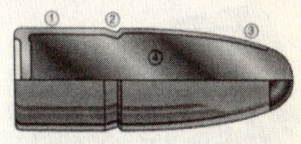
Soft Point bullets have optimum ballistic shape. They offer good penetration and mushroom well, even on smaller game. The Soft Point is an excellent all-around bullet particularly suitable for small and medium game. 1. Reinforced rear jacket. 2. Crimping groove for secure seating in the case. 3. Thin forward jacket. 4. Antimony hardened lead core.

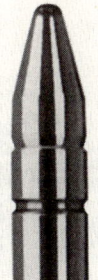
The design of the DK bullet is the result of Dynamit Nobel's extensive ballistics research.

Manufactured at considerable expense, DK bullets barely splinter, mushroom in a controlled manner, have a residue body of over 50 percent, and usually produce an exit hole. A true twin core that separates to perform two separate functions upon impact, penetration and a high degree of impact force, combine to give the DK a clear advantage over traditional bullets, especially for large game with heavy bones and muscles.

The RWS cone point bullet was designed and developed after exhaustive studies in the laboratory as well as in the field.

A carefully engineered matching of casing and core material and an aerodynamically favorable bullet shape have been paired to produce a controlled mushrooming to almost twice caliber size. The rear groove, which joins the lead core and casing, controls mushrooming and preserves effective residual body to give it killing power.

Due to external shape, the RWS cone point performs well in light brush, with minimal deflection.

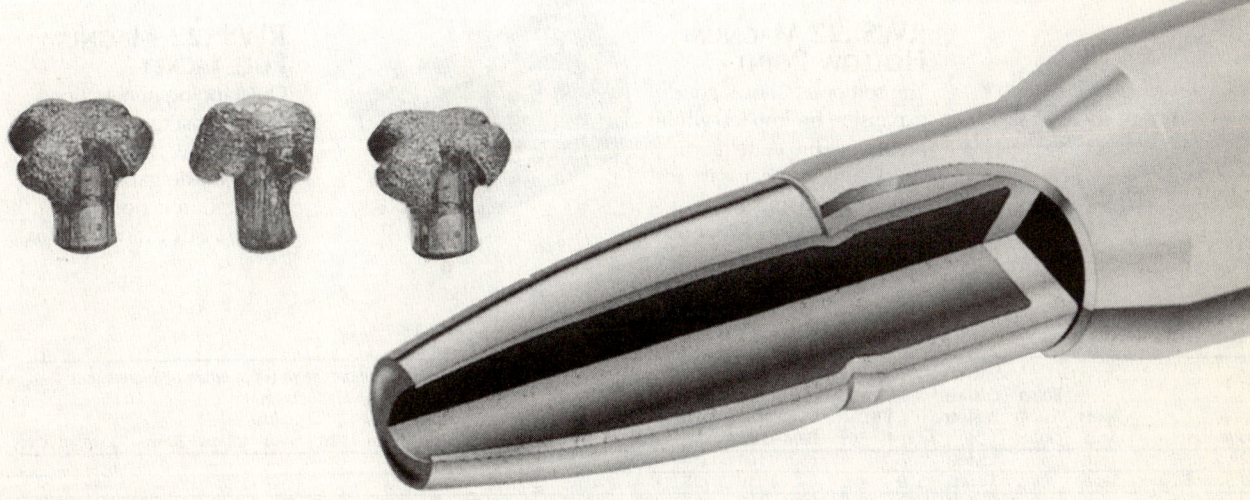

Norma Oryx
This bullet is designed to penetrate deep. The jacket and core are bonded together through a chemical process. This ensures a very high residual weight, even in tough targets. Despite the solid construction, mushrooming starts early. The Oryx bullet delivers excellent deep energy transfer and is suitable for big and medium sized game.

Price: box of 20 cartridges . . . . From $27 to 58
- Bonded bullet-lead core soldered into copper jacket
- Good penetration
- Exceptional expansion, combined with bonding, results in deep wound channel and minimal meat damage
- Very high weight retention

RWS Rimfire Cartridges

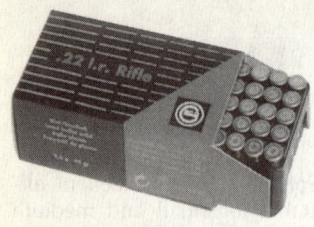

Geco .22 L.R. Rifle
Combining quality and cost effectiveness, this rimfire ammunition is made in the RWS Nuremberg factory to exacting standards. Perfect for informal target shooting and entry level competition.

Geco .22 L.R. Pistol
The same quality and affordability as the rifle version, but with a reduced velocity. For the pistol shooter looking for muzzle control.
Price: $2/box

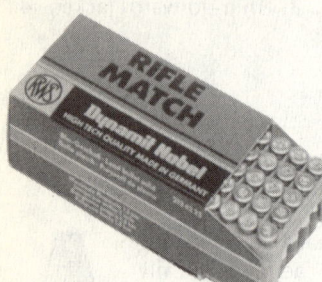

RWS .22 L.R. Rifle Match
Perfect for the club level target competitor. Accurate and affordable.
Price: $2/box

RWS .22 L.R. Target Rifle
An ideal training and field cartridge, the .22 Long Rifle Target also excels in informal competitions. The target .22 provides the casual shooter with accuracy at an economical price.
Price: $3/box

RWS .22 L.R. Subsonic Hollow Point
Subsonic ammunition is a favorite ammunition of shooters whose shooting range is limited to where the noise of a conventional cartridge would be a problem.
Price: $4/box

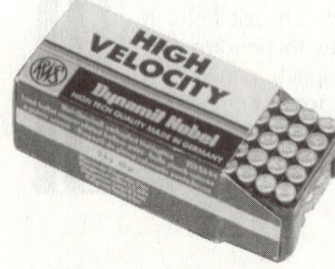

RWS .22 L.R. HV Hollow Point
A higher velocity hollow point offers the shooter greater shocking power in game, suitable for both small game and vermin.
Price: $5/box

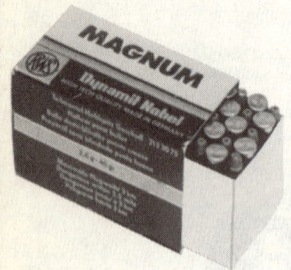

RWS .22 Magnum Hollow Point
The soft point allows good expansion on impact, while preserving the penetration characteristics necessary for larger vermin and game.
Price: $23/box

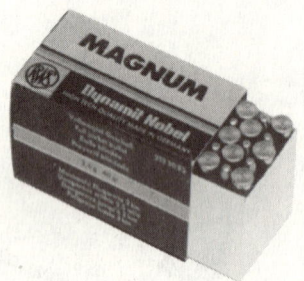

RWS .22 Magnum Full Jacket
Outstanding penetration characteristics of this cartridge allow the shooter to easily tackle game where penetration is necessary.
Price: $23/box

Technical Data

Cartridges	Bullet Style	Bullet Weight (Grains)	Max. Chamber Pressure (PSI)	Velocity (Ft./Sec.) Muzzle	50y	100y	Energy (Ft./Lbs.) Muzzle	50y	100y	Open Sight At	25 yds	50 yds	75 yds	100 yds	Scope Sighted In At	25 yds	50 yds	75 yds	100 yds
.22 L.R. R 50	Lead	40	25.600	1.070	970	890	100	80	70	--	--	--	--	--	--	--	--	--	--
.22 Short R 25	Lead	28	18.500	560	490	---	20	15	--	--	--	--	--	--	--	--	--	--	--
.22 L.R. Geco Rifle	Lead	40	25.600	1.080	990	900	100	8/5	70	50 yds.	+0.6		-3.1	-8.7	50 yds	+0.1		-2.5	-7.5
.22 L.R. Rifle Match	Lead	40	25.600	1.035	945	860	95	80	65	50 yds.	+0.7		-3.2	-9.0	50 yds	+0.1		-2.6	-7.8
.22 L.R. Target Rifle	Lead	40	25.600	1.080	990	900	100	85	70	50 yds.	+0.6		-3.1	-8.7	50 yds	+0.1		-2.5	-7.5
.22 L.R. Subsonic Hollow Point		40	25.600	1.000	915	835	90	75	60	50 yds.	+0.8		-3.4	-4.7	50 yds	+0.2		+2.8	-8.5
.22 L.R. HV Hollow point	Lead coppered	40	25.600	1.310	1.120	990	150	110	85		--	--	--	--	--	--	--	--	--
.22 Magnum	Soft Point	40	25.600	2.020	1.710	1.430	360	260	180	100 yds.	+0.6	+1.3	+1.1	0	100 yds	-0.3	+0.7	+0.8	0
.22 Magnum	Full Jacket	40	25.600	2.020	1.710	1.430	360	260	180	100 yds.	+0.6	+1.3	+1.1	0	100 yds	-0.3	+0.7	+0.8	0

Winchester Ammunition

WINCHESTER SUPREME & SUPER-X 270 WSM AND 7MM WSM WINCHESTER SHORT MAGNUM

Last year, Winchester's new 300 WSM won the "Ammunition of the Year". For 2002, Winchester will add the 270 and 7mm WSM. These new cartridges deliver incredible accuracy and magnum energy and velocity performance in a short-action cartridge, all with lower perceived recoil in lighter-weight rifles.

WINCHESTER SUPREME PLATINUM TIP HUNTING AMMUNITION

Winchester's new Platinum Tip Hollow Point Hunting Ammunition is ideal for deer hunting. Available in 12 gauge sabot slug shotshell and as a 50-caliber Muzzleloading sabot bullet, the Platinum Tip Hollow Point bullet has a reverse taper jacket that delivers superior accuracy, uniform expansion and on-target energy delivery.

WINCHESTER SUPER-X DRYLOK HI-VELOCITY STEEL WATERFOWL LOADS

Available in 12 gauge 3" and 3 1/2", these new steel shotshells give a performance boost, with 1550 feet-per-second muzzle velocity. Add the exclusive water-resistant Super-X Drylok wad system, and you have a traditional steel load delivering greater per-pellet energy on target for superior bird hunting in harsh conditions.

Z-Hat
Custom Dies and Ammunition

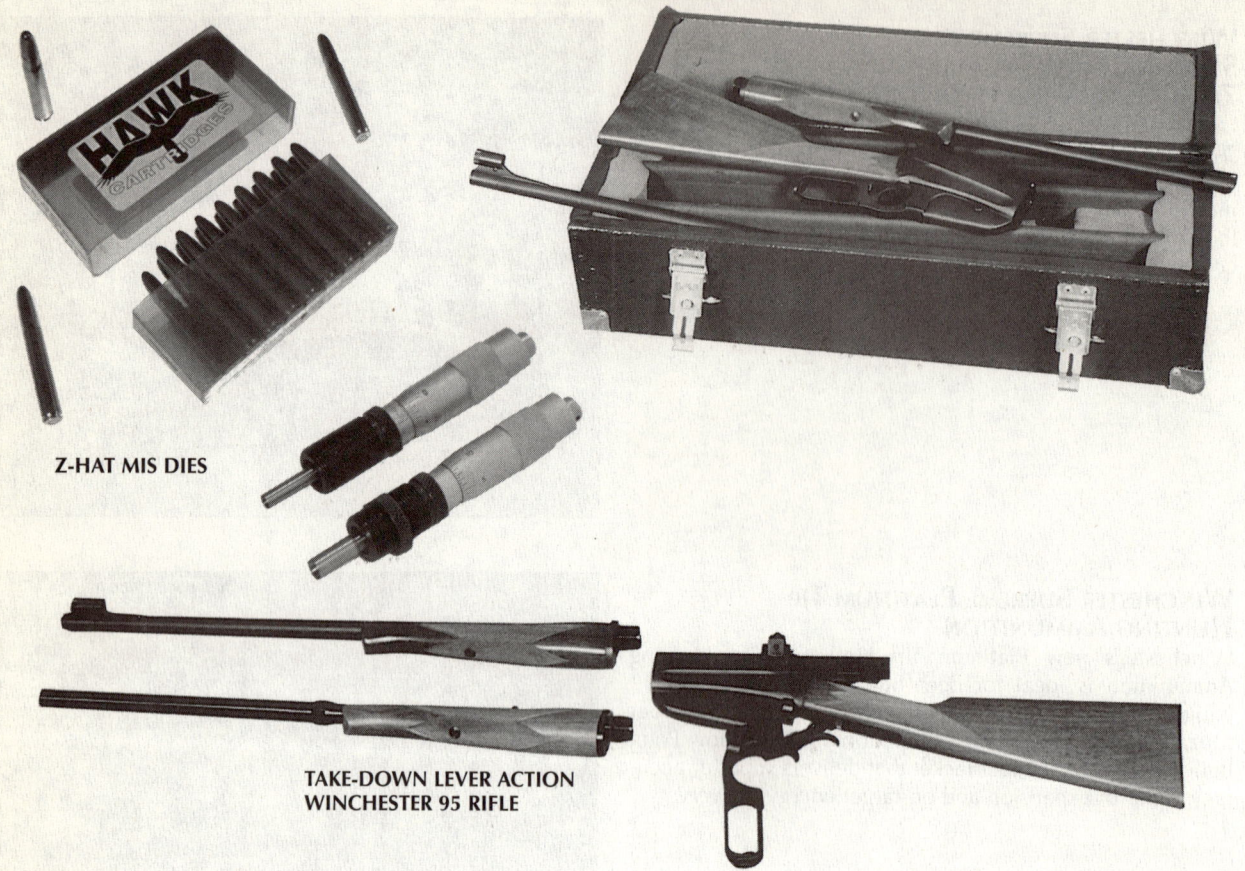

Z-HAT MIS DIES

TAKE-DOWN LEVER ACTION WINCHESTER 95 RIFLE

Fred Zeglin's work with Hawk wildcat cartridges, and his experience as a gunsmith, have resulted in a business that includes building and servicing rifles, developing loads and marketing premium-quality brass for Hawk cartridges and supplying shooters with match-grade loading dies.

The Z-Hat Micrometer Inline Seating (MIS) die is a universal in line bullet seater, similar to a "Vickerman" die. The universal seater comprises one die body and caliber sleeves for any caliber. It works with wildcats and obsolete rounds, as well as standard cartridges.

The MIS indexes on the datum line of the case shoulder and on the give of the bullet. This allows use of the MIS die with any caliber, .22 through .378 Wby. and 411 Hawk. 17 caliber is available on special order.

The Z-Hat takedown rifle conversion is a full thread system based on the 100-year-old Thomas Bland design. Simplicity of design insures longevity. This takedown involves the installation of a heavy contact plate on the barrel assembly, so that the barrel will always index to the same point. The 95 Winchester or Browning actions are fitted to the plate/barrel assembly, and a simple lock screw holds the assembly tightly aligned. Mutliple barrels are possible, each with its own complete forearm assembly, making it easy to switch barrels and calibers. The original factory barrel can be converted, as can any new barrel. This system, like the ability to use various calibers, has sight systems setup on one gun. For instance, Express sights on one barrel and a Scout Scope on the other. Zeglin is developing a version of this takedown design for the Winchester Model 70 bolt-action.

Takedowns are normally shipped in a high-quality aluminum travel case. Charcoal is standard; other colors are available. These custom cases, designed specifically for takedown rifles, hold the rifle snugly in transit. At the same time they look more like tool boxes than gun cases, so are less likely to attract unwanted attention from baggage handlers. More conventional shotgun style cases are available too.

Hawk Cartridges:
240 Hawk • 257 Hawk • 264 Hawk • 270 Hawk • 284 Hawk • 300 Hawk • 8mm Hawk • 338 Hawk • 358 Hawk • 9.3 Hawk • 375 Hawk • 411 Hawk

Z-Hat offers formed brass for all 12 Hawk cartridges, at $29.95 per 20. Loaded rounds are available at $69.95 per box, in .338, .358 and .375 Hawk. Custom loads for your rifle can be developed at Z-Hat (www.Rifle.Builder @ Z-Hat.com, or phone 307-577-7443).

Fred also offers custom sizing dies with Z-Hat custom rifles, and he builds a ring die that can size standard bullets to fit obsolete bore diameters.

Prices:
In-Line Seater set up for one cartridge $99
Caliber inserts 17

BALLISTICS

CENTERFIRE RIFLE BALLISTICS TABLES	**468**
	494
CENTERFIRE HANDGUN BALLISTICS TABLES	**495**
	504

Centerfire Rifle Ballistics

Comprehensive Ballistics Tables for Currently Manufactured Sporting Rifle Cartridges

No more collecting catalogs and peering at microscopic print to find out what ammunition is offered for a cartridge, and how it performs relative to other factory loads! *Shooter's Bible* has assembled the data for you, in easy-to-read tables, by cartridge. Of course, this section will be updated every year to bring you the latest information.

Notes: Data is taken from manufacturers' charts; your chronograph readings may vary. Listings are current as of February the year *Shooter's Bible* appears (not the cover year). Listings are not intended as recommendations. For example, the data for the .44 Magnum at 400 yards shows its effective range is much shorter. The lack of data for a 285-grain .375 H&H bullet beyond 300 yards does not mean the bullet has no authority farther out. Besides ammunition, the rifle, sights, conditions and shooter ability all must be considered when contemplating a long shot. Accuracy and bullet energy both matter when big game is in the offing. Barrel length affects velocity, and at various rates depending on the load. As a rule, figure 50 fps per inch of barrel, plus or minus, if your barrel is longer or shorter than 22 inches. Bullets are given by make, weight (in grains) and type.

Most type abbreviations are self-explanatory: **BT**=Boat-Tail, **FMJ**=Full Metal Jacket, **HP**=Hollow Point, **SP**=Soft Point – except in Hornady listings, where SP is the firm's Spire Point. **TNT** and **TXP** are trademarked designations of Speer and Norma. **XLC** identifies a coated Barnes X bullet. **HE** indicates a Federal High Energy load, similar to the Hornady **LM** (Light Magnum) and **HM** (Heavy Magnum) cartridges. **Arc** (trajectory) is based on a zero range published by the manufacturer, from 100 to 300 yards. If a zero does not fall in a yardage column, it lies halfway between – at 150 yards, for example, if the bullet's strike is "+" at 100 yards and "–" at 200.

.17 REMINGTON TO .222 REMINGTON

CARTRIDGE BULLET	RANGE, YARDS:	0	100	200	300	400
.17 REMINGTON						
Rem. 25 HP Power-Lokt	velocity, fps:	4040	3284	2644	2086	1606
	energy, ft-lb:	906	599	388	242	143
	arc, inches:		+1.8	0	-3.3	-16.6
.218 BEE						
Win. 46 Hollow Point	velocity, fps:	2760	2102	1550	1155	961
	energy, ft-lb:	778	451	245	136	94
	arc, inches:		0	-7.2	-29.4	
.22 HORNET						
Hornady 35 V-Max	velocity, fps:	3100	2278	1601	1135	929
	energy, ft-lb:	747	403	199	100	67
	arc, inches:	+2.8	0	-16.9	-60.4	
Rem. 45 Pointed Soft Point	velocity, fps:	2690	2042	1502	1128	948
	energy, ft-lb:	723	417	225	127	90
	arc, inches:		0	-7.1	-30.0	
Rem. 45 Hollow Point	velocity, fps:	2690	2042	1502	1128	948
	energy, ft-lb:	723	417	225	127	90
	arc, inches:		0	-7.1	-30.0	
Win. 34 Jacketed HP	velocity, fps:	3050	2132	1415	1017	852
	energy, ft-lb:	700	343	151	78	55
	arc, inches:		0	-6.6	-29.9	
Win. 45 Soft Point	velocity, fps:	2690	2042	1502	1128	948
	energy, ft-lb:	723	417	225	127	90
	arc, inches:		0	-7.7	-31.3	
Win. 46 Hollow Point	velocity, fps:	2690	2042	1502	1128	948
	energy, ft-lb:	739	426	230	130	92
	arc, inches:		0	-7.7	-31.3	

CARTRIDGE BULLET	RANGE, YARDS:	0	100	200	300	400
.221 REMINGTON FIREBALL						
Rem. V-Max boat-tail	velocity, fps:	2995	2605	2247	1918	1622
	energy, ft-lb:	996	753	560	408	292
	arc, inches:		+1.8	0	-8.8	-27.1
.222 REMINGTON						
Federal 50 Hi-Shok	velocity, fps:	3140	2600	2120	1700	1350
	energy, ft-lb:	1095	750	500	320	200
	arc, inches:		+1.9	0	-9.7	-31.6
Federal 55 FMJ boat-tail	velocity, fps:	3020	2740	2480	2230	1990
	energy, ft-lb:	1115	915	750	610	484
	arc, inches:		+1.6	0	-7.3	-21.5
Hornady 40 V-Max	velocity, fps:	3600	3117	2673	2269	1911
	energy, ft-lb:	1151	863	634	457	324
	arc, inches:		+1.1	0	-6.1	-18.9
Hornady 50 V-Max	velocity, fps:	3140	2729	2352	2008	1710
	energy, ft-lb:	1094	827	614	448	325
	arc, inches:		+1.7	0	-7.9	-24.4
Norma 50 Soft Point	velocity, fps:	3199	2667	2193	1771	
	energy, ft-lb:	1136	790	534	348	
	arc, inches:		+1.7	0	-9.1	
Norma 50 FMJ	velocity, fps:	2789	2326	1910	1547	
	energy, ft-lb:	864	601	405	266	
	arc, inches:		+2.5	0	-12.2	
Norma 62 Soft Point	velocity, fps:	2887	2457	2067	1716	
	energy, ft-lb:	1148	831	588	405	
	arc, inches:		+2.1	0	-10.4	
PMC 50 Pointed Soft Point	velocity, fps:	3044	2727	2354	2012	1651
	energy, ft-lb:	1131	908	677	494	333
	arc, inches:		+1.6	0	-7.9	-24.5

Centerfire Rifle Ballistics

.222 Remington to .223 Remington

Cartridge Bullet	Range, Yards:	0	100	200	300	400
Rem. 50 Pointed Soft Point	velocity, fps:	3140	2602	2123	1700	1350
	energy, ft-lb:	1094	752	500	321	202
	arc, inches:		+1.9	0	-9.7	-31.7
Rem. 50 HP Power-Lokt	velocity, fps:	3140	2635	2182	1777	1432
	energy, ft-lb:	1094	771	529	351	228
	arc, inches:		+1.8	0	-9.2	-29.6
Rem. 50 V-Max boat-tail	velocity, fps:	3140	2744	2380	2045	1740
	energy, ft-lb:	1094	836	629	464	336
	arc, inches:		+1.6	0	-7.8	-23.9
Win. 40 Ballistic Silvertip	velocity, fps:	3370	2915	2503	2127	1786
	energy, ft-lb:	1009	755	556	402	283
	arc, inches:		+1.3	0	-6.9	-21.5
Win. 50 Pointed Soft Point	velocity, fps:	3140	2602	2123	1700	1350
	energy, ft-lb:	1094	752	500	321	202
	arc, inches:		+2.2	0	-10.0	-32.3

.223 Remington

Cartridge Bullet	Range, Yards:	0	100	200	300	400
Black Hills 40 Nosler B. Tip	velocity, fps:	3600				
	energy, ft-lb:	1150				
	arc, inches:					
Black Hills 69 Sierra MK	velocity, fps:	2850				
	energy, ft-lb:	1245				
	arc, inches:					
Black Hills 73 Berger BTHP	velocity, fps:	2750				
	energy, ft-lb:	1226				
	arc, inches:					
Federal 50 Jacketed HP	velocity, fps:	3400	2910	2460	2060	1700
	energy, ft-lb:	1285	940	675	470	320
	arc, inches:		+1.3	0	-7.1	-22.7
Federal 50 Speer TNT HP	velocity, fps:	3300	2860	2450	2080	1750
	energy, ft-lb:	1210	905	670	480	340
	arc, inches:		+1.4	0	-7.3	-22.6
Federal 52 Sierra MatchKing BTHP	velocity, fps:	3300	2860	2460	2090	1760
	energy, ft-lb:	1255	945	700	505	360
	arc, inches:		+1.4	0	-7.2	-22.4
Federal 55 Hi-Shok	velocity, fps:	3240	2750	2300	1910	1550
	energy, ft-lb:	1280	920	650	445	295
	arc, inches:		+1.6	0	-8.2	-26.1
Federal 55 FMJ boat-tail	velocity, fps:	3240	2950	2670	2410	2170
	energy, ft-lb:	1280	1060	875	710	575
	arc, inches:		+1.3	0	-6.1	-18.3
Federal 55 Sierra GameKing BTHP	velocity, fps:	3240	2770	2340	1950	1610
	energy, ft-lb:	1280	935	670	465	315
	arc, inches:		+1.5	0	-8.0	-25.3
Federal 55 Trophy Bonded	velocity, fps:	3100	2630	2210	1830	1500
	energy, ft-lb:	1175	845	595	410	275
	arc, inches:		+1.8	0	-8.9	-28.7
Federal 55 Nosler Bal. Tip	velocity, fps:	3240	2870	2530	2220	1920
	energy, ft-lb:	1280	1005	780	600	450
	arc, inches:		+1.4	0	-6.8	-20.8
Federal 55 Sierra BlitzKing	velocity, fps:	3240	2870	2520	2200	1910
	energy, ft-lb:	1280	1005	775	590	445
	arc, inches:		+-1.4	0	-6.9	-20.9
Federal 62 FMJ	velocity, fps:	3020	2650	2310	2000	1710
	energy, ft-lb:	1225	970	735	550	405
	arc, inches:		+1.7	0	-8.4	-25.5
Federal 69 Sierra MatchKing BTHP	velocity, fps:	3000	2720	2460	2210	1980
	energy, ft-lb:	1380	1135	925	750	600
	arc, inches:		+1.6	0	-7.4	-21.9
Hornady 40 V-Max	velocity, fps:	3800	3305	2845	2424	2044
	energy, ft-lb:	1282	970	719	522	371
	arc, inches:		+0.8	0	-5.3	-16.6
Hornady 53 Hollow Point	velocity, fps:	3330	2882	2477	2106	1710
	energy, ft-lb:	1305	978	722	522	369
	arc, inches:		+1.7	0	-7.4	-22.7
Hornady 55 V-Max	velocity, fps:	3240	2859	2507	2181	1891
	energy, ft-lb:	1282	998	767	581	437
	arc, inches:		+1.4	0	-7.1	-21.4
Hornady 55 Urban Tactical	velocity, fps:	2970	2626	2307	2011	1739
	energy, ft-lb:	1077	842	650	494	369
	arc, inches:		+1.5	0	-8.1	-24.9
Hornady 60 Soft Point	velocity, fps:	3150	2782	2442	2127	1837
	energy, ft-lb:	1322	1031	795	603	450
	arc, inches:		+1.6	0	-7.5	-22.5
Hornady 60 Urban Tactical	velocity, fps:	2950	2619	2312	2025	1762
	energy, ft-lb:	1160	914	712	546	413
	arc, inches:		+1.6	0	-8.1	-24.7
Hornady 75 BTHP Match	velocity, fps:	2790	2554	2330	2119	1926
	energy, ft-lb:	1296	1086	904	747	617
	arc, inches:		+2.4	0	--8.8	-25.1
Hornady 75 BTHP Tactical	velocity, fps:	2630	2409	2199	2000	1814
	energy, ft-lb:	1152	966	805	666	548
	arc, inches:		-2.0	0	-9.2	-25.9
PMC 55 HP boat-tail	velocity, fps:	3240	2717	2250	1832	1473
	energy, ft-lb:	1282	901	618	410	265
	arc, inches:		+1.6	0	-8.6	-27.7
PMC 55 FMJ boat-tail	velocity, fps:	3195	2882	2525	2169	1843
	energy, ft-lb:	1246	1014	779	574	415
	arc, inches:		+1.4	0	-6.8	-21.1
PMC 55 Pointed Soft Point	velocity, fps:	3112	2767	2421	2100	1806
	energy, ft-lb:	1182	935	715	539	398
	arc, inches:		+1.5	0	-7.5	-22.9
PMC 64 Pointed Soft Point	velocity, fps:	2775	2511	2261	2026	1806
	energy, ft-lb:	1094	896	726	583	464
	arc, inches:		+2.0	0	-8.8	-26.1
PMC 69 BTHP Match	velocity, fps:					
	energy, ft-lb:					
	arc, inches:					
Rem. 50 V-Max, boat-tail	velocity, fps:	3300	2889	2514	2168	1851
	energy, ft-lb:	1209	927	701	522	380
	arc, inches:		+1.4	0	-6.9	-21.2
Rem. 55 Pointed Soft Point	velocity, fps:	3240	2747	2304	1905	1554
	energy, ft-lb:	1282	921	648	443	295
	arc, inches:		+1.6	0	-8.2	-26.2
Rem. 55 HP Power-Lokt	velocity, fps:	3240	2773	2352	1969	1627
	energy, ft-lb:	1282	939	675	473	323
	arc, inches:		+1.5	0	-7.9	-24.8
Rem. 55 Metal Case	velocity, fps:	3240	2759	2326	1933	1587
	energy, ft-lb:	1282	929	660	456	307
	arc, inches:		+1.6	0	-8.1	-25.5
Rem. 62 HP Match	velocity, fps:	3025	2572	2162	1792	1471
	energy, ft-lb:	1260	911	643	442	298
	arc, inches:		+1.9	0	-9.4	-29.9
Win. 40 Ballistic Silvertip	velocity, fps:	3700	3166	2693	2265	1879
	energy, ft-lb:	1216	891	644	456	314
	arc, inches:		+1.0	0	-5.8	-18.4
Win. 45 JHP	velocity, fps:	3600				
	energy, ft-lb:	1295				
	arc, inches:					

Centerfire Rifle Ballistics

.223 Remington to .220 Swift

CARTRIDGE BULLET	RANGE, YARDS:	0	100	200	300	400
Win. 50 Ballistic Silvertip	velocity, fps:	3410	2982	2593	2235	1907
	energy, ft-lb:	1291	987	746	555	404
	arc, inches:		+1.2	0	-6.4	-19.8
Win. 53 Hollow Point	velocity, fps:	3330	2882	2477	2106	1770
	energy, ft-lb:	1305	978	722	522	369
	arc, inches:		+1.7	0	-7.4	-22.7
Win. 55 Pointed Soft Point	velocity, fps:	3240	2747	2304	1905	1554
	energy, ft-lb:	1282	921	648	443	295
	arc, inches:		+1.9	0	-8.5	-26.7
Win. 55 Super Clean NT	velocity, fps:	3150	2520	1970	1505	1165
	energy, ft-lb:	1212	776	474	277	166
	arc, inches:		+2.8	0	-11.9	-38.9
Win. 55 FMJ	velocity, fps:	3240	2854			
	energy, ft-lb:	1282	995			
	arc, inches:					
Win. 64 Power-Point	velocity, fps:	3020	2656	2320	2009	1724
	energy, ft-lb:	1296	1003	765	574	423
	arc, inches:		+1.7	0	-8.2	-25.1
Win. 64 Power-Point Plus	velocity, fps:	3090	2684	2312	1971	1664
	energy, ft-lb:	1357	1024	760	552	393
	arc, inches:		+1.7	0	-8.2	-25.4

.5.6 x 52 R

Norma 71 Soft Point	velocity, fps:	2789	2446	2128	1835	
	energy, ft-lb:	1227	944	714	531	
	arc, inches:		+2.1	0	-9.9	

.22 PPC

A-Square 52 Berger	velocity, fps:	3300	2952	2629	2329	2049
	energy, ft-lb:	1257	1006	798	626	485
	arc, inches:		+1.3	0	-6.3	-19.1

.225 Winchester

Win. 55 Pointed Soft Point	velocity, fps:	3570	3066	2616	2208	1838
	energy, ft-lb:	1556	1148	836	595	412
	arc, inches:		+2.4	+2.0	-3.5	-16.3

.224 Weatherby Magnum

Wby. 55 Pointed Expanding	velocity, fps:	3650	3192	2780	2403	2056
	energy, ft-lb:	1627	1244	944	705	516
	arc, inches:		+2.8	+3.7	0	-9.8

.22-250 Remington

Federal 40 Sierra Varminter	velocity, fps:	4000	3320	2720	2200	1740
	energy, ft-lb:	1420	980	660	430	265
	arc, inches:		+0.8	0	-5.6	-18.4
Federal 55 Hi-Shok	velocity, fps:	3680	3140	2660	2220	1830
	energy, ft-lb:	1655	1200	860	605	410
	arc, inches:		+1.0	0	-6.0	-19.1
Federal 55 Sierra BlitzKing	velocity, fps:	3680	3270	2890	2540	2220
	energy, ft-lb:	1655	1300	1020	790	605
	arc, inches:		+0.9	0	-5.1	-15.6
Federal 55 Sierra GameKing BTHP	velocity, fps:	3680	3280	2920	2590	2280
	energy, ft-lb:	1655	1315	1040	815	630
	arc, inches:		+0.9	0	-5.0	-15.1
Federal 55 Trophy Bonded	velocity, fps:	3600	3080	2610	2190	1810
	energy, ft-lb:	1585	1155	835	590	400
	arc, inches:		+1.1	0	-6.2	-19.8
Hornady 40 V-Max	velocity, fps:	4150	3631	3147	2699	2293
	energy, ft-lb:	1529	1171	879	647	467
	arc, inches:		+0.5	0	-4.2	-13.3
Hornady 50 V-Max	velocity, fps:	3800	3349	2925	2535	2178
	energy, ft-lb:	1603	1245	950	713	527
	arc, inches:		+0.8	0	-5.0	-15.6
Hornady 53 Hollow Point	velocity, fps:	3680	3185	2743	2341	1974
	energy, ft-lb:	1594	1194	886	645	459
	arc, inches:		+1.0	0	-5.7	-17.8
Hornady 55 V-Max	velocity, fps:	3680	3265	2876	2517	2183
	energy, ft-lb:	1654	1302	1010	772	582
	arc, inches:		+0.9	0	-5.3	-16.1
Hornady 60 Soft Point	velocity, fps:	3600	3195	2826	2485	2169
	energy, ft-lb:	1727	1360	1064	823	627
	arc, inches:		+1.0	0	-5.4	-16.3
Norma 53 Soft Point	velocity, fps:	3707	3234	2809	1716	
	energy, ft-lb:	1618	1231	928	690	
	arc, inches:		+0.9	0	-5.3	
PMC 55 HP boat-tail	velocity, fps:	3680	3104	2596	2141	1737
	energy, ft-lb:	1654	1176	823	560	368
	arc, inches:		+1.1	0	-6.3	-20.2
PMC 55 Pointed Soft Point	velocity, fps:	3586	3203	2852	2505	2178
	energy, ft-lb:	1570	1253	993	766	579
	arc, inches:		+1.0	0	-5.2	-16.0
Rem. 50 V-Max boat-tail (also in EtronX)	velocity, fps:	3725	3272	2864	2491	2147
	energy, ft-lb:	1540	1188	910	689	512
	arc, inches:		+1.7	+1.6	-2.8	-12.8
Rem. 55 Pointed Soft Point	velocity, fps:	3680	3137	2656	2222	1832
	energy, ft-lb:	1654	1201	861	603	410
	arc, inches:		+1.9	+1.8	-3.3	-15.5
Rem. 55 HP Power-Lokt	velocity, fps:	3680	3209	2785	2400	2046
	energy, ft-lb:	1654	1257	947	703	511
	arc, inches:		+1.8	+1.7	-3.0	-13.7
Rem. 60 Nosler Partition (also in EtronX)	velocity, fps:	3500	3045	2634	2258	1914
	energy, ft-lb:	1632	1235	924	679	488
	arc, inches:		+2.1	+1.9	-3.4	-15.5
Win. 40 Ballistic Silvertip	velocity, fps:	4150	3591	3099	2658	2257
	energy, ft-lb:	1530	1146	853	628	453
	arc, inches:		+0.6	0	-4.2	-13.4
Win. 50 Ballistic Silvertip	velocity, fps:	3810	3341	2919	2536	2182
	energy, ft-lb:	1611	1239	946	714	529
	arc, inches:		+0.8	0	-4.9	-15.2
Win. 55 Pointed Soft Point	velocity, fps:	3680	3137	2656	2222	1832
	energy, ft-lb:	1654	1201	861	603	410
	arc, inches:		+2.3	+1.9	-3.4	-15.9

.220 Swift

Federal 52 Sierra MatchKing BTHP	velocity, fps:	3830	3370	2960	2600	2230
	energy, ft-lb:	1690	1310	1010	770	575
	arc, inches:		+0.8	0	-4.8	-14.9
Federal 55 Sierra BlitzKing	velocity, fps:	3800	3370	2990	2630	2310
	energy, ft-lb:	1765	1390	1090	850	650
	arc, inches:		+0.8	0	-4.7	-14.4
Federal 55 Trophy Bonded	velocity, fps:	3700	3170	2690	2270	1880
	energy, ft-lb:	1670	1225	885	625	430
	arc, inches:		+1.0	0	-5.8	-18.5
Hornady 40 V-Max	velocity, fps:	4200	3678	3190	2739	2329
	energy, ft-lb:	1566	1201	904	666	482
	arc, inches:		+0.5	0	-4.0	-12.9
Hornady 50 V-Max	velocity, fps:	3850	3396	2970	2576	2215
	energy, ft-lb:	1645	1280	979	736	545
	arc, inches:		+0.7	0	-4.8	-15.1

Centerfire Rifle Ballistics
.220 Swift to .243 Winchester

CARTRIDGE BULLET	RANGE, YARDS:	0	100	200	300	400
Hornady 50 SP	velocity, fps:	3850	3327	2862	2442	2060
	energy, ft-lb:	1645	1228	909	662	471
	arc, inches:		+0.8	0	-5.1	-16.1
Hornady 55 V-Max	velocity, fps:	3680	3265	2876	2517	2183
	energy, ft-lb:	1654	1302	1010	772	582
	arc, inches:		+0.9	0	-5.3	-16.1
Hornady 60 Hollow Point	velocity, fps:	3600	3199	2824	2475	2156
	energy, ft-lb:	1727	1364	1063	816	619
	arc, inches:		+1.0	0	-5.4	-16.3
Norma 50 Soft Point	velocity, fps:	4019	3380	2826	2335	
	energy, ft-lb:	1794	1268	887	605	
	arc, inches:		+0.7	0	-5.1	
Rem. 50 Pointed Soft Point	velocity, fps:	3780	3158	2617	2135	1710
	energy, ft-lb:	1586	1107	760	506	325
	arc, inches:		+0.3	-1.4	-8.2	
Rem. 50 V-Max boat-tail	velocity, fps:	3780	3321	2908	2532	2185
(also in EtronX)	energy, ft-lb:	1586	1224	939	711	530
	arc, inches:		+0.8	0	-5.0	-15.4
Win. 40 Ballistic Silvertip	velocity, fps:	4050	3518	3048	2624	2238
	energy, ft-lb:	1457	1099	825	611	445
	arc, inches:		+0.7	0	-4.4	-13.9
Win. 50 Pointed Soft Point	velocity, fps:	3870	3310	2816	2373	1972
	energy, ft-lb:	1663	1226	881	625	432
	arc, inches:		+0.8	0	-5.2	-16.7

6mm PPC

A-Square 68 Berger	velocity, fps:	3100	2751	2428	2128	1850
	energy, ft-lb:	1451	1143	890	684	516
	arc, inches:		+1.5	0	-7.5	-22.6

6x70 R

Norma 90 Nosler Bal. Tip	velocity, fps:	2461	2231	2013	1809	
	energy, ft-lb:	1211	995	810	654	
	arc, inches:		+2.7	0	-11.3	

.243 Winchester

Black Hills 55 Nosler B. Tip	velocity, fps:	3800				
	energy, ft-lb:	1763				
	arc, inches:					
Black Hills 90 Nosler B. Tip	velocity, fps:	2950				
	energy, ft-lb:	1836				
	arc, inches:					
Federal 70 Nosler Bal. Tip	velocity, fps:	3400	3070	2760	2470	2200
	energy, ft-lb:	1795	1465	1185	950	755
	arc, inches:		+1.1	0	-5.7	-17.1
Federal 70 Speer TNT HP	velocity, fps:	3400	3040	2700	2390	2100
	energy, ft-lb:	1795	1435	1135	890	685
	arc, inches:		+1.1	0	-5.9	-18.0
Federal 80 Sierra Pro-Hunter	velocity, fps:	3350	2960	2590	2260	1950
	energy, ft-lb:	1995	1550	1195	905	675
	arc, inches:		+1.3	0	-6.4	-19.7
Federal 85 Sierra GameKing BTHP	velocity, fps:	3320	3070	2830	2600	2380
	energy, ft-lb:	2080	1770	1510	1280	1070
	arc, inches:		+1.1	0	-5.5	-16.1
Federal 90 Trophy Bonded	velocity, fps:	3100	2850	2610	2380	2160
	energy, ft-lb:	1920	1620	1360	1130	935
	arc, inches:		+1.4	0	-6.1	-19.2
Federal 100 Hi-Shok	velocity, fps:	2960	2700	2450	2220	1990
	energy, ft-lb:	1945	1615	1330	1090	880
	arc, inches:		+1.6	0	-7.5	-22.0
Federal 100 Sierra GameKing BTSP	velocity, fps:	2960	2760	2570	2380	2210
	energy, ft-lb:	1950	1690	1460	1260	1080
	arc, inches:		+1.5	0	-6.8	-19.8
Federal 100 Nosler Partition	velocity, fps:	2960	2730	2510	2300	2100
	energy, ft-lb:	1945	1650	1395	1170	975
	arc, inches:		+1.6	0	-7.1	-20.9
Hornady 58 V-Max	velocity, fps:	3750	3319	2913	2539	2195
	energy, ft-lb:	1811	1418	1093	830	620
	arc, inches:		+1.2	0	-5.5	-16.4
Hornady 75 Hollow Point	velocity, fps:	3400	2970	2578	2219	1890
	energy, ft-lb:	1926	1469	1107	820	595
	arc, inches:		+1.2	0	-6.5	-20.3
Hornady 100 BTSP	velocity, fps:	2960	2728	2508	2299	2099
	energy, ft-lb:	1945	1653	1397	1174	979
	arc, inches:		+1.6	0	-7.2	-21.0
Hornady 100 BTSP LM	velocity, fps:	3100	2839	2592	2358	2138
	energy, ft-lb:	2133	1790	1491	1235	1014
	arc, inches:		+1.5	0	-6.8	-19.8
Norma 80 FMJ	velocity, fps:	3117	2750	2412	2098	
	energy, ft-lb:	1726	1344	1034	782	
	arc, inches:		+1.5	0	-7.5	
Norma 100 FMJ	velocity, fps:	3018	2747	2493	2252	
	energy, ft-lb:	2023	1677	1380	1126	
	arc, inches:		+1.5	0	-7.1	
Norma 100 Soft Point	velocity, fps:	3018	2748	2493	2252	
	energy, ft-lb:	2023	1677	1380	1126	
	arc, inches:		+1.5	0	-7.1	
PMC 80 Pointed Soft Point	velocity, fps:	2940	2684	2444	2215	1999
	energy, ft-lb:	1535	1280	1060	871	709
	arc, inches:		+1.7	0	-7.5	-22.1
PMC 85 HP boat-tail	velocity, fps:	3275	2922	2596	2292	2009
	energy, ft-lb:	2024	1611	1272	991	761
	arc, inches:		+1.3	0	-6.5	-19.7
PMC 100 Pointed Soft Point	velocity, fps:	2743	2507	2283	2070	1869
	energy, ft-lb:	1670	1395	1157	951	776
	arc, inches:		+2.0	0	-8.7	-25.5
PMC 100 SP boat-tail	velocity, fps:	2960	2742	2534	2335	2144
	energy, ft-lb:	1945	1669	1425	1210	1021
	arc, inches:		+1.6	0	-7.0	-20.5
Rem. 75 V-Max boat-tail	velocity, fps:	3375	3065	2775	2504	2248
	energy, ft-lb:	1897	1564	1282	1044	842
	arc, inches:		+2.0	+1.8	-3.0	-13.3
Rem. 80 Pointed Soft Point	velocity, fps:	3350	2955	2593	2259	1951
	energy, ft-lb:	1993	1551	1194	906	676
	arc, inches:		+2.2	+2.0	-3.5	-15.8
Rem. 80 HP Power-Lokt	velocity, fps:	3350	2955	2593	2259	1951
	energy, ft-lb:	1993	1551	1194	906	676
	arc, inches:		+2.2	+2.0	-3.5	-15.8
Rem. 90 Nosler Bal. Tip	velocity, fps:	3120	2871	2635	2411	2199
(also in EtronX)	energy, ft-lb:	1946	1647	1388	1162	966
	arc, inches:		+1.4	0	-6.4	-18.8
Rem. 100 PSP Core-Lokt	velocity, fps:	2960	2697	2449	2215	1993
(also in EtronX)	energy, ft-lb:	1945	1615	1332	1089	882
	arc, inches:		+1.6	0	-7.5	-22.1
Rem. 100 PSP boat-tail	velocity, fps:	2960	2720	2492	2275	2069
	energy, ft-lb:	1945	1642	1378	1149	950
	arc, inches:		+2.8	+2.3	-3.8	-16.6
Speer 100 Grand Slam	velocity, fps:	2950	2684	2434	2197	
	energy, ft-lb:	1932	1600	1315	1072	
	arc, inches:		+1.7	0	-7.6	-22.4

Centerfire Rifle Ballistics

.243 Winchester to .26-06 Remington

CARTRIDGE BULLET	RANGE, YARDS:	0	100	200	300	400
Win. 55 Ballistic Silvertip	velocity, fps:	4025	3597	3209	2853	2525
	energy, ft-lb:	1978	1579	1257	994	779
	arc, inches:		+0.6	0	-4.0	-12.2
Win. 80 Pointed Soft Point	velocity, fps:	3350	2955	2593	2259	1951
	energy, ft-lb:	1993	1551	1194	906	676
	arc, inches:		+2.6	+2.1	-3.6	-16.2
Win. 95 Ballistic Silvertip	velocity, fps:	3100	2854	2626	2410	2203
	energy, ft-lb:	2021	1719	1455	1225	1024
	arc, inches:		+1.4	0	-6.4	-18.9
Win. 100 Power-Point	velocity, fps:	2960	2697	2449	2215	1993
	energy, ft-lb:	1945	1615	1332	1089	882
	arc, inches:		+1.9	0	-7.8	-22.6
Win. 100 Power-Point Plus	velocity, fps:	3090	2818	2562	2321	2092
	energy, ft-lb:	2121	1764	1458	1196	972
	arc, inches:		+1.4	0	-6.7	-20.0

6mm Remington

CARTRIDGE BULLET	RANGE, YARDS:	0	100	200	300	400
Federal 80 Sierra Pro-Hunter	velocity, fps:	3470	3060	2690	2350	2040
	energy, ft-lb:	2140	1665	1290	980	735
	arc, inches:		+1.1	0	-5.9	-18.2
Federal 100 Hi-Shok	velocity, fps:	3100	2830	2570	2330	2100
	energy, ft-lb:	2135	1775	1470	1205	985
	arc, inches:		+1.4	0	-6.7	-19.8
Federal 100 Nosler Partition	velocity, fps:	3100	2860	2640	2420	2220
	energy, ft-lb:	2135	1820	1545	1300	1090
	arc, inches:		+1.4	0	-6.3	-18.7
Hornady 100 SP boat-tail	velocity, fps:	3100	2861	2634	2419	2231
	energy, ft-lb:	2134	1818	1541	1300	1088
	arc, inches:		+1.3	0	-6.5	-18.9
Hornady 100 SPBT LM	velocity, fps:	3250	2997	2756	2528	2311
	energy, ft-lb:	2345	1995	1687	1418	1186
	arc, inches:		+1.6	0	-6.3	-18.2
Rem. 75 V-Max boat-tail	velocity, fps:	3400	3088	2797	2524	2267
	energy, ft-lb:	1925	1587	1303	1061	856
	arc, inches:		+1.9	+1.7	-3.0	-13.1
Rem. 100 PSP Core-Lokt	velocity, fps:	3100	2829	2573	2332	2104
	energy, ft-lb:	2133	1777	1470	1207	983
	arc, inches:		+1.4	0	-6.7	-19.8
Rem. 100 PSP boat-tail	velocity, fps:	3100	2852	2617	2394	2183
	energy, ft-lb:	2134	1806	1521	1273	1058
	arc, inches:		+1.4	0	-6.5	-19.1
Win. 100 Power-Point	velocity, fps:	3100	2829	2573	2332	2104
	energy, ft-lb:	2133	1777	1470	1207	983
	arc, inches:		+1.7	0	-7.0	-20.4

.240 Weatherby Magnum

CARTRIDGE BULLET	RANGE, YARDS:	0	100	200	300	400
Wby. 87 Pointed Expanding	velocity, fps:	3523	3199	2898	2617	2352
	energy, ft-lb:	2397	1977	1622	1323	1069
	arc, inches:		+2.7	+3.4	0	-8.4
Wby. 90 Barnes-X	velocity, fps:	3500	3222	2962	2717	2484
	energy, ft-lb:	2448	2075	1753	1475	1233
	arc, inches:		+2.6	+3.3	0	-8.0
Wby. 95 Nosler Bal. Tip	velocity, fps:	3420	3146	2888	2645	2414
	energy, ft-lb:	2467	2087	1759	1475	1229
	arc, inches:		+2.7	+3.5	0	-8.4
Wby. 100 Pointed Expanding	velocity, fps:	3406	3134	2878	2637	2408
	energy, ft-lb:	2576	2180	1839	1544	1287
	arc, inches:		+2.8	+3.5	0	-8.4
Wby. 100 Partition	velocity, fps:	3406	3136	2882	2642	2415
	energy, ft-lb:	2576	2183	1844	1550	1294
	arc, inches:		+2.8	+3.5	0	-8.4

.25-20 Winchester

CARTRIDGE BULLET	RANGE, YARDS:	0	100	200	300	400
Rem. 86 Soft Point	velocity, fps:	1460	1194	1030	931	858
	energy, ft-lb:	407	272	203	165	141
	arc, inches:		0	-22.9	-78.9	-173.0
Win. 86 Soft Point	velocity, fps:	1460	1194	1030	931	858
	energy, ft-lb:	407	272	203	165	141
	arc, inches:		0	-23.5	-79.6	-175.9

.25-35 Winchester

CARTRIDGE BULLET	RANGE, YARDS:	0	100	200	300	400
Win. 117 Soft Point	velocity, fps:	2230	1866	1545	1282	1097
	energy, ft-lb:	1292	904	620	427	313
	arc, inches:		+2.1	-5.1	-27.0	-70.1

.250 Savage

CARTRIDGE BULLET	RANGE, YARDS:	0	100	200	300	400
Rem. 100 Pointed SP	velocity, fps:	2820	2504	2210	1936	1684
	energy, ft-lb:	1765	1392	1084	832	630
	arc, inches:		+2.0	0	-9.2	-27.7
Win. 100 Silvertip	velocity, fps:	2820	2467	2140	1839	1569
	energy, ft-lb:	1765	1351	1017	751	547
	arc, inches:		+2.4	0	-10.1	-30.5

.257 Roberts

CARTRIDGE BULLET	RANGE, YARDS:	0	100	200	300	400
Federal 120 Nosler Partition	velocity, fps:	2780	2560	2360	2160	1970
	energy, ft-lb:	2060	1750	1480	1240	1030
	arc, inches:		+1.9	0	-8.2	-24.0
Hornady 117 SP boat-tail	velocity, fps:	2780	2550	2331	2122	1925
	energy, ft-lb:	2007	1689	1411	1170	963
	arc, inches:		+1.9	0	-8.3	-24.4
Hornady 117 SP boat-tail LM	velocity, fps:	2940	2694	2460	2240	2031
	energy, ft-lb:	2245	1885	1572	1303	1071
	arc, inches:		+1.7	0	-7.6	-21.8
Rem. 117 SP Core-Lokt	velocity, fps:	2650	2291	1961	1663	1404
	energy, ft-lb:	1824	1363	999	718	512
	arc, inches:		+2.6	0	-11.7	-36.1
Win. 117 Power-Point	velocity, fps:	2780	2411	2071	1761	1488
	energy, ft-lb:	2009	1511	1115	806	576
	arc, inches:		+2.6	0	-10.8	-33.0

.25-06 Remington

CARTRIDGE BULLET	RANGE, YARDS:	0	100	200	300	400
Federal 90 Sierra Varminter	velocity, fps:	3440	3040	2680	2340	2030
	energy, ft-lb:	2365	1850	1435	1100	825
	arc, inches:		+1.1	0	-6.0	-18.3
Federal 100 Barnes XLC	velocity, fps:	3210	2970	2750	2540	2330
	energy, ft-lb:	2290	1965	1680	1430	1205
	arc, inches:		+1.2	0	-5.8	-17.0
Federal 100 Nosler Bal. Tip	velocity, fps:	3210	2960	2720	2490	2280
	energy, ft-lb:	2290	1940	1640	1380	1150
	arc, inches:		+1.2	0	-6.0	-17.5
Federal 115 Nosler Partition	velocity, fps:	2990	2750	2520	2300	2100
	energy, ft-lb:	2285	1930	1620	1350	1120
	arc, inches:		+1.6	0	-7.0	-20.8
Federal 115 Trophy Bonded	velocity, fps:	2990	2740	2500	2270	2050
	energy, ft-lb:	2285	1910	1590	1310	1075
	arc, inches:		+1.6	0	-7.2	-21.1
Federal 117 Sierra Pro Hunt.	velocity, fps:	2990	2730	2480	2250	2030
	energy, ft-lb:	2320	1985	1645	1350	1100
	arc, inches:		+1.6	0	-7.2	-21.4
Federal 117 Sierra GameKing BTSP	velocity, fps:	2990	2770	2570	2370	2190
	energy, ft-lb:	2320	2000	1715	1465	1240
	arc, inches:		+1.5	0	-6.8	-19.9

Centerfire Rifle Ballistics
.26-06 Remington to 6.5x55 Swedish

CARTRIDGE BULLET	RANGE, YARDS:	0	100	200	300	400
Hornady 117 SP boat-tail	velocity, fps:	2990	2749	2520	2302	2096
	energy, ft-lb:	2322	1962	1649	1377	1141
	arc, inches:		+1.6	0	-7.0	-20.7
Hornady 117 SP boat-tail LM	velocity, fps:	3110	2855	2613	2384	2168
	energy, ft-lb:	2512	2117	1774	1476	1220
	arc, inches:		+1.8	0	-7.1	-20.3
PMC 117 PSP	velocity, fps:					
	energy, ft-lb:					
	arc, inches:					
Rem. 100 PSP Core-Lokt	velocity, fps:	3230	2893	2580	2287	2014
	energy, ft-lb:	2316	1858	1478	1161	901
	arc, inches:		+1.3	0	-6.6	-19.8
Rem. 120 PSP Core-Lokt	velocity, fps:	2990	2730	2484	2252	2032
	energy, ft-lb:	2382	1985	1644	1351	1100
	arc, inches:		+1.6	0	-7.2	-21.4
Speer 120 Grand Slam	velocity, fps:	3130	2835	2558	2298	
	energy, ft-lb:	2610	2141	1743	1407	
	arc, inches:		+1.4	0	-6.8	-20.1
Win. 90 Pos. Exp. Point	velocity, fps:	3440	3043	2680	2344	2034
	energy, ft-lb:	2364	1850	1435	1098	827
	arc, inches:		+2.4	+2.0	-3.4	-15.0
Win. 115 Ballistic Silvertip	velocity, fps:	3060	2825	2603	2390	2188
	energy, ft-lb:	2391	2038	1729	1459	1223
	arc, inches:		+1.4	0	-6.6	-19.2

.257 Weatherby Magnum

CARTRIDGE BULLET	RANGE, YARDS:	0	100	200	300	400
Federal 115 Nosler Partition	velocity, fps:	3150	2900	2660	2440	2220
	energy, ft-lb:	2535	2145	1810	1515	1260
	arc, inches:		+1.3	0	-6.2	-18.4
Federal 115 Trophy Bonded	velocity, fps:	3150	2890	2640	2400	2180
	energy, ft-lb:	2535	2125	1775	1470	1210
	arc, inches:		+1.4	0	-6.3	-18.8
Wby. 87 Pointed Expanding	velocity, fps:	3825	3472	3147	2845	2563
	energy, ft-lb:	2826	2328	1913	1563	1269
	arc, inches:		+2.1	+2.8	0	-7.1
Wby. 100 Pointed Expanding	velocity, fps:	3602	3298	3016	2750	2500
	energy, ft-lb:	2881	2416	2019	1680	1388
	arc, inches:		+2.4	+3.1	0	-7.7
Wby. 115 Nosler Bal. Tip	velocity, fps:	3400	3170	2952	2745	2547
	energy, ft-lb:	2952	2566	2226	1924	1656
	arc, inches:		+3.0	+3.5	0	-7.9
Wby. 115 Barnes X	velocity, fps:	3400	3158	2929	2711	2504
	energy, ft-lb:	2952	2546	2190	1877	1601
	arc, inches:		+2.7	+3.4	0	-8.1
Wby. 117 RN Expanding	velocity, fps:	3402	2984	2595	2240	1921
	energy, ft-lb:	3007	2320	1742	1302	956
	arc, inches:		+3.4	+4.31	0	-11.1
Wby. 120 Nosler Partition	velocity, fps:	3305	3046	2801	2570	2350
	energy, ft-lb:	2910	2472	2091	1760	1471
	arc, inches:		+3.0	+3.7	0	-8.9

6.53 (.257) Scramjet

CARTRIDGE BULLET	RANGE, YARDS:	0	100	200	300	400
Lazzeroni 85 Nosler Bal. Tip	velocity, fps:	3960	3652	3365	3096	2844
	energy, ft-lb:	2961	2517	2137	1810	1526
	arc, inches:		+1.7	+2.4	0	-6.0
Lazzeroni 100 Nosler Part.	velocity, fps:	3740	3465	3208	2965	2735
	energy, ft-lb:	3106	2667	2285	1953	1661
	arc, inches:		+2.1	+2.7	0	-6.7

6.5x50 Japanese

CARTRIDGE BULLET	RANGE, YARDS:	0	100	200	300	400
Norma 156 Alaska	velocity, fps:	2067	1832	1615	1423	
	energy, ft-lb:	1480	1162	904	701	
	arc, inches:		+4.4	0	-17.8	

6.5x52 Carcano

CARTRIDGE BULLET	RANGE, YARDS:	0	100	200	300	400
Norma 156 Alaska	velocity, fps:	2428	2169	1926	1702	
	energy, ft-lb:	2043	1630	1286	1004	
	arc, inches:		+2.9	0	-12.3	

6.5x55 Swedish

CARTRIDGE BULLET	RANGE, YARDS:	0	100	200	300	400
Federal 140 Hi-Shok	velocity, fps:	2600	2400	2220	2040	1860
	energy, ft-lb:	2100	1795	1525	1285	1080
	arc, inches:		+2.3	0	-9.4	-27.2
Federal 140 Trophy Bonded	velocity, fps:	2550	2350	2160	1980	1810
	energy, ft-lb:	2020	1720	1450	1220	1015
	arc, inches:		+2.4	0	-9.8	-28.4
Federal 140 Sierra MatchKg. BTHP	velocity, fps:	2630	2460	2300	2140	2000
	energy, ft-lb:	2140	1880	1640	1430	1235
	arc, inches:		+16.4	+28.8	+33.9	+31.8
Hornady 129 SP LM	velocity, fps:	2770	2561	2361	2171	1994
	energy, ft-lb:	2197	1878	1597	1350	1138
	arc, inches:		+2.0	0	-8.2	-23.2
Hornady 140 SP LM	velocity, fps:	2740	2541	2351	2169	1999
	energy, ft-lb:	2333	2006	1717	1463	1242
	arc, inches:		+2.4	0	-8.7	-24.0
Norma 139 Vulkan	velocity, fps:	2854	2569	2302	2051	
	energy, ft-lb:	2515	2038	1636	1298	
	arc, inches:		+1.8	0	-8.4	
Norma 140 Nosler Partition	velocity, fps:	2789	2592	2403	2223	
	energy, ft-lb:	2419	2089	1796	1536	
	arc, inches:		+1.8	0	-7.8	
Norma 156 TXP Swift A-Fr.	velocity, fps:	2526	2276	2040	1818	
	energy, ft-lb:	2196	1782	1432	1138	
	arc, inches:		+2.6	0	-10.9	
Norma 156 Alaska	velocity, fps:	2559	2245	1953	1687	
	energy, ft-lb:	2269	1746	1322	986	
	arc, inches:		+2.7	0	-11.9	
Norma 156 Vulkan	velocity, fps:	2644	2395	2159	1937	
	energy, ft-lb:	2422	1987	1616	1301	
	arc, inches:		+2.2	0	-9.7	
Norma 156 Oryx	velocity, fps:	2559	2308	2070	1848	
	energy, ft-lb:	2269	1845	1485	1183	
	arc, inches:		+2.5	0	-10.6	
PMC 139 Pointed Soft Point	velocity, fps:	2850	2560	2290	2030	1790
	energy, ft-lb:	2515	2025	1615	1270	985
	arc, inches:		+2.2	0	-8.9	-26.3
PMC 140 HP boat-tail	velocity, fps:	2560	2398	2243	2093	1949
	energy, ft-lb:	2037	1788	1563	1361	1181
	arc, inches:		+2.3	0	-9.2	-26.4
PMC 140 SP boat-tail	velocity, fps:	2560	2386	2218	2057	1903
	energy, ft-lb:	2037	1769	1529	1315	1126
	arc, inches:		+2.3	0	-9.4	-27.1
PMC 144 FMJ	velocity, fps:	2650	2370	2110	1870	1650
	energy, ft-lb:	2425	1950	1550	1215	945
	arc, inches:		+2.7	0	-10.5	-30.9
Rem. 140 PSP Core-Lokt	velocity, fps:	2550	2353	2164	1984	1814
	energy, ft-lb:	2021	1720	1456	1224	1023
	arc, inches:		+2.4	0	-9.8	-27.0

Centerfire Rifle Ballistics

6.5x55 Swedish to .270 Winchester

CARTRIDGE BULLET	RANGE, YARDS:	0	100	200	300	400
Speer 140 Grand Slam	velocity, fps:	2550	2318	2099	1892	
	energy, ft-lb:	2021	1670	1369	1112	
	arc, inches:		+2.5	0	-10.4	-30.6
Win. 140 Soft Point	velocity, fps:	2550	2359	2176	2002	1836
	energy, ft-lb:	2022	1731	1473	1246	1048
	arc, inches:		+2.4	0	-9.7	-28.1

.260 REMINGTON

CARTRIDGE BULLET	RANGE, YARDS:	0	100	200	300	400
Federal 140 Sierra GameKing BTSP	velocity, fps:	2750	2570	2390	2220	2060
	energy, ft-lb:	2350	2045	1775	1535	1315
	arc, inches:		+1.9	0	-8.0	-23.1
Federal 140 Trophy Bonded	velocity, fps:	2750	2540	2340	2150	1970
	energy, ft-lb:	2350	2010	1705	1440	1210
	arc, inches:		+1.9	0	-8.4	-24.1
Rem. 120 Nosler Bal. Tip	velocity, fps:	2890	2688	2494	2309	2131
	energy, ft-lb:	2226	1924	1657	1420	1210
	arc, inches:		+1.7	0	-7.3	-21.1
Rem. 125 Nosler Partition	velocity, fps:	2875	2669	2473	2285	2105
	energy, ft-lb:	2294	1977	1697	1449	1230
	arc, inches:		+1.71	0	-7.4	-21.4
Rem. 140 PSP Core-Lokt	velocity, fps:	2750	2544	2347	2158	1979
	energy, ft-lb:	2351	2011	1712	1448	1217
	arc, inches:		+1.9	0	-8.3	-24.0
Speer 140 Grand Slam	velocity, fps:	2750	2518	2297	2087	
	energy, ft-lb:	2351	1970	1640	1354	
	arc, inches:		+2.3	0	-8.9	-25.8

6.5/284

CARTRIDGE BULLET	RANGE, YARDS:	0	100	200	300	400
Norma 120 Nosler Bal. Tip	velocity, fps:	3117	2890	2674	2469	
	energy, ft-lb:	2589	2226	1906	1624	
	arc, inches:		+1.3	0	-6.2	
Norma 140 Nosler Part.	velocity, fps:	2953	2750	2557	2371	
	energy, ft-lb:	2712	2352	2032	1748	
	arc, inches:		+1.5	0	-6.8	

.264 WINCHESTER MAGNUM

CARTRIDGE BULLET	RANGE, YARDS:	0	100	200	300	400
Rem. 140 PSP Core-Lokt	velocity, fps:	3030	2782	2548	2326	2114
	energy, ft-lb:	2854	2406	2018	1682	1389
	arc, inches:		+1.5	0	-6.9	-20.2
Win. 140 Power-Point	velocity, fps:	3030	2782	2548	2326	2114
	energy, ft-lb:	2854	2406	2018	1682	1389
	arc, inches:		+1.8	0	-7.2	-20.8

.270 WINCHESTER

CARTRIDGE BULLET	RANGE, YARDS:	0	100	200	300	400
Black Hills 130 Barnes X	velocity, fps:	2950				
	energy, ft-lb:	2184				
	arc, inches:					
Black Hills 130 Nosler B. Tip	velocity, fps	2950				
	energy, ft-lb:	2184				
	arc, inches:					
Federal 130 Hi-Shok	velocity, fps:	3060	2800	2560	2330	2110
	energy, ft-lb:	2700	2265	1890	1565	1285
	arc, inches:		+1.5	0	-6.8	-20.0
Federal 130 Sierra Pro-Hunt.	velocity, fps:	3060	2830	2600	2390	2190
	energy, ft-lb:	2705	2305	1960	1655	1390
	arc, inches:		+1.4	0	-6.4	-19.0
Federal 130 Sierra GameKing	velocity, fps:	3060	2830	2620	2410	2220
	energy, ft-lb:	2700	2320	1980	1680	1420
	arc, inches:		+1.4	0	-6.5	-19.0
Federal 130 Nosler Bal. Tip	velocity, fps:	3060	2840	2630	2430	2230
	energy, ft-lb:	2700	2325	1990	1700	1440
	arc, inches:		+1.4	0	-6.5	-18.8
Federal 130 Barnes XLC	velocity, fps:	3060	2840	2620	2420	2220
	energy, ft-lb:	2705	2320	1985	1690	1425
	arc, inches:		+1.4	0	-6.4	-18.9
Federal 130 Trophy Bonded	velocity, fps:	3060	2810	2570	2340	2130
	energy, ft-lb:	2705	2275	1905	1585	1310
	arc, inches:		+1.5	0	-6.7	-19.8
Federal 140 Trophy Bonded	velocity, fps:	2940	2700	2480	2260	2060
	energy, ft-lb:	2685	2270	1905	1590	1315
	arc, inches:		+1.6	0	-7.3	-21.5
Federal 140 Tr. Bonded HE	velocity, fps:	3100	2860	2620	2400	2200
	energy, ft-lb:	2990	2535	2140	1795	1500
	arc, inches:		+1.4	0	-6.4	-18.9
Federal 150 Hi-Shok RN	velocity, fps:	2850	2500	2180	1890	1620
	energy, ft-lb:	2705	2085	1585	1185	870
	arc, inches:		+2.0	0	-9.4	-28.6
Federal 150 Sierra GameKing	velocity, fps:	2850	2660	2480	2300	2130
	energy, ft-lb:	2705	2355	2040	1760	1510
	arc, inches:		+1.7	0	-7.4	-21.4
Federal 150 Sierra GameKing HE	velocity, fps:	3000	2800	2620	2430	2260
	energy, ft-lb:	2995	2615	2275	1975	1700
	arc, inches:		+1.5	0	-6.5	-18.9
Federal 150 Nosler Partition	velocity, fps:	2850	2590	2340	2100	1880
	energy, ft-lb:	2705	2225	1815	1470	1175
	arc, inches:		+1.9	0	-8.3	-24.4
Hornady 130 SP	velocity, fps:	3060	2800	2560	2330	2110
	energy, ft-lb:	2700	2265	1890	1565	1285
	arc, inches:		+1.8	0	-7.1	-20.6
Hornady 130 SST LM	velocity, fps:	3215	2998	2790	2590	2400
	energy, ft-lb:	2983	2594	2246	1936	1662
	arc, inches:		+1.2	0	-5.8	-17.0
Hornady 140 SP boat-tail	velocity, fps:	2940	2747	2562	2385	2214
	energy, ft-lb:	2688	2346	2041	1769	1524
	arc, inches:		+1.6	0	-7.0	-20.2
Hornady 140 SP boat-tail LM	velocity, fps:	3100	2894	2697	2508	2327
	energy, ft-lb:	2987	2604	2261	1955	1684
	arc, inches:		+1.4	0	6.3	-18.3
Hornady 150 SP	velocity, fps:	2800	2684	2478	2284	2100
	energy, ft-lb:	2802	2400	2046	1737	1469
	arc, inches:		+1.7	0	-7.4	-21.6
Norma 130 SP	velocity, fps:	3140	2862	2601	2354	
	energy, ft-lb:	2847	2365	1953	1600	
	arc, inches:	0	+1.3	0	-6.5	
Norma 150 SP	velocity, fps:	2799	2555	2323	2104	
	energy, ft-lb:	2610	2175	1798	1475	
	arc, inches:	0	+1.9	0	-8.3	
PMC 130 Barnes X	velocity, fps:	2910	2717	2533	2356	2186
	energy, ft-lb:	2444	2131	1852	1602	1379
	arc, inches:		+1.6	0	-7.1	-20.4
PMC 130 SP boat-tail	velocity, fps:	3050	2830	2620	2421	2229
	energy, ft-lb:	2685	2312	1982	1691	1435
	arc, inches:		+1.5	0	-6.5	-19.0
PMC 130 Pointed Soft Point	velocity, fps:	2816	2593	2381	2179	1987
	energy, ft-lb:	2288	1941	1636	1370	1139
	arc, inches:		+1.8	0	-8.0	-23.2
PMC 150 Barnes X	velocity, fps:	2700	2541	2387	2238	2095
	energy, ft-lb:	2428	2150	1897	1668	1461
	arc, inches:		+2.0	0	-8.1	-23.1
PMC 150 SP boat-tail	velocity, fps:	2850	2660	2477	2302	2134
	energy, ft-lb:	2705	2355	2043	1765	1516
	arc, inches:		+1.7	0	-7.4	-21.4

Centerfire Rifle Ballistics
.270 Winchester to 7mm Mauser (7x57)

CARTRIDGE BULLET	RANGE, YARDS:	0	100	200	300	400
PMC 150 Pointed Soft Point	velocity, fps:	2547	2368	2197	2032	1875
	energy, ft-lb:	2160	1868	1607	1375	1171
	arc, inches:		+2.4	0	-9.5	-27.5
Rem. 100 Pointed Soft Point	velocity, fps:	3320	2924	2561	2225	1916
	energy, ft-lb:	2448	1898	1456	1099	815
	arc, inches:		+2.3	+2.0	-3.6	-16.2
Rem. 130 PSP Core-Lokt	velocity, fps:	3060	2776	2510	2259	2022
	energy, ft-lb:	2702	2225	1818	1472	1180
	arc, inches:		+1.5	0	-7.0	-20.9
Rem. 130 Bronze Point	velocity, fps:	3060	2802	2559	2329	2110
	energy, ft-lb:	2702	2267	1890	1565	1285
	arc, inches:		+1.5	0	-6.8	-20.0
Rem. 130 Swift Scirocco	velocity, fps:	3060	2838	2677	2425	2232
	energy, ft-lb:	2702	2325	1991	1697	1438
	arc, inches:		+1.4	0	-6.5	-18.8
Rem. 140 Swift A-Frame	velocity, fps:	2925	2652	2394	2152	1923
	energy, ft-lb:	2659	2186	1782	1439	1150
	arc, inches:		+1.7	0	-7.8	-23.2
Rem. 140 PSP boat-tail	velocity, fps:	2960	2749	2548	2355	2171
	energy, ft-lb:	2723	2349	2018	1724	1465
	arc, inches:		+1.6	0	-6.9	-20.1
Rem. 140 Nosler Bal. Tip	velocity, fps:	2960	2754	2557	2366	2187
	energy, ft-lb:	2724	2358	2032	1743	1487
	marc, inches:		+1.6	0	-6.9	-20.0
Rem. 140 PSP C-L Ultra	velocity, fps:	2925	2667	2424	2193	1975
	energy, ft-lb:	2659	2211	1826	1495	1212
	arc, inches:		+1.7	0	-7.6	-22.5
Rem. 150 SP Core-Lokt	velocity, fps:	2850	2504	2183	1886	1618
	energy, ft-lb:	2705	2087	1587	1185	872
	arc, inches:		+2.0	0	-9.4	-28.6
Rem. 150 Nosler Partition	velocity, fps:	2850	2652	2463	2282	2108
	energy, ft-lb:	2705	2343	2021	1734	1480
	arc, inches:		+1.7	0	-7.5	-21.6
Speer 130 Grand Slam	velocity, fps:	3050	2774	2514	2269	
	energy, ft-lb:	2685	2221	1824	1485	
	arc, inches:		+1.5	0	-7.0	-20.9
Speer 150 Grand Slam	velocity, fps:	2830	2594	2369	2156	
	energy, ft-lb:	2667	2240	1869	1548	
	arc, inches:		+1.8	0	-8.1	-23.6
Win. 130 Power-Point	velocity, fps:	3060	2802	2559	2329	2110
	energy, ft-lb:	2702	2267	1890	1565	1285
	arc, inches:		+1.8	0	-7.1	-20.6
Win. 130 Power-Point Plus	velocity, fps:	3150	2881	2628	2388	2161
	energy, ft-lb:	2865	2396	1993	1646	1348
	arc, inches:		+1.3	0	-6.4	-18.9
Win. 130 Silvertip	velocity, fps:	3060	2776	2510	2259	2022
	energy, ft-lb:	2702	2225	1818	1472	1180
	arc, inches:		+1.8	0	-7.4	-21.6
Win. 130 Ballistic Silvertip	velocity, fps:	3050	2828	2618	2416	2224
	energy, ft-lb:	2685	2309	1978	1685	1428
	arc, inches:		+1.4	0	-6.5	-18.9
Win. 140 Fail Safe	velocity, fps:	2920	2671	2435	2211	1999
	energy, ft-lb:	2651	2218	1843	1519	1242
	arc, inches:		+1.7	0	-7.6	-22.3
Win. 150 Power-Point	velocity, fps:	2850	2585	2336	2100	1879
	energy, ft-lb:	2705	2226	1817	1468	1175
	arc, inches:		+2.2	0	-8.6	-25.0
Win. 150 Power-Point Plus	velocity, fps:	2950	2679	2425	2184	1957
	energy, ft-lb:	2900	2391	1959	1589	1276
	arc, inches:		+1.7	0	-7.6	-22.6
Win. 150 Partition Gold	velocity, fps:	2930	2693	2468	2254	2051
	energy, ft-lb:	2860	2416	2030	1693	1402
	arc, inches:		+1.7	0	-7.4	-21.6

.270 Winchester Short Magnum

CARTRIDGE BULLET	RANGE, YARDS:	0	100	200	300	400
Win. 130 Bal. Silvertip	velocity, fps:	3275	3041	2820	2609	2408
	energy, ft-lb:	3096	2669	2295	1964	1673
	arc, inches:		+1.1	0	-5.5	-16.1
Win. 140 Fail Safe	velocity, fps:	3125	2865	2619	2386	2165
	energy, ft-lb:	3035	2550	2132	1769	1457
	arc, inches:		+1.4	0	-6.5	-19.0
Win. 150 Power Point	velocity, fps:	3150	2867	2601	2350	2113
	energy, ft-lb:	3304	2737	2252	1839	1487
	arc, inches:		+1.4	0	-6.5	-19.4

.270 Weatherby Magnum

CARTRIDGE BULLET	RANGE, YARDS:	0	100	200	300	400
Federal 130 Nosler Partition	velocity, fps:	3200	2960	2740	2520	2320
	energy, ft-lb:	2955	2530	2160	1835	1550
	arc, inches:		+1.2	0	-5.9	-17.3
Federal 130 Sierra GameKing BTSP	velocity, fps:	3200	2980	2780	2580	2400
	energy, ft-lb:	2955	2570	2230	1925	1655
	arc, inches:		+1.2	0	-5.7	-16.6
Federal 140 Trophy Bonded	velocity, fps:	3100	2840	2600	2370	2150
	energy, ft-lb:	2990	2510	2100	1745	1440
	arc, inches:		+1.4	0	-6.6	-19.3
Wby. 100 Pointed Expanding	velocity, fps:	3760	3396	3061	2751	2462
	energy, ft-lb:	3139	2560	2081	1681	1346
	arc, inches:		+2.3	+3.0	0	-7.6
Wby. 130 Pointed Expanding	velocity, fps:	3375	3123	2885	2659	2444
	energy, ft-lb:	3288	2815	2402	2041	1724
	arc, inches:		+2.8	+3.5	0	-8.4
Wby. 130 Nosler Partition	velocity, fps:	3375	3127	2892	2670	2458
	energy, ft-lb:	3288	2822	2415	2058	1744
	arc, inches:		+2.8	+3.5	0	-8.3
Wby. 140 Nosler Bal. Tip	velocity, fps:	3300	3077	2865	2663	2470
	energy, ft-lb:	3385	2943	2551	2204	1896
	arc, inches:		+2.9	+3.6	0	-8.4
Wby. 140 Barnes X	velocity, fps:	3250	3032	2825	2628	2438
	energy, ft-lb:	3283	2858	2481	2146	1848
	arc, inches:		+3.0	+3.7	0	-8.7
Wby. 150 Pointed Expanding	velocity, fps:	3245	3028	2821	2623	2434
	energy, ft-lb:	3507	3053	2650	2292	1973
	arc, inches:		+3.0	+3.7	0	-8.7
Wby. 150 Nosler Partition	velocity, fps:	3245	3029	2823	2627	2439
	energy, ft-lb:	3507	3055	2655	2298	1981
	arc, inches:		+3.0	+3.7	0	-8.

7-30 Waters

CARTRIDGE BULLET	RANGE, YARDS:	0	100	200	300	400
Federal 120 Sierra GameKing BTSP	velocity, fps:	2700	2300	1930	1600	1330
	energy, ft-lb:	1940	1405	990	685	470
	arc, inches:		+2.6	0	-12.0	-37.6

7mm Mauser (7x57)

CARTRIDGE BULLET	RANGE, YARDS:	0	100	200	300	400
Federal 140 Sierra Pro-Hunt.	velocity, fps:	2660	2450	2260	2070	1890
	energy, ft-lb:	2200	1865	1585	1330	1110
	arc, inches:		+2.1	0	-9.0	-26.1
Federal 140 Nosler Partition	velocity, fps:	2660	2450	2260	2070	1890
	energy, ft-lb:	2200	1865	1585	1330	1110
	arc, inches:		+2.1	0	-9.0	-26.1
Federal 175 Hi-Shok RN	velocity, fps:	2440	2140	1860	1600	1380
	energy, ft-lb:	2315	1775	1340	1000	740
	arc, inches:		+3.1	0	-13.3	-40.1

Centerfire Rifle Ballistics

7mm Mauser (7x57) to 7x65 R

CARTRIDGE BULLET	RANGE, YARDS:	0	100	200	300	400
Hornady 139 SP boat-tail	velocity, fps:	2700	2504	2316	2137	1965
	energy, ft-lb:	2251	1936	1656	1410	1192
	arc, inches:		+2.0	0	-8.5	-24.9
Hornady 139 SP boat-tail LM	velocity, fps:	2830	2620	2450	2250	2070
	energy, ft-lb:	2475	2135	1835	1565	1330
	arc, inches:		+1.8	0	-7.6	-22.1
Hornady 139 SP LM	velocity, fps:	2950	2736	2532	2337	2152
	energy, ft-lb:	2686	2310	1978	1686	1429
	arc, inches:		+2.0	0	-7.6	-21.5
Norma 150 Soft Point	velocity, fps:	2690	2479	2278	2087	
	energy, ft-lb:	2411	2048	1729	1450	
	arc, inches:		+2.0	0	-8.8	
PMC 140 Pointed Soft Point	velocity, fps:	2660	2450	2260	2070	1890
	energy, ft-lb:	2200	1865	1585	1330	1110
	arc, inches:		+2.4	0	-9.6	-27.3
PMC 175 Soft Point	velocity, fps:	2440	2140	1860	1600	1380
	energy, ft-lb:	2315	1775	1340	1000	740
	arc, inches:		+1.5	-3.6	-18.6	-46.8
Rem. 140 PSP Core-Lokt	velocity, fps:	2660	2435	2221	2018	1827
	energy, ft-lb:	2199	1843	1533	1266	1037
	arc, inches:		+2.2	0	-9.2	-27.4
Win. 145 Power-Point	velocity, fps:	2660	2413	2180	1959	1754
	energy, ft-lb:	2279	1875	1530	1236	990
	arc, inches:		+1.1	-2.8	-14.1	-34.4

7x57 R

Norma 150 FMJ	velocity, fps:	2690	2489	2296	2112	
	energy, ft-lb:	2411	2063	1756	1486	
	arc, inches:		+2.0	0	-8.6	
Norma 154 Soft Point	velocity, fps:	2625	2417	2219	2030	
	energy, ft-lb:	2357	1999	1684	1410	
	arc, inches:		+2.2	0	-9.3	

7mm-08 Remington

Federal 140 Nosler Partition	velocity, fps:	2800	2590	2390	2200	2020
	energy, ft-lb:	2435	2085	1775	1500	1265
	arc, inches:		+1.8	0	-8.0	-23.1
Federal 140 Nosler Bal. Tip	velocity, fps:	2800	2610	2430	2260	2100
	energy, ft-lb:	2440	2135	1840	1590	1360
	arc, inches:		+1.8	0	-7.7	-22.3
Federal 140 Tr. Bonded HE	velocity, fps:	2950	2660	2390	2140	1900
	energy, ft-lb:	2705	2205	1780	1420	1120
	arc, inches:		+1.7	0	-7.9	-23.2
Federal 150 Sierra Pro-Hunt.	velocity, fps:	2650	2440	2230	2040	1860
	energy, ft-lb:	2340	1980	1660	1390	1150
	arc, inches:		+2.2	0	-9.2	-26.7
Hornady 139 SP boat-tail LM	velocity, fps:	3000	2790	2590	2399	2216
	energy, ft-lb:	2777	2403	2071	1776	1515
	arc, inches:		+1.5	0	-6.7	-19.4
PMC 140 PSP	velocity, fps:					
	energy, ft-lb:					
	arc, inches:					
Rem. 120 Hollow Point	velocity, fps:	3000	2725	2467	2223	1992
	energy, ft-lb:	2398	1979	1621	1316	1058
	arc, inches:		+1.6	0	-7.3	-21.7
Rem. 140 PSP Core-Lokt	velocity, fps:	2860	2625	2402	2189	1988
	energy, ft-lb:	2542	2142	1793	1490	1228
	arc, inches:		+1.8	0	-7.8	-22.9
Rem. 140 PSP boat-tail	velocity, fps:	2860	2656	2460	2273	2094
	energy, ft-lb:	2542	2192	1881	1606	1363
	arc, inches:		+1.7	0	-7.5	-21.7
Rem. 140 Nosler Bal. Tip	velocity, fps:	2860	2670	2488	2313	2145
	energy, ft-lb:	2543	2217	1925	1663	1431
	arc, inches:		+1.7	0	-7.3	-21.2
Rem. 140 Nosler Partition	velocity, fps:	2860	2648	2446	2253	2068
	energy, ft-lb:	2542	2180	1860	1577	1330
	arc, inches:		+1.7	0	-7.6	-22.0
Speer 145 Grand Slam	velocity, fps:	2845	2567	2305	2059	
	energy, ft-lb:	2606	2121	1711	1365	
	arc, inches:		+1.9	0	-8.4	-25.5
Win. 140 Power-Point	velocity, fps:	2800	2523	2268	2027	1802
	energy, ft-lb:	2429	1980	1599	1277	1010
	arc, inches:		+2.0	0	-8.8	-26.0
Win. 140 Power-Point Plus	velocity, fps:	2875	2597	2336	2090	1859
	energy, ft-lb:	2570	1997	1697	1358	1075
	arc, inches:		+2.0	0	-8.8	26.0
Win. 140 Fail Safe	velocity, fps:	2760	2506	2271	2048	1839
	energy, ft-lb:	2360	1953	1603	1304	1051
	arc, inches:		+2.0	0	-8.8	-25.9
Win. 140 Ballistic Silvertip	velocity, fps:	2770	2572	2382	2200	2026
	energy, ft-lb:	2386	2056	1764	1504	1276
	arc, inches:		+1.9	0	-8.0	-23.8

7x64 Brenneke

Federal 160 Nosler Partition	velocity, fps:	2650	2480	2310	2150	2000
	energy, ft-lb:	2495	2180	1895	1640	1415
	arc, inches:		+2.1	0	-8.7	-24.9
Norma 154 Soft Point	velocity, fps:	2821	2605	2399	2203	
	energy, ft-lb:	2722	2321	1969	1660	
	arc, inches:		+1.8	0	-7.8	
Norma 170 Vulkan	velocity, fps:	2756	2501	2259	2031	
	energy, ft-lb:	2868	2361	1927	1558	
	arc, inches:		+2.0	0	-8.8	
Norma 170 Oryx	velocity, fps:	2756	2481	2222	1979	
	energy, ft-lb:	2868	2324	1864	1478	
	arc, inches:		+2.1	0	-9.2	
Norma 170 Plastic Point	velocity, fps:	2756	2519	2294	2081	
	energy, ft-lb:	2868	2396	1987	1635	
	arc, inches:		+2.0	0	-8.6	
Rem. 175 PSP Core-Lokt	velocity, fps:	2650	2445	2248	2061	1883
	energy, ft-lb:	2728	2322	1964	1650	1378
	arc, inches:		+2.2	0	-9.1	-26.4
Speer 160 Grand Slam	velocity, fps:	2600	2376	2164	1962	
	energy, ft-lb:	2401	2006	1663	1368	
	arc, inches:		+2.3	0	-9.8	-28.6
Speer 175 Grand Slam	velocity, fps:	2650	2461	2280	2106	
	energy, ft-lb:	2728	2353	2019	1723	
	arc, inches:		+2.4	0	-9.2	-26.2

7x65 R

Norma 170 Plastic Point	velocity, fps:	2625	2390	2167	1956	
	energy, ft-lb:	2602	2157	1773	1445	
	arc, inches:		+2.3	0	-9.7	
Norma 170 Vulkan	velocity, fps:	2657	2392	2143	1909	
	energy, ft-lb:	2666	2161	1734	1377	
	arc, inches:		+2.3	0	-9.9	
Norma 170 Oryx	velocity, fps:	2657	2378	2115	1871	
	energy, ft-lb:	2666	2135	1690	1321	
	arc, inches:		+2.3	0	-10.1	

Centerfire Rifle Ballistics
.284 Winchester to 7mm Remington Magnum

CARTRIDGE BULLET	RANGE, YARDS:	0	100	200	300	400
.284 Winchester						
Win. 150 Power-Point	velocity, fps:	2860	2595	2344	2108	1886
	energy, ft-lb:	2724	2243	1830	1480	1185
	arc, inches:		+2.1	0	-8.5	-24.8
.280 Remington						
Federal 140 Sierra Pro-Hunt.	velocity, fps:	2990	2740	2500	2270	2060
	energy, ft-lb:	2770	2325	1940	1605	1320
	arc, inches:		+1.6	0	-7.0	-20.8
Federal 140 Trophy Bonded	velocity, fps:	2990	2630	2310	2040	1730
	energy, ft-lb:	2770	2155	1655	1250	925
	arc, inches:		+1.6	0	-8.4	-25.4
Federal 140 Tr. Bonded HE	velocity, fps:	3150	2850	2570	2300	2050
	energy, ft-lb:	3085	2520	2050	1650	1310
	arc, inches:		+1.4	0	-6.7	-20.0
Federal 150 Hi-Shok	velocity, fps:	2890	2670	2460	2260	2060
	energy, ft-lb:	2780	2370	2015	1695	1420
	arc, inches:		+1.7	0	-7.5	-21.8
Federal 150 Nosler Partition	velocity, fps:	2890	2690	2490	2310	2130
	energy, ft-lb:	2780	2405	2070	1770	1510
	arc, inches:		+1.7	0	-7.2	-21.1
Federal 160 Trophy Bonded	velocity, fps:	2800	2570	2350	2140	1940
	energy, ft-lb:	2785	2345	1960	1625	1340
	arc, inches:		+1.9	0	-8.3	-24.0
Hornady 139 SPBT LMmoly	velocity, fps:	3110	2888	2675	2473	2280
	energy, ft-lb:	2985	2573	2209	1887	1604
	arc, inches:		+1.4	0	-6.5	-18.6
Norma 170 Vulkan	velocity, fps:	2592	2346	2113	1894	
	energy, ft-lb:	2537	2078	1686	1354	
	arc, inches:		+2.4	0	-10.2	
Norma 170 Oryx	velocity, fps:	2690	2416	2159	1918	
	energy, ft-lb:	2732	2204	1760	1389	
	arc, inches:		+2.2	0	-9.7	
Norma 170 Plastic Point	velocity, fps:	2707	2468	2241	2026	
	energy, ft-lb:	2767	2299	1896	1550	
	arc, inches:		+2.1	0	-9.1	
Rem. 140 PSP Core-Lokt	velocity, fps:	3000	2758	2528	2309	2102
	energy, ft-lb:	2797	2363	1986	1657	1373
	arc, inches:		+1.5	0	-7.0	-20.5
Rem. 140 PSP boat-tail	velocity, fps:	2860	2656	2460	2273	2094
	energy, ft-lb:	2542	2192	1881	1606	1363
	arc, inches:		+1.7	0	-7.5	-21.7
Rem. 140 Nosler Bal. Tip	velocity, fps:	3000	2804	2616	2436	2263
	energy, ft-lb:	2799	2445	2128	1848	1593
	arc, inches:		+1.5	0	-6.8	-19.0
Rem. 150 PSP Core-Lokt	velocity, fps:	2890	2624	2373	2135	1912
	energy, ft-lb:	2781	2293	1875	1518	1217
	arc, inches:		+1.8	0	-8.0	-23.6
Rem. 165 SP Core-Lokt	velocity, fps:	2820	2510	2220	1950	1701
	energy, ft-lb:	2913	2308	1805	1393	1060
	arc, inches:		+2.0	0	-9.1	-27.4
Speer 145 Grand Slam	velocity, fps:	2900	2619	2354	2105	
	energy, ft-lb:	2707	2207	1784	1426	
	arc, inches:		+2.1	0	-8.4	-24.7
Speer 160 Grand Slam	velocity, fps:	2890	2652	2425	2210	
	energy, ft-lb:	2967	2497	2089	1735	
	arc, inches:		+1.7	0	-7.7	-22.4
Win. 140 Fail Safe	velocity, fps:	3050	2756	2480	2221	1977
	energy, ft-lb:	2893	2362	1913	1533	1216
	arc, inches:		+1.5	0	-7.2	-21.5
Win. 140 Ballistic Silvertip	velocity, fps:	3040	2842	2653	2471	2297
	energy, ft-lb:	2872	2511	2187	1898	1640
	arc, inches:		+1.4	0	-6.3	-18.4
7mm Remington Magnum						
A-Square 175 Monolithic Solid	velocity, fps:	2860	2557	2273	2008	1771
	energy, ft-lb:	3178	2540	2008	1567	1219
	arc, inches:		+1.92	0	-8.7	-25.9
Federal 140 Nosler Partition	velocity, fps:	3150	2930	2710	2510	2320
	energy, ft-lb:	3085	2660	2290	1960	1670
	arc, inches:		+1.3	0	-6.0	-17.5
Federal 140 Trophy Bonded	velocity, fps:	3150	2910	2680	2460	2250
	energy, ft-lb:	3085	2630	2230	1880	1575
	arc, inches:		+1.3	0	-6.1	-18.1
Federal 150 Hi-Shok	velocity, fps:	3110	2830	2570	2320	2090
	energy, ft-lb:	3220	2670	2200	1790	1450
	arc, inches:		+1.4	0	-6.7	-19.9
Federal 150 Sierra GameKing BTSP	velocity, fps:	3110	2920	2750	2580	2410
	energy, ft-lb:	3220	2850	2510	2210	1930
	arc, inches:		+1.3	0	-5.9	-17.0
Federal 150 Nosler Bal. Tip	velocity, fps:	3110	2910	2720	2540	2370
	energy, ft-lb:	3220	2825	2470	2150	1865
	arc, inches:		+1.3	0	-6.0	-17.4
Federal 160 Barnes XLC	velocity, fps:	2940	2760	2580	2410	2240
	energy, ft-lb:	3070	2695	2360	2060	1785
	arc, inches:		+1.5	0	-6.8	-19.6
Federal 160 Sierra Pro-Hunt.	velocity, fps:	2940	2730	2520	2320	2140
	energy, ft-lb:	3070	2640	2260	1920	1620
	arc, inches:		+1.6	0	-7.1	-20.6
Federal 160 Nosler Partition	velocity, fps:	2950	2770	2590	2420	2250
	energy, ft-lb:	3090	2715	2375	2075	1800
	arc, inches:		+1.5	0	-6.7	-19.4
Federal 160 Trophy Bonded	velocity, fps:	2940	2660	2390	2140	1900
	energy, ft-lb:	3070	2505	2025	1620	1280
	arc, inches:		+1.7	0	-7.9	-23.3
Federal 165 Sierra GameKing BTSP	velocity, fps:	2950	2800	2650	2510	2370
	energy, ft-lb:	3190	2865	2570	2300	2050
	arc, inches:		+1.5	0	-6.4	-18.4
Federal 175 Hi-Shok	velocity, fps:	2860	2650	2440	2240	2060
	energy, ft-lb:	3180	2720	2310	1960	1640
	arc, inches:		+1.7	0	-7.6	-22.1
Federal 175 Trophy Bonded	velocity, fps:	2860	2600	2350	2120	1900
	energy, ft-lb:	3180	2625	2150	1745	1400
	arc, inches:		+1.8	0	-8.2	-24.0
Hornady 139 SPBT	velocity, fps:	3150	2933	2727	2530	2341
	energy, ft-lb:	3063	2656	2296	1976	1692
	arc, inches:		+1.2	0	-6.1	-17.7
Hornady 139 SPBT HMmoly	velocity, fps:	3250	3041	2822	2613	2413
	energy, ft-lb:	3300	2854	2458	2106	1797
	arc, inches:		+1.1	0	-5.7	-16.6
Hornady 154 Soft Point	velocity, fps:	3035	2814	2604	2404	2212
	energy, ft-lb:	3151	2708	2319	1977	1674
	arc, inches:		+1.3	0	-6.7	-19.3
Hornady 154 SST	velocity, fps:	3035	2850	2672	2501	2337
	energy, ft-lb:	3149	2777	2441	2139	1867
	arc, inches:		+1.4	0	-6.5	-18.7
Hornady 162 SP boat-tail	velocity, fps:	2940	2757	2582	2413	2251
	energy, ft-lb:	3110	2735	2399	2095	1823
	arc, inches:		+1.6	0	-6.7	-19.7

Centerfire Rifle Ballistics

7mm Remington Magnum to 7mm Weatherby Magnum

CARTRIDGE BULLET	RANGE, YARDS:	0	100	200	300	400
Hornady 175 SP	velocity, fps:	2860	2650	2440	2240	2060
	energy, ft-lb:	3180	2720	2310	1960	1640
	arc, inches:		+2.0	0	-7.9	-22.7
Norma 140 Nosler Bal. Tip	velocity, fps:	3150	2936	2732	2537	
	energy, ft-lb:	3085	2680	2320	2001	
	arc, inches:		+1.2	0	-5.9	
Norma 150 Scirocco	velocity, fps:	3117	2934	2758	2589	
	energy, ft-lb:	3237	2869	2535	2234	
	arc, inches:		+1.2	0	-5.8	
Norma 170 Vulkan	velocity, fps:	3018	2747	2493	2252	
	energy, ft-lb:	3439	2850	2346	1914	
	arc, inches:		+1.5	0	-2.8	
Norma 170 Oryx	velocity, fps:	2887	2601	2333	2080	
	energy, ft-lb:	3147	2555	2055	1634	
	arc, inches:		+1.8	0	-8.2	
Norma 170 Plastic Point	velocity, fps:	3018	2762	2519	2290	
	energy, ft-lb:	3439	2880	2394	1980	
	arc, inches:		+1.5	0	-7.0	
PMC 140 Barnes X	velocity, fps:	3000	2808	2624	2448	2279
	energy, ft-lb:	2797	2451	2141	1863	1614
	arc, inches:		+1.5	0	-6.6	18.9
PMC 140 Pointed Soft Point	velocity, fps:	3099	2878	2668	2469	2279
	energy, ft-lb:	2984	2574	2212	1895	1614
	arc, inches:		+1.4	0	-6.2	-18.1
PMC 140 SP boat-tail	velocity, fps:	3125	2891	2669	2457	2255
	energy, ft-lb:	3035	2597	2213	1877	1580
	arc, inches:		+1.4	0	-6.3	-18.4
PMC 160 Barnes X	velocity, fps:	2800	2639	2484	2334	2189
	energy, ft-lb:	2785	2474	2192	1935	1703
	arc, inches:		+1.8	0	-7.4	-21.2
PMC 160 Pointed Soft Point	velocity, fps:	2914	2748	2586	2428	2276
	energy, ft-lb:	3016	2682	2375	2095	1840
	arc, inches:		+1.6	0	-6.7	-19.4
PMC 160 SP boat-tail	velocity, fps:	2900	2696	2501	2314	2135
	energy, ft-lb:	2987	2582	2222	1903	1620
	arc, inches:		+1.7	0	-7.2	-21.0
PMC 175 Pointed Soft Point	velocity, fps:	2860	2645	2442	2244	2957
	energy, ft-lb:	3178	2718	2313	1956	1644
	arc, inches:		+2.0	0	-7.9	-22.7
Rem. 140 PSP Core-Lokt	velocity, fps:	3175	2923	2684	2458	2243
	energy, ft-lb:	3133	2655	2240	1878	1564
	arc, inches:		+2.2	+1.9	-3.2	-14.2
Rem. 140 PSP boat-tail	velocity, fps:	3175	2956	2747	2547	2356
	energy, ft-lb:	3133	2715	2345	2017	1726
	arc, inches:		+2.2	+1.6	-3.1	-13.4
Rem. 150 PSP Core-Lokt	velocity, fps:	3110	2830	2568	2320	2085
	energy, ft-lb:	3221	2667	2196	1792	1448
	arc, inches:		+1.3	0	-6.6	-20.2
Rem. 150 Nosler Bal. Tip	velocity, fps:	3110	2912	2723	2542	2367
	energy, ft-lb:	3222	2825	2470	2152	1867
	arc, inches:		+1.2	0	-5.9	-17.3
Rem. 150 Swift Scirocco	velocity, fps:	3110	2927	2751	2582	2419
	energy, ft-lb:	3221	2852	2520	2220	1948
	arc, inches:		+1.3	0	-5.9	-17.0
Rem. 160 Swift A-Frame	velocity, fps:	2900	2659	2430	2212	2006
	energy, ft-lb:	2987	2511	2097	1739	1430
	arc, inches:		+1.7	0	-7.6	-22.4
Rem. 160 Nosler Partition	velocity, fps:	2950	2752	2563	2381	2207
	energy, ft-lb:	3091	2690	2333	2014	1730
	arc, inches:		+0.6	-1.9	-9.6	-23.6
Rem. 175 PSP Core-Lokt	velocity, fps:	2860	2645	2440	2244	2057
	energy, ft-lb:	3178	2718	2313	1956	1644
	arc, inches:		+1.7	0	-7.6	-22.1
Speer 145 Grand Slam	velocity, fps:	3140	2843	2565	2304	
	energy, ft-lb:	3174	2602	2118	1708	
	arc, inches:		+1.4	0	-6.7	
Speer 175 Grand Slam	velocity, fps:	2850	2653	2463	2282	
	energy, ft-lb:	3156	2734	2358	2023	
	arc, inches:		+1.7	0	-7.5	-21.7
Win. 140 Fail Safe	velocity, fps:	3150	2861	2589	2333	2092
	energy, ft-lb:	3085	2544	2085	1693	1361
	arc, inches:		+1.4	0	-6.6	-19.5
Win. 140 Ballistic Silvertip	velocity, fps:	3100	2889	2687	2494	2310
	energy, ft-lb:	2988	2595	2245	1934	1659
	arc, inches:		+1.3	0	-6.2	-17.9
Win. 150 Power-Point	velocity, fps:	3090	2812	2551	2304	2071
	energy, ft-lb:	3181	2634	2167	1768	1429
	arc, inches:		+1.5	0	-6.8	-20.2
Win. 150 Power-Point Plus	velocity, fps:	3130	2849	2586	2337	2102
	energy, ft-lb:	3264	2705	2227	1819	1472
	arc, inches:		+1.4	0	-6.6	-19.6
Win. 150 Ballistic Silvertip	velocity, fps:	3100	2903	2714	2533	2359
	energy, ft-lb:	3200	2806	2453	2136	1853
	arc, inches:		+1.3	0	-6.0	-17.5
Win. 160 Partition Gold	velocity, fps:	2950	2743	2546	2357	2176
	energy, ft-lb:	3093	2674	2303	1974	1682
	arc, inches:		+1.6	0	-6.9	-20.1
Win. 160 Fail Safe	velocity, fps:	2920	2678	2449	2331	2025
	energy, ft-lb:	3030	2549	2131	1769	1457
	arc, inches:		+1.7	0	-7.5	-22.0
Win. 175 Power-Point	velocity, fps:	2860	2645	2440	2244	2057
	energy, ft-lb:	3178	2718	2313	1956	1644
	arc, inches:		+2.0	0	-7.9	-22.7

7mm Remington Short Ultra Mag

Rem. 140 PSP C-L Ultra	velocity, fps:	3175	2934	2707	2490	2283
	energy, ft-lb:	3133	2676	2277	1927	1620
	arc, inches:		+1.3	0	-6.0	-17.7
Rem. 150 PSP Core-Lokt	velocity, fps:	3110	2828	2563	2313	2077
	energy, ft-lb:	3221	2663	2188	1782	1437
	arc, inches:		+2.5	+2.1	-3.6	-15.8
Rem. 160 Partition	velocity, fps:	2960	2762	2572	2390	2215
	energy, ft-lb:	3112	2709	2350	2029	1744
	arc, inches:		+2.6	+2.2	-3.6	-15.4

7mm Winchester Short Magnum

Win. 140 Bal. Silvertip	velocity, fps:	3225	3008	2801	2603	2414
	energy, ft-lb:	3233	2812	2438	2106	1812
	arc, inches:		+1.2	0	-5.6	-16.4
Win. 150 Power Point	velocity, fps:	3200	2915	2648	2396	2157
	energy, ft-lb:	3410	2830	2335	1911	1550
	arc, inches:		+1.3	0	-6.3	-18.6
Win. 160 Fail Safe	velocity, fps:	2990	2744	2512	2291	2081
	energy, ft-lb:	3176	2675	2241	1864	1538
	arc, inches:		+1.6	0	-7.1	-20.8

7mm Weatherby Mag.

Federal 160 Nosler Partition	velocity, fps:	3050	2850	2650	2470	2290
	energy, ft-lb:	3305	2880	2505	2165	1865
	arc, inches:		+1.4	0	-6.3	-18.4

Centerfire Rifle Ballistics

7mm Weatherby Magnum to 7.62x39 Russian

CARTRIDGE BULLET	RANGE, YARDS:	0	100	200	300	400
Federal 160 Sierra GameKing BTSP	velocity, fps:	3050	2880	2710	2560	2400
	energy, ft-lb:	3305	2945	2615	2320	2050
	arc, inches:		+1.4	0	-6.1	-17.4
Federal 160 Trophy Bonded	velocity, fps:	3050	2730	2420	2140	1880
	energy, ft-lb:	3305	2640	2085	1630	1255
	arc, inches:		+1.6	0	-7.6	-22.7
Hornady 154 Soft Point	velocity, fps:	3200	2971	2753	2546	2348
	energy, ft-lb:	3501	3017	2592	2216	1885
	arc, inches:		+1.2	0	-5.8	-17.0
Hornady 154 SST	velocity, fps:	3200	3009	2825	2648	2478
	energy, ft-lb:	3501	3096	2729	2398	2100
	arc, inches:		+1.2	0	-5.7	-16.5
Hornady 175 Soft Point	velocity, fps:	2910	2709	2516	2331	2154
	energy, ft-lb:	3290	2850	2459	2111	1803
	arc, inches:		+1.6	0	-7.1	-20.6
Wby. 139 Pointed Expanding	velocity, fps:	3340	3079	2834	2601	2380
	energy, ft-lb:	3443	2926	2478	2088	1748
	arc, inches:		+2.9	+3.6	0	-8.7
Wby. 140 Nosler Partition	velocity, fps:	3303	3069	2847	2636	2434
	energy, ft-lb:	3391	2927	2519	2159	1841
	arc, inches:		+2.9	+3.6	0	-8.5
Wby. 150 Nosler Bal. Tip	velocity, fps:	3300	3093	2896	2708	2527
	energy, ft-lb:	3627	3187	2793	2442	2127
	arc, inches:		+2.8	+3.5	0	-8.2
Wby. 150 Barnes X	veloctiy, fps:	3100	2901	2710	2527	2352
	energy, ft-lb:	3200	2802	2446	2127	1842
	arc, inches:		+3.3	+4.0	0	-9.4
Wby. 154 Pointed Expanding	velocity, fps:	3260	3028	2807	2597	2397
	energy, ft-lb:	3634	3134	2694	2307	1964
	arc, inches:		+3.0	+3.7	0	-8.8
Wby. 160 Nosler Partition	velocity, fps:	3200	2991	2791	2600	2417
	energy, ft-lb:	3638	3177	2767	2401	2075
	arc, inches:		+3.1	+3.8	0	-8.9
Wby. 175 Pointed Expanding	velocity, fps:	3070	2861	2662	2471	2288
	energy, ft-lb:	3662	3181	2753	2373	2034
	arc, inches:		+3.5	+4.2	0	-9.9

7mm Dakota

CARTRIDGE BULLET	RANGE, YARDS:	0	100	200	300	400
Dakota 140 Barnes X	velocity, fps:	3500	3253	3019	2798	2587
	energy, ft-lb:	3807	3288	2833	2433	2081
	arc, inches:		+2.0	+2.1	-1.5	-9.6
Dakota 160 Barnes X	velocity, fps:	3200	3001	2811	2630	2455
	energy, ft-lb:	3637	3200	2808	2456	2140
	arc, inches:		+2.1	+1.9	-2.8	-12.5

7mm STW

CARTRIDGE BULLET	RANGE, YARDS:	0	100	200	300	400
A-Square 140 Nos. Bal. Tip	velocity, fps:	3450	3254	3067	2888	2715
	energy, ft-lb:	3700	3291	2924	2592	2292
	arc, inches:		+2.2	+3.0	0	-7.3
A-Square 160 Nosler Part.	velocity, fps:	3250	3071	2900	2735	2576
	energy, ft-lb:	3752	3351	2987	2657	2357
	arc, inches:		+2.8	+3.5	0	-8.2
A-Square 160 SP boat-tail	velocity, fps:	3250	3087	2930	2778	2631
	energy, ft-lb:	3752	3385	3049	2741	2460
	arc, inches:		+2.8	+3.4	0	-8.0
Federal 140 Trophy Bonded	velocity, fps:	3330	3080	2850	2630	2420
	energy, ft-lb:	3435	2950	2520	2145	1815
	arc, inches:		+1.1	0	-5.4	-15.8
Federal 150 Trophy Bonded	velocity, fps:	3250	3010	2770	2560	2350
	energy, ft-lb:	3520	3010	2565	2175	1830
	arc, inches:		+1.2	0	-5.7	-16.7
Federal 160 Sierra GameKing BTSP	velocity, fps:	3200	3020	2850	2670	2530
	energy, ft-lb:	3640	3245	2890	2570	2275
	arc, inches:		+1.1	0	-5.5	-15.7
Rem. 140 PSP Core-Lokt	velocity, fps:	3325	3064	2818	2585	2364
	energy, ft-lb:	3436	2918	2468	2077	1737
	arc, inches:		+2.0	+1.7	-2.9	-12.8
Rem. 140 Swift A-Frame	velocity, fps:	3325	3020	2735	2467	2215
	energy, ft-lb:	3436	2834	2324	1892	1525
	arc, inches:		+2.1	+1.8	-3.1	-13.8
Speer 145 Grand Slam	velocity, fps:	3300	2992	2075	2435	
	energy, ft-lb:	3506	2882	2355	1909	
	arc, inches:		+1.2	0	-6.0	-17.8
Win. 140 Ballistic Silvertip	velocity, fps:	3320	3100	2890	2690	2499
	energy, ft-lb:	3427	2982	2597	2250	1941
	arc, inches:		+1.1	0	-5.2	-15.2
Win. 150 Power-Point	velocity, fps:	3250	2957	2683	2424	2181
	energy, ft-lb:	3519	2913	2398	1958	1584
	arc, inches:		+1.2	0	-6.1	-18.1
Win. 160 Fail Safe	velocity, fps:	3150	2894	2652	2422	2204
	energy, ft-lb:	3526	2976	2499	2085	1727
	arc, inches:		+1.3	0	-6.3	-18.5

7mm Remington Ultra Mag

CARTRIDGE BULLET	RANGE, YARDS:	0	100	200	300	400
Rem. 140 PSP Core-Lokt	velocity, fps:	3425	3158	2907	2669	2444
	energy, ft-lb:	3646	3099	2626	2214	1856
	arc, inches:		+1.8	+1.6	-2.7	-11.9
Rem. 140 Nosler Partition	velocity, fps:	3425	3184	2956	2740	2534
	energy, ft-lb:	3646	3151	2715	2333	1995
	arc, inches:		+1.7	+1.6	-2.6	-11.4
Rem. 160 Nosler Partition	velocity, fps:	3200	2991	2791	2600	2417
	energy, ft-lb:	3637	3177	2767	2401	2075
	arc, inches:		+2.1	+1.8	-3.0	-12.9

7.21 (.284) Firehawk

CARTRIDGE BULLET	RANGE, YARDS:	0	100	200	300	400
Lazzeroni 140 Nosler Part.	velocity, fps:	3580	3349	3130	2923	2724
	energy, ft-lb:	3985	3488	3048	2656	2308
	arc, inches:		+2.2	+2.9	0	-7.0
Lazzeroni 160 Swift A-Fr.	velocity, fps:	3385	3167	2961	2763	2574
	energy, ft-lb:	4072	3565	3115	2713	2354
	arc, inches:		+2.6	+3.3	0	-7.8

7.5x55 Swiss

CARTRIDGE BULLET	RANGE, YARDS:	0	100	200	300	400
Norma 180 Soft Point	velocity, fps:	2651	2432	2223	2025	
	energy, ft-lb:	2810	2364	1976	1639	
	arc, inches:		+2.2	0	-9.3	

7.62x39 Russian

CARTRIDGE BULLET	RANGE, YARDS:	0	100	200	300	400
Federal 123 Hi-Shok	velocity, fps:	2300	2030	1780	1550	1350
	energy, ft-lb:	1445	1125	860	655	500
	arc, inches:		0	-7.0	-25.1	
Federal 124 FMJ	velocity, fps:	2300	2030	1780	1560	1360
	energy, ft-lb:	1455	1135	875	670	510
	arc, inches:		+3.5	0	-14.6	-43.5
Norma 150 Soft Point	velocity, fps:	2953	2622	2314	2028	
	energy, ft-lb:	2905	2291	1784	1370	
	arc, inches:		+1.8	0	-8.3	
Norma 180 Soft Point	velocity, fps:	2575	2360	2154	1960	
	energy, ft-lb:	2651	2226	1856	1536	
	arc, inches:		+2.4	0	-9.9	
PMC 123 FMJ	velocity, fps:	2350	2072	1817	1583	1368
	energy, ft-lb:	1495	1162	894	678	507
	arc, inches:		0	-5.0	-26.4	-67.8

Rifles • 479

Centerfire Rifle Ballistics

7.62x39 Russian to .301 Winchester

CARTRIDGE BULLET	RANGE, YARDS:	0	100	200	300	400
PMC 125 Pointed Soft Point	velocity, fps:	2320	2046	1794	1563	1350
	energy, ft-lb:	1493	1161	893	678	505
	arc, inches:		0	-5.2	-27.5	-70.6
Rem. 125 Pointed Soft Point	velocity, fps:	2365	2062	1783	1533	1320
	energy, ft-lb:	1552	1180	882	652	483
	arc, inches:		0	-6.7	-24.5	
Win. 123 Soft Point	velocity, fps:	2365	2033	1731	1465	1248
	energy, ft-lb:	1527	1129	818	586	425
	arc, inches:		+3.8	0	-15.4	-46.3

.30 Carbine

Federal 110 Hi-Shok RN	velocity, fps:	1990	1570	1240	1040	920
	energy, ft-lb:	965	600	375	260	210
	arc, inches:		0	-12.8	-46.9	
Federal 110 FMJ	velocity, fps:	1990	1570	1240	1040	920
	energy, ft-lb:	965	600	375	260	210
	arc, inches:		0	-12.8	-46.9	
Magtech 110 FMC	velocity, fps:	1990	1654			
	energy, ft-lb:	965	668			
	arc, inches:		0			
PMC 110 FMJ	velocity, fps:	1927	1548	1248		
	energy, ft-lb:	906	585	380		
	arc, inches:		0	-14.2		
Rem. 110 Soft Point	velocity, fps:	1990	1567	1236	1035	923
	energy, ft-lb:	967	600	373	262	208
	arc, inches:		0	-12.9	-48.6	
Win. 110 Hollow Soft Point	velocity, fps:	1990	1567	1236	1035	923
	energy, ft-lb:	967	600	373	262	208
	arc, inches:		0	-13.5	-49.9	

.30-30 Winchester

Federal 125 Hi-Shok HP	velocity, fps:	2570	2090	1660	1320	1080
	energy, ft-lb:	1830	1210	770	480	320
	arc, inches:		+3.3	0	-16.0	-50.9
Federal 150 Hi-Shok FN	velocity, fps:	2390	2020	1680	1400	1180
	energy, ft-lb:	1900	1355	945	650	460
	arc, inches:		+3.6	0	-15.9	-49.1
Federal 170 Hi-Shok RN	velocity, fps:	2200	1900	1620	1380	1190
	energy, ft-lb:	1830	1355	990	720	535
	arc, inches:		+4.1	0	-17.4	-52.4
Federal 170 Sierra Pro-Hunt.	velocity, fps:	2200	1820	1500	1240	1060
	energy, ft-lb:	1830	1255	845	575	425
	arc, inches:		+4.5	0	-20.0	-63.5
Federal 170 Nosler Partition	velocity, fps:	2200	1900	1620	1380	1190
	energy, ft-lb:	1830	1355	990	720	535
	arc, inches:		+4.1	0	-17.4	-52.4
Hornady 150 Round Nose	velocity, fps:	2390	1973	1605	1303	1095
	energy, ft-lb:	1902	1296	858	565	399
	arc, inches:		0	-8.2	-30.0	
Hornady 170 Flat Point	velocity, fps:	2200	1895	1619	1381	1191
	energy, ft-lb:	1827	1355	989	720	535
	arc, inches:		0	-8.9	-31.1	
Norma 150 Soft Point	velocity, fps:	2329	2008	1716	1459	
	energy, ft-lb:	1807	1344	981	709	
	arc, inches:		+3.6	0	-15.5	
PMC 150 Starfire HP	velocity, fps:	2100	1769	1478		
	energy, ft-lb:	1469	1042	728		
	arc, inches:		0	-10.8		
PMC 150 Flat Nose	velocity, fps:	2159	1819	1554		
	energy, ft-lb:	1552	1102	804		
	arc, inches:		0	-9.0		
PMC 170 Flat Nose	velocity, fps:	1965	1680	1480		
	energy, ft-lb:	1457	1065	827		
	arc, inches:		0	-10.7		
Rem. 55 PSP (sabot) "Accelerator"	velocity, fps:	3400	2693	2085	1570	1187
	energy, ft-lb:	1412	886	521	301	172
	arc, inches:		+1.7	0	-9.9	-34.3
Rem. 150 SP Core-Lokt	velocity, fps:	2390	1973	1605	1303	1095
	energy, ft-lb:	1902	1296	858	565	399
	arc, inches:		0	-7.6	-28.8	
Rem. 170 SP Core-Lokt	velocity, fps:	2200	1895	1619	1381	1191
	energy, ft-lb:	1827	1355	989	720	535
	arc, inches:		0	-8.3	-29.9	
Rem. 170 HP Core-Lokt	velocity, fps:	2200	1895	1619	1381	1191
	energy, ft-lb:	1827	1355	989	720	535
	arc, inches:		0	-8.3	-29.9	
Speer 150 Flat Nose	velocity, fps:	2370	2067	1788	1538	
	energy, ft-lb:	1870	1423	1065	788	
	arc, inches:		+3.3	0	-14.4	-43.7
Win. 150 Hollow Point	velocity, fps:	2390	2018	1684	1398	1177
	energy, ft-lb:	1902	1356	944	651	461
	arc, inches:		0	-7.7	-27.9	
Win. 150 Power-Point	velocity, fps:	2390	2018	1684	1398	1177
	energy, ft-lb:	1902	1356	944	651	461
	arc, inches:		0	-7.7	-27.9	
Win. 150 Silvertip	velocity,fps:	2390	2018	1684	1398	1177
	energy, ft-lb:	1902	1356	944	651	461
	arc, inches:		0	-7.7	-27.9	
Win. 150 Power-Point Plus	velocity, fps:	2480	2095	1747	1446	1209
	energy, ft-lb:	2049	1462	1017	697	487
	arc, inches:		0	-6.5	-24.5	
Win. 170 Power-Point	velocity, fps:	2200	1895	1619	1381	1191
	energy, ft-lb:	1827	1355	989	720	535
	arc, inches:		0	-8.9	-31.1	
Win. 170 Silvertip	velocity, fps:	2200	1895	1619	1381	1191
	energy, ft-lb:	1827	1355	989	720	535
	arc, inches:		0	-8.9	-31.1	

.300 Savage

Federal 150 Hi-Shok	velocity, fps:	2630	2350	2100	1850	1630
	energy, ft-lb:	2305	1845	1460	1145	885
	arc, inches:		+2.4	0	-10.4	-30.9
Federal 180 Hi-Shok	velocity, fps:	2350	2140	1940	1750	1570
	energy, ft-lb:	2205	1825	1495	1215	985
	arc, inches:		+3.1	0	-12.4	-36.1
Rem. 150 PSP Core-Lokt	velocity, fps:	2630	2354	2095	1853	1631
	energy, ft-lb:	2303	1845	1462	1143	806
	arc, inches:		+2.4	0	-10.4	-30.9
Rem. 180 SP Core-Lokt	velocity, fps:	2350	2025	1728	1467	1252
	energy, ft-lb:	2207	1639	1193	860	626
	arc, inches:		+1.5	-4.0	-21.3	-54.8
Win. 150 Power-Point	velocity, fps:	2630	2311	2015	1743	1500
	energy, ft-lb:	2303	1779	1352	1012	749
	arc, inches:		+2.8	0	-11.5	-34.4

.307 Winchester

Win. 180 Power-Point	velocity, fps:	2510	2179	1874	1599	1362
	energy, ft-lb:	2519	1898	1404	1022	742
	arc, inches:		+1.5	-3.6	-18.6	-47.1

Centerfire Rifle Ballistics
.30-40 Krag to .308 Winchester

CARTRIDGE BULLET	RANGE, YARDS:	0	100	200	300	400
.30-40 Krag						
Rem. 180 PSP Core-Lokt	velocity, fps:	2430	2213	2007	1813	1632
	energy, ft-lb:	2360	1957	1610	1314	1064
	arc, inches, s:		0	-5.6	-18.6	
Win. 180 Power-Point	velocity, fps:	2430	2099	1795	1525	1298
	energy, ft-lb:	2360	1761	1288	929	673
	arc, inches, s:		0	-7.1	-25.0	
.308 Winchester						
Black Hills 150 Nosler B. Tip	velocity, fps:	2800				
	energy, ft-lb:	2611				
	arc, inches:					
Black Hills 165 Nosler B. Tip	velocity, fps:	2650				
	energy, ft-lb:	2573				
	arc, inches:					
Black Hills 168 Barnes X	velocity, fps:	2650				
	energy, ft-lb:	2620				
	arc, inches:					
Federal 150 Hi-Shok	velocity, fps:	2820	2530	2260	2010	1770
	energy, ft-lb:	2650	2140	1705	1345	1050
	arc, inches:		+2.0	0	-8.8	-26.3
Federal 150 Nosler Bal. Tip.	velocity, fps:	2820	2610	2410	2220	2040
	energy, ft-lb:	2650	2270	1935	1640	1380
	arc, inches:		+1.8	0	-7.8	-22.7
Federal 150 FMJ boat-tail	velocity, fps:	2820	2620	2430	2250	2070
	energy, ft-lb:	2650	2285	1965	1680	1430
	arc, inches:		+1.8	0	-7.7	-22.4
Federal 150 Barnes XLC	velocity, fps:	2820	2610	2400	2210	2030
	energy, ft-lb:	2650	2265	1925	1630	1370
	arc, inches:		+1.8	0	-7.8	-22.9
Federal 155 Sierra MatchKg. BTHP	velocity, fps:	2950	2740	2540	2350	2170
	energy, ft-lb:	2995	2585	2225	1905	1620
	arc, inches:		+13.2	+23.3	+28.1	+26.5
Federal 165 Sierra GameKing BTSP	velocity, fps:	2700	2520	2330	2160	1990
	energy, ft-lb:	2670	2310	1990	1700	1450
	arc, inches:		+2.0	0	-8.4	-24.3
Federal 165 Trophy Bonded	velocity, fps:	2700	2440	2200	1970	1760
	energy, ft-lb:	2670	2185	1775	1425	1135
	arc, inches:		+2.2	0	-9.4	-27.7
Federal 165 Tr. Bonded HE	velocity, fps:	2870	2600	2350	2120	1890
	energy, ft-lb:	3020	2485	2030	1640	1310
	arc, inches:		+1.8	0	-8.2	-24.0
Federal 168 Sierra MatchKg. BTHP	velocity, fps:	2600	2410	2230	2060	1890
	energy, ft-lb:	2520	2170	1855	1580	1340
	arc, inches:		+17.7	+31.0	+37.2	+35.4
Federal 180 Hi-Shok	velocity, fps:	2620	2390	2180	1970	1780
	energy, ft-lb:	2745	2290	1895	1555	1270
	arc, inches:		+2.3	0	-9.7	-28.3
Federal 180 Sierra Pro-Hunt.	velocity, fps:	2620	2410	2200	2010	1820
	energy, ft-lb:	2745	2315	1940	1610	1330
	arc, inches:		+2.3	0	-9.3	-27.1
Federal 180 Nosler Partition	velocity, fps:	2620	2430	2240	2060	1890
	energy, ft-lb:	2745	2355	2005	1700	1430
	arc, inches:		+2.2	0	-9.2	-26.5
Federal 180 Nosler Part. HE	velocity, fps:	2740	2550	2370	2200	2030
	energy, ft-lb:	3000	2600	2245	1925	1645
	arc, inches:		+1.9	0	-8.2	-23.5
Hornady 110 Urban Tactical	velocity, fps:	3170	2825	2504	2206	1937
	energy, ft-lb:	2454	1950	1532	1189	916
	arc, inches:		+1.5	0	-7.2	-21.2
Hornady 150 SP boat-tail	velocity, fps:	2820	2560	2315	2084	1866
	energy, ft-lb:	2648	2183	1785	1447	1160
	arc, inches:		+2.0	0	-8.5	-25.2
Hornady 150 SP LM	velocity, fps:	2980	2703	2442	2195	1964
	energy, ft-lb:	2959	2433	1986	1606	1285
	arc, inches:		+1.6	0	-7.5	-22.2
Hornady 155 A-Max	velocity, fps:	2815	2610	2415	2229	2051
	energy, ft-lb:	2727	2345	2007	1709	1448
	arc, inches:		+1.9	0	-7.9	-22.6
Hornady 165 SP boat-tail	velocity, fps:	2700	2496	2301	2115	1937
	energy, ft-lb:	2670	2283	1940	1639	1375
	arc, inches:		+2.0	0	-8.7	-25.2
Hornady 165 SPBT LM	velocity, fps:	2870	2658	2456	2283	2078
	energy, ft-lb:	3019	2589	2211	1877	1583
	arc, inches:		+1.7	0	-7.5	-21.8
Hornady 168 BTHP Match	velocity, fps:	2700	2524	2354	2191	2035
	energy, ft-lb:	2720	2377	2068	1791	1545
	arc, inches:		+2.0	0	-8.4	-23.9
Hornady 168 BTHP Match LM	velocity, fps:	2640	2630	2429	2238	2056
	energy, ft-lb:	3008	2579	2201	1868	1577
	arc, inches:		+1.8	0	-7.8	-22.4
Hornady 168 A-Max Match	velocity fps:	2620	2446	2280	2120	1972
	energy, ft-lb:	2560	2232	1939	1677	1450
	arc, inches:		+2.6	0	-9.2	-25.6
Hornady 168 A-Max	velocity, fps:	2700	2491	2292	2102	1921
	energy, ft-lb:	2719	2315	1959	1648	1377
	arc, inches:		+2.4	0	-9.0	-25.9
Hornady 178 A-Max	velocity, fps:	2965	2778	2598	2425	2259
	energy, ft-lb:	3474	3049	2666	2323	2017
	arc, inches:		+1.6	0	-6.9	-19.8
Hornady 180 A-Max Match	velocity, fps:	2550	2397	2249	2106	1974
	energy, ft-lb:	2598	2295	2021	1773	1557
	arc, inches:		+2.7	0	-9.5	-26.2
Norma 150 Nosler Bal. Tip	velocity, fps:	2822	2588	2365	2154	
	energy, ft-lb:	2653	2231	1864	1545	
			+1.6	0	-7.1	
Norma 150 Soft Point	velocity, fps:	2861	2537	2235	1954	
	energy, ft-lb:	2727	2144	1664	1272	
	arc, inches:		+2.0	0	-9.0	
Norma 165 TXP Swift A-Fr.	velocity, fps:	2700	2459	2231	2015	
	energy, ft-lb:	2672	2216	1824	1488	
	arc, inches:		+2.1	0	-9.1	
Norma 180 Plastic Point	velocity, fps:	2612	2365	2131	1911	
	energy, ft-lb:	2728	2235	1815	1460	
	arc, inches:		+2.4	0	-10.1	
Norma 180 Nosler Partition	velocity, fps:	2612	2414	2225	2044	
	energy, ft-lb:	2728	2330	1979	1670	
	arc, inches:		+2.2	0	-9.3	
Norma 180 Alaska	velocity, fps:	2612	2269	1953	1667	
	energy, ft-lb:	2728	2059	1526	1111	
	arc, inches:		+2.7	0	-11.9	
Norma 180 Vulkan	velocity, fps:	2612	2325	2056	1806	
	energy, ft-lb:	2728	2161	1690	1304	
	arc, inches:		+2.5	0	-10.8	
Norma 180 Oryx	velocity, fps:	2612	2305	2019	1755	
	energy, ft-lb:	2728	2124	1629	1232	
	arc, inches:		+2.5	0	-11.1	
Norma 200 Vulkan	velocity, fps:	2461	2215	1983	1767	
	energy, ft-lb:	2690	2179	1747	1387	
	arc, inches:		+2.8	0	-11.7	

Centerfire Rifle Ballistics

.308 Winchester to .30-06 Springfield

CARTRIDGE BULLET	RANGE, YARDS:	0	100	200	300	400
PMC 147 FMJ boat-tail	velocity, fps:	2751	2473	2257	2052	1859
	energy, ft-lb:	2428	2037	1697	1403	1150
	arc, inches:		+2.3	0	-9.3	-27.3
PMC 150 Barnes X	velocity, fps:	2700	2504	2316	2135	1964
	energy, ft-lb:	2428	2087	1786	1518	1284
	arc, inches:		+2.0	0	-8.6	-24.7
PMC 150 Pointed Soft Point	velocity, fps:	2643	2417	2203	1999	1807
	energy, ft-lb:	2326	1946	1615	1331	1088
	arc, inches:		+2.2	0	-9.4	-27.5
PMC 150 SP boat-tail	velocity, fps:	2820	2581	2354	2139	1935
	energy, ft-lb:	2648	2218	1846	1523	1247
	arc, inches:		+1.9	0	-8.2	-24.0
PMC 165 Barnes X	velocity, fps:	2600	2425	2256	2095	1940
	energy, ft-lb:	2476	2154	1865	1608	1379
	arc, inches:		+2.2	0	-9.0	-26.0
PMC 168 HP boat-tail	velocity, fps:	2650	2460	2278	2103	1936
	energy, ft-lb:	2619	2257	1935	1649	1399
	arc, inches:		+2.1	0	--8.8	-25.6
PMC 180 Pointed Soft Point	velocity, fps:	2410	2223	2044	1874	1714
	energy, ft-lb:	2320	1975	1670	1404	1174
	arc, inches:		+2.8	0	-11.1	-32.0
PMC 180 SP boat-tail	velocity, fps:	2620	2446	2278	2117	1962
	energy, ft-lb:	2743	2391	2074	1790	1538
	arc, inches:		+2.2	0	-8.9	-25.4
Rem. 150 PSP Core-Lokt	velocity, fps:	2820	2533	2263	2009	1774
	energy, ft-lb:	2648	2137	1705	1344	1048
	arc, inches:		+2.0	0	-8.8	-26.2
Rem. 150 PSP C-L Ultra	velocity, fps:	2620	2404	2198	2002	1818
	energy, ft-lb:	2743	2309	1930	1601	1320
	arc, inches:		+2.3	0	-9.5	-26.4
Rem. 150 Swift Scirocco	velocity, fps:	2820	2611	2410	2219	2037
	energy, ft-lb:	2648	2269	1935	1640	1381
	arc, inches:		+1.8	0	-7.8	-22.7
Rem. 165 PSP boat-tail	velocity, fps:	2700	2497	2303	2117	1941
	energy, ft-lb:	2670	2284	1942	1642	1379
	arc, inches:		+2.0	0	-8.6	-25.0
Rem. 165 Nosler Bal. Tip	velocity, fps:	2700	2613	2333	2161	1996
	energy, ft-lb:	2672	2314	1995	1711	1460
	arc, inches:		+2.0	0	-8.4	-24.3
Rem. 165 Swift Scirocco	velocity, fps:	2700	2513	2233	2161	1996
	energy, fps:	2670	2313	1994	1711	1459
	arc, inches:		+2.0	0	-8.4	-24.3
Rem. 168 HPBT Match	velocity, fps:	2680	2493	2314	2143	1979
	energy, ft-lb:	2678	2318	1998	1713	1460
	arc, inches:		+2.1	0	-8.6	-24.7
Rem. 180 SP Core-Lokt	velocity, fps:	2620	2274	1955	1666	1414
	energy, ft-lb:	2743	2066	1527	1109	799
	arc, inches:		+2.6	0	-11.8	-36.3
Rem. 180 PSP Core-Lokt	velocity, fps:	2620	2393	2178	1974	1782
	energy, ft-lb:	2743	2288	1896	1557	1269
	arc, inches:		+2.3	0	-9.7	-28.3
Rem. 180 Nosler Partition	velocity, fps:	2620	2436	2259	2089	1927
	energy, ft-lb:	2743	2371	2039	1774	1485
	arc, inches:		+2.2	0	-9.0	-26.0
Speer 150 Grand Slam	velocity, fps:	2900	2599	2317	2053	
	energy, ft-lb:	2800	2249	1788	1404	
	arc, inches:		+2.1	0	-8.6	-24.8
Speer 165 Grand Slam	velocity, fps:	2700	2475	2261	2057	
	energy, ft-lb:	2670	2243	1872	1550	
	arc, inches:		+2.1	0	-8.9	-25.9
Speer 180 Grand Slam	velocity, fps:	2620	2420	2229	2046	
	energy, ft-lb:	2743	2340	1985	1674	
	arc, inches:		+2.2	0	-9.2	-26.6
Win. 150 Power-Point	velocity, fps:	2820	2488	2179	1893	1633
	energy, ft-lb:	2648	2061	1581	1193	888
	arc, inches:		+2.4	0	-9.8	-29.3
Win. 150 Power-Point Plus	velocity, fps:	2900	2558	2241	1946	1678
	energy, ft-lb:	2802	2180	1672	1262	938
	arc, inches:		+1.9	0	-8.9	-27.0
Win. 150 Partition Gold	velocity, fps:	2900	2645	2405	2177	1962
	energy, ft-lb:	2802	2332	1927	1579	1282
	arc, inches:		+1.7	0	-7.8	-22.9
Win. 150 Ballistic Silvertip	velocity, fps:	2810	2601	2401	2211	2028
	energy, ft-lb:	2629	2253	1920	1627	1370
	arc, inches:		+1.8	0	-7.8	-22.8
Win. 150 Fail Safe	velocity, fps:	2820	2533	2263	2010	1775
	energy, ft-lb:	2649	2137	1706	1346	1049
	arc, inches:		+2.0	0	-8.8	-26.2
Win. 168 Ballistic Silvertip	velocity, fps:	2670	2484	2306	2134	1971
	energy, ft-lb:	2659	2301	1983	1699	1449
	arc, inches:		+2.1	0	-8.6	-24.8
Win. 168 HP boat-tail Match	velocity, fps:	2680	2485	2297	2118	1948
	energy, ft-lb:	2680	2303	1970	1674	1415
	arc, inches:		+2.1	0	-8.7	-25.1
Win. 180 Power-Point	velocity, fps:	2620	2274	1955	1666	1414
	energy, ft-lb:	2743	2066	1527	1109	799
	arc, inches:		+2.9	0	-12.1	-36.9
Win. 180 Silvertip	velocity, fps:	2620	2393	2178	1974	1782
	energy, ft-lb:	2743	2288	1896	1557	1269
	arc, inches:		+2.6	0	-9.9	-28.9

.30-06 Springfield

CARTRIDGE BULLET	RANGE, YARDS:	0	100	200	300	400
A-Square 180 M & D-T	velocity, fps:	2700	2365	2054	1769	1524
	energy, ft-lb:	2913	2235	1687	1251	928
	arc, inches:		+2.4	0	-10.6	-32.4
A-Square 220 Monolithic Solid	velocity, fps:	2380	2108	1854	1623	1424
	energy, ft-lb:	2767	2171	1679	1287	990
	arc, inches:		+3.1	0	-13.6	-39.9
Black Hills 150 Nosler B. Tip	velocity, fps:	2900				
	energy, ft-lb:	2770				
	arc, inches:					
Black Hills 165 Nosler B. Tip	velocity, fps:	2750				
	energy, ft-lb:	2770				
	arc, inches:					
Black Hills 168 Hor. Match	velocity, fps:	2700				
	energy, ft-lb:	2718				
	arc, inches:					
Black Hills 180 Barnes X	velocity, fps:	2650				
	energy, ft-lb:	2806				
	arc, inches:					
Federal 125 Sierra Pro-Hunt.	velocity, fps:	3140	2780	2450	2140	1850
	energy, ft-lb:	2735	2145	1660	1270	955
	arc, inches:		+1.5	0	-7.3	-22.3
Federal 150 Hi-Shok	velocity, fps:	2910	2620	2340	2080	1840
	energy, ft-lb:	2820	2280	1825	1445	1130
	arc, inches:		+1.8	0	-8.2	-24.4
Federal 150 Sierra Pro-Hunt.	velocity, fps:	2910	2640	2380	2130	1900
	energy, ft-lb:	2820	2315	1880	1515	1205
	arc, inches:		+1.7	0	-7.9	-23.3

Centerfire Rifle Ballistics

.30-06 Springfield

CARTRIDGE BULLET	RANGE, YARDS:	0	100	200	300	400
Federal 150 Sierra GameKing BTSP	velocity, fps:	2910	2690	2480	2270	2070
	energy, ft-lb:	2820	2420	2040	1710	1430
	arc, inches:		+1.7	0	-7.4	-21.5
Federal 150 Nosler Bal. Tip	velocity, fps:	2910	2700	2490	2300	2110
	energy, ft-lb:	2820	2420	2070	1760	1485
	arc, inches:		+1.6	0	-7.3	-21.1
Federal 150 FMJ boat-tail	velocity, fps:	2910	2710	2510	2320	2150
	energy, ft-lb:	2820	2440	2100	1800	1535
	arc, inches:		+1.6	0	-7.1	-20.8
Federal 165 Sierra Pro-Hunt.	velocity, fps:	2800	2560	2340	2130	1920
	energy, ft-lb:	2875	2410	2005	1655	1360
	arc, inches:		+1.9	0	-8.3	-24.3
Federal 165 Sierra GameKing BTSP	velocity, fps:	2800	2610	2420	2240	2070
	energy, ft-lb:	2870	2490	2150	1840	1580
	arc, inches:		+1.8	0	-7.8	-22.4
Federal 165 Sierra GameKing HE	velocity, fps:	3140	2900	2670	2450	2240
	energy, ft-lb:	3610	3075	2610	2200	1845
	arc, inches:		+1.5	0	-6.9	-20.4
Federal 165 Nosler Bal. Tip	velocity, fps:	2800	2610	2430	2250	2080
	energy, ft-lb:	2870	2495	2155	1855	1585
	arc, inches:		+1.8	0	-7.7	-22.3
Federal 165 Trophy Bonded	velocity, fps:	2800	2540	2290	2050	1830
	energy, ft-lb:	2870	2360	1915	1545	1230
	arc, inches:		+2.0	0	-8.7	-25.4
Federal 165 Tr. Bonded HE	velocity, fps:	3140	2860	2590	2340	2100
	energy, ft-lb:	3610	2990	2460	2010	1625
	arc, inches:		+1.6	0	-7.4	-21.9
Federal 168 Sierra MatchKg. BTHP	velocity, fps:	2700	2510	2320	2150	1980
	energy, ft-lb:	2720	2350	2010	1720	1460
	arc, inches:		+16.2	+28.4	+34.1	+32.3
Federal 180 Hi-Shok	velocity, fps:	2700	2470	2250	2040	1850
	energy, ft-lb:	2915	2435	2025	1665	1360
	arc, inches:		+2.1	0	-9.0	-26.4
Federal 180 Sierra Pro-Hunt. RN	velocity, fps:	2700	2350	2020	1730	1470
	energy, ft-lb:	2915	2200	1630	1190	860
	arc, inches:		+2.4	0	-11.0	-33.6
Federal 180 Nosler Partition	velocity, fps:	2700	2500	2320	2140	1970
	energy, ft-lb:	2915	2510	2150	1830	1550
	arc, inches:		+2.0	0	-8.6	-24.6
Federal 180 Nosler Part. HE	velocity, fps:	2880	2690	2500	2320	2150
	energy, ft-lb:	3315	2880	2495	2150	1845
	arc, inches:		+1.7	0	-7.2	-21.0
Federal 180 Sierra GameKing BTSP	velocity, fps:	2700	2540	2380	2220	2080
	energy, ft-lb:	2915	2570	2260	1975	1720
	arc, inches:		+1.9	0	-8.1	-23.1
Federal 180 Barnes XLC	velocity, fps:	2700	2530	2360	2200	2040
	energy, ft-lb:	2915	2550	2220	1930	1670
	arc, inches:		+2.0	0	-8.3	-23.8
Federal 180 Trophy Bonded	velocity, fps:	2700	2460	2220	2000	1800
	energy, ft-lb:	2915	2410	1975	1605	1290
	arc, inches:		+2.2	0	-9.2	-27.0
Federal 180 Tr. Bonded HE	velocity, fps:	2880	2630	2380	2160	1940
	energy, ft-lb:	3315	2755	2270	1855	1505
	arc, inches:		+1.8	0	-8.0	-23.3
Federal 220 Sierra Pro-Hunt. RN	velocity, fps:	2410	2130	1870	1630	1420
	energy, ft-lb:	2835	2215	1705	1300	985
	arc, inches:		+3.1	0	-13.1	-39.3
Hornady 150 SP	velocity, fps:	2910	2617	2342	2083	1843
	energy, ft-lb:	2820	2281	1827	1445	1131
	arc, inches:		+2.1	0	-8.5	-25.0
Hornady 150 SP LM	velocity, fps:	3100	2815	2548	2295	2058
	energy, ft-lb:	3200	2639	2161	1755	1410
	arc, inches:		+1.4	0	-6.8	-20.3
Hornady 150 SP boat-tail	velocity, fps:	2910	2683	2467	2262	2066
	energy, ft-lb:	2820	2397	2027	1706	1421
	arc, inches:		+2.0	0	-7.7	-22.2
Hornady 165 SP boat-tail	velocity, fps:	2800	2591	2392	2202	2020
	energy, ft-lb:	2873	2460	2097	1777	1495
	arc, inches:		+1.8	0	-8.0	-23.3
Hornady 165 SPBT LM	velocity, fps:	3015	2790	2575	2370	2176
	energy, ft-lb:	3330	2850	2428	2058	1734
	arc, inches:		+1.6	0	-7.0	-20.1
Hornady 168 HPBT Match	velocity, fps:	2790	2620	2447	2280	2120
	energy, ft-lb:	2925	2561	2234	1940	1677
	arc, inches:		+1.7	0	-7.7	-22.2
Hornady 180 SP	velocity, fps:	2700	2469	2258	2042	1846
	energy, ft-lb:	2913	2436	2023	1666	1362
	arc, inches:		+2.4	0	-9.3	-27.0
Hornady 180 SPBT LM	velocity, fps:	2880	2676	2480	2293	2114
	energy, ft-lb:	3316	2862	2459	2102	1786
	arc, inches:		+1.7	0	-7.3	-21.3
Norma 150 Nosler Bal. Tip	velocity, fps:	2936	2713	2502	2300	
	energy, ft-lb:	2872	2453	2085	1762	
	arc, inches:		+1.6	0	-7.1	
Norma 150 Soft Point	velocity, fps:	2972	2640	2331	2043	
	energy, ft-lb:	2943	2321	1810	1390	
	arc, inches:		+1.8	0	-8.2	
Norma 180 Alaska	velocity, fps:	2700	2351	2028	1734	
	energy, ft-lb:	2914	2209	1645	1202	
	arc, inches:		+2.4	0	-11.0	
Norma 180 Nosler Partition	velocity, fps:	2700	2494	2297	2108	
	energy, ft-lb:	2914	2486	2108	1777	
	arc, inches:		+2.1	0	-8.7	
Norma 180 Plastic Point	velocity, fps:	2700	2455	2222	2003	
	energy, ft-lb:	2914	2409	1974	1603	
	arc, inches:		+2.1	0	-9.2	
Norma 180 Vulkan	velocity, fps:	2700	2416	2150	1901	
	energy, ft-lb:	2914	2334	1848	1445	
	arc, inches:		+2.2	0	-9.8	
Norma 180 Oryx	velocity, fps:	2700	2387	2095	1825	
	energy, ft-lb:	2914	2278	1755	1332	
	arc, inches:		+2.3	0	-10.2	
Norma 180 TXP Swift A-Fr.	velocity, fps:	2700	2479	2268	2067	
	energy, ft-lb:	2914	2456	2056	1708	
	arc, inches:		+2.0	0	-8.8	
Norma 200 Vulkan	velocity, fps:	2641	2385	2143	1916	
	energy, ft-lb:	3098	2527	2040	1631	
	arc, inches:		+2.3	0	-9.9	
Norma 200 Oryx	velocity, fps:	2625	2362	2115	1883	
	energy, ft-lb:	3061	2479	1987	1575	
	arc, inches:		+2.3	0	-10.1	
PMC 150 X-Bullet	velocity, fps:	2750	2552	2361	2179	2005
	energy, ft-lb:	2518	2168	1857	1582	1339
	arc, inches:		+2.0	0	-8.2	-23.7
PMC 150 Pointed Soft Point	velocity, fps:	2773	2542	2322	2113	1916
	energy, ft-lb:	2560	2152	1796	1487	1222
	arc, inches:		+1.9	0	-8.4	-24.6
PMC 150 SP boat-tail	velocity, fps:	2900	2657	2427	2208	2000
	energy, ft-lb:	2801	2351	1961	1623	1332
	arc, inches:		+1.7	0	-7.7	-22.5

Centerfire Rifle Ballistics

.30-06 SPRINGFIELD

CARTRIDGE BULLET	RANGE, YARDS:	0	100	200	300	400
PMC 150 FMJ	velocity, fps:	2773	2542	2322	2113	1916
	energy, ft-lb:	2560	2152	1796	1487	1222
	arc, inches:		+1.9	0	-8.4	-24.6
PMC 165 Barnes X	velocity, fps:	2750	2569	2395	2228	2067
	energy, ft-lb:	2770	2418	2101	1818	1565
	arc, inches:		+1.9	0	-8.0	-23.0
PMC 180 Barnes X	velocity, fps:	2650	2487	2331	2179	2034
	energy, ft-lb:	2806	2472	2171	1898	1652
	arc, inches:		+2.1	0	-8.5	-24.3
PMC 180 Pointed Soft Point	velocity, fps:	2550	2357	2172	1996	1829
	energy, ft-lb:	2598	2220	1886	1592	1336
	arc, inches:		+2.4	0	-9.7	-28.2
PMC 180 SP boat-tail	velocity, fps:	2700	2523	2352	2188	2030
	energy, ft-lb:	2913	2543	2210	1913	1646
	arc, inches:		+2.0	0	-8.3	-23.9
Rem. 55 PSP (sabot) "Accelerator"	velocity, fps:	4080	3484	2964	2499	2080
	energy, ft-lb:	2033	1482	1073	763	528
	arc, inches:		+1.4	+1.4	-2.6	-12.2
Rem. 125 Pointed Soft Point	velocity, fps:	3140	2780	2447	2138	1853
	energy, ft-lb:	2736	2145	1662	1269	953
	arc, inches:		+1.5	0	--7.4	-22.4
Rem. 150 PSP Core-Lokt	velocity, fps:	2910	2617	2342	2083	1843
	energy, ft-lb:	2820	2281	1827	1445	1131
	arc, inches:		+1.8	0	-8.2	-24.4
Rem. 150 Bronze Point	velocity, fps:	2910	2656	2416	2189	1974
	energy, ft-lb:	2820	2349	1944	1596	1298
	arc, inches:		+1.7	0	-7.7	-22.7
Rem. 150 Nosler Bal. Tip	velocity, fps:	2910	2696	2492	2298	2112
	energy, ft-lb:	2821	2422	2070	1769	1485
	arc, inches:		+1.6	0	-7.3	-21.1
Rem. 150 Swift Scirocco	velocity, fps:	2910	2696	2492	2298	2111
	energy, ft-lb:	2820	2421	2069	1758	1485
	arc, inches:		+1.6	0	-7.3	-21.1
Rem. 165 PSP Core-Lokt	velocity, fps:	2800	2534	2283	2047	1825
	energy, ft-lb:	2872	2352	1909	1534	1220
	arc, inches:		+2.0	0	-8.7	-25.9
Rem. 165 PSP boat-tail	velocity, fps:	2800	2592	2394	2204	2023
	energy, ft-lb:	2872	2462	2100	1780	1500
	arc, inches:		+1.8	0	-7.9	-23.0
Rem. 165 Nosler Bal. Tip	velocity, fps:	2800	2609	2426	2249	2080
	energy, ft-lb:	2873	2494	2155	1854	1588
	arc, inches:		+1.8	0	-7.7	-22.3
Rem. 180 SP Core-Lokt	velocity, fps:	2700	2348	2023	1727	1466
	energy, ft-lb:	2913	2203	1635	1192	859
	arc, inches:		+2.4	0	-11.0	-33.8
Rem. 180 PSP Core-Lokt	velocity, fps:	2700	2469	2250	2042	1846
	energy, ft-lb:	2913	2436	2023	1666	1362
	arc, inches:		+2.1	0	-9.0	-26.3
Rem. 180 PSP C-L Ultra	velocity, fps:	2700	2480	2270	2070	1882
	energy, ft-lb:	2913	2457	2059	1713	1415
	arc, inches:		+2.1	0	-8.9	-25.8
Rem. 180 Bronze Point	velocity, fps:	2700	2485	2280	2084	1899
	energy, ft-lb:	2913	2468	2077	1736	1441
	arc, inches:		+2.1	0	-8.8	-25.5
Rem. 180 Swift A-Frame	velocity, fps:	2700	2465	2243	2032	1833
	energy, ft-lb:	2913	2429	2010	1650	1343
	arc, inches:		+2.1	0	-9.1	-26.6
Rem. 180 Nosler Partition	velocity, fps:	2700	2512	2332	2160	1995
	energy, ft-lb:	2913	2522	2174	1864	1590
	arc, inches:		+2.0	0	-8.4	-24.3
Rem. 220 SP Core-Lokt	velocity, fps:	2410	2130	1870	1632	1422
	energy, ft-lb:	2837	2216	1708	1301	988
	arc, inches, s:		0	-6.2	-22.4	
Speer 150 Grand Slam	velocity, fps:	2975	2669	2383	2114	
	energy, ft-lb:	2947	2372	1891	1489	
	arc, inches:		+2.0	0	-8.1	-24.1
Speer 165 Grand Slam	velocity, fps:	2790	2560	2342	2134	
	energy, ft-lb:	2851	2401	2009	1669	
	arc, inches:		+1.9	0	-8.3	-24.1
Speer 180 Grand Slam	velocity, fps:	2690	2487	2293	2108	
	energy, ft-lb:	2892	2472	2101	1775	
	arc, inches:		+2.1	0	-8.8	-25.1
Win. 125 Pointed Soft Point	velocity, fps:	3140	2780	2447	2138	1853
	energy, ft-lb:	2736	2145	1662	1269	953
	arc, inches:		+1.8	0	-7.7	-23.0
Win. 150 Power-Point	velocity, fps:	2920	2580	2265	1972	1704
	energy, ft-lb:	2839	2217	1708	1295	967
	arc, inches:		+2.2	0	-9.0	-27.0
Win. 150 Power-Point Plus	velocity, fps:	3050	2685	2352	2043	1760
	energy, ft-lb:	3089	2402	1843	1391	1032
	arc, inches:		+1.7	0	-8.0	-24.3
Win. 150 Silvertip	velocity, fps:	2910	2617	2342	2083	1843
	energy, ft-lb:	2820	2281	1827	1445	1131
	arc, inches:		+2.1	0	-8.5	-25.0
Win. 150 Partition Gold	velocity, fps:	2960	2705	2464	2235	2019
	energy, ft-lb:	2919	2437	2022	1664	1358
	arc, inches:		+1.6	0	-7.4	-21.7
Win. 150 Ballistic Silvertip	velocity, fps:	2900	2687	2483	2289	2103
	energy, ft-lb:	2801	2404	2054	1745	1473
	arc, inches:		+1.7	0	-7.3	-21.2
Win. 150 Fail Safe	velocity, fps:	2920	2625	2349	2089	1848
	energy, ft-lb:	2841	2296	1838	1455	1137
	arc, inches:		+1.8	0	-8.1	-24.3
Win. 165 Pointed Soft Point	velocity, fps:	2800	2573	2357	2151	1956
	energy, ft-lb:	2873	2426	2036	1696	1402
	arc, inches:		+2.2	0	-8.4	-24.4
Win. 165 Fail Safe	velocity, fps:	2800	2540	2295	2063	1846
	energy, ft-lb:	2873	2365	1930	1560	1249
	arc, inches:		+2.0	0	-8.6	-25.3
Win. 168 Ballistic Silvertip	velocity, fps:	2790	2599	2416	2240	2072
	energy, ft-lb:	2903	2520	2177	1872	1601
	arc, inches:		+1.8	0	-7.8	-22.5
Win. 180 Power-Point	velocity, fps:	2700	2497	2304	2118	1942
	energy, ft-lb:	2913	2492	2121	1793	1507
	arc, inches:		+2.7	0	-11.3	-34.4
Win. 180 Power-Point Plus	velocity, fps:	2770	2563	2366	2177	1997
	energy, ft-lb:	3068	2627	2237	1894	1594
	arc, inches:		+1.9	0	-8.1	-23.6
Win. 180 Silvertip	velocity, fps:	2700	2469	2250	2042	1846
	energy, ft-lb:	2913	2436	2023	1666	1362
	arc, inches:		+2.4	0	-9.3	-27.0
Win. 180 Partition Gold	velocity, fps:	2790	2581	2382	2192	2010
	energy, ft-lb:	3112	2664	2269	1920	1615
	arc, inches:		+1.9	0	-8.0	-23.2
Win. 180 Fail Safe	velocity, fps:	2700	2486	2283	2089	1904
	energy, ft-lb:	2914	2472	2083	1744	1450
	arc, inches:		+2.1	0	-8.7	-25.5

Centerfire Rifle Ballistics
.300 H&H Magnum to .300 Winchester Magnum

CARTRIDGE BULLET	RANGE, YARDS:	0	100	200	300	400
.300 H&H Magnum						
Federal 180 Nosler Partition	velocity, fps:	2880	2620	2380	2150	1930
	energy, ft-lb:	3315	2750	2260	1840	1480
	arc, inches:		+1.8	0	-8.0	-23.4
Win. 180 Fail Safe	velocity, fps:	2880	2628	2390	2165	1952
	energy, ft-lb:	3316	2762	2284	1873	1523
	arc, inches:		+1.8	0	-7.9	-23.2
.308 Norma Magnum						
Norma 180 TXP Swift A-Fr.	velocity, fps:	2953	2704	2469	2245	
	energy, ft-lb:	3486	2924	2437	2016	
	arc, inches:		+1.6	0	-7.3	
Norma 200 Vulkan	velocity, fps:	2903	2624	2361	2114	
	energy, ft-lb:	3744	3058	2476	1985	
	arc, inches:	0	+1.8	0	-8.0	
.300 Winchester Magnum						
A-Square 180 Dead Tough	velocity, fps:	3120	2756	2420	2108	1820
	energy, ft-lb:	3890	3035	2340	1776	1324
	arc, inches:		+1.6	0	-7.6	-22.9
Black Hills 180 Nosler B. Tip	velocity, fps:	3100				
	energy, ft-lb:	3498				
	arc, inches:					
Black Hills 180 Barnes X	velocity, fps:	2950				
	energy, ft-lb:	3498				
	arc, inches:					
Federal 150 Sierra Pro Hunt.	velocity, fps:	3280	3030	2800	2570	2360
	energy, ft-lb:	3570	3055	2600	2205	1860
	arc, inches:		+1.1	0	-5.6	-16.4
Federal 150 Trophy Bonded	velocity, fps:	3280	2980	2700	2430	2190
	energy, ft-lb:	3570	2450	2420	1970	1590
	arc, inches:		+1.2	0	-6.0	-17.9
Federal 180 Sierra Pro Hunt.	velocity, fps:	2960	2750	2540	2340	2160
	energy, ft-lb:	3500	3010	2580	2195	1860
	arc, inches:		+1.6	0	-7.0	-20.3
Federal 180 Barnes XLC	velocity, fps:	2960	2780	2600	2430	2260
	energy, ft-lb:	3500	3080	2700	2355	2050
	arc, inches:		+1.5	0	-6.6	-19.2
Federal 180 Trophy Bonded	velocity, fps:	2960	2700	2460	2220	2000
	energy, ft-lb:	3500	2915	2410	1975	1605
	arc, inches:		+1.6	0	-7.4	-21.9
Federal 180 Tr. Bonded HE	velocity, fps:	3100	2830	2580	2340	2110
	energy, ft-lb:	3840	3205	2660	2190	1790
	arc, inches:		+1.4	0	-6.6	-19.7
Federal 180 Nosler Partition	velocity, fps:	2960	2700	2450	2210	1990
	energy, ft-lb:	3500	2905	2395	1955	1585
	arc, inches:		+1.6	0	-7.5	-22.1
Federal 190 Sierra MatchKg. BTHP	velocity, fps:	2900	2730	2560	2400	2240
	energy, ft-lb:	3550	3135	2760	2420	2115
	arc, inches:		+12.9	+22.5	+26.9	+25.1
Federal 200 Sierra GameKing BTSP	velocity, fps:	2830	2680	2530	2380	2240
	energy, ft-lb:	3560	3180	2830	2520	2230
	arc, inches:		+1.7	0	-7.1	-20.4
Federal 200 Nosler Part. HE	velocity, fps:	2930	2740	2550	2370	2200
	energy, ft-lb:	3810	3325	2885	2495	2145
	arc, inches:		+1.6	0	-6.9	-20.1
Federal 200 Trophy Bonded	velocity, fps:	2800	2570	2350	2150	1950
	energy, ft-lb:	3480	2935	2460	2050	1690
	arc, inches:		+1.9	0	-8.2	-23.9
Hornady 150 SP boat-tail	velocity, fps:	3275	2988	2718	2464	2224
	energy, ft-lb:	3573	2974	2461	2023	1648
	arc, inches:		+1.2	0	-6.0	-17.8
Hornady 165 SP boat-tail	velocity, fps:	3100	2877	2665	2462	2269
	energy, ft-lb:	3522	3033	2603	2221	1887
	arc, inches:		+1.3	0	-6.5	-18.5
Hornady 180 SP boat-tail	velocity, fps:	2960	2745	2540	2344	2157
	energy, ft-lb:	3501	3011	2578	2196	1859
	arc, inches:		+1.9	0	-7.3	-20.9
Hornady 180 SST	velocity, fps:	2960	2764	2575	2395	2222
	energy, ft-lb:	3501	3052	2650	2292	1974
	arc, inches:		+1.6	0	-7.0	-20.1
Hornady 180 SPBT HM	velocity, fps:	3100	2879	2668	2467	2275
	energy, ft-lb:	3840	3313	2845	2431	2068
	arc, inches:		+1.4	0	-6.4	-18.7
Hornady 190 SP boat-tail	velocity, fps:	2900	2711	2529	2355	2187
	energy, ft-lb:	3549	3101	2699	2340	2018
	arc, inches:		+1.6	0	-7.1	-20.4
Norma 150 Nosler Bal. Tip	velocity, fps:	3250	3014	2791	2578	
	energy, ft-lb:	3519	3027	2595	2215	
	arc, inches:		+1.1	0	-5.6	
Norma 165 Scirocco	velocity, fps:	3117	2921	2734	2554	
	energy, ft-lb:	3561	3127	2738	2390	
	arc, inches:		+1.2	0	-5.9	
Norma 180 Soft Point	velocity, fps:	3018	2780	2555	2341	
	energy, ft-lb:	3641	3091	2610	2190	
	arc, inches:		+1.5	0	-7.0	
Norma 180 Plastic Point	velocity, fps:	3018	2755	2506	2271	
	energy, ft-lb:	3641	3034	2512	2062	
	arc, inches:		+1.6	0	-7.1	
Norma 180 TXP Swift A-Fr.	velocity, fps:	2920	2688	2467	2256	
	energy, ft-lb:	3409	2888	2432	2035	
	arc, inches:		+1.7	0	-7.4	
Norma 200 Vulkan	velocity, fps:	2887	2609	2347	2100	
	energy, ft-lb:	3702	3023	2447	1960	
	arc, inches:		+1.8	0	-8.2	
Norma 200 Oryx	velocity, fps:	3018	2755	2506	2271	
	energy, ft-lb:	4046	3371	2791	2292	
	arc, inches:		+1.5	0	-7.0	
PMC 150 Barnes X	velocity, fps:	3135	2918	2712	2515	2327
	energy, ft-lb:	3273	2836	2449	2107	1803
	arc, inches:		+1.3	0	-6.1	-17.7
PMC 150 Pointed Soft Point	velocity, fps:	3150	2902	2665	2438	2222
	energy, ft-lb:	3304	2804	2364	1979	1644
	arc, inches:		+1.3	0	-6.2	-18.3
PMC 150 SP boat-tail	velocity, fps:	3250	2987	2739	2504	2281
	energy, ft-lb:	3517	2970	2498	2088	1733
	arc, inches:		+1.2	0	-6.0	-17.4
PMC 180 Barnes X	velocity, fps:	2910	2738	2572	2412	2258
	energy, ft-lb:	3384	2995	2644	2325	2037
	arc, inches:		+1.6	0	-6.9	-19.8
PMC 180 PSP	velocity, fps:	2853	2643	2446	2258	2077
	energy, ft-lb:	3252	2792	2391	2037	1724
	arc, inches:		+1.7	0	-7.5	-21.9
PMC 180 SP boat-tail	velocity, fps:	2900	2714	2536	2365	2200
	energy, ft-lb:	3361	2944	2571	2235	1935
	arc, inches:		+1.6	0	-7.1	-20.3
Rem. 150 PSP Core-Lokt	velocity, fps:	3290	2951	2636	2342	2068
	energy, ft-lb:	3605	2900	2314	1827	1859
	arc, inches:		+1.6	0	-7.0	-20.2

Rifles • 485

Centerfire Rifle Ballistics

.300 Winchester Magnum to .300 Weatherby Magnum

CARTRIDGE BULLET	RANGE, YARDS:	0	100	200	300	400
Rem. 180 PSP Core-Lokt	velocity, fps:	2960	2745	2540	2344	2157
	energy, ft-lb:	3501	3011	2578	2196	1424
	arc, inches:		+2.2	+1.9	-3.4	-15.0
Rem. 180 PSP C-L Ultra	velocity, fps:	2960	2727	2505	2294	2093
	energy, ft-lb:	3501	2971	2508	2103	1751
	arc, inches:		+2.7	+2.2	-3.8	-16.4
Rem. 180 Nosler Partition	velocity, fps:	2960	2725	2503	2291	2089
	energy, ft-lb:	3501	2968	2503	2087	1744
	arc, inches:		+1.6	0	-7.2	-20.9
Rem. 180 Nosler Bal. Tip	velocity, fps:	2960	2774	2595	2424	2259
	energy, ft-lb:	3501	3075	2692	2348	2039
	arc, inches:		+1.5	0	-6.7	-19.3
Rem. 180 Swift Scirocco	velocity, fps:	2960	2774	2595	2424	2259
	energy, ft-lb:	3501	3075	2692	2348	2039
	arc, inches:		+1.5	0	-6.7	-19.3
Rem. 190 PSP boat-tail	velocity, fps:	2885	2691	2506	2327	2156
	energy, ft-lb:	3511	3055	2648	2285	1961
	arc, inches:		+1.6	0	-7.2	-20.8
Rem. 200 Swift A-Frame	velocity, fps:	2825	2595	2376	2167	1970
	energy, ft-lb:	3544	2989	2506	2086	1722
	arc, inches:		+1.8	0	-8.0	-23.5
Speer 180 Grand Slam	velocity, fps:	2950	2735	2530	2334	
	energy, ft-lb:	3478	2989	2558	2176	
	arc, inches:		+1.6	0	-7.0	-20.5
Speer 200 Grand Slam	velocity, fps:	2800	2597	2404	2218	
	energy, ft-lb:	3481	2996	2565	2185	
	arc, inches:		+1.8	0	-7.9	-22.9
Win. 150 Power-Point	velocity, fps:	3290	2951	2636	2342	2068
	energy, ft-lb:	3605	2900	2314	1827	1424
	arc, inches:		+2.6	+2.1	-3.5	-15.4
Win. 150 Fail Safe	velocity, fps:	3260	2943	2647	2370	2110
	energy, ft-lb:	3539	2884	2334	1871	1483
	arc, inches:		+1.3	0	-6.2	-18.7
Win. 165 Fail Safe	velocity, fps:	3120	2807	2515	2242	1985
	energy, ft-lb:	3567	2888	2319	1842	1445
	arc, inches:		+1.5	0	-7.0	-20.0
Win. 180 Power-Point	velocity, fps:	2960	2745	2540	2344	2157
	energy, ft-lb:	3501	3011	2578	2196	1859
	arc, inches:		+1.9	0	-7.3	-20.9
Win. 180 Power-Point Plus	velocity, fps:	3070	2846	2633	2430	2236
	energy, ft-lb:	3768	3239	2772	2361	1999
	arc, inches:		+1.4	0	-6.4	-18.7
Win. 180 Ballistic Silvertip	velocity, fps:	2950	2764	2586	2415	2250
	energy, ft-lb:	3478	3054	2673	2331	2023
	arc, inches:		+1.5	0	-6.7	-19.4
Win. 180 Fail Safe	velocity, fps:	2960	2732	2514	2307	2110
	energy, ft-lb:	3503	2983	2528	2129	1780
	arc, inches:		+1.6	0	-7.1	-20.7
Win. 180 Partition Gold	velocity, fps:	3070	2859	2657	2464	2280
	energy, ft-lb:	3768	3267	2823	2428	2078
	arc, inches:		+1.4	0	-6.3	-18.3

.300 Remington Short Ultra Mag

Rem. 150 PSP C-L Ultra	velocity, fps:	3200	2901	2672	2359	2112
	energy, ft-lb:	3410	2803	2290	1854	1485
	arc, inches:		+1.3	0	-6.4	-19.1
Rem. 165 PSP Core-Lokt	velocity, fps:	3075	2792	2527	2276	2040
	energy, ft-lb:	3464	2856	2339	1828	1525
	arc, inches:		+1.5	0	-7.0	-20.7

CARTRIDGE BULLET	RANGE, YARDS:	0	100	200	300	400
Rem. 180 Partition	velocity, fps:	2960	2761	2571	2389	2214
	energy, ft-lb:	3501	3047	2642	2280	1959
	arc, inches:		+1.5	0	-6.8	-19.7

.300 Winchester Short Magnum

Federal 180 Grand Slam	velocity, fps:	2970	2740	2530	2320	2130
	energy, ft-lb:	3525	3010	2555	2155	1810
	arc, inches:		+1.5	0	-7.0	-20.5
Federal 180 Trophy Bonded	velocity, fps:	2970	2730	2500	2280	2080
	energy, ft-lb:	3525	2975	2500	2085	1725
	arc, inches:		+1.5	0	-7.2	-21.0
Win. 150 Bal. Silvertip	velocity, fps:	3300	3061	2834	2619	2414
	energy, ft-lb:	3628	3121	2676	2285	1941
	arc, inches:		+1.1	0	-5.4	-15.9
Win. 180 Fail Safe	velocity, fps:	2970	2741	2524	2317	2120
	energy, ft-lb:	3526	3005	2547	2147	1797
	arc, inches:		+1.6	0	-7.0	-20.5
Win. 180 Power Point	velocity, fps:	2970	2755	2549	2353	2166
	energy, ft-lb:	3526	3034	2598	2214	1875
	arc, inches:		+1.5	0	-6.9	-20.1

.300 Weatherby Magnum

A-Square 180 Dead Tough	velocity, fps:	3180	2811	2471	2155	1863
	energy, ft-lb:	4041	3158	2440	1856	1387
	arc, inches:		+1.5	0	-7.2	-21.8
A-Square 220 Monolythic Solid	velocity, fps:	2700	2407	2133	1877	1653
	energy, ft-lb:	3561	2830	2223	1721	1334
	arc, inches:		+2.3	0	-9.8	-29.7
Federal 180 Sierra GameKing BTSP	velocity, fps:	3190	3010	2830	2660	2490
	energy, ft-lb:	4065	3610	3195	2820	2480
	arc, inches:		+1.2	0	-5.6	-16.0
Federal 180 Trophy Bonded	velocity, fps:	3190	2950	2720	2500	2290
	energy, ft-lb:	4065	3475	2955	2500	2105
	arc, inches:		+1.3	0	-5.9	-17.5
Federal 180 Tr. Bonded HE	velocity, fps:	3330	3080	2850	2750	2410
	energy, ft-lb:	4430	3795	3235	2750	2320
	arc, inches:		+1.1	0	-5.4	-15.8
Federal 180 Nosler Partition	velocity, fps:	3190	2980	2780	2590	2400
	energy, ft-lb:	4055	3540	3080	2670	2305
	arc, inches:		+1.2	0	-5.7	-16.7
Federal 180 Nosler Part. HE	velocity, fps:	3330	3110	2810	2710	2520
	energy, ft-lb:	4430	3875	3375	2935	2540
	arc, inches:		+1.0	0	-5.2	-15.1
Federal 200 Trophy Bonded	velocity, fps:	2900	2670	2440	2230	2030
	energy, ft-lb:	3735	3150	2645	2200	1820
	arc, inches:		+1.7	0	-7.6	-22.2
Hornady 150 SST	velocity, fps:	3375	3123	2882	2652	2434
	energy, ft-lb:	3793	3248	2766	2343	1973
	arc, inches:		+1.0	0	-5.4	-15.8
Hornady 180 SP	velocity, fps:	3120	2891	2673	2466	2268
	energy, ft-lb:	3890	3340	2856	2430	2055
	arc, inches:		+1.3	0	-6.2	-18.1
Hornady 180 SST	velocity, fps:	3120	2911	2711	2519	2335
	energy, ft-lb:	3890	3386	2936	2535	2180
	arc, inches:		+1.3	0	-6.2	-18.1
Rem. 180 PSP Core-Lokt	velocity, fps:	3120	2866	2627	2400	2184
	energy, ft-lb:	3890	3284	2758	2301	1905
	arc, inches:		+2.4	+2.0	-3.4	-14.9
Rem. 190 PSP boat-tail	velocity, fps:	3030	2830	2638	2455	2279
	energy, ft-lb:	3873	3378	2936	2542	2190
	arc, inches:		+1.4	0	-6.4	-18.6

Centerfire Rifle Ballistics
.300 Weatherby Magnum to .303 British

CARTRIDGE BULLET	RANGE, YARDS:	0	100	200	300	400
Rem. 200 Swift A-Frame	velocity, fps:	2925	2690	2467	2254	2052
	energy, ft-lb:	3799	3213	2701	2256	1870
	arc, inches:		+2.8	+2.3	-3.9	-17.0
Speer 180 Grand Slam	velocity, fps:	3185	2948	2722	2508	
	energy, ft-lb:	4054	3472	2962	2514	
	arc, inches:		+1.3	0	-5.9	-17.4
Wby. 150 Pointed Expanding	velocity, fps:	3540	3225	2932	2657	2399
	energy, ft-lb:	4173	3462	2862	2351	1916
	arc, inches:		+2.6	+3.3	0	-8.2
Wby. 150 Nosler Partition	velocity, fps:	3540	3263	3004	2759	2528
	energy, ft-lb:	4173	3547	3005	2536	2128
	arc, inches:		+2.5	+3.2	0	-7.7
Wby. 165 Pointed Expanding	velocity, fps:	3390	3123	2872	2634	2409
	energy, ft-lb:	4210	3573	3021	2542	2126
	arc, inches:		+2.8	+3.5	0	-8.5
Wby. 165 Nosler Bal. Tip	velocity, fps:	3350	3133	2927	2730	2542
	energy, ft-lb:	4111	3596	3138	2730	2367
	arc, inches:		+2.7	+3.4	0	-8.1
Wby. 180 Pointed Expanding	velocity, fps:	3240	3004	2781	2569	2366
	energy, ft-lb:	4195	3607	3091	2637	2237
	arc, inches:		+3.1	+3.8	0	-9.0
Wby. 180 Barnes X	velocity, fps:	3190	2995	2809	2631	2459
	energy, ft-lb:	4067	3586	3154	2766	2417
	arc, inches:		+3.1	+3.8	0	-8.7
Wby. 180 Nosler Partition	velocity, fps:	3240	3028	2826	2634	2449
	energy, ft-lb:	4195	3665	3193	2772	2396
	arc, inches:		+3.0	+3.7	0	-8.6
Wby. 200 Nosler Partition	velocity, fps:	3060	2860	2668	2485	2308
	energy, ft-lb:	4158	3631	3161	2741	2366
	arc, inches:		+3.5	+4.2	0	-9.8
Wby. 220 RN Expanding	velocity, fps:	2845	2543	2260	1996	1751
	energy, ft-lb:	3954	3158	2495	1946	1497
	arc, inches:		+4.9	+5.9	0	-14.6

.300 Dakota

Dakota 165 Barnes X	velocity, fps:	3200	2979	2769	2569	2377
	energy, ft-lb:	3751	3251	2809	2417	2070
	arc, inches:		+2.1	+1.8	-3.0	-13.2
Dakota 200 Barnes X	velocity, fps:	3000	2824	2656	2493	2336
	energy, ft-lb:	3996	3542	3131	2760	2423
	arc, inches:		+2.2	+1.5	-4.0	-15.2

.300 Pegasus

A-Square 180 SP boat-tail	velocity, fps:	3500	3319	3145	2978	2817
	energy, ft-lb:	4896	4401	3953	3544	3172
	arc, inches:		+2.3	+2.9	0	-6.8
A-Square 180 Nosler Part.	velocity, fps:	3500	3295	3100	2913	2734
	energy, ft-lb:	4896	4339	3840	3392	2988
	arc, inches:		+2.3	+3.0	0	-7.1
A-Square 180 Dead Tough	velocity, fps:	3500	3103	2740	2405	2095
	energy, ft-lb:	4896	3848	3001	2312	1753
	arc, inches:		+1.1	0	-5.7	-17.5

.300 Remington Ultra Mag

Federal 180 Trophy Bonded	velocity, fps:	3250	3000	2770	2550	2340
	energy, ft-lb:	4220	3605	3065	2590	2180
	arc, inches:		+1.2	0	-5.7	-16.8
Rem. 150 Swift Scirocco	velocity, fps:	3450	3208	2980	2762	2556
	energy, ft-lb:	3964	3427	2956	2541	2175
	arc, inches:		+1.7	+1.5	-2.6	-11.2
Rem. 180 Nosler Partition	velocity, fps:	3250	3037	2834	2640	2454
	energy, ft-lb:	4221	3686	3201	2786	2407
	arc, inches:		+2.4	+1.8	-3.0	-12.7
Rem. 180 Swift Scirocco	velocity, fps:	3250	3048	2856	2672	2495
	energy, ft-lb:	4221	3714	3260	2853	2487
	arc, inches:		+2.0	+1.7	-2.8	-12.3
Rem. 180 PSP Core-Lokt	velocity, fps:	3250	2988	2742	2508	2287
	energy, ft-lb:	3517	2974	2503	2095	1741
	arc, inches:		+2.1	+1.8	-3.1	-13.6
Rem. 200 Nosler Partition	velocity, fps:	3025	2826	2636	2454	2279
	energy, ft-lb:	4063	3547	3086	2673	2308
	arc, inches:		+2.4	+2.0	-3.4	-14.6

.30-378 Weatherby Magnum

Wby. 165 Nosler Bal. Tip	velocity, fps:	3500	3275	3062	2859	2665
	energy, ft-lb:	4488	3930	3435	2995	2603
	arc, inches:		+2.4	+3.0	0	-7.4
Wby. 180 Barnes X	velocity, fps:	3450	3243	3046	2858	2678
	energy, ft-lb:	4757	4204	3709	3264	2865
	arc, inches:		+2.4	+3.1	0	-7.4
Wby. 200 Nosler Partition	velocity, fps:	3160	2955	2759	2572	2392
	energy, ft-lb:	4434	3877	3381	2938	2541
	arc, inches:		+3.2	+3.9	0	-9.1

7.82 (.308) Warbird

Lazzeroni 150 Nosler Part.	velocity, fps:	3680	3432	3197	2975	2764
	energy, ft-lb:	4512	3923	3406	2949	2546
	arc, inches:		+2.1	+2.7	0	-6.6
Lazzeroni 180 Nosler Part.	velocity, fps:	3425	3220	3026	2839	2661
	energy, ft-lb:	4689	4147	3661	3224	2831
	arc, inches:		+2.5	+3.2	0	-7.5
Lazzeroni 200 Swift A-Fr.	velocity, fps:	3290	3105	2928	2758	2594
	energy, ft-lb:	4808	4283	3808	3378	2988
	arc, inches:		+2.7	+3.4	0	-7.9

7.65x53 Argentine

Norma 180 Soft Point	velocity, fps:	2592	2386	2189	2002	
	energy, ft-lb:	2686	2276	1916	1602	
	arc, inches:		+2.3	0	-9.6	

.303 British

Federal 150 Hi-Shok	velocity, fps:	2690	2440	2210	1980	1780
	energy, ft-lb:	2400	1980	1620	1310	1055
	arc, inches:		+2.2	0	-9.4	-27.6
Federal 180 Sierra Pro-Hunt.	velocity, fps:	2460	2230	2020	1820	1630
	energy, ft-lb:	2420	1995	1625	1315	1060
	arc, inches:		+2.8	0	-11.3	-33.2
Federal 180 Tr. Bonded HE	velocity, fps:	2590	2350	2120	1900	1700
	energy, ft-lb:	2680	2205	1795	1445	1160
	arc, inches:		+2.4	0	-10.0	-30.0
Hornady 150 Soft Point	velocity, fps:	2685	2441	2210	1992	1787
	energy, ft-lb:	2401	1984	1627	1321	1064
	arc, inches:		+2.2	0	-9.3	-27.4
Hornady 150 SP LM	velocity, fps:	2830	2570	2325	2094	1884
	energy, ft-lb:	2667	2199	1800	1461	1185
	arc, inches:		+2.0	0	-8.4	-24.6
Norma 150 Soft Point	velocity, fps:	2723	2438	2170	1920	
	energy, ft-lb:	2470	1980	1569	1228	
	arc, inches:		+2.2	0	-9.6	
PMC 180 SP boat-tail	velocity, fps:	2450	2276	2110	1951	1799
	energy, ft-lb:	2399	2071	1779	1521	1294
	arc, inches:		+2.6	0	-10.4	-30.1

Centerfire Rifle Ballistics

.303 British to .338 Winchester Magnum

CARTRIDGE BULLET	RANGE, YARDS:	0	100	200	300	400
Rem. 180 SP Core-Lokt	velocity, fps:	2460	2124	1817	1542	1311
	energy, ft-lb:	2418	1803	1319	950	687
	arc, inches, s:		0	-5.8	-23.3	
Win. 180 Power-Point	velocity, fps:	2460	2233	2018	1816	1629
	energy, ft-lb:	2418	1993	1627	1318	1060
	arc, inches, s:		0	-6.1	-20.8	

7.7x58 Japanese Arisaka

Norma 180 Soft Point	velocity, fps:	2493	2291	2099	1916	
	energy, ft-lb:	2485	2099	1761	1468	
	arc, inches:		+2.6	0	-10.5	

.32-20 Winchester

Rem. 100 Lead	velocity, fps:	1210	1021	913	834	769
	energy, ft-lb:	325	231	185	154	131
	arc, inches:		0	-31.6	-104.7	
Win. 100 Lead	velocity, fps:	1210	1021	913	834	769
	energy, ft-lb:	325	231	185	154	131
	arc, inches:		0	-32.3	-106.3	

.32 Winchester Special

Federal 170 Hi-Shok	velocity, fps:	2250	1920	1630	1370	1180
	energy, ft-lb:	1910	1395	1000	710	520
	arc, inches:		0	-8.0	-29.2	
Rem. 170 SP Core-Lokt	velocity, fps:	2250	1921	1626	1372	1175
	energy, ft-lb:	1911	1393	998	710	521
	arc, inches:		0	-8.0	-29.3	
Win. 170 Power-Point	velocity, fps:	2250	1870	1537	1267	1082
	energy, ft-lb:	1911	1320	892	606	442
	arc, inches:		0	-9.2	-33.2	

8mm Mauser (8x57)

Federal 170 Hi-Shok	velocity, fps:	2360	1970	1620	1330	1120
	energy, ft-lb:	2100	1465	995	670	475
	arc, inches:		0	-7.6	-28.5	
Norma 196 Alaska	velocity, fps:	2395	2112	1850	1611	
	Energy, ft-lb:	2714	2190	1754	1399	
	Arc, inches:		0	-6.3	-22.9	
Norma 196 Soft Point (JS)	velocity, fps:	2526	2244	1981	1737	
	energy, ft-lb:	2778	2192	1708	1314	
	arc, inches:		+2.7	0	-11.6	
Norma 196 Vulkan (JS)	velocity, fps:	2526	2276	2041	1821	
	energy, ft-lb:	2778	2256	1813	1443	
	arc, inches:		+2.6	0	-11.0	
PMC 170 Pointed Soft Point	velocity, fps:	2360	1969	1622	1333	1123
	energy, ft-lb:	2102	1463	993	671	476
	arc, inches:		+1.8	-4.5	-24.3	-63.8
Rem. 170 SP Core-Lokt	velocity, fps:	2360	1969	1622	1333	1123
	energy, ft-lb:	2102	1463	993	671	476
	arc, inches:		0	-7.6	-28.6	
Win. 170 Power-Point	velocity, fps:	2360	1969	1622	1333	1123
	energy, ft-lb:	2102	1463	993	671	476
	arc, inches:		0	-8.2	-29.8	

8mm Remington Magnum

A-Square 220 Monolythic Solid	velocity, fps:	2800	2501	2221	1959	1718
	energy, ft-lb:	3829	3055	2409	1875	1442
	arc, inches:		+2.1	0	-9.1	-27.6
Rem. 200 Swift A-Frame	velocity, fps:	2900	2623	2361	2115	1885
	energy, ft-lb:	3734	3054	2476	1987	1577
	arc, inches:		+1.8	0	-8.0	-23.9

.338-06

A-Square 200 Nos. Bal. Tip	velocity, fps:	2750	2553	2364	2184	2011
	energy, ft-lb:	3358	2894	2482	2118	1796
	arc, inches:		+1.9	0	-8.2	-23.6
A-Square 250 SP boat-tail	velocity, fps:	2500	2374	2252	2134	2019
	energy, ft-lb:	3496	3129	2816	2528	2263
	arc, inches:		+2.4	0	-9.3	-26.0
A-Square 250 Dead Tough	velocity, fps:	2500	2222	1963	1724	1507
	energy, ft-lb:	3496	2742	2139	1649	1261
	arc, inches:		+2.8	0	-11.9	-35.5

.338 Winchester Magnum

A-Square 250 SP boat-tail	velocity, fps:	2700	2568	2439	2314	2193
	energy, ft-lb:	4046	3659	3302	2972	2669
	arc, inches:		+4.4	+5.2	0	-11.7
A-Square 250 Triad	velocity, fps:	2700	2407	2133	1877	1653
	energy, ft-lb:	4046	3216	2526	1956	1516
	arc, inches:		+2.3	0	-9.8	-29.8
Federal 210 Nosler Partition	velocity, fps:	2830	2600	2390	2180	1980
	energy, ft-lb:	3735	3160	2655	2215	1835
	arc, inches:		+1.8	0	-8.0	-23.3
Federal 225 Sierra Pro-Hunt.	velocity, fps:	2780	2570	2360	2170	1980
	energy, ft-lb:	3860	3290	2780	2340	1960
	arc, inches:		+1.9	0	-8.2	-23.7
Federal 225 Trophy Bonded	velocity, fps:	2800	2560	2330	2110	1900
	energy, ft-lb:	3915	3265	2700	2220	1800
	arc, inches:		+1.9	0	-8.4	-24.5
Federal 225 Tr. Bonded HE	velocity, fps:	2940	2690	2450	2230	2010
	energy, ft-lb:	4320	3610	3000	2475	2025
	arc, inches:		+1.7	0	-7.5	-22.0
Federal 225 Barnes XLC	velocity, fps:	2800	2610	2430	2260	2090
	energy, ft-lb:	3915	3405	2950	2545	2190
	arc, inches:		+1.8	0	-7.7	-22.2
Federal 250 Nosler Partition	velocity, fps:	2660	2470	2300	2120	1960
	energy, ft-lb:	3925	3395	2925	2505	2130
	arc, inches:		+2.1	0	-8.8	-25.1
Federal 250 Nosler Part HE	velocity, fps:	2800	2610	2420	2250	2080
	energy, ft-lb:	4350	3775	3260	2805	2395
	arc, inches:		+1.8	0	-7.8	-22.5
Hornady 225 Soft Point HM	velocity, fps:	2920	2678	2449	2232	2027
	energy, ft-lb:	4259	3583	2996	2489	2053
	arc, inches:		+1.8	0	-7.6	-22.0
Norma 225 TXP Swift A-Fr.	velocity, fps:	2740	2507	2286	2075	
	energy, ft-lb:	3752	3141	2611	2153	
	arc, inches:		+2.0	0	-8.7	
Norma 250 Nosler Partition	velocity, fps:	2657	2470	2290	2118	
	energy, ft-lb:	3920	3387	2912	2490	
	arc, inches:		+2.1	0	-8.7	
PMC 225 Barnes X	velocity, fps:	2780	2619	2464	2313	2168
	energy, ft-lb:	3860	3426	3032	2673	2348
	arc, inches:		+1.8	0	-7.6	-21.6
Rem. 200 Nosler Bal. Tip	velocity, fps:	2950	2724	2509	2303	2108
	energy, ft-lb:	3866	3295	2795	2357	1973
	arc, inches:		+1.6	0	-7.1	-20.8
Rem. 210 Nosler Partition	velocity, fps:	2830	2602	2385	2179	1983
	energy, ft-lb:	3734	3157	2653	2214	1834
	arc, inches:		+1.8	0	-7.9	-23.2
Rem. 225 PSP Core-Lokt	velocity, fps:	2780	2572	2374	2184	2003
	energy, ft-lb:	3860	3305	2815	2383	2004
	arc, inches:		+1.9	0	-8.1	-23.4

Centerfire Rifle Ballistics

.338 Winchester Magnum to .348 Winchester

CARTRIDGE BULLET	RANGE, YARDS:	0	100	200	300	400
Rem. 225 Swift A-Frame	velocity, fps:	2785	2517	2266	2029	1808
	energy, ft-lb:	3871	3165	2565	2057	1633
	arc, inches:		+2.0	0	-8.8	-25.2
Rem. 250 PSP Core-Lokt	velocity, fps:	2660	2456	2261	2075	1898
	energy, ft-lb:	3927	3348	2837	2389	1999
	arc, inches:		+2.1	0	-8.9	-26.0
Speer 250 Grand Slam	velocity, fps:	2645	2442	2247	2062	
	energy, ft-lb:	3883	3309	2803	2360	
	arc, inches:		+2.2	0	-9.1	-26.2
Win. 200 Power-Point	velocity, fps:	2960	2658	2375	2110	1862
	energy, ft-lb:	3890	3137	2505	1977	1539
	arc, inches:		+2.0	0	-8.2	-24.3
Win. 200 Ballistic Silvertip	velocity, fps:	2950	2724	2509	2303	2108
	energy, ft-lb:	3864	3294	2794	2355	1972
	arc, inches:		+1.6	0	-7.1	-20.8
Win. 230 Fail Safe	velocity, fps:	2780	2573	2375	2186	2005
	energy, ft-lb:	3948	3382	2881	2441	2054
	arc, inches:		+1.9	0	-8.1	-23.4
Win. 250 Partition Gold	velocity, fps:	2650	2467	2291	2122	1960
	energy, ft-lb:	3899	3378	2914	2520	2134
	arc, inches:		+2.1	0	-8.7	-25.2

.340 Weatherby Magnum

		0	100	200	300	400
A-Square 250 SP boat-tail	velocity, fps:	2820	2684	2552	2424	2299
	energy, ft-lb:	4414	3999	3615	3261	2935
	arc, inches:		+4.0	+4.6	0	-10.6
A-Square 250 Triad	velocity, fps:	2820	2520	2238	1976	1741
	energy, ft-lb:	4414	3524	2781	2166	1683
	arc, inches:		+2.0	0	-9.0	-26.8
Federal 225 Trophy Bonded	velocity, fps:	3100	2840	2600	2370	2150
	energy, ft-lb:	4800	4035	3375	2800	2310
	arc, inches:		+1.4	0	-6.5	-19.4
Wby. 200 Pointed Expanding	velocity, fps:	3221	2946	2688	2444	2213
	energy, ft-lb:	4607	3854	3208	2652	2174
	arc, inches:		+3.3	+4.0	0	-9.9
Wby. 200 Nosler Bal. Tip	velocity, fps:	3221	2980	2753	2536	2329
	energy, ft-lb:	4607	3944	3364	2856	2409
	arc, inches:		+3.1	+3.9	0	-9.2
Wby. 210 Nosler Partition	velocity, fps:	3211	2963	2728	2505	2293
	energy, ft-lb:	4807	4093	3470	2927	2452
	arc, inches:		+3.2	+3.9	0	-9.5
Wby. 225 Pointed Expanding	velocity, fps:	3066	2824	2595	2377	2170
	energy, ft-lb:	4696	3984	3364	2822	2352
	arc, inches:		+3.6	+4.4	0	-10.7
Wby. 225 Barnes X	velocity, fps:	3001	2804	2615	2434	2260
	energy, ft-lb:	4499	3927	3416	2959	2551
	arc, inches:		+3.6	+4.3	0	-10.3
Wby. 250 Pointed Expanding	velocity, fps:	2963	2745	2537	2338	2149
	energy, ft-lb:	4873	4182	3572	3035	2563
	arc, inches:		+3.9	+4.6	0	-11.1
Wby. 250 Nosler Partition	velocity, fps:	2941	2743	2553	2371	2197
	energy, ft-lb:	4801	4176	3618	3120	2678
	arc, inches:		+3.9	+4.6	0	-10.9

.330 Dakota

		0	100	200	300	400
Dakota 200 Barnes X	velocity, fps:	3200	2971	2754	2548	2350
	energy, ft-lb:	4547	3920	3369	2882	2452
	arc, inches:		+2.1	+1.8	-3.1	-13.4
Dakota 250 Barnes X	velocity, fps:	2900	2719	2545	2378	2217
	energy, ft-lb:	4668	4103	3595	3138	2727
	arc, inches:		+2.3	+1.3	-5.0	-17.5

.338 Remington Ultra Mag

		0	100	200	300	400
Federal 250 Trophy Bonded	velocity, fps:	2860	2630	2420	2210	2020
	energy, ft-lb:	4540	3850	3245	2715	2260
	arc, inches:		+0.8	0	-7.7	-22.6
Rem. 250 Swift A-Frame	velocity, fps:	2860	2645	2440	2244	2057
	energy, ft-lb:	4540	3882	3303	2794	2347
	arc, inches:		+1.7	0	-7.6	-22.1
Rem. 250 PSP Core-Lokt	velocity, fps:	2860	2647	2443	2249	2064
	energy, ft-lb:	4540	3888	3314	2807	2363
	arc, inches:		+1.7	0	-7.6	-22.0

.338-378 Weatherby Magnum

		0	100	200	300	400
Wby. 200 Nosler Bal. Tip	velocity, fps:	3350	3102	2868	2646	2434
	energy, ft-lb:	4983	4273	3652	3109	2631
	arc, inches:	0	+2.8	+3.5	0	-8.4
Wby. 225 Barnes X	velocity, fps:	3180	2974	2778	2591	2410
	energy, ft-lb:	5052	4420	3856	3353	2902
	arc, inches:	0	+3.1	+3.8	0	-8.9
Wby. 250 Nosler Partition	velocity, fps:	3060	2856	2662	2475	2297
	energy, ft-lb:	5197	4528	3933	3401	2927
	arc, inches:	0	+3.5	+4.2	0	-9.8

8.59 (.338) Titan

		0	100	200	300	400
Lazzeroni 200 Nos. Bal. Tip	velocity, fps:	3430	3211	3002	2803	2613
	energy, ft-lb:	5226	4579	4004	3491	3033
	arc, inches:		+2.5	+3.2	0	-7.6
Lazzeroni 225 Nos. Partition	velocity, fps:	3235	3031	2836	2650	2471
	energy, ft-lb:	5229	4591	4021	3510	3052
	arc, inches:		+3.0	+3.6	0	-8.6
Lazzeroni 250 Swift A-Fr.	velocity, fps:	3100	2908	2725	2549	2379
	energy, ft-lb:	5336	4697	4123	3607	3143
	arc, inches:		+3.3	+4.0	0	-9.3

.338 A-Square

		0	100	200	300	400
A-Square 200 Nos. Bal. Tip	velocity, fps:	3500	3266	3045	2835	2634
	energy, ft-lb:	5440	4737	4117	3568	3081
	arc, inches:		+2.4	+3.1	0	-7.5
A-Square 250 SP boat-tail	velocity, fps:	3120	2974	2834	2697	2565
	energy, ft-lb:	5403	4911	4457	4038	3652
	arc, inches:		+3.1	+3.7	0	-8.5
A-Square 250 Triad	velocity, fps:	3120	2799	2500	2220	1958
	energy, ft-lb:	5403	4348	3469	2736	2128
	arc, inches:		+1.5	0	-7.1	-20.4

.338 Excaliber

		0	100	200	300	400
A-Square 200 Nos. Bal. Tip	velocity, fps:	3600	3361	3134	2920	2715
	energy, ft-lb:	5755	5015	4363	3785	3274
	arc, inches:		+2.2	+2.9	0	-6.7
A-Square 250 SP boat-tail	velocity, fps:	3250	3101	2958	2684	2553
	energy, ft-lb:	5863	5339	4855	4410	3998
	arc, inches:		+2.7	+3.4	0	-7.8
A-Square 250 Triad	velocity, fps:	3250	2922	2618	2333	2066
	energy, ft-lb:	5863	4740	3804	3021	2370
	arc, inches:		+1.3	0	-6.4	-19.2

.348 Winchester

		0	100	200	300	400
Win. 200 Silvertip	velocity, fps:	2520	2215	1931	1672	1443
	energy, ft-lb:	2820	2178	1656	1241	925
	arc, inches:		0	-6.2	-21.9	

Centerfire Rifle Ballistics

.357 Magnum to .375 H&H Magnum

CARTRIDGE BULLET	RANGE, YARDS:	0	100	200	300	400
.357 Magnum						
Federal 180 Hi-Shok HP Hollow Point	velocity, fps:	1550	1160	980	860	770
	energy, ft-lb:	960	535	385	295	235
	arc, inches:		0	-22.8	-77.9	-173.8
Win. 158 Jacketed SP	velocity, fps:	1830	1427	1138	980	883
	energy, ft-lb:	1175	715	454	337	274
	arc, inches:		0	-16.2	-57.0	-128.3
.35 Remington						
Federal 200 Hi-Shok	velocity, fps:	2080	1700	1380	1140	1000
	energy, ft-lb:	1920	1280	840	575	445
	arc, inches:		0	-10.7	-39.3	
Rem. 150 PSP Core-Lokt	velocity, fps:	2300	1874	1506	1218	1039
	energy, ft-lb:	1762	1169	755	494	359
	arc, inches:		0	-8.6	-32.6	
Rem. 200 SP Core-Lokt	velocity, fps:	2080	1698	1376	1140	1001
	energy, ft-lb:	1921	1280	841	577	445
	arc, inches:		0	-10.7	-40.1	
Win. 200 Power-Point	velocity, fps:	2020	1646	1335	1114	985
	energy, ft-lb:	1812	1203	791	551	431
	arc, inches:		0	-12.1	-43.9	
.356 Winchester						
Win. 200 Power-Point	velocity, fps:	2460	2114	1797	1517	1284
	energy, ft-lb:	2688	1985	1434	1022	732
	arc, inches:		+1.6	-3.8	-20.1	-51.2
.358 Winchester						
Win. 200 Silvertip	velocity, fps:	2490	2171	1876	1610	1379
	energy, ft-lb:	2753	2093	1563	1151	844
	arc, inches:		+1.5	-3.6	-18.6	-47.2
.35 Whelen						
Federal 225 Trophy Bonded	velocity, fps:	2600	2400	2200	2020	1840
	energy, ft-lb:	3375	2865	2520	2030	1690
	arc, inches:		+2.3	0	-9.4	-27.3
Rem. 200 Pointed Soft Point	velocity, fps:	2675	2378	2100	1842	1606
	energy, ft-lb:	3177	2510	1958	1506	1145
	arc, inches:		+2.3	0	-10.3	-30.8
Rem. 250 Pointed Soft Point	velocity, fps:	2400	2197	2005	1823	1652
	energy, ft-lb:	3197	2680	2230	1844	1515
	arc, inches:		+1.3	-3.2	-16.6	-40.0
.358 Norma Magnum						
A-Square 275 Triad	velocity, fps:	2700	2394	2108	1842	1653
	energy, ft-lb:	4451	3498	2713	2072	1668
	arc, inches:		+2.3	0	-10.1	-29.8
Norma 250 TXP Swift A-Fr.	velocity, fps:	2723	2467	2225	1996	
	energy, ft-lb:	4117	3379	2748	2213	
	arc, inches:		+2.1	0	-9.1	
Norma 250 Woodleigh	velocity, fps:	2799	2442	2112	1810	
	energy, ft-lb:	4350	3312	2478	1819	
	arc, inches:		+2.2	0	-10.0	
.358 STA						
A-Square 275 Triad	velocity, fps:	2850	2562	2292	2039	1764
	energy, ft-lb:	4959	4009	3208	2539	1899
	arc, inches:		+1.9	0	-8.6	-26.1
9.3x57						
Norma 232 Vulkan	velocity, fps:	2329	2031	1757	1512	
	energy, ft-lb:	2795	2126	1591	1178	
	arc, inches:		+3.5	0	-14.9	
Norma 286 Alaska	velocity, fps:	2067	1857	1662	1484	
	energy, ft-lb:	2714	2190	1754	1399	
	arc, inches:				+4.3	0-17.0
9.3x62						
A-Square 286 Triad	velocity, fps:	2360	2089	1844	1623	1369
	energy, ft-lb:	3538	2771	2157	1670	1189
	arc, inches:		+3.0	0	-13.1	-42.2
Norma 232 Vulkan	velocity, fps:	2625	2327	2049	1792	
	energy, ft-lb:	3551	2791	2164	1655	
	arc, inches:		+2.5	0	-10.8	
Norma 232 Oryx	velocity, fps:	2625	2294	1988	1708	
	energy, ft-lb:	3535	2700	2028	1497	
	arc, inches:		+2.5	0	-11.4	
Norma 286 Plastic Point	velocity, fps:	2362	2141	1931	1736	
	energy, ft-lb:	3544	2911	2370	1914	
	arc, inches:		+3.1	0	-12.4	
Norma 286 Alaska	velocity, fps:	2362	2135	1920	1720	
	energy, ft-lb:	3544	2894	2342	1879	
	arc, inches:		+3.1	0	-12.5	
9.3x64						
A-Square 286 Triad	velocity, fps:	2700	2391	2103	1835	1602
	energy, ft-lb:	4629	3630	2808	2139	1631
	arc, inches:		+2.3	0	-10.1	-30.8
9.3x74 R						
A-Square 286 Triad	velocity, fps:	2360	2089	1844	1623	
	energy, ft-lb:	3538	2771	2157	1670	
	arc, inches:		+3.6	0	-14.0	
Norma 232 Vulkan	velocity, fps:	2625	2327	2049	1792	
	energy, ft-lb:	3551	2791	2164	1655	
	arc, inches:		+2.5	0	-10.8	
Norma 232 Oryx	velocity, fps:	2526	2191	1883	1605	
	energy, ft-lb:	3274	2463	1819	1322	
	arc, inches:		+2.9	0	-12.8	
Norma 286 Alaska	velocity, fps:	2362	2135	1920	1720	
	energy, ft-lb:	3544	2894	2342	1879	
	arc, inches:		+3.1	0	-12.5	
Norma 286 Plastic Point	velocity, fps:	2362	2135	1920	1720	
	energy, ft-lb:	3544	2894	2342	1879	
	arc, inches:		+3.1	0	-12.5	
.375 Winchester						
Win. 200 Power-Point	velocity, fps:	2200	1841	1526	1268	1089
	energy, ft-lb:	2150	1506	1034	714	
	arc, inches:		0	-9.5	-33.8	
.375 H&H Magnum						
A-Square 300 SP boat-tail	velocity, fps:	2550	2415	2284	2157	2034
	energy, ft-lb:	4331	3884	3474	3098	2755
	arc, inches:		+5.2	+6.0	0	-13.3
A-Square 300 Triad	velocity, fps:	2550	2251	1973	1717	1496
	energy, ft-lb:	4331	3375	2592	1964	1491
	arc, inches:		+2.7	0	-11.7	-35.1
Federal 250 Trophy Bonded	velocity, fps:	2670	2360	2080	1820	1580
	energy, ft-lb:	3955	3100	2400	1830	1380
	arc, inches:		+2.4	0	-10.4	-31.7
Federal 270 Hi-Shok	velocity, fps:	2690	2420	2170	1920	1700
	energy, ft-lb:	4340	3510	2810	2220	1740
	arc, inches:		+2.4	0	-10.9	-33.3

Centerfire Rifle Ballistics

.375 H&H Magnum to .378 Weatherby

CARTRIDGE BULLET	RANGE, YARDS:	0	100	200	300	400
Federal 300 Hi-Shok	velocity, fps:	2530	2270	2020	1790	1580
	energy, ft-lb:	4265	3425	2720	2135	1665
	arc, inches:		+2.6	0	-11.2	-33.3
Federal 300 Nosler Partition	velocity, fps:	2530	2320	2120	1930	1750
	energy, ft-lb:	4265	3585	2995	2475	2040
	arc, inches:		+2.5	0	-10.3	-29.9
Federal 300 Trophy Bonded	velocity, fps:	2530	2280	2040	1810	1610
	energy, ft-lb:	4265	3450	2765	2190	1725
	arc, inches:		+2.6	0	-10.9	-32.8
Federal 300 Tr. Bonded HE	velocity, fps:	2700	2440	2190	1960	1740
	energy, ft-lb:	4855	3960	3195	2550	2020
	arc, inches:		+2.2	0	-9.4	-28.0
Federal 300 Trophy Bonded Sledgehammer Solid	velocity, fps:	2530	2160	1820	1520	1280
	energy, ft-lb:	4265	3105	2210	1550	1090
	arc, inches, s:		0	-6.0	-22.7	-54.6
Hornady 270 SP HM	velocity, fps:	2870	2620	2385	2162	1957
	energy, ft-lb:	4937	4116	3408	2802	2296
	arc, inches:		+2.2	0	-8.4	-23.9
Hornady 300 FMJ RN HM	velocity, fps:	2705	2376	2072	1804	1560
	energy, ft-lb:	4873	3760	2861	2167	1621
	arc, inches:		+2.7	0	-10.8	-32.1
Norma 300 Soft Point	velocity, fps:	2549	2211	1900	1619	
	energy, ft-lb:	4329	3258	2406	1747	
	arc, inches:		+2.8	0	-12.6	
Norma 300 TXP Swift A-Fr.	velocity, fps:	2559	2296	2049	1818	
	energy, ft-lb:	4363	3513	2798	2203	
	arc, inches:		+2.6	0	-10.9	
Norma 300 Barnes Solid	velocity, fps:	2493	2061	1677	1356	
	energy, ft-lb:	4141	2829	1873	1234	
	arc, inches:		+3.4	0	-16.0	
PMC 270 PSP	velocity, fps:					
	energy, ft-lb:					
	arc, inches:					
PMC 270 Barnes X	velocity, fps:	2690	2528	2372	2221	2076
	energy, ft-lb:	4337	3831	3371	2957	2582
	arc, inches:		+2.0	0	-8.2	-23.4
PMC 300 Barnes X	velocity, fps:	2530	2389	2252	2120	1993
	energy, ft-lb:	4263	3801	3378	2994	2644
	arc, inches:		+2.3	0	-9.2	-26.1
Rem. 270 Soft Point	velocity, fps:	2690	2420	2166	1928	1707
	energy, ft-lb:	4337	3510	2812	2228	1747
	arc, inches:		+2.2	0	-9.7	-28.7
Rem. 300 Swift A-Frame	velocity, fps:	2530	2245	1979	1733	1512
	energy, ft-lb:	4262	3357	2608	2001	1523
	arc, inches:		+2.7	0	-11.7	-35.0
Speer 285 Grand Slam	velocity, fps:	2610	2365	2134	1916	
	energy, ft-lb:	4310	3540	2883	2323	
	arc, inches:		+2.4	0	-9.9	
Speer 300 African GS Tungsten Solid	velocity, fps:	2609	2277	1970	1690	
	energy, ft-lb:	4534	3453	2585	1903	
	arc, inches:		+2.6	0	-11.7	-35.6
Win. 270 Fail Safe	velocity, fps:	2670	2447	2234	2033	1842
	energy, ft-lb:	4275	3590	2994	2478	2035
	arc, inches:		+2.2	0	-9.1	-28.7
Win. 300 Fail Safe	velocity, fps:	2530	2336	2151	1974	1806
	energy, ft-lb:	4265	3636	3082	2596	2173
	arc, inches:		+2.4	0	-10.0	-26.9

.375 Dakota

		0	100	200	300	400
Dakota 270 Barnes X	velocity, fps:	2800	2617	2441	2272	2109
	energy, ft-lb:	4699	4104	3571	3093	2666
	arc, inches:		+2.3	+1.0	-6.1	-19.9
Dakota 300 Barnes X	velocity, fps:	2600	2316	2051	1804	1579
	energy, ft-lb:	4502	3573	2800	2167	1661
	arc, inches:		+2.4	-0.1	-11.0	-32.7

.375 Weatherby

		0	100	200	300	400
A-Square 300 SP boat-tail	velocity, fps:	2700	2560	2425	2293	2166
	energy, ft-lb:	4856	4366	3916	3503	3125
	arc, inches:		+4.5	+5.2	0	-11.9
A-Square 300 Triad	velocity, fps:	2700	2391	2103	1835	1602
	energy, ft-lb:	4856	3808	2946	2243	1710
	arc, inches:		+2.3	0	-10.1	-30.8

.375 JRS

		0	100	200	300	400
A-Square 300 SP boat-tail	velocity, fps:	2700	2560	2425	2293	2166
	energy, ft-lb:	4856	4366	3916	3503	3125
	arc, inches:		+4.5	+5.2	0	-11.9
A-Square 300 Triad	velocity, fps:	2700	2391	2103	1835	1602
	energy, ft-lb:	4856	3808	2946	2243	1710
	arc, inches:		+2.3	0	-10.1	-30.8

.375 Remington Ultra Mag

		0	100	200	300	400
Rem. 270 Soft Point	velocity, fps:	2900	2558	2241	1947	1678
	energy, fps:	5041	3922	3010	2272	1689
	arc, inches:		+1.9	0	-9.2	-27.8
Rem. 300 Swift A-Frame	velocity, fps:	2760	2505	2263	2035	1822
	energy, ft-lb:	5073	4178	3412	2759	2210
	arc, inches:		+2.0	0	-8.8	-26.1

.375 A-Square

		0	100	200	300	400
A-Square 300 SP boat-tail	velocity, fps:	2920	2773	2631	2494	2360
	energy, ft-lb:	5679	5123	4611	4142	3710
	arc, inches:		+3.7	+4.4	0	-9.8
A-Square 300 Triad	velocity, fps:	2920	2596	2294	2012	1762
	energy, ft-lb:	5679	4488	3505	2698	2068
	arc, inches:		+1.8	0	-8.5	-25.5

.378 Weatherby

		0	100	200	300	400
A-Square 300 SP boat-tail	velocity, fps:	2900	2754	2612	2475	2342
	energy, ft-lb:	5602	5051	4546	4081	3655
	arc, inches:		+3.8	+4.4	0	-10.0
A-Square 300 Triad	velocity, fps:	2900	2577	2276	1997	1747
	energy, ft-lb:	5602	4424	3452	2656	2034
	arc, inches:		+1.9	0	-8.7	-25.9
Wby. 270 Pointed Expanding	velocity, fps:	3180	2921	2677	2445	2225
	energy, ft-lb:	6062	5115	4295	3583	2968
	arc, inches:		+1.3	0	-6.1	-18.1
Wby. 270 Barnes X	velocity, fps:	3150	2954	2767	2587	2415
	energy, ft-lb:	5948	5232	4589	4013	3495
	arc, inches:		+1.2	0	-5.8	-16.7
Wby. 300 RN Expanding	velocity, fps:	2925	2558	2220	1908	1627
	energy, ft-lb:	5699	4360	3283	2424	1764
	arc, inches:		+1.9	0	-9.0	-27.8
Wby. 300 FMJ	velocity, fps:	2925	2591	2280	1991	1725
	energy, ft-lb:	5699	4470	3461	2640	1983
	arc, inches:		+1.8	0	-8.6	-26.1

Centerfire Rifle Ballistics

.38-40 Winchester to .44 Remington Magnum

CARTRIDGE BULLET	RANGE, YARDS:	0	100	200	300	400
.38-40 Winchester						
Win. 180 Soft Point	velocity, fps:	1160	999	901	827	
	energy, ft-lb:	538	399	324	273	
	arc, inches:		0	-23.4	-75.2	
.38-55 Winchester						
Win. 255 Soft Point	velocity, fps:	1320	1190	1091	1018	
	energy, ft-lb:	987	802	674	587	
	arc, inches:		0	-33.9	-110.6	
.450/.400 (3")						
A-Square 400 Triad	velocity, fps:	2150	1910	1690	1490	
	energy, ft-lb:	4105	3241	2537	1972	
	arc, inches:		+4.4	0	-16.5	
.450/.400 (3 1/4")						
A-Square 400 Triad	velocity, fps:	2150	1910	1690	1490	
	energy, ft-lb:	4105	3241	2537	1972	
	arc, inches:		+4.4	0	-16.5	
.404 Jeffery						
A-Square 400 Triad	velocity, fps:	2150	1901	1674	1468	1299
	energy, ft-lb:	4105	3211	2489	1915	1499
	arc, inches:		+4.1	0	-16.4	-49.1
.405 Winchester						
Hornady 300 Flatpoint	velocity, fps:	2200	1851	1545	1296	
	energy, ft-lb:	3224	2282	1589	1119	
	arc, inches:		+4.6	0	-19.5	
.416 Taylor						
A-Square 400 Triad	velocity, fps:	2350	2093	1853	1634	1443
	energy, ft-lb:	4905	3892	3049	2371	1849
	arc, inches:		+3.2	0	-13.6	-39.8
.416 Hoffman						
A-Square 400 Triad	velocity, fps:	2380	2122	1879	1658	1464
	energy, ft-lb:	5031	3998	3136	2440	1903
	arc, inches:		+3.1	0	-13.1	-38.7
.416 Remington Magnum						
A-Square 400 Triad	velocity, fps:	2380	2122	1879	1658	1464
	energy, ft-lb:	5031	3998	3136	2440	1903
	arc, inches:		+3.1	0	-13.2	-38.7
Federal 400 Trophy Bonded Sledgehammer Solid	velocity, fps:	2400	2150	1920	1700	1500
	energy, ft-lb:	5115	4110	3260	2565	2005
	arc, inches:		0	-6.0	-21.6	-49.2
Federal 400 Trophy Bonded	velocity, fps:	2400	2180	1970	1770	1590
	energy, ft-lb:	5115	4215	3440	2785	2245
	arc, inches:		0	-5.8	-20.6	-46.9
Rem. 400 Swift A-Frame	velocity, fps:	2400	2175	1962	1763	1579
	energy, ft-lb:	5115	4201	3419	2760	2214
	arc, inches:		+1.3	-3.3	-17.0	-41.9
.416 Rigby						
A-Square 400 Triad	velocity, fps:	2400	2140	1897	1673	1478
	energy, ft-lb:	5115	4069	3194	2487	1940
	arc, inches:		+3.0	0	-12.9	-38.0
Federal 400 Trophy Bonded	velocity, fps:	2370	2150	1940	1750	1570
	energy, ft-lb:	4990	4110	3350	2715	2190
	arc, inches:		0	-6.0	-21.3	-48.1
Federal 400 Trophy Bonded Sledgehammer Solid	velocity, fps:	2370	2120	1890	1660	1460
	energy, ft-lb:	4990	3975	3130	2440	1895
	arc, inches:		0	-6.3	-22.5	-51.5
Federal 410 Woodleigh Weldcore	velocity, fps:	2370	2110	1870	1640	1440
	energy, ft-lb:	5115	4050	3165	2455	1895
	arc, inches:		0	-7.4	-24.8	-55.0
Federal 410 Solid	velocity, fps:	2370	2110	2870	1640	1440
	energy, ft-lb:	5115	4050	3165	2455	1895
	arc, inches:		0	-7.4	-24.8	-55.0
Norma 400 TXP Swift A-Fr.	velocity, fps:	2350	2127	1917	1721	
	energy, ft-lb:	4906	4021	3266	2632	
	arc, inches:		+3.1	0	-12.5	
Norma 400 Barnes Solid	velocity, fps:	2297	1930	1604	1330	
	energy, ft-lb:	4687	3310	2284	1571	
	arc, inches:		+3.9	0	-17.7	
.416 Rimmed						
A-Square 400 Triad	velocity, fps:	2400	2140	1897	1673	
	energy, ft-lb:	5115	4069	3194	2487	
	arc, inches:		+3.3	0	-13.2	
.416 Dakota						
Dakota 400 Barnes X	velocity, fps:	2450	2294	2143	1998	1859
	energy, ft-lb:	5330	4671	4077	3544	3068
	arc, inches:		+2.5	-0.2	-10.5	-29.4
.416 Weatherby						
A-Square 400 Triad	velocity, fps:	2600	2328	2073	1834	1624
	energy, ft-lb:	6004	4813	3816	2986	2343
	arc, inches:		+2.5	0	-10.5	-31.6
Wby. 350 Barnes X	velocity, fps:	2850	2673	2503	2340	2182
	energy, ft-lb:	6312	5553	4870	4253	3700
	arc, inches:		+1.7	0	-7.2	-20.9
Wby. 400 Swift A-Fr.	velocity, fps:	2650	2426	2213	2011	1820
	energy, ft-lb:	6237	5227	4350	3592	2941
	arc, inches:		+2.2	0	-9.3	-27.1
Wby. 400 RN Expanding	velocity, fps:	2700	2417	2152	1903	1676
	energy, ft-lb:	6474	5189	4113	3216	2493
	arc, inches:		+2.3	0	-9.7	-29.3
Wby. 400 Monolithic Solid	velocity, fps:	2700	2411	2140	1887	1656
	energy, ft-lb:	6474	5162	4068	3161	2435
	arc, inches:		+2.3	0	-9.8	-29.7
10.57 (.416) Meteor						
Lazzeroni 400 Swift A-Fr.	velocity, fps:	2730	2532	2342	2161	1987
	energy, ft-lb:	6621	5695	4874	4147	3508
	arc, inches:		+1.9	0	-8.3	-24.0
.425 Express						
A-Square 400 Triad	velocity, fps:	2400	2136	1888	1662	1465
	energy, ft-lb:	5115	4052	3167	2454	1906
	arc, inches:		+3.0	0	-13.1	-38.3
.44-40 Winchester						
Rem. 200 Soft Point	velocity, fps:	1190	1006	900	822	756
	energy, ft-lb:	629	449	360	300	254
	arc, inches:		0	-33.1	-108.7	-235.2
Win. 200 Soft Point	velocity, fps:	1190	1006	900	822	756
	energy, ft-lb:	629	449	360	300	254
	arc, inches:		0	-33.3	-109.5	-237.4
.44 Remington Magnum						
Federal 240 Hi-Shok HP	velocity, fps:	1760	1380	1090	950	860
	energy, ft-lb:	1650	1015	640	485	395
	arc, inches:		0	-17.4	-60.7	-136.0

Centerfire Rifle Ballistics
.44 Remington Magnum to .460 Short A-Square

CARTRIDGE BULLET	RANGE, YARDS:	0	100	200	300	400
Rem. 210 Semi-Jacketed HP	velocity, fps:	1920	1477	1155	982	880
	energy, ft-lb:	1719	1017	622	450	361
	arc, inches:		0	-14.7	-55.5	-131.3
Rem. 240 Soft Point	velocity, fps:	1760	1380	1114	970	878
	energy, ft-lb:	1650	1015	661	501	411
	arc, inches:		0	-17.0	-61.4	-143.0
Rem. 240 Semi-Jacketed Hollow Point	velocity, fps:	1760	1380	1114	970	878
	energy, ft-lb:	1650	1015	661	501	411
	arc, inches:		0	-17.0	-61.4	-143.0
Rem. 275 JHP Core-Lokt	velocity, fps:	1580	1293	1093	976	896
	energy, ft-lb:	1524	1020	730	582	490
	arc, inches:		0	-19.4	-67.5	-210.8
Win. 210 Silvertip HP	velocity, fps:	1580	1198	993	879	795
	energy, ft-lb:	1164	670	460	361	295
	arc, inches:		0	-22.4	-76.1	-168.0
Win. 240 Hollow Soft Point	velocity, fps:	1760	1362	1094	953	861
	energy, ft-lb:	1650	988	638	484	395
	arc, inches:		0	-18.1	-65.1	-150.3

.444 Marlin

Rem. 240 Soft Point	velocity, fps:	2350	1815	1377	1087	941
	energy, ft-lb:	2942	1755	1010	630	472
	arc, inches:		+2.2	-5.4	-31.4	-86.7
Hornady 265 FP LM	velocity, fps:	2335	1913	1551	1266	
	energy, ft-lb:	3208	2153	1415	943	
	arc, inches:		+2.0	-4.9	-26.5	

.45-70 Government

Black Hills 405 FPL	velocity, fps:	1250				
	energy, ft-lb:					
	arc, inches:					
Federal 300 Sierra Pro-Hunt. HP FN	velocity, fps:	1880	1650	1430	1240	1110
	energy, ft-lb:	2355	1815	1355	1015	810
	arc, inches:		0	-11.5	-39.7	-89.1
PMC 350 FNSP	velocity, fps:					
	energy, ft-lb:					
	arc, inches:					
Rem. 300 Jacketed HP	velocity, fps:	1810	1497	1244	1073	969
	energy, ft-lb:	2182	1492	1031	767	625
	arc, inches:		0	-13.8	-50.1	-115.7
Rem. 405 Soft Point	velocity, fps:	1330	1168	1055	977	918
	energy, ft-lb:	1590	1227	1001	858	758
	arc, inches:		0	-24.0	-78.6	-169.4
Win. 300 Jacketed HP	velocity, fps:	1880	1650	1425	1235	1105
	energy, ft-lb:	2355	1815	1355	1015	810
	arc, inches:		0	-12.8	-44.3	-95.5
Win. 300 Partition Gold	velocity, fps:	1880	1558	1292	1103	988
	energy, ft-lb:	2355	1616	1112	811	651
	arc, inches:		0	-12.9	-46.0	-104.9

.450 Nitro Express (3 1/4")

A-Square 465 Triad	velocity, fps:	2190	1970	1765	1577	
	energy, ft-lb:	4952	4009	3216	2567	
	arc, inches:		+4.3	0	-15.4	

.450 #2

A-Square 465 Triad	velocity, fps:	2190	1970	1765	1577	
	energy, ft-lb:	4952	4009	3216	2567	
	arc, inches:		+4.3	0	-15.4	

.458 Winchester Magnum

A-Square 465 Triad	velocity, fps:	2220	1999	1791	1601	1433
	energy, ft-lb:	5088	4127	3312	2646	2121
	arc, inches:		+3.6	0	-14.7	-42.5
Federal 350 Soft Point	velocity, fps:	2470	1990	1570	1250	1060
	energy, ft-lb:	4740	3065	1915	1205	870
	arc, inches:		0	-7.5	-29.1	-71.1
Federal 400 Trophy Bonded	velocity, fps:	2380	2170	1960	1770	1590
	energy, ft-lb:	5030	4165	3415	2785	2255
	arc, inches:		0	-5.9	-20.9	-47.1
Federal 500 Solid	velocity, fps:	2090	1870	1670	1480	1320
	energy, ft-lb:	4850	3880	3085	2440	1945
	arc, inches:		0	-8.5	-29.5	-66.2
Federal 500 Trophy Bonded	velocity, fps:	2090	1870	1660	1480	1310
	energy, ft-lb:	4850	3870	3065	2420	1915
	arc, inches:		0	-8.5	-29.7	-66.8
Federal 500 Trophy Bonded Sledgehammer Solid	velocity, fps:	2090	1860	1650	1460	1300
	energy, ft-lb:	4850	3845	3025	2365	1865
	arc, inches:		0	-8.6	-30.0	-67.8
Federal 510 Soft Point	velocity, fps:	2090	1820	1570	1360	1190
	energy, ft-lb:	4945	3730	2790	2080	1605
	arc, inches:		0	-9.1	-32.3	-73.9
Hornady 500 FMJ-RN HM	velocity, fps:	2260	1984	1735	1512	
	energy, ft-lb:	5670	4368	3341	2538	
	arc, inches:		0	-7.4	-26.4	
Norma 500 TXP Swift A-Fr.	velocity, fps:	2116	1903	1705	1524	
	energy, ft-lb:	4972	4023	3228	2578	
	arc, inches:		+4.1	0	-16.1	
Norma 500 Barnes Solid	velocity, fps:	2067	1750	1472	1245	
	energy, ft-lb:	4745	3401	2405	1721	
	arc, inches:		+4.9	0	-21.2	
Rem. 450 Swift A-Frame PSP	velocity, fps:	2150	1901	1671	1465	1289
	energy, ft-lb:	4618	3609	2789	2144	1659
	arc, inches:		0	-8.2	-28.9	
Speer 500 African GS Tungsten Solid	velocity, fps:	2120	1845	1596	1379	
	energy, ft-lb:	4989	3780	2828	2111	
	arc, inches:		0	-8.8	-31.3	
Speer African Grand Slam	velocity, fps:	2120	1853	1609	1396	
	energy, ft-lb:	4989	3810	2875	2163	
	arc, inches:		0	-8.7	-30.8	
Win. 510 Soft Point	velocity, fps:	2040	1770	1527	1319	1157
	energy, ft-lb:	4712	3547	2640	1970	1516
	arc, inches:		0	-10.3	-35.6	

.458 Lott

A-Square 465 Triad	velocity, fps:	2380	2150	1932	1730	1551
	energy, ft-lb:	5848	4773	3855	3091	2485
	arc, inches:		+3.0	0	-12.5	-36.4
Hornady 500 RN	velocity, fps:	2300	2022	1776	1551	
	energy, ft-lb:	5872	4537	3502	2671	
	arc, inches:		+3.4	0	-1.43	

.450 Ackley

A-Square 465 Triad	velocity, fps:	2400	2169	1950	1747	1567
	energy, ft-lb:	5947	4857	3927	3150	2534
	arc, inches:		+2.9	0	-12.2	-35.8

.460 Short A-Square

A-Square 500 Triad	velocity, fps:	2420	2198	1987	1789	1613
	energy, ft-lb:	6501	5362	4385	3553	2890
	arc, inches:		+2.9	0	-11.6	-34.2

Rifles • 493

Centerfire Rifle Ballistics

.450 Dakota to .700 Nitro Express

CARTRIDGE BULLET	RANGE, YARDS:	0	100	200	300	400
.450 Dakota						
Dakota 500 Barnes Solid	velocity, fps:	2450	2235	2030	1838	1658
	energy, ft-lb:	6663	5544	4576	3748	3051
	arc, inches:		+2.5	-0.6	-12.0	-33.8
.460 Weatherby Magnum						
A-Square 500 Triad	velocity, fps:	2580	2349	2131	1923	1737
	energy, ft-lb:	7389	6126	5040	4107	3351
	arc, inches:		+2.4	0	-10.0	-29.4
Wby. 450 Barnes X	velocity, fps:	2700	2518	2343	2175	2013
	energy, ft-lb:	7284	6333	5482	4725	4050
	arc, inches:		+2.0	0	-8.4	-24.1
Wby. 500 RN Expanding	velocity, fps:	2600	2301	2022	1764	1533
	energy, ft-lb:	7504	5877	4539	3456	2608
	arc, inches:		+2.6	0	-11.1	-33.5
Wby. 500 FMJ	velocity, fps:	2600	2309	2037	1784	1557
	energy, ft-lb:	7504	5917	4605	3534	2690
	arc, inches:		+2.5	0	-10.9	-33.0
.500/.465						
A-Square 480 Triad	velocity, fps:	2150	1928	1722	1533	
	energy, ft-lb:	4926	3960	3160	2505	
	arc, inches:		+4.3	0	-16.0	
.470 Nitro Express						
A-Square 500 Triad	velocity, fps:	2150	1912	1693	1494	
	energy, ft-lb:	5132	4058	3182	2478	
	arc, inches:		+4.4	0	-16.5	
Federal 500 Woodleigh Weldcore	velocity, fps:	2150	1890	1650	1440	1270
	energy, ft-lb:	5130	3965	3040	2310	1790
	arc, inches:		0	-9.3	-31.3	-69.7
Federal 500 Woodleigh Weldcore Solid	velocity, fps:	2150	1890	1650	1440	1270
	energy, ft-lb:	5130	3965	3040	2310	1790
	arc, inches:		0	-9.3	-31.3	-69.7
Federal 500 Trophy Bonded	velocity, fps:	2150	1940	1740	1560	1400
	energy, ft-lb:	5130	4170	3360	2695	2160
	arc, inches:		0	-7.8	-27.1	-60.8
Federal 500 Trophy Bonded Sledgehammer Solid	velocity, fps:	2150	1940	1740	1560	1400
	ft-lb:	5130	4170	3360	2695	2160
	arc, inches:		0	-7.8	-27.1	-60.8
.470 Capstick						
A-Square 500 Triad	velocity, fps:	2400	2172	1958	1761	1553
	energy, ft-lb:	6394	5236	4255	3445	2678
	arc, inches:		+2.9	0	-11.9	-36.1
475 #2						
A-Square 480 Triad	velocity, fps:	2200	1964	1744	1544	
	energy, ft-lb:	5158	4109	3240	2539	
	arc, inches:		+4.1	0	-15.6	
.475 #2 Jeffery						
A-Square 500 Triad	velocity, fps:	2200	1966	1748	1550	
	energy, ft-lb:	5373	4291	3392	2666	
	arc, inches:		+4.1	0	-15.6	
.495 A-Square						
A-Square 570 Triad	velocity, fps:	2350	2117	1896	1693	1513
	energy, ft-lb:	6989	5671	4552	3629	2899
	arc, inches:		+3.1	0	-13.0	-37.8
.500 Nitro Express (3")						
A-Square 570 Triad	velocity, fps:	2150	1928	1722	1533	
	energy, ft-lb:	5850	4703	3752	2975	
	arc, inches:		+4.3	0	-16.1	
.500 A-Square						
A-Square 600 Triad	velocity, fps:	2470	2235	2013	1804	1620
	energy, ft-lb:	8127	6654	5397	4336	3495
	arc, inches:		+2.7	0	-11.3	-33.5
.505 Gibbs						
A-Square 525 Triad	velocity, fps:	2300	2063	1840	1637	
	energy, ft-lb:	6166	4962	3948	3122	
	arc, inches:		+3.6	0	-14.2	
.577 Nitro Express						
A-Square 750 Triad	velocity, fps:	2050	1811	1595	1401	
	energy, ft-lb:	6998	5463	4234	3267	
	arc, inches:		+4.9	0	-18.5	
.577 Tyrannosaur						
A-Square 750 Triad	velocity, fps:	2460	2197	1950	1723	1516
	energy, ft-lb:	10077	8039	6335	4941	3825
	arc, inches:		+2.8	0	-12.1	-36.0
.600 Nitro Express						
A-Square 900 Triad	velocity, fps:	1950	1680	1452	1336	
	energy, ft-lb:	7596	5634	4212	3564	
	arc, inches:		+5.6	0	-20.7	
.700 Nitro Express						
A-Square 1000 Monolithic Solid	velocity, fps:	1900	1669	1461	1288	
	energy, ft-lb:	8015	6188	4740	3685	
	arc, inches:		+5.8	0	-22.2	

Centerfire Handgun Ballistics

Centerfire Handgun Ballistics

Data shown here is taken from manufacturers' charts; your chronograph readings may vary. Barrel lengths for pistol data vary, and depend in part on which pistols are typically chambered in a given cartridge. Velocity variations due to barrel length depend on the baseline bullet speed and the load. Velocity for the .30 Carbine, normally a rifle cartridge, was determined in a pistol barrel. Listings are current as of February the year *Shooter's Bible* appears (not the cover year). Listings are not intended as recommendations. For example, the data for the .25 Auto gives velocity and energy readings to 100 yards. Few handgunners would call the little .25 a 100-yard cartridge.

Abbreviations: Bullets are designated by loading company, weight (in grains) and type, with these abbreviations for shape and construction: **BJHP**=Brass-Jacketed Hollowpoint; **FN**=Flat Nose; **FMC**=Full Metal Case; **FMJ**=Full Metal Jacket; **HP**=Hollowpoint; **L**=Lead; **LF**=Lead-Free; **+P**=a more powerful load than traditionally manufactured for that round; **RN**=Round Nose; **SFHP**=Starfire (PMC) Hollowpoint; **SP**=Softpoint; **SWC**=Semi Wadcutter; **TMJ**=Totally Metal Jacket (Speer); **WC**=Wadcutter; **CEPP**, **SXT** and **XTP** are trademarked designations of Lapua, Winchester and Hornady, respectively.

.25 Auto to .32 S&W Long

CARTRIDGE BULLET	RANGE, YARDS:	0	25	50	75	100
.25 Auto						
Federal 50 FMJ	velocity, fps:	760	750	730	720	700
	energy, ft-lb	65	60	60	55	55
Hornady 35 JHP/XTP	velocity, fps:	900		813		742
	energy, ft-lb	63		51		43
Magtech 50 FMC	velocity, fps:	760		707		659
	energy, ft-lb	64		56		48
PMC 50 FMJ	velocity, fps:	754	730	707	685	663
	energy, ft-lb	62				
Rem. 50 Metal Case	velocity, fps:	760		707		659
	energy, ft-lb	64		56		48
Speer 35 Gold Dot	velocity, fps:	900		816		747
	energy, ft-lb	63		52		43
Speer 50 TMJ (and Blazer)	velocity, fps:	760		717		677
	energy, ft-lb	64		57		51
Win. 45 Expanding Point	velocity, fps:	815		729		655
	energy, ft-lb	66		53		42
Win. 50 FMJ	velocity, fps:	760		707		
	energy, ft-lb	64		56		
30 Luger						
Win. 93 FMJ	velocity, fps:	1220		1110		1040
	energy, ft-lb	305		255		225
.30 Carbine						
Win. 110 Hollow SP	velocity, fps:	1790		1601		1430
	energy, ft-lb	783		626		500
.32 Auto						
Federal 65 Hydra-Shok JHP	velocity, fps:	950	920	890	860	830
	energy, ft-lb	130	120	115	105	100
Federal 71 FMJ	velocity, fps:	910	880	860	830	810
	energy, ft-lb	130	120	115	110	105
Hornady 60 JHP/XTP	velocity, fps:	1000		917		849
	energy, ft-lb	133		112		96
Hornady 71 FMJ-RN	velocity, fps:	900		845		797
	energy, ft-lb	128		112		100

CARTRIDGE BULLET	RANGE, YARDS:	0	25	50	75	100
Magtech 71 FMC	velocity, fps:	905		855		810
	energy, ft-lb	129		115		103
Magtech 71 JHP	velocity, fps:	905		855		810
	energy, ft-lb	129		115		103
PMC 60 JHP	velocity, fps:	980	849	820	791	763
	energy, ft-lb	117				
PMC 71 FMJ	velocity, fps:	870	841	814	791	763
	energy, ft-lb	119				
Rem. 71 Metal Case	velocity, fps:	905		855		810
	energy, ft-lb	129		115		97
Speer 60 Gold Dot	velocity, fps:	960		868		796
	energy, ft-lb	123		100		84
Speer 71 TMJ (and Blazer)	velocity, fps:	900		855		810
	energy, ft-lb	129		115		97
Win. 60 Silvertip HP	velocity, fps:	970		895		835
	energy, ft-lb	125		107		93
Win. 71 FMJ	velocity, fps:	905		855		
	energy, ft-lb	129		115		
.32 S&W						
Rem. 88 LRN	velocity, fps:	680		645		610
	energy, ft-lb:	90		81		73
Win. 85 LRN	velocity, fps:	680		645		610
	energy, ft-lb	90		81		73
.32 S&W Long						
Federal 98 LWC	velocity, fps:	780	700	630	560	500
	energy, ft-lb:	130	105	85	70	55
Federal 98 LRN	velocity, fps:	710	690	670	650	640
	energy, ft-lb:	115	105	100	95	90
Lapua 83 LWC	velocity, fps:	240		189		149
	energy, ft-lb:	154		95		59
Lapua 98 LWC	velocity, fps:	240		202		171
	energy, ft-lb:	183		130		93
Magtech 98 LRN	velocity, fps:	705		670		635
	energy, ft-lb:	108		98		88

Centerfire Handgun Ballistics

.32 S&W Long to 9mm Luger

CARTRIDGE BULLET	RANGE, YARDS:	0	25	50	75	100
Magtech 98 LWC	velocity, fps:	682		579		491
	energy, ft-lb:	102		73		52
Norma 98 LWC	velocity, fps:	787	759	732		683
	energy, ft-lb:	136	126	118		102
PMC 98 LRN	velocity, fps:	789	770	751	733	716
	energy, ft-lb:	135				
PMC 100 LWC	velocity, fps:	683	652	623	595	569
	energy, ft-lb:	102				
Rem. 98 LRN	velocity, fps:	705		670		635
	energy, ft-lb:	115		98		88
Win. 98 LRN	velocity, fps:	705		670		635
		115		98		88

.32 Short Colt

Win. 80 LRN	velocity, fps:	745		665		590
	energy, ft-lb	100		79		62

.32-20

Black Hills 115 FPL	velocity, fps:	800				
	energy, ft-lb:					

.32 H&R Magnum

Black Hills 85 JHP	velocity, fps	1100				
	energy, ft-lb	228				
Black Hills 90 FPL	velocity, fps	750				
	energy, ft-lb					
Black Hills 115 FPL	velocity, fps	800				
	energy, ft-lb					
Federal 85 Hi-Shok JHP	velocity, fps	1100	1050	1020	970	930
	energy, ft-lb	230	210	195	175	165
Federal 95 LSWC	velocity, fps	1030	1000	940	930	900
	energy, ft-lb	225	210	195	185	170

9mm Makarov

Federal 90 Hi-Shok JHP	velocity, fps	990	950	910	880	850
	energy, ft-lb	195	180	165	155	145
Federal 90 FMJ	velocity, fps	990	960	920	900	870
	energy, ft-lb	205	190	180	170	160
Hornady 95 JHP/XTP	velocity, fps	1000		930		874
	energy, ft-lb	211		182		161
Speer 95 TMJ Blazer	velocity, fps	1000		928		872
	energy, ft-lb	211		182		161

9mm Luger

Black Hills 115 JHP +P	velocity, fps:	1300				
	energy, ft-lb:	431				
Black Hills 115 FMJ	velocity, fps:	1150				
	energy, ft-lb:	336				
Black Hills 115 EXP JHP	velocity, fps:	1250				
	energy, ft-lb:	400				
Black Hills 124 JHP +P	velocity, fps:	1250				
	energy, ft-lb:	430				
Black Hills 124 JHP	velocity, fps:	1150				
	energy, ft-lb:	363				
Black Hills 147 JHP subsonic	velocity, fps:	975				
	energy, ft-lb:	309				
Black Hills 147 FMJ subsonic	velocity, fps:	975				
	energy, ft-lb:	309				
Federal 115 Hi-Shok JHP	velocity, fps:	1160	1100	1060	1020	990
	energy, ft-lb:	345	310	285	270	250
Federal 115 FMJ	velocity, fps:	1160	1100	1060	1020	990
	energy, ft-lb:	345	310	285	270	250
Federal 124 FMJ	velocity, fps:	1120	1070	1030	990	960
	energy, ft-lb:	345	315	290	270	255
Federal 124 Hydra-Shok JHP	velocity, fps:	1120	1070	1030	990	960
	energy, ft-lb:	345	315	290	270	255
Federal 124 TMJ TMF Primer	velocity, fps:	1120	1070	1030	990	960
	energy, ft-lb:	345	315	290	270	255
Federal 124 Truncated FMJ Match	velocity, fps:	1120	1070	1030	990	960
	energy, ft-lb:	345	315	290	270	255
Federal 124 Nyclad HP	velocity, fps:	1120	1070	1030	990	960
	energy, ft-lb:	345	315	290	270	255
Federal 124 FMJ +P	velocity, fps:	1120	1070	1030	990	960
	energy, ft-lb:	345	315	290	270	255
Federal 135 Hydra-Shok JHP	velocity, fps:	1050	1030	1010	980	970
	energy, ft-lb:	330	315	300	290	280
Federal 147 Hydra-Shok JHP	velocity, fps:	1000	960	920	890	860
	energy, ft-lb:	325	300	275	260	240
Federal 147 Hi-Shok JHP	velocity, fps:	980	950	930	900	880
	energy, ft-lb:	310	295	285	265	255
Federal 147 FMJ FN	velocity, fps:	960	930	910	890	870
	energy, ft-lb:	295	280	270	260	250
Federal 147 TMJ TMF Primer	velocity, fps:	960	940	910	890	870
	energy, ft-lb:	300	285	270	260	245
Hornady 115 JHP/XTP	velocity, fps:	1155		1047		971
	energy, ft-lb:	341		280		241
Hornady 124 JHP/XTP	velocity, fps:	1110		1030		971
	energy, ft-lb:	339		292		259
Hornady 147 JHP/XTP	velocity, fps:	975		935		899
	energy, ft-lb:	310		285		264
Lapua 116 FMJ	velocity, fps:	365		319		290
	energy, ft-lb:	500		381		315
Lapua 120 FMJ CEPP Super	velocity, fps:	360		316		288
	energy, ft-lb:	505		390		324
Lapua 120 FMJ CEPP Extra	velocity, fps:	360		316		288
	energy, ft-lb:	505		390		324
Lapua 123 HP Megashock	velocity, fps:	355		311		284
	energy, ft-lb:	504		388		322
Lapua 123 FMJ	velocity, fps:	320		292		272
	energy, ft-lb:	410		342		295
Lapua 123 FMJ Combat	velocity, fps:	355		315		289
	energy, ft-lb:	504		397		333
Magtech 115 JHP +P	velocity, fps:	1246		1137		1056
	energy, ft-lb:	397		330		285
Magtech 115 FMC	velocity, fps:	1135		1027		961
	energy, ft-lb:	330		270		235
Magtech 115 JHP	velocity, fps:	1155		1047		971
	energy, ft-lb:	340		280		240
Magtech 124 FMC	velocity, fps:	1109		1030		971
	energy, ft-lb:	339		292		259
Norma 123 Full jacket	velocity, fps:	1099	1032	980		899
	energy, ft-lb:	331	292	263		221
Norma 123 Full jacket	velocity, fps:	1280	1170	1086		972
	energy, ft-lb:	449	375	323		259
PMC 95 SFHP	velocity, fps:	1250	1239	1228	1217	1207
	energy, ft-lb:	330				
PMC 115 FMJ	velocity, fps:	1157	1100	1053	1013	979
	energy, ft-lb:	344				
PMC 115 JHP	velocity, fps:	1167	1098	1044	999	961
	energy, ft-lb:	350				
PMC 124 SFHP	velocity, fps:	1090	1043	1003	969	939
	energy, ft-lb:	327				

Centerfire Handgun Ballistics

9mm Luger to .380 Auto

CARTRIDGE BULLET	RANGE, YARDS:	0	25	50	75	100
PMC 124 FMJ	velocity, fps:	1110	1059	1017	980	949
	energy, ft-lb:	339				
Rem. 101 Lead Free Frangible	velocity, fps:	1220		1092		1004
	energy, ft-lb:	334		267		226
Rem. 115 FN Enclosed Base	velocity, fps:	1135		1041		973
	energy, ft-lb:	329		277		242
Rem. 115 Metal Case	velocity, fps:	1135		1041		973
	energy, ft-lb:	329		277		242
Rem. 115 JHP	velocity, fps:	1155		1047		971
	energy, ft-lb:	341		280		241
Rem. 115 JHP +P	velocity, fps:	1250		1113		1019
	energy, ft-lb:	399		316		265
Rem. 124 JHP	velocity, fps:	1120		1028		960
	energy, ft-lb:	346		291		254
Rem. 124 BJHP	velocity, fps:	1125		1031		963
	energy, ft-lb:	349		293		255
Rem. 124 BJHP +P	velocity, fps:	1180		1089		1021
	energy, ft-lb:	384		327		287
Rem. 124 Metal Case	velocity, fps:	1110		1030		971
	energy, ft-lb:	339		292		259
Rem. 147 JHP subsonic	velocity, fps:	990		941		900
	energy, ft-lb:	320		289		264
Rem. 147 BJHP	velocity, fps:	990		941		900
	energy, ft-lb:	320		289		264
Speer 115 JHP Blazer	velocity, fps:	1145		1024		943
	energy, ft-lb:	335		268		227
Speer 115 FMJ Blazer	velocity, fps:	1145		1047		971
	energy, ft-lb:	341		280		241
Speer 115 FMJ	velocity, fps:	1200		1060		970
	energy, ft-lb:	368		287		240
Speer 115 Gold Dot HP	velocity, fps:	1200		1047		971
	energy, ft-lb:	341		280		241
Speer 124 FMJ Blazer	velocity, fps:	1090		989		917
	energy, ft-lb:	327		269		231
Speer 124 FMJ	velocity, fps:	1090		987		913
	energy, ft-lb:	327		268		230
Speer 124 TMJ-CF (and Blazer)	velocity, fps:	1090		989		917
	energy, ft-lb:	327		269		231
Speer 124 Gold Dot HP	velocity, fps:	1150		1030		948
	energy, ft-lb:	367		292		247
Speer 124 Gold Dot HP	velocity, ft-lb:	1220		1085		996
	energy, ft-lb:	410		324		273
Speer 147 TMJ Blazer	velocity, fps:	950		912		879
	energy, ft-lb:	295		272		252
Speer 147 TMJ	velocity, fps:	985		943		906
	energy, ft-lb:	317		290		268
Speer 147 TMJ-CF (and Blazer)	velocity, fps:	985		960		924
	energy, ft-lb:	326		300		279
Speer 147 Gold Dot	velocity, fps:	985		960		924
	energy, ft-lb:	326		300		279
Win. 105 Jacketed FP	velocity, fps:	1200		1074		989
	energy, ft-lb:	336		269		228
Win. 115 Silvertip HP	velocity, fps:	1225		1095		1007
	energy, ft-lb:	383		306		259
Win. 115 Jacketed HP	velocity, fps:	1225		1095		
	energy, ft-lb:	383		306		
Win. 115 FMJ	velocity, fps:	1190		1071		
	energy, ft-lb:	362		293		
Win. 115 Brass Enclosed Base WinClean	velocity, fps:	1190		1088		
	energy, ft-lb:	362		302		
Win. 124 FMJ	velocity, fps:	1140		1050		
	energy, ft-lb:	358		303		
Win. 124 Brass Enclosed Base WinClean	velocity, fps:	1130		1049		
	energy, ft-lb:	352		303		
Win. 147 FMJ FN	velocity, fps:	990		945		
	energy, ft-lb:	320		292		
Win. 147 SXT	velocity, fps:	990		947		909
	energy, ft-lb:	320		293		270
Win. 147 Silvertip HP	velocity, fps:	1010		962		921
	energy, ft-lb:	333		302		277
Win. 147 JHP	velocity, fps:	990		945		
	energy, ft-lb:	320		291		
Win. 147 Brass Enclosed Base WinClean	velocity, fps:	990		945		
	energy, ft-lb:	320		291		

9 x 23 Winchester

Win. 124 Jacketed FP	velocity, fps:	1460		1308		
	energy, ft-lb:	587		471		
Win. 125 Silvertip HP	velocity, fps:	1450		1249		1103
	energy, ft-lb:	583		433		338

.38 S&W

Rem. 146 LRN	velocity, fps:	685		650		620
	energy, ft-lb:	150		135		125
Win. 145 LRN	velocity, fps:	685		650		620
	energy, ft-lb:	150		135		125

.38 Short Colt

Rem. 125 LRN	velocity, fps:	730		685		645
	energy, ft-lb:	150		130		115

.38 Long Colt

Black Hills 158 RNL	velocity, fps:	650				
	energy, ft-lb:					

.380 Auto

Black Hills 90 JHP	velocity, fps:	1000				
	energy, ft-lb:	200				
Black Hills 95 FMJ	velocity, fps:	950				
	energy, ft-lb:	190				
Federal 90 Hi-Shok JHP	velocity, fps:	1000	940	890	840	800
	energy, ft-lb:	200	175	160	140	130
Federal 90 Hydra-Shok JHP	velocity, fps:	1000	940	890	840	800
	energy, ft-lb:	200	175	160	140	130
Federal 95 FMJ	velocity, fps:	960	910	870	830	790
	energy, ft-lb:	190	175	160	145	130
Hornady 90 JHP/XTP	velocity, fps:	1000		902		823
	energy, ft-lb:	200		163		135
Magtech 85 JHP + P	velocity, fps:	1082		999		936
	energy, ft-lb:	221		188		166
Magtech 95 FMC	velocity, fps:	951		861		781
	energy, ft-lb:	190		156		128
Magtech 95 JHP	velocity, fps:	951		861		781
	energy, ft-lb:	190		156		128
PMC 90 FMJ	velocity, fps:	910	872	838	807	778
	energy, ft-lb:	165				
PMC 90 JHP	velocity, fps:	917	878	844	812	782
	energy, ft-lb:	168				
PMC 95 SFHP	velocity, fps:	925	884	847	813	783
	energy, ft-lb:	180				
Rem. 88 JHP	velocity, fps:	990		920		868
	energy, ft-lb:	191		165		146

Centerfire Handgun Ballistics

.380 Auto to .38 Special

CARTRIDGE BULLET	RANGE, YARDS:	0	25	50	75	100
Rem. 95 FN Enclosed Base	velocity, fps:	955		865		785
	energy, ft-lb:	190		160		130
Rem. 95 Metal Case	velocity, fps:	955		865		785
	energy, ft-lb:	190		160		130
Rem. 102 BJHP	velocity, fps:	940		901		866
	energy, ft-lb:	200		184		170
Speer 88 JHP Blazer	velocity, fps:	950		920		870
	energy, ft-lb:	195		164		148
Speer 90 Gold Dot	velocity, fps:	990		907		842
	energy, ft-lb:	196		164		142
Speer 95 TMJ Blazer	velocity, fps:	945		865		785
	energy, ft-lb:	190		160		130
Speer 95 TMJ	velocity, fps:	950		877		817
	energy, ft-lb:	180		154		133
Win. 85 Silvertip HP	velocity, fps:	1000		921		860
	energy, ft-lb:	189		160		140
Win. 95 SXT	velocity, fps:	955		889		835
	energy, ft-lb:	192		167		147
Win. 95 FMJ	velocity, fps:	955		865		
	energy, ft-lb:	190		160		
Win. 95 Brass Enclosed Base WinClean	velocity, fps:	955		881		
	energy, ft-lb:	192		164		

.38 Special

CARTRIDGE BULLET	RANGE, YARDS:	0	25	50	75	100
Black Hills 125 JHP +P	velocity, fps:	1050				
	energy, ft-lb:	306				
Black Hills 158 CNL	velocity, fps:	800				
	energy, ft-lb:					
Federal 110 Hydra-Shok JHP	velocity, fps:	1000	970	930	910	880
	energy, ft-lb:	245	225	215	200	190
Federal 110 Hi-Shok JHP +P	velocity, fps:	1000	960	930	900	870
	energy, ft-lb:	240	225	210	195	185
Federal 125 Nyclad HP	velocity, fps:	830	780	730	690	650
	energy, ft-lb:	190	170	150	130	115
Federal 125 Hi-Shok JSP +P	velocity, fps:	950	920	900	880	860
	energy, ft-lb:	250	235	225	215	205
Federal 125 Hi-Shok JHP +P	velocity, fps:	950	920	900	880	860
	energy, ft-lb:	250	235	225	215	205
Federal 125 Nyclad HP +P	velocity, fps:	950	920	900	880	860
	energy, ft-lb:	250	235	225	215	205
Federal 129 Hydra-Shok JHP+P	velocity, fps:	950	930	910	890	870
	energy, ft-lb:	255	245	235	225	215
Federal 130 FMJ	velocity, fps:	950	920	890	870	840
	energy, ft-lb:	260	245	230	215	205
Federal 148 LWC Match	velocity, fps:	710	670	630	600	560
	energy, ft-lb:	165	150	130	115	105
Federal 158 LRN	velocity, fps:	760	740	720	710	690
	energy, ft-lb:	200	190	185	175	170
Federal 158 LSWC	velocity, fps:	760	740	720	710	690
	energy, ft-lb:	200	190	185	175	170
Federal 158 Nyclad RN	velocity, fps:	760	740	720	710	690
	energy, ft-lb:	200	190	185	175	170
Federal 158 SWC HP +P	velocity, fps:	890	870	860	840	820
	energy, ft-lb:	280	265	260	245	235
Federal 158 LSWC +P	velocity, fps:	890	870	860	840	820
	energy, ft-lb:	270	265	260	245	235
Federal 158 Nyclad SWC-HP+P	velocity, fps:	890	870	860	840	820
	energy, ft-lb:	270	265	260	245	235
Hornady 125 JHP/XTP	velocity, fps:	900		856		817
	energy, ft-lb:	225		203		185
Hornady 140 JHP/XTP	velocity, fps:	825		790		757
	energy, ft-lb:	212		194		178
Hornady 140 Cowboy	velocity, fps:	800		767		735
	energy, ft-lb:	199		183		168
Hornady 148 HBWC	velocity, fps:	800		697		610
	energy, ft-lb:	210		160		122
Hornady 158 JHP/XPT	velocity, fps:	800		765		731
	energy, ft-lb:	225		205		188
Lapua 123 HP Megashock	velocity, fps:	355		311		284
	energy, ft-lb:	504		388		322
Lapua 148 LWC	velocity, fps:	230		203		181
	energy, ft-lb:	254		199		157
Lapua 150 SJFN	velocity, fps:	325		301		283
	energy, ft-lb:	512		439		388
Lapua 158 FMJLF	velocity, fps:	255		243		232
	energy, ft-lb:	332		301		275
Lapua 158 LRN	velocity, fps:	255		243		232
	energy, ft-lb:	332		301		275
Magtech 125 JHP +P	velocity, fps:	1017		971		931
	energy, ft-lb:	287		262		241
Magtech 148 LWC	velocity, fps:	710		634		566
	energy, ft-lb:	166		132		105
Magtech 158 LRN	velocity, fps:	755		728		693
	energy, ft-lb:	200		183		168
Magtech 158 LFN	velocity, fps:	800		776		753
	energy, ft-lb:	225		211		199
Magtech 158 SJHP	velocity, fps:	807		779		753
	energy, ft-lb:	230		213		199
Magtech 158 LSWC	velocity, fps:	755		721		689
	energy, ft-lb:	200		182		167
Magtech 158 FMC-Flat	velocity, fps:	807		779		753
	energy, ft-lb:	230		213		199
PMC 125 SFHP +P	velocity, fps:	950	918	889	863	838
	energy, ft-lb:	251				
PMC 125 JHP +P	velocity, fps:	974	938	906	878	851
	energy, ft-lb:	266				
PMC 132 FMJ	velocity, fps:	841	820	799	780	761
	energy, ft-lb:	206				
PMC 148 LWC	velocity, fps:	728	694	662	631	602
	energy, ft-lb:	175				
PMC 158 LRN	velocity, fps:	820	801	783	765	749
	energy, ft-lb:	235				
PMC 158 JSP	velocity, fps:	835	816	797	779	762
	energy, ft-lb:	245				
PMC 158 LFP	velocity, fps:	800		761		725
	energy, ft-lb:	225		203		185
Rem. 101 Lead Free Frangible	velocity, fps:	950		896		850
	energy, ft-lb:	202		180		162
Rem. 110 SJHP	velocity, fps:	950		890		840
	energy, ft-lb:	220		194		172
Rem. 110 SJHP +P	velocity, fps:	995		926		871
	energy, ft-lb:	242		210		185
Rem. 125 SJHP +P	velocity, ft-lb:	945		898		858
	energy, ft-lb:	248		224		204
Rem. 125 FN Enclosed Base	velocity, fps:	1025		976		935
	energy, ft-lb:	292		264		243
Rem. 125 BJHP	velocity, fps:	975		929		885
	energy, ft-lb:	264		238		218
Rem. 130 Metal Case	velocity, fps:	950		913		879
	energy, ft-lb:	261		240		223

Centerfire Handgun Ballistics
.38 Special to .357 Magnum

CARTRIDGE BULLET	RANGE, YARDS:	0	25	50	75	100
Rem. 148 LWC Match	velocity, fps:	710		634		566
	energy, ft-lb:	166		132		105
Rem. 158 LRN	velocity, fps:	755		723		692
	energy, ft-lb:	200		183		168
Rem. 158 SWC +P	velocity, fps:	890		855		823
	energy, ft-lb:	278		257		238
Rem. 158 SWC	velocity, fps:	755		723		692
	energy, ft-lb:	200		183		168
Rem. 158 LHP +P	velocity, fps:	890		855		823
	energy, ft-lb:	278		257		238
Speer 125 JHP +P Blazer	velocity, fps:	945		898		858
	energy, ft-lb:	248		224		204
Speer 125 Gold Dot +P	velocity, fps:	945		898		858
	energy, ft-lb:	248		224		204
Speer 158 TMJ +P (and Blazer)	velocity, fps:	900		852		818
	energy, ft-lb:	278		255		235
Speer 158 LRN Blazer	velocity, fps:	755		723		692
	energy, ft-lb:	200		183		168
Speer 158 Trail Blazer LFN	velocity, fps:	800		761		725
	energy, ft-lb:	225		203		184
Speer 158 TMJ-CF +P (and Blazer)	velocity, fps:	900		852		818
	energy, ft-lb:	278		255		235
Win. 110 Silvertip HP	velocity, fps:	945		894		850
	energy, ft-lb:	218		195		176
Win. 110 Jacketed FP	velocity, fps:	975		906		849
	energy, ft-lb:	232		201		176
Win. 125 Jacketed HP	velocity, fps:	945		898		
	energy, ft-lb:	248		224		
Win. 125 Jacketed HP +P	velocity, fps:	945		898		858
	energy, ft-lb:	248		224		204
Win. 125 Jacketed FP	velocity, fps:	850		804		
	energy, ft-lb:	201		179		
Win. 125 Silvertip HP + P	velocity, fps:	945		898		858
	energy, ft-lb:	248		224		204
Win. 125 Jacketed FP WinClean	velocity, fps:	775		742		
	energy, ft-lb:	167		153		
Win. 130 FMJ	velocity, fps:	800		765		
	energy, ft-lb:	185		169		
Win. 130 SXT +P	velocity, fps:	925		887		852
	energy, ft-lb:	247		227		210
Win. 148 LWC Super Match	velocity, fps:	710		634		566
	energy, ft-lb:	166		132		105
Win. 150 Lead	velocity, fps:	845		812		
	energy, ft-lb:	238		219		
Win. 158 Lead	velocity, fps:	800		761		725
	energy, ft-lb:	225		203		185
Win. 158 LRN	velocity, fps:	755		723		693
	energy, ft-lb:	200		183		168
Win. 158 LSWC	velocity, fps:	755		721		689
	energy, ft-lb:	200		182		167
Win. 158 LSWC HP +P	velocity, fps:	890		855		823
	energy, ft-lb:	278		257		238

.38-40

Black Hills 180 FPL	velocity, fps:	800				
	energy, ft-lb:					

.38 Super

Federal 130 FMJ +P	velocity, fps:	1200	1140	1100	1050	1020
	energy, ft-lb:	415	380	350	320	300
PMC 115 JHP	velocity, fps:	1116	1052	1001	959	923
	energy, ft-lb:	318				
PMC 130 FMJ	velocity, fps:	1092	1038	994	957	924
	energy, ft-lb:	348				
Rem. 130 Metal Case	velocity, fps:	1215		1099		1017
	energy, ft-lb:	426		348		298
Win. 125 Silvertip HP +P	velocity, fps:	1240		1130		1050
	energy, ft-lb:	427		354		306
Win. 130 FMJ +P	velocity, fps:	1215		1099		
	energy, ft-lb:	426		348		

.357 Sig

Federal 125 FMJ	velocity, fps:	1350	1270	1190	1130	1080
	energy, ft-lb:	510	445	395	355	325
Federal 125 JHP	velocity, fps:	1350	1270	1190	1130	1080
	energy, ft-lb:	510	445	395	355	325
Federal 150 JHP	velocity, fps:	1130	1080	1030	1000	970
	energy, ft-lb:	420	385	355	330	310
Hornady 124 JHP/XTP	velocity, fps:	1350		1208		1108
	energy, ft-lb:	502		405		338
Hornady 147 JHP/XTP	velocity, fps:	1225		1138		1072
	energy, ft-lb:	490		422		375
PMC 124 SFHP	velocity, fps:	1350	1263	1190	1132	1083
	energy, ft-lb:	502				
PMC 124 FMJ/FP	velocity, fps:	1350	1242	1158	1093	1040
	energy, ft-lb:	512				
Rem. 104 Lead Free Frangible	velocity, fps:	1400		1223		1094
	energy, ft-lb:	453		345		276
Rem. 125 Metal Case	velocity, fps:	1350		1146		1018
	energy, ft-lb:	506		422		359
Rem. 125 JHP	velocity, fps:	1350		1157		1032
	energy, ft-lb:	506		372		296
Speer 125 TMJ (and Blazer)	velocity, fps:	1350		1177		1057
	energy, ft-lb:	502		381		307
Speer 125 TMJ-CF	velocity, fps:	1350		1177		1057
	energy, ft-lb:	502		381		307
Speer 125 Gold Dot	velocity, fps:	1375		1203		1079
	energy, ft-lb:	525		402		323
Win. 105 JFP	velocity, fps:	1370		1179		1050
	energy, ft-lb	438		324		257
Win. 125 FMJ FN	velocity, fps:	1350		1185		
	energy, ft-lb	506		390		

.357 Magnum

Black Hills 125 JHP	velocity, fps:	1500				
	energy, ft-lb:	625				
Black Hills 158 CNL	velocity, fps:	800				
	energy, ft-lb:					
Federal 110 Hi-Shok JHP	velocity, fps:	1300	1180	1090	1040	990
	energy, ft-lb:	410	340	290	260	235
Federal 125 Hi-Shok JHP	velocity, fps:	1450	1350	1240	1160	1100
	energy, ft-lb:	580	495	430	370	335
Federal 130 Hydra-Shok JHP	velocity, fps:	1300	1210	1130	1070	1020
	energy, ft-lb:	490	420	370	330	300
Federal 158 Hi-Shok JSP	velocity, fps:	1240	1160	1100	1060	1020
	energy, ft-lb:	535	475	430	395	365
Federal 158 JSP	velocity, fps:	1240	1160	1100	1060	1020
	energy, ft-lb:	535	475	430	395	365
Federal 158 LSWC	velocity, fps:	1240	1160	1100	1060	1020
	energy, ft-lb:	535	475	430	395	365

Centerfire Handgun Ballistics

.357 Magnum to .40 S&W

CARTRIDGE BULLET	RANGE, YARDS:	0	25	50	75	100
Federal 158 Hi-Shok JHP	velocity, fps:	1240	1160	1100	1060	1020
	energy, ft-lb:	535	475	430	395	365
Federal 158 Hydra-Shok JHP	velocity, fps:	1240	1160	1100	1060	1020
	energy, ft-lb:	535	475	430	395	365
Federal 180 Hi-Shok JHP	velocity, fps:	1090	1030	980	930	890
	energy, ft-lb:	475	425	385	350	320
Federal 180 Castcore	velocity, fps:	1250	1200	1160	1120	1080
	energy, ft-lb:	625	575	535	495	465
Hornady 125 JHP/XTP	velocity, fps:	1500		1314		1166
	energy, ft-lb:	624		479		377
Hornady 125 JFP/XTP	velocity, fps:	1500		1311		1161
	energy, ft-lb:	624		477		374
Hornady 140 Cowboy	velocity, fps:	800		767		735
	energy, ft-lb:	199		183		168
Hornady 140 JHP/XTP	velocity, fps:	1400		1249		1130
	energy, ft-lb:	609		485		397
Hornady 158 JHP/XTP	velocity, fps:	1250		1150		1073
	energy, ft-lb:	548		464		404
Hornady 158 JFP/XTP	velocity, fps:	1250		1147		1068
	energy, ft-lb:	548		461		400
Lapua 150 FMJ CEPP Super	velocity, fps:	370		527		303
	energy, ft-lb:	664		527		445
Lapua 150 SJFN	velocity, fps:	385		342		313
	energy, ft-lb:	719		569		476
Lapua 158 SJHP	velocity, fps:	470		408		359
	energy, ft-lb:	1127		850		657
Magtech 158 SJSP	velocity, fps:	1235		1104		1015
	energy, ft-lb:	535		428		361
Magtech 158 SJHP	velocity, fps:	1235		1104		1015
	energy, ft-lb:	535		428		361
PMC 125 JHP	velocity, fps:	1194	1117	1057	1008	967
	energy, ft-lb:	399				
PMC 150 JHP	velocity, fps:	1234	1156	1093	1042	1000
	energy, ft-lb:	512				
PMC 150 SFHP	velocity, fps:	1205	1129	1069	1020	980
	energy, ft-lb:	484				
PMC 158 JSP	velocity, fps:	1194	1122	1063	1016	977
	energy, ft-lb:	504				
PMC 158 LFP	velocity, fps:	800		761		725
	energy, ft-lb:	225		203		185
Rem. 110 SJHP	velocity, fps:	1295		1094		975
	energy, ft-lb:	410		292		232
Rem. 125 SJHP	velocity, fps:	1450		1240		1090
	energy, ft-lb:	583		427		330
Rem. 125 BJHP	velocity, fps:	1220		1095		1009
	energy, ft-lb:	413		333		283
Rem. 158 SJHP	velocity, fps:	1235		1104		1015
	energy, ft-lb:	535		428		361
Rem. 158 SP	velocity, fps:	1235		1104		1015
	energy, ft-lb:	535		428		361
Rem. 158 SWC	velocity, fps:	1235		1104		1015
	energy, ft-lb:	535		428		361
Rem. 165 JHP Core-Lokt	velocity, fps:	1290		1189		1108
	energy, ft-lb:	610		518		450
Rem. 180 SJHP	velocity, fps:	1145		1053		985
	energy, ft-lb:	542		443		388
Speer 125 Gold Dot	velocity, fps:	1450		1240		1090
	energy, ft-lb:	583		427		330
Speer 158 JHP Blazer	velocity, fps:	1150		1104		1015
	energy, ft-lb:	535		428		361
Speer 158 Gold Dot	velocity, fps:	1235		1104		1015
	energy, ft-lb:	535		428		361
Speer 170 Gold Dot SP	velocity, fps:	1180		1089		1019
	energy, ft-lb:	525		447		392
Win. 110 JFP	velocity, fps:	1275		1105		998
	energy, ft-lb:	397		298		243
Win. 110 JHP	velocity, fps:	1295		1095		
	energy, ft-lb:	410		292		
Win. 125 JFP WinClean	velocity, fps:	1370		1183		
	energy, ft-lb:	521		389		
Win. 145 Silvertip HP	velocity, fps:	1290		1155		1060
	energy, ft-lb:	535		428		361
Win. 158 JHP	velocity, fps:	1235		1104		1015
	energy, ft-lb:	535		428		361
Win. 158 JSP	velocity, fps:	1235		1104		1015
	energy, ft-lb:	535		428		361
Win. 180 Partition Gold	velocity, fps:	1180		1088		1020
	energy, ft-lb:	557		473		416

.40 S&W

CARTRIDGE BULLET	RANGE, YARDS:	0	25	50	75	100
Black Hills 155 JHP	velocity, fps:	1150				
	energy, ft-lb:	450				
Black Hills 165 EXP JHP	velocity, fps:	1150				
	energy, ft-lb:	483				
Black Hills 180 JHP	velocity, fps:	1000				
	energy, ft-lb:	400				
Federal 135 Hydra-Shok JHP	velocity, fps:	1190	1050	970	900	850
	energy, ft-lb:	420	330	280	245	215
Federal 155 FMJ Ball	velocity, fps:	1140	1080	1030	990	960
	energy, ft-lb:	445	400	365	335	315
Federal 155 Hi-Shok JHP	velocity, fps:	1140	1080	1030	990	950
	energy, ft-lb:	445	400	365	335	315
Federal 155 Hydra-Shok JHP	velocity, fps:	1140	1080	1030	990	950
	energy, ft-lb:	445	400	365	335	315
Federal 165 FMJ	velocity, fps:	1050	1020	990	960	935
	energy, ft-lb:	405	380	355	335	320
Federal 165 FMJ Ball	velocity, fps:	980	950	920	900	880
	energy, ft-lb:	350	330	310	295	280
Federal 165 Hydra-Shok JHP	velocity, fps:	980	950	930	910	890
	energy, ft-lb:	350	330	315	300	290
Federal 180 High Antim. Lead	velocity, fps:	990	960	930	910	890
	energy, ft-lb:	390	365	345	330	315
Federal 180 TMJ TMF Primer	velocity, fps:	990	960	940	910	890
	energy, ft-lb:	390	370	350	330	315
Federal 180 FMJ Ball	velocity, fps:	990	960	940	910	890
	energy, ft-lb:	390	370	350	330	315
Federal 180 Hi-Shok JHP	velocity, fps:	990	960	930	910	890
	energy, ft-lb:	390	365	345	330	315
Federal 180 Hydra-Shok JHP	velocity, fps:	990	960	930	910	890
	energy, ft-lb:	390	365	345	330	315
Hornady 155 JHP/XTP	velocity, fps:	1180		1061		980
	energy, ft-lb:	479		388		331
Hornady 180 JHP/XTP	velocity, fps:	950		903		862
	energy, ft-lb:	361		326		297
Magtech 155 JHP	velocity, fps:	1025		1118		1052
	energy, ft-lb:	500		430		381
Magtech 180 JHP	velocity, fps:	990		933		886
	energy, ft-lb:	390		348		314
Magtech 180 FMC	velocity, fps:	990		933		886
	energy, ft-lb:	390		348		314

Centerfire Handgun Ballistics
.40 S&W TO .44 SPECIAL

CARTRIDGE BULLET	RANGE, YARDS:	0	25	50	75	100
PMC 155 SFHP	velocity, fps:	1160	1092	1039	994	957
	energy, ft-lb:	463				
PMC 165 JHP	velocity, fps:	1040	1002	970	941	915
	energy, ft-lb:	396				
PMC 165 FMJ	velocity, fps:	1010	977	948	922	899
	energy, ft-lb:	374				
PMC 180 FMJ/FP	velocity, fps:	985	957	931	908	885
	energy, ft-lb:	388				
PMC 180 SFHP	velocity, fps:	985	958	933	910	889
	energy, ft-lb:	388				
Rem. 141 Lead Free Frangible	velocity, fps:	1135		1056		996
	energy, ft-lb:	403		349		311
Rem. 155 JHP	velocity, fps:	1205		1095		1017
	energy, ft-lb:	499		413		356
Rem. 165 BJHP	velocity, fps:	1150		1040		964
	energy, ft-lb:	485		396		340
Rem. 180 JHP	velocity, fps:	1015		960		914
	energy, ft-lb:	412		368		334
Rem. 180 FN Enclosed Base	velocity, fps:	985		936		893
	energy, ft-lb:	388		350		319
Rem. 180 Metal Case	velocity, fps:	985		936		893
	energy, ft-lb:	388		350		319
Rem. 180 BJHP	velocity, fps:	1015		960		914
	energy, ft-lb:	412		368		334
Speer 155 TMJ Blazer	velocity, fps:	1175		1047		963
	energy, ft-lb:	475		377		319
Speer 155 TMJ	velocity, fps:	1200		1065		976
	energy, ft-lb:	496		390		328
Speer 155 Gold Dot	velocity, fps:	1200		1063		974
	energy, ft-lb:	496		389		326
Speer 165 TMJ Blazer	velocity, fps:	1100		1006		938
	energy, ft-lb:	443		371		321
Speer 165 TMJ	velocity, fps:	1150		1040		964
	energy, ft-lb:	484		396		340
Speer 165 Gold Dot	velocity, fps:	1150		1043		966
	energy, ft-lb:	485		399		342
Speer 180 HP Blazer	velocity, fps:	985		951		909
	energy, ft-lb:	400		361		330
Speer 180 FMJ Blazer	velocity, fps:	1000		937		886
	energy, ft-lb:	400		351		313
Speer 180 FMJ	velocity, fps:	1000		951		909
	energy, ft-lb:	400		361		330
Speer 180 TMJ-CF (and Blazer)	velocity, fps:	1000		951		909
	energy, ft-lb:	400		361		330
Speer 180 Gold Dot	velocity, fps:	1025		957		902
	energy, ft-lb:	420		366		325
Win. 140 JFP	velocity, fps:	1155		1039		960
	energy, ft-lb:	415		336		286
Win. 155 Silvertip HP	velocity, fps:	1205		1096		1018
	energy, ft-lb:	500		414		357
Win. 165 SXT	velocity, fps:	1130		1041		977
	energy, ft-lb:	468		397		349
Win. 165 FMJ FN	velocity, fps:	1060		1001		
	energy, ft-lb:	412		367		
Win. 165 Brass Enclosed Base WinClean	velocity, fps:	1130		1054		
	energy, ft-lb:	468		407		
Win. 180 JHP	velocity, fps:	1010		954		
	energy, ft-lb:	408		364		
Win. 180 FMJ	velocity, fps:	990		936		
	energy, ft-lb:	390		350		
Win. 180 SXT	velocity, fps:	1010		954		909
	energy, ft-lb:	408		364		330
Win. 180 Brass Enclosed Base WinClean	velocity, fps:	990		943		
	energy, ft-lb:	392		356		

10 MM AUTO

CARTRIDGE BULLET		0	25	50	75	100
Federal 155 Hi-Shok JHP	velocity, fps:	1330	1230	1140	1080	1030
	energy, ft-lb:	605	515	450	400	360
Federal 180 Hi-Shok JHP	velocity, fps:	1030	1000	970	950	920
	energy, ft-lb:	425	400	375	355	340
Federal 180 Hydra-Shok JHP	velocity, fps:	1030	1000	970	950	920
	energy, ft-lb:	425	400	375	355	340
Federal 180 High Antim. Lead	velocity, fps:	1030	1000	970	950	920
	energy, ft-lb:	425	400	375	355	340
Hornady 155 JHP/XTP	velocity, fps:	1265		1119		1020
	energy, ft-lb:	551		431		358
Hornady 180 JHP/XTP	velocity, fps:	1180		1077		1004
	energy, ft-lb:	556		464		403
Hornady 200 JHP/XTP	velocity, fps:	1050		994		948
	energy, ft-lb:	490		439		399
PMC 170 JHP	velocity, fps:	1200	1117	1052	1000	958
	energy, ft-lb:	543				
PMC 180 SFHP	velocity, fps:	950	926	903	882	862
	energy, ft-lb:	361				
PMC 200 TC-FMJ	velocity, fps:	1050	1008	972	941	912
	energy, ft-lb:	490				
Rem. 180 Metal Case	velocity, fps:	1150		1063		998
	energy, ft-lb:	529		452		398
Speer 200 TMJ Blazer	velocity, fps:	1050		966		952
	energy, ft-lb:	490		440		402
Win. 175 Silvertip HP	velocity, fps:	1290		1141		1037
	energy, ft-lb:	649		506		418

.41 REMINGTON MAGNUM

CARTRIDGE BULLET		0	25	50	75	100
Federal 210 Hi-Shok JHP	velocity, fps:	1300	1210	1130	1070	1030
	energy, ft-lb:	790	680	595	540	495
PMC 210 TCSP	velocity, fps:	1290	1201	1128	1069	1021
	energy, ft-lb:	774				
Rem. 210 SP	velocity, fps:	1300		1162		1062
	energy, ft-lb:	788		630		526
Win. 175 Silvertip HP	velocity, fps:	1250		1120		1029
	energy, ft-lb:	607		488		412

.44 COLT

CARTRIDGE BULLET		0	25	50	75	100
Black Hills 230 FPL	velocity, fps:	730				
	energy, ft-lb:					

.44 RUSSIAN

CARTRIDGE BULLET		0	25	50	75	100
Black Hills 210 FPL	velocity, fps:	650				
	energy, ft-lb:					

.44 SPECIAL

CARTRIDGE BULLET		0	25	50	75	100
Black Hills 210 FPL	velocity, fps:	700				
	energy, ft-lb:					
Federal 200 SWC HP	velocity, fps:	900	860	830	800	770
	energy, ft-lb:	360	330	305	285	260
Federal 250 CastCore	velocity, fps:	1250	1200	1150	1110	1080
	energy, ft-lb:	865	795	735	685	645
Hornady 180 JHP/XTP	velocity, fps:	1000		935		882
	energy, ft-lb:	400		350		311
Magtech 240 LFN	velocity, fps:	750		722		696
	energy, ft-lb:	300		278		258

Centerfire Handgun Ballistics

.44 Special to .45 Automatic (ACP)

CARTRIDGE BULLET	RANGE, YARDS:	0	25	50	75	100
PMC 180 JHP	velocity, fps:	980	938	902	869	839
	energy, ft-lb:	383				
PMC 240 SWC-CP	velocity, fps:	764	744	724	706	687
	energy, ft-lb:	311				
PMC 240 LFP	velocity, fps:	750		719		690
	energy, ft-lb:	300		275		253
Rem. 246 LRN	velocity, fps:	755		725		695
	energy, ft-lb:	310		285		265
Speer 200 HP Blazer	velocity, fps:	875		825		780
	energy, ft-lb:	340		302		270
Speer 200 Trail Blazer LFN	velocity, fps:	750		714		680
	energy, ft-lb:	250		226		205
Speer 200 Gold Dot	velocity, fps:	875		825		780
	energy, ft-lb:	340		302		270
Win. 200 Silvertip HP	velocity, fps:	900		860		822
	energy, ft-lb:	360		328		300
Win. 240 Lead	velocity, fps:	750		719		690
	energy, ft-lb	300		275		253
Win. 246 LRN	velocity, fps:	755		725		695
	energy, ft-lb:	310		285		265

.44 Remington Magnum

CARTRIDGE BULLET	RANGE, YARDS:	0	25	50	75	100
Black Hills 240 JHP	velocity, fps:	1260				
	energy, ft-lb:	848				
Black Hills 300 JHP	velocity, fps:	1150				
	energy, ft-lb:	879				
Federal 180 Hi-Shok JHP	velocity, fps:	1610	1480	1370	1270	1180
	energy, ft-lb:	1035	875	750	640	555
Federal 240 Hi-Shok JHP	velocity, fps:	1180	1130	1080	1050	1010
	energy, ft-lb:	740	675	625	580	550
Federal 240 Hydra-Shok JHP	velocity, fps:	1180	1130	1080	1050	1010
	energy, ft-lb:	740	675	625	580	550
Federal 240 JHP	velocity, fps:	1180	1130	1080	1050	1010
	energy, ft-lb:	740	675	625	580	550
Federal 300 CastCore	velocity, fps:	1250	1200	1160	1120	1080
	energy, ft-lb:	1040	960	885	825	775
Hornady 180 JHP/XTP	velocity, fps:	1550		1340		1173
	energy, ft-lb:	960		717		550
Hornady 200 JHP/XTP	velocity, fps:	1500		1284		1128
	energy, ft-lb:	999		732		565
Hornady 240 JHP/XTP	velocity, fps:	1350		1188		1078
	energy, ft-lb:	971		753		619
Hornady 300 JHP/XTP	velocity, fps:	1150		1084		1031
	energy, ft-lb:	881		782		708
Magtech 240 SJSP	velocity, fps:	1180		1081		1010
	energy, ft-lb:	741		632		623
PMC 180 JHP	velocity, fps:	1392	1263	1157	1076	1015
	energy, ft-lb:	772				
PMC 240 JHP	velocity, fps:	1301	1218	1147	1088	1041
	energy, ft-lb:	900				
PMC 240 TC-SP	velocity, fps:	1300	1216	1144	1086	1038
	energy, ft-lb:	900				
PMC 240 SFHP	velocity, fps:	1300	1212	1138	1079	1030
	energy, ft-lb:	900				
PMC 240 LSWC-GCK	velocity, fps:	1225	1143	1077	1025	982
	energy, ft-lb:	806				
Rem. 180 JSP	velocity, fps:	1610		1365		1175
	energy, ft-lb:	1036		745		551
Rem. 240 SP	velocity, fps:	1180		1081		1010
	energy, ft-lb:	721		623		543
Rem. 240 SJHP	velocity, fps:	1180		1081		1010
	energy, ft-lb:	721		623		543
Rem. 275 JHP Core-Lokt	velocity, fps:	1235		1142		1070
	energy, ft-lb:	931		797		699
Speer 240 JHP Blazer	velocity, fps:	1200		1092		1015
	energy, ft-lb:	767		636		549
Speer 240 Gold Dot HP	velocity, fps:	1400		1255		1139
	energy, ft-lb:	1044		839		691
Speer 270 Gold Dot SP	velocity, fps:	1250		1142		1060
	energy, ft-lb:	937		781		674
Win. 210 Silvertip HP	velocity, fps:	1250		1106		1010
	energy, ft-lb:	729		570		475
Win. 240 Hollow SP	velocity, fps:	1180		1081		1010
	energy, ft-lb:	741		623		543
Win. 240 JSP	velocity, fps:	1180		1081		
	energy, ft-lb:	741		623		
Win. 250 Partition Gold	velocity, fps:	1230		1132		1057
	energy, ft-lb:	840		711		620

.44-40

CARTRIDGE BULLET	RANGE, YARDS:	0	25	50	75	100
Black Hills 200 RNFP	velocity, fps:	800				
	energy, ft-lb:					
Hornady 205 Cowboy	velocity, fps:	725		697		670
	energy, ft-lb:	239		221		204
Magtech 225 LFN	velocity, fps:	725		703		681
	energy, ft-lb:	281		247		232
PMC 225 LFP	velocity, fps:	725		723		695
	energy, ft-lb:	281		261		242
Win. 225 Lead	velocity, fps:	750		723		695
	energy, ft-lb:	281		261		242

.45 Automatic (ACP)

CARTRIDGE BULLET	RANGE, YARDS:	0	25	50	75	100
Black Hills 185 JHP	velocity, fps:	1000				
	energy, ft-lb:	411				
Black Hills 200 Match SWC	velocity, fps:	875				
	energy, ft-lb:	340				
Black Hills 230 FMJ	velocity, fps:	850				
	energy, ft-lb:	368				
Black Hills 230 JHP	velocity, fps:	850				
	energy, ft-lb:	368				
Black Hills 230 JHP +P	velocity, fps:	950				
	energy, ft-lb:	460				
Federal 165 Hydra-Shok JHP	velocity, fps:	1060	1020	980	950	920
	energy, ft-lb:	410	375	350	330	310
Federal 185 Hi-Shok JHP	velocity, fps:	950	920	900	880	860
	energy, ft-lb:	370	350	335	315	300
Federal 185 FMJ-SWC Match	velocity, fps:	780	730	700	660	620
	energy, ft-lb:	245	220	200	175	160
Federal 200 Exp. FMJ	velocity, fps:	1030	1000	970	940	920
	energy, ft-lb:	470	440	415	395	375
Federal 230 FMJ	velocity, fps:	850	830	810	790	770
	energy, ft-lb:	370	350	335	320	305
Federal 230 Hi-Shok JHP	velocity, fps:	850	830	810	790	770
	energy, ft-lb:	370	350	335	320	300
Federal 230 Hydra-Shok JHP	velocity, fps:	850	830	810	790	770
	energy, ft-lb:	370	350	335	320	305
Federal 230 FMJ	velocity, fps:	850	830	810	790	770
	energy, ft-lb:	370	350	335	320	305
Federal 230 TMJ TMF Primer	velocity, fps:	850	830	810	790	770
	energy, ft-lb:	370	350	335	315	305

Centerfire Handgun Ballistics
.45 Automatic (ACP) to .454 Casull

CARTRIDGE BULLET	RANGE, YARDS:	0	25	50	75	100
Hornady 185 JHP/XTP	velocity, fps:	950		880		819
	energy, ft-lb:	371		318		276
Hornady 200 JHP/XTP	velocity, fps:	900		855		815
	energy, ft-lb:	358		325		295
Hornady 200 HP/XTP +P	velocity, fps:	1055		982		925
	energy, ft-lb:	494		428		380
Hornady 230 FMJ/RN	velocity, fps:	850		809		771
	energy, ft-lb:	369		334		304
Hornady 230 FMJ/FP	velocity, fps:	850		809		771
	energy, ft-lb:	369		334		304
Hornady 230 HP/XTP +P	velocity, fps:	950		904		865
	energy, ft-lb:	462		418		382
Magtech 185 JHP +P	velocity, fps:	1148		1066		1055
	energy, ft-lb:	540		467		415
Magtech 200 LSWC	velocity, fps:	950		910		874
	energy, ft-lb:	401		368		339
Magtech 230 FMC	veloctiy, fps:	837		800		767
	energy, ft-lb:	356		326		300
Magtech 230 FMC-SWC	velocity, fps:	780		720		660
	energy, ft-lb:	310		265		222
PMC 185 JHP	velocity, fps:	903	870	839	811	785
	energy, ft-lb:	339				
PMC 200 FMJ-SWC	velocity, fps:	850	818	788	761	734
	energy, ft-lb:	321				
PMC 230 SFHP	velocity, fps:	850	830	811	792	775
	energy, ft-lb:	369				
PMC 230 FMJ	velocity, fps:	830	809	789	769	749
	energy, ft-lb:	352				
Rem. 175 Lead Free Frangible	velocity, fps:	1020		923		851
	energy, ft-lb:	404		331		281
Rem. 185 JHP	velocity, fps:	1000		939		889
	energy, ft-lb:	411		362		324
Rem. 185 BJHP	velocity, fps:	1015		951		899
	energy, ft-lb:	423		372		332
Rem. 185 BJHP +P	velocity, fps:	1140		1042		971
	energy, ft-lb:	534		446		388
Rem. 230 FN Enclosed Base	velocity, fps:	835		800		767
	energy, ft-lb:	356		326		300
Rem. 230 Metal Case	velocity, fps:	835		800		767
	energy, ft-lb:	356		326		300
Rem. 230 JHP	velocity, fps:	835		800		767
	energy, ft-lb:	356		326		300
Rem. 230 BJHP	velocity, fps:	875		833		795
	energy, ft-lb:	391		355		323
Speer 185 Gold Dot	velocity, fps:	1050		956		886
	energy, ft-lb:	453		375		322
Speer 200 JHP Blazer	velocity, fps:	975		917		860
	energy, ft-lb:	421		372		328
Speer 200 Gold Dot +P	velocity, fps:	1080		994		930
	energy, ft-lb:	518		439		384
Speer 230 FMJ (and Blazer)	velocity, fps:	845		804		775
	energy, ft-lb:	363		329		304
Speer 230 TMJ-CF (and Blazer)	velocity, fps:	845		804		775
	energy, ft-lb:	363		329		304
Speer 230 Gold Dot	velocity, fps:	890		845		805
	energy, ft-lb:	405		365		331
Win. 170 JFP	velocity, fps:	1050		982		928
	energy, ft-lb:	416		364		325
Win. 185 Silvertip HP	velocity, fps:	1000		938		888
	energy, ft-lb:	411		362		324
Win. 185 FMJ FN	velocity, fps:	910		861		
	energy, ft-lb:	340		304		
Win. 185 Brass Enclosed Base WinClean	velocity, fps:	910		835		
	energy, ft-lb:	340		286		
Win. 230 JHP	velocity, fps:	880		842		
	energy, ft-lb:	396		363		
Win. 230 FMJ	velocity, fps:	835		800		
	energy, ft-lb:	356		326		
Win. 230 SXT	velocity, fps:	880		846		816
	energy, ft-lb:	396		366		340
Win. 230 JHP subsonic	velocity, fps:	880		842		808
	energy, ft-lb:	396		363		334
Win. 230 Brass Enclosed Base WinClean	velocity, fps:	835		802		
	energy, ft-lb:	356		329		

.45 Winchester Magnum

		0	25	50	75	100
Win. 260 Partition Gold	velocity, fps:	1200		1105		1033
	energy, ft-lb:	832		705		616
Win. 260 JHP	velocity, fps:	1200		1099		1026
	energy, ft-lb:	831		698		607

.45 Schofield

		0	25	50	75	100
Black Hills 180 FNL	velocity, fps:	730				
	energy, ft-lb:					
Black Hills 230 RNFP	velocity, fps:	730				
	energy, ft-lb:					

.45 Colt

		0	25	50	75	100
Black Hills 250 RNFP	velocity, fps:	725				
	energy, ft-lb:					
Federal 225 SWC HP	velocity, fps:	900	880	860	840	820
	energy, ft-lb:	405	385	370	355	340
Hornady 255 Cowboy	velocity, fps:	725		692		660
	energy, ft-lb:	298		271		247
Magtech 250 LFN	velocity, fps:	750		726		702
	energy, ft-lb:	312		293		274
PMC 250 LFP	velocity, fps:	800		767		736
	energy, ft-lb:	355		331		309
Rem. 225 SWC	velocity, fps:	960		890		832
	energy, ft-lb:	460		395		346
Rem. 250 RLN	velocity, fps:	860		820		780
	energy, ft-lb:	410		375		340
Speer 200 FMJ Blazer	velocity, fps:	1000		938		889
	energy, ft-lb:	444		391		351
Speer 230 Trail Blazer LFN	velocity, fps:	750		716		684
	energy, ft-lb:	287		262		239
Win. 225 Silvertip HP	velocity, fps:	920		877		839
	energy, ft-lb:	423		384		352
Win. 255 LRN	velocity, fps:	860		820		780
	energy, ft-lb:	420		380		345
Win. 250 Lead	velocity, fps:	750		720		692
	energy, ft-lb:	312		288		266

.454 Casull

		0	25	50	75	100
Federal 300 Trophy Bonded	velocity, fps:	1630	1540	1450	1380	1300
	energy, ft-lb:	1760	1570	1405	1260	1130
Hornady 240 XTP-MAG	velocity, fps:	1900		1679		1483
	energy, ft-lb:	1923		1502		1172
Hornady 300 XTP-MAG	velocity, fps:	1650		1478		1328
	energy, ft-lb:	1813		1455		1175
Magtech 260 SJSP	velocity, fps:	1800		1577		1383
	energy, ft-lb:	1871		1437		1104

Centerfire Handgun Ballistics

.454 Casull to .50 Action Express

Cartridge Bullet	Range, Yards:	0	25	50	75	100
Speer 300 Gold Dot HP	velocity, fps:	1625		1477		1343
	energy, ft-lb:	1758		1452		1201
Win. 250 JHP	velocity, fps:	1300		1151		1047
	energy, ft-lb:	938		735		608
Win. 260 Partition Gold	velocity, fps:	1800		1605		1427
	energy, ft-lb:	1871		1485		1176
Win. 300 JFP	velocity, fps:	1625		1451		1308
	energy, ft-lb:	1759		1413		1141

.475 Linebaugh

Cartridge Bullet		0	25	50	75	100
Hornady 400 XTP-MAG	velocity, fps:	1300		1179		1093
	energy, ft-lb:	1501		1235		1060

.480 Ruger

Cartridge Bullet		0	25	50	75	100
Hornady 325 XTP-MAG	velocity, fps:	1350		1191		1076
	energy, ft-lb:	1315		1023		835
Speer 325 SP	velocity, fps:	1350		1224		1124
	energy, ft-lb:	1315		1082		912

.50 Action Express

Cartridge Bullet		0	25	50	75	100
Speer 300 Gold Dot HP	velocity, fps:	1550		1361		1207
	energy, ft-lb:	1600		1234		970
Speer 325 UCHP	velocity, fps:	1400		1232		1106
	energy, ft-lb:	1414		1095		883

RELOADING

BULLETS
Barnes	506
Berger	512
Federal	513
Hornady	514
Nosler	517
Sierra	521
Speer	524
Swift	529
Woodleigh	531

POWDERS
Accurate	532
Alliant	533
Hodgdon	535
IMR	536
Ramshot	537
Vihtavuori	538

RELOADING
Dillon	539
Forster	541
Hornady	543
Lyman	544
MEC	549
MTM	551
RCBS	552
Redding	556

Barnes Bullets

In 1989 Barnes introduced the X-Bullet. It has since supplanted the company's lead-core softpoints (still made) as a premier big game bullet. Now the X-Bullet is also available for handguns, muzzleloaders and shotguns, and for rifles with a special blue dry-film lubricant–the XLC. The XLC promises higher velocities at modest pressures.

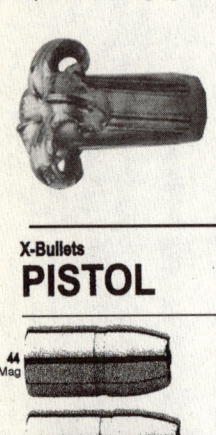

308 Cal. 180 Gr. XBT
RECOVERED FROM A MOOSE
98% WGT. RETENTION.

X-Bullets PISTOL

	Dia.	Bullet Weight	Desr.	Sect. Dens.	Ballist. Coeff.	Cat. #
44 Mag	.429"	200 GR	"X" PB	.155	.172	42920
	.429"	225 GR	"X" PB	.175	.195	42922
45	.451"	250 GR	"X" PB	.176	188	45123
50 AE	.500"	275 GR	"X" PB	.157	.183	50025

Expander MZ MUZZLELOADER

	Dia.	Bullet Weight	Desr.	Sect. Dens.	Ballist. Coeff.	Cat. #
50 Cal	.451"	250 GR	MZ	.176	.189	45125
	.451"	300 GR	MZ	.211	.207	45130
54 Cal	.500"	275 GR	MZ	.157	.184	50027
	.500"	325 GR	MZ	.186	.204	50032

Expander SGS SHOTGUN

	Dia.	Bullet Weight	Desr.	Sect. Dens.	Ballist. Coeff.	Cat. #
	.575"	438 GR	SGS	.189	.214	57500

COATED X-BULLETS RIFLE

Cal.	Dia.	Bullet Weight	Desr.	Sect. Dens.	Ballist. Coeff.	Cat. #
22	.224"	45 GR	"XLC" BT	.128	.203	22452
	.224"	50 GR	"XLC" S	.142	.220	22454
	.224"	53 GR	"XLC" S	.151	.231	22455
6mm	.243"	85 GR	"XLC" BT	.206	.401	24352
25	.257"	100 GR	"XLC" BT	.216	.420	25754
6.5	.264"	120 GR	"XLC" BT	.246	.441	26451
	.264"	140 GR	"XLC" S	.287	.522	26453
270	.277"	130 GR	"XLC" BT	.242	.466	27754
7mm	.284"	140 GR	"XLC" BT	.248	.477	28455
	.284"	160 GR	"XLC" S	.283	.508	28458
30	.308"	130 GR	"XLC" BT	.196	.374	30851
	.308"	150 GR	"XLC" BT	.226	.428	30854
	.308"	165 GR	"XLC" BT	.247	.505	30857
	.308"	180 GR	"XLC" S	.271	.511	30858
	.308"	180 GR	"XLC" BT	.271	.552	30859
338	.338"	185 GR	"XLC" BT	.231	.437	33854
	.338"	210 GR	"XLC" BT	.263	.471	33856
	.338"	225 GR	"XLC" S	.281	.482	33855
375	.375"	235 GR	"XLC" S	.239	.400	37553
	.375"	270 GR	"XLC" S	.275	.503	37557
416	.416"	400 GR	"XLC" S	.330	.546	41658
470 NIT	.474"	500 GR	"XLC" S	.326	.318	47550
500 NIT	.509"	570 GR	"XLC" S	.335	.316	50957

Barnes Bullets

X-BULLETS RIFLE

	Dia.	Bullet Weight	Desr.	Sect. Dens.	Ballist. Coeff.	Cat. #
22	.224"	50 GR	"X" S	.142	.220	22450
	.224"	53 GR	"X" S	.151	.231	22453
6mm	.243"	85 GR	"X" BT	.206	.401	24310
	.243"	90 GR	"X" S	.218	.382	24315
	.243"	95 GR	"X" S	.230	.398	24320
25	.257"	90 GR	"X" BT	.195	.343	25710
	.257"	100 GR	"X" S	.216	.401	25715
	.257"	100 GR	"X" BT	.216	.420	25717
	.257"	115 GR	"X" S	.249	.429	25722
6.5	.264"	120 GR	"X" S	.246	.441	26402
	.264"	130 GR	"X" S	.266	.479	26403
	.264"	140 GR	"X" S	.287	.522	26405
270	.277"	120 GR	"X" S	.223	.406	27712
	.277"	120 GR	"X" BT	.223	.423	27713
	.277"	130 GR	"X" S	.242	.428	27715
	.277"	130 GR	"X" BT	.242	.466	27717
	.277"	140 GR	"X" S	.261	.462	27725
	.277"	140 GR	"X" BT	.261	.497	27727
	.277"	150 GR	"X" S	.279	.491	27735
7mm	.284"	120 GR	"X" BT	.213	.411	28417
	.284"	130 GR	"X" BT	.230	.444	28420
	.284"	140 GR	"X" S	.248	.436	28425
	.284"	140 GR	"X" BT	.248	.477	28426
	.284"	150 GR	"X" S	.266	.488	28427
	.284"	150 GR	"X" BT	.266	.529	28428
	.284"	160 GR	"X" S	.283	.508	28435
	.284"	175 GR	"X" S	.310	.530	28445
30	.308"	110 GR	"X" S	.166	.322	30800
	.308"	130 GR	"X" BT	.196	.374	30808
	.308"	140 GR	"X" BT	.211	.398	30810
	.308"	150 GR	"X" S	.226	.386	30815
	.308"	150 GR	"X" BT	.226	.428	30817
	.308"	165 GR	"X" S	.247	.456	30825
	.308"	165 GR	"X" BT	.247	.505	30827
	.308"	180 GR	"X" S	.271	.511	30835
	.308"	180 GR	"X" BT	.271	.552	30840
	.308"	200 GR	"X" S	.301	.550	30845
30/30	.308"	150 GR	"X" FN	.226	.269	30819
8mm	.323"	180 GR	"X" S	.246	.382	32305
	.323"	200 GR	"X" S	.274	.429	32310
	.323"	220 GR	"X" S	.301	.462	32315
338	.338"	160 GR	"X" S	.200	.337	33878
	.338"	175 GR	"X" S	.218	.392	33880

Reloading • 507

Barnes Bullets

X-BULLETS RIFLE

Dia.	Bullet Weight	Desr.	Sect. Dens.	Ballist. Coeff.	Cat. #
.338"	185 GR	"X" BT	.231	.437	33881
.338"	200 GR	"X" S	.250	.440	33882
.338"	210 GR	"X" BT	.263	.471	33883
.338"	225 GR	"X" S	.281	.482	33885
.338"	250 GR	"X" S	.313	.521	33890
.348"	200 GR	"X" FN	.234	.291	34800
.348"	220 GR	"X" FN	.260	.315	34802
.358"	180 GR	"X" S	.201	.298	35810
.358"	225 GR	"X" S	.250	.405	35825
.358"	250 GR	"X" S	.279	.458	35835
.366"	250 GR	"X" S	.267	.428	36605
.366"	286 GR	"X" S	.305	.468	36615
.375"	210 GR	"X" S	.213	.341	37575
.375"	250 GR	"X" S	.254	.450	37582
.375"	270 GR	"X" S	.275	.503	37585
.375"	300 GR	"X" S	.305	.555	37590
.411"	300 GR	"X" S	.254	.401	41180
.411"	325 GR	"X" S	.275	.478	41182

X-BULLETS RIFLE

Dia.	Bullet Weight	Desr.	Sect. Dens.	Ballist. Coeff.	Cat. #
.411"	350 GR	"X" S	.296	.536	41185
.411"	400 GR	"X" S	.338	.562	41190
.416"	300 GR	"X" S	.247	.394	41680
.416"	325 GR	"X" S	.268	.467	41682
.416"	350 GR	"X" S	.289	.521	41685
.416"	400 GR	"X" S	.330	.546	41690
.423"	350 GR	"X" S	.279	.481	42382
.423"	400 GR	"X" S	.319	.537	42385
.458"	300 GR	"X" S	.204	.340	45802
.458"	350 GR	"X" S	.283	.402	45805
.458"	400 GR	"X" S	.272	.457	45815
.458"	450 GR	"X" S	.306	.488	45818
.458"	500 GR	"X" S	.341	.526	45822
.458"	250 GR	"X" FN	.170	.172	45831
.458"	300 GR	"X" FN	.206	.204	45832

Barnes Bullets

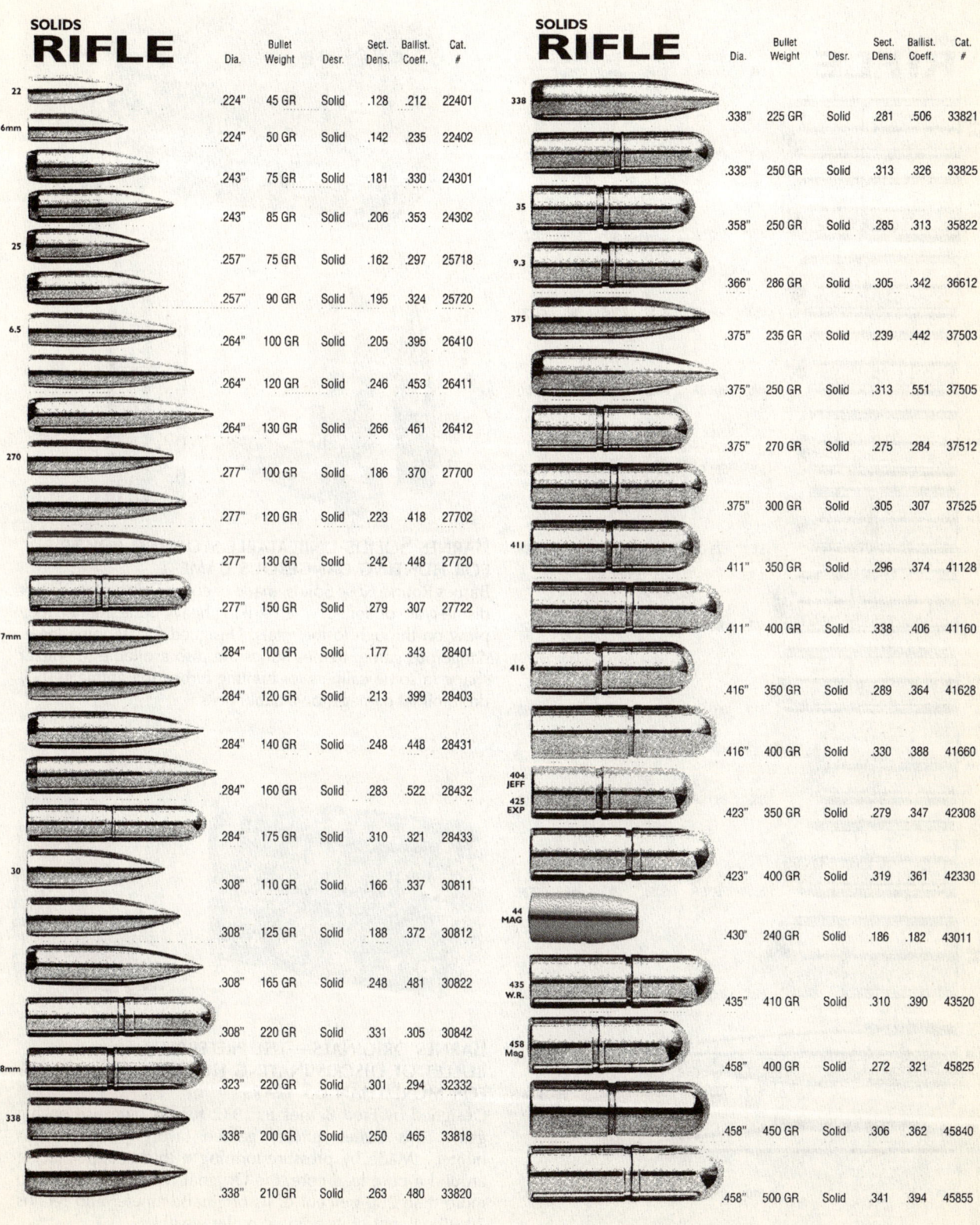

SOLIDS RIFLE

	Dia.	Bullet Weight	Desr.	Sect. Dens.	Ballist. Coeff.	Cat. #
22	.224"	45 GR	Solid	.128	.212	22401
6mm	.224"	50 GR	Solid	.142	.235	22402
	.243"	75 GR	Solid	.181	.330	24301
	.243"	85 GR	Solid	.206	.353	24302
25	.257"	75 GR	Solid	.162	.297	25718
	.257"	90 GR	Solid	.195	.324	25720
6.5	.264"	100 GR	Solid	.205	.395	26410
	.264"	120 GR	Solid	.246	.453	26411
	.264"	130 GR	Solid	.266	.461	26412
270	.277"	100 GR	Solid	.186	.370	27700
	.277"	120 GR	Solid	.223	.418	27702
	.277"	130 GR	Solid	.242	.448	27720
	.277"	150 GR	Solid	.279	.307	27722
7mm	.284"	100 GR	Solid	.177	.343	28401
	.284"	120 GR	Solid	.213	.399	28403
	.284"	140 GR	Solid	.248	.448	28431
	.284"	160 GR	Solid	.283	.522	28432
	.284"	175 GR	Solid	.310	.321	28433
30	.308"	110 GR	Solid	.166	.337	30811
	.308"	125 GR	Solid	.188	.372	30812
	.308"	165 GR	Solid	.248	.481	30822
	.308"	220 GR	Solid	.331	.305	30842
8mm	.323"	220 GR	Solid	.301	.294	32332
338	.338"	200 GR	Solid	.250	.465	33818
	.338"	210 GR	Solid	.263	.480	33820

SOLIDS RIFLE

	Dia.	Bullet Weight	Desr.	Sect. Dens.	Ballist. Coeff.	Cat. #
338	.338"	225 GR	Solid	.281	.506	33821
	.338"	250 GR	Solid	.313	.326	33825
35	.358"	250 GR	Solid	.285	.313	35822
9.3	.366"	286 GR	Solid	.305	.342	36612
375	.375"	235 GR	Solid	.239	.442	37503
	.375"	250 GR	Solid	.313	.551	37505
	.375"	270 GR	Solid	.275	.284	37512
	.375"	300 GR	Solid	.305	.307	37525
411	.411"	350 GR	Solid	.296	.374	41128
	.411"	400 GR	Solid	.338	.406	41160
416	.416"	350 GR	Solid	.289	.364	41628
	.416"	400 GR	Solid	.330	.388	41660
404 JEFF / 425 EXP	.423"	350 GR	Solid	.279	.347	42308
	.423"	400 GR	Solid	.319	.361	42330
44 MAG	.430"	240 GR	Solid	.186	.182	43011
435 W.R.	.435"	410 GR	Solid	.310	.390	43520
458 Mag	.458"	400 GR	Solid	.272	.321	45825
	.458"	450 GR	Solid	.306	.362	45840
	.458"	500 GR	Solid	.341	.394	45855

Reloading

Barnes Bullets

SOLIDS RIFLE

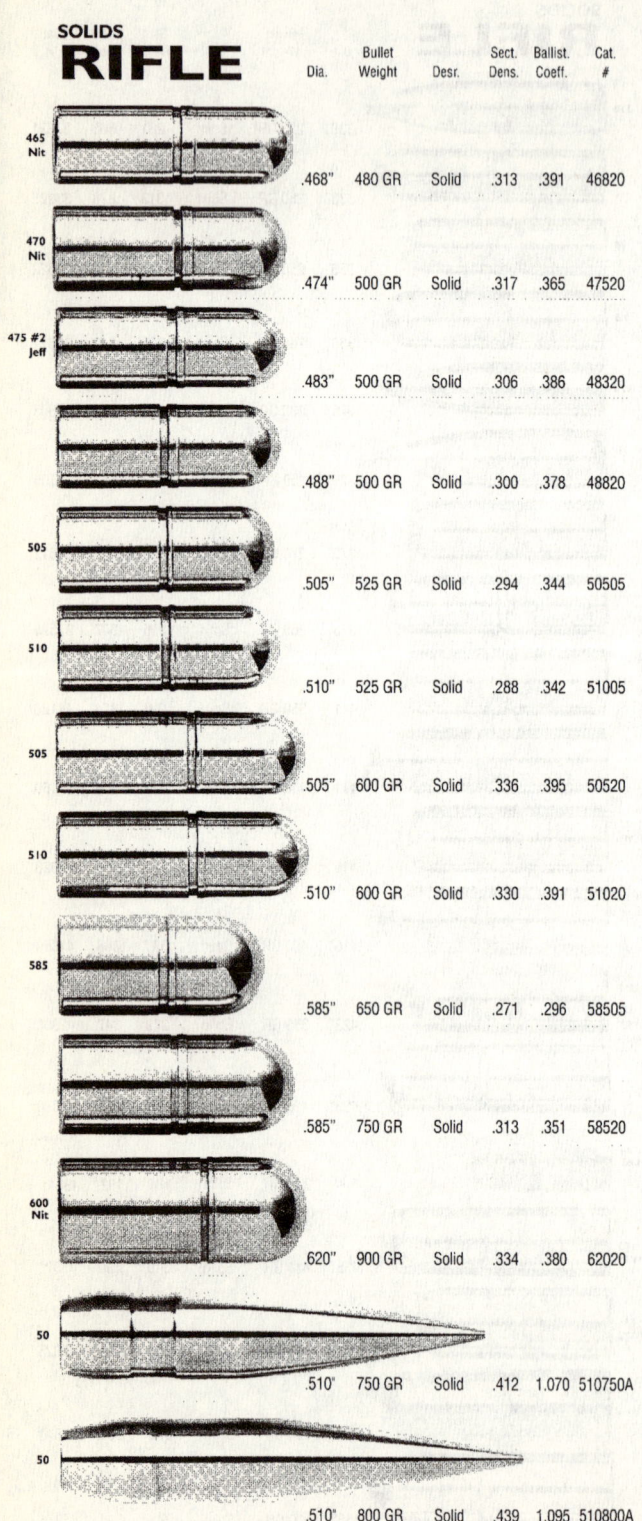

	Dia.	Bullet Weight	Desr.	Sect. Dens.	Ballist. Coeff.	Cat. #
465 Nit	.468"	480 GR	Solid	.313	.391	46820
470 Nit	.474"	500 GR	Solid	.317	.365	47520
475 #2 Jeff	.483"	500 GR	Solid	.306	.386	48320
	.488"	500 GR	Solid	.300	.378	48820
505	.505"	525 GR	Solid	.294	.344	50505
510	.510"	525 GR	Solid	.288	.342	51005
505	.505"	600 GR	Solid	.336	.395	50520
510	.510"	600 GR	Solid	.330	.391	51020
585	.585"	650 GR	Solid	.271	.296	58505
	.585"	750 GR	Solid	.313	.351	58520
600 Nit	.620"	900 GR	Solid	.334	.380	62020
50	.510"	750 GR	Solid	.412	1.070	510750A
50	.510"	800 GR	Solid	.439	1.095	510800A

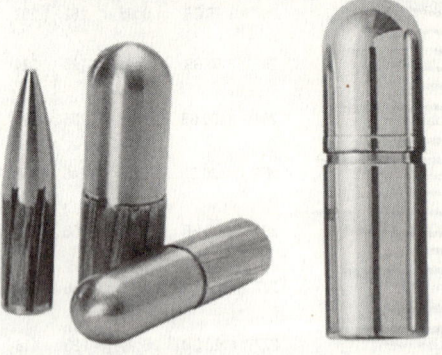

BARNES SOLIDS—UNBEATABLE STOPPING POWER FOR HUNTING DANGEROUS GAME

Barnes Round Nose Solids, made of copper/zinc alloy, do not disintegrate or deflect when striking heavy bone. Rather, they plow on through to the vitals. Designed for stopping large, dangerous game, Barnes Solids are also available in Spitzer shape in some calibers for hunting furbearing animals. They do minimal damage to valuable pelts.

BARNES ORIGINALS—THE PREFERRED BULLET OF DISCRIMINATING HUNTERS FOR MORE THAN 65 YEARS

Designed by Fred Barnes in 1932 for his own use on big game, this bullet quickly gained favor among serious hunters. Made by pressure-forming a thick copper jacket around a pure lead core, the Original typically expands to more than 200 percent of its original diameter and retains 70-90 percent of its original bullet weight.

Barnes Bullets

ORIGINALS RIFLE

	Dia.	Bullet Weight	Desr.	Jacket Thick.	Sect. Dens.	Ballist. Coeff.	Cat. #
6mm	.243"	115 GR	R.N.S.P.	.030"	.290	.322	24330
270	.277"	180 GR	R.N.S.P.	.032"	.335	.372	27750
7mm	.284"	195 GR	S.S.P.	.032"	.345	.570	28450
30	.308"	250 GR	R.N.S.P.	.032"	.376	.417	30860
348 Win	.348"	220 GR	F.N.S.P.	.032"	.260	.301	34805
	.348"	250 GR	F.N.S.P.	.032"	.295	.327	34810
375 Win	.375"	220 GR	F.N.S.P.	.032"	.223	.246	375W10
	.375"	255 GR	F.N.S.P.	.032"	.259	.290	375W20
38/55	.375"	255 GR	F.N.S.P.	.032"	.259	.290	38/5510
	.377"	255 GR	F.N.S.P.	.032"	.256	.290	38/5520
401 Win	.406"	250 GR	R.N.S.P.	.032"	.217	.241	40610
425	.435"	410 GR	R.N.S.P.	.049"	.310	.344	43510
	.458"	300 GR	S.S.P.	.032"	.204	.291	457010
45/70	.458"	300 GR	F.N.S.P.	.032"	.204	.227	457020
	.458"	400 GR	S.S.P.	.032"	.272	.389	457030

ORIGINALS RIFLE

	Dia.	Bullet Weight	Desr.	Jacket Thick.	Sect. Dens.	Ballist. Coeff.	Cat. #
	.458"	400 GR	F.N.S.P.	.032"	.272	.302	457040
458 Mag	.458"	600 GR	R.N.S.P.	.049"	.409	.454	45860
465 Nit	.468"	480 GR	R.N.S.P.	.049"	.318	.362	46810
470 Nit	.475"	500 GR	R.N.S.P.	.049"	.317	.352	47510
	.475"	600 GR	R.N.S.P.	.049"	.380	.422	47530
475 #2 JEFF	.488"	500 GR	R.N.S.P.	.049"	.300	.333	48810
50/110 Win	.510"	300 GR	F.N.S.P.	.032"	.165	.183	5011010
	.510"	450 GR	F.N.S.P.	.032"	.247	.274	5011020
50	.510"	600 GR	R.N.S.P.	.049"	.336	.365	51010
	.510"	700 GR	R.N.S.P.	.049"	.392	.436	51030
577 Nit	.585"	750 GR	R.N.S.P.	.049"	.313	.346	58510
600 Nit	.620"	900 GR	R.N.S.P.	.049"	.334	.371	62010

Reloading

Berger Bullets

Berger's match bullets are well-known for their superior performance in benchrest matches. Now Berger offers a variety of bullets from .17 to .30. All feature J4 jackets with wall concentricity tolerance of .0003. Lead cores are 99.9% pure and swaged in dies to within .0001 of round. Berger's line includes several profiles: Low Drag, Very Low Drag, Length Tolerant, Maximum-Expansion, besides standard flat-base and standard boat-tail.

ITEM	WEIGHT	TWIST
.172 17 Cal.	15 Gr. MEF	12
.172 17 Cal.	18 Gr. MEF	12
.172 17 Cal.	20 Gr.	12
.172 17 Cal.	22 Gr.	11
.172 17 Cal.	25 Gr.	10
.172 17 Cal.	30 Gr.	9
.172 17 Cal.	37 Gr. VLD	6
.204 20 Cal.	36 Gr. MEF	12
.224 22 Cal.	30 Gr MEF	15
.224 22 Cal.	35 Gr. MEF	15
.224 22 Cal.	40 Gr. MEF	15
.224 22 Cal.	45 Gr.	15
.224 22 Cal.	50 Gr.	14
.224 22 Cal.	52 Gr.	14
.224 22 Cal.	55 Gr.	14
.224 22 Cal.	60 Gr.	12
.224 22 Cal.	62 Gr.	12
.224 22 Cal.	64 Gr.	12
.224 22 Cal.	70 Gr. VLD	9
.224 22 Cal.	70 Gr. LTB	10
.224 22 Cal.	73 Gr. LTB	9
.224 22 Cal.	75 Gr. VLD	9
.224 22 Cal.	80 Gr. VLD	8
.243 (6mm) Cal.	60 Gr.	14
.243 (6mm) Cal.	62 Gr	14
.243 (6mm) Cal.	65 Gr	13
.243 (6mm) Cal.	65 Gr. Short	14
.243 (6mm) Cal.	65 Gr. BT	13
.243 (6mm) Cal.	66 Gr. LD	13
.243 (6mm) Cal.	68 Gr.	13
.243 (6mm) Cal.	69 Gr. LD	12
.243 (6mm) Cal.	70 Gr.	13
.243 (6mm) Cal.	71 Gr. BT	12
.243 (6mm) Cal.	74 Gr.	13
.243 (6mm) Cal.	80 Gr.	12
.243 (6mm) Cal.	88 Gr. LD	10
.243 (6mm) Cal.	90 Gr. BT	10
.243 (6mm) Cal.	95 Gr. VLD	9
.243 (6mm) Cal.	105 Gr. LTB	9
.243 (6mm) Cal.	105 Gr. VLD	8
.243 (6mm) Cal.	115 Gr. VLD	7
.257 25 Cal.	72 Gr.	15
.257 25 Cal.	78 Gr.	13
.257 25 Cal.	82 Gr.	14
.257 25 Cal.	87 Gr.	13
.257 25 Cal.	95 Gr.	12
.257 25 Cal.	110 Gr.	12
.257 25 Cal.	115 Gr. VLD	10
.264 (6.5mm) Cal.	140 Gr. VLD	9
.284 (7mm) Cal.	168 Gr. VLD	10
.284 (7mm) Cal.	180 Gr. VLD	9
.308 30 Cal.	110 Gr.	19
.308 30 Cal.	125 Gr.	19
.308 30 Cal.	135 Gr.	16
.308 30 Cal.	150 Gr.	15
.308 30 Cal.	155 Gr. LTB	14
.308 30 Cal.	155 Gr. VLD	14
.308 30 Cal.	168 Gr. LTB	13
.308 30 Cal.	168 Gr. VLD	13
.308 30 Cal.	175 Gr. VLD	13
.308 30 Cal.	185 Gr. VLD	12
.308 30 Cal.	190 Gr. VLD	12
.308 30 Cal.	210 Gr. VLD	11

Federal Rifle and Handgun Bullets

Classic® Centerfire Rifle
Hi-Shok® Soft Point
It's a proven performer on small game and thin-skinned medium game. It has an aerodynamic tip for a flat trajectory. The exposed soft point expands rapidly for hard hits, even as velocity slows at longer ranges.

Hi-Shok® Soft Point Round Nose
For generations, hunters have made this bullet the choice for deer and bear in heavy cover. Its large exposed tip, good weight retention and specially tapered jacket provide controlled expansion for deep penetration.

Hi-Shok® Soft Point Flat Nose
This is the bullet hunters traditionally choose when headed into thick cover. It expands reliably and penetrates deep on light to medium game. The flat nose prevents accidental discharge in tubular magazines.

Speer® Hot-Cor® Soft Point
For larger game, Vernon Speer recognized the importance of bullet integrity. Nearly 40 years ago, he developed the Hot-Cor®, a bullet with a molten lead core poured into the jacket. Today, this still gives you excellent bullet integrity, combining nearly 200% expansion with deep penetration.

Full Metal Jacket Boat-Tail
These accurate, non-expanding bullets give you a flat shooting trajectory, leave a small exit hole in game, and puts clean holes in paper - great for sharpening your shooting eye. And they're famous for smooth, reliable feeding into semi-automatics too.

Classic® Handgun Bullet Styles
Lead Round Nose
A great economical training round for practicing at the range. It dates back to the early part of this century. This bullet is 100% lead with no jacket. It provides excellent accuracy and is very economical.

Full Metal Jacket
A good choice for range practice and reducing lead fouling in the barrel. The jacket extends from the nose to the base, preventing bullet expansion and barrel leading. It is used primarily as military ammunition and for recreational shooting.

Hi-Shok® Jacketed Soft Point
It's a proven performer on small to medium-sized game.

Lead Semi-Wadcutter
The most popular all-around choice for target and personal defense. a versatile design which cuts clean holes in targets and efficiently transfers energy.

Hi-Shok® Jacketed Hollow Point
It's an ideal personal defense round in revolvers and semi-autos. Creates quick, positive expansion with proven accuracy. Specially designed jacket ensures smooth feeding into autoloading firearms.

Semi-Wadcutter Hollow Point
A good combination for both small game and personal defense. Hollow point design promotes uniform expansion.

Premium® Handgun Bullet Styles
Hydra-Shok®
The choice of law enforcement agencies nationwide. Federal's unique center-post design delivers controlled expansion, and the notched jacket provides efficient energy transfer to penetrate barriers while retaining stopping power. The deep penetration of this jacketed bullet satisfies even the FBI's stringent testing requirements.

Premium® Personal Defense®
We hope you never have to use our Premium Personal Defense ammunition in a critical situation. But, if you do, you'll appreciate the increased muzzle velocity and energy compared to standard loads, and the rapid bullet expansion that delivers instant stopping power. You'll also appreciate that recoil is significantly reduced. In addition, our unique clear packaging lets you see the ammo before you open the box.

Premium Expanding Full Metal Jacket
An ideal choice for agencies that don't permit hollow point ammunition, this revolutionary barrier-penetrating design combines a scored metal nose over an internal rubber tip that collapses on impact. It never fills with barrier material and assures expansion on every shot. A lead core at the base maintains weight retension.

CastCore
Premium CastCore gives you a heavyweight, flat nosed, hard cast-lead bullet that smashes through bone, without breaking apart.

Trophy Bonded Bear Claw
The Trophy Bonded Bear Claw handgun bullet has a fusion-bonded jacket and core for up to 95% weight retention, better penetration and more knockdown power.

Hornady Rifle Bullets

RELOADING

RIFLE BULLETS

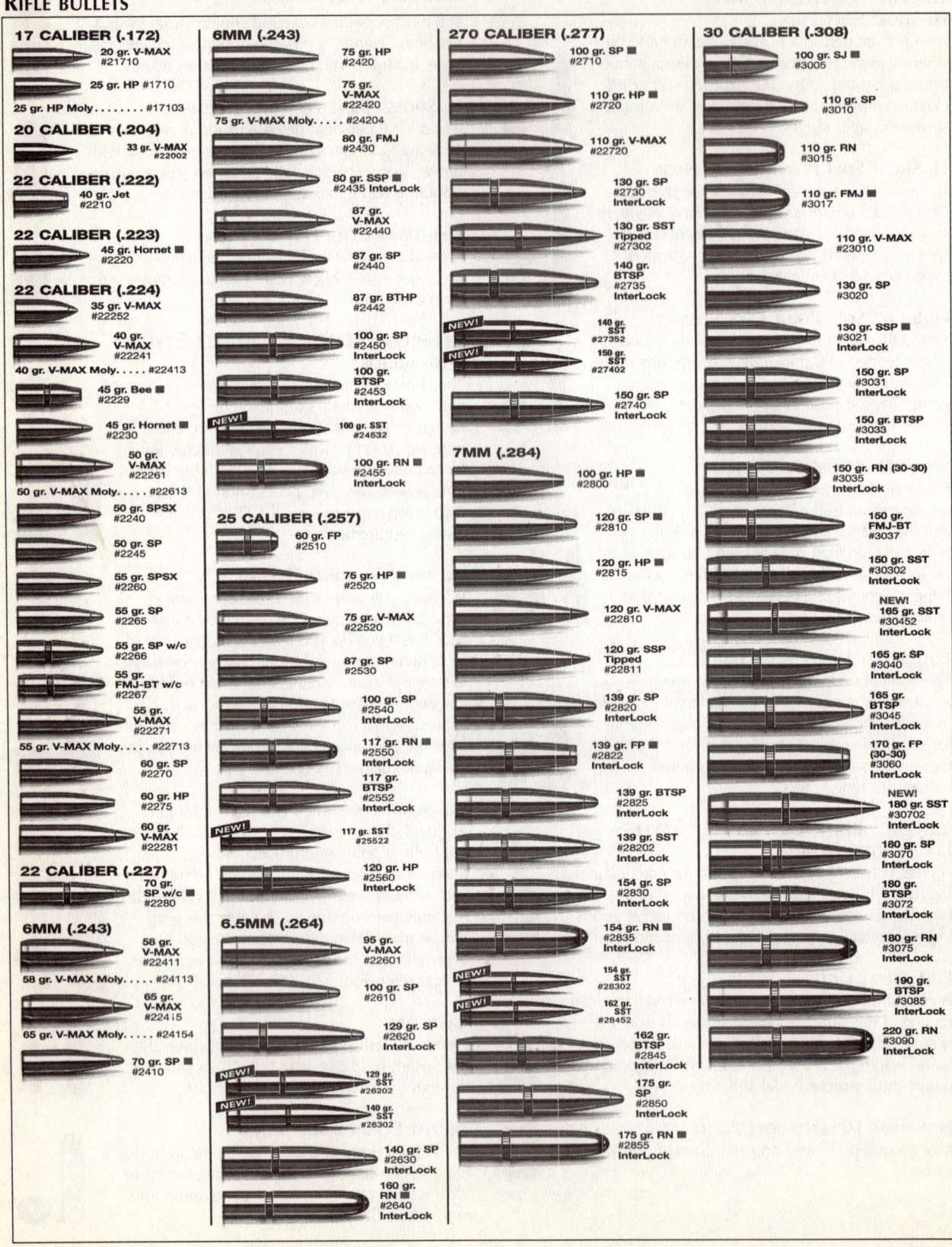

Hornady Rifle Bullets

RIFLE BULLETS (CONTINUED)

7.62 X 39 (.310)
- 123 gr. SP #3140
- 123 gr. FMJ #3147

303 CAL. AND 7.7 JAP (.312)
- 150 gr. SP #3120 InterLock
- 174 gr. RN #3130 InterLock
- 174 gr. FMJ-BT #3131

32 SPECIAL (.321)
- 170 gr. FP #3210 InterLock

8MM (.323)
- 125 gr. SP #3230
- 150 gr. SP #3232 InterLock
- 170 gr. RN #3235 InterLock
- 220 gr. SP #3238 InterLock

338 CALIBER (.338)
- 200 gr. SP #3310 InterLock
- 200 gr. FP (33 Win) #3315 InterLock
- 225 gr. SP #3320 InterLock
- NEW! 225 gr. SST #33202
- 250 gr. RN #3330 InterLock
- 250 gr. SP #3335 InterLock

348 CALIBER (.348)
- 200 gr. FP #3410 InterLock

35 CALIBER (.358)
- 180 gr. SSP #3505 InterLock
- 200 gr. SP #3510 InterLock
- 200 gr. RN #3515 InterLock

35 CALIBER (.358)
- 250 gr. SP #3520 InterLock
- 250 gr. RN #3525 InterLock

375 CALIBER (.375)
- 220 gr. FP (375 Win.) #3705 InterLock
- 225 gr. SP #3706
- *270 gr. SP #3710 InterLock
- *270 gr. RN #3715 InterLock
- *300 gr. RN #3720 InterLock
- *300 gr. BTSP #3725 InterLock
- *300 gr. FMJ-RN #37277
- NEW! 300 gr. FP #41050

416 CALIBER (.416)
- *400 gr. RN #4165 InterLock
- *400 gr. FMJ-RN #41677

44 CALIBER (.430)
- 265 gr. FP #4300 InterLock

45 CALIBER (.458)
- *300 gr. HP #4500
- *350 gr. FP #4503 InterLock
- †350 gr. RN #4502 InterLock
- *500 gr. RN #4504 InterLock
- *500 gr. FMJ-RN ENC #45077

MATCH BULLETS

22 CALIBER (.224)
- 52 gr. BTHP #2249
- 53 gr. HP #2250
- 68 gr. BTHP #2278
- 75 gr. BTHP #2279
- 75 gr. BTHP Moly .... #22793

22 CALIBER A-MAX (.224)
- 52 gr. A-MAX #22492
- 75 gr. A-MAX #22792
- 75 gr. A-MAX Moly .... #22794

6MM A-MAX
- 105 gr. A-MAX #24562
- 105 gr. A-MAX Moly .... #24564

6.5MM A-MAX
- 140 gr. A-MAX #26332
- 140 gr. A-MAX Moly .... #26334

7MM
- 162 gr. A-MAX #28402
- 162 gr. A-MAX Moly .... #28404

30 CALIBER BTHP
- 168 gr. BTHP #30501
- 168 gr. BTHP Moly .... #30503

30 CALIBER A-MAX
- 155 gr. A-MAX #30312
- 155 gr. A-MAX Moly .... #30314
- 168 gr. A-MAX #30502
- 168 gr. A-MAX Moly .... #30504
- 178 gr. A-MAX #30712
- 178 gr. A-MAX Moly .... #30714

50 CALIBER (.510)
- 750 gr. A-MAX UHC #5165
- (Packaged 20 per box.)

Hornady Pistol Bullets

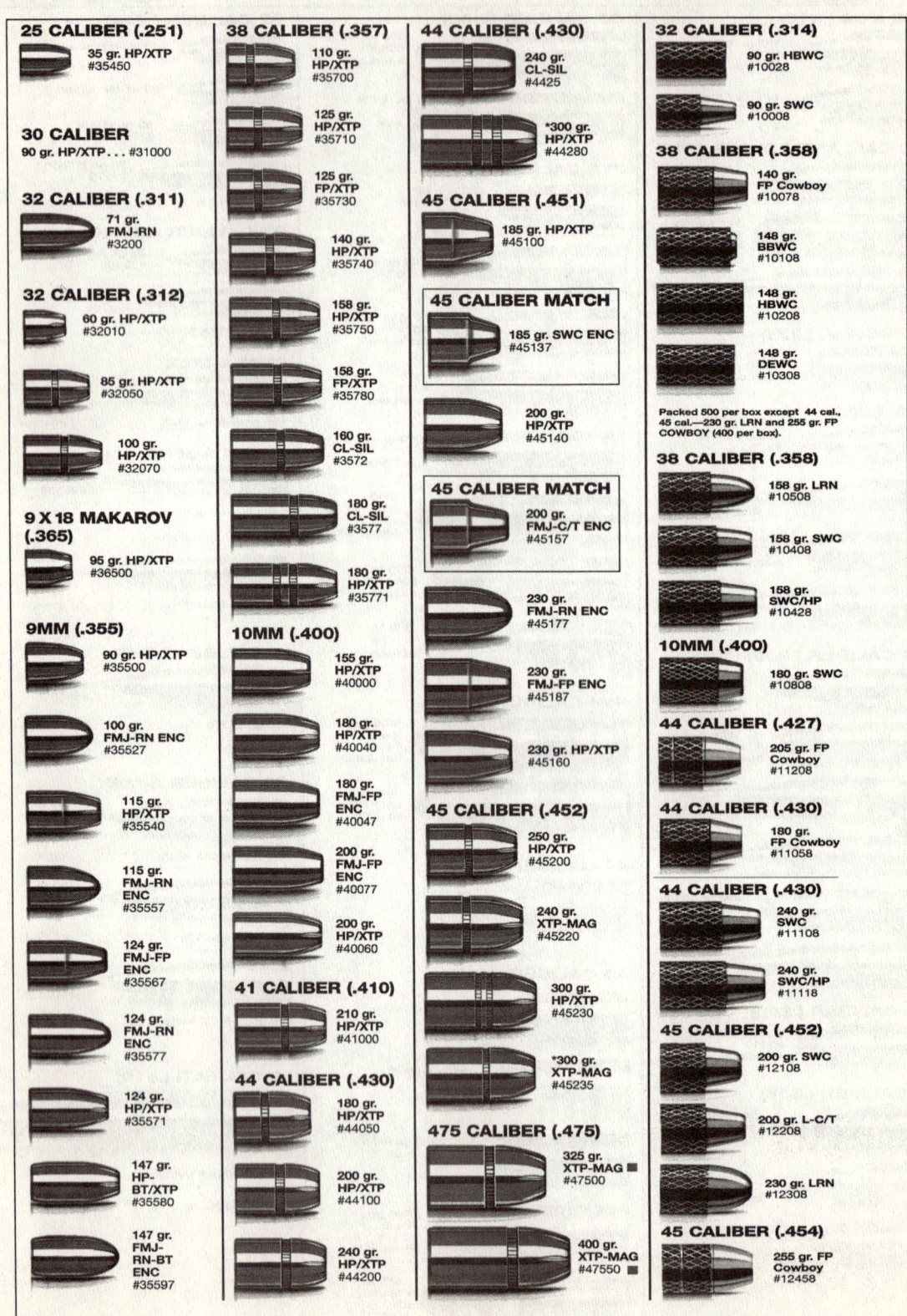

Nosler Bullets

Nosler J4 Competition
Nosler has blended the renowned accuracy of J4 bullet jacket with its own ultra-precise lead alloy cores to create a new performance standard for the popular .30 caliber match bullets.

Cal. Dia.	BULLET WEIGHT AND STYLE	SECT. DENS.	BAL. COEF.	PART#
22 .224"	69 GR. HPBT 250 QUANTITY BULK PACK (NEW!)	.196	.359	53065
	80 GR. HPBT 250 QUANTITY BULK PACK (NEW!)	.228	.440	53080
30 .308"	155 GR. HPBT 250 QUANTITY BULK PACK	.233	.450	53155 53169
	168 GR. HPBT 250 QUANTITY BULK PACK	.253	.462	53164 53168

Bullets for Pistols

Cal. Dia.	BULLET WEIGHT AND STYLE	SECT. DENS.	BAL. COEF.	PART#
9mm .355"	115 GR. HOLLOW POINT 250 QUANTITY BULK PACK	.130	.110	44848
38 .357"	115 GR. HOLLOW POINT PRACTICAL PISTOL™ 250 QUANTITY BULK PACK	.129	.110	44835
	135 GR. PRACTICAL PISTOL™ 250 QUANTITY BULK PACK	.151	.149	44836
10mm .400"	135 GR. HOLLOW POINT 250 QUANTITY BULK PACK	.121	.093	44852
	150 GR. HOLLOW POINT 250 QUANTITY BULK PACK	.134	.106	44860
45 .451"	185 GR. HOLLOW POINT 250 QUANTITY BULK PACK	.130	.142	44847
	230 GR. FULL METAL JACKET	.162	.183	42064

Bullets for Revolvers

Cal. Dia.	BULLET WEIGHT AND STYLE	SECT. DENS.	BAL. COEF.	PART#
38 .357"	125 GR. HOLLOW POINT 250 QUANTITY BULK PACK	.140	.143	44840
	158 GR. HOLLOW POINT 250 QUANTITY BULK PACK	.177	.182	44841
	180 GR. SILHOUETTE 250 QUANTITY BULK PACK	.202	.210	44851
41 .410"	210 GR. HOLLOW POINT	.178	.170	43012
44 .429"	200 GR. HOLLOW POINT 250 QUANTITY BULK PACK	.155	.151	44846
	240 GR. HOLLOW POINT 250 QUANTITY BULK PACK	.186	.173	44842
	240 GR. SOFT POINT 250 QUANTITY BULK PACK	.186	.177	44868
	300 GR. HOLLOW POINT	.233	.206	42069
45 Colt .451"	250 GR. HOLLOW POINT	.176	.177	43013

Partition-HG™

50 cal/250 GR. JHP	.429"	50441
50 cal/260 GR. JHP	.451"	50260
54 cal/260 GR. JHP	.451"	54261
50 cal/300 GR. JPP	.451"	50281
54 cal/300 GR. JPP	.451"	54281

S.H.O.T.S.™

50 cal/250 grain JHP	.451"	50251
50 cal/300 grain JHP	.429"	50301
54 cal/250 grain JHP	.451"	54251

High volume shooters can now get Nosler's specially designed plastic muzzleloading sabots in 50-count Bulk Packs:

50 cal. sabots for 44 cal. bullets	50095
50 cal. sabots for 45 cal. bullets	50096
54 cal. sabots for 45 cal. bullets	50097

Nosler Bullets

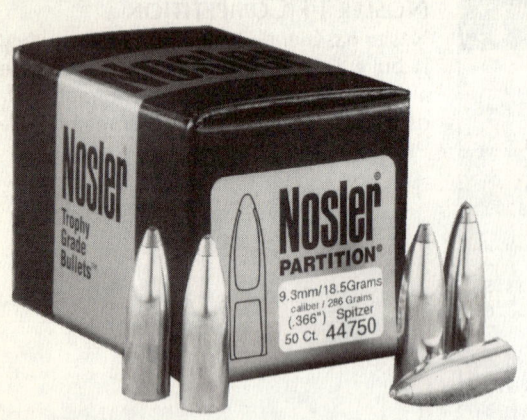

Nosler Partition® Bullets

The Nosler Partition® bullet earned its reputation among professional guides and serious hunters for one reason: it doesn't fail. The patented Partition® design offers a dual core that is unequalled in mushrooming, weight retention and hydrostatic shock.

Cal. Dia.	Bullet Weight and Style	Sect. Dens.	Bal. Coef.	Part#
22 .224"	60 GR. SPITZER	.171	.228	16316
6mm .243"	85 GR. SPITZER	.206	.315	16314
	95 GR. SPITZER	.230	.365	16315
	100 GR. SPITZER	.242	.384	35642
25 .257"	100 GR. SPITZER	.216	.377	16317
	115 GR. SPITZER	.249	.389	16318
	120 GR. SPITZER	.260	.391	35643
6.5mm .264"	100 GR. SPITZER	.205	.326	16319
	125 GR. SPITZER	.256	.449	16320
	140 GR. SPITZER	.287	.490	16321
270 .277"	130 GR. SPITZER	.242	.416	16322
	150 GR. SPITZER	.279	.465	16323
	160 GR. SEMI SPITZER	.298	.434	16324
7mm .284"	140 GR. SPITZER	.248	.434	16325
	150 GR. SPITZER	.266	.456	16326
	160 GR. SPITZER	.283	.475	16327
	175 GR. SPITZER	.310	.519	35645
30 .308"	150 GR. SPITZER	.226	.387	16329
	165 GR. SPITZER	.248	.410	16330
	170 GR. ROUND NOSE	.256	.252	16333
	180 GR. PROTECTED POINT	.271	.361	25396
	180 GR. SPITZER	.271	.474	16331
	200 GR. SPITZER	.301	.481	35626
	220 GR. SEMI SPITZER	.331	.351	16332
8mm .323"	200 GR. SPITZER	.274	.426	35277
	210 GR. SPITZER	.263	.400	16337
338 .338"	225 GR. SPITZER	.281	.454	16336
	250 GR. SPITZER	.313	.473	35644
35 .358"	225 GR. SPITZER	.251	.430	44800
	250 GR. SPITZER	.279	.446	44801
9.3mm .366"	286 GR. SPITZER (18.5 GRAM)	.307	.482	44750
375 .375"	260 GR. SPITZER	.264	.314	44850
	300 GR. SPITZER	.305	.398	44845
416 .416"	400 GR. SPITZER	.330	.390	45200
45-70 .458"	300 GR. PROTECTED POINT	.204	.199	45325
38 .357" (PARTITION-HG™)	180 GR. HOLLOW POINT	.202	.201	35180
44 .429" (PARTITION-HG™)	250 GR. HOLLOW POINT	.194	.200	44250
45 .451" (PARTITION-HG™)	260 GR. HOLLOW POINT	.182	.174	45260
	300 GR. PROTECTED POINT	.211	.199	45350

Nosler Bullets

Nosler Ballistic Tip® Hunting Bullets

Nosler has replaced the familiar lead point of the Spitzer with a tough polycarbonate tip. The purpose of this new Ballistic Tip® is to resist deforming in the magazine and feed ramp of many rifles. The Solid Base® design produces controlled expansion for excellent mushrooming and exceptional accuracy.

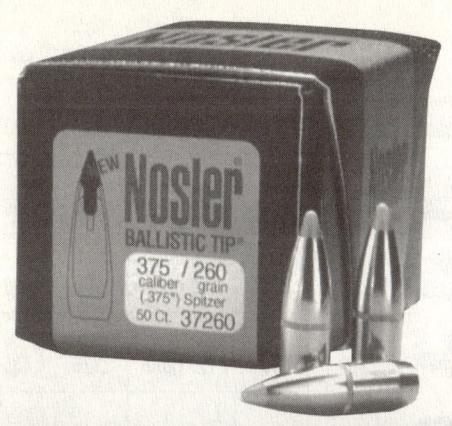

Varmint Bullets

Cal. Dia.	BULLET WEIGHT AND STYLE	SECT. DENS.	BAL. COEF.	PART#
22 .224"	40 GR. SPITZER (ORANGE TIP) 250 CT. VARMINT PAK™	.114	.221	39510 / 39555
22 .224"	45 GR. HORNET (SOFT LEAD TIP)	.128	.144	35487
22 .224"	50 GR. SPITZER (ORANGE TIP) 250 CT. VARMINT PAK™	.142	.238	39522 / 39557
22 .224"	55 GR. SPITZER (ORANGE TIP) 250 CT. VARMINT PAK™	.157	.267	39526 / 39560
6mm .243"	55 GR. SPITZER (PURPLE TIP) 250 CT. VARMINT PAK™	.133	.276	24055 / 39565
6mm .243"	70 GR. SPITZER (PURPLE TIP) 250 CT. VARMINT PAK™	.169	.310	39532 / 39570
6mm .243"	80 GR. SPITZER (PURPLE TIP)	.194	.339	24080
25 .257"	85 GR. SPITZER (BLUE TIP)	.183	.331	43004

Hunting Bullets

Cal. Dia.	BULLET WEIGHT AND STYLE	SECT. DENS.	BAL. COEF.	PART#
6mm .243"	90 GR. SPITZER (PURPLE TIP)	.218	.365	24090
6mm .243"	95 GR. SPITZER (PURPLE TIP)	.230	.379	24095
25 .257"	100 GR. SPITZER (BLUE TIP)	.216	.393	25100
25 .257"	115 GR. SPITZER (BLUE TIP)	.249	.453	25115
6.5mm .264"	100 GR. SPITZER (BROWN TIP)	.205	.350	26100
6.5mm .264"	120 GR. SPITZER (BROWN TIP)	.246	.458	26120

Cal. Dia.	BULLET WEIGHT AND STYLE	SECT. DENS.	BAL. COEF.	PART#
270 .277"	130 GR. SPITZER (YELLOW TIP)	.242	.433	27130
270 .277"	140 GR. SPITZER (YELLOW TIP)	.261	.456	27140
270 .277"	150 GR. SPITZER (YELLOW TIP)	.279	.496	27150
7mm .284"	120 GR. FLAT POINT (SOFT LEAD TIP)	.213	.195	28121
7mm .284"	120 GR. SPITZER (RED TIP)	.213	.417	28120
7mm .284"	140 GR. SPITZER (RED TIP)	.248	.485	28140
7mm .284"	150 GR. SPITZER (RED TIP)	.266	.493	28150
30 .308"	125 GR. SPITZER (GREEN TIP)	.188	.366	30125
30 .308"	150 GR. SPITZER (GREEN TIP)	.226	.435	30150
30 .308"	165 GR. SPITZER (GREEN TIP)	.248	.475	30165
30 .308"	180 GR. SPITZER (GREEN TIP)	.271	.507	30180
8mm .323"	180 GR. SPITZER (GUNMETAL TIP)	.247	.394	32180
338 .338"	180 GR. SPITZER (MAROON TIP)	.225	.372	33180
338 .338"	200 GR. SPITZER (MAROON TIP)	.250	.414	33200
35 .358"	225 GR. WHELEN (BUCKSKIN TIP)	.251	.421	35225
9.3mm .366"	250 GR. SPITZER (OLIVE TIP) Available Mid-year	.267	.494	36250
375 .375"	NEW! 260 GR. SPITZER (SAFARI TIP)	.264	.473	37260

Reloading • 519

Nosler Bullets

Cal.	Dia.	Bullet Weight	Sect. Dens.	Bal. Coef.	Part #
22	.224"	40 grain	.114	.221	51005
22	.224"	50 grain	.142	.238	51010
22	.224"	55 grain	.157	.267	51031
6mm	.243"	55 grain	.133	.276	51030
6mm	.243"	95 grain	.230	.379	51040
25	.257"	85 grain	.183	.331	51045
25	.257"	115 grain	.249	.453	51050

Cal.	Dia.	Bullet Weight	Sect. Dens.	Bal. Coef.	Part #
270	.277"	130 grain	.242	.433	51075
7mm	.284"	140 grain	.248	.485	51105
7mm	.284"	150 grain	.266	.493	51110
30	.308"	150 grain	.226	.435	51150
30	.308"	168 grain	.253	.490	51160
30	.308"	180 grain	.271	.507	51170
338	.338"	200 grain	.250	.414	51200

Fail Safe

Cal.	Dia.	Bullet Weight	Sect. Dens.	Bal. Coef.	Part #
270	.277"	140 grain	.261	.322	53140
7mm	.284"	140 grain	.248	.323	53150
7mm	.284"	160 grain	.283	.382	53160
30	.308"	150 grain	.226	.308	53170
30	.308"	165 grain	.248	.314	53175
30	.308"	180 grain	.271	.391	53180
338	.338"	230 grain	.288	.436	53230
375	.375"	270 grain	.274	.393	53350
375	.375"	300 grain	.305	.441	53360

Ballistic Silvertip, Fail Safe and Partition Gold bullets are made by Nosler for loading in Winchester ammunition in a project known as Combined Technology.

Partition Gold

Cal.	Dia.	Bullet Weight	Sect. Dens.	Bal. Coef.	Part #
270	.277"	150 grain	.279	.465	52100
7mm	.284"	160 grain	.283	.475	52150
30	.308"	150 grain	.226	.387	52200
30	.308"	180 grain	.271	.474	52230
338	.338"	250 grain	.313	.473	52280

Partition Gold Moly-Free

Cal.	Dia.	Bullet Weight	Sect. Dens.	Bal. Coef.	Part #
270	.277"	150 grain	.279	.465	52101
7mm	.284"	160 grain	.283	.475	52151
30	.308"	150 grain	.226	.387	52201
30	.308"	180 grain	.271	.474	52231
338	.338"	250 grain	.313	.473	52281

Sierra Bullets
Rifle Bullets

.22 Caliber Hornet (.223/5.66MM Diameter)
- 40 gr. Hornet Varminter #1100
- 45 gr. Hornet Varminter #1110

.22 Caliber Hornet (.224/5.69MM Diameter)
- 40 gr. Hornet Varminter #1200
- 45 gr. Hornet Varminter #1210

.22 Caliber (.224/5.69MM Diameter)
- 40 gr. HP Varminter #1385
- 40 gr. BlitzKing #1440
- 45 gr. SPT Varminter #1310
- 50 gr. SMP Varminter #1320
- 50 gr. SPT Varminter #1330
- 50 gr. Blitz Varminter #1340
- 50 gr. BlitzKing #1450
- 52 gr. HPBT MatchKing #1410
- 53 gr. HP MatchKing #1400
- 55 gr. Blitz Varminter #1345
- 55 gr. SMP Varminter #1350
- 55 gr. FMJBT GameKing #1355
- 55 gr. SPT Varminter #1360
- 55 gr. SBT GameKing #1365
- 55 gr. HPBT GameKing #1390
- 55 gr. BlitzKing #1455
- 60 gr. HP Varminter #1375
- 63 gr. SMP Varminter #1370
- 69 gr. HPBT MatchKing #1380

7"-10" TWST BBLS

6MM .243 Caliber (.243/6.17MM Diameter)
- 55 gr. BlitzKing #1502
- 60 gr. HP Varminter #1500
- 70 gr. HPBT MatchKing #1505
- 70 gr. BlitzKing #1507
- 75 gr. HP Varminter #1510
- 80 gr. Blitz Varminter #1515
- 80 gr. SPT SSP Pro-Hunter #7150
- 85 gr. SPT Varminter #1520
- 85 gr. HPBT GameKing #1530
- 90 gr. FMJBT GameKing #1535
- 100 gr. SPT Pro-Hunter #1540
- 100 gr. SBT GameKing #1560
- 107 gr. HPBT MatchKing #1570

7"-8" TWST BBLS

.25 Caliber (.257/6.53MM Diameter)
- 75 gr. HP Varminter #1600
- 87 gr. SPT Varminter #1610
- 90 gr. HPBT GameKing #1615
- 100 gr. SPT Pro-Hunter #1620
- 100 gr. SBT GameKing #1625
- 100 gr. HPBT MatchKing #1628
- 117 gr. SBT GameKing #1630
- 117 gr. SPT Pro-Hunter #1640
- 120 gr. HPBT GameKing #1650

6.5MM .264 Caliber (.264/6.71MM Diameter)
- 85 gr. HP Varminter #1700
- 100 gr. HP Varminter #1710
- 107 gr. HPBT MatchKing #1715

6.5MM .264 Caliber (cont.) (.264/6.71MM Diameter)
- 120 gr. SPT Pro-Hunter #1720
- 120 gr. HPBT MatchKing #1725
- 140 gr. SBT GameKing #1730
- 140 gr. HPBT MatchKing #1740
- 142 gr. HPBT MatchKing #1742
- 160 gr. SMP Pro-Hunter #1750

.270 Caliber (.277/7.04MM Diameter)
- 90 gr. HP Varminter #1800
- 110 gr. SPT Pro-Hunter #1810
- 130 gr. SBT GameKing #1820
- 130 gr. SPT Pro-Hunter #1830
- 135 gr. HPBT MatchKing #1833
- 140 gr. HPBT GameKing #1835
- 140 gr. SBT GameKing #1845
- 150 gr. SBT GameKing #1840

7MM .284 Caliber (.284/7.21MM Diameter)
- 100 gr. HP Varminter #1895
- 120 gr. SPT Pro-Hunter #1900
- 130 gr. HPBT MatchKing #1903
- 130 gr. SPT SSP Pro-Hunter #7250
- 140 gr. SBT GameKing #1905
- 140 gr. SPT Pro-Hunter #1910
- 150 gr. SBT GameKing #1913
- 150 gr. HPBT MatchKing #1915
- 160 gr. SBT GameKing #1920
- 160 gr. HPBT GameKing #1925
- 168 gr. HPBT MatchKing #1930

Sierra Bullets

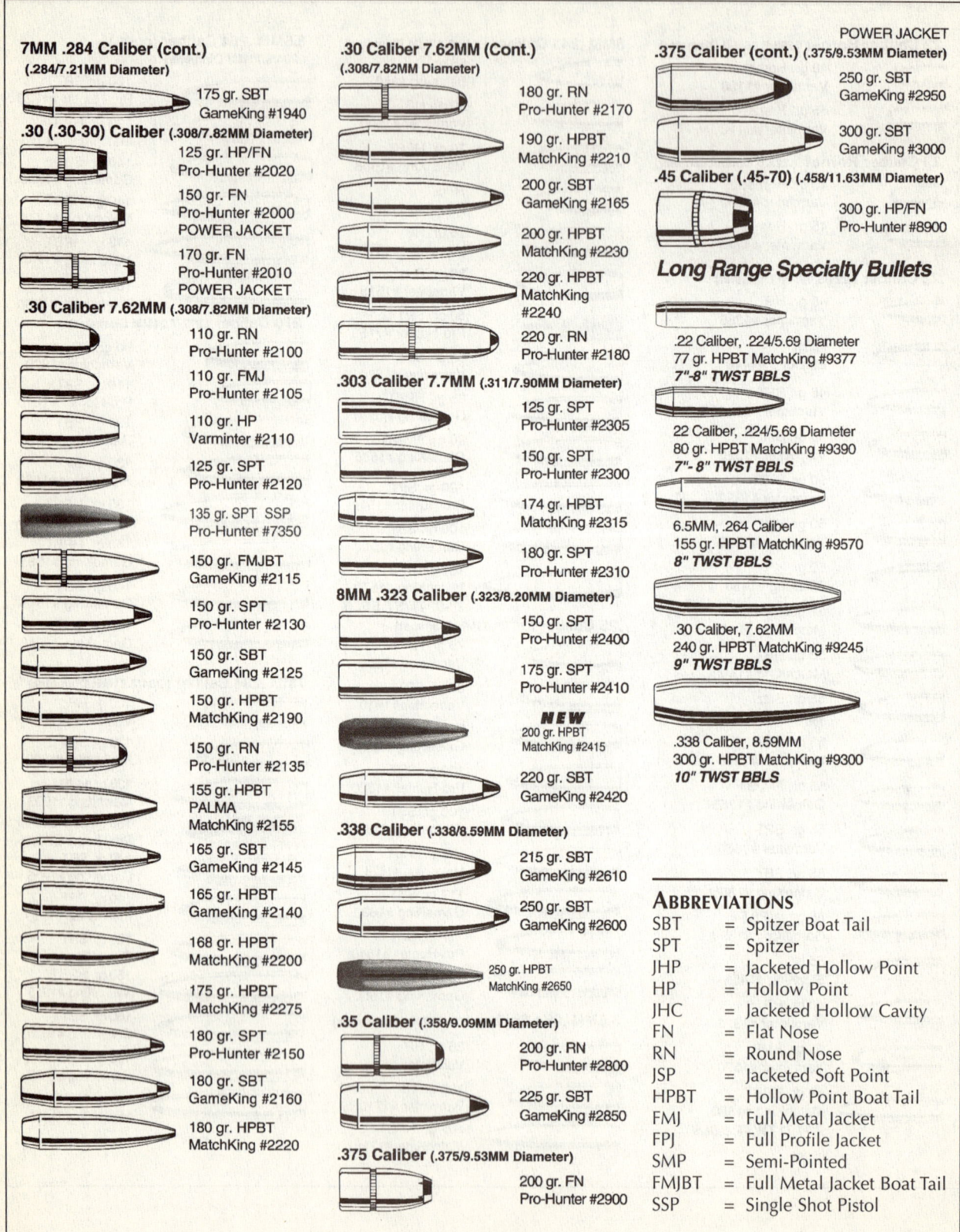

Sierra Bullets
Handgun Bullets

.25 Caliber (.251/6.38MM Diameter)
50 gr. FMJ
Tournament Master #8000

.30 Caliber (.308/7.82MM Diameter)
85 gr. RN
Sports Master #8005

.32 Caliber 7.65MM (.312/7.92MM Diameter)
71 gr. FMJ
Tournament Master #8010

.32 Mag. (.312/7.92MM Diameter)
90 gr. JHC
Sports Master #8030
POWER JACKET

9MM .355 Caliber (.355/9.02MM Diameter)
90 gr. JHP
Sports Master #8100
POWER JACKET

95 gr. FMJ
Tournament Master #8105

115 gr. JHP
Sports Master #8110
POWER JACKET

115 gr. FMJ
Tournament Master #8115

125 gr. JHP Sports Master
#8125 POWER JACKET

125 gr. FMJ
Tournament Master #8120

130 gr. FMJ
Tournament Master #8345

.38 Caliber (.357/9.07MM Diameter)
110 gr. JHC Blitz
Sports Master #8300
POWER JACKET

125 gr. JSP
Sports Master #8310

125 gr. JHC
Sports Master #8320
POWER JACKET

.38 Caliber (cont.) (.357/9.07MM Diameter)
140 gr. JHC
Sports Master #8325
POWER JACKET

158 gr. JSP
Sports Master #8340

158 gr. JHC
Sports Master #8360
POWER JACKET

170 gr. JHC
Sports Master #8365
POWER JACKET

170 gr. FMJ Match
Tournament Master #8350

180 gr. FPJ Match
Tournament Master #8370

9MM Makarov (.363/9.22MM Diameter)
95 gr. JHP
Sports Master #8200
POWER JACKET

100 gr. FPJ
Tournament Master #8210

10MM .400 Caliber (.400/10.16MM Diameter)
135 gr. JHP
Sports Master #8425
POWER JACKET

150 gr. JHP
Sports Master #8430
POWER JACKET

165 gr. JHP
Sports Master #8445
POWER JACKET

180 gr. JHP
Sports Master #8460
POWER JACKET

190 gr. FPJ
Tournament Master #8480

.41 Caliber (.410/10.41MM Diameter)
170 gr. JHC
Sports Master #8500
POWER JACKET

210 gr. JHC
Sports Master #8520
POWER JACKET

.44 Caliber (.4295/10.91MM Diameter)
180 gr. JHC
Sports Master #8600
POWER JACKET

.44 Caliber (cont.) (.4295/10.91MM Diameter)
210 gr. JHC
Sports Master #8620
POWER JACKET

220 gr. FPJ Match
Tournament Master #8605

240 gr. JHC
Sports Master #8610
POWER JACKET

250 gr. FPJ Match
Tournament Master #8615

300 gr. JSP
Sports Master #8630

.45 Caliber (.4515/11.47MM Diameter)
185 gr. JHP
Sports Master #8800
POWER JACKET

185 gr. FPJ Match
Tournament Master #8810

200 gr. FPJ Match
Tournament Master #8825

230 gr. JHP
Sports Master #8805
POWER JACKET

230 gr. FMJ Match
Tournament Master #8815

240 gr. JHC
Sports Master #8820
POWER JACKET

300 gr. JSP
Sports Master #8830

Abbreviations

SBT	=	Spitzer Boat Tail
SPT	=	Spitzer
JHP	=	Jacketed Hollow Point
HP	=	Hollow Point
JHC	=	Jacketed Hollow Cavity
FN	=	Flat Nose
RN	=	Round Nose
JSP	=	Jacketed Soft Point
HPBT	=	Hollow Point Boat Tail
FMJ	=	Full Metal Jacket
FPJ	=	Full Profile Jacket
SMP	=	Semi-Pointed
FMJBT	=	Full Metal Jacket Boat Tail
SSP	=	Single Shot Pistol

Speer Handgun Bullets

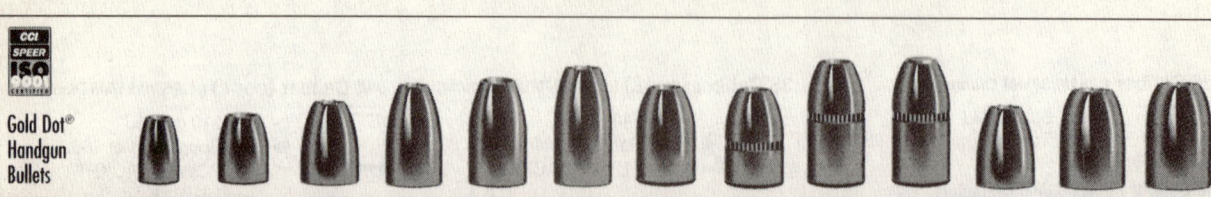

Gold Dot® Handgun Bullets

Caliber & Type	25 Auto Gold Dot HP	32 Auto Gold Dot HP	380 Auto Gold Dot HP	9mm Gold Dot HP	9mm Gold Dot HP	9mm Gold Dot HP	357 SIG 38 Super Gold Dot HP	38/357 Gold Dot HP	38/357 Gold Dot HP	357 Mag Gold Dot SP	9x18mm Makarov Gold Dot HP	40/10mm Gold Dot HP	40/10mm Gold Dot HP
Diameter	.251"	.312"	.355"	.355"	.355"	.355"	.355"	.357"	.357"	.357"	.364"	.400"	.400"
Weight (grs.)	35	60	90	115	124	147	125	125	158	170	90	155	165
Ballist. Coef.	0.091	0.118	0.101	0.125	0.134	0.164	0.141	0.140	0.168	0.185	0.107	0.123	0.138
Part Number	3985	3986	3992	3994	3998	4002	4360	4012	4215	4230	3999	4400	4397
Box Count	100	100	100	100	100	100	100	100	100	100	100	100	100

Gold Dot® Handgun Bullets

Caliber & Type	40/10mm Gold Dot HP	44 Special Gold Dot HP	44 Mag Gold Dot HP	44 Mag Gold Dot SP	44 Mag Gold Dot SP	45 Gold Dot HP	45 Gold Dot HP	45 Gold Dot HP	454 Casull GDHP	475 Linebaugh Gold Dot SP	480 Ruger GDSP	50 Action Express GDHP
Diameter	.400"	.429"	.429"	.429"	.429"	.451"	.451"	.451"	.451"	.475"	.475"	.500"
Weight (grs.)	180	200	240	240	270	185	200	230	300	400	325	300
Ballist. Coef.	0.143	0.145	0.175	0.175	0.193	0.109	0.138	0.143	0.233	0.242	0.191	0.155
Part Number	4406	4427	4455	4456	4461	4470	4478	4483	3974	3976	3978	4493
Box Count	100	100	100	100	50	100	100	100	50	50	50	50

* 475 Linebaugh is a registered trademark of Timothy B. Sundles.

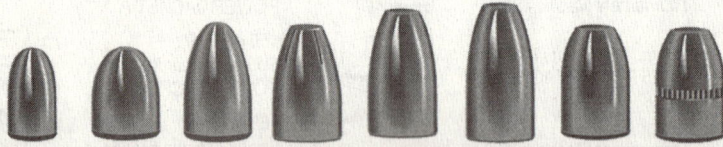

Uni-Cor Handgun Bullets

Caliber & Type	25 Auto TMJ	380 Auto TMJ	9mm TMJ	9mm SP	9mm TMJ	9mm TMJ	357 SIG 38 Super TMJ	38/357 TMJ
Diameter	.251"	.355"	.355"	.355"	.355"	.355"	.355"	.357"
Weight	50	95	115	124	130	147	125	125
Ballist. Coef.	0.110	0.131	0.177	0.115	0.165	0.208	0.147	0.146
Part Number	3982	4001	3995	3997	4010	4006	4362	4015
Box Count	100	100	100	100	100	100	100	100

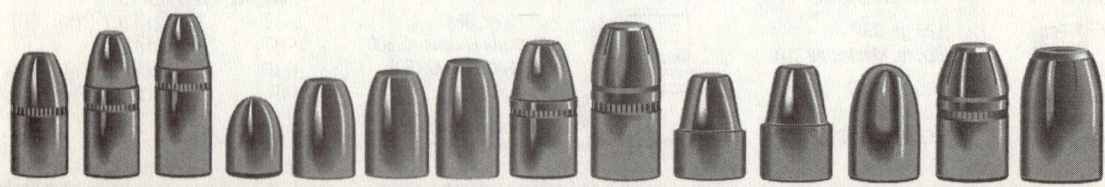

Caliber & Type	38/357 TMJ	357 Mag Sil. Match TMJ	357 Mag Sil. Match TMJ	9x18mm Makarov TMJ	40/10mm TMJ	40/10mm TMJ	40/10mm TMJ	44 Mag Sil. Match TMJ	44 Mag SP	45 Match TMJ	45 Match TMJ	45 Auto TMJ	45 Colt 454 Casull SP	50 Action Express HP
Diameter	.357"	.357"	.357"	.364"	.400"	.400"	.400"	.429"	.429"	.451"	.451"	.451"	.451"	.500"
Weight	158	180	200	95	155	165	180	240	300	185	200	230	300	325
Ballist. Coef.	0.173	0.230	0.236	0.127	0.125	0.135	0.143	0.206	0.213	0.090	0.128	0.153	0.199	0.149
Part Number	4207	4229	4231	4375	4399	4410	4402	4459	4463	4473	4475	4480	4485	4495
Box Count	100	100	100	100	100	100	100	50	100	100	100	100	50	50

Speer Handgun Bullets

JACKETED HANDGUN BULLETS

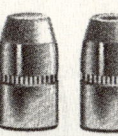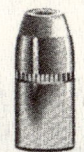

Caliber & Type	32 JHP	32 JHP	38/357 JHP	38/357 JSP	38/357 JHP	38/357 JHP	38/357 JHP-SWC	38/357 JHP
Diameter	.312"	.312"	.357"	.357"	.357"	.357"	.357"	.357"
Weight	85	100	110	125	125	140	146	158
Ballist. Coef.	0.121	0.167	0.122	0.140	0.135	0.152	0.159	0.158
Part Number	3987	3981	4007	4011	4013	4203	4205	4211
Box Count	100	100	100	100	100	100	100	100

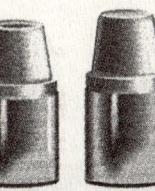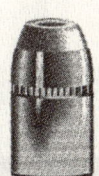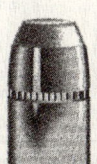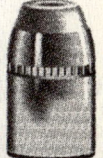

Caliber & Type	38/357 JSP	41 Mag JHP-SWC	41 Mag JSP-SWC	44 Mag JHP	44 Mag JHP-SWC	44 Mag JSP-SWC	44 Mag JHP	44 Mag JSP	45 JHP	45 JHP
Diameter	.357"	.410"	.410"	.429"	.429"	.429"	.429"	.429"	.451"	.451"
Weight	158	200	220	200	225	240	240	240	225	260
Ballist. Coef.	0.158	0.113	0.137	0.122	0.146	0.157	0.165	0.164	0.169	0.183
Part Number	4217	4405	4417	4425	4435	4447	4453	4457	4479	4481
Box Count	100	100	100	100	100	100	100	100	100	100

LEAD HANDGUN BULLETS

Want to shoot more for less money? Speer lead handgun bullets give you an economical alternative to jacketed bullets. Swaged, not cast, construction means you get the same quality–box after box. No worries about voids or slag that can cause flyers with cast bullets. Each Speer lead handgun bullet is coated with a clean lubricant to reduce fouling. Available in a variety of styles in calibers from 32 to 45.

LEAD HANDGUN BULLETS

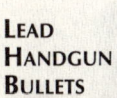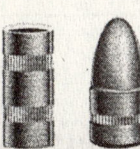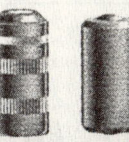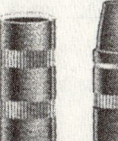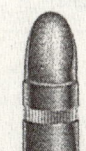

Caliber & Type	32 HB-WC	9mm RN	38 BB-WC	38 DE-WC	38 HB-WC	38 SWC	38 HP-SWC	38 RN	44 SWC	45 SWC	45 RN	45 SWC
Diameter	.314"	.356"	.358"	.358"	.358"	.358"	.358"	.358"	.430"	.452"	.452"	.452"
Weight (grs.)	98	125	148	148	148	158	158	158	240	200	230	250
Part Number	--	4601	4605	--	4617	4623	4627	4647	4660	4677	4690	4683
Bulk Part No.	4600	4602	4606	4611	4618	4624	4628	4648	4661	4678	4691	4684

Speer Rifle Bullets

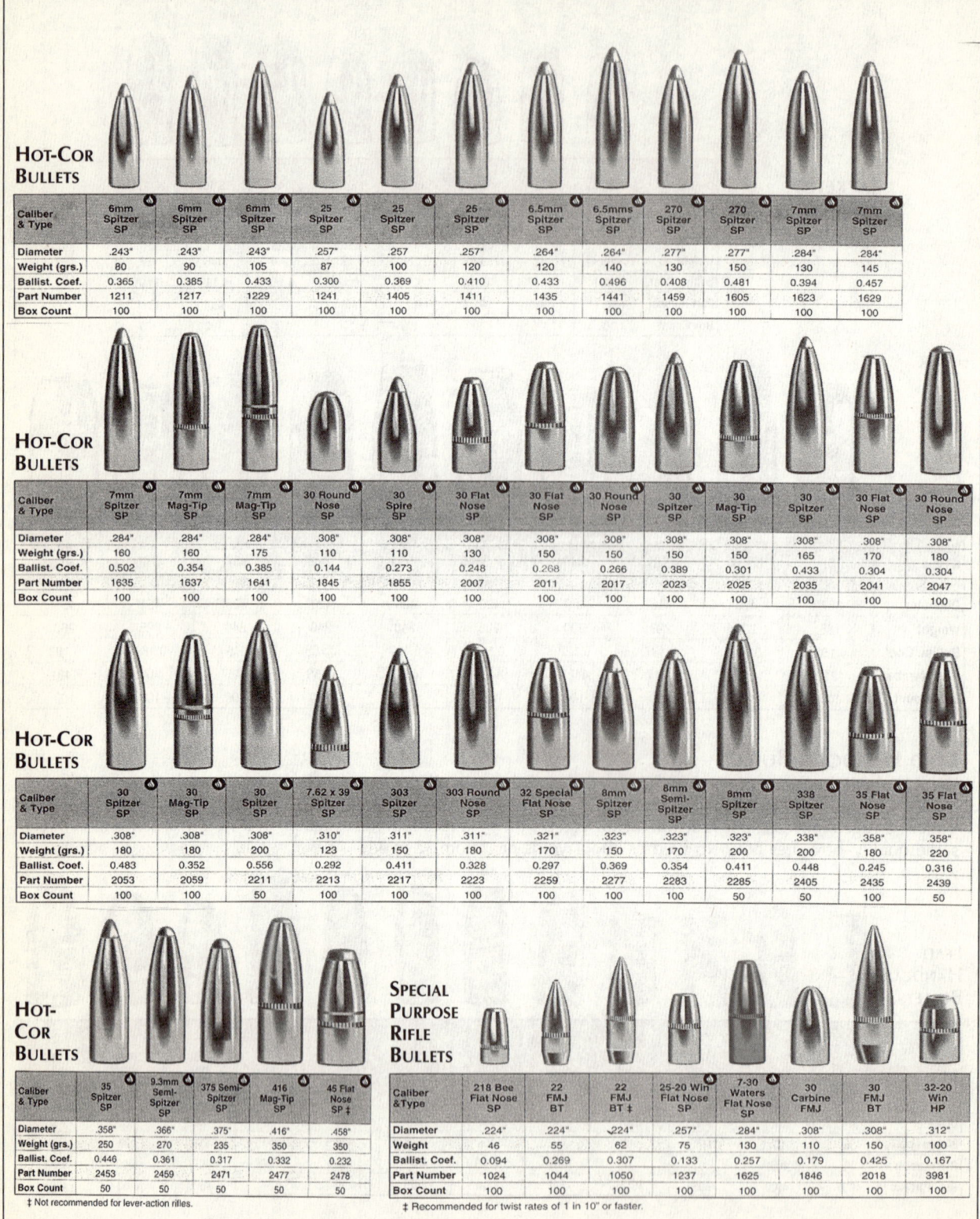

Hot-Cor Bullets

Caliber & Type	6mm Spitzer SP	6mm Spitzer SP	6mm Spitzer SP	25 Spitzer SP	25 Spitzer SP	25 Spitzer SP	6.5mm Spitzer SP	6.5mms Spitzer SP	270 Spitzer SP	270 Spitzer SP	7mm Spitzer SP	7mm Spitzer SP
Diameter	.243"	.243"	.243"	.257"	.257"	.257"	.264"	.264"	.277"	.277"	.284"	.284"
Weight (grs.)	80	90	105	87	100	120	120	140	130	150	130	145
Ballist. Coef.	0.365	0.385	0.433	0.300	0.369	0.410	0.433	0.496	0.408	0.481	0.394	0.457
Part Number	1211	1217	1229	1241	1405	1411	1435	1441	1459	1605	1623	1629
Box Count	100	100	100	100	100	100	100	100	100	100	100	100

Hot-Cor Bullets

Caliber & Type	7mm Spitzer SP	7mm Mag-Tip SP	7mm Mag-Tip SP	30 Round Nose SP	30 Spire SP	30 Flat Nose SP	30 Flat Nose SP	30 Round Nose SP	30 Spitzer SP	30 Mag-Tip SP	30 Spitzer SP	30 Flat Nose SP	30 Round Nose SP
Diameter	.284"	.284"	.284"	.308"	.308"	.308"	.308"	.308"	.308"	.308"	.308"	.308"	.308"
Weight (grs.)	160	160	175	110	110	130	150	150	150	150	165	170	180
Ballist. Coef.	0.502	0.354	0.385	0.144	0.273	0.248	0.268	0.266	0.389	0.301	0.433	0.304	0.304
Part Number	1635	1637	1641	1845	1855	2007	2011	2017	2023	2025	2035	2041	2047
Box Count	100	100	100	100	100	100	100	100	100	100	100	100	100

Hot-Cor Bullets

Caliber & Type	30 Spitzer SP	30 Mag-Tip SP	30 Spitzer SP	7.62 x 39 Spitzer SP	303 Spitzer SP	303 Round Nose SP	32 Special Flat Nose SP	8mm Spitzer SP	8mm Semi-Spitzer SP	8mm Spitzer SP	338 Spitzer SP	35 Flat Nose SP	35 Flat Nose SP
Diameter	.308"	.308"	.308"	.310"	.311"	.311"	.321"	.323"	.323"	.323"	.338"	.358"	.358"
Weight (grs.)	180	180	200	123	150	180	170	150	170	200	200	180	220
Ballist. Coef.	0.483	0.352	0.556	0.292	0.411	0.328	0.297	0.369	0.354	0.411	0.448	0.245	0.316
Part Number	2053	2059	2211	2213	2217	2223	2259	2277	2283	2285	2405	2435	2439
Box Count	100	100	50	100	100	100	100	100	100	50	50	100	50

Hot-Cor Bullets

Caliber & Type	35 Spitzer SP	9.3mm Semi-Spitzer SP	375 Semi-Spitzer SP	416 Mag-Tip SP	45 Flat Nose SP ‡
Diameter	.358"	.366"	.375"	.416"	.458"
Weight (grs.)	250	270	235	350	350
Ballist. Coef.	0.446	0.361	0.317	0.332	0.232
Part Number	2453	2459	2471	2477	2478
Box Count	50	50	50	50	50

‡ Not recommended for lever-action rifles.

Special Purpose Rifle Bullets

Caliber & Type	218 Bee Flat Nose SP	22 FMJ BT	22 FMJ BT ‡	25-20 Win Flat Nose SP	7-30 Waters Flat Nose SP	30 Carbine FMJ	30 FMJ BT	32-20 Win HP
Diameter	.224"	.224"	.224"	.257"	.284"	.308"	.308"	.312"
Weight	46	55	62	75	130	110	150	100
Ballist. Coef.	0.094	0.269	0.307	0.133	0.257	0.179	0.425	0.167
Part Number	1024	1044	1050	1237	1625	1846	2018	3981
Box Count	100	100	100	100	100	100	100	100

‡ Recommended for twist rates of 1 in 10" or faster.

Speer Rifle Bullets

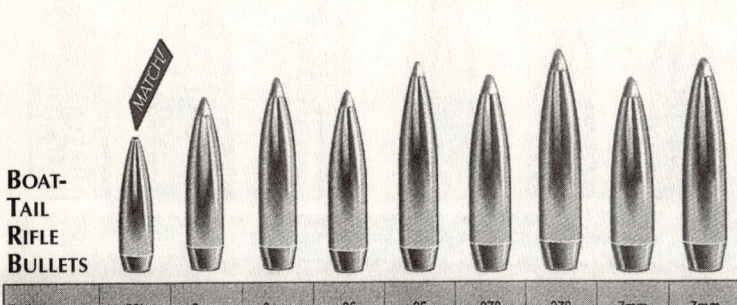

BOAT-TAIL RIFLE BULLETS

Bullet Caliber & Type	22" Match HPBT	6mm Spitzer SPBT	6mm Spitzer SPBT	25 Spitzer SPBT	25 Spitzer SPBT	270 Spitzer SPBT	270 Spitzer SPBT	7mm Spitzer SPBT	7mm Spitzer SPBT
Diameter	.224"	.243"	.243"	.257"	.257"	.277"	.277"	.284"	.284"
Weight (grs.)	52	85	100	100	120	130	150	130	145
Ballist. Coef.	0.253	0.404	0.430	0.393	0.435	0.449	0.496	0.411	0.502
Part Number	1036	1213	1220	1408	1410	1458	1604	1624	1628
Box Count	100	100	100	100	100	100	100	100	100

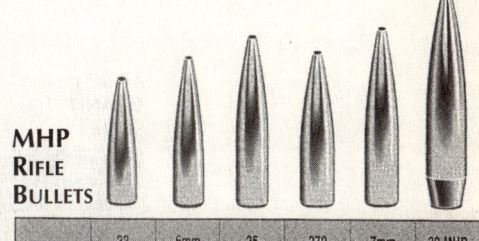

MHP RIFLE BULLETS

Caliber & Type	22 MHP HP	6mm MHP HP	25 MHP HP	270 MHP HP	7mm MHP HP	30 MHP Match HPBT
Diameter	.224"	.243"	.257"	.277"	.284"	.308"
Weight	50	70	87	90	110	168
Ballist. Coef.	0.234	0.296	0.325	0.289	0.355	0.504
Part Number	1031	1207	1247	1457	1615	2039
Box Count	100	100	100	100	100	100

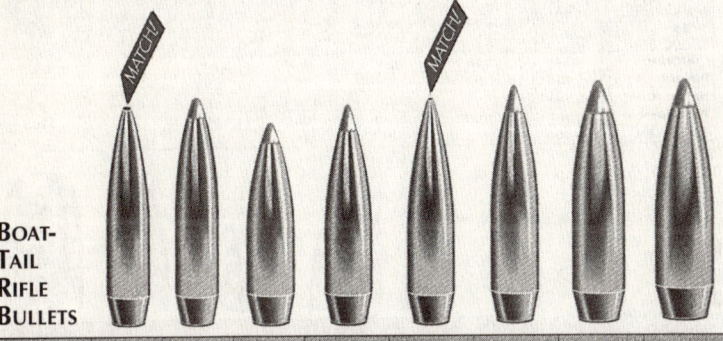

BOAT-TAIL RIFLE BULLETS

Bullet Caliber & Type	7mm* Match HPBT	7mm Spitzer SPBT	30 Spitzer SPBT	30 Spitzer SPBT	30" Match HPBT	30 Spitzer SPBT	338 Spitzer SPBT	375 Spitzer SPBT
Diameter	.284"	.284"	.308"	.308"	.308"	.308"	.338"	.375"
Weight (grs.)	145	160	150	165	168	180	225	270
Ballist. Coef.	0.465	0.556	0.423	0.477	0.480	0.540	0.484	0.429
Part Number	1631	1634	2022	2034	2040	2052	2406	2472
Box Count	100	100	100	100	100	100	50	50

*Match bullets are not recommended for use on game animals.

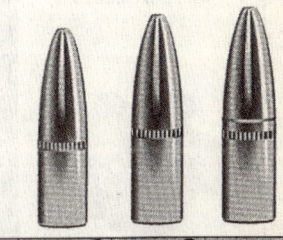

GRAND SLAM

Bullet Caliber & Type	6mm GS SP	25 GS SP	6.5mm GS SP
Diameter	.243"	.257"	.264"
Weight (grs.)	100	120	140
Ballist. Coef.	0.351	0.328	0.385
Part Number	1222	1415	1444
Box Count	50	50	50

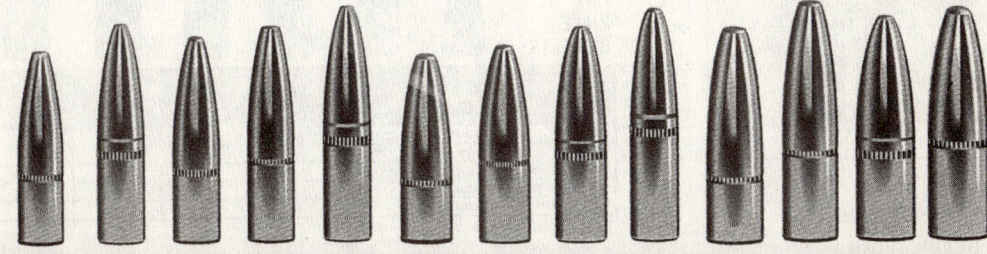

GRAND SLAM

Bullet Caliber & Type	270 Grand Slam SP	270 Grand Slam SP	7mm Grand Slam SP	7mm Grand Slam SP	7mm Grand Slam SP	30 Grand Slam SP	30 Grand Slam SP	30 Grand Slam SP	30 Grand Slam SP	338 Grand Slam SP	338 Grand Slam SP	35 Grand Slam SP	375 Grand Slam SP
Diameter	.277"	.277"	.284"	.284"	.284"	.308"	.308"	.308"	.308"	.338"	.338"	.358"	.375"
Weight (grs.)	130	150	145	160	175	150	165	180	200	225	250	250	285
Ballist. Coef.	0.345	0.385	0.327	0.387	0.465	0.305	0.393	0.416	0.448	.0382	0.431	0.335	0.354
Part Number	1465	1608	1632	1638	1643	2026	2038	2063	2212	2407	2408	2455	2473
Box Count	50	50	50	50	50	50	50	50	50	50	50	50	50

Speer Rifle Bullets

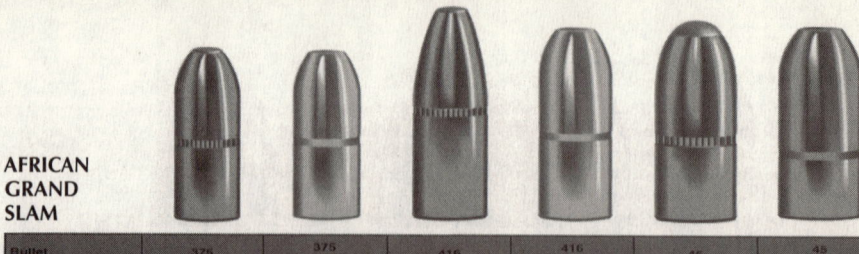

AFRICAN GRAND SLAM

Bullet Caliber & Type	375 AGS SP	375 AGS Tungsten Solid	416 AGS SP	416 AGS Tungsten Solid	45 AGS SP	45 AGS Tungsten Solid
Diameter	.375"	.375"	.416"	.416"	.458"	.458"
Weight (grs.)	300	300	400	400	500	500
Ballist. Coef.	0.323	0.258	0.318	0.262	0.285	0.277
Part Number	2470	2474	2475	2476	2485	2486
Box Count	25	25	25	25	25	25

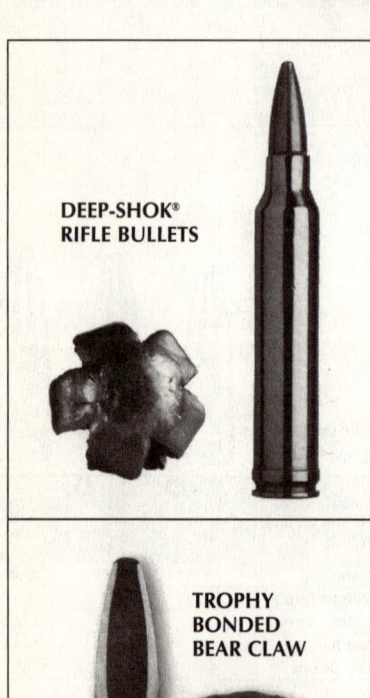

DEEP-SHOK® RIFLE BULLETS

TROPHY BONDED BEAR CLAW

JACKETED RIFLE BULLETS

Caliber & Type	22 Spire SP	22 Spitzer SP	22 Spitzer SP	22 HP	22 Spitzer SP	22 Semi-Spitzer SP	6mm HP
Diameter	.224"	.224"	.224"	.224"	.224"	.224"	.243"
Weight	40	45	50	52	55	70	75
Ballist. Coef.	0.144	0.167	0.231	0.225	0.255	0.214	0.234
Part Number	1017	1023	1029	1035	1047	1053	1205
Box Count	100	100	100	100	100	100	100

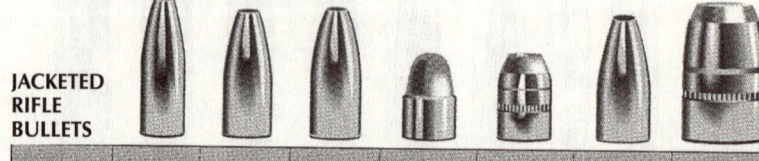

JACKETED RIFLE BULLETS

Caliber & Type	25 HP	270 HP	7mm HP	30 Plinker RN SP	30 HP	30 HP	45 Flat Nose SP
Diameter	.257"	.277"	.284"	.308"	.308"	.308"	.458"
Weight	100	100	115	100	110	130	400
Ballist. Coef.	0.255	0.225	0.257	0.124	0.136	0.263	0.214
Part Number	1407	1447	1617	1805	1835	2005	2479
Box Count	100	100	100	100	100	100	50

TNT RIFLE BULLETS

Caliber & Type	22 TNT HP	6mm TNT HP	25 TNT HP	6.5mm TNT HP	270 TNT HP	7mm TNT HP	30 TNT HP
Diameter	.224"	.243"	.257"	.264"	.277"	.284"	.308"
Weight	50	70	87	90	90	110	125
Ballist. Coef.	0.223	0.282	0.310	0.281	0.275	0.338	0.326
Part Number	1030	1206	1246	1445	1446	1616	1986
Box Count	100	100	100	100	100	100	100

DEEP-SHOK® RIFLE BULLETS
- Compound-profile, fluted jacket
  - Reliable, controlled expansion over a wide range of hunting conditions
- Boat Tail design
  - Higher ballistic coefficient for better energy retention at long range
- Hot-Cor
  - Eliminates oxide layers that lead to core slippage
- Large heel lock
  - Mechanically locks the core to the jacket
- Available in 165 gr. and 180 gr. - 30 cal.

TROPHY BONDED® BEAR CLAW® RIFLE BULLETS
- Fusion-bonded core
  - Fusion bonding ensures retained weights in excess of 95 percent.
- Solid copper shank
  - Ensures deep penetration
- Protected soft point
  - Long jacket protects lead tip against recoil damage
- Available from .224 55 gr. to .458 500 gr.

Swift
A-Frame and Scirocco Bullets

Scirocco™ Rifle Bullets

Cal.	Scirocco™ Bullet	Dia.	Wt. (gr.)	Profile	Sect. Den.	Ball. Coef.
270		.277"	130	BTS	.242	.450
7mm		.284"	150	BTS	.266	.515
30		.308"	150	BTS	.226	.430
		.308"	165	BTS	.248	.470
		.308"	180	BTS	.271	.520

BTS=Boat Tail Spitzer

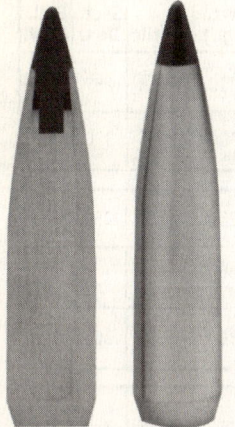

Swift Scirocco™ Bonded 30 Cal. (.308") 180-gr. Polymer Tip/Boat Tail Spitzer
Tapered jacket and proprietary bonding process produce controlled mushrooming with high weight retention. Ideally suited to fast, flat-shooting calibers.

The Swift Bullet Company

The Swift Bullet Company has two types of big game bullets.

The **Scirocco** design starts with a tough, pointed, polymer tip that reduces air resistance, prevents tip deformation, and blends symmetrically into the curved radius of its secant ogive nose section. A moderate 15-degree boat-tail base reduces drag and eases seating. The thick base prevents bullet deformation during launch. **Scirocco's** shape creates two other significant advantages. One is an extremely high ballistic coefficient. The other, derived from the secant ogive nose, is a comparatively long bearing surface for a sharply pointed bullet, a feature that improves rotational stability.

Inside, the **Scirocco** has a bonded-core construction with a pure lead core encased in a tapered, progressively thickening jacket of pure copper. Pure copper was selected because it is more malleable and less brittle than less expensive gilding metal. Both jacket and core are bonded together by Swift's proprietary bonding process so that the bullet expands without breakup as if the two parts were the same metal. In tests, the new bullet mushroomed effectively at velocities as low as 1440 fps, yet stayed together at velocities in excess of 3,000 fps, with over 70 percent weight retention.

Swift's **A-Frame** bullet, with its mid-section wall of copper, is still earning praise for its deep-driving dependability in tough game. Less aerodynamic than the Scirocco, it produces a broad mushroom while carrying almost all its weight through muscle and bone. Available in a wide range of weights and diameters, it is also a bonded-core bullet.

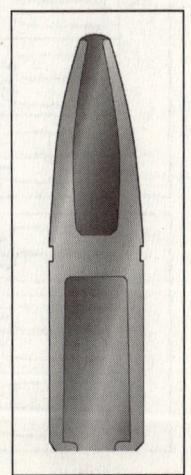

A-Frame Bullet Design

The Swift A-Frame, noted for deep penetration in tough game, is loaded in Remington Premier ammunition.

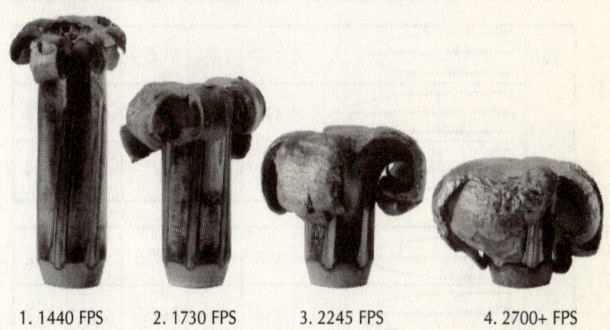

1. 1440 FPS   2. 1730 FPS   3. 2245 FPS   4. 2700+ FPS

Swift Scirocco™ Expands dependably over a wide range of velocities, and maintains high jacket/core integrity.

Swift
A-Frame Rifle Bullet Specifications

Cal.	A-Frame Bullet	Dia.	Wt. (gr.)	Profile	Sect. Den.	Ball. Coef.
.25		.257"	100	AF/SS	.216	.318
		.257"	120	AF/SS	.260	.382
6.5 mm		.264"	120	AF/SS	.246	.344
		.264"	140	AF/SS	.287	.401
.270		.277"	130	AF/SS	.242	.323
		.277"	140	AF/SS	.261	.414
		.277"	150	AF/SS	.279	.444
7mm		.284"	140	AF/SS	.248	.335
		.284"	160	AF/SS	.283	.450
		.284"	175	AF/SS	.310	.493
.30		.308"	165	AF/SS	.249	.367
		.308"	180	AF/SS	.271	.400
		.308"	200	AF/SS	.301	.444
8mm		.323"	200	AF/SS	.274	.357
		.323"	220	AF/SS	.301	.393
.338		.338"	225	AF/SS	.281	.384
		.338"	250	AF/SS	.313	.427
		.338"	275	AF/SS	.344	.469
.35		.358"	225	AF/SS	.251	.312
		.358"	250	AF/SS	.279	.347
		.358"	280	AF/SS	.312	.388
9.3 mm		.366"	250	AF/SS	.267	.285
		.366"	300	AF/SS	.320	.342
.375		.375"	250	AF/SS	.254	.271
		.375"	270	AF		
		.375"	300	AF/SS	.305	.325
.416		.416"	350	AF/SS	.289	.321
		.416"	400	AF/SS	.330	.367
.458		.458"	400	AF/FN	.272	.258
		.458"	450	AF/SS	.307	.325
		.458"	500	AF/SS	.341	.361
.470		.475"	500	AF/RN	.329	.364

Handgun Bullet Specifications

Cal.	A-Frame Bullet	Dia.	Wt. (gr.)	Profile	Sect. Den.	Ball. Coef.
.44		.430"	240	AF/HP	.185	.119
		.430"	280	AF/HP	.216	.139
		.430"	300	AF/HP	.232	.147
.45		.452"	265	AF	.210	.135
		.452"	300	AF/HP	.210	.135
		.452"	325	AF	.210	.135

Woodleigh Premium Bullets

WELDCORE SOFT NOSE
Woodleigh Weldcore Soft Nose bullets are made from 90/100 gilding metal (90% copper: 10% zinc) 1.6 mm thick. Maximum retained weight is obtained by fusing the pure lead to the gilding metal jacket, hence the name "Weldcore."

FULL METAL JACKET
Made from gilding metal-clad steel 2mm thick, jackets on fmj bullets are heavy at the nose for extra impact resistance. The jacket then tapers towards the base to assist rifling engraving.

Calibre Diameter	Type	Weight Grain	SD	BC
700 Nitro .700"	SN	1000	.292	.340
	FMJ	1000	.292	.340
600 Nitro .620"	SN	900	.334	.371
	FMJ	900	.334	.334
577 Nitro .585"	SN	750	.313	.346
	FMJ	750	.313	.351
	SN	650	.271	.292
	FMJ	650	.271	.292
577 B.P. .585"	SN	650	.271	.320
500 Nitro .510"	SN	570	.313	.474
	FMJ	570	.313	.434
500 B.P. .510"	SN	440	.242	.336
500 Jeffery .510"	PP	535	.304	.460
	SN	535	.304	.460
	FMJ	535	.304	.422
	FMJ	600	.330	.330
505 Gibbs .505"	PP	600	.336	.450
	SN	525	.294	.445
	FMJ	525	.294	.408
	FMJ	600	.366	.450
475 No2 Jeffery .488"	SN	500	.300	.420
	FMJ	500	.300	.416
475 No2 .483"	SN	480	.303	.400
	FMJ	480	.303	.410
476 W.R. .476"	SN	520	.328	.420
	FMJ	520	.328	.455
475 Nitro .476"	SN	480	.227	.307
	FMJ	480	.227	.257
470 Nitro .474"	SN	500	.318	.411
	FMJ	500	.318	.410
465 Nitro .468"	SN	480	.318	.410
	FMJ	480	.318	.407
450 Nitro .458"	SN	480	.327	.419
	FMJ	480	.327	.410
458 Mag. .458"	SN	500	.341	.430
	SN	550	.375	.480
	FMJ	500	.341	.405
	FMJ	550	.375	.426
	PP	400	.272	.420
	RN	350	.238	.305
45/70 .458"	FN	405	.276	.250
11.3x62 Schuler .440"	SN	401	.296	.411
425 W.R. .435"	SN	410	.310	.344
	FMJ	410	.310	.336
404 Jeffery .423"	SN	400	.319	.354
	FMJ	400	.319	.358
	SN	350	.279	.357
10.75x68mm .423"	SN	347	.277	.355
	FMJ	347	.277	.307
416 Rigby .416"	SN	410	.338	.375
	FMJ	410	.338	.341
	PP	340	.281	.425
	SN	450	.372	.402

Calibre Diameter	Type	Weight Grain	SD	BC
450/400 Nitro .411" or .408"	SN	400	.338	.384
	FMJ	400	.338	.433
375 Mag. .375"	PP	235	.239	.331
	RN	270	.275	.305
	SP	270	.275	.380
	PP	270	.275	.352
	RN	300	.305	.340
	SP	300	.305	.425
	PP	300	.305	.420
	FMJ	300	.305	.307
	RN	350	.354	.354
	PP	350	.354	.440
405 Win., .411"	SN	300	.254	.194
9.3mm .366"	SN	286	.305	.331
	FMJ	286	.305	.324
	SN	250	.267	.296
360 No2 .366"	SN	320	.341	.378
	FMJ	320	.341	.362
358 Cal .358"	SN	225	.250	.277
	FMJ	225	.250	.298
	SN	250	.285	.365
	SN	310	.346	.400
	FMJ	310	.346	.378
338 Mag .338"	PP	225	.281	.425
	SN	250	.313	.332
	PP	250	.313	.470
	FMJ	250	.313	.326
	SN	300	.375	.416
	FMJ	300	.375	.398
333 Jeffery .333"	SN	250	.328	.400
	SN	300	.386	.428
	FMJ	300	.386	.419
318 W.R. .330"	SN	250	.328	.420
	FMJ	250	.328	.364
8mm .323"	SN	196	.268	.370
	SN	220	.302	.363
	SN	250	.343	.389
303 British .312	SN	174	.257	.342
	PP	215	.316	.359
308 Cal .308"	FMJ	220	.331	.359
	RN	220	.331	.367
	PP	180	.273	.376
	PP	165	.250	.320
	PP	150	.226	.301
Win Mag.	PP	180	.273	.435
	PP	200	.301	.450
275 H&H .287"	PP	160	.275	.474
	PP	175	.301	.518
7mm .284"	PP	140	.247	.436
	PP	160	.282	.486
	PP	175	.312	.530
270 Win .277"	PP	130	.241	.409
	PP	150	.278	.463

SP = Semi-point • PP = Protected Point • FN = Flat Nose
• RN = Round Nose • FMJ = Full Metal Jacket
All PP, FN, RN, SP, SN bullets are Weldcore Softnose

98% & 95%
RETAINED WEIGHT
300 WIN MAG 180GR PP

458 X 500GN SN
RECOVERED FROM BUFFALO

270 WIN 150GN PP
86% RETAINED WEIGHT

94% RETAINED WEIGHT
300 WIN MAG 180GR PP

500/465 RECOVERED
FROM BUFFALO

Accurate Powder

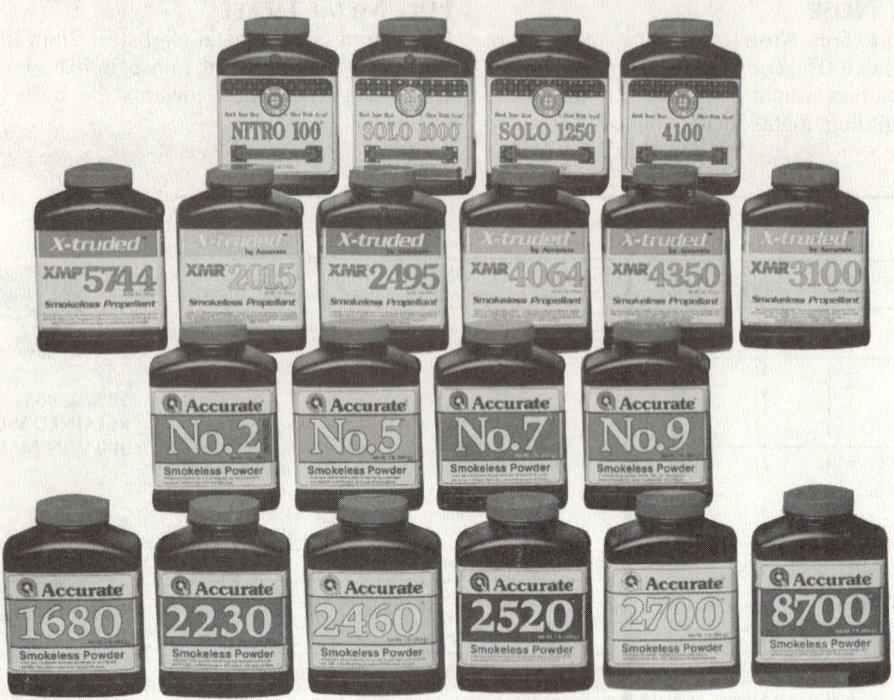

Accurate Powder Specifications

	NG*	Avg. Length	Avg. Grain Diameter	Bulk Density**	Comparative Powders***
Ball Propellants					
No. 2 Imp.	14.0%	N/A	0.018	0.650	Bullseye, HP38, 231
No. 5	18.0%	N/A	0.027	0.950	Unique, 540, 800X
No. 7	12.0%	N/A	0.012	0.985	Blue Dot, HS7, 630
No. 9	10.0%	N/A	0.015	0.935	2400, H110, 296
1680	10.0%	N/A	0.014	0.950	680, 4227, 4198
2230	10.0%	N/A	0.022	0.980	H335, BL-C2, 3031, 748
2460	10.0%	N/A	0.022	0.990	748, H335, BL-C2, 3031
2520	10.0%	N/A	0.022	0.970	4895
2700	10.0%	N/A	0.022	0.960	4350, 760, 4320
New MAGPRO	9.0%	N/A	0.030	0.970	-
8700	10.0%	N/A	0.030	0.960	870, 5010
X-truded Propellants					
XMP-5744	20.0%	0.048	0.033	0.880	Beyond Comparision
XMR-2015	-	0.039	0.031	0.880	H322, N201, 3031
XMR-2495	-	0.068	0.029	0.900	4895
XMR-4064	-	0.050	0.035	0.900	IMR-4064, 748, BL-C2
XMR-4350	-	0.083	0.038	0.920	IMR-4350
XMR-3100	-	0.083	0.038	0.920	4831, 785
Shotshell Propellants					
Nitro 100	21.0%	0.010	0.058	0.505	700X, Red Dot
Solo 1000	-	0.010	0.052	0.510	Green Dot
Solo 1250	-	0.010	0.051	0.550	PB
Solo 4100	10.0%	-	0.011	0.960	No. 9, 2400, 296

*NG-NItroglycerin (glyceryl trinitrate) **g/cc ***For comparison only, not a loading recommendation

Alliant Smokeless Powders

Alliant Rifle, Shotgun and Pistol Powders

Powder	Relative Quickness	Principal Purpose	Secondary Uses
BULLSEYE®	100%	Handgun Loads	12 ga. Light Target Loads
RED DOT®	94.1%	Light & Standard 12 & 16 ga. Target Loads	Handgun Loads
AMERICAN SELECT®	81.0%	12 ga. Target Loads	Cowboy Action Handgun Loads
GREEN DOT®	77.9%	Handicap Trap Loads	20 & 28 ga. Target Loads
UNIQUE®	61.6%	All-around Shotshell Powder, 12, 16 & 20 ga.	Handgun Loads
POWER PISTOL®	58.6%	High Performance 9mm, .40 S&W & 10mm	Moderate Pistol Cartridges
HERCO®	56.1%	Heavy Shotshell Loads 10, 12 16, 20 & 28 ga.	Heavy Handgun Loads
BLUE DOT®	37.8%	Magnum Shotshell Loads 10, 12, 16, 20 & 28 ga.	Magnum Handgun Loads
STEEL™	34.0%	Non-Toxic Hunting Shotshell	2 oz. Turkey Loads
2400®	27.00%	Magnum Handgun Loads	.22 Hornet & 218 Bee
RELOADER® 7	19.4%	Light Rifle	45-70 Gov't
RELOADER® 15	13.7%	Medium Rifle	Silhouette Rifle
RELOADER® 19	11.3%	Standard Rifle	Light Magnum Rifle
RELOADER® 22	11.1%	Magnum Rifle	Heavy Bullet Stand Rifle
RELOADER® 25	10.5%	Heavy Magnum Rifle	Magnum Rifle

Hodgdon Smokeless Powder

PYRODEX PELLETS
Both rifle and pistol pellets eliminate powder measures, speeds shooting for black powder enthusiasts.

EXTREME H4198
H4198 was developed especially for small and medium capacity cartridges.

EXTREME H322
This powder fills the gap between H4198 and BL-C9(2). Performs best in small to medium capacity cases.

EXTREME BENCHMARK
A fine choice for small rifle cases like the .223 Rem and PPC competition rounds. Appropriate also for the 300-30 and 7x57.

SPHERICAL BL-C2
Best performance is in the 222, .308 other cases smaller than 30/06.

SPHERICAL H335®
Similar to BL-C(2), H335 is popular for its performance in medium capacity cases, especially in 222 and 308 Winchester.

EXTREME VARGET
Features small extruded grain powder for uniform metering, plus higher velocities/normal pressures in such calibers as .223, 22-250, 306, 30-06, 375 H&H

EXTREME H4895®
4895 gives desirable performance in almost all cases from 222 Rem. to 458 Win. Reduced loads, to as low as 3/5 maximum, still give target accuracy.

SPHERICAL H380®
This number fills a gap between 4320 and 4350. It is excellent in 22/250, 220 Swift, the 6mm's, 257 and 30/06.

SPHERICAL H414®
In many popular medium to medium-large calibers, pressure velocity relationship is better.

EXTREME H4350
This powder gives superb accuracy at optimum velocity for many large capacity metallic rifle cartridges.

EXTREME H4831®
Outstanding performance with medium and heavy bullets in the 6mm's, 25/06, 270 and Magnum calibers. Also available with shortened grains (H4831SC) for easy metering.

EXTREME H1000 EXTRUDED POWDER
Fills the gap between H4831 and H870. Works especially well in overbore capacity cartridges (1,000-yard shooters take note).

EXTREME H50 BMG
Designed for the 50 Browning Machine Gun cartridge. Highly insensitive to extreme temperature changes.

CLAYS
Tailored for use in 12 ga., 7/8, 1-oz. and 1 1/8-oz. loads. Also performs well in many handgun applications, including .38 Special, .40 S&W and 45 ACP. Perfect for 1 1/8 and 1 oz. loads.

NEW FOR 2002 RETUMBO
A true magnum rifle powder, designed for such cartridges as the 300 Rem. Ultra Mag., 30-378 Weatherby, the 7mm STW and other cases with large capacities and small bores. Shooters can expect up to 40-100 feet per second more velocity than other magnum powders.

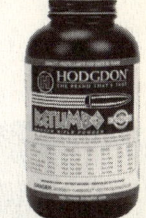

NEW FOR 2002 TRIPLE SEVEN
A new muzzleloading propellant that does not use sulfur, keeping shooter's hand clean. No offensive odor and cleaning is as easy as running a water soaked patch down the barrel followed by 3 or 4 dry patches!

UNIVERSAL CLAYS
Loads nearly all of the straight-wall pistol cartridges as well as 12 ga. 1.25 oz. thru 28 ga. 3/4 oz. target loads.

INTERNATIONAL CLAYS
Ideal for 12 and 20 ga. autoloaders who want reduced recoil.

TITEWAD
This 12 ga. flattened spherical shotgun powder is ideal for 7/8, 1 and 1 1/8 oz. loads, with minimum recoil and mild muzzle report.

HS-6 AND HS-7
HS-6 and HS-7 for Magnum field loads are unsurpassed, since they do not pack in the measure. They deliver uniform charges and are dense to allow sufficient wad column for best patterns.

LONGSHOT
A new spherical powder for heavy shotgun loads.

HP38
A fast pistol powder for most pistol loading. Especially recommended for mid-range 38 specials.

TITEGROUP
Excellent for most straight-walled pistol cartridges, incl. 38 Spec., 44 Spec., 45 ACP. Low charge weights, clean burning; position insensitive and flawless ignition.

H110
A spherical powder made especially for the 30 M1 carbine. H110 also does very well in 357, 44 spec., 44 Mag. or 410 ga. shotshell. Magnum primers are recommended for consistent ignition.

H4227
An extruded powder similar to H110, it is the fastest burning in Hodgdon's line. Recommended for the 22 Hornet and some specialized loading in the 45-70 caliber. Also excellent in magnum pistol and .410 shotgun.

LIL' GUN
This powder was developed specifically for the .410 shotgun but works very well in rifle cartridges like the .22 Hornet and in the .44 magnum.

IMR Powders

E.I. DuPont de Nemours began its corporate life in 1802, on Delaware's Brandywine River. The varied product line that evolved over the next couple of centuries could hardly have been imagined by its founder, French immigrant Eleuthere Irenee DuPont.

"I can make better black powder than what your country has in its magazines," DuPont told Alexander Hamilton. The enterprising engineer got the help he needed to build a plant in Wilmington. The new propellant satisfied U.S. ordnance officers, and DuPont put down roots. Gunpowder was the firm's primary product for most of the 19th century. In the 1880s, DuPont built a plant at Carney's Point to boost capacity. During World War I, 25,000 people went to work at this facility on the Brandywine, providing more than 80 percent of the military powders used by the Allies (the British, French, Danes, and Russians as well as U.S. troops.

Soon after the transition from black to smokeless powders at the close of the 19th century, "MR" began appearing on canisters of DuPont powders. It meant "military rifle." The IMR line of "improved military rifle" powders came along in the 1920s, when four-digit numbers replaced two-digit numbers in DuPont designations. MR 10 and the like died out. IMR fuels, beginning with 4198, supplanted them. The first had relatively fast burn rates, because in those days, rifle cartridges were small. In 1934, DuPont introduced IMR 4227. In the early 1940s, IMR 4895 came along, specifically for the .30-06 in the M1 Garand service rifle. About that time the first slow IMR propellant made its debut. Developed for 20mm cannons, IMR 4831 would become one of the most popular powders for high-capacity rifle cartridges developed by wildcatters like Roy Weatherby and P.O. Ackley. Incidentally, label numbers have nothing to do with burning rate. According to long-time DuPont engineer Larry Werner, powder is labeled chronologically. The highest numbers indicate the most recent propellants.

You'll find differences in charts ranking the burn rates of IMR and other smokeless powders. The reason: powders can behave differently as you change case shape and bore diameter, fuel charge and bullet weight. IMR gives all its powders a Relative Quickness value, assigning IMR 4350 an arbitrary value of 100. According to Larry Werner, quick-burning IMR 4227 has an RQ of 180; IMR 4198 comes in at 165 and IMR 3031 at 135. IMR 4064, 4320 and 4895 are listed at 120, 115 and 110 respectively, though some loading manuals suggest a different order. IMR 4831 and 7828 burn more slowly. "Closed bomb" tests are used to gauge burn rate. A unit charge of powder ignited in a chamber of known volume produces a pressure curve that's then compared to the curves from other propellants.

DuPont's MR line included single-base (nitrocellulose) and double-base (nitrocellulose with nitroglycerine) powders. "The nitro gives you more energy per grain," explains Larry, "and it reduces the tendency for the grains to pick up moisture. Its drawback is more residue. Double-base powders generally don't burn as clean. To get the full effect of nitroglycerine, you really need 8 to 12 percent in the mix, but some powders claimed to be double-base contain less." All commercial ball powders are double-base, he says. The current IMR line includes only single-base propellants.

IMR powders are no longer made by DuPont. The IMR trademark belongs to EXPRO, another chemical firm. The transfer has its roots in the Depression, which DuPont weathered. But scathing political attacks from certain U.S. senators accused the company of war-mongering. As Hitler tuned his war machine and the U.S. prepared to re-arm, DuPont boosted its production capacity. "But the company was fed up with the treatment it had received from Congress," Larry remembers. Rather than build new plants, it contracted to operate government facilities for one dollar a year. That way, it could not be said to have had a stake in the hostilities. Of course, the government had no powder works that could match DuPont's, so the firm supervised construction of seven factories modeled on the Carney's Point plant. Another was built in Canada. At the height of the Second World War, these facilities shipped a million pounds of powder a day.

In the summer of 1978, DuPont contracted with Valleyfield Chemical Products in Quebec to produce its commercial smokeless propellants. (The Valleyfield plant was the Canadian factory built during World War II. It had been operated by CIL, or Canadian Industries, Ltd., a branch of the government.) In 1982, Valleyfield Chemical sold to Welland Chemical, which became EXPRO.

In December, 1986, DuPont sold its smokeless powder business to EXPRO. The IMR Powder Company became a testing and marketing firm for EXPRO propellants. IMR's laboratory and offices in Plattsburg, New York, now develop ballistics data for IMR powders and package and distribute them to dealers. EXPRO, with an annual manufacturing capacity of more than 10 million pounds, also makes other powders, including Alliant. Though DuPont owned 70 percent of Remington for decades, it has from time to time provided powder for competing ammunition firms.

Powders sold with the IMR label have changed since the 1940s, and America's powder industry is nothing like E.I. DuPont de Nemours found it back in 1802. Still, target shooters and hunters remain indebted to the enterprise of the young French immigrant – and to those men and women who have made and used MR and IMR powders in our country's defense.

Ramshot Powders

Western Powders, Inc. recently introduced a line of nine spherical powders for shooters. They are all double-base propellants, meaning they contain nitrocellulose and nitroglycerine. While some spherical or ball powders are known for leaving plenty of residue in barrels, Ramshots people say these new fuels burn very clean. They meter easily, as do all ball powders. Plastic cannisters are designed for spill-proof use and include basic loading data on the labels.

RAMSHOT COMPETITION is for the clay target shooter. A fast-burning powder comparable to 700-X or Red Dot it performs well in a variety of 12-gauge target loads, offering low recoil, consistent pressures and clean combustion.

RAMSHOT TRUE BLUE was designed for small to medium-size handgun cartridges. Similar to Winchester 231 and Hodgdon HP-38, it has enough bulk to nearly fill most cases, thereby better positioning the powder for ignition.

RAMSHOT ZIP, a fast-burning target powder for cartridges like the .38 Special and .45 ACP, gives competitors uniform velocities.

RAMSHOT SILHOUETTE is ideal for the 9mm handgun cartridge, from light to heavy loads. It also works well in the .40 Smith & Wesson and combat loads for the .45 Auto.

RAMSHOT ENFORCER is a match for high-performance handgun hulls like the .40 Smith & Wesson. It is designed for full-power loading and high velocities.Ramshot X-Terminator, a fast-burning rifle powder, excels in small-caliber, medium-capacity cartridges. It has the versatility to serve in both target and high-performance varmint loads.

RAMSHOT TAC was formulated for tactical rifle cartridges, specifically the .223 and .308. It has produced exceptional accuracy with a variety of bullets and charge weights.

RAMSHOT BIG GAME is a versatile propellant for cartridges as diverse as the .30-06 and the .338 Winchester, and for light-bullet loads in small-bore magnums.

RAMSHOT MAGNUM is the slowest powder of the Western line, and does its best work in cartridges with lots of case volume and small to medium bullet diameter. It is the powder of choice in 7mm and .30 Magnums.

www.ramshot.com

Vihtavuori

Kaltron-Pettibone markets Vihtavuori propellants (and Lapua ammunition in the U.S.) The powders, only recently available Stateside, have become popular with American shooters, who applaud their consistency. Their burning rates complement those of powders from IMR, Accurate, Hodgdon and Alliant (the ReLoder series). Here's a synopsis. Note that "similar" in these descriptions does NOT connote interchangeability!

N110: very fast, for rifle cartridges like the .22 Hornet and .25-20, and for powerful handgun rounds like the .357 and .44 Magnums; similar powders include H110, Winchester 296, Alliant 2400.

N120: a fast powder that requires high pressure for complete and efficient burn; similar to IMR 4227 and best used in small-capacity .22 centerfires.

N130: a bit slower than 4227 but still quick; a standard propellant in the .22 and 6mm PPC.

N133: slow enough for use in medium-capacity .22 cartridges like the .223; also useful in the .45-70 and similar cartridges with little or no neck restriction; similar to IMR 4198.

N135: a versatile powder of medium burn rate, ideal in the .308 and close derivatives, as well as the .30-06; applications from the various 17-calibers to the .458 Winchester; similar to RL-12.

N140: . . slightly slower than N135, but useful in the same cartridges and any that would be served with RL-15 or IMR 4320; a fine choice for the .30-06 and .375 H&H.

N150: a medium-slow powder for light-bullet loads in the .270 and the 30-caliber magnums; an excellent alternative to Winchester 760, Hodgdon H414, IMR 4350.

N160: a workhorse powder for magnum cases and high-velocity rounds on the .308 and .30-06 hulls; similar to RL-19, IMR 4831, Accurate 3100; useful in the .243, .270, 7mm Remington and .300 and .338 Winchester Magnums.

N165: a slow powder for "overbore" magnum cases and for heavy-bullet loads in the medium-bore magnums; ideal for high-performance .300s with all bullet weights; similar to H4831 and RL-22.

N170: the slowest-burning of Vihtavuori's propellants, for small-bore magnums like the .257 Weatherby and .264 Winchester; similar to H1000 and RL-25.

Unlike the single-base (nitrocellulose) N100 series, the N500 series of Vihtavuori powders has a nitroglycerin component (up to 25 percent, by impregnation). There's also a special stabilizer, a flame reducing agent, a wear-reducing agent and coating agents that ensure progressive burning in the case to provide uniform and efficient pressure curves. These high-energy double-base powders are available in three burning rates, equivalent to the 100-series powders with the same last digits. N540 is applicable in the same cartridges as N140. N550 is a match for N150. N560 is the slowest, an ideal propellant for the .270 Winchester and 6.5x55 Swedish Mauser.

Vihtavuori also makes single-base powders for the .50 BMG. The 24N41 is slightly faster than the 20N29. Eight Vihtavuori pistol powders complete the 2003 line:

N310: as fast as Bullseye, for small-capacity cartridges like the .25 ACP up to the 9mm Luger.

N320: slightly faster than Winchester 231, a versatile powder for the most popular of pistol rounds, including the .38 Special, .357 Magnum, .45 ACP, .44 Magnum and .45 Long Colt.

N330: useful in medium- to large-capacity cases from the .38 Special to the various .44s and .45s; similar to Green Dot.

N340: slow enough for high-performance loads in the .357 and .44 Magnums, also useful in the .38 Super and .30 Luger; similar to Winchester 540.

N350: a slow powder for magnum and heavy-bullet handgun loads; burning rate like that of Blue Dot or Hi-Skor 800-X.

3N37: between N340 and N350 in burn rate; recommended for competitive shooters.

3N38: a competition powder specifically for high-speed loads in the .38 Super and 9mm Luger.

N105 Super Magnum: a very slow pistol powder for heavy-bullet loads in magnum cases; almost as slow as N110.

Dillon Precision Reloaders

Dillon Precision is a leader in the shotgun shooting sports market with its SL 900 progressive shotshell reloader. Based on Dillon's proven XL 650 O-frame design, it incorporates the same powerful compound linkage. The automatic case insert system, fed by an electric case collator, ranks high among the new features of this reloader. Adjustable shot and powder bars come as standard equipment. Both the powder and shot bars are case-activated, so no powder or shot can spill when no shell is at that station. Should the operator forget to insert a wad during the reloading process, the SL 900 will not dispense shot into the powder-charged hull. Both powder and shot systems are based on Dillon's adjustable powder bar design, which is accurate to within a few tenths of a grain. These systems also eliminate the need for fixed-volume bushings. Simply adjust the measures to dispense the exact charges required.

The Dillon SL 900 is the first progressive shotshell loader on which it is practical to change gauges. An interchangeable toolhead makes it quick and easy to change from one gauge to another. The SL 900 also has an extra large, remote shot hopper that holds an entire 25-pound bag of shot, making it easy to fill with a funnel. The unique shot reservoir/dispenser helps ensure that a consistent volume of shot is delivered to each shell.

For shotgunners who shoot and load for multiple gauges or different kinds of shooting, the SL 900's interchangeable toolhead feature makes quick work of changing from one gauge to another. It uses a collet-type sizing die that re-forms the base of the shotshell to factory specifications—a feature that ensures reliable feeding in all shotguns. The heat-treated steel crimp die forms and folds the hull before the final taper crimp die radiuses and blends the end of the hull and locks the crimp into place.

Model RL550B Progressive Loader
- Accommodates over 120 calibers
- Interchangeable toolhead assembly
- Auto/Powder priming systems
- Uses standard 7/8" by 14 dies
- Loading rate: 500-600 rounds per hour

Price: $326

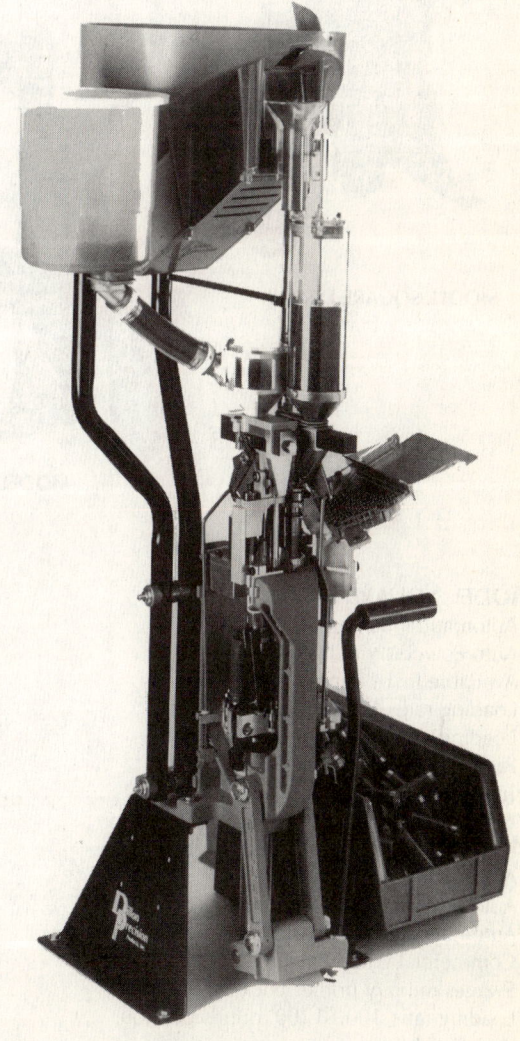

Model SL900
Price: $820

Dillon Precision Reloaders

MODEL SQUARE DEAL B

MODEL XL 650

MODEL AT-500

MODEL SUPER 1050 AND RL 1050

MODEL SQUARE DEAL B
- Automatic Indexing
- Auto Powder/Priming Systems
- Available in 14 handgun calibers
- Loading rate: 400-500 rounds per hour
- Loading dies standard
- Factory adjusted, ready-to-use

Price: $253

MODEL SUPER 1050 AND RL 1050
- Automatic indexing
- Auto powder/priming systems
- Automatic casefeeder
- Commercial grade machine
- Swages military primer pockets
- Loading rate: 1000-1200 rounds per hour
- Weighs 54 lbs.
- Eight stations

Price: 1300

MODEL XL 650
- Rotary indexing plate for primers
- Automatic indexing
- Uses standard 7/8" x 14 dies
- Loading rate: 800-1000 rounds per hour
- Five-station interchangeable toolhead

Price: $444

MODEL AT-500
- Loads over 40 calibers
- Uses standard 7/8" by 14 dies
- Upgradeable to Model RL 550B
- Interchangeable toolhead
- Switch from one caliber to another in 30 seconds
- Universal shellplate

Price: 194

Forster Reloading

CO-AX® BENCH REST® RIFLE DIES

HAND CASE TRIMMER

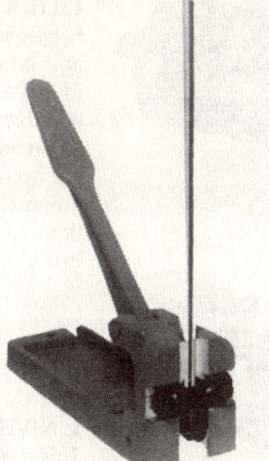
PRIMER SEATER

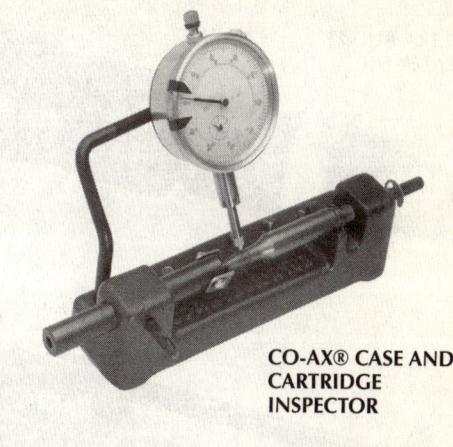
CO-AX® CASE AND CARTRIDGE INSPECTOR

PRIMER POCKET CLEANER

CO-AX® BENCH REST® RIFLE DIES
Bench Rest Rifle Dies are glass-hard and polished mirror-smooth with special attention given to headspace, tapers and diameters. Sizing die has an elevated expander button to ensure better alignment of case and neck.
Bench Rest® Die Set $74
Ultra Bench Rest Die Set 98
Full Length Sizer 34
Bench Rest Seating Die 41

HAND CASE TRIMMER
Shell holder is a Brown & Sharpe-type collet. Case and cartridge conditioning accessories include inside neck reamer, outside neck turner, deburring tool, hollow pointer and primer pocket cleaners. The case trimmer trims all cases, ranging from 17 to 458 Winchester caliber.
Price: 63

PRIMER SEATER WITH "E-Z-JUST" SHELLHOLDER
The Bonanza Primer Seater is designed so that primers are seated co-axially (primer in line with primer pocket). Mechanical leverage allows primers to be seated fully without crushing. With the addition of one extra set of disc shell holders and one extra Primer Unit, all modern cases, rim or rimless, from 222 up to 458 Magnum, can be primed. Shell holders are easily adjusted to any case by rotating to contact rim or cannelure of the case.
Primer Seater 72

"CLASSIC 50" CASE TRIMMER (NOT SHOWN)
Handles more than 100 different big bore calibers–500 Nitro Express, 416 Rigby, 50 Sharps, 475 H&H, etc. Also available: .50 BMG Case Trimmer, designed specifically for reloading needs of .50 Cal. BMG shooters.
Price: "Classic 50" Case Trimmer $88
.50 BMG Case Trimmer 94

CO-AX® CASE AND CARTRIDGE INSPECTOR
One tool to perform three vital measurements. Accurate performance from ammunition is absolutely dependent on uniformity of both the bullet and the case. Achieving that uniformity is not possible without an accurate, reliable measuring device. Forster's exclusive Co-Ax® Case & Cartridge Inspector provides the ability to ensure uniformity by measuring three critical dimensions: • Neck wall thickness • Case neck concentricity • Bullet runout.

Measurements are in increments of one-thousandth of an inch. The Inspector is unique because it checks both the bullet and case alignment in relation to the centerline (axis) of the entire cartridge or case.
Price: 84

PRIMER POCKET CLEANER
The Primer Pocket Cleaner helps ensure consistent ignition and reduce the incidence of misfires by removing powder and primer residue frm the primer pockets of your cases. This simple took is easy to use: Just hold the case mouth over the Primer Pocket Center with one hand while you quickly and easily clean the primer pockets by turning the Case Trimmer Handle.
Price: 7

Forster Reloading

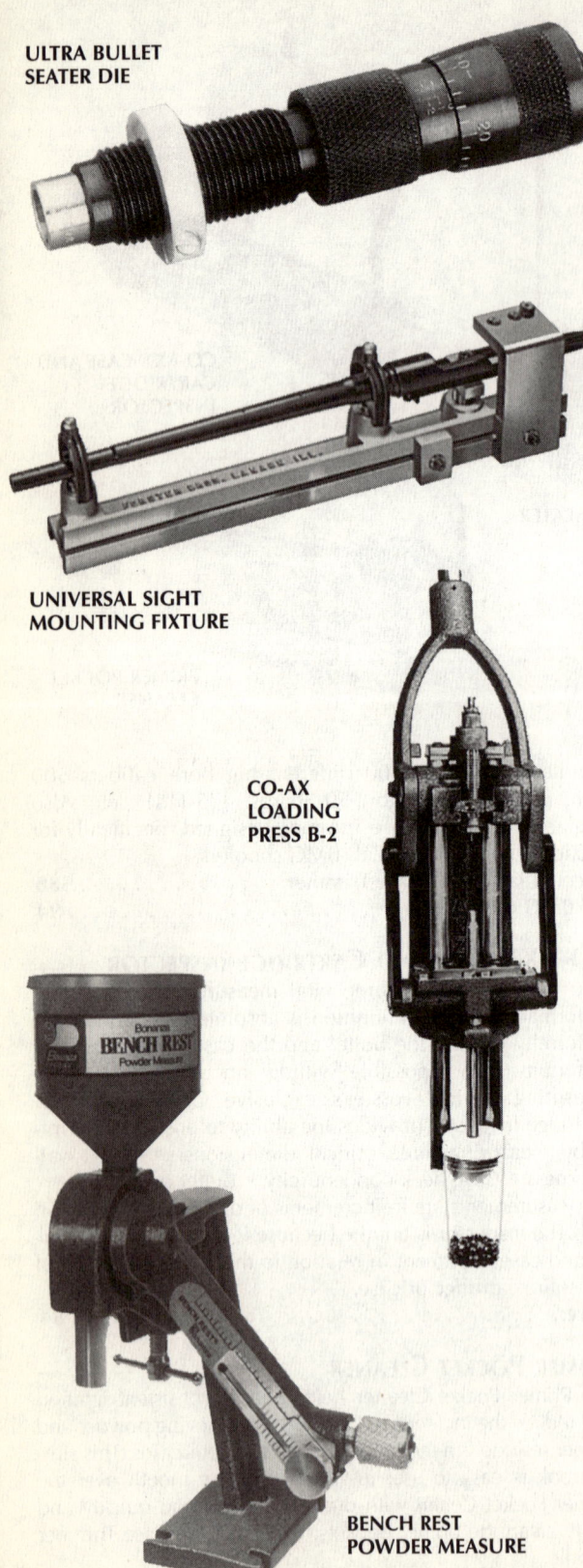

ULTRA BULLET SEATER DIE

UNIVERSAL SIGHT MOUNTING FIXTURE

CO-AX LOADING PRESS B-2

BENCH REST POWDER MEASURE

Ultra Bullet Seater Die
Forster's new Ultra Die is available in 56 calibers, more than any other brand of micrometer-style seater. Adjustment is identical to that of a precision micrometer—the head is graduated to .001" increments with .025" bullet movement per revolution. The cartridge case, bullet and seating stem are completely supported and perfectly aligned in a close-fitting chamber before and during the bullet seating operation.
Price: **$66**

Universal Sight Mounting Fixture
This product fills the exacting requirements needed for drilling and tapping holes for the mounting of scopes, receiver sights, shotgun beads, etc. The fixture handles any single-barrel gun—bolt-action, lever-action or pump-action—as long as the barrel can be laid into the "V" blocks of the fixture. Rifles with tube magazines are drilled in the same manner by removing the magazine tube. The fixture's main body is made of aluminum casting. The two "V" blocks are adjustable for height and are made of hardened steel ground accurately on the "V" as well as the shaft.
Price: **376**

CO-AX® Loading Press Model B-2
Designed to make reloading easier and more accurate, this press offers the following features: Snap-in and snap-out die change • Positive spent primer catcher • Automatic self-acting shell holder • Floating guide rods • Working room for right- or left-hand operators • Top priming device seats primers to factory specifications • Uses any standard 7/8"X14 dies • No torque on the head • Perfect alignment of die and case • Three times the mechanical advantage of a "C" press
Price: **304**

Bench Rest Powder Measure
When operated uniformly, this measure will throw uniform charges from 2 1/2 grains Bullseye to 95 grains #4320. No extra drums are needed. Powder is metered from the charge arm, allowing a flow of powder without extremes in variation while minimizing powder shearing. Powder flows through its own built-in baffle, entering the charge arm uniformly.
Price: **114**

Hornady

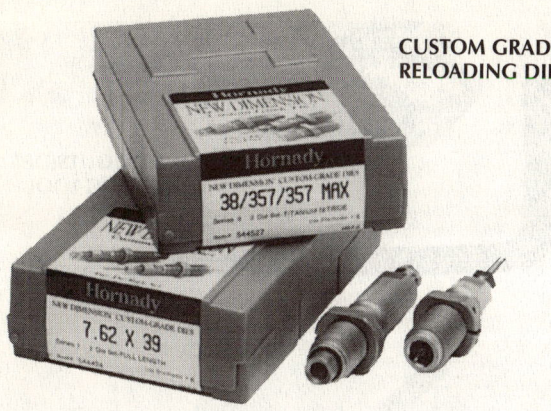

CUSTOM GRADE RELOADING DIES

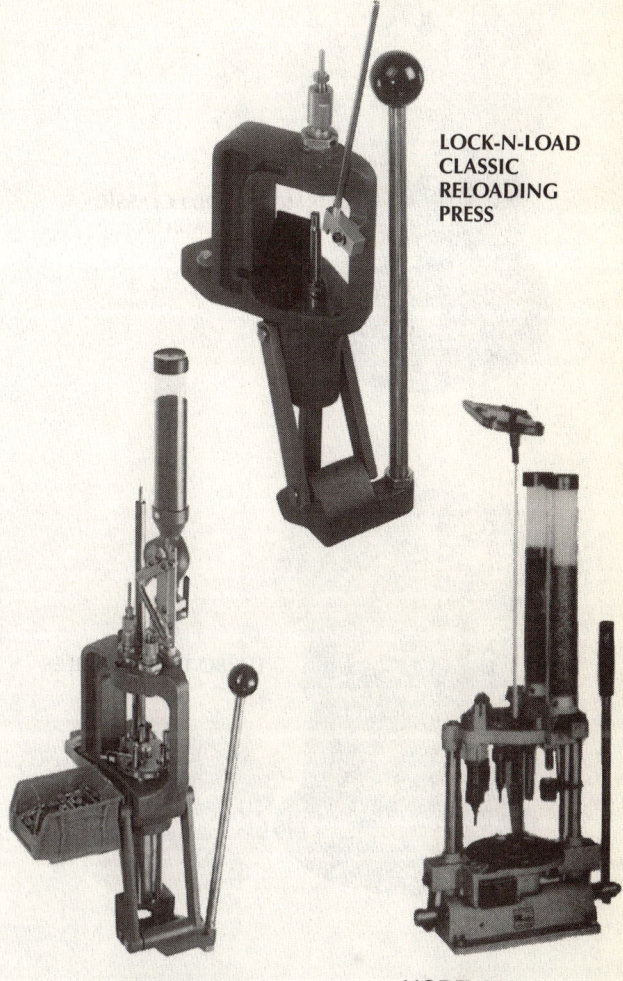

LOCK-N-LOAD CLASSIC RELOADING PRESS

LOCK-N-LOAD   MODEL 366

Custom Grade Reloading Dies
Features an Elliptical Expander that minimizes friction and reduces case neck stretch, plus the need for a tapered expander for "necking up" to the next larger caliber. Other recent design changes include a hardened steel decap pin that will not break, bend or crack even when depriming stubborn military cases. A bullet seater alignment sleeve guides the bullet and case neck into the die for in-line benchrest alignment. All New Dimension Reloading Dies include: collar and collar lock to center expander precisely; one-piece expander spindle with tapered bottom for easy cartridge insertion; wrench flats on die body, Sure-Loc™ lock rings and collar lock for easy tightening; and built-in crimper.

Prices:
New Dimension Custom Grade Reloading Dies:
- Series I Two-die Rifle Set $30
- Series II Three-die Rifle Set 32
- Series II Three-die Pistol Set (w/Titanium Nitride) . . 42
- 50 Caliber BMG Dies (Two-Die Set) 273

Lock-N-Load Classic Press
Lock-N-Load is available on Hornady's single stage and progressive reloader models. This bushing system locks the die into the press like a rifle bolt. Instead of threading dies in and out of the press, you simply lock and unlock them with a slight twist. Dies are held firmly in a die bushing that stays with the die and retains the die setting. The Lock-N-Load Classic Press features an easy-grip handle, an O-style frame made of high-strength alloy, and a positive priming system that feeds, aligns and seats the primer smoothly and automatically.

Prices: Lock-N-Load Classic Press Kit 275
Also Available: Lock-N-Load
  50 BMG Press Kit 525

Lock-N-Load Auto Progressive Press
The Lock-N-Load Automatic Progressive reloading press featuring the Lock-N-Load bushing system offers the flexibility to add a roll or taper crimp die. Dies and powder measure are inserted into Lock-N-Load die bushings, which lock securely into the press. The bushings remain with the die and powder measure and can be removed in seconds. They also fit on other presses. Other features include: deluxe powder measure, automatic indexing, off-set handle, power-pac linkage, case ejector.

Price:
Lock-N-Load Auto Progressive Press (includes five die bushings, shellplate, primer catcher, Positive Priming System, powder drop, Deluxe Powder Measure, automatic primer feed) $380

Model 366 Auto Shotshell Reloader
The 366 Auto features full-length resizing with each stroke, automatic primer feed, swing-out wad guide, three-state crimping featuring Taper-Loc for factory tapered crimp, automatic advance to the next station and automatic ejection. The turntable holds 8 shells for 8 operations with each stroke. Automatic charge bar loads shot and powder, dies and crimp starters for 6 point, 8 point and paper crimps.

Price:
Model 366 Auto Shotshell Reloader:
  12, 20, 28 gauge or .410 bore 472

Lyman Reloading Tools

MODEL 1200 CLASSIC TURBO TUMBLER

"IINSIDE/OUTSIDE" DEBURRING TOOL

TURBO TWIN TUMBLER

MASTER CASTING KIT

MODEL 1200 CLASSIC TURBO TUMBLER
This sturdy case tumbler features a redesigned base and drive system, plus a stronger suspension system and built-in exciters for better tumbling action and faster cleaning
Model 1200 Classic $80
Model 1200 Auto-Flo 100
Also available:
   Model 600 70
   Model 2200 Auto-Flo 125
   Model 3200 Auto-Flo 185

"IINSIDE/OUTSIDE" DEBURRING TOOL
This tool features an adjustable cutting blade that adapts easily to the mouth of any rifle or pistol case from 22 caliber to 45 caliber with a simple hex wrench adjustment. Inside deburring is completed by a conical internal section with slotted cutting edges, thus providing uniform inside and outside deburring in one simple operation. The deburring tool is mounted on an anodized aluminum handle that is machine-knurled for a sure grip.
Deburring Tool. 14

TURBO TWIN TUMBLER
The Twin features Lyman 1200 Pro Tumbler with an extra, 600 bowl system. Reloaders may use each bowl interchangeably for small or large capacity loads. 1200 Pro Bowl System has a built-in sifter lid for easy sifting of cases and media at the end of the polishing cycle. The Twin Tumbler features the Lyman Hi-Profile base design with built-in exciters and anti-rotation pads for faster, more consistent tumbling action.
Turbo Twin Tumbler 110V. $80

MASTER CASTING KIT
Designed especially to meet the needs of blackpowder shooters, this kit features Lyman's combination round ball and maxi ball mould blocks. It also contains a combination double cavity mould, mould handle, mini-mag furnace, lead dipper, bullet lube, a user's manual and a cast bullet guide. Kits are available in 45, 50 and 54 caliber.
Master Casting Kit 170

Lyman Reloading Tools

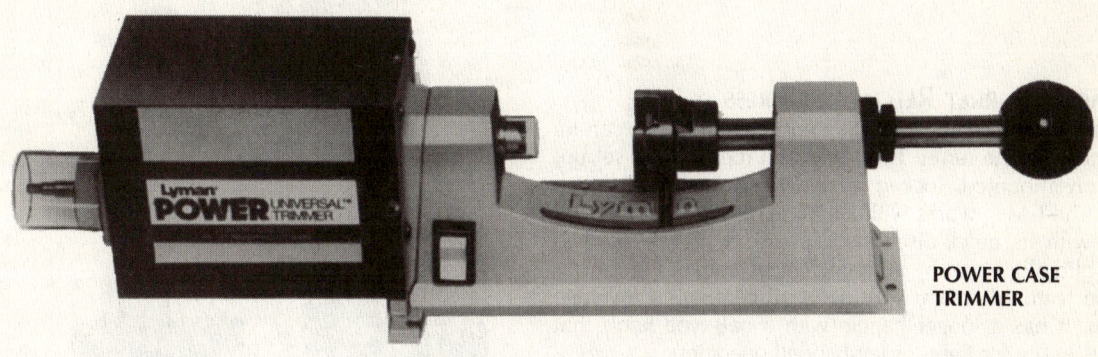

POWER CASE TRIMMER

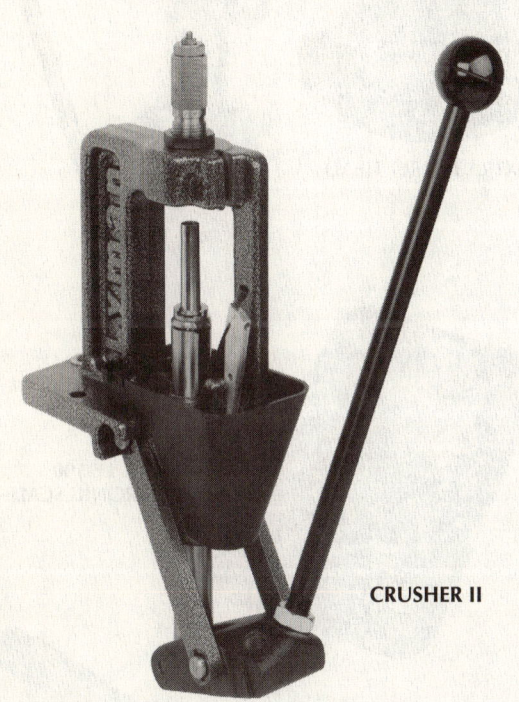

CRUSHER II

Power Case Trimmer
The Lyman Power Trimmer is powered by a fan-cooled electric motor designed to withstand the severe demands of case trimming. The unit, which features the Universal™ Chuckhead, allows cases to be positioned for trimming or removed with fingertip ease. The Power Trimmer package includes Nine-Pilot Multi-Pack. Two cutter heads and a pair of wire end brushes for cleaning primer pockets are included. Other features include safety guards, on-off rocker switch, heavy cast base with receptacles for nine pilots, and bolt holes for mounting on a work bench. Available for 110 V or 220 V systems.
Prices: 110 V Model $200
220 V Model 200

Acculine Outside Neck Turner
(NOT SHOWN)
To obtain perfectly concentric case necks, Lyman's Outside Neck Turner assures reloaders of uniform neck wall thickness and outside neck diameter. The unit fits Lyman's Universal Trimmer and AccuTrimmer. In use, each case is run over a mandrel, which centers the case for the turning operation. The cutter is carefully adjusted to remove a minimum amount of brass. Rate of feed is adjustable and a mechanical stop controls length of cut. Mandrels are available for calibers from .17 to .375; cutter blade can be adjusted for any diameter from .195" to .405".
Outside Neck Turner w/extra blade, 6 mandrels $30
Individual Mandrels 4

Crusher II Pro Kit
Includes press, loading block, case lube kit, primer tray, Model 500 Pro scale, powder funnel and Lyman Reloading Handbook.
Starter Kit 165

Lyman Crusher II Reloading Press
The only press for rifle or pistol cartridges that offers the advantage of powerful compound leverage combined with a true Magnum press opening. A unique handle design transfers power easily to the center of the ram. A 4 1/2-inch press opening accommodates even the largest cartridges.

Crusher II Press
With Priming Arm and Catcher 117

Lyman Reloading Tools

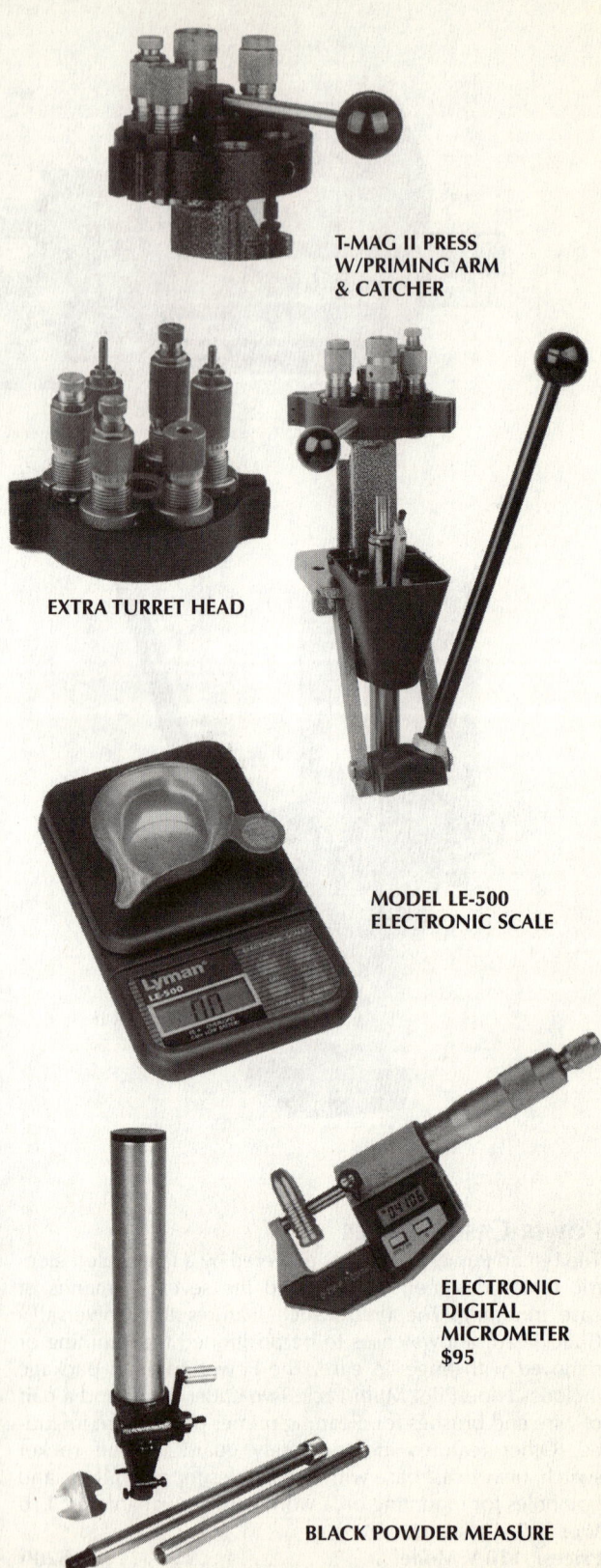

T-MAG II PRESS W/PRIMING ARM & CATCHER

EXTRA TURRET HEAD

MODEL LE-500 ELECTRONIC SCALE

ELECTRONIC DIGITAL MICROMETER $95

BLACK POWDER MEASURE

T-MAG II TURRET RELOADING PRESS
With the T-Mag II, up to six different reloading dies can be mounted on one turret. This means all dies can be set up, precisely mounted, locked in and ready to reload at all times. The T-Mag works with all 7/8 x 14 dies. The T-Mag II turret with its quick-disconnect release system is held in rock-solid alignment by a 3/4-inch steel stud.

Also featured is Lyman's Crusher II compound leverage system. It has a longer handle with a ball-type knob that mounts easily for right- or left-handed operation.

T-Mag II Press w/Priming Arm & Catcher $165
Extra Turret Head 38

Also available:
Expert Kit that includes T-MAG II Press, Universal Case Trimmer and pilot Multi-Pak, Model 500 powder scale and Model 50 powder measure, plus accessories and Reloading Manual. Available in calibers 30-06, 270 and 308
Price: 390

ELECTRONIC SCALE MODEL LE-1000
Accurate to 1/10 grain, Lyman's LE: 1000 measures up to 1000 grains of powder and easily converts to the gram mode for metric measurements. The push-button automatic calibration feature eliminates the need for calibrating with a screwdriver. The scale works off a single 9V battery or AC power adapter (included with each scale). Its compact design allows the LE-1000 to be carried to the field easily. A sculpted carrying case is optional. 110 Volt or 220 Volt.
Model LE-1000 Electronic Scale 260
Model LE-300 Electronic Scale 167
Model LE-500 Electric Scale 184

55 CLASSIC BLACK POWDER MEASURE
Lyman's 55 Classic Powder Measure is ideal for the Cowboy Action Competition or the growing number of black powder cartridge shooters. The one-pound-capacity aluminum reservoir and brass powder meter eliminate static. The internal powder baffel assures highly accurate and consistent charges. The 24" powder compacting drop tube allows the maximum charge in each cartridge. Drop tube works on calibers 38 through 50 and mounts easily to the bottom of the measure. Clamp on back allows easy mounting of the measure at a convenient height, when using long drop tubes.
55 Classic Powder Measure (std model-no tubes) 108
55 Classic Powder Measure (with drop tubes) 125
Powder Drop Tubes Only 29

Lyman Reloading Tools

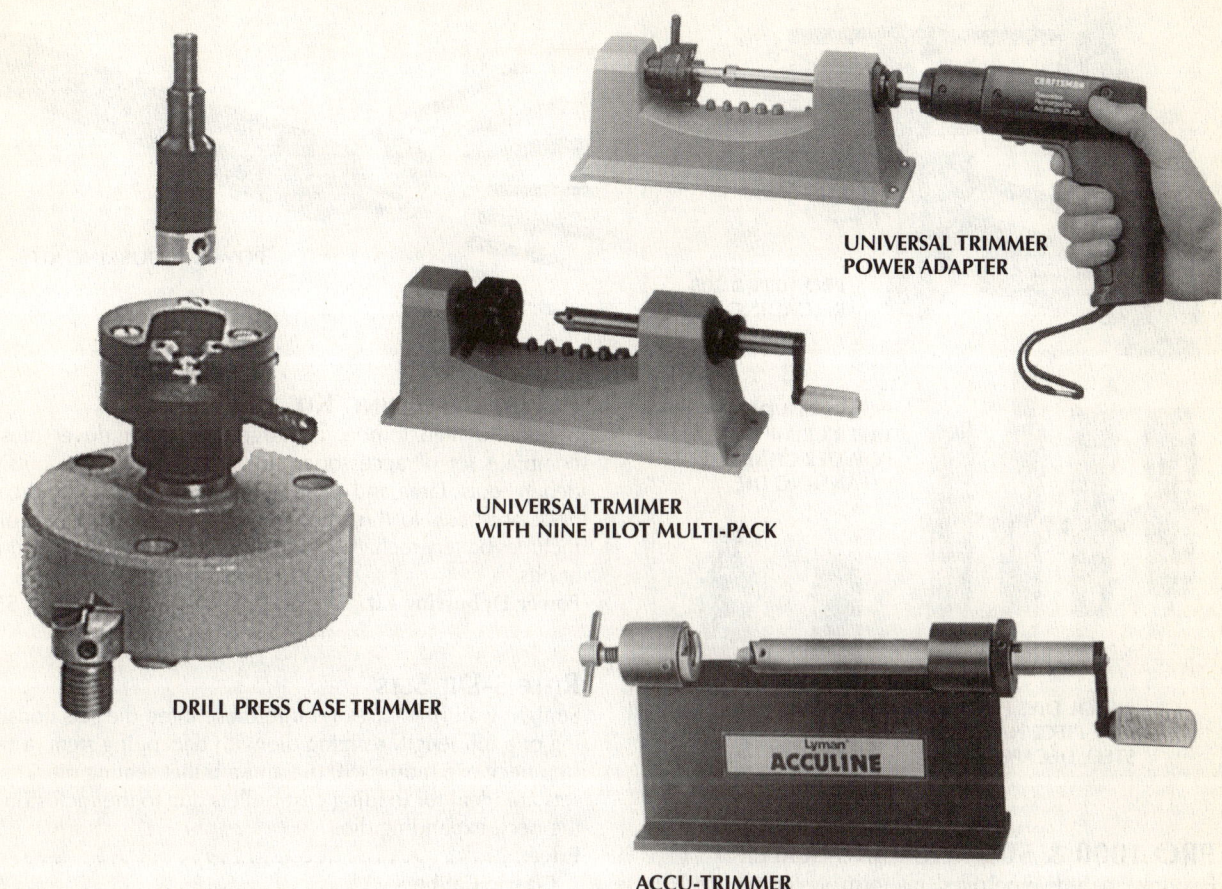

UNIVERSAL TRIMMER POWER ADAPTER

UNIVERSAL TRMIMER WITH NINE PILOT MULTI-PACK

DRILL PRESS CASE TRIMMER

ACCU-TRIMMER

DRILL PRESS CASE TRIMMER
Intended for competitive shooters, varmint hunters, and other sportsmen who use large quantities of reloaded ammunition, this drill press case trimmer consists of the Universal™ Chuckhead, a cutter shaft adapted for use in a drill press, and two quick-change cutter heads. Its two major advantages are speed and accuracy. An experienced operator can trim several hundred cases an hour, and each will be trimmed to a precise length.
Drill Press Case Trimmer $50

ACCU-TRIMMER
Lyman's Accu Trimmer can be used for all rifle and pistol cases from 22 to 458 Winchester Magnum. Standard shell-holders are used to position the case, and the trimmer incorporates standard Lyman cutter heads and pilots. Mounting options include bolting to a bench, C-clamp or vise.
Accu Trimmer w/9-pilot multi-pak 45

UNIVERSAL TRMIMER WITH NINE PILOT MULTI-PACK
This trimmer with patented chuckhead accepts all metallic rifle or pistol cases, regardless of rim thickness. To change calibers, simply change the case head pilot. Other features include coarse and fine cutter adjustments, an oil-impregnated bronze bearing, and a rugged cast base to assure precision alignment and years of service. Optional carbide cutter available. Trimmer Stop Ring includes 20 indicators as reference marks.
Replacement carbide cutter $42
Trimmer Multi-Pack (incl. 9 pilots: 22, 24, 27,
   28/7mm, 30, 9mm, 35, 44 and 4A) 68
Nine Pilot Multi-Pack 12
Power Pack Trimmer 78
Universal Trimmer Power Adapter 20

ELECTRONIC DIGITAL CALIPER (NOT SHOWN)
Lyman's 6" electronic caliper gives a direct digital readout for both inches and millimeters and can perform both inside and outside depth measurements. Its zeroing function allows the user to select zeroing dimensions and sort parts or cases by their plus or minus variation. The caliper works on a single, standard 1.5 volt silver oxide battery and comes with a fitted wooden storage case.
Electronic Caliper 100
Also Available:
   4" Pocket Electronic Caliper 83

Lyman Reloading Tools

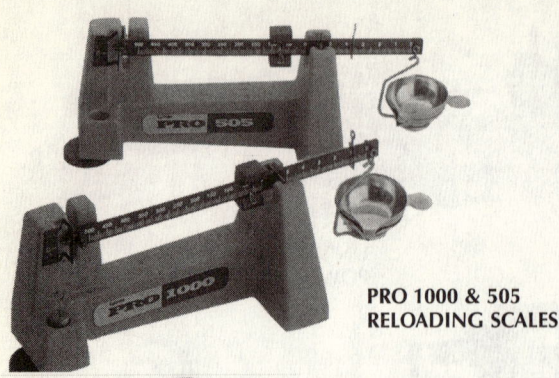

PRO 1000 & 505 RELOADING SCALES

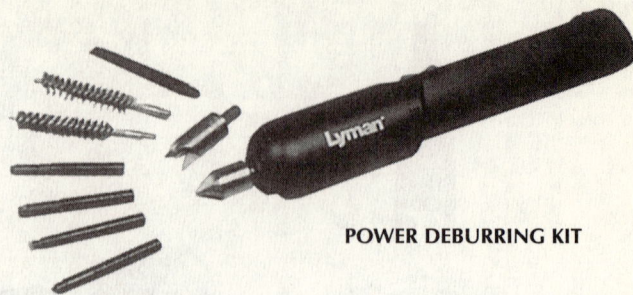

POWER DEBURRING KIT

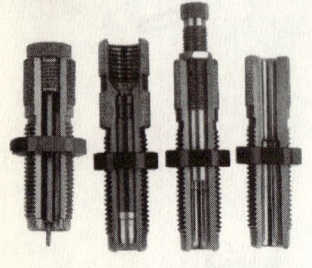

PREMIUM 4-DIE SET WITH TAPER CRIMP AND POWDER CHARGE EXPANDING DIE

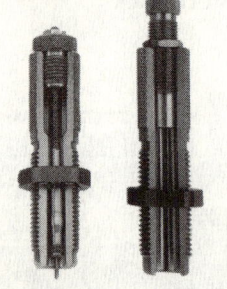

PISTOL DIES FEATURE ONE PIECE HARDENED STEEL DECAPPING ROD

PRO 1000 & 505 RELOADING SCALES
Features include improved platform system; hi-tech base design of high-impact styrene; extra-large, smooth leveling wheel; dual agate bearings; larger damper for fast zeroing; built-in counter weight compartment; easy-to-read beam.
Pro 1000 Scale. $63
Pro 500 Scale. 45

RIFLE DIE SETS
Lyman precision rifle dies are manufactured on computer controlled equipment ensuring that each die is chambered perfectly and has a smooth finish. Each sizing die for bottle-necked rifle cartridges is then carefully vented. This vent hole is precisely placed to prevent air traps that can damage cartridge cases. Each sizing die is polished, then heat treated for toughness. It receives a final hand polish for extra smoothness. Fine adjustment threads on the bullet seating stem allow for precision adjustments of bullet seating depth. Lyman dies fit all popular presses using industry standard 7/8 x 14 threads, including RCBS, Lee, Hornady, Dillon, Redding and others.

RIFLE 2-DIE SETS
Set consists of a full length resizing die with decapping stem and neck expanding button and a bullet seating die for loading jacketed bullets in bottlenecked rifle cases. For those who load cast bullets, use a neck expanding die, available separately.
Price:. 30

POWER DEBURRING KIT
Features a high torque, rechargeable power driver plus a complete set of accessories, including inside and outside deburr tools, large and small reamers and cleaners and case neck brushes. No threading or chucking required. Set also includes battery recharger and standard flat and phillips driver bits.
Power Deburring Kit. $55

RIFLE 3-DIE SETS
Straight wall rifle cases require these three die sets consisting of a full length resizing die with decapping stem, a two step neck expanding (M) die and a bullet seating die. These sets are ideal for loading cast bullets due to the inclusion of the neck expanding die.
Price:. 40
 Classic Calibers 50
 Classic Neck Size Dies 21

PREMIUM CARBIDE 4-DIE SETS FOR PISTOLS
Lyman 4-Die Sets feature a separate taper crimp die and powder charge/expanding die. The powder charge/expand die has a special hollow 2-step neck expanding plug which allows powder to flow through the die from a powder measure directly into the case. The powder charge/expanding die has a standard 7/8 x 14 thread and will accept Lyman's 55 Powder Measure, or most other powder measures.
Price:. 55

3-DIE CARBIDE PISTOL DIE SETS
Lyman originated the Tungsten Carbide (T-C) sizing die and the addition of extra seating screws for pistol die sets and the two step neck expanding die. Multi-Deluxe Die sets offer these features; a one-piece hardened steel decapping rod and extra seating screws for all popular bullet nose shapes; all-steel construction.
Price:. 42

STANDARD PISTOL DIE SETS
These 3-die pistol sets are designed for bottleneck pistol cases. The full length sizing die is precision machined from solid steel. 3-Die sets also feature Lyman's two step neck expanding die.
Price:. 32

MEC Shotshell Reloaders

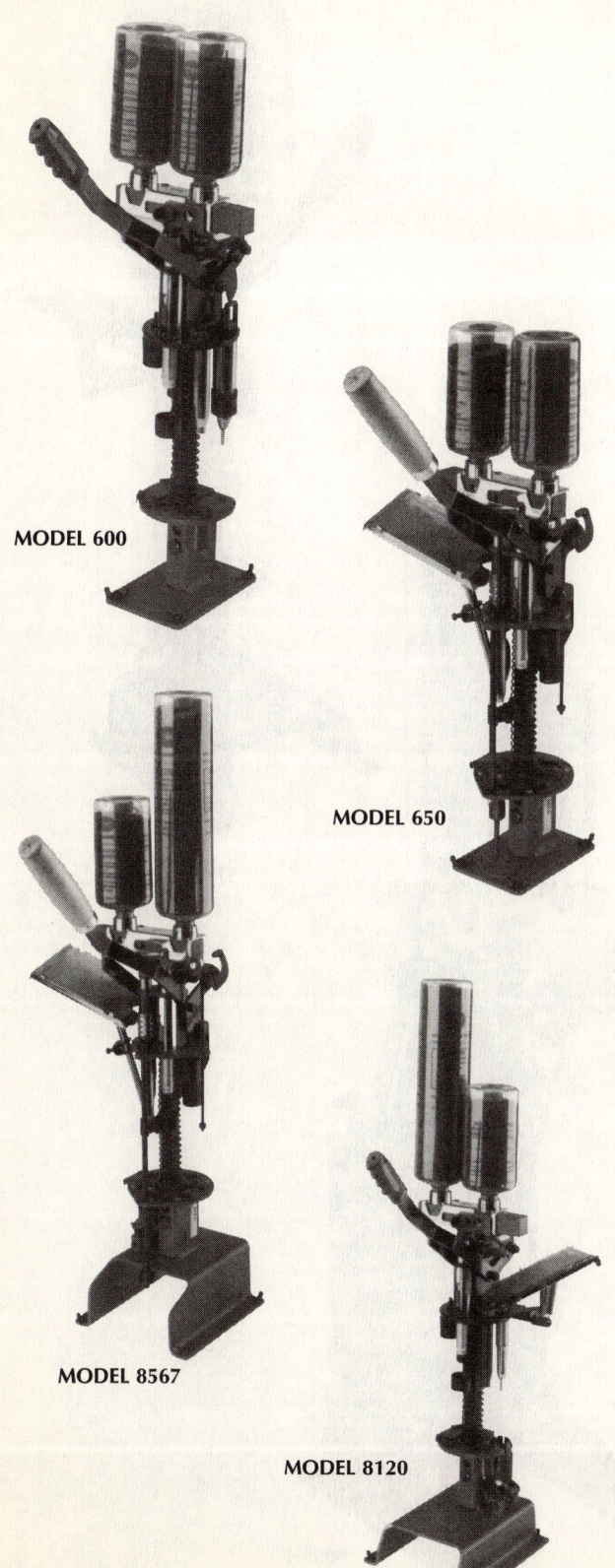

MODEL 600
MODEL 650
MODEL 8567
MODEL 8120

MODEL 600 JR. MARK V
This single-stage reloader features a cam-action crimp die to ensure that each shell returns to its original condition. MEC's 600 Jr. Mark 5 can load 6 to 8 boxes per hour and can be updated with the 285 CA primer feed. Press is adjustable for 3" shells.
Price:....................................$107

MODEL 650
This reloader works on 6 shells at once. A reloaded shell is completed with every stroke. The MEC 650 does not resize except as a separate operation. Automatic Primer feed is standard. Simply fill it with a full box of primers and it will do the rest. Reloader has 3 crimping stations: the first one starts the crimp, the second closes the crimp, and the third places a taper on the shell. Available in 12, 16, 20 and 28 gauge and .410 bore. No die sets are available.
Price:....................................211

MODEL 8567 GRABBER
This reloader features 12 different operations at all 6 stations, producing finished shells with each stroke of the handle. It includes a fully automatic primer feed and Auto-Cycle charging, plus MEC's exclusive 3-stage crimp. The "Power Ring" resizer ensures consistent, accurately sized shells without interrupting the reloading sequence. Simply put in the wads and shell casings, then remove the loaded shells with each pull of the handle. Optional kits to load 3" shells and steel shot make this reloader tops in its field. Resizes high and low base shells. Available in 12, 16, 20, 28 gauge and .410 bore. No die sets are available.
Price:....................................303

MODEL 8120 SIZEMASTER
Sizemaster's "Power Ring" collet resizer returns each base to factory specifications. This generation resizing station handles brass or steel heads, both high and low base. An 8-fingered collet squeezes the base back to original dimensions, then opens up to release the shell easily. The E-Z Prime auto primer feed is standard equipment (not offered in .410 bore). Press is adjustable for 3" shells and is available in 10, 12, 16, 20, 28 gauge and .410 bore. Die sets are available at: $88.67 ($104.06 in 10 ga.)
Price:....................................162

Reloading • 549

MEC Reloading

STEELMASTER SINGLE STATE
The only shotshell reloader equipped to load steel shotshells as well as lead ones. Every base is resized to factory specs by a precision "power ring" collet. Handles brass or steel heads in high or low base. The E-Z prime auto primer feed dispenses primers automatically and is standard equipment. Separate presses are available for 12 gauge 2 3/4", 3", 12 gauge 3 1/2" and 10 gauge.

8639 Steelmaster 10 &12 ga 175
8755 Steelmaster 12 ga. 3 1/2" only 196

MEC 9000 SERIES SHOTSHELL RELOADER
MEC's 9000 Series features automatic indexing and finished shell ejection for quicker and easier reloading. The factory set speed provides uniform movement through every reloading stage. Dropping the primer into the reprime station no longer requires operator "feel." The reloader requires only a minimal adjustment from low to high brass domestic shells, any one of which can be removed for inspection from any station. Can be set up for automatic or manual indexing. Available in 12, 16, 20 and 28 gauge and .410 bore. No die sets are available.

MEC 9000H 888
MEC 9000H without pump 480
MEC 9000G Series 368
Also Available: MEC Super Sizer
Resize shotgun shells back to factory specs!
Price: 61

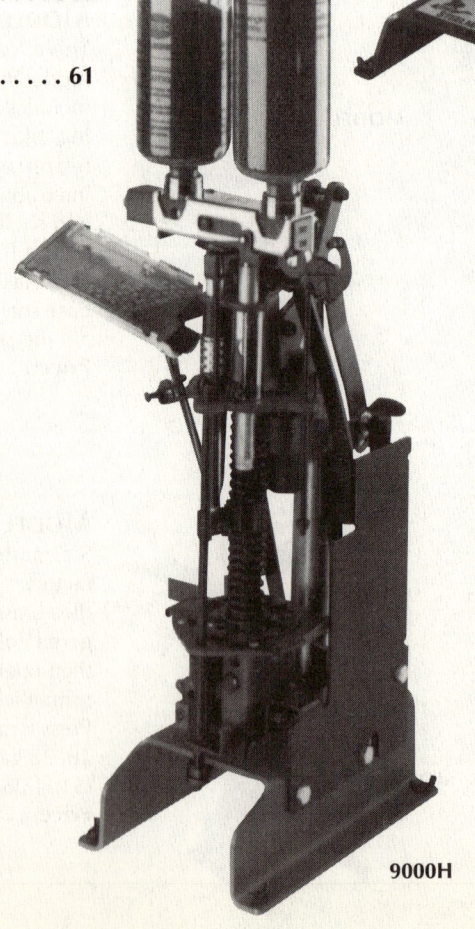

STEEL MASTER

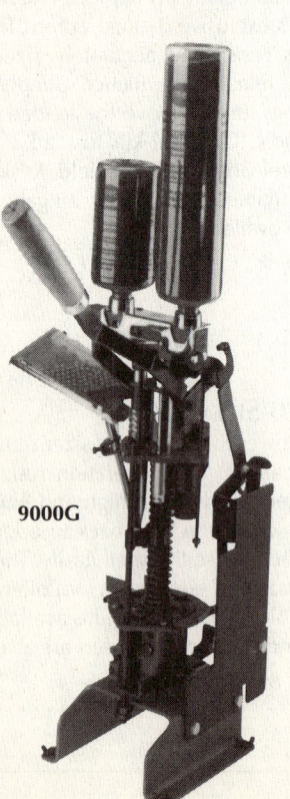

9000G

9000H

550 • 2003 Shooter's Bible

www.StoegerIndustries.com

MTM Reloading

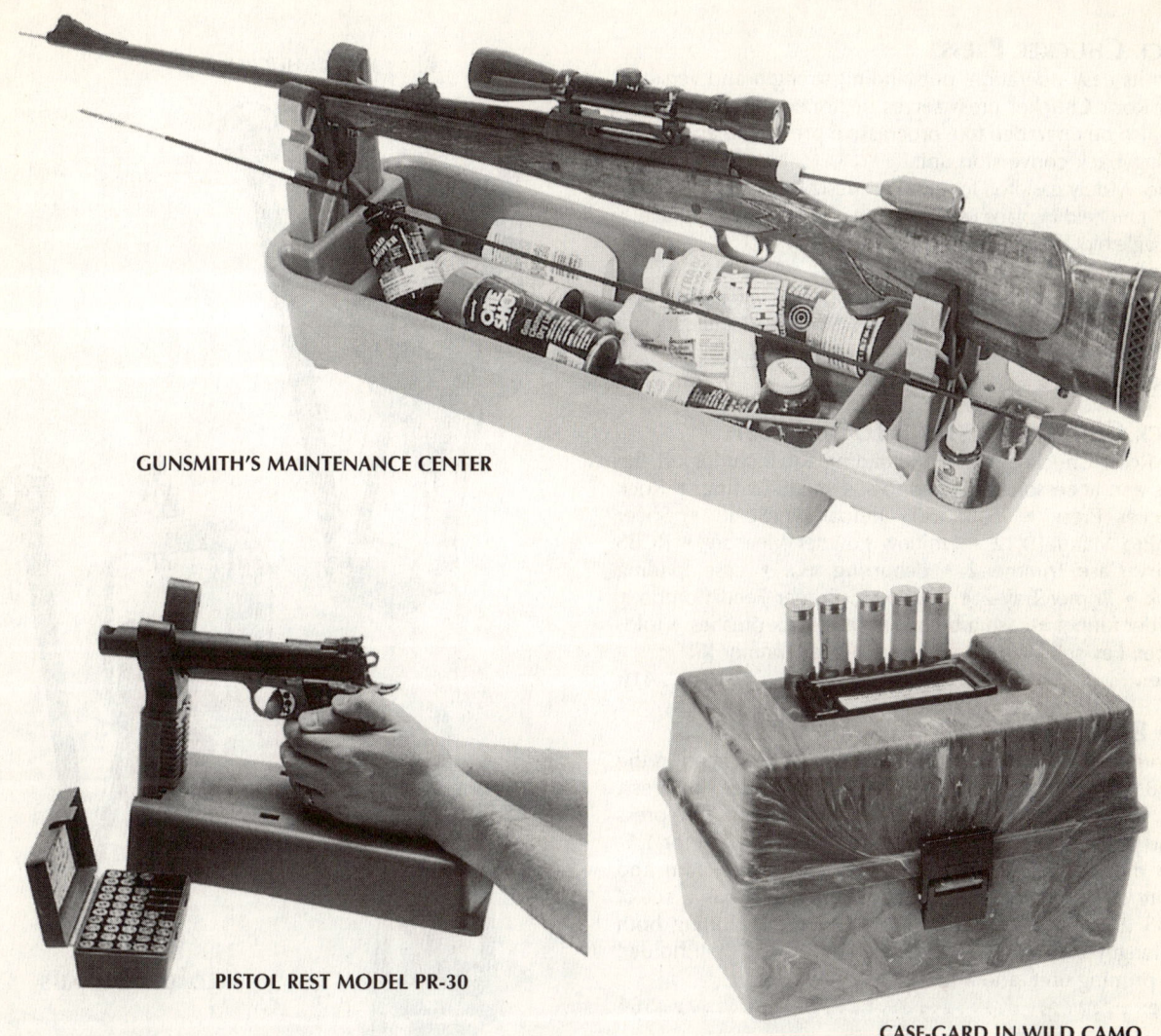

GUNSMITH'S MAINTENANCE CENTER

PISTOL REST MODEL PR-30

CASE-GARD IN WILD CAMO

GUNSMITH'S MAINTENANCE CENTER
MTM's Gunsmiths Maintenance Center (RMC-5) is designed for mounting scopes and swivels, bedding actions or for cleaning rifles and shotguns. Multi-positional forks allow for eight holding combinations, making it possible to service firearm level, upright or upside down. The large middle section keeps tools and cleaning supplies in one area. Individual solvent compartments help to eliminate accidental spills. Cleaning rods stay where they are needed with the two built-in holders provided. Both forks (covered with a soft molded-on rubber pad) grip and protect the firearm. The RMC-5 is made of engineering- grade plastic for years of rugged use. Not Shown: Extensive line of plastic ammo boxes, reloading trays, pistol cases, target holders, clay target throwers, arrow and tackle boxes.
Dimensions: 29.5" X 9.5"
Model RMC-5-30 . . . . $31

PISTOL REST MODEL PR-30
MTM's PR-30 Pistol Rest will accommodate any size handgun, from a Derringer to a 14" Contender. A locking front support leg adjusts up or down, allowing 20 different positions. Rubber padding molded to the tough polypropylene fork protects firearms from scratches. Fork clips into the base when not in use for compact storage.
Dimensions: 6" x 11" x 2.5
Pistol Rest Model PR-30 . . . . $17

CASE-GARD IN WILD CAMO
The CASE-GARD SF-100 holds 100 shotshells in two removable trays. Designed primarily for hunters, this dust and moisture resistant carrier features a heavy-duty latch, fold-down handle, integral hinge and textured finish.
Price: SF-100 12 or 20 ga.
    Wild Camo Shotshell Box 17

RCBS Reloading Tools

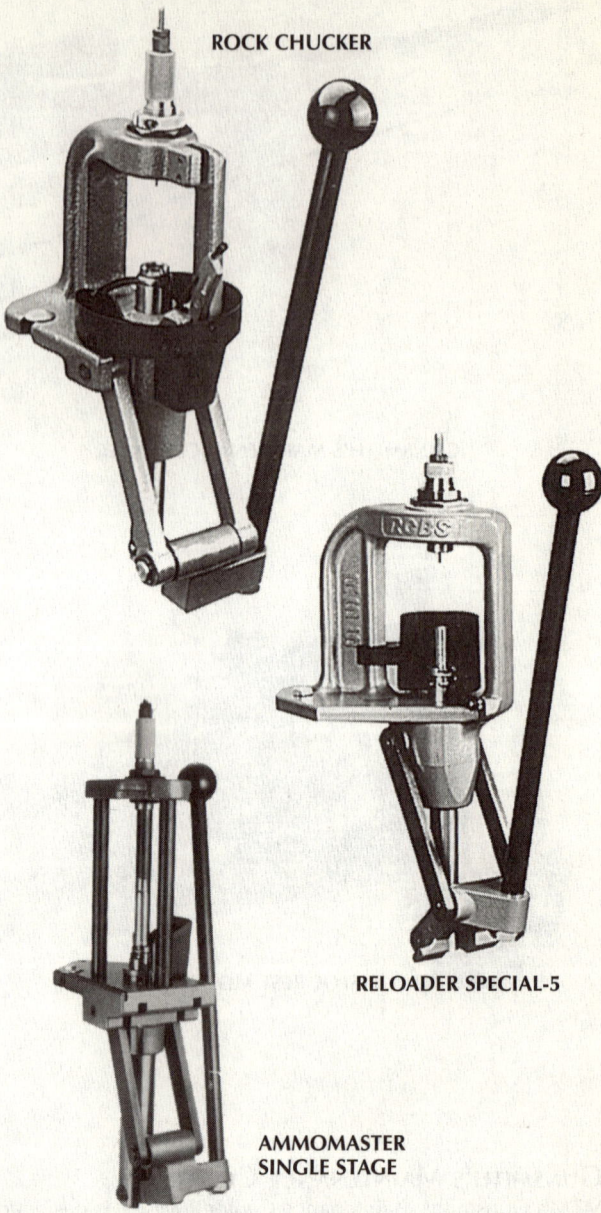

ROCK CHUCKER

RELOADER SPECIAL-5

AMMOMASTER
SINGLE STAGE

ROCK CHUCKER PRESS
With its easy operation, outstanding strength and versatility, a Rock Chucker press serves beginner and pro alike. It can also be upgraded to a progressive press with an optional Piggyback conversion unit.
- Heavy-duty cast iron for easy case-resizing
- 1" ram held in place by 12.5 sq. in. of rambearing surface
- Toggle blocks of ductile iron
- Compound leverage system
- 7/8"-14 thread for all standard reloading dies and accessories
- Milled slot and set screws accept optional RCBS automatic primer feed

Price:.................................$146

ROCK CHUCKER MASTER RELOADING KIT
The Rock Chucker Master Reloading Kit includes all the tools and accessories needed to start handloading: • Rock Chucker Press • RCBS 505 Reloading Scale • Speer TrimPro Manual #12 • Uniflow Powder Measure • RCBS Rotary Case Trimmer-2 • deburring tool • case loading block • Primer Tray-2 • Automatic Primer Feed Combo • powder funnel • case lube pad • case neck brushes • fold-up hex key set • Trim Pro Manual Case Trimmer Kit

Price:..................................416

.50 BMG PACK
Shooters who favor the .50 BMG have all they need in the .50 BMG Pack from RCBS®. The Pack includes the press, dies, and accessory items needed, all in one box. The press is the powerful Ammo Master® Single Stage rigged for 1.5-inch dies. It has a massive 1.5-inch solid steel ram and plenty of height for the big .50. The kit also has a set of RCBS .50 BMG, 1.5-inch reloading dies, including both full-length sizer and seater. Other items are a shell holder, ram priming unit, and a trim die.

Price:..................................564

AMMOMASTER RELOADING SYSTEM
The AmmoMaster offers any handloader the freedom to configure a press to his particular needs and preferences. It covers the complete spectrum of reloading, from single stage through fully automatic pro-gressive reloading, from .25 Auto to .50 caliber. The AmmoMaster Auto has all the features of a five-station press.

Single Stage..............................213

RELOADER SPECIAL-5
The Reloader Special press features a comfortable ball handle and a primer arm so that cases can be primed and resized at the same time.
- Compound leverage system
- Solid aluminum black "O" frame offset for unobstructed access
- Corrosion-resistant baked-powder finish
- Can be upgraded to progressive reloading with an optional Piggyback II conversion unit
- 7/8" - 14 thread for all standard reloading dies and accessories

Price:.................................$116
Reloading Starter Kit 268

PIGGYBACK III CONVERSION KIT
(NOT SHOWN)
- The Piggyback III conversion unit moves from single-stage reloading to 5-station, manual-indexing, progressive reloading in one step
- Increases output from 50 rounds an hour to well over 400

The Piggyback III will work with the RCBS Rock Chucker, Reloader Special-3, and Reloader Special-5.

Price:..................................281

RCBS Reloading Tools

APS PRIMER STRIP LOADER

APS BENCH-MOUNTED PRIMING TOOL

APS PRESS-MOUNTED PRIMING TOOL

RELOADING SCALE MODEL 5-0-5

TRIM PRO™ CASE TRIMMER

APS BENCH-MOUNTED PRIMING TOOL
The APS Bench-Mounted Priming Tool was created for reloaders who prefer a separate, specialized tool dedicated to priming only. The handle of the bench-mounted tool is designed to provide hours of comfortable loading. Handle position can be adjusted for bench height.
Price:..$96

APS PRIMER STRIP LOADER
For those who keep a supply of CCI primers in conventional packaging, the APS primer strip loader allows quick filling of empty strips. Each push of the handle seats 25 primers.
Price:...27

POW'R PULL BULLET PULLER (NOT SHOWN)
The RCBS Pow'r Pull bullet puller features a three-jaw chuck that grips the case rim—just rap it on any solid surface like a hammer, and powder and bullet drop into the main chamber for re-use. A soft cushion protects bullets from damage. Works with most centerfire cartridges from .22 to .45 (not for use with rimfire cartridges).
Price:...29

RELOADING SCALE MODEL 5-0-5
This 511-grain capacity scale has a three-poise system with widely spaced, deep beam notches to keep them in place. Two smaller poises on right side adjust from 0.1 to 10 grains, larger one on left side adjusts in full 10-grain steps. The first scale to use magnetic dampening to eliminate beam oscillation, the 5-0-5 also has a sturdy die-cast base with large leveling legs for stability. Self-aligning agate bearings support the hardened steel beam pivots for a guaranteed sensitivity to 0.1 grains.
Price:...$89

APS PRESS-MOUNTED PRIMING TOOL
This APS press-mounted priming tool provides the same features as the bench-mounted tool, except it attaches to any single-stage press that accepts standard 7/8" x 14 dies.
Price:...61

TRIM PRO™ CASE TRIMMER
Cartridge cases are trimmed quickly and easily with a few turns of the RCBS Trim Pro case trimmer. The lever-type handle is more accurate to use than draw collet systems. A flat plate shell holder keeps cases locked in place and aligned. A micrometer fine adjustment bushing offers trimming accuracy to within .001". Made of die-cast metal with hardened cutting blades. The power model is like having a personal lathe, delivering plenty of torque. Positive locking handle and in-line power switch make it simple and safe.
Price: Power 110 Vac Kit 242
   Manual..................................95
Also available:
Trim Pro Case Trimmer Stand 19
   Case Holder Accessory 39

Reloading • 553

RCBS Reloading Tools

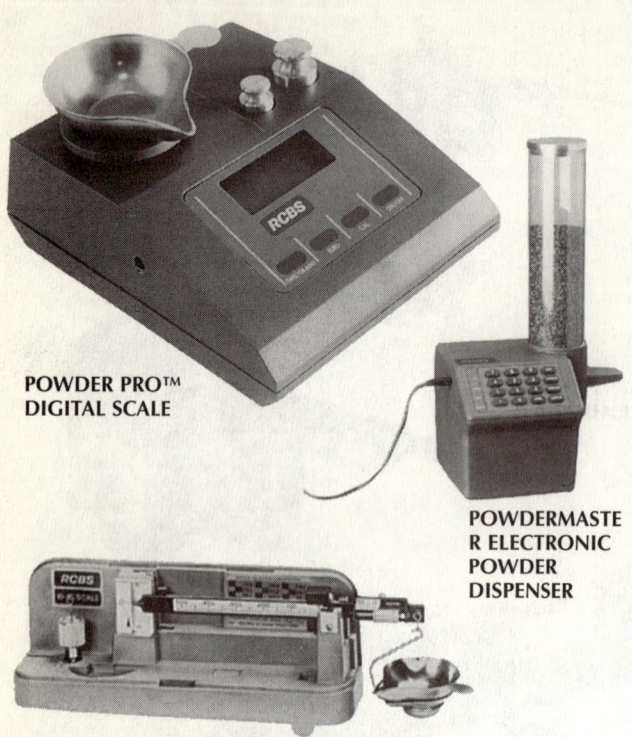

POWDER PRO™ DIGITAL SCALE

POWDERMASTER ELECTRONIC POWDER DISPENSER

RELOADING SCALE MODEL 10-10 UP TO 1010 GRAIN CAPACITY

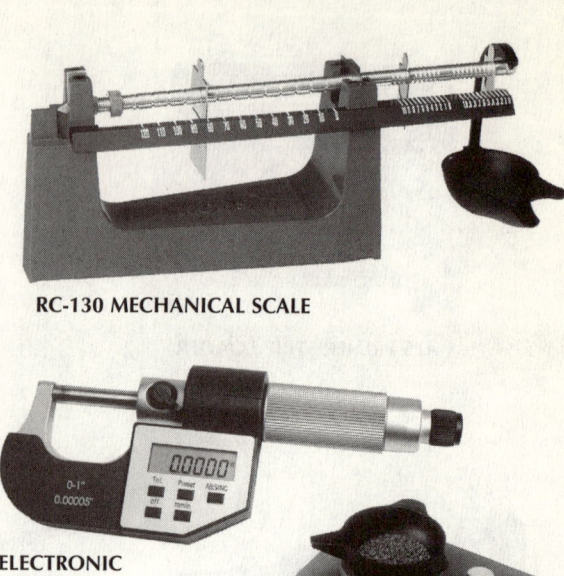

RC-130 MECHANICAL SCALE

ELECTRONIC DIGITAL MICROMETER

PARTNER ELECTRONIC POWDER SCALE

Powder Pro™ Digital Scale
The RCBS Powder Pro Digital Scale has a 1500-grain capacity. Powder, bullets, even cases can be weighed with accuracy of 0.1 grain. Includes infra-red data port for transferring information to the Powdermaster Electronic Powder Dispenser and electronic powder trickler.
Price: 110 VAC $235

Powdermaster Electronic Powder Dispenser
Works in combination with the RCBS Powder Pro Digital Scale and with all types of smokeless powder. Can be used as a power trickler as well as a powder dispenser. Accurate to one-tenth of a grain.
Price: 252

Reloading Scale Model 10-10 Up To 1010 Grain Capacity
Normal capacity is 510 grains, which can be increased without loss of sensitivity by attaching the included extra weight. Features include micrometer poise for quick, precise weighing, special approach-to-weight indicator, easy-to-read graduation, magnetic dampener, agate bearings, anti-tip pan, and dustproof lid snaps on to cover scale for storage. Sensitivity is guaranteed to 0.1 grains.
Price: 141

RC-130 Mechanical Scale
The RC130 features a 130 grain capacity and maintenance-free movement, plus a magnetic dampening system for fast readings. A 3-poise design incorporates easy adjustments with a beam that is graduated in increments of 10 grains and one grain. A micrometer poise measures in 0.1 grain increments with acuracy to ±0.1 grain.
Price: $39

Powder Checker (not shown)
Operates on a free-moving rod for simple, mechanical operation with nothing to break. Standard 7/8x14 die body can be used in any progressive loader.
Price: 28

Electronic Digital Micrometer
•Instant reading • Large, easy to read numbers for error reduction with instant inch/millimeter conversion • Zero adjust at any position • thimble lock for measuring like objects • replaceable silver oxide cell – 1.55 Volt • auto off after 5 minutes for longer battery life • adjustment wrench included • fitted wooden storage cases
Price: 103

Partner Electronic Powder Scale
Accurate for +/- one-tenth of a grain up to 350 grains and +/- two-tenths from 350 to 750 grains. Large LCD display is angled for easy reading over a wide range of positions. Powered by 9-volt battery.

Price: 169

RCBS Reloading Tools

TURRET PRESS

PRO 2000 PROGRESSIVE PRESS

GRAND SHOTSHELL PRESS

TURRET HEAD

RCBS Turret Press
Handloaders who want to speed up the loading process without giving up the level of control offered by a single-stage press can boost their output fourfold with the RCBS Turret Press. With pre-set dies in the six-station turret head, the Turret Press can increase production from 50 to 200 rounds per hour with a simple manual operation.

The frame, links, and toggle block of the press are constructed of strong, reliable, cast iron. The handle offers compound leverage for full-length sizing of any caliber from .25 ACP to .460 Wea-therby Magnum. Priming is accomplished with a reliable tube feed priming system.

Six stations allow the handloader to customize his set-up with the options of using a lube die in station one and seating and crimping bullets in separate operations. The quick-change turret head makes caliber changes fast and easy. Dies can be left in the turret head to eliminate set-up and tear-down time. This press accepts all standard 7/8 - 14 dies and shell holders and comes with the RCBS lifetime warranty.

Price: RCBS Turret Press $202
Turret Deluxe Reloading Kit 383

RCBS Pro 2000 Progressive Press
Constructed of strong and reliable cast iron, the Pro 2000 features five reloading stations. It can be set up with a lube die in station one, sizing dies in station two and three, a Powder Checker or Lock Out Die in station four and seating die in station five. Bullet seating and crimping can also be done in separate operations in station four and five.

The case-actuated powder measure assures repeatability of dispensing powder and eliminates spillage. A Micrometer Adjustment Screw allows precise return to previously recorded powder charges. All dies are standard 7/8-14, including the Expander Die.

The press incorporates RCBS's exclusive APS Priming System. Using preloaded plastic priming strips, it eliminates handling of primers and loading tube priming. Compound leverage in the press allows effortless full-length sizing in any caliber, from .32 Auto to the .460 Weatherby Magnum. The press is covered by the RCBS Lifetime Warranty.

Prices:
RCBS Pro 2000 Progressive Press 492
Pro 2000 Deluxe Reloading Kit 844

RCBS Grand Shotshell Press
Features: The combination of the Powder system and shot system and Case Holders allows the user to reload shells without fear of spillage. The powder system is case-actuated: no hull, no powder. Cases are easily removed with universal 12 and 20 gauge case holders allowing cases to be sized down to the rim. **Priming system:** Only one primer feeds at a time. Steel size ring: Provides complete resizing of high and low base hulls. Holds 25 lbs of shot and 1 1/2 lbs. of powder. Lifetime warranty.
Price 649

Redding Reloading Tools

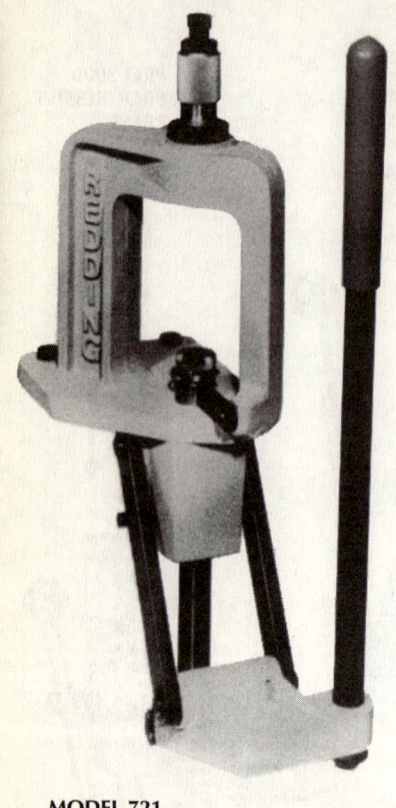

MODEL 721

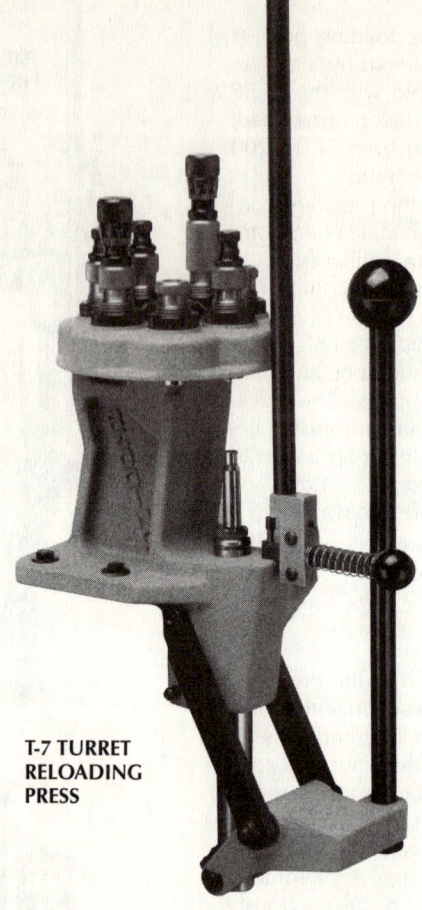

T-7 TURRET
RELOADING
PRESS

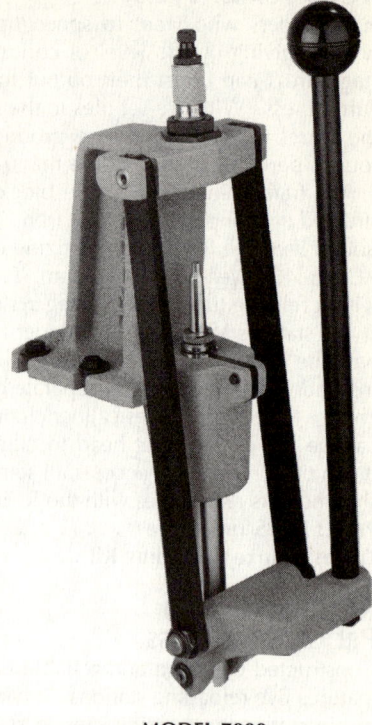

MODEL 7000

Model 721 "The Boss" Press
This "O" type reloading press features a rigid cast iron frame whose 36° offset provides the best visibility and access of comparable presses. Its "Smart" primer arm moves in and out of position automatically with ram travel. The priming arm is positioned at the bottom of ram travel for lowest leverage and best feel. Model 721 accepts all standard 7/8-14 threaded dies and universal shell holders.

Model 721 "The Boss" $140
    With Shellholder and 10A Dies 180
Also available:
Boss Pro-Pak Reloading Kit.
Includes Boss Reloading Press, #2 Powder and Bullet Scale, Powder Trickler, Reloading Dies 375
    w/o dies and shellholder 324
Boss Deluxe Reloading Kit.
Includes all items in the Pro-Pak plus:
Match-Grade Model 3BR Powder Measure
    and Model 1400 case trimmer. 569
Big Boss Reloading Press.
All the features of the Boss with a heavier frame. ... 170

Ultramag Model 7000
Unlike other reloading presses that connect the linkage to the lower half of the press, the Ultramag's compound leverage system is connected at the top of the press frame. This allows the reloader to develop tons of pressure without the usual concern about press frame deflection. Huge frame opening will handle 50 x 3 1/4-inch Sharps with ease.

No. 700 Press, complete. $315
No. 700K Kit, includes shell holder and
    one set of dies 356

T-7 Turret Reloading Press
Features: 7 station turret head, heavy duty cast iron frame, 1" diameter ram, optional "Slide Bar Automatic Primer Feeder System". This feeder eliminates handling of primers during sizing and speeds up reloading operations.

T-7 Turret Press 299
Kit, including press, shellholder and dies. 339
Slide Bar Automatic Primer Feeder System 39

Redding Reloading Dies

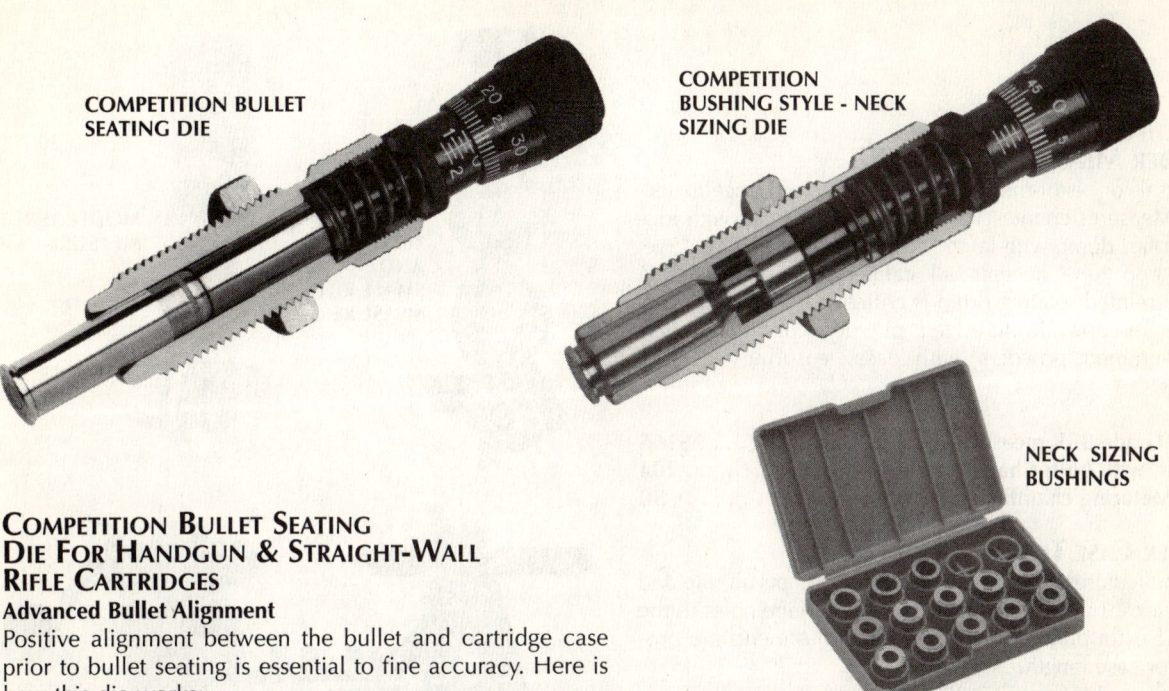

COMPETITION BULLET SEATING DIE

COMPETITION BUSHING STYLE - NECK SIZING DIE

NECK SIZING BUSHINGS

Competition Bullet Seating Die For Handgun & Straight-Wall Rifle Cartridges

Advanced Bullet Alignment
Positive alignment between the bullet and cartridge case prior to bullet seating is essential to fine accuracy. Here is how this die works:

The precision fitting seating stem is allowed to move well down into the chamber of the die to accomplish early bullet contact. The spring loading of the seating stem provides the positive alignment bias between its tapered nose and the bullet ogive. Thus spring loading and bullet alignment are maintained as the bullet and cartridge case move upward until the actual seating of the bullet begins.

Redding's Advanced Bullet Alignment feature assures the straightest possible bullet alignment for handgun and straight-wall rifle cartridges.

Micrometer Adjustment
The micrometer adjustment simplifies setting and recording bullet seating depth. By recording the micrometer setting of reloads one can return to that same overall length by simply "dialing it in." The micrometer is calibrated in .001" increments, is infinitely adjustable and has a "zero" set feature that allows setting desired load to zero if desired.

Separate Crimp
Competition shooters generally prefer bullet crimping as a separate operation from bullet seating. A superior crimp will be acomplished by using a Redding "Profile Crimp" or "Taper Crimp" die.

Progressive Press Compatible
The Competition Seating Die for straight-wall cartridges has been made compatible with all popular progressive reloading presses. The industry standard 7/8 x 14 threaded die bodies have been slightly extended to allow full thread engagement of the lock ring. An oversize bell-mouth chamfer with smooth radius has been added to the bottom of the die to ease case and bullet entry in progressive presses.
Price:..$80
Competition bullet seating dies for bottleneck cases
  Category I.......................................105
  Category II......................................128

Competition Bushing Style - Neck Sizing Die

This die allows you to fit the neck of your case perfectly in the chamber. As in the Competition Seating Die, the cartridge case is completely supported and aligned with the sizing bushing and remains supported in the sliding sleeve as it moves upward while the resizing bushing self-centers on the case neck.

The micrometer adjustment of the bushing position delivers precise control to the desired neck length. All dies are supplied without bushings.
Category I................................$105
Category II................................127

Redding Neck Sizing Bushings

Redding Neck Sizing Bushings are available in two styles. Both share the same external dimensions (1/2" O.D. x 3/8" long) and freely interchange in all Redding Bushing style Neck Sizing Dies.

They are available in .001" size increments throughout the range of .185" thru .365", covering all calibers from .17 to .338.

By selecting the correct bushing, the right amount of neck tension is provided to properly hold the bullet.
Part No. 73185 thru 73365.....................14
Heat treated steel. The sizing diameters are hand-polished with a surface hardness of Rc 60-62 to reduce sizing effort.
Part No. 76185 thru 76365.....................24
Heat treated steel as above but with the addition of a Titanium Nitride surface treatment to further increase the effective surface hardness and reduce sizing friction.

Redding Reloading Tools

Match-Grade Powder Measure Model 3BR

Universal- or pistol-metering chambers interchange in seconds. Measures charges 100 grains. Unit is fitted with lock ring for fast dump with large "clear" plastic reservoir. "See-thru" drop tube accepts all calibers from 22 to 600. Precision-fitted rotating drum is critically honed to prevent powder escape. Knife-edged powder chamber shears coarse-grained powders with ease, ensuring accurate charges.

Prices:
Match Grade 3BR measure $165
3BR Kit, with both Chambers 204
Pistol Metering chamber (0-10 grains). 50

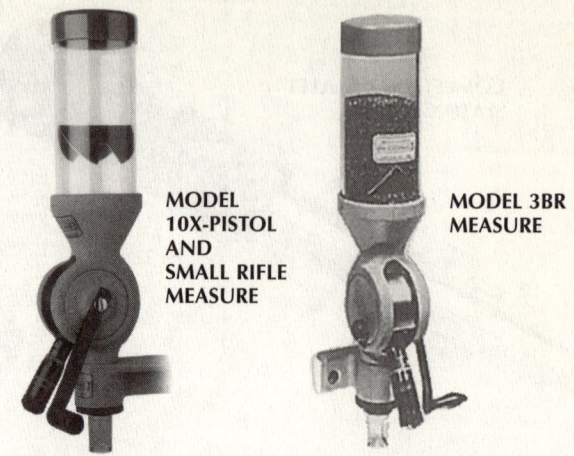

MODEL 10X-PISTOL AND SMALL RIFLE MEASURE

MODEL 3BR MEASURE

Master Case Trimmer Model 1400

This unit features a universal collet that accepts all rifle and pistol cases. The frame is cast iron with storage holes in the base for extra pilots. Coarse and fine adjustments are provided for case length.
- Six pilots (22, 6mm, 25, 270, 7mm and 30 cal.)
- Universal collet
- Two neck cleaning brushes (22 thru 30 cal.)
- Two primer pocket cleaners (large and small)
- Tin coated replaceable cutter
- Accessory power screwdriver adaptor

Prices:
No. 1400 Master Case Trimmer complete 99
No. 1500 Pilots 5

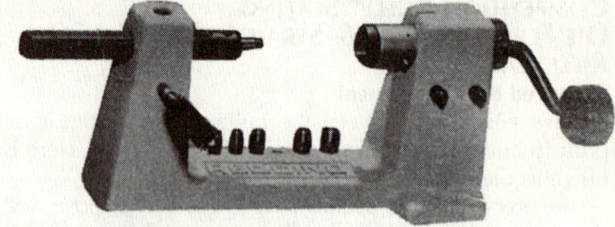

MODEL 1400 TRIMMER

Competition Model BR-30 Powder Measure (not shown)

This powder measure features a drum and micrometer that limit the overall charging range from a low of 10 grains to a maximum of 50 grains. The diameter of Model 3BR's metering cavity has been reduced, and the metering plunger has a unique hemispherical shape, creating a powder cavity that resembles the bottom of a test tube. The result: irregular powder settling is alleviated and charge-to-charge uniformity is enhanced.

Price:
Competition Model BR-30 Powder Measure 198

Standard Powder and Bullet Scale Model RS-1

For the beginner or veteran reloader. Only two counterpoises need to be moved to obtain the full capacity range of 1/10 grain to 380 grains.
Model No. RS-1 56
Also available:
Master Powder & Bullet Scale.
Same as standard model, but includes a magnetic dampened beam swing for extra fast readings.
Price:
505-grain capacity 84

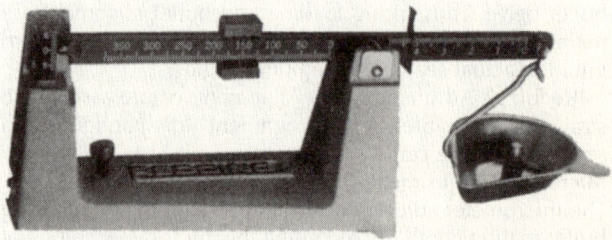

MODEL RS-1 SCALE

Competition Model 10x-Pistol And Small Rifle Powder Measure

This powder measure uses all of the special features of Competition Model BR-30, combined with new drum and metering unit designed to provide the most uniform metering of small charge weights. To achieve the best metering possible at the targeted charge weight of approximately 10 grains, the diameter of the metering cavity is reduced and the metering plunger is given a unique hemispherical shape. Charge range: 1 to 25 grains.

To provide increased versatility, the 10X-Pistol Powder Measure has a drum assembly that can be easily changed from right to left-handed operation. In addition to offering left-handed reloaders increased ease of operation, this feature adapts the 10X-Pistol Powder Measure to progressive reloading presses.

No. 03400 Competition Model 10X-Pistol
Price: Powder Measure. $198

Redding Reloading Accessories

"Instant Indicator" Headspace And Bullet Comparator

The Instant Indicator checks the headspace from the case shoulder to the base. Bullet seating depths can be compared and bullets can be sorted by checking the base of bullet to give dimension. Case length can be measured. Available for 28 cartridges from .222 Rem to .338 Win. Mag.

Price: w/Dial Indicator $119
w/o Dial Indicator 89

"EZ Feed" Shellholders

Redding shellholders are of a Universal "snap-in" design recommended for use with all Redding dies and presses, as well as all other popular brands. They are precision mach-ined to very close tolerances and heat treated to fit cases and eliminate potential resizing problems. The outside knurling makes them easier to handle and change.

Price: 8

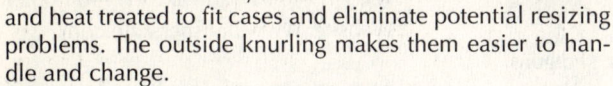

Form & Trim Dies

Redding trim dies file trim cases without unnecessary resizing because they are made to chamber dimensions. For case forming and necking brass down from another caliber, Redding trim dies can be the perfect intermediate step before full length resizing.

Prices:
Series A 29
Series B 38
Series C 44
Series D 53

Neck Sizing Dies

These dies size only the necks of bottleneck cases to prolong brass life and improve accuracy. These dies size only the neck and not the shoulder or body, fired cases should not be interchanged between rifles of the same caliber. Available individually or in Deluxe Die Sets.

Prices:
Series A 33
Series B 44
Series C 54
Series D 62

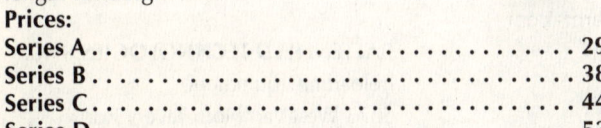

Pistol Trim Dies

Redding trim dies for pistol calibers allow trimming cases without excessive resizing. Pistol trim dies require extended shellholders.

Series A 29
Series B 38
Series C 44
Series D 53

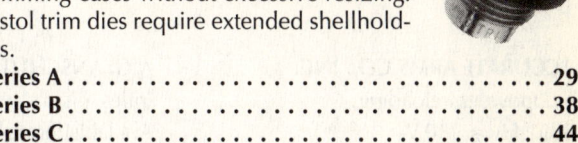

Profile Crimp Dies

For handgun cartridges which do not headspace on the case mouth. These dies were designed for those who want the best possible crimp. Profile crimp dies provide a tighter, more uniform roll type crimp, and require the bullet to be seated to the correct depth in a previous operation.

Series A 26
Series B 32
Series C 37
Series D 41

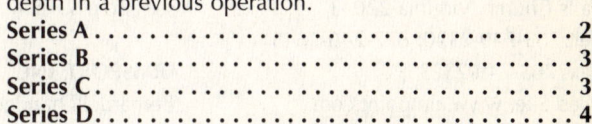

Carbide Size Button Kits

Make inside neck sizing smoother and easier without lubrication. Now die sets can be upgraded with a carbide size button kit. Available for bottleneck cartridges 22 thru 338 cal. The carbide size button is free-floating on the decap rod, allowing it to self-center in the case neck. Kits contain: carbide size button, retainer and spare decapping pin. These kits also fit all Type-S dies

Price: 24

Extended Shell Holders

Extended shellholders are required when trimming short cases under 1 1/2" O.A.L. They are machined to the same tolerances as standard shellholders except they're longer.

Price: 13

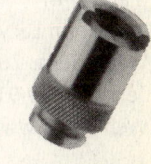

Taper And Crimp Dies

Designed for handgun cartridges which headspace on the case mouth where conventional roll crimping is undesirable. Also available for some revolver cartridges, for those who prefer the uniformity of a taper crimp. Now available in the following rifle calibers: 223 Rem., 7.62MM x 39, 30-30, 308 Win, 30-06, 300, Win Mag

Prices:
Series A 26
Series B 32
Series C 37
Series D 41

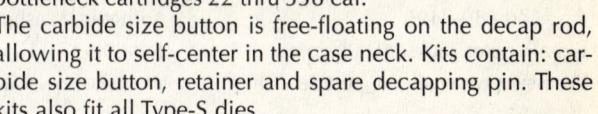

Directory of Manufacturers & Suppliers

The following manufacturers, suppliers and distributors of firearms, reloading equipment, sights, scopes, ammo and accessories all appear with their products in the "Specifications" and/or "Manufacturers' Showcase" sections of this edition of Shooter's Bible.

ACCURATE ARMS CO., INC.
(gunpowder, reloading)
5891 Hwy. 230 W
McEwen, Tennessee 37101
Tel: 931-729-4207; 800-416-3006
Fax: 931-729-4211
Web Site: www.accuratepowder.com

AIMPOINT
(sights, scopes, mounts)
7702 Leesburg Pike
Falls Church, Virginia 22043
Tel: 703-749-2320; 877-246-7646
Fax: 703-749-2323
Web Site: www.aimpoint.com
E-mail: sales@aimpoint.com

ALLIANT POWDER
(gunpowder)
Route 114, P.O. Box 6 Bldg. 229
Radford, Virginia 24143-0096
Tel: 540-639-7805; 800-276-9337
Fax: 540-639-8496
E-mail: peter_jackson@atk.com
Web site: www.alliant_powder.com

AMERICAN DERRINGER CORP.
(handguns)
127 North Lacy Drive
Waco, Texas 76705
Tel: 817-799-9111 Fax: 817-799-7935
Web site: www.amderringer.com

AMERICAN HUNTING RIFLES, INC.
(AHR rifles)
P.O. Box 300
Hamilton, MT 59840
Tel: 406-961-1410
Web site: www.hunting-rifles.com

AMERICAN SECURITY PRODUCTS
(AMSEC) (safes)
11925 Pacific Avenue
Fontana, California 92337
Tel: 800-423-1881 Fax: 909-681-9056
(see p. 75 in Manufacturer's Showcase)

A.G. ANSCHUTZ GMBH
(rifles, pistols)
Available through Champion's Choice Inc.

AO SIGHT SYSTEMS
(formerly Ashley Outdoors)
2401 Ludelle St.
Forth Worth, Texas 76105
Tel: 817-536-0136; 888-744-4880
Fax: 800-734-7939
Web site: www.aosights.com
(see also p. 77 in Manufacturer's Showcase)

ARMSPORT, INC.
(Bernardelli handguns, shotguns)
P.O. Box 523066
Miami, Florida 33152-3066
Tel: 305-635-7850 Fax: 305-633-2877

ARNOLD ARMS
(rifles)
P.O. Box 1011
Arlington, Washington 98223
Tel: 800-371-1011 Fax: 360-435-7304
Web site: www.arnoldarms.com

ASHLEY OUTDOORS
(See AO Sight Systems)

Austin & Halleck
2150 South 950 East
Provo UT 84606-6285
Tel: 801-371-0412 Fax: 801-374-9998

AUTO-ORDNANCE CORP.
Available through Kahr Arms

AXTELL RIFLE CO.
The Riflesmith
353 Mill Creek Rd.
Sheridan MT 59749
Tel: 406-842-5814
Website: www.riflesmith.com

AYA
(shotguns)
Available through New England Custom Gun Service

LES BAER CUSTOM, INC.
29601 34th St.
Hillsdale IL 61257
Tel: 309-658-2716 Fax: 309-658-2610

BANSNER'S ULTIMATE RIFLES L.L.C.
Mark Bansner (custom guns)
P.O. Box 839
261 East Main St.
Adamstown PA 19501
Tel: 717-484-2370 Fax: 717-484-0523
Website: www.bansnersrifle.com

BARNES BULLETS
P.O. Box 215
750 N. 2600 W.
American Fork, Utah 84003
Lindon, Utah 84042
Tel: 385-756-4222; 800-574-9200
Fax: 385-756-2465
E-mail: email@barnesbullets.com
Web site: www.barnesbullets.com

BATTENFIELD TECHNOLOGIES, INC.
(reloading equipment)
5875 West Van Horn Tavery Rd.
Columbia, Missouri 65203
Tel: 573-445-6363 Fax: 800-992-8312
Web site: www.midwayusa.com

BENELLI U.S.A. CORP.
(shotguns)
17603 Indian Head Hwy, Suite 200
Accokeek, Maryland 20607-2501
Tel: 301-283-6981 Fax: 301-283-6988
Web site: www.benelliusa.com
E-mail benusa1@aol.com

BERETTA U.S.A. CORP.
(handguns, rifles, shotguns; Sako, Tikka)
17601 Beretta Drive
Accokeek, Maryland 20607
Tel: 301-283-2191 Fax: 301-283-0189
Web site: www.berettausa.com
E-mail: cwilliams@berettausa.com

Directory of Manufacturers & Suppliers

BERGER BULLETS, INC.
4275 N. Palm St.
Fullerton CA 92835
Tel: 714-447-5456 Fax: 714-447-5407
www.bergerbullets.com
Web site: www.bergerbullets.com

BERNARDELLI
(handguns, shotguns)
Available through Armsport

BERSA
(handguns)
Available through Eagle Imports Inc.

ROGER BIESEN
(custom guns)
W. 5021 Rosewood
Spokane, Washington 99208
Tel: 509-328-9340

BLACK HILLS AMMUNITION
P.O. Box 3090
3050 Eglin
Rapid City, South Dakota 57709-3090
Tel: 605-348-5150 Fax: 605-348-9827
Web site www.black-hills.com
E-mail: black-hills.com

BLACKPOWDER PRODUCTS, INC.
(CVA & Winchester Blackpowder)
5988 Peachtree Corners East
Norcross GA 30071
Tel: 770-449-4687 Fax: 770-242-8546
www.bpiguns.com

BLASER USA, INC.
(rifles)
Available through Sig Arms

BLUE BOOK PUBLICATIONS, INC.
(books)
8009 34th Ave. South, Suite 175
Minneapolis, Minnesota 55425
Tel: 952-854-5229; 800-877-4867
Fax: 952-853-1486
Web site: www.bluebookinc.com
E-mail: bluebook@bluebookinc.com
(see P. 78 in Manufacturer's Showcase)

BONANZA
(reloading tools)
See Forster Products

BOND ARMS INC.
(handguns)
204 Alpha Lane
P.O. Box 1296
Granbury, Texas 76048
Tel: 817-573-4445 Fax: 817-573-5636
(see p. 76 in Manufacturers' Showcase)

KENT BOWERLY
(custom guns)
710 Golden Pheasant Drive
Redmond, Oregon 97756
Tel: 541-923-3501

BRENNEKE OF AMERICA LTD.
(Rottweil ammunition)
81 Eades Drive
Irvine, Kentucky 40336-9463
Tel: 606-723-1045 Fax: 606-723-3253

ED BROWN PRODUCTS, INC.
(custom gunmaker)
P.O. Box 492
Perry, Missouri 63462
Tel: 573-565-3261 Fax: 573-565-2791
Web site: www.edbrown.com

BROWNING
(handguns, rifles, shotguns,
blackpowder guns)
One Browning Place
Morgan, Utah 84050
Tel: 801-876-2711 Fax: 801-876-3331
Web site: www.browning.com

BROWN PRECISION, INC.
(custom rifles)
7786 Molinos Avenue P.O. Box 270 W.
Los Molinos, California 96055
Tel: 530-384-2506 Fax: 530-384-1638

BSA OPTICS, INC.
3911 SW 47th Ave., Ste 914
Ft. Lauderdale, Florida 33314
Tel: 954-581-2144 Fax: 954-581-3165
Web site: www.bsa.optic.com
E-mail: bsaoptic@bellsouth.net

BURRIS COMPANY, INC.
(scopes)
331 East Eighth Street P.O. Box 1899
Greeley, Colorado 806321-1899
Tel: 970-356-1670; 888-228-7747
Fax: 970-356-8702
Web site: www.burrisoptics.com

BUSHNELL
(scopes)
Performance Optics
9200 Cody
Overland Park, Kansas 66214
Tel: 913-752-3400 Fax: 913-752-3550
Web site: www.bushnell.com

CABELA'S INC.
(blackpowder rifles)
812 13th Ave.
Sidney, Nebraska 69160
Tel: 308-254-5505 Fax: 308-254-6669

CCI/SPEER-BLOUNT, INC.
(ammunition, bullets)
2299 Snake Rive Ave., P.O. Box 856
Lewiston, Idaho 83501
Tel: 208-746-2351 Fax: 208-746-3904
Web site: www.cci-ammunition.com
www.speer-bullets.com

CHAMPION'S CHOICE INC.
Anschutz
201 International Blvd.
LaVergne TN 37086
Tel: 615-793-4066 Fax: 615-793-4070

CHRISTENSEN ARMS
(rifles)
192 E. 100 N.
Fayette, Utah 84630
Tel: 801-528-7199
Web site: www.christensenarms.com

DAVID CHRISTMAN, JR.
(custom gunmaker)
216 Rundell Loop Rd.
Delhi LA 71232
Tel: 318-878-1395

CIMARRON FIREARMS CO.
(revolvers, rifles)

Directory of Manufacturers & Suppliers

Available through Traditions Effects
Wed site: www.cimarron-firearms.com
E-mail:cimarron@fbg.net

CLARK CUSTOM GUNS INC.
Jim Clark, Jr.
336 Shootout Lane
Princeton LA 71067
Tel: 888-458-4126
www.clarkcustomguns.com

JIM COFFIN
(custom guns)
1224 NW Fernwood Circle
Corvallis, Oregon 97330-2909
Tel: 541-754-7662 Fax: 541-754-0255

COLT BLACKPOWDER ARMS CO.
(handguns)
110 8th street
Brooklyn, New York 11215
Tel: 718-499-4678 Fax: 718-768-8056

COLT'S MANUFACTURING CO., INC.
(handguns, rifles)
P.O. Box 1868
Hartford, Connecticut 06144-1868
Tel: 800-962-COLT Fax: 860-244-1467
Web site: www.colt.com

CONNECTICUT SHOTGUN MFG. CO.
(A.H. Fox shotguns)
35 Woodland Street, P.O. Box 1692
New Britain, Connecticut 06051-1692
Tel: 860-225-6581 Fax: 860-832-8707

COOPER FIREARMS of Montana, Inc.
P.O. Box 114
Stevensville, Montana 59870
Tel: 406-777-5534
Web site: www.cooperfirearms.com

CVA
(blackpowder arms)
5988 Peachtree Corners East
Norcross, Georgia 30071
Tel: 800-320-8767 Fax: 770-242-8546
Web site: www.cva.com
E-mail: sales@cva.com

CZ-USA
(pistols, rifles)
P.O. Box 171073
Kansas City, Kansas 66117-0073
Tel: 913-321-1811; 800-955-4486
Fax: 913-321-2251
Web site: www.cz-usa.com
E-mail: cz-usa@qvl.net

DAKOTA ARMS
(rifles, shotguns)
HC 55, Box 326
Sturgis, South Dakota 57785
Tel: 605-347-4686 Fax: 605-347-4459;
508-302-4784
Web site: www.dakotarms.com
E-mail: dakarms@sturgis.com
CHARLES DALY (pistols, shotguns)
Available through K.B.I., Inc.

DAYTONA SHOTGUNS
Renato Gamba U.S.A. Inc.
375 Park Ave.
New York NY 10152
Tel: 212-618-1391 Fax: 212-618-1396

DESERT EAGLE
(handguns)
Available through Magnum Research Inc.

DESERT MOUNTAIN MFG.
(rifle rests)
44950 Elk Mountain Rd.
Banks, Oregon 97106
Tel: 800-477-0762 Fax: 406-387-5361
Web site: www.bench-master.com
(see p. 78 in Manufacturers' Showcase)

DGS, INC.
(Dale A. Storey custom guns)
1117 E. 12th Street
Casper, Wyoming 82601
Tel: 307-237-2414

DILLON PRECISION PRODUCTS, INC.
(reloading equipment)
8009 East Dillon's Way
Scottsdale, Arizona 85260-9865
Tel: 800-223-4570; 602-948-8009
Fax: 602-998-2786
Web site: www.dillonprecision.com

DIXIE GUN WORKS
(blackpowder guns)
P.O. Box 684
Union City, Tennessee 38281
Tel: 731-885-0374; 800-238-6785
Fax: 901-885-0440
Web site: www.dixiegunworks.com
E-mail: dixieguns@iswt.com

DOCTER SCOPES
Available through Eldorado Cartridge Corp.

DOWNSIZER CORPORATION
(handguns)
P.O. Box 710316
Santee, California 92072-0316
Tel: 619-448-5510 Fax: 619-448-5780
Web site: www.downsizer.com

DYNAMIT NOBEL/RWS
(Rottweil shotguns and ammunition,
Steyr Mannlicher)
81 Ruckman Road
Closter, New Jersey 07624
Tel: 201-767-1995 Fax: 201-767-1589

EAGLE IMPORTS, INC.
(Bersa, Llama and Firestorm handguns)
1750 Brielle Avenue, Unit B1
Wanamassa, New Jersey 07712
Tel: 732-493-0302 Fax: 732-493-0301

D'ARCY ECHOLS
(custom rifles)
98 West 300 South, P.O. Box 421
Millville, Utah 84326
Tel: 435-755-6842

ELDORADO CARTRIDGE CORP.
(PMC ammo, Docter scopes and
Verona shotguns)
PO Box 62508
Boulder City NV 89005
Tel: 702-294-0025 Fax: 702-294-0121
www.pmcammo.com

E.M.F. COMPANY, INC.
(Dakota handguns; Uberti handguns,
blackpower arms, rifles)
1900 East Warner Avenue, Suite 1-D
Santa Ana, California 92705

Directory of Manufacturers & Suppliers

Tel: 714-261-6611 Fax: 714-756-0133
Web site: www.emf-company.com

ENTRÉPRISE ARMS
(handguns)
15861 Busines Center Drive
Irwindale, California 91706-2062
Tel: 626-962-8712 Fax: 626-962-4692
Web site: www.entreprise.com

EUROARMS OF AMERICA INC.
(blackpowder arms)
P.O. Box 3277
Winchester, Virginia 22604
Tel: 540-662-1863

EUROPEAN AMERICAN ARMORY CORP.
(E.A.A. handguns, rifles)
P.O. Box 1299
Sharpes, Florida 32959
Tel: 800-536-4442 Tel: 321-639-4942
Fax: 321-639-7006
Web site: www.eaacorp.com

FABARMS
(shotguns)
Available through Heckler & Koch

FEDERAL CARTRIDGE CO.
(ammunition, ballistics)
900 Ehlen Drive
Anoka, Minnesota 55303-7503
Tel: 800-322-2342; 763-323-2300
Fax: 763-323-2506
Web site: www.federalcartridge.com

KENT "BUZZ" FLETCHER
(custom gunmaker)
117 Siler Rd.
Taos NM 87571
Tel: 505-758-3486

FLODMAN GUNS SWEDEN
640 60 Akers styckebruk
Jarsta, Sweden
Tel: 46 159308 61 Fax: 46 159300 61
www.flodman.com

FIRESTORM PISTOLS
Available through Eagle Imports

FIOCCHI OF AMERICA
(ammunition)
6930 Fremont Rd.
Ozark, Missouri 65721
Tel: 800-721-AMMO; 417-725-4118
Fax: 417-725-1039
Web Site: www.fiocchiusa.com

FLINTLOCKS, ETC.
(Pedersoli replica rifles)
160 Rossiter Road, P.O. Box 181
Richmond, Massachusetts 01254
Tel: 413-698-3822 Fax: 1-888-GUNCLIP
Web site: www.GUNMAGS.com

FORREST INC.
(magazines)
P.O. Box 326
Lakeside, California 92040
Tel: 619-561-5800 Fax: 888-GUNCLIP
Web site: www.GUNCLIP.COM
(see p. 76 in Manufacturers' Showcase)

FORSTER PRODUCTS
(reloading)
310 East Lanark Avenue
Lanark, Illinois 61046
Tel: 815-493-6360 Fax: 815-493-2371
Web site: forsterproducts.com
E-mail: infor@forsterproducts.com

A.H. FOX (shotguns)
Available through Connecticut Shotgun Mfg. Co.

FRANCHI
(shotguns)
Available through Beretta

FRANCOTTE
(rifles)
Available through Armes de Chasse

FREEDOM ARMS
(handguns)
314 Hyw. 239, P.O. Box 150
Freedom, Wyoming 83120-0150
Tel: 307-883-2468 Fax: 307-883-2005
Web site: www.freedomarms.com
E-mail: freedom@freedomarms.com

GIBBS RIFLE COMPANY
211 Lawn Street
Martinsburg, West Virginia 25401
Tel: 304-262-1651 Fax: 304-262-1658
E-mail: support@gibbsrifle.com

GLASER SAFETY SLUG, INC.
(ammunition, gun accessories)
P.O. Box 8223
Foster City, California 94404
Tel: 800-221-3489 Fax: 510-785-6685
(see p. 77 in Manufacturers' Showcase)

GLOCK, INC.
(pistols)
6000 Highland Parkway
Smyrna, Georgia 30082
Tel: 770-432-1202 Fax: 770-433-8719

GARY GOUDY
(custom gunmaker)
1512 S. 5th St.
Dayton WA 99328
Tel: 509-382-2726

CHARLES GRACE
(custom gunmaker)
1305 Arizona Avenue
Trinidad, Colorado 81081

GRIZZLY INDUSTRIAL, INC.
3 locations:
Bellingham, Washington
Williamsport, Pennsylvania
Springfield, Missouri
Tel: 800-523-4777 Fax: 800-438-5901
Web site: www.grizzly.com
(see p. 75, 76, 77, 78, 79 in Manufacturers' Showcase)

GSI (GUN SOUTH INC.)
(Mauser rifles; Merkel shotguns)
7661 Commerce Lane, P.O. Box 129
Trussville, Alabama 35173
Tel: 800-821-3021; 205-655-8299
Fax: 205-655-7078
Web site: www.gsifirearms.com
E-mail: infor@gsifirearms.com

H&R 1871 INC.
Available through New England Firearms

Directory of Manufacturers & Suppliers

H-S PRECISION
(rifles, pistols)
1301 Turbine Drive
Rapid City, South Dakota 57703
Tel: 605-341-3006 Fax: 605-342-8964
Web site: www.hsprecision.com

HÄMMERLI U.S.A.
(handguns)
19296 Oak Grove Circle
Groveland, California 95321
Tel: 209-962-5311 Fax: 209-962-5931

HARRIS ENGINEERING, INC.
(bipods)
999 Broadway
Barlow, Kentucky 42024
Tel: 270-334-3633 Fax: 270-334-3000
Web site: www.cyberteldabs.com/
harris/main/htm
(see p. 79 in Manufacturers' Showcase)

HARRINGTON & RICHARDSON
(handguns, rifles, shotguns)
Available through H&R 1871 Inc.

HECKLER & KOCH
(handguns, rifles; and Fabarms shotguns)
21480 Pacific Blvd.
Sterling, Virginia 20166
Tel: 703-450-1900 Fax: 703-450-8160
Web site: www.hecklerkoch-usa.com

HENRY REPEATING ARMS CO.
(rifles)
110 8th Street
Brooklyn, New York 11215
Tel: 718-499-5600 Fax: 718-768-8056
Web site: www.henryrepeatingcom

DARWIN HENSLEY
(custom rifles)
63133 E. Barlow Trail Rd.
Brightwood, Oregon 97011
Tel: 503-622-5411

HERITAGE MANUFACTURING
(handguns)
4600 NW 135 St.
Opa Locka, Florida 33054
Tel: 305-685-5966 Fax: 305-687-6721

Web site: www.heritagemfg.com

HI-POINT FIREARMS
(handguns)
MKS Supply, Inc.
8611-A North Dixie Drive
Dayton, Ohio 45414
Tel/Fax: 877-425-48671
Web site: www.hi-pointfirearms.com

HIGH STANDARD MFG. CO., INC.
5200 Mitchelldale Suite E-17
Houston TX 77092
Tel: 800-272-7816; 713-462-4200
Fax: 713-681-5665

HILL COUNTRY RIFLE CO.
5726 Morningside Dr.
New Braunfels, Texas 78132
Tel: 830-609-3139
Web site: www.hillcountryrifle.com

BOB HISSERICH
(custom gunmaker)
StockWorks Rifles
1843 S. Los Alamos
Mesa, Arizona 85204
Tel: 480-545-2994 Fax: 480-507-7560
Web site: www.stockworks.net

HODGDON POWDER CO., INC.
(gunpowder)
6231 Robinson, P.O. Box 2932
Shawnee Mission, Kansas 66201
Tel: 913-362-9455 Fax: 913-362-1307
Web site: www.hodgdon.com
E-mail: info@hodgdon.com

PATRICK HOLEHAN
(custom rifles)
5758 E. 34th St.
Tucson, Arizona 85711
Tel: 520-745-0622
E-mail: plholehan@juno.com

HORNADY MFG. CO.
(ammunition, reloading)
P.O. Box 1848; 3625 Old Potash Hwy.
Grand Island, Nebraska 68803
Tel: 308-382-1390 Fax: 308-382-5761
Web site: www.hornady.com

HOWA
(rifles)
Available through Legacy Sports

STEVEN DODD HUGHES
(custom rifles)
P.O. Box 545
Livingston, Montana 59047
Tel: 406-222-9377

IMR POWDER CO. INC.
622 Malone Ridge Road
Washington PA 15301
Tel: 724-228-8949 Fax: 724-228-9498
www.imrpowder.com

ISRAEL ARMS, INTL.
1085 Gessner Rd. Suite F
Houston TX 77055
Tel: 713-789-0745 Fax: 713-914-9515

ITHACA GUN CO.
(shotguns)
891 Route 34-B
Kings Ferry, New York 13081
Tel: 315-364-7171 Fax: 315-364-5134
Web site: www.ithacagun.com

JARRETT RIFLES INC.
(custom rifles)
383 Brown Road
Jackson, South Carolina 29831
Tel: 803-471-3616 Fax: 803-471-9246
Web site: www.jarrettrifles.com

JOHANNSEN
(Express Rifle)
Available through New England
Custom Guns

KAHLES
(scopes)
2 Slater Rd.
Cranston, Rhode Island 02920
Tel: 800-426-3089
Web site: www.kahlesoptics.com
Fax: 401-734-5888

KAHR ARMS
(handguns, Auto-Ordnance)
630 Route 303, POB 220

Directory of Manufacturers & Suppliers

Blauvelt, New York 10913
Tel: 914-353-7770 Fax: 914-353-7830
Web site: www.kahr.com
E-mail: kahrhq@compuserve.com

K.B.I., INC.
(rifles, handguns, shotguns; Charles Daly rifles, shotguns; FEG handguns)
P.O. box 6625
Harrisburg, Pennsylvania 17112-0625
Tel: 717-540-8518 Fax: 717-540-8567
Web site: www.kbi-inc.com or
www.charlesdaly.com
E-mail: sales @kbi-inc.com

KEL-TEC CNC IND INC.
(handguns)
P.O. Box 236009
Cocoa, Florida 32926
Tel: 321-631-0068 Fax: 231-631-1169
Web site: www.kel-tec.com
E-mail: aimkeltec@aol.com

KIMBER MANUFACTURING, INC.
(handguns, rifles)
1 Lawton Street
Yonkers, New York 10705
Tel: 914-964-0771; 888-243-4522
E-mail: info@kimberamerica.com

KNIGHT RIFLES
(blackpowder rifles)
P.O. Box 130, 21852 Hwy. J46
Centerville, Iowa 52544-0130
Tel: 515-856-2626 Fax: 515-856-2628
Web site: www.knightrifles.com
E-mail: knightrifles@lisco.net

KRIEGHOFF INTERNATIONAL INC.
(rifles, shotguns)
337A Route 611, P.O. Box 549
Ottsville, Pennsylvania 18942
Tel: 610-847-5173 Fax: 610-847-8691

KYNOCH AMMUNITION
Kynamco Limited - The Old Railway Station
Mildenhall, IP28 7DT England
Tel: +44 (0) 1638 711999
Fax: +44 (0) 1638 515251

L.A.R. MANUFACTURING, INC.
(Grizzly rifles)
4133 West Farm Rd.
West Jordan, Utah 84088-4997
Tel: 801-280-3505 Fax: 801-280-1972
Web site: www.largrizzly.com
E-mail: guns@largrizzly.com

LASERAIM TECHNOLOGIES INC.
(sights)
721 Main St., P.O. Box 3548
Little Rock, Arkansas 72203-3548
Tel: 501-375-2227 Fax: 501-372-1445

LEGACY SPORTS INTL.
(Howa & Mauser rifles)
206 S. Union St.
Alexandria VA 22314
Tel: 703-548-4837 Fax: 703-549-7826
www.legacysports.com

LENARTZ MUZZLOADING
(blackpowder guns)
8001 Whitneyville Rd.
Alto, Michigan 49302

LEUPOLD & STEVENS, INC.
(scopes, mounts)
14400 N.W. Greenbriar Parkway,
P.O. Box 688
Beaverton, Oregon 97075
Tel: 503-646-9171 Fax: 503-526-1475
Web site: www.leupold.com

PAUL A. LINDKE
(custom gunmaker)
11367 Spenceville Rd.
Penn Valley CA 95946
Tel: 530-432-2698

LLAMA
(handguns)
Available through Eagle Imports

LONE STAR RIFLE CO., INC.
11231 Rose Road
Conroe, Texas 77303
Tel: 409-856-3363
Web site: www.lonstarrifle.com

LYMAN PRODUCTS CORP.
(blackpowder guns, reloading tools)
475 Smith Street
Middletown, Connecticut 06457
Tel: 800-225-9626; 860-632-2020
Fax: 860-632-1699
Web site: www.lymanproducts.com
E-mail: lymansales@cshore.com

MAGNUM RESEARCH INC.
(handguns, rifles)
7110 University Avenue N.E.
Minneapolis, Minnesota 55432
Tel: 612-574-1868 Fax: 612-574-0109
Web site: www.magnumresearch.com

MAGTECH AMMUNITION CO.INC
6845 20th Ave. South
Suite 120
Centerville MN 55038
Tel: 800-466-7191 Fax: 651-429-9485

MARKESBERY MUZZLELOADERS, INC.
(blackpowder guns)
7785 Foundation Drive, Suite 6
Florence, Kentucky 41042
Tel: 606-342-5553 Fax: 606-342-2380
Web site: www.markesbery.com

MARLIN FIREARMS COMPANY
(rifles, shotguns, blackpowder)
100 Kenna Drive, P.O. Box 248
North Haven, Connecticut 06473
Tel: 203-239-5621 Fax: 203-234-7991
Web site: www.marlinfirearms.com

MAROCCHI
(Conquista shotguns)
Available through Precision Sales Int'l.

MAUSER RIFLES
Available through Legacy Sports Intl.

MEC INC.
(reloading tools)
c/o Mayville Engineering Co.
715 South Street
Mayville, Wisconsin 53050
Tel: 800-797-4MEC; 920-387-4500
Fax: 920-387-5802
Web site: www.mecreloaders.com
E-mail: reloaders@mayvl.com

Directory of Manufacturers & Suppliers

MERKEL
(shotguns, rifles)
Available through GSI (Gun South Inc.)
Web site: www.gsifirearms.com

DAVID MILLER
(custom rifles)
3131 E. Greenlee Rd.
Tucson, AZ 85716

M.O.A. CORP.
(handguns)
2451 Old Camden Pike
Eaton, Ohio 45302
Tel: 937-456-3669 Fax: 937-456-9331
Web site: moaguns.com

O.F. MOSSBERG & SONS, INC.
(shotguns, rifles)
7 Grasso Avenue, P.O. Box 497
North Haven, Connecticut 06473
Tel: 203-230-5300 Fax: 203-230-5420
Web site: www.mossberg.com

MTM MOLDED PRODUCTS
(cases, reloading accessories)
P.O. Box 13117
Dayton, Ohio 45413
Tel: 937-890-7461 Fax: 937-890-1747
Web site: www.intmcase-grad.com
(see also p. 80 in Manufacturers' showcase)

NAVY ARMS COMPANY, INC.
(handguns, rifles, blackpowder guns)
689 Bergen Blvd
Ridgefield, New Jersey 07657-14999
Tel: 201-945-2500 Fax: 201-945-6859
Web site: www.navyarms.com

NELSON'S CUSTOM GUNS, INC.
Stephen Nelson
7430 NW Valley View Dr.
Corvallis OR 97330
Tel: 541-745-5232

NEW ENGLAND ARMS CORP./FAIR TECHNI MEC
(Rizzini shotguns)
6 Lawrence Lane, P.O. Box 278
Kittery Point, Maine 03905
Tel: 207-439-0593 Fax: 207-439-6726

NEW ENGLAND CUSTOM GUN LTD.
(Johannsen Rifle, AYA shotguns and Schmidt-Bender Scopes)
428 Willow Brook Rd.
Plainfield, NH 03781
Tel: 603-469-3450 Fax 603-469-3471

NEW ENGLAND FIREARMS CO. INC.
(handguns, rifles, shotguns)
60 Industrial Rowe
Gardner, Massachusetts 01440
Tel: 978-632-9393 Fax: 978-632-2300

NEW ULTRA LIGHT ARMS, LLC
1024 Grafton Road
Morgantown, West Virginia 26508
Tel: 304-292-0600 Fax: 304-292-9662

NIKON INC.
(scopes)
1300 Walt Whitman Road
Melville, New York 11747-3064
Tel: 631-547-4200 Fax: 631-547-4040
Web site: www.nikonusa.com

DAVE NORIN
(custom gunmaker)
2010 Washington St.
Waukegan IL 60085
Tel: 847-662-4034

NORTH AMERICAN ARMS
(handguns)
2150 South 950 East
Provo, Utah 84606-6285
Tel: 800-821-5783; 801-374-9990
Fax: 801-374-9998
Web site: www.naaminis.com

NOSLER BULLETS, INC.
(bullets)
P.O. Box 671, 107 SW Columbia
Bend, Oregon 97709
Tel: 541-382-3921 Fax: 541-388-4667
Web site: www.nosler.com

OLIN/WINCHESTER
(ammunition, primers, cases)
427 No. Shamrock St.
East Alton, Illinois 62024-1174
Tel: 618-258-3692 Fax: 618-258-3609

Web site: www.winchester.com

PARA-ORDNANCE MFG, INC.
(handguns)
PO Box 1
Oakhurst, CA 93644
Tel: 559-683-3060 Fax: 559-683-3061
Web site: www.paraord.com
E-mail: info@paraord.com

PEDERSOLI, DAVIDE
(replica arms)
Available through Flintlocks Etc.
Web site: www.davide-pedersoli.com

PENTAX
(scopes)
P.O. Box 6509 (80155)
35 Inverness Drive East
Englewood, Colorado 80112
Tel: 303-799-8000 Fax: 303-790-1131
Web site: www.pentax.com

PERAZZI U.S.A.
1010 W. 10th St.
Azusa CA 91702
Tel: 626-334-1234 Fax: 626-334-0344
PerazziUSA@aol.com

PMC CARTRIDGES
Available through Eldorado Cartridge Corp.

PRAIRIE GUN WORKS
(rifles)
1-761 Marion St.
Winnipeg, Manitoba, Canada R2J0K6
Tel: 204-231-2976 Fax: 204-231-8566
Web site: www.prairiegunworks.com

PRECISION SALES INTERNATIONAL
(Marocchi shotguns)
P.O. Box 1776
Westfield, Massachusetts 01086
Tel: 413-562-5055 Fax: 413-562-5056
Web site: www.precision-sales.com

JAMES PURDEY & SONS
(shotguns)
844 Madison Ave.
New York, New York 10021

Directory of Manufacturers & Suppliers

Tel: 212-639-1500 Fax: 212-452-9675

J.C. RACK SYSTEMS
Available through Versatile Rack Co.

RAMSHOT PROPELLANT
(gunpowder)
Western Powders, P.O. Box 158
Miles City, Montana 59301
Tel: 406-232-0422 Fax: 406-232-0430
Web site: www.westernpowders.com

RCBS-BLOUNT, INC.
(reloading equipment)
605 Oro Dam Blvd.
Oroville, California 95965
Tel: 916-533-5191 Fax: 916-533-1647
Web site: www.rcbs.com

REDDING RELOADING EQUIPMENT
(reloading tools)
1089 Starr Road
Cortland, New York 13045
Tel: 607-753-3331 Fax: 607-756-8445
Web site: www.redding-reloading.com
E-mail: techline@redding-reloading.com

REDFIELD-BLOUNT, INC.
(scopes)
P.O. Box 38
Onalaska, Wisconsin 54650
Tel: 608-781-5800 Fax: 608-781-0368
Web site: www.redfieldoptics.com

GARY REEDER CUSTOM GUNS
2710 N. Steves Blvd.
Flagstaff, Arizona 86044, Suite 22
Tel: 520-526-3313 Fax: 520-526-1287
Web site: www.reedercustomguns.com
(see p. 77, 79 in Manufacturers' Showcase)

REMINGTON ARMS COMPANY, INC.
(rifles, shotguns, blackpowder arms, ammunition)
870 Remington Drive, P.O. Box 700
Madison, North Carolina 27025-0700
Tel: 800-243-9700 Fax: 336-548-7741
Web site: www.remington.com

RIFLES, INC.
3580 Leal Rd.
Pleasanton TX 78064
Tel: 830-569-2055 Fax: 830-569-2297

RAY RIGANIAN
(custom gunmaker)
324 N. Central Ave., Unit B
Glendale CA 91203
Tel: 818-502-2678

RIZZINI
(shotguns)
Available through New England Arms
Web site: www.rizzini.it

ROSSI FIREARMS
(handguns, rifles, shotguns)
BrazTech Intl.
16175 NW 49th Ave.
Miami, Florida 33014
Tel: 305-624-1115 Fax: 305-623-7506
Web site: www.rossiusa.com

ROTTWEIL BRENNEKE
(see Brenneke)

RUGER
(handguns, rifles, shotguns, blackpowder guns) See Sturm, Ruger & Co., Inc.

RWS
Available through Dynamit Nobel

SAFARI ARMS
(handguns)
c/o Olympic Arms, Inc.
620 Old Pacific Hwy SE
Olympia, Washington 98513
Tel: 360-459-7940 Fax: 360-491-3447
Web site: www.olyarms.com

SAKO
(rifles, actions, scope mounts, ammo)
Available through Beretta U.S.A. Corp.

SAUER
(rifles)
c/o Paul Company, Inc.
27385 Pressonville Road
Wellsville, Kansas 66092
Tel: 913-883-4444 Fax: 913-883-1515

SAVAGE ARMS
(handguns, rifles, shotguns)
100 Springdale Road
Westfield, Massachusetts 01085
Tel: 413-568-7001
Fax: 413-562-7764
Web site: www.savagearms.com

SCHMIDT AND BENDER INC.
(scopes)
Schmidt & Bender U.S.A.
P.O. Box 134
Meriden, New Hampshire 03770
Tel: 800-468-3450 Fax: 603-469-3471
Web site: www.schmidt-bender.de

ANTHONY SCHUELKE
(custom guns)
1606 N. Baxter Ave.
Glencoe, Minnesota 55336
Tel: 320-864-3905

SHILOH RIFLE MANUFACTURING
(Blackpowder guns)
PO Box 279
Big Timber MT 59011
Tel: 406-932-4454 Fax: 406-932-5627
Shilohrifle@men.net

SIERRA BULLETS
(bullets)
P.O. Box 818
1400 West Henry Steet
Sedalia, Missouri 65301
Tel: 888-223-3006; 660-827-6300
Fax: 660-827-4999
Web site: www.sierrabullets.com
E-mail: sierra@sierrabullets.com

SIGARMS INC.
(Sig-Sauer shotguns, handguns, Blaser rifles)
18 Industrial Dr.
Exeter, New Hampshire 03833
Tel: 603-772-2302 Fax: 603-772-1481
Web site: www.sigarms.com

SIGHTRON, INC.
(scopes)
100 Jeffrey Way, Suite A
Youngville NC 27596

Directory of Manufacturers & Suppliers

Tel: 919-562-3000 Fax: 919-556-0157
www.sightron.com

GENE SIMILLION
(custom guns)
220 S. Wisconsin
Gunnison, Colorado 81230
Tel: 970-641-1126

SIMMONS-BLOUNT, INC.
(scopes, sporting equipments)
201 Plantation Oak Drive
Thomasville, GA 31792
Tel: 912-227-9053 Fax: 912-227-9054
Web site: www.simmonsoptics.com

SISK RIFLES
(cusom rifles)
Charlie Sisk
16607 Port O'Call
Crosby, Texas 77532
Tel: 281-328-5458

SKB SHOTGUNS
(shotguns)
4325 S. 120th Street
Omaha, Nebraska 68137-1253
Tel: 800-752-2767 Fax: 402-330-8040
Web site: www.skbshotguns.com
E-mail: SKB@radiks.net

SMITH & WESSON
(handguns)
2100 Roosevelt Avenue, P.O. Box 2208
Springfield, Massachusetts 01102-2208
Tel: 413-781-8300; 800-331-0852
Fax: 413-747-3317
Web site: www.smith-wesson.com

SPEER
(bullets)
Available through CCI/Speer-Blount, Inc.

SPRINGFIELD INC.
(handguns, rifles, Aimpoint scopes, & sights)
420 West Main Street
Geneseo, Illinois 61254
Tel: 800-680-6866; 309-944-5631
Fax: 309-944-3676
Web site: www.springfield-armory.com

STEYR-MANNLICHER
(rifles)
Available throughDynamit/Nobel
Web site: www.dnrws.com

STOEGER INDUSTRIES
(shotguns)
17603 Indian Head Hwy., Suite 200
Accokeek, Maryland 20607
Tel: 301-283-6300 Fax: 301-283-6586
Web site: jtroiani@stoegerindustries.com

DALE STOREY
(custom gunmaker) (See DGS, Inc.)

MARK STRATTON
(custom gunmaker)
13704 Beverly Park Rd.
Lynnwood, Washington 98037
Tel: 425-745-8309
Web Site: www.gunmaker.net
E-mail: octbarrel@aol.com

STURM, RUGER AND COMPANY, INC.
(Ruger handguns, rifles, shotguns, blackpower, revolvers)
200 Ruger Road
Prescott, Arizona 86301
Tel: 520-541-8820 Fax: 520-541-8850
Web site: www.ruger-firearms.com

SWAROVSKI OPTIK NORTH AMERICA
(scopes)
2 Slater Road
Cranston, Rhode Island 02920
Tel: 800-426-3089; 401-734-1800
Fax: 401-734-5888; 877-287-8517
Web site: www.swarovskioptik.com

SWIFT BULLET CO.
(bullets)
201 Main Street
P.O. Box 27
Quinter, Kansas 67752
Tel: 785-754-3959 Fax: 785-754-2359

SWIFT INSTRUMENTS, INC.
(scopes, mounts)
952 Dorchester Avenue
Boston, Massachusetts 02125
Tel: 800-446-1116 Fax: 617-436-3232

Web site: www.swift-optics.com

SZECSEI & FUCHS
(custom rifles)
450 Charles Street
Windsor, Ontario N8X 371 Canada
Tel: 001 519 966 1234

TASCO WORLDWIDE, INC.
(scopes, mounts)
2889 Commerce Parkway
Miramar, Florida 33025
Tel: 800-368-2726; 954-252-3600
Fax: 954-252-3705
Web site: www.tascosales.com
E-mail: dduquesne@tascosales.com

TAURUS INT'L, INC.
(handguns)
16175 N.W. 49th Avenue
Miami, Florida 33014-6314
Tel: 800-327-3776; 305-624-1115
Fax: 305-623-7506
Web site: www.taurususa.com

TAYLOR'S & CO. INC.
(rifles, carbines)
304 Lenoir Drive
Winchester, Virginia 22603
Tel: 540-722-2017 Fax: 540-722-2018
Web site: www.taylorsfirearms.com
E-mail: info@taylorsfirearms.com

THOMPSON & CAMPBELL
(custom rifles)
Cromarty – The Black Isle
Ross-Shire IV11 8YB Scotland
Tel: +44 (0) 1381 600 536
Fax: +44 (0) 1381 600 767

THOMPSON/CENTER ARMS
(handguns, rifles, reloading, blackpowder arms)
Farmington Road, P.O. Box 5002
Rochester, New Hampshire 03867
Tel: 603-332-2394 Fax: 603-332-5133
Web site: www.tcarms.com

TIKKA
(rifles, shotguns))
Available through Beretta U.S.A.

Directory of Manufacturers & Suppliers

TRADITIONAL EFFECTS CO.
Cimarron
PO Box 333
Red Rock TX 78662
Tel: 512-303-0636
www.traditionaleffects.com

TRADITIONS PERFORMANCE FIREARMS
(blackpowder arms)
1375 Boston Post Road
P.O. Box 776
Old Saybrook, Connecticut 06475-0776
Tel: 860-388-4656 Fax: 860-388-4657
Web site: www.traditionfirearms.com
E-mail: info@traditionsfirearms.com

TRIJICON
(rifle scopes)
49385 Shafer Ave. P.O. Box 930059
Wixom, Michigan 48393
Tel: 248-960-7700; 800-338-0563
Fax: 248-960-7725
Web site: www.trijikon-inc.com

TRIUS PRODUCTS, INC.
(traps, targets)
221 South Miami Avenue, P.O. Box 25
Cleves, Ohio 45002
Tel: 513-941-5682 Fax: 513-941-7970
(see p. 77 in Manufacturers' Showcase)

UBERTI USA, INC.
(handguns, rifles, blackpowder guns)
17603 Indian Head Hwy, Suite 200
Accokeek, MD 20607
Tel: 301-283-6300

U.S. REPEATING ARMS CO.
(Winchester rifles, shotguns)
275 Winchester Ave.
Morgan, Utah 84050-9326
Tel: 801-876-3440 Fax: 801-876-3737
Web site: www.winchesterguns.com

VERSATILE RACK CO.
5761 Anderson Street
Vernon, California 90058
Tel: 323-588-0137 Fax: 323-588-5067
Web site: www.versatilegunrack.com
E-mail: versatile@earthlink.net

(see p. 76 in Manufacturer'Showcase)

VERONA SHOTGUNS
Available through Eldorado Cartridge

VIHTAVUORI POWDER
1241 Ellis St.
Bensenville IL 60106
Tel: 630-350-1116 Fax: 630-350-1606

VOLQUARTSEN CUSTOM, LTD.
(pistols, rifles)
24276 240th Street
Carroll, Iowa 51401-8537
Tel: 712-792-4238 Fax: 712-792-2542
Web site: www.volquartsen.com
E-mail: vcl@netins.com
(see p. 79 in Manufacturers' Showcase)

WALTHER U.S.A.
(handguns)
2100 Roosevelt Ave.
Springfield, Massachusetts 01104
Tel: 800-372-6454 Fax: 413-747-3592
Web site: www.walther-usa.com

AL WARD
(custom gunmaker)
12731 Friar Tuck Rd.
Grass Valley CA 95949
Tel: 530-477-0108

WEATHERBY, INC.
(rifles, shotguns, ammunition)
3100 El Camino Real
Atascadero, California 93422
Tel: 800-227-2016; 805-466-1767
Fax: 805-466-2527
Web Site: www.weatherby.com

WEAVER-BLOUNT, INC.
(scopes)
201 Plantation Oak Drive
Thomasville, Georgia 31792
Tel: 912-227-9053 Fax: 912-227-9054
Wev site: www.weaveroptics.com

WILDEY F.A. INC.
(handguns)
45 Angevine Road
Warren, Connecticut 06754
Tel: 860-355-9000 Fax: 860-354-7759
Web site: www.wildeyguns.com

WILD WEST GUNS, INC.
(Summit rifles)
7521 Old Seward Hwy., Unit A
Anchorage, Alaska 99518
Tel: 800-992-4570 Fax: 907-344-4005
Web site: www.wildwestguns.com
E-mail: wwguns@ak.net

WILLIAMS GUN SIGHT CO.
7389 Lapeer Road
P.O. Box 329
Davison, Michigan 48423
Tel: 800-530-9028; 810-653-2131
Fax: 810-658-2140
Web site: www.williamsgunsight.com

WINCHESTER
(ammunition, primers, cases, ballistics)
Available through Olin/Winchester
Web site: www.winchester.com

WINCHESTER FIREARMS
(rifles, shotguns)
Available through U.S. Repeating Arms Co.
Web site: www.winchester-guns.com

WINCHESTER MUZZLELOADING
Available through Blackpowder Prods.

WOODLEIGH BULLETS
Huntingtons
601 Oro Dam Blvd.
Oroville CA 95965
Fax: 530-534-1212

CARL ZEISS OPTICAL, INC.
13017 N. Kingston Ave.
Chester VA 23836
Tel: 804-530-8300

Z-HAT CUSTOM DIES
(reloading)
4010A S. Poplar, Suite 72
Casper, Wyoming 82601
Tel: 307-577-7443
Web site: www.z-hat.com
E-mail: RifleBuilder@z-hat.com

Gunfinder Index

To help you find the model of your choice, the following index includes every firearm found in the Shooter's Bible 2002, listed by type of gun.

RIFLES
Centerfire Bolt Action

AMERICAN HUNTING RIFLE	112
AXTELL RIFLE CO.	82
LES BAER CUSTOM	83
MARK BANSNER	84
BERETTA	
Mato Rifle	119
BLASER	
Model R 93	121
Long Range	121
ED BROWN CUSTOM TACTICAL	
Model 72	122
Model 702	123
BROWNING	
A-Bolt II Eclipse, Stainless Stalker	125
A-Bolt II Hunter	125
A-Bolt II Medallion (LH)	125
BROWN PRECISION	
High Country, Youth	127
Pro-Hunter, Pro-Varminter	127
Tactical Elite	128
CHARLES DALY	149
CHRISTENSEN	
CarbonChallenger Series	129
CarbonTactical Series	129
CarbonOne Series	129
CarbonRanger	129
COOPER ARMS	
Varmint Extreme Series (Models 21, 22)	133
CZ	
Model CZ 527 Lux	136
Model CZ 527 Premium	136
Model CZ 550 Lux Series (Varmint, Premium, American, Safari Magnum)	135
Model 452-2E-ZMK Series (Lux, Varmint, American)	134
DAKOTA ARMS	
Dakota 76 Series	137
Dakota 97 Varmint, Lightweight & Long Range Hunter	138
Long Bow Tactical	138
EUROPEAN AMERICAN ARMORY	139
GIBBS RIFLE COMPANY	
Quest II Extreme	141
Model M71/84	141
H-S PRECISION	
Pro-Series 2000 (Professional Hunter, Varmint Takedown, Heavy Tactical)	144, 145
HOWA	
Lightning Bolt Action	146
JARRETT	
Standard Hunting Rifle	146
The Wind Walker	146
The Walkabout	147
50 Caliber Model	147
JOHANNSEN EXPRESS	
Safari, Classic Safari, Tradition	148
KIMBER	
Model 84M Series	150
LAZZERONI	
Models L2000ST/SA/SP/DG	152
Ballistics	153
MAGNUM RESEARCH	
Mountain Eagle	155
Tactical Rifle	155
NEW ULTRA LIGHT ARMS	
Model 20 Series	167
PRAIRIE GUN WORKS	
LRT-2 Series (Ultralight, Benchrest, Varmint, Tactical, PGW/Gibbs)	169
REMINGTON	
Model Seven Series	173
Model 700	171-176
Model 710	173
RIFLES, INC.	
Classic	179
Lightweight Strata SS	179
Safari	179
RUGER	
Model 77 Series	186-188
SAKO	
Model 75 Series (Hunter, Stainless Synthetic)	189
Deluxe, Stainless	192
75 Actions	192
TRG-22, TRG-S	193
SAUER	
Model 202 Supreme	194
SAVAGE	195-199
Model 10FMC Scout	198
TIKKA	
Sporter	208
Continental Varmint & Long-Range Hunting	208
Whitetail Hunter, Left Hand	207
Whitetail Battue, Hunter Deluxe, Synthetic	207
THOMPSON & CAMPBELL	
Inver Rifle, Cromie Rifle, Jura Rifle	205
WEATHERBY	
Mark V	210-213
WINCHESTER	
Model 70	215-217

Centerfire Lever Action

BROWNING	
Model Lightning BLR	126
CIMARRON	
Henry	113
1873 Winchester	113
EMF	
Yellowboy Model 1866	139
Model 1873 Sporting Rifle & Carbine	139
MARLIN	
Model 336 Cowboy Gun	159
Model 444P & 1895G	161
Model 1894 P	160
NAVY ARMS	163-164
WILD WEST GUNS	
CoPilot .457 Magnum & .50 Alaskan	214
Alaskan Guide	214
TAYLOR'S RIFLES	204
UBERTI	209
WINCHESTER	
Model 94 Standard Walnut	218
Model 94 Legacy	218
Model 94 Trail's End	218
Model 94 Ranger	218
Model 94 Walnut Trapper Carbine	208

Centerfire Semiautomatic & Slide Action

AUTO-ORDNANCE	
Thompson Model M1 Carbine	117
Thompson Model 1927 A1 Deluxe, Lightweight and Commando	117
BROWNING	
BAR Mark II Safari & Lightweight	126
COLT	
Match Target, Lightweight	132
HECKLER & KOCH	
.45 ACP Autoloading Carbine	142
.223 Autoloading	142
Model SLB 2000	142
REMINGTON

Gunfinder Index

Models 7400 & 7600	176
RUGER	
Model PC9 Auto	182
Mini-14/5 Carbine, 14/5R Ranch	183
Model Mini-Thirty, Mini-14	183
SPRINGFIELD	
M1A Standard	202
M1 A-A1 Scout	202

Centerfire Single Shot

HARRINGTON & RICHARDSON	
Ultra Single Shot Rifles	140
L.A.R.	
Grizzly Big Boar Competitor	151
LONE STAR	
Silhouette, Sporting, Cowboy Action	154
MOSSBERG	
Model SSI-One Single Shot Rifle/Shotgun	162
NEW ENGLAND FIREARMS	
Synthetic Handi-Rifle	166
Super Light Youth Handi-Rifle	166
ROSSI	181
RUGER	
No. 1A Light & 1S Medium Sporters	185
No. 1B Standard/1V Special Varminter	185
No. 1H Tropical	185
No. 1RSI International	185
THOMPSON/CENTER	
Encore	206

Rimfire Bolt Action & Single Shot

ANSCHUTZ	
Model 2013 Supermatch	113
Model 1907	113
Model 1912 Sport	114
Model 54, 18 MSR Silhouette	115
Model 1827 "Fortner"	115
Model 1903	115
Model 2013 Benchrest	114
CZ	
452 American	134
JARRETT	
Rimfire Rifle	147
KBI/CHARLES DALY	
Model CDGA Empire and Field Grades	149
KIMBER	
Model 82C Series (Classic, SVT, Super-America, HS)	150
MARLIN	
Model 15YN "Little Buckaroo"	158
Models 25MN & 25N	157
Model 70 PSS	156

Model 17 & 17 US	157
REMINGTON	
Models 40-XR	177
ROGUE RIFLE CO.	180
RUGER	
77/22 Rimfire Series	186
SAKO	
Finnfire (Scout, Hunter, Varmint)	191
SAVAGE	
Mark I-G Single Shot	200
Model 93G Magnum, 93F Magnum, FVSS	200
Mark II-FV Heavy Barrel, Mark II-FSS Mark II-LV	200

Rimfire Lever Action

BROWNING	
Model BL-22	124
HENRY REPEATING ARMS	
Henry Rifle	143
U.S. Survival	143
Golden Boy	143
MARLIN	
Golden 39AS	158
1897 Cowboy	158
WINCHESTER	
Model 9422 Traditional	219
Model 9422, Legacy, Trapper	219

Rimfire Semiautomatic & Slide Action

BROWNING	
22 Semiauto Grades I & VI	124
Buckmaster	124
BROWN PRECISION	
Custom Team Challenger	127
HENRY	
Pump Action .22	143
KBI/CHARLES DALY	
22 Caliber	149
MARLIN	
Models 60, 60SS	156
Models 7000	156
Model 70PSS "Papoose"	156
REMINGTON	
Model 597 Series	178
Model 552 BDL Speedmaster	177
Model 572 BDL Fieldmaster	177
RUGER	
Model 10/22 Series	182
SPRINGFIELD	
Model M-6 Scout Combo	202

THOMPSON/CENTER	
Model T/C 22LR Classic	206

Double Rifles, Actions & Drillings

BERETTA	
Express Rifles (5506, 455)	118
Silver/Gold Sable II Over/Under	120
KRIEGHOFF	
Classic Side-by-Side	151
MERKEL	
Safari Double Rifles	162
PURDEY	
Double Barrel Rifle .577 NITRO	170
SAKO	
Actions	190
SZECSEI & FUCHS	
Double Barrel Rifles	203

Replica Rifles

CIMARRON FIREARMS	
1885 High Wall	130
Billy Dixon 1874 Sharps Sporting Rifle	130
Quigley 1874 Sharps Sporting Rifle	130
Silhouette 1874 Sharps Sporting Rifle	130
EMF	
1860 Henry	139
1866 Yellowboy Carbine/Rifle	139
1873 Sporting Rifle & Carbine	139
LONE STAR	
Silhouette, Sporting, Cowboy Action	154
NAVY ARMS	
1866 "Yellowboy" Rifle & Carbine	163
1873 Springfield Cavalry Carbine	164
1873 Winchester Sporting	164
1874 Sharps Cavalry Carbine	164
1874 Sharps Sniper	164
1892 Model (brass frame, short rifle)	163
Henry Iron Frame, Military, Trapper	163
Remington-Style Rolling Block Buffalo Rifle	165
Sharps Plains & Buffalo	165
PEDERSOLI	
Kodiak Mark IV Double Rifle	168
Rolling Block Target	168
Sharps Carbine Model 766	168
Mortimer Target	168
TAYLOR'S	
Henry, 1866 Yellowboy Carbine	204
1873 Winchester Rifle, 1873 Sporting Rifle	204
UBERTI	
Henry Carbine, Rifle	209
Model 1866 Yellowboy Carbine	209
Model 1871 Rolling Block Baby Carbine	209
Model 1873 Sporting Rifle	209
WINCHESTER	

Gunfinder Index

Model 1895 ... 220

Competition Target Rifles

ANSCHUTZ (See under RIMFIRE BOLT ACTION)

BROWN PRECISION
Custom Team Challenger ... 127

CHRISTENSEN
Carbon Challenger ... 129

COLT
Match Target ... 132

MAGNUM RESEARCH
Magnum Lite Rimfire w/Barracuda Stock ... 155

REMINGTON
Model 40-XR BR Target Rimfire ... 177

RUGER
Model 1022T ... 182

SAVAGE
Model M112BT Competition ... 198

Rifle/Shotgun Combinations
(See SHOTGUNS Shotgun/Rifle Combinations)

SHOTGUNS
Autoloading

BENELLI
Legacy ... 223, 224
Super Black Eagle ... 223, 224
Executive Series (grades I, II, III) ... 225
M1 Series ... 226
Montefeltro Super 90 ... 226
Super Black Eagle/Slug ... 223
Sport Model ... 224

BERETTA
Model AL391 Series (Gold, Synthetic,
 Trap, Youth) ... 231
Model 1201 FP Riot ... 230
Pintail, Pintail Rifled Slug ... 230
Extrema 3.5 ... 227

BROWNING
Gold Sporting Clays, ... 232
Gold Hunter & Stalker ... 232
Gold Deer & Camo ... 232
Gold Light ... 232

CHARLES DALY
Superior Sport ... 239
Field Hunter Series ... 239

FRANCHI
Variomax, 612, 620 ... 242
AL48 & Deluxe ... 242

HECKLER & KOCH
Gold Lion, Classic Lion, Silver Lion
 (Fabarm Series) ... 245

REMINGTON
Model 11-87 Premier, Deer Gun ... 262
Model 11-87 SPS/SPS
 Camo/SPST Turkey ... 262
Model 1100 LT-20 ... 262
Model SP-10 Magnum, Camo ... 263

STOEGER
2000, Deluxe ... 272

WEATHERBY
SAS Series (Shadow Grass, Mossy Oak,
 Field Synthetic) ... 273

WINCHESTER
Super X2 Series (Turkey, Sporting Clays) ... 275

Bolt Action

MOSSBERG
Model 695 Series ... 253

SAVAGE
Model 210 FT "Master Shot" Slug Gun ... 268

Over-Under

BERETTA
Model 682 Gold Competition Skeet & Trap ... 227
Model 682 Gold Competition Sporting ... 227
Model 686 Onyx ... 227
Model 686 Ultralight ... 228
Model 687 Silver Pigeon Sporting ... 228
Model 687L Silver Pigeon Sporting ... 228
Model 687EL Gold Pigeon Field ... 228
Model 687 Diamond Pigeon ... 228
Trident Skeet DT10 ... 229
Whitewing ... 229
S686 Silver Pigeon ... 229

BROWNING
Citori Field Models ... 233-235
Citori Light Sporting
Citori Special Trap & Skeet
Citori Model 425, Ultra Sporter
Citori Sporting Hunter
Citori White Upland Special
Ultra XT Trap & Skeet Models

CHARLES DALY
Field Hunter ... 237
Superior Sporting ... 237
Empire EDL Hunter ... 237
Diamond Competition ... 237
Country Squire ... 238

FLODMAN ... 241

FRANCHI
Alcion Sport ... 243
Veloce ... 243

HECKLER & KOCH
Silver Lion ... 245

KIMBER
Augusta ... 238

KRIEGHOFF

Models K-80 Live Bird, Trap, Skeet,
 Sporting Clays ... 248
Model K-20 ... 248

MAROCCHI
Conquista Series ... 249

MERKEL
Models 2000 Series ... 250
Models 303 Sidelocks ... 250
Model 2002 ... 250

NEW ENGLAND ARMS/RIZZINI
Models 500, 600, 702, 900 ... 254

PERAZZI
Competition Series (Electrocibies, Double
 Trap, Pigeon, Mirage, Olympic, Pigeon,
 Skeet, Special/Sporting); Game Models;
 SC3, SCO High Grades ... 257-258

PURDEY
Over & Under Gun ... 259

REMINGTON
Model 300 Ideal ... 263

RIZZINI
Premier Sporting & Upland ... 265
Artemis EL High Grade ... 265
Emilio Rizzini Over/Under ... 265

RUGER
Red Label ... 267
Sporting Clays ... 267
Woodside O/U ... 267

SIG ARMS
TR-40 Silver ... 268

SKB
Model 505 ... 269
Model 585 Upland ... 270
Model 785 Series
 (field, skeet, sporting clays, trap) ... 270

STOEGER
Condor I Single Trigger ... 272
Condor Supreme Deluxe SS ... 272

WEATHERBY
Athena Grades IV & V ... 273
Orion Grades I, II, III ... 273
Orion Super Sporting Clays ... 273
Orion Grade II Classic Field ... 273

WINCHESTER
Supreme Over/Under ... 277
Model 9410 Lever Action ... 277

Side-By-Side

AYA
Boxlock Models ... 222
Sidelock Models ... 222
Countryman ... 222

BERETTA

Gunfinder Index

Model 470 Silver Hawk	230
DAKOTA ARMS	
American Legend	240
CHARLES DALY	
Field Hunter	238
Superior, Diamond	238
A.H. FOX	
Custom Boxlock Models	240
IGA (see STOEGER)	
MERKEL	
Models 47E, 147E, 147EL	251
Model 280EL	251
Models 360EL	251
PURDEY	
Game Gun	259
SKB	
Model 385	269
Model 485	269
STOEGER/IGA	
Coach Gun	271
Uplander, Supreme	271

Single Barrel

BROWNING	
BT-99	236
HARRINGTON & RICHARDSON	
.410 Tamer Shotgun	244
Model Ultra Slug Hunter	244
Topper Series Models 098 & Junior Classic	244
N.W.T.F.	244
KRIEGHOFF	
Model KS-5	249
NEW ENGLAND FIREARMS	255-256
Pardner/Pardner Youth	
Special Purpose Waterfowl SS	
Survivor Series	
Tracker Slug Gun	
Tracker II Rifled Slug Gun	
Turkey Gun	
PERAZZI	
American Trap Series	257
ROSSI	
Field Grade 12 ga.	266
Youth Model .410	266
Matched Pair Combos	266

Slide Action

BROWNING	
BPS Magnum Series	236
BPS Field Model	236
CHARLES DALY	
Field Hunter Series	239

ITHACA	
Model 37 Deerslayer II	246
Model 37 Turkeyslayer	246
Classic 37, English Version	246
MOSSBERG	
Model 500 Crown Grade/Combos	252
Model 500 Mariner	252
Model 500 Sporting	252
Model 500/590 Special Purpose	252
Model 835 Ulti-Mag	253
REMINGTON	
Model 870 Express Combo/Deer/Turkey/ Super Magnum	260
Model 870 SP Marine Magnum	261
Model 870 Express Youth	261
Model 870 Wingmaster Series	260
WINCHESTER	
Model 1300 Deer, Field, Turkey	276
Model 1300 New Camp Defender Series	277
Model 1300 Ranger, Deer, Ladies'/Youth	276

Rifle/Shotgun Combination

CHARLES DALY	
Superior Combination	238
SAVAGE	
Model 24F	268

HANDGUNS

Pistols - Competition/Target

AUTO-ORDNANCE	
Model 1911A1 (WWII Parkerized, Standard, Deluxe)	279
BROWNING	
Buck Mark 5.5 Target, Challenge, Bullseye	287
ED BROWN	
Class A Limited	262
CHARLES DALY	
1911 A-1 45ACP	288
Superior Grade, Field Target	288
HAMMERLI	
Model 160 Free	302
SP20 New Face	302
Model EP10 Free Pistol	302
X-ESSE Sport	302
HECKLER & KOCH	
USP 45 Expert	308
HIGH STANDARD	
Olympic Rapid Fire	305
Olympic Military	306
Citation, Supermatic Citation MS	306
Supermatic Trophy	306
Victor 22LR	306
H-S PRECISION	
Pro Series 2000	308

KIMBER	
Gold Match	311
Ultra Ten II	312
Polymer Series	312
MAGNUM RESEARCH	
Lone Eagle Single Shot	314
RUGER	
Mark II Target Series	325
SIG ARMS	
Trailside PL 22 Series	331
SMITH & WESSON	
Model 41 Rimfire	334
Model 22A Sport	334
THOMPSON/CENTER	
Encore	348
UBERTI	
1871 Rolling Block Target	349
WALTHER	
GSP Expert	350

Pistols - Derringers

AMERICAN DERRINGER	
Model 4, Model M-4 Alaskan Survival	279
Lady Derringer	279
BOND ARMS	
450 Super Defender, Texas Defender, Cowboy Defender	285
DOWNSIZER	
Model WSP	294

Pistols Semiautomatic
(See also Pistols Competition/Target)

AUTO-ORDNANCE	
1911 AL	279
BENELLI See European American Armory	
BERETTA	
Model 21 Bobcat	282
Model 84 Cheetah	283
Model 85, 86, 87 Cheetah	283
Model 92 Series	284
Elite	281
Model 950 BS Jetfire	282
Model 3032 Tomcat	280
Model 8040 Mini-Cougar	280
Models 8000/8040/8045 Cougar	280
Model 9000 Series	281
Neos	282
BERSA	
Thunder 380, 380 Deluxe	285
ED BROWN	
Kobra, Class A	286

Reference • 573

Gunfinder Index

BROWNING	
Buck Mark	287
CHARLES DALY	
1911 A-1, Double Action	288
COLT	
Defender & Gold Cup Model O	290
Model O Series 1991 and XSE	290
Gov't 1991 Matte, Stainless, Commander	290
CZ	
Model 75 Series (Standard, Champion)	292
Model 75/85 Kadet (CZ83, CZ100, 97B, CZ 85 Combat	293
ENTREPRISE	
Elite P425	295
Tactical P325 Plus	295
Boxer P500	295
EUROPEAN AMERICAN ARMORY	
Witness DA	296
Witness Compact	296
FIRESTORM	
Mini Firestorm, Govt.	298
GLOCK	
Model 17	300
Model 19 Compact	300
Model 20	300
Model 22, 23 Compact	300
Model 26, 27 Subcompacts	301
Models G33, G34, G35 Subcompacts	301
Models G32, G29, G309	301
HECKLER & KOCH	
Mark 23 Special	304
Model HK USP 9 & 40 Universal	303
Model P7M8 Self-Loading	303
Model USP45 Universal Self-Loading	303
Model USP45 Expert	304
Model USP45 Compact Universal	303
HI-POINT FIREARMS	
Models 9mm, 9mm Compact & 380 Polymer	307
9mm Comp Gun	307
HIGH STANDARD (see Competition/Target)	
ISRAEL ARMS	
Models M-5000, M-999	308
KAHR ARMS	
Models P40, P9	309
KBI	
FEG Model PJK-9HP	309
FEG Model SMC Auto	309
KEL-TEC	
P-32, P11 9mm Luger	310
Sub Rifle 2000	310
KIMBER	
Model Custom .45 Series	
(Target, Gold Match)	311
Compact & Pro Carry, Ultra Ten, Ultra Carry	312
CDP Series	312
LLAMA	
Government Model (table)	313
Micro-Max (table)	313
Mini-Max (table)	313
MAGNUM RESEARCH	
Mark XIX Component System	314
Baby Eagle	314
Desert Eagle	314
M.O.A.	
Maximum	315
NORTH AMERICAN ARMS	
Guardian 32	317
PARA-ORDNANCE	
P Series Pistols (P10, P12, P13, P16), tables	318
LDA Series (Single Stack, Limited)	319
RUGER	
Mark II Series	325
P-Series Pistols (P93, P94, P90, P95, P89)	327
Mark II 22/45	325
SAFARI ARMS	
Cohort, Enforcer, Matchmaster	328
SAVAGE ARMS	
"Striker" Models 510F, 516	329
Super Striker	329
SIG ARMS	
Models P226	330
Models P229, P232, P239	330
Trailside PL 22	331
P210 Sports Series	331
SMITH & WESSON	
Model 410, 910	332
Model 22A Sport	334
Model 41 Rimfire SA	334
Model 457	328
Model 4000 Series	332
Model 3913 LadySmith	333
Model 4500 Series	332
Model 5900 Series	332
Sigma Series SW40F, SW380, SW99	333
TSW Tactical Series (3953TSW, 4013TSW4053TSW)	335
Traditional DA Model 4513TSW	335
SPRINGFIELD	
Model 1911-A1 Series (Champion, Trophy Match)	342
Ultra Compact Series	342
TAURUS	
Models PT 22, PT 25	343
Model PT-92	344
Model PT-911 Compact	343
Model PT 945	344
Model PT-938 Compact	343
Model PT 940	344
THOMPSON/CENTER	
Encore	348
UBERTI	
1871 Rolling Block Target	349
WALTHER	
Model P 99 Compact	350
Model PP, PPK & PPK/E	350
WILDEY	
Hunter & Survivor	350
Guardsman	350

REVOLVERS

CIMARRON FIREARMS	
1872 Open Top	289
1858 Army .44	289
Model P Jr.	289
1836 Paterson	289
COLT	
Cowboy SA, Anaconda, Python	291
EMF/DAKOTA	
Hartford Pinkerton	294
1873 Hartford Buntline	294
Model 1873 Dakota SA	294
Model 1890 Remington Police	294
Model 1875 SA Remington	294
EUROPEAN AMERICAN ARMORY	
Big Bore Bounty Hunter	297
Windicator DA	296
FREEDOM ARMS	
Model 97 Premier Grade	299
Model 83 Premier, Field Grade	299
Model 83 Silhouette/Competition	299
HERITAGE MFG.	
Rough Rider SA	305
MAGNUM RESEARCH	
BFR Revolver	315
NAVY ARMS	
1873 SA Army	316
1875 Schofield	316
Bisley Model SA	316
New Model Russian	316
NORTH AMERICAN ARMS	
Mini-Master Series	317
Mini Revolvers	317
ROSSI	
Models R352, R462	320
RUGER	
Bisley SA Target	326
GP-100, 357 Mag.	325

Gunfinder Index

Model	Page
Model SP101 (Spurless, Heavy Barrel)	325
New Bearcat (SBC-4)	326
Mark II Series	325
New Model Blackhawk, Convertible	323
New Model Single-Six	324
New Model Super Blackhawk	323
Fixed Sight New Model Single-Six	323
Redhawk Models (Stainless & Blued)	321
Super Redhawk Stainless DA	321
Bisley-Vaquero	322
Vaquero SA	322

SMITH & WESSON
Model 10 Military & Police	339
Model 37 Chiefs Special Airweight	336
Model 60 .38 Chiefs Special Stainless	336
Model 60LS LadySmith	336
Model 317 Airlite, LadySmith	337
Model 64 M & P Stainless	339
Model 65 M & P, LadySmith	339
Model 66 Combat Magnum	340
Model 340 Airlite	338
Model 360 Airlite SC	338
Model 386 Mountain Lite Airlite	338
Model 610 Classic Hunter	341
Model 625	341
Model 629 Classic/Classic DX, Powerport	341
Model 629	341
Model 640 Centennial	337
Model 649 Bodyguard	337
Model 657	341
Model 686, 686 Plus	340
Model 696	340

TAURUS
Model 44	346
Model 82	346
Model 85 Series	346
Model 454 Casull "Raging Bull"	246
Model 445 DA	347
Model 605	347
Model 608 DA	347
Model 94, 941	347

UBERTI REPLICAS
1873 Cattleman	349
Dragoon	349
Walker	349
1875 Outlaw	349

BLACKPOWDER
Muskets, Carbines & Rifles

AUSTIN & HALLECK
Mountain Rifle	352
Models 320, 420	352

CABELA'S
Blue Ridge Rifle	353
Kodiak Express Double Rifle 390	353
Traditional Hawken	353

COLT BLACKPOWDER
Colt Model 1861 Musket	354

CVA
Firebolt 209 Ultramag	358
Hunterbolt 209 Magnum	358
Eclipse 209	358
Mountain Rifle	359
Bobcat	359
Stag Horn Rifle	358
St. Louis Hawken,	359
Youth Hunter	357
Plainsman	357

DIXIE
1858 Two-Band Enfield Rifle	363
1859 Sharps New Model Carbine/Military Rifle	361
1862 Three-Band Enfield Rifled Musket	363
1873 Springfield Rifle/Carbine & Officer's Model	362
1874 Sharps Lightweight Hunter	361
1874 Sharps Silhouette	361
Hawken	361
Early American Jaeger	361
Kodiak Mark IV Double Barrel Rifle	362
Pennsylvania Rifle	362
U.S. Model 1816 Flintlock Musket	363
U.S. Model 1861 Springfield Percussion Rifle/Musket	363
Waadtlander Model	362

EUROARMS
Cook & Brother Confederate Carbine	365
Cook & Brother Field Model 2301	365
C.S. Richmond Musket Model 2370	365
J.P. Murray Carbine 2315	365
London Armory Co. 2-Band & Rifle Musket	365

GONIC
Model 93 Series (Magnum, Mountain, Classic, Thumbhole, Deluxe)	368
Standard	368

KNIGHT MUZZLELOADERS
Disc Extreme	370
American Knight	369
Model Wolverine - 209	369
Knight .45 Original Disc	370
Master Hunter II Disc	370

LENARTZ MUZZLELOADING
Model RDI-50	371

LYMAN
Great Plains Rifle, Hunter	372

MARKESBERY MUZZLELOADERS
Black Bear, Brown Bear, Grizzly Bear	373
Colorado Rocky Mountain Series	374
Polar Bear	374

NAVY ARMS
1859 Sharps Cavalry Carbine	378
Berdan 1859 Sharps Rifle	379
Brown Bess Musket/Carbine	379
1803 Harpers Ferry	379
Parker-Hale 1858 Enfield Rifle	379
Parker-Hale 1861 Musketoon	379
1861 Springfield	378
1862 C.S. Richmond Rifle	378
Smith Carbine	378

PEDERSOLI
Tryon Percussion	380

REMINGTON
Model 700 ML & MLS	381

RUGER
Model 77/50 RSBBZ Series	382

SAVAGE
Model 10	383

SHILOH SHARPS | 383 |

THOMPSON/CENTER
Black Diamond	385
Black Mountain Magnum	384
Encore 209x50 Magnum Rifle	385
Hawken (50 & 54 Cal.)	385
Fire Storm	384

TRADITIONS
Buckskinner Carbine	388
Deerhunter Rifle Series	387
Lightning Bolt-Action Series	389
Hawken Woodsman	388
Pennsylvania Rifle	388
Shenandoah Rifle	388
Panther	387
Tracker 209 In-Line	387
E-Bolt 209 Rifle	387

WINCHESTER
Model X-150	389

Pistols

CVA
Hawken, Kentucky	356

DIXIE
LePage Percussion Dueling	360
Mang Target	360
Charles Moore English Dueling	360
Queen Anne	360
Screw Barrel Pistol	360

LYMAN MUZZLELOADERS
Plains Pistol	370

NAVY ARMS
1850 Harpers Ferry	375

PEDERSOLI
"Pistol Le Page" International Flintlock Target	378
"Mang in Gräz" Percussion	378

TRADITIONS
Buckhunter Pro In-Line	383
Kentucky	383
William Parker	383
Pioneer, Trapper	383

Revolvers

COLT BLACKPOWDER
Colt 1849 Pocket	350
Colt 1851 Navy	350

Reference • 575

Gunfinder Index

Colt 1860 Army, Cavalry Model	351
Colt 1861 Navy	351
Colt Third Model Dragoon	350
Colt Model 1860 Army Fluted Cylinder	351
Colt Walker 150th Anniversary Model	350
Trapper Model 1862 Pocket Police	351

CVA

1851 Navy Brass Frame	356
1858 Remington	356

EMF HARTFORD

Model 1851 Sheriff's	364
Model 1860 Army	364
Model 1862 Police	364
1863 Texas Dragoon	364
1847 Walker	364
1849 Baby Dragoon	364
1848 Dragoon	364
1851 Navy	364

EUROARMS

Remington 1858 New Army Models 1010, 1020, 1040	366
Rogers & Spencer Models 1005, 1006	366
Rogers & Spencer London Gray Model 1007	366

NAVY ARMS

Colt 1847 Walker	375
1851 Navy "Yank"	376
1858 New Model Army Remington Models	377
1860 Army	376
1862 New Model Police	375
Le Mat (Army, Navy, Cavalry, 18th Georgia, Beauregard)	375
Reb Model 1860	376
Reb 60 Sheriff's	377
Rogers & Spencer Models	375
Spiller & Burr	376

RUGER

Old Army Cap & Ball	382

UBERTI

1851 & 1861 Navy	390
1858 Remington New Army 44	390
1860 Army	390
Paterson	390

Shotguns

CVA

Trapper Single Barrel	357

KNIGHT MUZZLELOADERS

Model TK2000	369